D1045289

A Comprehensive Dictionary of

PSYCHOLOGICAL

and

PSYCHOANALYTICAL

TERMS

Board of Consulting Editors

✔   ✔   ✔

"The question is," said Alice, "whether you *can* make words mean so many different things."
"The question is," said Humpty Dumpty, "which is to be master —that's all."

✔   ✔   ✔

A Comprehensive Dictionary of

PSYCHOLOGICAL

and

PSYCHOANALYTICAL

TERMS

A GUIDE TO USAGE

BY

HORACE B. ENGLISH
The Ohio State University

AND

AVA CHAMPNEY ENGLISH

✗ ✗ ✗

Ad-i-ad-o-cho-kin-e-sis
Is a term that will bolster my thesis
　　That 'tis idle to seek
　　Such precision in Greek
When confusion it only increases.

✗ ✗ ✗

DAVID McKAY COMPANY, INC.
NEW YORK

A COMPREHENSIVE DICTIONARY OF PSYCHOLOGICAL AND PSYCHOANALYTICAL TERMS

NINTH PRINTING, DECEMBER 1968

LIBRARY OF CONGRESS CATALOG CARD NUMBER 57–10524

Printed in the United States of America

Preface

The extraordinary growth of psychology has brought with it a profusion of new terms and many potentially confusing shifts in the meaning of old ones. Even the latest unabridged dictionaries inadequately represent the language of psychology. The scholar, scarcely less than the neophyte, needs a guide to current and to historical technical usage.

This dictionary has been prepared in the belief that knowledge of the conventional or accepted meanings of words can decrease friction in the processes of *communicating facts and ideas*. A dictionary cannot spare the reader the task of discerning how a particular author uses a term, but it can indicate what usages are available. It can prevent needless confusion and controversy about terms. It can help to stabilize terminology. Above all, it can help us to say just what we mean more clearly—and less pretentiously.

It is a common opinion that a dictionary is merely a record of frequently used meanings. This is wrong on two counts. In the first place, since every use of a term in a new context gives it a new meaning, there are as many meanings as there are contexts. The task of the dictionary is thus to be representative, to set forth nuclear definitions that stand for the myriad individual meanings. The nuclear definitions emerge from a kind of cluster analysis. For some terms a single meaning—a G factor, as it were—can represent the individual usages. For others, analysis brings to light several clusters of meaning. A particular art is required to phrase a definition that will represent, not just a single author's meaning, but the "center of gravity" of a whole cluster.

In the second place, goodness of terminology is not merely statistical, even in this refined sense; it is psychological and social. Our goals are clarity of thinking and effectiveness of communication. Misleading terminology does not become better by being widely diffused; it merely does greater damage.

A lexicographer should not essay the role of a King Canute vainly attempting to sweep back a tide of usage. When a term or a meaning has attained a certain currency, into the dictionary it must go despite any lexical imperfections. This does not mean, however, that the lexicographer need be the "harmless drudge" of Dr. Sam Johnson's derisive self-description; he may assume a more positive role as critic, interpreter, and guide.

It is now more than thirty years since the beginning of my work with psychological dictionaries. That experience has given me certain perspectives about the growth trends in our professional vocabulary which I have thought I should share with colleagues. In editorial comments, duly distinguished from the definitions proper, I have tried to show where and why certain usages lead to confusion; when possible, I have suggested a better usage. These comments are aimed at terminological issues. Thus the comment on **reinforcement** is concerned, not with the validity of the empirical hypotheses that have been so named, but with lexical and semantic difficulties.

Within such limits, however, I have exposed my opinions with perhaps indecent plainness. I have been openly critical of the morbid fascination of "prestige" terms designed rather to show that one belongs to the proper inner circle than to express a clear idea. In the face of the neologistic fertility that plagues psychology and certain neighboring disciplines, I have not hesitated to suggest terminological contraception, or even—dare we say?—verbocide. And I emphatically refuse to follow the example of a certain admirable psychiatric dictionary in helping writers to *find* fancy terms, presumably with a view to using them. (E.g., the entry "love of knowledge" refers you to "epistemophilia.") If they are widely used, the lexicographer must condone the crime by defining these monstrosities; but to encourage their use is to compound the felony.

Condensed statements of an empirical theory often masquerade as definitions. When the pseudo definition is then given a name that refers to undoubted facts, it becomes what I have called theory-begging, a variant of the logical fallacy of question-begging. I have probably overlooked more instances of such theory-begging than I have detected, but I have thought it my duty to warn of this insidious error whenever found. (For brief discussions of these and related points see the articles **arbitrary definition, bogus erudition, neologism, rational coinage, theory-begging, traditional terminology**.)

Full agreement with such frankly subjective comments is hardly to be expected. If they help to clarify issues, that is enough.

I cannot hope that my theoretical and systematic biases have been entirely suppressed even in the definitions proper. But I have been at great pains not to load the terminological dice so that those of another theoretical persuasion should have no acceptable way of expressing their different views. A definition is not thought of as a way of closing an argument, but rather as a way of making certain that people are talking about the same thing.

SCOPE

The aim has been to include all terms frequently used in a special or technical sense by psychologists. These are, first and foremost, the terms which denote mental and behavior phenomena, and the concepts and constructs used in ordering these phenomena. (But words whose meanings seem to be merely those of everyday speech, such as *bite* and *sorrow*, are ordinarily omitted.) Where their reference is not self-evident, terms naming psychological laws, theories, theorems, tests, procedures, and instruments are identified.

How far to go afield into other disciplines for terms that are often used technically by psychologists is a most difficult problem. One must somewhere draw a line, but in most cases decision can only be arbitrary. It is to be hoped that users of this book will find a helpful selection of definitions from mathematics, from the natural and the social sciences, and from medicine.

Psychoanalysis or depth psychology, although logically a school of psychology, has pursued until recently an independent course of development and has evolved its own vocabulary. Like psychologists, psychoanalysts have been notably productive of new concepts and of new terms to name them.

Such terms must obviously be defined in the vocabulary of those who use them. The matter is not quite so simple, however. Many psychoanalytical terms are standard psychological expressions given a new meaning. On the other side, more and more psychologists are borrowing—and modifying—psychoanalytical terms. Clearly a considerable interchange of both concepts and terms is under way.

Accordingly, meanings from both disciplines have been given for many terms. Where it has seemed possible to do so without elaborate explanation or theorizing, the relationship between usages has been stated. More detailed articulation of the two vocabularies is perhaps premature, and in any event beyond the scope of a defining dictionary. It is to be hoped, however, that the inclusion of both in one dictionary will facilitate interfertilization and be of value to scholars in both fields.

Most psychiatric terms are descriptions or interpretations of psychological phenomena, hence they belong in this dictionary. The Standard Nomenclature of the American Psychiatric Association has been followed in applicable instances, but it has been necessary to define also such obsolescent terms as dementia praecox and the working expressions of psychiatrists not included in the official nomenclature.

Commonly used symbols, abbreviations and initials used as abbreviations, and the commoner combination terms are included. Foreign terms are covered only when at least half-naturalized in English. Pronunciation appears only for words that seem likely to give some trouble. Inflected forms and parts of speech are indicated when they are irregularly formed.

In the effort at comprehensiveness an extensive search was made of the literature. Inevitably, however, many terms will be missing. It is consoling to remember that noninclusion of a term will not prevent its continuing use, provided it meets a need. Nonetheless, it is hoped that omissions will be called to the editor's attention.

TREATMENT

This is a defining dictionary, a collection of meanings, not an encyclopedic compilation of facts. The line is difficult to draw, since meanings in the last analysis refer to facts. Factual material has been included, therefore, whenever a brief and noncontroversial illustration seemed likely to make the meaning clearer or more easily understood. Such material must, however, be recognized as merely illustrative.

Sources are not routinely identified but the specialized terms or usages of a branch of science, a school, or an individual are so labeled. Meanings of a term are stated in the language of those who use it. Thus a term used chiefly by those adopting a mentalistic point of view receives a mentalistic definition. If it is used also by behaviorists, a second definition in behavior language is given. (See the article **traditional terminology**.) Agreement with the point of view is not implied. Nor does a definition imply factual existence of the phenomena or the soundness of the theory it refers to. For example, **psychokinesis** means "the direct influence by a subject on a physical system without any known intermediate physical instrumentation," even though a majority of psychologists seriously doubt the existence of such an influence.

The degree of technicality needed in a definition depends on who is to use it; one man's overtechnicality is another's exact and economical statement. To take a prime example, certain statistical terms appear only in contexts where the high specialist alone has any concern with them. They can be more accurately and briefly defined in specialized technical language. Statistical terms that are found in more general psychological writings, on the other hand, deserve definition in terms the nonstatistician can understand. The same principle holds in other specialties.

Two statements of a meaning are sometimes given, a relatively simple one for the layman, a second more accurate and technical for the specialist. The result is that bristling technicalities are found cheek-by-jowl with rather basic English. Perhaps the juxtaposition may show the possibilities of simpler writing. Jargon has been eliminated whenever it has been detected.

STRUCTURAL PLAN

Alphabetization. For a condensed statement of how this dictionary is organized see Explanatory Notes on page xii. A further statement about word order may be made. The proper alphabetization of terms compounded of more than one word is troublesome. They should be found where the user is most likely to seek them. Intensive use of other technical dictionaries, however, as well as our own struggles, has convinced me that no satisfactory rule for placement of compound terms can be formulated. Placement is therefore somewhat arbitrary or subjective; I hope it will not usually seem whimsical.

In general, a compound is entered under the most distinctive of its components. Nouns, being usually more distinctive than adjectives, are given preference as the entry word. But in many entries, such as **abient behavior** (or **response**), it is the adjective that is the distinctive word; and in others, such as **quota sampling,** distinctiveness depends on the user's purpose. The only safe rule seems to be: *if you do not find a term where you first look for it, turn to a synonym, to a variant spelling, or to another distinctive word of a compound term.*

Cross-referencing and grouping. Wherever possible, related terms should be brought together for definition and comparison. Listing them under the most distinctive word of a compound often does just that: e.g., **generalization/response** and **generalization/stimulus** are contiguous. More often the iron law of alphabetization causes related terms to be entered on widely separated pages. Extensive use of cross-referencing has therefore been made in order to bring together terms that need to be defined in relation to each other. An example is the article **person,** with its comparison of organism, self, psyche, and other related terms. Words that are thus explained or defined under another heading are printed in small capitals.

A list of general articles which define a group of terms or which comment on problems of terminology in various areas of psychology appears on pages x–xi.

ACKNOWLEDGMENTS

We acknowledge with thanks the permission of authors and publishers to quote or freely paraphrase certain definitions from the following works:

KURTZ, A. K., and EDGERTON, H. A. *Statistical Dictionary*. New York: John Wiley and Sons, 1939.

Diagnostic and Statistical Manual of Mental Disorders. Compiled by the Committee on Nomenclature and Statistics. Washington, D. C.: American Psychiatric Association, 1952.

ROBBINS, S. D. *A Dictionary of Speech Pathology*. Cambridge, Mass.: Sci-Art Publishing Co., 1951.

BRENNAN, J. G., BURNHAM, R. W., and NEWHALL, S. M. "Color Terms and Definitions," *Psychological Bulletin*, 45 (1948), 207–230.

ENGLISH, H. B. *A Student's Dictionary of Psychological Terms*. 4th ed. New York: Harper and Brothers, 1934.

HILGARD, ERNEST R. *Introduction to Psychology* (glossary). New York: Harcourt, Brace and Co., 1953.

At various times the following have assisted in compiling the dictionary: Margit Badt, Claude Bartlett, Ronald Johnson, Pi Yu Ko, Edward Ostrander, Donald L. Papin, Marie Zimmerman; and Drs. Mary Beam, William Brett, Marion E. Hook, Edwin C. Lewis, and J. P. Smith.

Professional colleagues have been most generous in counsel and other assistance. Nearly all my associates in the Department of Psychology have been drawn upon, but the help of Drs. H. A. Toops, Donald Meyer, R. J. Wherry, and G. A. Kelly calls for special acknowledgment. In addition, so many psychologists throughout the country have given of their counsel that it is a real embarrassment to know how to acknowledge them all: if any are missing from the following list who should be there, let it be put down to poor record keeping rather than lack of gratitude:

Dorothy Adkins	S. Diamond	M. H. Krout	J. R. Royce
R. A. Alexander			J. L. Rubins
R. M. Allen	Robert Fisher	R. T. Lennon	Harry Ruja
G. Allport	Joshua Fishman		E. R. Ryden
Anne Anastasi	I. S. Fusfeld	N. Maier	
	Ericka Fromm	S. S. Marzolf	Herbert Saltzstein
R. Bauernfeind		W. J. McKeachie	L. G. Schmidt
S. J. Beck	M. S. Gadel		Harold Schlosberg
E. G. Boring	Cecil A. Gibb	T. M. Newcomb	Charles Simon
D. Brower	W. E. Gregory	C. E. Noble	D. Snygg
Egon Brunswik		P. Nordlie	Julian Stanley
	D. B. Harris		
D. T. Campbell	Lois Harzfeld	R. Perloff	W. S. Taylor
H. Cantril	D. O. Hebb	Carolyn Pratt	E. S. Tolman
J. B. Carroll	H. Helson	Carolyn Price	
Charles Collins		E. S. Primoff	W. S. Verplanck
Isidor Chein	M. Jackson		W. Van Spanckeren
A. W. Combs	B. T. Jensen	V. Raimy	
Stuart Courtis	R. S. Jones	D. Rapaport	Lucien Warner
Lee Cronbach		G. Razran	Leroy Wolins
	J. R. Kantor	D. Rife	P. T. Young
H. P. David	Ethel Kawin	H. D. Rinsland	
H. A. Delp	W. R. Knievel	S. D. Robbins	Sheila Zipf
Don Devoe	May Krantz		

The Board of Consulting Editors has been most helpful in matters of general policy. Had it been possible to make fuller use of their wisdom, a better book would have been possible.

The grant by The Ohio State University of a quarter's tenure of a research professorship has greatly facilitated completion of the book.

Dorothy U. Lewis and Virginia R. Terris of the Longmans Green editorial staff have been of invaluable assistance, especially in maintaining consistency of style and form.

To my wife Ava C. English who, as assistant editor, labored for three years over the growing manuscript, goes much of the credit for such clarity as we have achieved. Her insistent demand that a definition be made to mean something straightforward often contributed also to correctness. The definitions of musical terms are almost wholly her responsibility.

A PLEA FOR COLLABORATION

"Ignorance, madam, sheer ignorance" was Dr. Sam Johnson's explanation of a flagrant error. I must plead the same excuse for many errors of commission and omission. But I hope readers will not let these errors stand uncorrected. I shall welcome extensive critical comments setting us right, but shall also be grateful for two or three lines on a postcard calling attention to errors of any kind. Communications will be acknowledged, and used for the improvement of later editions.

HORACE B. ENGLISH

Department of Psychology,
The Ohio State University,
Columbus, Ohio.
October, 1957.

General Articles

Listed below are articles containing material that has bearing considerably beyond the entry term. Most of these general articles define or compare a group of related terms. Others contain comment on terminological problems, either for psychology in general or for a special area of psychology.

ability
accuracy
achievement quotient
acquired behavior
act
adiadochokinesis
adjustment
affect
age
aggressiveness
agoraphobia
agrammatism
aim
algesia
analytical psychology
anger
anthropomorphism
antisocial
anxiety
applied psychology
aptitude
arbitrary definition
Aristotelian classification
association
attitude
attribute
audiogenic
avoidance motive
awareness
awareness/unconscious
behavior
behavioral
bogus erudition
centile: *see also* partile
centralist psychology
chance
class: *see also* rank
clinic
cognition
color primaries
conceptual nervous system
conditioned response
conditioning
conscious
consciousness
control/scientific
covert behavior
cross-validation
cyclothymic
decibel
defense

deficiency/mental
degenerate
depth psychology
desire: *n.* and *v.*
determine
development
diathesis/traumatophilic
differentiate
disposition
distal vs. proximal
drive
dualism
eclecticism
ego
emotion
entropy
equivocation
evaluation
event
experience
experiment
factor analysis
factor/group
factor theory
factuality/levels of
false negative
false positive: *see* false
  negative
family
fiducial limits
field theory
figure-ground
folie à deux
formal culture or discipline
formalism: *see also*
  eclecticism
formication
forms/comparable
function
functional disorder
fundamentals/psychological
*Geisteswissenschaftliche
  Psychologie*
generalization/stimulus
geneticism
genotype
Gestalt psychology
goal
gradient
habit
heredity

heterosexuality
homosexual
hydrophobophobia
identification
idiophrenic
illusion
image/mental
immoral
implicit
incentive
indecency
information
innate
instinct
intellectual
intelligence
intelligence quotient
interest/doctrine of
introversion
irradiation
leadership
learning/laws of
learning theory
libido
love
luminance
male
mathematical model
  psychology
matter
maturation
meaning
measurement
mechanism
mechanomorphism
medical practice
mental
message
method
mind
miscegenation
model
mode/refined calculation
molar behavior
monism
morals
motion/apparent
motivation
movement
narcissism
nature

Explanatory Notes

Alphabetization: 1. All terms (including abbreviations and symbols) are arranged in one alphabetical list. Terms compounded of more than one word are alphabetized as though forming a single word, word-breaks being ignored. Symbols are entered as though spelled out in English: e.g., Σ as sigma. In general, the simpler of two spellings determines alphabetization: e.g., **esthetics,** not aesthetics. American spellings are given preference over British.

2. Phrases are usually entered under the *most distinctive* word, more often a noun than an adjective. A slant (/) indicates an inverted phrase: e.g., hearing/colored.

3. *If you do not find a term where you first look for it, turn to a synonym, to a variant spelling, or to another distinctive word of the phrase.*

Source Labels: Restricted usage by a school, individual, or branch of science is marked by an italicized label, in parentheses, preceding the definition. (If the restriction applies to only one meaning, it follows the number prefixed to that meaning.) Foreign terms are similarly labeled.

Definitions: 1. Relatively distinct meanings of a term are preceded by arabic numerals. Occasionally, highly distinct meanings appear in separate entries. Distinct aspects of a single meaning are set off by letters.

2. Only one part of speech is defined unless the others have distinct meanings. If, for instance, you don't find torpid, try **torpor.**

Cross References: 1. **Bold face type** (in addition to distinguishing entry words and their inflected forms—respectively at the beginning and at the end of the article) indicates that the term so printed is technically used and is defined in its proper alphabetical place. (But technical terms in the definitions of other terms are not always in bold face.) An asterisk before a word indicates that entry is made under that word: e.g., **film *color** under **color/film.** An equals sign (=) means that two terms are virtually equivalent. Note that the cross-referring word will not always have the same inflectional form as the entry. E.g., the cross-referring word in many places is the adjective **abnormal,** whereas the entry is the noun **abnormality.**

2. SMALL CAPITALS are used within an entry to show that this term is defined (or informally explained) there instead of in its own alphabetical position. E.g., the entry **Hering theory of vision** refers you to **color theories** where (the) HERING THEORY (printed thus) is defined and compared with others.

Usage Notes and Comments: An arrowhead (➤) indicates that the discussion or explanation that follows is not strictly a part of the preceding definition. The symbol ¶ divides discussions of a single meaning into paragraphs. Where the discussion applies to several meanings the regular paragraph indentation is used.

Abbreviations

abbr.—abbreviation, -ated
abstr. n.—abstract noun
adj.—adjective
adv.—adverb
advert.—advertising
ambig.—ambiguous
Amer.—American
anal.—analysis, analytical
anat.—anatomy
Ant.—antonym
anthrop.—anthropology
anthropom.—anthropometry
approx.—approximate
archeol.—archeology
aud.—audition

beh.—behavior, behaviorism
biol.—biology
bot.—botany
Brit.—British

cap.—capitalized,
  capital (letter)
chem.—chemistry
colloq.—colloquial
commun.—communication(s)
comp.—comparative
Contr. w.—contrast(ed)
  with
Cp.—compare

Distg. fr.—distinguish(ed)
  from

econ.—economics
educ.—education
e.g.—for example
elec.—electricity
embryol.—embryology
eng.—engineering
esp.—especially
esth.—esthetics
etymol.—etymology
exper.—experiment(al)

factor anal.—factor analysis
Fr.—French

fr.—from

gen.—general
genet.—genetics
geom.—geometry
Ger.—German
Gk.—Greek
gram.—grammar

hist.—historic(al)
human eng.—human
  engineering

i.e.—that is
indiv. psychol.—individual
  psychology
info. theory—information
  theory
ital.—italic

L.—Latin

math.—mathematics
meas.—measurement
mech.—mechanics
med.—medicine
metaph.—metaphysics
morph.—morphology

n.—noun
N.B.—note well
neurol.—neurology

obs.—obsolete
obsoles.—obsolescent
ophthal.—ophthalmology

parapsych.—parapsychology
pathol.—pathology
pers. n.—personal noun
philos.—philosophy
philos. of educ.—philosophy
  of education
phys.—physics
physiol.—physiology
pl.—plural
pop.—popular (usage)

prefd.—preferred
prep.—preposition
pron.—pronounced,
  pronunciation
psychiat.—psychiatry, -tric
psychoan.—psychoanalysis *
psychol.—psychology
psychopathol.—psycho-
  pathology
psychophys.—psychophysics
psychophysiol.—psycho-
  physiology
psychother.—psychotherapy

recom.—recommended
Ror.—Rorschach (test)

s., sing.—singular
sociol.—sociology
soc. sci.—social science
sp.—spelled
specif.—specifically
speech pathol.—speech
  pathology
Stan. Psychiat.—Standard
  Psychiatric
  (Nomenclature) **
stat.—statistics, -ical
structural psychol.—structural
  psychology
syn.—synonym(s), -ous

tech.—technical
theol.—theology
theor.—theoretical(ly)
topol.—topological,
  topology

v.—verb
Var.—variant
vis.—vision
viz.—namely
vs.—versus

w.—with

zool.—zoology

* See article **psychoan.** for explanation of use of this abbreviation.
** See article **Standard Psychiatric Nomenclature.**

Key to Pronunciation

Pronunciation is given only when a word presents difficulty.

a	at, lap	k	kill, seek	t̶h̶	then, father
ā	able, cane				
ã	air, fare	l	let, ball	u	up, son
ä	art, far			ū	use, cute
		m	me, trim	u̇	put, book
b	bed, rob			ü	rule, move
		n	no, tin		
ch	chin, much	ng	long, bring	v	vat, save
		N	as in *Fr. bon*		
d	did, bad			w	will, way
		o	hot, top		
e	let, ten	ō	open	y	yet, you
ē	eat, see	ô	order, all	Y	as in *Fr. lune, Ger.*
ėr	earn, term	œ	as in *Fr. deux*		*für*
			or *Ger. König*		
f	fat, off	oi	oil, boy	z	zero, haze
		ou	out, now	zh	leisure, measure
g	get, bag				
		p	pet, tap	ə	occurs only in un-
h	how, ahead				accented syllables
H	as *ch* in *Ger. ach*	r	run, dear		and represents the
					sound of
i	is, pin	s	say, pass	a]	as in *a*bout
ī	ice, bite			e]	as in op*e*n
		t	top, it	i]	as in san*i*ty
j	jam, joy	th	thin, both	o]	as in lem*o*n
				u]	as in foc*u*s

A single stroke (′) marks the primary stress, a double stroke (″) the secondary.

A

A: 1. any number (*cp. x,* any value). 2. = **amplitude,** esp. the maximum amplitude of a wave (*cp. a*). 3. (*C. Hull*) = **reaction** or **response** *amplitude.* 4. (*Ror.*) a response scored as **animal content. 5.** (not *ital.*) = **albedo.**

Å = **angstrom unit.**

*A*ₒbⱼ: (*Ror.*) code for a report of seeing in the **inkblots** objects derived from, or connected with, the body of an animal.

a: 1. the **amplitude** of a wave at any moment. 2. an incentive substance, e.g., a food pellet.

a-: prefix meaning *without, lacking, not, absent from, deprived of.* (Preferably used only in words of Greek or Latin origin.)

$a_1, a_2, a_3 \ldots a_n$: successive observations or measurements of same variable.

AA or **A.A.** = 1. achievement *age. 2. Alcoholics Anonymous.

abac (ā'bak, or pronounce as four letters, a-b-a-c): a type of computing diagram designed to decrease the labor involved in statistical analysis. ➤The several values of the variables that are related in an equation are projected by lines across the graph so that the points of intersection indicate the values of the function corresponding to the values of the variables.—*Syn.* **net table.**—*Distg. fr.* **nomograph.**

abasement: *n.* humiliation; degradation.

abasia (ə·bā'zhə): see **astasia-abasia.**

ABBA order: counterbalanced order when just two conditions, A and B, are to be compared.

abdominal reflex: a concave bowing or bending away of the belly when stroked.

abducens (ab·dū'senz): the VIth cranial nerve, which innervates the external rectus muscle of the eye.—*Syn.* ABDUCENT NERVE.

abduction: *n.* movement of a limb away from the **axis** of the body. ➤*Contr. w.* ADDUCTION, movement toward the axis.

ABEPP = American Board of Examiners in Professional Psychology, created by the APA.

aberration: *n.* departure from the normal or typical, esp. if somewhat unexpected or severe; a difference from the normal.

aberration/chromatic: (*optics*) the separation of the component rays of a mixed light due to the fact that different wave lengths are bent different amounts as they pass through a lens. ➤When white light passes thus through a lens, it is spread out in a band of all the colors of the spectrum. A lens can be corrected to prevent chromatic aberration.

aberration/mental: 1. (*pop.*) a temporary

lapse from normal behavior. **2.** mental disorder, kind not specified.

aberration of light: (*optics*) passage of light through an optical system (lenses, translucent bodies, etc.) by any pathway other than the most efficient; particularly, passage in such fashion that the rays do not converge upon one point.

aberration/spherical: (*optics*) the distortion of light rays due to the curvature of a lens.

abient behavior or **response** (ab'i·ənt): literally, behavior that goes away from something; behavior tending to remove the organism from exposure to a stimulus, whether by retreat from the situation or by such action as removes or cancels the stimulus.—*Syn.* **avoidance behavior,** WITHDRAWAL BEHAVIOR, **defense reaction** (all more limited).—*Ant.* **adient behavior.** —*n.* **abiency,** the property of responses that remove an animal from a situation or stimulus.

abilities/primary mental or **PMA: 1.** hypothetical units, various combinations of which constitute all distinguishable abilities; the elements that make up the **ability** patterns; specifically **2.** the seven **unit traits,** derived by L. L. and T. G. Thurstone by factor analysis, which together are held to account for most of the variance in ability. These units are called: **Verbal Comprehension (V), Word Fluency (W), Number (N), Space (S), Associative Memory (M), Perceptual Speed (P),** and **Reasoning** or **Induction (R)** or **(I).** The PMA TEST measures these seven traits.

ability: *n.* actual power to perform an act, physical or mental, whether or not attained by training and education. ➤GENERAL ABILITY is concerned with all sorts of tasks, but especially those of a cognitive or intellectual sort. *Syn.* **intelligence.** SPECIAL ABILITY has to do with a defined kind of task. Each special ability should, when possible, be so defined as not to overlap with other special abilities.

Ability implies that the task can be performed *now,* if the necessary external circumstances are present; no further training is needed. APTITUDE (which formerly carried implications of **innateness**) has now been specialized in technical writing to refer to the fact that the individual can be brought by a specified amount of training to a specified level of **ability,** either general or special, but usually the latter. CAPABILITY is the maximum effectiveness a person can attain with optimum training. CAPACITY is

1

a loose synonym for ability or for APTITUDE, often with implications of innateness; it is sometimes a synonym for CAPABILITY (latter *prefd.*). TALENT is a high degree of ability or of aptitude. GIFT and ENDOWMENT are popular terms for high ability, largely innate. COMPETENCE is fitness either for a particular kind of task or fitness in general (GENERAL ABILITY). Ability is sometimes contrasted with **personality** but, in the broader sense of that term, ability is a part of personality.—See also **skill**, **achievement**. The several kinds of special abilities are listed under the qualifying word, e.g., **mechanical ability**.

ability/general: see **general ability**.

ability grouping: (*educ.*) subdividing a group of pupils into smaller groups of relatively equal **ability**, either in some one subject or in **general ability**.—*Syn.* homogeneous grouping, SECTIONING ACCORDING TO ABILITY. ➤In the TWO-TRACK PLAN, two levels of ability in any given school grade are recognized; in the THREE-TRACK PLAN, three levels, etc. It is now recognized that ability alone is an inadequate basis for assignment to school classes.

ability/initial or **/final:** the ability of a learner at the beginning or at the end of a specified period of study or practice.

ability test: a **test of maximum performance** designed to reveal the level of present ability to function. ➤*Cp.* **aptitude test**, which is designed to reveal the probable future level of ability to function after a given amount of further **maturation** and **learning**; and **achievement test**, which is designed to reveal how much the testee has learned. All three are tests of maximum performance, but the emphasis lies respectively upon *present* level, probable *future* level, and *past* achievement.

abiogenesis (ab″i·ō·jen′ə·sis): *n.* origination of life out of nonliving matter.—*adj.* **abiogenetic** (-jə·net′ik).

Abklingen (äp′kling·ən): *n.* (*Ger.*) the fading out of a tone; by extension, the fading out of any other sensation.

ablation: *n.* surgical removal of a bodily part or organ.

abmodality: *n.* (*stat.*) variation from type; variation from some measure of **central tendency**.

abnormality: *n.* **1.** departure from the **norm**, however defined.—*Syn.* NONNORMALITY (*prefd.*). **2.** (*stat.*) departure from the *mean *interval of a distribution.—*Syn.* **deviation** (*prefd.*). **3.** extreme and harmful departure from the usual, or from a condition of **integration** or **adjustment**.—*Syn.* **pathology, morbidity, disease**. ➤The effort to restrict the term **abnormality** to its purely quantitative meanings, as in (**1**) or (**2**), is unlikely to succeed. A

beneficial departure from the norm is not easily accepted as abnormal; in popular usage **abnormal** means distorted, if not morbid, and **abnormal psychology** is firmly fixed as meaning the study of pathological departures from the usual.—*adj.* **abnormal**, which is also used with the definite article as an abstract or collective noun.

abnormal psychology: the division of the science of psychology that investigates disordered behaviors, deficiencies in behavior capacities, and the persons exhibiting them. ➤The effort to construe the word **abnormal** statistically, and thus to bring marked superiority also under the category **abnormal psychology**, has not succeeded.—*Syn.* **psychopathology**.—See **psychology/divisions and schools of, IX**.

aboral (ab·ô′rəl): *adj.* away from the mouth.

aboulia = **abulia**.

abreaction (ab″ri·ak′shən): *n.* **1.** (*psychoan.*) eliminating or weakening a **complex**, or lessening the emotional tension caused by **conflict** and **repression**, by reliving—in feeling, action, or imagination—the situation that originally caused the conflict.—*Syn.* catharsis, which is now less commonly spoken of. **2.** loosely, the relief of emotional tension by thinking about the originating situation.—*v.* **abreact**.

abscissa (ab·sis′ə): *n.* (*math.*) **1.** the horizontal reference axis of a two-dimensional chart.—*Syn.* X AXIS, BASE LINE. **2.** the shortest distance of a point *P* along a line parallel with the *X* axis to the vertical axis (or *Y* axis) of a two-dimensional chart.—*Syn.* x DISTANCE, x VALUE.—*Ant.* **ordinate**.—See **axis**.

abscission (ab·sizh′ən; -sish′-): *n.* separateness or distinction between two dynamic interacting systems. ➤E.g., two waterfalls in the same river are interactive, and both are constantly changing; yet, despite the changefulness, they maintain distinctness, or **abscission**. *Distg. fr.* **categorical** difference, which obtains between stable objects (such as knife and spoon). Modern theory tends, however, to conceive of a stable object as merely a slowly changing dynamic system, so the distinction between abscission and category is only relative.

absence: *n.* a short period (often found in epilepsy or hysteria) of apparent unconsciousness, characterized by suspended or merely automatic activity and by **amnesia** for events during the period.

absent-mindedness: *n.* a habitual tendency to be so absorbed with one's thoughts as to be unaware of one's surroundings. ➤*Distg. fr.* **daydreaming** (the absentminded person is thinking); and *fr.* the tendency to withdraw from contact with reality as in **schizophrenia**.—*Cp.* **abstrac-**

tion (3), a temporary absent-mindedness.

absolute: *adj.* **1.** completely independent of anything else, or of something that might be expected to be of influence; logically unconditioned; not relative.—*n.* **2.** a thing or value that does not vary with time or in relation to circumstances. ➤E.g., a moral injunction that is considered to hold at all times and in all places is a moral absolute.

absolute error: see **error/absolute.**

absolute impression: an unanalyzed judgment that assigns an object to a place in a quantitative series without explicit comparison with other members of the series: e.g., the absolute impression, *a bright day*, which rests only on an implied and vague standard of comparison.—*Distg. fr.* **comparative judgment** and from **absolute judgment.**

absolute judgment: in a series of comparisons of paired items, the judgment that is sometimes made about the first of a pair without waiting for the second of the pair to be shown. ➤*S* clearly makes his judgment on the basis of the way the series as a whole is running; he "knows" what is coming next. The term is a misnomer, as the judgment is comparative, not absolute. ANTICIPATION JUDGMENT is more descriptive.—*Distg. fr.* **absolute impression** and **absolute judgment procedure.**

absolute judgment procedure: a psychophysical method (now little used) in which each stimulus of a series is judged by itself without an explicit standard for comparison. Essentially it uses the **absolute impression.**—*Distg. fr.* **absolute judgment.** —*Syn.* METHOD OF SINGLE STIMULI.

absolute limen or **threshold:** see **threshold/absolute.**

absolute measurement: 1. obtaining a quantitative representation of a thing or a variable by means of units or subdivisions derived from the variable itself. ➤*Contr. w.* RELATIVE MEASUREMENT, which requires comparison with other variables. Most measurements in psychology are relative.—See **absolute *scale. 2.** measurement without regard to the plus or minus sign.

absolute pitch: see **pitch/absolute.**

absolute scaling: transforming the obtained values of a set of observations into a scale that permits direct comparison with a set of observations on a different scale.

absolute sensitivity: sensory *acuity (1) measured by the minimum **stimulus value** that is just barely perceptible; the **absolute *threshold.**

absolute value: see **value/absolute.**

absolute zero: see **zero/absolute.**

absolutism: *n.* **1.** the doctrine that there is a reality complete in itself, not depending in any way upon anything else, self-contained and unconditional. **2.** the tendency to think in terms of **absolutes (2),** i.e., of things, principles, laws, or relationships that do not change with time and circumstances.—*Syn.* ABSOLUTIST (or ABSOLUTISTIC) ATTITUDE.— *Ant.* **relativity attitude.**

absorption: *n.* **1.** high level of attention to one object, with inattention to others.— *Syn.* **abstraction (3),** which emphasizes the withdrawal of attention from other objects, whereas absorption emphasizes the focusing of attention. **2.** attention to **autistic** thoughts to the exclusion of reality.— *v.* **absorb.**

abstract (ab'strakt): *adj.* **1.** characterizing any quality of something considered apart from the thing itself, or from the other qualities with which it is associated; and pertaining to terms that refer to such a quality. ➤The basic idea is separation, distinctness, selection. See **abstract idea. 2.** lacking the necessary or judicious relation with concrete reality; inapplicable to a concrete or practical situation; excessively separated from relationship with things or with other qualities. ➤**Abstract** in this sense means much the same as *impracticable.* But its further extension to mean *abstruse* or *difficult* is unnecessary and improper.

abstract (ab·strakt': note accent): *v.* **1.** to consider a quality apart from the object, or apart from other qualities with which it is actually found; to separate, mentally or in words, a quality or aspect of a thing from its concomitants: He *abstracted* the color as the only relevant characteristic.—*n.* **abstraction. 2.** to make a brief noncritical summary of the contents of a book or other writing.—*n.* **abstract** (ab'strakt).

abstract ability: the ability to comprehend relationships and to react, not merely to concrete objects, but to concepts and abstract symbols.

abstract attitude: see **concrete attitude.** —*Syn.* CONCEPTUAL ATTITUDE, CATEGORICAL ATTITUDE (neither *prefd.*).

abstract behavior: see **concrete attitude.**

abstract idea or **quality:** an idea considered apart from its application to, or embodiment in, a particular instance: e.g., honesty, considered apart from specific honest acts or persons, is an abstract idea or quality. ➤Since it is impossible to **abstract** (i.e., "draw away") the abstract idea without having experienced more than one instance, the *abstract* idea is also a *general* idea, and the often-used term *abstract general idea* is somewhat redundant. —*Cp.* **concept.**

abstract intelligence: see **intelligence/ abstract.**

abstraction: *n.* **1.** the process of selecting or isolating a certain aspect from a concrete whole, as a part of the process of evaluation or communication. ➤*Distg. fr.* **analy-**

sis, in which the totality is broken up (mentally) into all its parts, whereas **ab-straction** deals with the isolation of one part.—*Syn.* **abstracting.**—*adj.* **abstrac-tive. 2.** an idea or concept resulting from the process of abstracting; a verbal state-ment that utilizes abstract terms. ➤Some-times used derogatorily for an idea that has lost relationship with concrete facts: a mere *abstraction.* **3.** attention to one's own thoughts, with failure to attend to what goes on about one. ➤*Distg. fr.* **absent-mindedness,** which is a habitual way of acting.

abstraction factor: (*W. C. Halstead*) a hypothesized **unit factor** of **ability** that underlies the total ability to comprehend similarities, to compare, and to classify.— *Syn.* A FACTOR.

absurdities test: one in which the task is to detect the **absurdity** in a given pic-ture or writing.

absurdity: *n.* something that is contradic-tory (usually quite obviously) to accepted fact or general truth.—*adj.* **absurd.**

abulia (ə·bū′li·ə; -bü-): *n.* diminished ability to will effectively, or to make up one's mind.—*Var.* **aboulia.**—*adj.* **abulic.**

academic: *adj.* **1.** (usually cap.) related to the Platonic philosophy. **2.** having to do with formal schooling, particularly with those aspects involving study of books. **3.** unrelated to practical issues; theoretical (derogatory). **4.** pertaining to ideas and abstractions.

academic aptitude: see **aptitude/aca-demic.**

academic persistence: see **persistence/ academic.**

acalculia (ā″kal·kū′li·ə; ak″əl-): *n.* a form of **aphasia** characterized by loss of ability to carry out even very simple mathematical calculations.—*Syn.* NUMBER BLINDNESS.

acatamathesia (ə·kat″ə·mə·thē′zhə): *n.* impaired ability to comprehend perceived objects or situations; esp., inability to com-prehend the meaning of speech.

acataphasia (-fā′zhə): *n.* a sensory **aphasia** characterized by loss of power to use the phrasing and sentence structure of com-mon speech.—*Syn.* **aphasia/syntactical.**

acathexis (ak·ə·thek′səs): *n.* lack of **cathexis.**

accelerate: *n.* see **acceleration/educa-tional.**

acceleration: *n.* **1.** speeding up. **2.** rate of increase in change. ➤UNIFORM or CON-STANT or ZERO ACCELERATION means that there is the same amount of increase from one time unit to the next, e.g., when a wheel revolves three times in the first sec-ond, six in the next, nine in the third, twelve in the fourth. POSITIVE A. means that, with each successive time unit, the amount of in-crease increases, e.g., when the speed of revolution in successive seconds is 3, 6, 10, 15, 21. NEGATIVE A. is still acceleration; there is an increase (not a decrease) in rate of change which is less with each unit of time, e.g., when the number of revolutions in successive seconds is 21, 26, 30, 33, 35, 36. *Distg. fr.* DECELERATION, in which the speed decreases. Deceleration also may be POSITIVE, NEGATIVE, or CONSTANT. CONSTANT DECELERATION is illustrated by the series 36, 35, 34, 33; POSITIVE DECELERATION by the series 35, 34, 32, 29, 25; NEGATIVE DECELERA-TION by the series 35, 30, 26, 23, 21.

acceleration/bodily: the increase in the speed with which an individual is trans-ported through space. ➤The motion may be ANGULAR or RADIAL, as well as forward or backward.

acceleration/developmental: growth in some function at faster than normal rate; or the attainment of a higher level of devel-opment in some function than others of the same age have attained.—*Ant.* **retardation.** —*pers. n.* developmental **accelerate** (see **acceleration/educational**).

acceleration/educational: any process whereby a pupil makes educational progress faster than is usual, whether measured by advancement in school grade (*Amer.*) or standard (*Brit.*), or by actual educational achievement. ➤The means to such faster progress are many; the term **acceleration** should not be restricted to faster progress by grade-skipping.

An ACCELERATE is a pupil who has made faster progress than usual or expected. Con-fusion arises when the functions referred to are not carefully defined. A child of **mental *age (MA)** two years above his **chronological *age (CA)** is a DEVELOP-MENTAL ACCELERATE. If he is assigned to a class one year in advance of his CA, one year behind his MA, he is **accelerated** in respect to CA, **retarded** in respect to MA. Most children of superior intelligence are educationally retarded in relation to their aptitude—somewhat so if progress is meas-ured by educational achievement, severely so if it is measured by grade placement. On the other hand, most pupils of low scho-lastic aptitude are actually accelerated in grade placement (but not in achievement) in relation to their ability.—*Syn.* GRADE ACCELERATION.—*Ant.* **retardation.**

acceleration/scholastic = acceleration/ educational.

accent/subjective: rhythm read into a series of impressions (the beats of a metro-nome, a group of parallel lines) whose units lack **objective (3)** differences; also, meta-phorically, for any nonobjective emphasis. —*Cp.* **ictus,** which may be objective or subjective.—*Syn.* SUBJECTIVE RHYTHM.

acceptance: *n.* **1.** a receptive or positive attitude toward an idea or judgment; an approving reception.—*Syn.* **belief. 2.** an attitude or a relationship that recognizes the worth of a person without implying approval of particular behaviors, and without implying personal affection. ➤In counseling, an ACCEPTANCE REMARK conveys interest in, and understanding of—but not agreement or disagreement with—the counselee's statement, even when the latter expresses hostility or negative feeling.

acceptance/region of: see **critical region.**

acceptance therapy: a term for **release therapy,** proposed as more descriptive.

accessible: *adj.* **1.** open to approach or entrance; get-at-able. **2.** (*K. Lewin*) of a region in the **life space** that is open to psychological freedom of movement, or that can be reached either by locomotion or communication. **3.** ready to respond, or to respond **overtly,** to social stimuli. ➤A patient is **inaccessible** when he does not respond in any overt way to words or other social stimuli.

accessory: *adj.* additional or contributory. ➤Said especially of those parts of a sense organ which help to make reception of a **stimulus** more efficient, as distinguished from the essential parts.

accident: *n.* **1.** an event whose causes are unknown and therefore unpredictable. **2.** an event whose causes lie outside the system to which the event belongs. ➤If the cause of an event becomes known and understood, it is seen to form part of the system, hence, the effect is no longer to be called an accident. Meaning (2) is thus merely a more precise statement of (1). Since an event may belong to many systems of greater or less comprehensiveness, it may be accidental in relation to one system, nonaccidental in relation to a more comprehensive one. **Determinism** is the doctrine that in a final sense no event is accidental, i.e., without cause.—*Cp.* **chance. 3.** an event that was not intended or desired, especially one in which there is damage to persons or property.

accidental: *adj.* **1.** pertaining to an **accident;** characterizing an event as an accident. **2.** unpredictable. ➤This is properly a corollary of (1) but has itself come to be a defining meaning of the term.

accidental error: an unpredictable departure from the **true value** of a measurement. ➤In practice, the **mean** of a large series of measurements of whatever is being measured is taken to be the true value; the accidental error is the difference from this mean when all controllable factors have been eliminated or allowed for. It is assumed to be due to **random** or **chance** factors, whether in the person making the measure-

ment, in the measuring instrument, or in the thing or process measured.—*Distg. fr.* **constant** **error* or systematic **error.*—*Syn.* **chance** **error,* **variable error, random error.**

accident proneness: special susceptibility to accident. ➤Accident proneness may be conceived of as highly general, i.e., found in many sorts of situations; or as rather specific to such situations as driving automobiles or tending machinery. The term merely describes; it does not explain. Some accident proneness is said to be in a category of INTENTIONAL or PURPOSEFUL ACCIDENTS, that is, of "accidents" that satisfy some need of the individual.

acclimation (ak″lə·mā′shən): *n.* **1.** adaptation to climate. **2.** adaptation to continuous (as against repeated) stimulation. **3.** figuratively, mental and social adjustment to a new social environment.—*Syn.* ACCLIMATIZATION (ə·klī″mə·ti·zā′shən).

acclimatization = **acclimation.**

accommodation: *n.* **1.** movements that prepare a sense organ for receiving impressions distinctly; esp., **2.** adjustment of the focus of the eye for different distances. ➤The HYDRAULIC THEORY OF ACCOMMODATION asserts that this is accomplished by a properly balanced transfer of fluid, brought about by the ciliary muscle, from the front to the peripheral regions of the lens (or the reverse). **3.** the effect of a new experience in modifying the **schema** by which a person perceives or thinks. **4.** = **accommodation/ social. 5.** = **adaptation/sensory** (not *recom.*).

accommodation/absolute: (*vis.*) accommodation (2) of either eye separately.

accommodation/binocular: accommodation (2) of both eyes for a given distance.

accommodation/consensual: the simultaneous **accommodation** (2) of both eyes upon stimulation of either one.

accommodation/social: changes, in one or more of the parties to a social or interpersonal conflict, that reduce or eliminate the conflict: e.g., conciliation, compromise, giving in, revising the conception of the interpersonal relationship or of the nature of the conflict, etc. ➤There is usually an implication that the **accommodation** is made for the sake of social harmony.

accommodation time: the time elapsed from the beginning of stimulation to the achieving of visual **accommodation.**

accomplishment quotient: *obsoles.* for **achievement quotient.**

accomplishment test = **achievement test.**

accretion (ə·krē′shən): *n.* growth by addition. ➤This is the term for **growth** in nonorganic structures. The changes in an organism are never merely additive; the multiplication of cells and the increased size of organs and tissues always involve a change in structural pattern and in the dynamic interaction of functions.

accretion learning: the acquisition of highly unrelated facts or responses by dint of frequency of association.

acculturation: *n.* **1.** the processes whereby children learn the behavior patterns characteristic of their social group, esp. of the larger social group or **culture. 2.** the processes, witting or unwitting, whereby individuals assume the behavior patterns of an **in-group** sufficiently to be accepted into the group or to get along in it without friction, etc. **3.** acquisition, through contact, by peoples of one **culture** of cultural elements from another: e.g., the adoption of firearms and horses by the American Indian.—*Cp.* **diffusion, assimilation/cultural.**—*adj.* **accultural.**

accuracy: *n.* **1.** correspondence between a statement (or a measure) and a fact, thing, or event. **2.** in testing, the ratio between the number of items correct and the number attempted. ➤*Syn.* **Correctness** is correspondence with standards or requirements. **Precision** is measurement utilizing fine units. It is possible to be precise, yet neither correct nor accurate. **Accuracy** is freedom from all error, **reliability** from **variable errors** (but not necessarily from **constant errors**). Unless characterized as **absolute,** accuracy is relative and refers to the *degree of correspondence.*—*adj.* **accurate.**

accuracy compulsion: (*Ror.*) a tendency of the subject to be overly accurate with regard to the **form** qualities of the **content:** to make many corrections, to reject many of his own associations, to be helplessly dissatisfied with each response he gives and yet unable to improve it.

accuracy score: 1. the number or proportion of test items that are correctly answered by the subject. **2.** the degree of **accuracy** attained in performing a task.

accuracy test: see **test/accuracy.**

accurateness: *n.* the abstract quality of being accurate.

acenesthesia (ā″sen·es·thē′zhə): *n.* loss or lack of the normal perception of one's own body.—*Var.* **acoenaesthesia.**—See **cenesthesia.**

ACE (test): the American Council on Education test of intelligence, designed for higher secondary school and college students.

acetylcholine (as″ə·təl·kō′lēn): *n.* a substance released during activation of some or all nerves, and known to be related to the excitation of somatic muscles and some types of glands.

achievement: *n.* **1.** success in bringing an effort to the desired end. **2.** the end gained; the thing accomplished. **3.** the degree or level of success attained in some specified area (esp. scholastic) or in general.

achievement/academic or **/scholastic:** the attained ability to perform school tasks. It may be general, or specific to a given subject matter.

achievement age: achievement described in an **age equivalent.**—See **age/achievement.**

achievement battery: a collection of tests designed to measure the level of skill or knowledge attained in several areas of activity. ➤Used especially, but not exclusively, for tests of academic achievement. Each test or subunit of the **battery** covers a particular area of achievement.

achievement drive: the tendency to work with energy and persistence at something deemed important; ambition manifested in action. It is a scoring category in **TAT** tests.

achievement quotient or **AQ:** the ratio between the actual level of scholastic performance and that which is expected. Actual performance is measured by **achievement age** or **educational *age,** expected performance alternatively by **chronological *age** or **mental *age.** ➤The two methods of computation are by no means equivalent. The synonym **accomplishment quotient** is similarly ambiguous. Since these ratios tend to be unreliable, the easiest solution is to use neither the ratio nor the terms. The relation of school achievement to mental level (**MA**) may be phrased in terms of **underachievement** and **overachievement** (which see); of school achievement to chronological age in terms of **acceleration** or **retardation.**

achievement test: a measure of proficiency level gained by testing the performance actually displayed in a given field: e.g., journeyman's skill in plumbing, third-grade level in arithmetic (or other school subjects). ➤See **educational *age.** An achievement test is a kind of **ability test.** It is so constructed as to bring to light the relative excellence of the individual's past learning.

Achilles jerk: the reflex ankle jerk stimulated by a gentle tap on the Achilles tendon. —*Syn.* ANKLE REFLEX, ACHILLES TENDON REFLEX.

achondroplasia (ă·kon″drō·plā′zhə): *n.* defective development of the ends of the long bones, producing a peculiar type of dwarfism.

achromatic (ak″rō·mat′ik): *adj.* **1.** lacking in **chroma,** i.e., in **hue** and **saturation;** of a "colorless color," a visual datum on the dimension running from black through gray to white. **2.** of a lens system corrected for chromatic *aberration.—*n.* achromaticity (ə·krō″mə·tis′ə·ti).

achromatic color: a visual quality characterized by its degree of brightness or lightness, and showing no hue or saturation: e.g., gray, white, clear, silver.

achromatic color response or *C'*: a Rorschach category for reports mentioning black, gray, white, or lack of color.—*Distg. fr.* achromatic response.

achromatic response: a Rorschach category for reports mentioning texture or anything that is described as achromatic. ➤*Fc, c, C'* are all achromatic response coding symbols; thus, this category is more inclusive than achromatic color response.

achromatic stimulus: a visual stimulus that characteristically evokes an achromatic color.—*Syn.* NEUTRAL (COLOR) STIMULUS (not *prefd.*), ACHROMATIC LIGHT.

achromatop(s)ia (ə·krō″mə·top′(s)i·ə): *n.* vision in which all lights are seen as achromatic, i.e., without hue.—*Syn.* ACHROMATISM (*ambig.*, not *recom.*), total color blindness (which see).

acme: *n.* 1. the peak or height of feeling; culmination. 2. the climax of orgasm.

acmesthesia (ak″mes·thē′zhə): *n.* perceiving sharp points by touch but without feeling pain.—*Var.* acmaesthesia.—*Syn.* ACUESTHESIA.

acne: *n.* a chronic inflammatory condition of the skin of the face, back, and chest, marked by many pimples. ➤It is prevalent between puberty and age 30, and is often aggravated during menstruation or gastrointestinal upsets.

acoasm (ak′ō·az·əm): *n.* an auditory hallucination in which indefinite sounds, such as ringing or hissing, are heard.—*Var.* acouasm, acousma (ə·küz′mə).

acoenaesthesia = acenesthesia.

acoria (ə·kō′ri·ə): *n.* a sensation of hunger that is not relieved by taking food.—*Var.* akoria.

acou-, -acousia, -acousis: combining forms meaning *hearing.*

acoumeter (ə·kü′mə·tər) = audiometer. —*Var.* acumeter.

acousma = acoasm.

acoustic: *adj.* concerned with sound waves. ➤*Cp.* auditory, concerned with hearing, although the two are sometimes used as synonyms.

acoustics (ə·kü′stiks): *n.* 1. (*pl.*) the qualities of a room, hall, etc., that affect the distinctness with which sounds are heard or transmitted. 2. (*sing.*) the science of sound (usually limited to the physics of sound).—*Distg. fr.* audition.—*adj.* acoustic.

acquaintance index or volume: a list of all the persons an individual remembers as

having spoken to, or as having spoken to him, during a certain period.

acquaintance with: knowledge gained by personal experience. ➤*Contr. w.* comprehension, which is gained indirectly or through verbal means.

acquired behavior or response = ACQUIRED BEHAVIOR DIFFERENCES. ➤Strictly speaking, there is no behavior that is merely acquired; every behavior depends on both inheritance and acquisition through experience. Therefore, the qualifying adjectives, innate and acquired respectively, can refer only to the *differences* in behavior—the differences between the behavior of one individual and of another, or between behavior in childhood and in adulthood, etc. Whether one talks or not is a question not of heredity alone nor of experience alone, but of both; the differences, however, in manner or amount of talking may be ascribable *primarily* to heredity (in which case they may be called INNATE BEHAVIOR DIFFERENCES), or they may be ascribable *primarily* to experience (in which case they may be called ACQUIRED BEHAVIOR DIFFERENCES). The shortened forms INNATE BEHAVIOR or ACQUIRED BEHAVIOR should be used only when the context makes fully clear that only *differences* are meant.—See character/acquired, heredity, maturation, learning.

acquired character or characteristic: see character/acquired.

acquisition: *n.* 1. gaining, adding, or incorporating something on the part of an organism; or that which is gained. ➤For psychology the term is a loose synonym for learning or maturation, or both. It includes the addition of new ideas or information, and the gaining of new modes of response or alteration of old ones. 2. an increase in the strength of the tendency to respond after the administration of a reward.—*v.* acquire.

acquisitive: *adj.* having a strong desire to possess or to hoard.—*n.* acquisitiveness.

acro- (ak′rō-): combining form meaning *topmost* or *extremity*; hence, the crown of the head, or the fingers and toes, or a high place: e.g., acromegaly, a disease of the extremities; acrophobia, a fear of high places.—See neologism.

acromegaly (-meg′ə·li): *n.* a form of hyperpituitary gigantism characterized also by increased size of hands, feet, face, and some internal organs.—*Var.* acromegalia (-mə·gā′li·ə).—*adj.* acromegalic (-mə·gal′ik).

acromicria (-mik′ri·ə): *n.* underdevelopment of extremities and skull as compared to development of other body organs.

acromicria/congenital = mongolism.

acroparesthesia (-par″es·thē′zhə): *n.* recurrent numbness, esp. of the extremities.

acrophobia: *n.* pathological fear of being in high places.—See **phobia.**

act: *n.* **1.** a psychological unit in the continuous interplay between a living organism and its environment; a unit of psychological activity; a concrete instance of what an organism or a person does. ➤The continuous interplay may be described as either conscious process or behavior. **2.** (*neobehaviorism*) a set of behaviors having a unity defined by the kind of effect they have upon the external world. ➤E.g., eating is composed of the separate behaviors of moving the jaws in sundry ways, salivating, and swallowing, but it has unity insofar as it leads to ingesting food. Different ways of eating are then considered equivalent acts. It is difficult to stipulate how "effects in the external world" are to be distinguished without implying that they are purposive—for which reason many of this school prefer to speak of **molar behavior** (thus emphasizing merely the complexity of a set of related behaviors) and to define what constitutes the unity of the set in terms of correlation of occurrence. **3.** (*act psychology*) an integration of **cognition, feeling,** and **conation** as inseparable aspects, not separable parts, in a person's interaction with environment. ➤This is the usage also of many who would not class themselves as **act psychologists.** The emphasis upon the unity of the act distinguishes act psychology from **stimulus-response psychology.**

For many psychologists, **act** is the fundamental concept of psychology; it is correspondingly difficult to define. It is a unit of behavior, of conduct, of what a person does. But how does this unit differ from the unit of physiological activity? The two chief answers—**dualism** and **emergentism** —are clearly metaphysical. It is too often forgotten that the denial of a distinction— **monism**—is no less so.

If we turn from the effort at a fundamental definition to its actual use in context, **act** is distinguishable from a number of other terms. They are here treated in relation to act; in their own proper places they are further discussed.

Action is properly an abstract name for the fact of acting; but (esp. in the plural) it is often merely an untechnical term for act. Sometimes it carries an implication of volition or intent. It is also used for a complex of acts: walking is an **action** composed of the *acts* of stepping.

Activity is a general name for the functioning of an organism, including the physiological as well as the psychological (in whatever way these are to be distinguished). As a collective noun, activity often has a quantitative modifier: intense *activity,* intermittent *activity.*

Behavior, originally a collective term for acts and still so used, received a specially limited meaning in **behaviorism.** The emphasis upon integration of cognition, feeling, and conation was pushed aside as meaningless, and the fundamental identity of behavior with physiological activity—a flagrantly metaphysical doctrine—was asserted. Yet concretely, a specific behavior refers to the same event as an act; and act psychology—and in general stimulus-response psychology—use the term so, without the limitations introduced by behaviorism.

Conduct is an act or action judged by social standards, particularly by moral standards.

Movement is applied to the change of position of a bodily part as a result of organic functioning. Usually there is no necessary reference to environment. In contrast, an act always implies a changed relationship between organism and environment, and the act is usually named for its consequences outside the organism. By some, however, this difference is denied; movement is considered to be the executive aspect of an act, or simply to be the act.

Reaction is also a synonym; but whereas act somewhat emphasizes the role of the organism, reaction emphasizes that the act is elicited by an event outside the organism, the stimulus. Reaction is more naturally used for very simple acts.

Response refers sometimes to the whole act, but sometimes to parts of the act, generally with the implication that such parts are separable and at least relatively independent: e.g., a motor or glandular *response,* a perceptual *response,* less often, a thinking or affective *response.*

act: *v.* to do; to operate; to function; to perform; to respond to environment; to be· have.—See **act** *n.*

ACTH: *n.* adrenocorticotropic hormone: a **hormone** produced in the pituitary which acts on the cortex of the adrenals. ➤It is used in the treatment of various diseases, and experimentally in some psychological disorders.

acting out: manifesting the purposive behavior appropriate to an older situation in a new situation which symbolically represents it. ➤*Cp.* **transference,** which is a form of acting out; and **catharsis,** which attributes curative value to acting out under certain conditions.

action: *n.* **1.** an abstract term for the fact of **acting. 2.** = **act. 3.** behavior with **volition** or **intent. 4. organismic** movements correlated with conscious process. **5.** a unified sequence or complex of **acts** or **behaviors. 6.** any physiological process.

➤This use is rare, but is implied in combinations, such as heart *action,* **action current.**—See **act** *n.*

action current: change in electric potential of a nerve or muscle during physiological activity.—See **EEG, EDR.**—*Syn.* **action potential.**

action/law of determined: the **Gestalt** theorem that an object moves only within the limits prescribed by the whole **field** of which it is a part.

action/mass = **mass activity.**—See also **mass action theory.**

action potential: the measure, in terms of electric potential, of the **action current;** often used as a synonym for the latter.

action quotient = **activity quotient.**

action research: use of scientific research principles for the study of **actions** that are aimed at a comprehensive goal. ➤Generally, the research is done by some of the participants in the program of action. In **action research** the activities studied are undertaken in the hope of achieving certain useful results, and the research is designed to effect improvement in the ongoing process, not merely in some future process. In pure experiment, by contrast, activities are prescribed primarily to obtain data that may be analyzed for scientific or technological generalization. When, however, practical programs of action are modified in such fashion as to facilitate research analysis, the distinction is one of degree.

action-specific energy: see **energy/action-specific.**

action/stream of: the never-ceasing succession of **acts** and activities of a living organism. Emphasis is upon the connectedness or continuity of action rather than upon the distinguishable **action units** in the flow.—*Cp.* **consciousness/stream of.**

action system or **mechanism: 1.** the efferent nerves and the muscles or glands participating in a specific response. **2.** the entire set of **organismic** or **personal** structures involved in accomplishing a certain behavioral result—e.g., the visual and kinesthetic receptors, the nerves, the muscles, and the brain structures involved in kicking a football. ➤Emphasis is upon the executive aspect, but some reference to the cognitive factors guiding execution may be included. The term is generally used where fairly complex activities, with alternative means to the same end, are involved.—*Cp.* **disposition, habit, sentiment,** all of which are action systems in this sense.

action unit: a unit of behavior; an episode that begins with a specific **need** and ends in **goal** achievement.—*Syn.* **act.**

activation: *n.* making active or reactive; preparing for action. ➤Used of one organ or system acting upon another, and therefore distinguished from **stimulation,** which should be restricted to external influence. The LEVEL OF ACTIVATION of the whole system is the degree of **tension.**

activation theory (of emotion): the theory that defines emotion as one end of the continuum of **activation:** when the several organismic systems are interacting vigorously with each other, we have emotion; when there is little interaction, we have sleep.

active: *adj.* **1.** acting; working; functioning. **2.** causing action; pertaining to a cause of action. **3.** characterized by much activity or movement or change. **4.** of an attitude or role characterized by spontaneity, initiative, vigor. **5.** pertaining to, or resembling, the behavior of the male in sex activities; hence, of malelike activities in **homosexuality.** *Contr. w.* **reactive.**

active analysis or **active psychotherapy:** see **therapy/active.**

activism: *n.* **1.** (*educ.*) the doctrine that **activity** is necessary to learning. **2.** the set of doctrines on which **activist psychology** is based.—See **psychology/divisions and schools of, V.**

activist psychology: see **reactive.**

activity: *n.* **1.** anything an organism does or that happens within an organism; anything requiring expenditure of energy by an organism. **2.** a bodily process or group of processes as studied in physiology; a physiological **function.** ➤In this sense it contrasts with **behavior,** or **act,** which designates a psychological **function.** This would be a useful meaning if it could be consistently maintained—which is unlikely. **3.** a group of responses possessing at least a low degree of organization toward a specific result, generally with the implication that the character of the behavior is determined more largely from within the organism than by stimulation: e.g., the *activity* of putting a meal on the table.—See **activity** under **act. 4.** (*educ.*) an organized behavior, approved by the teacher as contributing to the child's development, but engaged in by the child because of intrinsically satisfying elements or because it leads to a goal sought by the child. ➤This actually covers many classroom behaviors organized about traditional subject matter, but the term usually refers to behaviors organized about some other focus.—*Cp.* **activity school. 5.** (*educ.*) large-muscle **overt** bodily activity, in contrast with small-muscle, or **covert,** activity.

activity analysis or **inventory:** list of the acts actually performed by a given person or in a given type of situation or job. ➤The list is intended to be as objective and as free from theory as possible, a mere unvarnished description. It is often a summary of **activity sampling**.

activity cage: a revolving wire drum, like the familiar squirrel treadmill, provided with a mechanical revolution-counter to measure certain movements of the animal; or any analogous instrument.—*Syn*. ACTIVITY WHEEL.

activity concept: a generalization that learning takes place only when the person is active. ➤This is too often misunderstood to imply the necessity of **overt** activity.

activity cycles: rhythms, or regular variations, in the amount of bodily activity displayed over a period of time.

activity drive or **need**: 1. the tendency of an animal to engage in physical activity, even in the absence of extra-organic stimulus. 2. tendency of an animal to exercise any of its capacities: muscular, sensory, or intellectual; tendency to be active.

activity/extracurricular: see **extracurricular activity**.

activity/learning: see **learning process** (2) and (3).

activity/mass: see **mass activity**.

activity quotient: the ratio of activity words to qualitative words in a person's speech or writing; in practice, the ratio of the total number of verbs to the total number of adjectives. ➤This ratio is proposed as a measure of emotionality.—*Syn*. ACTION QUOTIENT.

activity rating: the proportion of a person's time given to quiet activities in relation to total activities.

activity sampling: a technique for determining exactly what a person does at a given task or during a given time. ➤Emphasis is upon objective and relatively detailed description, often including the time order in which responses are made. A **behavior check list** may or may not be used.

activity school: one in which the learning of the pupils is organized around their purposeful pursuit of certain activities or projects rather than around the traditional subjects and skills.—See **activity (4)**.

activity wheel = **activity cage**.

actone (ak′tōn): *n*. 1. (*H. A. Murray*) an adaptive act that is peculiar to the individual or to the specific occasion. 2. a single reflexlike simple response.

actor: one who acts or performs; a **person** in *active* relation to environment.—*Syn*. **person** (which see).

act psychology: 1. (*F. Brentano*) the point of view that every psychic or mental phenomenon "intends," i.e., refers to, an object other than itself, and that the referring (not the object) is the distinctive subject matter of psychology. The act of referring may take the form of cognizing, liking-disliking, or

evaluating. 2. the view that psychology studies the act, or that special kind of act called a **psychic act**.—See **act**, esp. (2). ➤If explicit attention is given to the actor as well, act psychology combines with **personalism**. If attention is given to the object of the act as a special kind of object, act psychology joins with **phenomenology**. Act psychology may be **reactive** (in which case it merges with stimulus-response psychology), but it is more often the doctrine of those viewing psychology in active terms. —See **psychology/divisions and schools of**, III.

act/pure-stimulus or **r**: (*C. Hull*) an act that does not bring the organism nearer the goal but sets up the **proprioceptive** stimuli that actually initiate **operant** response. ➤This is Hull's substitute for many of the processes others call instrumental **ideas**.

act regression: a reversion to a previously **extinguished CR** when a barrier is interposed in the road of a CR related to the extinguished CR.—See **extinction**.

actual: *adj*. 1. existing in fact, as opposed to the potential, possible, or theoretical. 2. existing in the present, as opposed to the future and the past. ➤*Cp*. **real**. In several European languages, the word cognate with **actual** has the second meaning; this has influenced the meaning of the English word in combinations that are translations of foreign terms.—See also **actual** **neurosis* for a different meaning.

actuarial: *adj*. 1. pertaining to the **probability** statistics employed in insurance; hence, 2. of generalizations that embody and state relationships in terms of **probability** or relative frequency of occurrence. ➤An actuarial principle takes the form: *Thirty persons in a thousand show this behavior*. *Distg. fr.* scientific **law**. While probability statistics are generally employed in the formulation of laws, the law itself is stated in **categorical** absolutes: *All* cats have fur.

actuarial table: a tabulation showing the proportion of people in a population who reach *x* years of age.—*Syn*. MORTALITY TABLE.

acuesthesia (ak″yü·es·thē′zhə) = **acmesthesia**.—*Var*. **acuaesthesia**.

acuity: *n*. sharpness or keenness of **perception**.—See also **acuity/sensory** and **acuity/visual**.—*Cp*. **sensitivity**.—*adj*. **acute**.

acuity grating: a block of alternate black and white lines very close together, used to determine the **minimum separable**—that is, how far apart the retinal image of two objects must be to be seen as two.

acuity/sensory: 1. the ability to respond to **sense data** of low intensity, duration, or extent. ➤Included is the ability to respond to "*something* there" when one is unable to discriminate *what* is there. 2. the degree to which the subject can distinguish between sense data that differ in intensity, extent, duration, position, temporal order, or quality; = **sensory discrimination.** 3. the ability to distinguish details of a sensory pattern, to resolve a sensory pattern: to hear the second overtone, to see the small speck of red in a fabric.—*Cp.* **visual *acuity.

acuity/visual:** the ability of the human visual mechanism to distinguish small spatial separations or intervals between portions of the visual field. The closer two points can be distinguished as two, the higher the acuity. ➤Many kinds of test objects are used to measure acuity, the most familiar being the **Snellen** (letter) **chart.** Visual acuity is determined not by one but by many factors in the visual mechanism: e.g., myopia, diplopia, astigmatism all affect it adversely. ¶The commonest statement of visual acuity is in terms of a ratio between the distance at which the tested eye can make a given discrimination and that at which a normal eye can make it. Thus, $20/15$ means that one can see at 20 feet what a normal eye can see at 15 (better-than-normal vision); $20/20$ means normal visual acuity; $20/40$ means that one can see at 20 feet what a normal eye can see at 40, etc. ¶Note that acuity has a somewhat special meaning in visual acuity, since it is restricted to the discrimination of space intervals, whereas in other uses it refers to discrimination of stimuli of low quantity.—See **acuity/sensory.**

acumeter (ə·kū′mə·tər) = **audiometer.**

-acusia, -acusis: combining forms meaning *hearing.*

acute: *adj.* 1. keenly sensitive, either to thought or to sensory impressions. 2. of pains of great sharpness and intensity. 3. of a disease or symptom with sudden onset and of relatively short duration: *acute* hallucinosis. ➤*Contr. w.* CHRONIC conditions, which are long-persisting. SUBACUTE is applied to intermediate forms.—*n.* **acuity** for (1); **acuteness** for (2) and (3).

acute brain disorders: (*Stan. Psychiat.*) a symptom complex due to temporary, reversible, diffuse impairment of brain tissue function: e.g., the disordered behavior due to overuse of barbiturates.

AD or **A.D.** = average deviation (see **deviation/mean** and **variability).**

Ad: (*Ror.*) scoring code for parts of living animals.

-ad: (*anat.*) suffix to indicate *toward, in the direction of.* ➤This suffix is often preferable to **-al** or **-ic,** which are general and vague. E.g., **cephalic** may mean *pertaining to, forming part of, characteristic of,* or *in the region of, the head*; **cephalad** means more specifically *toward the head, on the head side.* **Dextral** means almost anything *pertaining to the right side,* **dextrad** means precisely *toward the right side.*

adaptability: *n.* ability to make appropriate responses to changed or changing circumstances.—*Syn.* **docility.**—*adj.* **adaptable.**

adaptation: *n.* 1. originally, change in structure or behavior that has survival value; now, more generally, any beneficial change to meet environmental demand. 2. settling down to the conditions for work or learning, with the elimination of unnecessary preparatory behavior. 3. = **social *adaptation.** 4. = **sensory *adaptation.** 5. the progressive lessening of clearness of an object steadily attended to. ➤This is a phenomenon of **attention.** *Distg. fr.* the receptor phenomenon of **sensory *adaptation.** 6. a confusing synonym for **habituation.**

See also **adaptability,** and discussion under **adjustment.**—*adj.* **adaptative, adaptive** (*prefd.*), usually referring to the effect of adaptation, **adaptational,** to the processes.—*v.* **adapt,** to modify something as a means to **adaptation** (1); reflexively, to change oneself for better **adaptation** (1). (The noun is preferably spelled **adaptation,** not *adaption.*)

adaptation board: a test in which pegs must be placed in holes in such a way as to copy a pattern presented in a different spatial orientation.

adaptation/brightness: decrease in the **brilliance** of objects due to increase in the general **illumination** of the visual field; reduced responsiveness to a given **brightness** level due to intense general illumination. ➤The reduced responsiveness lasts for some time after the intense illumination is reduced.—*Syn.* PHOTOPIC ADAPTATION, LIGHT ADAPTATION.—See **adaptation/sensory** (2).

adaptation/chromatic: 1. the process whereby the visual mechanism reaches equilibrium when stimulated by chromatic light; the gradual lessening of sensitivity to **hue** and/or **saturation** consequent upon continued stimulation by chromatic stimuli. 2. the alteration of hue and/or saturation due to prior exposure to light of another wave length.—*Syn.* CHROMATIC (or COLOR) FATIGUE.—*Cp.* **adaptation/sensory** (2) and **Purkinje phenomenon.**

adaptation/darkness or **/dark:** see **dark adaptation.**

adaptation level or **AL:** (*H. Helson*) the hypothesized neutral point or region of organic functioning at which stimuli coinciding with AL are indifferent or ineffective, stimuli above AL have a given character, and stimuli below AL have an opposite or complementary quality. ➤AL represents the pooled effect of three classes of factors: (a) stimuli immediately responded to, or in the focus of attention; (b) stimuli having background or contextual influence; and (c) residuals from past experience with similar stimuli. Quantitatively, AL is a log mean of these three classes of factors, weighted according to relevant dimensions of effectiveness, e.g., size, nearness, intensity, quality, affective value, significance, etc.

adaptation/negative: 1. reduced responsiveness of sensory function consequent upon continued stimulation; esp., 2. the raising of the sensory **threshold** by continued stimulation. 3. the gradual weakening of the motor response as a result of continued stimulation. ➤This phenomenon is not merely, though it may be in part, the result of reduced sensory responsiveness. Muscular fatigue and many other factors also contribute. 4. = *experimental *extinction (*prefd.*). 5. = adaptation (5).

adaptation/photopic=adaptation/brightness (*prefd.*).

adaptation/scotopic = dark adaptation (*prefd.*).—See **adaptation/sensory** (1).

adaptation/sensory: 1. the maintenance of sensory effectiveness under changing conditions of stimulation; = POSITIVE ADAPTATION, esp. DARKNESS ADAPTATION, whereby the eye partially maintains acuity under reduced illumination. 2. reduced responsiveness of sensory function consequent upon continued stimulation; = NEGATIVE ADAPTATION. ➤*Distg. fr.* **refractory phase,** which is a phenomenon of the nerve rather than of the sense organ.

The two meanings are almost opposite in reference to the sensory function, but not in reference to **adaptation** (1). Reduced responsiveness is in many cases adaptive. Thus, reduced responsiveness to odors is usually helpful; and **brightness *adaptation** (which is reduced responsiveness) is adaptive quite as much as its opposite, DARKNESS ADAPTATION (which is the maintenance of responsiveness).

adaptation/social: 1. accepting and meeting the usual demands of society, and of one's personal relations with others, without undue strain or friction. 2. the processes by which a group or institution comes into such relation with its environment as to survive and prosper.—*Cp.* adaptation (1).—*Syn.* adjustment/social (*prefd.*).

adaptation time: the time from the beginning of a continuous and steady stimulation to the moment when no further change in sensory responsiveness occurs.

adaptation/visual: see visual adaptation.

adapted information: (*J. Piaget*) conversational remarks that show adaptation to

the point of view of a specific hearer or hearers and are designed for exchange of thought. ➤Said to be a sign of growing maturity in childhood.

adaption: a corruption of **adaptation.**

adaptive: *adj.* pertaining to improvement, or to that which aids **adjustment** or **adaptation,** esp. **adaptation** (1).—See **adaptation** (1–4).

adaptive behavior: any behavior that helps the organism meet environmental demands. ➤Two criteria frequently implied are capacity to profit from past experience, and capacity to initiate new and more complex experiences.—*Syn.* adaptation (1), adjustment.

adaptometer (ad″ap·tom′ə·tər): *n.* a device for measuring degree of **sensory** *adaptation (2).

addend (ad′end; ə·dend′): *n.* a code number for each category of a variable such that the sum of the numbers for every possible combination of categories constitutes a distinctive code number for the combination. ➤Thus, suppose we categorize individuals as adult or nonadult, male or nonmale, high-scoring on a test or non-high-scoring. If we assign a code number of *1* to adult, *2* to male, *4* to high-scoring, every possible combination of the three categories can be represented by a unique number: *1* for adult but not male or high-scoring; *3* for adult male, but not high-scoring (adding *1* and *2*); *6* for male, high-scoring, but not adult (adding *2* and *4*); *5* for adult, high-scoring, but not male (adding *1* and *4*); *7* for all three categories (adding *1, 2, 4*). **Addends** may also be used for combinations of categories of more than one variable. The addends are not magnitudes but merely a convenient coding device.

addiction: *n.* slavery to a pernicious habit, esp. the taking of certain drugs.—See **drug addiction.**

Addison's disease: a chronic debilitating disorder of the **adrenals.**

additional score: (*Ror.*) **content** reported as an afterthought, or **content** withdrawn after being given.—*Contr. w.* main score.

addition facts: the 100 statements of the possible combinations, two at a time, of one-digit numbers, from $0 + 0 = 0$ to $9 + 9 = 18$, including permutations.

additive: *adj.* capable of being treated by the arithmetical process of addition; or of a result reached by addition. ➤Perhaps the commonest error in science is the adding of things that cannot be added. There are several mathematical restrictions on adding (e.g., the units must be of the same category). And there is the restriction that things can be added only for a given measuring purpose, or if they are alike in respect to some dimension: cabbages and kings can be added only if the purpose is to find the number of heads in an aggregate. The ADDITIVE ASSUMPTION, that any two can be added to any other two to make four, is usually unwitting.

additive *W*: (*Ror.*) an **inkblot** response in which the subject reports details which he eventually combines into a **whole response.**

adduction: see **abduction.**

adenoids: *n. pl.* spongy tissues between the back of the nose and the throat. If enlarged, they interfere with breathing and lead to lowering of the behavior level.

adenoma (ad"ə·nō'mə): *n.* one kind of tumor.

adequate response: see **response adequacy.**

adequate stimulus: see **stimulus/adequate.**

adhesion principle: name given by K. Lewin to the non-Gestalt conception of psychological causation that one event brings about the revival of a second because they have been stuck together.—*Cp.* **contiguity, cohesion.**

***ad hoc* hypothesis** (ad' hok'): (*L. ad hoc: for this purpose, for this case only*) a hypothesis designed to account for the discrepancy between a basic theory and a particular finding that could not otherwise be fitted into the theory. ➤Such hypotheses need not be invalid, but if they are numerous the explanation loses simplicity.—*Cp.* **parsimony.**

adiadochokinesis (ad"i·ad·ō"kō·kin·ē'səs): *n.* 1. inability to make rapidly alternating movements. 2. incessant movement. ➤Alas, all this struggle for a precise word, only to have it end up in a contradiction.

> Ad-i-ad-o-cho-kin-e-sis
> Is a term that will bolster my thesis
> That 'tis idle to seek
> Such precision in Greek
> When confusion it only increases.

adient behavior or **response** (ad'i·ənt): behavior that exposes the organism to more of a given stimulus, either by approach or by action that maintains the stimulus. ➤*Contr. w.* **abient behavior,** which leads away from the stimulus.—*Syn.* POSITIVE BEHAVIOR (*ambig.*), APPROACH-(ING) RESPONSE.

adiposogenital syndrome (ad"i·pō"sō·-jen'ə·təl sin'drō·mi): obesity and childlike sex development in adolescence, caused by disorder of the anterior **pituitary.**

adjusted: *adj.* 1. pertaining to **adjustment** (1, 2, 4). 2. (*stat.*) corrected.—See **smoothing.**

adjustment: *n.* 1. a static equilibrium between an organism and its surroundings in which there is no stimulus change evoking

a response, no need is unsatisfied, and all the continuative functions of the organism are proceeding normally. ➤Such complete adjustment is never attained; it is a theoretical end of a continuum of degrees of partial adjustment. 2. a condition of harmonious relation to the environment wherein one is able to obtain satisfaction for most of one's needs and to meet fairly well the demands, physical and social, put upon one; = RELATIVE ADJUSTMENT (the only actual kind). 3. the process of making the changes needed, in oneself or in one's environment, to attain relative adjustment.—*Syn.* **adaptation, accommodation, conformity.** ➤Adaptation emphasizes modification to meet changed circumstances and flexibility in doing so; **accommodation** is social and suggests conciliation and compromise; **conformity** means the bringing of something into harmony with a standard or principle; **adjustment** emphasizes (more than does adaptation) the bringing of things into proper or harmonious relationship, perhaps more by skill or judgment than by mere flexibility. 4. (*stat.*) = **smoothing.**—*adj.* **adjusted,** for (1), (2), (4); **adjustive,** for (3).—*v.* **adjust,** for (3) and (4).

adjustment/emotional: a state of relatively stable and moderate emotional responsiveness.

adjustment/interpersonal: see **adjustment/social.**

adjustment inventory: see **inventory/adjustment.**

adjustment level: the degree to which an individual has effected a harmonious relation with his environment.—See **adjustment,** esp. (2).

adjustment mechanism: see **mechanism** (4).

adjustment of observations or **of measurements:** 1. correction of observed values to make proper allowance for disturbed conditions: e.g., the allowance made in a mental-age scale for the fact that most of the seriously defective children were not included in the standardization. 2. utilizing the principle of **least squares** to obtain the most probable value to represent a series of independent measurements of the same magnitude.—See **smoothing.**

adjustment/personal = **adjustment** (2).

adjustment procedure or **method:** The subject adjusts a stimulus object until it seems to him equal (or in other prescribed relationship) to a criterion object: i.e., he reproduces the criterion; hence also called METHOD OF REPRODUCTION. A threshold of the error is computed by taking the average deviation from objective equality; hence the name METHOD OF AVERAGE (or MEAN) ERROR.—Also *syn.* ADJUSTMENT OF EQUIVALENT-STIMULUS METHOD. ➤In all these terms, **procedure** (although less usual) is preferred to **method**.

adjustment scale: a scale for the rating of an individual's **adjustment (2).** ➤Different kinds of reactions to certain verbally described standard or typical situations are given a descriptive or a numerical value. The situations are such as to require emotional and social responses. The rating can be made by self or others.

adjustment/social: 1. a person's harmonious relationship with his social environment.—See **adjustment (2). 2.** the process of modifying the demands and the behaviors of persons interacting with each other so that they can achieve and maintain a certain desired relationship. The modification may be mutual or one-sided.—*Syn.* **accommodation/social.**—*v.* **adjust.**

adjustment/statistical = **correction (4).**

adjustment/vocational: see **vocational adjustment.**

Adlerian psychology: the body of doctrine set forth by A. Adler. Its essential principle is that behavior is controlled by an effort, usually unwitting, to compensate for deficiency or inferiority, whether physical, psychological, or social.

administration: *n.* **1.** the determination of purposes and policies in an enterprise.—*Cp.* **management** and **executive.** In practice, administrative and executive functions are often combined, thus blurring a useful distinction. **2.** the giving out of something, or the supervision of some activity: *administration* of drugs, treatment, tests.—*v.* **administer.**

adolescence: *n.* the period from the beginning of **puberty** to the attainment of **maturity;** the transitional stage during which the youth is becoming an adult man or woman. ➤A few authors speak of **adolescence** as beginning with the close, not with the initiation, of puberty. The period is defined in terms of development in many different functions which may be reached at different times. Hence only conventional limits may be stated; these are usually given as ages 12–21 for girls, 13–22 for boys. —*adj.* and *pers. n.* **adolescent.**

adolescent spurt: an acceleration in the growth rate, esp. in height, that occurs shortly before, or in the early years of, adolescence. It does not appear in all children.

adoption: *n.* the voluntary acceptance of a child of other parents as one's own; esp., such acceptance as sanctioned by a legal process.

adrenal (ad·rē'nəl): *adj.* **1.** located near the kidney. **2.** pertaining to the **adrenal glands** or their secretions.

adrenal cortex: the outermost layer of the **adrenal glands** which is the source of **cortin.**

adrenal glands: endocrine glands, lying just above the kidneys, which produce **cortin** and **adrenalin.**—*Syn.* ADRENALS, SUPRARENAL GLANDS.

adrenalin (ə·dren'əl·in): *n.* a **hormone** secreted by the central or medullary portion of the **adrenal glands.** ➤Its chief effects seem to be: stimulating the liver to production of blood sugar, increasing the coagulation rate of the blood, and increasing the sensitivity of the muscles to neural impulses, thus facilitating contraction.— *Syn.* EPINEPHRINE, ADRENIN. Epinephrine is, properly, the hormone secreted by the adrenals; adrenalin and adrenin are names of proprietary products, but the three terms are often used interchangeably.

adrenals = **adrenal glands.**

adrenergic (ad″ren·ėr'jik): *adj.* **1.** acting like **adrenalin. 2.** characterizing the hypothesized action of certain nerve fibers that produce at their terminals a substance called **sympathin,** similar to adrenalin.

adrenin = **adrenalin.**

adrenocorticotropic hormone = **ACTH.**

adult (ə·dult'; ad'ult): *adj.* fully grown or matured in all respects or in any specified respect. Human adulthood is generally attained in the early twenties.—*pers. n.* **adult.** —*abstr. n.* **adulthood.**

adult education: organized effort for furthering the culture or the vocational skill of mature persons, no matter at what point their schooling (in the usual sense) may have been interrupted.

adultomorphism: *n.* interpretation of children's behavior in adult terms.—*Syn.* ENELICHOMORPHISM.—*Cp.* **anthropomorphism.**

advantage by illness: the gratification secured from being ill. ➤E.g., the ill person need not work—this is a direct, PRIMARY, or PARANOSIC, GAIN. SECONDARY GAIN, or EPINOSIC ADVANTAGE, is the gratification received from a neurotic illness, secondary to an original illness. Thus a person suffering from the deprivation of the close personal attention that in childhood characterized his relation with his mother may regain that relation by becoming ill.—*Syn.* GAIN BY ILLNESS.

advantage/principle of: Of two or more incompatible responses to the same situation, one has an advantage over the others and occurs more frequently.—*Cp.* **prepotent response.**

adversive movement: a rotation of the eyes, head, or trunk about the long axis of the body.

advice: *n.* in counseling, careful and considered recommendation to a counselee as to a course of conduct.—*v.* **advise.**

advocacy (ad'və·kə·si): *n.* propaganda in which the propagandist's purpose is openly announced, and deliberate distortion is

avoided.—*Cp.* **propaganda.**—*v.* and *pers.*
n. **advocate.**

Adx: (*Ror.*) symbol for the response of see-ing a part or detail (*d*) of an animal (*A*) where most persons would see the whole. ➤Originally called OLIGOPHRENIC RESPONSE.

-ae-: alternative spelling for *-e-* in many Greek or Latin words. Most words in *ae* are spelled *e* in this dictionary.

aero- (ãr'ō-; ã'ər·ō-): combining form denoting *air, aerial;* or *gas, gasses.*

aero-otitis media (-ō·tī'təs mē'di·ə): traumatic inflammation of the middle ear initiated by a difference between the pres-sure within the middle ear and that of the surrounding air.

aerophagia (-fã'ji·ə): *n.* (*Gk.* for *air-eat-ing*) au.omatic gulping of air.—*Syn.* AER-OPHAGY (-of'ə·ji).

aesthesiometer: see **esthesiometer.**

aesthetics: see **esthetics.**

aetiology: see **etiology.**

A factor = abstraction factor.

affect (af'ekt): *n.* 1. a class name for feel-ng, emotion, mood, temperament. ➤Historically, three modes of mental func-tion were usually distinguished: **cogni-tion, conation** (or **volition**), and **affect** (more often called **affection**). Some writers, however, combined conation and affection. Many contemporary theorists hold that there is no separate affect-state, but only an affective or feeling aspect of a cog-nitive state or process. 2. a class name for a particular kind of feeling or emotion, gen-erally one with a name: e.g., joy or excite-ment; practically = an **emotion.** 3. a par-ticular instance of **feeling** or emotion; a single feeling-response to a particular object or idea. 4. a feeling-state or psychic tension, accompanied by noticeable bodily activity. ➤This probably refers to the same events as do (2) and (3). 5. = **affection** (1). 6. the general reaction toward something as liked or disliked.—*Syn.* **valence.** 7. the dynamic or essential quality of an emotion; the energy of an emotion.

Any combination of these meanings is likely to be found. ¶Note that the common verb *affect* (ə·fekt') differs in both pro-nunciation and meaning. *Distg.* also *fr.* **effect** *n.* and *v.*—*adj.* (also for **affection**) **affective.**—*v.* feel, emote.

affect/appropriateness of: the degree to which emotional responses are congruent with those normally to be expected in a given situation.

affectation: *n.* an artificial or assumed man-ner intended to impress.—*adj.* **affected.**

affect conversion: see **conversion of affect.**

affect/displacement of: a shift of feeling or emotion from the object originally arous-ing it to some **associated** object. ➤Psy-choanalysts hold that in dreams the **affect**

often shifts to unimportant elements, even to an opposed object, as a result of the ac-tivity of the **censorship;** and in general that the **displacement** is a **defense re-action** whereby **affect** seems (to the sub-ject or to others) to be aroused by a socially approved rather than a disapproved situation. Marked disparity between the **affect** and the ostensible cause is con-sidered a sign of at least partial **displace-ment.**—*Syn.* AFFECTIVE DISPLACEMENT.

affect/externally aroused: emotion result-ing from factors exterior to the individual.

affect/fixation of: see fixation (2).

affect/floating: see floating **affect.**

affect hunger: craving for **affection** (2). ➤Since **affect** does not mean **affection** in this sense, AFFECTION HUNGER is preferred.

affect/internally aroused: emotion result-ing from internal factors.

affect/inversion of: see **inversion of affect.**

affection: *n.* 1. a general term for **feeling** and **emotion,** as distinguished from **cog-nition** or **volition.**—See **affect** (1). 2. = love, esp. in moderate degree or when lack-ing overt sex elements.—*adj.* **affective, affectional,** pertaining to feeling; **affec-tionate,** manifesting love.

affection/masked: (*W. Stekel*) a show of tender behavior that disguises hostility and hatred. ➤The term usually connotes a **de-fense reaction** against one's own uncon-scious hostility, but it may also refer to a conscious attempt to deceive.

affective (af·ek'tiv): *adj.* pertaining to **affect, feeling,** or **affection** (1). ➤Often used in combinations: **affective tone, affective *fixation,** etc.—*Distg. fr.* **affec-tionate.**

affective arousal theory: (*D. C. McClel-land*) a theory that defines **motive** as the arousal of pleasure and pain, and that at-tempts to give an objective definition of these states.

affective experience: an event in a per-son's life strongly colored by feeling, whether pleasant or unpleasant.

affective failure: inadequacy in **emotional *adjustment.**

affective flattening: see **flattening of affect.**

affective psychosis: a severely disabling disorder of **mood** or feeling, with resultant disturbance of thought and behavior con-gruent with the **affect.** The **affect** is dis-proportionate to objective circumstances. **Manic-depressive psychosis** and **psy-chotic *depressive reaction** are the chief forms.—*Syn.* (*Stan. Psychiat.*) PSYCHOTIC AFFECTIVE REACTIONS.

affective ratio: (*Ror.*) the ratio of the total number of responses to the colored inkblot cards (Nos. VIII, IX, X) to the total num-ber of responses to the achromatic cards

(Nos. I through VII). ➤The normal range is from 0.40 to 0.60. The affective ratio is a measure of the degree to which color increases responsiveness and is held to be an index of **affectivity (1)**.

affective reaction type: (*psychiat.*) any disorder in which the principal symptoms are **affective** or emotional.—See **affective psychosis.**

affective tolerance: the ability to maintain a reasonably effective adjustment to **emotive** situations; personal control free from overreacting.—*Syn.* AFFECT TOLERANCE (*prefd.*).

affective tone: 1. the generalized **feeling** tone of an experience. ➤The term is occasionally restricted to pleasantness-unpleasantness; more often it covers as well excitement, antagonism, optimism, etc. **2.** the subjective aspect of acceptance-rejection behavior.

affectivity (af″ek·tiv′ə·ti): *n.* **1.** the tendency to react easily with feeling and emotion. ➤The general abstract noun should not, in the absence of data, be taken to imply a unitary generalized **trait.**—*Syn.* **emotionality. 2.** a highly generalized emotional experience, i.e., one that cannot be identified with any particular emotion. **3.** the amount of feeling manifested at any particular time. **4.** that property of the stimulus situation which evokes feeling. ➤An unfortunate extension of meaning.— *Approx. syn.* (for 4) EMOTIVE STRENGTH, **emotivity.**

afferent (af′ər·ənt): *adj.* concerned with the transmission of **neural impulse** toward the central part of the **nervous system.** —*Contr. w.* **efferent.**

afferent influx: neural influx; **afferent** (neural) impulse. ➤**Afferent influx** is tautological.

afferent-stimulus interaction: (*C. Hull*) postulate that the interaction of stimuli produces behavior effects distinct from a mere summation of their results taken separately. ➤This postulate was believed by Hull to be a behavioristic parallel, for perception, of the **gestalt** principle.

affiliative need: the need to be associated with another person or persons, whether for cooperative effort, companionship, love, or sexual satisfaction.—*Syn.* AFFILIATION NEED, NEED FOR AFFILIATION.—*Cp.* **social need, status need.**

a fortiori (ā fôr·shi·ô′rī; -ri): *adj.* (*L., from yet firmer ground*) of a conclusion that follows with even greater logical necessity than another already accepted.

afterbrain = **medulla.**

aftercontraction: *n.* a muscular contraction occurring a noticeable time after the stimulation has ceased.

afterdischarge: *n.* a neural impulse con-

tinued after removal of the stimulus.—*Cp.* **aftercontraction.**

aftereffect: *n.* **1.** any psychological phenomenon that follows removal of a stimulus, either immediately or after a brief delay. **2.** = **aftersensation. 3.** the hypothetical process whereby the satisfyingness of an act "works back" and strengthens the presumed **psychoneural** connections involved; and a similar process whereby dissatisfyingness has a weakening effect. ➤Some authorities postulate only a positive **aftereffect.**—See **law of *effect.**

aftereffect/figural: see figural aftereffect.

afterimage = **aftersensation** (*prefd.*).

afterimage/memory: see memory afterimage.—*Distg. fr.* afterimage.

after-only design: see **before-after design.**

afterpotential or **aftercurrent:** *n.* the **action current** that follows the **spike.** ➤This part of the **action current** is considered an index of rate of conduction in the fibers.

aftersensation: *n.* **sense impressions** or **sense data,** usually coming in rhythmic pulses, after stimulation of eye or skin has ceased. ➤In vision, they are POSITIVE if the image is brighter than the surrounding field, NEGATIVE if less bright. Usually, but not necessarily, the negative aftersensation is roughly complementary in hue as well; but in preferred usage *negative* and *positive* as applied to the aftersensation refer only to brightness relations. As aftersensations are of peripheral origin, that term is preferred to the somewhat more common AFTERIMAGES, a term that suggests a central origin.—*Cp.* Purkinje afterimage.

agapism (ag′ə·piz·əm): *n.* the doctrine that exalts the value of love, especially in its general nonsexual sense.—*adj.* agapistic.

AGCT or **A.G.C.T.** = **Army General Classification Test.**

age: *n.* **1.** the length of time an organism has lived; unless qualified, = chronological age (CA) = life age.—See **life *age. 2.** = **age equivalent,** always with a qualifying expression: e.g., **mental *age, education *age, carpal *age. 3.** a stage or period in a person's life: infancy, middle age, old age.— See **development/levels of.**

Conventionally, **age** of mammals is taken as beginning at birth unless otherwise stated. For young children it is stated in months, for others in years or years and months: e.g., 8–7 (not 8.7) for eight years and seven months. (If the decimal point is used, the figure following must be a decimal fraction of a year; but this is so often violated that ages so stated must be interpreted with caution. With children's **ages,** the error is not negligible.)

At the younger ages a serious miscalculation is apt to result if **ordinal** numbers (instead of **cardinals**) are used in calculating age. The first year is clearly the year *before* the first birthday anniversary. Equally clearly, the fourth year is the year before the fourth anniversary, i.e., it begins with the third birthday anniversary. However, it is commonly reckoned, even in some professional writings, to begin at the fourth anniversary—a 33⅓ per cent error! It is, therefore, recommended that ages be stated in cardinal numbers: age 1, age 6, age 20, etc. In computing for IQ or in averaging, it is safer to convert all ages to months.

age/accomplishment (*obsoles.*) = **achievement** *age.

age/achievement: a given level of **achievement** (which see) stated as the age at which that level is normally attained. ➤Preferred for use only when the achievement has been measured by tests.—*Syn.* (when the achievement is in school subjects) **age/educational.**

age/anal: see **anal stage.**

age/anatomical: the level of development of bodily structures (if unspecified, of the bony structures) expressed as the **life** *age at which this level is, on the average, attained. ➤The **carpal** *age is often taken as an *index* of general bony development, but it should not be used as a direct equivalent.

age/attainment: *obsoles.* for **achievement** *age.

age/base or **/basal:** on an **age equivalent** test, the highest level at which a subject passes *all* the test items assigned to that level and passes (or is assumed to pass) all tests at a lower level. Additional credits are given for passes of items assigned to higher levels.—*Syn.* BASAL or BASE YEAR, BASAL MENTAL AGE (likely to be misunderstood).

age calibration: standardizing a test in **age equivalents.**

age/carpal: the level of bony development judged by the relative completeness of the calcium deposit in the carpal (wrist) bones as seen in X-ray photographs. The photographs are rated in terms of the **age equivalent.**—*Cp.* **ossification ratio.** ➤Carpal age is the commonest index of **anatomical** *age, but it should not be regarded as identical.

age/chronological or **CA:** the time elapsed since birth.—*Syn.* **age/life** (*prefd.*).

age/conceptional: **age** reckoned from the presumed moment of **conception** as the zero point of development. ➤It is useful in considering the development of **prematures** or in extrapolating toward a **true** *zero score in developmental measures. The presumed moment of conception is some-

times calculated from the last day, sometimes from the first day, of the last menstrual period prior to pregnancy. If the day of copulation is reliably known, conception is reckoned to have taken place within 48 hours.—*Cp.* **ovulation** *age, **copulation** *age, **menstrual** *age.—*Syn* FERTILIZATION AGE.

age/copulation or **/insemination:** the age of the **fetus** dated from the known day of copulation. This **age** is about 10 days shorter than the mean **menstrual** *age of the fetus.

age/dental: measure of dental development reached by a particular child, based on the number of permanent teeth erupted, expressed in terms of the age at which the average child attains that level.

age/developmental: 1. any measure of development, especially when stated in **age equivalent. 2.** a combination of all available **age-equivalent** indices of development.—*Cp.* **organismic** *age. **3.** a measure of development in functions other than the intellectual. ➤This usage is arbitrary but common. The functions measured or estimated should be specified: **anatomic** *age, **emotional** *age, **social** *age, etc.—*Distg. fr.* **development/levels of.**

age/educational or **EA:** a pupil's average accomplishment in school subjects measured in terms of the average for a given **life** *age in school. ➤E.g., if a child performs school tasks at the level of 10-year-olds, his EA is 10 years. There is no accepted list of school subjects which are, or should be, included in the average; hence educational ages are often far from comparable. The EA should always be determined by achievement tests or similar procedures, otherwise it merely duplicates classification according to grade in school.—See **achievement** *age.

age/emotional: a measure of the person's development in emotion, by comparison with the average emotional development at a given **life** *age. ➤The concept is much more vague than would be expected from the term. There is presently no **scale** for emotional age analogous to those for **mental** or **educational** *age, and no substantial agreement on what emotional development consists of.

age equivalent: the relative level of development in any trait or characteristic expressed as equal to the **life** *age at which the given level is normally or on the average attained. ➤Thus the anatomical development characteristic of 6-year-olds is designated as **anatomical** *age 6. See also **mental** *age, **educational** *age.—*Cp.* **age equivalent scale.**

age (equivalent) scale: a scale in which the units of measurement are the differences between successive **age equivalents,** each such difference being taken *as if* equal to any other. ➤Thus a child whose anatomical development is like that of the average of 8-year-olds is said to be one year older anatomically than the child whose development is that of 7-year-olds. —*Syn.* AGE SCALE.

age/fertilization = age/conceptional.

age-grade distribution or **table:** a table showing the number or per cent of children of each age in each school grade.

age-grade scaling: standardizing a test by reference to a population of children who are at the normal age for their school grade.

age/grip: strength of grip in a child, as measured on a hand dynamometer, expressed in terms of the age at which the average child attains the same strength of grip.

age/growth: composite of various physical-growth measures, stated in an **age equivalent.**

age/height: measurement of height attained by a child, expressed in terms of the age at which the average child of the same sex reaches that height.

age/intelligence = age/mental.

age/life or **CA:** the time elapsed since birth; the length of time an organism has lived since birth, hatching, or some other agreed-upon beginning point. ➤With human beings, birth is taken as the beginning point unless otherwise specified.—*Cp.* **conceptional** *age. **Life age** is preferred to its synonym CHRONOLOGICAL AGE, since **age equivalents** are also stated in terms of chronology; but the abbreviation is **CA,** not LA. See **age** for conventions of writing age numerically.

age/lunar: age expressed in lunar months of 28 days each.

age-mates: *n. pl.* the children of about the same age with whom a child associates, and from whom he commonly derives some of his standards. ➤The use of **peer group** as a synonym has led to confused thinking.

age/maximal: in the administration of an **age scale,** the lowest year in which all tests are failed.

age/maximal growth: the age at which a person reaches his greatest growth. Fractions of the total time taken to reach maximal growth are treated as equal units.

age/menstrual: the age of the **fetus** calculated from the first day of the mother's last menstrual period prior to the onset of pregnancy.—*Syn.* MENSTRUATION AGE.

age/mental or **MA:** the level of development in **intelligence,** expressed as equivalent to the life age at which the average child attains that level.—See **age equivalent scale.** ➤The term should be quite

technically interpreted in terms of the results of a particular specified **mental test** (2). It is of very doubtful value where normal adults are in question.—*Syn.* INTELLIGENCE AGE (more descriptive but uncommon). The abbreviation **MA** is preferred to **M.A.**

agenitalism: *n.* lack of testes or ovaries. ➤If the condition dates from an early age the **secondary** *sex characters do not develop normally.

age norm: 1. the representative performance or developmental status of children of a given age level in any measured characteristic; the **norm (1)** for a given age. **2.** the chronological age at which a particular score is typically achieved.

age/normal: (*educ.*) the typical **life** *age for entering a school grade.

agent: *n.* **1.** a person, thing, or force that acts, or is capable of acting, on something else.—See **person. 2.** a person who acts, or is empowered to act, for another. **3.** in tests for telepathy, the person whose mental states are to be apprehended by the **percipient.**

agent/excitatory = stimulus.

age/ontogenetic = life *age.

age/organismic: the average of all measures of a child's development, scored in **age equivalents.** It usually includes **mental** *age, carpal *age, dental *age, height *age, weight *age, one or more kinds of educational *age, and social *age.

age/ovulation: the age of the fetus, calculated from the time when the egg is thought to have been discharged from the ovary.

age/physiological: level of physiological development stated in terms of the age at which it is normally attained. ➤It is often assumed to be measured by the **ossification ratio,** but this measures not physiological but **anatomical** *age. No very precise criteria for physiological age have been developed: it is estimated, not measured. (An estimate based on whether the individual has entered or passed puberty is too limited.)—*Cp.* **mental** *age.

age-progress curve: a growth curve or learning curve showing improvement as related to **life** *age.

age ratio: the chronological age of the child at one testing divided by chronological age at a later testing. ➤Since (in general) the first test score predicts better the second test score in proportion as the interval between tests in short, and also in proportion to the age of the child, the age ratio is a rough measure of the test's predictive power. E.g., prediction from ages 5 to 6 (ratio ⅚) is likely to be better than from ages 3 to **4** (ratio ¾), but worse than from ages 8 **to 9** (ratio ⅞).

age/reading: an **age-equivalent** scoring of reading performance.

age scale = **age-equivalent scale.**

age score: a test score in which the individual's test performance is expressed as the age at which most individuals reach the same level of performance; an **age-equivalent** score.

age/sex: the level of development of the sex organs, measured either anatomically or physiologically, and stated in **age equivalents.**

age/skeletal = **age/carpal.**

age/social: the level of development in social understandings and techniques, measured by comparison with the average social development of children at the several life ages.—See **age equivalent.**

age/test: the score on an **age-equivalent scale.**

age/true: the actual **age** of a person from conception. ➤*Syn.* conceptional *age. It is of importance chiefly in studying the development of prematures and fetuses.

ageusia (ə·gū′si·ə): *n.* absence or impairment of the sense of taste.—*adj.* **ageusic.**

age/weight: the weight reached by a growing child, expressed in terms of the age at which the average child of the same sex attains that weight.

agglutination: *n.* 1. the formation of a word by combining several root words: e.g., manlike. ➤Several languages, e.g., Turkish, depend more upon agglutination than on inflection. All languages have some agglutination. 2. representing the meaning of several words by a single sound or speech element, usually in internal speech. ➤The agglutinating word may be a combination of parts of the words represented: "partial failure" may become "pailure."

aggregate (ag′ri·gət): *n.* 1. that which is brought together; a plurality of units, terms, objects, or persons that are to be treated without regard to the interaction (if any) between them: e.g., an uncatalogued collection of seashells. ➤*Some* similarity, whether intrinsic or adventitious, characterizes units or they would not be an **aggregate**, but their relative distinctness is emphasized. *Contr. w.* gestalt. 2. = SOCIAL AGGREGATE, for which **aggregation** is preferred. 3. (*math.*) the total or sum of a number of values or quantities.—*v.* **aggregate** (-gāt).

aggregate/attention: see **attention aggregate.**

aggregation: *n.* (*sociol.*) a plurality of persons assembled in one place but having only a minimum of social organization or unity of purpose.—*Syn.* SOCIAL AGGREGATE (not *prefd.*), **assemblage, crowd.**

aggregation theory: (*W. C. Halstead*) a neurological conception of **intelligence** as a property of the coordinated functioning of diverse sensory and motor fields discretely distributed throughout the cortex.

aggression: *n.* 1. hostile action; action that causes fear or flight in another animal, or that—failing such effect—brings the aggressor into forceful contact with the other animal; or any psychological equivalent for such attack.—*Syn.* AGGRESSIVE BEHAVIOR. ➤What constitutes a "psychological equivalent" requires careful study of the usual behavior of the species or individual; in man, an attempt to destroy or appropriate possessions of another is one such equivalent. 2. by postulation in the **frustration-aggression hypothesis,** any behavior whatever resulting from **frustration.** 3. (*A. Adler*) any manifestation of the **"will-to-power."** 4. (*S. Freud*) a manifestation in conscious behavior of the hypothesized **death instinct.** 5. that quality which makes an act one of **aggression** in the previous meanings.—*adj.* **aggressive;** but this serves also as *adj.* for **aggressiveness** (which see) and perpetuates a confusion.—*v.* **aggress.**

aggression/direct: aggression against the person or object producing **frustration.**—*Cp.* aggression.—*Contr. w.* displaced *aggression.

aggression/displaced: aggression against a person or object other than that which was (or is) the source of **frustration.** The aggression may be disguised.—*Contr. w.* **aggression/direct.**—See **displacement.**

aggressive: *adj.* characterized by **aggression** or by **aggressiveness.**

aggressiveness: *n.* 1. tendency to display **aggression;** or the quality found in aggressive acts. ➤This was the original meaning, but it has been so weakened in the senses that follow as to have lost almost all connotation of hostility. Hence, for this meaning, either **aggression** (5) or **aggressivity** are substituted. 2. a tendency to push forward one's own interests or ideas, despite opposition.—*Cp.* initiative, which does not imply the presence of opposition. 3. tendency to seek dominance in a social group. 4. tendency to be enterprising, energetic, active.—*adj.* **aggressive,** which is unfortunately ambiguous as between **aggressiveness** and **aggression.**—*v.* **to be aggressive, to show aggressiveness.** Note that **aggress** is the verb for **aggression,** not for **aggressiveness.**

aggressivity: *n.* the tendency toward **aggression.**

aggrith: see **ulstrith.**

aging: *n.* the continuous process, beginning at conception and ending with death, wherein the structures and functions of an immature organism first become mature and then deteriorate. ➤Some functions age more rapidly than others, as do some individuals.

agitated melancholia: a psychotic syndrome of **depression** with **anxiety.** It is characteristically found late in life.

agitation: *n.* a condition of tense and irrepressible activity, usually rather "fussy" and anxious.

agitolalia (aj″ə·tō·lā′li·ə): *n.* cluttered and excessively rapid speech with sounds slurred, omitted, or distorted.—*Syn.* AGITOPHASIA, **cluttering.**

agitophasia = agitolalia.

aglossia (ə·glos′i·ə): *n.* complete absence of articulate speech due to structural defect of lips, tongue, teeth, or palate.—*Syn.* ORGANIC MUTISM.

agnosia (ag·nō′zhə): *n.* **1.** inability to interpret sensory impressions; imperfect perceiving; specifically, loss of ability to recognize and identify familiar objects through a particular sense organ. **2.** attitude of suspended judgment with respect to a *particular* truth claim. ➤*Distg. fr.* AGNOSTICISM, which is the generalized attitude of suspended judgment, especially in respect to religious beliefs.—*adj.* **agnostic,** (for **1**) **agnosic.**

agnosia/ideational: faulty recognition of objects or symbols, based on faulty elaboration of sensory impressions which are themselves dissociated from one another.

agnosia/visual: 1. functional ***blindness. 2.** disturbance in ability to recognize objects in the visual field, due to brain lesions.—*Syn.* OPTIC AGNOSIA.

agnosticism: see agnosia (2).

A.G.O.: Adjutant General's Office. ➤Used in connection with psychological tests, etc., sponsored by the A.G.O.

agonist (ag′ə·nist): *n.* (*physiol.*) a contracting muscle that acts in opposition to another muscle, its **antagonist.**—*adj.* **agonistic.**

agoraphobia (ag″ə·rə·fō′bi·ə): *n.* a **phobia** of open spaces. ➤An unnecessary term. If one knows Greek, it is misleading: the *agora* was a busy marketplace, and that is not what the **agoraphobic** fears. If one does not know Greek, the substitution of a Greek **neologism** for English merely adds to vocabulary burden.

agrammatism (ə·gram′ə·tiz·əm): *n.* loss of ability to speak grammatically or coherently following brain injury, or in schizophrenia. ➤A form of **dyslogia.**—*Syn.* AGRAMMALOGIA, AGRAMMATALOGIA, AGRAMMATICA, AGRAMMAPHASIA, **acataphasia,** syntactical ***aphasia,** and doubtless other combinations. (Writers in the field of speech disorder patently do not suffer from **oligologia.**)

➤graphia (ə·graf′i·ə): *n.* a form of **aphasia** due to cerebral lesion and characterized by impairment in the ability to write.—*Cp.* **alexia.**—*adj.* **agraphic.**

agraphia/congenital: a degree of difficulty in learning to write that is out of line with other manifestations of ability.

agreement and differences/canon of or **/method of:** one of Mill's working principles of **induction,** combining the **canons of *agreement** and **of *differences:** whatever is uniformly present when a phenomenon is present, absent when it is absent, is a cause or part-cause of that phenomenon.—*Syn.* JOINT METHOD.—See **concomitant variations/method of, residues/method of.**

agreement/canon of or **/method of:** one of Mill's working principles of **induction** which regards as the cause, or an indispensable part of the cause, that aspect of all the events being considered in which they are alike.—See **agreement and differences/canon of.**—*Cp.* **concomitant variations, differences/canon of, residues/method of.**

agreement/coefficient of: (*J. Dunlap*) a measure of degree of agreement among ratings or rankings:

$$\text{coef. of } \mathbf{agreement} = 100 \left[1 - \frac{\Sigma T - \Sigma B}{\dfrac{N}{2(H-L)}} \right]$$

where $T =$ top 50% of rankings, $B =$ bottom 50% of rankings, $(H - L) =$ range between highest and lowest possible rank.

agrypnia (ā·grip′ni·ə; ə·grip′-): *n.* **insomnia.**

aha experience (ä·hä′): the moment in which the features of a situation perceived or thought about seem suddenly to fit together in a unitary pattern; a sudden insight or solution of a problem.—Also spelled **ah-hah** or **ah-ah experience.**

ahistorical: *adj.* of the point of view or method that emphasizes the study of present behavior in relation to present conditions both within and without the organism, and minimizes the use of the facts of the individual's past as a means of understanding his present.—See **psychology/divisions and schools of, VIII.**

Ahlfeld breathing movements, Ahlfeld's sign (äl′felt): rhythmic contractions of the **fetal** thorax felt through the mother's body after about the third month of pregnancy. ➤These movements are considered an example of **anticipatory *maturation.**

ahypnia (ā·hip′ni·ə; ə·hip′-): *n.* pathological **insomnia.**—*Syn.* AHYPNOSIS.

ahypnosis = ahypnia.

aid/audio-visual: any sound-plus-sight device to supplement regular instruction. ➤The word *aid* is significant. A sound motion picture, e.g., should be thought of as an aid to teaching, not as a substitute for it.— *Cp.* audio aid.

aided-recall technique: an interview procedure in which the respondent is assisted in giving answers by a list of reminders bearing on the question. ➤This procedure is at the opposite pole from **open-ended questioning.**

aid/visual: see **visual aids.**

aim: *n.* **1.** that which is to be attained by voluntary action. **2.** a conscious or symbolic representation of the end sought. **3.** the state or action desired in connection with a goal object. ➤Freud clearly distinguished between the sexual or INSTINCTUAL OBJECT (generally a person) and the sexual or INSTINCTUAL AIM, which is an activity (not only coitus but many other kinds of sexual behavior, normal and anomalous). Later the notion of aim was slightly altered and two forms are recognized: the INTERNAL AIM, which is the satisfied state or condition of the organism, and the EXTERNAL AIM, which is the activity. (These are respectively what one aims *at* and what one aims *to do.*) ❡The concept can be broadened to all other kinds of goaloriented behavior. Thus, in thirst, the goal or incentive object is water; the INTERNAL AIM is the state of properly "watered" tissues; the EXTERNAL AIM is the act of drinking. For many theorists, the internal aim is defined as **homeostasis,** the state of over-all organismic stability that existed before the particular motivational system was aroused. Clarity is lost when external aim is extended to include not only the behavior but the accessory objects—as when a new hat is considered part of the external aim. Preferred usage would speak of wearing the new hat as the EXTERNAL AIM, of attracting the attention of one's rivals as the OBJECT, of the satisfied internal state as the INTERNAL AIM. End, **goal, incentive, intent, objective, purpose,** are related terms, sometimes used as synonyms, sometimes to express a contrast or difference.

aim/external: see **aim (3).**

aim-inhibited: *adj.* (*psychoan.*) characterizing action in which recognition of the **drive** involved is repressed, as in the pleasure of sociability without recognizing that there is a sexual element in the pleasure.

aim/internal: see **aim (3).**

aim-transference: *n.* a shift of the **external *aim** from one life situation to another in which it is more likely to be achieved. ➤E.g., a boy who cannot hope to be a football hero is encouraged to play the saxophone.

akinesia (ak″i·nē′zhə): *n.* loss or impairment of motor function, esp. of voluntary

movement.—*adj.* **akinesic** (not *akinetic,* which means *without motion*).

akinesthesia (ā·kin″es·thē′zhə; ə·kin″-): *n.* insensitivity to movements of one's own body.

akoasm = **acoasm.**

akoria = **acoria.**

AL: 1. = **adaptation level. 2.** = absolute limen or **absolute *threshold.**

-al: suffix meaning *pertaining to, of the nature of.*

alalia (ə·lā′li·ə): *n.* complete absence of articulate speech, arising from **functional** causes.—*adj.* **alalic** (-lal′ik).

alar plate (ā′lər): (*neurol.*) either of two dorsolateral zones of the embryonic **neural tube.**

albedo (al·bē′dō): *n.* the whiteness or diffuse reflecting power of a surface; the ratio of the light reflected from a surface to the light falling thereon.

albedo perception: a form of **perceptual *constancy** in which wide variations in illumination are disregarded and the **albedo** taken by itself is reacted to. ➤Thus a glossy white paper, when viewed under low illumination, is judged as very white (having high albedo) despite the fact that it then matches a fairly dark gray.

albinism (al′bi·niz·əm): *n.* congenital absence of pigment from the skin, hair, choroid coat, and iris.—*adj.* **albinic, albinotic** (al″bin·ot′ik).—*pers. n.* **albino** (al·bī′nō).

alcoholic: *n.* **1.** a chronic compulsive drinker; a person who cannot abstain from drinking; a sufferer from **alcoholism (2).** **2.** an unfortunate euphemism for *drunkard,* a person frequently intoxicated. ➤The line between **(1)** and **(2)** is not easy to draw, but the distinction lies in the **compulsive** nature of the alcoholic's drinking. The alcoholic remains an alcoholic despite ordinary change of external circumstances; the drunkard may be reformed (though not easily, as a rule) if the provoking circumstances are improved.

alcoholic dementia = **Korsakow's psychosis.**

alcoholic psychosis: a severe mental disorder (to be distinguished from ordinary intoxication) due to excessive or chronic drinking of alcohol, with acute inflammation of the brain or chronic impairment of brain tissue. The acute forms are **delirium tremens** or ALCOHOLIC HALLUCINATIONS; the chronic form is **Korsakow's psychosis.** But alcoholic damage of the brain may also trigger the onset of other psychoses.

alcoholism: *n.* **1.** (*pop.*) a tendency to excessive use of alcohol. **2.** (*Stan. Psychiat.*) a personality disturbance whose most prominent symptom is chronic compulsive drinking. **3.** a pathological condition of body or mind, resulting chiefly from excessive chronic drinking: e.g., **Korsakow's psychosis.** ➤Note that (3) deals with drinking as a cause, (2) with drinking as an effect or symptom.—*adj.* and *pers. n.* **alcoholic,** best reserved for (2).

alertness: *n.* the personal quality of being quickly attentive to ideas when presented, and to environmental changes; rapid receptivity; ability to react quickly and accurately to tasks of relatively low intellectual difficulty. ➤A **unitary** **trait* of **alertness** is questioned by many.

alertness test: a misleading synonym for **intelligence test.**

alexia (ə·lek'si·ə): *n.* a form of **sensory** **aphasia* characterized by loss of ability to read written or printed language despite unimpairment of vision or intelligence.—*Syn.* **visual *aphasia,** WORD BLINDNESS (*prefd.*). —*Cp.* **strephosymbolia.**

alg-: combining form meaning *pain.* ➤HYP(O)ALGIA = deficient pain; HYPERALGIA = excessive pain; PARALGIA = mistaken feeling of pain.

algebraic: *adj.* **1.** pertaining to the operations of algebra. **2.** pertaining to arithmetic operations that take into account the plus or minus signs of the values operated on; or to a value that has a plus or minus sign prefixed, i.e., to an ALGEBRAIC VALUE.—*adv.* **algebraically.**

algedonic (al"jə·don'ik): *adj.* pertaining to the pleasantness-unpleasantness dimension in experience.

algesia (al·jē'zi·ə): *n.* pain; the pain sense. ➤**Algesia** or **algesis** is the capacity for feeling pain. It sometimes refers to a heightened capacity (properly, **hyperalgesia**). **Algesthesia** is an actual pain experience; **algesthesis** is the sensibility to pain, i.e., the pain sense. But practically no one can remember and carefully use these terms in their distinguished meanings. Why not simply say *capacity for pain* (for algesia or algesis), *pain sensation* (for algesthesia), *pain sense* or *pain sensitivity* (for algesthesis)?—*Syn.* ALGESIS.—*Ant.* **analgesia.**—*adj.* **algetic.**

algesimeter (al"jə·sim'ə·tər): *n.* a device for measuring pain sensitivity to a sharp pricking stimulus.—*Syn.* ALGESIOMETER (al'·jē"zi·om'ə·ter).—*Cp.* ALGOMETER (-gom'-ə·tər), a device using a blunt stimulus, but also sometimes called algesimeter.

algesiometer = **algesimeter.**

algesis = **algesia.**

algesthesia: see **algesia.**

algesthesis: see **algesia.**

-algia, -alg(o)-: combining elements meaning *pain.*

algolagnia (al"go·lag'ni·ə): *n.* sexual excitement aroused either by experiencing or inflicting pain, i.e., either **masochism** or **sadism.**—*adj.* **algolagnic.**

algometer (al·gom'ə·tər): see **algesimeter.**

algophilia (al"gō·fil'i·ə): *n.* PLEASURE IN PAIN (*prefd.*).—*Cp.* **algolagnia, masochism.**

algophobia: *n.* a PHOBIA FOR PAIN (*prefd.*).

alienation: *n.* **1.** loss or lack of **relationship,** esp. where or when relationship is to be expected. ➤The term is very general; it may be used of statistical, experimental, or interpersonal relationships. **2.** a state wherein familiar persons and situations appear strange. ➤It is the opposite of *déjà vu.*

alienation/coefficient of or **k:** a measure of departure from perfect correlation; a measure of the error of prediction from scores in one variable to scores in another when the **correlation coefficient** is known. ➤The formula $k = \sqrt{1 - r^2}$ indicates how much less the error of prediction would be than would result from a guess.—*Cp. E,* index of **forecasting efficiency.*

alienation/mental: *obsoles.* for **insanity;** a general term for nontemporary mental disorder of such nature as to render the patient subject to special legal provisions, such as restraint, guardianship, or legal responsibility.—See also **self-alienation.**

alien drive: see **drive/alien.**

alienist (āl'yən·ist): *n.* a physician qualified in a court as an expert witness concerning the mental responsibility, etc., of other persons appearing before the court as parties to legal action or as witnesses. ➤An alienist (in law) need not be a **psychiatrist,** and the term is not one of preference except in medicolegal discussion.

alimentary: *adj.* pertaining to food or to the digestion of food.—*n.* **alimentation.**

alimentary canal: the passage in the body, from mouth to anus, which serves the functions of digestion and absorption of food and elimination of residual waste.

allachesthesia = **allesthesia.**

allele (ə·lēl'): *n.* = **allelomorph.**

allelomorph (ə·lē'lə·morf; ə·lel'-): *n.* either of two genes that are alternative in Mendelian inheritance, a given mature cell receiving one or the other but not both. ➤E.g., brown or blue eyes are allelomorphic characters.—*Syn.* ALLELE.

allergy: *n.* hypersensitivity to a specific substance which, under similar conditions, would be harmless to most people.—*adj.* **allergic.**

allesthesia (al"es·thē'zhə): *n.* referral of a tactile sensation to a point remote from the source of stimulation.—*Syn.* ALLACHESTHESIA (al"ə·kes-).

alley problem: the problem of why two actually parallel lines extending into the distance seem to approach each other.

alliaceous: *adj.* of a class of smells of which garlic is the typical example.

allied reflexes: two or more simultaneous or closely successive **reflexes** that combine into a harmonious unit.

allness: *n.* (*semantics*) a reaction in which one's generalization about a class of objects is implicitly assumed to represent *all* the characteristics of the class. ➤The statement: "You can't tell me anything about labor unions!" means: "They are all alike and they are what I know about them; there is no other truth." **Allness** is dogmatic over-generalization.

allo-: combining form meaning *outside of, other than.*

allochiria (-kī′ri·ə): *n.* referring a touch to the other side of the body from that stimulated.—*Var.* **allocheiria.**

allochthonous (ə·lok′thə·nəs): *adj.* having a source or cause outside its own system: e.g., a behavior activated as the result of the frustration of another behavior is called ALLOCHTHONOUS BEHAVIOR.—*Var.* **alloctho-nous.**

alloeroticism: *n.* turning the **erotic** tendency away from the self and toward others; the opposite of **autoeroticism.**—*Syn.* ALLOEROTISM.

alloerotism = **alloeroticism.**

allomorphs: *n. pl.* similar sounds that have the same meaning: e.g., the final sounds in *asked, baked,* and *kept,* which all mean *past time.*

allophemy (al·of′ə·mi) = **heterophemy.**

allophones (al′ō·fōnz): *n. pl.* a group of closely similar elementary speech sounds in any language, differences between which do not convey different meanings. ➤E.g., in English the word *pin* may be pronounced with or without a certain aspirated sound as if *h* followed the *p.* This difference (between [*p*‘] and [*p*] does not alter the meaning—the two sounds are **allophones** of the same **phoneme.** In some other languages these two sounds are distinct **phonemes.**

alloplasty (-plas″ti): *n* (*psychoan.*) the process, in the developing individual, by which the **libido** adapts itself to the environment, i.e., turns outward from the self and toward other objects and persons. ➤*Contr. w.* AUTOPLASTY, the earlier phase during which the psychic structures are being molded within the individual.—*adj.* **alloplastic.**

allopsychic: *adj.* of a psychic process referring to the external world. ➤An ALLO-PSYCHIC DELUSION is a projection of one's own impulses and feelings into others: a husband, being filled with jealousy, believes his wife is jealous.—*Contr. w.* AUTOPSYCHIC, of a psychic process referring to one's own personality (e.g., belief in one's own prowess).

all-or-none law: 1. the principle that a single **neuron** reacts either with maximum intensity or not at all, regardless of the in-

tensity of the stimulus or other excitation. **2.** (*psychoan.*) the principle that **instinctual** reactions are not graded in intensity but are manifested in full strength or not at all. ➤This principle holds only when **instinctual** is taken in its psychoanalytic sense; it is obviously not true, for example, that instinctive fear, in its ordinary sense, is **all-or-none.**

allotropic type: (*A. Meyer*) a personality that tends to be preoccupied with what "others" think, or mean, or do.

Allport A-S Reaction Study: an inquiry form that asks whether certain overt behaviors (believed to be diagnostic of **ascendance-submission**) are characteristic of the subject's usual conduct.

Allport-Vernon Study of Values: a questionary designed to reveal relative interest in six value areas: the theoretical, the social, the religious, the esthetic, the economic (here meaning interest in the acquisition of material things), and the political (here meaning interest in interpersonal power relations). ➤The ALLPORT-VERNON-LINDZEY STUDY is a revision of the above.

alogia (ə·lō′ji·ə): *n.* **1.** inability to speak, resulting from a brain lesion. **2.** a form of **mutism,** resulting from a lack of ideas, shown by idiots or imbeciles.

Alpha, Beta, Gamma hypotheses: (*K. Dunlap*) the three possibilities regarding the influence of frequency of repetition: **Alpha,** that frequency promotes learning; **Beta,** that frequency as such has no influence; **Gamma,** that it hinders learning.

alphabet content: (*Ror.*) code used when letters of the alphabet are reported in response to the inkblots.

alphabet/manual: conventional positions of one or both hands, and the fingers, which symbolize the different letters of the alphabet. It is used to supplement **sign language** in communicating with the deaf, or by deaf-mutes in communicating with others.—See **finger spelling.**

alpha coefficient: (*L. J. Cronbach*) a coefficient that represents the mean of all possible **chance-half *correlations.** It has the same formula as one of the Kuder-Richardson formulas:

$$r_{1T} = \left(\frac{n}{n-1}\right)\frac{\sigma_t{}^2 - \Sigma pq}{\Sigma t^2}$$

where $\sigma_t{}^2$ is the **variance** of the whole test, p is the per cent who pass, and q the per cent who fail each item. The products of these per cents are obtained for each item and then summed.

Alpha Examination or Test: a battery of eight types of general intelligence tests given to soldiers in World War I.—*Cp.* **Beta Test.**

alpha movement: see **motion/apparent.**

alpha rhythm: the most common wave form of the EEG from the adult cortex. The oscillations are smooth, regular, and come at 8-12 a second when the subject is at rest. —*Syn.* BERGER RHYTHM or WAVE, ALPHA WAVE.

Alpine race: see race.

alt.: *abbr.* for *alternating, alternate.*

alter: *n.* the person's concept of other selves or persons, as distinct from himself.

alter ego: *n.* (*L., the other I*) a friend so close that he seems a second self.

alternate forms: see forms/comparable.

alternate-response test: see test/alternate-response.

alternating personality = dual personality (see multiple *personality and dissociation).

alternating psychosis: manic-depressive psychosis with alternation of excitement and depression. ➤The term is merely descriptive and is no longer used as a classification. —See cyclothymic and circular psychosis.

alternating response: a response, A, which follows another, B, and is in turn followed by B in a series A, B, A, B: e.g., the alternating movements made in walking.

alternation cycle: serial behavior in which one type of response, *Rx,* having been made to a stimulus a certain number of times, shifts to another response, *Ry.* ➤E.g., *Rx Rx Rx* || *Ry Ry* || *Rx Rx Rx* || *Ry Ry* || . . . . One ALTERNATION PHASE need not be symmetrical with the other; thus in the above example *Ry* does not occur as often as *Rx.*

alternation phase: see alternation cycle.

altitude of intelligence: a dimension of intelligence, defined by the difficulty level of the problems the testee can solve. ➤Other proposed dimensions are EXTENT OF INTELLIGENCE, measured by the variety of problems the testee can solve; and SPEED, measured by the time required to solve standard problems.

altrigendrism: *n.* tendency to engage in natural, wholesome, nonerotic activity between persons of both sexes. ➤The concept needs a name, but the euphemistic employment of *gender* for *sex* is unfortunate. —See heterosexual for discussion of related terms.—*Syn.* (*proposed*) INTERSEX COMRADESHIP.

altruism: *n.* affection and concern for others, in contrast to self-love and selfishness.—*Ant.* egoism.—*adj.* altruistic.

Alzheimer's disease (älts'hī·mərz): a relatively rare presenile deterioration of the brain which causes speech difficulties and early senility.

amalgamation: *n.* fusion of diverse peoples by intermarriage.

amaurosis (am"ô·rō'səs): *n.* 1. loss of sight due to defect of the optic nerve, but with-

out perceptible change in the eye itself. 2. partial or absolute blindness from whatever cause.—*adj.* amaurotic (-rot'ik).

amaurotic idiocy: a form of *congenital *amaurosis, associated with severe mental defect and leading to early death.

ambi-: combining form meaning *both,* sometimes *both equal:* e.g., AMBIEYED, having both eyes the same, with neither one dominant.

ambidextral: *adj.* pertaining to use of both sides (of the body); ambilateral.—*Cp.* dextral, sinistral.—*Distg. fr.* ambidextrous.—*n.* ambidextrality.

ambidextrous: *adj.* skillful with both hands or with both sides of the body; somewhat more loosely, = ambidextral, able to perform motor acts equally well (or equally badly) with either side of the body; having no preference for right or left side in motor function.—*n.* ambidextrousness.—*pers. n.* ambidexter.

ambiequal: *adj.* (*Ror.*) of a person having well-balanced extratensive and introversive tendencies.

ambiguity/intolerance of: a behavior syndrome characterized by discomfort when faced with complex or uncertain situations that do not easily yield to understanding and/or control, and by a tendency to retreat rather than to attempt to understand or cope with the situation. ➤The "retreat" may take the form of a demand that some one in authority shall resolve or explain the ambiguity, or shall simplify the situation; hence the correlations found between the authoritarian personality and this syndrome.—*Cp.* ambiguity tolerance.

ambiguity tolerance: willingness to accept a state of affairs capable of alternate interpretations, or of alternate outcomes: e.g., feeling comfortable (or at least not feeling uncomfortable) when faced by a complex social issue in which opposed principles are intermingled. ➤Low ambiguity tolerance is shown by the desire to have everything reduced to black and white. Note that the ambiguity is supposed to be a function of the object, not of the person's inability to perceive; but low ambiguity tolerance seems to lessen ability to perceive incongruous features.—*Cp.* intolerance of *ambiguity.

ambiguous (am·big'yū·əs): *adj.* 1. pertaining to a statement, or to a situation, that has two meanings, or is capable of two interpretations; loosely, = equivocal, having several meanings. ➤The doubleness of meaning is implicitly attributed to the statement, situation, or object, however much it may later be proved to have been due to the observer. *Distg. fr.* ambivalent, which applies to a *person* who has two attitudes. Ambiguous *figures are those that can be seen in two or more ways, as in so-called illusions of **reversible** *per-spective. **2.** (*pop*.) vague; obscure; difficult to understand (each of which is better than **ambiguous** for these meanings). —*n*. **ambiguity** (am″bi·gū′ə·ti).

ambiguous figure: see **figure/ambiguous.**

ambiguous perspective: see **reversible** *perspective.

ambiguous stimulus: one that can mean more than one thing; a stimulus object that has a double signaling value. ➤E.g., the sound *rān* can mean "rain" or "reign," the choice depending either on objective context or on personal set.

ambilateral: *adj*. having equal facility in using the organs of either side of the body, esp. eyes, arms, and legs.—*Distg. fr*. **ambidextrous.**—*n*. **ambilaterality.**

ambisexual: *adj*. lacking in sex dominance; having the character of being suitable to both sexes. ➤Most **traits** are ambisexual: that is, they belong to both sexes. Early childhood is said to be a period in which sex differentiation plays little part, hence is ambisexual.—*Distg. fr*. **asexual,** lacking sex; and *fr*. **bisexual,** having the peculiar differentiating characters of both sexes. (But **bisexual** is often used as synonym for **ambisexual.**)

ambivalence (am·biv′ə·ləns): *n*. **1.** tendency to be pulled in psychologically opposite directions, as between denial-affirmation, acceptance-rejection, love-hate, etc.—*Syn*. BI-POLARITY OF FEELING, **ambiversion** (chiefly with special meaning). **2.** coexistence within a person, to a similar degree, of opposed traits, attitudes, or sentiments: e.g., relatively equal strength of tendency to dominate, and to submit to, other persons. **3.** capacity to see two (or more) sides to an issue, or to perceive individuals as having more than one aspect or value; COGNITIVE AMBIVALENCE.—*Syn*. AMBIVALENCY; (for **3**) **tolerance of** *ambiguity.—*adj*. **ambivalent.**

ambivalency = ambivalence.

ambiversion: *n*. tendency to a balance between **introversion** and **extraversion.**—*pers. n*. **ambivert.**

amblyopia (am″bli·ō′pi·ə): *n*. dimness of vision for which no organic defect in the refractive system of the eye has been discovered. ➤It is often associated with total **color blindness,** with **albinism,** and with excessive use of tobacco and other drugs.—*adj*. **amblyopic** (-op′ik).—*pers. n*. **amblyope** (am′bli·ōp).

amblyoscope: *n*. an instrument that presents two stereoscopic images to determine the point at which they fuse.—*Var*. **amblyscope.**

Amblystoma (am·blis′tō·mə): *n*. a small amphibian, a genus of salamander, much

used in embryological studies. (Sometimes misspelled **Ambystoma.**)

ambrosiac: *adj*. of a class of smells of which musk is an example.

ambulatory psychotherapy: treatment of behavior-disordered persons who are able to be at large.

ameliorate: *v*. to make better; to improve.

ament (ā′ment; -mənt): *n*. a person who has **amentia.**

amentia (ə·men′shi·ə) = **deficiency/mental.**

amentia/isolation: see **isolation amentia.**

amentia/subcultural: mental *deficiency that differs only quantitatively from the normal. ➤Many authorities hold this to be true of all mental deficiency.

Ames demonstration: a series of situations, each of which gives full play to a cue to the perception of depth. By eliminating conflicting cues, various distortions of depth perception are produced.

ametropia (am″ə·trō′pi·ə): *n*. any chronic defect in the refractive mechanism of the eye that makes images fail to focus directly on the retina.—*adj*. **ametropic** (-trop′ik).

amimia (ə·mim′i·ə): *n*. loss or impairment of capacity to communicate by gestures or signs. MOTOR AMIMIA refers to inability to make (or to imitate) appropriate gestures, SENSORY AMIMIA to failure to perceive or to interpret (correctly) the gestures of others.

amitosis (am″ə·tō′səs): *n*. cell division in which the nucleus divides without a splitting of the **chromosomes.**—*Contr. w*. **mitosis.**—*adj*. **amitotic** (-tot′ik).

amixia (ā·mik′si·ə): *n*. any restriction that prevents general intercrossing in a species, thus often leading to inbreeding. ➤In human beings, restriction of marriage to one race, caste, class, or tribal division is **amixia.**—*Cp*. **miscegenation.**

ammeter (am′ē·tər): *n*. an instrument for measuring in amperes the amount of electric current.

amnesia (am·nē′zhə): *n*. **1.** lack of memory; inability to recall past experiences, especially where recall is to be expected. **2.** pathological inability, not associated with known damage to the brain, to remember events connected with the subject's past life. ➤Recovery is presumed possible in amnesia but may be delayed for many years. Amnesia may be TOTAL or PARTIAL, and in the latter case may be SELECTIVE or CIRCUMSCRIBED according to time, place, or type of experience. But even in total amnesia not everything learned is forgotten, though the circumstances of learning may be.

Several terms describe the temporal course of the disorder. In ANTEROGRADE AMNESIA, there is failure to recall anything that happened (in a circumscribed period) *after* the onset. The patient had evidently been conscious but does not remember what occurred. In RETROACTIVE AMNESIA, recall of the events in a circumscribed period *preceding* the onset is lost. RETROGRADE AMNESIA, strictly speaking, is inability to recall now what previously the patient had been able to recall. Often, however, it is merely a synonym for retroactive amnesia. PROGRESSIVE AMNESIA involves loss of more and more memories; RETROGRESSIVE AMNESIA means that the disorder is lessening, that lost memories are gradually being recovered (a confusing but accepted usage).—*adj.* **amnesic** (-sik, -zic), **amnestic** (-nes'tik).

amnesia/anterograde: see **amnesia (2).**

amnesia/autohypnotic: an artificial, self-induced forgetting. (**Amnesia** is here used in its etymological sense of **forgetting**.)

amnesia/catathymic (kat″ə·thī′mik): amnesia limited to a given experience or to a closely circumscribed group of experiences: e.g., many women have no memory, after a brief time, of the pains of childbirth.

amnesia/circumscribed: see **amnesia (2).**

amnesia/episodic: loss of memory for important episodes only.

amnesia/hypnotic: any forgetting that is induced by suggestion of the hypnotist. ➤A wider term than **amnesia/post-hypnotic.**

amnesia/infantile: (*psychoan.*) inability, due to **repression,** to recall certain events that happened during the first few years of life. ➤According to psychoanalytic theory, certain **symbolic** behaviors give evidence that memory for these events persists. Under **analysis** many of the events can be recalled.

amnesia/localized = partial amnesia (*prefd.*). See **amnesia (2).**

amnesia/posthypnotic: inability to recall in the waking state what happened under hypnosis. When rehypnotized, however, the subject generally remembers from the previous state. This form of amnesia is usually deliberately induced by the hypnotist.

amnesia/retrograde or /**retroactive:** see **amnesia (2).**

amnesic (am·nē′zik): *adj.* pertaining to **amnesia.**—*Var.* **amnestic** (-nes′tik).

amniotic (am″ni·ot′ik): *adj.* pertaining to the AMNION, the membrane or sac that encloses the fetus. ➤The AMNIOTIC FLUID is the liquid surrounding the fetus. The AMNIOTIC STATE is the intrauterine state.

amoeba (ə·mē′bə) *n.*, *pl.* **amoebae, -as:** one of the simplest of single-celled organisms, very widely distributed. It has no mouth or locomotor organs; it moves by sending out temporary projections called PSEUDOPODIA; and it absorbs nutrients by flowing around them.—*adj.* **amoebic,** related to or caused by amoebas (e.g., amoebic dysentery); **amoeboid,** like an

amoeba (e.g., amoeboid movements).—*Var.* **ameba.**

amok = **amuck.**

amorality: *n.* **1.** conduct to which distinctions of ethical right and wrong do not apply. **2.** an attitude that ignores, denies, or transcends moral considerations.—See **immoral.**—*adj.* **amoral.**—*pers. n.* **amoralist,** one who believes himself to be above morality.

amorous: *adj.* pertaining to love, or to love-making that involves a strong **erotic** element, including caresses. ➤*Syn.* AMATORY, AMATIVE. The emphasis upon the sexual is somewhat less in amatory, still less in amative, but the terms are often used interchangeably.

ampere (am′pir): *n.* the standard unit of amount of electric current.—*Cp.* **volt, watt.**

amphi- (am′fi-): combining form meaning *on both sides, of both kinds.* ➤*Distg. fr.* **ambi-,** which means *taking two things together* (but the distinction is not always observed: e.g., **ambilateral** should be *amphilateral*).

amphierotism: *n.* a condition in which a person conceives of himself as having the **erotic** nature of both sexes. ➤*Cp.* **bisexuality,** which refers to anatomy and physiology.

amphigenous inversion (am·fij′ə·nəs): a condition in which the individual finds it acceptable to have sex relations with both sexes.

amphimixis (am″fi·mik′səs): *n.* **1.** the fact that both parents contribute to the inheritance of their offspring. **2.** (*psychoan.*) the mingling of **genital** and **anal erotism.**

amplitude: *n.* **1.** the amount or value of a wave or a fluctuating magnitude or variable. **2.** = MAXIMUM AMPLITUDE, or A, the maximum height of a **periodic** curve or wave; half the distance between the highest and lowest points on the curve or wave. **3.** = EFFECTIVE AMPLITUDE, the square root of the mean of all the squares of the values assumed by a periodic variable during one phase: i.e., essentially, the average height of the curve or wave throughout the phase. ➤The effective amplitude of a sound wave is the primary determiner of loudness. The amplitude of a light wave is related to intensity, although the relation is complicated by other variables.

ampulla (am·pul′ə): see **vestibule.**

amuck (ə·muk′): *adj.* characterized by a state of frenzy; of an emotional outburst with homicidal tendencies.—*Var.* **amok.**

amusia (ə·mū′zi·ə): *n.* loss or impairment of the ability to recognize or reproduce musical sounds. ➤It is analogous to **aphasia** in relation to speech.

amygdaloid nucleus (ə·mig′də·loid): a small almond-shaped mass of subcortical gray matter, under the tip of the temporal lobe, which is part of the olfactory system.

amyostasia (ə·mī"ō·stā'zhə): *n.* muscle **tremor** (*prefd.*).—*adj.* **amyostatic.**

amytal (am'i·tal): *n.* trade name for one of the barbiturate drugs, used as a sedative and hypnotic. ➤Under amytal, many patients can be led to discuss their problems more freely.

An or *At:* (*Ror.*) scoring code for **anatomy response.**

an-, a-: prefix meaning *un-, without, lacking, not.* (Preferably used only with words of Greek or Latin origin.)

anabolism (ə·na'bə·liz·əm): see **metabolism.**

anaclisis (ə·nak'lə·sis): *n.* dependence on another or others for support, esp. for emotional support.—*Syn.* emotional *dependence (*prefd.*).—*adj.* **anaclitic** (an·-ə·klit'ik), **anaclinic.**

ʃnaclitic object choice: (*psychoan.*) choice, whether witting or unwitting, of a love object resembling the person on whom the individual was dependent for comfort in infancy.

anacrotic pulse (an"ə·krot'ik): a pattern in which a small pressure precedes the principal pulse pressure.

ʃnacusia (an"ə·kū'zhə): *n.* total deafness. —*Var.* **anacousia, anacusis.**—*adj.* **anacusic.**

anaesthesia: see **anesthesia.**

anaglyph (an'ə·glif): *n.* a picture printed in two complementary colors not quite exactly superimposed and viewed through transparencies of the two colors, one to each eye. The result is **stereoscopic vision.** —*adj.* **anaglyphic.**

anaglyptoscope (-glip'tō·scōp): *n.* a device for showing the effect of shadows upon perspective by reversing the lighting of an object.—*Var.* **anaglyphoscope.**

anagogic (an"ə·goj'ik): *adj.* **1.** pertaining to ideals, or to the ideal or spiritual significance of psychic content or behavior. **2.** (*C. Jung*) pertaining to the moral tendencies of the **unconscious.**

anagogic interpretation: (*anal. psychol.*) dream interpretation which supposes a dream to reflect, not only conflict involving infantile wishes, but also, at a deeper level, the idealistic strivings of the unconscious.

anal (ā'nəl): *adj.* pertaining to the **anus.**

anal character: (*psychoan.*) a pattern of personality traits believed to be due to the habits, attitudes, and values formed when the child was learning control of defecation. ➤Believed to be associated with the pleasure of ANAL EXPULSION are the tendencies to conceit, suspicion, ambition, and loveless generosity; associated with the pleasure of ANAL RETENTION of feces are the tendencies to meticulousness, parsimony or

avarice, orderliness, and obstinacy. Since a child may have both pleasures, any or all of these tendencies may be combined in the anal character. Where marked, the anal character is regarded as an infantile **fixation** resulting from the child's inability to reconcile anal pleasures with social demands.

anal erotism or **eroticism:** sexual excitement, or the tendency thereto, aroused by stimulation of the anus, or by the complex of activities associated with defecation.— See also **anal stage, anal character.**

anal-expulsive or **-retentive:** see **anal character.**

analgesia (an·əl·jē'zi·ə): *n.* insensibility to pain.—*Syn.* ANALGIA, ANALGESTHESIA.— *adj.* **analgesic,** which is also used as a noun for something that relieves pain.

anality: *n.* the anal component in **libido.**

analogies test: a test of ability to supply or to recognize the fourth term which bears the same relation to the third as the second does to the first: e.g., *banana* is to *peel* as *oyster* is to *what?*

analog/libido: see **libido analog.**

analogue (an'ə·log): *n.* **1.** (*biol.*) an organ that is similar in function or in superficial appearance to another, but not in origin or in basic structure. **2.** (*logic*) that which resembles some other specific item.—*Var.* **analog.**—*adj.* **analogous.**

analogy (ə·nal'ə·ji): *n.* **1.** (*biol.*) correspondence in function between organs having a different structure or origin.—*Contr.* *w.* **homology. 2.** (*logic*) resemblance in relationships. ➤The use of argument by **analogy,** or ANALOGICAL THINKING, to *prove* something is invalid; for discovery, analogies may be invaluable. **3.** an explanation proceeding by point-by-point comparison of something with something else, i.e., by pointing to the many ways two things are **analogous** or similar.—*adj.* **analogous** (ə·nal'ə·gus).

analogy/response by: the principle that the organism, in a situation for which there is no previously learned response, responds as he would to a familiar situation that resembles the new one.—*Syn.* PRINCIPLE OF ANALOGY, law of *assimilation.

anal reflex: a reflex contraction of the anal sphincter muscle.

anal-sadistic stage: (*psychoan.*) a period in pregenital development that is dominated by **anal erotism** and by **sadism.**

anal stage: (*psychoan.*) the period in an infant's life when he is supposed to be preoccupied with the pleasurable feelings connected with the anus and with the process of defecation. ➤Expulsion and retention of feces are both said to bring pleasure. Either **anal-expulsive** or **anal-retentive** pleasure may be complicated by anxiety caused by toilet training, resulting in the development of **anal character.**

anal triad: (*S. Freud*) the three character traits growing out of mismanaged anal interests in infancy and childhood and constituting the **anal character:** obstinacy, stinginess, pedantic orderliness.

analysand (ə·nal'ə·zand): *n.* one who is being treated by **analysis (3).**

analysator = analyzer.

analysis: *n.* 1. (*logic*) a method of studying phenomena which breaks up the object of study into smaller units, either by physical separation or by thinking separately about the distinguished parts or qualities of the object. ➤*Syn.* STRUCTURAL or REDUCTIVE ANALYSIS. The search for **elementary** components of mental process by means of analytic introspection is the distinguishing characteristic of **structural psychology.** Currently, reductive analysis in psychology generally takes the form of an attempt to state psychological phenomena in stimulus-response terms and to reduce these further to physiological terms. See **reductionism.** 2. (*logic*) a method of varying the conditions under which a phenomenon takes place, as a means of determining its nature. ➤*Syn.* FUNCTIONAL ANALYSIS. In **Gestalt,** the term is narrowed to the study of the influence of member parts upon the whole. 3. the technique and practice of **psychoanalysis;** sometimes, loosely, also for the theory. ➤The chief procedures are the study of dreams and of the unconstrained **associations,** or revery, of the patient as expressed in words. This study is guided by a large number of canons of interpretation. 4. = **analytic psychology,** the school of C. Jung. (For this meaning, sometimes capitalized.)—*adj.* **analytic, analytical.**— *v.* **analyze.**

analysis/active: (*psychoan.*) a method in which the analyst does not confine himself to recording and interpreting free associations but intervenes actively, seeking to evoke significant associations, and giving advice on the basis of the **manifest content** of dreams as he intuitively interp ets them without the help of the **analys nd.**

analysis/activity: the breaking down of a complex behavior into smaller, more specific units. ➤Used esp. in curriculum studies.— *Cp.* **job analysis.**

analysis/aspective: finding that aspect of a given trait that is common to most people (in a given culture) who show that particular trait. ➤E.g., while the trait of courage doubtless differs from individual to individual, we may seek (though we may fail to find) a common quality characteristic of most courageous people.

analysis/child: treatment of a child accord-

ing to **psychoanalytic** principles, but utilizing play diagnosis and less formal techniques than the usual **analysis.**

analysis/content: see **content analysis.**

analysis/deep or **/depth:** an investigation that goes beneath the surface of the personality; specif., an investigation of **repressed** or **unconscious** factors.

analysis/didactic or **/training:** a psychoanalysis carried out with a view to educating an analyst for his work. It is preceded or accompanied by instruction, and generally is much shorter than the usual analysis.

analysis/existential: see **existential analysis.**

analysis/factor: see **factor analysis.**

analysis/functional: varying the conditions antecedent to a phenomenon with a view to determining which ones are necessary for its existence. ➤The term comes from **Gestalt** theory but the process is implied in all **induction.**

analysis/item: see **item analysis.**

analysis/job: see **job analysis.**

analysis/latent structure: see **latent structure analysis.**

analysis/lay: the practice of psychoanalysis by one without a medical degree. ➤Since the lay analyst frequently has extensive professional training, the word "lay" is misleading.

analysis/multivariate: any of a number of methods or techniques (such as **multiple-factor analysis** and **analysis of covariance**) that are employed to identify, or show the effect of, many variables when acting together.

analysis/occupational: see **job analysis.**

analysis of covariance: the extension of the methods used in the **analysis of variance** to include two or more related variables. ➤Adjustments are made in the experimental variable on the basis of its known correlation with one or more other variables that might affect the experimental outcome.

analysis of variance: a method for determining whether the differences (expressed as **variance**) found in a dependent variable, when it is exposed to the influence of one or more experimental variables, exceed what may be expected by chance. The *F* test is a measure of the probability of the beyond-chance difference. Each variable in turn can be treated as the dependent variable.

analysis/passive: a psychoanalysis in which the analyst makes little effort to direct the flow of the **analysand's** report. —*Ant.* **analysis/active.**

analysis/phonetic: breaking a sound sequence into smaller units: e.g., breaking a pronounced word into syllables, or syllables into still smaller units such as the initial *p*- and the final -*ant* of *pant*.

analysis/propaganda: appraisal of **propaganda** in terms of its motivation, sources or agencies, techniques, and content.—*Cp*. **content analysis.**

analysis/reductive: 1. see **analysis** (1). 2. (*psychoan*.) an **analysis** (3) carried far enough to reveal to both the analyst and the analysand the true cause of the latter's maladjustment.

analysis/regression: see **regression analysis.**

analysis/sequential: a procedure in which a certain set of calculations or operations is performed after each observation (or group of observations), and on the basis of that calculation decision is made whether to accept the hypothesis being tested, to accept its alternative, or to suspend judgment till more data are secured.

analysis/training = analysis/didactic.

analyst: *n*. 1. any professional practitioner of **analysis** (3); the person who elicits and interprets the reports of the **analysand**. (This is the preferred meaning). 2. an adherent of the school of C. Jung; an **analytical psychologist,** better called an ANALYTICAL PSYCHIATRIST. 3. an adherent of Freud or of the neo-Freudian school; a **psychoanalyst.** (This is the commonest meaning.)

analytic(al): see **analysis.**

analytical method: (*educ*.) a method of teaching reading in which a whole is broken into smaller and (presumably) familiar or more readily learned elements. Usually these are phonic elements, and the method more specifically the **phonic method.**

analytical psychologist: 1. a psychologist who emphasizes the method of **analysis** (3). 2. a practitioner of the analytical psychology of C. Jung.—See **analytical psychology** (2).—*Syn*. ANALYTICAL PSYCHIATRIST (*prefd.*).

analytic(al) psychology: 1. the systematic attempt to reduce the phenomena of psychology to their elements.—See **analysis** (1). 2. C. Jung's system of **psychoanalysis,** in contrast with Freud's. ➤This is an unfortunate appropriation of a psychological term—already well-established and carrying the more inclusive meaning implied in the words themselves—by a psychiatrist for his own highly special theory. Such trespass, if not ignorant, is arrogant. The confusion it causes is further compounded in the personal noun, **analytical psychologist.** Just as psychologists should not, and do not, claim to be psychiatrists, so psychiatrists should not call themselves psychologists.— *Syn*. JUNGIAN PSYCHOLOGY (*prefd.*), ANALYTICAL PSYCHIATRY.—See **psychology/divisions and schools of,** III.

analytical type: proposed term for a classification of persons who tend to attack problems by analyzing them into elements, to approach problems from relatively isolated points of view, to seek for details, to desire definiteness.—*Contr. w.* **synthesizing type.**—*Cp*. **type, elementarism.**

analytic approach or **method:** one that assumes that a complex process can be understood by breaking it into its components, and that the complex can best be improved by improving its parts.—*Cp*. **elementarism, atomism.**

analytic situation: the analytic session and the way it tends to determine the patient's behavior. ➤The most important part of the situation is the client's attitude toward the analyst.

analyzer: *n*. (*neurol*.) a functional unit consisting of **receptor, afferent** nerves, and **central** connections.—*Syn*. ANALYSATOR. ➤*Cp*. **nervous arc,** which includes an **efferent** nerve as well. The term was proposed by Pavlov as a name for the nerve structures that give us differential sensitivity.

analyzer/tridimensional: an apparatus for recording the extent, direction, and place in time of the movement of a bodily member.

anamnesis (an″əm·nē′səs): *n*. 1. recalling to mind; recollection. 2. those events in his personal and family history prior to the onset of a disorder which the patient remembers and considers possibly relevant. ➤The expansion of the term to include facts from the person's history or biography obtained in other ways is disapproved; HISTORY is entirely adequate for that.— *Contr. w.* **catamnesis.**—*adj.* **anamnestic** (-nes′tik).

anancastia (an″ən·kas′ti·ə): *n*. a condition in which a person feels himself forced to think, act, or feel against his own will, as in **obsessions, compulsions, phobias.**—*Var*. **anankastia.**—*adj.* **anancastic.**

anaphia (an·ā′fi·ə; -af′i·ə): *n*. lack of, or defect in, the sense of touch.—*adj.* **anaptic** (-ap′tik).

anaphrodisiac (an·af″rō·diz′i·ak): *adj*. pertaining to, or causing lack of, sexual or erotic feeling.—*n*. **anaphrodisia.**

anaphylaxis (an″ə·fi·lak′səs): *n*. excessive susceptibility; esp., hypersensitivity to proteins introduced into the body (one form of allergy).—*adj.* **anaphylactic.**

anaphylaxis/psychic: hypersensitivity to a kind of experience, developed as the result of a psychic **trauma,** which eventuates in neurotic symptoms when a similar experience occurs in later years.

anarthria (an·är′thri·ə): *n*. 1. (*prefd.*) complete inability to produce articulate speech. 2. defective articulation; **dysarthria.** —*adj.* **anarthric.**

anastomosis (ə·nas″tə·mō'səs): *n.* (*neurol.*) the joining of two tissues, esp. of two nerves, by means of small fibers.—*Cp.* synapse.—*v.* anastomose.

anatomical index = ossification ratio.

anatomy: *n.* 1. the size, shape, and proportions of an organism and of its parts or organs. 2. the science that studies the structure of plants and animals.—*Syn.* (for 2) morphology.—*adj.* anatomical.

anatomy responses or *An* or *At*: (*Ror.*) a scoring category for internal body details such as are seen only in dissection or by X ray.—*Contr. w. Hd.*

-ance, -ancy: suffix meaning *act* or *fact of doing; state; quality; condition.*

anchorage: *n.* 1. = perceptual *anchoring. 2. standards with reference to which judgment takes place. ➤Such anchorage need not be explicitly adopted or consciously recognized.—*Syn.* anchoring point.—*Cp.* criterion.—*v.* anchor.

anchoring of ego: the process whereby a person finds security and satisfaction in relationships with persons, or groups of persons, or even with things; the security and sense of being oneself most wholly when related to familiar friends or possessions.—*Syn.* identification.

anchoring/perceptual: a process by which a perceptual response is determined not merely by the properties of the object but by a **frame of reference** supplied by the observer. ➤E.g., the size of an object as seen is determined by what it is thought to be. A somewhat shapeless blot in a picture which is accepted as representing a sheep will be perceived in the appropriate proportions; the same blot identified as an elephant will be perceived as much larger. Frequently a special feature of the percept attains special prominence and other features are related to it.—*Syn.* anchorage.

anchoring point: a reference point from which other items in a series are judged: e.g., the point that divides ranked items into *preferred* and *not preferred* is such an **anchoring point.**

anchoring/social: the process whereby a person's judgments or his attitudes toward a variety of objects are determined, not directly by his own perception of the facts nor by his reflection on them, but by what he interprets as the attitudes or judgments of a **reference group.** The reference group may have either positive or negative influence.

anchylosis = ankylosis.

ancillary (an'sə·ler″i): *adj.* auxiliary; helping; subordinate.

ancillary statistic: a statistic which, while giving no information directly about the **parameter** that is being estimated, does help to determine, and possibly improve, the accuracy of the sample used to estimate the parameter.

andro-: combining form meaning *man, masculine.*

androgen (an'drō·jən): *n.* a hormone, secreted in both sexes but more abundantly in males, that influences the development of maleness, either of structure or behavior.—*adj.* androgenic.

androgenic: *adj.* causing maleness; characterizing experiences or **hormones** that contribute to maleness.

androgynous (an·droj'ə·nəs): *adj.* said of a male presenting many of the characteristic structures (or by extension, the behaviors) of the female. ➤Sometimes loosely used for **hermaphroditic.** For behavior, **effeminate** is more appropriate, though it has unfortunate derogatory overtones. The parallel condition in females is called **gynandrous.**—*n.* androgyny.—*pers. n.* androgyne (an'drō·jin; -jīn).

andromania = nymphomania.

and-summation hypothesis: a term used by **Gestalt** psychologists to characterize the view that wholes may be constructed by the mere addition of distinct parts, in contrast with their own view that elements becoming part of a whole lose their distinct identity.—*Syn.* **bundle,** or **mosaic, hypothesis.**

anecdotal evidence: casually observed incidents. ➤The evidence is seldom reportable in sufficient detail to be trusted for generalizations, but it is often a source of hypothesis for further investigation.—See **anecdotal record, critical incident technique.**

anecdotal record: a record of casually observed events that seem to the reporter to have possible significance. ➤It is frequently used in schools. Although the possibility of error, especially of overgeneralization, is very great, important clues and hypotheses may be suggested. It is to be distinguished from systematic observation according to a plan, and from **experiment.**—*Cp.* **diary.**

anechoic (an″ə·kō'ik): *adj.* free from echo; said especially of a room or similar enclosure.

anemia: *n.* a deficiency of blood. ➤The deficiency may be in quantity, either general or in certain parts, or in quality. When unqualified, a deficiency in red blood cells or hemoglobin is usually meant.—*adj.* **anemic.**

anencephalia (an″ən·sef·ā'li·ə): *n.* (*anat.*) absence of the brain. ➤Not to be used figuratively.—*Syn.* ANENCEPHALY (-sef'ə·li). —*adj.* **anencephalic** (-sef·al'ik), **anencephalous** (-sef'ə·ləs).

anencephaly = anencephalia.

aneneia (an″en·ē'yə) = deaf-mutism.

anergasia (an″ər·gā'zhi·ə): *n.* loss of functional activity.—*adj.* **anergastic.**

anergia (an·ẽr′ji·ə): *n.* lack of energy; inactivity. ➤See **bogus erudition,** of which this wholly unnecessary term is an example. —*Syn.* ANERGY (an′ər·ji).—*adj.* **anergic** (-ẽr′jik).

anergy = **anergia.**

anesthesia (an″es·thē′zhə): *n.* loss of sensitivity to stimuli, whether because of use of a drug, of neural lesions, or of functional disorder. It may be local or general.— *Var.* **anesthesis, anaesthesia.**—*adj.* **anesthetic.**—*n.* **anesthetic,** a drug that induces anesthesia.

anesthesia/glove or /shoe or /stocking: insensitivity to touch in the area indicated. ➤The anesthetic region ends sharply at the wrist, ankle, or stocking top. The distribution of sensory nerves is such that no possible local injury could give rise to an anesthesia limited in this fashion. The sensory nerve that supplies the hand, e.g., supplies the lower arm as well. Either some of the hand would not be affected or parts of the arm would also. It is thus demonstrably a symptom of a **functional disorder,** generally of **hysteria.**

anesthesis = anesthesia.

aneurism (an′ū·riz·əm): *n.* abnormal dilation of an artery or vein. ➤Brain **aneurisms** often give rise to nervous or mental symptoms.—*Var.* **aneurysm.**

anger: *n.* an emotional reaction—aroused by being interfered with, injured, or threatened—that is characterized by certain distinctive facial grimaces, by marked reactions of the **autonomic nervous system,** and by overt or concealed symbolic activities of attack or offense. ➤**Anger** is a passing emotional disturbance; **rage** is anger out of control **Hostility** is a condition of enmity, more or less enduring, marked by angry feeling, as are also **animus** (which see for other meanings) and **animosity.** All three name a relatively simple **attitude** or **sentiment.** Hatred and **hate** connote a more highly complex sentiment, in which a variety of reaction tendencies toward the object are organized in conformity with the central attitude of **anger,** e.g., joy felt at the discomfiture of the person hated.

angina (an·ji′nə; an′jə·nə): *n.* **1.** any inflammatory disease, esp. in the throat region, characterized by spasms of choking or suffocation, as in croup or quinsy. **2.** = ANGINA PECTORIS, a heart disease marked by spasms of pain and suffocation in the chest. —*adj.* **anginal.**

angio- (an′ji·ō-): combining form meaning *blood vessel:* e.g., ANGIONEUROSIS, a neurosis with symptoms in the circulatory system.

angle/facial: see **facial angle.**
angle/visual: see **visual angle.**

angstrom unit: (*phys.*) a unit of wave length equal to one ten-thousandth of a **micron.**—*Var.* **Ångström.**—*abbr.* A., A.U., Å., Å.U.

anguish: *n.* great mental or physical distress; agony.

angular gyrus: (*neurol.*) a *cerebral *convolution that forms the posterior portion of the lower **parietal** region. In the left hemisphere it is associated with speech function.

angular perspective: the relation between angles formed by lines in the field of vision and angles formed by the images of the lines on the retina.

anhedonia (an″hi·dō′ni·ə): *n.* absence of pleasure or unpleasure where normally expected.

aniconia (an″i·kō′ni·ə): *n.* absence of mental **imagery.**—*adj.* **aniconic** (-kon′ik).

anima: *n.* **1.** the **soul.** **2.** (*C. Jung*) that part of the **psyche** which is in communication with the **unconscious.**—*Contr. w.* **persona. 3.** (*C. Jung*) the femininity component of the **soul-image,** in contrast with the masculinity component, ANIMUS. Anima is often used as if it were the feminine component of men only, and animus as the masculine component of women only. But both men and women are said to have both components.

animal: *n.* a living organism, typically capable of locomotion and not capable of photosynthesis. ➤In psychology, animal often means the **subject** of an experiment, whether human or subhuman.—*Syn.* **person, individual, organism** (technically the last includes plants, but in psychology nearly always means an animal).

animal behavior: the responses of subhuman animals to stimuli.

animal content or *A:* (*Ror.*) a scoring category for a reference to any animal species other than man.

animal magnetism: (*hist.*) Mesmer's term for the supposed force that was held to induce **hypnosis** by passing from operator to subject.

animal psychology: **1.** the study of the behavior of animals; esp., the comparative study of different animal species. **2.** any study using subhuman animal subjects. ➤In many such studies the purpose is the derivation of general psychological principles.—See **psychology/divisions** and **schools of, IX.**

animatism: see **animism.**

animism: *n.* **1.** an implicit belief that certain important objects in the environment are living or that they manifest purpose.— *Syn.* ANIMATISM, used by anthropologists to distinguish this primitive belief from meanings (**2, 3, 4**). But in reference to childish belief, **animism** is more commonly used, various stages being distinguished. **2.** doctrine that various classes of objects— or all—have souls. **3.** doctrine that soul or mind has a real or causal influence in the activity of a living creature. **4.** = **interactionism.**—*adj.* **animistic.**—*pers. n.* **animist.**

animosity: *n.* strong hatred or ill will; open or active hostility.—See **anger**

animus: *n.* **1.** animating spirit or disposition; intention. **2.** a spirit or feeling of active hostility; **animosity.**—*Syn.* see **anger.** **3.** see **anima (3).**

aniseikonia (an"ə·sī·kō'ni·ə): *n.* a condition in which the two retinal images are different in size and shape.—*adj.* **aniseikonic** (-kon'ik).

anis(o)- (an·ī'sō-): combining form meaning *unequal, dissimilar.*

anisocoria (-kō'ri·ə): *n.* inequality of size of the pupils of the two eyes.

anisometropia (-mə·trō'pi·ə): *n.* inequality in the refractive power of the two eyes.—*adj.* **anisometropic** (-trop'ik).

anisotropy (an"ī·sot'rō·pi): *n.* **1.** the change in apparent length of a line when it is rotated from vertical to horizontal. **2.** the change in appearance of objects when given a different orientation in space: e.g., the difficulty of reading type upside down. —*adj.* **anisotropic** (an·ī"sō·trop'ik).

ankle clonus (klō'nəs; klon'əs): jerky, abnormal reflex flexion of the ankle.

ankle reflex = **Achilles jerk.**

ankylosis (ang"ki·lō'səs): *n.* a condition in which the cartilage or bones of a joint have grown together.—*Var.* **anchylosis.**—*adj.* **ankylosed, ankylotic** (-lot'ik).—*v.* **ankylose.**

anlage (än'lä·ge): *n.* (*Ger.*) in embryology, the foundation group of cells from which an organ will develop; metaphorically, traits and experiences that may be expected to develop later into a definite mental condition; a predisposing condition.

nnoyance: *n.* a feeling or attitude in which certain aspects of the environment are reacted to with distaste or rejection.—*v.* **annoy.**

annoyer: *n.* an incident or object, esp. a minor one, to which one tends to react with rejection or distaste; an irritating condition which the organism seeks to terminate or remove.—*Contr. w.* **satisfier.**

annulment: *n.* (*psychoan.*) the process of rendering painful ideas "nonexistent" or ineffective for behavior. ➤In **annulment** it is said the ideas are converted into daydreams; in **repression** they are entirely banished from awareness.

anode (an'ōd): *n.* the positive pole or electrode in an electric battery.—*adj.* **anodic** (an·od'ik), **anodal** (-ō'dəl).

anodyne (an'ō·dīn): *n.* a substance or treat-

ment that reduces pain.—*Syn.* **analgesic.** —*adj.* **anodyne.**

anoegenetic (an"ō·i·jə·net'ik): *adj.* applied by Spearman to three fundamental processes that do not yield new knowledge: **reproduction, disparition,** clearness-variation.—*Cp.* **noegenetic.**

anoesia = **anoia.**

anoetic (an"ō·et'ik): *adj.* **1.** not self-evident. **2.** not leading to, or not pertaining to, knowledge or cognition: feeling may be considered anoetic. **3.** passively receptive of what is presented, without conscious or·ganization.—*n.* **anoesis** (an"ō·ē'sis).

anoia (an·oi'ə): *n.* idiocy.—*Syn.* **ANOESIA** (an"ō·ē'zhə).—See **deficiency/mental.**

anomaloscope (ə·nom'ə·lə·skōp): *n.* spectral apparatus for the determination of color weakness by the use of the **Rayleigh equation.**

anomalous differences: differences, in a series of observations, from what is to be expected. ➤Such differences set the experimenter to work to find their cause.

anomalous trichromatism: see **trichromatism.**

anomaly: (ə·nom'ə·li): *n.* that which is markedly irregular, exceptional, deviating from the typical, but not necessarily diseased or pathological. ➤**Anomaly** is often a good substitute for a more derogatory word, such as **perversion:** e.g., **sexual anomaly** for *sex perversion.*—*adj.* **anomalous.**

anomaly/sex or **/sexual:** see both **sex anomaly** and **sexual anomaly.**

anomia (ə·nō'mi·ə): *n.* a form of **aphasia** in which names of objects cannot be recalled.—*adj.* **anomic** (-nom'ik).

anomy (an'ə·mi): *n.* the state of being without organization or system, esp. without natural law or uniformity.—*Var.* **anomie.**

anopia (an·ō'pi·ə): *n.* **1.** absence of sight, esp. that resulting from defect of the eyes. **2.** = **anopsia (2).**

anopsia (-op'si·ə): **1.** failure to use vision. **2.** upward **strabismus.**

anorexia (an"ô·rek'si·ə): *n.* lack of ap petite for food.—*Contr. w.* **bulimia.**—*adj* **anorectic, anorectous.**

anorthopia (an"ôr·thō'pi·ə): *n.* **1.** a disturb ance in vision in which objects are seen **as** distorted. **2.** = **strabismus** (*prefd.*).

anosmia (an·oz'mi·ə): *n.* lack of sensitivity to smells.—*Syn.* **anosphresia.**—*adj.* **anosmic, anosmatic** (an"əz·mat'ik).

anosognosia (an"ə·sog·nō'zhə): *n.* failure, or refusal, to recognize that one has sensory or motor defects or a disease: e.g., refusal to recognize one's own hearing impairment or paralysis. ➤The concept is doubtless important, but does it need a pretentious name?

anosphresia (an"əs·frē'zha): *n.* insen-

sitivity to odors.—*Syn.* **anosmia** (*prefd.*).
anoxemia (an″ok·sē′mi·ə): *n.* deficiency of
oxygen in the blood.—*adj.* **anoxemic.**
anoxia (an·ok′si·ə): *n.* deficiency in the supply of oxygen to the tissues.—*Cp.* **anoxemia.**
Anregung (än′rä·gùng): *n.* (*Ger., stirring
up*) something that stirs an organism
to activity. ➤It can cover anything from a
stimulus to an **incentive.** But English, too,
has vague terms for this; need we say it in
German?
Anschauung (än′shou·ùng): *n.* (*Ger.,*
literally, *gazing upon*) **1.** (*philos.*) direct
awareness, as in simple **sensing** or in **intuition. 2.** (*D. B. Klein*) a highly generalized attitude or control principle that manifests itself in a kind of behavior. ➤It differs from **attitude** in not being directed
at an object and not having a **valence.**
Thus, **sharpening** is an *Anschauung* that
denotes a tendency to be hypersensitive to
details, to exaggerate small changes. The
details may be of any sort and may be
either liked or disliked. ¶The term is not
easy for English tongues and does not seem
very appropriate; it is included here because the concept is not otherwise named,
and in the hope that a better term will be
suggested. Perhaps **schema** will do.
answer key: a device that displays in convenient form the correct (or incorrect) answers to a test; a scoring key.
ant.: *abbr.* for **anterior.**
antagonistic: *adj.* acting in opposition.—
See esp. **antagonistic muscles, color antagonists.**
antagonistic colors: see **color antagonists.**
antagonistic cooperation: (*sociol.*) the
suppression of antagonisms by persons or
groups in the effort to achieve a common
objective.
antagonistic muscles: muscles, arranged
in pairs, that pull in opposite directions
upon a moving part such as a bone: flexor
and extensor muscles are antagonistic.—
Syn. ANTAGONISTS, ASSOCIATED ANTAGONISTS.
—*Ant.* **agonists.**
ante-: prefix meaning *before* (in time), *in
front of* (in space).
antecedent: *n.* **1.** that which goes before or
precedes. **2.** (*logic*) the "if" clause in **hypothetical reasoning** (which see for illustration).
antecedent/necessary: (*logic*) an event
which necessarily precedes another event
and without which the latter cannot occur.
—*Syn.* **cause.**
antecedent-to-response analysis: the
analysis of a brief period of organismic
activity as consisting of a sequence: manipulatable antecedent conditions→hypothesized
intervening variables→response. ➤Nearly

all **behavior theory** is based on this pattern.
antedating goal response/fractional or
r$_G$ or **f.a.g.r.**: a hypothetical **antedating
reaction** that occurs progressively earlier
in a response chain during acquisition of a
classical *conditioned response, and
thus provides stimuli which may become
conditioned to ensuing responses. ➤The
fractional antedating goal response is put
forward as an explanation of latent learning.—*Syn.* FRACTIONAL ANTICIPATORY GOAL
RESPONSE.
antedating reaction or **response:** a response that occurs earlier in a repeated
sequence of events than it originally occurred in that sequence; esp., a response
that occurs prior to the stimulus that originally evoked it. ➤If R$_3$ was originally the
response to S$_3$ in the series S$_1$, S$_2$, S$_3$, it is
called an antedating response when it is
evoked by S$_1$ or S$_2$. **Aversive** or **avoidance**
responses are antedating.—*Syn.* **anticipatory response,** but this is ambiguous and
theory begging.—*Cp.* **expectancy,** a hypothetical construct to explain the phenomenon.
anterior: *adj.* before (in time), or in front
(in space).—*Contr. w.* **posterior.** ➤In
anatomy, **anterior** and **posterior** are used
ambiguously. In embryology, they refer respectively to the head (or **cephalic**) and
tail (or **caudal**) ends. But in man, with
his upright posture, the front aspect is the
ventral, the back aspect is the **dorsal.**
Superior and **inferior** thus tend to replace **anterior** and **posterior** (though by
no means uniformly); but **ventral** and
dorsal are preferred for the front and back
sides of an upright animal.
**anterior-posterior development/princi-
ple of** = **cephalocaudad development/
principle of.**
anterograde: *adj.* working or proceeding
forward.
anterograde amnesia: see **amnesia.**
anthropo-, -anthropy (an′thrə·pō-; -pi):
combining forms meaning *human* or *humanlike.*
anthropocentrism: *n.* the assumption, usually unargued or even unwitting, that man
is the central fact of the universe, to which
all other facts have reference.—*adj.* **an-
thropocentric.**
anthropoid: *adj.* resembling man; esp., pertaining to the larger apes (gorilla, gibbon,
chimpanzee, orangutan) but not to the
monkeys.—*Distg. fr.* **Anthropoidea,** which
includes monkeys and man, as well as apes.
(But the plural form **anthropoids** is sometimes used as synonym for **Anthropoidea.**)
Anthropoidea (-poi′di·ə): *n. pl.* (*zool.*) the
suborder of primates that includes the mon-

keys, apes, and man.—See **primate.**—*Cp.* **anthropoid.**

anthropology: *n.* **1.** the science of man. **2.** the comparative study of the chief divisions of man, including somatic characteristics, social habits and customs, linguistics, and prehistory. ⇥In the broad sense of **(1),** it includes both sociology and psychology. In the narrower sense of **(2),** anthropology is distinct from, but utilizes, the concepts of human anatomy, psychology, and sociology. The two main divisions are **physical** and **cultural** **anthropology.—See also **anthropometry, ethnology, ethnography.**

anthropology/cultural: that branch of anthropology devoted to study of the culture of **nonliterate** peoples, and of the culture of so-called civilized peoples by methods adapted from those devised for nonliterate groups. ⇥As *distg. fr.* archeology, which studies material remains, cultural anthropology depends upon description of the social behavior of peoples by those who have observed it, preferably by trained field workers. More and more the limitation to nonliterate peoples is disappearing, and cultural anthropology is becoming a general **sociology.**—*Syn.* SOCIAL ANTHROPOLOGY.

anthropology/physical: **1.** the study of the **somatic,** especially the **anthropometric,** characteristics of the individual members of different societies or ethnic groups, and the relationships between these characteristics and the culture. **2.** the study of the biological evolution of the varieties of man.—*Syn.* SOMATOLOGY (rare).

anthropology/social = **anthropology/cultural.**

anthropometric (body) **type** = **body type.**

anthropometry (an″thrō·pom′ə·tri): *n.* **1.** the science, or the technique, of measuring the physical proportions and shape of the individual human being. **2.** the determination of the relative frequency with which the chief physical characteristics occur in different social groups.—*adj.* **anthropometric** (-pō·met′rik).

anthropomorphic: *adj.* formed like a human being; having human characteristics.—*n.* **anthropomorphism.**

anthropomorphism: *n.* the ascribing of distinctively human characteristics to gods, animals, or inanimate objects. ⇥Its use is often derogatory, implying that someone has merely assumed that animals can do what the critic believes them not capable of. However, when a distinguished critic objects to "purpose" in a description of human behavior, because that is **anthropomorphism,** he himself is guilty of **zoomorphism** (or THERIOMORPHISM), the opposite error of depicting man with only the character-

istics of subhuman species, or of denying him any higher characteristics. How, indeed, should human behavior be described if not as **anthropomorphic?**—*Cp.* the similarly opposed pair, **enelicomorphism** and **pedomorphism** (see the latter).

anthroponomy (-pon′ə·mi): *n.* the science of human **behavior;** man as studied by **behaviorists.** ⇥This was suggested by W. Hunter as a better term than **behaviorism,** but it did not have "take."

anthropopathy (-pop′ə·thi): *n.* the attribution of human feelings to nonhumans whether gods or subhuman animals.—*Syn* **anthropomorphism.**

anti- (an′ti-): prefix meaning **1.** *against, opposed to.* **2.** *preventing,* or *counteracting* **3.** *the opposite* or *reverse.*

anticathexis (-kath·ek′səs): *n.* (*psychoan.*) **1.** the prevention of satisfaction (or **cathexis**) by the action of internal or psychic forces originating in ego or superego. **2.** the shift to an emotional charge of opposite sign, e.g., from love to hate, or vice versa.—*Syn.* (for **2**) **counterinvestment.**

anticipation: *n.* **1.** adjusting to a coming stimulus situation of which one is forewarned.—*Syn.* **set, anticipatory response** (*not* **anticipation response**). **2.** a mental attitude of readiness (usually favorable readiness) for a coming event.—*Syn.* **expectancy.**

anticipation error: in serial learning experiments, making a response before it is due. ⇥ANTICIPATORY ERROR (which is more often used) is ambiguous.—See **anticipatory response (2).**

anticipation image: see **imagination (2).**

anticipation/level of = **aspiration/level of.**

anticipation method = **prompting method.**

anticipation response: **1.** = **anticipation error.** **2.** = **anticipatory response (2).**

anticipatory goal reaction: a goal-directed action prompted by the general situation but occurring in advance of the specific stimulus or **cue** that originally evoked it. —*Syn.* **antedating reaction** (*prefd.* when part of a repeated sequence).

anticipatory goal response/fractional = **antedating goal response/fractional.**

anticipatory response: **1.** a partial response that is made when the full movement is inhibited or delayed: e.g., the incomplete writing movements of the fingers while thinking, pen in hand, of what to write. **2.** responding before receiving the appropriate stimulus: e.g., a runner responds to other stimuli than the starter's pistol and jumps the gun. ⇥ANTICIPATION RESPONSE is proposed for this meaning, in order to distinguish it from **(1).** Both **(1)** and **(2)** are to be distinguished from

preparatory response, one that brings the organism closer to a final **consummatory response:** e.g., cutting the steak preparatory to eating it. **3.** = **antedating reaction** (*prefd.*).

antidromic conduction (-drom'ik): see **conduction/antidromic.**

anti-intellectualism: *n.* the attitude or doctrine that minimizes the importance of intellect and knowledge, and places first importance on feeling or action.

antimetropia (-mə·trō'pi·ə): *n.* the condition of having one eye nearsighted and the other farsighted.

antinomy (an·tin'ə·mi): *n.* (*logic*) a contradiction between two principles, each of them taken to be true or valid; or between the inferences drawn from such principles.

antipathy (an·tip'ə·thi): *n.* aversion or dislike; distaste.

anti-Semitism: *n.* a form of prejudice that ascribes faults to Jews as a group; the complex of discriminatory actions that accords with the prejudice.—See **ethnocentrism.**

antisocial: *adj.* **1.** harmful to society. **2.** averse to social intercourse or to being with people; unsociable. **3.** hostile to social organizations or codes.—*Distg. fr.* **unsocial,** lacking in social attributes; and *fr.* **nonsocial,** which means that the term **social** is irrelevant.

antisocial reaction: (*Stan. Psychiat.*) a personality disorder that brings the individual chronically into trouble with society. It manifests itself in lack of loyalty to, or identification with, authority; or in hostility to authority, to society in general, to social or moral codes.

antonym test: a test in which the task is to give the opposite of a presented word.

anus (ā'nəs): *n.* the lower opening of the **alimentary canal.**—*adj.* **anal** (ā'nəl).

anxiety: *n.* **1.** an unpleasant emotional state in which a present and continuing strong **desire** or **drive** seems likely to miss its goal. **2.** a fusion of fear with the anticipation of future evil. **3.** marked and continuous fear. **4.** a continuous fear of low intensity. **5.** a feeling of threat, especially of a fearsome threat, without the person's being able to say what he thinks threatens. **6.** (*beh. theory*) a secondary *drive for which the establishing operation is the acquisition of a specific **avoidance response,** and the symptom of which is that the stimulation of the anxiety response depresses the rate of the responses usual in the situation and produces other behaviors inappropriate to the situation.—*adj.* **anxious.**
➤Meaning (1), with its emphasis upon a present desire or drive but with a future reference, seems to have been the commonest English usage. The affective state is no more fear than it is disappointment, and

is perhaps a distinct quality. **Anxiety** came, however, to be the translation of the German *Angst* as used in psychiatry, for which meaning (2) is approximate. Especially in psychiatry and psychology, therefore, the word has almost lost its reference to a present desire or drive; in its place is reference to a sympathetically induced feeling aroused by the anticipation of a vaguely fearsome future.

Meanings (3) and (4) are popular but also appear in technical writings—both of them, contradictory as they are. Meaning (5) is popular but is also essentially the usage of psychoanalytically inclined writers, who attribute the sense of threat to conscious or unconscious **conflict.** For meaning (1), **fear** is often used where **anxiety** is more accurate; but in (3) and (4) **anxiety** is used where **fear** is more appropriate.

When a term is frequently employed in behavioristic learning theory, in psychoanalysis, and in nearly every field of psychology between them, the variety and shadings of meaning become very troublesome. **Anxiety** must be read with great vigilance for an author's meaning or, more often than not, his several meanings.

anxiety/basic: (*K. Horney*) feelings (originating in childhood) of loneliness, helplessness, and counterhostility in the face of the environment, which is conceived as hostile. ➤This is a more inclusive construct than Freud's **objective** *anxiety.

anxiety/discharge of: (*psychoan.*) relief of unconscious tension by the actions of everyday life.—*Distg. fr.* **anxiety/resolution of.**

anxiety/dramatization of: the re-enactment of the sources of **anxiety,** in symbolic form and in the presence of the therapist.

anxiety/ego: (*psychoan.*) a response to something that is apprehended as a threat to the **ego.** ➤*Distg. fr.* **fear,** which is a response to external threats. The threat associated with ego anxiety comes from the pressure of **instinctual** demands that are opposed to reality or to prohibitions of the **superego.** Ego anxiety is the root of all **ego defense.**

anxiety equivalent: (*psychoan.*) an intense functional disturbance of the body (e.g., palpitation of the heart, difficult breathing, contractures) that takes the place of conscious fear or anxiety.

anxiety/erotized: a paradoxical reaction in which a person heads toward the threatening situation and enjoys doing so.

anxiety fixation: (*psychoan.*) maintenance, into a later phase of development, of **anxiety** associated with dangerous situa· tions of an earlier phase.

anxiety/free-floating: a chronic state of anxiety (5) which attaches to almost any situation or activity of the individual. ➤It is clear that the individual's fear that something disagreeable (or worse) will happen is not founded on any rational appraisal of the situation, though he may find ostensible grounds for the fear.

anxiety hysteria: a disorder characterized by manifest *anxiety, sometimes also by conversions (which see).

anxiety indicator: any unintended behavior which, by its inappropriateness to the situation, reveals the existence and at least the general source of anxiety.

anxiety/instinctual: fear of the intensity of one's own organic impulses, i.e., of one's instincts in the psychoanalytic sense.

anxiety/manifest: (psychoan.) an apparent or conscious anxiety, believed to be symptomatic of repression.—Cp. conversion of affect.—Distg. fr. anxiety/primal. —Syn. OVERT ANXIETY.

anxiety neurosis: a neurosis characterized by anxiety, or dread, without apparent object or cause. ➤It is doubted whether a separate neurosis distinct from anxiety hysteria is to be recognized.

anxiety/neurotic: a free-floating *anxiety, or general apprehensiveness, without objective justification.—Cp. anxiety/objective.

anxiety object: (psychoan.) a person or object, symbolizing the original cause, upon which anxiety is displaced.

anxiety/objective: anxiety with an intelligible cause or occasion.

anxiety/oral: see oral anxiety.

anxiety/organic: anxiety that originates in organic pain and real physical disease, although it may nonetheless be neurotic in character.

anxiety/primal: (S. Freud) the anxiety assumed to arise in the infant in connection with separation from the mother at birth. ➤In Freud's later writing, this is the cause of repression, whereas manifest *anxiety is the result.

anxiety reaction: (Stan. Psychiat.) a condition of diffuse anxiety characterized by anxious expectation and frequently associated with somatic symptoms. The anxiety is not restricted, as in phobia, to definite situations or objects.—Syn. ANXIETY STATE.

anxiety/real = anxiety/objective.

anxiety/resolution of: (psychoan.) the process through which the unconscious roots of anxiety are brought to light and mastered by the subject. ➤Distg. fr. discharge of *anxiety, which reduces tension but leaves the causes of anxiety untouched.

anxiety tolerance: the ability to continue one's usual activities without too great loss of effectiveness despite anxiety, whether it

be objective anxiety or resulting from conflict.

anxious: adj. 1. disturbed over a possible future ill. 2. causing anxiety.—See anxiety.

anxious mania: a mixed form of manic-depressive psychosis in which, instead of depressed activity, there is excitable anxiety.

AP = action potential.

Ap: (Ror.) scoring code for Erfassungstypus.

APA, A.P.A.: 1. American Psychological Association. 2. American Psychiatric Association.

apareunia (ap"ə·rü'ni·ə): n. inability to have coitus.

apathy (ap'ə·thi): n. lack of feeling or interest in situations that usually provoke such reactions; listlessness; indifference.— adj. apathetic.

ape: n. 1. a chimpanzee, gorilla, or orangutan; an anthropoid. 2. any monkey.—See primate.

aperiodic reinforcement: see reinforcement/aperiodic.

aperture (ap'ər·chər): n. 1. an opening or gap. 2. in a camera, telescope, etc., the diameter of the opening through which light passes.

aphakia (ə·fā'ki·ə): n. loss or lack of the lens of the eye.—adj. aphakial, aphakic (ə·fak'ik).

aphasia (ə·fā'zhə): n. loss or impairment of the ability to use language because of lesions in the brain. ➤Aphasia may be SENSORY (inability to understand words; = word blindness or word deafness) or MOTOR (inability to speak, or to speak the words intended; = anarthria). Many varieties are distinguished according to the specific impairment: e.g., SYNTACTICAL APHASIA, inability to arrange words properly; BRADY-PHASIA, groping speech; and many others. The term is highly general and tends to be loosely used, but authorities insist on restriction to cases resulting from brain lesion. Hence, it does not include stammering or stuttering, which are functional, nor difficulties resulting from defects in the vocal organs.—adj. aphasic.—pers. n. aphasiac (-zi·ak).

aphasia area or zone: the area of the brain most likely to be affected in aphasia. ➤In right-handed persons it is the left lateral surface of the cerebrum in the neighborhood of the Sylvian fissure.

aphasia/auditory: inability, due to brain damage, to comprehend spoken words.— Syn. WORD DEAFNESS (not prefd.), sensory *aphasia.

aphasia/functional: ➤Since aphasia is defined as organic, this expression is a contradiction.

aphasia/global: total aphasia; motor and sensory aphasia combined.

aphasia/motor: see aphasia.

aphasia/nominal: inability to speak or to recognize the name of a person or object.

aphasia/semantic: aphasia characterized by inability to grasp the meaning of a phrase as a whole, though each word may be recognized.

aphasia/sensory: see aphasia.

aphasia/syntactic(al): aphasia characterized by faulty sentence structure.—Syn. ASYNTACTICISM.

aphasia/verbal: aphasia characterized by defective power of pronouncing words.

aphasia/visual: loss of ability to understand the written word.—Syn. alexia.

aphemia (ə·fē'mi·ə): n. (obsoles.) knowing what one wants to say but being unable to utter the words. >The condition may be functional or organic. Motor *aphasia is aphemia due to brain lesion.—adj. aphemic (ə·fem'ik).

aphonia (ə·fō'ni·ə): n. loss of voice arising either from organic or from psychic causes, but not from brain lesion.—Syn. APHONY (af'ə·ni).—adj. aphonic (ə·fon'ik).

aphony = aphonia.

aphoria (ā·fôr'i·ə): n. (P. Janet) a condition of weakness or lack of energy that does not yield to training or exercise and is regarded as a manifestation of neurosis.

aphrasia (ə·frā'zhə): n. functional inability, or refusal, to speak or understand connected speech, although the person may say or understand detached words.—Distg. fr. aphasia, which is always organic. (But usage is inconsistent.)

aphrenia (ə·frē·ni·ə): n. (psychiat.) loss of function of the conscious mind.—Distg. fr. dementia.

aphrodisia (af"rō·diz'i·a): n. sex excitation.

aphrodisiac (af"rō·diz'i·ak: 1. adj. exciting the sexual impulse.—2. n. any drug that arouses sexual impulses.

aphthongia (af·thon'ji·ə): n. a form of motor *aphasia characterized by a spasm of certain speech muscles.

aplasia (ə·plā'zhə): n. (med.) failure of a tissue to develop.—adj. aplastic (ā·plas'-tik).

apnea (ap·nē'ə): n. partial privation of breath; breathlessness caused by forced respiration or excess oxygen in the blood.— Var. apnoea.—adj. apneal, apneic (-nē'ik).

Apollonian: see Dionysian.

apopathetic (ap"ō·path·et'ik): adj. of behavior not overtly directed toward others but clearly influenced by their presence, e.g., showing off.

apoplexy: n. sudden loss of consciousness and motor control, caused by cerebral hemorrhage or thrombosis.—adj. apoplectic.

a posteriori (ā' pōs·tir·i·ô'rī): (L., from behind) working back from effects to causes, i.e., inductively; of knowledge gained by observing facts; of reasoning that starts from observed facts.—Cp. empirical (1) and a priori.

apostilb: n. (vis.) one tenth of a millilambert.

apparatus (ap"ə·rā'təs; -rat'əs) n., pl. apparatus, -ratuses: in psychology, any instrument designed to cause stimulation or to facilitate the measurement of the stimulus, or the response, or other psychological process.—Syn. instrument.

apparent: adj. 1. of that which can be (easily) seen or understood. 2. of that which is perceived but does not correspond with a given criterion of the real: e.g., apparent motion, for which the eliciting stimulus is something other than objects moving in space. >Apparent in this sense is synonymous with one meaning of illusory or subjective, but all three terms are infected with epistemological theorizing. 3. characterizing the qualities, or quantity, directly attributed to an object in perceiving, in contrast with what can be learned about it indirectly and by measurement: e.g., the apparent size of the moon, as contrasted not only with its diameter as measured in astronomy, but also with the relative size of the image on the retina. >This meaning is preferred.

apparent motion: see motion/apparent.

apparent visual kinetics: the visual perception of a motion as caused by something other than that which is moving. >E.g., when a marble strikes another marble, the motion of the second is seen as caused by the first. Contrast with a cloud, which is perceived as moving of itself.

apparition: n. a visual hallucination of a person; a ghost.

appeal: n. 1. a communication that arouses emotions or motives in others. 2. an incentive, as used in advertising or propaganda. >A SHORT-CIRCUIT APPEAL is based on currently established motives; a LONG-CIRCUIT APPEAL uses reasoning and seeks to build up a motive.

appeasement behavior: behaviors (other than flight) that terminate or ward off attack by another animal of the same species.

apperception: n. 1. the final stage of attentive perception in which something is clearly apprehended and thus is relatively prominent in awareness.—Cp. attention. 2. the process by which the apprehended qualities of an object are articulated with similar, or related, already existing knowledge and attitude in such a way as to be understood. >The already existing knowledge to which the present content is articulated is the APPERCEPTIVE MASS, or schema (3). Though the term is now little used, the doctrine that understanding and learning depend upon discovering relationships between the facts presented and the learner's already existing experience is the basis of practically all educational theory, and of much educational practice. Apperception is defined in terms of the outmoded psychology of **mental content,** but the facts referred to are important and deserve restatement in terms of behavior or performance.—*adj.* **apperceptive,** of the data or process; **apperceptional,** of the study.— *v.* **apperceive,** to perceive and react to, with some awareness of the relations involved.

apperception/tendentious: (*A. Adler*) perceiving the world in the pattern which is congruent with one's "will to power."— *Syn.* **autism.**

apperceptive mass: see **apperception.**

appersonation: *n.* a **delusion** in which a person appropriates the character and circumstances of another (usually eminent) person.—*Syn.* APPERSONIFICATION (not *prefd.*).

appet (ap'ət): *n.* (*K. Dunlap*) the distinctive **affective** content which, in conjunction with anticipatory thinking, constitutes a **desire.**

appetite: *n.* 1. a **motivation (2)** or **motive** derived from internal organic conditions. ➤It is not dependent on, though often influenced by, external stimuli. The chief appetites are hunger, thirst, sex, need for air, for elimination, for activity, for rest. 2. the mental processes, sensory and affective, dependent on such organic conditions. ➤**Aversions,** which are internally derived in a similar way, are conceived as NEGATIVE APPETITES. It has been proposed to restrict appetite to secondary needs (not *hunger* but *hunger for caviar* is an appetite) but the proposal seems not to have caught on. 3. (*W. McDougall*) the welling up of the energy of an instinct.—*Cp.* **appet.**—See **desire.**

appetitive (ap'ə·tī"tiv): *adj.* pertaining to **appetite.**

applicational transfer: see **transfer/applicational.**

applied psychology: 1. (*obsoles.*) the employment in practical situations of the principles developed in other divisions of **psychology.** 2. the science or art of securing desired conduct in oneself or others. It deals with, or utilizes, all the physical, physiological, psychological, or social conditions as these relate to the person's effectiveness in the desired conduct. ➤The subdivisions of applied psychology are usually named by referring to the practical goal: business psychology, psychology of sport, educational psychology, etc. PSYCHOTECHNOLOGY is the body of *principles* dealt with in applied psychology; it is thus a somewhat less general term but is often more descriptive. PSYCHOTECHNICS refers to the

actual skills and specific procedures of the *art* of applied psychology.

The adjective *applied* gives a somewhat misleading impression of the relation between pure and applied psychology. It seems to imply that the latter proceeds by borrowing from the fund of principles or laws provided by the former. (*Cp.* sense 1.) Such utilization of pure psychology does occur, but more often the principles of psychotechnology are independently derived in the effort to solve practical problems. The resulting principles are usually less general since they are restricted to statements of how a particular kind of purpose can be attained (to save time, e.g., in inspecting ball bearings; to teach citizenship); whereas the principles of pure psychology are intended to describe *all* of a specified class of phenomena. Thus, if there is a distinctive class of phenomena called **motives,** the principles stating how motives are evoked would be true in all cases, including how to evoke motives for learning arithmetic in the fourth grade. But the universal statements, though valid for such a situation, might not have great effectiveness in directing a teacher's efforts. The psychotechnology of motives would direct attention to principles that enable motives to be controlled for particular kinds of purposes. Utility, not universality, of description is the criterion in psychotechnology. But, like pure psychology, applied psychology and psychotechnology are orderly and scientific. —See **psychology/divisions and schools.**

appraisal (of behavior): *n.* a judgment concerning the fact or facts, guided by theory but limited essentially to the behavior at hand. ➤*Contr. w.* **fact, context, interpretation, generalization,** and **evaluation.** The judgment that a child is tired rather than uninterested is an **appraisal;** it asserts that the acts observed belong to a certain category, but it does not generalize concerning his habitual behavior nor compare it with standards, as in **evaluation.**—See **factuality/levels of.**

appreciable: *adj.* possessing sufficient magnitude to be noticeable, or of practical use; perceptible.

appreciation: *n.* judgment or report on the value, meaning, or significance of something. —*Syn.* **evaluation.** In introspective studies, *contr w.* **description.**

apprehension: *n.* 1. the awareness of a relatively simple object; or the relatively simple process of becoming aware of presented facts. ➤**Apprehension** involves a greater ideational content than is usually included in **perceiving,** yet it does not quite reach the level of thorough understanding meant by **comprehension.** As contrasted with **judgment.** apprehension is direct and immediate, judgment is mediate. One *perceives* a shout, *apprehends* a danger, *judges* that it is unwise to proceed. The verb **apprehend** is limited to this meaning. 2. fear of some future event.—*Cp.* **anxiety (2).** ➤This use is ambiguous: **apprehensiveness** is preferred for this meaning.—*v.* **apprehend.**

apprehension-span test = **attention-span test.**

apprehensiveness: *n.* fear, usually rather mild fear, of a future event or outcome.— *Cp.* **anxiety (2).** *Prefd. syn.* for **apprehension (2).**

apprentice: *n.* a worker, in process of learning a trade, who has not yet reached the stage where he is competent to work without supervision. ➤The trade hierarchy is **novice, apprentice, journeyman, expert.**

apprenticeship: *n.* any form of systematic vocational education in which the learner participates, under the direction of skilled workers, in the actual work of various occupations.

approach-approach conflict: a conflict arising when an individual is drawn toward two goals, both satisfying but at least partially incompatible.

approach-avoidance conflict: a situation in which the stimulus to approach and the stimulus to avoid are in approximately the same "locality"—literally in space, or psychologically in the **life space.**

approach/conceptual: see **conceptual approach.**

approach(ing) response = **adient response.**

approach motive: see **avoidance motive.**

approach type: (*Ror.*) a dimension by means of which the inkblot responses are classified according to whether they are made predominantly to the **whole,** or to **details** (including rare details). ➤In scoring the response it is said: *The approach type is to details.*

approbation: *n.* a judgment that something is good according to some standard: moral, esthetic, literary, etc.

approximation: *n.* the making of a nearly correct estimate; or the estimate itself.

approximation-and-correction: see **learning/trial-and-error.**

approximations procedure or **method:** a variation of trial-and-error learning, in which the desired performance is encouraged by rewarding any responses that approximate, or are part of, the correct performance.—*Cp.* **trial-and-error learning.**

Appunn's lamella (äp'ünz lə·mel'ə): a strip of soft steel (adjustable in length) that vibrates very slowly, thus producing very low tones.

appurtenance: *n.* (*Gestalt*) the property of parts of a field of mutually influencing each other: e.g., in color contrast, the mutual influence of two colors.

apraxia (ə·prak'si·ə): *n.* loss of ability to perform purposeful movements, in the absence of paralysis or sensory disturbance, caused by lesions in the cortex.—*adj.* **apraxic, apractic.**

apraxia/amnestic: inability to carry out an act upon command.

apraxia/ideational: faulty conception of a movement as a whole: individual acts are correct but the proper sequence for goal attainment is disturbed.—*Syn.* IDEOMOTOR APRAXIA.

apraxia/ideokinetic: confusion, in performing complicated acts, in which individual movements can be correctly carried out by the muscles but movements irrelevant to the goal are substituted for the appropriate ones: e.g., the patient may reach out his hand when the appropriate act is to stand up.—*Syn.* MOTOR APRAXIA.

apraxia/motor = **apraxia/ideokinetic.**

apraxia/sensory: 1. = **astereognosis.** 2. confusion about what to do with familiar objects. ➤Not good usage.

a priori (ā"pri·ô'rī; ä"pri·ô'ri): (*L., from the earlier part*) 1. reasoning that deduces consequences from definitions, or that deduces effects from previously known or assumed causes. 2. knowledge or forms of thinking held to belong to the mind prior to experience, especially such as must be assumed in order to make experience possible. ➤The two meanings tend to consolidate and the term to take on, in science, somewhat contemptuous connotation of *lacking adequate factual support.* In that sense it is opposed, not to the **a posteriori,** but to the **empirical (1).**

aprosexia (ap"rō·sek'si·ə): *n.* inability to give sustained attention.

A.P.S. = the American Psychopathological Society.

aptitude: *n.* the capacity to acquire proficiency with a given amount of training, formal or informal. ➤SPECIAL APTITUDE does not necessarily mean very high aptitude, but rather aptitude of a special kind: e.g., *aptitude for mechanics.* GENERAL APTITUDE means the capacity to acquire proficiency in many activities. ¶Since all measurement is necessarily of present performance, an APTITUDE TEST is merely one form of **ability test.** It is a measure of present characteristics that has been found to be predictive of capacity to learn. Thus an **intelligence test** is a test of fairly general present **ability,** but also of capacity to learn. Hence it is both a **general ability** and a **general aptitude** test. But the distinction remains: **ability** is present and actual, **aptitude** is potential, though the same test may measure both. ¶There is a tendency to restrict **aptitude** to *measured* present characteristics that permit prediction of the *amount* of ability attainable with a given *amount* of training, i.e., to restrict **aptitude** to a quantified **variable.**— See **ability,** where related terms are discussed.

aptitude/academic or **/scholastic:** the personal characteristics that make likely a given degree of success in academic pursuits. It is estimated in quantitative terms (e.g., a two-to-one chance of surviving the freshman year with passing grades) and on the basis of factual data (e.g., the high school record, or score on an **academic** *aptitude test).—See **aptitude.**

aptitude test: a set of tasks so chosen and standardized that they yield an estimate of a person's future performance on other tasks not necessarily having evident similarity to the test tasks. ⇢See **aptitude.** Aptitude tests do not differ in form from achievement tests; but the former consist of tasks that predict future learning, whereas the latter consist of tasks sampling the adequacy of past learning.

aptitude test/academic: a test that estimates the fitness of a testee to profit from a course of scholastic study. ⇢*Distg. fr.* academic **achievement test,** though the two may overlap.

aptitude/vocational: see **vocational aptitude.**

AQ = achievement (or **accomplishment**) quotient. (Sometimes **A.Q.,** not *prefd.*).

aqueduct/cerebral: see **cerebral aqueduct.**

aqueous humor (ā'kwi·əs; ak'-): a transparent fluid filling the space between the **cornea** and the crystalline **lens** of the eye.

Ar A = arithmetic age.—See **age equivalent.**

arachnoid (membrane) (ə·rak'noid): the middle of three membranes covering the brain and spinal cord.

Arapesh (ar'ə·pesh): *n.* a **nonliterate** tribe in New Guinea, described by M. Mead as a society based on tight **in-group** solidarity and on the very great suppression of aggressive behavior.

arbitrary: *adj.* involving a choice between possibilities that depends on preference or discretion rather than on rule or principle. ⇢It is a term of reproach only when the choice is merely capricious or insisted on to the exclusion of other alternatives equally proper.

arbitrary definition: the form of **neologism** that consists of giving to a familiar word a special meaning not easily seen as an extension of the older one. ⇢There are many examples in the vocabulary of psy-

chology, some of which, one fears, come under the heading of **bogus erudition.** While it has been my duty, if not my pleasure, to record such usage when I find it, I have sometimes allowed my opinion of it to show with what Fowler calls "indecent plainness."

Terminology is not altogether a matter of usage. More basic is the principle of association by analogy. A usage that compels a reader figuratively to stand on his head in order to read it as the author says he intended it to be read, a usage that affronts every idea that naturally springs to his mind as the familiar outline of the word is spread before him—such a usage is impolite to the reader, if not downright sinful. It attempts communication with others while denying its fundamental presupposition: that a word shall, once learned, have reliable and dependable meanings.

It is ironic that in a discipline calling itself **information theory** the word **information** means, not *that which informs* (which is what ordinary men mean by the term), but rather a *measure of uncertainty.* This *seems* to say that he who is best informed knows least. It is even more ironic that in **communications theory** so little thought is given to using terms that will communicate.

A word's meanings must indeed be suffered to grow or expand; otherwise language would wither and die. (See **rational coinage.**) But the growth should not, must not, be a cancerous excrescence that saps vitality from the parent body; nor should new meanings attempt, like negativistic children, to contradict their parents.

arbitrary responses: (*Ror.*) responses that do not, in any respect, take into consideration the particular features of the **inkblot** card to which the answer is ostensibly assigned.

arborization: *n.* the treelike endings of the fine fibers of the **axon.**—*Cp.* **synapse.**

arbor vitae (är'bər vī'tē): the treelike arrangement of white matter seen when the cerebellum is cut at right angles to the right-left axis.

arc: see **nervous arc.**

archaic: *adj.* (*C. Jung*) characterizing the hypothetical mental remnants of man's prehistoric past, largely unconscious, which reappear in dreams, symptomatic acts, and unconscious impulses.—*Cp.* **archetypes.**

archetype: *n.* **1.** the original model or type. **2.** (*C. Jung.*) = **image/primordial.**

architectonic: *adj.* orderly or systematic in arrangement.

area: *n.* **1.** (*geog.*) any specified part of the earth or other astronomical unit; esp., a part of the earth's surface. **2.** (*neurol.*) a particular region in the brain, marked off either by topographical features or as the

brain center for a certain **function. 3.** a particular kind or grouping of phenomena on which certain persons tend to focus their interests; an INTEREST AREA: e.g., the area of attitudes; or, the broader area of social psychology. ➤For the metaphorical use, see **domain.**

areal factor: an index of personality obtained by measuring the space required for manual, postural, or gestural responses, esp. in handwriting and drawing.

areal growth: increase in body mass or volume.

area of intelligence: (*E. L. Thorndike*) the total intelligence, shown graphically by plotting the successive **ranges** of intelligence at each level of **altitude.**

area sampling: a **survey** procedure that takes *all* of a specified kind of respondents from each of several areas carefully selected to represent the different geographical regions involved: e.g., all adult males living in block 15 in a certain city. ➤*Contr. w.* **quota** **sampling*, which tries to get representative samples of the several **categories** of respondents.

area study: research and teaching centered around a particular geographic area rather than around particular subject matters: e.g., study of the language, culture, climate, economics, history, and government of an area such as Japan. —*Distg. fr.* **area sampling.**

argument: *n.* (*math.*) a value, assigned to an **independent** **variable* in an equation, that determines a specific value for the **dependent** **variable.*

argumentative: *adj.* tending to argue, discuss, and dispute excessively.

argument-completion: *n.* an inquiry technique in which the subject is given enough of the argument or story to focus his attention upon a given issue but is left free to complete it in his own way.

Argyll-Robertson pupil (är·gīl′): a pupil that contracts normally in **accommodation** (2) but inadequately to light. ➤An important symptom of a particular brain **lesion,** generally of syphilitic origin.

aristogenic: *adj.* characterized by excellent **genetic** potentiality.

Aristotelian classification: a system of classifying or defining by **genus** and **species.** Any object is first assigned to the larger group (the genus) to which it belongs by virtue of possessing the essential characteristic of that group; it is then assigned to the subgroup (the species) on the basis of having the characteristics that mark off the species. ➤Genus and species are used in their logical sense, not in the narrow biological sense. ¶Some field theorists minimize the usefulness of such classification on the ground that the important issue is not whether an object "belongs" to

a certain abstract class, but how it relates to other objects in the field of which it is a part. Aristotelian classification says that candy is a sweet substance (it belongs to that genus); field theory inquires how candy reacts with tooth enamel in children's mouths.—*Cp.* **Galilean method, field theory,** Aristotelian method.—See psychology/divisions and schools of, VIII.

Aristotelian method: 1. the method of inquiry that stresses the relation between a general **class** or **category** and a particular object or group of objects constituting a subclass. Both **induction** and **deduction** are employed. **2.** the method of explaining particular facts by appealing to already established principles or laws. ➤The method stresses **deduction.**—*Cp.* **Aristotelian classification.** The term is generally one of reproach; much "logic-chopping" and circular reasoning have been associated with it. Yet modern science makes very extensive use of the method in both the above meanings.—See **mathematico-deductive method.**

Aristotle's dictum: see *dictum de omni et nullo.*

Aristotle's experiment: the **illusory** impression that a single object is double when it is brought in contact with the crotch formed by the crossed fingers.—*Syn.* ARISTOTLE'S ILLUSION.

arithmetic(al) (ar″ith·met′ik·əl): *adj.* **1.** pertaining to the operations of addition, subtraction, multiplication, and division. **2.** increasing or decreasing by a constant difference.—*Contr. w.* **geometric, algebraic.**

arithmetic(al) average or **mean:** see **mean/arithmetic.**

arithmetic/fundamentals of: the computation processes most used in everyday life: addition, subtraction, multiplication, division, fractions, percentage, and simple interest.

arithmetic value = **value/absolute.**

arithmomania (ə·rith″mō·mā′ni·ə): *n.* **1.** an obsessive tendency to count objects; a pathological tendency to count. **2.** figuratively and humorously, an excessive preoccupation with numerical relations, to the neglect of concrete facts and significance. ➤It is said to characterize some psychologists.

armchair psychology: 1. the attempt to found a systematic psychology on the facts of common experience.—*Syn.* **empirical psychology** (1). **2.** reflection on the significance of experience.—*Syn.* **rational psychology. 3.** a term used derogatorily for any attempt at theorizing except in closest relation to laboratory findings.

armor/character: see **character armor.**

armor-plating: *n.* (*W. Reich*) the characteristic traits that determine the modes of expression permitted **id** impulses when they emerge into the conscious; the individual or personal modes of distortion of id tendencies; the idiosyncratic or habitual **defense** process.

Army General Classification Test or **AGCT**: a test of intelligence used in the U.S. Army during World War II and after. ➤It is appropriate for use with literate adults and covers a wide range of ability.

army tests: 1. (*obsoles.*) the **Alpha** and **Beta tests** of intelligence, used in 1917–18. **2.** any tests used on army personnel.

aromatic: *adj.* of a class of smells: e.g., nutmeg, camphor.

arousal function: the function of a sensory event of giving tone to the **cortex,** of arousing the cortex to vigilance or readiness. ➤The arousal impulses stem from sensory stimulation. They are believed to reach the cortex by a different route, to be more widely diffused in the cortex, and to last longer than ordinary *sensory *messages. It is probable that the arousal function from different classes of sensory events has differentiated effects on different functional divisions of the cortex.—*Syn.* VIGILANCE FUNCTION.—*Contr. w.* cue function.

arousal index: a name for *all* the influences, known or merely inferred, that determine how ready an animal is to respond at a certain time to a certain kind of situation. ➤Included are sensory excitability and various activities (such as those of the suprarenal glands) that are known or believed to facilitate the release of bodily energy in muscular or glandular response. The term is needed chiefly because in any given case very little is known in detail about these activities; yet, as observed fact, differences in the ease of arousing a response exist from moment to moment.—*Cp.* discharge index, recovery quotient.

arpeggio paradox: (*G. Humphrey*) Many persons, conditioned to respond differentially to a certain tone, do not so respond when that tone is played as part of a rapid sequence of tones, as in an arpeggio.—*Syn.* HUMPHREY'S PARADOX.

Ar Q = arithmetic quotient.

Ar R = arithmetic ratio.

arrangement of the neurosis: see **neurosis/arrangement of.**

array: *n.* (*stat.*) **1.** a row or a column in a **two-way** table. **2.** a series of values in order of magnitude.—*Syn.* RANK LIST.

arrest of development: see **development/ arrest in.**

arrhythmia (ə·rith'mi·ə): *n.* lack of rhythm, esp. of normal rhythm; irregularity.—*adj.* **arrhythmic, arrhythmous.**

art: *n.* **1.** a product of human exertion that excites admiration and pleasure because of its beauty or of the skill in its execution; or, the activity in producing such a product.— *Ant.* nature. **2.** the body of principles that

govern practice in activities requiring considerable skill or knowledge.—*Syn.* **technology. 3.** skilled or knowledgeable practice; actual application in contrast with knowledge. **4.** practice guided by **minimal cues** and a sense of fitness rather than primarily by the *direct* application of scientific findings. ➤Most human relationships and a good deal of psychotherapy is an art in this sense; the scientific knowledge of the practitioner is important but often operates indirectly.

arteriosclerosis: (är·tir″i·ō·sklər·ō'sis): *n.* thickening of the walls of the arteries. ➤CEREBRAL ARTERIOSCLEROSIS often leads to destructive breakdown of brain tissue.

-arthria: combining form meaning *speech disorder resulting from paralysis.*

arthr(o)-: combining form meaning *joint, articulation.*

Arthur Scale: a **point scale** of **performance tests** for measuring intelligence in children. Language can be eliminated in administering the test to the deaf or to those of a foreign speech.

articular sensation: a sensation arising from the movements of the joints.

articulation: *n.* **1.** the production of consonantal sounds by modifying the stream of breath through movements of tongue, teeth, lips, and soft palate; specif., forming words in this way; the production of speech sounds; utterance. **2.** the way bones fit together at a joint. **3.** bringing different ideas into meaningful relation to each other so that they function together; specif., such meaningful relating of parts in a curriculum. **4.** the breaking of a sequence or pattern of action into sharply distinct units. ➤It involves the establishment of sharp and distinct boundaries between different parts of a pattern. Note that (3) and (4) are quite opposite.

articulation test: a test for accuracy in pronouncing speech sounds, both singly and in connected speech.

artifact: *n.* **1.** an object made by man, as distinguished from a **natural** object; esp. (*archeol.*) an object made by primitive man. **2.** the outcome of an investigation that does not reveal the true principles involved but only the results of an arbitrary treatment of the data. ➤E.g., if one were to compute the average weight for college males after having arbitrarily excluded all persons over 6 feet, the results would be an artifact.—*Var.* artefact.—*adj.* **artifactual, artifactitious** (*not* artificial).

artificialism: *n.* (*J. Piaget*) a tendency, found in children, to regard natural phenomena as caused by human agency: e.g., to believe that the mother causes the plant to bloom.

artificial isolation: a condition in which, by a specially assumed attitude or as a ĸsult of particular experimental arrangements (or both), a certain relatively simple stimulus-response mechanism may be set in play without being affected to the usual extent by the relations of the mechanism with the rest of the organism.

A-S = ascendance-submission.

asapho-: combining form denoting *mumbled speech.*

asapholalia (as"ə·fō·lā'li·ə): *n.* indistinct speech; mumbling.

A scale: *n.* a questionary designed to yield a measure of the tendency to be intolerant of ambiguity, of any kind of vagueness or lack of definiteness.

ascendance: *n.* a tendency to take the lead in determining the behavior of another person or of a group.—*Contr. w.* **submission.** —See also **ascendance-submission.**—*Var.* **ascendancy, -ency, ascendence.**—*adj.* **ascendant, ascendent.**

ascendance-submission or **A-S:** a bipolar continuum from the maximum tendency to dominate to the maximum tendency to be dominated in face to face relations. ➤The **Allport A-S Reaction Study** is an inventory for this **trait** or **dimension.**

ascendancy = ascendance.—*Var.* **-ency.**

ascendancy/social: see **social ascendancy.**

ascending vs. descending series: (*exper.*) In the determination of a **threshold** by the **method of** *limits,* the ascending series presents for judgment stimuli that are progressively more different from the probable threshold value; the descending series presents stimuli closer and closer to the threshold.

asceticism: *n.* a mode of life in which sensuous pleasures are voluntarily renounced, esp. with a view to serving a higher moral or religious ideal.—*adj.* and *pers. n.* **ascetic.**

asemasia = asemia.

asemia (ə·sē'mi·ə): *n.* inability to use or understand symbols of any sort—words, figures, gestures, signs, etc.—for communication.—*Syn.* ASEMASIA (as"i·mā'zhə).—*Cp.* **asymbolia.**—*adj.* **asemic** (-sem'ik).

asexual (ā·sek'shü·əl): *adj.* **1.** sexless. **2.** (*biol.*) of reproduction that takes place independently of sexual processes.

as if hypothesis: 1. thinking or acting in terms of an unproved assumption, either to see what would happen if it were true or in order to cause the assumption to become true. **2.** tentatively treating a behavior *as if* it belonged in a certain classification, although it lacks some of the attributes hitherto deemed essential to the class. ➤Thus Tolman says a rat acts *as if* he had acquired a visual-image map of the maze, although it is quite clear that any "map" the rat employs will be in many respects quite unlike that of a human being. The as if hypothesis raises the question whether, in certain unanalyzed ways, the two are not fundamentally alike. This kind of thinking differs from **anthropomorphism** in not postulating a **global** similarity. **3.** (*A. Adler*) the process of acting *as if* the goal of complete superiority were attained—a self-deception.

asitia (ə·sish'i·ə): *n.* disgust at the sight or thought of food.

Asn: symbol for strength of **association.**

asocial (ā·sō'shəl): *adj.* **1.** indifferent to social customs or rules. **2.** lacking social value or meaning.—*Distg. fr.* **unsocial, antisocial** (which see).

asonia (ə·sō'ni·ə): *n.* lack of normal ability to discriminate pitch differences.—*Syn.* **tone *deafness.**

aspective analysis: see **analysis/aspective.**

asphyxia (as·fik'si·ə): *n.* **coma** resulting from lack of oxygen.—*Distg. fr.* **anoxia** and **apnea.**—*v.* **asphyxiate.**

aspiration: *n.* **1.** ardent desire to accomplish what one sets out to do; longing for realization of higher values, such as ideals, religious experience, and the like. **2.** the act of breathing, esp., of breathing in; a breath.

aspiration/level of: the standard by which a person judges his own performance as a success or a failure, or as being up to what he expects of himself. ➤*Distg. fr.* **achievement,** and *fr.* **ambition,** which is what one strives for and which may be higher (or lower) than the level of aspiration. ¶The level of aspiration is found by asking the subject before a performance how well he expects to do. LEVEL OF ANTICIPATION would be more descriptive for this. Experimental work has mostly concerned itself with the effect of perceived success or failure upon the level of aspiration, but this is not essential to the concept. In nonexperimental contexts, level of aspiration usually means a level of performance which the subject judges, at least before the event, will be acceptable to his image of himself, i.e., to his **ego (4).**

A/S ratio: (*D. O. Hebb*) = **association-sensation ratio.**

assault/criminal: 1. illegal violence against a person. **2.** a violent sex attack; rape.

A-S scale: an opinion scale for estimating tendencies to anti-Semitism.

assemblage: *n.* a collection of objects or of persons, esp. a miscellaneous or fortuitous collection.—*Cp.* **assembly.**

assembly: a number of persons present or congregated in a space sufficiently limited that they can be seen or heard from one point. ➤If the group is loosely organized or if the gathering is fortuitous, **assemblage** is more specific, but **assembly** does not necessarily imply an organized group.

assessment program: a method of evaluating personality in which an individual, living in a group under partly controlled physical and social conditions, meets and solves a variety of lifelike problems, including stress problems, and is observed and rated by a team of observers.

assets-liabilities technique: a counseling procedure in which the client is led to list his personality assets and liabilities, and to consider how the latter can be removed or converted into assets.

assign: *n.* a verbal sign that gets its meaning, not from direct perceptual experience, but from other words or symbols. ➤Abstract words are necessarily assigns; but many concrete words do not receive their meaning from direct experience. E.g., the word *mermaid* is necessarily only an assign.

assignment therapy: the attempt to help individuals in their behavior adjustment by regrouping them in small work or play groups, generally after making a **sociometric** measurement of the over-all group. ➤The technique is especially applicable in correctional institutions.

assimilation: *n.* **1.** (*physiol.*) conversion of food into the substance of the body. **2.** a learning process, esp. a thorough learning, in which what is studied is made part of oneself, as food is made part of the body. **3.** a process by which an unpleasant fact is faced and brought into tolerable relation with the rest of one's experience: *a newly crippled person sometimes succeeds in assimilating his new limitations.—Ant.* **repression** or **suppression,** in which the facts are not thus faced. **4.** a process of perceiving or **apperceiving** in which the new content is so similar to a familiar content that the two seem almost identical: = ASSIMILATION LEARNING. ➤When a salient but minor similarity is overeffective, the assimilation of the new to the old may cause a distortion: the new is seen as more similar to the old than it is in fact. (*C. Jung*) the process of altering the object or situation to fit the needs of the **self.** ➤If the alteration is merely in the way the situation is perceived, it is **autism.**—*Cp.* DISSIMILATION, which (for Jung) is the process by which the *self* changes to conform to the situation. **6.** (*speech*) the modification of letter sounds to conform, in mouth position and/or sound, to the sounds of neighboring letters.

assimilation/cultural: the process by which persons and groups acquire the sociopsychological characteristics of other persons and groups, and are incorporated with them in a common cultural life. ➤*Cp.* **acculturation,** a broader term implying the adoption of ideologies, institutions, and materials from another group, as well as a considerable degree of cultural assimilation. —*Syn.* SOCIAL ASSIMILATION.

assimilation/law of: the principle that the organism responds to a new type of situation as it responded to similar situations in the past.—*Syn.* **principle of** *analogy.

assimilation/social = assimilation/cultural.

assimilative illusion: see **illusion/associative.**

assimilative learning: see **assimilation** (4).

assimilative material: subject matter to be studied not for its own sake but because it is helpful in promoting thorough learning of something else: e.g., illustrative material.

associate: *n.* **1.** any psychological phenomenon linked with another in learning. —*Cp.* association (1).—See **right associates procedure.**—*Syn.* association (6). **2.** a person with whom one has considerable dealings, generally of a cooperative nature.—*v.* **3.** to form an **association** (all meanings). **4.** to be reminded of an item by means of association. **5.** to bring things into some sort of relationship, objective or subjective; to assert or to call attention to a relationship.

associated movements: those movements an animal makes when struggling against an external interference with a specific other movement: e.g., grinding the teeth when one's hands are forcibly held.

associate points: all the points in the field of vision which are referred to a single point in external space.—*Syn.* **congruent points.**

association: *n.* **1.** a functional relationship between psychological phenomena established in the course of individual experience and of such nature that the presence of one tends to evoke the other; or the establishing of such a relationship; or the process whereby the relationship is established.— *Syn.* **connection.** ➤This is the basic meaning of a term with a long history and many shadings of meaning and usage, the most important of which are given below. ¶The two phenomena related are ASSOCIATES; they may be any sort of phenomena studied by psychology. In historical **associationism,** sensations (percepts) and ideas were associated; in **behavior** and **functional psychology,** stimuli are associated to responses, or acts to acts. **2.** the mental bond of connection between two associated ideas. ➤The bond is said to consist of relations between the two ideas. But it is usually not clear whether the actual objective relation is thought to cause the bond (a chair's objective similarity to a stool causes a bond); or that the two *ideas* are related, thus creating a bond (the idea of chair is similar to the idea of stool); or that thinking about the objective and/or subjective relation causes a bond. This usage, although mainly historical, is still current, but is too confused to permit clarification. **3.** the hypothetical nerve bond, assumed to be the basis for the functional relations of **(1).** This is better called **neural linkage.** **4.** = ASSOCIATING, in any of the above senses.—*Syn.* **learning, conditioning. 5.** = ASSOCIATIVE RECALL, the evoking of one psychological phenomenon by its associate. ➤In context, this meaning is usually clear; where it is not, associative recall should be used. **6.** that which is psychologically connected with some other datum; the second member of an associational sequence; the second ASSOCIATE (see **1** above). ➤It may be a relatively long train of ideas or of overt behavior: e.g., the ideas suggested by the word *father.* **7.** *giving* the second ASSOCIATE upon presentation of the first. ➤This is particularly the usage in an **association test** where the verbal associate of something is requested. **8.** the strength of the hypothetical linkage between two items associated. **9.** (*stat.*) the tendency of two variables to vary together: the *association* between poverty and ill-health.—See **association/coefficient of.**—*Syn.* **correlation, covariance. 10.** = **social *association.**

The variety of usage of **association** makes necessary great care both in reading and in using it.

association/affective: a linkage of ideas on the basis of common feeling tone.

association area or **center:** (*obsoles.*) the anterior portion of the **cerebral *cortex.** ➤It was so called because it was believed to be the area in which **association (3)** took place.—See **associative center.**

association/backward: connecting an item with one that preceded it, immediately or more remotely, in the learning period.—*Cp.* **association/forward** and **/remote.**

association by contiguity: see **association/laws of.**

association/coefficient of: a measure of correlation between variables each of which is expressed in only two categories, e.g., boys-girls, pass-fail, etc. It does not assume continuous variation.

association/constrained: see **constrained association.**

association/controlled: a procedure in which specific instructions limit the kind of **association (6)** that will be an acceptable response: e.g., to name the opposite of a word pronounced.—*Cp.* **association/free.**

association cortex = **association area.**

association/evidential: an **association (6)** that reveals something about the personality structure or the unconscious trends of a person. ➤It is generally conceded that, strictly speaking, all associations are evidential but that some—especially those of **free *association** and of dreams—are

more so than others. Some psychoanalysts concede that the structure of personality is not wholly revealed by evidential associations.

association experiment: see **association test.**

association/false: (*psychoan.*) unconscious, evasive associations, usually not wholly false but misleading because they give only part of the true picture. ➤E.g., a certain tree may be reported as associated with the playmate with whom one built a house in the tree; but it will not be reported as associated with the father who angrily destroyed the tree house.

association fibers: nerve fibers that connect different regions in the same hemisphere of the brain. ➤It is not implied that they serve the function of psychological **association.**

association/forward: connection of an item with one that followed it, immediately or more remotely, in the learning period.— *Cp.* **association/backward** and **/remote.**

association/free: an unconstrained sequence of ideas or of words. ➤In the association experiment (see **association test**), a word is spoken and the subject speaks another word as quickly as possible. In psychoanalysis, the analysand is asked to begin with some item in a dream, or some remark he has made, and relate whatever comes to mind. *Free* means *free from instructions*; the association is postulated to be determined by the reactor's psychic makeup.

association-frequency table: a list showing the frequency of certain replies to the words of the **Kent-Rosanoff list,** or to an analogous **association test.**

association group: people who associate freely with one another, or would feel free to do so.—*Syn.* **social *class** (*approx.*).

association/immediate and **/mediate:** An association is termed **immediate** when a second associate is connected directly with a first; it is called **mediate** when the linkage is by means of intervening terms or associates. ➤If *black* suggests *white,* and *white* in turn suggests *paper,* the association of *black* and *white* is immediate; of *black* with *paper* is mediate.— *Distg.* **mediate** from **remote *association.** In the former, the intervening items play an essential role; in the latter, this is not implied.

associationism: *n.* **1.** a theory that starts with supposedly irreducible **mental elements** and asserts that learning and the development of higher processes consist mainly in the combination of these elements. ➤The theory has many forms;—*cp.* **sensationism. 2.** the point of view of those who define the variables or constructs of learning theory and experimentation in terms of stimulus and response, and the relationships of temporal contiguity between them.—*Syn.* **contiguity theory.**— See **psychology/divisions and schools of, VIII.**—*adj.* **associational,** pertaining to the process; **associationistic,** pertaining to the theory.—*pers. n.* **associationist.**

association/laws of: (*hist.*) generalizations stating how the functional relationships between **percepts** and **ideas** are established and made manifest. ➤See **association (1)** and **associationism.** Originally there were four such laws: the LAW OF SIMILARITY, of DIFFERENCE (or CONTRAST), of SUCCESSION, and of COEXISTENCE; these were eventually summarized in the **law of *contiguity.** A typical statement of this law is as follows: If two experiences have occurred simultaneously or in close succession, the reoccurrence of one of them tends to reinstate the other or its imaginal representation. **2.** generalizations of the way connections are formed between stimulus and response. ➤Although the generalizations of sense **(2)** are associationistic, it is better to confine the term **laws of association** to the traditional meaning of sense **(1).**

association mass = apperceptive mass: see **apperception.**

association method: the study of the **associative** responses to various stimuli as a means of revealing behavior tendencies or personality.—See **association test.**

association/negative: (*stat.*) the relationship between two items, such that one is more frequently present when the other is absent.—*Ant.* **association/positive.**

association/neural: 1. the process by which nervous impulses of independent origin are brought together for a joint resultant. **2.** the hypothetical nerve pathways between **action systems;** or the forming of such pathways. ➤These pathways belong to the **conceptual nervous system.**

association of ideas: (*hist.*) the process whereby **percepts** or **ideas** are joined together in the mind to form new compound ideas.—See **associationism (1), association psychology.**

association/positive: (*stat.*) a more-than-chance likelihood that an item will be present if a certain other item is present, or absent if the other is absent.—*Ant.* **association/negative.**

association psychology: a pre-experimental psychology whose basic principle was the **association of ideas.**—*Contr. w.* faculty psychology.—*Cp.* **association (1)** and **associationism (1).**

association/psychosis of = *folie à deux.*

association reaction time: the time required to respond to an object or idea with an **associate.** ➤Used especially in the **association test** (which see).

association reflex: Bekhterev's term for **conditioned response.**

association/remote: connection of an item

to one that was distant from it in the learning period: e.g., in the series A-B-C-D, the connection between A and D.—*Cp.* **stimulus generalization,** which is said by Hull to include this phenomenon.

association/retroactive: see **retroactive association.**

association-sensation ratio: the ratio of the size of the total **association cortex** to the total **sensory cortex.** ➤It is said to be an interspecies index of ability to learn. The term is often written in the form **association/sensation ratio.**

association/serial: the learning of items in the order in which they are presented. —*Syn.* SERIAL LEARNING.

association/social: the process of bringing persons together in groups; or the group itself if it possesses some permanence.

association test or **experiment:** a procedure designed to discover the nature of the subject's **associations (6)** to certain stimuli. ➤Any kind of stimulus and any kind of response may be employed, but most often they are verbal; the subject responds to a word with a word which for him is an **associate.** If no further limitation is prescribed, the test is a CHANCE-WORD ASSOCIATION TEST or FREE ASSOCIATION TEST. It is established, however, that the response is not really chance or really free, but is determined by prior experience; hence it may reveal much about the subject's history, attitudes, or personality structure. In CONTROLLED ASSOCIATION, certain limits are placed on the subject's response although a range of choice is always left to him. The **association reaction time** may or may not be recorded.

association time: 1. = association reaction time. **2.** (*hist.*) the total **association reaction time** minus the **simple *reaction time.** ➤It was assumed that subtracting the time required for the neural impulse to reach the brain and to travel from brain to muscle (supposedly measured by simple reaction time) would leave the time required to make the **association (3)** in the brain. This assumption is now denied on several counts.

association word: see **association test.**

associative: *adj.* pertaining to, or based on, **association,** esp. **(1).** The word occurs in several special phrases, e.g., **associative *illusion.**

associative bond or **coupling:** the hypothetical mechanism that underlies an **association (1).**

associative center or **region:** (*neurol.*) a hypothesized center for the integration of neural impulses transmitted to it from the various sensory mechanisms. ➤Such centers are now believed to be restricted to that part of the cerebral cortex anterior to the precentral motor cortex and that part of the posterior cerebral cortex which is bounded by the tactile, auditory, and visual sensory areas. It is roughly comparable to the **intrinsic,** as opposed to the **extrinsic,** *****cortex.** The function of integration (somewhat differently conceived) was formerly attributed to the anterior cortex, which was therefore called the ASSOCIATION AREA. **Associative center** is now preferred, to avoid implication that only the anterior cortex is referred to.

associative chain theory: hypothesis that each action in a sequential series is the response to the previous act. ➤*Cp.* **circular behavior.** The hypothesis is challenged on the ground that the act is a total, and that each response relates to the whole, not merely to the preceding response.

associative facilitation: the effect of prior **associations (1)** in making easier the formation of new ones.—*Cp.* **transfer.**

associative inhibition: 1. the weakening or blocking of an **associative bond** when its **cue** item becomes associated to a new response. **2.** the difficulty of forming associative bonds because of prior associations; = ASSOCIATIVE INTERFERENCE. ➤Neither **(1)** nor **(2)** happens inevitably; hence a LAW OF ASSOCIATIVE INHIBITION is not generally accepted.—*Approx. syn.* **transfer/negative.**

associative interference = **associative inhibition (2).**

associative learning: the principle that items experienced together enter into a connection, so that one tends to reinstate the other. ➤Originally, the **association** was said to be between ideas, but it is now said to be between words, or between stimuli and responses.—*Cp.* **association test, conditioning.**—*Syn.* **redintegration.**

associative memory: 1. recalling a past experience by thinking of something connected with it, so that the present idea will bring back its former **associations. 2.** the function of recalling by **association.**—*Syn.* (for **2**) **memory.** (The adjective **associative** seems redundant for this meaning.)

associative shifting/principle of: (*E. L. Thorndike*) If two stimuli are effectively presented together, one of them will in time come to substitute for the other in evoking the response proper to the latter. ➤Mere *simultaneous* occurrence of the two stimuli is held not to be enough to meet the requirement of being "effectively presented together," though it has not been easy to say what more is needed.—See **belongingness (2).** Thorndike believes that **conditioning** is a special case of this principle.

associative spread: the learning of things that are connected with a task that is purposefully pursued; = CONCOMITANT LEARNING.

associative strength: the tendency of a certain class of responses to follow any of a certain class of stimuli, as measured by the relative frequency of that succession.

associative thinking: thinking that attempts to bring to bear on a present problem all the *present* factors that are relevant. ➤**Free** *****association** is often used as a synonym, but has a broader meaning, since it includes those chains of associations that travel backward in time, and also much that is—or at least seems—irrelevant.

assonance (as'ō·nəns): *n.* similarity of vowel sounds, as in *scream, beach.*

assortment/genetic = **segregation (2).**

assumed mean = **mean/assumed.**

assumption: *n.* (*logic*) a judgment accepted as if true in a train of reasoning, though it has not been proved. ➤The term includes both **hypothesis** and **postulate.** But in many cases the assumption is not explicitly formulated (a TACIT ASSUMPTION) or even consciously recognized (an IMPLICIT ASSUMPTION). Implicit assumptions especially are fruitful sources of error.

assurance: *n.* **1.** an attitude of faith in oneself. **2.** giving confidence and a feeling of security to another person.

astasia-abasia (ə·stā'zhə-ə·bā'zhə): *n.* **functional** inability to stand (**astasia**) or to walk (**abasia**), although the limbs can be used for other purposes.

astereognosis (ə·ster"i·og·nō'səs): *n.* a. form of **agnosia** consisting in inability to recognize objects by the sense of touch. It is thought to be caused by lesion in the central **parietal lobe.**—*Syn.* STEREOAGNOSIS, tactile **agnosia.**

asthenia: *n.* weakness; debility. ➤Often used in combination words: **neurasthenia, psychasthenia.**—*adj.* **asthenic,** characterizing states of depression; or characterizing a type of physique, the **asthenic type** (which see).

asthenic feeling: a feeling in which **overt** activity is depressed or inhibited: grief, despair, depression, etc.

asthenic type or **physique:** (*E. Kretschmer*) the classification of long slender body structure, said to be associated with **schizoid** tendencies.—See **body types.**

asthenopia (as"thə·nō'pi·ə): *n.* weakness or rapid tiring of the ocular muscles or of the eye in general.—*adj.* **asthenopic** (-nop'ik).

astigmatism (ə·stig'mə·tiz·əm): *n.* **1.** a defect in the curvature of a lens so that the image of any object viewed through the lens is distorted: i.e., the light rays from any given point do not all focus at a point; specif. **2.** such defect in the curvature of the cornea (and sometimes of the lens) of the eye. ➤REGULAR ASTIGMATISM can be corrected by cylindrical lenses, but most astigmatism is more or less irregular and only partially correctable. Very few eyes are entirely free from it.—*adj.* **astigmatic**

(as"tig·mat'ik). (Note: the noun is not *stigmatism*.)

astridecile (ə·strī'də·sīl): *n.* (*stat.*) an interval placed exactly astride the decile point. Astridecile 0 ranges from 1 to 5, 2 ranges from 6 to 15, 9 ranges from 85 to 95, 10 from 96 to 100.

astrology: *n.* the pseudo science of the influence of stars on human affairs.

asylum: *n.* an obsolescent term for an institution for the care of the insane. ➤*Syn.* STATE HOSPITAL, HOME, SANITARIUM. While the use of euphemisms is generally to be deplored, the still-current attitude of the public toward mental disorder prevents the employment of an openly descriptive name.

asymbolia (as"im·bō'li·ə): *n.* **1.** a specific form of **asemia** characterized by inability to use or understand a particular set or sets of signs or symbols, such as those used in mathematics, chemistry, music, etc. **2.** = **asemia**, inability to use or understand symbols of any kind, including words.

asymmetrical relation: (*logic*) one that does not hold when the terms are inverted: A is father of B; *x* is larger than *y.—Ant.* **symmetrical relation.**

asymmetry (ā·sim'ə·tri): *n.* **1.** lack of correspondence between two aspects or parts of a unit, especially between the two sides of a body: e.g., one arm longer or stronger than the other. **2.** (*stat.*) lack of similarity between the two halves of a **distribution curve** divided at the **mean** or **median.**— *Syn.* **skew, skewness.**—*adj.* **asymmetric(al).**

asymptomatic: *adj.* **1.** without symptoms. **2.** of a person whose behavior or outward bodily appearance does not point to any disorder but who is known from laboratory findings to have a disease.

asymptote (as'im·tōt): *n.* a straight line which a regular curve constantly ap-

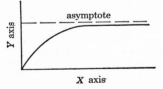

proaches but never reaches, or reaches only at infinity.—*adj.* **asymptotic** (-tot'ik), of the relation, or of either line.

asynchronous (ā·sing'krə·nəs): *adj.* not corresponding in time; not simultaneous; not keeping together in time.—*n.* **asynchronism, asychrony.**

asynergia (as"i·nèr'ji·ə): *n.* inability to carry out complex motor acts that require harmonious coordination of different muscle groups.—*Var.* **asynergy** (ə·sin'ər·ji).— *adj.* **asynergic** (-èr'jik).

At: (*Ror.*) = **anatomy response.**

atactic = **ataxic.**

ataractic drug: a tranquilizer.

atavism (at'ə·viz·əm): *n.* **1.** (*genet.*) reappearance in an organism of a character absent in its immediate ancestors but present in more remote ones; esp., a throwback to a more primitive character; hence **2.** a primitive mode of behaving. ➤Because of unscientific use of the term, geneticists more frequently speak of **reversion.**—*adj.* **atavistic.**—*pers. n.* **atavist.**

ataxia (ə·tak'si·ə): *n.* marked incoordination in voluntary muscular movements. ➤In LOCOMOTOR ATAXIA (or TABES DORSALIS), there is loss of the coordination needed in walking: the patient cannot sense his own movements because of damage in the **posterior roots.**—*adj.* and *pers. n.* **ataxic, atactic.**

ataxiameter (ə·tak"si·am'ə·tər): *n.* **1.** any apparatus for measuring involuntary movement of the body or its parts; esp. **2.** an apparatus for measuring involuntary sway when standing erect with eyes closed.

ataxia/psychic or **/mental:** lack of correspondence between the ideas expressed and the emotions displayed: e.g., immoderate laughter when describing a serious accident.

ataxia/static: incoordination of movements while attempting to maintain a fixed position.

ataxic (ə·tak'sik): *adj.* pertaining to **ataxia.** —*Syn.* ATACTIC (-tak'tik).

ataxic writing: writing marked by extreme incoordination, whether because of lack of skill or of organic disorder.

ateliosis (ə·tē"li·ō'sis): *n.* a pituitary infantilism marked by arrested growth and childish face and voice, but without deformity.

atel(o)- (at'ə·lō-): combining form meaning *incomplete, unfinished,* and used esp. to denote a developmental defect.

athetoid (ath'ə·toid): *adj.* pertaining to, or resembling, **athetosis.**

athetosis (ath"ə·tō'səs): *n.* a derangement, resulting principally from brain lesion, marked by slow, recurring, weaving movements of arms and legs, and by facial grimaces.—*adj.* **athetoid.**

athletic type: (*E. Kretschmer*) the classification of a body structure in which there is well-balanced proportion between limbs and trunk. It is said to be associated with normal personality. ➤See **body types. Athletic** is sometimes used as the adjectival form of this term, without its usual implication of skillful functioning in sports.

athletosome (ath·let'ə·sōm): *n.* (*E. Kretschmer*) a person of **athletic type.**

athymia (ə·thim'i·ə; ə·thī'-): *n.* **1.** lack of **affect** or feeling. **2.** absence of the **thymus** gland.—*adj.* **athymic** (ə·thī'mik; -thim'-).

atmosphere effect: the determination of a response by the habits associated with specific words of the stimulus. ➤E.g., meaning to write "the prices of ham and coffee," one writes "the prices of ham and eggs." Or again, seeing "never" in a conclusion, many will respond "doubtful" because "never" suggests an overstatement.

atmosphere/psychic: the **global** or overall effect of a situation, particularly upon motivation or feeling. ➤It is a summation of all the stimuli that affect the person, including very many minimal cues or stimuli not separately noticed, and especially including emotive stimuli not ostensibly related to the task in hand.

atomism (at′ə·miz·əm): *n.* **1.** a term, used chiefly by opponents, for the view that psychological phenomena should be reduced by analysis to their elementary components, which components are prior to, and independent of, the whole; and that psychology works best with small and/or simple bits of **mental content** or **behavior.** ➤Historical **associationism, sensationism,** and early **behaviorism** were all **atomistic.**— *Cp.* **molar behavior.**—*Syn.* **elementarism** (*prefd.*), **reductionism.**—See **psychology/ divisions and schools of,** VII. **2.** (*sociol.*) the theory that social groups are to be understood in terms of the individuals who comprise them.—*adj.* **atomistic.**

atom/social: (*sociometry*) the pattern of reciprocal attraction and repulsion sustained by an individual with the several members of a group; the individual and his relations of reciprocal attraction-repulsion. ➤The **social atom** includes all the persons in the group but gives only their relations with the **reference** person, not with each other.

atonia = **atony.**

atony (at′ō·ni): *n.* **1.** (*physiol.*) reduction of normal muscular tone or tension. **2.** (*phonetics*) lack of accent or stress.—*Syn.* ATONIA (ə·tō′ni·ə), ATONICITY (at″ō·nis′ə·ti).—*adj.* **atonic** (ə·ton′ik).

atrophy (at′rə·fi): *n.* wasting away; degeneration; decrease in size.—*adj.* **atrophied, atrophic** (-trof′-).

atropin (at′rō·pēn; -pin): *n.* a drug acting chiefly to relax smooth muscles, esp. those of the pupil, intestines, and bladder.—*Var.* atropine.

attachment: *n.* **1.** a state of being emotionally attracted to a person and highly dependent upon that person for emotional satisfaction. **2.** (*anat.*) that by which an organ or tissue is fastened to something else: the *attachment* of a muscle to a bone. **3.** the functional connection of a response to a stimulus: the *attachment* of flight-avoidance to the red signal. ➤This is a highly metaphorical expression but is often interpreted literally, somewhat as in mean-

ing (2). Only as a figure of speech can a come-and-go event (a response) be "attached" to another ephemeral event (a stimulus)—or to anything. The term attachment, while properly emphasizing the relative permanence of the functional relation, tends to suggest that the underlying mechanism is a simple linkage—which is not known to be the case.—*Syn.* **bond.**

attack: *n.* **1.** the use of force against someone or something, generally with intent to harm.—*Cp.* **aggression. 2.** a sudden manifestation of some disorder: mania, epilepsy, hysteria, etc. ➤Marked change in motor behavior is the outstanding symptom.—*v.* **attack.**

attack/negative: taking the "wrong" side in a discussion in order to stimulate thinking or to bring out the implications of the wrong position. ➤Although the term is new, the technique was an important device in the Socratic dialogs.

attainment = **achievement.**

attend: *v.* **1.** to make any kind of response to any stimulus. **2.** to make preferential response to only certain concurrent stimuli. —See **attention.**

attensity: *n.* (*E. B. Titchener*) the attention-attracting attribute of a **sensation** or **sense datum.**—*Syn.* sensory clearness.

attention: *n.* **1.** the active selection of, and emphasis on, one component of a complex experience, and the narrowing of the range of objects to which the organism is responding; the maintenance of a **perceptual set** for one object and disregard for others. **2.** an adjustment of a sense organ for optimal stimulation. **3.** (*structural psychol.*) the state of a **mental content** when it is clear or vivid; or the state of **consciousness** when one content is clearer or more vivid than the rest. **4.** the attitude of taking notice of, and responding to, another's behavior, esp. to his demands: the child demands *attention.*

In the psychology of consciousness, attention tended to be a central concept. A variety of phrase-terms reflect this fact: DURATION OF ATTENTION, FLUCTUATION OF ATTENTION, INERTIA OF ATTENTION, PRIMARY ATTENTION, SECONDARY ATTENTION, etc. They seem sufficiently self-explaining, except to the historical scholar. Contemporary psychology tends to use the term nontechnically.

attention/act of: the process whereby part of the field of awareness becomes clearer or more emphasized.

attention aggregate: a group of persons having essentially the same attitude toward an object or event: e.g., the reverential attitude of Roman Catholics toward the papacy.

attention/field of: 1. everything to which

the organism attends at any given time. ➤Depending on theory, it may or may not be more limited than **field of** *consciousness.** **2.** those stimuli or ideas that lie at the **focus of** *attention.** ➤This results in giving one name to what some think are two phenomena.

attention/focus of: that component of a complex experience which, at any moment, is most vivid. The *process* is called FOCAL ATTENTION.

attention-getting mechanism: a technique for gaining attention (if not favorable recognition) when one feels neglected. ➤The term is generally employed for behaviors that are otherwise maladjustive. E.g., a child will continue behavior for which he is consistently punished so long as it brings with it the satisfaction of being noticed.

attention level: the relative **intensity** or **clarity** of a **mental content.** ➤As many as five levels have been described: complete nonattention or **unconsciousness** (to be distinguished from the **psychoanalytic** usage), **subconsciousness,** marginal *attention,** general **attention,** focal attention or **apperception.**

attention/margin of: those components of a complex experience that are less clearly or vividly apprehended. The *process* is called MARGINAL ATTENTION.

attention/range of: see **attention/span of.**

attention reflex: a change in the size of the pupil upon sudden fixing of attention.

attention/span of: 1. the number of distinct objects that can be perceived in a single "momentary" presentation. It is usually determined by the number of items one can see and report when the objects are exposed for 0.1 sec.—*Cp.* **tachistoscope.** —*Syn.* RANGE OF ATTENTION. **2.** the length of time a person can attend to one thing.

attenuation: *n.* **1.** making thin or slender; hence, reducing the strength, amount, or value of something. **2.** (*stat.*) the reduction of the **correlation coefficient** because the measurements used are not reliable. ➤SPEARMAN'S CORRECTION FORMULA for attenuation seeks to estimate what the correlation would be if the measures were perfectly reliable; apparently it often overcorrects.

attitude: *n.* an enduring, learned predisposition to behave in a consistent way toward a given class of objects; a persistent mental and/or neural state of readiness to react to a certain object or class of objects, not as they are but as they are conceived to be. It is by the consistency of response to a class of objects that an attitude is identified. The readiness state has a directive effect upon feeling and action related to the object.

➤This definition is recommended as being most in line with current usage and research. The term is, however, also loosely employed. Coming from the same root as **aptitude,** it originally meant a posture of the body suitable for a certain action and, by extension, a "posture of the mind." Thus it meant a sort of preparatory or suspended action, consisting at least in part of partial or minute **symbolic** (esp. **subverbal**) acts. This notion is influential, if not nuclear, in the evolution of the term's meanings.

M. Calkins first used **attitude** technically, for such basic relations of the self to its objects as receptivity, activity, sympathy, egoism. Later it was used to translate the *Ger. Bewusstseinslagen,* i.e., for such affectively toned states as expectancy or certainty. Closely related are phrases such as the critical attitude, the religious attitude, the scientific attitude, the inquiring spirit, the acceptant attitude, a rigid attitude, the attitude of security, the attitude of pride. In all of these the object is highly generalized, but a common affective pattern and a certain class of overt behaviors are associated with it. This meaning is still current and there is no adequate substitute for it.

It is perhaps unfortunate, then, that the term tends to be more often used, esp. in attitude research explicitly so-called, for instances where the object is much more narrowly limited: approval of dating practices, approval of disarmament, disapproval of drinking. Some writers further limit it to expressions along the one dimension of approval-disapproval, but this seems arbitrary: **interests** and any emotional category can also be associated with a class of objects.

Attitude is one of many terms that refer to an aspect of personality inferred to account for persistent and consistent behavior toward a family of related situations or objects. **Set** emphasizes motor readiness and relatively rigid response. **Habit** usually refers to a somewhat more complex structure and has a stronger **affective** component (not always explicit) than **set.** **Sentiments** are complex attitudes in which the affective aspect plays a central role. **Value** systems are of much the same character but with a more explicit judgment factor. At one end, attitudes are not well distinguished from emotional **temperamental** tendencies; at the other end from **ideology** or **belief.** See also **opinion.** Where the *object* is very general, the term **trait** tends to replace **attitude.**

Specific attitudes are named in terms of the object with which they are concerned, often qualified to indicate the feeling-component as well: an *attitude* of interest in chemistry.—*adj.* **attitudinal.**

attitude cluster: a group of related attitudes which tend in any population to be covariant: i.e., scores on one attitude tend (in the population as a whole) to be accompanied by corresponding scores on the other attitudes. ➤The several attitudes, however, are so independent that a particular person may be relatively high on one, low on the others.

attitude/conceptual: see **conceptual attitude.**

attitude/concrete: see **concrete attitude.**

attitude/constancy: see **constancy attitude.**

attitude/ergic: see **ergic attitude.**

attitude generality: see **generality/attitude.**

attitude/object: see **stimulus attitude** (2).

attitude poll: see **opinion/public.**

attitude/private vs. public: A respondent in an **attitude** inquiry may manifest two contradictory attitudes: one that is publicly avowed, the other held privately. ➤E.g., a member of a certain church is publicly averse to dancing, though privately admitting he sees no harm in it. Both attitudes are real. An attitude is readiness to act, and this readiness takes into account the total situation. In this case, the public attitude takes into account not only the dancing but also the other members of the church and its rules and principles.

attitude scale: an instrument for eliciting from respondents indications of the **attitudes** or **opinions** they hold. ➤Characteristically, the stimuli are verbal statements concerning some issue, principle, person, or object, with each of which the respondent expresses agreement or disagreement; but questions, and even nonverbal stimuli, may be used to elicit the responses that the attitude determines. ¶In the THURSTONE (type of) ATTITUDE SCALE, a number of statements represent different degrees of strength of the attitude. Thus the statement "All wars are totally unjustified" represents a stronger pacifist attitude than "Wars of defense, if unavoidable, are morally justified." Statements are selected to form a series of equal steps along the dimension of attitude-strength. The respondent indicates simple agreement or disagreement.

The LIKERT (type of) ATTITUDE SCALE asks for degree of agreement with each statement; the statements themselves need not be equally spaced to show strength of attitude. ¶In the GUTTMAN or CORNELL SCALE OF ATTITUDES, the statements are so composed that agreement with one implies agreement with all others "lower" on the scale, "higher" and "lower" being in terms

of attitude strength rather than logical inclusiveness.

attitude/social: 1. an **attitude** toward a social object. 2. an attitude held in common by many persons. 3. an attitude favorable to societal rather than individual ends. 4. an attitude that is communicable; = VERBALIZED ATTITUDE (more descriptive). 5. an attitude influenced by social factors. ➤This meaning makes a distinction where distinction scarcely exists; all attitudes are social in this sense. If it is meant that the attitude is one absorbed from the social context, CULTURAL ATTITUDE would be more descriptive.

The term **social attitude** is chiefly useful to make clear that one is not using it in the older sense of a mere posture or **set.** —See **attitude.**

attitude survey: an attempt to discover the attitudes that characterize any group of persons.—See **attitude scale** and **survey.**

attitude test = **attitude scale.**

attitude type: (*C. Jung*) a classification of individuals according to their general way of reacting to stimuli, i.e., whether they turn response inward **(introversion)** or outward **(extraversion).**—*Syn.* GENERAL ATTITUDE TYPE.

attitude universe: the set of responses comprised in a given attitude. ➤These responses are not similar in response quality but in terms of their congruence with the whole attitude. A favorable attitude toward dogs may be manifested by feeding and petting a dog or by cursing a man who abuses a dog. Feeding and cursing in this case belong to the same attitude universe.

attitudinal pathoses: (*F. C. Thorne*) those personality disorders in which the major symptom is a pathological pattern of **attitudes.**

attitudinizing: *n.* assuming certain attitudes or postures in order to impress others. ➤The use of this term to describe the **cataleptoid** positions of **catatonic** patients is unfortunate, since it is not known whether the postures are socially oriented.

attraction: *n.* a characteristic attributed to an activity or object when it is such that a person tends to engage in the activity or to approach and interact with the object. ➤Although attraction is attributed to the object, it is actually an *interactive* property or relation, determined by the needs or desires of the person, as well as by the characteristics of the object or activity.—*Syn.* positive **valence.**—*Ant.* negative **valence, repulsion.**

attractive nuisance: (*law*) a hazard or danger having the property of attracting persons to it: e.g., the sign "Wet Paint."

attribute (at′rə·būt): *n.* 1. (*logic*) any quality or character that is predicated of a subject. **2.** (*metaph.*) an essential quality. **3.** (*structural psychol.*) the simplest characters discovered by analysis of sensation. ➤Of these, quality and intensity are universally conceded; extensity, duration, local sign, and others are disputed. **4.** (*beh. theory*) an elementary dimension or property of sensory behavior (not of physical objects), defined by the kind of discriminatory response made by the subject. ➤The reference is probably to the same phenomena defined in (3). The test for an attribute is that it remains invariant or constant when other attributes change, or (what comes to the same thing) that it has distinct thresholds from other attributes. The discriminatory response which defines the attribute is, in the first instance, a human verbal response; all other discriminatory responses are operationally anchored to the verbal for their interpretation. When we say an animal in an experiment shows such discriminatory responses, we define what he is discriminating by reference to what human beings call differences of color intensity, or pitch, or painfulness (i.e., differences in attributes).—*Syn.* **dimension;** also (when modified by context) **variable.**—*adj.* **attributive.**

attribute/tonal: see **tonal attribute.**

attrition: *n.* **1.** a wearing away; hence, a loss or decline. **2.** a loss in number of the elements of a **population** with the passage of time. ➤Generally the term is used for the loss in number of persons when no one specific cause for the loss is given. Thus, one speaks of the attrition of the entering class in a university over a 4-year period. In therapy, the loss of clients who fail to complete a course of treatment is called attrition.—*Ant.* (for the scholastic instance) **persistence/academic.**

atypical (ā·tip′i·kəl): *adj.* differing to a marked degree in one or more characteristics from others of a given class; not conforming to type. ➤A relative term. Among children in general, the blind child is atypical. Among blind children, the child born without eyes is atypical. A blind rage (temper tantrum) is typical in early childhood, but its persistence is atypical.—*Syn.* **anomalous.**

A.U. or **Å.U.:** *abbr.* for **angstrom unit.**

Aubert-Förster phenomenon (ō·bär′-fĕrst′ər): Small near objects can be distinguished over a larger portion of the retina than larger more distant objects that subtend the same visual angle.

Aubert phenomenon (ō·bär′): apparent displacement of a vertical line in the direction opposite to the tilt of the head when viewed without other **figural** object in the visual field. ➤With some persons only a slight displacement is found.

A-U-D: a type of test item offering the choice, *agree, undecided, disagree.*

audibility: *n.* that property of a sound by which it can be heard under given conditions. ➤*Distg. fr.* **intelligibility** or **discriminability** of a sound: audibility requires merely that the sound be heard.—*adj.* **audible.**

audibility limit: 1. the least sound that can be heard by an individual; the **absolute *threshold** for sound. **2.** the highest or lowest vibration frequency that can be heard as a tone: the UPPER or the LOWER AUDIBILITY LIMIT. ➤The RANGE OF AUDIBILITY is the tonal distance between these limits, which for normal ears may extend over 8 or even 10 octaves, or from about 20 to 20,000 cycles or double vibrations per second.

audibility range: see **audibility limit.**

audible: *adj.* capable of being heard.

audience: *n.* an assembly of hearers or viewers reacting, usually passively, to a speaker or performer. ➤Until the advent of broadcasting, a group in physical proximity was meant, and the performer was interacting with his audience.

audile (ô′dil; -dīl): *adj.* **ear-minded;** of a person who tends to understand better by hearing than by seeing.—*Syn.* AUDITIVE.—*n.* a person who is ear-minded.—*Syn.* AUDITIVE, **auditory type.**

audimutism (ô″di·mū″tiz·əm): *n.* muteness without deafness.—*Syn.* AUDIMUTITAS (-mū′-ti·təs).

audimutitas = **audimutism.**

auding: *n.* a term proposed for *listening to speech,* as a parallel to *reading.*

audi(o)- (ô′di·ō-): combining form meaning *related to hearing.*

audio aid: any audible device used to supplement regular instruction; in practice, a recording of sounds—music, natural sounds, public addresses, etc. ➤Often included in the classification **audio-visual *aids.** The audio aid should be integrated with, not substituted for, other means of instruction.

audio frequency: a measure, in wave frequency, of the range within which an instrument will emit audible **tones.**

audiogenic: *adj.* produced or caused by sound. ➤AUDIOGENIC SEIZURES are convulsions brought on by prolonged exposure to intense high-frequency sounds. (So far not observed in radio or TV listeners, but experimentally induced in rats, mice, and rabbits.)

audiogram: *n.* a graphic record, for each ear separately, of hearing acuity at selected pitches throughout the normal range of audibility.

audiogravic illusion (-grav′ik): an error in sound localization that is a corollary of a illusion of bodily position. ➤If a subject, deprived of visual **cues,** is caused experimentally to have the illusion that the body is tilted in relation to gravity, sounds are localized as they would be if the body were actually so tilted.

audiogyral illusion (-ji'rəl): an error in sound localization made by a subject who has been first blindfolded and then rapidly rotated.

audiometer (ô"di·om'ə·tər): *n.* an instrument for testing **acuity** of hearing. ➤Recent types make use of a vacuum-tube oscillator regulated to produce a series of tones at various points throughout the audibility range, each at various intensity levels above the normal **absolute *threshold.** Measurements of hearing loss are obtained in terms of **decibels** or of percentage of normal sensitivity.—*Syn.* ACU-METER, etymologically sounder but less common.—*n.* **audiometry.**

audio oscillator: an instrument that produces a continuous sound, and can be adjusted to emit any of a wide range of frequencies.

audition: *n.* the sense, or act, of hearing. ➤Properly, **audition** is the sense or capacity, **hearing** the act or process; but the distinction is not well observed.

auditive: *n.* a person who learns better by hearing than by seeing.—*Syn.* ear-minded person.

auditory: *adj.* pertaining to the sense by which one hears, or to the hearing process. ➤*Cp.* au**r**al, pertaining to the ear; **otic,** pertaining to the receptor cells for hearing in the inner ear; **acoustic,** pertaining to the sound vibrations; **hearing,** often used as a synonym but preferably referring to the *process* rather than to the sense.—*n.* **audition.** (The related verb *audit* has special meanings.)

auditory acuity: sensitivity of hearing. ➤It is measured by the physical intensity of sound waves. The term is usually used as equivalent to the AUDITORY THRESHOLD, which is the stimulus energy that is heard in 50 per cent of the trials at a given pitch level.

auditory flicker: see **flicker/auditory.**

auditory masking: see **masking.**

auditory nerve: that portion of the VIIIth cranial nerve which carries the **neural impulse** resulting from sound from the ear to the brain.

auditory projection area: the region in the posterior portion of the superior temporal convolution to which proceed the nervous impulses set up in the inner ear by sounds. —See **sensory areas.**

auditory regression: see **recruitment of loudness.**

auditory space: the area in physical space within which objects can be localized by means of hearing.

auditory span: the number of letters, words, or numbers that can be immediately repeated after one hearing.

auditory threshold: see **threshold; auditory acuity.**

auditory type: a person who is **ear-minded.** —*Syn.* **audile.**

Aufgabe (ouf'gä·be): *n.* (*Ger., task*) a task or problem, set up by instructions self-imposed or otherwise, which gives direction to mental process or behavior.—*Cp.* **set.**

aura (ô'rə): *n.* **1. sensations** or **hallucinations** preceding an **epileptic** seizure. **2.** (*parapsych.*) alleged emanations from a person's body that are visible to others who are sufficiently "sensitive."

aural (ô'rəl): *adj.* pertaining to the ear.— See **auditory.**

auralize: *v.* to utilize the auditory sense or auditory content in imagination or thinking; the auditory counterpart of **visualize.**

aural microphonic: the electric response generated in the **cochlea** when it is stimulated by sound waves. It is combined with the action potential of the auditory nerve in the **Wever-Bray effect.**

aurist = otologist.

Ausfrage **method** (ous'frä·ge): a method of supplementary interrogation, in which the subject is freely questioned after he has rendered his **protocol.**

Aussage **experiment** or **test** (ous'sä·ge): a test of the ability to make a faithful report of what one has observed for only a brief interval.

Austrian school: a group of philosophical psychologists, led by Brentano, who define the science in terms of **acts** rather than of **content,** and—like the **functionalists**— emphasize the mind-in-action. ➤**Empirical psychology,** applied as a name to this school, is apt to be misleading.

autacoid (ô'tə·koid): *n.* a secretion passed into circulating fluid in the body and influencing other tissues. ➤Originally, autacoid was the group name for **hormones** and **chalones,** but **hormone** tends to replace the other two.—*Var.* **autocoid.**

autarchy (ô'tär·ki): *n.* sovereign power. ➤The term is sometimes applied to the period when no rules are imposed on the infant and all his needs are satisfied.— *pers. n.* **autarch.**

authoritarian atmosphere: a descriptive term for the quality of personal relationships produced within a group by a leader who uses autocratic or authoritarian techniques.—*Contr. w.* the **democratic** and the **laissez-faire atmospheres.**

authoritarian character: one who craves

unquestioning obedience and subordination. ➤This is the defining quality, but various other qualities are believed to be generally associated with it, such as a servile acceptance of superior authority, scorn for weakness, **rigidity**, rejection of **out-groups**, conventionality, desire to have everything clearly marked off and determined **(intolerance of *ambiguity)**, cynicism.

authoritarianism: *n.* **1.** the method of control of others in which one person sets the tasks, prescribes procedures, and judges results without permitting others to share in the decision process. **2.** belief in the principle of **authority** in social relations. **3.** belief in authority as a source of truth. **4.** a personal tendency to crave or demand obedience and subordination; or the complex of traits said to be associated with that tendency.—See **authoritarian character.**

authoritarian personality: the whole pattern of personality characteristics said to be common to those of **authoritarian character** (which see).

authoritative imperative: (*psychoan.*) a directive from the **superego** which subconsciously directs the person's behavior.

authoritativeness: *n.* behaving in a peremptory, imperative, bossy manner. ➤Such behavior is usually, though not necessarily, associated with **authoritarianism (1).**

authority: *n.* **1.** a relation between two or more persons such that the commands, suggestions, or ideas of one of them influence the others. **2.** = AUTHORITY FIGURE; the person who—by virtue of his status, role, or recognized superiority in knowledge, strength, etc.—exerts the influence in the **authority (1)** relation. **3.** a pronouncement by an expert. **4.** the credibility claimed for a pronouncement because of the expertness and reliability of its author.

authority/social: **1.** a relation in which the source of **authority (1)** is a social group or an institution. **2.** the acceptance of a code of conduct or a value system because it is held by a group (the **reference group**) with which the individual identifies himself, or because it is enforced by the group or institution regarded as having **authority (1).**

autism (ô′tiz·əm): *n.* **1.** a tendency in one's thinking or perceiving to be regulated unduly by personal desires or needs, at the expense of regulation by objective reality; apprehending the world as closer to one's wishes than it really is. **2.** finding pleasure in fantasies that represent reality in wish-fulfilling terms, even when these are not believed.—*adj.* **autistic** (which see for another meaning).

autistic: *adj.* **1.** characterized by **autism. 2.** of thinking directed unduly toward one-

self. **3.** characterizing a shut-in, introverted personality. ➤Usage **(3)** is becoming less common and is not recommended.

autistic gesture: a muscular **automatism**, essentially the same as a tic but involving more muscles. ➤It is so named because the gesture is supposed to express **symbolically** a personal wish.

autistic type: see **subjective type.**

aut(o)-: combining form meaning **1.** *pertaining to the self*; or **2.** *self-propelled.*

autoanalysis = **self-analysis.**

autocatalytic curve = **logistic curve.**

autocatharsis: *n.* a therapeutic technique in which the patient is encouraged to rid himself of disturbing unconscious elements by writing out his experiences or impressions.

autocentric: *adj.* self-centered.

autochthonous (ô·tok′thə·nəs): *adj.* **1.** sprung from the soil; or of a people believed to have originated in a given area; hence, of the "original" inhabitants.—*Syn.* **native. 2.** of anything originating from within an organ or organism in relative independence of outside influence: e.g., **appetites** (such as hunger) which depend on the metabolic changes of the body; inspirations and obsessive ideas, which seem to arise spontaneously.—Suggested *syn.* **autogenic,** self-generated, intraorganic. For *autochthonous determinants of perception,* see **behavioral determinants. 3.** of an idea or impulse that seems literally to have come from outside, to be thrust upon one by some evil agency. ➤Since in most cases the ideas are false, we may speak of AUTOCHTHONOUS DELUSION. This usage is a curious inversion of etymology and of the meaning of (2). An idea that breaks in upon a current of thought is first called autochthonous because it appears to come "from within," being suggested neither by association nor by passing events. But such ideas often seem so "foreign" that they are disowned, or attributed to demonological possession or other outside agency. The corollary is then mistaken for the defining attribute by persons using a term too alien for them to manage. This is a good example of why simpler terms are better.

autochthonous behavior or **response:** behavior activated by a stimulus that is regularly effective and belongs in the system of that behavior, or by a motive or drive regularly associated with the behavior.—*Ant.* **allochthonous** behavior.

autochthonous gestalt: a perceptual unity believed to arise from factors indigenous to the organism rather than to the stimulus factors: e.g., an objectively homogeneous pattern of dots seen as making a figure, or a rhythm imposed on the sound of a metronome.

autochthonous idea: see **autochthonous** (3).

autocompetition: *n.* the attempt to better one's own previous performance.

autocriticism: *n.* thoughtful and objective evaluation of oneself: of one's ideas, ideals, or behavior.

autoeroticism: *n.* arousal and/or gratification of sex feeling by one's own acts or ideas without the participation of another person. ➤**Masturbation** is only one form of autoeroticism.—*Cp.* narcissism.—*Var.* autoerotism.—*Ant.* alloerotism.—*adj.* autoerotic.

autoerotism = autoeroticism.

autogenic = autogenous.

autogenic reinforcement: a strengthening of the tendency to a certain response by factors within the organism, so that response is more vigorous, reliable, or rapid. ➤**Reinforcement** has here its earlier meaning and is not to be confused with the reinforcement of **conditioned response** theorizing.

autogenous (ô·toj'ə·nəs): *adj.* self-generated; self-originated. — *Syn.* AUTOGENIC (ô″tō·jen'ik), **endogenous**, which means originating within but has a somewhat more biological connotation.—*Contr. w.* **sociogenous**, having a social origin.—*n.* **autogeny.**

autohypnosis: *n.* self-induced **hypnosis.**

autointoxication: *n.* poisoning by uneliminated toxin generated within the body.

autokinesis (-kə·nē'səs): *n.* **1.** movement initiated by stimuli within the organism itself, i.e., by **proprioceptive** stimulation. **2.** a shift in judgment or perception as a result of **set, attitude,** or other subjective factors. —See **autokinetic** effect.—*adj.* **autokinetic.**

autokinetic effect or **illusion:** the apparent movement of a small stationary spot of light seen in darkness. The movement is usually a slow drift that may extend up to 20°.—*Syn.* CHARPENTIER'S ILLUSION.

automatic: *adj.* **1.** operating by itself; not requiring constant oversight or human control. **2.** relatively independent of external stimulus: the heartbeat is *automatic.* **3.** of acts that occur without reflection, intention, or high degree of attention.—See **automatic behavior, automatism.**

automatic behavior: acts that normally require intention and attention but are carried on without them, e.g., **automatic writing.** —*Syn.* automatism (1).

automatic speaking: speaking without voluntary control. ➤The speaker does not intend the meaning, if any, of the word sequences; often there is no apparent meaning.

automatic speech: words connected in a series (e.g., the alphabet, the number series, days of the week, etc.) that can ordinarily be spoken automatically by most persons.— *Contr. w.* propositional speech.

automatic writing: 1. writing while attending almost wholly to the content rather than to the movements or the resulting handwriting. **2.** the writing of more or less meaningful material without the conscious direction of the writer. ➤The writing is generally done without the writer's seeing what is being written and while he is preoccupied with other affairs. He does not know what he has written nor even that he has been writing.—See **automatism** and **dissociation.**

automation: see **automaton.**

automatism (ô·tom'ə·tiz·əm): *n.* **1.** an act performed without reflection or intent, often without realizing that it is taking place. ➤The term is applied to **reflexes** and to thoroughly habitual acts, esp. those of language. Often, however, it is restricted to acts performed without attention that normally require it, e.g., **automatic writing. 2.** (*P. Janet*) a system of psychological and physiological phenomena, arising from a traumatic experience, that grows by annexing other phenomena originally independent. ➤These annexed behaviors are the secondary symptoms that mark the **neurotic.** This concept resembles, but is more restricted than, that of the **complex (2).**

automatism/sensory: the production of illusions or hallucinations during prolonged sensory fixation, e.g., the hallucinations seen in crystal gazing.

automatization: *n.* the process whereby an act becomes routine, automatic, smooth and easy, without conscious effort or direction. ➤*Distg. fr.* AUTOMATION, which refers to making machinery do work without direct human control.

automatograph (-mat'ə·graf): *n.* a device for recording involuntary or undirected movements. ➤The JASTROW AUTOMATOGRAPH records movements of the hand when the fingers rest lightly on a plate.—*Cp.* **planchette.**

automaton (ô·tom'ə·ton): *n.* a machine that performs humanlike activities. ➤The expression *man is an automaton* is curiously circular.—*n.* AUTOMATION, the utilization of automatons.

automorphic perception: the tendency to think of others as being like oneself, ignoring differences and emphasizing likenesses.— *Cp.* egocentrism.

autonomic (-nom'ik): *adj.* **1.** self-regulating; free from external control; characterizing a part of a larger whole that nonetheless has some relatively independent functions.— *Distg. fr.* automatic.—*Syn.* autonomous. **2.** pertaining to the **autonomic nervous system,** which was formerly supposed to be self-regulating, but is now known to be only relatively independent.—See **nervous system.**—*n.* **autonomic,** short for **autonomic nervous system.**

autonomic balance: normal interaction between the sympathetic and parasympathetic branches of the **autonomic nervous system.**

autonomic function: any physiological process under control of the **autonomic nervous system.**

autonomic locking: a continued **tonic** contraction of unstriped muscle long after the original excitation has ceased.

autonomic nervous system: a major division of the **nervous system,** concerned chiefly with the largely automatic regulation of smooth *muscles and of glands. ➔While the activities of the autonomic are mostly not subject to voluntary control, the system is not independent of the brain and spinal cord; rather it is conceived as a peripheral distribution system for certain **efferent** impulses from the brain and cord. The autonomic system consists primarily of a chain of **ganglia** more or less parallel with the cord, together with fibers from the cord or brain to the ganglia (PREGANGLIONIC), and other fibers from the ganglia to the tissues controlled (POSTGANGLIONIC). The autonomic has two major divisions: the SYMPATHETIC (or THORACOLUMBAR) and the PARASYMPATHETIC (or CRANIOSACRAL), which act roughly in opposite ways, most organs receiving a nerve supply from both divisions. —*Syn.* **vegetative nervous system** (not *recom.*), **autonomic,** AUTONOMIC DIVISION.

autonomous changes: the progressive changes when a person is asked to make, from memory, repeated reproductions of what he had earlier observed. If he is asked for a series of drawings of the same object, or to tell a certain story many times over, the reproductions show a trend toward greater coherence and simplicity.

autonomous complex: (*C. Jung*) a complex, first formed in the unconscious, which breaks through into the conscious at a later stage. ➔In contrast, some **constellations** are said to be first formed in consciousness and then repressed.

autonomy (ô·ton'·ə·mi): *n.* independence; self-regulation. ➔**Autonomy** is ascribed to a part of a larger whole that has some relatively independent functions.—*adj.* **autonomous, autonomic** (-nom'ik).

autonomy drive: (*A. Angyal*) the tendency for the individual to attempt to master the environment, to impose his purposes on it.

autonomy/functional: (*G. Allport*) the tendency of a developed motive system to become independent of the primary **drive** from which it originated. ➔The strength of the autonomous motive is conceived as no

longer dependent upon the primary drive. E.g., the motive of acquisition, said to be based originally on a hunger drive, may later become independent of hunger both as to objects sought and as to strength of motive.—*Syn.* AUTONOMY OF MOTIVES.

autonomy/group: the property of a group of being free from institutional or outside control.

autonomy of motives = autonomy/functional.

autonomy/organismic: (*A. Angyal*) the self-maintenance of any living being in virtue of its **intrinsic, endogenous** powers. —*Syn.* **homeostasis** (originally somewhat more limited, but now tending toward a broader meaning).

autophilia: *n.* self-love; **narcissism.**

autophobia: *n.* **1.** morbid dread of being alone. **2.** morbid fear of self.

autophony (ô·tof'ə·ni): *n.* a pathological condition in which the Eustachian tube remains continuously open. The sound of one's own voice travels directly from mouth to middle ear, producing an unpleasant rumble.

autoplasty: see **alloplasty.**

autopsychic: see **allopsychic.**

autopsychoses: *n. pl.* mental disorders in which the person's ideas about his self or personality play a dominant part. ➔This is not a formal class of psychoses.

autorivalry = autocompetition.

autoscope: *n.* a device to make minute and involuntary muscular movements visible, e.g., the **dowsing** (or divining) rod, the **automatograph.**

autosome (ô'tō·sōm): *n.* any **chromosome** other than those determining sex.

autosuggestion: *n.* **1. suggestion** arising from oneself; specif., **2.** the technique of trying to improve health or behavior by repeating verbal formulas till (supposedly) the induced belief effects the desired end: e.g., the Coué formula, "Every day in every way I am getting better and better."

autotelic (-tel'ik): *adj.* pertaining to those traits closely bound up with the central purposes of an individual, esp. self-preservation, self-defense, and self-development.

auxiliary (ôg·zil'yə·ri): *adj.* **1.** giving aid or support. **2.** subsidiary or secondary. **3.** additional; supplementary.

auxiliary ego: (*J. L. Moreno*) a person who consciously accepts another's expressions and purposes in order to strengthen and help him; hence esp., a secondary actor in a **psychodrama** who enacts the supporting roles from the standpoint of the major character. ➔E.g., the auxiliary ego may enact the role of the father as seen by the person who, as a part of therapy, is enacting himself in relation to his father. The auxiliary ego must have considerable psychological understanding of the person for whom he plays the supporting role.—*Cp.* **alter ego.**

auxiliary solution: (*K. Horney*) a partial and temporary solution to an **intrapsychic** conflict. ➤Five such solutions are listed: **self-alienation, externalization** of inner experiences, **compartmentalization,** automatic control of feelings, **intellectual-ization.**—*Cp.* **defense mechanisms.**

A-V = Allport-Vernon Study of Values.

availability principle: The more ready for functioning a response is, the more easily it can be called out.

avalanche conduction: neural conduction in which the impulse spreads out to many more neurons, thus producing an effect apparently disproportionate to the initial excitation.—*Cp.* **irradiation.**

average: *n.* **1.** any one of several measures of **central tendency.** The three most widely used averages are the arithmetic **mean,** the **median,** and the **mode. 2.** = ARITHMETIC AVERAGE, a value obtained by adding all the values algebraically and dividing by the number of cases.—*Syn.* **mean** (*prefd.*).—*adj.* **3.** typical or ordinary: the *average* citizen. ➤This usage should never be employed if there is likelihood that a numerical significance will be attached to it.

average/abstract: an average that may be substituted for the individual items in subsequent calculations. ➤This is a narrower concept than **central tendency** or **representative** measure. The abstract average may be used in calculations *in place of* any individual value.—*Ant.* **average/typical.**

average/calculated: an average that depends upon the magnitude of all the observations in a series.—*Contr. w.* **position *average.**

average/concrete = average/typical.

average/descriptive: an average compiled from data that are inexact or incomplete, and thus are usable only as a rough estimate of the true **central tendency.**

average deviation or **AD:** see **deviation/mean.**

average error: see **error/average.**—*Distg. fr.* **average** or mean *deviation.**

average error procedure = adjustment procedure.

average/geometric or **/harmonic:** see **mean.**

average/guessed = mean/assumed.

average/position: a measure of **central tendency** that is defined by its location in a definite arrangement of the observations: e.g., the **median** which is the middle of ranked observations.—*Contr. w.* **average/calculated.**

averages/law of: the principle that **chance** or **random *error** will occur as often in one direction away from the **true value** as in the other direction; hence, that in an average of many observations such errors will tend to cancel each other. ➤Thus the **mean** of many observations is often taken as the true value. **2.** the generalization that, in a random series of observations, the mean value is likely to occur more frequently than any other. **3.** the principle that the stability of any given statistic tends to increase as the number of items from which it is computed increases.

average/typical: any **average** that is really representative of the **variable.** ➤Many averages are decidedly not. The mean of a distribution that has a wide range of scores, although it serves many purposes, does not actually typify the other scores. No average, moreover, can be typical if the distribution is **bimodal.** (Consider, e.g., the average score on femininity in a population of college students of both sexes.)—*Syn.* CONCRETE AVERAGE.—*Contr. w.* abstract *average.**

average variation: see **deviation/mean.**

aversion: *n.* **1.** dislike, with impulse to turn away. **2.** a negative **appetite;** a turning away from something as a result of internal organic conditions.—*Cp.* **desire.**

A-V-L = Allport-Vernon-Livesey revision of the **Allport-Vernon Study of Values.**

avocation: *n.* a subordinate occupation; a secondary task to which one devotes time; a hobby. ➤Often incorrectly used for **vocation.**

avoidance-avoidance conflict: the situation in which an animal, if he moves away from one undesirable situation, moves toward another undesirable one. ➤The closer the animal approaches one situation, the higher becomes the AVOIDANCE GRADIENT toward that situation and the lower the AVOIDANCE GRADIENT toward the other.

avoidance learning or **training:** see **escape training.**

avoidance motive: a **motive** leading an animal to avoid. ➤One may well ask, "To avoid what?" It is hard to believe that there is a general motive to avoid—*just* to avoid. This term and its fellow, APPROACH MOTIVE, belong in the same category with the obsolete *instinct of self-preservation.* They elevate an abstraction into an entity. **Abience** and **adience** refer to the observable *fact* that a response leads from or toward a stimulus, but **avoidance motive** or APPROACH MOTIVE imply a communality in the *causes* of abient or adient responses. This is an unlikely hypothesis which, in any case, should not be embodied in a term that seems to have reference to a fact.—*Cp.* **theory-begging.**

avoidance reaction: see **avoidance motive** and **abient behavior.**

awake: *adj.* not sleeping.—See **sleep.**

aware-need: *n.* a **need** that is consciously recognized and verbalizable by the person. —*Syn.* **felt-need.**

awareness: *n.* **1.** the being conscious of something; the act of "taking account" of an object or state of affairs. ➤The term implies neither attention nor an assessment of the qualities or nature of the object; there can be SIMPLE AWARENESS without specific discrimination or recognition of objective characteristics, even though these characteristics must be deemed to have an effect.

The verb form, **to be aware of,** has gained much currency among those psychologists who are unwilling to speak of **consciousness,** yet who find need for a general term to refer to a unique kind of relation between the higher animals and certain parts of their environment. Possible synonyms are **knowing, cognition,** or **thinking** in its older use (i.e., with a very broad meaning). Each has its difficulties for a **behavior** psychology.—See **traditional terminology.** **2.** a translation of the *Ger. Bewusstheit,* a total knowledge-content that is not analyzed or analyzable.

awareness/unconscious: a personal activity or process, not directly inspectable and known only by inference, that nevertheless influences a person's behavior as if it were a conscious process. ➤This is as close as one can come to a clear statement of a muddled terminology. The term is on its face self-contradictory—since to be **aware** is to be conscious—but there seems no other expression for the hypothetical construct above defined, one that to many has seemed useful and even unavoidable.

awe: *n.* a compound emotion in which admiration and fear are blended.

awkward age: (*pop.*) early adolescence, or the period of the pubescent **spurt.** ➤Not all adolescents pass through such a period of awkwardness.

axes: *pl.* of **axis.**

axial (ak′si·əl): *adj.* **1.** pertaining to an **axis,** esp. to the main or **cephalocaudal** axis of a body; hence, **2.** pertaining to the spinal column.

axial gradient: a **gradient** with reference ·o an **axis** of an organism. ➤It is used of a gradient of **metabolism,** or of development.—*Cp.* **cephalocaudad development,** in which there is a gradient along the axis from head to tail; and **proximodistad development,** in which there is a gradient away from that axis.

axillary (ak′si·ler″i): *adj.* relating to the armpit.—*n.* **axilla** (ak·sil′ə).

axiological (ak″si·ō·loj′i·kəl): *adj.* interpretative; evaluative; employing moral standards in appraising data.—See **axiology.**

axiology (ak″si·ol′ə·ji): *n.* the scientific study of **values.**

axiom: *n.* a proposition susceptible of neither proof nor disproof but accepted as true by anyone who reflects upon it. ➤Often too loosely used for **postulate** or **assumption.**—*adj.* **axiomatic.**

axis (ak′sis) *n., pl.* **axes** (-sēs): (*geom.*) one of two or more straight lines meeting at a point called the origin, by reference to which any point in space can be located.

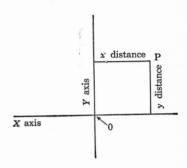

—*Syn.* **coordinate.** ➤The CARTESIAN CO-ORDINATES (or **axes**) are two lines at right angles, the *X* AXIS and the *Y* AXIS (usually pictured horizontally and vertically respectively). The shortest distance of any point *P* from the *X* axis is measured along a line *parallel* with the *Y* axis and is called the *y* VALUE; the shortest distance from the *Y* axis is called the *x* VALUE, i.e., the *x* value is the distance in a direciton parallel to the *x* axis. When we have the *x* value and the *y* value of the point *P,* the location of that point in the plane of the two axes is completely determined.

A third axis at right angles to the plane of the first two permits determination of all points in three-dimensional space. The principle can be extended to *n*-dimensional space, which cannot be visualized.—See also **axis of reference/anatomical, rotation** (2).—*adj.* **axial.**

axis cylinder: the central core of a nerve fiber.

axis of reference/anatomical: one of the three **axes** through an animal body, so placed that any bodily part can be located in reference to them. ➤The preferred system has head-tail or **cephalocaudal,** right-left or **dextrosinistral,** and back-belly or **dorsoventral** axes. VERTICAL AXIS and FRONT-BACK AXIS apply only to upright animals.

axis/principal: see **principal component method.**

axis/visual: see **visual axis.**

axon, axone (ak'sən; -sōn): see **neuron.**

axon reflex: a peripheral reflex, supposed to be mediated by a **collateral** branch of the **afferent** nerve discharging into an **effector.**

Ayres Handwriting Scale: a product *scale for evaluating legibility. ➤A large number of writing samples are assigned scores according to the average time required to read them. The testee's writing receives the score assigned to the sample it most resembles.

Ayres Spelling Scale: a test consisting of 1000 words of known spelling difficulty. ➤It is one of the earliest standardized **achievement tests.**

B

B: **1.** all of an animal's body except the nervous system. **2.** = **luminance. 3.** any number. **4.** (*C. Hull*) mean number of responses in a response cycle or in an alternation cycle.

b_{12} = **regression coefficient** of 1 on 2.

babble: *n.* speech sounds without meaning, as found in the vocalization of infants. —*Syn.* BABBLING.

Babinski reflex or **sign:** upward extension of the toes, instead of flexion, when the sole is lightly stroked. ➤This response is normal, though not invariable, in infancy but gives way later to the plantar response in which the toes are flexed when the sole is stroked. In certain organic disorders of the nervous system the Babinski reappears.

babyhood = **infancy** (which see).

backcross: *n.* a mating, or the offspring of a mating, between a pure-line plant or animal and a hybrid descended in part from the same pure line.

background: *n.* **1.** the surfaces and objects in a picture that are represented as in the rear or in the distance as opposed to the foreground. **2.** that portion of the visible surface being viewed which contains no **figure;** the **ground** (which see). **3.** a sensory experience that is functionally secondary to another sensory experience or perceived object, e.g., *background* music.—See **figure-ground. 4.** figuratively, the events preceding and/or surrounding a certain event that are helpful to understanding or interpreting it: the *background* of a political crisis.—*Cp.* **apperceptive mass, cognitive schema, context. 5.** the sum of a person's experiences, training, education, etc., either in general or as related to a particular task, vocation, or form of behavior; the regular and persistent influences that affect or have affected the person's development.

backlash: *n.* the effect upon the organism of its own **overt** responses; esp., this effect as playing a part in re-**excitation.**—*Cp.* **feedback.**

backward association: see **association/backward.**

backward conditioning: see **conditioning/backward.**

backwardness: *n.* **1.** mild mental inferiority; slow mental development. **2.** scholastic **retardation** that is not due to lack of intelligence.

backward reading: reading in reverse direction: e.g., reading *was* as *saw.*—*Cp.* **mirror writing.**—*Syn.* PALINLEXIA.

Baconian method: the method of **induction.**

bad-me: *n.* the child's early awareness of himself as disapproved by the adults about him. ➤The cluster of ideas and feelings thus named is said to be a nucleus for the development of later **anxiety.**

Bahnung (bä'nung): *n.* (*Ger.*) the increased ease of transmission of neural impulse in a specific nerve tract as a result of prior excitation.

balance: *n.* **1.** a state in which opposed forces or influences are equal; esp., the state in which upright posture is maintained by harmonious adjustment of muscles against gravity. **2.** a harmonious relationship between various behavior trends; absence of eccentricity.

balance/autonomic: see **autonomic balance.**

balance/experience: see **experience balance.**

balance of minus judgments: (*exper.*) the difference between per cent of plus and per cent of minus judgments when the comparison stimulus is objectively equal to the standard stimulus. ➤This is often used as a rough measure of the **time error.**

balancing factor: (*F. L. Wells*) a mode of behavior utilized to obtain a satisfaction not otherwise obtainable: e.g., a child's crying used as a way of coercing the parent. ➤*Distg. fr.* **sublimation,** which implies **repression** of the impulse toward direct satisfaction.

ball-and-field test: one of the Stanford-Binet tests in which the task is to show how one would go about searching for a ball in a circular field.

ballistic: see **movement/ballistic.**

balsamic: *adj.* of a class of smells like balsam. ➤Authorities differ as to the smells belonging in this class.

bandwagon effect: the pressure toward conformity felt by many persons when they perceive that the majority of a group with which they **identify** themselves (or would like to identify themselves) is taking a certain attitude or behaving in a certain way.

bar (bär): (*phys.*) a pressure of one dyne per square centimeter—*Syn.* BARYE (bar'i).

Barany test (bä'rä·ni): rotation of a subject, with his head in each of the planes that bring the three **semicircular *canals** vertical to the direction of rotation. The resulting **nystagmus** reveals whether the canals function properly.

bar chart or **diagram: 1.** a visual representation of quantities by means of narrow rectangles of uniform width, the length corresponding to the quantity. When the bars are contiguous and represent frequencies, the figure is called a **histogram.**—*Distg. fr.* **frequency polygon. 2.** a means of representing a whole by a single bar or column subdivided into two or more parts to show the proportional composition of the whole. ➤Distinction is sometimes made between a COLUMN DIAGRAM, in which the rectangles are vertical, and a **bar diagram,** in which they are horizontal, but the latter term is also used for both kinds.

baresthesia = baresthesis.

baresthesis (bar"es·the'sis): *n.* pressure sense.—*Var.* **baresthesia** (-the'zha).

barrier: *n.* **1.** a limit, boundary, or line of separation; a fence or wall. ➤In psychology the term is used metaphorically for anything that restricts or impedes action. It may be a literal physical barrier, such as a fence, or a physical obstacle, such as rain or heat. It may be a social obstacle, such as the scorn of associates or the threat of punishment. Or the barrier may be some internalized hindrance: a **conflict,** a moral scruple, a fear of failure. It is thus a very general term, though all these usages seem congruous with each other. **2.** see **incest barrier.**

barrier/schizophrenic: a division line or barricade between two parts of a patient's behavior, one part representing an orientation to reality, one part representing unconscious psychic process. ➤E.g., a patient may draw a picture in two distinct halves, the two manifesting little or no logical or graphic relationship. A similar incongruity of two overt or operant behaviors may also be observed.

bar(y)- (bar'i-): combining form meaning *heavy.*

barye = bar.

barylalia (-lā'li·ə): *n.* thick indistinct speech caused by poor articulation.

baryphony (bə·rif'ō·ni): *n.* **1.** difficulty of speech. **2.** a thick, heavy voice quality; a form of **dysphasia.**—*Var.* **baryphonia** (bar·i·fō'ni·ə).

basal age = age/base.

basal age level: see **age/base.**

basal ganglion *n., pl.* **ganglia, ganglions:** (*obsoles.*) a mass of gray matter in the subcortex; either the **corpus striatum,** or that body together with the **thalamus.**

basal (mental) age = age/base or **/basal.**

basal metabolic rate or **BMR:** the minimum rate at which heat is produced by a person at rest, preferably 14 to 18 hours after eating. It measures BASAL METABOLISM, the energy expenditure necessary to minimum vital functioning.

basal plates: (*neurol.*) portions of the embryonic **neural tube** from which the motor centers of the brain and the anterior columns of gray matter of the spinal cord develop.

basal year = age/base.

base (bās) *n., pl.* **bases** (-əz): **1.** the lowest point or foundation on which anything rests. **2.** the point or line, in an operation or action, from which a start is made: e.g., a price from which other prices are calculated is *the base.* **3.** (*math.*) a constant figure with reference to which a mathematical table is constructed.—*Cp.* **basis.**—*adj.* **basal.**

Basedow's disease (bä'zə·dōz) = **exophthalmic goiter.**

base line = abscissa. See **axis.**

base year = age/base or **/basal.**

basi-, baso- (bā'si-, -sō-): combining form meaning *the base, at* or *near a base,* or *walking.*

basic personality type: (*A. Kardiner*) the configuration of personality characteristics that is shared by a majority of the members of a social group as the outcome of shared experience; the central and fundamental attitudes and values of the majority of a society.

basic skills: those activities learned in school which are necessary for the carrying on of other school activities, esp., the mechanics of reading, spelling, writing, and the primary processes of arithmetic. ➤These skills are also deemed fundamental for practical life, but their position as unique in this respect is challenged.

basilar membrane (bas'ə·lər): a delicate membrane in the **cochlea** of the inner ear whose motions in some fashion stimulate the **auditory** nerve.

basis (bā'sis) *n., pl.* **bases** (-sēz): a loosely used term for a concept or thesis that supports a theory, belief, line of reasoning, or procedure. ➤*Contr. w.* **base,** which tends to be used in a literal scene as physical support; **basis** has more figurative meanings. Note pronunciation of the plural form *bā'sēz*, not *bā'səz*, the latter being plural of **base.**—*adj.* **basic.**

basophobia (bā"sə·fō'bi·ə):*n.* pathological fear of walking or of standing erect.—*Var.* **basiphobia.**

bathy-: combining form meaning *deep:* *bathyanesthesia.*

battery (of tests): see **test battery.**

battle exhaustion = **combat fatigue.**

Bayes' principle or **theorem:** (*stat.*) an algebraic statement of the probability that a given event is a consequence of a specified one of a number of mutually exclusive antecedent conditions which might have given rise to the event.

B **coefficient:** the ratio (multiplied by 100) of the average of the intercorrelations of a subgroup of variables to the average of their intercorrelations with the other variables in the group. This gives a measure of the correlational similarities of the subgroup variables.—*Syn.* COEFFICIENT OF BELONGING.

beats: *n. pl.* (*acoustics*) periodic intensity fluctuations corresponding in frequency to the difference in vibration frequencies of simultaneous tones that have slightly different frequencies.—*Cp.* **difference tone.** —For *binaural beats* see **binaural shift.**

beat tone = **intertone.**

before-after design: an experimental program in which both experimental and control groups have both a pretest and a posttest. ➤When the procedure involves only a posttest, it is called an AFTER-ONLY DESIGN.

beh.: *abbr.* for **behavior** or **behaviorism.**

behave: *v.* to make any kind of *organismic *response; (for an organism) to do anything in relation to environment.—See **behavior.**

behavior: *n.* 1. loosely but frequently, anything an animal does. The term is used either for a particular doing or for doings collectively. 2. an act, or acts collectively.— See **act.** 3. a response, or responses collectively. 4. a movement (muscular or glandular), a complex of movements, or movements collectively. 5. (*pop.*) = **conduct.** ➤Since, for most psychologists, behavior is the central concept of their science, its limitation is important; it is also difficult. Traditional **mentalists** limit it to an activity directly correlated with psychic process. (For the kinds of correlation, see **mind-body problem.**)

For most contemporary psychologists, the problem is how to distinguish behavior as studied by psychology from those activities (unfortunately also sometimes called behavior) studied by physiology. (*a*) It is sometimes proposed to define behavior as the activities of the organism as a whole.

Depending on the interpretation of the last phrase, this probably includes either all activities or none. Activities "in a frame of reference of the organism itself" seems equally undifferentiating. (*b*) It is proposed that behavior refers to a *whole response,* in contrast with physiological activities as part-responses. This is inacceptable to many physiologists. (*c*) **Emergentism** views behavior as the new event which is generated by an **integration** of physiological activities, or as a certain **gestalt** or gestalt property in organic functioning. (This view is implicit in the actual usage of many psychologists who would be surprised to find it attributed to them.) (*d*) The least controversial (but ultimately unsatisfactory) attempt at distinction is simply to enumerate those events which seem clearly psychological or physiological respectively: thinking, talking, perceiving, on the one hand; secreting bile, breathing, on the other. (*e*) Many psychologists simply make no attempt to distinguish behavior from what is studied in physiology, though they obviously think there is at least a **heuristic** distinction.

Actually, nearly all who use the term **behavior** seem to be referring to the same or nearly the same phenomena, despite their differences in conceiving these phenomena. —*Cp.* **behaviorism, neobehaviorism, behavior unit.**—*adj.* **behavioral** (which see).

For compounds with **behavior,** when a particular kind of behavior is referred to, see the qualifying term, e.g., **circular behavior.** Note also that, in such compounds, **behavior** is often interchangeable with **act, movement, process, reaction, response.**

behavior/abnormal: see **abnormality.**

behavior/abstract: see **abstract attitude.**

behavior/adaptive: see **adaptation.**

behavior adjustment: see **adjustment;** **behavior determinant.**

behavioral: *adj.* pertaining to or characterizing **behavior.** ➤Used to distinguish the study of responses (by objective methods) from the study of subjective processes; but also to characterize the psychological in contrast with the physiological.—See **behavioral science.**—*Distg. fr.* **behavioristic.**

behavior(al) criterion: see **criterion behavior.**

behavioral determinants of perception: (*J. Bruner* and *C. Goodman*) those organismic factors or functions that coact with the local functions in the sense organ (autochthonous determinants) in determining perception. ➤The **behavioral determinants** may be feelings, wishes, values, prior experience. They are said to affect perception by relative dominance, accentuation, fixation, and by determining selection among alternative perceptual objects. The AUTOCHTHONOUS DETERMINANTS reflect directly the characteristic physiological properties of the sense organ. The distinction between autochthonous and behavioral determinants corresponds roughly with the distinction between sensory and perceptual determinants, but the expression behavioral determinant leaves open the case for factors not ordinarily thought of as inherently perceptual.—*Distg. fr.* **behavior determinants.**

behavioral environment: the organized or patterned aspect of the surroundings to which a person responds. ➤There is much to which a person does not respond, so far as can be ascertained, by emitting behavior, e.g., traffic noises of customary level of loudness. A different concept is implied in the term **adequate** or **inadequate** *stimulus.**

behavioral equivalence: the fact that a certain class of stimuli will evoke, for certain persons or under certain circumstances, the same kind of response.

behavioral oscillation: see **oscillation/behavioral.**

behavioral science: any science that studies the behavior of man and the lower animals in their physical and social environment by experimental and observational methods similar to those of other natural sciences. The recognized **behavioral sciences** include psychology, sociology, social anthropology, and those parts of other social sciences similar to these in outlook and method.

behavioral stimulus field = **behavioral environment.**

behavioral unit=behavior unit.

behavior/animal: see **animal behavior.**

behavior/apopathetic: see **apopathetic.**

behavior/appeasement: see **appeasement behavior.**

behavior cards: a diagnostic set of questions relating to delinquent behavior to be answered by the child by sorting into *yes* and *no* boxes.

behavior check list: a list of behaviors or acts on which to check how often any of these have been observed in a particular situation and/or in particular persons. ➤It is a special form of **activity analysis,** distinguished by the fact that the list is carefully prepared beforehand to include all acts concerning which information is desired.—*Cp.* **activity sampling.**

behavior clinic: see **clinic.**

behavior contagion: imitation of behavior when the initiator of the behavior gives no sign of inviting imitation.—See **contagion/social.**

behavior-description record: data, presented in narrative form, that aim to give an exact account of just what a person

observably does in a given period of time. **behavior determinant:** (*E. C. Tolman*) any variable having a causal relation to behavior. ➤Tolman distinguishes INITIATING DETERMINANTS (environmental stimuli and physiological states), IMMANENT DETERMINANTS (objectively defined purposes or cognitions), CAPACITIES (preferably called **abilities**), and BEHAVIOR ADJUSTMENTS. He speaks only of **covert** preparatory acts that modify the organism's readiness or motivation, but some **overt** preparatory acts are also determinants.—*Distg. fr.* **behavioral determinants of perception.**

behavior disorder: abnormality of conduct believed not to be associated with specific organic cause or symptoms. ➤In general, the term is used for abnormalities that affect general and social adjustment rather than for specific disorders such as a tic.—*Cp.* **functional disorder.**

behavior dynamics: see **dynamics/behavior.**

behavior/extrinsic: see **intrinsic behavior.**

behavior field: everything in, or related to, the objective world that influences responses at a given period in an organism's history. ➤A very broad construct. Excluded are the properties of the organism's reactive equipment; but even these, *as thought about* by the subject, may be included in the behavior field.—*Cp.* **field.**

behavior function: see **mental function.**

behavior/instinctive: see **instinct.**

behavior integration: see **integration of behavior.**

behaviorism: *n.* the view that psychology as a science studies only behavior. ➤For the difficulties of defining **behavior,** see that term. ¶For early behaviorists, behavior meant very specific muscular or glandular responses. They held that the behavior of walking consists in, or may be reduced to, the contraction of certain muscles. (Opponents call this **atomism,** or a "psychology of muscle twitches.") The basic contention was that only the **objectively** observable can be the data of science. For this reason, **consciousness** was excluded (since it is usually defined as **subjective**), or it was held to be only a sort of **covert** language response. ¶Although most behaviorists have been rigid and vocal upholders of **mechanism** and **determinism,** these are philosophical positions and are not integral to behaviorism as science. The denial of heredity (which marked the early phase of behaviorism) is even less a doctrine truly corollary to the central thesis.

Today it is almost true that no one is a behaviorist, or that nearly everyone is, and the term has lost most of its distinctive reference. (But see **behavior theory and** neobehaviorism.)—See **psychology/divisions and schools of, III, IV, VIII.** For its effect on terminology, see **traditional terminology.**—*adj.* **behaviorist,** pertaining to or characterizing the doctrine; **behavioristic,** having some of the characteristics of behaviorism (but *cp.* **behavioristics**).

behaviorist: *n.* **1.** an adherent of the doctrine of **behaviorism. 2.** (*jocular*) a psychologist who by preference studies learning and motivation in *Rattus norvegicus albinus,* or comparable animal species.

behavioristic: *adj.* pertaining to, or resembling, behaviorism. ➤It should not be used as a synonym for **behavioral** (which see).

behavioristics: *n.* an attempt to describe behavior using only the language of physical science.—See **physicalism.**

behavior/manipulative: see **manipulation.**

behavior/matched-dependent = **imitation.**

behavior method: the systematic study of **behavior** as response to stimulus; the study of stimuli, and of responses to stimuli, in human or other animal species. Behavior method does not use **introspection** nor deal with **mental processes** or **contents.** ➤The term is adopted by those who do not wish to be identified with some of the negations and philosophical postulates associated with **behaviorism,** but do accept its methods and goal.—See **behavior theory.**

behavior object: see **object/behavior.**

behavior/operant: see **operant.**

behavior pattern: see **pattern/behavior-(al).**

behavior potential: (*J. Rotter*) the strength of a tendency to respond in a particular situation or class of situations as a function of the **expectancy** of **reinforcement** and of the **reinforcement value** of what is expected.

behavior problem or **behavior/problem:** see **problem behavior.**

behavior psychology = **behaviorism** or **behavior theory.**

behavior rating: see **rating/behavior.**

behavior-rating schedule: a form that provides specific questions about how the ratee behaves in a variety of situations, together with a framework specifying the alternatives to be used in replying. ➤E.g.: "How restrictive of the child's play is the mother? Directs minute details of play—interferes with child's play much of the time—consistently avoids volunteering suggestions." The questions deal with **behavior,** not with **traits.** The schedule may be self-rating or other-rating.

behavior ratio: the ratio of the respective strengths of opposed response tendencies at a **choice-point:** e.g., strength of tendency to turn right compared with strength of tendency to turn left.

behavior record: data, presented in narrative form, which aim to give an exact account of just what a person observably does in a given period of time.

behavior repertoire: see **repertoire/behavior.**

behavior sampling: see **sampling/behavior.**

behavior segment: the smallest descriptive unit of response to a stimulus.—*Syn.* BEHAVIOR ATOM, **behavior unit.**—See **atomism.**

behavior setting: (*R. Barker, H. Wright*) a stable and recognizably distinct part of the physical and social milieu of a community which provides time and place for a characteristic pattern of behavior, e.g., a specific church service with its pattern of meditating, listening, singing, responding in concert, etc. ➤The personnel and the materiel of a behavior setting may change without substantially altering the behavior setting, e.g., new members or new pews may not change the Presbyterian Sunday service.

behavior space: 1. (*topol. psychol.*) the complex set of conditions and relations which determine behavior at a given time. ➤It consists (*a*) of the perceived objects, and the perceived relations between them that are present in the situation; of the person's memories and inferences in relation to these objects and relations; of the perceived **self** in the situation; and (*b*) of a controlling and activated system of beliefs and values. —*Cp.* **life space. 2.** (*E. C. Tolman*) the space in which objects are perceived by the actor at any one time. The objects are perceived as being in a place at a distance and direction from the viewer.

behavior support: a specific environmental condition that is necessary if a given act is to be finished.

behavior system: see **system/activity.**

behavior theory: a general point of view, rather than a particular theory, that conceives of the task of psychology as the determination of the relation of stimulus to response, both of these as measured in physical units. ➤Most adherents, however, make use of hypothetical states of the organism as **intervening *variables.** Investigation is largely of motivation and learning, especially of infrahuman animals, although the data of psychophysics and of sensory-discrimination experiments are sometimes made use of.—See **behavior method.**—*Near syn.* **neobehaviorism.**

behavior unit: a segment of the total behavior stream that is natural, i.e., it possesses some degree of inherent unity that is not arbitrarily imposed by the observer or theorizer. ➤The units have been classified as **atomistic, molecular,** and **molar.** —See **molar behavior** for discussion.— *Syn.* BEHAVIORAL UNIT, BEHAVIOR SEGMENT.

Behn-Rorschach Test: a set of inkblots that parallels the original **Rorschach Test.**

Bekanntheitsqualität (be·känt′hīts·kä·li·· tät″): *n.* (*Ger.* for *quality of being known*) the attribute of familiarity of a sense datum. It may be present even when the object cannot be **recognized.**

bel: see **decibel.**

belief: *n.* an emotional acceptance of a proposition or doctrine upon what one implicitly considers adequate grounds. ➤The grounds for belief, however, are often not examined, nor does the believer imply that others need have the same grounds. Beliefs have varying degrees of subjective certitude.—*Cp.* **assumption, opinion, conviction.**—*Distg. fr.* **faith.**—*Ant.* DISBELIEF, **doubt.**

belief-value matrix: (*E. C. Tolman*) the set of classifications or categorizations (including **valences** and **expectancies**) with which a person interacts with the environment.—*Cp.* **schema.**

Bellevue Scale = Wechsler-Bellevue Scale.

bell-shaped curve = frequency curve/ normal.

belongingness: *n.* **1.** a feeling-attitude of being identified with, being a part of, being accepted by, and having a secure position in, the group. **2.** (*E. L. Thorndike*) the property of any object of being, for a given individual, an integral part of a larger unit or of being closely related to another object with which it forms a larger unit.

belongingness/principle of: (*E. L. Thorndike*) A bond is more readily formed between two items if the learner recognizes that they belong together in some way.

Bender Gestalt Test: a test consisting of nine simple designs, presented individually on cards, which the subject is asked to copy. ➤Analysis of the errors in perception of spatial relations permits use of the test for screening more serious forms of psychological disturbances, although educational status influences errors.—*Syn.* BENDER VISUAL MOTOR GESTALT TEST.

beneceptor (ben″i·sep′tər): *n.* a **receptor** for stimuli that tend to promote the wellbeing of the organism.—*Contr. w.* **nociceptor.**—*adj.* **beneceptive.**

benign: *adj.* **1.** of a diseased condition from which a favorable outcome may be expected, although it may be a very serious and distressing state.—*Ant.* **malignant. 2.** by extension, of psychological disturbances in which the prognosis is favorable.—*n.* **benignity** (bi·nig′nə·ti).

benzedrine (ben′zə·drēn): *n.* a synthetic

drug used for decongestion of nasal tissues, and as a stimulant to the central nervous system.

berdache (bèr·dash′): *n.* one who adopts the dress and the manner of living of a person of opposite sex.

Berger rhythm or **wave = alpha rhythm.**

berserk (bèr′sèrk; bèr·sèrk′): *adj.* in a state of violent rage or frenzy.

Beschreibung (be·shrī′bung): *n.* (*Ger., description*) a method of **introspection** that confines the report to a statement of the psychological **attributes** of the object of awareness. ➤These attributes were strictly defined by Titchener and his associates. *Beschreibung* is contrasted with *Kundgabe,* the giving of information *about* the object, e.g., where it is, what it means.

best-answer test: see **test/selective answer.**

best fit: (*stat.*) a fit of a straight line or a curve to a set of observations so as to conform to some criterion of **goodness of** *fit,* usually that of **least squares method.**

bestiality = zoerasty.

best-reason test: see **test/best-reason.**

beta coefficient = beta weight.

Beta Examination or **Test** (bā′tə; bē-): a series of group intelligence tests, designed by U.S. Army in World War I, for soldiers nonliterate in English.

Beta hypothesis: see **Alpha, Beta, Gamma hypotheses.**

beta movement: see **motion/apparent.**

beta regression coefficient or **weight = beta weight.**

beta response: an eyelid response somewhat delayed after presentation of the conditioned stimulus. ➤It is contrasted with the ALPHA RESPONSE, a similar response given more quickly. It is believed that the beta response is the true CR, that the alpha response is a UR that has been sensitized during training.

beta rhythm: a brain-wave pattern in the **EEG** in which the waves are somewhat shallower and faster than in the **alpha rhythm.**

beta weight or β-**weight:** the amount that each variable must be multiplied in order to make the **multiple *correlation** with a criterion a maximum; the coefficient or multiplier of one of the independent variables in a **multiple *regression equation,** the variables being in **standard *scores.** ➤Given a set of predictors (e.g., age, intelligence test score, high school marks), the beta weights are those multipliers of each predictor that will yield the highest multiple correlation of the predictors with such a criterion as college marks.—*Syn.* BETA COEFFICIENT, BETA PARTIAL REGRESSION

COEFFICIENT, BETA REGRESSION COEFFICIENT or WEIGHT, STANDARD REGRESSION COEFFICIENT.

betweenbrain = diencephalon.

Betz cells: *n. pl.* large pyramidal cell bodies in the **motor area.**

Bewusstseinslagen (be·vûst′zīns·lä″gen): *n. pl.* (*Ger.*) name given by the Wuerzburg school to conscious **attitudes** (such as doubt, uneasiness, effort, vacillation, ignorance), held to be unanalyzable into sensory elements.

Bezold-Brücke phenomenon (bā′tsolt-brY′ke): a shift in hue wherein colors tinged with red or green shift toward yellow or blue when the intensity or luminance is sharply increased.

bi-: prefix meaning *double, both, twofold.*

bias: *n.* 1. the tendency to favor a certain position or conclusion.—See **prejudice.** 2. the tendency to err in a certain direction. ➤A BIASED SAMPLE is unrepresentative of all the cases concerning which an inference is to be drawn. 3. any factor in an experimental procedure which systematically introduces error, such error being a **constant *error.**—*adj.* biased or biassed.

bias/interviewer: see **interviewer bias.**

biblio-: combining form meaning *book, of books: bibliography, bibliotherapy.*

bibliotherapy: *n.* the utilization of reading for cure or amelioration of psychic disorder; more broadly, the use of reading to promote mental hygiene.

Bidwell's ghost = Purkinje afterimage.

bifactoral theory of conditioning = learning/factor theory of (2).

bifactor method: a method of factoring which first extracts a factor common or general in all the tests and then extracts group factors among several clusters of tests. ➤The method assumes the existence of a **general *factor** (but tests that assumption); the **multiple-factor** method does not assume a general factor, though it may find one. In general, for a given test only one group **factor loading** is extracted.

bifurcation (bī″fər·kā′shən): *n.* a dividing into two parts.—*adj.* and *v.* **bifurcate.**

biglottism (bī′glot·iz·əm): see **bilingual.**

bilateral: *adj.* 1. having, or arranged about, two sides, as *bilateral* symmetry. 2. pertaining to both right and left sides.—*n.* **bilaterality.**

bilingual: *adj.* 1. speaking as mother tongues two languages learned at about the same time. ➤*Distg. fr.* BIGLOTTAL (*n.* BIGLOTTISM), having facility in a second language. 2. loosely but commonly, speaking two languages with approximately equal facility.—*n.* **bilingualism.**

bimanual: *adj.* of performance that uses or requires two hands.—*Distg. fr.* **ambidextrous.**

bimodal (bī·mō′dəl): *adj.* (*stat.*) of a distribution that has two points (**modes**) at which the frequencies, or numbers of cases, are considerably greater than on either side of those points.—*Cp.* **multimodal.**—*n.* **bimodality, bimodalism.**

binary (bī′nə·ri): *adj.* 1. composed of two elements or parts; double; dual: a *binary* relation has two terms. 2. (*math.*) of a system of numeration using two as a base: e.g., a *binary* logarithm.—See also **binary number system.**

binary (number) system: Compared with the usual decimal system—which has nine digits and a zero—the binary system has only one digit, 1, and a zero. Thus, the first ten whole numbers of the b. n. s. (with their everyday equivalents in parentheses) are: 0 (0), 1 (1), 10 (2), 11 (3), 100 (4), 101 (5), 110 (6), 111 (7), 1000 (8), 1001 (9), 1010 (10). The b. n. s. is used in many electronic computers and in **information theory.**

binaural (bin·ôr′əl): *adj.* of both ears functioning together.—*Ant.* uniaural (*prefd.*), **monaural.**

binaural ratio: the ratio of sound intensities at the two ears.

binaural shift: a periodic shift in localization of the sound, heard when two tones of slightly different frequency are conducted separately to each ear, the rate of fluctuation corresponding to the frequency difference.—*Syn.* BINAURAL BEAT.

binaural space: the totality of points in space from which, under stated constant conditions, sounds are heard as having a distinguishable location.

Binet or **Binet-Simon scale** (bē·nā′sē·-mōn′): a series of tests for the measurement of intelligence in school children, first issued in France in 1905 by A. Binet and since adapted for use in many other cultures. ➤A **Binet** is technical slang for a test or test score using a scale of the Binet type—in the U.S., usually the **Stanford-Binet.**

binocular (bin·ok′ū·lər; bī·nok′-): *adj.* pertaining to both eyes functioning together. —*Ant.* uniocular, monocular.

binocular disparity = disparity/retinal.

binocular rivalry = retinal rivalry.

binocular vision: see **vision/binocular.**

binomial (bī·nō′mi·əl): *n.* an algebraic expression that contains two terms. ➤The BINOMIAL EXPANSION is the binomial raised to any power, n: e.g., $(p - q)^2$ or $(p + q)^5$. The binominal expansion is the algebraic approximation of the **normal *frequency curve.**—*adj.* having two terms or aspects or dimensions.

bio- (bī′ō-): combining form meaning *living* or *life.*

bio-analysis: *n.* the attempt to apply psychoanalytic procedures and principles to the study of physiological phenomena.

biochemistry: *n.* the chemistry of plant and animal life.

biodynamics: *n.* the branch of physiology that deals with the active vital processes of organisms.—*Contr. w.* **biostatics.**

bioelectric potential: the electric charge carried by any bodily part at a particular time. ➤The charge depends upon the resistance of the involved part, upon its metabolic activity (which is associated with the production of an electric charge), and upon any electric current reaching the part, whether from another part of the body or from an external source.—*Cp.* **electroencephalogram, electromyogram,** and **electrodermal response.**

biogenesis: *n.* the origin and evolution of living beings; or a theory concerning such origin and evolution.—*adj.* **biogenetic.**

biogenetic law = **recapitulation/theory of.**

biogenic: *adj.* originating in biological sources. ➤*Contr. w.* **psychogenic,** originating in psychological processes. Biogenic thus usually means *unlearned,* or coming into existence without learning although subject to modification by learning.—*Distg. fr.* **biogenetic,** pertaining to **biogenesis.**

biograms: *n. pl.* partial autobiographies by members of a selected social group, written under specific directions as to content and form, and for the purpose of obtaining mass data.

biographical method: the systematic analysis of all recorded data about a person, with a view to discovering causal relationships or correlations between events and personal development.

biological memory: see **memory/racial.**

biologic curve = **frequency curve/normal.**

biologism (bī·ol′ō·jiz·əm): *n.* application of the methods of biology to the study of behavior and experience, in the belief that these methods are all-sufficient.

biology: *n.* the science of life. ➤Taken narrowly, biology includes zoology and botany with their several divisions. Taken broadly, it also includes all scientific disciplines dealing with living beings, esp. anthropology, sociology, and psychology. A purely verbal inconsistency results when authors define psychology as a biological science and yet contrast biological with psychological considerations, concepts, methods, etc. This is avoided by speaking of the psychological, on the one hand, and of the physiological (or anatomical), on the other.

biomechanics = **human engineering.**

biometry (bī·om′ə·tri): *n.* **1.** the science of statistical methods applied to living structures and functions, esp. as developed by K. Pearson and his students.—*Syn.* BIO-METRICS. **2.** calculation of the probable human life span.—*adj.* **biometric.**

bionegativity: *n.* (*A. Angyal*) a condition in which the integration of the organism is so disturbed that the *normal* functioning of a part impedes instead of promotes total functioning. ➤It is not mere disorganization but a specific malorganization.

bionomic factors: those influences or factors external to the organism that limit its development: e.g., lack of oxygen at high altitudes, resulting in a people with large lung capacity.

bionomics = **ecology.**

biopsy (bī′op·si): *n.* (*med.*) microscopic examination, for diagnostic purposes, of a bit of tissue taken from the living organism.—*adj.* **biopsic.**

biopsychic: *adj.* of psychological phenomena in relation to the life of the organism.

biopsychology: *n.* **1.** psychology as a branch of biology. **2.** psychology as related to biology. **3.** = **psychobiology.**

biosocial: *adj.* **1.** pertaining to the interaction of biological and social phenomena. **2.** characterizing a phenomenon or event as being both biological and social at the same time, often inherently both. **3.** of social phenomena that are determined chiefly by biological factors, e.g., the social upheaval following the Black Death.

biosphere: *n.* **1.** collectively, all the regions in the world or in the air surrounding it wherein living beings may be found. **2.** the world described as an environment for living beings.

biostatics: *n.* the study of the structure of organisms as it relates to their functions.—*Contr. w.* **biodynamics.**

biostatistics = **statistics/vital.**

biotechnology = **human engineering.**

biotype: *n.* **1.** (*biol.*) a group of organisms of common descent who share a certain complex of hereditary factors: e.g., all Jersey cows form a biotype. ➤Within the limits of the biotype there is much individual variation. **2.** (*E. Jaensch*) either of two kinds of persons, each characterized by a kind of **eidetic imagery** said to be associated with a physiological basis: the **B type,** associated with a tendency to Basedow's disease (exophthalmic goiter); and the **T type,** associated with a tendency to tetany. **3.** any category of persons distinguished in **biotypology.**—*adj.* **biotypic.**

biotypology: *n.* the classification of man—considered as a constellation of interacting anatomical, physiological, and psychological characters—into distinct groups or **types.**

biparental: *adj.* pertaining to both parents.

bipolar: *adj.* **1.** characterizing a variable, trait, or factor that extends from an extreme or maximum value through zero to an extreme opposite: e.g., from a maximum of self-effacement to a maximum of exhibitionism by way of a zero or neutral value. ➤The opposites must be opposite not merely in the meaning of the words but in the facts of behavior—i.e., the two kinds of behavior must be negatively correlated. Thus leadership and followership, although semantically opposite, do not constitute a bipolar variable since there is a positive correlation between them: good leaders tend to make fairly good followers. ¶Not all traits, moreover, have two poles. Intelligence has but one. Stupidity is not a distinct trait but merely relative lack of intelligence. **2.** tending to behave in opposed ways: e.g., to love and to hate someone, either simultaneously or in alternation.—*Cp.* **ambivalence,** nearly synonymous but with an interesting difference in meaning.—See also **polarity, polar opposites, polar continuum.**—*n.* **bipolarity.**

bipolar factor: see **bipolar (1).**

bipolar (nerve) cell: a neuron with two prolongations (the **axon** and **dendrite**) in opposite directions. ➤In a typical sensory nerve the long axon seems continuous with the dendrite, the cell body being off to the side.

birth control: voluntary regulation of the number and spacing of offspring. ➤Technically, the term includes artificially induced abortion (premature expulsion of the embryo after conception), as well as **contraception** (voluntary prevention of conception). But in actual fact the birth-control movement has devoted itself to the effort to substitute contraception for the extremely prevalent abortion. Birth control includes measures to facilitate conception when desired, as well as to prevent unwanted conception.—*Syn.* PLANNED PARENT-HOOD (*prefd.*).

birth cry: the reflex vocalization that usually immediately follows birth and announces the beginning of respiration.

birth injury: transient or permanent injury to the infant during the birth process, esp. **brain damage.** Many motor disabilities are attributed to such injury.—*Distg. fr.* **birth trauma.**

birthmark: *n.* **1.** a congenital disfigurement or blemish.—*Cp.* **nevus,** the most common type. **2.** any sharply distinguishing physical characteristic alleged to result from a mother's unusual experience during pregnancy. ➤Inasmuch as it is clearly thought of as a *before-birth* mark, the term is as inexpressive as the phenomenon is doubtful.

birth/multiple: see **multiple birth.**

birth order: the relative order of birth of the children in a single family.

birth/premature: a live birth occurring between 28 and 38 weeks of pregnancy. A birth weight of less than 5½ pounds is considered a sign of premature birth.

birth rate: the number of births (more often of live births) per thousand of the total population per year or other unit of time.

birth symbolism: (*psychoan.*) a symbolic representation, usually far from obvious, of the separation from the first **libido object,** i.e., of the newborn from its mother. ➤According to psychoanalysis, many neurotic symptoms are **symbols** of this first great deprivation.—*Cp.* **birth trauma (2).**

birth theories/infantile: the ideas and fantasies of young children about birth. ➤Strictly speaking, these theories are not **infantile** but *childish,* though some psychoanalytic theorists suppose them to originate before speech develops. They are spontaneous, original (and often amusing) solutions to the child's curiosity, and are to be distinguished from the folklore about birth which passes from child to child, and from the adult myths (of the stork, etc.) fobbed off on children.

birth trauma: 1. literally, but seldom, an injury received during birth.—*Syn.* **birth injury** (*prefd.*) **2.** (*psychoan.*) the effect upon the psyche of the stress of being born. ➤Usually emphasis is not upon the actual pain of being delivered but upon the infant's having to begin adaptation to a strange and seemingly hostile environment. Some speak of the trauma of being torn unwilling from the security of the first home (the uterus) and from the first object of the **libido.** The result is the seed-anxiety from which (according to some psychoanalysts) all **anxiety neuroses** and many other neurotic symptoms grow.

bisection scaling method = **halving method.**

biserial r: see **correlation/biserial.**

bisexuality: *n.* **1.** possession of the **somatic** or psychological characteristics (generally only of the **secondary** *sex characters*) of both sexes.—*Syn.* **hermaphroditism. 2.** excessive impartiality in sexual attraction to both sexes; = **ambieroticism.**

bit: *n.* (*info. theory*) a unit measure of amount of **information (3):** the **bit** is that amount which, put into a given assemblage consisting of a known number of alternative outcomes for a certain event, reduces the alternatives by one half. ➤If we are tossing a coin, the chances of getting head or tail are even. To reduce the alternatives by half (i.e., to specify that the coin will fall head, not tail) requires one bit of information. The formula is *bit* = log₂ *k,* where *k* is the number of alternatives.

The term bit is taken from the first two

and the last letters of *binary digit*. It does not mean *a small amount,* as the ordinary word bit suggests. Moreover, it must always be taken as relative to the assemblage in which it operates. Hence one bit is incommensurable with a bit from a different assemblage. A bit is **information,** as strictly interpreted in **information theory.**

bivariate: *adj.* having two variables; relating to two variables. ➤A BIVARIATE POPULATION—or, more properly, a BIVARIATE SAMPLE—is one selected, intentionally or otherwise, on two variables.

bivariate frequency table = scatter diagram.

black: *n.* an **achromatic color** of minimum **lightness** (maximum darkness) which represents one limit of the series of grays; the complement or antagonist of white (the other extreme of the gray series). ➤Black is typically a response to low **luminance** in conjunction with relatively high surrounding, or preceding, luminance.

blackbox: *n.* a formal **model** used in formulating **hypothetical** *constructs: given a certain **input,** what must be hypothesized as taking place in the blackbox to account for the **output.** ➤In psychology, the organism (or just the nervous system) may be conceived as a blackbox, nothing being known about what is inside. The correlations between input and output on many occasions enable certain inferences to be made, not about what the mechanism inside is but how it works. Such conceptualizing is familiar in psychology—only the analogy to a blackbox is new.

blackout threshold: the point or level at which a person "blacks out," or loses consciousness; esp., the level of oxygen deprivation at which such loss of consciousness occurs.

Blacky pictures: a **projective** test that asks a child to tell a story about the situations depicted in a series of cartoons of a dog family. ➤The stories are supposed to reveal the strength of certain psychoanalytic mechanisms. E.g., one cartoon invites, but does not require, a story depicting the Oedipus situation.

Blakeman's test: a test according to which **regression** is **linear** if $N (\eta^2 - r^2) < 11.37$.

blamavoidance need (blăm"ə·void'əns): *(H. A. Murray)* the need to avoid blame by inhibiting asocial impulses; need to fear censure, ostracism, or punishment; need to be well-behaved.

blamescape need: *(H. A. Murray)* the need to escape blame by flight or by concealment of guilt.

blanket group: in classification, a division composed of all those cases that do not fit any other division.

blank experiment or **trial:** a trial in

which irregular stimulus conditions are inserted in an experimental series to prevent the subject from reacting automatically or from guessing what is coming. The results of the blank are not counted in the series. —*Syn.* PUZZLE TRIAL (not *prefd.*).

blast-injection technique: the induction of convulsions in an animal by prolonged exposure to air blasts.—See **audiogenic seizure.**

blend: *n.* **1.** an unanalyzed fusion of elements.—*Cp.* **fusion** and **pattern.** **2.** *(Ror.)* a response for which there is more than one direct **determinant.**

blepharospasm (blef'ə·rō·spaz"əm): *n.* involuntary blinking of the eyelids, similar to a **tic.** ➤An example of **bogus erudition.**—*Syn.* EYELID SPASM *(prefd.).*

blind: *adj.* **1.** deprived of vision; having **visual** *acuity less than $20/200$ in the better eye after attempted correction; unable to read printed matter, even with the aid of glasses.—*n.* **blindness,** which see. **2.** see **blind analysis.**

blind alley: a passageway whose only exit is at the point of entrance.—*Syn.* BLIND.

blind-alley job: one that provides little scope for mature ability and does not lead to better jobs.

blind analysis: a diagnosis of a person, from a set of test scores or other **protocol,** without knowing who the person is or seeing him. ➤When the blind analysis yields correct diagnosis, or when two or more blind analyses coincide, it is often taken as evidence for test **validity;** but this criterion has severe limitations.—*Syn.* BLIND DIAGNOSIS, BLIND INTERPRETATION, BLIND TEST. —See also **blind matching.**

blindism: *n.* a term that refers to any of various repetitive hand and/or body movements—rubbing the eyes, waving the fingers before the face, swaying the body, etc.— which tend to become persistent mannerisms in blind children.

blind learning: learning of a task through repetition but with a minimum understanding of the relationships involved in the task. ➤*Contr. w.* meaningful *learning. —*Syn.* rote *learning.

blind-matching technique: the procedure (chiefly used in validation studies) in which, given one description of each or several persons (or events), it is required to select another of the same person (or event) from an independent set of descriptions.

blindness: *n.* a condition in which one is unable to see, or unable to see well enough to use vision for the ordinary conduct of affairs. ➤It is ordinarily defined as less than $20/200$ acuity in the better eye after correction (see **acuity/visual**); or as having the visual field contracted so that it subtends an angular distance no greater than

20 degrees. A PARTIALLY SEEING person has better vision but is markedly handicapped, usually with not better than $20/70$ vision in the better eye after correction.

blindness/cerebral: inability to see, due to a lesion in the visual area of the cerebrum.

blindness/color: see **color blindness.**

blindness/day: an abnormal condition of the central area of the retina in which bright light is uncomfortable to the individual and he sees better in dim light.— *Syn.* **nyctalopia, hemeralopia,** both *ambig.*—*Ant.* night *blindness.

blindness/functional: inability to see, although the eyes and local nervous mechanism are intact. ➤If there is reason to attribute the blindness to a specific lesion in the brain, it should be called ENCEPHALITIC, or CEREBRAL, BLINDNESS.—*Syn.* **psychogenic** *blindness, which implies a specific mode of causation.—See **functional disorder.**

blindness/hysterical: inability to see, caused by **hysteria;** more generally = **blindness/psychogenic.**

blindness/mental: (*pop.*) a refusal to face reality.

blindness/night: severely lessened ability to see under reduced intensity of light.— *Syn.* **hemeralopia, nyctalopia,** both used in confusing ways.

blindness/psychic: 1. inability to see, although the **receptor** and the pathways to the brain are normal.—*Syn.* **blindness/functional** (*prefd.*). **2.** = **blindness/cerebral** (*prefd.*). **3.** = **blindness/psychogenic.** ➤Psychic blindness is an ambiguous and unnecessary term.

blindness/psychogenic: blindness brought on by psychological causes in the absence of damage to the specific organs of vision. —See **psychogenic.**

blindness/red-green: see **red-green blindness.**

blind spot: an area in the retina, where the optic nerve leaves the eyeball, that is nearly but not wholly insensitive to light; (metaphorically) persistent inability to consider something impartially.

blinking reflex: a closing of the eyelids induced by bright light or by a shift in attention. ➤It is, in general, slower than the **winking reflex.**

block: *n.* **1.** an external obstacle that prevents a response.—*Syn.* **barrier. 2.** (*neurol.*) a barrier to the transmission of **excitation** in nerve tissue. ➤The location of the barrier is usually indicated, e.g., SPINAL BLOCK, a barrier somewhere in the spinal cord. The block may be due to a lesion or to a local anesthetic, the latter being usually meant in NERVE BLOCK. **3.** a sudden stoppage of thought or action, not accountable for in

terms of the present objective situation nor in terms of genuine forgetting. ➤While it is common to speak of an EMOTIONAL BLOCK, it is not evident that all blocks are caused by high emotional tension. In psychoanalysis, some blocks are attributed to an emotion-*preventing* **repression.**—See **emotional blocking. 4.** the sudden stoppage of the flow of speech in stuttering.— *n.* (for the process) **blocking.**—*v.* **block,** to impede or wholly prevent any activity.

block design: (*exper. design*) Experimental subjects are divided into several classes or categories considered to be homogeneous for the purpose in hand, and representatives of each are exposed to all the kinds or degrees of experimental treatment. ➤The group of subjects of a given category receiving a given treatment is a BLOCK. The term originally came from agricultural research where each square plot (or block) of land received differential treatment.— *Cp.* the much simpler **control group** design.

block design test: a type of performance test, using colored blocks, in which the subject must try to match standard designs. ➤As well as being a test of intelligence, it is held to be diagnostic of brain injury and/or of deterioration in some types of **functional psychosis.**

block diagram = **histogram.**

blocking/emotional: see **emotional blocking.**

blood group or **type:** a classification of human blood based on the effect of various kinds of blood serums in causing agglutination of the red corpuscles. ➤Each person's blood belongs to a specific inherited type. Different biological stocks show characteristic percentages of persons of given types, but no blood group is found exclusively in any one stock.

blood pressure: the pressure exerted by the blood against the walls of the arteries. ➤Changes in blood pressure correlate with many physiological and psychological activities.

bloom: *n.* (*vis.*) a hazy appearance near the highlight of a glossy specimen.

blue: *n.* the color seen by a normal eye when stimulated by a wave length of approximately 478.5 millimicrons; or any similar color.

blue blindness = **tritanopia.**

blue-yellow blindness: a rare type of partial **color blindness,** in which blue and yellow stimuli are confused because the color gamut is reduced to reds, greens, and grays.

blushing: *n.* an involuntary reddening, especially of the face, associated with feelings of embarrassment, confusion, or shame. ➤*Contr. w.* FLUSH, a similar reddening

associated with anger or with a fever.—*v.*
blush.
BMR = **basal metabolic rate.**
board school: (*Brit.*) a nondenominational
school supported by local rates (taxes) and
controlled by a local school board. In the
U.S. these would be called public schools.
body: *n.* **1.** the central part of an organism,
not including appendages or head; in vertebrates, the trunk. **2.** an anatomically coherent mass of tissue, usually an organ:
adrenal *body,* etc. **3.** the total organized
being or individual which has existence in
space, either living or now dead but still
retaining the characteristic living form. ➤In
this sense, body nearly always suggests a
metaphysical distinction between body and
mind or soul (see **mind-body problem**)
that is foreign to scientific psychology.
Organism, or **soma,** is therefore more
satisfactory in most contexts. See **person.**
4. (*stat.*) the remainder of a **frequency
curve** or frequency distribution after the
tails are cut off.—*Contr. w.* **tail.**
body build: the observable structure of an
animal (usually human), and the pattern
of relationships among the several members and features of the body. ➤Usually
only **macroscopic** features are dealt with—
height, weight, length of fingers, etc. Sometimes features such as skin color are included. The dimensions along which measurements are to be taken differ among
investigators.—See **body *type, constitutional type.**
body build/index of or **I.B.:** (*H. J. Eysenck*) one hundred times the height divided
by six times the transverse chest diameter.
➤For adult English males the mean approximates 100. A LEPTOMORPH is a person
one standard deviation or more above the
mean; a MESOMORPH is within one SD of
the mean; a EURYMORPH is one or more SD
below the mean.—See **constitutional type.**
body cell: a cell other than a **germ cell;** a
somatic cell.
body concept: an evaluative representation
of one's own body, with special emphasis
upon how one thinks it looks to others.
➤The concept includes body functioning as
well as structure. It is a person's answer to
the question: what sort of a body do I
have? The answer is often far from the objective fact.
body image: 1. the picture or mental representation one has of his own body at rest
or in motion at any moment. It is derived
from internal sensations, postural changes,
contact with outside objects and people,
emotional experiences, and fantasies. **2.**
= **body concept. 3.** the sum of all the relations implying the body as one term, or
fundament. ➤The body need not be specifically imaged or spoken of; thus the rela-

tion *in front,* meaning *in front of my body,*
does not require that one imagine the body.
body jerk: a sudden tensing of the trunk
and flailing movements of the limbs, usually without specific external stimulus. It is
characteristic of the newborn and of young
infants, but not infrequent in adult sleep.
body mechanics: 1. a collective term for the
mechanical functioning of the movable
parts of the body, esp. the bones and
muscles (e.g., the working of the arm as a
complex set of levers); or the study of
bodily movements in terms of the laws of
mechanics. **2.** more generally, the bodily
functions considered as being mechanical:
the heart as a pump, the flow of blood as
hydraulic, the absorption of food as osmosis, etc. **3.** the functional relationship between various parts of the body in physical
activities.
body memory: metaphorical expression for
learned responses that take place automatically and without apparent conscious
control or even awareness, as when one
says, "My legs remembered where to go."
➤Body memory is responsive to the present situation and is not dissociated, as in
automatism.
body protest: physical symptoms that express a protest against the circumstances—
esp. stress conditions—in which an individual is placed.
body schema: 1. the over-all pattern of
one's direct or sensory awareness of his own
body, excluding kinesthetic reports on outer-
directed movements; the pattern of **coenesthesia. 2.** the characteristic way in which
a person is aware of his own body. ➤While
coenesthesia is at the base of this awareness,
other body-related experiences are also influential in its formation. The **body image**
is an actual experience; the **body schema**
is a pattern, an acquired structure that
codetermines the body image in a given
situation.
body size/general: (*H. J. Eysenck*) a score
calculated by multiplying the **standard
score** for height by the standard score for
transverse chest measurement. ➤A MACRO-
SOMATIC is a person whose general body
size is one or more SD above the mean; a
MESOSOMATIC is within one SD of the mean;
and a MICROSOMATIC is one or more SD
below the mean.—*Cp.* **body build/index
of,** in which height is *divided* by chest
diameter, not multiplied as here.
body type: see **type/body.**
Bogardus scale (bō·gär′dəs) = **Social
Distance Scale.**
Bogen cage: a performance test requiring
solution of a **maze**like problem in three
dimensions.
bogus erudition: the unnecessary use of
technical words when simpler words ex-

pressing the same idea are available. ➤It is both pretentious and naïve, to quote H. W. Fowler, for a writer "to think that what has just impressed him because he knows a little about it may be trusted to impress his readers." If, he continues, your term "convinces the reader he is an ignoramus, he will not like it nor you." Moreover, if you try too hard to parade your erudition, it may slip and show you're bogus. Such a Greek **neologism** as **traumatic *di-athesis** is a prime example. Indeed, many Latin and Greek neologisms (esp. in medicine) were introduced at least partly to bewilder and impress the layman.

The desire to use a newly acquired prestige term leads to such a meaningless phrase as "the replication of a hypothesis." It reveals itself also in a stereotyped employment of useful technical terms, esp. if they are new or unusual. **Frame of reference,** though never a happily constructed phrase, once had a fairly explicit meaning. It is now so overworked as to be little more than a cliché. Phrase terms constructed by piling up nouns as adjectives, though occasionally useful, are too often merely an attempt to be learnedly impressive.

The most unfortunate form of bogus erudition is use of a technical term in a vague or general sense. This adds to the offense of pretentiousness that of depriving more accurate writers of a convenient expression for a legitimate meaning. **Differentiate** means "to make to differ," and it is needed in that sense. When elegant variationism leads a writer to say **differentiate** when he means **distinguish** or **discriminate,** a useful distinction is blurred or lost.

If terms born of bogus erudition become current, it is the duty of a lexicographer to record their ostensible intellectual content; it is not his duty to conceal his contempt of their parentage. Nonetheless, discretion having got the better of valor, only the more extreme examples have been editorially marked as **bogus erudition.**—See also **arbitrary definition.**

Bolgar-Fisher World Test: a projective test in which the subject constructs a "world"—i.e., a village, town, farm, airport, etc.—utilizing what he needs from 232 modellike items in 15 categories: houses, trees, cars, dogs, people, etc. ➤The theme and the type of construction are believed to reflect the subject's orientation to reality.

bond: *n.* whatever it is in the organization of an organism that accounts for the fact that a given response consistently follows a given stimulus, or that a given idea follows a given stimulus or other idea; the hypothetical linkage inferred to account for a regular stimulus-response sequence or for an association. ➤The term is intended to be entirely noncommittal as to the nature of the linkage. It is not even necessary to assume (as most psychologists do, however) that the bond is a neuroanatomical structure.—*Syn.* **connection,** ASSOCIATIVE BOND.

bone conduction: transmission of sound vibrations to the **internal *ear** via the bones of the skull. ➤The BONE-CONDUCTION TEST determines how well a person can hear sounds so conducted. It indicates whether hearing loss is due to defective conduction in the middle ear.

borderline: *adj.* **1.** of a phenomenon that is not easily assigned to one or the other of two distinguishable classes between which it falls.—*n.* **2.** (*tech. slang*) a person near the dividing line between normal mental ability and **mental *deficiency.**

borderline defect or **intelligence:** see deficiency/mental.

boredom: *n.* a psychological state resulting from any activity that lacks motivation, or from enforced continuance in an uninteresting situation. It is characterized by slack attention and some aversion from continuing the activity or situation.

Borstal system (bôr'stəl): a method of treating juvenile delinquents in Britain, emphasizing especially close, but friendly, supervision after release from detention.

boulimia = **bulimia.**

boundary: *n.* (*topol. psychol.*) any hindrance to moving from one region of the **life space** to another; a **region** separating one system from another; a region between two systems within which information exchange or energy exchange is less than it is within either of the systems; a relation between psychological forces. ➤A boundary need not be an impenetrable **barrier.** Since the regions are defined by activities, the boundary is any hindrance to change in activity; and a boundary becomes more passable by whatever induces such change. —See **boundary/group.**

boundary/class: either the upper or lower limit of a statistical class. ➤The distance between the two limits is the **class interval.**

boundary/group: 1. the qualifications determining social group membership. **2.** any factor determining a **region** of the **life space** of a social group; a factor that sets limits around certain activities of a group. ➤E.g., a club has its business meeting and its social hour. Each is a region, and certain conventions keep these from more than limited overlap. The conventions are **boundaries.**

bound energy: (*psychoan.*) psychic energy that is under control of **ego** processes, related to reality, and not wastefully expended on impulsive action or on **wish fulfillment.**

bound memory: an aftereffect of a particular past experience which is not now present as an **image** or **idea** but which modifies the person's awareness of present objects; that property of a **perception** which is not directly attributable to immediate sensing.

bouton (bü′tən): see **synaptic knob.**

bow movement: see **motion/apparent.**

BP or **B.P.** = **blood pressure.**

Brace Test: a **battery** of motor-ability tests for adolescents.

brachy- (brak′i-): combining form meaning *short* or *too short.*

brachycephalic (-sef·al′ik): having a relatively short (or broad) head, with a **cephalic index** of more than 81.—See **cephalic index.**—*Var.* **brachycephalous** (-sef′ə·ləs).—*n.* **brachycephaly** (-sef′ə·li).

brady- (brad′i-): combining form meaning *slow* or *sluggish.*

bradyarthria (-är′thri·ə): *n.* abnormally hesitating and monotonous speech caused by brain lesions.

bradykinetic (-kin·et′ik): *adj.* characterized by slowness of movement.—*n.* **bradykinesia** (ē′zhə), **bradykinesis** (-ē′səs).

bradylalia (-lā′li·ə): *n.* slowness of speech but with correct articulation, usually of functional origin.

bradylexia (-lek′si·ə): *n.* pathological slowness in reading; a form of **dyslexia.**

bradylogia (-lō′ji·ə): *n.* abnormally slow speech, due to slowness of thinking, in mental deficiency.

bradyscope: *n.* an instrument for presenting visually a series of objects or pictures at a slow but regulated rate of speed. ➔*Cp.* **tachistoscope,** which presents such a series at a rapid rate.

Braidism (brād′iz·əm) = **hypnotism.**

Braille (brāl): *n.* a system of writing and printing for the blind, using different combinations of raised points for letters and signs.—*Var.* **braille.**

brain: *n.* that portion of the **central nervous system** enclosed within the skull. ➔It includes the **cerebrum, midbrain, cerebellum, pons, medulla.** It is not a synonym for **mind** (if that term is to be retained); from any possible view the brain, though the most important, is not the sole organ of mind.—*Syn.* **encephalon.**

brain center: 1. an area to which **afferent** nerves come (AFFERENT or SENSORY CENTER or PROJECTION AREA), or from which **efferent** nerves start (MOTOR CENTER), or an intermediate "station" between these (ASSOCIATIVE CENTER). **2.** a hypothetic group of neurons in the brain that are interconnected to perform a specific function. ➔The concept belongs to the **conceptual nervous system** and in general implies a doctrine of brain localization not wholly in accord

with contemporary knowledge. The physiological or behavior functions to be related to the group of neurons are seldom established as true functional units. The neural grouping is almost certainly not permanent; after brain damage new connections are often established (see **equipotentiality**). And the implied specificity of localization neglects unduly the codetermination of functions by other parts of the brain, or even of the brain as a whole. ¶The relation of these hypothetical brain centers to operationally defined **neural centers (2)** is not clear; the two are certainly not merely identical. It is recommended that **neural center** not be used as synonym for **brain center.**—See **cell assembly.**

brain damage: 1. any structural injury to the brain, whether by surgery, accident, or disease. **2.** any brain injury before, during, or very soon after birth; early injury to the brain. ➔Early brain damage frequently (but not always) results in lowered intellectual performance and/or in perceptual and motor impairment.—*Syn.* **birth injury** (more general). **Birth trauma** (which see) usually has a special meaning and should not be used for brain damage.

brain dominance: see **dominance (6, 7).**

brain-field theory: see **isomorphism.**

brain lesion: a localized **macroscopic** damage to the brain; destruction of brain tissue.

brain localization: hypothesis that various mental or behavior phenomena are associated with specific and definitely localized areas in the brain. ➔This hypothesis is now generally hedged about with many limitations.—See **brain center.**

brain potential: the electrical potential of the brain; the level of electric activity in the brain.—See **electroencephalogram.**

brain-spot hypothesis: (*hist.*) theory that mental disorders are strictly **organic.**—*Contr. w.* **mind-twist hypothesis.**

brain stem: the axial portion of the brain; the part left when **cerebrum** and **cerebellum** are excluded.

brain storm: (*pop.*) **1.** an emotional crisis. **2.** an idea, original with oneself, that one greets with emotional fervor.

brainwashing: a metaphorical term for the process of inducing a person to depart radically from his former behavior patterns and standards, and to adopt those imposed on him by his captors.

brain waves: 1. spontaneous fluctuations in the electrical activity of the brain, particularly in the **cerebral cortex.**—See **electroencephalogram. 2.** (*pop.*) bright, new ideas; inspiration.

b **reaction:** in reaction-time experiments, a reaction requiring discrimination or choice.

break down: *v.* (*stat.*) to subdivide a population of persons or of items so that the subgroups will be different in respect to a particular variable.

breakdown/nervous: a lay term for any incapacitating mental disorder, or for such condition (short of **psychosis**) requiring hospitalization.

break phenomenon: a sudden shift from one movement to another more or less opposed to it (e.g., from a right-left to an up-and-down movement of the eye) that occurs when the first movement becomes fatigued.

breakthrough: *n.* (*psychother.*) a relatively sudden manifestation of new and more constructive attitudes and actions after a period of resistance or inability to adopt such a course.

breeding/selective: the mating of animals selected because they display a desired trait, followed by the further mating of those among their offspring that show the same trait.

brief-stimulus therapy or **BST:** mild shock therapy.

brightness: *n.* **A.** (*vis.*) **1.** the **intensity** attribute of all visual **sense data;** the correlate of **luminosity.** ➤This is the older usage, one that is still current. Two kinds of **brightness** are, however, sometimes distinguished: **lightness** and **brightness (2). 2.** that attribute of a **film** or **glowing color** by which it can be placed in a series ranging from very dim to brighter-than-white under similar conditions of viewing. ➤*Cp.* **lightness,** which is the attribute by means of which an **object color** can be placed in the series from black to white. **3.** *obs.* for **saturation.**—*Ant.* DIMNESS, DARKNESS.— *adj.* **bright. B.** (*intel.*) **4.** relative degree of **intelligence** as compared with others in one's "natural group," esp. of a child compared with others of his **life *age.** ➤For children, this is often stated in terms of **IQ. 5.** relatively high degree of intelligence. ➤For children, usually taken as IQ 125 or above.—*Ant.* **dullness.**—*adj.* **bright,** having a superior degree of brightness.

brightness adaptation: see **adaptation/ brightness.**

brightness contrast: the relative difference in **brightness** between two objects, expressed as the ratio of the absolute brightness difference to the greater brightness.

brightness/sound or **/tonal:** see **density/ tonal.**

brightness threshold/absolute: the intensity of the least visual stimulus (of any specified wave-length composition) sufficient to be recognized as brighter than the adjacent unstimulated visual field. It may be taken under various conditions and does not exclude the effect of processes normally active in the sense organ.—See **threshold/ absolute.**

brightness/tonal: see **density/tonal.**

bril: *n.* a measure of the brightness of light in which 100 bril is arbitrarily equated to 1 millilambert and smaller and lesser brightnesses are obtained by the halving method.

brilliance: *n.* **1.** obsolescent term for visual **intensity,** or for the property by which a color is located on the scale from white to black.—See **brightness. 2.** high degree of intelligence; **brightness (5). 3.** striking or spectacular performance of any sort.

Broca's area or **convolution** (brō′kəz): the brain center most critically involved in speaking; the caudad portion of the inferior frontal convolution in the left cerebral hemisphere (in right-handed individuals).

Brodmann's area 18: a portion of the cortex, adjacent to the **striate body,** known to be involved in complex visual processes. —*Cp.* **prestriate.**

Brodmann's area 17: a cortical area (with well-developed layers in the **occipital lobe)** that is the major terminus of the visual pathway.

broken home = **family/broken.**

broken series: a **discrete** series.

Brown-Spearman (or **Brown's) formula** = **Spearman-Brown formula.**

Brunet tests (brü·nā′): a developmental scale of baby tests, drawn from the studies of C. Buhler and Gesell, which contains items for ages as low as one month.

Brunswik ratio: an expression of the **constancy** that prevails under given experimental conditions. For visual intensity of surfaces viewed under differing illumination the ratio is $(R\text{-}S)/(A\text{-}S)$, where S is the per cent of reflectance for the stimulus match, A is the **albedo** (or per cent of reflectance) of the object to be matched, R is the per cent of reflectance of the subject's matching sample. The THOULESS RATIO uses the logs of the three variables.

bruxism (bruks′iz·əm): *n.* grinding of the teeth during sleep.

B **score:** an achievement score expressed in a **grade equivalent:** one figure indicates school grade, another follows a decimal point and indicates the month of the school year. ➤E.g., 4.3 = the level of achievement that is normal for the third month of the fourth grade. It would be more consistent with other usage (see **life *age**) if it were written 4–3 or, better yet, IV–3.

BST = **brief-stimulus therapy.**

B type: (*F. Jaensch*) contraction for BASEDOW TYPE, a person with a tendency to **exophthalmic goiter** who has **eidetic imagery** that is natural in color and under relatively voluntary control.

buccal (buk'əl): *adj.* pertaining to the mouth cavity.

buffer items: items interspersed between others in a test or experiment to keep the others from having too much influence on each other. ➤Ordinarily they are not scored; but it is possible to have **buffer items** which interpose adequately between others, yet which themselves present a significant task.

bugger: *n.* (*colloq.*) **sodomite.**

Buhler (baby) tests: a series of tests of infant development, extending from birth to school entrance.

uild/macrosplanchnic: see **macrosplanchnic build.**

ʌulb = **medulla oblongata.**—*adj.* **bulbar.**

ulbocavernous reflex = **virile reflex.**

-bulia (-bū'li·ə): combining form meaning *will* or *volition.*

bulimia (bū·lim'i·ə; bü-): *n.* excessive appetite for food.—*Var.* **boulimia.**—*adj.* **bulimic.**

bulky color = **color/volume.**

bundle hypothesis: a term used by critics to characterize the view that a complex total consists of a mere summation of its elementary components.—*Contr. w.* **Gestalt.** —See also **analysis/reductive.**—*Syn.* MO-SAIC HYPOTHESIS, **and-summation.**

Bunsen-Roscoe law: the generalization that the threshold for light is a function of duration multiplied by intensity. It holds only for very short durations (about 50 *msec.*)

β-weight = **beta weight.**

C

C: **1.** symbol for any **constant. 2.** = **contingency coefficient. 3.** (not *ital.*) = **class. 4.** (*Ror.*) scoring code for **color response. 5.** (*E. L. Thorndike*) symbol for any activity, state, or condition of an animal's neurons. **6.** (*C. Hull*) symbol for the larger **habit strength** or the larger **reaction potential** in behavior withdrawal. **7.** symbol for control conditions (see **control/scientific**).

C': (*Ror.*) scoring code for a response determined solely by black, gray, or white.— See **achromatic color response.**

C. or cent. = centigrade.

C_A = **coefficient of** *association.*

C_D = **drive** condition.

$C_{des}:$ (*Ror.*) scoring code for **color description.**

$C_{sum}:$ (*Ror.*) scoring code for the sum of the weights for **color response.**

$C_{sym}:$ (*Ror.*) scoring code for **color symbolism.**

c: **1.** symbol for the value of a **correction. 2.** (*Ror.*) scoring symbol when the shading of the inkblot is seen as a flat surface. **3.** symbol for **C factor. 4.** (as a subscript) = **criterion variable.**

CA = chronological age or **life** *age.* (Formerly written **C.A.**)

cachexia (kə·kek'si·ə): *n.* an extreme stage of malnutrition caused by some serious disease.—*adj.* **cachexic, cachectic.**—*Var.* **cachexis.**

cachexis = **cachexia.**

cac(o)- (kak'ō-): a combining form meaning *bad, diseased:* e.g., CACOPHONY, a harsh sound; CACOGEUSIA, sensation of a bad taste.

calcarine (kal'kə·rin; -rīn): *adj.* designating a spur-shaped **fissure,** on the medial surface of the **occipital lobe,** which separates

the latter into superior and inferior portions.

calibration: *n.* **1.** the careful marking off of the division points that make up the scale of a measuring instrument, such as a thermometer. **2.** translation of the values yielded by an instrument into terms of a known standard.

California infant scale: (*N. Bayley*) a series of tests that measure sensorimotor development in infants.

calling = **vocation.**

callosum or corpus callosum (kə·lō'səm): *n.* (*neurol.*) a mass of white matter, at the floor of the longitudinal fissure, which links the two cerebral hemispheres.

camouflage: *n.* the attempt to disguise objects by coloring them to blend into their background or to assume deceptive configurations. ➤Color and shading are so applied as to destroy the pattern by which the object is usually recognized, its several parts being absorbed by patterns of the adjacent background. **Camouflage** is also metaphorical for any attempt to disguise one's psychological qualities or behavior.— *Syn.* PROTECTIVE COLORATION, usually applied to the deceptive coloration of some animal forms.

campimeter (kam·pim'ə·tər): *n.* a flat chart upon which is projected the map of the visual field.—*Cp.* **perimeter.**

canalboat children: children living on canalboats and thus deprived of normal schooling. ➤Often referred to in discussion of the **nature-nurture problem.**

canal/central: the small tube, filled with cerebrospinal fluid, that runs within the spinal cord for its entire length. ➤*Distg. fr.* SPINAL or VERTEBRAL CANAL, the canal in the bony spinal column that contains the whole spinal cord.—*Syn.* CANAL CENTRALIS.

canal/cochlear: see **scala media.**

canalization: *n.* **1.** restricting a particular behavior pattern within narrower limits: e.g., settling down to taking the same path home, after a period of trying out various alternatives.—*Distg. fr.* **sublimation,** which implies a shift to a different behavior pattern. **2.** (*G. Murphy*) establishing and progressively strengthening a preference for one among several potential ways of satisfying a **drive;** or the established preference itself: e.g., in the U.S. the hunger drive is **canalized** into a high preference for ice cream (among other preferences); among Eskimos, for blubber.—*Cp.* **sentiment,** which is a complex canalization.—*Syn.* DRIVE SPECIALIZATION.—*Distg. fr.* **secondary *reinforcement.**—*v.* **canalize.**

canalization/neural: the formation or fixation of a definite set of connections so that the **neural current** passes more readily.

canal/spinal: see **spinal canal.**

canals/semicircular: three roughly semicircular tubes in the inner ear, set at nearly right angles to each other in three planes and containing the receptors for the **static sense.**

canal/tympanic: one of the two spiral tubes in the **cochlea,** extending from the round window to the apex and connecting with the **scala vestibuli.**—*Syn.* **scala tympani.**

canal/vestibular: see **scala vestibuli.**

cancellation test: one in which the task is to strike out quickly one or more specified symbols (letter, digit, word, geometrical figure, etc.) irregularly distributed among others.

candle: *n.* the unit of luminous intensity of a source of light. ➤It was originally measured by comparison with a standard international candle. Since 1948, a candle is one-sixtieth of the **luminance** per square centimeter of a complete radiator at the temperature of solidification of platinum.—*Syn.* CANDLE POWER.

candle power = **candle.**

canon: *n.* a formula or rule recommended as likely to lead to the discovery of truth. ➤Canons are not axiomatic, nor are they natural laws; they are working procedures. —*Cp.* **Mill's canons, principle of *parsimony.**

capability: see **ability.**

capacitance (kə·pas'i·təns): *n.* the quantity of electricity, per volt of pressure, that a condenser will hold. It is usually measured in microfarads.

capacity: *n.* **1.** the power of containing or absorbing. ➤ELECTRICAL CAPACITY = **capacitance.** CRANIAL CAPACITY is the volume of the skull. **2.** a loose synonym for **ability** (which see).

capacity variable: a constitutional factor, differing from person to person, that exists before a given learning period, and is capable of influencing the learning.

cardiac: *adj.* pertaining to the heart.

cardiac neurosis: behavior disorder associated with disorder of the heart.

cardinal number: one of the primary numbers used in simple counting: one, two, three, etc.

cardinal value: (*G. Fechner*) that value in a quantitative series of sensations at which the **difference *threshold** begins to increase in proportion to the stimulus.

cardi(o)-: combining form meaning *heart*.

cardiochronograph: *n.* an instrument that draws successive lines whose height is proportional to the duration of each heart cycle, so that the heart rate per minute is immediately apparent.

cardiograph: *n.* an instrument for recording action of the heart. ➤A CARDIOGRAM is the graphic record obtained from the cardiograph.

cardiovascular: *adj.* pertaining to the heart, veins, and arteries as a system: in other words, to the circulatory system of the blood.

card-sorting test: a test requiring the testee to sort cards bearing certain marks or signs into homogeneous piles. ➤In its usual form, the examiner specifies the categories: e.g., "all the crosses in one pile, all the circles in another." In another form, the testee must himself determine what categories will make a good sorting.

Carl hollow-square test: a performance test for **intelligence** that consists of assembling irregularly shaped wooden blocks into a solid square pattern.

carpal: *adj.* pertaining to the wrist.

carpal age: see **age/carpal.**

Cartesian coordinates: see **axis.**

case: *n.* a specific instance, example, or item; or, a kind of instance or circumstance; or, an individual about whom data are gathered or sought.

case history or **study:** a collection of all available evidence—social, psychological, physiological, biographical, environmental, vocational—that promises to help explain a single individual or a single social unit such as a family. ➤It is especially used in psychopathology, guidance, and social work. Since it emphasizes the single case or instance, it differs in *aim* from an experiment and from statistical studies. But the case study often incorporates data from experiments or tests, and a series of case studies may be subjected to statistical study and generalization.

casework: *n.* the function of professional (social) workers who, through social services and personal counseling, attempt to help individuals and families improve their personal and family adjustments.

caste: *n.* a group of persons set apart—originally by occupation, later by religious sanctions and by economic or legal privilege—so that its members are nonmarrying with outsiders and are limited in other associations.

caste/color: social separatism based on skin color. ➤In U. S., applied esp. to Negrowhite relations. Color caste is less rigid than the Indian caste system, but is generally more rigid than social class.

castration: *n.* **1.** surgical removal of the testes, or of testes and penis; by extension, **ovariotomy.**—*Distg. fr.* **sterilization. 2.** (highly metaphorical) any rude external deprivation of a cherished possession or part of oneself.—*Cp.* **castration complex.**—*n.* **castrate,** a eunuch.—*v.* **castrate.**

castration complex: (*psychoan.*) in the male, the repressed or unacknowledged fear (or mixture of desire and fear) of losing one's genitals; in the female, the fantasy (generally laden with guilt anxiety) of once having had a penis, but of having lost it. ➤It is said by many psychoanalysts to be an almost universal source of anxiety—the CASTRATION ANXIETY—in young children of either sex.

casuistry: *n.* reasoning about how the general principles of ethics apply to a particular case. ➤The word has derogatory implications because such reasoning, necessary though it is, too often degenerates into a quibbling justification of whatever one wants to do.

CAT = Children's Apperception Test.

C-A-T (*pron.* as separate letters): see **College Ability Tests.**

cat(a)-, cath-: a prefix of varied meanings: *downward, away, completely, in accordance with,* or *against*; in speech pathology terms, *repeating.*

catabolism (kə·tab′ō·liz·əm): see **metabolism.**—*Var.* **katabolism.**

catalepsy: *n.* **1.** a state in which body and limbs are held muscularly rigid for a considerable period. **2.** = WAXY FLEXIBILITY, or CEREA FLEXIBILITAS, a state in which the limbs maintain the position imparted to them by another. ➤Catalepsy is a frequent symptom in **hysteria, epilepsy, schizophrenia,** and deep **hypnosis.**—*adj.* **cataleptic.**

cataleptoid: *adj.* resembling **catalepsy.**

catalexia (kat″ə·lek′si·ə): *n.* a form of **dyslexia** characterized by a tendency to reread words and phrases.

catalyst: *n.* **1.** (*chem.*) a substance that alters the speed of a chemical reaction but itself emerges unchanged. **2.** metaphorically, an agency that markedly influences the social process without being an integral part thereof; a person without personal

stake in a group's behavior who, by participation in discussion, helps the group define its means and ends.

catamnesis (kat″am·nē′səs): *n.* the history of a patient following onset of an illness; a follow-up history. ➤The term is variously used with reference to the period following onset of an illness, following the first examination by a physician, or following discharge from treatment.—*Contr. w.* **anamnesis.**—*adj.* **catamnestic.**

cataphasia (-fā′zhə): *n.* a form of **aphasia** characterized by frequent and uncontrollable repetitions of the same words or phrases without reference to their meaning. —*Syn.* VERBIGERATION, CATAPHRASIA.

cataplexy: *n.* immobility induced by fear or shock.—*Distg. fr.* **catalepsy.**—*adj.* **cataplectic.**

catastrophic reaction: response to severe shock or to a threatening situation with which the individual is unprepared to cope. The behavior is inadequate, vacillating, inconsistent, and generally retarded, and the person reports that he feels himself buffeted by circumstances.

catatonia (-tō′ni·ə): *n.* a pathological condition characterized by marked motor anomalies—either generalized inhibition of overt response (shown as stupor, negativism, mutism, waxy flexibility, or catalepsy), or generalized excessive motor activity and excitement. ➤The disorder is generally considered a form of **schizophrenia.**—*Syn.* (*Stan. Psychiat.*) SCHIZOPHRENIC REACTION (CATATONIC TYPE).—*adj.* **catatonic.**

catatonic dementia praecox: see **schizophrenia/catatonic.**

catatonic rage: uncontrolled impulse to destroy occurring in certain **schizophrenic** conditions.

categorical: *adj.* **1.** pertaining to a **category,** or to a division or classification based on qualitative rather than quantitative differences. **2.** (*logic*) absolute; unqualified; without regard to circumstances.—*Ant.* dependent, **hypothetical,** conditional. ➤The two meanings are not closely related: classification by categories (hence categorical **1**) need not be absolute or unconditional (hence need not be categorical **2**).

categorical attitude = abstract attitude. ➤See **concrete attitude.** Since **categorical** has associations with absolute and rigid, **abstract attitude** is preferred.

categorical behavior: the behavior of classifying objects. ➤It involves ability to understand the **abstractions** implied. A CATEGORICAL BEHAVIOR TEST may test for the number of categories a person can discern in a set of objects, or the rigidity with which a classificatory system, once adopted, is maintained despite its greater or less suitability to the actual objects.

categorical frequency: (*stat.*) the number

of cases falling within each **category** or **class**.

categorical imperative: an unqualified ethical demand or command, permitting no exception or limitation. ➤Kant's categorical imperative was that one should act as if on the basis of a rule that can be made universal.

categorical series: a series in which each group of items differs from the other groups qualitatively, not merely quantitatively; a series of **categories**.

category: *n.* **1.** (*logic*) a class to which a certain description or assertion uniquely applies; a group of objects (in the widest sense) having a certain set of attributes in common and differing from all other groups in that respect. **2.** (*stat.*) a division or group of data based on qualitative rather than quantitative differences. ➤*Contr. w.* **class**, which is, properly, a grouping based on quantitative differences; but the two terms are often used without distinction. **3.** (*philos.*) an ultimate form of thought; one of the fundamental ideas underlying all thinking: e.g., (for Aristotle) position in space or time; (for Kant) unity, plurality, universality.—*adj.* **categorical** (which see for two distinct meanings).

catelectrotonic: *adj.* pertaining to a negative electrotonic change in a neural element, which renders it more susceptible to **excitation**.—*n.* **catelectrotonus**.

catharsis: *n.* **1.** (*esth.*) the purification or purging of emotions by art. ➤Artistotle's original statement was ambiguous and led to two interpretations: that emotional tensions are lessened by expressing them in esthetic experience; or they are refined by sharing in emotions universalized and artistically portrayed. **2.** (*psychoan.*) release of tension and anxiety by emotionally reliving the incidents of the past, especially those that have been repressed, and honestly facing the causes of difficulty.—*Cp.* **abreaction**. **3.** the folk belief that uninhibited, expressive behavior in one situation (esp. in early life) reduces the need for expression in similar situations later. **4.** loosely, the relaxation of emotional tension or anxiety by any kind of expressive reaction. **5.** still more loosely, any satisfying emotional experience not directly related to adaptive behavior.

Sublimation, often used as a synonym, probably refers to a different process.—*adj.* **cathartic**.

cathection: *n.* the process of attaching something to, or investing something with, affect or psychic energy.

cathexis (kə·thek'səs): *n., pl.* **cathexes** (-sēz): **1.** the **affective** value of an object, idea, or action: its energizing value.—*Syn.* **valence**. **2.** a connection between a **drive** and a **goal** or type of goal object. ➤Literally, **cathexis** means *channel*. A particular

drive is conceived as being led along a channel to a goal. The goal is **cathected** when a drive is thus connected with it.— *Distg. fr.* **canalization**. **3.** (*psychoan.*) the **libido** or psychic energy that has been fixed upon or invested in an object—whether a person, an inanimate thing, a social group, or a cause (OBJECT CATHEXIS); one's own ego processes or self (EGO CATHEXIS); or wish-fulfillment processes (FANTASY CATHEXIS).—*Syn.* **investment**.

Despite the differences in phrasing, it is probable that the three definitions refer to the same process or processes.—*Cp.* **cathection**, which is the process of attaching the "psychic charge," whereas cathexis is the psychic energy when thus attached; but the latter term is used for both.—*adj.* **cathected, cathectic**.—*v.* **cathect, cathecticize**.

cathode: *n.* the negative pole or electrode of an electrolytic cell, vacuum tube, etc.— *Ant.* **anode**.

cathode-ray oscilloscope: an instrument in which a beam of electrons is deflected by an electrostatic field and the result made visible.

caudad vs. **caudal** (kô'dad; kô'dəl): *adj.* The former means *toward* or *at* the tail end, the latter *pertaining to* the tail or tail end.—See **-ad**.—*Contr. w.* **cephalad, cephalic**.

caudal: see **caudad**.

caudate nucleus: a mass of gray matter buried within each cerebral hemisphere: a part of the **corpus striatum**.

causal: *adj.* pertaining to the relation of cause and effect.—*Cp.* **causative**.

causal explanation: see **explanation (1)**.

causalgia (kôs·al'ji·ə): *n.* burning pain, not caused by heat, localized by the sufferer in peripheral areas.—*Syn.* THERMALGIA.

causality: *n.* the abstract quality that is the relation of cause and effect; or the doctrine that asserts the reality, and attempts to define the nature, of such relation. ➤Issues of **causality** are philosophical; issues of **causation** are factual.—*adj.* **causal**.

causal texture: (*E. C. Tolman* and *E. Brunswik*) the property of environmental events of being regularly dependent upon each other; the property of the environment of being made up of events that are mutually dependent. ➤Every event is conceived as being linked with every other, but the degree of dependence may range from the negligible to apparently complete or absolute dependence of one event upon a specified other or others. Moreover, at each critical point there may be, not invariable sequence (the classical conception of **causation**), but a probability of a specified occurrence.—*Cp.* **stochastic process**.

causation: *n.* the relation obtaining when a given event or phenomenon, called **the**

cause, invariably precedes a certain other event, called the **effect.** ➤The issue with causation is **empirical:** Do the facts as observed warrant the inductive generalization that A invariably precedes B? If so, A is the cause of B, and causation is asserted. This assertion is not intended to imply the metaphysical reality of causality as a link between A and B (though some philosophers say that it does imply it, whether the scientist means it or not).—*adj.* **causative,** pertaining to the cause; **causal,** pertaining to the relation.

causation/historical: explaining present behavior in terms of previous experiences.— *Contr. w.* systematic *causation.

causation/principle of multiple: 1. recognition of the fact that no one cause is the sole determiner of an event. **2.** the theory that the many factors leading to an event *interact,* that it is misleading to consider any one factor as if it were an independent part-cause.

causation/systematic(al): explaining present behavior in terms of present conditions; considering an event to be a function of the total situation at a given time.—*Contr. w.* **causation/historical.**

causative: *adj.* pertaining to the phenomenon that is expected to produce, or to have produced, a certain effect. ➤**Causative** points to a concrete thing or event, the **cause; causal** points to a relation.

cause: *n.* that which produces an **effect;** the condition that must precede if a given change is to occur. ➤Philosophically, there is debate about the nature of the **causal** relation. Scientifically, a cause is an **induction** from the fact of regular relationship between an antecedent and an **effect.**—*Syn.* (field theory) HISTORICAL CAUSE.—*Cp.* **cause/structural.**

cause and effect: a basic relationship that can be stated as an inductive conclusion or scientific law: viz., that any of a particular class of phenomena (the **cause)** invariably precedes, and is invariably followed by, any of a certain other class of phenomena (the **effect).**

cause-and-effect test: see **test/cause-and-effect.**

cause/structural: (*field theory*) all the elements in a **field** having an important determining effect upon another element in the field. ➤In field theory it is held that a given phenomenon is determined by the field of which it is a part—by all of the field to some extent, but some parts have negligible effect. The contrast is thus with what field theorists speak of as HISTORICAL CAUSATION or HISTORICAL EXPLANATION, the explanation of a phenomenon in terms of preceding phenomena. The two approaches are not contradictory: historical causation

(the classic cause-and-effect causation) may be appealed to, to explain how a certain element became a part of the field it is in.

CAVD: a battery of four tests of intelligence (completion, arithmetical problems, vocabulary, following directions) developed by E. L. Thorndike and his associates.

caveat lector: (*L.*) "let the reader beware!" ➤A caution almost universally needed for psychological terms referring to concepts and constructs.—See **theory-begging.**

ccw: *abbr.* for counterclockwise (rotation).

CE = **constant error.**

CEEB: *abbr.* for College Entrance Examination Board.

ceiling: *n.* (*stat.*) **1.** the maximum score on a test minus an allowance for **chance** *error.* ➤The CEILING EFFECT is a limitation upon scores as a testee approaches the maximum possible score. By chance, one may fail a few items within one's ability **range** and pass a few above it. As ability begins to coincide with maximum difficulty of the test, it is still possible to fail items by chance but there are no compensating chance successes. Thus, at its upper end, any test becomes less discriminating. **2.** in measures having no ascertainable perfect score, the highest score actually obtained by a specified group.

cell: *n.* **1.** the fundamental structural unit of organized living bodies. **2.** (*stat.*) a compartment formed by the intersection of a horizontal and a perpendicular **array.**—*Syn.* (for 2) **class, compartment.**—*adj.* **cellular.**

cell assembly: a hypothetical system of neurons, organized as a result of repeated stimulation into a complex closed circuit that functions as a unit. ➤As postulated by D. O. Hebb, there are alternative pathways each having the same function, so that disablement of part of the system does not necessarily cause it to cease functioning. An **engram** is a very simple cell assembly.

cell body: see **neuron.**

cell/visual: see **visual cells.**

cemf: *abbr.* for counterelectromotive force.

cenesthesia: see **coenesthesia.**—*Var.* cenesthesis.

cen(o)- = **coen(o)-.**

cenotrope (sē'nō·trōp; sen'ō-): *n.* a behavior pattern or habit shown by all members of a large group having the same biological equipment and the same sorts of experience. ➤The term was proposed as a, substitute for **instinct,** which has misleading implications.—*Var.* **coenotrope.**

censorship: *n.* (*psychoan.*) the factor or factors (in the **ego, ego ideal,** or **superego)** that regulate the emergence of ideas and desires into consciousness and maintain repression.—*Syn.* **censor** (not *prefd.* because it tends, even more than censorship, to personify the factors). **2.** (*sociol.*) restraint by some institutional agency upon the public dissemination of information, viewpoints, or artistic and literary products.

census data: in psychological and sociological surveys, information concerning an individual's age, sex, residence, occupation, or similar identifying items.

cent: *n.* a pitch unit equaling the 1200th part of an octave.

cent.: *abbr.* for centigrade.

center: *v.* to direct one's attention or effort at a center or goal; to concentrate on a central element or factor. ➤*Ant.* DISPERSE. To **decenter** may be either to disperse or to shift to a new center.

center/afferent: see **brain center.**

center/brain: see **brain center.**

center (or **central**) **clipping:** the opposite of **peak clipping** (which see).

center/correlation: see **correlation center.**

center/cortical: a **brain center** in the cortex.—See **brain center.**

center/higher: see **higher brain center, center/nerve.**

centering: *n.* (*K. Goldstein*) the perfect integration of the organism with its environment.

center/lower: a **nerve center,** usually one in the brain below the cortex or cerebrum, sometimes one in the spinal cord.

center/motor: see **brain center.**

center/nerve or **/neural: 1.** any portion of the nervous system that marks the transition from **afferent** to **efferent** impulse. ➤It may be a single **neuron** or an elaborate interconnected group of neurons. When not specified, a brain center is usually meant, but there are also spinal centers.—*Distg. fr.* **ganglion** (which see). **2.** a locus in the nervous system, usually in the brain and cord, defined by the fact that its electrical excitation causes determinate effects and that its destruction leads to gross modifications of certain functions. ➤These centers are classified and named from their locations—BRAIN, SPINAL, CEREBRAL or SUBCEREBRAL, CORTICAL or SUBCORTICAL, CEREBELLAR, AUTONOMIC, etc., CENTERS. It is not held that these centers are the only ones serving a particular function. They are to be clearly distinguished, by their operational definition, from the hypothetical centers of meaning (3). **3.** a hypothetical group of neurons in the brain that act as a unit in determining specific functions.—*Syn.* **brain center** (which see for discussion).
➤Since **nerve** is often taken to refer to peripheral nerves, many prefer the form **neural center** to **nerve center.** It is recommended that **neural center** be re-

served for meanings (1) and (2), and that **brain center** be used for meaning (3).

center of gravity method = **centroid method.**

center/sensory: see **brain center (1).**

center/spinal: see **center/neural (1)** or **(2).**

centesimal grade = **percentile.**

centi-: combining form meaning *division by 100, a hundredth part of.* ➤*Cp.* **hecto-,** which means multiplication by 100. Similar distinctions are **deci-** vs. **deca-** (for 10), and **milli-** vs. **kilo-** (for 1000).

centile: 1. = **percentile,** any one of the point scores dividing a **ranked distribution** into divisions each of which contains 1/100 of all the scores. ➤This usage is the logical extension of the proper usage for **tertile, quartile,** and other **partile** scores. But **percentile** has assumed the same meaning (so that centile is not required) and **centile** has come to be used as in (2) below. It is recommended that **percentile** replace centile for meaning (1). **2.** any one of the 100 groups or divisions separated by the percentile scores; or the rank order of any such division. ➤The scores are arranged in order of magnitude or merit and an equal number of scores assigned each of the 100 groups or divisions. The groups are given a number or rank order beginning with the lowest 1/100 (the 1st centile or CENTILE RANK), rising to the highest 1/100 (100th centile or CENTILE RANK). Note that centile ranks run from 1 to 100, whereas the percentiles (points) run from 1 to 99. ¶Each centile division by definition contains the same number of cases; normally the range of scores from top to bottom of the division differs from one centile to another. This contrasts with the statistical **class,** wherein the score range is the same from class to class but the number of cases usually differs. The two ways of dividing a population are thus based on two different statistical assumptions: for the centile, the equivalence of the achievement attained by a given proportion of the cases in the total group; for the **class,** the equivalence of a given proportion of the total score range.

It is to be noted that the nomenclature of **centile** and **percentile** is not entirely consistent with that of other **partile** terms, nor is usage consistent with respect to these two. A percentile is a *point* and, while that point has a rank so that "percentile rank" has a logical meaning, it has a different numerical significance from CENTILE RANK. Yet the two are often interchanged. Let the reader beware (even in reading presumably careful statistics).

See **partile** for discussion of the rationale.

central: *adj.* **1.** pertaining to the middle or

main portion of a body or structure, in distinction from outlying portions or members.—*Contr. w.* **distal, peripheral. 2.** in the nervous system, pertaining either to the spinal cord and brain in contrast with peripheral nerves, or to the cerebral cortex (as most central of all) in contrast with the rest of the nervous system.—See **brain centers.** ➤CENTRAL FUNCTIONS are those attributed (at least primarily) to the brain, in contrast with PERIPHERAL FUNCTIONS, determined chiefly by factors at the periphery of the body.—See **centralist psychology.** —*adj.* and *adv.* **centrad,** toward the center. **3.** characterizing those parts of the personality structure which most strongly cohere, which are most likely to be cofunctional with other parts, and which cannot be changed without profound change in personality. ➤Lewin speaks of the **central** layers (of the personality structure) as those most easily changed by changes elsewhere *within* the structure, and of the **inner** layers as those least easily affected by changes from *without.* Many authors include both those concepts under **central** or **inner,** which are used as synonyms. **4.** said of the values, habits, ideas, and traditions considered essential to, and representative of, a group.

central canal: see **canal/central.**

central integrative field factor: the total organized experience of the individual. It is the basis upon which new experiences are tested and incorporated.

centralist psychology: a point of view that gives major importance in explanation of behavior to events that take place in the brain, in contrast with PERIPHERALIST PSYCHOLOGY, which stresses the role of events taking place at the periphery of the body. ➤It is agreed that the datum to be explained is **behavior.** Peripheralists define behavior as an event taking place in an **effector** organ—either a muscle or a gland. (This is essentially the position of **behaviorism.**) Most centralists deny that behavior is merely an effector response. Even the basic datum, they say, includes activity in the higher centers. But some centralists accept the peripheral definition of behavior, while insisting that central factors must be emphasized in explaining it.

Both groups postulate that external events have a part in determining behavior, but peripheralists usually attribute a greater part of the **variance** to external events. Thus, in the study of vision, peripheralists stress the physical stimulus and the sense organ functions; centralists stress more strongly the role of brain function. **Color contrast** and **color constancy,** for example, are said to be primarily phenomena due to brain activity. ¶Since the events in

the brain that are appealed to in explaining behavior are almost wholly inferential, many centralists (but not all) use some of the traditional psychological concepts—they speak, e.g., in terms of **cognition, expectancy, attitudes.** Peripheralists, when they talk in terms of brain action at all, describe it in such neurophysiological terms as the **EEG.** Centralism also more readily makes room for such concepts as motive, voluntary action, etc. Peripheralists are more likely to use such terms as **drive** and **need,** conceived as being chiefly peripheral in the wider sense that includes internal bodily activity.

While the respective preferences for centralism or peripheralism are undoubtedly strong, it should be noted that the difference is chiefly one of the *relative importance* attributed to central factors. Probably no psychologist questions that behavior is triply determined: by external events, by the activity of receptor and effector organs at the periphery, and by brain activity.

See **psychology/divisions and schools of, V.**

centrality: *n.* **1.** the degree to which a pattern or configuration has a sharply marked center; the degree to which all the other elements concerned in any relation focus upon a central element; or the summed distances of all the elements from the center. **2.** the closeness of a given element to the center.

centrality/individual: a property of the individual in relation to a particular social group: it is measured by the ease with which he can communicate with the other members of the group. ➤All forms of communication are included. Although the centrality is an attribute of the individual, it is an attribute dependent in part on the nature and attitudes of the group members.

central motive state: a hypothetical activity in the central nervous system, not part of the present efferent excitation, that plays a determinative part in behavior.

central nervous system or **c.n.s.:** in vertebrates, the brain and spinal cord.—See **nervous system.**

central process: an activity of the brain and spinal cord, esp. of the higher brain centers, in contrast with **peripheral** and **autonomic** processes.

central region: see **central (2).**

central tendency/index of or **/measure of:** a statistic, calculated from a set of distinct and independent observations or measurements of a certain item or entity, and intended to typify those observations. ➤The implication is that, in the absence of errors of chance or of measurement, the several observations would all be equal and would be the **true** *score of that which is observed. The measure of central tendency is said to represent, or to be a good approximation to, that true score. The statistics most commonly used for a measure of central tendency are the mean, the median, and the mode.—*Syn.* REPRESENTATIVE VALUE (*prefd.* as having a broader connotation).

central tendency of judgment: the tendency, in successive estimates or judgments, to eliminate the more extreme estimates.

central thought test: see **test/central thought.**

central vision: see **vision/central.**

centrifugal (sen·trif'ū·gəl): *adj.* moving or flying out from a center.—*Contr. w.* **centripetal.** ➤Often used figuratively. In the nervous system, **efferent** is a synonym.

centrifugal factor: 1. the tendency to make gestures away from the body and toward the environment. **2.** the tendency in speech away from self-reference. ➤That these two factors are the same or that either is a unitary factor is not to be assumed.

centrifugal swing: the tendency of an animal, at a choice point, to continue along that path which most nearly continues the previous direction of travel.

centripetal (sen·trip'ə·təl): *adj.* moving or directed inward toward a center.— *Contr. w.* **centrifugal.**

centripetal individuation: the principle that reduction of the stimulus strength may restrict response to a smaller number of muscles in a group than would respond to stronger stimulation.

centroid factors: (*factor anal.*) the factors extracted by Thurstone's **centroid method,** as distinguished from the **principal axis,** or **principal components, method.**

centroid method: (*factor anal.*) a method of extracting factors from a correlation **matrix** in which the first axis passes through the center of gravity of the system. ➤The axes are all **orthogonal** but may be **rotated** to **oblique** positions.— *Syn.* CENTER OF GRAVITY METHOD.

cephalad (sef'əl·ad): *adj.* toward the head. —See -ad.—*Distg. fr.* **cephalic.**—*Contr. w.* **caudad,** toward the tail end.

cephalic (sef·al'ik): *adj.* pertaining to the head.—*Cp.* **cephalad.** See -ad.

cephalic index: a ratio obtained by dividing the maximum breadth of the head by its maximum length (measured from front to back) and multiplying by 100. Long, medium, and broad (or short) heads are called, respectively, DOLICHOCEPHALIC, MESOCEPHALIC, and BRACHYCEPHALIC. The respective cephalic index numbers are up to 75.9, 76.0–80.9, and 81.0 or over.

cephalization (sef"əl·i·zā'shən): *n.* (*biol.*) concentration of important organs and functions in the head region of the body: in-

creasing dominance during development by the organs in the head.

cephal(o)- (sef'ə·lō-): combining form meaning *the head.*

cephalocaudad development/principle of: the hypothesis that physical growth, esp. embryological growth, tends to begin in the head end and to progress toward the tail end. ➤The principle is usually generalized to include also the tendency of growth to proceed from shoulder and thigh toward fingers and toes (PROXIMO-DISTAD DEVELOPMENT). The final syllable is often miswritten -al, which means *concerned with* head and tail, whereas the principle deals with *direction* of growth, head and tail being merely reference points.—See -ad.— *Syn.* ANTERIOR-POSTERIOR DEVELOPMENT; LAW OF DEVELOPMENTAL DIRECTION.

cephalocaudal: *adj.* pertaining to, or extending between, the head and the tail.— *Cp.* **axis of reference/anatomical.**

cephalometry (sef"ə·lom'ə·tri): *n.* measurement of the size and shape of the head. —*n.* **cephalometer.**—*adj.* **cephalometric** (sef"ə·lō·met'rik).

-ceptor: a suffix meaning a **receptor** of the kind indicated by the preceding syllables: e.g., CHEMOCEPTOR, a receptor for chemical stimuli.

CER = conditioned emotional response.

cerea flexibilitas (si'ri·ə flek"sə·bil'i·təs): see **catalepsy.**

cerebellum or **little brain:** *n.* one of the major divisions of the brain, caudad to the **cerebrum** and attached to the dorsal aspect of the **brain stem.**—*adj.* **cerebellar.**

cerebral (ser'ə·brəl): *adj.* pertaining to the **cerebrum.**

cerebral aqueduct: an elongated slender cavity in the **midbrain** which connects the third and fourth **ventricles.**—*Syn.* AQUEDUCT OF SYLVIUS.

cerebral arteriosclerosis/psychosis with: a disorder, with varied mental symptoms, consequent upon disease of the blood vessels in the brain.

cerebral cortex = **cortex cerebri.**

cerebral dominance: see **dominance (6)** and **(7).**

cerebral hemispheres = **hemispheres** of the cerebrum.

cerebral integration: 1. the hypothesized function of the cerebrum as the organ that correlates the activities of the whole body, maintaining organismic unity. ➤The unifying function is a fact; the degree of unity achieved is controversial. **2.** the functional interrelating in the cerebrum of impulses from other parts of the brain or from the body generally. ➤Subcerebral centers also have an interrelating function.

cerebral palsy: paralysis due to a **lesion** in the brain. ➤Congenital cerebral palsy

is found at birth: its most usual form is SPASTIC DIPLEGIA, in which both legs show sudden uncontrollable muscular contractions. It is often associated with **convulsions**, sometimes with **mental *deficiency.**
cerebral syphilis/psychosis with: mental disorder with little deterioration, due to infection of the covering tissues, etc., of the brain. ➤*Distg. fr.* **paresis**, which results from infection of the true brain substance.
cerebral type: 1. a person with very large head, small limbs, and poor musculature.— *Distg. fr.* **macrocephaly. 2.** (*pop.*) a person who tends to be guided by rational considerations or who is much interested in problem-solving.
cerebration (ser"ə·brā'shən): *n.* physiological activity in the **cerebrum;** hence (jocularly) mental activity, esp. thinking.
cerebro- (ser'ə·brō-): a combining form meaning *cerebrum* or (loosely) *brain.*
cerebrospinal axis: the brain and spinal cord.
cerebrospinal fluid: lymph filling all the spaces in the cranial cavity and the spinal canal not occupied by solid tissues and blood vessels.
cerebrospinal nervous system: all the **neurons** of the body except those of the **autonomic** system. It includes the nerves of the brain and the cord and their peripheral connections.—See **nervous system.**
cerebrotonia: *n.* (*W. H. Sheldon*) a personality **type** correlated with the **ectomorphic** bodily type and marked by restraint, inhibition, alert attentiveness, and in general by predominance of the intellective processes.
cerebrovascular accident: a sudden event, of injurious nature, involving the cerebral arteries or veins. e.g., cerebral hemorrhage.
cerebrum (ser'ə·brəm; sə·rē'brəm): *n.* the main division of the brain in vertebrates, consisting of two hemispheres. ➤It is the latest part of the brain to evolve and is probably of critical importance in mental activity or discriminatory behavior. Cerebrum is sometimes used for the **cortex** of the cerebrum, sometimes for the entire **brain;** both usages are incorrect.
ceremony: *n.* **1.** a system of rites and practices sanctified by custom and having symbolic meaning. **2.** a set or sequence of behaviors determined by rule and having emotional significance beyond the act itself: e.g., a child's ceremony of putting a doll to bed in a precisely ordered fashion.
certainty or **certitude:** great confidence in a truth; the highest degree of belief. ➤Certainty is either a state of the believer or a property of the thing believed. Certitude is the attitude or state of mind.—*Cp.* **probability.**—*adj.* **certain.**
certifiable (ser'ti·fī"ə·bəl): *adj.* a medico-

legal term indicating that a person, by reason of mental pathology, needs some form of guardianship. ➤*Cp.* COMMITTABLE, of a person who shows enough mental disorder or deficiency to be placed, by court order, under some degree of restraint in an institution.
certification/legal: a statement by an official body that a person or institution has complied with, or met, certain standards of excellence. ➤Under COMPULSORY CERTIFICATION for psychologists, no person may represent himself to be a psychologist unless certified by a legally established board. This does not, however, restrict psychological practice to those thus certified. When practice is restricted, **licensure** is the proper term.
certitude: see **certainty.**
cervical (sėr'vik·əl): *adj.* (*anat.*) pertaining to the neck, or to the neck of an organ.
—*n.* **cervix.**
CF: (*Ror.*) scoring code for an **inkblot** response determined by color and form together, with color dominant.
C* factor** or ***c: n. **1.** a factor of "cleverness" (quickness, originality, liveliness in thinking) uncovered in some factor analyses.—*Contr. w.* **perseveration. 2.** the character factor that accounts for readiness to forgo an immediate gain for a greater but remote gain.
CFF = critical *flicker frequency.*
C **group** = control group.
C.G.S. or **cgs** = centimeter-gram-second. The C.G.S. SYSTEM, using these measures, is the accepted system for physical measurement of **macroscopic** objects.
chain/behavior: a sequence of behaviors that proceeds semiautomatically in a determinate order: e.g., reciting a memorized poem. ➤The last previous response provides the necessary **cue** that determines which behavior comes next, but the whole preceding portion of the sequence forms an essential part of the stimulus. In HETEROGENEOUS CHAINS, external stimuli also influence the response: e.g., in walking, the (visually or tactually perceived) contour of the ground determines size of step, etc.—*Syn.* CHAIN REACTION, CHAIN REFLEX (when the constituents are truly **reflex**).
chaining: *n.* the process of learning a **behavior *chain.***
chalone (kal'ōn): see **hormone.**
chance: *n.* **1.** (*pop.*) the fact that an event has no known cause and is therefore unpredictable. ➤An unnecessary usage. **2.** the extent to which an event occurring within a limited system of events is due to causes lying wholly outside that system. ➤From the standpoint of that kind of system which is a **person,** it is **chance** when one is struck by lightning. However, to the extent

that the person *chooses* dangerous shelter in a thunderstorm (e.g., a tree in an open field), it is not chance. Even with so capricious an event as lightning, degrees of chance are distinguishable.—*Syn.* (*pop.*) LUCK; **accident. 3.** the occurrence of a **random** event; or the likelihood that the event will occur according to the theory of **probability**: e.g., the occurrence of a run of three heads in coin tossing. ➤See **probability.** The event is conceived, not as causeless, but as caused by a very large number of independent factors which, though individually unknown, produce combined effects that can be predicted. Chance in this sense has a statable, quantitative value. (In contrast, meaning (2) is unrelated to probability.)—*adj.* **chance.**

chance/correction for: see **correction for chance.**

chance difference: (*stat.*) any difference between two measures attributable to **random** influences. ➤The assertion is essentially the negative one that the difference is *not* due to **constant error**, to **bias**, or to a **true** difference between the variables measured.—See **significance/statistical.**

chance error: see **error/chance.**

chance halves correlation: see **correlation/chance halves.**

chance variation: a variation, in the inherited **characters** of an organism, that has no known antecedents. ➤Chance variation is the basis for Darwin's **natural selection.**—*Syn.* RANDOM VARIATION.

chance-word association or **reaction:** see **association test.**

change: *n.* **1.** any alteration in a structure, a process, or an event. **2.** an observed difference in a given perception with the passage of time.

change of life = **menopause.**

channel: *n.* (*info. theory*) a complete system for transmitting a **signal** from an **input** location to an **output** location. ➤The channel includes the properties not only of the apparatus or equipment in the system, but of the **code** or language used. The channel may be an organism, in which case the sense organ is the input location and the motor mechanism is the output location. But it may also be purely mechanical, as in telephony; or it may be an institution, such as a newspaper or news service, or any combination of physical, organic, and social transmitting media.

channel capacity: (*info. theory*) the maximum transmission of **information** that a channel can provide. ➤It is measured in **bits** by $\log_2 c$, where c is the number of classes of input messages that can be discriminated by the channel.—*Syn.* MAX T.

character: *n.* **1.** (*logic, biol.*) any observable mark, quality, or property by which any thing, person, species, or event may be known as different from something else.—*Syn.* **trait, characteristic (2)** (which see for difference in usage). **2.** all such marks taken collectively; hence, the nature of the thing or event: the *character* of the stimulus situation. **3.** all the mental or behavior traits of a person; the sum total of psychological traits. ➤This meaning was formerly current in English; it remains a meaning in the *Fr. caractère* and the *Ger. Charakter,* and in such combinations as **character analysis** and **anal character.** But in most contexts **personality** is now more usual for this meaning. **4.** an integrated system of traits or behavior tendencies that enables one to react, despite obstacles, in a relatively consistent way in relation to mores and moral issues. ➤This is the standard, though wavering, current psychological usage. It is distinguished from **personality** by its emphasis upon (*a*) the volitional aspect, and (*b*) morality. **5.** a person delineated in literature: the leading *character.* **6.** status or role: in his *character* as a psychologist. **7.** (*colloq.*) a conspicuously different person; an eccentric.

Compound terms characterizing a particular kind or quality of character are listed under the qualifying term: e.g., **anal character.**

character/acquired: 1. changes in the body or **somatic** (7) cells as a result of environmental influences or of the organism's own activities.—*Syn.* ACQUIRED MODIFICATION (*prefd.*). **2.** a difference between individual organisms or groups of organisms that is attributed to differences in their contact with the physical or social environment. ➤The term was introduced in discussions of genetic transmission and should be restricted to that context. When the context is that of the organism's **development,** after the transmission has taken place, the term inevitably *suggests* that a given organic structure or behavior is due solely to environment—and no such structure or behavior is conceivable. The above definition is phrased to avoid such an implication, but the apparent meaning of the term itself will generally override the definition, no matter how careful. It is suggested therefore that ACQUIRED DIFFERENCE (of behavior or of structure) be usually substituted for **acquired character.** ¶The hypothesis that characteristics acquired by a parent can be transmitted to the offspring (see **Lamarckianism**) meets little acceptance.—See **genotype, heredity, acquired behavior.**

character/anal: see **anal character.**

character analysis: 1. = **characterology.** **2.** the psychoanalysis of a well-adjusted person undertaken for training purposes or to gain insight into the theory of psychoanalysis.—*Syn.* didactic *analysis (*prefd.*). ➤Character analysis seldom means what the words imply, an analysis of **character.**

character armor: (*W. Reich*) the system of **defenses** that enables a person consciously to take a certain role in interpersonal relationships which he could not otherwise sustain; a personality syndrome serving as a generalized defense. ➤E.g., a child may somehow conceal hatred of a parent and thus be able to play the role of a dutiful child.

character/authoritarian: see **authoritarian character.**

character disorder: a disorder manifested chiefly by vacillation and inconstancy of volitional behavior.

character formation: 1. the processes of forming **character** (4). 2. (*psychoan.*) = **personality formation.**

characteristic: *adj.* 1. peculiar to an individual instance or person; pertaining to that which describes an individual so that he may be distinguished from others.—*n.* 2. properly, a unique feature—one found only in the particular instance; loosely, any discernible or inferred attribute, property, or part that contributes to making something what it is.—*Syn.* **character** (1). 3. (*math.*) the integral part of a logarithm.

characteristic/acquired = **character/acquired.**

characterize: *v.* 1. to be a distinguishing or notable feature of something. 2. to point out the distinctive feature or features; to delineate.—*Cp.* **definition.**

character/moral = **character** (4).

character/neurotic: see **neurotic character.**

characterology: *n.* 1. a branch of psychology that investigates **personality** and **character** (3).—*Syn.* PERSONALITY STUDY (*prefd.*). 2. the diagnosis of personal traits from such visible physical features as color of skin, eyes, hair, size and shape of nose, length of fingers, distribution of fat, etc. ➤Characterology has too often been the field of charlatans; the term is probably too far gone to be rescued. Serious students of body build and its correlation with behavior prefer other terms.—See **body** *type.**

character/oral: see **oral character.**

character/paranoid: see **paranoid character.**

character research: the scientific investigation of the distribution of **character** (4) in the population, and the environmental and educational factors influencing its development.

characters/linked: see **linkage** (2).

character structure: 1. the sum or the **integration** of **character** (4) traits. 2.

(*psychoan.*) the traits that result from the efforts of the **superego** to control the **id.** ➤This meaning differs from (1) in the terms used to define it, rather than in the facts referred to.

character test: any means for predicting character from samples of actual behavior. ➤*Distg. fr.* ETHICAL KNOWLEDGE TEST, in which the testee reveals how well he knows the rules for moral behavior; and *fr.* ETHICAL JUDGMENT TEST, a measure of his ability to say how the rules apply to concrete situations as described.

character training: the development of habits, attitudes, moral values, and ideals through instruction, guidance, and example, and by providing situations in which moral decisions are made.

character trait: see **trait/character.**

character type: see **character.** Specific kinds of character are listed under the qualifying term: e.g., **anal character.**

character/unit: (*genet.*) a trait genetically transmitted in relative independence of other unit characters; a variation caused by a one-**gene** difference: e.g., (in man) pigmentation vs. albinism. ➤Strictly speaking, only the **genes** are transmitted, but the term is used for traits closely dependent upon the genes.

charge of affect = **cathexis.**

charlatan: *n.* one who claims expert knowledge of a profession or trade without having it; a quack or faker.

Charlier's checks: a method for checking the accuracy of computations.

Charpentier's bands (shär·päN′tyāz): radii of black seen upon the white when a white sector on a black ground is slowly rotated. ➤More rapid rotation causes various hues (FECHNER'S COLORS) to appear.

Charpentier's law: The product of the area of the image on the fovea and the light intensity is a constant for stimuli of **threshold** value.

chart: *n.* a systematic arrangement of facts in graphic form designed to bring out relations, esp. quantitative relations.—*Syn.* diagram, *statistical *diagram, figure.— See under qualifying term for combinations with **chart:** e.g., **correlation chart.**—*v.* **chart.**

check: *n.* 1. a further testing or verification of any sort to insure the accuracy and precision of an observation, measurement or computation.—*v.* 2. to conduct such a testing. 3. to stop suddenly; to restrain or control.

check list: a record form on which to indicate how often certain items have been observed. The list is prepared beforehand and serves as a reminder of what one is to watch for.—See **behavior check list.**

check reading: verification that a mechanical **indicator** is at the normal or desired position: glancing at a speedometer to determine speed is check reading.

cheiro- = chiro-.

chemical sense: a sense whose stimulus is a chemical substance that reacts with a substance in the receptor, as in smell or taste.

chem(o)-: a combining form that means *pertaining to chemical action.*

chemoreceptors: *n. pl.* sense organs responsive to chemical changes: the receptors for taste, smell, and possibly pain.

Cheyne-Stokes respiration (chān′ stōks′): highly irregular and labored breathing found in premature babies and in certain diseases.

chi or χ (kī): a Greek letter used in formulas.

chiaroscuro (ki·ä′rə·skū′ro): *n.* the distribution of light and shade in a two-dimensional pattern or picture that yields the impression of visual depth.

chiasm/(optic) (kī′az·əm): a place where the two optic nerves join and again diverge. Fibers from the nasal halves of the two retinas cross over to the opposite side before passing upward to the cerebral hemispheres.

Chicago School = **functional psychology.**

child *n., pl.* **children: 1.** a person who has not reached maturity. **2.** a person between birth and puberty. **3.** a person between infancy and puberty. **4.** the offspring of a human parent. ➤See **development/levels of** for classification of infant, child, adolescent, etc. For different kinds of children, see qualifying term: e.g., **gifted child, handicapped child.**

child-centered: *adj.* **1.** of a home in which the child's needs are placed ahead of others' needs. ➤The implication that the child is coddled, protected, indulged, is not necessary, but is often made. **2.** of a school organized about the satisfaction of the child's present needs rather than about preparation for adult life. Usually such a school emphasizes overt activities, and subordinates bookish work.

child development: an interdisciplinary study of the changes that take place in a child as he passes from birth to maturity, or (more commonly) from the end of infancy at one year to the beginning of adolescence at thirteen years. ➤As compared with **child psychology,** there is more emphasis upon physical growth, somewhat more emphasis upon sociological data and the social arrangements that bear differently upon the child at different ages, sharper emphasis upon temporal change, and less upon the learning processes by which change is brought about.

child guidance clinic: see **clinic/child guidance.**

childhood: *n.* **1.** the period from birth to puberty. **2.** the period between infancy and adolescence. ➤Note that **child (1)** has a greater range than **childhood.**—See also **development/levels of.**

child marriage: a marriage contracted by a girl under 15 or a boy under 17. ➤*Contr. w.* YOUTHFUL MARRIAGE, where the respective age limits are 17 and 19; and with EARLY MARRIAGE, which occurs in the early twenties.

child-parent fixation: an attitude of emotional attachment to either parent so firm as to interfere seriously with forming attachments to others. The feeling may be either love or hate or, more often, **ambivalence.** —*Cp.* **Oedipus complex** and **Electra complex** for certain special forms.

child psychology: a subdivision of psychology that treats of the behavior (or mental processes) of children. It may deal with the normal or the abnormal, and may be either pure or applied psychology.—*Cp.* **child development,** a somewhat more inclusive term.

Children's Apperception Test or **CAT:** a set of pictures to be described by the child. The descriptions are analyzed, as in the TAT.

child study: an older term for **child development:** the more or less systematic study of children's growth and development.

chimera (kī·mir′ə): *n.* an organism made up of tissues having different genetic constitutions: e.g., an apple limb grafted on a crab apple tree.

chir(o)- (kī′rō-): a combining form meaning *hand: chirography,* handwriting.—*Var.* **cheiro-.**

chi square or χ² (kī): a means of estimating whether a given distribution differs from expected values to such a degree as to be evidence for the operation of nonchance factors. It is the sum of the quotients obtained by dividing the square of each difference between an actual and the expected frequency by the expected frequency.—*Syn* SQUARE CONTINGENCY.—*Cp.* **F test.**

chi-square test of goodness of fit: a formula by which to estimate the probability that a given set of data conforms to what would be expected to be observed if a certain law or cause were in operation; a measure of the **goodness of** *fit of a curve to the distribution of the actual observations.

chlor (klôr): *n.* the color that was called green in older formulations of the three-color theory, and that in popular terminology would now be called greenish-yellow or (by women) chartreuse.

choc (shok): (*Fr.* for *shock*) a poorly coordinated response elicited by stimuli for which the animal has no ready-prepared adaptation.

choice: *n.* selection among two or more alternative objects or acts, usually after a period of deliberation. ➤It is implied that the alternatives are effectively presented, and are perceived or thought of as possible.

choice/anaclitic object: see **anaclitic object choice.**

choice experiment or **reaction:** one in which the subject is required to make a different prescribed response to each of several prespecified stimuli. ➤With animal (and often with human) subjects, the correct choices are rewarded and the incorrect punished. The experiment may be used to measure rate of learning or speed of reaction. For the latter see **reaction time.**

choice point: 1. that point in a **maze** or other apparatus from which it is possible for the animal to proceed in more than one direction, or to make more than one kind of response. 2. more generally, any point or state of affairs that requires a choice of alternative action.

choice situation/simple: the presentation of two attractive but incompatible goals, either of which, when chosen, leaves one with the feeling that the other might equally well have been selected.

choleric (kol'ər·ik): *adj.* quick-tempered; touchy; easily aroused to anger.—*n.* **choler.**

cholesterol (kə·les'tə·rōl): *n.* a substance, found in many body tissues, that can be activated to form vitamin D.

cholinergic (kō"lin·ėr'jik): *adj.* 1. stimulated or activated by **acetylcholine;** pertaining to the physiological functions of acetylcholine. 2. pertaining to a group of nerve fibers whose action upon effectors is accomplished by the release of acetylcholine.

cholinesterase (-es'tər·ās): *n.* an **enzyme,** found in the blood and in various tissues, that plays an important part in chemical transmission of nervous impulses.

chord (kôrd): *n.* (*music*) a combination of two or more tones which, when sounded simultaneously, form a **harmony (3).**

chorda tympani (côr'də tim'pə·ni): a branch of the facial nerve that carries nerve impulses from taste receptors.

chorea (kô·rē'ə): *n.* a neurological disorder characterized by jerky involuntary movements, or spasms of short duration, involving a considerable set of muscles. ➤*Distg. fr.* **tic,** which involves a small set of muscles. Two chief forms are ACUTE or SYDENHAM'S CHOREA (popularly called ST. VITUS' DANCE), in which there is irritability, restlessness, and sometimes delirium; and HUNTINGTON'S CHOREA, a rare form of insanity, quickly fatal.—*adj.* **choreal, choreic, choreatic. Choreiform** refers to movements similar to those of chorea.

chorea/Parkinsonian: see **Parkinson's disease.**

chorea/Sydenham's: a form of **chorea** that follows infection.—*Syn.* ST. VITUS' DANCE, CHOREA MINOR.

choreoathetosis (kô"ri·ō·ath"ə·tō'səs): *n.* an abnormal condition in which cortically initiated impulses produce involuntary jerking of limbs and **athetoid** movements.

choroid (kôr'oid): *n.* the delicate vascular membrane just back of the **retina.**—*Syn.* CHOROID COAT, CHOROID MEMBRANE.—*adj.* **choroid(al)** (kôr·oid'əl).

chroma (krō'mə): *n.* the dimension in the **Munsell color system** that corresponds most closely to **saturation.**—*adj.* **chromatic.**

chroma/sound: see **tonality.**

chromatic (krō·mat'ik): *adj.* 1. pertaining to color or **hue,** in contrast with the white-gray-black **(achromatic)** series. 2. pertaining to the **chromatic** *scale. 3. pertaining to **chroma.**

chromatic aberration: see **aberration/chromatic.**

chromatic adaptation: see **adaptation/chromatic.**

chromatic color: a color having **saturation** and **hue.** ➤*Contr. w.* achromatic color, one of the black-gray-white series.

chromatic dimming: the lessening of **saturation** when the intensity of a light is suddenly diminished after some seconds of fixation. The hue may even pass over into its **complementary** *color.

chromaticity: *n.* an aspect of the color stimulus, physically specified in terms of wave length and purity. ➤*Distg. fr.* CHROMATICNESS, the psychological correlate of chromaticity, which is specified in **hue** and **saturation.**

chromaticity diagram: a plane diagram representing all the **hues.**—See **color surface.**

chromaticness: see **chromaticity.**

chromatic scale: see **scale/chromatic.**

chromatic valence: the **hue**-producing power of any component stimulus in a color mixture. ➤When stimuli are so mixed that they yield gray, they are said to be equated in chromatic valence.

chromatism: *n.* a colored **photism** (which see).

chromat(o)-: combining form meaning *color, hue.*—*Var.* **chrom(o)-.**

chroma/tonal = **tonality.**

chromatopseudopsia: *n.* a pretentious name for **color blindness.**

chromatopsia (krō"mə·top'si·ə): *n.* a condition in which drugs or disease cause a visual stimulus to be perceived with a color (or colors) added to what is normally perceived in the stimulus. ➤The effect is much as if one wore colored spectacles (but without the **chromatic** *adaptation of glasses). E.g., dosage with santonin causes everything to look yellowish.—*Syn.* CHROMOPSIA.

chromesthesia: *n.* a form of **synesthesia** characterized by a persistent (usually involuntary) "seeing" of colors upon hearing sounds (or the visual symbols of sounds), various sounds having specific associated colors; in a more general sense, the association of colors with any form of sensation. The "seen" colors do not have illusory quality: they are more like **memory images.** (See **image** 3.)—*Syn.* COLORED HEARING.

chrom(o)- = chromat(o)-.

chromopsia (krō·mop'si·ə) = **chromatopsia.**

chromosome: *n.* (*genet.*) one of the minute deeply staining bodies in the nucleus of a cell, believed to play an important or determinative part in heredity. The **genes** are carried in the chromosomes.

chromosomes X and Y: the sex-determining chromosomes. In most species, females have two X chromosomes, males an X and a Y (or in some species, only an X).

chronaxie (krō'nak·si): *n.* an index of the excitability of tissue in terms of the time required for the passage of an electric current of twice the intensity necessary barely to excite the tissue. ➤It is held that nerve conduction depends on the similarity of the chronaxies of the neurons involved.—*Var.* **chronaxy, chronaxia** (krō·nak'si·ə).

chronic: see **acute.**

chronic brain disorder: (*Stan. Psychiat.*) a symptom complex resulting from relatively permanent, largely irreversible, diffuse impairment of brain-tissue function: e.g., **mongolism, paresis.** ➤The underlying pathological process may subside or respond to treatment. But some of the damage remains and there is usually some behavior change, though the post**remission** changes may be mild impairments of memory, judgment, etc., rather than **psychotic** or **neurotic** reactions.

chron(o)- (kron'ō-): combining form meaning *time.* ➤Its use should be confined to combination with words of Greek origin. In other contexts *temporal,* or simply *time,* serves adequately.

chronograph: see **chronoscope.**

chronological age or **CA = age/life.**

chronometer/fall: see **fall chronometer.**

chronoscope (kron'ō·skōp): *n.* a precise clockwork stopped at the end of each time interval measured. ➤A CHRONOMETER is a precise clockwork that runs continuously. A CHRONOGRAPH is an instrument (not always a clockwork) that makes a graphic record of time sequences.—*adj.* **chronoscopic.**—*n.* **chronoscopy** (krō·nos'kə·pi).

chronostereoscopic effect (-ster"i·ō·skop'-ik): an effect in which an oscillating pendulum appears to describe a funnel or cone when observed **binocularly** with a smoked glass before one of the eyes.

CI = intelligence/coefficient of.

cilia (sil'i·ə) *n. pl., sing.* **cilium: 1.** hairlike processes, found on the surfaces of certain cells, which propel fluids over the cell surfaces. **2.** the eyelashes.—*adj.* **ciliary, ciliate, ciliated.**

ciliary body or **muscle** (sil'i·er"i): the muscle of **accommodation** (2).

cingulate gyrus: a convolution of the middle surface of the **cerebrum** just above, and arching over, the **corpus callosum.** —*Syn.* GYRUS CINGULI, CALLOSAL GYRUS, GYRUS CALLOSUS.

cingulectomy (sing"gū·lek'tə·mi): *n.* surgical undercutting of the mesial surface of the **cortex.** It is an alternative and presumably less radical form of psychosurgery than frontal **lobotomy.**

circuit/reverberating: 1. a repetitive discharge of motor impulses maintained by **feedback** to nerve centers in the cord which are transiently autonomous. **2.** a hypothesized set or system of neurons in the brain capable of maintaining activity within the system for some time after an initial excitation from outside the system: within the system, cells are interrelated in complex circuits so that one cell fires another which may again fire the first, and so on until some change in conditions brings about discharge into cells outside the system.—*Cp.* **cell assembly.** This **circuit** is a part of the **conceptual nervous system.**

circular behavior: 1. a cycle of behaviors that provides the stimulus for its own repetition. ➤It is sometimes said that the last behavior in the sequence provides the stimulus for repeating the cycle; actually, the whole sequence is that stimulus, the last response being merely the *temporal* cue to begin again.—*Cp.* **chain/behavior.**—*Syn.* CIRCULAR REACTION, CIRCULAR RESPONSE. **2.** the tendency of one person's behavior to provoke in others a response that stimulates continuation of the initiating behavior: e.g., anger provokes anger, which in turn angers the first person further; or **integrative** behavior elicits integrative behavior, and so encourages more integrative action.

circular definition: see **definition.**

circular insanity or **psychosis:** a rare form of **manic-depressive psychosis** in which periods of depression and excitement follow each other without interruption. ➤The term is no longer used as a classification.

circularity: (*logic*) resting one element of one's thinking upon another element that is seen to depend (eventually) on the first: A is true because of B, which is true because of C, which is true because of A.—

Syn. CIRCULAR REASONING.—For *circular definition,* see **definition.** (A reader who finds circular definitions in this dictionary will confer a favor by notifying the editor or publisher.)

circular reaction/hypothesis of: (*speech*) the hypothesis that children transmute **babbling** into speech partly because the adult imitates the child's babbled sound in a context that gives it a meaningful association.

circular reasoning = **circularity.**

circular reflex or **response** = **circular behavior.**

circumstances: *n. pl.* **1.** a group of concurrent stimuli that together evoke a response or related responses.—*Syn.* **situation.** **2.** a relatively narrow range of concurrent external conditions affecting an organism. ➤*Contr. w.* **environment,** which is the total range of such circumstances existing over a span of time.

circumstantiality: *n.* a characteristic of conversation that proceeds indirectly to its goal idea, with many tedious details and parenthetical and irrelevant additions. ➤This type of behavior is shared with certain psychotics by many otherwise normal and worthy people.

claim/neurotic: (*K. Horney*) the irrational feeling, based on a sense of unique superiority, that others ought to see to it that one's wishes or needs are fulfilled. ➤If partially conscious, the feeling is justified by **rationalizations.** If not satisfied, the **neurotic claim** produces anger, vindictiveness, and feelings of unjust treatment.

clairaudience: *n.* alleged power to "hear" without the use of ears or by any known sensory mechanism. ➤Often improperly included under **clairvoyance.**—*Cp.* **cryptesthesia.**

clairvoyance: *n.* **1.** alleged power to "see" objective events without the use of eyes or of any known sensory process. **2.** any form of "perceiving" without known sensory process.—*Syn.* (for **2**) **cryptesthesia** (which see).

clan: *n.* a form of social group, consisting of families who claim common descent. ➤It was restricted originally to descent through the female line (a **gens** being the parallel patrilineal group), but the distinction is now seldom observed.

clang: *n.* a sound composed of a fundamental tone and its overtones. ➤All normal musical tones are clangs. Their distinctive quality, or **timbre,** is due chiefly to the relative prominence of certain overtones.— *Var.* (*Ger.*) **Klang.**

clang association: one in which one word recalls another word because of their similarity in sound.

clarification remark: restatement by a counselor, in what is hoped to be clearer

terms, of the substance of what the counselee has said. ➤The clarification remark studiously avoids any expression of the counselor's attitude or feeling, but may attempt to restate an expression of attitude by the counselee, provided it is explicit.—*Cp.* **nondirective procedure.**

clarification/sudden: (*N. Cameron*) a strong feeling and belief that all ambiguity has been removed and that one is quite certain of what needs to be done.

clasping reflex: a response of grasping or holding something in the fingers; a **grasping reflex.**

class: *n.* **1.** (*logic*) a group or aggregate of items—things, persons, abstractions—all of which manifest certain characters that collectively are the marks setting this group off from all others. **2.** = **class/social. 3.** (*educ.*) a group of persons gathered together for more or less simultaneous instruction. **4.** (*biol.*) the group of animals or plants between phylum and order. **5.** (*stat.*) one of the divisions that result when related data are arranged in order of magnitude and arbitrarily divided into nonoverlapping groups or parts, each having an equal **range** of scores. ➤As a means of grouping or categorizing data, **class** may be contrasted with **rank.** The class assumes that scores of about the *same magnitude* are (or may be) for specifiable purposes equivalent. The rank assumes the equivalence for specifiable purposes of those scores attained by an *equal proportion* of the population. Thus each class has the same range of scores or **class interval**—i.e., the score difference from top to bottom of each class is the same—but the number of cases in the several classes generally differs greatly. In contrast, the number of cases in each rank is by definition the same, but the range of scores differs from rank to rank. In further contrast, the highest class, but the lowest rank, is conventionally designated as the first.—See **rank** for further discussion of that term.

Both class and rank are quantitative divisions; a division of data based on logical or qualitative similarities is called a **category. Classification** is used for all three types of division.

class analysis chart: a chart that shows the relative performance of members of a class on the several parts of an achievement **test battery.**

class-free test: see **test/culture-free.**

classic: *adj.* (*hist. of sci.* and *jocular*) characterizing a doctrine once generally believed to be true, which the writer believes to be false.—*Cp.* the expression: a *classic* blunder. —*Syn.* TRADITIONAL. ➤This meaning is not to be confused with the usage in art and literature.

classical conditioning: see **conditioning.**

classical psychoanalysis: that part of the movement which emphasizes the **libido** and Freud's instinct theory (see **instinct 4**).

classification: *n.* **1.** process of grouping objects into mutually exclusive **classes, ranks,** or **categories;** or the group so classified. ➤ A CROSS-CLASSIFICATION uses more than one basis for grouping, so that an item can be placed in more than one class; it is permissible only in very special cases. **2.** (*info. theory*) a variable of an **ensemble;** a dimension having several states or classes, or a continuum of magnitudes. For a given classification, each **element** of an ensemble must be in one class only, or at one point only on the continuum. But not all the elements need to be classifiable by all the classifications.

classification/Aristotelian: see **Aristotelian classification.**

classification table: a table that facilitates classification by the way the variables are tallied: e.g., a table so arranged that the rows stand for the tens, the columns for the units. The **cell** at the intersection of row 4 and column 7 denotes a score or observation of 47.—*Syn.* CLASSIFIER.

classification test: 1. one in which the testee's task is to sort objects into appropriate categories. The categories may be either prescribed or left to the testee's choice. **2.** a test designed to help in the proper classification of individuals for any stated purpose.

classifier = **classification table.**

class index = **class mark.**

class interval or *i*: (*stat.*) the width of a **class (5);** the range of values or the number of score units between the upper and lower boundaries of a class.—*Syn.* STEP INTERVAL, INTERVAL, CLASS SIZE, CLASS.

class limits: the upper and lower limits of a given **class interval;** the highest and the lowest values that can be included in the class interval.—*Syn.* CLASS RANGE.

class mark: the midpoint of a **class interval.**—*Syn.* CLASS INDEX.

class/opportunity: see **opportunity class.**

class range = **class limits.**

classroom test: a test prepared, generally by the teacher, for a particular local classroom situation.—*Contr. w.* **standardized *test.**

class/social: a grouping or division of a society, made up of persons having certain common social characteristics which are taken to qualify them for participation on roughly equal terms with others of the group in important social relations, and to restrict (but not prohibit) many kinds of social interaction with those outside the group. ➤Particularly affected by social class are marriage and certain clubs and social functions. Classes are usually formed on a combination of criteria: similarities in educa-

tion, vocation, complexion, value systems, custom, family—but today chiefly in wealth. There is usually a recognition by all of a hierarchy of upper, middle, and lower classes (sometimes with subdivisions), but this hierarchy is not necessarily one of worth or power.—*Cp.* **caste.**

class/special: one with special provisions for any or all types of **atypical** children.— See **special class.**

class structure: the way in which a given society is divided into **social *classes.**

class-theoretical: *adj.* of a system of classification in which the **categories** are conceived as existing in nature or in reality, not as merely invented or designed. ➤The classification of chemical elements by Mendeleev is said to be an example. Those who do not believe in a class-theoretical classification hold that this chemical classification, though valid and useful, is (like all the others) arbitrary.—*Cp.* **class theory.**

class theory: 1. the philosophical view that an object has the properties it has *because* it belongs to a certain class. ➤Chiefly used derogatorily by **field theorists. 2.** the philosophical position that an event may be explained by stating the attributes or properties of the objects involved.

class/ungraded: (*educ.*) a class of children in one room, of mixed age and school achievement, taught in very small groups or individually. ➤Not to be used euphemistically for a **class** organized for the mentally deficient.

claustral complex: (*H. Murray*) the enduring effects of the uterine experience that influence (unconsciously) the course of later development and behavior.

claustrophobia: *n.* pathological fear of being in a confined place.—See **phobia.**

cleanliness training: teaching a child to keep himself clean. ➤Often a euphemism for bowel training.

clearness: *n.* **1.** (*structural psych.*) an elementary attribute of a sensation, or of a sensed or imagined object. ➤It characterizes the sensation or sense datum when nothing prevents its full apprehension, when it is salient or standing out from its background. It is conceived as being, or being the result of, attention.—*Syn.* **attensity, vividness.**—*Ant.* INDISTINCTNESS. **2.** a property of perceived or conceived objects, or of propositions, of being definite, distinct, comprehensible, not obscure; or that property in relatively high degree. **3.** (*phenomenology*) the definiteness with which one component of a **phenomenal** or **cognitive *field** can be distinguished from another; the sharpness of boundary between two objects in the field.

clerical test: a test of ability in such tasks as filing, simple bookkeeping, checking, and routine arithmetical operations. Tasks such as stenography and machine calculation are sometimes included.

Clever Hans: (*Ger., der kluge Hans*) one of the **Elberfeld horses.**

cleverness: *n.* quickness in apprehending what is required in a particular situation. —For *cleverness factor,* see **C factor.**

cliché: *n.* a stereotyped or hackneyed verbal expression. ➤It is the best key wherewith to gain entrance to a closed mind.

click: *n.* (*speech*) any of a class of sounds, usually formed by withdrawing the tongue from against teeth or palate, that produce a clicking sound: e.g., the sound usually written as *tsk,* the click used to urge a horse forward.

client: *n.* (*psychol.*) a person who comes for counseling or psychotherapy; a counselee.

client-centered therapy or **counseling:** see **therapy/client-centered.**

climacteric (klī·mak'tər·ik; klī"mak·ter'-ik): *n.* the **menopause.** ➤Sometimes applied to the period of analogous physiological change in men, and less appropriately to **puberty.**

climate/psychological: figuratively, the prevailing characteristics of a person's environment, taken not analytically but globally. ➤The INTELLECTUAL CLIMATE consists in the conditions of life as they offer great or little opportunity for intellectual development. The EMOTIONAL CLIMATE is the sum of the prevailing circumstances as they affect emotional response, or as they reflect emotions directed at the subject. The CULTURAL CLIMATE is made up of the conditions that affect the person's cultural growth. The SOCIAL CLIMATE is the totality of social stimuli, particularly those that tend to cause a person to feel accepted or rejected.

clinic: *n.* a place and organization to which persons come for individualized diagnosis and treatment of some physical or mental disorder. ➤Although **clinical** referred originally to bedside treatment, a clinic is now more generally a place for patients who can walk. In medicine, it is sometimes a demonstration diagnosis for medical students. Popularly, a clinic is likely to mean the out-patient department of a hospital, especially one with reduced fees; but an organization of specialists in private practice is also a clinic. ¶All of this has somewhat influenced the meaning of PSYCHOLOGICAL CLINIC: it is a place to which persons come for specialized *individual* help from one psychologist or from a team of psychologists. (Such a clinic may also have affiliated medical or social work personnel.) Any kind of psychological diagnosis and treatment may be included.

A BEHAVIOR CLINIC specializes in the treatment of behavior maladjustments. Brain-damaged and mentally deficient children may also be treated in such clinics. Treatment of **behavior problems** of children nearly always includes helping the parents. The behavior clinic may deal with adult, as well as child, clients.

A PSYCHOEDUCATIONAL CLINIC is designed to supplement the work of schools with children presenting especially difficult problems. Diagnosis and treatment may be concerned with adjustment to school, special learning problems, behavior problems, vocational adjustment.

The **child guidance *clinic** is likely to be less oriented to the problems arising in school and more to behavior problems and to incipient mental illness. Frequently the clinic is under psychiatric direction.

The extension of the general idea of clinic in such a term as EDUCATIONAL CLINIC for a place where educational "ailments" are given individual diagnosis and treatment is reasonable; but further extension to short "refresher" courses for in-service education, e.g., "football-coaches clinic," is unfortunate.—See **clinical.**

clinical: *adj.* **1.** pertaining to a **clinic. 2.** characterizing the method of studying the individual as a unique whole. Specific behaviors are observed and specific traits may be inferred, but the goal is that of understanding (and helping) the particular individual.—*Syn.* **idiographic;** but **clinical** is broader, since it covers remediation as well as description. **3.** relying upon the **intuitive** judgment of the clinician rather than upon measurement; the intuitive integration of measurement findings with direct observation. ➤In medicine, the contrast exists between clinical observation and laboratory tests. But in psychology the "laboratory tests" are often called *clinical tests,* in contrast to observation, which employs no tests.

clinical group(ing): a category for the classification of persons who present a fairly homogeneous pattern of symptoms, e.g., **reactive depression.** The category is based on clinical observations, usually without the refinement of **cluster analysis** or similar statistical treatment.—See **cluster.**

clinical psychology: that branch of psychology which deals with the psychological knowledge and practice employed in helping a client who has some behavior or mental disorder to find better adjustment and self-expression. It includes training and actual practice in diagnosis, treatment, and prevention, as well as research for the expansion of knowledge.—*Distg. fr.* **psychiatry,** which is a medical specialty.

clinical type (of feeble-mindedness): a feeble-minded person whose symptoms conform to any of several recognized patterns of physical symptoms, e.g., a **microcephalic,** a **mongolian.**—*Cp.* **constitutional type.**

clinic/child guidance: a **clinic** for professional guidance and help of children with major problems of adjustment. ➤Nearly all such clinics stress help by a "team" consisting of two or more of the following: pediatrician, child psychiatrist, clinical child psychologist, social worker.

clique (klēk): *n.* a tightly organized group of persons, esp. one that tends to exclusiveness.

clitoris (klī'tə·ris; klit-): *n.* a small organ of erectile tissue, part of the external female genitals, stimulation of which is an important source of sex pleasure.—*adj.* **clitoral.**

cloaca theory (klō·ā'kə): a belief, frequently held by children, that birth takes place through the anus.

clonus (klō'nəs): *n.* involuntary rapid contractions and relaxations of a muscle.—*Cp.* **tonus; ankle clonus.**—*adj.* **clonic** (klon'-).

closure/law of: (*Gestalt*) the principle that behavior or mental process tends toward as complete, stable, or "closed" a state as circumstances permit: e.g., an asymmetrical figure tends to be perceived as symmetrical, an unfinished act to be completed, an incomplete musical chord to be resolved, a meaningless object or situation to be perceived as having meaning.

clouded state/epileptic: a dazed or deeply confused state that sometimes precedes or follows epileptic convulsions.

clouding effect: (*C. Jung*) the barrier that keeps a person of one psychological type from understanding a person of a different type.

clouding of consciousness: a confused condition marked by impaired perception, attention, and orientation. ➤Clouding is normal in sleepy states, and also characterizes most forms of **delirium** and many **psychoses.**

clue: see **cue.**

cluster: *n.* (*stat.*) **1.** a subgroup of variables each of which is more closely correlated with other members of the subgroup than with the other variables in the larger group. **2.** less strictly, variables all of which have high positive correlations with each other, and most of which have higher correlations with those in the **cluster** than with others not therein. ➤A cluster being first defined as in (1), on purely mathematical grounds, other variables are added or subtracted on psychological grounds to obtain the cluster of (2).—*Cp.* **surface *trait.**

cluster analysis: (*stat.*) a technique for determining **clusters;** esp. for determining them by inspection of the **matrix.**

cluster correlation: see **correlation/ cluster.**

clutter: *n.* **1.** a disorderly crowding together. **2.** in radar reading, signals returned from objects not significant for the purpose in hand, e.g., from clouds. ➤It is distinguished from **noise.** However, it is suggested that clutter be extended to mean noise (as defined in **communications theory**).—See **noise (3).**

cluttering: *n.* speech so rapid, under pressure of excitement, that enunciation is indistinct, words are run together, and syllables are slighted or dropped out.—*Syn.* **agitolalia** (not *prefd.*).

cm: *abbr.* for *centimeter.*

cmps: *abbr.* for *centimeters per second.*

Cn: (*Ror.*) scoring code for **color naming.**

c.n.s.: 1. = **central *nervous system. 2.** = **conceptual nervous system.** ➤C.n.s. should not be used for (2) except when context makes the reference quite unambiguous.

co-: combining form meaning *together with, joint, equally.*—*Var.* **col-, com-, con-.**

coacting group: persons working side by side and receiving only "contributory" social stimuli from each other. There is no direct communication or interaction—the individuals are primarily concerned with some task rather than with one another. ➤*Syn.* SHOULDER-TO-SHOULDER GROUP. Some writers contrast the coacting with the **face-to-face group,** the latter being thought of as interacting with each other. More often, the face-to-face group is con. ceived as including the coacting group.

coaction compass: (*Ror.*) a schema for showing, by means of rectangular coordinate axes, the relation between control and affect factors in personality.

coarctated (cō"ärk·tā'təd): *adj.* narrowed; pressed together; articulated or joined by a narrow union; constricted. ➤The term is used metaphorically in a variety of ways: for inhibited behavior, esp. for ego-limited behavior; for the narrowed range of experience open to the preschizophrenic; for a constricted range of both **extratensive** and **introversive** tendencies (*Ror.*). (In *Ror.* terminology, *distg. fr.* COARTATIVE, which means weak in both tendencies rather than constricted.)—*Var.* **coartated.**—*n.* **coarctation.**

coccyx (kok'siks): *n.* (*anat.*) the lowest bone of the spinal column, adjoining the **sacrum** and formed of four fused rudimentary vertebrae; the rudimentary tail found in man and the tailless apes.—*adj.* **coccygeal** (kok·sij'i·əl).

cochlea (kok'li·ə): *n.* the spiral bony tube in the inner ear which contains the organ of hearing.—*adj.* **cochlear.**

cochlear-palpebral reflex: response to auditory stimulus by closing the eyelids if they are open, or further tightening if they are closed.

coconsciousness: *n.* a dissociated system of mental activities, described in cases of divided personality, wherein what seems a subpersonality is aware directly of the ideas and actions of the "normal" personality and may greatly influence them, but does not at all points share the normal desires or purposes of the individual.—*Cp.* **personality/multiple.**

code: *n.* **1.** a set of **symbols** employed to convert a given set of data or items into a quantitative or qualitative series. ➤Each item or class of items in the original series receives a CODE SYMBOL in terms of a systematic plan, i.e., in such fashion as to represent some relationship between the items. Thus, each manifestation of anger might be given a code number according to its supposed relative strength. Or each behavior exhibited in a given time might be given a code letter to indicate its classification or categorization. (In **communications theory, coding, encoding,** and **decoding** have special meanings. See also **ulstrith** for a particular kind of code.) **2.** a system of rules and standards for conduct; a compilation of such rules.—*Cp.* **code/professional.**—*v.* **codify, code.**

code capacity: (*info. theory*) the maximum possible rate at which information can be sent through a **code channel.**

code channel: (*info. theory*) a system whereby a sequence of **signals** related to a given **code** is transmitted at a given rate.

code/moral: see **moral code.**

code/professional: a set of rules that prescribes the specific ethics, the ideals and standards of personal conduct, approved or required of members of a professional group. ➤Particular techniques or methods are seldom included, nor are standards of knowledge and skill, but there is usually prohibition from attempting what clearly lies beyond the training or skill of the practitioner.

codetermine: *v.* to share in the cause of an event. ➤The term is often used in this dictionary without statement of the other factors involved: e.g., a stimulus *codetermines* response.

code test: 1. one in which the task is to translate from one set of symbols to another set, according to a given code that is unfamiliar at the start of the test: e.g., in the form known as LETTER-DIGIT TEST, substitution in a printed message of 1 for *a,* 2 for *b,* etc., to 26 for *z.*—See also **digit-symbol test.**—*Syn.* SUBSTITUTION TEST. **2.** an achievement test to measure how well a standard code, e.g., the Morse code, has been learned.

coding: *n.* **1.** (*stat.*) transforming a set of obtained scores into a more convenient set of scores. ➤E.g., all persons aged 0 to 35.9 months may be represented by the median value 18 months; all from 36 to 71.9 months by the median value 54 months, etc. More complex forms of coding are also used. **2.** (*commun. theory*) in a communication system, the process whereby a **message** is translated into a **signal,** or a signal into a message: coding is either **encoding** or **decoding,** or both.

coding key: a list of the classes or categories of data, together with the symbols assigned to each. ➤E.g., each kind of error may be given a symbol to be employed in tabulating the number and kind of error in a given performance or product.

coef.: *abbr.* for **coefficient.**

coefficient: *n.* **1.** (*math.*) a constant value by which other values are to be multiplied. **2.** (*stat.*) a value expressing the degree to which some characteristic or relation is to be found in specified instances. ➤E.g., the **coefficient of *correlation** is a value expressing the degree to which two variables vary concomitantly. The root meaning of "working with" is nearly gone; the word is little more than a synonym for **index.** (But often, by purely arbitrary convention, the terms **coefficient of** and **index of** refer to different formulas.)

For combination terms with **coefficient,** see the other member: **correlation coefficient, alienation coefficient,** etc.

coenesthesia (sē"nəs·thē'zhi·ə; sen"əs-): *n.* collective term for sense impressions from within the organism. These are attended to only *en masse* or not at all, but they form the basis for feelings of health, briskness, relaxation, etc.—*Var. sp.* **cen-, -aes-, -sis.** —*Syn.* COMMON SENSATION, **common sensibility.**

coen(o)-: combining form meaning *common.*—*Var.* **cen(o)-.**

coenotrope: see **cenotrope.**

coercion: *n.* the act of compelling another by physical force, or otherwise, to act or refrain from acting.—*Syn.* **compulsion, restraint, constraint.**—See **constraint** for discussion.—*v.* **coerce.**

cognition: *n.* **1.** a generic term for any process whereby an organism becomes aware or obtains knowledge of an object. ➤Although it is part of the **traditional terminology** and has subjective connotations, many neobehaviorists use the term. It includes **perceiving, recognizing, conceiving, judging, reasoning.** Some older authorities held that **sensing** was not strictly cognitive (holding that a distinct cognizing process followed upon sensing), but in modern usage sensing is usually included under cognition. In most systems, **cognition, affection,** and **conation** are the three categories under

which all mental processes are classified.—
Syn. **noesis. 2.** the product of cognizing;
the knowledge obtained. (Not *recom.*) **3.**
the awareness of objects. ➤This usage
usually results from failure to distinguish
(1) from **(2)**. (Not *recom.*) **4.** (*beh.*) a
hypothetical stimulus-stimulus association
or perceptual organization inferred to account for **expectancies.**—*adj.* **cognitive.**
—*v.* **cognize.**

cognition/paranormal: the process of obtaining knowledge without the normal
processes of perceiving and thinking.—See
paranormal.

cognitive awareness level (of a construct):
(*G. A. Kelly*) the degree to which the
construct is expressed in socially effective
symbols, has accessible alternatives, and is
not contradicted by other constructs.

cognitive clearness: the clearness and distinctness with which one is aware of the
relationships of an object. ➤*Contr. w.*
sensory **clearness** or **attensity,** the elementary attribute of a sensation, posited
by **content psychology** as the result of
attending.

cognitive map: (*E. C. Tolman*) a hypothesized representation by an organism of the
means-end relationships by which a goal
can be attained, or of certain portions of
such relationships. It is composed of a set
of one or more beliefs and **expectancies.**
➤It is held that, in many kinds of behavior,
we must infer a process intervening between
a **cue** and a response which, even in lower
animals, is functionally equivalent to what
human beings call an expectation. Tolman
holds that in learning a maze an animal
usually learns, not a series of movements,
but a **cognitive map:** i.e., he learns the
spatial relationships between parts of the
maze in relation to the goal object. This
"map" thereafter elicits and selects different responses to suit varying circumstances as they arise. Thus, a rat who has
learned to run a maze correctly will swim
the same maze correctly, although he has
to use a wholly different set of responses.
The concept of the cognitive map is generalized to almost any problem-solving behavior.—*Cp.* **expectancy, schema.**

cognitive need: whatever it is that causes
an organism to examine objects; a drive
or motive that is satisfied when the person
apprehends the nature of an object.—*Syn.*
curiosity (*prefd.* as less pretentious).

**cognitive organization = cognitive
schema.**

cognitive schema: the complex pattern, inferred as having been imprinted in the
organismic structure by experience, that
combines with the properties of the presented stimulus object or of the presented
idea to determine how the object or idea is
to be perceived and conceptualized. ➤The

term is a broad one: it may be applied to
a very small pattern, such as that which
determines that a certain thing shall be
perceived as a shoe; or to large over-all
patterns, such as that of **ethnocentric**
prejudice which causes one to perceive the
behavior of persons from another social
group in an unfavorable light; or such as
the way in which one conceives time as
divided into past, present, and future. **2.**
(*E. C. Tolman*) the implicit **assumptions**
and **expectancies** that a person makes
about the external world, or the analogous
construct for subhumans, that must be assumed effective in order to account for the
specific nature of an individual's behavior.
➤It is probable that the referents for
meanings **(1)** and **(2)** are the same.—*Syn.*
apperceptive mass (more limited in
scope); **cognitive map** (having a special
usage); **set** (very much more limited, but
perhaps referring to the same kind of pattern); **frame of reference; cognitive
structure; cognitive organization;** COG-
NITIVE PATTERN (less explicit).

cognitive-sign principle: the principle that
learning consists in becoming aware of a
relation between a stimulus and a goal, or
between a stimulus and a goal-oriented response, rather than in learning a set of
responses.

cognitive structure: 1. (*K. Lewin*) the
way the individual sees the physical and
social worlds, including all his facts, concepts, beliefs, and expectations, and the pattern of their interactions.—Partial *syn.*
ideology, but cognitive structure is much
more inclusive. **2.** = **cognitive schema**
(which see). ➤Meanings **(1)** and **(2)** differ
chiefly in the greater complexity of **(1)**.
This is especially true for E. C. Tolman's
use of cognitive structure, which is nearly
the same as **cognitive map.**

cognitive theory (of learning): an interpretation of the facts of learning that, more
freely than other theories, postulates central
brain processes as intermediary, that *what*
is learned is a cognitive structure rather
than a response, and (generally) that learning comes as a result of a restructuring of
the individual's way of perceiving (**insight**).—*Ant.* **stimulus-response** theory
(of learning).

cognizance need: (*H. A. Murray*) the need
to observe, inquire, explore, and investigate;
the need to acquire facts.

cognize: *v.* to know; to take account of
the properties and relations of an object.—
n. **cognition,** which see.

coherence criterion: a means of judging
whether a testee's "correct" response is to
be accepted as a true or insightful **performance** of the task set. ➤In an **object
assembly** test, the testee may be unable to
see meaning in the completed assembly

which he has produced (he does not meet the PATTERN COHERENCE CRITERION); in a **similarities test** he may be unable to tell how two things are similar though he correctly says they are (here he fails to meet the VERBAL COHERENCE CRITERION).

coherent: *adj.* hanging together; forming a unit within which parts are not in conflict.—*v.* **cohere.**

cohesion/figural: see **figural cohesion.**

cohesion/ or **cohesiveness/group:** 1. the over-all attraction of a group for each of its members. ➤This ignores the influence of the forces outside the group that may tend to keep it together.—*Cp.* the following. 2. the total field of forces, inside and outside the group, which tend to keep it intact. 3. = group **morale.** 4. the feeling of belongingness on the part of members of a group.—*adj.* **cohesive.**

cohesion/law of: 1. a principle of learning according to which acts that occur at the same time or in close succession tend to form a unity, thus becoming a complex act of a higher order.—*Cp.* **contiguity/law of** and **conditioned response.** 2. the principle that the parts of a **gestalt** tend to assume greater coherence and stability.— *Syn.* **closure** (which refers to the process, **cohesion** to the result).

cohesive forces: (*Gestalt*) those psychic tendencies that tend to the formation and maintenance of a **gestalt.**

coincidence: *n.* 1. the occurrence at the same time of two events having distinct causes.—*adj.* **coincidental.** 2. (*math.*) a point for point correspondence of two geometrical figures.—*adj.* **coincident.**

coincidental method: a method of estimating the size of a radio or TV audience for a particular program by making telephone calls while the program is in progress.

coition, coitus (kō·ish'ən, kō'i·təs): *n.* the introduction of the male sex organ into the body of another, generally with orgasm. ➤**Coition** is the process in general, **coitus** the specific act.—*Syn.* SEX(UAL) INTERCOURSE, COPULATION, and (as usually used) COHABITATION.—*adj.* **coital.**

cold emotion: a bodily state that resembles true emotion, resulting from the injection of hormones. Bodily changes occur that are like those of some emotional states, but the subject reports no experience of true emotion.

coldness = frigidity.

cold spot: a minute area on the skin or mucous membrane, sensitive to stimuli that are below body temperature, and yielding **sense data** of coolth.

collaboration: *n.* (*H. S. Sullivan*) a stage, beyond mere acceptance of the conditions necessary for joint activity (which is co-

operation), in which there is sensitivity to the needs of the other person.

collapse: *n.* 1. (*med.*) extreme prostration or depression, with failure of circulation. 2. (*med.*) an abnormal falling in of the walls of any organ. 3. an extreme loss of motivation to any but routine activities; failure of hope, ambition, and most desires.

collateral: *n.* 1. a secondary or side item. 2. a kinsman not in the direct line of descent: cousin, uncle, niece, etc. 3. one of the secondary branches of the **axon.**—*adj.* **collateral.**

collective: *adj.* pertaining to a group, usually to a group as a whole.

collective behavior: see **mind/collective,** esp. (3).

collective consciousness: (*hist.*) the supposed fusion or integration of individual consciousnesses into a single **group mind.**

collective mind: see **mind/collective.**

collective monolog: a monolog stimulated by a hearer's presence although he is not directly addressed and his point of view is not taken into account. ➤While primarily a phenomenon of childhood, it is sometimes approximated by adults.

collective psychology: 1. (*obs.*) the study of the **collective consciousness.** 2. a part of **social psychology** dealing either with (*a*) the effect on the individual's behavior of being part of a social group, or with (*b*) the behavior of a group as such, or with both (*a*) and (*b*).—*Syn.* GROUP PSYCHOLOGY (*pref'd.*).

collective representation: (*E. Durkheim*) that portion of the individual's experience which he shares with others and which is attributable to the fact of social association. ➤Religion, e.g., is a **collective representation.**—*Syn.* (*C. Jung*) COLLECTIVE IDEAS.

collective unconscious: see **unconscious/ collective.**

collectivity: *n.* 1. any category of human beings. It is the most general classification of more than one person and includes such subclassifications as class, caste, public, mass, nationality, electorate, crowd, mob, audience, group, etc. 2. a collection of human beings, as distinguished from **group** by a lesser degree of organization.

College Ability Tests, or **C-A-T** (*pron.* as separate letters): a series of tests of intellectual readiness for the college level.—See **School and College Ability Tests.**—*Distg. fr.* California Achievement Test, sometimes abbreviated to C.A.T.

colliculus (kə·lik'ū·ləs) *n., pl.* **colliculi** (-lī): (*anat.*) a small elevation or prominence; specif., any one of the four prominences of the **corpora quadrigemina** (which see). ➤The posterior (or caudad) pair are the INFERIOR COLLICULI; the anterior (or cephalad) pair are the SUPERIOR COLLICULI.

colligation: *n.* a combination in which the units are separately recognizable. ➤*Contr. w.* **fusion,** in which the units are not separately identifiable by direct inspection. **Pattern** is a near synonym, but emphasizes somewhat more the unity of the combination. In **constellation** or **gestalt** the unity is still more strongly connoted. A printed word may be, with a shift of purpose or attention, alternatively a mere **colligation** of letters or a meaningful **gestalt.**

colligation/coefficient of: (*stat.*) a crude measure of relationship between two dichotomous qualitative variables, the measure being a function of the square roots of the products of frequencies in opposite cells of the fourfold table.

colloidal gold test: a chemical test of the cerebrospinal fluid, used in diagnosis of syphilis of the nervous system.—*Syn.* LANGE'S TEST.

color: *n.* 1. the perceived characteristic of light other than the spatial and temporal characteristics. ➤It includes **chromatic color** (popularly called color proper), which is the sensory component of visual experience in the chromatic series (characterized by **lightness, hue,** and **saturation**); and **achromatic color,** which is the sensory component of visual experience in the black-gray-white series (characterized by zero saturation and, hence, absence of hue). 2. any particular hue or achromatic color: the *color* magenta, or the *color* black.

color/achromatic: see **achromatic color.**

colorant: *n.* a dye or pigment.

color antagonism or **complementarism:** the fact that the mixture of any colors results in greater or less loss of **hue;** specif., that certain colors when mixed in a given proportion yield **achromatic color.**—See **color complementaries.**

color antagonists = **color complementaries.**

color/aperture: color perceived as filling a hole in a (usually neutral) screen. It is seen as **film color.**—*Syn.* REDUCED COLOR.

color attribute: the elementary or basic discriminable differences between colors: **hue, brightness,** and **saturation.**—See **attribute.**—*Syn.* COLOR DIMENSION.

color blindness: inability to distinguish colors on the part of a person able to see shapes and forms. ➤It may be TOTAL (*syn.* **achromatopsia, achromatism**) or PARTIAL. Of the latter, the commonest form is inability to distinguish certain reds and greens from each other or from gray. Complete inability to discriminate hues is apparently very rare; most so-called cases of color blindness are really cases of COLOR WEAKNESS—i.e., relative inability to discriminate between all hues **(achromatopsia)** or between certain specified hues (e.g., RED-GREEN

COLOR WEAKNESS).—See **anomalous *tri-chromatism.**

A number of color blindness tests have been devised to determine the presence or extent of color weakness. Of these the most common but least adequate is the **Holmgren,** in which a skein of dyed worsted is to be matched with the proper skein from a varicolored assortment.

Naming of the many varieties of color blindness is heavily infected with **theory-begging:** i.e., the same phenomenon is given a different name according to the **color theory** accepted by the writer.

color/bulky = **color/volume.**

color/chromatic: see **chromatic color.**

color circle: a disk with sectors of the primary or fundamental colors arranged in spectral order and of such angular width that the disk when rotated yields a gray. ➤The arrangement of colors on a circular band (see **color cycle**) is also called a **color circle.**

color complementaries or **complements:** pairs of colors which, mixed in a given proportion, yield gray. ➤By extension, white and black are often treated as complementaries. Either member of the pair is called a complement, or complementary, to the other.—*Syn.* COLOR ANTAGONISTS.

color complementarism = **color antagonism.**

color constancy: the fact that colors of an ordinary object are relatively independent of changes in illumination or of other viewing conditions. ➤A red pencil is usually seen as red, even though the illumination is green.

color contrast: the effects on the perception of color of being seen in temporal or spatial juxtaposition with another color. ➤When two **color complementaries** are juxtaposed, the effect is to intensify the difference between them—this is the primary meaning of **contrast.** But this intensification of difference is only one effect of color juxtaposition. The general effect is that each color is seen as if a little of the color complementary of its neighboring color had been mixed with it. Thus, red seen next to green looks even more red (as if the green had thrown a bit more red into its red neighbor), and the green appears more green. But red next to blue looks as if it had a bit of blue's complementary (yellow) mixed with it, and the blue looks as if it had a dash of green (the complement of the red). ¶If one color is a neutral gray, it receives a little of the chromatic color's complementary: red on gray makes the gray slightly green. When one speaks of CONTRASTING COLORS, however, one usually means colors far apart on the color circle. ¶**Color contrast** may include contrast in brightness as well as in hue. The contrast may be SIMULTANEOUS (two colors next each other in space) or SUCCESSIVE (one color presented very shortly after the other).

color cycle: a schematic representation of all the **hues** in fully saturated form. ➤The hues are arranged in a circular band in spectral order, with the nonspectral purples and magenta placed between blue and red. When the proportion of each hue is adjusted so that the band when rotated yields an **achromatic** mixture, it is sometimes called a **color circle.**

color deficiency: general term for relative inability to discriminate chromaticity or hue. It includes **monochromatism, dichromatism, anomalous *trichromatism.—** *Syn.* **color blindness.**

color description or C_{des}: (*Ror.*) statements about an inkblot in which color is mentioned only incidentally, e.g., as part of describing a form.—*Distg. fr.* **color naming.**

color determinant: (*Ror.*) the color (considered as such and not merely as a defining component of some other feature such as form) as **(Rorschach) *determinant** of response to the inkblot cards. Color may be chromatic or achromatic.

color dynamics: (*Ror.*) a term proposed as better than **color shock** to describe the dynamic effects, both positive and negative, of color.

colored hearing = chromesthesia.

color equation: see **color mixture.**

color/film: see **film color.**

color-form test: a set of geometric forms (cubes, circles, etc.) painted in different colors which subjects must sort into categories of their own devising. ➤It is classed as a test of **concept formation.**

color fundamental: 1. a color presumed, in a given **color theory,** to correspond with a *basic* color vision response. 2. any of the three spectral colors—red, green, and a certain blue-violet—the mixture of which (as light stimuli, not as pigments—see **color mixture**) in varying ratios yields every possible hue and in higher **saturation** than can be obtained from any other three colors. ➤The first meaning, that of the authoritative Inter-Society Color Council, reflects theory as well as facts. The second, based on the useful distinctions made by Titchener, reflects factual differences.—See **color primaries** for a discussion of ways of classifying colors as invariable, primary, or principal.

color/glowing = color/illuminant.

color/hard: see **hard colors.**

color hue = hue.

color/illuminant or **/illumination:** a glowing color; one coming directly from a light (in contrast with a reflected color).— *Syn.* GLOW, GLOWING COLOR.

colorimeter (kul·ər·im'ə·tər): *n.* a color-matching instrument for equating a known color stimulus mixture to an unknown color stimulus, so that the latter is specified in terms of the former.—*n.* **colorimetry,** the matching of colors by means of a colorimeter.

colorimetric primaries (kul"ər·i·met'rik): the three **color fundamentals** of a **trichromatic color theory.** They may be additively mixed to match any unknown color.—*Distg. fr.* the artist's primary pigments (see **color primaries** 2).

color induction: see **induced color.**

color insistence: the impressiveness or attention-catching power of a color. ➤It is associated especially with the **brightness** of **achromatic** colors and the **saturation** of **chromatic** colors.

color invariables: four colors that do not alter in hue when seen in the middle **color zone.** ➤They are yellow, blue, a bluish green, and a bluish or cerise red.—*Distg. fr.* INVARIABLE HUES, those hues which do not change with change in **luminance** of the stimulus.—See **color primaries** for discussion.

color/mirrored: color seen as if in a mirror behind the reflecting surface.

color mixture: the presentation of two or more color stimuli to the same area of the retina at the same time or in close succession, for the purpose of eliciting their combined effect. ➤Mixture may be accomplished in various ways: simultaneous projection, rapid alternation, or diffusive combination of the several stimuli concerned. COLOR EQUATIONS, formed on the analogy of chemical equations, state the results. ¶Mixture of pigments is not mixture of stimuli and often has different results. E.g., mixture of blue and yellow pigments gives green, mixture of blue and yellow lights gives a colorless light.

color naming or C_n: (*Ror.*) the naming or listing of colors as a direct primary response by the subject.—*Distg. fr.* **color description.**

color/neutral = achromatic color.

color notation: see **Munsell color system.**

color primal: 1. = **color principal.** 2. = **color fundamental.** 3. = **color invariable.** ➤Of the four classifications of color, the only one this term has not been used for is **color primary.** It is recommended that it be abandoned.

color primaries or **primary colors:** 1. loosely, those colors which, in any system, are of special importance for the classification of colors. 2. certain pigments that can be mixed to give, though in reduced **color saturation,** all the hues: white, black, red, yellow, blue.

➤Three other color classifications may be contrasted here: (*a*) PRINCIPAL COLORS:

the four colors—red, yellow, green, blue—which to direct inspection are turning points in the series of hues. Each of these is the terminal point of two continuous series leading toward two of the others: red to blue and red to yellow; yellow to red and yellow to green; green to yellow and green to blue; blue to green and blue to red. A principal is perceived as having no admixture of neighboring hues. Each principal can thus be represented as the corner of a four-sided figure, conventionally a square. —*Syn.* UNITARY HUE. (*b*) **Color invariables:** the four colors seen in the central zone as blue, yellow, a slightly purplish red, a somewhat bluish green, which do not change to a different **hue** in the **middle** zone of the retina. The red and the green simply lose **hue** in the middle zone and are seen as gray, the blue and yellow are unchanged. All other colors are seen in the middle zone as if the red or green component were changed to gray, thus changing the total toward yellow or blue with reduced saturation.— *Distg.* **color invariables** from **invariable hues.** (*c*) **Color fundamentals:** those colors that correspond to the hypothetical *basic processes* or responses which, combined in varied proportions, make possible the whole range of **chromatic** (or color) perception. These colors are variously identified in different color theories.—*Syn.* **colorimetric primaries** (for trichromatic theory). Often called **primary colors,** they are not the same (in any theory) as those colors long since called *primary* by painters. Hence, this use of **color primaries** is to be discouraged in favor of adherence to **(2)** above. ¶The above usages follow Titchener and in each case reflect operational distinctions. Many other terms, each defined in its alphabetical place, reflect **color theories** as well as fact.

color/principal: see discussion under **color primaries.**

color purity: the degree to which a color approaches maximum **saturation;** the degree to which a spectral color is unmixed with **achromatic color.** ➤A PURE COLOR is one of nearly maximum saturation. In the case of spectral colors, this condition is attained when the stimulus is of a single wave length or very nearly so.

color pyramid, solid, or **spindle:** a schematic three-dimensional representation of all possible colors in their directly perceptible relations of **hue, brightness,** and **saturation.** ➤The base is either a COLOR TRIANGLE, SQUARE, or CIRCLE, according to the view taken about what constitutes the basic hues. If we use a triangle, it has at its corners the three **color fundamentals** with intermediate or blended hues along its sides. If we use a circle, it has all the colors of the spectrum, together with the purples,

grading into each other as in a spectrum (the assumption here being that no hue is more basic than another). The square has the four **color principals** at the corners.

The colors on the periphery of the plane surface forming the base (whether triangle, circle, or square) are of maximum satura-

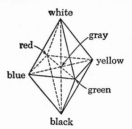

tion. As we move from the periphery toward the center, the colors are less and less saturated but of equal brightness. The color surface forming the base represents schematically the relations of the hues to each other and is often used separately.

At the ends of the vertical axis of the solid figure are white and black. Grays of varying brightness are ranged along the axis. On the sides of the figure from the poles toward the periphery of the base are all the **color tints** and the **color shades.** Between the side surfaces at any point and the axis lie the tints or shades in reduced saturation from their maximum.

color/reduced = color/aperture.

color response or *C*: (*Ror.*) a response determined by the color of the **inkblot** card, or by color and form.

color response/symbolic: (*Ror.*) an inkblot response in which a symbolic meaning is attributed to a color: e.g., "red stands for attraction."

color saturation: the degree to which any color possessing a hue differs from a gray of the same **brightness.**—*Syn.* (in the Munsell system) **chroma.** ➤Saturation depends primarily (but not exclusively) upon the purity of the light-wave: i.e., a single wave length gives rise to a COMPLETELY SATURATED color; the more the light waves are of mixed length, the less is the saturation. For structural psychology, saturation is an elementary **attribute.**

colors/flight of: see **flight of colors.**

color shade: 1. one of a series of colors, of any fixed **hue** and **saturation,** which vary only in **brightness (1). 2.** more narrowly, one of the darker members of this series, in contrast with the lighter members which are called **tints** if they possess perceptible hue.—*Syn.* SHADE.

color shock: (*Ror.*) a response showing

disturbance when a colored card is introduced in the inkblot series.

color solid: 1. = **color pyramid. 2.** a figure representing the brightness and saturation attributes of all the colors.

color sorting test: a test for **color blindness.**—See **Holmgren test.**

color/spectral: see **spectral.**

color spindle: see **color pyramid.**

color square: see **color pyramid.**

colors/soft: the blue-green colors; those which tend to segregate least from a gray field of equal luminosity, and which show the **Liebmann effect** in its most pronounced form.

color/strong: a color of high **saturation.**

color/subjective: a chromatic color sometimes perceived when viewing a moving achromatic stimulus, such as a rotating disk with a black-and-white pattern.

color surface: the plane surface obtained by cutting through the **color pyramid,** usually at right angles to the axis of brightness. Such a surface represents all possible hues and saturations at a given level of brightness.—*Distg. fr.* **surface *color.**

color/surface: one that is seen as lying on the surface of an object. ➤The color is compact in texture, resistant to the gaze, and well localized. Examples are the color of a wall, of a book cover, of the surface of a soap bubble.—*Cp.* **color/volume.**—*Distg. fr.* **color surface.**

color temperature: the temperature of a blackbody, or complete radiator, at which it yields a color matching that of a given sample of radiant energy. ➤The blackbody colors form a single series of relatively unsaturated visual qualities, ranging from red, through orange, white, pale blues, and violets, as the temperature is increased. The temperature is measured on the absolute, or **Kelvin, scale.**

color theories: efforts to state how the energy of light is so transformed into neural impulse as to condition the perceiving of the several colors. ➤Trireceptor theories, of which the Young-Helmholtz theory was the earliest, hold that all colors are reducible to combinations of three basic or **fundamental color** components, for each of which a basic neural impulse is yielded by a specific receptor in the retina. Mc-Dougall's theory modifies this in important details, especially by adopting the duplicity theory of von Kries, which holds that the retina has two separate sets of receptors—the **rods** for faint lights (which yield only **achromatic** impressions) and the **cones** for ordinary vision. Hering's theory, a four-color theory, holds that all colors are reducible to two pairs of opposed or **antagonistic *colors,** with a chemical substance of reversible action in the retina for

each pair. Mueller's theory supplements this with certain cerebral processes. The Ladd-Franklin theory holds that certain mechanisms in the retina have undergone a progressive evolution. The primal receptor yielded achromatic impressions only. From this were differentiated added mechanisms for blue and yellow, the latter giving rise still later to mechanisms for red and green. More recently, a larger number of qualitatively different receptors has been proposed.

color tint or **tone: 1. hues** lighter than median gray, in contrast with the darker **color shades. 2.** = **hue.** (Not *recom.*) **3.** = **saturation.** (Not *recom.*)

color/tone = **timbre.**

color triangle: the plane figure that sets forth certain color relations. The triangle is the base of the **color pyramid** (which see).

color value: a dimension in the Munsell color system roughly corresponding with **lightness.**

color/volume: color seen as organized, transparent, and filling a tridimensional space: e.g., the color of a block of clear ice, a jar of jelly, a room full of smoke.—*Syn.* bulky color.

color/weak: a color with low **color saturation.**

color weakness: a defect in color vision marked by diminished, rather than complete, lack of color sensitivity for a certain range of **hues.** ➤The term is preferred by some to **color blindness** on the ground that, in most cases at least, complete inability to respond to certain hues is not proved.—See **anomalous *trichromatism.**

color wheel: a device for mixing colors by rapid rotation of a disk composed of sectors of different size and color. Usually the sizes of the sectors can be varied.

color zones: regions of the retina that yield different color responses. ➤For normal persons and conditions, in the central zone all colors can be seen. In the middle zone, yellows, blues, and achromatic colors can be seen; but invariable red and green (see **color invariables**) are seen as gray, and other reds and greens are seen as slightly yellow or blue. In the extreme periphery all colors are seen as members of the achromatic series. The zones merge into each other gradually.—*Syn.* retinal zones, chromatic zones.

column: n. 1. (*stat.*) a series of numbers arranged vertically in a table.—*Syn.* y-array, vertical **array.**—*Distg. fr.* row, which is a horizontal series. **2.** (*neurol.*) a nerve bundle extending longitudinally for some distance in the cord or lower brain.

column diagram: 1. see **bar chart. 2.** = **histogram.**

com-: a prefix meaning *with, together,* sometimes *very.*

coma: *n.* a state of suspension of all or nearly all behavior and most reflexes. The patient does not respond even to severely painful stimuli.—*adj.* COMATOSE.

combat fatigue: a disorder brought on by the exhaustion and anxiety of combat; a gross **stress reaction.** ➤Formerly, misleadingly called SHELL SHOCK. Combat fatigue is somewhat of a euphemism. While usually transient, it may progress to a permanent neurotic reaction.

combination: *n.* (*math.*) one of the different sets or groupings in which a number of objects or items can be placed or assigned in such a way that no two sets contain the same items throughout, though a given item may appear in more than one set. The order of the items does not affect the **combination** (as it does affect **permutation** and **variation**). The letters *a b c* have the following combinations: *a + b, a+c, b+c, a+b+c.*—*Syn.* **group, set.**

combination principle: 1. Two or more stimuli presented together may combine to elicit a response. 2. Responses made together tend to recur together whenever the stimulus for either one is presented.—*Cp.* **conditioning/R-R.**

combination tone: a **difference tone** or a **summation tone.**—*Syn.* RESULTANT TONE.

commensurable: *adj.* (*math.*) of two or more quantities that can be measured by the same unit of measurement.—*Ant.* **incommensurable.**

commissural fibers (kə·mish'yū·rəl): a tract connecting corresponding areas in the **hemispheres** or other bilateral divisions of the brain or cord. ➤*Distg. fr.* ASSOCIATION FIBERS or TRACTS, which connect regions within the same hemisphere.—*Syn.* COMMISSURE (kom'i·shùr).

commissure = **commissural fibers.**

committable: *adj.* see **certifiable.**

common factor = **factor/group.**

common factor space: (*factor anal.*) a geometrical space having as many dimensions as there are common factors.

common factor variance = **communality.**

common fate/law of: (*Gestalt*) 1. Incongruous objects in the **phenomenal *field** tend to be so apprehended that they can be assimilated into the common structure or dominant **gestalt** of the field. 2. Elements of a gestalt change more readily when all the elements change in the same way (have a common fate).

common field: see **shared field.**

common marker: see **marker test.**

common sensation = **coenesthesia.**

common sense: 1. the seat or center in which all the other senses were supposed to be united. 2. opinions supposed to be common to all men. ➤Usually contrasted with ordered doctrine or philosophy, it is itself but a tissue of ill-assorted fragments of philosophy. Reliance on common sense is usually a confession that one has fallen back on prejudices which he refuses to examine. Common sense confirms and also rejects some part of every reasoned set of doctrines, scientific or philosophical. 3. good judgment; ability to select the right course of action in practical affairs without resort to elaborate theory or general principles.

common sensibility: a term of rather variable meaning, denoting vague and diffuse sensibility (chiefly visceral), but also including fused tactual-kinesthetic components, and usually an affective component; sensations derived from the body as a whole and without precise localization.—*Syn.* coenesthesia.

common trait: see **trait/common.**

commotional shock: the physical and mental effect of sudden changes in atmospheric pressure; true shell shock, as opposed to the neurosis miscalled **shell shock.**

communality (kom″ū·nal'ə·ti): *n.* (*factor anal.*) that proportion of the **variance** of a variable which is describable in terms of factors common to some of the other variables in the set; the sum of squares of the **factor loadings** of one of a given set of variables.—*Syn.* COMMON FACTOR VARIANCE. —*Ant.* **uniqueness.**

communication: *n.* 1. (*phys.*) the transmission of an effect from one place to another without transport of material: e.g., a sound wave transmitted from its origin to the ear drum. 2. the process whereby physical energy acts upon a sensory receptor: a stimulus is *communicated* to an organism. —*Syn.* **excitation** (*pref'd.*). 3. transmitting, or transmitting and receiving, **information, signals,** or **messages** by means of gestures, words, or other **symbols,** from one organism to another. The information must refer to something that can be distinguished from other things by both organisms. 4. the **information** or **message** which is to be, or has been, transmitted. 5. (*commun. theory*) the total process whereby one system (a **source**) influences another system (a **destination**) by manipulation of the alternative signals carried in a **channel** connecting them. ➤In psychology the source system and the destination system are organisms. 6. (*K. Lewin*) a high degree of dynamic dependence between two personal **regions** so that the changes in one bring about proportional changes in the other.

communication/consummatory: a behavior directed at others that is reduced **or** discontinued solely as a result of its own occurrence, the expression being its own consummation. ➤*Contr. w.* instrumental *communication, in which the tendency to continue or to discontinue depends upon how it is received. Since a person usually perceives some effect of his communication, an instrumental element in most cases contaminates the consummatory element. Designed (apparently) as a positivistic synonym for **expressive behavior,** consummatory communication is so narrowly conceived as to eliminate a great deal of what is usually termed expressive behavior. But consummatory communication seemingly denotes a distinguishable class of behaviors.

communication content: see **content/ communication.**

communication/human: 1. (*commun. theory*) the subscience that investigates the relations between persons who select messages **(sources)** and persons who interpret and are affected by them **(destinations).** 2. the study of **mass media** of communication and their effects on mass audiences, other cultures, etc. ➤This usage somewhat arbitrarily restricts the meaning of the term.

communication/instrumental: an attempt by one person to influence another whom he addresses in such a way as to reduce discrepancies between them; communicating in order to change a person's ideas or actions.—*Contr. w.* **communication/consummatory.**

communication/mass: the influencing of many persons by means of **mass media.**

communication model: (*C. E. Shannon*) a display of the steps or stages in a communication:

noise
↓
source of message ➤ encoding ➤ communication channel
↓
destination of message ◄ decoding

communications theory: a technology (not a theory) that deals with **communication** in all its aspects—physical, psychological, sociological. ➤The parallels between processes of communication in machines, organisms, and institutions are described; and common terms for parallel processes are invented, or adapted from old ones. Since **information** is what is communicated, there is much overlap with **information theory** (which see).

communication unit: (*commun. theory*) a complex unit consisting of **source, transmitter, receiver,** and **destination.** ➤In the model for **human *communication** the source and the destination are persons. The former selects messages and by means

of the **transmitter** (the motor system of the individual) **encodes** the message and starts it on its way through the communication **channel** in the form of **signals** (words, gestures, etc.). These signals are picked up by the **receiver** (a sense organ and its brain connections) of the person who is the **destination.** The signals are **decoded** (receive a meaning) as a **central** process in the destination. ¶There are several variations on this model. In one such model the person (in this connection called a **mediator**) is the whole unit, being both the destination of messages from another system and the source of messages transmitted to a third system.

communion: *n.* fellowship, characterized by a sense of personal closeness or oneness.

community: *n.* 1. members of a species living in close proximity and having some sort of social organization. ➤Some authors maintain that there is no community without shared interests "wide enough to include their lives." (R. M. MacIver.) 2. a group of persons, whether or not in physical contact, who are aware of themselves as sharing a common ideology, interest, property, etc.; or the fact of sharing something in common. ➤That which is held in common is usually specified, e.g., *community of ideas.*

community of content theory: the theory that there are many specific stimuli common to ostensibly different situation complexes, and that these common stimuli account for the consistency or correlation of responses to the situations. ➤It postulates that to each stimulus a specific response is regularly made, the obtained correlation of responses in the complex situation being proportional to the number of common stimulus-response bonds. The theory is a special form of the **multiple-factor** theory.—*Cp.* also **identical elements.**

community of ideas: a sharing of the same reactions, attitudes, and notions by a given group of persons; likemindedness. ➤Asked to name a color, e.g., a large percentage of persons will reply "red."

companion/imaginary: an imaginary playmate, often endowed by the child with a complete personality and perceived with hallucinatory vividness.

comparability (kom″pə·rə·bil′ə·ti): *n.* 1. the quality or attribute of two or more things of being alike in some specific respects and different in others, of having the same effects in stipulated respects. 2. a characteristic of two sets of scores or measures that yield equivalent meanings; or the characteristic of the measuring instrument or system by which such scores are obtained: e.g., degrees of temperature in centigrade and Fahrenheit, two psychophysical procedures for determining a threshold, two forms of the same test. ➤It is not necessary that the two instruments yield the same scores for a given phenomenon, but there must be a point-for-point correspondence. The term **comparable measures** or **scores** has been given a stricter meaning.

comparable form: see **form/comparable.**

comparable measures or **scores: 1.** measures that have a common arbitrary zero point and a common unit of measurement. **2.** loosely, scores that have the same significance for a given purpose: e.g., the **MA** on a Binet and on a group test of intelligence may, under certain circumstances, be regarded as having the same meaning.—See **form/comparable, commensurate.**

comparative judgment: a report that compares one stimulus with another stimulus with reference to a certain dimension: one stimulus is said to be more intense, more colored, more pleasant, more to the right, heavier, or the like.

comparative judgment/law of: the postulate that, in any perceptual discrimination or any comparative judgment of two items, the psychological difference between the items is indirectly measured by the relative frequency with which the difference is perceived and reported under similar conditions of observation. ➤The principle is held to be entirely general and is implicit in such things as the national ratings of football teams according to the frequencies with which "experts" judge one team better than others (though such ratings do not embody all the necessary mathematical refinements for its application). The principle is the basis for scoring items on an **attitude scale.**

comparative psychology: the branch of psychology that compares the minds or behavior of different animal species, or of different races or peoples of man, or of different stages of the individual. ➤The last is more often, and better, called **developmental psychology. Comparative** and **animal psychology** overlap considerably but not completely; the two terms should be kept distinct. **Genetic psychology,** so far as it studies the evolution of mind or behavior through a series of species, is essentially comparative. But if a distinction be made, such genetic psychology is interested in the unity or similarity thus found, comparative psychology in the differences.

comparison/method of paired: see **paired comparison.**

comparison stimulus: (*psychophys.*) one of a set of stimuli each of which is to be compared with an invariant, or **standard, stimulus.**

compartment: *n.* (*stat.*) the box formed by the intersection of a row and a column in a **two-way table.** ➤The position of the

compartment is specified first by the row, then by the column.—*Syn.* **cell.**

compartmentalization: *n.* **1.** the tendency to keep thoughts or feelings distinct that should be kept in relation: e.g., keeping one's moral code as based on religion in a compartment distinct from one's business code, without allowing either to influence the other. **2.** (*K. Horney*) the experiencing of oneself as a sum of disconnected parts, and of one's personality traits as isolated and dissociated from each other; psychic fragmentation. ➤It is said to constitute an attempt to relieve tension and to avoid awareness of inner contradictions, and is therefore (in Horney's system) an **auxiliary solution** or **defense mechanism.**

compassion: *n.* literally, a suffering with another; a strong fellowship in feeling.

compatibility: *n.* **1.** (*logic*) a relation between two statements that are not contradictory or contrary to each other so that both may be true. ➤It is not implied that either is actually true. **2.** a relation between any two things or events such that they can coexist. **3.** a relation between two persons such that they may associate freely and harmoniously.—*Ant.* **incompatibility.**

compeer: *n.* an equal in some specified respect or respects.—*Syn.* **peer.**

compensate: *v.* to make up for; to counterbalance; to make equivalent in value or effect. For psychological uses, see **compensation.**

compensating error: see **error/compensating.**

compensation: *n.* **1. in sensation,** the process whereby one stimulus partly or wholly cancels another, or two stimuli mutually cancel. **2. in vision,** an **adaptation** phenomenon whereby shadows appear less dark and high lights less bright. ➤This usage is confusing. **3.** = COMPENSATORY MOVEMENT, a movement that restores an organ or part to its normal or neutral position, or that restores the "balance of forces" within in the organism when these are disturbed by other movements: e.g., leaning forward when going uphill. **4.** metaphorically, but now semitechnically, = COMPENSATORY BEHAVIOR, action that aims to make amends for some lack or loss in personal characteristics or status; or action that achieves partial satisfaction when direct satisfaction is blocked. ➤Speaking of **compensation** implies nothing about the mechanism of its motivation. Nor does it characterize a personality **trait:** it refers only to the compensatory activity itself. ¶The effort to compensate takes diverse directions: (*a*) VICARIOUS, or SUBSTITUTE, COMPENSATION in which the person strives to develop a contrasting or substitute ability, e.g., a student compensates for lack of athletic ability by

seeking scholastic recognition; (*b*) COM-
PENSATION IN KIND, which is characterized
by determination to overcome the handicap
by unusually zealous effort, as in the tale of
Demosthenes and the pebbles; (*c*) denial of
value in the lacking quality: the "sour
grapes" attitude; (*d*) taking refuge in
dream and fantasy consolation.

Thus, it appears that compensatory behavior may include motor responses, affect,
and cognition. Freud described compensation as an effort to exclude a painful awareness of any deficiency of behavior or personality, Adler as an effort to overcome an
inferiority complex.—*Distg. fr.* **overcompensation.**—*adj.* **compensating, compensatory** (com·pen'sə·tô"ri).—*v.* **compensate.**

competence: *n.* **1.** ability for a particular job
or vocation. **2.** (*law*) state in which one is
capable legally of making choices, hence, is
legally responsible for his actions. ➤An
INCOMPETENT may be a minor or an insane
or mentally deficient person.—*Syn.* COMPE-
TENCY.

competition: *n.* **1.** a striving on the part
or two or more persons for the same object, esp. for the goal of being superior.
➤Personal opposition, usually mutual, is
implied: i.e., one works against the com-
petitor's success as well as for one's own.—
Syn. **rivalry,** which connotes only the
struggle to achieve as well as, or better than,
others, without necessary personal opposition.—*Distg. fr.* personal or interpersonal
conflict, in which there is direct struggle
with others. **2.** = SELF-COMPETITION, striving to surpass one's own previous performances.—*adj.* **competitive.**—*v.* **compete.**

competitiveness: *n.* a tendency to be
easily stimulated to **competition** or
rivalry.

complacency: *n.* **1.** (*pop.*) smug self-satis-
faction. **2.** a state of adjustment, or a
dynamic balance between organism and environment, typified by established habits
and responses that are in a quiescent stage.
➤The COMPLACENCY PRINCIPLE holds that
organisms tend toward complacency except
when disturbed from outside.—*Cp.* **adjustment.**—*Syn.* **homeostasis.**

complaint habit: habitual reporting of
aches and pains or other symptoms for
which no physical cause is found. ➤*Syn.*
hypochondriasis, which sounds more impressive but says no more.

complement: *n.* (*math.*) the difference between a number and any specified power of
10 that is greater than the number. ➤E.g.,
93 is the complement of 7 in relation to 10^2
or 100.

complementarism = color antagonism.

complementary color: see **color complementaries.**

complete learning procedure: an experimental procedure in which the items of a
series are presented, one at a time, at a uniform rate, and the person is asked to reproduce the series. If error is made, the entire series is again presented, and so on till
errorless reproduction is accomplished.—
Syn. COMPLETE MEMORIZING PROCEDURE.

completeness compulsion: (*Ror.*) tendency of the subject to utilize systematically
all the possibilites and aspects of an inkblot card.

completeness of response theory: (*J.
Peterson*) a theory that those responses
most in conformity with both objective and
intraorganic conditions lead to more complete release of tension, are less impeded,
and hence are more likely to be repeated
and learned. ➤This is an alternative theory
to the **law of** *effect.—Cp.* also **closure/
law of.**

completion test: see **test/completion.**

complex (kəm·pleks'; kom'-): *adj.* made
up of components that are either interdependent or in a relationship of subordination
to other components.—*Distg. fr.* **compound,** in which the parts are coordinate.
(This useful distinction is too often ignored.)
—*Contr. w.* **simple, elementary.**

complex (kom'pleks): *n.* **1.** any grouping of
related factors or elements in mental constitution.—*Syn.* (*approx.*) **disposition. 2.**
(*psychoan.*) a system of emotionally toned
ideas that have been **repressed** and give
rise to morbid behavior. ➤Brief for RE-
PRESSED COMPLEX, this is by far the
most frequent usage. **3.** a system of related
ideas with common **affective** ties such that
the arousal of one part of the system brings
the whole to bear upon the situation and results in acts of a defined nature. ➤Such a
system differs from that of (2) in not being
necessarily repressed. If the response is
primarily **affective,** it may be called a
sentiment; if predominantly conative, a
trend or SYSTEM OF DESIRES; if intellectual,
a **constellation.** (But note that the unifying ties are affective in all three.) Some
authors call all such systems, if normal,
sentiments.

Specific named complexes are listed under
the qualifying word, e.g., **Oedipus complex.**

complex/father = **Electra complex.**

complex indicator: in an **association test,**
any behavior that may arise from a *repressed *complex or a voluntarily suppressed emotion: e.g., very fast or very slow
reactions, emotional behavior in general,
certain kinds of odd replies.

complex reaction: in a **reaction time** experiment, the situation in which the subject is instructed to make some discrimination or choice.—*Ant.* SIMPLE REACTION.

compliance: *n.* a yielding to the desires, suggestions, or proposals of another person. ➤The term is somewhat more inclusive than **obedience** and has less implication of resistance or of yielding unwillingly. One *obeys* an order, **complies** with a suggestion; but the difference lies in the reactor, not in the source.—*adj.* **compliant.** —*v.* **comply.**

compliance/neurotic: a **compulsive** overvaluation of submissiveness and self-effacement.

compliant character: (*K. Horney*) a person who tends to neurotic *compliance.

complication: *n.* **1.** a combination of sense data from different senses, e.g., taste and smell of food. **2.** an intricate combination that is hard to untangle. **3.** a diseased condition that occurs during the progress of another disease.

complication experiment: see **prior entry/law of.**

components/instinctual: (*psychoan.*) partial impulses, often quite at variance with each other, that are joined to form a unified (though not necessarily internally consistent) instinctual tendency. ➤E.g., the partial impulses of cruelty to others and cruelty to self are said by many analysts to be combined (with other impulses) in the sex instinct.

composite: *n.* a whole composed of features or traits belonging to different individuals or different experiences. ➤A COMPOSITE PORTRAIT is made by superimposing the photographs of many persons.

composite family = extended family (see **family**).

composite figure, image, or **person:** a dream figure made up of traits belonging to more than one real person.

composite score: the mean of an individual's scores from several tests after they have been expressed in terms of a common unit; a summation of his weighted scores.

composition scale: a scale used in evaluating the excellence of written compositions. It consists of a series of literary extracts each of which has been assigned a numerical score value by the pooled judgment of experts. The composition to be evaluated receives the score of that extract which it most nearly equals in excellence.

compos mentis (kom'pǝs men'tǝs): *adj.* (*L.*) of sound mind; not insane or mentally deficient; **competent.**—*Ant. non compos mentis.*

compound: *n.* that which is formed of coordinate or independent parts.—*Syn.* **composite.**—*Cp.* **fusion, colligation, system; complex** (*adj.*).

compound eye: see **eye/compound.**

compound reaction: see **reaction time.**

comprehend: *v.* **1.** to understand; esp., to understand what a symbol refers to or what an object of thought implies. ➤As compared with **apprehend, comprehend** involves more complete or more complex knowing. **2.** to bring together several facts or ideas under a single head.—*adj.* (for **2**) **comprehensive.**—*n.* **comprehension.**

comprehensibility: *n.* the ease with which a complex object or verbal expression can be understood. ➤While it depends on the person who is to understand, comprehensibility is conceived as a property of the object.

comprehension: *n.* knowledge or understanding of an object, situation, event, or verbal statement. ➤**Comprehension** involves fuller and more explicit knowledge of relationships and general principles than does **apprehension.** In European languages, **comprehension** (or knowledge about) contrasts more sharply with direct **acquaintance with** or **apprehension.** (*Cp. Ger. wissen* vs. *kennen; Fr. savoir* vs. *connaître.*)

comprehension test: 1. a measure of one's understanding of what is needed in a given imaginary practical situation: e.g., what one should do if it is raining when one leaves for school. **2.** a reading test that measures the respondent's ability to obtain information by reading a passage, the respondent usually being required to answer questions about its content. Reading rate and pronunciation are ignored.

comprehensive examination: an examination in school or college subjects that cuts across the boundaries of particular courses and seeks to determine the integrated learning achievement over a relatively large scholastic area and during a considerable time, generally more than one year.

comprehensive solution: (*K. Horney*) the avoidance of conflict by believing oneself actually to be the **idealized** *self—a **neurotic** *solution that leaves one constantly at odds with reality but protects against intrapsychic disharmony.—*Cp.* **auxiliary solution.**

compression: *n.* **1.** using a symbol to convey more than one meaning at one and the same time. ➤*Distg. fr.* **ambiguity,** in which the symbol presumably means only one thing at a time but one cannot tell which thing. **2.** = **condensation.**

compromise formation: (*psychoan.*) a conscious activity that reflects both the work of **repression** and the **instinctual** impulses seeking expression. ➤Repressed impulses may be modified enough to pass **censorship,** the modified form being called a compromise formation. But the term is also used for deflections and distortions of behavior due to **conflict.** COMPROMISE DIS-

TORTION is an analogous process in psychosis.

compulsion: *n.* **1.** compelling or forcing a person to act against his inclination; the state of being compelled.—*Syn.* see **constraint. 2.** that which impels a person to act against his inclination; or such action. ➤Compulsion may be an external force (including an irresistible suggestion) or it may be internal or subjective.—*Cp.* **coercion, compulsiveness, obsessive-compulsive reaction.**—*adj.* **compulsory,** pertaining to a state of affairs involving compulsion; **compulsive,** of a person who is overconscientious or strongly impelled by inner compulsion despite inappropriateness of the action. See also **compulsiveness.**

compulsion/completeness: see **completeness compulsion.**

compulsion/inner or **/internal:** action despite conscious intent to the contrary. ➤Stress is upon a feeling of inability to resist a strong suggestion, either one from without that somehow becomes internalized or one that seems to be generated from within.—*adj.* **compulsive** (not *compulsory*).

compulsion/repetition: see **repetition compulsion.**

compulsive behavior: see **compulsiveness.**

compulsiveness: *n.* the tendency to repeat over and over a certain kind of behavior, despite its inappropriateness, and to be unable to inhibit the behavior. ➤Originally the term referred to motor behavior, but persons manifesting such behavior nearly always have **obsessions** as well: i.e., they feel compelled to attend to certain unwanted ideas or to certain aspects of the environment. Hence, an **obsessive-compulsive** syndrome or neurosis was recognized, and compulsiveness came to be used for obsessive cognition as well as for a motor behavior. Compulsive behavior is generally highly stylized or ritualistic. The person often regards his behavior as irrational, but cannot inhibit it.—*Syn.* COMPULSIVITY, (*Stan. Psychiat.*) **obsessive-compulsive reaction.**—*Cp.* **compulsive personality.**—*adj.* and *pers. n.* **compulsive.**—*n.* **compulsion,** for the actual impulse or for the deed to which it leads, **obsession** referring to the ideas that are compulsively entertained.

compulsive personality: (*Stan. Psychiat.*) a personality pattern characterized by chronic, excessive, or obsessive concern with adherence to standards of conscience or of conformity. ➤The person may be overinhibited, overconscientious, and may have an inordinate capacity for work. Typically he is rigid and lacks a normal capacity for relaxation.—*Cp.* **obsessive-compulsive reaction, compulsiveness.**

compulsivity = **compulsiveness.**

con-: variant of **com-.**

conation (kō·nā′shən): *n.* **1.** that aspect of mental process or behavior by which it tends to develop into something else; an intrinsic "unrest" of the organism. ➤Conation is almost the opposite of **homeostasis. 2.** a **conscious** tendency to act; a conscious striving. ➤Historically, conation was coordinate with **cognition** and **affection,** and was often conceived as a **mental** *faculty.** It is now seldom used for a specific form of behavior, rather for an aspect found in all. Impulse, desire, volition, purposive striving, all emphasize the conative aspect.—*adj.* **conative, conate** (*distg. fr.* **connate**).

conative perseveration: a tendency to persist with **unfinished business.**

conatus (kō·nā′təs): *n.* (*L.*) (*Spinoza*) the striving toward self-preservation and self-affirmation.

conceivable: *adj.* of a statement or judgment that may be true, often with the implication that it is not very likely. ➤The term seldom means literally that something can be conceived; anything can be.

conceive: *v.* **1.** to receive embryonic life into one's body; to become pregnant. **2.** to receive into one's mind; to entertain an idea or notion; to imagine; to gain an idea by reasoning.—*Contr. w.* **perceive. 3.** to frame, to have, or to use, a **concept.** ➤This, the modern technical meaning, is often contaminated by (2) from which it is derived. —*adj.* **conceptional** (for 1); **conceptual** (for 2 and 3); **conceivable,** pertaining to what can be imagined as actual or real.— *n.* **conception, concept formation** (somewhat narrower), **concept** (which see).

concentration: *n.* **1.** exclusive and persistent attention to a limited object or aspect of an object. **2.** the selection of a related group of academic subjects or college courses for special and more detailed study. ➤Designed to insure that the student knows one subject well, it is contrasted in curriculum studies with DISTRIBUTION, designed to insure a broad general knowledge. **3.** (*I. P. Pavlov*) the restriction within a small cortical area of the hypothetical neural processes of **excitation** and **inhibition.**

concept: *n.* **1.** any object of awareness together with its significance or meaning; anything one can think about that can be distinguished from other "things." **2.** a general meaning, an idea, or a property, that can be predicated of two or more individual items. **3.** knowledge that is not directly perceived through the senses but is the result of the manipulation of sensory impressions. ➤Thus one may directly perceive in Dobbin certain properties, but for a concept one must also apprehend these properties as constituting part of the general notion of "horsiness." A concept requires both **abstraction** and **generalization**—the first to isolate the property, the second to recognize that it may be ascribed to several objects. But we distinguish a class concept or a **general *concept** from an abstract ***concept**, depending upon our desire to emphasize one or the other aspect of conceiving. The verbal expression of a concept is a **term;** but some hold, on theoretical grounds, that the concept *is* the verbal or other symbol.—See **conceptualization, conception, construct.**—*adj.* **conceptual.** —*v.* **conceive.**

concept/abstract: a quality apprehended as common to a class of individual items: e.g., sweetness, durability, excellence.—See **abstraction.**

concept/class = **concept/general.**

concept/conditional-genetic: see **concepts/mathematical.**

concept/dynamic: (*K. Lewin*) see **concepts/mathematical.**

concept extension: use of a concept for a wider set of data than that for which it was introduced. ➤A dangerous but not necessarily invalid procedure.

concept formation: see **conception (2).**

concept/general: the idea that represents a number of individual instances, all of which have something in common. "Dog" is a general concept; it represents any dog, or dogs in general. It *implies* the abstract ***concept** of "dogginess," but the latter may remain very vague. Many who speak of "dogs in general" would have difficulty in explaining what "dogginess" is.—*Syn.* GENERAL IDEA, CLASS CONCEPT.

conception: *n.* 1. the process of **conceiving** (all senses). 2. the process of forming **concepts;** CONCEPT FORMATION. 3. = **concept.** (A needless variant.) 4. a related group of concepts; a general point of view expressed or expressible in many concepts, e.g., the biological *conception* of life in contrast with the *concept* of natural selection. ➤The distinction is not rigid since every concept may be considered as having subconcepts and may therefore be called a conception.

concepts/mathematical: (*K. Lewin*) **topological** concepts such as boundary, region, vector, in contrast with DYNAMIC or CONDITIONAL-GENETIC CONCEPTS such as force, tension, resistance, fluidity.

conceptual approach: an approach to science or scientific problems that emphasizes the selection (or invention) and clarification of its concepts.—*Contr. w.* **empirical, experimental, statistical,** and **historical** approaches, although the **conceptual approach** may actually combine all these.

conceptual attitude = **abstract attitude** (*prefd.*)—See **concrete attitude.**

conceptualization: *n.* 1. a particular act of **conceiving.** 2. discovering the appropriate **concepts** that will put a group of facts into a rational or useful order; or the ordering of data by means of concepts.—*v.* (for 2) **conceptualize.**

conceptual matrix: (*F. T. Bugenthal*) a **schema** that includes both the phenomenal self and the components of the perceptual field that are not-self, together with their relations.

conceptual nervous system: any **model** or system of **constructs** that translates the facts of behavior into the language of neural anatomy and physiology. It is hypothesized as the kind of nervous system to be expected in the light of the ascertained behavior facts, and of some general principle of correlation between the nervous system and behavior. ➤The properties ascribed to the **conceptual nervous system,** though they do not conflict with any known properties of the observed nervous system, are merely translations of the properties of behavior, and hence add nothing directly to the understanding of behavior. See **model** for the value and limitations of such transformation of symbols. ¶Unless its use is carefully guarded, the conceptual nervous system becomes a vast neurological tautology, a satisfying pseudosolution with which one rests, instead of the intended stimulation to search for solutions.

conceptual space: the system of abstractly conceived relationships that (when put in order) constitute the **space** of geometry, in contrast with directly perceived space.

conclusion: *n.* a judgment reached, or alleged to be reached, by reasoning.

concomitant: *n.* any phenomenon that accompanies another. ➤The word as such is noncommittal on the relationship between the two phenomena. It may even imply denial of causal relation: it is a mere *concomitant.*

concomitant variations method or **canon:** one of Mill's working principles of **induction** according to which things that vary together are probably connected, either as cause and effect or as having a cause in common. ➤**Correlation** is a measure of concomitant variation.—See **agreement and differences/canon of, residues/ method of.**

concordance/coefficient of: (*stat.*) an estimate of general agreement among judges in ranking a group of individuals: the squared deviations of the summed rankings of each individual from the mean of the rankings of the group, divided by the sum of the squared deviations that would result from perfect agreement among the rankers.

concrete: *adj.* 1. pertaining to a specific or particular item or thing, as a whole; characterizing an individual fact at a particular moment; the opposite of **abstract**. **2.** (less technically) of an exposition wherein general laws or principles are illustrated by individual instances.

concrete attitude: tendency to react to the immediately given object or situation without considering its relationships or classification. ➤*Contr. w.* ABSTRACT ATTITUDE, in which the person reacts not so much to sensory impressions of the situation as to **abstract** qualities, to objects as classified or conceptualized. The person with an abstract attitude, when he has no ready concepts that fit, will seek to find or construct them. The contrast between concrete and abstract attitude may characterize either a reaction to a given situation or a prevailing trend in a person's behavior.

concrete intelligence: see **intelligence/concrete.**

concretizing: *n.* the process of supplying concrete illustration, application, or proof for an abstraction.

concurrent deviations/coefficient of or **/method of:** an indication of the extent to which a change in one quantity is accompanied by a change in another quality, in either the same or the opposite direction.

concussion: *n.* disorder of nervous function, produced by a severe blow to the head or spinal column, and manifesting symptoms such as shock, unconsciousness, temporary or permanent paralysis.

condensation: *n.* (*psychoan.*) representation of more than one element of the **latent content** by a single detail in the manifest content (see **dream content**); or, the production of a new mental process to represent two or more processes in the **unconscious.**

condition: *n.* **1.** the state of anything, esp. whether it is good or bad, or much or little; a complex of variables. **2.** the antecedent, or part of the antecedent, without which an event does not occur. ➤Distinction is made between a NECESSARY CONDITION (a part-cause) and a SUFFICIENT CONDITION.—*v.* **3.** to act as part, or all, of the cause of anything. **4.** to establish a **conditioned response (3)**; to bring it about that a certain response is evoked by a certain stimulus. ➤It is the response that is said to be conditioned—i.e. to be made conditional upon the stimulus. To speak of the stimulus as being conditioned to the response is misleading. **5.** (loosely) to cause an organism to learn, or to change in any way its responsiveness to stimuli. ➤Though very widespread, this usage should be avoided.—See **conditioning** for general discussion.—*adj.* **conditioned.**

conditional: *adj.* subject to conditions; con-

tingent; occurring only if certain circumstances are found. ➤In phrase combinations, often synonymous with **conditioned.**

conditionalism: *n.* (*C. Jung*) = **determinism.**

conditional reflex: I. P. Pavlov's term, now seldom used, for **conditioned response.**

conditioned: *adj.* **1.** dependent, or caused to be dependent, on something else. **2.** characterizing a response made dependent upon a previously neutral stimulus by the experimental procedure of **conditioning. 3.** (*lab. slang*) characterizing an animal as having reached a certain criterion stage in the procedure of conditioning. ➤The expression, "the animal is conditioned," has very curious implications if taken seriously. **4.** characterizing a stimulus that, by conditioning, has come to elicit a certain response; or a stimulus that has, by conditioning, become related to another stimulus. ➤A widely held theory holds that, strictly speaking, the dynamics of conditioning consists in attaching an **R** to an **S**; this usage is therefore objected to. But it is implied in the firmly entrenched **conditioned stimulus,** and as defined it has a clear operational meaning.

For phrases with **conditioned,** see also **conditioning.**

conditioned avoidance: see **conditioned (instrumental) avoidance response.**

conditioned emotion: see **emotion/conditioned.**

conditioned inhibition: (*I. P. Pavlov*) the suppression of the **CR** when the **CS** is repeatedly paired with an indifferent stimulus and the **US** (or **reinforcement**) is not given. The indifferent stimulus becomes the suppressor. ➤The phenomenon is not that of simple **extinction,** for the **CS,** when not paired with the suppressor, elicits **CR.**—*Syn.* INHIBITORY CONDITIONING, NEGATIVE CONDITIONING.

conditioned (instrumental) avoidance response: a conditioned response that prevents the appearance of a **noxious** stimulus. ➤There is a signal that a noxious stimulus is coming and a learned response that avoids the stimulus.—*Distg. fr.* **conditioned (instrumental) escape response** in which the noxious stimulus is already present and the learned response terminates it.

conditioned (instrumental) escape response: a learned response that separates the organism from a noxious stimulus. ➤*Distg. fr.* **conditioned (instrumental) avoidance response.** The avoidance response *prevents* the occurrence of, the escape response *terminates,* the stimulus, or removes the animal from its impact.

conditioned instrumental response: see **conditioning (2).**

conditioned reactive inhibition: see **inhibition/conditioned reactive.**

conditioned reflex: (*obsoles.*) **conditioned response.**

conditioned response: 1. the new or modified response that is elicited by a given stimulus after **conditioning.** ➤See that term for basic consideration of usage.—*Syn.* (*I. P. Pavlov*) CONDITIONED or CONDITIONAL REFLEX, (*V. M. Bekhterev*) ASSOCIATION REFLEX. 2. the hypothetical mechanism or connection between stimulus and response established by **conditioning.** ➤The evidence for the connection is found in change in the frequency, the amplitude, or the latency of the response. The strength of the **CR** refers to the strength of the hypothetical connection, not to the vigor of the response. —*Syn.* **bond** or **association,** but both tend to have special meanings or to imply certain theories. 3. term used for the sequence of stimulus-leading-to-response when emphasis is upon acquisition of the sequence by conditioning. ➤Some authors use **CR** for meanings (2) and (3), **R**$_C$ when they wish to emphasize the response (meaning 1).

conditioned response/anticipatory: a response intervening between the **CS** and the **US,** or between the **CS** and the **CR** when the **US** is not presented. ➤E.g., when the **US** is shock, marked changes in breathing follow the **CS.** They have been interpreted as **expectancy** reactions to the shock.

conditioned response/classical: see **conditioning (1).**

conditioned response/trace: a **CR** that does not occur until after the cessation of the **CS.** ➤If the interval is less than a minute, it is called a SHORT TRACE RESPONSE; if over a minute, it is a LONG TRACE RESPONSE. The delay in response is established by delaying the presentation of the **US** by a corresponding interval.

conditioned stimulus or **CS** or **S**$_C$: an originally ineffective stimulus for a given response that, by the experimental procedure of conditioning, has become capable of eliciting that response.—See **conditioning (1)** and **(2).**—*Syn.* **substitute** stimulus, which is more general and does not imply the experimental procedure of conditioning.

conditioning: *n.* 1. = CLASSICAL CONDITIONING, the complex of organismic processes involved in the experimental procedure, or the procedure itself, wherein two stimuli are presented in close temporal proximity. One of them has a reflex or previously acquired connection with a certain response, whereas the other is not an **adequate** *stimulus to the response in question. Consequent upon such paired presentation of the two stimuli, usually many times repeated, the second stimulus acquires

the potentiality of evoking a response very like the response provoked by the other stimulus. ➤The first-mentioned stimulus is called the UNCONDITIONED STIMULUS (US or S$_U$), the second-mentioned is the CONDITIONED STIMULUS (CS or Sc). The original response is the UNCONDITIONED RESPONSE (UR or R$_U$), the newly acquired response for the CS is the CONDITIONED RESPONSE (CR or R$_C$). ¶In the classical experiments of Pavlov, a signal such as a bell was paired with the presentation of food, the signal acquiring the potentiality of evoking a salivation response very much like the salivation that reflexly follows the stimulus of food.—*Syn.* PAVLOVIAN CONDITIONING, TYPE-S CONDITIONING, RESPONDENT CONDITIONING. 2. = INSTRUMENTAL CONDITIONING: the complex of organismic processes involved in the experimental procedure (or the procedure itself) wherein a stimulus, having evoked a response that brings into view a rewarding stimulus, thereafter is more likely to evoke that response; or alternatively, the complex of processes or the experimental procedure wherein the stimulus, having evoked a response that prevents or removes a **noxious** or punishing stimulus, thereafter is more likely to evoke that response. ➤The response that brings the rewarding stimulus or that prevents or removes the punishing stimulus is called the conditioned response, and the stimulus that evokes the CR is called the conditioned stimulus. The stimulus called forth by the conditioned response is called the unconditioned stimulus or the **reinforcement.** (See **reinforcement** for a different usage.) E.g., a caged animal sees a lever bar (CS) and depresses it (CR). This brings into view a food pellet, the unconditioned stimulus (US) or reinforcement. (The response to the unconditioned stimulus —in the above example, eating the pellet—is usually included with the US as part of the reinforcement.)—*Syn.* TYPE-R CONDITIONING, OPERANT CONDITIONING, OPERANT LEARNING. 3. = learning in general.

➤The terminology dealing with conditioning and reinforcement and their relation to learning is badly confused and infected with **theory-begging.** The employment of **conditioning** as a synonym for all kinds of learning (as in **3** above) makes two assumptions: that conditioning means only one process; and that this process is the only, or at least the basic, process in learning. Both assumptions are speculative. The term conditioning is best reserved for those forms of learning that bear *close resemblance* to the experimental design of conditioning.

But to which experimental design? The use of the same word **conditioning** glosses over the very great differences, at least at the descriptive level, between the classical and the instrumental forms. They differ greatly in experimental plan, temporal sequence, outcome, and, many believe, in organismic dynamics. In classical conditioning, the US is presented by the experimenter and *precedes* and evokes the response; in instrumental conditioning, the US is brought into view by the animal's response and *follows* it, being called in this connection the **reinforcement.** ¶In classical conditioning, the conditioned and unconditioned responses are the same or very similar; in instrumental conditioning they characteristically bear no resemblance to each other. In the former, proximity of *stimuli* is the characteristic feature (hence, TYPE-S) ; in the latter, the nature of the conditioned *response* as bringing a reward is essential (hence, TYPE-R). In classical conditioning a new stimulus-response sequence is established; in instrumental conditioning an already functioning sequence is strengthened.

Even if it should be established (as it has not yet been) that instrumental and classical conditioning have the same organismic dynamics, it would be sounder nomenclature to give different names to two radically different experimental plans. The layman and the beginning student almost invariably get the notion that the two processes are basically identical—otherwise why invent a new technical term, conditioning, and apply it to both?

Classical conditioning is the original model of conditioning described by I. P. Pavlov. Many would therefore restrict the term **conditioning** to this model. It has been suggested that instrumental conditioning be renamed REINFORCEMENT LEARNING. But **reinforcement** has a different meaning in classical conditioning. It is therefore here suggested that instrumental conditioning be called OPERANT LEARNING. We should then have **learning** as the general term, **conditioning** or RESPONDENT CONDITIONING (for sense 1) and **operant learning** (for sense 2) as two experimentally described varieties of learning, with a place left for such other varieties as may be empirically delineated (insight learning, canalization, etc.). If it is felt that instrumental conditioning *must* be called conditioning, because of the *mystique* attached to that word, the qualifier **instrumental** or **operant** should always be stated or clearly implied. (But this dictionary must reflect current usage of **conditioning** for both procedures, usually without making distinction.)—See **conditioned** for other terminological problems.

The symbols US, UR, CS, CR are very commonly used, the last being ambiguous

just as conditioned response ambiguously refers to the *bond* established between S and R or to the R elicited by a CS. The alternative symbols S_U, R_U, S_C, and R_C are clearer and leave CR for the bond; but this notation is less often used.—*v.* **condition:** to train, or to expose an animal to the experimentally delineated conditions or conditioning; or, to learn as a result of such exposure.

conditioning/approximation: an experimental procedure in which the animal is trained **(operant learning)** to make an unusual response to a certain stimulus by causing him to be rewarded for acts progressively more like the act to be learned until that act finally occurs and is rewarded. —*Syn.* **shaping.**

conditioning/avoidance: see **conditioned (instrumental) avoidance response.**

conditioning/backward: experimental procedure in which the **conditioned stimulus** follows the cessation of the **unconditioned.** ➤On theoretical grounds, it is sometimes held that the physiological activity initiated by the CS must precede or accompany that of the US, but conditioning may still take place when the time sequence of the two external stimuli is reversed, possibly by virtue of unobserved intervening activities.

conditioning/classical: see **conditioning** (1).

conditioning/configural: that in which the CS is a pattern of stimuli rather than an isolated simple stimulus. ➤The distinction is merely relative, since virtually all stimuli are patterned.

conditioning/counter: the procedure of conditioning a second and conflicting response to a CS that is not simultaneously being **reinforced.**

conditioning/decorticate: conditioning in the absence of the cerebral cortex.

conditioning/delayed: the CR that is established when the interval between the onset of the CS and of the US is greater than several seconds.—*Cp.* **conditioned response/trace.**

conditioning/escape: see **conditioned (instrumental) escape response.**

conditioning/higher order: a form of **classical *conditioning** in which the CS of the earlier conditioning procedure serves as the US for a later procedure. SECOND ORDER, THIRD ORDER, and HIGHER ORDER CONDITIONINGS are postulated.—*Syn.* CONDITIONING/SECONDARY.

conditioning/inhibitory: see **conditioned inhibition.**

conditioning/instrumental = **conditioning** (2).

conditioning/latency of = **latency** (2).

conditioning/negative: see **conditioned inhibition.**

conditioning/operant = instrumental conditioning.—See conditioning (2).

conditioning/Pavlovian = conditioning (1).

conditioning/pseudo-: see pseudoconditioning.

conditioning/remote: the procedure in which the conditioned stimulus does not immediately precede the response but is separated from it by a considerable time. ➤The term is somewhat loosely used to include trace *conditioned response and backward *conditioning.—See simultaneous *conditioning.

conditioning/respondent = conditioning (1).

conditioning/R-R: the experimental procedure whereby one response is made a necessary part of the conditions for the occurrence of another response.

conditioning/secondary or /second-order: the process whereby a stable CR may serve as a base for further conditioning, the achievement of a conditioned goal acting as a secondary *reinforcement.

conditioning/semantic: the procedure in which the response previously conditioned to a word is elicited either by the object that the word names or by another word meaningfully related to the conditioned stimulus word. ➤Better called SEMANTIC TRANSFER.—Distg. fr. primary stimulus *generalization, in which the new stimulus is perceptually similar to the original conditioned stimulus.

conditioning/sensory: the presentation simultaneously or in close succession of two stimuli, e.g., a light and a tone, enough times that one stimulus (demonstrably) can be substituted for the other in eliciting some specific response. ➤See type-S conditioning under conditioning (2). Sensory conditioning differs from classical *conditioning in that no particular response is made mandatory by the experimental conditions during the simultaneous presentations of the stimuli. The term refers to a specific experimental procedure and outcome, and does not imply (what some theorists deny) that a stimulus can be conditioned to a stimulus.

conditioning/simultaneous: the experimental situation in which the CS occurs with the US, or precedes it by a brief interval (up to 5 seconds) and continues until the US is presented. ➤The latter is the better experimental arrangement for training, and the term is often restricted to this design.

conditioning/trace: see conditioned response/trace.

conditioning/type-R = conditioning (2).

conditioning/type-S = conditioning (1).

conduct (kon′dukt): n. 1. behavior of a person, over a short or a prolonged period of time, and including any number of individual actions. 2. behavior as guided by foresight, esp. by ethical or moral standards.—See act.

conduction: n. 1. transmission of neural impulse through one neuron from dendrite to axon termination, or from one neuron to another (synaptic *conduction), or from a neuron to an effector organ. 2. transmission of a wave through a medium from one place to another.—v. conduct (kən·dukt′).

conduction/antidromic: passage of a neural impulse in a direction opposite to the normal, that is, from axon to dendrite.

conduction deafness = deafness/conduction.

conduction/synaptic: stimulation of a neuron in consequence of excitation delivered to its synaptic endings by impulses traveling in other neurons.

conduction unit: 1. the entire nerve mechanism for transmission of neural impulse from a particular place in the body to another particular place. ➤The term includes the neural mechanisms for reflexes, habits, conditioned responses, and for various covert responses. 2. (E. L. Thorndike) the mechanism inferred when an organism tends more or less consistently to react in a specific way under specific circumstances; the hypothesized mechanism for an action system.

conductivity: n. 1. capacity of a substance to transmit energy. 2. capacity of a nerve tract to transmit neural impulse.

cones: n. pl. minute bodies in the retina which transform the energy of light rays into the specific neural impulses for color and light vision.—Cp. rods.

confabulation: n. 1. unsystematic falsification of memory. 2. (Ror.) a category for unorganized and rambling inkblot responses. ➤Even when certain details are evidently perceived together, that fact may not appear at the time because of ill-organized linguistic response.

confact: n. an overt response to the similarity between the present situation and certain previously experienced situations; an overt response as if to an abstract concept. ➤It is not implied that the concept is verbally formulated.

confidence coefficient = risk level.—See also fiducial limits.

confidence interval: the distance in sigma units between the fiducial limits (which see).

confidence level = risk level.—See also fiducial limits.

confidence limits = fiducial limits.

configural analysis or scoring: see pattern analysis.

configuration = gestalt (which see).

configuration/factor: see **factor configuration.**

configuration principle: Any system of events functions as a unit in adjusting to events outside itself.

configuration/word: see **word configuration.**

confirmation: (*E. C. Tolman*) a principle proposed in place of **reinforcement** as a factor in learning: when an **expectancy** is confirmed—i.e., when a behavior actually leads toward a goal as expected—the expectancy acquires a higher probability value.

confirming reaction: the hypothetical activity that takes place in the nervous system when the organism is stimulated by a **satisfier.** ➤The objectively observed effect is a tendency to repeat the behaviors closely connected with obtaining satisfaction.—*Syn.* YES REACTION, OK REACTION.

conflict: *n.* **1.** the simultaneous functioning of opposing or mutually exclusive impulses, desires, or tendencies; or the state of a person when opposed impulses or response tendencies have been activated.—*Syn.* INTRAPSYCHIC, INTRAPERSONAL, or MENTAL CONFLICT. **2.** = **conflict/interpersonal.**

conflict/actual: (*psychoan.*) a presently functioning opposition between impulses, or between a conscious and an unconscious desire. ➤The actual conflict is regarded as a transformation of a ROOT CONFLICT originating in early infancy. E.g., there may be in infancy an unresolved **Oedipus** conflict (the root) which later gives rise to conflict over following the father's vocation (the actual or present conflict). The word *actual* in this term is an unhappy translation of the *Ger. aktuel,* meaning *now present.*

conflict / approach - approach: see **approach-approach conflict.**

conflict/approach-avoidance: see **approach-avoidance conflict.**

conflict/basic: (*K. Horney*) **1.** the intrapsychic conflict between basic **neurotic *trends. 2.** the intrapsychic conflict between two **compulsive** drives or solutions, e.g., between self-effacing and expansive solutions. **3.** the conflict within the **pride system** between the proud and the despised self. It is generally characterized by partial involvement of the self, and resultant hatred for the **actual *self.**

conflict/central: (*K. Horney*) intrapsychic conflict between the totality of healthy constructive forces within the **real *self** and the totality of neurotic obstructive forces (the **idealized *self**). ➤This conflict involves the entire self, is more severe than **basic *conflict,** and usually is experienced only after **psychoanalysis** has made clear the opposition of forces.

conflict/cultural: the push and pull of divergent **cultures** upon the behavior of individuals or groups.

conflict/inner = **conflict (1).**

conflict/interpersonal: 1. a relation between two or more persons who seek goals that cannot be simultaneously attained under the prevailing conditions. **2.** a conflict within the individual that has its roots in his relations with others. ➤Such conflict can be described as both inter- and intrapersonal: this usage is confusing.

conflict/intrapersonal or **/intrapsychic** = **conflict (1).**

conflict/mental = **conflict (1).**

conflict/root: see **conflict/actual.**

conflict situation: a situation in which a person is acted upon by two opposing forces of approximately equal strength: e.g., an order to perform a disagreeable task and threat of punishment if it is not performed.

confluence: *n.* a flowing together of what has been apart; the combined influence of the separate parts or elements of a situation. ➤The term is used in many specific contexts: in perception, e.g., for such a phenomenon as the combining of separate parts of the Müller-Lyer figure to cause a space illusion that is not given by any one element; by Adler, for the choice of a goal as result of more than one motive; by R. B. Cattell, for a group of responses that serve originally conflicting goals; in genetics, for the combined influence of heredity and environment.

conformance: *n.* (*M. Jahoda*) change of attitude or belief chiefly because of social pressure. ➤*Distg. fr.* **consentience** in which belief is changed by relevant argument. *Cp.* **convergence (5), compliance.** —*Syn.* **conformity/social.**

conformity: *n.* correspondence to a recognized or required pattern or standard.

conformity/social: 1. behaviors or attitudes that are regulated by the norms, prescribed roles, standards, or consensus of a group in which a person is a member; or behaviors and attitudes that resemble the **modal** behaviors and attitudes of the other members of the group.—*Ant.* **deviance. 2.** a hypothetical trait or general tendency on the part of an individual to accede to social pressure.

confound: *v.* **1.** (*exper.*) to mingle data from distinct sources of variation; to represent by a single number variation that comes from distinct sources. ➤This occasionally results from an effort to simplify, more often from imperfect experimental design. It is usually very difficult, often impossible, to unscramble confounded variation after the fact. **2.** to design an experiment so that irrelevant variables are counterbalanced. ➤The purpose of the design—to free the dependent variable from irrelevant influences—is not suggested by **confound.**—*Syn.* (for 2) **counterbalance** (*prefd.*).—*n.* **confounding.**

confusion: *n.* a state characterized by bewilderment, emotional disturbance, lack of clear thinking, and (sometimes) perceptual disorientation. ➤In mild form, it is experienced by everyone, but it is also a common early symptom of psychosis.—*Cp.* **clouding of consciousness.**

confusion control: any device to insure that it is the experimental variable that determines the answer given in a **recognition** test. ➤E.g., in seeking to determine whether a given radio program increases the recognition of a sponsor's product, the recognition test is given to a sample before the program as well as after. The logic is that of the **control group.**

congenital: *adj.* present in an individual at birth. ➤*Distg. fr.* **innate.** The **congenital** is not necessarily determined by heredity; indeed, the term is sometimes used to mean *present at birth but not innate.*—*Syn.* **connate.**

congeries (kən·jir'ēz; -i·ēz): *n.* a mere collection, whether of objects or of organisms.—See **group/social.**—*Syn.* **aggregation.**

congregation: *n.* an assemblage of persons gathered in a common (relatively limited) area.

congruent (kong'grü·ənt): *adj.* of two or more objects, or properties of objects, that may coexist in some limited area or totality. ➤*Distg. fr.* **congruous,** which refers to propositions about the objects.

congruent points: a pair of points in the two retinas referred to the same point in the external stimulus.—*Distg. fr.* **identical points.**

congruous: *adj.* (*logic*) of two or more noncontradictory propositions that refer to the same data.—*Distg. fr.* **congruent.**

conjugate movement: coordinated movement of the two eyes.

conjugation: *n.* 1. a joining together; a uniting of two distinct things. 2. a union of two unicellular organisms prior to reproduction by fission. 3. the union of the nuclei of male and female **gametes.**—*adj.* and *v.* **conjugate.**

conjunctiva (kon"jungk·tī'və): *n.* the mucous membrane that forms the inner lining of the eyelid and the outer cover of the eyeball.—*adj.* **conjunctival.**

conjunctival reflex: closing the eyelid when the **cornea** is touched.—*Syn.* LID REFLEX, CORNEAL REFLEX.

conjunctive motivation: (*H. S. Sullivan*) motivation that seeks to harmonize diverse situations or factors.

conjunctivity: *n.* (*H. A. Murray*) coordination of action and thought; the organiza-

tion of trends and purposes.—*Ant.* DISJUNCTIVITY.

connate (kon'āt): *adj.* **congenital.**

connection: *n.* any linkage between two or more psychological phenomena; specif. but not exclusively, the linkage of a stimulus with a response such that the one leads to the other. ➤Occasionally, an entire chain of linkages is spoken of as a **connection.** The term is a general one and need not commit to any theory about the nature of the connection, nor to **connectionism** as a point of view (though it is often so used). —*Syn.* **bond.**—*Cp.* **association, integration, fusion, colligation.**

connectionism: *n.* the doctrine that the basis of all behavior is a **connection** or bond that links a stimulus to a response, that learning consists in the acquisition and strengthening of such connections, and that all complex behaviors are describable as combinations of stimulus-response connections.—See **psychology/divisions and schools of, VII.**

connector: *n.* a nerve element between a receptor nerve and an **effector** nerve.

connotation: *n.* the meaning of a term defined by abstract qualities or properties common to a class of objects or instances designated by that term.—*Contr. w.* **denotation** (which see).—*v.* **connote.**

consanguineous (con"sang·gwin'i·əs): *adj.* 1. descended from the same ancestor, generally from one not greatly remote (such as a parent or grandparent). 2. of marriages between related persons: cousins, brother-sister, etc.—*n.* **consanguinity** (con"sang·gwin'ə·ti).—*Syn.* CONSANGUINE (con·sang'-gwin).

conscience: *n.* 1. in earlier theological discussions, an innate or divinely implanted **faculty** enabling one to judge correctly on moral issues. ➤The **superego,** though acquired by earthly means, is conceived in psychoanalysis as functioning in substantially the same way as conscience. 2. the more-or-less integrated functioning of a person's system of moral values in the approval or disapproval of his own acts or proposed acts.

conscious: *adj.* 1. characterizing a person as able to react to environment; as having sensations, feelings, thoughts, and strivings; as being aware. 2. pertaining to the process of being aware or knowing. 3. = **mental** or **psychic** (which see). 4. **subjective;** observable by **introspection.**—*n.* 5. (*psychoan.*) a division of the **psyche** that includes those parts of mental life of which the person is momentarily aware. (As a noun, nearly always with the definite article.)

➤Long abuse in philosophical and popular discussion has endowed this term with many meanings. Originally it meant "knowing with" and referred to the doctrine that, in knowing any object, one always simultaneously knows one's knowing, or knows one's self as knowing. When this doctrine faded, the term was applied to any knowing or cognitive process (meaning **2**). But it was soon extended to include the feelings and the strivings—in short, to the **mental** in its broadest connotation (meaning **3**). The broader usage tends always to be modified in the direction of the narrower, but not consistently. *To be conscious* does mean primarily *to know*; yet it seems perverse to say we are not conscious when we feel or strive. (Some theorists neatly solve this difficulty by holding that knowing, feeling, and striving are never separate but are merely aspects of an integral **act**.)

The earlier meaning of "knowing with" survived in the idea (see **4**) that **conscious** refers to a mental process simultaneously observed by introspection. Earlier **behaviorism**, however, denied both the factual reality of a special class of phenomena called conscious, or **subjective**, and the scientific usefulness of introspective observation. But it has proved difficult to maintain the complete denial of subjective observation; all psychologists use it, relating it to objective observation by various theoretical interpretations. (Behaviorists generally interpret it as subverbal behavior.)

It appears that many behaviors can be directly observed only by the person who behaves. With changing circumstances some of these behaviors may become objectively observable. Or, under other circumstances, the behaviors may cease to be observable even subjectively. In either case, the subjective, or conscious, behavior does not gain or lose any property when subjected to a different kind of observation or when it ceases to be observed. In short, in this view, conscious does not refer to a dynamic property of a behavior but merely to the possibility of its being observed and reported in a certain way. It is entirely consistent with this position to hold that the most important psychological behaviors are those called conscious—that is, usually observable only in introspection—while insisting that being conscious adds nothing to the dynamic effectiveness of those behaviors. This interpretation of conscious behavior has not received a special name, but it is widely held —often unwittingly, it seems. In view of the semantic difficulties of conscious, it may be better to speak of subjective behavior (though subjective also has its confusions).

The question of how conscious process (in any of its meanings) is related to bodily process not only raises metaphysical issues

but confuses the usage.—See **mind-body problem.**

In the psychoanalytic use (**5**) the conscious is not conceived as merely a place in the **psyche**; it is an agency in dynamic relation with the **preconscious** and the **unconscious.** The whole psychoanalytic position hinges on the doctrine that the unconscious is not merely that which is not conscious; and this position has implications for the meaning of the conscious. An already confused semantic situation is thus further confused.—*n.* **consciousness.**

conscious behavior: ➤The term is impossible to define without begging basic issues of theory and/or metaphysics. Some theorists hold that being **conscious** is the distinguishing character of behavior (as compared with physiological activity). **Conscious behavior** in this view is redundant (though perhaps forgivable to make a point), and **unconscious** behavior is merely an unfortunate synonym for physiological activity. Certain **neobehavorists** hold that conscious behavior is (**overt**) behavior accompanied by verbal behavior, usually **covert.** (This has the curious corollary that the covert verbal behavior is not itself conscious, unless it is in turn accompanied by another covert verbal behavior, and so on in infinite regression.) ¶For all its terminological deficiencies, the expression has served a generation of psychologists, possibly helping them to feel that somehow they were bridging the gap between **mentalism** and **behaviorism.** (It is not quite that easy.)

conscious experience: (*pop.*) a vague designation for the activities of perceiving, thinking, emoting, choosing and deciding, etc., usually with some implication that this experience has formative influence on the individual. ➤The difficulties of the terms **conscious** and **experience** are compounded when they are used together.—*Cp.* also **conscious behavior.**

conscious need: see **felt need.**

consciousness: *n.* **1.** that which experiences; the **mind** or **self.** ➤An unnecessary usage, but once very prevalent.—See **person. 2.** the sum total of the individual's lifetime experiences, or the sum total at any given moment. ➤There is often an unnoticed glide between these two meanings. **Experiences,** in this usage, may be equated with conscious processes or **mental contents.** Some authors suppose the totality of experience, merely as cohering mental content, to be the agent of conscious process— that is, they combine (**1**) and (**2**). **3.** the sum total of the processes of being **aware,** or of taking account of, or reacting to, objects; the sum total of **acts.** ➤This is probably the commonest usage today; it is this consciousness that is lost when asleep or in coma. It is difficult, however, to say how those processes or acts which are summed to constitute consciousness differ from merely physiological processes which are not part thereof. See **act. 4.** that which can be **introspected. 5.** the subjective correlate of certain of the higher neural activities. **6.** a verbal—or, more often, a subverbal—commentary on one's own behavior. ➤Behaviorists contend that it is this to which other psychologists *refer* when they use the term, however they define it. **7.** (*psychoan.*) = the **conscious (5).**

➤Consciousness has many other shades of meaning, few of them explicitly defended or consistently used. Because of stubbornly persistent confusions, the term has lost usefulness and should be replaced in technical discussion. (But some of its informal usages are probably unavoidable—even by psychologists.) Its denial on semantic grounds does *not* imply the essentially metaphysical denial of a class of phenomena which, albeit with much confusion, was formerly described or denoted by the term. But that class of phenomena—if there is one—will be more clearly delimited if a less confused term is employed to name it.—See **act, conscious, psychic, self, person.**

consciousness/field of: that of which a person is aware at any one time; the objects to which one is reacting differentially. —*Syn.* FIELD OF AWARENESS, (often) **field of *attention, phenomenal *field, behavior field.**

consciousness/fringe of: see **fringe of consciousness.**

consciousness/marginal: awareness that is unclear, faint. ➤The analogy is to the appearance of objects when not directly looked at.

consciousness/motor theory of: see **motor theory of consciousness.**

consciousness of kind: awareness of characteristics in other persons similar to one's own.

consciousness/stream of: (*W. James*) personal experience likened to a stream to emphasize its continuity, in contrast to its conception as a series of discrete states. ➤The term now appears more often in literature than in psychology.

consciousness/subliminal: any mental process too weak to be **introspected,** yet affecting behavior.

consensual eye reflex: contraction in the pupil of the shaded eye when a bright light is flashed in the other. ➤*Syn.* CONSENSUAL LIGHT REFLEX.

consensual validation: the determination that something is real, not illusory, by the fact of agreement between the perceiving of several persons.

consensus: *n.* **1.** a working together of more than one **sense;** the information gained by such a combination: e.g., that of taste and smell to yield **flavor,** or of vision and vestibular function to perceive bodily motion. **2.** the working together of the two eyes. **3.** a decision participated in by all the members of a group and representing the maximum area of common acceptance. ➤Acceptance does not imply agreement; one may accept a decision as the best obtainable, though believing that a better plan is conceivable.—*Syn.* SENSE OF THE MEETING. **4.** the state in a social group when the members have common cognitions, feelings, attitudes, or behaviors, and perceive this communality; or the degree of mutually recognized congruence in attitude toward an object or objects: PERCEIVED CONSENSUS. **5.** (*H. S. Sullivan*) an attribute of experience when it refers to what can be confirmed by the senses of more than one person; that which is objectively verifiable. —*adj.* **consensual.**

consent: *n.* voluntary concurrence with an action (by oneself or another) proposed by another person. ➤*Distg. fr.* ASSENT, the acceptance of another's judgment; and *fr.* DECISION, which is selection of a course of action, or of an answer in a problem situation, irrespective of suggestion from others.

consentience: *n.* (*M. Jahoda*) agreement with a position or attitude as a result of relevant evidence or other considerations. —*Cp.* **consent.**—*Distg. fr.* **conformance, convergence (5), compliance.**

consequence: *n.* **1.** (*logic*) the fact that two propositions, the ANTECEDENT and the CONSEQUENT, are so related logically that the former validates the latter. **2.** the fact that two phenomena are so related dynamically that the consequent always follows the antecedent. (But the reverse does not follow: a given phenomenon may have alternative antecedents, hence a particular antecedent may not be inferred from a consequent.)

conservation: *n.* proposed but little used synonym for **retention.** ➤Conservation is freer of theoretical implications.

conservation of effect/principle of = **use/law of.**

conservatism: *n.* tendency to adhere to established ways of behaving. ➤It is debatable to what extent the tendency is general or specific.

conserve/cultural: see **cultural conserve.**

consistency: *n.* sometimes used as an informal synonym for **reliability.**

consistency coefficient = **internal consistency coefficient.**

consistency coefficient/inter-item = **alpha coefficient.**

consistency index: 1. a means of determining the extent to which the members of a group give the same responses to the same stimulus or task after a stated time:

$$i = \sqrt{\frac{1}{N} \Sigma \cos \pi - \frac{(BC)^{1/2}}{(AD)^{1/2} + (BC)^{1/2}}}$$

where A = no. of responses both times; D = no. of responses omitted or denied both times; B and C = no. of responses present one time and not the other, respectively; i = consistency index. 2. = coefficient of *reliability, esp. the internal consistency coefficient. ➤This usage is confusing.

consistency/internal: a criterion of the utility of a test which consists in determining the extent to which the items are homogeneous in the sense of measuring the same variable. ➤One procedure—usually not practicable—is to find the average intercorrelation between items. As a substitute, it is common to correlate each item with the total score, perhaps correcting for overlap.—*Cp.* **cumulative scale.** The **internal consistency coefficient** (which see) has a somewhat more restricted meaning.

consolidation theory: (*learning*) the theory that the psychophysiological changes that constitute learning continue for a time after the cessation of the learning activities. —*Syn.* PERSEVERATION THEORY (of learning).

consonance: *n.* (*music*) a combination of tones that blend or fuse pleasantly; one end of the consonance-**dissonance** dimension.

consonant: *n.* a speech sound, or a letter representing the sound, that is produced by some obstruction to the breath.—*Cp.* **vowel.**

consonant association: in the association experiment, replying with a word similar in sound to the stimulus word.—*Syn.* **clang association.**

constancy: *n.* In view of the many uses of **constancy,** a qualifier should generally be supplied. See the following entries, but esp. **constancy/object.**

constancy attitude: the attitude that there are certain "true" one-to-one relationships between variables which it is the purpose of an experiment to lay bare. ➤E.g., it might assume a direct and invariate relationship between speed of performance and accuracy. The contrasting RELATIVITY ATTITUDE would take the view that there is no one or "true" relationship, that the relationship of speed and accuracy may vary with the difficulty of the task.

constancy/brightness: see **constancy/object.**

constancy/form: see **constancy/object.**

constancy hypothesis: the postulate that there is a strict parallelism or correspondence between the local or **proximal** stimulus and the sensory response (or sensation), so that the sensory response always occurs unaltered to the same stimulus no matter what the attendant circumstances. ➤The theory is attributed by Gestalt theorists to their opponents; in its strict form it is probably held by no one.—*Distg. fr.* **object *con**stancy,** which has almost the opposite meaning.—See **constancy attitude.**

constancy/object or /**perceptual:** the fact that perceptual objects retain a certain standard (or normal) appearance, in considerable independence of surrounding stimuli and also of the component stimuli making up the perceptual pattern. ➤A chair is seen as a chair despite considerable differences in the stimulus pattern on the retina as the viewer changes position relative to it; an orange is seen as that color even when seen in a blue light. ¶The constancy is not perfect but a matter of degree. The degree of constancy, moreover, depends in part upon the stimulus. COLOR, FORM, MAGNITUDE, and WEIGHT CONSTANCIES are named, but any perceptual quality may have some sort of constancy. ¶ Note that **object constancy** is contradictory to the **constancy hypothesis.**

constancy of organism: the hypothesized tendency of the organism to return to its "average state" after stimulation.—*Syn.* homeostasis.

constancy of the IQ: the degree to which changes are found from year to year in a given child's IQ as determined by a specified scale. ➤**Constancy of the IQ** is not interpreted by psychologists—as some laymen have thought—as meaning that each person is endowed with a fixed or constant potentiality for intellectual growth. The term refers simply to the *amount* of change found in test scores when the test is repeated after a considerable interval (6 months or more).

constancy/perceptual: see **constancy/object:**

constant: *n.* a value that remains unchanged under all conditions relevant to the investigation.—*Ant.* **variable.**—*adj.* constant.

constant/absolute or /**numerical:** a quantity that retains the same value or magnitude in all situations. E.g., π has the same value (viz., 3.1416) in every circle and in all mathematical computations.

constant/arbitrary: a quantity to which any one of various values may be assigned, the assigned value then remaining fixed throughout an investigation.

constant error: 1. a departure from the correct or true value of a measure, or of a representative value, that results from a distorting factor working relatively consistently in a given direction. ➤E.g., some subjects persistently judge as larger the right-hand member of a pair of nearly equal objects (= constant **space error**) ; and most persons persistently attribute to themselves a greater degree of approved qualities than others do. **2.** the effect on a single measure of an invariable distorting factor.—*Distg. fr.* **variable error.**—*Syn.* CUMULATIVE ERROR, SYSTEMATIC ERROR, BIASED ERROR.

constant method = **constant stimulus method.**

constant process: a method of computing a threshold that assumes that the best measure is the median of the theoretical normal **ogive** which comes nearest to the observed distribution.—*Syn.* MÜLLER-URBAN METHOD, URBAN PROCESS.—*Contr. w.* **constant stimulus method.**

constant R method: an obsolete abbreviation for **constant stimulus method.** (R = Reiz, *Ger.* for *stimulus.*)

constant/statistical: see **statistical constant.**

constant stimulus method: a **psychophysical method** for determining accuracy of discrimination or judgment. ➤A "standard," or invariable, object or stimulus of any sort—the constant stimulus (formerly *abbr.* as constant R)—is presented for comparison in some given respect with each of a series of similar stimuli, presented in chance order. From the percentage of correct judgments rendered on each comparison stimulus, a **threshold** is mathematically determined.—*Syn.* METHOD OF RIGHT AND WRONG CASES.

constellation: *n.* **1.** any fairly inclusive and organized grouping of phenomena. **2.** a complex organization of ideas that is charged with emotion and tends toward certain kinds of action. ➤The constellation is a **sentiment** with emphasis upon the cognitive component. The term is occasionally used in psychoanalysis for a structure that resembles a **complex** but is unrepressed.

constellation/family: see **family constellation.**

constitution: *n.* **1.** the nature of anything; the organized totality of qualities in relation to each other. **2.** specif., the enduring and relatively constant *bodily* qualities, or the *bodily* and *mental* qualities, of an organism considered as constituting a unity. ➤Most usages conform to one of the above definitions. But there the agreement ends. One group of authors (chiefly medical) use **constitution** for the hereditary characters of an organism. Another group take the opposite line; for them, **constitution** is the **phenotype.**—See **constitutional type.**

constitutional: *adj.* **1.** pertaining to a person's **constitution** or nature; hence, char-

acterizing an enduring personal attribute. **2.** of behavior considered as determined primarily by **constitution (2)** rather than by situational factors. ➤CONSTITUTIONAL DISORDERS are those believed to be rooted in some enduring organic impairment or **deficiency.** They are thus contrasted with **functional disorders** and with temporary troubles. Often the unstated assumption is that the impairment is hereditary. ORGANIC DISORDER is less ambiguous.—See **functional disorders.**

constitutional (psychopathic) inferior: a person with some severely handicapping queerness not due directly to feeblemindedness or physical handicap. There is inadaptability, ineptness, poor judgment, lack of stamina, social unattractiveness, odd emotional response (or lack of response).—*Syn.* (*Stan. Psychiat.*) **inadequate personality.**

constitutional type: 1. a constellation of enduring personal qualities—anatomical; or anatomical, physiological, and psychological—believed to constitute a natural grouping, and forming the basis of a classification of individuals.—See **type. 2.** a pattern of behavior characteristics (as in 1) supposed to be correlated with a pattern of bodily characters. ➤See **body *type.** For a concrete illustration of one among many systems of constitutional types, see **ectomorphic. 3.** *abbr.* form for MENTAL DEFECTIVE, CONSTITUTIONAL TYPE: a person whose deficiency is supposed to arise from defective morphological development of the brain.—*Syn.* (for 3) **clinical type** (not *recom.*).

constitution-specific: *adj.* of behavior determined in major part by **genotypical** factors not general in the species. ➤The constitutional-specific may be common to small groups: e.g., it may be familial. *Contr. w.* **species-specific.**

constrained association: in an **association test,** a defined relation of the response to the stimulus word; the opposite of **free *association.**

constraint (kən·strānt') : *n.* compelling another, or oneself, to act or to refrain from action. ➤*Syn.* **restraint, compulsion, coercion,** all of which share the idea of force exerted against will, wish, or consent. Such force need not be physical. In restraint or constraint, sometimes in compulsion, it may be exerted either by the self or by others; coercion is usually exercised against others. Compulsion and coercion are likely to be exerted by persons, constraint and restraint by impersonal agents as well. Constraint implies forcible restriction and confinement of action; restraint implies its actual hindrance.—*Cp.* **compulsion.**—*v.* **constrain.**

constriction: *n.* **1.** lack of spontaneity or freedom in response; inflexibility.—*Cp.* **rigidity. 2.** more specif. (particularly in projective tests), the quality of being narrowly determined by *external* factors, thus giving prosaic, stereotyped, and limited responses to the stimulus material. **3.** (*Ror.*) a category for a person who, though of at least average intelligence, gives more than 50 per cent *F* responses.

construct (kon'strukt): *n.* a property ascribed to at least two objects as a result of scientific observation and comparison; a concept, formally proposed, with definition and limits explicitly related to empirical data. ➤As compared with **concept**, a construct is a planfully designed **model**, with full awareness of the relationships between the data and the model. A construct is likely, moreover, to be a fully articulated model, with relationships indicated in detail. Although a concept may be very complex and intricate, it is likely to be somewhat globally characterized. But any fully scientific concept is a construct; the distinction between the two terms seems chiefly a matter of degree.

A proposal that seems to be gaining ground is the restriction of **construct** to an inferred entity or **hypothetical *construct.** That is, it is to be conceived as actually existing and as giving rise to measurable phenomena, including phenomena other than the observables that led to hypothesizing the construct. In this sense, construct contrasts with **intervening *variable** (which see).

construct/constellatory: (*G. A. Kelly*) a construct which determines that the members of the construct shall also belong to another realm or construct. ➤E.g., the construct *Afghan* does not inherently carry the meaning of *treacherous* (a different construct) but may cause some persons to think of an individual Afghan as treacherous. **Stereotyped** or **typological** thinking uses constellatory constructs.

construct/core: (*G. A. Kelly*) a construct that governs in part the way in which a person maintains himself in his environment.

construct/empirical: see **empirical construct.**

construct/hypothetical: a **construct** referring to an entity or process that is inferred as actually existing (though not at present fully observable) and as giving rise to measurable phenomena, including phenomena other than the observables that led to hypothesizing the construct. ➤The hypothetical construct is said to have "surplus meaning." Thus, an attitude, inferred from the behavior of stating one's preferences on an attitude questionary, is con-

ceived as having certain other, predictable consequences: a person with a strong attitude of support for civil liberties will manifest predictable behavior in respect to ethnic segregation. A **habit,** a **conditioned response,** a **belief,** a **sentiment** are all usually conceived as hypothetical constructs. The construct may be either a **hypothetical *process variable** or a **hypothetical *state variable.** It contrasts with **intervening *variable** (which see).

construction need: (*H. A. Murray*) the need to organize and build things, to produce.

constructive: *adj.* **1.** done by construction; characterizing that which is put together. **2.** pertaining to a **construct.** ➤CONSTRUCTIVE EXPLANATION searches for or designs constructs as the central element in scientific explanation. **3.** (*semipop.*) beneficial; tending to build up rather than tear down.

constructive explanation: see **constructive (2).**

constructive play: play activity in which the results show a greater degree of structure than the materials out of which they are made.

construct/pre-emptive: (*G. A. Kelly*) a construct whose **elements** belong to it exclusively; an "all-or-none" or "nothing-but" construct. ➤For many people, sin is a pre-emptive construct: if a given act is a sin, it is nothing else but a sin.

construct/preverbal: (*G. A. Kelly*) one that has no word symbol, or none that is consistent. ➤It may or may not have originated before the person learned to talk.

construct/regnant: (*G. A. Kelly*) a superordinate construct that assigns its **elements** (2) uniquely to subordinate constructs.

consultant/psychological: a person providing advice and counsel to organizations on their psychological problems. ➤The term has broader connotations than **consulting psychologist,** which has come to mean helping with the problems of individuals.

consulting psychologist: a professional psychologist with special education and qualifications who studies individuals to determine their educational and vocational needs, or to assist them in correcting maladjusted behavior or mental ill-health. ➤Usually a consulting psychologist serves on a fee basis, but is sometimes employed by an organization to give counsel to persons within or served by it.—*Distg. fr* **consultant/psychological.**

consummatory response: a response that following a series of **preparatory responses,** brings the organism into adjustment with the initiating situation, thus concluding the act or series of responses.

contact: *n.* any kind of social interaction

➤PRIMARY CONTACT is face to face and personal; SECONDARY CONTACT lacks intimacy and involves only a relatively small part of the personalities of the interacting individuals: e.g., ordinary contact with a salesclerk.

contagion/mass: the spread of behaviors among large numbers of people who are not gathered in one place or not identified with one another. ➤Such behaviors are said to be inhibited to a lesser degree by forces of moral prohibition or legal condemnation.

contagion/social: the spontaneous imitation, by other persons in a group, of a behavior initiated by one member but without overtly shown intention to stimulate such imitation.—*Distg. fr.* direct **influence,** in which a person manifestly intends to affect the behavior of another or others.

contamination: *n.* **1.** (*exper.* and *testing*) allowing the variable that is to be validated to influence the variable used for validation. ➤E.g., if a pupil's class standing is determined in part by the teacher's knowledge of his score on a test, there will be a spuriously high correlation between class standing and test score, and the class standing is a CONTAMINATED CRITERION of the test's validity (and of the validity of other tests having high correlation with the first test). Similarly, the experimenter's knowledge of which subjects belong to the experimental and which to the control group may lead him to **contaminate** his results by unwittingly treating the two groups differently, thus destroying the usefulness of comparing them. **2.** (*Ror.*) combining into one response two associations with the inkblot that would ordinarily be distinct: e.g., a certain part of an inkblot "looks like a field of green turnips on fire."—*v.* **contaminate.**

contamination of speech: amalgamation of part of one word with part of another: e.g., "gruesor" as a combination of *gruesome* and *sorrowful.*

contemporaneity principle: (*K. Lewin*) the postulate that only present facts can influence present behavior.—*Syn.* AHISTORICAL PRINCIPLE. ➤Past events have influence only as they modified (in the past) the constituent factors of the present.

content (kən·tent'): *adj.* satisfied with what one has; not desiring a change, at least not enough to do anything to bring one about.

content (kon'tent): *n.* all that is contained in something; whatever constitutes something. ➤In the singular, the several constituents are taken collectively (but not necessarily as an *organized* totality): the dream *content.* In the plural, reference is to the single items distributively: the *contents* of a purse.—See **content/conscious.**

content analysis: discovering and listing according to a systematic plan the ideas, feelings, truth claims, and personal references in a communication; the objective tabulation of the frequency with which certain elements occur in a certain communication. ➤The elements tabulated may be certain syntactical forms (verbs vs. nouns, past vs. present tense, etc.), certain kinds of meanings (words expressing distaste, words drawn from the vocabulary of a trade), or certain levels of complexity (simple gestures, complex gestures). The communication may be in words, pictures, gestures, musical signs, singing, etc. A definite set of categories is provided, along with a set of rules for deciding how to categorize each element of content. The process of assigning an element to one or more categories is called **coding.** Only the **manifest** *content of the communication is analyzed; interpretation of **latent** *content is a distinct process. Thus, the occurrence of words referring to anger may be tabulated as part of content analysis; but the inference that the author was angry is not analysis but interpretation.

content/animal or *A*: see **animal content.**

content/communication: the body of **meanings** that are transmitted by means of **symbols** from one person to another.

content/conscious or /**mental:** that which is "in the mind"; that of which one is aware at any moment; that which can be introspectively reported; a mental item or datum, or all the mental data collectively present at one time. ➤In **structural** (or **content**) **psychology,** psychology is defined as the scientific study of such content. Some authors make the content identical with the object of consciousness together with its qualities; others contrast these two, only the qualities being mental content. For Titchener, mental content was a **process;** others use process for the mental **act** that results in apprehending a content. The differences are not primarily in the area of semantics—i.e., to what facts we agree to refer by the term—but in that of philosophical postulates.

content/founded: see **Gestaltqualität.**

content/latent: see **content/manifest.**

content/manifest: (*psychoan.*) **1.** any idea, feeling, or impulse considered as the conscious expression of an unreportable or **repressed** motive, which in this connection is spoken of as the LATENT CONTENT. ➤The term stems from the interpretation of dreams, in which the dream story or picture is the manifest content. But any conscious process may be spoken of as manifest content when it is desired to emphasize its relation to unconscious process.—*Cp.* **dream content. 2.** that which is directly stated in a communication, in contrast with the inferred significance or LATENT CONTENT. ➤When "the lady doth protest too much," her direct words of protest are the manifest content, her unacknowledged feelings the latent content. A latent content may also be intentionally suggested: a diplomatic communication is often intended to mean more than it says.

content/mental: see **content/conscious.**

content psychology: the study of mental content, of that which is in the mind or in consciousness, of that which can be introspectively observed. ➤**Structural psychology** and **phenomenology** are two different forms of content psychology. The data are sensations, thoughts, probably feelings (but some believe feelings are not content), and perhaps volitions. Mental contents were the central target of **behaviorism**, which denied their existence or at least their scientific validity. Much of the older content psychology is now being revived but in a matrix of response-oriented psychology.

content response: (*Ror.*) what the subject reports that he "sees" on the inkblot card. ➤Content response is a scoring category used to distinguish the "objects" reported as "seen" from what is said about them or the manner in which they are reported.

content subject: (*educ.*) a field for study in which mastery consists mainly in acquiring information and understanding, in contrast with "skill subjects" such as reading or handwriting.

context: *n.* 1. the words and phrases used with a particular verbal symbol that help to determine what it conveys. 2. according to the CONTEXT THEORY, those psychological processes which "surround," or are associated with, a given mental process. —See **meaning/context theory of.** 3. the particular circumstances which, at any given time, surround a person or an event and influence his behavior.—*Syn.* (for 3) **surround** (when highly specific circumstances are meant); **environment** (as a very general term). 4. (*G. A. Kelly*) = CONTEXT OF A CONSTRUCT, all those **elements**—i.e., things, objects, or events—that a user *ordinarily* sorts out and discriminates by means of a **construct.**

context/law of: 1. the principle that words, phrases, or statements take on meaning in relation to the situation in which they are found; or, more generally, that the perceived qualities of any item are in part determined by its **surrounds.** 2. the generalization that the degree of **retention** is a function of the similarity between the original learning situation and the retention situation.

contiguity: *n.* nearness of two objects in space or time; or, nearness of two experi-

ences or behaviors in time.—*adj.* **contiguous.**

contiguity/law of: the general principle that togetherness in time is a necessary condition under which psychological phenomena become dynamically connected—i.e., under which learning occurs. The principle is differently stated, in various systematic accounts of learning: (*a*) If two psychological phenomena occur at the same time or in close succession, the recurrence of one tends to bring back the other.—*Syn.* principle of **redintegration.** (*b*) A stimulus acquires effectiveness in eliciting a response when it occurs at the same time as the response. If it is held that such simultaneity is the sufficient condition, this constitutes the CONTIGUITY THEORY OF LEARNING. (*c*) If a stimulus is presented with another when the latter is evoking its characteristic response, the first stimulus acquires capacity to evoke that response.—See **associationism, conditioning,** both of which embody contiguity as a necessary condition.—*Distg. fr.* **continuity.**

contiguity theory of learning: see **contiguity/law of,** *b.*

continence: *n.* 1. self-restraint from excessive or illicit sex activity. 2. the ability to retain urine or other discharges.—*Ant.* **incontinence.**

contingency: *n.* (*stat.*) the extent to which the values of a variable depend on another variable or variables.

contingency coefficient or *C*: a measure of the extent to which one set of data is found associated with another set more often than is to be expected by chance when each is expressed in several categories. As a measure of **correlation,** it does not assume that the successive categories are intervals on a continuous variable; they may be qualitative categories. The **mean square contingency coefficient,** ϕ^2, measures the same correlation. The two coefficients are related according to the formula:

$$C = [\phi^2(1 + \phi^2)]^{1/2}, \text{ where } \phi^2 = \frac{x^2}{N}.$$

contingency method: (*stat.*) a method of measuring the degree to which two variables occur together, by taking a function of the differences between the actual frequencies in the cells of a two-way table and the frequencies that would be expected if the two variables were independent.

contingency table: a **two-way table** showing the frequencies of occurrence of the **classes** or categories indicated by the horizontal row and by the vertical column of the cells.—*Syn.* CROSS-CLASSIFICATION TABLE.

contingency table/compound: a contingency table that has two or more variables in at least one of its two principal dimensions.

contingent: *adj.* dependent upon some other event which may or may not happen; possible, but not certain, to occur. ➤*Contr. w.* **conditioned,** dependent upon something that has occurred. (Hence, the conditioned must also actually occur.) The contingent lies between the **necessary** and the **independent.**

continuity: *n.* the state of being **continuous;** uninterrupted succession, connection, or relation; a variable every moment of which is connected with neighboring moments by infinitesimal steps. The **continuity** may be in space, time, or logical relationship.—See **continuum.**

continuity of the germ plasm: the doctrine that in higher organisms the specific reproductive cells are derived from other reproductive cells (not from cells differentiated into other bodily structures), and that environmental influences on other bodily tissues do not affect the hereditary potentials of the germ cells.

continuity/personality: 1. the fact that in the development of personality many traits change slowly and by imperceptible degrees, so that at any time the individual is recognizably the same. ➤This continuity is consistent with the fact that behavior is often constrained by circumstances rather than determined primarily by personal traits. Continuity of total personality is consistent also with radical change in a few traits. **2.** the theory that in a large population the distribution of a personality trait is **continuous**—i.e., that variation is by very many small steps; or the theory that personalities differ by continuous variation.— *Contr. w.* **discontinuity, typology. 3.** = TRAIT CONTINUITY, the view that one trait grades over into another by a continuous series.

continuity/principle of: a generalization that, to pass from one designated state to another, it is necessary to pass through all intermediate states or conditions. ➤This requires specification of what is "intermediate," a requirement of some difficulty in psychology.—*Distg. fr.* **continuity theory.**

continuity theory of learning: the hypothesis that, in discrimination learning, there is an increment of learning (whether measurable or not) for every rewarded response to the stimulus. ➤Opposed to the **discontinuity** (or noncontinuity) **theory,** which holds that no *relevant* learning takes place until the animal hits upon, and attends to, that aspect of the total situation which is related to the required discrimination.

continuity/trait: see **continuity/personality (3).**

continuous: *adj.* changing by infinitesimal increments, i.e., by steps so small as to be separately unnoticeable; capable of being infinitely subdivided without break or irregularity. ➤An unbroken line, straight or curved, is **continuous** and is often used to represent other **continuous** variables.—See **continuum.**—*Ant.* discrete, discontinuous.

continuous reinforcement or **reward:** see **reinforcement/intermittent.**

continuous series: see **continuum.**

continuous variable = **continuum.**

continuous variation: a change that is **continuous** at all times. ➤It is usually represented by an unbroken line or, if regular, by the equation of the line. See **continuum.**

continuum *n., pl.* **continua, continuums:** a **variable** such that between any two values, no matter how close together they may be, it is always possible to have a third value; a CONTINUOUS VARIABLE.—See **continuous.** ➤**Continuum** is used when it is desired to refer to the **variable** itself: Pleasantness and unpleasantness form a single *continuum*. **Continuous variation,** nearly synonymous, is used to emphasize the change in the variable: There is a *continuous variation* from red to yellow. A CONTINUOUS SERIES has consecutive steps or values, each measurably distinct but believed to be separated (or connected—which in this context means the same thing) by an infinite number of intervening steps, so that the series is to be conceived as part of a continuum or continuous variation. ¶Virtually all psychological measures are, on the surface, **discontinuous;** many but not all are believed to form a continuous series—i.e., to represent a variable that is actually **continuous.** Most statistical procedures assume such continuous variation and may not properly be used unless the data do come from a continuous series.

continuum/polar: see **polar continuum.**

contour: *n.* the outline or boundary of a plane figure or solid body. ➤Used metaphorically when psychological processes are described in geometric terms.

contraception: *n.* voluntary limitation of offspring by artificially preventing the sperm cell from fertilizing the ovum. ➤A form of **birth control** not to be confused with **abortion.**

contractility: *n.* a fundamental property of living tissue whereby it draws together as a result of stimulation.—*Cp.* **irritability,** which includes **contractility,** as well as glandular or chemical activity.

contraction: *n.* the shortening of a muscle. ➤Such contraction is TETANIC when it is continuous, PHASIC when it occurs at regular intervals (in phases), TONIC when it merely maintains the parts of the organism in their normal position or condition, ready for more definite intense contraction. A con-

tracted muscle is said to be under **tension**.
—*Ant*. **relaxation**.—*v*. **contract** (-trakt′).
contract plan: a method of organizing a
school whereby the subject matter for the
year is subdivided into a number of relatively extensive instructional units to be
completed at stated intervals by each pupil,
working largely by himself. A given unit
contract may provide only for minimum
essentials or may include additional work
for faster learners.

contracture (kən·trak′chər): *n*. failure,
temporary or permanent, of a muscle to
relax or to return to its former normal
length.

contradiction: *n*. **1**. (*logic*) the relation
between two propositions such that if one
is false the other is true, and (therefore
necessarily) vice versa. **2**. a statement that
is directly opposed to a previous statement.
➤If the two statements are made by the
same person, they are SELF-CONTRADICTORY.
—*Cp*. **contrary**.—*adj*. **contradictory**.

contradiction/law of or **/principle of:** the
logical principle that "a thing is not other
than itself"; or that "A is not non-A." It is
the second of the three fundamental **laws
of *thought**. It is more often called the
LAW OF NONCONTRADICTION.

contradictory: *n*. either of two propositions
so related that if one is true, the other is
false, and vice versa.

contralateral: *adj*. pertaining to the opposite side. ➤*Cp*. **ipsilateral**.

contralateral reflex = crossed reflex.

contrary (kon′trer·i): *adj*. of the relation
between two propositions such that if one
is true, the other cannot be true, though
both may be false. ➤*Distg. fr*. **contradictory**. Contrary is loosely used for any sort
of logical opposition or contrast.

contrast (kon′trast): *n*. **1**. heightened awareness of difference resulting from bringing
together two items of any sort, either
simultaneously or in close succession (SI-
MULTANEOUS or SUCCESSIVE CONTRAST). **2**.
= **color contrast**.—*v*. **contrast** (kən·-
trast′): to bring out or emphasize differences between two items by putting them
close together.

contrast/brightness or **/brilliance:**
heightening of the apparent difference in
brightness between two visual sense data
when they are presented together or in close
succession.

contrast/chromatic: heightening of the apparent difference in **hue** or **saturation** (or
both) when two visual sense data are presented together or in close succession.—See
color contrast.

contrast/color: see **color contrast**.

contrast flicker: flicker that is induced in
a physically constant field by a neighboring
flicker.

contrast illusion: see **illusion/associa-
tive**.

contrast/law of: one of the four laws of
association: that thinking about any special quality or character tends to remind
one of its opposite. Later **associationism**
regarded this as a special case of **contiguity**.

contrast/marginal: an accentuated type of
simultaneous **color contrast** that occurs in
regions close to the boundary between two
contrasting areas.

contrasuggestibility: *n*. the tendency of a
person to adopt an opposite attitude or
action from that suggested to him by
another.—*Distg. fr*. **countersuggestion**.—*Syn*. **negativism**, CONTRARY SUG-
GESTIBILITY.

contravention: *n*. a form of social interaction midway between competition and
conflict.

contrectation (kon″trek·tā′shən): *n*. tendency to approach, touch, and fondle another person, generally with genital tumescence.—*Syn*. (*pop*., and with many variant
meanings) petting.

control: *n*. **1**. = **experimental** or **scientific *control**. **2**. (*Ror*.) a characteristic
discerned in the subject's response to the
inkblots that is taken as an index to the
degree of non-**affective** determination of
behavior.

control analysis: (*psychoan*.) an **analysis**
(3) of a patient made by a trainee under
supervision of an experienced **analyst**.
➤*Distg. fr*. didactic ***analysis**, in which
the trainee is himself analyzed.

control center: see **sensory area**.

control/emotional = control/nervous.

control experiment: a repetition of an experiment, with or without intentional variations.—*Distg. fr*. **control/experimental**.—
See **control/scientific**.

control/experimental: 1. in the abstract,
intentional manipulation or modification of
the conditions under which observation is
to be made, including changes in the experimental or treatment variable. **2**. concretely,
any intentional modification of conditions
other than those of the experimental variable.—See **control/scientific**.

control group: a group as closely as possible equivalent to an experimental group,
and exposed to all the conditions of the
investigation except the experimental variable or treatment being studied. Such a
group should be representative of the population for which a generalization is to be
made.—See **control/scientific**.

control/hypnotic: the regulation of the
hypnotized person by the hypnotizer (who
is also sometimes called the control).

controlled association: see **association/
controlled**.

controlled-association test: see **association test**.

controlling idea: a thought that influences the associative sequence of further thoughts.

control/nervous or **/emotional**: more or less voluntary avoidance or regulation of excitement and **nervousness (2)**.

control/neural: regulation of a part of the body by a nerve center or special neural mechanism.

control/scientific: such regulation of conditions that the effect of a given supposed cause is clearly and unambiguously displayed.—*Syn.* EXPERIMENTAL CONTROL. ➤Included in this general meaning of scientific control is the systematic variation of the experimental (or treatment) variable (see **experiment**). When **control** is used concretely, however—i.e., for a particular control—it refers to any intentional modification of conditions *other than* in the experimental variable, such changes being made to insure that the effect being measured is really a function of the experimental variable.

From this concrete meaning of control we get **control group** and CONTROL EXPERIMENT, SERIES, or TEST. A control group consists of a number of persons who are not exposed to the experiment variable but are exposed to as many as possible of the other conditions in the experiment, the purpose being to insure that the effects under examination are *not* the result of differences in the persons. The control group should be representative of the **population** for which a generalization is to be made. ¶A CONTROL EXPERIMENT or SERIES or TEST is a repetition, with or without change in conditions other than those involved in repeating, to see whether the same cause-effect relations hold. The control experiment or series often includes checks on the functioning of the apparatus, the clarity of the instructions, changes in collateral conditions such as time of day. "Controll*ed* experiment" is redundant—all experiments are controlled. ¶The basic notion in control is negative; one seeks evidence that the experimental results are *not* due to irrelevant variables.

control series: see **control/scientific**.

control/social: regulation of conduct by social institutions and customs.

control/spirit: an alleged agency that determines behavior of a **medium** in **trance**. ➤Usually the "agency" claims, through the automatized activity of the medium, to be a departed spirit.

control/statistical: the correction of research data to allow for, or to eliminate, the *effects* of irrelevant factors that are known and measured but that cannot be directly removed.

control test: see **control/scientific**.

contusion: *n.* a bruise; an injury in which the skin is not broken.—*Distg. fr.* **concussion**.

convention: *n.* (*sociol.*) social custom, often recognized only tacitly, and not rigidly binding upon the members of a group; rules or prescriptions that lack the force of law or of the moral code but have the approval of the group. ➤A convention may be arbitrary chiefly in the interest of convenient uniformity, e.g., the graphing of the time units along the horizontal axis. But the word often implies unreasonable rigidity: slaves to *convention*.—*adj.* **conventional**.

conventionality: *n.* rigid and stereotyped adherence to social demands or pressures.

convergence: *n.* **1.** tendency toward one point; esp., position or movement of the eyes such that light from a single source falls on the two foveas; the turning of the eyes inward when viewing binocularly an object less than 20 feet away. **2.** inheritance of personal characteristics from both paternal and maternal ancestry. **3.** the postulate that no character may be deemed to result exclusively from either hereditary or acquired factors, but is the product of both. **4.** the coming together of nervous impulses from different sensory sources. **5.** (*M. Jahoda*) acceptance of an action that conflicts with a belief or attitude because the action is supported by what seem other and more powerful considerations. ➤E.g., acceptance of overemphasis upon football (believed to be antieducational) on the grounds that it will help college finances. *Cp.* **compliance, conformance, consentience**.

convergent vs. divergent phenomena: (*I. Langmuir*) **Convergent** events can be determined if we know the component causes. **Divergent** phenomena are indeterminate events due to a single happening. CHAIN REACTIONS are often made up of divergent phenomena. ➤The distinction resembles that of sufficient vs. necessary cause.

converse (kon'vērs): *n.* (*logic*) a proposition that results from the interchange of subject and predicate: *truth is beauty, and beauty is truth* are converse propositions. ➤Many fallacies result from assuming the truth of a converse proposition.—*adv.* **conversely**.

conversion: *n.* **1.** radical and relatively rapid change of belief or attitude, esp. of religious attitude, with or without a corresponding change in character or conduct. **2.** (*psychiat.*) the manifesting of a bodily symptom, such as paralysis or anesthesia, as a result of psychic conflict; = CONVERSION HYSTERIA. ➤Many psychiatrists now limit the term to bodily symptoms controlled by the central nervous system. Where the symptoms are controlled by the autonomic system, they speak of VEGETATIVE NEUROSIS or of PSYCHO-PHYSIOLOGIC AUTONOMIC AND VISCERAL DISORDER (*Stan. Psychiat.*). **3.** (*logic*) the interchange of subject and predicate of a proposition—a fallacious operation unless certain conditions are fulfilled.—See **converse.**

conversion of affect: (*psychoan.*) the symbolic representation of a psychic conflict, or of that which causes conflict, in motor or sensory manifestations. ➤The symbolic representation is considered to be a means whereby the repressed instinctual desire gains external expression. Often the expression is of such nature that it not only can itself evade **censorship** but help maintain it. It is a symptom of conversion hysteria (see **conversion** 2) but may be so mild as hardly to be classified as such.

conversion of scores: changing a series of scores into another series having a different unit of measurement: e.g., from inches to millimeters, or from **raw scores** to **derived scores.**

conversion reaction or **symptom:** see **conversion (2).**

conviction: *n.* belief with no shadow of doubt. ➤The believer may admit (in a distinct mental process) that demonstrative evidence is lacking, but he is "firmly convinced all the same."—*v.* **convince.**

convolution: *n.* one of the irregular folds of the outer surfaces of the cerebrum. ➤*Syn.* **gyrus.** The several **convolutions** form the conventional landmarks of brain topography. The term is sometimes applied also to a fold of the cerebellum, for which **folium** is preferred.

convulsion: *n.* pathological, involuntary, and extensive muscular contractions. ➤*Contr. w.* **spasm,** a localized contraction; **clonus,** a slow, repeated contraction; and **fit,** a succession of convulsions.

convulsive therapy or **treatment:** induced **convulsion** by drugs, esp. insulin, or by electric shock, as part of the treatment of mental disorder.—*Syn.* **shock therapy.**

coolth: *n.* the sensation of coolness.

cooperation: *n.* **1.** the working together of two or more units to produce some common or joint effect. ➤The units may be bodily organs (such as muscles), individuals in a social group, or forces operating together. **2.** a euphemism for obedience or compliance: *the subjects cooperated well* (i.e., they obeyed instructions).—*adj.* **cooperative,** of persons willing to work together, or actually doing so, in pursuit of a common goal.

cooperation/antagonistic: see **antagonistic cooperation.**

coordinate (kō·ôr′də·nit; -nāt): *adj.* **1.** equal in rank or position in a hierarchy;

neither subordinate nor superior. **2.** related to a system of **coordinates.**—*v.* (-nāt). **3.** see **coordination (1). 4.** to place elements in an order that corresponds with a prescribed pattern; to define a concept by its position in relation to other concepts, as one defines a point by reference to **axes** of co-ordination. **5.** to place a concept in a context of related facts and/or of other concepts.

coordinates: *n. pl.* **1.** points or lines by reference to which something is located in space. ➤Also used metaphorically for other than spatial locations: e.g., "most of an adolescent's behavior can be referred to the twin *coordinates* of parental control and his desire for independence." **2.** the abscissa value and the ordinate value of a point. ➤They are usually written in parentheses, the abscissa first, separated by a comma: e.g. (27, 16).—See **axis.**

coordinates/oblique: a system for uniquely locating any point in a plane by stating its distances from each of two lines that intersect obliquely.—*Syn.* OBLIQUE AXES.—*Distg. fr.* rectangular *coordinates.

coordinates/rectangular: a system of uniquely locating any point in a plane by stating its distance from each of two lines that intersect at right angles.—See **axis.**—*Syn.* CARTESIAN COORDINATES.—*Distg. fr.* oblique *coordinates.

coordination: *n.* **1.** the harmonious combination or working together of parts, esp. of parts or aspects of an act or of muscular movements (MUSCULAR or MOTOR COORDINATION). **2.** the arrangement of data in classes that are at the same level of subordination to a more inclusive class.—*v.* **coordinate.**

coordination/eye: the working together of the two eyes to attain a fused visual impression of a single object.

coorientation: *n.* (*T. M. Newcomb*) simultaneous possession of (**cognitive** and/or **cathectic**) attitudes by two or more individuals toward one another and toward some object(s), with mutual awareness of the possession of these attitudes. The attitudes need not be congruent; the individuals simply are oriented to the same objects.

coping behavior: (*A. Maslow*) action that enables one to adjust to the environmental circumstances, to get something done. ➤*Contr. w.* EXPRESSIVE BEHAVIOR, which is behavior for its own sake or for enjoyment. **Coping behavior** and **operant *behavior** refer to nearly, but not quite, the same kinds of activity.

copro-: a combining form meaning *excrement, filth, obscenity.*

coprolagnia (kop″rō·lag′ni·ə): *n.* sex excitement induced by sight or thought of feces.

coprolalia (-lā′li·ə): *n.* irresistible desire to use obscene words.

coprophagy (kɔp·rofʹə·ji): *n.* the eating of excrement, or, more generally, of filth.—*Syn.* COPROPHAGIA.

coprophilia: *n.* inordinate interest in feces.

coprophobia: *n.* fear of feces; or, more generally, of dirt or contamination. ➤In psychoanalysis, it is regarded as a defense against an unconscious love of excrement, or against a socially unacceptable desire.

copulation: *n.* sexual union; **coitus.**—*v.* **copulate.**

copy: *n.* **1.** an imitation or reproduction of an object or act. **2.** the pattern or model that is to be reproduced.—*v.* **3.** to make responses as like those of another person as possible, with conscious recognition of the similarity.—*Syn.* **imitate** (which may be unwitting).—*n.* **copying.**

copy theory: 1. the metaphysical theory that mental contents copy the qualities of the extramental or "real" world. **2.** the theory that memory consists of having images that copy previous mental contents. **3.** the theory that what we perceive is a replica of real objects.—*Syn.* PASSIVE REGISTRATION THEORY.

➤The term is so shot through with old metaphysics as to be unusable for psychology. But, although few philosophers or psychologists now hold to the first theory, it is so firmly rooted in "common sense" and popular vocabulary that it influences even those who reject it; both senses **(2)** and **(3)**, for example, reflect the metaphysics of **(1)**. Most psychologists postulate that there is something not wholly dependent upon the observer that plays a part in determining what is observed; but psychology need not assume that perception *copies* that independent factor. But *cp.* **isomorphism.**

cord = **spinal cord.**

cord block = spinal block.—See **block.**

core: *n.* (*counseling*) the essential element of a **counselee's** remark. It may be a feeling-attitude or a meaning, possibly not recognized by the counselee himself.

core curriculum: a course of study in which the contributions of some, or all, of the conventional subject matters (mathematics, history, languages, etc.) are related to a central "core," or topic of large scope, as the unifying activity. ➤The CORE COURSE is generally required of all pupils in a given grade or standard.

corium: *n.* the outer portion of the **derma;** or the whole of the derma.

cornea: *n.* the transparent outermost layer of the eye.

corneal reflection: a technique for studying eye movements by photographing a light reflected from the surface of the cornea.

Cornell method (of scale analysis): L. Guttman's method of determining **scalability.**

corollary: *n.* **1.** something proved as an indirect outcome of proving something else; hence, a law or principle, not itself directly proved, deduced from another. **2.** a natural consequence.—*adj.* **corollary.**

corpora: *n., pl.* of **corpus.**

corporal: *adj.* pertaining to the body. ➤E.g., CORPORAL PUNISHMENT is the infliction of pain on the body.—*Syn.* **somatic** (which see); bodily.—*Distg. fr.* **corporeal.**

corpora quadrigemina (kwod″ri·jemʹi·nə): *n. pl.* (*anat.*) the two pairs of rounded elevations on the dorsal surface of the midbrain, each of which is called a COLLICULUS. The INFERIOR COLLICULI contain centers for auditory reflexes; the SUPERIOR COLLICULI contain centers for visual reflexes.

corporate behavior = **group behavior (2).**

corporeal (kôr·pôrʹi·əl): *adj.* having a body; material rather than spiritual.—*Distg. fr.* **corporal.**

corpus *n., pl.* **corpora:** (*L.*) a body; or a distinct organ of a body. ➤A qualifying Latin word is added to name the particular organ, e.g., **corpus striatum,** and the term **corpus** is sometimes dropped: **corpus striatum** becomes **striatum.**

corpus callosum: see **callosum.**

corpuscle: *n.* **1.** a minute particle. **2.** a cell floating in blood or lymph. **3.** a small multicellular organ: e.g., the TOUCH CORPUSCLES in the skin.—*adj.* **corpuscular.**

corpus striatum (strī·āʹtəm) *n., pl.* **corpora striata** (-tə): a portion of the base of each cerebral hemisphere, composed of the caudate and lenticular nuclei and the **internal capsule.**—*Syn.* STRIATE BODY, STRIATUM, BASAL GANGLIA (which sometimes includes the thalamus).

correct associates method = **right associates procedure.**

correction: *n.* **1.** any change that remedies a mistake or error. **2.** helping a person to make his behavior conform to standards. ➤The colloquial use of this word for **punishment** implies a debatable conception of the value of punishment in helping a person to improve his behavior. **3.** fitting with lenses to correct visual defect. ➤VISION AFTER CORRECTION refers to amount of vision after maximum improvement from lenses, e.g., *vision after correction, 20/30.* **4.** (*stat.*) manipulation of a value or series of values, by means of an accepted principle, in order to minimize chance errors. **5.** the amount to be added or subtracted from a value to make it more accurate.

correction for attenuation: (*C. Spearman*) see **attenuation.**

correction for chance: deducting from the scores obtained on a test the amount which presumably might have been due to chance or pure guessing. ➤Thus 25 points might be subtracted from each score obtained on a 50-item true-false test, since half of the answers could be right by chance. The procedure rests on the false assumption that guessing and chance are the same. Moreover, it does not affect the rank order of the scores (though it may change the rank of an individual); it merely overemphasizes the relative size of the differences.

correctness: *n.* conformity to standards or requirements.—*Cp.* **accuracy** for related terms.

correlate: *n.* **1.** either of two things reciprocally related; a correlative. **2.** a principle or conclusion that is logically related to some other principle; by extension, a fact of which one feels sure because of other knowledge: *It is a correlate of his known honesty that he does not embezzle.*—See **eduction of correlates; correlation.**—*v.* **3.** to put a thing in relation to something else. **4.** to be in relation to something; to have a correlation coefficient different from zero. **5.** to compute a **correlation coefficient.**

correlated: *adj.* **1.** of either of two variables that does not have a zero correlation with the other; not statistically independent. —*Ant.* UNCORRELATED. **2.** of a variable whose coefficient of correlation with another has been computed.

correlation: *n.* **1.** (*logic*) relationship or dependence; the fact that two things or variables are so related that change in one is accompanied by a corresponding or parallel change in the other. ➤Positive change in one variable may accompany either positive or negative change in the other variable, or vice versa. **2.** (*stat.*) the tendency to concomitant variation; the degree to which two (or more) variables vary together. ➤The parallelism between the variables is usually imperfect; the measure of the degree of concomitance is the **correlation coefficient.** —*Syn.* **covariation. 3.** = correlation coefficient. **4.** (*neurol.*) the combination of neural impulses in specialized centers.—*Distg. fr.* **neurological** *correlation (which see).* **5.** the act or process of bringing two things into orderly relationship, or of considering them together in order to discern relationships; or the process of computing a statistical correlation. **6.** (*educ.*) an effort by teachers to have the pupils see the interrelationships between elements taught in separate subject matter classes. ➤It contrasts with **core curriculum,** in which the correlation is the basis of curriculum organization.

correlation/biserial or r_{bis}: a correlation in which one variable has only two divisions, classes, or steps, and the other has many classes: e.g., the correlation of height

tabulated in two classes, *tall* or *short*, with income tabulated in twenty income classes. It is assumed that the underlying distributions of both variables are **continuous** and **normal.**

correlation/bivariate = **correlation/ simple.**

correlation by ranks = **correlation/rank difference.**

correlation center: a place in the nervous system where two **afferent** impulses unite to exercise joint influence on an **efferent** impulse.

correlation/chance-halves: a method of estimating the reliability of a test or other variable by splitting it into comparable halves, correlating the scores of the two halves, and applying the **Spearman-Brown** (prophesy) **formula** to estimate the correlation. ➤There are various methods of choosing the halves to be as representative of the whole as possible; the most common is the ODD-EVEN METHOD, one half being composed of the even-numbered items, the other of the odd-numbered.—See **coefficient of *equivalence; reliability coefficient.**—*Syn.* SPLIT-HALVES CORRELATION.

correlation chart = **correlation table.**

correlation cluster: a group of variables with all possible correlations between them significantly positive. ➤This is the statistical basis for inferring a **surface *trait** or **syndrome.**—See **cluster analysis.**

correlation coefficient: (*stat.*) a number that indicates the strength of the tendency of two or more variables to vary concomitantly. ➤Perfect correspondence between the two is expressed by +1.00; perfect inverse correspondence is expressed by −1.00; complete lack of correspondence, i.e., independence of the two variables, is expressed by 0.00. Fractional values of the coefficient are not to be read as per cents. ¶The **product-moment *correlation** or *r* is most frequently used, and this coefficient is meant unless the context shows that an alternative method of computation has been employed.

correlation coefficient/first-order: see **first-order correlation coefficient.**

correlation/curvilinear: correlation in which **regression** is not **linear;** correlation in which regression is represented by a curved, rather than by a straight, regression line.—*Syn.* SKEW CORRELATION.—*Ant.* linear *correlation.—*Distg. fr.* correlation ratio.

correlation diagram = **scatter diagram.**

correlation/direct = **correlation/positive.**

correlation/footrule or *R*: (*C. Spearman*) a coefficient of correlation based on gains in rank: $R = 1 - \dfrac{6\Sigma g}{N^2 - 1}$, where *g* is a gain by any individual from his rank in the first variable to the second. ➤The method is relatively crude, and is appropriate only when the number of cases is small. If ranks are used, the rank difference formula is generally preferred.—See **correlation/rank difference.**

correlation graph = scatter diagram.

correlation/index of: 1. a measure of relationship: it is the square root of the proportion of the **variance** of a dependent variable that can be imputed to **eta,** the curvilinear relationship between it and the independent variable. This index is never less than r nor greater than η. **2.** a confusing synonym for **correlation coefficient.**

correlation/indirect = negative *correlation.

correlation/inverse = correlation/negative.

correlation/linear: a **correlation** in which the **regression** line is a straight line, so that for any increase in the magnitude of one variable there will be a proportional change in the magnitude of the other variable. ➤Many equations for computing a **coefficient of *correlation** require that the regression be linear. The requirement is seldom perfectly fulfilled. Where departure from a linear form is too great, alternative equations are—or should be—used.

correlation matrix: see **matrix/correlation.**

correlation/multiple or **R:** the dependence where two (or more) "causal" or "prediction" variables are related to, or are employed to predict, the **dependent** or **criterion *variable;** the correlation between a variable and two or more other variables taken together. It is the highest possible correlation between the criterion and two or more independent variables. One formula, based on the **total *correlations,** is

$$R_{1.23} = \sqrt{\frac{r_{12}^2 - 2r_{12}\,r_{13}\,r_{23} + r_{13}^2}{1 - r_{23}^2}}$$

—*Cp.* **beta regression weight.**

correlation/negative: a **correlation** between two **variables** which indicates that large values of one variable tend to be associated with small values of the other variable, and vice versa.—*Syn.* INVERSE CORRELATION.

correlation/net = correlation/partial.

correlation/neurological: the hypothesis that a specific neural event—the neurological correlate—corresponds with each mental or behavior event, that neurological and psychological phenomena run parallel courses.

correlation/part: the **linear *correlation** between a dependent variable and certain independent variables after the effect of several other independents has been removed

from the dependent variable; the correlation between A and C, D, E when the variance of A due to variables L, M, and N has been removed. ➤*Distg. fr.* **partial *correlation.** Part correlation is the relation of a variable to several others, partial correlation is the relation of a variable to one other. (But in both cases, certain other influences are ruled out.)—*Cp.* **multiple *correlation.**

correlation/partial: the net correlation between two variables when the influence of one or more other variables on their relation has been eliminated or allowed for. ➤E.g., the relation between intelligence and mathematical achievement, when the influence of age has been eliminated, is a partial correlation. The correlation coefficient between variables 1 and 2, when the influence of variables 3, 4 . . . n is to be allowed for, is given in the formula:

$$r_{12\cdot34\ldots n} =$$

$$\frac{r_{12\cdot34\ldots(n-1)} - r_{1n\cdot34\ldots(n-1)}\,r_{2n\cdot34\ldots(n-1)}}{\sqrt{1 - r^2_{1n\cdot34\ldots(n-1)}}\,\sqrt{1 - r^2_{2n\cdot34\ldots(n-1)}}}$$

—*Distg. fr.* **part *correlation,** which is the correlation between independent variables and a variable purged of variation due to other variables.

correlation/perfect: such relation between two variables that any change in one is exactly paralleled by a change in the other; a correlation where $r = 1.00$. (Or $r = -1.00$ when the correlation is negative.)

correlation/point-biserial or **r_p:** the **product-moment *correlation** between a continuous variable and another variable represented by a **dichotomy:** e.g., the relation of height (a continuous variable) to sex (a dichotomy).—*Cp.* **correlation/biserial.**

correlation/polychoric: the correlation between two variables that are plotted in a table containing more than four cells, when it is assumed that both variables, though expressed quantitatively, are really continuous and normally distributed.—*Contr. w.* **correlation/tetrachoric.**

correlation/positive: a relation between two **variables** such that large values of one variable tend to be associated with large values of the other variable, and small values of the one tend to be associated with small values of the other.—*Syn.* DIRECT CORRELATION.—*Ant.* **negative *correlation.**

correlation/primary: that **correlation** between two **variables** which apparently cannot be ascribed to the influence of some third variable.—*Ant.* **secondary *correlation.**

correlation/product-moment or **r:** the most usual method of computing **correlation,** based on **product-moments.** One form of the formula is: $r = \Sigma xy/N\sigma_x\sigma_y$. (This formula assumes **rectilinear** *****regression** lines.)—*Syn.* PEARSONIAN CORRELATION.

correlation/Q: see *P* technique.

correlation/rank difference or ρ: a coefficient of correlation based on the differences in ranking assigned the individuals in two variables: $\rho = 1 - \dfrac{6\Sigma d^2}{N(N^2 - 1)}$, where d is a rank difference.

correlation ratio: a measure of the degree to which the **regression** line is nonlinear. ➤It is a function of the ratio of the **variances** of the arrays of a variable to the variance of that variable; or of the ratio of the standard deviation of the weighted means of the arrays to the standard deviation of the individual measures. It is symbolized by η (the Greek letter *eta*, pron. ā′tə).—*Distg. fr.* **curvilinear** *****correlation.**

correlation/rectilinear = **correlation/ linear.**

correlation/secondary: the **correlation** between two variables which is due to the operation of some third variable contributing to the variability of both of the variables concerned.—*Ant.* **primary** *****correlation.**

correlation/simple: **correlation** between two variables on the basis of magnitude.— *Syn.* BIVARIATE CORRELATION.

correlation/split-half = **correlation/ chance halves** (*prefd.*).

correlation/spurious: correlation between two variables, the magnitude of which results, in whole or in part, from the method of obtaining or handling the data rather than from any real relationship.

correlation table: a schema for showing the quantitative relationship of two variables. ➤Scores or other values of one variable are represented by horizontal rows, those of the other by vertical columns. In the square formed by the intersection of a row with a column are recorded the cases whose scores are represented by row and column respectively. Thus a person scoring 10 on one test, 20 on another, would be recorded in the square formed by the intersection of row 10 with column 20.—*Syn.* DOUBLE-ENTRY TABLE, TWO-WAY TABLE, DOUBLE-FREQUENCY TABLE. A SCATTER DIAGRAM or PLOT is a correlation table in which the entry is made by dots or tallies instead of numbers; hence, the terms are sometimes used as synonyms.

correlation/tetrachoric or r_t (tet″rə·kô′rik): the correlation between two variables, both assumed to be continuous and normally distributed, but each expressed in terms of two classes only.

correlation/total: the ordinary form of correlation in which each variable is represented by the whole series of individual scores; the correlation between two variables in their original form (not **residuals**).— *Syn.* ZERO ORDER CORRELATION, GROSS CORRELATION, ENTIRE CORRELATION.—*Distg. fr.* **partial** *****correlation.**

correlation/zero: a correlation having no linear association or relationship; one having a **correlation coefficient** of zero.—*Distg. fr.* **zero order** *****correlation.**

correlation/zero order = **correlation/ total.**—*Distg. fr.* **zero** *****correlation.**

correlative: *adj.* having a mutual relationship.

correspondence: *n.* (*stat.*) a relationship between two variables such that each observed value of one variable is paired with a value of the other.

correspondence/coefficient of = **forecasting efficiency/index of.**

correspondence theory: 1. (*phys.*) the theory that whatever is true of classical mechanics is true of atomic mechanics, or vice versa, and that a unifying formula by which to translate the laws of one into the other is to be sought for. ➤A formula has been proposed and apparently works. 2. (*psychol.*) the theory that whatever is true of **molecular behavior** is true of **molar behavior,** and that a unifying principle is to be sought for.

corresponding retinal points: 1. = identical **points.** 2. = **congruent points.** ➤Because of the confusion, the term should be avoided.

cortex: *n.* (*anat.*) the thin outer layer of an organ. When unqualified, the word refers to the cerebral cortex or **cortex cerebri** (which see).—*adj.* **cortical.**

cortex/adrenal: see **adrenal cortex.**

cortex cerebelli (ser″ə·bel′ĭ): the gray matter that forms the outermost layer or coating of the cerebellum. ➤Note that **cortex** (used alone) refers to the **cortex cerebri.**

cortex cerebri (ser′ə·brī): the surface layers of **gray matter** of the cerebral **hemispheres.** ➤The cortex is the most recent evolutionary development of the nervous system and is the organ most critically and differentially involved in behavior and mental processes. But to speak of it as *the* organ of behavior (or of consciousness) is to ignore the many other organs that play important roles.—*Syn.* **cortex,** CEREBRAL CORTEX, CORTICAL CEREBRUM.

cortex/contralateral: the **cortex** on the opposite side of the body from the **peripheral** nerves in question.

cortex/extrinsic: see **thalamus/extrinsic.**

cortex/intrinsic: see **thalamus/extrinsic.**

cortex/motor: (*neurol.*) those portions of

the cortex from which motor fibers originate.—See **brain center.**

cortex/precentral: the **convolution** anterior and adjacent to the **central** *fissure
and superior to the **lateral** *fissure; or all
the cortex thus bounded.

cortex/sensory: that portion of the cortex
which receives nervous impulses from the
sense organs.

cortical: *adj.* pertaining to a **cortex.**

cortical control: the influence exerted by
the cortex upon the activities of the **lower**
*centers.

cortical gray: the median gray that is perceived in complete darkness by the dark-
adapted eye. ➤The name derives from the
theory that the perception is due to the
metabolic action of the cortex.—*Syn.* IDIO-
RETINAL LIGHT (*prefd.*).

corticalization: *n.* increase in the degree of
dependence of an organism upon cerebral
cortical mechanisms. ➤**Corticalization** may
be general or may refer to a particular type
of adaptive response. It is one of the most
important indices of evolutionary development.—See **encephalization.**

cortical relay nuclei: nuclei that receive
fibers directly from the ascending afferent
systems and project them to the cerebral
cortex.

corticotrophin: *n.* a hormone, secreted by
the anterior pituitary, which regulates the
activity of the adrenal cortex.

cortin: *n.* a substance, containing several
hormones, extracted from the cortex of the
adrenal glands.

Corti/organ of (kôr′ti): a spiral structure
in the **cochlea** of the inner ear containing
the **receptor** cells for hearing.

Corti/rods of (kôr′ti). minute, rodlike
structures forming the arches in the **organ
of** *Corti in the inner ear.—*Syn.* PILLARS
OF CORTI.

cortisone: *n.* one of the hormones produced by the adrenal cortex, also produced
synthetically.

cos: symbol for cosine.

cosatiation: *n.* the **satiation** of one **drive**
or **need** by the satisfaction of another.—
Distg. fr. **sublimation.**

cosmology: *n.* philosophic theory that treats
of the ultimate character of the universe.

cosmos: *n.* the universe as an orderly system.—*adj.* **cosmic.**

cot: symbol for cotangent.

co-twin control/method of: a procedure
in which one **identical** *twin is subjected
to special treatment or training while the
other twin, with the same heredity, is not.
➤The method is designed to throw light on
the limitations placed by heredity upon
trainability; or, conversely, to discover how
far development will proceed without special training.

counselee: *n.* a person who receives **counseling.**

counseling: *n.* a relationship in which one
person endeavors to help another to understand and to solve his adjustment problems. The area of adjustment is often indicated: educational counseling, vocational
counseling, social counseling, etc. ➤The
term covers a wide area of procedures:
advice-giving, psychoanalysis, information-
giving, interpretation of test scores, en-
couraging the counselee to think out his
difficulties or to work through his emotions,
etc. While usually applied to helping normal
counselees, it merges by imperceptible degrees into **psychotherapy.** Everyone occasionally undertakes counseling, but the
word **counselor** is preferably restricted to
professionally trained persons. ¶Counseling
is a two-way affair involving both counselor
and counselee. Unfortunately, both noun
and verb **counsel** retain an older meaning
of advice-giving, which is now conceived as
only part of the counseling process.—*Var.*
counselling.

counseling/directive: the procedure when
a counselor endeavors to control, directly
or indirectly, the topics about which the
counselee speaks, describes the choices which
face him, and/or advises him what to do.
—See **nondirective procedure.**

counseling interview: see **interview/
counseling.**

counseling ladder: the series of steps taken
by a counselor in guiding the thinking of a
client. Each step is usually one that the
counselor believes to be suggested by the
client's previous remarks or attitudes.

counseling/nondirective: see **nondirective procedure.**

counseling psychologist: a professional
psychologist who specializes in **counseling.**
➤His training equips him to deal with personal problems not classified as mental illness, though they may be sequels or corollaries of mental or physical illness, e.g., the
academic, social, or vocational problems
of students.—*Syn.* PSYCHOLOGICAL COUN-
SELOR.

counseling/semantic: counseling based on
the assumption that the counselee is prevented from forming a true picture of
reality by the emotional connotations and
tensions associated with word meanings.

counseling/therapeutic: the alleviation of
behavior difficulties by **counseling.** ➤De-
spite the apparent medical implications of
the word **therapeutic** (which make the
term unfortunate), it denotes activities that
are in no sense medical, and is designed to
remedy conditions that are not directly
medical.

counseling/vocational: see **vocational
counseling.**

counselor: *n.* a professionally trained person who does **counseling.** ➤It may include other professionally trained persons, e.g., vocational guidance specialists, ministers, social workers, as well as counseling psychologists.

counselor/psychological = counseling psychologist.

counter-: a combining form meaning **1.** opposite, contrary to: e.g., *counteract, counterinvestment.* **2.** opposed to but complementary; reciprocal: e.g., *counterpart.*

counteraction need: (*H. A. Murray*) the need, following failure, to strive again and to overcome weakness.

counterbalanced procedure: a method of canceling out the influence of irrelevant variables that cannot be experimentally removed. The independent or experimental variables are presented in different trials with contrasting degrees of the irrelevant variables. ➤E.g., in a long experiment comparing variables *a* and *b,* it may be impossible to avoid fatigue (or boredom). But *a* can be presented early in the series (fatigue absent) and late in the series (fatigue relatively high) in comparison with *b,* presented in the middle of the series. Thus, the order *a-b-b-a* enables comparison of the effects of *a* with *b,* fatigue being ruled out. —*Syn.* COUNTERBALANCING.

counterbalancing = counterbalanced procedure.

countercathexis = counterinvestment.

countercompulsion: *n.* (*psychoan.*) a compulsion developed to resist another compulsion: e.g., a compulsion to keep silent at all times as resistance to a compulsion to speak at unseemly times or in unseemly ways.

counterego: *n.* (*W. Stekel*) the hypothetical unconscious part of the **psyche** which acts antagonistically to the **ego.** ➤*Cp.* **id,** but the two seem not quite identical.

counteridentification: *n.* the *analyst's *identification of himself with the **analysand,** in response to the latter's identification with him.

counterinvestment: *n.* (*psychoan.*) attaching to a conscious idea a feeling opposite to that which the same idea carries when repressed in the unconscious. ➤E.g., repressed hatred for a person is replaced on the conscious level with a feeling of love.— *Syn.* ANTICATHEXIS, COUNTERCATHEXIS.

countersuggestion: *n.* a suggestion intended to inhibit a previous suggestion.

countertransference: *n.* (*psychoan.*) the arousal of the analyst's repressed feelings by the analytic situation; esp. (but not always) the transference by the analyst of his repressed feelings upon the **analysand.** —*Cp.* **transference.**

counterwill: *n.* (*O. Rank*) the ability to say "no" to others (or to one's own impulses). ➤This ability is, for Rank, the nucleus of personality.

courage: *n.* **1.** a personal attitude of meeting and dealing with dangers, obstacles, or difficulties rather than withdrawing from them. **2.** a specific emotion that accompanies the behavior of confronting danger. —*adj.* **courageous.**

Courtis growth curve: a representation of normal growth in **isochron** units.

couvade (kü·väd'): *n.* (*Fr.*) the custom among some peoples of having the father take to bed while his child is being born, acting as if suffering the pangs of childbirth.

covariance: *n.* the tendency of two variables to change together, as measured by the mean of the products of the paired deviations of the two variables, taken from their respective means: $\Sigma xy/N$.—*Cp.* **variance.**—*Syn.* **product-moment.**

covariance/analysis of: see **analysis of covariance.**

covariation = correlation (2).

cover memory: (*psychoan.*) a trivial incident of childhood retained because of its association with an emotionally important idea, which it helps to keep **repressed:** e.g., memory of a very happy holiday which helps to repress recognition that the childhood was in general miserable.—*Syn.* SCREEN MEMORY.

covert (kuv'ərt): *adj.* concealed; disguised; hidden: a *covert* threat.—See **covert behavior.**

covert behavior or **response:** an act that cannot be directly observed by another person. It may be inferred from the readings of an instrument or from other behaviors of the subject, or it may be accepted on the strength of the subject's own report. ➤The last is variously called **introspection, subjective** report or subjective observation, or IMPLICIT VERBAL RESPONSE. ¶OVERT RESPONSE is a muscular or glandular change that can be observed by another person. The distinction between **overt** and **covert,** resting as it does on the possibility of observation by an outsider, is hardly a basic psychological distinction (which must rest upon differences between the responses). ¶A basic distinction, however, was asserted by **behaviorism.** Traditional psychology used many terms—such as **thinking,** for example—which had, or seemed to have, **dualistic** implications rejected by behaviorism. Yet the terms obviously referred to something. If the phenomenon was not a directly observable (i.e., **overt**) response, it must be a nondirectly observable (i.e., **covert**) response. In this sense, overt and covert become almost synonymous with **objective** and **subjective,** respectively; and the word covert, instead of being a frank admission that empirical data are lacking, becomes an assertion of the theory that the allegedly subjective phenomena are merely objective phenomena that we cannot see. There is thus danger of **theory-begging.**

Implicit, often used as a synonym for covert, is an unhappy term for the facts referred to; it is properly an antonym for **explicit,** not for overt.

covert speech: see **internal speech.**

c.p.: *abbr.* for **candle power.**

cps: *abbr.* for cycles per second.

CR: 1. = **conditioned response. 2.** = **critical ratio.**

cramp: *n.* a severe contraction of a muscle group, maintained for some time, generally accompanied by discomfort.—*Cp.* **contracture.**

cranial: *adj.* pertaining to the **cranium.**

cranial capacity: cubic content of the **cranium.**

cranial conduction = **bone conduction.**

cranial division: part of the **craniosacral division** of the **autonomic nervous system.**

cranial index: the **cephalic index,** except that the bare skull is measured instead of the head with intact covering tissues.

cranial nerves: twelve pairs of nerves arising directly from the cerebrum. They are numbered I to XII and also individually named: e.g., *auditory nerve* (the VIIIth nerve).—*Syn.* CEREBRAL NERVES.—*Distg. fr.* **spinal nerves.**

cranial reflex: a **reflex** mediated by one of the cranial nerves and its connections in the brain.—*Distg. fr.* **spinal reflex.**

craniometry: *n.* measurement of the **cranium.**

craniosacral division: see **autonomic nervous system.**

cranium: *n.* that part of the skull which contains the brain.—*adj.* **cranial.**

craving: *n.* a strong **desire** or **impulse** for a particular **satisfier;** a state in which the organism is restless and tends to be attentive only to stimuli that are related to the satisfier. ➤The term implies a **tissue *need** as the basis of the craving.—See **desire.**

craving/segmental: (*E. J. Kempf*) a craving arising in a localized segment or organ of the autonomic system, most often in one of the **viscera.**

crawling: *n.* human locomotion with trunk on the ground, head and shoulders raised, the arms pulling the body forward, with or without pushing movements of the legs.—*Cp.* **creeping.**

craze: *n.* an exaggerated enthusiasm for a new mode of behavior, dress, etc., usually uncritically adopted. It may be an individual or a group phenomenon.

C reaction: a response of the human embryo to external stimulation, in which the body is bent into a **C** shape.

creatinine (kri·at'ə·nēn): *n.* a substance normally present in blood and urine, and excreted in the urine at a constant rate.

creatinine-height index: the amount in milligrams of urinary creatinine, divided by height in centimeters cubed. ➤The index is used in appraisal of nutritional status.

creative imagination: 1. a new pattern or sequence of images or ideas that serves as a solution to a problem. 2. = **creativeness.** —*Syn.* CONSTRUCTIVE IMAGINATION, CREATIVE THOUGHT. ➤*Contr. w.* **fancy** or **fantasy** (which do not solve problems) and with **reproductive *imagination** (which revives old patterns).

creative instability: the capacity to break out into new lines of activity that have never before occurred to the organism.

creativeness: *n.* ability to find new solutions to a problem or new modes of artistic expression; bringing into existence a product new to the individual (not necessarily new to others).—*Var.* **creativity.**

creative resultants/principle of: (*W. Wundt*) the hypothesis that the combination of mental processes engenders processes not found in a mere summation. Thus certain elements, themselves not spatial, may engender awareness of space.—*Cp.* **Gestalt** and **emergentism,** which take a similar but broader position.—*Syn.* PRINCIPLE OF CREATIVE SYNTHESIS.

creative synthesis: (*W. Wundt*) the doctrine of **creative resultants.** ➤The term is sometimes used with the same meaning as Wundt's but with broader application.— See **emergentism** and **psychology/divisions and schools of, VII.**

credibility: *n.* compatability of a statement with accepted facts; compatability of one's perception of a situation with what is generally accepted as true or possible.—*Ant.* **incredibility.**—*adj.* **credible.**

credit hour: (*U.S.*) a unit for measuring the quantity of academic achievement in a college or university. It represents the equivalent of one hour's attendance a week for a semester or a quarter at lecture or recitation, with at least passing marks. The amassing of a given number of such credit hours is the chief requirement for graduation in most undergraduate colleges.—*Cp.* **point-hour ratio.**

credulity (krə·dü'lə·ti): *n.* the tendency to believe on very slight grounds.—*Distg. fr.* **credibility.**—*Syn.* CREDULOUSNESS.—*Ant.* INCREDULITY.—*adj.* **credulous** (krej'ü·ləs).

creeping: *n.* human locomotion on hands and knees with the trunk free and roughly parallel to the surface.—*Cp.* **crawling.**

Crespi effect: an increase in a learned response that is more than proportional to the increase in incentive over that of the training period.

cretinism (krē'tin·iz·əm): *n.* a condition arising from thyroid insufficiency in fetal life or early infancy, marked by great retardation in mental and physical growth and by physical **stigmata.**—*adj.* **cretinous.**—*pers. n.* **cretin.**

criminality: *n.* the abstract quality of criminal action. ➤Criminality is a legal, not a psychological, expression. It is doubtful that any special pattern of psychological characteristics constitutes criminality.

criminal type: a person with strong tendency to antisocial behavior. ➤The implied notion that a pattern of (possibly inherited) behavior traits characterizes the criminal is so doubtful that the term should be abandoned.—*Cp.* **degenerate type, type.**

criminology: *n.* the systematic study of crime and criminals, with particular reference to the personality factors and social conditions leading toward, or away from, crime.

crisis: *n.* a turning point.—See **critical (3).**

criterion *n.*, *pl.* **criteria, criterions:** 1. a comparison object, or a rule, standard, or test for making a judgment, esp. a qualitative judgment; the basis for assignment to a **class** or **category.** 2. a behavior goal by which progress is judged. 3. the variable, comparison with which constitutes a measure of **validity; a** validating variable. ➤A **criterion** is an external basis for judgment; a **standard** is, properly, a quantitative level within a test or similar measure. E.g., a score of 63 on a certain test is a **standard** for seventh graders as based on the **criterion** of the performance of the seventh grades in 1000 public schools. Usually a criterion is a single variable or a composite treated as single.—*Cp.* **type,** which is a pattern. 4. (*stat.*) the **dependent** *variable, the variable to be predicted.

criterion analysis: 1. a factor analysis that includes the **criterion variable** in the test **matrix** being factored. 2. a method of factor **rotation,** developed by H. J. Eysenck, utilizing two distinct homogeneous groups presumed to differ in the factor accounting for the greatest variance in the factor matrix.

criterion behavior: that specific behavior which is in any way a standard by which another behavior is judged. ➤*Distg. fr.* BEHAVIOR(AL) CRITERION, a criterion that is behavioral rather than subjective on the one hand or physical on the other.

criterion contamination: see **contamination.**

criterion group: a group of individuals of known standing or worth according to some criterion characteristic or characteristics (e.g., seniority in a job, leadership as rateα by associates, age, sex, membership in a given church, etc.) which are believed to be reflected in their scores on a given test or other measure of performance. The test scores of the criterion group serve as a standard for evaluating the test scores of other persons, or for the usefulness of the test relative to the criterion.

criterion measure or **score:** (*stat.*) a score in the dependent variable, or in the variable to be predicted, or in the variable that serves as a **criterion (3)**; esp., a score that is to be predicted by a **regression equation.**

criterion overlap: 1. the extent to which a presumably independent criterion is dependent upon the variable to be judged. 2. the extent to which two or more criteria, supposed to be different, actually are measures of the same thing.

criterion variable: 1. the variable used to test another, or by which another is judged. 2. the **dependent** *variable.**

critical: *adj.* 1. pertaining to **criticism,** i.e., to careful and unbiased evaluation. 2. tending toward unfavorable or skeptical evaluation. ➤Search for fault rather than for worth is implied—the notion of carefulness remains, but that of lack of bias is lost. 3. pertaining to **crisis,** a turning point in the course of events. 4. = **crucial** (*prefd.*), pertaining to a point in the state of affairs (the **crux**) which, if properly considered, determines choice.—*Syn.* see **crucial.**—*Ant.* UNCRITICAL, connoting failure to be careful; NONCRITICAL, deliberately withholding judgment, not being at a crisis, or not adequate for choice (NONCRUCIAL *prefd.* for the last).

critical flicker frequency: see **flicker.**

critical fusion frequency: see **flicker.**

critical incident technique: a method of investigation by gathering observations of human or other animal activity that are complete enough in themselves to permit inferences about the performer, and occur in a situation where the intent and consequences seem fairly clear to the observer.—*Cp.* **anecdotal evidence** and **anecdotal record.**

critical ratio or **CR** or **cr:** the ratio of a **statistic** to its **standard error.** It is a measure of statistical **significance** or **stability,** of how likely it is that the obtained statistic is materially affected by chance. ➤The most commonly used is the CR OF A DIFFERENCE. A difference is usually regarded as not sufficiently stable unless the CR is about 3. When the sample is small, *t* (which includes CR as a special case) must be used; it is coming to be preferred in all cases.

critical region: that range of values or

scores which, if it characterizes a sample, leads to the rejection (at any given level of probability) of the hypothesis the sample is intended to test.—*Ant.* REGION OF ACCEPTANCE.—*Syn.* REGION OF REJECTION (*prefd.*). —See **fiducial limits.**

critical score: one that divides ranked scores into distinct groups with reference to some purpose or criterion: e.g., a pass-fail division point.—*Syn.* **cutting score,** which see.

criticism: *n.* 1. careful unbiased examination of the meaning, implications, internal consistency, value, etc., of anything. 2. (*pop.*) statement of the reasons for finding fault.

critique (kri·tēk'): *n.* a detailed and systematic **criticism** (1).

cross-adaptation: *n.* the effect of **sensory** *adaptation to one stimulus upon sensitivity to other stimuli.

cross-check questioning: seeking the same information by an alternative form of question, as a means of insuring that the answer is correct.

cross-classification: *n.* a schema that uses more than one basis for grouping, so that an item may belong in more than one **class.** ➤In general, this is to be carefully avoided.

cross-classification table = **contingency table** (*prefd.*).

cross-conditioning: *n.* 1. conditioning to an irrelevant stimulus that happens to coincide in time with an unconditioned stimulus. 2. the conditioning of oft-repeated responses (particularly **tonic** and **postural** responses) to some very common, almost universal, stimulus condition. Such responses become practically constant features of the individual's behavior. ➤Some restrict the term to the special case where the **CS** is **proprioceptive.**

cross-correspondence: *n.* (*parapsych.*) the appearance in the **automatic writing** of one **medium** of messages that can be interpreted only in the light of a message received by another medium.

cross-cultural method: an attempt to discover the specific dynamic effects upon behavior of a particular environmental stimulus by observing more than one **culture.** ➤E.g., the effect of a certain child-rearing practice (or of its absence) may be studied in a nonliterate people, in the U.S., among Buddhists in Ceylon, among Moslems in Afghanistan. It does not seek so much to compare cultures as to compare the effects of a certain practice, using cultures as a sort of experimental variation of conditions.

cross-culture test: see **test/culture free.**

crossed reflex: one in which the stimulus and the response are on opposite (**contra-**lateral) sides of the body.—*Ant.* **direct reflex.**

cross-education = **transfer/bilateral.**

crossing over: (*genet.*) the process whereby some of the linked genes separate and enter into different gametes and thus effect new combinations.

cross-parent identification: strong affection for, and tendency to imitate, the parent of unlike sex.—See **identification.**

cross-section method: the study of a large number of variables (persons, anatomical structures, psychological functions) as they all are at a single period of time. ➤In studies of **development,** the average of many persons for a given variable at a given age is taken as an age **norm,** and generalized development is pictured in terms of progress from one norm to another.— *Contr. w.* the LONGITUDINAL METHOD, wherein the changes in the same person are studied over a considerable period of time.

cross-validation: *n.* 1. determining the **validity** of a procedure found to work with one sample by trying it out on a second sample of the population in question. 2. specif., testing the discriminating power of a set of test items, which have been selected because they make the required discriminations with one group, by finding whether they make the required discrimination with a second (independent) sample of the population. ➤If a set of items is chosen for a test because each of them correlates with the scholastic success of one group of students, the test must be cross-validated by being tried with a fresh sample. A demonstration of the discriminating power of the test for the original sample is CIRCULAR VALIDATION. Selecting items on the basis of several independent samples may be called VALIDATION GENERALIZATION; it improves selection but is not **cross-validation,** which tests selection after it is made.

crowd: *n.* a temporary face-to-face group of persons, relatively unorganized but with its members in some degree responsive to one another. ➤*Cp.* **mob,** a crowd dominated by strong excitement directed toward a single object. Discussions of CROWD PSYCHOLOGY stress irrational behavior, but this is not necessary to the meaning of crowd.

crowding: *n.* (*learning*) requiring a person to react to too many tasks or problems in a limited time.

CRT = cathode-ray tube.

crucial: *adj.* pertaining to a **crux:** i.e., to any datum, fact, or argument that will determine choice or decision for a person who gives it proper consideration. ➤A CRUCIAL EXPERIMENT (or *experimentum crucis,* for those who prefer Latin) is one that is definitive in establishing the truth or falsity of a hypothesis. ¶**Crucial, critical,** and **decisive** are often used interchangeably but may be distinguished: **crucial** refers to the data, **critical** to the evaluation, **decisive** to the action taken as a result of the evaluation: *decisive* action results from *critical* consideration of *crucial* data.

crude: *adj.* pertaining to data that are inexact, approximate, or not yet analyzed. ➤The CRUDE SCORE is a **raw** *score.

cruelty: *n.* 1. causing the suffering of another without proper reason. 2. enjoying the sufferings of another. ➤It is not clear how far these two represent the same psychic dynamism. Unwitting or unconscious cruelty is sometimes spoken of. By extension, one may be said to be cruel to oneself. Cruelty should not be, but often is, equated with **sadism** (which see).

crus cerebri = **peduncle/cerebral.**

crush: *n.* 1. a short-lived but intense attachment on the part of a child or adolescent to another (usually older) person; esp., such attachment to an older person of the same sex. 2. any short-lived infatuation. (An unnecessary usage.)

crutch/learning: any artificial learning aid or **mnemonic** device.

crux: *n.* (*L., a cross*) the point in a logical discussion that separates the correct or the valid from the incorrect or invalid; the actual facts or data by means of which choice or decision between competing hypotheses is validly and definitely made.—See **critical (4), crucial.**

crypt-, crypto- (kript-): combining form meaning *secret* or *hidden.*

cryptesthesia (krip″tes·thē′zhə): *n.* (*parapsych.*) the power to perceive without use of any known sensory mechanism. ➤This is the general term for **paranormal** perception. It includes **clairvoyance,** paranormal "seeing" (used also, however, in a more general sense as *syn.* for **cryptesthesia**); **clairaudience,** paranormal "hearing"; **telesthesia,** any paranormal perception at a distance; and at least some forms of **telepathy** and **telegnosis.** *Cp.* also **telekinesis.** PREMONITIONS are paranormal "warnings" of events to come, often not formed in words.

cryptogenic: *adj.* of unknown origin. ➤A wonderful term to flash when reluctant to admit ignorance!

cryptomnesia (krip″tom·nē′zhə): *n.* apparently creative thinking in which organized ideas from past experience seem to be novel. The past experience itself is not recalled and may be unrecallable or **repressed.**— *Cp.* **intuition.**

cryptorchism (-tor′kiz·əm): *n.* an anatomic anomaly in which the testes do not descend as is usual during the last weeks of fetal life, but remain enclosed in the body cavity.

crystal gazing: induction of a **hypnoidal** state by gazing fixedly into a crystal ball. The subject may report seeing more or less coherent happenings within the ball.—*Syn.* SCRYING.

CS = **conditioned stimulus.**

Cs.: *abbr.* for **conscious.**

C **scale:** (*J. P. Guilford*) a scale of 11 units, with a mean of 5.0 and an SD of 2.0, representing linear distances from the mean, into which rank scores may be transformed.

CTMM: *abbr.* for California Test of Mental Maturity.

cue: *n.* 1. a signal for an action; that specific portion of a perceptual field or pattern of stimuli to which an animal has learned to respond. ➤It is usual to restrict **cue** to that which produces an **operant** response, but it is also used for that which arouses **expectancy.** 2. an identifying mark that permits discrimination or recognition of a stimulus pattern. ➤Cue is particularly appropriate when the mark is an obscure part of the stimulus or an accidental concomitant. If the cue stimulus is very faint and not specifically attended to, it is called a MINIMAL CUE.—*Cp.* CLUE, a stimulus which, when thought about, guides response.

cue function: the **message** function of a sensory event; the function of the sensory event in guiding behavior.

cue reduction: the process whereby a part of the stimulus elicits the response formerly elicited by the whole or larger part of the stimulus.

cue/response-produced: an aspect of the stimulus situation produced by an organism's own behavior.

cue reversal: an experimental design in which the stimulus that leads to reward and the stimulus that leads to nonreward are reversed.

cul-de-sac: *n.* (*Fr.*) a blind alley; a path that has no exit except the entrance.

Culler's phi process: (*psychophys.*) a method of finding a **DL** in which the DL is equated to the PE's of the **ogive** distribution, thereby taking into account the willingness of the subject to make doubtful judgments.

cult: *n.* 1. a specific complex of beliefs, rites, and ceremonies maintained by a social group in association with some particular person or object. The cult object is usually considered as having magical or religious significance. 2. the group of persons thus associated. ➤Often used derogatorily for any group of persons strongly committed to a certain belief.—*Var.* **cultus.**

cultural anthropology: see **anthropology/ cultural.**

cultural area = **culture area.**

cultural climate: see **climate/psychological.**

cultural conserve: (*J. L. Moreno*) something that conserves cultural values (e.g., a book or a film). ➤It differs from a machine which accomplishes his labor, and from a robot which is an imitation of man.

cultural determinism: the view that emphasizes the important part played by **culture (1)** in the development of personality, esp. in influencing the frequency with which certain traits will be found within the various cultural groups. ➤Strictly speaking, the term should be CULTURAL DETERMINATION; cultural determinism should be reserved for the view that *only* culture determines personality. This view, however, is not held by anyone, though it is sometimes implied.

cultural education: education that promotes **culture (3)** and that prepares for the "duties of citizenship." ➤What constitutes a cultural education as thus defined is controversial; most of its advocates agree that education that merely prepares for earning a livelihood does not well serve that aim.

cultural items: test items that reflect the kind of learning experiences prevalent in a specific culture or subculture, in contrast with items that reflect more widely distributed experiences.

cultural lag: 1. preservation of large elements in a **culture (1)** after conditions have so changed that they are not adaptive. **2.** = CULTURAL RESIDUE, the elements preserved after the culture as a whole has changed.

cultural norm: an accepted standard of behavior in a society. ➤Norms differ from **mores** in having a quantitative connotation. They define not only what one should do but how much, how well, how often.

cultural process: any social process by which a **culture (1)** is instituted, maintained, and transmitted.

cultural relativism: 1. the view that judgments of beauty, goodness, health, etc., have meaning in relation to a cultural context and cannot be taken to have a universal or absolute meaning. ➤*Contr. w.* CULTURAL ABSOLUTISM, which maintains that certain values hold in all cultures, being based on reason or on revelation by God. **2.** the view that psychological principles derived from research in one culture cannot be directly applied to other cultures.

cultural science psychology: a school of psychologists (chiefly German) who hold that the goal of psychology is not explanatory, as in a natural science such as physics, but interpretative, as in a social science

such as history.—*Syn.* *Geisteswissenschaftliche Psychologie.*

cultural transmission = **acculturation.** ➤The term emphasizes those aspects of learning by means of which children acquire the behaviors of a **culture.**

culture: *n.* **1.** the pattern of all those arrangements, material or behavioral, whereby a particular society achieves for its members greater satisfactions than they can achieve in a state of nature. It includes social institutions and "knowledge, belief, art, morals, custom, and any other capabilities and habits acquired by man as a member of society." (*E. B. Tyler*) **2.** a group of persons having a common culture in sense **(1). 3.** cultivation of the intellectual and esthetic aspects of life, as distinguished from the more purely pragmatic: e.g., good taste in personal conduct, knowledge of the intellectual heritage of the race, appreciation of art and letters and of beauty in nature, and a reasonably consistent personal philosophy of life.

culture area: a geographic area within which all the peoples have in common important **culture complexes** peculiar to that area.—*Syn.* CULTURE AREA.

culture complex: a pattern of social activities or beliefs so closely related to each other in a given community as to form a unity. ➤E.g., all the activities associated with growing maize in a nonliterate culture, including the practical arts of soil preparation, sowing, harvesting, storage, preparing and eating the crop; but also the rites and ceremonies, the traditions and anecdotes, that arise in a maize culture.

culture conflict: the **conflict** arising when social groups of differing **culture (1)** live in close contact. ➤The conflict may be intergroup, as when a noisy Hindu wedding procession conflicts with the weekly Moslem prayer service in India. Or it may be internal: a difficulty of absorption by one group of "indigestible" elements from the culture of the other group, e.g., the practice of private land ownership borrowed by a people whose culture is essentially communal.

culture-epoch theory: 1. hypothesis that there is a typical evolution in human culture which all societies tend to follow: from hunting to pastoral to agricultural, etc. **2.** belief that the individual child tends in his mental development to pass through the cultural stages or levels typical of the race, and that education should be so timed as to take account of these phases. ➤Both views are outmoded.—*Cp.* **recapitulation theory.**

culture-fair: see **test/culture-free.**

culture/formal: see **formal culture.**

culture-free test: see **test/culture-free.**

culture hero: a legendary superhuman or demigod, exemplifying some of the values most highly cherished in a given culture.

culture pattern: 1. a coherent group of elements forming part of a culture; a **culture complex** (*prefd.*). **2.** the mutual relations between the parts of a whole culture; = CULTURAL PATTERN (*prefd.*).

culture/personal = **culture** (3).

culture trait: an element of **culture:** it may be a material object (such as a plow), a technique (plowing), or a belief (that plowing is women's work).—*Cp.* **culture complex.**

culturology: *n.* the systematic study of the origin, development, diffusion, and transmission of **culture.**

cultus = **cult.**

cumulation: *n.* addition by successive summation, a new sum being calculated whenever a new quantity is included.

cumulative: *adj.* **1.** of that which has been piled together or summed; esp., of that reached by successive additions. **2.** (*stat.*) of a method of representing a series or a distribution in which the sum of all the figures taken from the beginning to a certain point is added to succeeding figures up to the next point, and so on, the last point representing all cases in the series or distribution. ➤The successive sums are known as CUMULATIVE TOTALS or SUMS, CONTINUED SUMS, PROGRESSIVE TOTALS.—*Distg. fr.* **moving total.**—See **cumulative frequency curve.**

cumulative error = **constant *error.**

cumulative (frequency) curve: a graphic representation of the summed number or percentages of cases falling at and below (or at and above) successive scores or values of a variable. ➤The number or percentage is represented by distance from the *X* axis along the vertical lines representing the successive scores. The frequency on each line is that of all the cases at or beyond that score point, hence the frequency progressively increases or decreases. If it is a normal distribution, the curve resulting from joining the points thus located is a continuously rising curve with a double bend, and is one of the family of curves called **ogive.**—*Syn.* ACCUMULATION GRAPH, SUMMATION CURVE, S CURVE.

cumulative percentage curve: a **cumulative frequency curve** in which the entry values are percentages.

cumulative scale: a scale in which the items can be arranged in an order so that a testee who responds positively to any particular item also responds positively to all items of lower rank order. ➤*Syn.* GUTTMAN SCALE, SCALOGRAM. SCALOGRAM ANALYSIS is the procedure for obtaining such scales. Cumulative scaling has been most used for opinion scales but has general applicability. It is designed to insure that test items lie approximately along a single dimension, i.e., test the same thing.—*Cp.* **latent structure analysis.**

cuneus (kū′ni·əs): *n.* the triangular lobe on the inner surface of the cerebral hemisphere behind the parieto-occipital and above the calcarine fissure.—*adj.* **cuneate.**

cunnilinctus: *n.* the application of the mouth to the external genitalia of the female. —*Var.* **cunnilingus.**

cunnus: *n.* the external genitalia of the female.

curiosity: *n.* the tendency to investigate, to seek to observe the novel, to obtain information.

curiosity/infantile: (*psychoan.*) the assumption by a child of babyish investigatory behavior of apparent casualness in order to be permitted to observe sex parts or behavior.

current/neural: see **neural current.**

cursive: *adj.* of writing in which letters are joined so that a word can be written without lifting the pen.—*Cp.* **uncial.**

cursory enumeration test: the task of naming as many objects as possible in a specified time, either entirely freely or of a special kind.—*Cp.* **association/free.**

curve: *n.* **1.** any line between two contiguous surfaces; a line located with reference to a system of **coordinates.** ➤Such a line need not be curved (bent) in the popular sense, but may also be a straight line or a series of shorter straight lines end to end, each in a different direction from the preceding (a BROKEN LINE). **2.** a representation by a line of the series of values of a single variable, or of the **covariation** of two treated as one variable. ➤When representing a **continuous** variable an unbroken line or curve is used. **3.** (*student slang*) the normal *frequency curve.** ➤Academic tasks or examinations are said to be graded "on the curve."

curve/accelerated: a curve that has progressively greater (or lesser) increments from moment to moment; a curve that changes direction more and more (or less and less) rapidly as it moves away from a given point.—See **acceleration.**

curve/bell-shaped = **frequency curve/ normal.**

curve/binomial = **frequency curve/ normal.**

curve/distribution: a graphic representation of the actual frequency with which anything occurs.—*Syn.* **frequency curve.** The **probability *curve,** which represents the expected frequency; and the **normal *frequency curve** (which see) are special kinds of distribution curves.—See also **frequency.**

curve fitting or **smoothing:** the process of

finding the regular, or "smooth," curve that most closely represents an obtained set of data. The process may be a visual, freehand fitting of a line to plotted points, or a more rigorous mathematical determination.—*Syn.* EMPIRICAL CURVE FITTING.

curve/frequency = **curve/distribution.**

curve/Gaussian = **normal *frequency curve.**

curve/normal frequency: see **frequency curve/normal.**

curve of error: 1. = **normal *frequency curve. 2.** a curve showing the distribution of errors as found in an investigation.

curve of means = **regression curve.**

curve of normal error = **normal *frequency curve.**

curve of rest: the graphic representation of the gradual change in the **electrodermal response** during a period of no specific stimulation.

curve/probability: a curve showing the expected frequency of occurrence of anything. When not qualified, the **normal *frequency curve** is meant, but other frequencies are also to be expected.

curve/regression: see **regression curve.**

curve/smoothed: a curve in which erratic or sudden changes in slope or direction, arising from or associated with its representing only a small population, have been removed. ➤Generally the smoothing is done by eye, aided perhaps by such devices of the draftsman as French curves or lead rulers; but it may also be the plotted result of **curve fitting.** The result in the former case is a relatively SMOOTH CONTINUOUS CURVE, but this latter term is better restricted to a curve that is "naturally" smooth.

curvilinear: *adj.* of a line that is bent, i.e., that changes direction from moment to moment; or of data that can be represented by such a line. ➤*Distg. fr.* **rectilinear,** of a line that maintains a constant direction.

Distg. also *fr.* a BROKEN LINE, which is an end-to-end series of elements, each having a different direction from the preceding. NONLINEAR or NONRECTILINEAR are less specific and are not properly used as synonyms for curvilinear. See **curve.**

curvilinear relation or **relationship:** a relationship of two variable quantities portrayed by some curve other than a straight line.—*Ant.* **linear relationship.**

custodial case: a person who needs close supervision or restraint (usually in a special institution such as a mental hospital, prison, etc.) by reason of mental disorder or deficiency, criminality, delinquency.—*Distg. fr.* **committable** and **certifiable** (which see).

custom: *n.* **1.** a usual mode of acting; or a complex general practice prevailing in a social group, or learned by an individual under social influences. ➤**Habit** is a close synonym, more often applied to individual behavior and not restricted to socially learned behavior. Custom is more general than habit; indeed a custom is a complex pattern of habits. But the distinction is not sharp. It is the custom (not a habit) to be hospitable to strangers; it is either custom or habit to eat with a fork; it is a habit (not custom) to stir the coffee each time before taking a sip. **2.** the whole set or body of regular practices prevalent in a social group, inclusive of both **folkways** and **mores.**—*Cp.* **tradition, culture.**

cutaneous: *adj.* pertaining to the skin; more specif., to the skin as a sense organ.

cutaneous sense: any of the senses whose receptors lie in the skin or immediately beneath it (or in the external mucous membranes): contact, pressure, warmth, cold, pain, and perhaps others.—*Syn.* DERMAL SENSE.

cutting score: a dividing point in a series of scores that have been ranked in order of magnitude so that, for a stated purpose, all above that point receive one treatment, all below, another. ➤A given series may have several cutting scores: e.g., academic marks may have a cutting score at B+ for scholarship grants, another at D for passfail.—*Syn.* **critical score.**

CV: 1. = controlled variable (see **variable/independent**). **2.** = **variation/coefficient of.**

CVS Abbreviated Intelligence Test: the Comprehension and Similarities series from the **Wechsler-Bellevue,** plus Thorndike's 15-word vocabulary test.

cw: *abbr.* for clockwise (rotation).

cyan (sī'ən): *n.* a bluish green or peacock color.

cyanosis: *n.* blueness of the skin, caused by insufficient oxygen in the blood.—*adj.* **cyanotic.**

cybernetics (sī″bər·net′iks): *n.* (*Gk.* for *steersman*) (*N. Wiener*) the scientific study of **messages** and of regulatory or control mechanisms (esp. those involving **feedback**), whether found in machines, persons, social groups, or institutions. ➤Cybernetics emphasizes the control mechanisms, **communication theory** and **information theory** the messages, but the three overlap very greatly.

From this loosely defined group comes a

suggestion that psychic processes are to be regarded as messages, having the same *general* properties as other messages. This would seem to constitute a somewhat different definition of the **psychic,** undercutting the distinction physical versus psychic. See **psychology/divisions and schools of, V.**

cycle: *n.* **1.** a series of events regularly recurring as a whole; a complete recurring series of changes within a larger series; a CYCLIC CHANGE; esp., **2.** one complete vibration in a sound or light wave.—*Syn.* DOUBLE VIBRATION or D.V.—*adj.* **cyclic(al),** occurring in a regular order.—*Distg. fr.* **periodic,** occurring at regular intervals (hence, more specific than **cyclic**); and *fr.* **cycloid** (which see).

cyclic disorder: one that comes and goes with some regularity.

cyclofusional movement: a slight rotation of the eyeballs to gain fused or single binocular vision.

cycloid: *adj.* of a person who shows relatively marked but normal swings of mood. —See **cyclothymia.**

cyclopean eye: a theoretical single eye in the median plane of the forehead. ➤In discussions of coordinate eye movements, it is often helpful to imagine the two eyes working as if they were a cyclopean eye.

cyclophoria: see **heterophoria.**

cycloplegia: *n.* paralysis of the muscle controlling the pupillary opening of the eye, resulting in a wide-open pupil. It may be due to injury or to drugs such as atropin.—*adj.* **cycloplegic.**

cyclothymia (sī″klō·thī′mi·ə): *n.* a personality pattern marked by alternating periods of elation and sadness, activity and in-

activity, excitement and depression. ➤The alternations do not usually follow a regular cycle, and periods of average activity may intervene. Except when the depression is too great, the person tends to be outgoing, friendly, superficially generous, readily responsive to competition, and emotionally responsive to his environment. The sadness and depression on the one hand, and the elation and hyperactivity on the other, seem to express internal factors rather than a response to external events. CYCLOTHYMIC PERSONALITY is officially recommended (*Stan. Psychiat.*) for persons who, though not psychotic, manifest abnormal swings in mood and in activity level. It is therefore recommended that CYCLOID PERSONALITY be used as characterization of the person whose swings are within the normal range. The behavior of cyclothymia resembles that of **manic-depressive psychosis;** whether the dynamics are the same is unsettled.—*adj.* **cycloid,** emphasizing mood swings within normal limits; **cyclothymic.**—*pers. n.* **cyclothyme.**

cyclothymic personality: see **cyclothymia.**

cylinder/axis: see **axis cylinder.**

cynic: *n.* one who doubts the actuality of altruistic or idealistic motivation.—*Distg. fr.* the **skeptic,** whose doubts are intellectual.

cyto- (sī′tō-): combining form meaning *cell* (of an organism).

cytoarchitecture: *n.* the spatial pattern of the cells within a region or organ.

cytology: *n.* the branch of biology that studies cells.

cytoplasm: *n.* (*biol.*) the substance of the organic cell, exclusive of the nucleus.

D

D: **1.** (*stat.*) symbol for the difference between the tenth and the ninetieth **percentiles** of a **frequency distribution:** a measure of dispersion which includes the middle four-fifths of the cases. **2.** (*stat.*) symbol for a measure of similarity between sets of scores: $D_{12}{}^2 = \sum\limits_{j=1}^{k} (x_{j1} - x_{j2})^2$ where j = any of the variates a, b, c, which are k in number; 1, 2 = the two sets of scores or the two individuals having each a set of scores to be compared; and x_{j1}, x_{j2} = the scores of persons 1 or 2 on variate j. **3.** (*stat.*) difference between two scores of the same individual. **4.** = **drive** or **drive stimulus** (the latter also symbolized by S_D). **5.** (*K. Spence*) symbol for the distance or difference in logarithmic units between

the stimulus on which an animal is tested and that on which it is trained. **6.** (*C. Hull*) the strength of dominant primary drive operative in the primary motivation to action after formation of the habit involved. Hull gives the formulas

$$D = D' \times \Sigma, \text{ and } \Sigma = \frac{D}{D'};$$

$$\text{hence, } D = D' \times \frac{D}{D'}$$

(which seems obvious). **7.** (*Ror.*) scoring code for a response that reports associations of a usual sort with the large parts of the inkblot.

$$\overline{D} \text{ (}C. \text{ Hull}\text{)} = 100 \, \frac{D + D}{D + Md}$$

Ꭰ: (*C. Hull*) the strength of all the non-dominant drives operative at a given moment.

Ꭰ': (*C. Hull*) symbol for drive proper; the strength of primary drive operative during the formation of a habit.

Ꭰ%: (*psychophys.*) in judgments of time interval that are objectively equal, the per cent of judgments "shorter than the standard" minus the per cent of judgments "longer than the standard."

ꭰ: 1. = (*stat.*) **deviation. 2.** = (*stat.*) deviation of a **class** from the mean of a population. **3.** = (*stat.*) a difference in rank of an individual on two tests. **4.** = **diopter. 5.** = **drive. 6.** (*Ror.*) scoring code for a response reporting small details of an often-reported kind. **7.** = the number of **j.n.d.**'s lying between two stimulus aggregates.

ꭰ' = (*C. Hull*) $\dot{D} - D$.

Ꭰaltonism: *n.* red-green **color blindness.**

ꭰamp: *v.* to check or restrict; esp., to lessen progressively or suddenly the amplitude of a vibration. ➤The **damping** may be due to external pressure or to internal friction. Thus, a tuning fork **damps** itself even in a vacuum through friction of the molecules of which it is made.—*n.* **damping.**

ꭰanger situation: (*psychoan.*) any situation that arouses **anxiety.**

ꭰAP Test = Draw-a-Person Test.

ꭰark: *adj.* characterizing a state of low illumination, or an object that reflects little light; characterizing a color of low brilliance or brightness.

ꭰark adaptation: the adjustment of the eye to low intensity of light; the gradual increase in ability to see faint lights or faintly illuminated objects when general illumination is reduced; or the state finally reached after several minutes of lessened light stimulation.—*Syn.* DARKNESS ADAPTATION, SCOTOPIC ADAPTATION.

ꭰarkness adaptation = dark adaptation.

Ꭰarwinian reflex: the tendency of very young infants to grasp a pliable cylinder of appropriate size and to hang suspended from it.—*Syn.* SUSPENSION REFLEX.—*Distg. fr.* grasping reflex.

Ꭰarwinism: *n.* **1.** the theory set forth by Charles Darwin that living forms (species, genera, orders, etc.) have evolved chiefly as the result of **natural selection. 2.** more generally and loosely, an evolutionary theory or point of view. **3.** still more loosely, in psychology, emphasis upon the adaptive utility of behavior; practically = **functionalism.**

Ꭰaseinanalyse (däs″ĭn·än·ə·lē′ze): *n.* (*Ger.*) = **existential analysis.**

ꭰAT = **Differential Aptitude Tests.**

ꭰata (dā′tə; dat′ə): *n.* **1.** the plural of **datum** (which see). **2.** the collective mass of factual material used as basis for discus-

sion and inference of conclusions. ➤The plural form **data** is often, though incorrectly, construed as singular: *the body of data is impressive* is correct; but the expression *the data is* should be avoided.

data/observational: data obtained from nonexperimental observation. ➤There is no implication that the observation is unscientific.

data processing: the description of every discriminable aspect of a process by an appropriately refined mathematical index so that complex processes may be expressed in mathematical equations.—*Syn.* PROGRAMING (not *recom.*).

data/raw: data not yet submitted to logical or statistical analysis.

data sheet: a form that makes possible a systematic and orderly recording of pertinent data.

datum (dā′təm) *n., pl.* **data:** (*L., that which is given*) **1.** that which is given in sensing; the perceived. **2.** in arguments, that which is used as a starting point. **3.** loosely, a fact.—See also **data.**

Davis-Eells Games: an intelligence test for children, consisting of pictures accompanied by orally presented verbal material. The problems are drawn from common experiences familiar to children in urban groups.

dawdling: *n.* delay in starting an unpleasant task and interruption of the task behavior by many irrelevant actions.

day blindness: see **blindness/day.**

daydream: *n.* a revery while awake. ➤Usually the unfulfilled wishes of the dreamer are imagined as fulfilled. Wishes are not disguised and fulfillment is imagined as direct, without repression. Daydreaming is not inherently pathological.

daylight vision = **photopic vision.**

day residues: (*psychoan.*) experiences from the preceding day which partly determine the **manifest content** of a dream.—See **dream content.**

db = **decibel.**

d.c. = **direct current.**

Ꭰd: (*Ror.*) scoring code for an **inkblot** response that mentions unusual details.

dd: (*Ror.*) scoring code for tiny-detail response to an **inkblot.**

Ꭰds: (*Ror.*) scoring code for an associative response for which the stimulus is a minor white space of the **inkblot** card.

ꭰdW: (*Ror.*) a scoring code used when a minor detail of a figure (*Dd*) suggests a percept, the subject interpreting the entirety as though it had the form of the *Dd.* ➤*Cp.* **DW,** in which the detail is a more important one.

de: (*Ror.*) scoring code for **edge detail.**

de-: prefix meaning *down, off, away, deprivation,* or *undoing.*

deaf-mute: *n.* a person unable to hear or speak.—See **mutism.**—*Syn.* MUTE. ➤The expression DEAF AND DUMB is regarded as contemptuous.—*n.* **deaf-mutism.**

deafness: *n.* **1.** (*pop.*) complete or partial loss of hearing. **2.** (*tech.*) inability to hear, even with a hearing aid, well enough for the ordinary purposes of life. ➤Specialists strongly urge the term HARD-OF-HEARING or DEAFENED PERSONS for those in whom hearing, though defective even to the point where an auditory aid must be worn, is functional or useful in everyday life.—*Syn.* SURDITY (rare), AUDITORY IMPAIRMENT, HYPACUSIA.—*adj.* **deaf, deafened.**—*v.* **deafen,** which is also used for temporary impairing.

deafness/adventitious: deafness acquired as a result of injury or disease. ➤It may be both adventitious and **congenital** if the injury occurred during the prenatal period or at delivery.

deafness/central or /**cortical:** deafness due to impairment of the cortical center for hearing: a form of **organic *deafness.** —*Distg. fr.* functional *deafness.

deafness/conduction: deafness or impaired hearing due to defect in the structure of the outer ear, the eardrum, or the middle ear, as a result of which the sound wave is obstructed on its way to the inner ear.— *Distg. fr.* **nerve *deafness,** in which the impaired conduction is due to loss of function of sensory cells in the inner ear or of the auditory nerve.

deafness/congenital: that existing at birth, whether due to **heredity** or to prenatal injury.—See **deafness/adventitious.**

deafness/functional: 1. that due to some disorder of the working of the auditory mechanism, either the sense organ or its neural connections, without known or permanent change in structure. **2.** that due to the person's inability to respond to the activity of the unimpaired peripheral and central auditory mechanism.—*Syn.* PSYCHIC DEAFNESS, HYSTERICAL DEAFNESS.—*Cp.* **deafness/organic, functional disorder.**

deafness/hysterical = **deafness/functional.**

deafness/nerve: that due to impaired function of the **auditory nerve.** ➤*Distg. fr.* **deafness/conduction.**

deafness/organic: that due to some structural defect of the sensory apparatus for hearing, including the auditory nerve mechanism and the cortical area for hearing.— *Distg. fr.* **deafness/functional.** See also **functional disorder.**

deafness/psychic = **deafness/functional.**

deafness/tonal gap or /**tonal island:** hearing that is deficient only in certain limited portions of the pitch range, remaining relatively normal elsewhere.

deafness/tone: deficient ability to discrim inate differences in pitch, though the sound themselves are heard. ➤The term is no precise but applies to inability to recogniz a difference of something less than a whol tone. It is often applied to inability to tel one tune from another, resulting either from poor pitch discrimination or from othe causes.—*Syn.* ASONIA (not *recom.*).

deafness/word = **aphasia/auditory.**

death feigning (fān′ing): **tonic immobility** of an animal in the presence of a threat.

death instinct: (*S. Freud*) a hypothesizec general instinct of denial, rejection, anc death; a collective name for all the primi tive or instinctual tendencies that lead away from full expression and pleasure towarc constriction, and (in full form) towarc death.—*Syn.* THANATOS.—*Ant.* **Eros, lif instinct.**

debility: *n.* weakness in a body or a bodily part; esp., lack of vigor in a vital function

deca-, deka-: prefix meaning *multiplied b) ten.*—*Distg. fr.* **deci-,** *division by ten.*—*Cp* **centi-.**

deceleration: see **acceleration.**

decency: *n.* propriety of speech and conduct; conformity to social standards of what is appropriate for public display.—*Ant.* **indecency.**—*Cp.* **obscenity.**

decenter: *v.* to react to a certain aspect of a perceptual total in a way that was previously adaptive but is not so in the present circumstances. ➤Various levels of **decentering,** or freedom from it, are distinguished. —See **recenter.**

decerebration: *n.* removal of the **cerebrum.** —*adj.* and *v.* **decerebrate.**

deci- (des′i-): combining form meaning *divided by ten, a tenth of.*—*Distg. fr.* **deca-.** —*Cp.* **centi-.**

decibel or **db** (des′ə·bel): *n.* **1.** a unit for measuring the difference between the perceived intensity or loudness of a certain sound and that of a standard sound. ➤Conventionally, the standard sound is that of an air wave exerting a pressure of .0002 **dynes** per square centimeter. This is roughly the average human intensity **threshold** for a tone of 1000 c.p.s. The decibel is 10 times log₁₀ of the ratio between this barely audible sound and the comparison sound. A human whisper is from 10 to 18 decibels above this zero, ordinary conversation about 60, a boiler shop about 100. As the decibel is a logarithmic unit, it is not to be interpreted that a boiler shop is only ten times as loud as a whisper. **2.** one tenth of a BEL, a logarithmic measure of the ratio betwen two physical intensities. A decibel is 10 times the log₁ of the ratio. ➤It is used in electric, in acoustic, and less often in light, measurement. Since the unit is logarithmic, the physical intensities increase geometrically in relation to the **db**. The **db** is a ratio measurement (often with an arbitrary standard as the denominator). In acoustics, the decibel is the ratio between two sound pressures or two energies. ¶It is to be noted that **decibel** denotes either a measure of audible sound (sense **1**) or a measure of the physical sound-wave intensity (sense **2**).

deciduous teeth: baby teeth; the impermanent first set of teeth.

decile: *n.* **1.** one of the nine points that divide a **ranked distribution** into ten divisions, each containing one-tenth of all the cases. **2.** = DECILE RANK, the rank order, counting from the bottom, of the 10 divisions thus made. ➤The 1st decile rank is the rank of those below the 1st decile point, the 9th decile rank below the 9th decile point. The 10th decile rank is of those at or above the 9th decile point—there is no 10th decile point.—See **partile** for discussion.

decision: *n.* **1.** the formulation of a course of action with intent to execute it. **2.** = DECISIVENESS, the quality of formulating plans and acting on them.

decision theory: a theoretical treatment using the mathematics of **game theory** to set forth the decisions that would be made if they were to be based on considerations of the consequences of possible error. ➤It is not assumed that actual decisions are necessarily so based; deviations from the theoretical expectation necessitate search for supplemental or alternate grounds for decision.

decisive: *adj.* **1.** pertaining to, or leading to, **decision.** ➤Decisive characterizes that which did lead to decision or choice; **crucial** characterizes some property of the situation that should lead to choice. **2.** of a person who makes decisions easily, quickly, and/or firmly.—*n.* **decisiveness,** the trait or abstract quality of being decisive; **decision,** the act.—*v.* decide.

Deckerinnerung (dek″er·in'ə·rủng) = (*Ger.*) **cover memory.**

decoding: *n.* **1.** (*commun. theory*) process whereby a **receiver** transforms **signals** into **messages** at the **destination.** ➤In the case of organisms the destination is a person, the receiver is the entire sensory apparatus, the signals are stimuli, the messages are the meanings elaborated by the organism. **2.** translating from an unfamiliar code into a familiar set of symbols or language.

decompensation: *n.* failure to **compensate** normally; activity intended to compensate but not succeeding.

deconversion: *n.* sudden loss of religious faith.

decorticate: *adj.* of an animal whose **cortex** has been removed.

decortication: *n.* removal of the **cortex,** or of portions of it.

decrement: *n.* decrease or loss in quantity of a function; the amount lost or decreased. ➤Decrement when overused becomes an example of **bogus erudition.** In most cases it means simply *decrease.*—*Cp.* **increment.**

decrement/work: see **work decrement.**

decussation: *n.* an X-like crossing over of nerve tracts, from one side of the body to the other, in their course to or from the higher centers.

dedifferentiation: *n.* loss of qualitative distinction of parts within any system; a return to a more homogeneous state.—*Syn.* regression (2).

deduction: *n.* the mode of reasoning that starts with premises or propositions and attempts to derive valid conclusions therefrom. ➤Inference is said to have two forms: **deductive** and **inductive.** The former begins with established truths or truth claims, the latter with fact or observation. ¶The DEDUCTIVE METHOD is sometimes contrasted with the **empirical** and the **experimental** methods. The contrast is imperfect for, while both are chiefly inductive, they also employ the deductive method. —*Contr.* also *w.* **intuition, induction.**

deduction/logical: see **logical deduction.**

deep: *adj.* **1.** (*anat.*) pertaining to underlying tissues or organs.—*Ant.* SHALLOW, SUPERFICIAL. **2.** characterizing tones of slow vibration rate. ➤*Pref.* to the *syn.* LOW, which may refer to intensity as well as rate.

deep reflex: a reflex in an underlying muscle, elicited by tapping the **tendon,** bone, or point of insertion of the muscle.

deep sensibility: a sense mode or system of sensibility for which the receptors are in deep-lying **cutaneous** and **subcutaneous** layers, or in muscles.

defecation: *n.* discharge of the contents of the intestine.

defect (dē·fekt', dē'fekt): *n.* failure to conform to a standard because of faulty functioning or arrangement. ➤*Distg. fr.* DEFICIENCY, which implies a specific lack (as of energy, of hemoglobin). The distinction is worth preserving, even though in many cases the two words are synonymous. **Defect** and (esp.) **defective** imply **malfunction:** compare the connotations of *defective motivation* and *deficient motivation.*—*Cp.* **deficient, defective.**

defect/functional: see **functional defect.**

defective: *adj.* **1.** faulty in structure, arrangement, or operation; having a **defect.** ➤*Distg. fr.* **deficient:** inadequate in quantity, or completely lacking.—*n.* **2.** a person who has a **defect** or, more commonly, a **deficiency,** esp. in intelligence.—See **mental *deficiency, mental defective.**

defective/high-grade: a person of limited intellectual ability who is able to adjust to concrete situations with a minimum of supervision, but has very limited ability to handle abstract situations. Most such individuals are between IQ 50 and 69.

defective/low-grade: a person who can function adequately only in a sheltered environment: he is unable to control his bodily functions and may constitute a threat to himself or others. Most such individuals are below IQ 50.

defective/mental: see **mental defective.**

defendance need: (*H. A. Murray*) the need to defend the self verbally against blame or criticism.

defense: *n.* any psychological instrumentality by which a person automatically protects his **self** or **ego** against unpleasantness, shame, anxiety, or loss of self-esteem. ➤Originally psychoanalytical, the term has been taken over very generally in psychiatry and psychology. The psychological instrumentality may be an *activity* (see **perceptual *defense, defense reaction,** and **ego defense**), or a psychological *structure* (see **defense mechanism**). The defense is usually (if not always) fully **unconscious**— that is, it is not intentionally acquired, and it operates automatically, without voluntary inception or control and without a conscious signal that it is operating. Its presence is betrayed by an otherwise unexplainable lack of relation between the circumstances and the behavior. Even quite unimaginative persons have ingenious defenses. Many names for special forms are current: **rationalization, projection, overcompensation, undoing, reaction-formation, symbolization.** Repression is perhaps the most general defense. Each of these is a defense against a special situation or action; DEFENSE CHARACTER or **character armor** is a generalized defense, a personality trait (or trait syndrome) that wards off anxiety.—*Var.* **defence.**

defense/isolation: see **isolation defense.**

defense mechanism: (*psychoan., pop.*) **1.** any enduring structure of the **psyche** that enables a person to avoid awareness of the unpleasant or the anxiety-arousing. **2.** = **defense reaction.** ➤This usage, while very common, blurs the distinction between the action and the mechanism for the action. ¶Many varieties of defense mechanism have been named, often overlapping greatly. See **defense** for general discussion. See also **ego defense (1)** for a more specific meaning.

defense/neurotic or **/pathogenic:** (*psychoan.*) a **defense** that blocks healthy expression of the instinctual or unconscious impulse, thus leading to a neurotic **breakthrough.** ➤Successful—i.e., nonneurotic—defense is said to allow expression through **sublimation** or some sort of compromise. —*Cp.* **ego defense (1).**

defense/perceptual: selective perceiving such that a person is protected from awareness of something unpleasant or threatening to the **ego.** ➤*Distg. fr.* **rationalization** or reinterpretation of what has been perceived. Perceptual defense is preventive: the unpleasant datum does not get through in its unpleasant form but is so misperceived that it is inoffensive. Thus, unpleasant or taboo words presented very rapidly may be misperceived as typographically similar but inoffensive words. (E.g., an excessively "nice" person perceives *stink* as *stick*.)

defense reaction: (*psychoan.*) **1.** any activity, including thinking or feeling, designed to shut out awareness of an unpleasant or shameful or anxiety-arousing fact, or one that threatens self-esteem. ➤The activity may be that of **repression, symbolic** expression (actually, symbolic distortion), or some other alteration of conscious process or overt behavior. A familiar example is **rationalization. 2.** an activity that acts as a barrier against doing something that threatens the **ego** or **superego.** ➤E.g., one may emphasize all forms of loving behavior toward a parent to keep oneself from hating the parent (which is prohibited by the **superego**). Note that in (**1**) the activity is to keep one from knowing, in (**2**) from doing.—*Cp.* **ego defense. 3.** the psychic structure that provides for a defense reaction; = **defense mechanism** (*pref'd.*).—See **defense** for general discussion.

defense reflex: an automatic protective movement such as dodging a missile or closing the eyelids. ➤It is often not strictly reflex. Since **defense** has taken on a different meaning (see **defense reaction** or **mechanism**), PROTECTIVE RESPONSE is recommended for the above.

defensiveness: *n.* **1.** excessive rejection of criticism of oneself, express or implied. ➤It may be manifested in what the observer sees as **defense reaction,** in reasoned but too emotional argument, or in counterattack. It may be exhibited also when persons with whom one **identifies** are criticized. **2.** behavior that shifts attention away from another behavior, notice of which would cause embarrassment, discomfort, or shame.

deference need: (*H. A. Murray*) the need to admire and follow a superior.

deficiency: see **defect.**

deficiency/mental: a term for all levels of subnormal **intellectual** development. ➤Logically, mental deficiency should mean lack in all sorts of mental functions; it is arbitrarily restricted, however, to intellectual deficiency and to such lack in other functions as is corollary to low intellectual development. There are several grades, conventionally distinguished as follows:

(*a*) BORDERLINE DEFICIENCY, in which the person is usually considered legally competent but slightly subnormal in intelligence. It includes persons of IQ 70–80 and such persons below IQ 70 as are deemed not to be morons.

(*b*) MORONITY, in which the usual range of IQ is 50–69. A MORON is defined as a person "who is capable of earning a living under favorable conditions, but is incapable, from mental defect existing from birth or from an early age, of competing on equal terms with his normal fellows; or of managing himself or his affairs with ordinary prudence." This statement (which follows the wording of an English Royal Commission) is vague and defines a psychological condition in sociological terms; but it has been very influential.

(*c*) IMBECILITY, in which the usual range of IQ is 25–49. An IMBECILE is capable of learning to guard himself against common dangers but cannot earn a living.

(*d*) IDIOCY, in which the IQ is below 25. IDIOTS are unable to guard themselves against common dangers and cannot be taught connected speech. ¶It should be noted that the intelligence quotients given are not defining; they represent only the usual range.

A variety of related terms is in use. FEEBLE-MINDEDNESS, in the U.S., covers all the grades except borderline deficiency; in Britain, it is synonymous with moronity. AMENTIA is a synonym for mental deficiency; but it is hard to distinguish aurally from **dementia,** and logically should apply only to idiocy. MENTAL DEFECT or MENTAL DEFECTIVENESS are used as synonyms but, since **defect** properly means faulty functioning, **mental deficiency** is preferred. (But note that the personal noun is **mental defective**). HYPOPHRENIA and OLIGOPHRENIA are seldom-used synonyms. SUBNORMAL is a general term without specific limits but seldom applied to anyone over IQ 80.

Standard Psychiatric Nomenclature proposes to limit mental deficiency to cases of deficiency existing since birth, without organic brain disease or known prenatal cause (hitherto called PRIMARY by many authorities). What was formerly called **secondary mental *deficiency** is now designated in the Psychiatric Nomenclature as CHRONIC BRAIN SYNDROME ASSOCIATED WITH CONGENITAL CRANIAL ANOMALY, OR WITH MONGOLISM. It seems better, however, to keep mental deficiency as a theory-free term, descriptive of the presenting symptoms of both primary and secondary forms.

deficiency/primary mental: lack of normal development in intelligence not caused by disease or injury after birth and believed to result, essentially, from genetic factors.

deficiency/secondary mental: failure of normal development in intelligence as a result of early brain disease or injury.— *Contr. w.* **deficiency/primary mental.**— *Syn.* EXOGENOUS MENTAL DEFICIENCY.

deficient: *adj.* inadequate in quantity, or wholly lacking. ➤*Distg. fr.* **defective,** meaning faulty, functioning improperly. While it may be true that most persons classed as feeble-minded function poorly (are mentally defective), the defining fact is their relative lack of intelligence; hence, the correct term is **mentally deficient.** But since "mental deficient" seems inacceptable as a noun, **mental defective** has become established as the personal noun form.— *abstr. n.* **deficiency.**

deficit motive: a motive contingent upon some lack in the organism; a motive extinguished by the reduction of tension.

deficit stimulus: a stimulus arising from some tissue lack.

definiendum: *n.* (*L.*) that which is, or needs to be, defined.

definite: *adj.* having well-marked limits or boundaries, physical or logical.

definite correction servo: see **sampling servo.**

definition: *n.* **1.** marking off boundaries between classes or groups of phenomena. **2.** marking off the boundaries of the meaning of a word, phrase, or other linguistic symbol; or the formulation that results. ➤FORMAL DEFINITION consists in stating the class that includes the objects defined and the characteristics by which they are distinguishable from others in that class; it is definition by **genus** and **species.** Definition by means of synonyms or of mere grammatical variants of the term itself is TAUTOLOGICAL DEFINITION. A CIRCULAR DEFINITION defines something in terms whose definitions refer back to itself: e.g., to define *neuron* as "the unit structure of the nervous system" while defining *nervous system* as "a complex of neurons" is circular. (A reader who finds circular definitions in this dictionary will confer a favor by notifying the editor or publisher.) An admittedly incomplete definition is called a DELIMITATION. DEFINITION BY ENUMERATION (which can seldom be complete) is often useful. ¶A definition should be phrased in more understandable terms than the DEFINIENDUM— i.e., than the term to be defined; but this depends on the audience.

definition/coordinating: restating a set of observable facts in terms of a mathematical system or model.

definition/functional: a definition in terms of use. ➤Although it is characteristic of low levels of intelligence to *depend* on such definition, it is both a useful and a valid form.—See **definition**.

definition/operational: see **operational definition**.

deflection: *n.* (*psychoan.*) a **defense reaction** in which attention is diverted from the unpleasant.

deflection strain: (*R. B. Cattell*) the effort required to sustain a learned behavior over an earlier or innately preferred behavior.

defloration: *n.* the perforation of the hymen during first coitus.

deformity: *n.* abnormal bodily formation, esp. one that is visible and is considered ugly. ➤It may or may not be correlated with defective functioning.

defusion (dē·fū′zhən): *n.* (*psychoan.*) the partial undoing of the fusion of **Eros** and **Thanatos**; a **regression** to a state in which the two **instinctual** trends are less completely harmonized.—*Ant.* **fusion (2).** —*Distg. fr.* **diffusion.**—*v.* **defuse.**

degenerate: *n.* a person who has changed markedly for the worse according to biological, moral, or societal standards; by extension, a person who falls seriously short of attaining such standards. ➤The associative overtones of the word are often offensively moralistic, esp. in journalism, where it usually means a person whose offense against sex mores is different from those commonly recognized and condoned.—*adj.* **degenerate.**—*abstr. n.* **degeneracy.**

degenerate type: a person displaying a number of loosely defined deviations from normal conduct. ➤The usual implications of the term—that a correlation exists between the deviations; that the type is hereditary, or that it is characterized by physical **stigmata**—are so highly questionable that the term should be avoided.

degeneration: *n.* alteration in an organ or an organism from better to worse, however defined. ➤It may refer to moral decay or criminality, mental **deterioration**, pathological destruction of tissue, change from more complex to more simple organization (as in parasitic worms).—*adj.* **degenerative; degenerate,** which should be used with caution against unfortunate implications in certain contexts (see **degenerate, degenerate type**).

degeneration/retrograde: (*neurol.*) degenerative changes that occur in the cell bodies of certain neurons if their axons are cut.

degeneration/social: a breakdown in society or in a social group; esp., the loss of moral, intellectual, and cooperative standards, without visible indication of the substitution of new or higher standards. ➤The notion of a falling off from a former state is explicit.

degrees of freedom or **df**: **1.** (*math.*) the number of elements that can vary while still permitting the fulfillment of a mathematical requirement. ➤E.g., let it be required that five numbers must add to a given number *x,* the value of the numbers not being restricted. Then four of them may vary freely, since the fifth can assume the necessary value so that the five will sum to *x.* In such a case there are $N - 1$, or four, degrees of freedom. **2.** (*stat.*) the number of observations (persons, test items, trials, scores—whatever a **sample** is composed of) minus the number of independent restrictions, i.e., of the number of prior calculations based on the sample, used in estimating a given **statistic.** ➤This is the mathematical meaning applied to the problem of sampling. The statistics of prediction based on a sample may be in error because part of the **variance** of the sample may be peculiar to that sample. Knowing the degree to which the sample is free or open to such variation permits a better *estimate* of what the prediction from another sample will be.

déjà (dā′zhə): *adv.* (*Fr.*) already. ➤In combination with various adjectives, it refers to an illusion of familiarity: DÉJÀ PENSÉE, of a new idea that seems familiar; DÉJÀ ENTENDU, of a new voice that sounds familiar; DÉJÀ VU, of a new scene that looks familiar.

dejection: *n.* lowness of spirits. ➤*Prefd.* to **depression** when referring to a temporary state of a normal person.—*adj.* **dejected.**

delayed reaction: **1.** (*hist.*) in a reaction-time experiment, reactions believed to depend upon higher cortical centers: discrimination reactions, choice reactions, etc. ➤The term implies the oversimplified theory that there is delay while an extra set of neurons is activated. **2.** = **delayed response.**

delayed response: an adaptive or goal-seeking response evoked a considerable time after the disappearance of its usual stimulus. ➤In the typical experiment, food is hidden while the animal watches, but he is restrained for varying periods before being allowed to seek the food.—*Distg. fr.* DELAYED REWARD REACTION (better called DELAYED REWARD LEARNING) in which the reward is not immediately forthcoming after an **instrumental** response. In the one case the stimulus disappears while the rewarding response is restrained, in the other the response disappears before its reward is forthcoming.—See also **predelay reinforcement**.

delayed reward: a situation in which the reward (or negative reward) follows the response of the subject by a considerable interval. ➤Used for situations comparable to **instrumental *conditioning**.

delayed reward reaction: see **delayed response.**

deliberation: *n.* comparison of alternatives, with a view to choice.—*adj.* **deliberate,** acting only after deliberation; **deliberative,** pertaining to the process.

delinquency: *n.* a relatively minor violation of legal or moral codes, esp. by children or adolescents. ➤JUVENILE DELINQUENCY is such behavior by a young person (usually under 16 or 18, depending on the state code) as to bring him to the attention of a court.—*adj.* and *pers. n.* **delinquent.**

delinquency area: an area with a high juvenile delinquency rate.

delinquent/defective: a person whose antisocial behavior is due largely to mental deficiency.

délire (dā·lir') : *n.* (*Fr.*) delusion; (rarely) **delirium.** ➤The French DÉLIRE D'INTERPRÉTATION is sometimes preferred to the Greek **paranoia.**

délire de toucher (dā·lir' də tü·shā') : (*Fr.*) a **compulsion** to touch objects.

delirium (di·lir'i·əm) : *n.* a confused mental condition, usually the result of shock or fever, characterized by **delusions, illusions, hallucinations,** and **incoherence.**—*adj.* **delirious.**

delirium/exhaustion: see **exhaustion delirium.**

delirium tremens (trē'mənz) : an acute delirium precipitated by alcohol, characterized by great anxiety, tremors, **hallucinations,** and **delusions.**

deltagraph: *n.* a graphic device for finding the statistical significance or stability of the differences of the mean without having to compute the individual *t* values.

delta movement: see **motion/apparent.**

delusion: *n.* a belief held in the face of evidence normally sufficient to destroy the belief. ➤A delusion must be considered a definitely abnormal phenomenon, even though a normal individual may hold it. Innumerable varieties are distinguished by naming the belief.—*Distg. fr.* **illusion** and **hallucination.**—*adj.* **delusive,** pertaining to the false belief; **delusional,** characterizing the condition of a person suffering from delusions; **delusory,** of data that seem to (but actually do not) support a conclusion, or of alleged facts that are fanciful and produced by delusion.

delusional speech: speech that is extensively contaminated by **delusions** of grandeur or of persecution.

delusion/expansive: see **expansive delusion.**

delusion of grandeur: exaggerated belief that one is of exalted station or accomplishment.—*Syn.* **megalomania,** IDEAS OF GRANDEUR.—*adj.* **grandiose.**

delusion of persecution: a **delusion** that other persons are deliberately and unfairly causing the person's efforts to fail or are in some way inflicting hardships on him. The delusion is often highly systematized as an elaborate conspiracy, minor and innocent happenings being interpreted as evidence.

delusion of reference: a false belief that behaviors actually having other significance have malign or derogatory reference to oneself.

demand: *n.* any aspect of the environment that puts the organism out of adjustment or **homeostatic** balance until a certain kind of response is made. Certain changes internal to the organism when they are perceived are also reacted to as a **demand.**—*Syn.* DEMAND TASK.

demand character: (*Gestalt*) an attribute that an object has for a particular organism which causes the organism to behave, or tend to behave, in a certain way: e.g., the full moon seems to demand romantic behavior from young lovers. ➤The **demand character** is itself in part a function of a **need-state.** A **valence** is aversion or attraction to an object; **demand character** is more general and includes behavior not directly related to the precipitating object.

demand/environmental: an aspect of the situation that is perceived as requiring some sort of action. ➤The range is from relatively simple **stimuli** to complex **problems.** The demand may elicit uneasy general activity and trial-and-error, or directed and oriented behavior, depending on whether the organism perceives a means to the required correction.

demand feeding = **self-demand schedule.**

demand task = **demand.**

dementia (di·men'shə) : *n.* lasting mental **deterioration;** esp., pathological decline in intellectual power and in appropriateness of emotional response. ➤*Distg. fr.* amentia (see **mental *deficiency**), a failure to develop.

dementia infantilis (in″fən·tē'ləs) : a degenerative disease in which some of the nerve cells in the cerebral lobes **atrophy.** It occurs around three years of age and leads to rapid loss of speech. Motor patterns are less affected.—*Syn.* HELLER'S DISEASE.

dementia paralytica = **paresis.**

dementia praecox: see **schizophrenia.**

dementia (praecox) simplex: see **schizophrenia/simple.**

dementia/senile: gradual but eventually severe loss in mental effectiveness, esp. intellectual but also emotional, found in old age. ➤Usually applied only to a loss that passes normal limits.

democratic atmosphere: a descriptive term for the quality of personal relationships produced within a group by a leader who uses democratic techniques, such as permitting the self-determination of policies by the group.—*Cp.* **authoritarian atmosphere, laissez-faire atmosphere.**

demography (di·mog'rə·fi): *n.* the study of human populations, including **vital *statistics,** geographic distribution, causes of increase and decrease, and the like.—*adj.* **demographic.**

demonstration: *n.* **1.** teaching by presenting concrete illustrations of the facts. **2.** conclusive proof.

demophobia (dē"mō·fō'bi·ə): *n.* morbid fear of crowds.

demoralize: *v.* to break down the habits, attitudes, and values of a person or a group; to break down **morale.**

dendrite: *n.* the receiving fiber or branch of the **neuron** (which see).—*adj.* **dendritic.**—*Syn.* DENDRON.

dendron = dendrite.

denervation (dē"nər·vā'shən): *n.* deprivation of a portion of the body of its nerve supply.

denotation: *n.* all of the objects or instances to which a term points or refers. ➤*Distg. fr.* **connotation,** the abstract qualities or properties common to the class of objects or instances designated by a term. The denotation of *U.S. citizen* is any of the 160 million persons who are U.S. citizens, or all of them; the connotation comprises the characteristics of the American citizen and the rights, privileges, and duties conferred by citizenship.—*adj.* **denotative.**—*v.* **denote.**

density: *n.* (*stat.*) the extent to which the entries of a correlation plot are grouped closely together; esp., the extent to which they are grouped about a **regression line.**

density/tonal: an elementary attribute or dimension of a tone, operationally defined by having different thresholds from those of pitch, volume, and loudness. It is the attribute of being compact or solid as a tone. ➤Density does not have a one-to-one relation to a physical dimension of the sound wave. A bugle tone is denser than that of an organ. It is probable that SOUND (or TONAL) BRIGHTNESS is only another name for this attribute.

dentate nucleus: a large mass of cells embedded within the **cerebellum.**

dentition: *n.* the development and cutting of teeth.

dependence: *n.* **1.** causal relationship between phenomena. ➤*Contr. w.* **dependency,** which (strictly speaking) refers to the actual causal relation in a concrete case. **2.** (*topol. psychol.*) the degree to which a change in one **region** causes a change in another. **3.** the extent to which members of a social group rely on each other in form-

ing their ideas about social reality.—*Ant.* INDEPENDENCE.

dependence/functional: a relation between two variables such that a change in one implies a corresponding change in the other.

dependence/oral: see **oral dependence.**

dependency: *n.* **1.** (*sociol.*) state or condition of requiring economic support or other aid from others, specif. from public agencies.—*Cp.* **dependence. 2.** a lack of self-reliance; the tendency to seek the help of others in making decisions or in carrying out difficult actions. **3.** = **dependence (1).** —*adj.* and *pers. n.* **dependent.**

dependency/emotional: habitual reliance upon another person for comfort, guidance, and decision.

dependency/morbid: (*K. Horney*) an extreme form of **self-effacement** in which there is a **compulsive** need for total emotional surrender to, and union with, a stronger person.

dependency/passive: a relationship which individuals of low self-esteem maintain with others by hinting at their own inferiority and thus arousing the others' concern for them.—*Syn.* DIRECT EXPLOITATIVE ATTITUDE.

dependent: *adj.* characterizing that which is influenced or determined by the occurrence or nonoccurrence of some other event. —See **variable/dependent.**

dependent variable: see **variable/dependent.**

depersonalization: *n.* a state in which a person loses the feeling of his own reality, or feels his own body to be unreal. Everything seems dreamlike, and actions of oneself or others are watched with indifferent detachment. There may be **delusions,** such as that the body is hollow or does not exist.

depolarization: *n.* causing something to lose its condition of polarity, i.e., of being organized with two opposed poles. ➤E.g., an audience-speaker relation is depolarized when a stray dog runs down the aisle.

depression: *n.* a state of inaccessibility to stimulation or to particular kinds of stimulation, of lowered initiative, of gloomy thoughts. ➤Depression may be a symptom in many mental disorders, esp. in **manic-depressive reaction** (or **psychosis**) and in **depressive reaction** (also called reactive depression). But persons quite without mental disorder may experience depression. For the normal case, DEJECTION is usually a preferred synonym.—*Contr. w.* **mania;** also *w.* **euphoria.**

depression/agitated: a pathological condition of restless overactivity, despair, and apprehensive or self-condemnatory delusions.

depression/psychotic: an older diagnostic category that included both **agitated** and retarded *depression.—See psychotic *depressive reaction.

depression/reactive = depressive reaction.

depression/retarded: a pathological condition in which ordinary activities are slowed down (some even omitted), and in which the patient is dejected and self-depreciatory, sometimes to the point of delusion.

depressive reaction: (*Stan. Psychiat.*) a psychoneurotic disorder precipitated by some loss sustained by the person, and usually transient. There is anxiety but it is allayed by depression and self-depreciation. —*Syn.* REACTIVE DEPRESSION. ➤*Distg. fr.* psychotic *depressive reaction in which the reaction to precipitating circumstances is more severe and less realistic.

depressive reaction/psychotic: (*Stan. Psychiat.*) a disorder marked by severe depression and gross misinterpretation of reality, including delusions and hallucinations. It is distinguished from manic-depressive psychosis chiefly by being precipitated by environmental factors and by the absence of marked cyclothymic swings in mood. It is distinguished from the depressive reaction by the greater severity and persistence of the symptoms.

depressor nerve: 1. any afferent nerve whose excitation depresses motor activity; esp. 2. one that depresses action of the arterial and capillary muscles, thus lowering blood pressure.

deprivation: *n.* loss of something desired. ➤Privation means *lack,* generally involuntary lack; deprivation means *loss* or taking away; frustration means *obstruction* (esp. by social or personal agency) of an ongoing goal-directed activity.

depth analysis: see depth psychology.

depth perception: 1. direct awareness of the distance of objects from the observer.— *Syn.* DISTANCE PERCEPTION, PERCEPTION OF DEPTH. 2. awareness of distance from front to back of an object, so that it is seen as three-dimensional.—*Syn.* stereoscopic vision (more specific).

depth psychology: any psychology that postulates dynamic psychic activities that are unconscious. It embraces all schools deriving from Freud, including many that depart widely from his teachings, and others of independent origin.—*Approx. syn.* psychoanalysis (which see), DEPTH ANALYSIS.

dereistic (dē″rē·is′tik): *adj.* pertaining to fantasy; imaginative; autistic.

derivation: *n.* 1. a hypothesis based on a theorem or other hypothesis; a corollary. 2. a behavior that is unnatural to the situation or object with which it occurs, and that gets its character from some other situation or behavior trend: e.g., a child's

rejection of a toy because a misliked neighbor has one like it. 3. (*psychoan.*) a behavior due to a conflict, esp. to an unconscious conflict. 4. (*V. Pareto*) an effort to justify one's actions; a rationalization; a fictitious motive.

➤All four usages can be defended as being related to the common meaning of derivation. Yet is there any context in which the idea cannot be more clearly conveyed in other terms, with less effort by the reader to discern what is meant?

derivation of formula: (*math.*) the procedure of obtaining a compact and mathematically elegant symbolical representation of a given rule or law; the process of expressing a law by operating mathematically with a group of conventional symbols; transforming certain given formulas according to rules in such a way as to lead to a new formula.

derivative: *n.* (*psychoan.*) distorted behavior that permits an id impulse to be expressed with less anxiety. ➤The distortion is believed to be the product of ego defenses working against the impulse.

derived measure or score: see score/derived.

derived properties/postulate of: the Gestalt principle that parts derive their properties from wholes.

derma: *n.* the skin; esp., the true skin that lies below the epidermis.—*Syn.* DERMIS.— *adj.* dermal.

dermal sense = cutaneous sense.

dermatitis: *n.* inflammation of the skin.

dermatographia: *n.* literally, skin writing; a condition in which stroking the skin lightly causes elevated reddish marks.— *Syn.* DERMOGRAPHIA.

dermatosis: *n.* any disease of the skin.

dermis = derma.

dermographia = dermatographia.

description: *n.* 1. a report of observed phenomena and of their relationships so far as the latter are observable. ➤It is debatable to what extent relations are observable. Description is distinguished from appraisal, appreciation, generalization, evaluation, and theorizing, in each of which the data are reorganized or related to other data in order to reveal their meaning, value, or significance. 2. (*introspective psychol.*) a statement of a psychological process in terms of what happens, with no addition of meaning (which see).—*Syn.* (*Ger.*) *Beschreibung.*

desensitization: *n.* (*counseling*) lessened emotional sensitivity with respect to some personal defect, some social inferiority, etc.

desexualization: *n.* the act of detaching, or apparently detaching, sexual energy from an object or activity; the act of removing from an activity any apparent connection with sexuality. ➤E.g., sexual **exhibitionism** may be sublimated in acting; or the sexual aspect of any act may be subtly concealed or overlaid.

design: *n.* 1. forethought or representation of a complex action to be carried out; a plan. 2. a purpose. 3. a schematic representation of the essential elements of something.—See **design/experimental.**—*v.* **design.**

design/experimental: the plan of an experiment, including selection of subjects, order of administration of the experimental treatment, the kind of treatment and the **procedures** by which it is administered, and the recording of the data (with special reference to the particular statistical analyses to be performed).

design/factorial: see **factorial design.**

design/representative: (*E. Brunswik*) an experimental plan that utilizes the **covariation** of a group of variables in the study of stimulus-response relationships. ➤The CLASSICAL DESIGN sought to hold constant all but the experimental and the dependent variables. Representative design seeks to give effect to all the relevant variables in such a way as to represent their frequency of occurrence and range of variation. It combines experimental with statistical manipulation of variables.

desire: *n.* a feeling of longing, usually with an element of active striving to alter a state of affairs that is lacking, excessive, or disordered, so as to accord with the purposes of the individual. ➤Except when qualified as **unconscious desire,** it refers to conscious process. The nearest behavioral term is **drive.**—*Syn.* want, craving, urge, wish, **need, appetite,** and (for negative desire) **aversion.**—See **desire** (*v.*).—*Cp.* also **valence.**

desire: *v.* to long for; to represent something to oneself as being a **satisfier** or a means to satisfaction; to feel that a particular thing or condition will satisfy or relieve a **need.** ➤*Syn.* **wish, crave, want.** WISH is weaker than desire and often carries the connotation that the wish is, or may well be, unattainable. CRAVE is stronger than desire and means to demand gratification of an urgent need, esp. of a physical appetite. WANT basically means *to lack;* it has come to be used for wish or desire but is somewhat stronger.—See **desire** (*n.*).

destination: *n.* (*commun. theory*) a system, including as a special case a responding animal, that accepts and is influenced by **messages** coming from the **receiver.** Within a communication unit, the **destination** and the **source** may be treated as a single system called a **mediator.**

destruction method: a method for determining the function of a portion of the nervous system by surgical removal of that portion. ➤The resulting behavior is, however, a function of the undestroyed portions; inference as to the function of the destroyed parts is complex.

destructiveness: *n.* a tendency to express **aggression** by mutilating or destroying environmental objects.

destrudo (des·trü′dō): *n.* (*psychoan.*) the expression of the hypothesized **death instinct.**

desurgency or *F*-: (*R. B. Cattell*) a **source** *trait marked (in its extreme form) by anxious, agitated, melancholy, brooding, seclusive behavior.—*Ant.* **surgency.**

detached affect: (*S. Freud*) an **affect** associated originally with an unbearable idea but now separated from the idea. The affect attaches itself to other ideas which thereby become **obsessions.**—*Distg. fr.* **displacement of *affect.**

detachment: *n.* 1. freedom from unnecessary details, esp. in trying to solve a problem. 2. freedom from emotional involvement in a problem or situation. 3. emotional distance from others; lack of sympathy, empathy, or concern. 4. the active avoidance of emotional closeness to any person, or to a person with whom emotional closeness is to be expected. ➤This is usually a neurotic symptom, a **defense reaction** against the inner or outer conflict such emotional closeness would involve, but it may also be a rationally chosen precaution.

detachment/emotional: a state in which little emotion is experienced, no matter what (within statable wide limits) happens. ➤Such detachment may be from external events, from what happens to others, or from what happens to oneself. The term usually implies the experiencing of less emotion than is appropriate.—*Cp.* **objectivity.**

detachment/intellectual: considering a problem on its merits without being influenced by previous notions or conclusions in similar cases.

detail/inside: see **inside detail.**

detail response: (*Ror.*) a scoring category for response to less than the entire inkblot. ➤A detail that is a major part of the pattern is symbolized as *D;* one that is minor is *d.* Details are also distinguished as USUAL and UNUSUAL (*B. Klopfer*), or as DETAIL and RARE DETAIL (*S. Beck*).

detector/lie: see **lie detector.**

deter: *v.* to restrain or discourage from action by means of threat, warning, or fear of consequences.—*adj., n.* **deterrent.**

deterioration: *n.* qualitative impairment of a physiological or mental function, or of personality as a whole. ➤Certain **psychoses,** marked by progressive impairment, are grouped together as DETERIORATIVE.

deterioration index or **quotient:** an index based on comparison of scores for the four "Hold" tests of the **Wechsler-Bellevue** (*information, vocabulary, picture completion, object assembly*), which show little or no age decline, with the four "Don't Hold" tests (*digit span, arithmetic, block design, digit symbol*), which show steep decline. The index, using standard scores, has the formula

$$DI = \frac{Hold - Don't\ Hold}{Hold}$$

deterioration/intellectual: see **intellectual deterioration.**

determinant: *n.* **1.** that which settles or decides; esp., a limiting term that makes a proposition more precise. **2.** that which causes an event to happen in a specified way.—*Syn.* **determiner,** *pref.* as having the notion of agency, and as less liable to confusion with (1). **3.** = **determinant/ Rorschach.**—*Distg. fr.* **determinate.**

determinant/behavior: see **behavior determinant.**

determinant/constitutional: the influence of the individual's total physiological make-up on his personality.

determinant/dream: (*psychoan.*) the principal factor in producing a particular dream and in giving it its essential quality. ➤Every dream, however, is **overdetermined**—i.e., has many **determiners.**

determinant/form: see **form determinant.**

determinant/organismic or **/personal:** those qualities or aspects of character of the animal that codetermine the nature of a behavior.—*Contr. w.* **determinant/ situational.** ➤**Determinant** usually applies to a rather limited range of behavior; **trait,** which has the same meaning, may signify a wider range.

determinant/Rorschach: any of the qualities of the inkblots that are important for a given person in determining what he will perceive in them: **color, form, shading,** and **movement** determinants. ➤Color, form, and shading are objective characteristics of the stimulus patterns. Movement, however, obviously is only imaginatively imputed to them. The Rorschach terms movement, color, shading, and form are used to describe the content of the *response,* as well as the objective *stimulus* for the response, usually with no confusion when they appear in context.

determinant/situational: 1. any energy impinging on an organism and having a part in determining its behavior.—*Ant.* **constitutional** or **organismic *determinant. 2.** an external event of more or less accidental character—one not directly attributable to one's own action nor to the culture—that influences behavior. ➤Getting caught in the rain on the way home is **situational;** but being exposed to the subway rush on the way home is said to be culturally (*sic!*) determined.

determinate: *adj.* **1.** having well-defined limits. **2.** (*math.*) having specific values that can be found by the indicated mathematical operations.—*n.* **determination.**—*v.* **determine.**

determination: *n.* **1.** assigning boundaries or limits; the assignment of a specific descriptive attribute or (more often) of a specific quantitative value to something: *determination* of (the object's) color, *determination* of intensity. **2.** the act of coming to a decision. **3.** the attitude or disposition to carry through a course of action despite obstacles.

determination/coefficient of: (*stat.*) the proportion of the **variance** of the **dependent *variable** determined directly by a specified **independent *variable.** It is measured by the square of the **path coefficient.** (It is the complement of the **coefficient of *nondetermination.**)— *Distg. fr.* **determination/index of.**

determination/index of: (*stat.*) **1.** the square of the **index of *correlation** of causally related variables. It expresses the proportion of the **variance** in the dependent variable that is determined by the independent variable.—*Distg. fr.* **determination/coefficient of. 2.** the squared correlation coefficients of **test-retest.**

determine: *v.* to fix boundaries; to decide by authority; to make a decision; to define. ➤In laboratory parlance, one may determine the threshold, i.e., measure it, fix its boundaries. But one does not determine the acceptability of a hypothesis, unless one means to do so by authoritative pronouncement. The use of *determine* to mean *discover* (often seen in research reports) is pedantic.

determined action/principle of: (*Gestalt*) the view that the part (of any phenomenon) is regulated by the whole.

determiner: *n.* **1.** that which brings it about that a certain event occurs as it does.—*Syn.* **cause, factor, determinant** (2). **2.** (*biol.*) a hypothetical unit, presence of which in the germ cell is a condition of the development of a specific hereditary trait; a **gene.** —See **heredity.**

determining or **directive tendency:** a state of the organism that results from accepting a goal direction and regulates behavior accordingly. ➤One may cease to be aware of the goal and may not realize that it is regulating behavior—i.e., the regulation may be unwitting or unconscious.—*Cp.* **set** (esp. **2**), a partial *syn.*

determinism: *n.* the doctrine that an event

is completely explicable in terms of its antecedents. ➤Applied to human actions it holds that, given complete knowledge of conditions, one would have complete knowledge of precisely how a person will—indeed *must*—act. In effect, if not in theory, some degree of determinism is postulated in all scientific, as well as practical, psychology. The several philosophical interpretations of this postulation *need* not, as such, influence psychology.—*Ant.* INDETERMINISM, LIBERTARIANISM.—*Distg. fr.* **mechanism,** which holds that the determining of an event can be explained in terms of physical mechanics (i.e., of the displacement of masses).—See **psychology/divisions and schools of, V, VI.**

determinism/cultural: see **cultural determinism.**

determinism/environmental = **environmentalism.**

detour behavior: any indirect action that leads toward a goal when direct progress is obstructed.—*Distg. fr.* direct action to remove the obstruction; and *fr.* **sublimation,** in which a substitute goal is accepted.

detour tests: those in which a desired goal is reached only by first moving away from the goal.

detraction: *n.* lessening of attention without shifting its focus.

detumescence: *n.* subsidence of swelling, esp. in the genital organs of either sex after erection.

deuteranomaly (dü″tər·ə·nom′ə·li): *n.* color vision in which, by comparison with normal vision, an unusual amount of green is required in a red-green mixture to match a given yellow.—See **Rayleigh's equation.** —*adj.* **deuteranomalous.**

deuteranopia (-nō′pi·ə): *n.* **1.** a somewhat uncommon form of **color blindness** for green.—*Syn.* GREEN BLINDNESS. **2.** inaccurate name for ordinary **red-green blindness.**

development: *n.* **1.** a sequence of continuous change in a system extending over a considerable time; specifically, such change, or related and enduring particular changes, as follow one another in an organism from its origin to maturity or to death. **2.** such sequence leading to irreversible change. **3.** such sequence leading to progressive change, to a higher degree of differentiation and complexity in the system. **4.** the outcome of change in any of the preceding senses. ➤The changes may be in structure, function, or organization; they may be in size, differentiation, complexity, integration, or efficiency. Originally **development,** as a qualitative phenomenon, was distinguished from **growth,** as quantitative or incremental; but present usage tends to make development inclusive of growth, or to employ them synonymously. ¶Sometimes

development and **learning** are thought of as distinct. *Cp.* the expression *development and learning,* though here again the former more often is made inclusive of the latter, at least of persisting changes due to learning. Changes attributable to **maturation** (which see) are also part of development. ¶By extension, development refers to analogous changes in social groups or in anything that can reasonably be compared to an organism, even to inanimate structures such as crystals. The term is thus very broad: its application ranges from molecular changes in crystals or bones to changes in purposes, ideals, or the structure of society; and it is applied both to supposedly genetic changes and to those attributable to nutrition or learning.—*Syn.* **growth** (2).—*adj.* **developmental.**—*v.* **develop.**

developmental direction/law of = **cephalocaudad development/principle of.**

developmental levels: see **development/levels of.**

developmental psychology: the branch of psychology that studies how individuals and classes of individual organisms develop psychologically. It deals with the characteristic behaviors found at various ages or stages of development, and with the general principles that describe the course of development, including the interaction of various developmental functions. It includes the psychologies of infancy, childhood, adolescence, maturity, and old age.—See **psychology/divisions and schools of, VIII, IX.**

developmental quotient: developmental *age divided by chronological age.

developmental scale: a test, check list, or inventory for estimating the stage of development attained by a given person. Various aspects of development may be combined or measured separately.

developmental sequence: that regular order of development in some specific structure or function which characterizes a species or other group. ➤The usual implication, that the sequence is genetically determined, is not necessary; implied only is that the sequence is found unless interfered with by abnormal conditions within or without the organism.

developmental stage: a period in an individual's life typically characterized by a specific cluster of **traits.** ➤E.g., the **oral libido stage** (*psychoan.*) is the period said to be dominated by the investment of **libido** chiefly in the mouth region; at the "gang age" or stage, children are supposed to be especially prone to form gangs; at puberty, when the sex glands are rapidly attaining full maturity, a number of other developments (e.g., rapid increase in stature) are asserted to take place. ¶Due to individual differences, the age placement of such stages is variable, and the association of certain traits with a given period is seldom very close. E.g., although most children gain sharply in height during or just before puberty, some do not.

developmental tasks: levels of achievement or of development that, in a given society and at a given age, are considered appropriate or necessary for socially acceptable functioning. Attainment of these levels thus contributes to the child's happiness and to success with later tasks, whereas failure is disapproved and contributes to unhappiness. ➤Developmental tasks may be almost purely anatomical (e.g., change of voice in the male); or they may be more psychological, even educational (e.g., interest in the opposite sex shortly after the usual age for puberty, or ability to keep up with agemates in reading).

developmental unit: 1. a unit that can be used at different stages of development to designate equal amounts of change. ➤An IQ is intended to be such a unit. Thus, a change of 6 points in IQ should be the same at age 5 as it is at age 9 (approximately true). **2.** a measure that takes the development occurring in any given time interval (e.g., a year) as the equal of that occurring in any other unit of time. ➤The development from age 5 to age 6 is equated with the development from age 7 to age 8 in an MA scale. Although this is the implication of the MA (or any other **age equivalent scale**), mental age units are regarded as equal only to a strictly limited degree or for specific purposes.

developmental zero: the point in time at which development of life actually begins; or the point conventionally agreed upon as the beginning. ➤Both theoretical and factual considerations point to the moment of impregnation of the ovum as the zero point.

development/arrest in: 1. ceasing to increase normally in physical and mental abilities or capacities. **2.** holding to habits and attitudes suitable to an earlier period of life.—*Cp.* **fixation (2), regression (2).**

development/levels of: arbitrary divisions of the life span defined in terms of chronological age. ➤The divisions are for convenience of reference; there is no implication that developmental phenomena form correlated clusters assignable to the several stages. The following age divisions represent a consensus of the members of the Division of Developmental Psychology, APA: (*a*) **infancy,** from birth to 1 year, including the **neonate,** or newborn (from birth to 1 month); (*b*) **childhood,** from 1 to 12 years, divided into EARLY CHILDHOOD

(1 to 6 years), MID-CHILDHOOD (6 to 10 years), LATE CHILDHOOD (*prefd.*) or **preadolescence** (10 to 12 yrs.); (*c*) **adolescence,** from 12 to 21 years, divided into EARLY ADOLESCENCE (12 to 14 years), MID-ADOLESCENCE (14 to 16 years), LATE ADOLESCENCE (16 to 21 years); (*d*) **maturity,** from 21 to 65 years; (*e*) OLD AGE, from 65 years on. ¶Actual usage is somewhat varying; some authors set their own limits, and others leave the limits of a word such as **childhood** to the reader's interpretation.—See also **developmental stage.**

deviant = **deviate.**

deviate: *n.* **1.** a person differing considerably from the average or the standard; esp. **2.** one whose behaviors or attitudes are not in accord with the prevailing patterns or the moral standards of the group; = SOCIAL DEVIATE. ➤Social disapproval is not implied but is in fact commonly directed at the deviate. Even superiority to the norm is often deplored.—See also **deviation/sexual.**—*adj.* **deviant.**—*n.* **deviation.**

deviation: *n.* **1.** departure from a straight line or, more generally, from any point of reference: from the correct, the average, the **standard,** or the **norm. 2.** (*stat.*) the amount by which a measure differs from a point of reference, generally from the **mean.**

deviation/absolute: the **absolute** value of the difference between an observation or score and any origin such as an arithmetic mean.—*Syn.* NUMERICAL DEVIATION.

deviation/average or **AD** = **deviation/ mean.**

deviation/behavior: conduct departing materially from social or ethical standards; conduct departing so far from the usual as to be socially disapproved.

deviation/concomitant = **deviation/concurrent.**

deviation/concurrent: a **deviation** in one variable in the same direction as the corresponding deviation (for the same individual) in another variable.—*Syn.* CONCOMITANT DEVIATION.

deviation IQ: a **standard** *score on an intelligence test that has a mean of 100 and an **SD** approximately that of the **Stanford-Binet** (roughly 16). ➤It is held that the deviation IQ can be interpreted as having the same meaning as the familiar IQ; but, since it is not a quotient between MA and CA, to call it an IQ is misleading.

deviation/mean or **m.d.:** the arithmetic **mean** of the differences from the mean of each value in a series: m.d. $= \dfrac{\Sigma d_M}{N}$. ➤This statistic is now generally replaced by the standard deviation. In a normal distribution it is equal to $.7979\sigma$.—*Syn.* AVERAGE DEVIATION, MEAN VARIATION, AVERAGE ERROR, AVERAGE DEPARTURE, AVERAGE DISCREPANCY,

AVERAGE VARIATION, MEAN ABSOLUTE ERROR. —*Distg. fr.* **median *deviation.**

deviation/median or **Md D:** the **median** of the absolute values of the deviations about some **measure of *central tendency.** —*Syn.* MEDIAN ERROR.

deviation/numerical = **deviation/absolute.**

deviation/quartile: see **quartile deviation.**

deviation score: (*stat.*) an individual score obtained by subtracting from any **gross score** the mean of all the gross scores. Another reference value may be substituted for the mean; in such case, the other value is specifically indicated. A deviation score from the mean is symbolized by x or y, from an arbitrary origin by x' or y'. Deviation scores are used in **product-moment *correlation** coefficients.

deviation/sexual: (*Stan. Psychiat.*) any persisting form of sexual behavior different enough from the normal of a given society to be judged pathological. ➤The line between the pathological and the merely different is a shifting one, but persistent sexual behavior that is forbidden by law (except prostitution) is generally considered deviant: e.g., **homosexuality, transvestism,** rape. But **fetishism** and forms of **sadism** and **masochism,** though not all illegal, are also to be classed as deviations. The term is to be used sparingly since it tends to a condemnatory connotation.—*Syn.* **sexual anomaly** (*prefd.*).—*pers. n.* **sexual deviant** or **deviate.**

deviation/standard (variously symbolized as **SD,** σ, SD_{dist}, σ_{dist}; *pron.* es·dē; σ, sig'-mə): a measure of the **dispersion** or **variability** of a whole distribution. It is computed by summing the squared differences of each measure from the mean, dividing by the number of measures, and extracting the square root:

$$SD \text{ or } \sigma = \sqrt{\frac{\Sigma x^2}{N}} = \sqrt{\frac{\Sigma(M-X)^2}{N}},$$

or (where N is small) $\sqrt{\dfrac{\Sigma x^2}{N-1}}$.

➤*Distg. fr.* **standard error of the mean,** or **SD**ₘ. In a normal distribution, 68.2 per cent of the scores fall between the limits of the mean, plus or minus 1 SD. For certain purposes the squared value of SD, called **variance,** is preferred. When the standard deviation is computed in terms of the class interval, σ' is used instead of σ.—*Syn.* INDEX OF VARIABILITY, DISPERSION, ROOT MEAN SQUARE DEVIATION, MEAN SQUARE ERROR, MEAN DISCREPANCY.—*Cp.* **score/standard, standard error, probable error.**

device: *n.* an instrument or a plan of procedure for obtaining some desired result.

devolution: *n.* undoing of **evolution;** a reversal of the evolutionary process.—*Cp.* **regression.**

dexterity: *n.* skillfulness, esp. of the hands. —*Syn.* DEXTROUSNESS.—*adj.* **dexterous, dextrous.**

dexterity test: a test of speed and accuracy in performing simple manual activities.

dextrad: *adv.* toward the right side.

dextral: *adj.* pertaining to the right side of the body.—*Contr. w.* **sinistral.**

dextrality: *n.* **1.** preferential use of the right hand or of the right side generally; right-sidedness. **2.** sidedness, whether right or left; **unidextrality.** ➤The proper antonym is **ambidextrality** or **ambilaterality** (having no preference as to sides), not **ambidextrousness** (skillful on both sides).

dextrosinistral: *adj.* of a person originally left-handed but retrained to use the right hand.

dextrousness = **dexterity.**

df: symbol for **degree(s) of freedom.**

DI or ***ΔI*:** increment of intensity or stimulus strength.

di: (*Ror.*) scoring code for **inside detail.**

di- (dī-): prefix meaning *two* or *double.*

dia-: (dī'ə-): prefix meaning *through* or *within.*

diadic (dī·ad'ik): *adj.* composed of two elements: e.g., a chord of two tones.—*Var.* **dyadic** (which see).

diadochokinesis (dī·ad″ə·kō·kin·ē′səs): normal ability to perform alternating movements, such as flexion and extension of a limb, in rapid succession.

diad/social: 1. a two-person group. **2.** a qualitative unit for classifying the dynamic social interrelations of pairs of persons. Certain dynamic relations are arbitrarily selected and each pattern of combination is a **diad.** ➤E.g., if only the relationship of liking-disliking is considered, the diads for a pair of persons A and B are: A likes B, B likes A; A likes B, B dislikes A; A dislikes B, B likes A; A dislikes B, B dislikes A. When more than four relationships are involved, the number and complexity of the diads becomes too great.

diag.: *abbr.* for *diagnosis, diagnostic.*

diagnosis: *n.* **1.** identification of disease or abnormality from symptoms presented, and from a study of its origin and course. **2.** any classification of an individual on the basis of observed characters. ➤EDUCATIONAL DIAGNOSIS, e.g., classifies a pupil on the basis of facts relevant to his school progress. —*adj.* **diagnostic.**

diagnosis/differential: distinguishing between two similar-appearing conditions by searching for a significant symptom or attribute found in only one. ➤It is extended by analogy from its medical use to conditions of any sort.

diagnostic test: one designed to locate the particular source of a person's difficulties in learning, esp. in school subjects, thus providing clues to what further measures of instruction, guidance, or study are needed. ➤The test must probe for difficulties and their global sources in great detail.—*Contr. w.* **achievement test, aptitude test.**

diagnostic value = **validity.**

diagnostic word test: a test to determine the intensity threshold at which speech can be understood. It uses words especially likely to be confused (phonetically balanced), presenting them in several grades of loudness.

diagram: *n.* **1.** a schematic drawing showing the spatial or the spacio-temporal relations of certain objects or parts to each other. **2.** a drawing that utilizes spatial relations to symbolize logical relations. ➤**Diagrammatic** (*adj.*) often carries the notion that only the essential relations are symbolized, but should not be used to mean *sketchy* or *incomplete.* **3.** = **scatter diagram.**

dialectic: *adj.* **1.** (*logic*) pertaining to reasoning or argument, or to a relatively extensive reasoned argument. **2.** pertaining to reasoning that depends primarily upon elucidation of the meaning of concepts. ➤While the term is usually somewhat disparaging, a very considerable part of any science must be judged to be dialectic.— *Contr. w.* **empirical (1, 6). 3.** (*G. Hegel*) of the law that action (THESIS) must inevitably be followed by counteraction (ANTITHESIS), and that by integration (SYNTHESIS). ➤Marx's **dialectic materialism** is based on this principle.—*n.* **dialectic.**

dialectic(al) materialism: the philosophy of Marx and Engels, which proceeds by the **dialectic** method from the premise that matter is the sole reality. ➤Psychology in Communist countries must work within the framework of this philosophy.

Diana complex: (*psychoan.*) the repressed wish of a female to be a male.—*Cp.* **masculine protest.**

dianetics: *n.* an attempt, resting upon uncontrolled observation and extremely free speculation, to explain behavior in terms of the person's experience not only before birth but before conception.

diary: *n.* a daily record of events. ➤The DIARY METHOD of observation attempts to record all happenings in a given period of time that relate to the object of observation. It is distinguished from the anecdotal method by the attempt to record everything. Since this is not possible, a diary record is merely an unusually complete **anecdotal record.**

diaschisis (dī·as′kə·səs): *n.* the temporary withdrawal of normal excitation from a group of nerves.

diastole (dī·as′tō·li): *n.* the rhythmic period of dilation of a chamber of the heart (usually the ventricles) during which it fills with blood; the correlate of **systole.**—*adj.* **diastolic** (dī″əs·tol′ik).

diathesis (dī·ath′ə·səs): *n.* predisposition to a particular disease or disorder.—*adj.* **diathetic.**

diathesis/traumatophilic (trô″mə·tō·fil′-ik) = **accident proneness.** ➤This term illustrates several of the worst features of a technical vocabulary. It uses Greek **neologisms** when reasonably unambiguous English words are available and when the Greek is less precise: **traumato-** is not quite "accident" but "injury to the body"; and to say that the accident-repeater *wants* to have an accident, as **-philic** implies, injects speculation into what pretends to be description. Also the predominantly medical and variable connotations of **diathesis** make it unsuitable for a name that should simply point to a phenomenon. Use of this term is a perfect example of **bogus erudition.**

diathetic (dī″ə·thet′ik): *adj.* (*E. Kretschmer*) of a dimension of personality ranging from humorous, vivacious, quick-witted, to quiet, calm, serious.

diatonic scale: see **scale/diatonic.**

dich(o)- (dī′kō-): combining term meaning *separation into two, a different one to each of two:* e.g., *dichotomy, dichotic.*

dichotic (dī·kot′ik): *adj.* (*aud.*) affecting the two ears differently, as by conveying one sound to one ear simultaneously with a different sound to the other ear.—*Distg. fr.* **diotic,** of like stimuli to the two ears.

dichotomy (dī·kot′ə·mi): *n.* division of a group into two classes on the basis of presence or absence of a certain character. ➤*Distg. fr.* **classification,** in which each class has its own defining character. DICHOTOMOUS CLASSIFICATION is either redundant for **dichotomy** or self-contradictory.—*adj.* **dichotomous.**

dichromatism (dī·krō′mə·tiz·əm): *n.* partial color blindness in which two of the four **principal** *colors (usually yellow and blue) are seen.—*Syn.* DICHROMOPSIA, DICHROMATOPSIA (dī″krō·mop′si·ə; -mə·top′si·ə).

dichromatopsia = **dichromatism.**

dicrotic (dī·krot′ik): *adj.* of a pulse curve that has a notch in the descending part of the wave.

dictum de omni et nullo: (*L.*) an axiom of reasoning which asserts that whatever is asserted or denied of *all* instances of a class may be asserted or denied of *each* instance: e.g., what is true of all men is true of every man.

didactic: *adj.* fitted to instruct or teach; pertaining to teaching, as contrasted with learning by direct observation or study. ➤DIDACTIC THERAPY tells the counselee what he should know, explaining the nature of his difficulty, etc. A DIDACTIC ANALYSIS is a teaching **analysis** for prospective analysts. (But since the purpose is chiefly to acquaint the analyst with the **mechanisms** at first hand, a didactic analysis more nearly resembles laboratory or clinical instruction than the lecture-discussion situation to which didactic is usually applied.)

diencephalon (di"en·sef'ə·lon): *n.* the posterior part of the **forebrain.** It includes the **thalamus, epithalamus,** and **hypothalamus.**—*Syn.* BETWEENBRAIN.—*adj.* **diencephalic** (di"en·sə·fal'ic).

diff.: *abbr.* for **difference.**

difference: *n.* **1.** noncorrespondence of analogous parts. **2.** the amount by which a number or quantity differs from another.

difference/feeling of: a vague belief that one is peculiar or unlike one's associates. ➤In pathological cases, it is often a marked **delusion.**

difference/group: any difference, whether qualitative or quantitative, by which a group can be distinguished from another group. ➤The difference need not be in collective behavior, or **syntality;** it may consist of the relative frequency with which certain behaviors are found, or even just of the number of persons in the groups. Group **means** or group **variability** may be compared. Group differences are often, curiously, treated under the heading of **individual *differences.**

difference/individual: any psychological **character, quality,** or **trait,** or difference in the amount of a character, by which an individual may be distinguished from others. ➤The topic of **individual differences** usually deals with the differences characteristic of individuals in different categories. It is thus also a study of **group *differences.**—*Cp.* **differential psychology.**

difference/just noticeable or **/least noticeable:** see **just noticeable difference.**

difference limen or **threshold:** see **threshold, threshold/difference.**

differences/anomalous: see **anomalous differences.**

differences/canon of or **/method of:** one of Mill's working principles of induction: Any differences between two effects that are otherwise similar are to be attributed to differences in their antecedents.—*Cp.* **agreement and differences/canon of.**

differences/supraliminal: see **supraliminal differences.**

difference tone: a third tone sometimes heard when two tones of similar quality and pitch are sounded together. Its frequency is the difference between the vibration frequencies of the two tones.—*Syn.* TARTINI'S TONE.

differentia *n.,* *pl.* **-tiae:** the characteristic by means of which any datum may be distinguished from others.

differential: *n.* **1.** a distinguishing feature which makes something different from other things. **2.** (*math.*) an arbitrary, constant increment, Δx, of the variable x. (There are other mathematical meanings based on Δx.) —*adj.* **differential,** relating to or creating a difference or differential.

differential analysis (of ability): search for the areas of a person's relative strengths and weaknesses in ability or aptitude.—*Syn.* DIFFERENTIAL DIAGNOSIS OF ABILITY (but see **diagnosis/differential**).

Differential Aptitude Tests or **DAT:** a battery of tests for use especially with high school students. It includes tests of verbal reasoning, numerical reasoning, abstract reasoning, space relation, mechanical reasoning, clerical speed and accuracy, and two language tests (spelling and sentences).

differential inhibition: see **inhibition/differential.**

differential psychology: the branch of psychology that investigates the kinds, amounts, causes, and effects of individual or group differences in psychological characteristics.—See **psychology/divisions and schools of, VII, IX.**

differential response: see **response/differential.**

differentiate: *v.* **1.** to compare in detail the whole series of differences between two things. **2.** to make different; to become different. ➤The use of **differentiate** for the meanings *to distinguish, to make distinction,* to **discriminate,** or *to perceive differences* is unnecessary and occasionally confusing. See **differentiation (7).**

differentiation: *n.* **1.** the process by means of which something becomes different, or is made different, either from its former condition or from some reference object. **2.** (*biol.*) the process by which a relatively homogeneous group of cells generates different kinds of cells and tissues. **3.** the process whereby relatively unspecialized activities develop into relatively more specialized activities. ➤The earlier activities or functions are somewhat metaphorically conceived as "generating" the later, just as (in **2**) the early or parent cells generate new and different cells. **4.** the process by which a psychological **field** changes progressively from relative homogeneity to relative heterogeneity, so that its various aspects or parts are more readily distinguished; or the attained condition of the field after such change, measured by the number of subparts in the field.—See **field.**—*Syn.* **individuation,** which emphasizes one aspect of differentiation. **5.** (*conditioning*) an experimental procedure in which an animal is trained to make a distinction, either (*a*) between two similar responses to a given situation, one being rewarded and the other nonrewarded or punished, until only the one response is made; or (*b*) between two similar stimuli, a required response to one being rewarded and the same response to the other being nonrewarded or punished, until the first stimulus regularly does and the second regularly does not elicit the response.—*Syn.* RESPONSE DIFFERENTIATION (for *a*) or STIMULUS DIFFERENTIATION (for *b*).—*Cp.* **approximation** *conditioning. ➤It is the experimental procedure that constitutes differentiation. The animal is not **differentiating,** he is **discriminating. 6.** (*math.*) the working out of a **differential (2). 7.** = **discrimination:** *differentiation between two colors.* ➤This usage is thoroughly bad and, despite acceptance by distinguished authors, smacks of **bogus erudition.** Differentiation is needed for the process of *making* or *becoming different*; it is not needed as a synonym for **discrimination.** Hallowed use in mathematics and biology is no excuse for its use in psychology, the more so when it is thereby given a meaning that is not analogically exact. Moreover, this usage suggests a curious metaphysic: that to *perceive* differently is to *make* different.—*v.* **differentiate,** to cause to be different; to perceive difference (an improper but common usage).

difficulty scale: see **scale/difficulty.**

difficulty value: the percentage of some specified group, such as students of a given age or grade, who answer a test item correctly.

diffraction: *n.* the bending of a portion of a light or sound wave around the edge of an obstacle. ➤The longer waves bend more, hence diffraction can be used to analyze the wave.

diffuse: *adj.* said of behavior that is not sharply directed at the goal (though it is goal-oriented); of behavior that lacks coordination.—*Syn.* **undifferentiated.**

diffused responses: widespread and ill-coordinated activity with little or no apparent relation to the stimulating conditions; undifferentiated activity.—*Cp.* **random activity.**

diffusion: *n.* (*sociol.*) the spread of culture traits, by borrowing or migration, from one area to another, or from one group to another in the same area.—*Cp.* **acculturation, assimilation/cultural.** — *Syn.* CULTURAL BORROWING.

diffusion circle: 1. = **dispersion circle. 2.** the area on the skin affected by a stimulus within the area.

diffusionism: see **diffusion theory.**

diffusion /motor: see **motor diffusion.**

diffusion response or *K:* (*Ror.*) a response elicited by the shading effects in the **inkblot:** reports of smoke, whirling water, etc.

diffusion theory: the view that **culture** has spread extensively from certain centers, notably ancient Egypt. ➤*Contr. w.* the so-called EVOLUTIONARY THEORY, that similar types of culture arise independently in different regions because of the fundamental identity of human nature.—*Syn.* DIFFUSIONISM.

digital: *adj.* **1.** pertaining to one of the numbers from 0 to 9. **2.** pertaining to fingers or toes.

digit-span test: a test in which the task is to repeat a series of digits following a single visual or auditory presentation. The number of digits varies, and the score is the longest series correctly recalled.

digit-symbol test: a **code** (or substitution) **test:** each digit is equated with a small geometric figure, and the task is to write the proper digit under each of the geometric figures presented in irregular order. ➤Increasing speed is taken to reflect increasing familiarity with the code, hence, learning.—*Syn.* SYMBOL SUBSTITUTION TEST (*prefd.*).

digraph: (dī′graf): *n.* a combination of two letters to represent one speech sound: the *ou* in bounce, the *ph* in graph.

dilapidation: *n.* deterioration; **dementia.**

dilatation: *n.* an enlargement of an organismic structure: e.g., the iris, a blood vessel, an intestine.—*Syn.* DILATION.

dilemma: *n.* a situation presenting two mutually exclusive alternatives (the HORNS OF THE DILEMMA), neither of which is completely satisfactory. ➤Said originally of an argument; now more often of a concrete situation, sometimes of one offering more than two choices.

dimension: *n.* **1.** any characteristic by which an object or event can be positioned in a quantitative series. ➤The term referred originally to length, breadth, or thickness (physical dimensions) but has now been extended. Thus an event, such as the perceiving of cloud figures, might be positioned in a series according to the greater or lesser rigidity of the perception. Many personality traits are described by their position on a **bipolar** dimension: e.g., **ascendance-submission.** For scientific description, dimensions should be independent and should collectively describe all of a coherent group of facts.—*Syn.* **attribute,** but **dimension** is broader and is largely superseding it. **2.** any measurable extent or magnitude.—*adj.* **dimensional.**

dimensional principle: the doctrine that most functions show **continuous** variation along a dimension. Apparent discontinuity is believed to be due to failure to discover connecting intermediate variations.

dimension/extensive: a dimension that meets the conditions of intensive *dimension, and in addition permits the operation of adding. ➤Thus heat is an **intensive dimension:** one object is greater or less or equal to another in heat, but the adding of two heated objects does not give heat equal to the sum of the two. In contrast, the addition of a foot-long object to another foot-long object gives two feet in length; the **dimension** permits of adding and is **extensive.** Few psychological measurements use an extensive dimension.

dimension/intensive: a **dimension** by means of which **objects** (in the widest sense) can be ordered as *more* or *less,* or *equal.* The ordering must be testable by manipulations within the dimension.—See **dimension/extensive.**

diminishing return: an improvement that is progressively smaller with each successive application of some favoring influence. ➤The POINT OF DIMINISHING RETURN usually refers to the point where the gain is practically not worth the effort involved—that is, to the point at which the diminishing becomes clearly noticeable rather than at which it actually begins. NEGATIVELY ACCELERATED IMPROVEMENT is a more accurate expression.

dimming effect: the enhancement of an **aftersensation** which is brought about by reducing the intensity of the stimulus field upon which the image is projected.

ding-dong theory: the hypothesis that languages originated in mimicry of natural sounds.—*Syn.* BOW-WOW THEORY, ONOMATOPOETIC THEORY.

Dionysian (dī″ō·nish'ən; -nis'i·ən): *adj.* **1.** pertaining to Dionysus; hence, wild, violent, orgiastic. **2.** emphasizing the emotional and romantic, in contrast with the intellectual, attitude toward life. ➤*Contr. w.* APOLLONIAN, of a classic, tempered, intellectually ordered way of life. Dionysus, the Greek god of wine and earthy enjoyment, represents the primitive and instinctual; Apollo, the sun god, represents the reasonable in man's life.

diopter (dī·op'tər): *n.* a unit used in measuring the power of a lens to bring parallel rays of light to a focus: it is the focal distance of the lens in meters divided into unity. The values are *plus* for convex lenses (which facilitate seeing near objects), *minus* for concave lenses (which facilitate seeing distant objects).—See **prism diopter.**—*Var.* **dioptre.**

diopter/prism: see **prism diopter.**

diotic: *adj.* (*aud.*) of a stimulus that affects both ears. ➤*Distg. fr.* **dichotic,** of stimuli different for the two ears.

diphonia (dī·fō'ni·ə): *n.* (*speech*) a vocal shift, without intent by the speaker, from one register to another (as in the adolescent boy).

diplacusis (dip″lə·kū'səs): *n.* the hearing of a single tone as if it were two tones slightly different in pitch, one with each ear.

diplegia (dī·plē'ji·ə): *n.* paralysis of similar parts on the two sides of the body.—*adj.* **diplegic.**

dipl(o)-: combining form meaning *double.*

diplopia (di·plō'pi·ə): *n.* seeing double. ➤Although the images on the two retinas are never (in ordinary vision) exactly the same, the differences may be considerable without being noticed. Troublesome diplopia may be due to failure to focus the eyes, or to intrusive attention to differences that are normally fused.—*Distg. fr.* **retinal rivalry.**—*adj.* **diplopic.**

dipsomania: *n.* recurrent uncontrollable craving for alcoholic drink, usually at relatively long intervals, believed to be symptomatic of more fundamental disorder.—*Cp.* **alcoholism.**

direct: *adj.* straight; immediate; without intermediary; without turning aside; by the shortest route.

direct apprehension: responding to the properties of a stimulus without (ostensible) involvement of any process other than those of reception—i.e., without full recognition, without involving **context** responses or **cognitive schemas.** ➤It is probable that apprehension is never completely direct as thus defined.

direct association: a connection between items without an intermediary.

directed movement or **response:** one observed as specifically related to a certain stimulus.—*Contr. w.* **random movement.** —*Syn.* **goal-directed behavior** which, however, is directed by a **drive state** as well as by stimulus.

directed thinking: thought processes governed by a formulated goal. ➤The goal is often set by another person, but it may also be self-chosen. Irrelevant mental activities are suppressed.

direction: *n.* metaphorically, any property of a means-to-an-end by which one means can be distinguished from another. In this extended sense, spatial location is only one form of direction.

directional factor: (*W. C. Halstead*) any medium or means through which intelligence is expressed or exteriorized at any given moment, including sensory and motor activities and special abilities, as well as the more complex overt problem-solving activities, etc.

direction in thinking: a persisting type of limited approach to a problem, such as searching for ways to get around a barrier (e.g., by going over or under) without exploring other approaches.—*Cp.* **mental *set, directed thinking.**

direction/law of identical visual: Objects seen in **binocular** vision are localized as if seen by a single or cyclopean eye located in the median plane of the head.

direction/line of: any line passing from the retina through the **nodal point** of the eye and to the object viewed. It determines the direction in which the object is seen.—*Syn.* (loosely used) LINE OF SIGHT or OF VISION, VISUAL LINE.—*Distg. fr.* **visual axis.**

directions test: a test of ability to follow directions. The testee is directed to perform in a prescribed order a series of tasks, each of which is by itself within his ability level.

directive counseling: see **counseling/directive.**

directive tendency = determining tendency.

direct reflex: a response for which effector and receptor are on the same side of the body.—*Ant.* **crossed reflex.**

direct sampling = **sampling/controlled.**

dirhinic stimulation (di·ri′nik): stimulation of both nostrils by the same scent.

dis-: prefix meaning *separation, parting, depriving, reversal, undoing.*

disability: *n.* 1. an impairment or defect of a bodily organ or member (esp. sense organs and/or organs of execution such as arms, legs, tongue). 2. a loss or lack in one or more functions severe enough to be a handicap.—*v.* **disable.**—*adj.* **disabled.**

disability/special: a handicapping impairment or lack in sense-organ or **operant** behavior functions, esp. such impairment as interferes with other functions: e.g., severe visual disability, esp. when it interferes with social learning or with reading.

disarranged-sentence test: a test whose task is to arrange a group of words to make a meaningful and grammatical sentence.—*Syn.* DISSECTED SENTENCES.

disassociation = **dissociation.**

disbelief: *n.* active rejection of a **belief.** ➤*Distg. fr.* UNBELIEF, lack of conviction.—*Cp.* **doubt.**

discernible: *adj.* noticeable or perceptible. ➤*Distg. fr.* DISCRIMINABLE or DISTINGUISH-ABLE, meaning noticeably different.

discernment: *n.* 1. sensitivity to, and understanding of, social signals. 2. effective perception, including the perception of differences.

discharge: *n.* 1. (*neurol.*) the passage of neural excitation from one neuron to others.—*Syn.* **firing.** 2. the hypothesized reduction of drive activity that occurs when a **consummatory response** is made. 3. the emission of a response.

discharge control: the hypothetical state of the nervous system that determines readi-ness for motor activities. ➤*Distg. fr.* **drive arousal.**—*Contr. w.* DISCRIMINATIVE CAPACITY, a collective term for all the hypothetical factors in the nervous system that enable the organism to distinguish between stimuli.

discharge index: a quantity representing all the motor activities by means of which an aroused state of bodily energy is discharged. —*Contr. w.* **drive reduction.**—*Cp.* **arousal index; recovery quotient.**

discharge of affect: (*psychoan.*) lessening of feeling through giving it expression, as when sorrow is lessened by tears and sobbing.—*Distg. fr.* **catharsis.**

discipline: *n.* 1. a definitely limited branch of knowledge. 2. the control exercised by a superior over a subordinate; esp., the direct control of conduct and punishment for misconduct. ➤**Discipline** should not, however, merely mean *punishment.* 3. the habit patterns that cause a subordinate to be ready to act promptly and consistently in the manner prescribed by the superior. 4. = SELF-DISCIPLINE, the ability to inhibit behavior inconsistent with relatively remote purposes. 5. formal or mental discipline: see **formal culture.**

discomfiture: *n.* 1. defeat; overthrow; the having of plans broken up or frustrated. 2. (*social work*) the giving up of struggle as a consequence of defeat.

discomfort-relief quotient or **DRQ:** in a verbal communication, the ratio of expressions indicating dissatisfaction with self or surroundings to those indicating satisfaction or a feeling of improvement.

discontinuity: *n.* a condition marked by gaps, breaks, or sharp alterations; lack of **continuity.**—See **continuum, discontinuity theory of learning.**—*adj.* **discontinuous** (which see).

discontinuity theory of learning: the hypothesis that, in discrimination learning, no learning of the **discriminandum** takes place until the animal hits upon, and attends to, that aspect of the total situation which is related to the required discrimination. ➤It is opposed to the **continuity theory,** which holds that a small increment of learning attends every rewarded response. The discontinuity theory is related to the doctrine of **insight** but, unlike that view, it accepts the possibility of gradual improvement *after* hitting upon the clue to the required discrimination.—*Syn.* NONCONTINUITY THEORY.

discontinuous: *adj.* not **continuous;** having breaks, irregularities, or sharp alterations. ➤Nearly all psychological *measures* are discontinuous: they are represented by the number series, which proceeds by steps (from 1 to 2, etc.). Many measures, however, are believed to be values of a *variable* that is actually continuous. In that case they are said to form a **continuous series** —the superficially discontinuous is actually continuous. But not all discontinuous measures belong to a continuous series, and in that case the use of statistics that imply continuous variation is improper.—See **continuum**.—*Syn.* **discrete.**

discord: *n.* **1.** absence of unity; disagreement.—*Ant.* **harmony (1, 2). 2.** (*music*) nontechnically = **dissonance.**

discover: *v.* to ascertain something not hitherto known, or not known to the discoverer. ➤**Determine** (which see) is often pedantically but ambiguously used as a synonym.

discrepancy: *n.* a difference between an assertion and the facts, or between two assertions.

discrepancy/mean = deviation/standard.

discrete: *adj.* separate; distinct; discontinuous; not grading imperceptibly into or with some other item; changing only by finite amounts. E.g., the units in a group of persons, or a collection of doorknobs, are discrete.—*Distg. fr.* discreet.—*Ant.* **continuous.**—*n.* **discreteness** (not **discretion**).

discretion: *n.* **1.** a complex trait that involves sensitive awareness of social judgments and a desire to avoid bringing adverse criticism upon oneself for the violation of social injunction. **2.** the tendency to delay action till the facts are known.—*adj.* **discreet** (not **discrete**, which has a different meaning).

discrimen: see **discriminanda.**

discriminability: *n.* abstract name for the property or properties that make it possible for objects or events to be distinctly perceived or marked off from others.

discriminal dispersion: the frequency distribution of **discriminal process** values about the modal value. ➤If the commonest response to a stimulus has the value x, other responses to that stimulus, greater or less than x, are generally distributed on a **normal *frequency curve.**

discriminal process: the specific activity of discriminating (to which a quantitative value is assigned) that is induced in an organism by a stimulus. ➤The term is neutral as to nature of the process—whether subjective, receptor, motor. But to any given stimulus the organism makes a response different from that to other stimuli, and to that response a quantity is assigned.

discriminanda *n. pl., s.* **discriminandum:** (*L.* for *those things which are to be discriminated*) (*E. C. Tolman*) the characteristics of objects that render it possible to make sensory **discriminations.**—*Syn.* DIS-CRIMINA (*s.* DISCRIMEN).

discriminant function: a formulation indicating how to combine a set of variables to

give a total that will show the maximum difference or discriminative power between two groups.

discriminate: *v.* to note differences.—See **discrimination.**—*Cp.* **differentiate, distinguish.**

discriminated operant: (*B. F. Skinner*) an emitted response for which a particular stimulus has become the occasion (in virtue of prior temporal association) but which is not a true **eliciting** stimulus. ➤The discriminated operant differs in dynamics (e.g., in **latency** or speed of response) from the **respondent** of the same system.

discriminating fineness: an index of the smallness of difference in a variable which a given test can measure.—*Syn.* **precision.** —See **discriminating power.**

discriminating power: a composite criterion of the usefulness of a test or test item. It includes an index (a) of how precisely the trait is measured (= **discriminating fineness**), (b) of the likelihood that the several items of the test will discriminate in the same direction as the trait (= **probability of the test**), (c) of the general level of the trait at which the test discriminates (= **discriminating *range**). It is often estimated from the relative frequency with which persons in the top 27 per cent and the bottom 27 per cent by an *independent* criterion succeed or fail the test or test item.

discriminating range: see **range/discriminating.**

discrimination: *n.* **1.** the process of detecting differences in objects; esp., SENSORY DISCRIMINATION, the detecting of **sensory** differences. **2.** reacting differently to different objects.—See **discrimination *learning. 3.** prejudicial treatment; any difference in action premised upon a **prejudice,** or upon the class or category by which an individual is typed, rather than upon his relevant characteristics: e.g., RACE DISCRIMINATION, treating a person in a given way because of his race or **ethnic group.**—*adj.* **discriminating,** usually with the meaning of making fine sensory discriminations or responding to small differences; **discriminative,** usually of logical or esthetic judgment; **discriminatory** (for 3).

discrimination/index of: a numerical expression of the extent to which a test or test item discriminates among testees possessing varying amounts of the trait the test is supposed to measure.—See **discriminating power, discriminating fineness.**

discrimination reaction: see **reaction time.**

discussion: *n.* **1.** an examination and comparison of the views of two or more persons each of whom seeks, not to persuade or convince or display his own excellence, but to illuminate the issue and to contribute to general understanding. ➤This ideal is seldom completely realized; discussion is mingled in varying degrees with argument, persuasion, exhibitionism, and striving for dominance, all of which are subversive of discussion. 2. an examination of a problem by one person who inquires into various facets and aspects, and expounds diverse views with some impartiality.

discussion leader: a person whose function is to promote free examination (i.e., **discussion**) of a group's views.—*Distg. fr.* lecturer, instructor, orator.

disease: *n.* an abnormal impairment, disorder, or derangement of any function of an individual, momentary or trivial instances being excluded. ➤No clear-cut line between disease and its opposite, health, can be drawn.

disease/mental: see **mental disease.**

disgust: *n.* a feeling or attitude of disdain, unpleasure, rejection, and/or incipient nausea.

disinhibition: *n.* 1. the temporary removal of an inhibition through the action of an unrelated stimulation. ➤E.g., a person who has been inhibiting a laugh in a social situation may lose control when a sudden noise (unrelated to the laugh-provoking situation) occurs. The phenomenon has been noted in the **extinction** of the classical CR. (See **conditioning.**) It has been interpreted as the inhibition of an inhibition. 2. the action of alcohol and other drugs in lessening the control by the cortex of impulsive or **vegetative** functions.

disintegration: *n.* loss of organization, system, or unity in any organized entity. ➤The term is general and may apply to inorganic or organic materials, systems of ideas, social organizations. PERSONALITY DISINTEGRATION is often found in serious mental disorders—the several functions cease to work harmoniously. Disintegration includes such phenomena as decay, decomposition, segregation, demoralization, disorganization.

disjunctive: *adj.* literally, pertaining to that which separates; hence, of parts that have been separated or are in some way opposed to each other.—*Ant.* CONJUNCTIVE.—*n.* **disjunctivity, disjunctiveness.**

disorder: *n.* 1. condition when a group of phenomena show no intelligible relations with one another. 2. = **disease.**

disorder/behavior: see **behavior disorder.**

disorder/cyclic: see **cyclic disorder.**

disorder/functional: see **functional disorder.**

disorder/organic: see **organic disorder.**

disorder/somatic: see **somatic disorder** and **functional disorder.**

disorder/speech or **/voice:** see **speech disorder.**

disorganization: *n.* loss or lack of orderly relations.—*Syn.* **disintegration,** which is a stronger term.

disorganization/personal: 1. temporary loss of ability for unified or harmonious behavior; **disorganized behavior.** 2. more or less enduring loss of system or organization in behavior tendencies; loss of hierarchical controls over behavior so that conflict cannot be resolved; loss of **character,** or of personality unity.

disorganized behavior: an act in which the separate parts directly interfere with each other or lead to different and conflicting goals. ➤To use **disorganized behavior** as a synonym for **emotion** is theory-begging.

disorientation: *n.* lack of normal **orientation**—i.e., of one's usual ability to relate to space, time, and surrounding objects.

disparate (dis'pǝ·rǝt): *adj.* 1. of two or more things so different in kind or quality that they cannot be compared. ➤*Contr. w.* **incommensurable,** not capable of being measured by the same units or on the same scale or dimension.—*n.* **disparity.** 2. separated in space or time.—*n.* **disparation.**

disparate retinal points: points on the retina far enough apart so that whatever is seen by means of those points has a different position in perceived space. ➤The exact antonym is **congruent points. Corresponding retinal points,** often used as an antonym, is ambiguous. In both **retinal *disparity** and **disparation,** the difference in images is caused by their falling on disparate points.

disparation: *n.* (*vis.*) the difference in the two retinal images of an object that is either nearer or farther than the point of fixation. ➤The object is seen double **(diplopia)** unless one image is suppressed, which it usually is.—*Distg. fr.* **retinal *disparity,** which is the difference in the images of a solid object viewed at the fixation point. —*adj.* **disparate.**

disparity: *n.* difference; inequality.—*adj.* **disparate.**

disparity/binocular = **disparity/retinal.**

disparity/retinal or **/visual:** the difference between the two images on the retina, resulting from the slightly different angle of the two eyes, when viewing a solid object at the fixation point; or the analogous effect when viewing a **stereogram.** ➤These images normally fuse into a single visual impression of a solid object. See **stereoscopic vision.**—*Syn.* BINOCULAR DISPARITY.—*Distg. fr.* **disparation,** which is the doubling of images *not* viewed at fixation.—*adj.* **disparate** (which see).

dispersion: *n.* (*stat.*) = SCATTER or VARIABILITY of observations: the extent to which a group of scores or measures differ from one another, or from some reference point such as the mean. It is measured by **average *deviation, standard *deviation, variance, interquartile range.**

dispersion circle: a circle of light or color seen when light from a point source passes through a lens system.—*Cp.* **chromatic *aberration.**—*Syn.* DIFFUSION CIRCLE.

dispersion/coefficient of: a measure of relative **variability** used in order to make allowance for unequal averages: it is 100 times any measure of variability divided by a **measure of *central tendency.**—*Syn.* **coefficient of *variation,** COEFFICIENT OF VARIABILITY.—*Distg. fr.* measure of dispersion, which is simply any index of **dispersion** (which see).

dispersion/response: the randomization or scattering and deviation of responses from the established pattern when the latter fails to yield satisfaction.—*Syn.* ERGIC DISPERSION.

displacement: *n.* **1.** movement of an object from its usual place to another. **2.** spatial distortion of an **eidetic image** by inversion, rearrangement of parts, etc. **3.** a substitute activity, from a different **activity *system,** resorted to when the usual **consummatory response** to a situation is prevented. ➤This probably refers to the same actual behaviors as in 4 and 5 below. **4.** the attachment of an **affect** to something other than its proper object. ➤E.g., hatred of a father is attached to a walking stick used by the father; anger aroused by punishment is transferred to a pet. It is a common phenomenon in dreams. **5.** a **Rorschach category** for attention to insignificant details of the **inkblot** in order to avoid making revelatory responses.

displacement/angles of: the angles by which the respective eyes deviate from the direction occupied in the primary position. ➤The VERTICAL DISPLACEMENT is the angle of the eye upward or downward from the primary position; the LATERAL DISPLACEMENT is the angle to right or left.

display: *n.* (*human eng.*) any device designed to present stimuli to any of the senses; or the device and the stimuli so presented: e.g., a book, a TV screen and loudspeaker, an instrument panel.

disposition: *n.* **1.** the arranging of elements or components in relation to each other; or the result of such arrangement, esp. when the components are conceived to have dynamic effects as a result of the arrangement: the *disposition* of troops for battle. **2.** a general term for any (hypothesized) organized and enduring part of the total psychological or psychophysiological organization in virtue of which a person is likely to respond to certain statable conditions with a certain kind of behavior: his *disposition*

is to think before acting.—*Cp.* **structure. 3.** (*biol.*) = **anlage. 4.** a relatively lasting emotional attitude; or the relative predominance in the total personality of a certain emotional attitude: a stubborn *disposition.* **5.** (*W. McDougall*) the sum of all innate tendencies or propensities.—*Contr. w.* **temperament** and **character.**

➤Although all behavior depends upon a certain dynamic or propulsive readiness of the organism, as well as upon the stimulating conditions, **disposition** gives sharp emphasis to the former. The resulting behavior may then be described, to adapt a distinction made by B. F. Skinner, as **emitted** by the organism rather than **elicited** by the stimulus. Specific dispositions are distinguished and named for the kind of behavior effects produced rather than for the specific movements.—*Cp.* **molar** and **distal.**

The construct of *a something to account for sameness of behavior despite variation in the environing situation* is a formal necessity. Thus it is necessarily and formally true that to enjoy a swim whether the water be hot or cold requires that the person have a certain disposition. But it need not be a specific *enjoyment of swimming* disposition. It may be a more general athleticism, or a relative indifference to temperature, or a combination of personal qualities each of which also plays its part in other situations. We cannot usually go directly from observed fact to a specific disposition to account for that fact. To constitute a useful construct, a disposition must be more general than the fact that led to its being inferred. The logical requirements for inference are not easily met.

The **faculties** of popular thinking and of **faculty psychology** are dispositions hypothesized without observing this necessary logic. On the other hand, **factor analysis** may be employed to discover (but not to confirm) nonoverlapping dispositions that do permit of prediction beyond the immediate fact.

TENDENCY is a close synonym and is perhaps less likely to have properties attributed to it that are not justified by the facts. Most **traits** are dispositions; but the trait concept also includes **abilities,** which are not conceived as dynamic and hence not as dispositions. **Habit (2)** is a special kind of disposition, as are **attitude, set, sentiment, motive,** and **drive.**

disposition rigidity = **perseveration (2).**

disruption: *n.* the sudden breakdown of organization. ➤*Cp.* **disintegration,** which is gradual.

dissected sentences = **disarranged sentences.**

dissimilation: *n.* **1.** = **catabolism. 2.** (*C. Jung*) the adjustment of a person to an object other than his **self.**—*Ant.* **assimilation (5)** (which see).—*Cp.* **autism.**

dissociation: *n.* a process whereby (or condition in which) a group of psychological activities possessing a certain unity among themselves lose most of their relationships with the rest of personality and function more or less independently: e.g., the **compartmentalization** of the "Sunday saint and weekday sinner," the **amnesia** of hypnosis or neurosis, and **multiple *personality.** ➤*Distg. fr.* the allover disintegration common in **schizophrenia:** in dissociation the segregated subsystems maintain or even increase their internal organization. —*Distg.* also *fr.* **complex,** in which the segregated group is restricted in its *manner* of relationship with other activities but is by no means cut off. (The form DISASSOCIATION is redundant.)—*Syn.* DISSOCIATIVE REACTION (*Stan. Psychiat.*), slightly broader in its denotation.

dissonance: *n.* (*music*) the harsh effect produced by two or more tones that do not blend well or harmonize; one end of the dissonance-consonance dimension.—See **harmony (4).**—*Ant.* **consonance.**

dist.: 1. = distal. 2. = distribution.

distal: *adj.* 1. (*anat.*) away from the center of the body, or from the point of origin or attachment of an organ or bodily member: the *distal* end of a bone.—*Ant.* **proximal.** 2. see **distal vs. proximal variables.**

distal vs. proximal variables: (*E. Brunswik*) in the total chain of events that constitute an act or behavior, those that are located at the boundary between a body and its surroundings are called **proximal,** those more remote from that boundary are called **distal.** ➤A PROXIMAL STIMULUS acts directly on the **receptor**—e.g., the light wave at the surface of the eyeball or as it impinges on the retina. A DISTAL STIMULUS is any of the events in the environment causally related to the proximal stimulus—e.g., the energy of light at the source or at a reflecting surface (the latter being less distal than the former). The distance of an object, *as* distance, is also a distal stimulus.

A PROXIMAL RESPONSE is the actual movement of the muscles; a DISTAL RESPONSE is the part of the executive aspect of an act that is measured by its effect in altering the environment beyond the boundaries of the organism or the environment-organism relation. The movements of writing are a proximal response, the words written are a distal response. Stepping movements are proximal, arrival at the far side of the street is distal.

The proximal is correlated with the distal (whether stimuli or responses are in question) but does not stand in one-to-one rela-

tion with it. This fact is the basis for what Brunswik calls **representative *design.**

distance/psychic or **/psychological:** 1. the linear distance between two psychological data represented in the same spatial schema. ➤E.g., on a graphic rating scale one kind or degree of shyness may be represented at one point, another kind or degree at another; their psychological distance is the linear separation of the points. 2. the degree of difficulty a person experiences in psychological relationships with another; or the subjective estimate of that difficulty. ➤The difficulty may be due to a sense of difference in manners, ideology, personality, or status; or to an awareness of inapproachability or unfriendliness. Psychic distance in this sense is topologically described as a function of the accessibility to one personality of the several **regions** of another personality, or of the amount of communication possible between their respective **central regions.**—*Distg. fr.* **valence,** which characterizes the desirability rather than the difficulty of the relationship.—See also **social distance.** 3. (*topol.*) the relative length of the path over which a psychic force travels; the minimum number of boundaries to be crossed in moving from one psychic **cell** to another. 4. the degree to which an artist succeeds in maintaining a dispassionate attitude toward the object portrayed. 5. (*A. Adler*) the means by which one avoids making reactions that would reveal how far one is falling short of attaining one's life aim. ➤*Cp.* **retreat from *reality.** Adler lists four forms: (*a*) RETROGRESSIVE MOVEMENTS (as in functional paralysis or suicide); (*b*) cessation from effort; (*c*) hesitation and **abulia;** (*d*) the fabrication of obstacles to be overcome before putting oneself to the crucial test.

distance receptor: a sense organ capable of being aroused by a stimulus at a distance. ➤Visual, auditory, and smell receptors are included; usually warmth or cold are not, though these can be felt at a slight distance from the stimulus object.—*Syn.* DISTANT RECEPTOR, TELE(O)CEPTOR, DISTOCEPTOR (*prefd.*).

distance/sense: see **sense distance.**
distance/social: see **social distance.**
distance vision: see **vision/distance.**
distant: *adj.* far away in space or time; figuratively, far removed psychologically from something: e.g., red and green are *distant* (i.e., very different) in color quality. —See also **distance/psychic, social distance.**
distinction: *n.* 1. that which makes possible discrimination between any two items. —*Distg. fr.* **distinctness.** 2. a characteristic of a person of recognized ability, e.g., one included in such reference works as *Who's*

Who or *American Men of Science.*—See **eminence** for the gradations from **distinction** to **illustriousness.**—*v.* **distinguish.** —*adj.* **distinguished** (not *distinct*).

distinctness: *n.* the quality in a perceived object of having its outlines and parts sharply marked off.—*Syn.* CLEARNESS.—*adj.* **distinct.**

distinguish: *v.* to recognize a difference between two or more items; esp., to perceive a difference.

distoceptor = distance receptor.

distorted room: an especially planned room that is set up to demonstrate some of the more common illusions of space perception.

distortion: *n.* **1.** a twisting out of shape. **2.** a twisting of retinal or of visual images so that they are not faithful to objective shape. **3.** a twisting of statements or of ideas—witting or unwitting—so that they are not faithful to fact or to the statements upon which they are ostensibly based. **4.** (*psychoan.*) a **defense mechanism** by means of which **dream content** inacceptable to the **superego** is disguised or modified.—*Cp.* **reaction formation.**

distortion/perceptual: 1. lack of correspondence between the way an object is commonly perceived and the way a given individual perceives it under given conditions. **2.** lack of correspondence between the physical facts and the way they are perceived. ➤The first meaning does not consider **illusions** and phenomena such as **color contrast** or **size constancy** to be distortions; the second does. The distinction, often not explicit, may be important in some contexts.

distractibility: *n.* a characteristic of a person whose attention is easily drawn to extraneous stimuli.

distraction: *n.* **1.** an undesired shift of attention. **2.** a stimulus that causes such a shift. ➤*Distg. fr.* **detraction,** a lessening of degree of attention without a shift; and *fr.* ABSTRACTION, attending to one's own thoughts with failure to attend to what goes on about one.

distractor: *n.* in **selective answer *tests,** one of the choices that are to be scored as incorrect. They are designed to be attractive to (hence, to *distract*) the respondent who does not know the correct answer.

distress-relief quotient: in a verbal communication, esp. that of a counseling client, the number of expressions of "distress" divided by the number of expressions of "relief." ➤"Distress" and "relief" are very broadly interpreted. Any expression of unhappiness, discontent, dissatisfaction, worry, lack of self-confidence, etc., is "distress"; and "relief" is similarly broad.

distributed learning or **practice:** see **practice/distributed.**

distributed repetition: see **practice/distributed.**

distribution: *n.* **1.** (*stat.*) a systematic grouping of data into classes or categories according to the frequency of occurrence of each successive value or range of values: e.g., a table that shows how many persons per hundred die at each year of age. ➤The distribution may be set forth in a numerical table or represented in graphic form: DISTRIBUTION CURVES, bar graphs, polygons, etc.—See **frequency (2). 2.** (*educ.*) see **concentration (2).**

distribution/binominal = normal frequency distribution.

distribution/cumulative frequency: a tabulation showing how many cases fall at or below each of the successive values (or class intervals) arranged in order of magnitude. ➤Each entry thus includes all those cases falling below that point, and the last entry includes all the cases. If distribution is normal, the CUMULATIVE FREQUENCY CURVE (also called summation curve) is an **ogive,** or S-shaped curve.

distribution-free: *adj.* (*stat.*) of methods of analyzing data that make no assumption concerning the **true** distribution; or, somewhat more narrowly, that do not assume that the true distribution is **normal.**—*Syn.* **nonparametric.**

distribution/frequency: see **frequency (2).**

distribution/grouped: a distribution in which the successive classes or categories are defined by a range of values greater than the unit of measurement: e.g., the distribution of heights by the classes 60 to 62.9 inches, 63 to 65.9 inches, 66 to 68.9 inches, etc.

distribution/normal = normal frequency distribution.

distribution/ranked: see **ranked distribution.**

distribution/rectangular: a frequency distribution which has approximately the same number of observations in all class intervals within a certain range (the frequency being zero outside this range), so that the **frequency polygon** is a rectangle.

disuse/principle of: a generalization that the tendency to make a specific learned response to a stimulus situation is weakened with the passage of time unless the tendency is exercised.

diuresis (dī″yu̇·rē′səs): *n.* increased secretion of urine.—*adj.* **diuretic** (-ret′ik).

diurnal (dī·ėr′nəl): *adj.* occurring each day; or, occurring in the daytime, not at night.

diurnal variation: changes from day to day.

divagation (div″ə·gā′shən): *n.* rambling and incoherent speech or thought; digression.

divergence: *n.* **1.** a moving apart, esp. in opinions or attitudes; or the state of being in disagreement where agreement is to be expected. **2.** (*vis.*) turning one eyeball outward with respect to the other when the latter is directed at an object. Either eye may be so affected, or, more commonly, one eye regularly diverges outwardly.— *Syn.* EXOTROPIA, divergent **strabismus,** DIVERGENT SQUINT, WALLEYE.

divergence/index of: (*stat.*) the difference between the **modes** of a **bimodal** frequency curve, divided by the SD of the more variable of the two components; or the difference divided by three times the SD.

divergence/modal: the difference between the **mean** and **mode.**

dizygotic twins (di"zī·got'ik) = **twins/ fraternal.**

DL = difference limen or **difference *threshold.**

Do: (*Ror.*) scoring code for **oligophrenic** detail.

docile (dos'əl): *adj.* **1.** easily managed or controlled or guided; tractable; performing actions, not from personal choice nor under coercion by external force or threat, but as a function of suggestion from others. **2.** willing to listen to advice and to be guided by it. **3.** teachable; able, or able and willing, to learn, either in general or in respect to some sort of task. (Used esp. of animals.) —*n.* **docility.**

doctrine: *n.* a teaching; esp., an elaborate and carefully formulated body of beliefs. ➤A doctrine does not include a statement of the facts that support it, but lack of such facts is not implied.—*Cp.* **dogma.** Although **doctrine** is more often applied to religious teaching, it is used loosely in science for a complex theory or system of hypotheses that emphasizes *what* is believed true rather than *why*.

dogma: *n.* a statement of belief for which supporting facts are admittedly not available. ➤A dogma is accepted on faith or from authority. In science, which rests upon factual evidence, dogma is a term of disapproval. Frequently any doctrine put forward by an opponent is labeled dogma. See **doctrine.**—*adj.* **dogmatic.**

dogmatic: *adj.* of individuals who seek to impose their views by authority; or of teaching that asks pupils to accept ideas without critical study of the evidence.—*n.* **dogmatism, dogma.**

dolicho- (dol'ik·ō-): combining form meaning *long, narrow.*

dolichocephalic (-sef·al'ik): having a long and narrow head, with a cephalic index under 75.9.—See **cephalic index.**—*Syn.* DOLICHOCEPHALOUS (-sef'ə·ləs).—*n.* **dolichocephaly** (-sef'ə·li).

dolichomorphic: *adj.* having a tall, thin bodily structure.

dolor (dō'lər): *n.* **1.** = **grief. 2.** = **pain.** ➤Neither usage seems needed.—*Var.* **dolour.**

domain: *n.* all the data and/or concepts governed by, or included within, a given principle or law; all the situations or circumstances within which a given variable is to be found. ➤**Field, area, sphere,** and **domain** were all originally spatial, but now may refer to a nonspatial grouping. **Domain** retains something of its original meaning as the "place" where a rule prevails. The other three are used somewhat generally and metaphorically—e.g., "responses in this area" may mean "similar responses" or "responses having similar effect"—but all retain something of a geometrical meaning.

domal sampling (dō'məl): a special form of **area sampling** in which there is a systematic selection of houses in an area (e.g., every fourth house in a certain block), and a specification of which persons in each house are to be included in the sample for interview (e.g., "heads of household," "housewives," "any male able to speak," etc.).

domesticated: *adj.* of an animal reared by man for his use or enjoyment and become dependent upon man for support.—*Ant.* wild, feral. ➤**Domestication** is an inherited tendency in some species.

dominance: *n.* **1.** in any psychological pattern or complex, whether **cognitive** or **conative**-motor, the relation of being more prominent or more important, of taking precedence, of being more pressing. ➤**Dominance** is not an explanation but a description of something to be explained. **2.** the fact that, of two or more responses that may be elicited in a given situation, one is more frequent than the others. **3.** tendency to seek control over others. ➤*Syn.* **ascendance,** prefd. because it lacks the implication of bearing down.—*Cp.* **domination.** **4.** (*genet.*) appearance, as a result of factors in the **gene pair,** of a somatic trait like that of one parent, unlike that of the other.—*Ant.* **recessiveness.**—See **dominant (3). 5.** preferential use of one side of the body (LATERAL DOMINANCE), of one eye, (OCULAR or EYE DOMINANCE), of one hand (MANUAL DOMINANCE), etc. **6.** control of the activity of one organ by another; esp., CEREBRAL or CORTICAL DOMINANCE, i.e., control of lower centers in brain and cord by the cerebrum or cortex respectively. **7.** = HEMISPHERICAL DOMINANCE: the fact that one cerebral hemisphere generally leads the other in control of bodily movement, resulting in **laterality** (esp. handedness). ➤CEREBRAL DOMINANCE is more common than HEMISPHERICAL DOMINANCE, but the latter is preferred as avoiding confusion with **(6)** above.—See **mixed cerebral *dominance.**

dominance/cerebral: see **dominance (6)** and **(7).**

dominance/eye: see **eye dominance.**

dominance feeling: the **affective** concomitant of one's awareness of his own dominant or ascendant role, or of its lack.

dominance/hemispherical: see **dominance (7).**

dominance hierarchy: see **hierarchy/dominance.**

dominance/lateral: see **dominance (5).**

dominance/mixed cerebral: the theory that speech disorders and some other maladjustments may be due wholly or partly to the fact that one cerebral hemisphere does not consistently lead the other in control of bodily movement. ➤See **dominance (7).** Normally, speech is controlled by the hemisphere that controls the favored hand. Attempts to train left-handed persons to use the right hand are said to upset the **dominance** of one hemisphere and thus to bring about confusion and uncertainty, not only between the hands but in the realm of speech and, therefore, of thinking.

dominance need: (*H. A. Murray*) the need to influence or control others; need for leadership.

dominance - submission = ascendance-submission.

dominant: *adj.* **1.** seeking or exercising **domination. 2.** (*music*) of the fifth tone of the diatonic scale. ➤A DOMINANT CHORD has this tone as its root. **3.** (*genet.*) of a gene that expresses itself—i.e., produces an observable effect in the offspring—when present, even though the **gene pair** also contains a **recessive** gene; or characterizing the observable effect (the DOMINANT TRAIT or CHARACTER) of such a gene or set of genes. ➤*Contr. w.* RECESSIVE GENE, which does not produce an observable trait unless both of the gene pair are recessive. As to the **phenotypic** trait (i.e., as to observable structure) the distinction of **dominant** or **recessive** is known not to be absolute: dominance varies from complete to very slight.—*n.* **dominance,** the fact of being dominant; **domination** (which see).—*v.* **dominate.**

dominant trait: see **dominant.**

dominant wave length: the wave length from the spectral band which yields a hue matching any given hue; or which, mixed with an appropriate amount of **achromatic color,** will match the given color.

domination: *n.* control of the behavior of others, esp. by coercion.—*v.* **dominate.**

dominator-modulator theory: theory that a separate dominating receptor exists for the

brightness aspect of vision, chromatic distinctions being introduced by receptors that modulate the dominant response.

Donder's law (don′dɔrz): the principle that the position of the eye in looking at a given object (or along a given line of vision) is independent of where one was looking just before—i.e., independent of the path taken in arriving at the new position.

Don Juan: a legendary figure symbolizing the man who pursues women for sexual conquest; a seducer (not a rapist).

doodling: *n.* apparently aimless writing or drawing while ostensibly talking or listening. ➤It may range from highly articulate prose to incomprehensible scrawled fragments, from coherent pictures to scribbled lines lacking apparent pattern. May be used as **projective** data.

Doolittle method: (*stat.*) a rapid and systematic method for solving for the unknowns in a set of normal equations. ➤The method is very useful in curve fitting and in the solution of multiple-correlation problems (see **Wherry-Doolittle**).

Doppler's effect or **principle:** the increase or decrease in the wave length when a source of light or sound recedes from or approaches the observer. If the motion is very rapid, relative to the speed of light or sound, the shift is noticed as a change in hue or pitch.

dorsad (dôr′sad): *adv.* toward the back.—*Cp.* **dorsal.**

dorsal (dôr′səl): *adj.* pertaining to the back; on or at the back.—*Contr. w.* **ventral.**—See **anterior.**

dorso-: a combining form denoting *the back* or *dorsal.*

dorsoventral: *adj.* (*anat.*) extending from **dorsal** to **ventral** sides of the body: e.g., *dorsoventral axis.*—See **axis of reference/anatomical.**

DOT = Dictionary of Occupational Titles.

dotage: *n.* senility.—*pers. n.* **dotard.**

dotting test: 1. a test in which the testee makes as many dots as possible in a unit of time.—*Syn.* **tapping test. 2.** a test in which the testee aims with a pen at a succession of small circles arranged in irregular pattern on a moving tape.—*Syn.* AIMING TEST.

double-alternation problem: an experimental design in which, for solution, the responses must follow the order *a-a-b-b,* in the absence of an immediate **cue** that it is time to shift. It is used in the study of symbolic processes with animals.

double-aspect theory: see **mind-body problem.**

double-entry table: (*stat.*) **1.** = **scatter diagram. 2.** any table in which the entries are identified by the value or heading of both the **rows** and the **columns.**

double-frequency table = scatter diagram.

double-language theory: see **mind-body problem.**

double personality: see **personality/multiple.**

double representation: perception of two hues and two brightnesses in or on an object when it is illuminated by a light of different color and **luminance** from that of the object. ➤The two hues and brightnesses do not mix, or mix incompletely.—See **object *constancy, film color.**

double stimulation: alternate name for classical **conditioning (1).**

double vibration or **d.v.:** see **vibration.**

double vision = diplopia.

doubt: *n.* a state of mind in which one neither believes nor disbelieves something, or does both alternately; absence of conviction. ➤Not properly used for **disbelief.**

doubtful judgment: (*psychophys.*) a response in which the subject reports inability to make the required discrimination, or to make it with sufficient assurance.—See **equality judgment.**

dowsing (douz'ing): *n.* prospecting for minerals or subterranean waters by means of a DIVINING ROD (a forked twig, the two ends of which are held in the hands), the twisting of the rod allegedly indicating the hidden substance.—*Var.* **dousing.**

DQ: 1. = deterioration quotient. 2. = developmental quotient.

DR or Δ*R:* symbol for increment of response.

dr: (*Ror.*) scoring code for **rare detail.**

drainage: *n.* (*W. McDougall*) a hypothesis explaining **facilitation** and **inhibition:** the supposition is that when two groups of neurons, anatomically closely connected, are simultaneously aroused the neural impulse is drained away from the usual discharge route of the less active into the discharge route of the more active.

dramamine: *n.* an antihistamine drug used to control motion sickness.

drama therapy: a dramatic re-enactment of scenes involving a person's adjustment problems (the client usually taking the role of himself), first as the event allegedly took place, then as it might have been more wisely managed.—*Syn.* **psychodrama.**

dramatism: *n.* dramatically stilted and pompous speech or behavior, symptomatic in some psychoses.

dramatization: *n.* (*psychoan.*) transformation of **repressed wishes** into symbolic form, generally into personifications.

Draw-a-Person Test: see **Machover Test.**

d **reaction:** in a reaction-time experiment, a procedure in which the subject withholds the prescribed response until he has identified which of two or more stimuli have

been presented. ➤The procedure is faulty and obsolete.—*Syn.* **cognitive** reaction.

dread: *n.* **1.** anxiety related to a specific danger situation; anticipation of an event with great fear. **2.** (*obsoles.*) awe or reverence.—*Cp.* **fear.**

dread/talion: see **talion.**

dream: *n.* a more-or-less coherent **imagery** sequence occurring during sleep.

dream analysis: the fundamental technique of psychoanalysis (but also used, sparingly, by others) wherein the client relates a dream and **free-associates** about its elements. ➤These associations, interpreted within the theoretical framework of the therapist, are guides to the client's underlying dynamics or motivations. In psychoanalysis elements of the dream are interpreted as symbols of **repressed** wishes or other unconscious processes. See **interpretation (2), dream theory.**—*Syn.* DREAM INTERPRETATION.

dream content: (*psychoan.*) The ideas, images, and events of the dream as remembered and related constitute its MANIFEST CONTENT; its underlying significance—or LATENT CONTENT—is made up of the **repressed wishes** that have been indirectly expressed in the manifest content. Together, they constitute the **dream content.**

dream ego: (*C. Jung*) that portion of the ego that indulges in dreaming.

dream/incest: see **incest dream.**

dream instigators = day residues.

dream interpretation: see **dream analysis.**

dream material = dream content.

dream/parallel: (*C. Jung*) a dream whose meaning, or **latent *content** (see also **dream content**) coincides with or supports the conscious attitude.

dream wish: (*psychoan.*) the representation of a **repressed wish** in a dream. ➤The manifest content may be a disguised or transformed wish, or a symbol of a **wish fulfillment.**—See **dream content.**

dream work: (*psychoan.*) the process by which the **instinctual** processes of the **id** are transformed into a dream. ➤Particular instinctual desires must be altered if they are to be acceptable to the **ego** and **superego.** The chief mechanisms of dream work are **condensation, displacement** of affect, **secondary *elaboration.**—See **dream content.**

drill: *n.* systematic repetition of an act with a view to learning. (Where the drill is imposed by another, the desire for learning may be found only in the drillmaster.)

drive, drive state or **D: 1.** a tendency, initiated by shifts in physiological balance, to be sensitive to stimuli of a certain class and to respond in any of a variety of ways that are related to the attainment of a certain goal. ➤**Drive** is currently used in innumerable contexts, often quite loosely. The above is believed to be the greatest common denominator for its most frequent usages. **2.** a hypothetical state of activity of an organism, or of some of its organs or tissues, that is a necessary condition before a given stimulus will elicit a class of behaviors. ➤E.g., a certain level of hunger (the drive) must be present before food (the stimulus) will elicit eating (the response). In addition, however, to being a necessary condition for a given S-R sequence, a drive sometimes enhances other ongoing activities (which presumably are controlled by their own drive). Some authors speak of all the concurrent physiological activities that enhance an S-R sequence as the **drive state;** others distinguish a general drive state from a specific drive.

The drive state may be manipulated by creating certain conditions: deprivation of food, altering temperature, etc. This may be called **drive arousal.**—*Cp.* **drive stimulus.**—*Syn.* **motive, need** (which see for discussion).

drive/acquired or **/secondary:** a drive aroused and/or satisfied in ways acquired by experience or learning; a drive that is not a part of the **species-specific** repertory of an animal.—*Contr. w.* **drive/primary.**—See **reinforcement/secondary.**

drive/alien = **drive/irrelevant.**

drive arousal: any combination of conditions, whether external and environmental or within the organism, that results in the arousal of a specified **drive.** ➤The DRIVE AROUSAL STIMULUS is an external stimulus that has the capacity of arousing the drive. E.g., the smell of food arouses the hunger drive. *Distg. fr.* **drive stimulus,** which is a **proprioceptive** effect of drive activity. —*Syn.* **drive-inducing operation.**

drive conversion: turning a **drive** toward a new goal; the process of acquiring a **secondary** *drive.

drive displacement: behavior, appropriate to one drive, that follows frustration of another drive; or the hypothetical mechanism that leads to such behavior. E.g., a food-satiated animal will eat when frustrated in sex.

drive-inducing operation: the procedure to be followed before beginning an experimental investigation to insure that a certain drive will be active in the animal.—*Syn.* **drive arousal.**

drive/irrelevant: When two or more drives are simultaneously active, the drive that is not reduced is called the **irrelevant drive.** —*Syn.* ALIEN DRIVE.

drive/learnable: see **learnable drive.**
drive/oral: see **oral drive.**
drive/primary: a drive which in its major

form is determined by the animal's heredity; a **species-specific** drive; a drive that depends upon a physiological need and that, independent of prior learning, instigates a special class of behavior. ➤All actual drives have been modified by prior learning; the primary drive is one that bears, even when modified, essential similarity to its original form.—*Cp.* **instinct,** for which **primary drive** is a close synonym.

drive reduction: the sequence of events within the organism that results in lessening the specific activity called a **drive.** ➤Drive reduction is accomplished usually by satisfaction of the associated needs, but also by removal of **drive arousal.**—*Cp.* **need reduction.**

drive-reduction hypothesis: 1. the hypothesis that all motivation is based upon the lessening of a **drive** or **need,** or of the **drive stimulus;** the hypothesis that the **motive** of all action is the reduction of *aroused* tissue activities or tissue-activity gradients. ➤This is sometimes called the TICKLE-ITCH-PAIN-REMOVAL THEORY because it views all motivation as like that to remove a tickling or painful stimulus from the skin. A less derisive synonym is the PRINCIPLE OF MINIMAL STIMULATION, which contrasts with the **principle of *optimal stimulation.**—*Syn.* NEED-REDUCTION HYPOTHESIS (less common but more accurate). **2.** the hypothesis that a stimulus-response sequence is **reinforced** or strengthened when the response results in lessening the concurrent **drive, drive state,** or **drive stimulus.** ➤In this meaning, **drive reduction** is envisaged as a means to learning rather than as a **motive.**

drive/secondary = **drive/acquired.**

drive/socialized: a drive that, as a result of teaching and/or other social experience, finds expression is socially accepted ways. The learning-teaching process by which this is accomplished is **socialization.**—*Cp.* **sublimation.**

drive specificity: the hypothesized connection of a **drive stimulus** with those particular skeletal responses which reduce that stimulus.

drive state: see **drive.**
drive stimulus or S_D: (*C. Hull*) a hypothetical specific afferent neural impulse resulting from the functioning of a **drive.** ➤It is an intervening *variable between the **need** state and a specific way of responding. The term is ill-chosen, since it suggests many meanings other than this specific one.

drive/visceral: see **visceral drive.**

dropout: *n.* (*colloq.*) a pupil who leaves school before completing a grade or before graduation.

Drosophila melanogaster (drə·sof'i·lə

mə·lan'ō·gas"tər): the fruit fly, an organism studied intensively in genetics.

DRQ = discomfort-relief quotient.

drug addiction: continued reliance upon the effects of a **narcotic** drug, with the result that progressively stronger doses are required to obtain these effects, and that there is both psychological and physiological distress when the drug is withdrawn. ➤*Distg. fr.* **drug habituation,** in which the tissues do not "demand" increasing doses.—*n.* **drug addict** (ad'ikt), a person who manifests such addiction.

drug habituation: reliance upon the effects of a drug, but without the need of increasing dosage as in **drug addiction.** ➤But HABIT-FORMING DRUG usually means one that leads to addiction.

drunkard: *n.* a person given to frequent intoxication with alcohol.—*Distg. fr.* **alcoholic.**

Ds: (*Ror.*) scoring code for an associative response for which the stimulus is a major white space of the inkblot card.

dualism: *n.* 1. any of several philosophical theories that admit of two fundamentally different sorts of principles or entities in the universe, usually conceived as mental and material. 2. a point of view in psychology that accepts a distinction of some sort between mental and physical phenomena. ➤It is not implied that mental and physical are fundamentally or metaphysically different. This form of dualism tries to be neutral on the philosophical issue. —*Contr. w.* **monism,** which maintains that all phenomena are basically of one sort, whether conceived as like the mental or like the material. No scientific criterion permits of choice between monism and dualism; to insist on either is both unscientific and naïve.—*Cp.* **mind-body problem.**—See **psychology/divisions and schools of, IV.**

dual or **double personality:** see **personality/multiple.**

ductless gland: see **gland.**

dull: *adj.* 1. literally, not sharp. 2. metaphorically, of colors that lack brilliance; of pain that is massive and diffuse; of tones that lack high partials; of literature or of social activities that are uninteresting, lacking in variety and novelty; of persons that are either unintelligent or uninteresting, prosaic.

dullard: *n.* a person of low intelligence, but not feeble-minded. ➤*Syn.* **dull normal,** a term with less derogatory implication.

dullness: *n.* see **brightness (5).**

dull normal: a person below average in intelligence but not feeble-minded. ➤The usual IQ is from 80 to 89. Preferred to **dullard,** which has a derogatory connotation.

dumbness: *n.* 1. inability to speak.—*Syn.*

mutism. 2. refusal to speak. ➤The word is used only colloquially to mean stupidity. —*adj.* **dumb.**

duodenum (dü"ō·dē'nəm): *n.* the upper part of the intestine, directly connected with the stomach.—*adj.* **duodenal.**

duplation: *n.* doubling.

duplicate form: see **form/comparable.**

duplicity theory (of vision): the theory that there are in the retina two distinct **receptor** mechanisms for light: **rods** for dim, **cones** for normal and intense, illumination.

dural sinus (dü'rəl sī'nəs): a space between layers of the **dura mater** that carries venous blood from the cerebral veins into the neck.

dura (mater) (dü'rə mā'tər): *n.* the thick outermost membrane that covers the brain and spinal cord.

durance: *n.* (*H. Murray*) a block of time within which a unitary life activity takes place. It may have several overlapping **proceedings.**

duration: *n.* 1. continuance in time. 2. an irreducible or unanalyzable attribute of **sense data** or of sensing processes that is basic to the perceiving of temporal duration.—*Syn.* PROTENSITY.

duty: *n.* 1. an action prescribed by an accepted authority, failure to perform which involves penalties. 2. an individual's own interpretation of what he should or should not do.

DV = dependent *variable.

D. V. or **d.v.:** *abbr.* for *double vibration*(s).

DW: (*Ror.*) scoring code used when part of the figure, *D,* suggests a percept, and the subject interprets the entirety as though it had the form suggested by *D.*

dyadic (dī·ad'ik): *adj.* pertaining to the number *two;* having a double or paired structure; arranged in pairs.—*Cp.* **binary.** —*n.* **dyad, diad** (dī'ad).—*Var.* **diadic.**

dyad/social: see **diad/social.**

dynaception: *n.* a process, analogous to sensory perception, whereby the organism responds to its own **need** state. ➤It is not clear how this process is related to **coenesthesia** or **proprioception.**

dynamic: *adj.* 1. relating to change. 2. relating to that which causes change. 3. forceful or potent. ➤The three meanings are generally combined in varying proportion. In popular use, "dynamic" is often a mere cliché to imply that something is happening of which the speaker approves. DYNAMIC PSYCHOLOGY or DYNAMICS concerns itself with causes of behavior (esp. with one behavior as cause of another, and with **motivation**). **Psychoanalysis** and the **neopsychoanalytic** schools are dynamic in this sense but, contrary to a common implication, are by no means the only forms of dynamic psychology.—*Distg. fr.* **dynamic theory.**—*n.* **dynamics** (which see).

dynamic effect law: (*R. B. Cattell*) the generalization that specific attentions and overt behaviors become habitualized in proportion as they facilitate attainment of a goal.—*Syn.* (*approx.*) **law of *effect.**

dynamic equilibrium: a system in which the distribution of forces maintains a regular pattern, even though the total amount of force be altered and despite the fact that the force at any point may change (in the latter case, with corresponding change at every other point in the system). Such an ideal **equilibrium** probably does not exist, but many systems maintain approximately regular balance over long periods.

dynamic psychology: 1. any treatment of psychology that emphasizes the **drives** and **motives;** or any psychology stressing cause-and-effect relationships. **2.** = **depth psychology.** ➤This usage, though fairly common, implies that only unconscious processes have dynamic effects—a view no one explicitly proposes.—See **psychology/divisions and schools of, III.**

dynamics: *n. pl.* **1.** the study of forces, originally of physical forces, acting on a body; hence, **2.** the forces, physical or other, operating in any **field.** ➤Often merely a pseudoerudite cant phrase.—*adj.* **dynamic** (which see).

dynamics/behavior: 1. the **motivations** or the **mechanisms** postulated as determining behavior. ➤The term is properly applicable to such humdrum motivation as a preference for cider vinegar; in actual use it is more often reserved for the more "exciting," not to say esoteric, motives. It seldom makes a clear reference to facts. **2.** the study of **motivation** as a division of psychology.

dynamics/group: see **group dynamics.**

dynamic situation principle: (*V. W. Voeks*) the generalization that the stimulus pattern of a situation is continually changing, due either to environmental influences or to organismic changes that affect what external stimulus elements are received and how they are received.

dynamic subsidiation: the sequence of subsidiary goals leading to a final goal. ➤A particular goal is conceived as being "servant" to a more inclusive goal, as when a child tries for applause by teaching tricks to his dog. Intermediate goals may be subsidiary to several more inclusive goals, forming a latticelike structure rather than a hierarchy.

dynamic theory or **psychic dynamism:** (*W. Koehler*) the theory that the action of the brain is determined by **dynamic conditions** (i.e., by constant interchanges of energy) rather than by static or fixed relations among the anatomic brain structures.

dynamis: *n.* (*C. Jung*) a principle that brings order out of chaos in the psyche. It is sometimes identified with the **animus** or masculine component of the psyche.

dynamism (dī′nə·miz·əm): *n.* **1.** a persisting or enduring mode of behaving in such a way as to bring, at least temporarily, satisfaction or relief of **tension:** e.g., the habit of closing one's eyes to relieve eyestrain. ➤A somewhat broader term than **habit,** stressing the adjustive and dynamic aspect of an act rather than its acquisition; yet habit is also adjustive and dynamic, and a dynamism is acquired as a habit is. **Mechanism,** as used in psychoanalysis, is a near synonym. **2.** (*H. S. Sullivan*) a persisting mode of individual behavior that is found in interpersonal relations. ➤CONJUNCTIVE DYNAMISMS (e.g., behavior due to the need for intimacy) tend to maintain the relation, DISJUNCTIVE DYNAMISMS (e.g., anxiety) to disrupt it. **3.** = **dynamic theory.**

dynamism/oral: (*H. S. Sullivan*) a relatively enduring configuration of energy found in interpersonal relations (a **dynamism**) organized about hunger and oral pleasure. It often includes linguistic elements that stabilize and give limits to the system.

dynamogenesis or **dynamogeny** (dī″nə·mō·jen′ə·sis; -moj′ə·ni): *n.* the fact that changes in sensory activity are correlated with changes in response. ➤Included are cases where nonspecific sensory activity, or change in the general level of sensory activity, has an influence. The PRINCIPLE OF DYNAMOGENESIS asserts that the response changes are proportional to the changes in sensory activity—a proposition difficult to prove in the absence of comparable measurements. The mere presence of other persons is sometimes spoken of as **dynamogenic.**—*Cp.* **social facilitation.**—*adj.* **dynamogenic.**

dynamograph: *n.* a recording **dynamometer.**

dynamometer (dī″nə·mom′ə·tər): *n.* an instrument for measuring the strength of muscular exertion; specif., the SQUEEZE DYNAMOMETER, which measures strength of grip.

dyne (dīn): *n.* the unit of force in the C.G.S. system: the force needed to accelerate a one-gram mass an increment of 1 centimeter per second per second.

dys- (dis-): prefix meaning *hard, bad, ill,* or *faulty.*—*Distg. fr.* **dis-,** although **dis-** is occasionally a spelling variant of **dys-:** *distrophy* (for **dystrophy**).

dysacousia (-ə·kü′zhə): *n.* discomfort, esp. disproportionate discomfort, caused by noise.—*Var.* **dysacusia.**

dysarthria (-är′thri·ə): *n.* impairment of articulation in speech, caused by disease in the central nervous system.—*adj.* **dysarthric.**

dysbasia (-bā′zhə) = **ataxia.**

dysbulia (-bū′li·ə; -bü-): *n.* difficulty in thinking and giving attention.

dyseneia (dis″ə·nā′yə): *n.* (*speech*) defective articulation that results from any form of deafness.

dysergastic reaction: (*A. Meyer*) behavior or mental disorders due to lack of circulation or nutrition in the brain: hallucination, disorientation, fears.

dysesthesia (-es·thē′zhə): *n.* diminished, excessive, or inappropriate sensitivity to pain.

lysfunction = **malfunction.**

dysgenic (dis·jen′ik): *adj.* 1. characterizing influences detrimental to the **heredity** of offspring. 2. characterizing a parental stock that is biologically deficient.—*Ant.* **eugenic.**

dysgraphia (-graf′i·ə): *n.* inability, due to brain lesion, to express ideas by means of writing or written symbols.

dyslalia (-lā′li·ə): *n.* 1. speech impairment due to defect in the organs of speech. 2. speech impairment due to functional and unknown causes.

dyslexia (-lek′si·ə): *n.* impairment of the ability to read, or to understand what one reads silently or aloud, independent of any speech defect.—*Distg. fr.* **alexia,** a type of visual **aphasia.**

dyslogia (-lō′ji·ə): *n.* difficulty, resulting from arrested mental development or feeblemindedness, in expressing ideas through speech.

dysmenorrhea (-men″ô·rē′ə): *n.* disordered menstruation.

dysmnesia (dis·nē′zhə): *n.* any disorder of memory.—*adj.* **dysmnesic.**

dysmnestic (-nes′tik): *adj.* pertaining to a psychosis marked by **dissociation** (which see).—*Syn.* DISSOCIATIVE PSYCHOSIS (*prefd.*).

dyspareunia (-pə·rü′ni·ə): *n.* 1. deficient capacity for sexual pleasure. 2. painful sexual intercourse.

dysphagia (-fā′ji·ə): *n.* inability to swallow, due to hysterical spasm.

dysphasia (-fā′zhə) = **aphasia.**

dysphemia (-fē′mi·ə): *n.* defective **articulation** of speech, due to functional causes.

dysphonia (-fō′ni·ə): *n.* impairment of voice quality.—*adj.* **dysphonic** (-fon′ik).

dysphoria (-fô′ri·ə): *n.* generalized feeling of anxiety, restlessness, and depression of spirits.—*Ant.* **euphoria.**

dysphrasia (-frā′zhə): *n.* difficulty in speaking or writing resulting from mental impairment.

dysphrenia (-frē′ni·ə): *n.* **mental disorder.** ➤An example of **bogus erudition.**

dysplasia (-plā′zhə): *n.* abnormal growth or development.—*adj., pers. n.,* **dysplastic.**

dysplastic body types: types of body structure that are too irregular to permit of regular classification.

dyspnea (disp′nē·ə): *n.* difficulty in breathing.—*Var.* **dyspnoea.**

dyspraxia (-prak′si·ə): *n.* impairment of coordination of movement.

dysrhythmia/cerebral (-riŧh′mi·ə): abnormal rhythm in **brain waves,** as revealed by the **EEG.**

dyssocial reaction (di·sō′shəl): (*Stan. Psychiat.*) behavior that manifestly disregards the social code and often conflicts with it, but is not antagonistic to social codes as such.—*Distg. fr.* **antisocial reaction.**—*Cp.* **pseudosocial child.**

dysthymia (-thī′mi·ə): *n.* a despondent mood; or the tendency to such a feeling state. ➤This is the basic meaning; some psychiatrists make it a syndrome of various symptoms with despondency as its central feature.—*Ant.* **euthymia.**—*adj.* **dysthymic.**

dystonia: lack of **tonus;** disordered tonus.

dystrophy (dis′trə·fi): *n.* faulty nutrition.—*adj.* **dystrophic** (-trof′ik).—*Syn.* DYSTROPHIA (-trō′fi·ə).

dystrophy/adiposogenital = **Froelich's syndrome.**

E

E: 1. (*phys.*) = energy in **joules.** 2. = environment. 3. = **excitatory tendency.** 4. = index of *forecasting efficiency. 5. = **probable error** (more often written **PE**). 6. = the experimenter (usually *ital.* E.; *pl.* Es; possessive E's, Es'). 7. = **error variance.**

$_sE_R$ = excitatory or **reaction potential.**

$_sE_R$ = (*C. Hull*) **reaction potential** resulting from **stimulus** *generalization; generalized reaction potential.

$_s\bar{E}_R$: (*C. Hull*) = **effective reaction potential.**

$_s\dot{\bar{E}}_R$: (*C. Hull*) momentary effective excitatory potential; the net **reaction potential** as modified by **oscillation.**

e: 1. (*math.*) the base of natural logarithms, 2.718281. 2. = **error.**

E.A. or **EA:** *abbr.* for **educational** *age.

ear/internal or **/inner** = **labyrinth** (1).

ear-minded: *adj.* 1. tending to apprehend ideas better when they are presented to the ear. **2.** tending to **imagery** that is predominantly **auditory.**—*Syn.* **audile.**

Ebbinghaus curve (eb'ing·hous): a form of the forgetting curve, typical with nonsense material, in which there is a sudden drop in the amount recallable shortly after the learning, followed by a much slower decline.

Ebbinghaus test = completion *test.

eccentric: *adj.* off-centered; deviating noticeably from the usual; peculiar in conduct. ➤The eccentric person is often recognized as mildly (but harmlessly) **psychotic**; eccentric behavior is often (but not always) an early symptom of the onset of mental disorders.—*n.* **eccentricity.**

eccentric projection: see **projection/eccentric.**

ecco analysis (ek'ō): (*commun. theory*) a questionary method of analyzing the patterns of communication found in an organization, as measured on such variables as timing, media, subject matter, and organizational level. ➤**Ecco** is formed from *e*pisodic *c*ommunication *c*hannels in *o*rganization. The term was chosen because of its similarity to a "communication echo."

E chart: the Snellen chart, used in testing visual **acuity.**

echo- (ek'ō-): a combining form meaning *repetition*; more specif., repetition of the words or actions of others: **echolalia, echopraxia.**

echolalia or **echophrasia** (-lā'li·ə; -frā'-zhə): *n.* the involuntary and senseless repetition of a word or sentence just spoken by another person. ➤*Distg. fr.* speech **perseveration (cataphasia).** Distinction is sometimes made between echolalia as a **functional disorder** (it may be as mild as the speech mannerism of repeating the last phrase of a speaker's remark—a sort of verbal nodding of the head), and echophrasia as a symptom of a **psychosis**; but the terms are often employed interchangeably.

echopathy (ē·kop'ə·thi): *n.* a morbid condition in which the person imitates the posture, gestures, speech, and actions of another.

echophrasia = echolalia.

echopraxia (-prak'si·ə): *n.* a tendency toward automatic imitation of another's movements.

echo principle: (*E. B. Holt*) the generalization that an animal will learn to "echo" an action of another animal, provided that it has perceived the other's behavior while both are simultaneously engaged in the same act.

echo reaction: the repeating by a child of sounds made by parents, etc., without any necessary awareness of their meaning.

E/C intervening variable: (*M. H. Marx*) a function assumed in order to account for the differences in the outcomes of the experimental (*E*) and the control (*C*) conditions. ➤This function is given a name that serves as a shorthand way of referring to the **operationally defined** stimulus situation differences and the operationally defined outcome differences. The name means or refers to these differences and nothing else whatever. The variable has no "surplus meaning."—*Cp.* **hypothetical *construct, intervening *variable.**

eclampsia (ek·lamp'si·ə): *n.* (*med.*) a convulsion; esp., a recurrent convulsion sometimes found in late pregnancy.

eclecticism: *n.* in theoretical system building, the selection and orderly combination of compatible features from diverse sources, sometimes from otherwise incompatible theories and systems; the effort to find valid elements in all doctrines or theories and to combine them into a harmonious whole. The resulting system is open to constant revision even in its major outlines.

➤A general temper of mind seems to determine the degree to which a systematizer seeks for the maximum of rational order and over-all consistency (with resulting temporary loss in inclusiveness and explanatory power), or for the maximum of understanding of particular issues (with some loss in the tightness of organization). For the latter approach, **eclecticism** is an established term; for the former no good name is current, but FORMALISM perhaps describes its chief attribute. Formalism leads to the advocacy of competing schools and theories; eclecticism, though often called a school, is essentially the denial of schools.

Eclecticism is to be distinguished from unsystematic and uncritical combination, for which the name is **syncretism.** The eclectic seeks as much consistency and order as is currently possible; but he is unwilling to sacrifice conceptualizations that put meaning into a wide range of facts for the sake of what he is apt to think of as a premature and unworkable *over-all* systematization. The formalist thus finds the eclectic's formulation too loose and uncritical. For his part, the eclectic finds formalism and schools too dogmatic and rigid, too much inclined to reject, if not facts, at least helpful conceptualizations of fact. Few psychologists, however, occupy a fixed position on the continuum that runs from eclecticism to formalism.—See **psychology/ divisions and schools of, I.**

ecmnesia (ek·nē'zhə): *n.* relative inability to recall recent events while retaining ability to recall remote ones. ➤A frequent symptom in old age.

ecology (ē·kol'ə·ji): *n.* **1.** the study of organisms in reference to their physical environment, esp. in reference to the ways they adapt to environment and the resulting geographic distribution. ➤In a broad sense, most of psychology is **ecological,** being concerned with responses to stimuli (which are environmental). **2.** (*K. Lewin*) the attempt to determine which parts of the physical and social environment (in a given period) are transformed into goals, barriers or boundaries, and the other psychological factors that constitute an individual's **life space.**—*pers. n.* **ecologist.**—*adj.* **ecologic-(al)** (ek″ō·loj′ik·əl; ē″kō-).

ecomania (ē″kō·mā′ni·ə): *n.* a symptom complex of irritable and domineering behavior in the family circle and of humility toward persons in authority.—*Cp.* **authoritarian character.**

economic: *adj.* applied to that part of psychoanalytic doctrine which is concerned with the origin, distribution, and consumption of psychic energy.

economy/principle of = parsimony/principle of.

ecphory (ek′fô·ri): *n.* the activation of a memory trace, or **engram.**—See **mneme.**

ECS = electroconvulsive shock.—See **electroshock therapy.**

ecstasy: *n.* **1.** overwhelming joy or rapture. **2.** see **trance.**

ECT: *abbr.* for **electroconvulsive therapy.**

ecto- (ek′tō-): combining form meaning *outside, external.*

ectoderm: *n.* the outermost of the three cell layers in the embryo. ➤It develops into the **ectomorphic** structures of skin and nervous system.—*Contr. w.* **endoderm, mesoderm.**—See **ectomorphic.**

ectomorphic: *adj.* pertaining to bodily structures developed from the embryonic **ectoderm.** ➤*Contr. w.* ENDOMORPHIC, pertaining to structures developed from the embryonic endoderm; and *w.* MESOMORPHIC, pertaining to those from the mesoderm.

➤W. H. Sheldon proposed to classify **body build** on the basis of the relative predominance of components belonging to one of these three developmental systems. The ECTOMORPHIC COMPONENTS consist chiefly of the outer layers of the skin and the nervous system; the ENDOMORPHIC COMPONENTS, of the linings of the digestive tract and its appendages and the viscera; the MESOMORPHIC COMPONENTS, of bones, muscles, and connective tissues. The respective body types are ECTOMORPHIC TYPE: relatively thin, with a large skin surface in comparison with weight; ENDOMORPHIC TYPE: relatively heavy, with highly developed viscera and relatively weak muscular and bony structure; MESOMORPHIC TYPE: a highly developed skeletal structure, thick skin, sturdy upright posture. For young males (who were his subjects), mixed types are represented by numbers standing for the relative contribution of each kind of component. Sheldon finds a correlation between the three body types thus delineated and three varieties of temperament or personality: respectively, **cerebrotonia, viscerotonia,** and **somatotonia.** The linked body type and personality pattern define the **constitutional type** to which a person belongs.

-ectomy (-ek′tə·mi): a combining form denoting *surgical removal: thyroidectomy.*

ectoplasm: *n.* a semisolid substance alleged to emanate from the human body in a **mediumistic** trance.

edema (ə·dē′mə): *n.* dropsy; excessive accumulation of fluid in the tissue spaces.—*adj.* **edematous** (ə·dem′ə·təs); **edemic** (-dem′ik).

edge detail or ***de:*** (*Ror.*) a response based on the contour of the edge of the **inkblot.**

edging: *n.* (*Ror.*) behavior in which the subject studies the **inkblot** card edgewise, usually with eyes narrowed.

Edipus: see **Oedipus.**

EDR = electrodermal response.

educability (ed″ū·kə·bil′ə·ti): *n.* capacity for learning, whether in general, in certain stated ways, or at stated levels. ➤The usual reference is to capacity for learning in school, which is sometimes defined as IQ 50 or MA 6.—*Syn.* **plasticity (1), docility** (both of which are, however, more commonly used for subhumans).—*adj.* **educable** (ed′ū·kə·bəl), pertaining to one with demonstrated capacity to learn.

education: *n.* progressive or desirable changes in a person as a result of teaching and study. ➤Occasionally applied also to changes that result from experience ("the school of hard knocks") but not to those resulting from **maturation,** so far as these can be abstracted.—*adj.* **educational,** which applies to anything related to education; **educative,** which applies only to what actually brings about educational changes.

educational age: see **age/educational.**

educational clinic: see **clinic.**

educational guidance: the art of assisting pupils to select the best program of studies in the light of their capacities, interests, plans, and general circumstances.—*Cp.* also **remedial instruction,** occasionally included under this term.

educational psychology: 1. the application of psychology to education. ➤This conception of the nature of **educational psychology** is obsolescent. **2.** that branch of psychology which investigates educational problems by means of psychological methods and concepts, many of them designed for the special purpose. ➤The older view implied that the task of educational psychology was merely that of selecting those psychological findings, made for other purposes, which seemed pertinent to education. The newer conception does not preclude such borrowing, but it assigns to educational psychology the task of independently deriving the psychological principles needed for investigating the problems of education.—*Cp.* **applied psychology.**

educational quotient or **EQ:** the **educational** *age of a pupil divided by his **life** *age, the quotient being arbitrarily multiplied by 100 for ease of reading:

$$EQ = \frac{EA}{CA} \times 100.$$

educational test: a test that measures the results or effects of school instruction and/ or of learning.—*Syn.* **achievement test.**— *Cp.* **instructional test.**

Educational Testing Service or **ETS:** a national testing and research agency established under the Carnegie Foundation.

education/cultural: see **cultural education.**

education/experimental: an educational program that welcomes trial of new procedures, esp. those that seem congruent with a controlling philosophy of education. ➤The term is frequently applied to trials in which there is no measurement of outcomes; hence, although they are **educational,** they are neither **experimental** in the true sense nor guaranteed to be **educative.** Where true experimental methods are used, EDUCATIONAL EXPERIMENTATION is more descriptive.

education/permissive: education that does not restrain or coerce the child's actions (at least, not for educational purposes) but allows him to learn by pursuing his own choice of activities. The planned provision of **educative** facilities is usually not ruled out, even though these have a directive function.

education/secondary: that period of formal schooling which follows elementary or elementary-intermediate education. In the U. S., it is interpreted as beginning as early as the seventh grade or as late as the ninth, and is usually considered terminated with the twelfth grade. Thus, for most children it corresponds roughly with the period of **adolescence.**

education/special: the education of pupils (such as the deaf, blind, mentally subnormal, gifted, etc.) who deviate so far, physically or mentally, from the comparatively homogeneous groups of normal pupils that the standard curriculum is not adaptable to their educational needs. The standard curriculum is modified in content, method of instruction, and expected rate of progress to provide optimum educational opportunity. ➤**Special education** is broader than **special class.**

education/vocational: see **vocational education.**

eduction: *n.* 1. (*C. Spearman*) the process whereby the knowledge of the nature of

two **fundaments** directly yields knowledge of their relation (EDUCTION OF RELATION); or where the knowledge of one fundament and a relation yields knowledge of the correlated fundament which stands in that relation to the first (EDUCTION OF CORRELATE). 2. (*H. S. Sullivan*) the **central processes** which lie between the **receptor** functions and the **effector** functions.

E.E.G. or **EEG:** *abbr.* for **electroencephalogram.**

effect: *n.* a phenomenon or event that invariably follows a certain other phenomenon and never occurs except in such sequence; a result.—*Distg. fr.* **affect** (*n.*).—*v.* to produce a result; to bring something about. ➤*Distg. fr.* AFFECT (*v.*), which is weaker and means merely to modify or influence a phenomenon.

effective habit strength: (*C. Hull*) "The **habit strength** throughout the entire zone of habit formation which is set up by a given reinforcement process; or, with modifications, the summation of the effects of two or more reinforcement processes."

effective range: (*stat.*) the range of a series of observations after scattered items widely removed from the others have been eliminated: a crude measure of **dispersion.**

effective reaction potential or $s\bar{E}_R$: (*C. Hull*) **reaction potential** minus total amount of inhibitory behavior.

effective stimulus: see **stimulus/effective.**

effect/law of or **/principle of:** an empirical generalization that an organism learns more quickly those reactions that are accompanied or followed by a satisfying state of affairs, and learns slowly or not at all those that result in an annoying state of affairs. ➤*Distg. fr.* **reinforcement hypothesis,** which is an explanatory theory.

effect/leveling: see **leveling effect.**

effector: *n.* a muscle or gland considered as the executive organ or organ of response; the terminus of a **nervous arc** (which see). The nerve fiber that discharges into the muscle or gland is an EFFECTOR NERVE. (This is to be distinguished from **efferent** nerve, which is more general.)

effect/spread of: the hypothesis that the effect of the satisfying or unsatisfying consequence of a response spreads to anything that also belongs to the situation, or that occurs in close temporal contiguity to the response.

effeminate: *adj.* resembling a woman in one or several respects, physical or psychological. ➤Used of normal degrees of departure from the usual masculine character.—*Cp.* **androgynous, effemination.**—*n.* **effeminacy.**

effemination: *n.* a state of being, or process of becoming, extremely womanlike in physical and mental make-up.

efferent (ef'ər·ənt): *adj.* **1.** leading out from a center; specif., **2.** of a nerve transmitting away from the **central nervous system.**—*Syn.* (for **2**) **motor nerve.**

efficiency: *n.* **1.** in a mechanism, the ratio of effect produced to energy expended. **2.** in psychology, by a metaphor often not recognized as such, the ratio of output to **effort** (1).

efficiency engineering: see **scientific management.**

efficiency/factor: see **factor efficiency.**

efficiency quotient or **EQ:** a score that compares a person's performance on the Wechsler-Bellevue test of intelligence with that of persons 20–24 years of age—at which age average performance on this test is maximal. The EQ is simply the 20–24 year IQ (as given in the standard tables) for the test score of the individual, whatever his age.

efficient cause: the sum total of the necessary antecedents of a given event.

efficient statistic: see **statistic/efficient.**

effort: *n.* **1.** the subjective experience that accompanies bodily movement when it meets resistance or when the muscles are fatigued. **2.** intensification of mental activity when it is obstructed in some way. **3.** work maintained by **will** or **volition** rather than by external **incentives.**

effort/least: see **least action/law of** and **least effort principle.**

effort syndrome: a group of symptoms—quick fatigue, palpitation or rapid heart beat, difficulty in breathing, dizziness—that do not result from pathology of organs or tissues and that are out of all proportion to the amount of exertion required.—*Syn.* SOLDIER'S HEART, NEUROCIRCULATORY ASTHENIA.

E-F scale: a scale of 30 items from **MMPI,** to measure **ethnocentric** and **authoritarian** attitudes.

egg: *n.* a reproductive cell produced by the female.—*Syn.* **ovum.**

ego (ē'gō): *n.* (*L.* for *I*) **1.** the "I," self, **person,** or individual, as distinguished from others; that which is postulated as the "center" to which all a person's psychological activities and qualities are referred. ➤This meaning is often used by those who believe that the ego is unknowable, that it is a mere formal or logical necessity.—See **person. 2.** (*psychoan.*) that aspect of the **psyche** which is conscious and most in touch with external reality. ➤According to Freud, the psyche is at first dominated wholly by the instinctual processes of the **id;** as a result of reality-perceiving, the **ego**—an aspect of the personality which is in contact with the external world by means of perception, thought, and reality-regulated striving—is gradually

differentiated. Later the ego is further differentiated and the **ego ideal** and the **superego** are distinguished. In this, the mature phase, the ego mediates between the superego and the id by building up **ego defenses.** Many later writers do not separate ego and id, speaking instead of **id-ego. 3.** the psychological processes that are oriented toward the **self;** the defining aspect of an individual who is preoccupied with his own interests, attainments, and qualities (*adj.* **egocentric**), is conceited of himself (*adj.* **egotistical**), and seeks his own welfare (*adj.* **egoistic**). ➤This usage is very common, even semipopular. It is contaminated by the other meanings, esp. the psychoanalytic, but without sharp distinctions.—*Approx. syn.* **self-regard. 4.** that aspect of the total **self** constituted by one's conception of what one is and of what one desires to become. ➤Despite the fact that this ego contains a large measure of self-deception, it is the object of self-love and **ego defense.**—*Approx. syn.* (*psychoan.*) **ego ideal.**

ego-alter theory: a theory that holds that social interaction is largely controlled by the individual's notion of himself (his **ego**) in relation with the other person as conceived (the **alter**) by the former.

ego analysis: (*psychoan.*) the investigation of ego strengths and weaknesses for the purpose of making therapeutic use of these integrative and defensive forces (esp. the former), instead of trying to break down **ego defenses** and release **id** instincts.—*Contr. w.* ID ANALYSIS, which concentrates on the difficulties arising from instinctual forces.

ego anxiety: see **anxiety/ego.**

ego/auxiliary: see **auxiliary ego.**

ego block: anything that prevents the enhancement of the **ego** (in any of its several senses). ➤It may be an inhibition that prevents the person from using his full capabilities; or it may be something that lessens his sense of dignity or importance.

ego/body: the experienced composite representation of the body that forms the core of the **ego** or **self;** the bodily self.

ego cathexis: a channeling of **libido** onto an object in the reality-oriented **ego** domain.

egocentric: *adj.* **1.** concerned with oneself; preoccupied with one's own concerns and relatively insensitive to the concerns of others, though not necessarily selfish.—*Approx. syn.* **introverted,** or (*Ror.*) **introversive.**—See **ego** (3) for related terms. **2.** of behavior, esp. of speech, that is controlled by one's own concerns and insensitive to the needs, expressions, or reactions of others. ➤Highly characteristic of children, such behavior also often colors the conduct and speech of adults.—*n*. **egocentrism. 3.** tending to behavior or belief so wholly one's own as to be peculiar, almost eccentric.—*n*. **egocentricity.**

egocentric predicament: the human difficulty or impossibility of knowing things or persons as they are in themselves, as distinguished from the way one necessarily knows and experiences them through one's own personality.

egocentric response: a response, in an **association** or **projective test,** that refers to oneself or one's personal affairs.

egocentric speech: 1. speech having no social reference or at least making no social demand, though it may be in the presence of others; talking to oneself. **2.** speech controlled by one's own needs and insensitive to the needs of others. ➤Both meanings refer to behavior common among children and often found, also, among adults.

ego complex: (*C. Jung*) a mental structure comprising those emotional reactions that are related to the **ego.** ➤*Syn.* **self-sentiment,** *prefd.* as avoiding the implication of **repression** usually associated with the word **complex.**

ego defense: (*psychoan.*) **1.** the retraining or sublimating or symbolic alteration of id impulses in order to protect the integrity of the **ego (2);** protecting the ego by effecting harmony between **id** and **superego. 2.** = **defense mechanism,** a looser and more general expression. **3.** = **defense reaction (2).**

ego development: the progressive awareness, experienced by a child, of himself as a distinct person, of his actual traits, and of those traits to which he aspires.

ego drive: motivation to activities that maintain self-esteem. ➤This includes **ego-defense** activities, but also activities that contribute positively to the sense of personal worth.

ego-dystonic (-dis·ton′ik): *adj.* inacceptable to the **ego.**—*Ant.* **ego-syntonic.** —*n*. **ego dystonia.**

ego erotism = **narcissism.**

ego extension: enlarging of the reality-oriented, integrative functions of the personality.

ego failure: (*psychoan.*) the failure to keep the impulses of the **id** in normal balance with the constraints and imperatives of the **superego** and the demands of reality.

ego function: (*psychoan.*) any activity of the **ego,** in contrast with an activity of the **id.** An ego function is adaptive (i.e., it is self-preservative and takes account of reality); at times it is **repressive** of id functions or **defensive** of the ego.

ego goal: a particular goal for one's personal development; a desired or purposed achievement of personality or character.

ego-id = **id-ego.**

ego ideal: (*psychoan.*) a part of the **ego** closely related with, but also to be distinguished from, the **superego.** ➤The ego ideal represents the sum of positive **identifications** with loving, reassuring parents (or parent substitutes, including society and God, so far as these are *positively* identified with). From the ego ideal proceed consciously held and actually desired standards of goodness and excellence, standards not of what one ought to be but of what one genuinely wants to be. The superego, in contrast, incorporates the punitive, stern, forbidding aspect of the parent. It is primarily concerned with *control* of impulse. As life experiences bring new persons into the individual's life, the ego ideal may develop; the superego, laid down in early childhood, does not change. In the main, the ego ideal provides positive striving for ideals, the superego functions as a forbidding **conscience.**

ego ideal/narcissistic: (*psychoan.*) a beloved image of one's own perfection and omnipotence, formed in childhood. Since it is unrealistic, in the healthy person it is gradually rejected.

ego instinct: (*psychoan.*) all impulses that serve the self-preservation of the individual.—*Contr. w.* **libido** (or instincts of the **id**).—*Distg. fr.* the **life** vs. **death instinct** dichotomy.

ego-integrative: *adj.* tending to harmonize one's impulses and strivings; tending toward organization of personality.

ego involvement: the relationship in which a task or situation is regarded as important to the **ego (3** or **4).** Action to maintain (or remove) the situation, or to perform the task, is set in motion or increased.

egoism: *n.* the view that in the final analysis self-interest is—or should be—the basis of motivation and of morality; or the behavior of one who acts accordingly.—*Ant.* **altruism.**

egoistic: *adj.* in love with oneself; tending to push one's own interests at the expense of others.—*Syn.* **egotistic.** ➤Both terms imply a high degree of self-centeredness, but **egoistic** seldom connotes the offensive conceit associated with **egotistic.** —See also **ego (3),** **egotic.**—*Ant.* **altruistic.**—*n.* **egoism.**—*pers. n.* **egoist.**

egoistic theory of dreams: (*psychoan.*) the view that the chief actor in a dream is always the dreamer himself.

ego level: (*F. Hoppe*) the supposed unitary level at which a person actually functions, in contrast to his **level of *aspiration;** the SELF-LEVEL.

ego libido: (*psychoan.*) psychic energy that is restricted to the **ego.** It is libido that has been withdrawn from, or never bestowed on, external objects or interests.—*Contr. w.* **object libido.**—*Syn.* **narcissism (1).**

egomorphism: *n.* **1.** (*L. Ackerson*) the tendency to read into the actions of others what we want to find there; more generally, the framing of a theoretical system that represents things the way we want them to be.—*Syn.* **autism. 2.** the tendency to use one's own motivational system as a standard of comparison for others. ➤One does not, necessarily, ascribe one's own motives to others (as in **projection** or **extrajection**); the egomorph may even complain because another has motives that differ from his own.

ego neurosis: (*psychoan.*) a neurosis with symptoms that are primarily disturbances of activities of the **ego** or the **conscious,** such as paralyses, loss of sensory functions or of memory, etc.

ego-object polarity: the tendency to maintain a sharp distinction between self and not-self.

egopathy (ē·gop′ə·thi): *n.* hostility deriving from the effort to exalt one's own **ego** by pushing others down.

ego regression (*psychoan.*) a return to a more primitive **id**-dominated level of **ego** development.

ego relevance: the recognized relation of some fact to the **ego (3, 4).**

ego resistance: (*psychoan.*) the resistance, shown by the **ego** during analysis, to recognition of the individual's repressed impulses, and to giving up neurotic or unhealthy defenses.

ego seeking: 1. seeking that which is for one's own advantage. **2.** seeking that which increases one's importance in one's own eyes. **3.** seeking that which accords with the **superego.**

ego strength: 1. ability of a person to maintain the **ego (2, 3). 2.** ability to maintain **adjustment** in general. ➤This usage seems to imply some vague theory concerning the relation of the ego (in which sense?) to adjustment. Sometimes mere resoluteness or character strength seems referred to.

ego structure: the enduring arrangements that codetermine **ego** behavior or ego processes.

ego/supportive: see **supportive ego.**

ego-syntonic (-sin·ton′ik): *adj.* consistent with consciously held ideals, or with the **ego ideal;** of a condition in which **ego** and **superego** are in agreement.—*Ant.* **ego-dystonic.**—*n.* **ego syntonia.**

ego threat: the pressure of **instinctual** impulses against the demands of the reality situation as perceived by the ego; by extension, the pressure of such impulses against the prohibitions of the **superego.**

egotic (ē·got′ik): *adj.* pertaining to the **ego;** pertaining to enjoyment of personal pleasures such as those of body or status. ➤Egotic is less derogatory in its implications of self-reference than **egotistic** or **egoistic** (which see).

egotistic(al): *adj.* conceited; entertaining a high opinion of one's own value.—See discussion under **egoistic.**—*Cp.* also **ego, egotic.**—*n.* **egotism.**—*pers. n.* **egotist.**

E **group = experimental group.**—*Contr. w. C* **group (control group).**

eidetic imagery (ī·det′ik): a peculiarly vivid type of **imagery:** it is practically as if the subject were actually perceiving, although in general he realizes that the imaged object is not literally present to the senses. ➤It is very common in childhood (perhaps universal) and is gradually lost by most persons.—*Cp. B* **type** and *T* **type.**—*pers. n.* **eidetic, Eidetiker.**

eidotropic (ī″dō·trō′pik): *adj.* characterizing perception in which a form is seen as more perfect or typical than it actually is. Thus, in a drawing, a simple but crucial line or two may give a vivid representation of an object.—*Cp.* **law of *closure, object *constancy.**

Eindringlichkeit (īn′dring·liH′kīt): *n.* (*Ger.* for *forcefulness* or *insistence*) an attribute (considered by some unanalyzable) of a perceived size, shape, color, etc., that brings it to attention.

Einfühlung (īn′fY·lüng): *n. Ger.* for **empathy.**

eingestellt (īn′gā·shtelt): *adj.* (*Ger.*) prepared to react in a certain general way to a stimulus situation.—See *Einstellung.*—*Syn.* **set** (*adj.*) (*prefd.*).

Einstellung (īn′shtel·úng): (*Ger.* for **attitude** or **set**) a relatively rigid and simple **attitude,** or **predisposition.** ➤The German root means *to put in place,* or *to adjust* (beforehand). As compared with **set,** *Einstellung* refers less to muscular arrangements and more to a kind of directed readiness for a particular kind of stimulus: one who has an *Einstellung* for the sound of a bell is surprised if instead he hears a buzzer.

ejaculation: *n.* forcible emission of semen at the height of the male **orgasm.**

ejaculatio praecox (i·jak″ū·lā′shi·ō prē′-koks): premature **ejaculation** (of semen) previous to, or at the beginning of, coitus.

ejection: *n.* ridding oneself of uncomfortable mental processes by denying that they are one's own and attributing them to someone else: "I don't dislike him; he dislikes me."—*Cp.* **projection, defense mechanism.**

EKG: *abbr.* for **electrocardiogram.**

elaboration/secondary: (*psychoan.*) the process whereby the fragments of **latent *content** in dream or phantasy are made more coherent and logical as they are put together in the **manifest *content.** The process is conceived to result from the reality demand of the **ego**; it begins during the dream and is continued in the later revival and report of the dream. It is one of four mechanisms in dream-making. *Cp.* **displacement (4), dramatization, condensation.**

élan (ā·läN'): *n.* (*Fr.*) ardor; eagerness. ➤Sometimes used as synonym for **horme** (which see). For Bergson the ÉLAN VITAL (vē·täl') was the creative and directive vital force or impulse of life, immanent in all organisms, and the cause of evolutionary progress.

elation: *n.* joyful behavior, esp. but not necessarily when disproportionate to the circumstances; high spirits over the turn of events, or achievement of a goal.

Elberfeld horses (el'bər·felt): a group of horses, including *der kluge Hans* (Clever Hans), who were trained to respond so that they seemed able to solve difficult arithmetical problems.

Electra complex (ē·lek'trə): (*psychoan.*) the repressed desire of a female for incestuous relations with her father. It is held by Freudians to be nearly universal.—*Cp.* the analogous **Oedipus complex** in males.

electric shock therapy = **electroshock therapy.**

electric skin response = **electrodermal response.**

electro- (i·lek'tro-): combining form meaning *electric* or *electricity.*

electrocardiogram or **EKG** (-kär'di·ə·gram): a graphic record of the spreading electric potential which accompanies the cycle of the heart beat. It permits study of the heart's performance.—*n.* **electrocardiography** (kär″di·og'rə·fi).

electroconvulsive therapy = **electroshock therapy.**

electrode: *n.* a device for transmitting electric current to a substance not usually regarded as an electric transmitter, e.g., to an animal tissue. The positive pole is the ANODE, the negative the CATHODE.

electrodermal response or **EDR:** electrical reactions on the skin as detected by a sensitive **galvanometer.** ➤The term applies either to the apparent resistance of the skin to the passage of a weak external electric current (FÉRÉ PHENOMENON), or to the production by the body of a weak current on the skin surface (TARCHANOFF PHENOMENON). The EDR correlates with emotion, effort, or strain, but the correlations are difficult to interpret.—*Syn.* PSYCHOGALVANIC REFLEX or PGR (*obsoles.*), ELECTRIC SKIN RESPONSE, GALVANIC SKIN RESPONSE or GSR.

electrodiagnosis: *n.* examination of muscles or nerves by applying electric currents. Diseased tissues give a specific reaction.—*Cp.* **chronaxie.**

electroencephalogram, electroencephalo-

graph or **EEG** (-en·sef'ə·lō·gram): graphic record of the wavelike changes in the electric potential observed when electrodes are placed on the skull or on the exposed brain.—*n.* **electroencephalography** (-en·sef″ə·log'rə·fi).

electromotive force or **emf:** (*phys.*) the force due to a difference in electric potential.

electromyogram, electromyograph or **EMG** (-mī'ə·gram): a record of the changes of electric potential in a muscle. —*n.* **electromyography** (-mī·og'rə·fi).

electronarcosis (-när·kō'səs): *n.* a form of shock treatment which induces a sleeplike **coma** after the initial shock.

electron-proton theory: (*A. P. Weiss*) the doctrine which holds that behavior reduces to nothing but (*a*) different kinds of electron-proton groupings into certain geometrical structures, and (*b*) motions that occur when one structure changes into another.

electrophysiology: *n.* the study of the function of organs and physiological systems with instruments designed to record **bioelectrical** phenomena.

electroretinogram or **ERG:** a graphic record of changes in the electric potential of the retina.

electroshock therapy or **EST:** treatment of a behavior disorder by electric shock to the brain.—See **shock therapy.**—*Syn.* ELECTROCONVULSIVE THERAPY.

electrotherapy: *n.* the use of repeated, brief, nonconvulsive electric shock as part of the treatment for mental or bodily ills. —*Distg. fr.* **electroshock therapy.**

element: *n.* **1.** a constituent part, esp. one that cannot be reduced to simpler terms under the conditions of the observation or investigation. ➤*Distg. fr.* **factor,** a force or influence that combines with others to produce an effect.—See **mental element. 2.** (*G. A. Kelly*) one of the things, objects, or events that are abstracted or segregated by a given person's use of a given **construct;** the field to which the construct applies. **3.** (*info. theory*) one of the items that are being considered or talked about as forming an **ensemble.** While the elements need not be indivisible, they are treated as unitary for the purposes of the ensemble of which they form parts. Examples of elements are letters, sentences, amino acids, persons, explosions, walking, any distinct event, etc. They may be treated formally as points in a sample space.—*adj.* **elementary,** simple; **elemental,** pertaining to an element.

elemental: see **element.**

elementalism: *n.* **1.** a point of view that regards it possible to analyze something into elements by making verbal distinctions in the absence of empirical or operational separation. **2.** a tendency to consider as a separate entity the simplest distinguishable aspect of a phenomenon.—*Syn.* **atomism** (usually derogatory).—See **elementarism** (1).

elementarism: *n.* **1.** a point of view holding that complex phenomena can be best (or only) understood when described or reduced to their elements (or simple, independent parts), and that a whole can be totally described or understood in terms of its parts considered as independent elements.—*Syn.* **reductionism, atomism.**—*Ant.* **holism, emergentism, Gestalt. 2.** any system of psychology that describes in terms of **mental elements,** but especially the system of Wundt and his followers.—See **psychology/divisions and schools of, VII.**

elementary: see **element.**

element/mental: see **mental element.**

element of a matrix: a single entry in a **matrix;** the number that occupies a **cell.** In the **correlation** *matrix, the elements are correlation coefficients.

elements/social: the simplest units of human behavior that are communicable to others.

Elgin check list: a list of behaviors found more frequently among psychotic patients than in the normal population.

elicit: *v.* to draw forth from something what is latent therein. →A stimulus is said to elicit a response (**respondent** behavior) from an organism. While the stimulus is evidently part of the cause, the term implies also that the nature of the organism contributes to the nature of the reply, though the details are unspecified.—*Distg. fr.* **emit,** in which the role of the organism as compared with that of the stimulus is still greater.

elimination: *n.* **1.** the voiding of feces and urine. **2.** decrease in a school population due to death or leaving school.

elision: *n.* (*speech*) the omission or partial pronunciation of one or more phonetic units: e.g., the omission of some or all consonants in the speech of young children.—*Syn.* LEIPOLALIA.

ellipsis: *n.* the omission of one or more words, leaving the whole to be constructed and understood by the hearer or reader. →In psychoanalysis, the omitted words when recovered by **analysis** are deemed highly significant.

emancipation: *n.* attainment of freedom from control, esp. from control of parents. Such emancipation may be manifest in independence of thought and feeling, as well as of overt behavior.

emasculation = **castration.** (Occasionally used metaphorically.)

embeddedness: *n.* (*W. Stern*) the property of being enclosed within the basic structure of personal life, of having numerous relations with other psychic phenomena, and of not being easily detached from them.—*Ant.* **salience** (1).

embolism (em′bō·liz·əm): *n.* stoppage of a blood vessel by a clot or obstruction in the bloodstream.—*adj.* **embolic** (em·bol′ik).

embol(o)-: a combining form denoting (*a*) *presence of embolism;* (*b*) in terms relating to speech, *interpolation* (of superfluous sounds, words, etc.): *embolalia.*

embryo: *n.* an organism in the very early phases of its prenatal development. →In mammals the **embryonic** period precedes the time the organism begins to resemble its adult form. In man, it is conventionally the first six weeks after conception.—*Cp.* **fetus,** the organism during the later stages of pregnancy.—*adj.* **embryonic** (-on′ik) (which see).

embryology: *n.* the study of organisms in the early stages of their development, before they begin to resemble the adult form.—See **embryo.**

embryonic: *adj.* pertaining to an **embryo,** or to the whole development of **embryo** and **fetus;** metaphorically, of anything in the early stages of its development.

emergency theory of emotions: the theory that, in the **autonomic nervous system** and the **effectors** connected with it, the organism is provided with a check-and-drive mechanism which puts it in readiness to meet emergencies with undivided energy output. With this action of the autonomic system certain emotions are said to stand in a very close relationship, that either of identity or of cause and effect.

emergent: *adj.* of a phenomenon that cannot be predicted (*a*) from its constituent parts, or (*b*) from the properties of the events antecedent to it. →Many accept the reality of (*a*) and not of (*b*).

emergent counseling technique = **client-centered** *therapy.

emergentism: *n.* theory that objects or phenomena have **emergent** properties; the view of EMERGENT EVOLUTION, which holds that combinations of elements may result in something new that was unpredictable from knowledge of those elements. →Specifically, it is hypothesized that life, or livingness, is such an emergent property; and that mind, or the property of being conscious, is an attribute of living matter when it reaches a certain state of complexity.—*Distg. fr.* **Gestalt theory,** which takes the wholeness property as given rather than as evolved from combinations of simpler elements.—*Syn.* EMERGENT EVOLUTION.—See **psychology/divisions and schools of, IV.**

emergent vitalism: the view that regards the life process as a unique phenomenon emerging from a complex organization of matter.—See **emergentism.**

emesis (em′ə·sis): *n.* vomiting.—*adj.* **emetic** (ə·met′ik).

emf: *abbr.* for **electromotive force.**

EMG = **electromyogram.**

eminence: *n.* recognized ability such as is attained by one person in 4,000. ➤*Cp.* **illustriousness,** the level reached by one in 1,000,000; and **distinction,** somewhat more vague and implying less ability than **eminence.**

emission: *n.* 1. giving out or sending forth. 2. the occurrence of a response that is not directly elicited by a stimulus. ➤An **emitted** response is not entirely random but the particular stimulus pattern to which it is related cannot be specified. This concept is important in the theory of **instrumental** *conditioning. 3. the excretion of semen, esp. the often quite normal NIGHT or NOCTURNAL EMISSION.—*v.* **emit.**

emit: *v.* 1. to give forth; to send out. 2. to make an **operant** response in the absence of any *specific* stimulus. ➤*Distg. fr.* **elicit,** used when a specific stimulus is the necessary condition for making a response. Emit implies nothing as to causation, except that it is unknown.—*Cp.* **spontaneous behavior.**—*n.* **emission.**

Emmanuel Movement: a proposal for mental health clinics in connection with churches, providing both psychological or psychiatric treatment and spiritual counseling.

Emmert's law: a generalization concerning the size of an **afterimage** or an **eidetic image** projected on a ground. The formula is $l' = \dfrac{la'}{a}$ where l' = linear distances in the image, l = linear distances in the stimulus object, a' = distance between eye and image, a = distance between eye and stimulus object.

emmetropic (em″ə·trop′ik): *adj.* having normal vision.—*Contr. w.* **hyperopia, myopia, astigmatism.**—*n.* **emmetropia** (-trō′pi·ə).

emote: *v.* to manifest **emotion**; to make a response that is classed as **emotional.**

emotion: *n.* a complex feeling-state accompanied by characteristic motor and glandular activities; or a complex behavior in which the visceral component predominates. ➤**Emotion** is virtually impossible to define (the above characterization fails to distinguish emotion sharply from certain other phenomena) except in terms of conflicting theories, though there is fair agreement in classifying as emotion such phenomena as fear, anger, joy, disgust, pity, affection, etc. Nearly all theories assign important roles to the activities of both the central nervous system and the autonomic, though they interpret these roles variously. Nearly all relate emotion in some way to motivation. All, except the most rigidly behavioristic, classify emotion as affective or assign a dominant role to a feeling element. ¶Many psychologists, although they do not recognize particular emotions, such as joy or anger, do recognize that certain behaviors may be described as being **emotional:** they speak of emotional response in general, or of an emotional struggle, even of an angry struggle, but not of *an emotion* of anger. On the other hand, even in professional discussion (e.g., of the role of emotion in social adjustment), emotion implies more than a *momentary* feeling reaction. Often emotion is used not for a single feeling but for a system of feelings, i.e., for a **sentiment.**

The following are typical meanings of the term; they are perhaps not so much definitions as abbreviated theories, or themes about which a theory is constructed: (*a*) a mental state, characterized by strong feeling and accompanied by motor expression, that is related to some object or external situation. (*b*) (*W. McDougall*) an excited state of mind that accompanies goal-directed effort. The qualitative differences between one such state and another are a function of the sensations aroused by the motor activities involved.—See **emotion/primary.** (*c*) (*J. Drever*) the affective state consequent upon obstruction or delay in instinctive behavior. (*d*) (*psychoan.*) the dynamic expression of instinct. (*e*) a disorganized response. (*f*) a total act organized about an autonomic-controlled complex of behaviors.

In addition to the many named varieties of emotion, an extraordinary variety of terms refer to behavior that is emotional and may be regarded as approx. synonyms: **feeling, affect, sentiment, mood, passion, cathexis, interest,** and nearly all the **motivational** terms. See also **emergency theory, James-Lange theory.**

—*adj.* **emotional,** used not only for emotion but for **feeling, feeling tone, mood,** and **passion,** and characterizing either the behavior or the person behaving; **emotive,** characterizing the instigating situation.—*n.* **emotionality** (which see); **emotivity.**—*v.* **emote,** an uncommon but acceptable term, needed by those who define emotion as overt behavior. (A few prefer the form **emove.**) **Feel** (*v.*), though it has other meanings, often means **emote.**

emotional: *adj.* 1. pertaining to the state or process of **emotion.** 2. having the attribute of **emotion.** ➤Some authorities question the existence of separate, distinct emotions; but they recognize an **emotional** quality which may attach to or pervade certain actions. Any response with the quality of emotion is an EMOTIONAL RESPONSE. **3.** characterizing a person as experiencing an **emotion** or manifesting emotional behavior; or a person who is easily or excessively given to emotion.—*Cp.* **emotionality.**

emotional adequacy: the feeling that one is able to do what is required of him. ➤The term means more than that emotions are adequate, but its limits are vague.—*Syn.* SELF-CONFIDENCE (*pref'd.*).

emotional blocking: inhibition of thinking or of other forms of adjustive response due to excessive emotions, usually of the fear group. ➤*Distg. fr.* simple BLOCKING, in which inability to recall something very familiar is apparently not caused by emotion, but may lead to it.

emotional breadth: the degree of variation in feeling displayed in a situation; the range of objects and situations to which a person will react emotionally, either in general or in a concrete situation.

emotional climate: see **climate/psychological.**

emotional decompensation: an uncontrollable emotional outburst that results from a cumulation of emotive stimulation; an explosive emotional response following many, often minor, incidents.

emotional disorder: a condition in which emotional reactions are disproportionate—either too intense or the reverse—to reality situations. ➤Intense fear under appropriate conditions is not **emotional disorder**; but consequent chronic anxiety or emotional depression is.

emotional exhaustion = **neurasthenia.**

emotional expansiveness: 1. tendency to display **emotion** in new situations, esp. when the shift is easily made. **2.** tendency to relatively superficial, light, jovial, and easily aroused emotion. It is akin to **euphoria.**

emotional expression: 1. all the muscular and glandular activities that occur during, or as part of, **emoting. 2.** those activities found in emoting that do not directly alter the person's relation to environment, but are socially perceived (a blush but not a kiss; a clenched fist but not a blow). ➤The term in either usage implies a distinction between the emotion and the activities by which it is expressed, whereas many theories hold that the activities are constituent parts, not mere signs, of emoting; but the usage is well established.

emotional flattening: see **flattening of affect.**

emotional immaturity: see **immaturity/emotional.**

emotional indicator: any observable sign or symptom of the **covert** activities of emotion.

emotional instability: the tendency to quick-changing and unreliable emotional response.—*Cp.* **emotionally unstable personality.**

emotionality: *n.* a characteristic of a person who reacts easily and strongly to **emotive** situations. ➤Generally the implication is of excessive reaction. *Cp.* **emotivity,** which is the capacity to **emote** but which implies that the emoting is under control. Neither term should imply a generalized trait of emotional sensitivity.

emotional lability: easy arousal and shift from one emotion to another.

emotionally unstable personality: (*Stan. Psychiat.*) a person who reacts with excitement and ineffectively in situations of minor stress and whose relation with other people is fraught with fluctuating emotional attitudes.—*Syn.* (*obsoles.*) PSYCHOPATHIC PERSONALITY WITH EMOTIONAL INSTABILITY.

emotional pattern: 1. an arrangement or a set of relationships, esp. of timing and of relative intensity, among the activities that characterize a given emotion. **2.** the mode of **emoting** that is characteristic for an individual under stated conditions, including various combinations of different emotions.

emotional release: the outpouring of **emotion** after a period of attempted suppression.—*Syn.* **catharsis, abreaction.**—*Cp.* **release therapy, suppression.**

emotional stability: characteristic of a person who does not react excessively to **emotive** situations.—*Contr. w.* **emotionality.**

emotional state: the condition of the organism during affectively toned experiencing, whether mild or intense.

emotional strength: intensity of feeling in a given situation.

emotion/conditioned: 1. an emotional response that has been acquired by the process or processes specified as **conditioning;** an emotional response acquired by sheer temporal contiguity with a certain situation, without understanding of the situation or reasoned relation between situation and response. **2.** any learned emotional response. ➤This is a **theory-begging** usage, since it implies that all learned emotional responses are acquired by operations similar to those of the **conditioning** experiment—an unverified speculation. Moreover, this usage keeps us from using **conditioned emotion** for pure **contiguity learning.**

emotion/derived: (*W. McDougall*) an emotion not directly correlated with a particular impulse but reflecting the course or outcome of any strong impulse: joy, sorrow, surprise, regret, hope, despair, chagrin, etc.

emotion/induced: see induction/sympathetic.

emotion/primary: (W. McDougall) the constellation of feelings associated with an instinct. ➤Designating an emotion as primary does not imply that it is unmodified or unmodifiable; the contrast is with derived *emotion and with compounds of emotions.

emotive: adj. of a situation or stimulus that evokes emotion or feeling.

emotivity: n. capacity for emotional response. ➤In contrast with emotionality, this term does not imply excess.

empathy: n. 1. (T. Lipps) attribution of the feelings or attitudes aroused by its surroundings (actual or depicted) to a natural object or a work of art: e.g., a column seems to brace itself doggedly under tooheavy pressure (as a man might do). NEGATIVE EMPATHY is empathy that takes place against a certain resistance or repugnance. ➤Distg. fr. the so-called PATHETIC FALLACY in literature, where inanimate objects are described figuratively in human terms (the cruel sea) without any implication that the object actually feels like a human. 2. apprehension of the state of mind of another person without feeling (as in sympathy) what the other feels. ➤While the empathic process is primarily intellectual, emotion is not precluded, but it is not the same emotion as that of the person with whom one empathizes. The parent may empathize with the child's puny rage, feeling pity or amusement, whereas in sympathy he would feel rage along with the child. The attitude in empathy is one of acceptance and understanding, of an implicit "I see how you feel."—Cp. projection, identification, sympathy.—v. empathize. —adj. empathic (em·path′ik).

emphasis principle: the generalization that anything that heightens attention to a significant cue in the learning situation, or that makes the animal respond specifically to such a cue, is favorable to learning.

empirical: adj. 1. related to facts or experience. 2. valuing facts and disparaging or subordinating theory or speculation. 3. proceeding without guidance from theory; trial-and-error investigation. ➤This is never possible in an absolute sense. 4. of a generalization not based on, nor as yet related to, a superior generalization or theory. 5. = experimental. 6. based on factual investigation.

➤The term is sometimes one of praise (avoiding "empty" speculation or "mere" theorizing); sometimes one of dispraise (lacking necessary rationality or theory, unsystematically gathering facts). Usage (5) seems unnecessary duplication. Usage (6) includes experiment and all other systematic collection of data: it is that most used (and useful) in modern psychology. Empirical contrasts with, but is not necessarily opposed to, a priori, rational, or deductive.

empirical construct: a construct hypothesized on the basis of observed facts; the construct hypothesized when different classes of operation lead to the same result: e.g., a mass (as in physics), a stimulus trace, a factor (as in factor analysis). ➤There is a class of operations in an anagrams test and a class of operations in a test of oral fluency. When subjected to factor analysis, these two classes yield approximately the same rating of an individual in respect to a factor x; x is an empirical construct.

empirical curve-fitting = curve fitting.

empirical equation or formula: an equation fitted to a particular set of observations or quantitative data, in contrast to one derived by deductive means. It is an attempt to describe a set of data by means of a mathematical equation that simplifies without excessive distortion. An EMPIRICAL CURVE represents the equation. The criterion is closeness of fit, not theoretical implication. —Cp. rational equation.

empirical law: a law based on data (i.e., on facts or observations) and expressing in general form the invariant relationships between two or more sets of data (i.e., two or more variables). ➤Contr. w. rational law, deductive law, a priori law, each of which designates a general statement of relations that does not, at least immediately, rest on data or observations.

empirical psychology: 1. (usually cap.) (F. Brentano) psychology conceived as the study of mind in action, of what mind accomplishes rather than of what it is, of mind as the producer of thinking or willing. ➤This conception is related to functional psychology and contrasts with content psychology. 2. a psychology sharply oriented to facts. ➤Such empirical psychology may be one that emphasizes getting facts as a precursor to theorizing, one that is chiefly a collection of facts without theorizing, or one that avoids philosophical issues and implications. 3. a psychology based on nonexperimental factual evidence.
    Bretano's Empirical Psychology, being chiefly speculative and philosophical, is almost the opposite of empirical psychology (2).—Cp. empirical.

empirical regression line: (stat.) the line that passes through the means of a two-way table.

empirical test: an effort to verify a proposition by reference to facts.—See test (1) and (2), and empirical (6).

empiricism: n. 1. the philosophical view that experience is the only source of knowledge; that all knowledge or certain kinds of knowledge (e.g., that of space-perceiving) originate in experience. ➤ONTOGENETIC THEORY of knowledge would be a less equivocal term (see **ontogenesis**).—*Contr. w.* **nativism** and **a priorism** (2). **2.** the view that science must deal exclusively with objectively observable fact. ➤**Behaviorism** is a form of empiricism in this sense. Some empiricists, however, accept the view that "observable fact" in any science is a matter of **experience:** the observed fact that an object has a certain density is given in experience. But the experience which is thus the fact for science is the experience of the observing scientist (not subjective experience) stated in **physicalist** terms.— See **scientific *empiricism, positivism. 3.** a science or an art based as little as possible on deduction from general principles and guided almost entirely by inductive generalizations, usually by generalizations having narrow range and not rationally related with each other. ➤EMPIRICAL MEDICINE was historically contrasted with RATIONAL MEDICINE. It was not based on knowledge of physiology; it trusted to induction from experience that certain drugs have certain effects.—See **psychology/divisions and schools of, I, VI.**

empiricism/scientific: 1. a somewhat diffuse philosophic movement that seeks to establish a science of sciences. ➤It holds that the instrument of all the sciences is the experience of the scientist himself used as a means of examining the several coherent bodies of fact that constitute the various sciences. Statements about experience (i.e., **empirical** propositions) must be **operationally defined.** The movement calls for studies of the language of science and the principles governing the building of theory around empirical facts. As applied in psychology, it is held that mentalistic concepts may be used if introduced by operational definitions anchored to changes along a physical or **physicalistic** continuum.—*Syn.* LOGICAL EMPIRICISM, LOGICAL POSITIVISM.—*Cp.* **physicalism, operationalism. 2.** an antitheoretical position holding that science is merely descriptive. ➤The older forms of **positivism** were sometimes called scientific empiricism.

employment test: any test designed to predict a person's probable satisfactoriness to his employer.

empyreumatic (em″pī·rü·mat′ik): *adj.* of a class of odors of which tar and tobacco smoke are typical.—*n.* **empyreuma** (-rü′-mə).

emulation: *n.* conscious effort to equal or excel the performance of another, implying a large element of imitation. ➤**Emulation** permits all to succeed, whereas **competition**

implies designation of a rank order or of the unique success of one person.—See **rivalry.**

enantiodromia (en·an″ti·ō·drō′mi·ə): *n.* (*C. Jung*) the view that everything eventually is transformed into its opposite.

encapsulation/psychological: (*K. Lewin*) behavior that shuts one off from all possible external stimulation in order to escape a tension-evoking situation, e.g., hiding the face to avoid seeing an accident. The term is also used figuratively.

encephalitis (en·sef″ə·lī′tis): *n.* **1.** any acute inflammation of the brain or its membranous coverings. **2.** specif., an infectious disease of the brain known as EPIDEMIC ENCEPHALITIS, ENCEPHALITIS LETHARGICA, or (because of its symptoms of drowsiness and apathy) less accurately as SLEEPING SICKNESS. (*Distg. fr.* the sleeping sickness of Africa.) The serious neurological and personality changes which persist after the patient has recovered from the acute stage are called POSTENCEPHALITIC.

encephalitis/lethargic = encephalitis (2).

encephalization (en·sef″ə·liz·ā′shən): *n.* **1.** the evolutionary processes that led to the formation of the brain. **2.** in the growth of an individual or in the evolution of species, the progressively greater control of bodily activities by the brain. ➤The term may be used in comparing species or in comparing kinds of behavior within a species. It is often used when ENCORTICALIZATION, the progressively greater control by the **cortex**, would be more specific and accurate.

encephal(o)- (en·sef′ə·lō-): combining form referring to the *brain*.

encephalography (-log′rə·fi): *n.* any examination of the brain and mapping of the result. The examination may be by X ray or by an **electroencephalograph.** Indirect methods of determining and mapping brain functions are not usually included.

encephalon (en·sef′ə·lon): *n.* that portion of the nervous system within the skull; the whole brain.

encephalopathy (-lop′ə·thi): *n.* brain disease. ➤Although *brain disease* sounds like a layman's expression, it means exactly what the two Greek roots of **encephalopathy** say.—See **bogus erudition.**

encephalopsychosis: *n.* mental disorder due to a brain disease that has a definite and limited location.

encoded: *adj.* of data translated into a code; of information arranged in such form that it can be communicated. E.g., a message is encoded when it is translated into telegraphic electric impulses; data are encoded when punched into an IBM card.

encoding: *n.* (*commun. theory*) **1.** process whereby a **message** is transformed into **signals** that can be carried by a communication **channel. 2.** process whereby a person transforms his intention into such behavior as can be a **signal** in a communication system. ➤The usual behaviors are oral or graphic language, but gestures, etc., may also serve. The entire **encoding** may involve several steps, e.g., a person writes out a telegram (first **encoding**) which is in turn transformed by another into electric signals (second **encoding**).

encopresis (en″kəp·rē′səs): *n.* involuntary defecation not due to local organic defect or illness. ➤In Western culture it is regarded as a symptom of faulty training when habitual in a child over two years old (but the term is seldom used by parents).

encorticalization: see **encephalization.**

enculturation: *n.* the process of adapting to and adopting a **culture.**—*Cp.* **socialization.**

encystment of the self: protective behaviors by which the **self** is shielded from inescapably disagreeable situations.—*Cp.* **defense mechanism.**—*Syn.* ENCAPSULATION OF SELF or PSYCHE.

end: *n.* **1.** a desired result of striving. **2.** the purpose implied in a goal or set of goals.

endbrain: *n.* (*neurol.*) the anterior subdivision of the embryonic brain, which develops into the **olfactory lobes,** the cerebral **hemispheres,** and the **corpora striata.**—*Syn.* TELENCEPHALON.

end brush: the finely branched termination of an **axon.**

end buttons: see **synaptic knob.**

end foot: (*neurol.*) a small terminal enlargement of nerve fibers that are in contact with **dendrites** of other nerve cells; the **synaptic** ending of a nerve fiber.—*Syn.* END BULB.—See **synaptic knob.**

endo-, ento-: combining form meaning *within, inside.*

endocathection: *n.* (*H. A. Murray*) the **cathection** of thought or emotion for its own sake; preoccupation with inner activities.—*Ant.* EXOCATHECTION, cathection directed outwardly.

endocrine (en′dō·krin, -krīn): *adj.* secreted or secreting internally; esp., of a **gland** that produces a **hormone,** i.e., a substance passed into the blood stream as a chemical regulator of physiological activity. Other tissues, not glandlike in structure, also have an ENDOCRINE FUNCTION.—*Ant.* **exocrine.**

endocrine gland: see **gland.**

endocrinology (en″dō·krin·ol′ə·ji): *n.* the study of the body's internal secretions, from whatever source, including those of the **endocrine glands.**

endocrinopathy (-op′ə·thi): *n.* any disorder of metabolism caused by disease of the **endocrine glands.**

endoderm: *n.* the innermost of the three cellular layers of the embryo that develops into the digestive tract and most of the viscera.—*Syn.* ENTODERM.—*Contr. w.* **ectoderm, mesoderm.**—See **ectomorphic.**

endogamy (en·dog′ə·mi): *n.* the custom o confining marriage within one's own limited social or kinship group (clan, caste, etc.) in contrast with EXOGAMY, which restrict marriage to one outside the group. In non literate cultures, the social and the kin ship group are likely to be identical. Mod ern society is exogamous as to close kin ship, loosely endogamous as to social groups

endogenic (en″dō·jen′ik): *adj.* **1.** originat ing from within a structure or system; esp originating within the body (**somatogeni** *prefd.*), or within the mind (**psychogeni** *prefd.*). **2.** pertaining to forms of menta deficiency that are **gene**-determine (*prefd.*).—*Syn.* ENDOGENOUS (en·doj′ə nəs).—*n.* endogeny (en·doj′ə·ni).

endolymph: *n.* the fluid within the **laby rinth** of the internal ear.

endomorphic: see **ectomorphic.**

endomusia (en″dō·mū′zhə): *n.* silent re production of a melody without overt sing ing movements.

endophasia (-fā′zhə) = **internal speech** (1).

endopsychic: *adj.* **1.** that which achieve changes in imagination, thinking, attitude etc. **2.** that which is within the mind; in **trapsychic.**—*Ant.* **exopsychic.**

end organ: 1. a sensory **receptor** or sens organ, constituted by the initial part of th **afferent** neuron and the attached non neural mechanism (if any), which is directl concerned with the initiation of a nervou impulse: e.g., the retina, the taste buds. **2** the **distal** end of any peripheral neuron **afferent** or **efferent.**

endowment: *n.* capacity for development physical or mental, so far as conditione by heredity. Superior capacity is usuall implied.—See **ability.**

end plate or **end plate/motor:** the spe cialized structure of a nerve fiber that make functional contact with the muscle cell.

end pleasure: the experience accompany ing relief from tension, particularly that o **orgasm.**

end spurt: a rise in muscular action jus before the end of a task, or before aban doning it because of exhaustion.

endtest: see **pretest.**

endurance: *n.* the capacity to bear pain o hardship, or to persist in a line of actio despite difficulties; or the actual persisting —*Ant.* TRANSIENCE.

enelicomorphism (en·el″ə·kō·môrf′iz·əm) see **pedomorphism.**

energy: *n.* **1.** (*phys.*) the capacity for doin work. **2.** the degree, strength, or vigor of psychological activity. ➤The relation between energy physically conceived and the energy of psychological activity is complex, and by any theory is not an identity.

energy/action-specific: the energy believed to be specifically available for the performance of a given act. ➤The term is unfortunate since the quantity of energy is variable.—*Cp.* **reflex reserve.**—*Syn.* SPECIFIC ACTION ENERGY.

energy/background: a loose synonym for **basal metabolic rate.**

energy/least or **/least expenditure of:** see **least action/law of.**

energy-level/basic = **basal metabolic rate.**

energy/mental or **/psychic:** ability to do mental work. ➤Whether **mental energy** is to be regarded as a metaphor or as referring to a literal fact depends upon one's conception of the **mind-body** relation.— See also **psychic energy hypothesis.**

energy/radiant: see **radiant energy.**

energy: *v.* **1.** to deprive of energy or vigor. **2.** to remove the nerves that supply a tissue or organ.—*Syn.* (for **2**) **denervate** (*prefd.*)—*Distg. fr.* **innervate.**—*n.* **enervation.**

engineering psychology: the study of man's behavior in using tools and machines, and of machine design in relation to man's behavioral capacities, abilities, and motivations.

engram (en'gram): *n.* a hypothesized, permanently altered state of a living tissue resulting from temporary excitation. ➤Each engram has a particular **locus,** though it may be widespread. It is usually hypothesized as being in the brain. The engram is the most general term for the **intervening *variable** inferred to explain retention. See **mneme.**

enriched curriculum: additional educational experiences for pupils who do not need to spend all their time on the usual curriculum; esp., such opportunity for gifted children, usually while they continue in regular classes.

ensemble: *n.* an aggregate; a group of items not necessarily having any relation to each other except that they are together.

entelechy (en·tel'ə·ki): *n.* **1.** (*obsoles.*) an act fulfilled and therefore perfect, in contrast with one in course of completion. **2.** the form that determines the way in which a "power" shall be expressed or actualized. Such a form is postulated in **vitalism** as the nonmaterial factor in living process.

enteroceptor = **interoceptor.**

entity: *n.* a self-maintaining portion of reality; a being, or part of a being, having some degree of autonomy. ➤Despite the fact that no psychological discussion has ever been free of entities, the word is nearly always used in reproach. When others infer some enduring X in the nature of the person to account for the apparent consistency of behavior from one occasion to another, they are said to invent an entity. An effort is often made to *explain* entities as processes (as physics has explained matter in terms of energy), but it is naïve metaphysics to suppose that this explains them away.

ento-, endo-: combining form meaning *within* or *inside.*

entoderm = **endoderm.**

entoptic: *adj.* **1.** within the eye. **2.** pertaining to visual experience that has no adequate *stimulus but is due to mechanical or chemical conditions in the eye.

entropy: *n.* **1.** (*phys.*) a theoretical property of a body or system measured as that part of the heat or energy invested in the body which cannot be taken out and is thus unavailable for work. ➤According to the Second Law of Thermodynamics, the entropy of the universe tends to increase with every transformation of energy so that the total available energy grows constantly less. **2.** (*psychoan.*) a measure of the degree to which psychic energy cannot be transferred after being invested or **cathected** in an object. ➤This usage is highly metaphorical but scrupulously maintains analogy with physical usage. **3.** (*info. theory*) = *H,* an index of the number of possible outcomes an event can have; a measure of the amount of randomness in the state of a system; the amount of **uncertainty** in the categorization of items in a specified assemblage or **ensemble,** measured by the number of operations (statements, decisions, tests, manipulations, etc.) needed to select and categorize each item. ➤Other terms than **uncertainty,** used to explain the meaning of *H,* are SELECTION, DISCRIMINATION, SPECIFICITY, SURPRISE. The toss of a die with six possible outcomes occurring at random has more **entropy** or *H* and less **information (3)** than that of a coin with two possible outcomes. It is important to note that *H* is defined only with respect to a particular ensemble; hence, the *H* of one ensemble is likely to be completely incommensurate with another *H.* ¶As used in information theory, entropy has no readily apparent relation to its root meaning of "turning in upon," nor to established use in physics. It is based upon a defensible analogy, but upon an analogy that is not apparent and has to be carefully explained. The reader thus is compelled to a rather difficult task of translation when he meets the word. It is not ambiguous but it is bad communication; not a terminological sin but terminological bad manners. There is some tendency to drop the term **entropy** in favor of *H.*

entropy/social: the doctrine that with every social change the energy available for further progress is less, so that in the end every society becomes static.

entry: *n.* (*stat.*) a term, symbol, or value that is written in a particular place in a statistical tabulation; esp., the value entered in a two-way cell.

enucleation (i·nü″kli·ā′shən): *n.* the removal of an organ or a tumor in its entirety, e.g., removal of the entire eyeball.

enumeration: *n.* the act or process of counting or listing a number of people, events, objects. Definition or **induction** by COMPLETE ENUMERATION is considered valid, by INCOMPLETE ENUMERATION is risky but often very helpful.

enuresis (en″yü·rē′səs): *n.* involuntary discharge of urine.—*adj.* **enuretic** (-ret′ik).

envelope lines: the upper and lower lines that join the tops and bottoms, respectively, of a series of equally spaced **ordinates** of a time curve, esp. of the curve representing a complex **sinusoidal** sound wave. If the time curve is plotted on Cartesian coordinates, the X axis is the lower line.

environment: *n.* the sum of the external conditions and factors potentially capable of influencing an organism. ➤Not the same as the sum of **stimuli**, since some of these are internal; and some parts of the environment (e.g., ultraviolet rays) influence the organism without being stimuli. **Milieu** is properly the organism and its immediate environment, but is often used for the latter alone.—*Cp.* **object, context, surround, situation.**

environmentalism: *n.* a point of view that stresses the role of the environment in determining behavior, in contrast with the influence of **heredity.**—*Distg. fr.* **peripheralism.**—See **psychology/divisions and schools of, VI.**

environmental-stress theory: the view that neurotic behavior is merely an exaggeration or accentuation, resulting from environmental pressures, of behaviors common to all human beings. It includes distortion of a whole pattern of behavior by exaggeration of one component.

environment/behavioral: see **behavioral environment.**

envy: *n.* an unpleasant feeling aroused by awareness that another possesses what one desires but lacks.—*Cp.* **envious *rivalry.**

enzygotic twins = **twins/identical.**

enzyme (en′zīm; -zim): *n.* one of several organic compounds, of special importance in digestion, that are capable of producing other compounds by catalytic action.

eonism = **transvestism.**

ependyma (ep·en′di·mə): *n.* (*neurol.*) the lining membrane of the **central *canal** and the cerebral **ventricles.**—*adj.* **ependymal** (-məl).

epi- (ep′i-): a prefix meaning *upon, beside, on the outside, above*: e.g., **epidermis, epiphenomenon.**

epicritic sensibility: (*H. Head*) one of two divisions of cutaneous sensing: it is responsive to light touch, warmth, and coolth, but not to pain or extremes of temperature sensed as such; localization is very delicate. ➤In the other division—the PROTOPATHIC SYSTEM, which Head regarded as genetically older—there is only gross localization or other discrimination, but extremes of temperature are sensed as such and there is ready susceptibility to pain. All these protopathic reactions have a marked affective quality. ¶The neurological separation of the two systems is no longer generally accepted, and the detailed distinctions between types of sensibility are doubted. But some authorities are still inclined to postulate an early-developing, coarsely discriminative, and markedly affective type of response (protopathic) out of which has evolved the more discriminative but less affective type (epicritic). Rivers generalized the distinction and speaks of higher mental activities (predominantly intellectual) as **epicritic**, the earlier and more instinctual as PROTOPATHIC.

epidemic: *adj.* metaphorically, of psychological and social phenomena that spread rapidly through a population: an *epidemic* of fear, an *epidemic* of suicide.

epidermis: *n.* the outer layer of the skin.

epigastric sensation: a peculiar, weak sinking feeling in the region of the stomach often associated with fear in normal persons and an occasional symptom in **hysteria.**

epigastric voice: hallucinatory "voices" localized in the stomach region.

epigenesis: *n.* the emergence, in the course of development, of new phenomena and new properties not contained in miniature in the egg or germ of the organism; or, more generally, the emergence of such new properties not contained in any earlier stage of the organism's life history; or the doctrine that such emergence takes place. ➤Syn. **emergentism,** which more strongly emphasizes that the new properties cannot be reached by summation, whereas **epigenesis** merely asserts that the interaction of zygote with environment results in properties not present in the former.—*Ant.* **preformism.** See also **environmentalism.**

epiglottis: *n.* the saddle-shaped structure that covers the entrance to the **larynx.**

epilepsy: *n.* the name given to a group of nervous diseases marked primarily by convulsions. ➤The attacks may be of any degree of frequency or severity. In PETIT MAL ("slight illness") there may be only a momentary dizziness or some **automatic** action of which the patient has no knowledge. JACKSONIAN EPILEPSY manifests no loss of awareness but a definite course or series of convulsions affecting a limited region. In GRAND MAL the convulsions are severe and widespread, with rather prolonged loss of awareness, often also a progressive **dementia.** In the EPILEPTIC EQUIVALENT, **confusion** or EPILEPTIC FUROR takes the place of convulsions, the furor characterized by brutal violence and **maniacal** attacks of which the patient preserves no memory.—*adj.*, *pers. n.* **epileptic.**

epilepsy/focal = Jacksonian epilepsy.— See epilepsy.

epilepsy/idiopathic: a convulsive disorder without known or specific organic cause.— *Syn.* ESSENTIAL EPILEPSY.

epilepsy/Jacksonian: see **epilepsy.**

epilepsy/masked: a type in which there is no convulsion, but instead a brief period of activity that appears normal but has no connection with what the patient does before or after, and of which he has no recollection.

epilepsy/symptomatic: epileptic convulsions as a symptom of another organic disorder.

epileptic equivalent: see **epilepsy.**

epileptic furor: see **epilepsy.**

epileptic stupor: a state often following the convulsions, in which the patient is conscious but unresponsive.

epileptiform seizure: 1. a convulsion resembling those of **epilepsy** but resulting from some particular localized brain condition, such as a tumor. **2.** pseudoepileptic behavior as found in **hysteria,** etc.

epileptoid personality: (*A. J. Rosanoff*) a person who is irritable, selfish, uncooperative, apathetic, stubborn, and given to violent temper. ➤Some **epileptics,** however, do not behave in this way; others with no sign of epilepsy do.

epinephrin(e) (-nef′rēn; -rin): see **adrenalin.**

epinosic (-nō′sik): see **advantage by illness.**

epiphenomenalism: *n.* (*metaphys.*) the doctrine that mental activities are mere by-products of neural processes and are without causal influence upon the course of events, either physical or mental.—See **psychology/divisions and schools of, IV.**

epiphenomenon: *n.* an event that accompanies another event but has no causal efficacy.

epiphysis (ə·pif′ə·sis): *n.* **1.** a bony process, attached to another by cartilage which later becomes bony (ossifies). The degree

of ossification is used as an index of growth. **2.** = EPIPHYSIS CEREBRI, the **pineal gland.** —*adj.* **epiphyseal** (ep″i·fiz′i·əl).

epiphysis cerebri = **pineal gland.**

episcotister (ep″i·skō·tis′tər; ə·pis″-): *n.* a rotating disc with open and closed sectors of adjustable angular width interposed between an observer and a visible object or beam of light.—See **Talbot-Plateau law.**—*Var.* episkotister.

episode: *n.* (*R. Barker, H. Wright*) a particular action sequence or segment of behavior limited in time and having a constant direction. The situation (person and milieu) determines the episode. It is a **molar** unit.

episode/interactive: see **interactive episode.**

epistemology (ə·pis″tə·mol′ə·ji): *n.* the philosophical study of the origin, nature, and limits of knowledge.—*Syn.* THEORY OF KNOWLEDGE.

epithalamus: *n.* (*neurol.*) that portion of the brain lying above the **thalamus.** It includes the habenula, **pineal body,** and posterior **commissure.**

epithelium (ep·ə·thē′li·əm) *n.*, *pl.* **epithelia:** a thin layer of tissue covering the surface of an organ of the body or viscera, or lining a hollow structure or organ.

epsilon movement: see apparent *motion.

EQ or **E.Q.: 1.** = educational quotient. **2.** = efficiency quotient.

equal and unequal cases/method of: a variant of the **constant stimulus method.**

equal-appearing intervals method: 1. = **equal sense differences method. 2.** (*L. Thurstone*) adaptation of the logical principles of the equal sense differences method to the task of **scaling** judgments of any kind (e.g., judgments about statements of opinion) by sorting the items to be judged into groups separated by **equal steps.**

equal form: see **form/comparable.**

equal-interval scale: see **equal steps/subjective.**

equality: *n.* absence of any discriminable quantitative difference between two or more data.—*Distg. fr.* equivalence.

equality judgment: (*psychophys.*) a judgment about two stimuli that is not of the form "greater" or "less." ➤Strictly speaking, the term is a misnomer, since two compared stimuli rarely if ever give the impression of exact equality.—*Syn.* **doubtful judgment** (*prefd.*).

equality/law of: (*Gestalt*) the principle that, to the degree to which the parts of a field approach equality or similarity, they tend to be perceived as being a group or unit.

equalization of excitation: (*K. Goldstein*) a gradual decrease of excitation and reaction at the point of stimulation accompanied by an increase in other parts of the functional system; a spread of excitation to functionally related parts of an action system.

equally noticeable: (*psychophys.*) pertaining to a difference between stimuli that will be noticed and reported as frequently as a certain other difference. Such differences are held to be psychologically equal. —*Cp.* just noticeable difference.

equal sense differences method: (*psychophys.*) a procedure in which the observer is instructed to find the midpoint B between two appreciably different sense data A and C. The sense distances AB and BC are regarded as equal. This sense distance may be taken as a unit of measurement. A sensation greater than C by the unit amount may then be found, to which a second unit may be added, etc.—See ratio *scale.—Syn.* METHOD OF SUPRALIMINAL DIFFERENCES, OF MEAN STIMULI, OF MEAN GRADATION, OF EQUAL-APPEARING INTERVALS.

equal steps/subjective: a series of items of any sort that differ quantitatively in such way that the difference or interval between any contiguous pair is judged equal to the difference between any other contiguous pair. The steps form an EQUAL-INTERVAL SCALE.

equated scores: scores from different forms of a test, or from two different tests of what is presumed to be the same variable, reduced to a common basis of scoring so that they can be directly compared. ➤Standard *scores, percentile scores, etc., may be treated as equated.

equation/empirical: see empirical equation.

equation/factor-specification: see factor-specification equation.

equation/method of = adjustment procedure.

equation/normal: see frequency curve equation.

equation/rational: see rational equation.

equi- (ē'kwi-): combining form meaning *equal, equally:* e.g., *equilateral, equilibrium.*

equifinality: *n.* the equivalence of one form of behavior with another in reaching a certain goal.

equilibration (ē"kwil·ə·brā'shən): *n.* adjusting a measuring instrument to equality with a standard measuring instrument.

equilibrium: *n.* 1. a stable condition in which opposing forces are balanced; or a condition in which departure from a central state is not great and is quickly rectified.—*Syn.* balance.—*Cp.* also homeostasis. 2. maintenance in the human body of upright posture. The PERCEPTION OF EQUILIBRIUM affords data with respect to the organism's center of gravity. 3. (*biol.*) in a species, lack of tendency to evolve into another.

equilibrium sense = static sense.

equilibrium/static: 1. a state in which the internal activities of a system are so in balance that no change in the relation of the system to other systems is being made. ➤The term is broader than stationary state. 2. maintenance of balance while not moving; esp., maintenance of upright posture.

equipoise (ē'kwi·poiz; ek'wi-): *n.* a state of balance or equilibrium.

equipotentiality: *n.* 1. equality in power or effectiveness of any sort. 2. a generalization that, at a sufficiently early stage, any part of the embryonic tissue can produce any or all parts of the developed organism, or at least all parts within a certain range: e.g., any part of the ectoderm can produce any ectodermal structure. 3. = equipotentiality/cerebral. 4. = equipotentiality of cues.

equipotentiality/cerebral: the theory that, within certain large cerebral areas (as defined by functions), one part is equally important for that function with any other part.—*Cp.* mass action (1).

equipotentiality of cues: (*E. Brunswik*) the generalization that one sensory cue may often substitute for another in a given perception: e.g., indistinctness of outline may take the place of relative size in the perception of distance.

equiv.: *abbr.* for equivalent, equivalence.

equivalence: *n.* 1. relation between two terms or two data such that one can be substituted for the other in a given context without making any substantial difference. 2. = STIMULUS EQUIVALENCE, a property of different but similar stimuli that evoke the same or closely similar responses. 3. = RESPONSE EQUIVALENCE, a property of different but similar responses made to the same or closely similar stimuli.—For the relation of equivalence to generalization and to transfer, see generalization/stimulus.

equivalence/behavioral: see behavioral equivalence.

equivalence belief: (*E. C. Tolman*) a hypothesized state or internal behavior of an animal whereby it acts toward a subgoal as it would in the presence of the goal, or as if the subgoal were the goal. ➤This is Tolman's substitute for secondary *reinforcement.

equivalence/coefficient of: 1. the correlation of two comparable *forms of a test taken by the same testees at essentially the same time. ➤Under such conditions the two forms may be considered to be split halves of the same test, and the coefficient of equivalence yields the same sort of information as the coefficient of *internal consistency. It is overoptimistic, however, to suppose that either of these terms will yield to the other, and we refrain from the vain suggestion of a third term to supplant both. 2. more loosely but commonly, the correlation of two forms of a test that are taken with a considerable (and specified!) interval between them to minimize differential practice effects. ➤This is more exactly called a COEFFICIENT OF STABILITY AND EQUIVALENCE. It is one of the meanings of reliability. Although not in common use, he symbol r_{eq} is suggested for the coefficient of equivalence.

quivalence/motor: see motor equivalence.

quivalence test: a measure to determine which properties of an object may not be altered without destroying the trained response to the object. The animal is first trained to a specific response to an object, then the properties are systematically altered. Those which continue to elicit the response are equivalent.

quivalent/anxiety: see anxiety equivalent.

quivalent/epileptic: see epilepsy.

quivalent form: see form/comparable.

quivalent/grade: see grade equivalent.

quivalent groups: groups that yield the same distribution (within stated allowable limits of deviation) on a given variable: e.g., two groups having the same maximum, minimum, and mean scores, and the same standard *deviation on a test of arithmetic.—Cp. equivalent-groups procedure.

quivalent-groups procedure: an experimental procedure in which the subjects are so divided that the groups are regarded as of equal merit or ability for the purposes in hand. The groups are then exposed to different experimental conditions and the differing effects (if any) are measured. In careful work it is usual to match the ability of each person in one group with that of a person in the other group (method of MATCHED PAIRS).—Syn. MATCHED-GROUPS PROCEDURE.

quivalents/method of: the procedure of *reproduction adapted to the comparison of sensibility in two distinct organs.

equivalent stimulus/method of adjustment of: see adjustment procedure.

equivocal: adj. susceptible of several possible interpretations.—Syn. ambiguous.— n. equivocation, which see.

equivocation (i·kwiv″ə·kā′shən): 1. (logic) the fallacy of having two or more meanings for a single term or proposition; or a statement having two or more meanings.— Syn. ambiguity. 2. (pop.) the use of words

or expressions that can have more than one meaning, usually with intent to mislead; hence, prevarication. 3. (info. theory) the loss in amount of information (3) that occurs between input and output. ➤This usage is confusing. It is true that what is ordinarily called equivocation causes loss of information; to that extent the new term is a permissible analogy. But not all loss of information in an ordinary sense is due to equivocation in an ordinary sense. This usage requires us to commit the logical fallacy of simple conversion upon our normal associations with the word.— See rational coinage.—v. equivocate.— adj. equivocal (i·kwiv′ə·kəl).

$_sE_R$: ➤Symbols of this general form are listed as if written E.

erection: n. swelling of the penis, clitoris, or other erectile tissue from engorgement with blood.

erethism (er′ə·thiz·əm): n. an exaggerated degree of irritability or sensibility in any part, or all, of the body.—adj. erethismic, erethistic, erethitic.

Erfassungstypus (er·fäs′ûngs·tē″pəs): n. (Ger. for type of comprehending or grasping) the heading under which Rorschach responses are classified according to the way in which the subject goes about his task. Scoring code: AP.

ERG = electroretinogram.

erg (ērg): n. 1. (phys.) unit of work in C.G.S. system: the work necessary to move the point of application of 1 dyne of force 1 centimeter. 2. (R. B. Cattell) "an innate psychophysical disposition which permits its possessor to acquire reactivity to certain classes of objects more readily than others, to experience a specific emotion in regard to them, and to start on a course of action which ceases more completely at a specific goal activity than at any other." ➤A more precisely formulated term than instinct, and one free from the connotations accumulated by the latter over decades of misuse.—Cp. metanerg.—adj. ergic.

ergasia (ər·gā′zhä): n. (A. Meyer) the totality of psychobiological functioning. ➤The term stresses the activities that belong to the whole person.—Approx. syn. BEHAVIOR TOTALITY.

ergic (ēr′jik): adj. 1. having to do with striving, purpose, or motive.—Syn. purposive, (sometimes) dynamic. 2. of innately determined striving.—See erg.— Contr. w. metanergic.

ergic affect: (R. B. Cattell) the feeling associated with a specific erg.—Syn. primary *emotion.

ergic attitude: (R. B. Cattell) an attitude considered as a vector expressive of an erg.

ergic dispersion = dispersion/response.

erg(o)- (ėr'gō-): combining form meaning *work*.

ergodic sequence (ər·god'ik): (*info. theory*) a system of symbols in which the order is subject to probability estimation, and in which the effect of one symbol upon the others is limited to a certain finite maximum that can be ascertained: a sentence is an *ergodic sequence*. ➤In the foregoing six-word illustrative sentence, each word (or symbol) influences the following words, but even when we reach *ergodic* the final word is not yet completely determined by the others, i.e., the sentence could have been finished in other ways. An *ergodic sequence* has redundancy.—*Cp.* **redundancy.**

ergograph: *n.* an instrument for recording the amount of movement in a restricted muscle group or bodily member—hand, finger, eyelid, etc.—during continuous work.

Erlebnistyp (er·lāp'nəs·tēp): *n.* (*Ger.*) experience type.

Ernstspiel (ernst'shpēl): *n.* (*Ger.* for *serious play*) behavior that reflects serious concerns of the player, yet, as play, is free to take any form and has no social consequence.

erogenous: *adj.* giving rise to **sexual, libidinal,** or **erotic** behavior or feeling.—*Syn.* **erotogenic** (not *recom.*).

Eros (ir'os; er-): *n.* the Greek god of love; in psychoanalysis, the **libido.** ➤Freud sometimes uses **Eros** for all the self-preservative instincts (including sexual), in contrast with **Thanatos,** the total of death instincts.

erotic (i·rot'ik): *adj.* **1.** pertaining to sex sensations or to their stimuli; pertaining to sensations arising from the sex organs and from certain other tissues that have become closely associated with sex. **2.** pertaining to feelings or emotions aroused by sex sensations or related to them. **3.** pertaining to the drive or motive that has sexual satisfaction as its primary goal but that is often diverted to secondary satisfactions. **4.** pertaining to the love life in all its manifestations.—See **sex** for discussion of related terms.—*n.* **eroticism, erotism.**

eroticism = **erotism.**

eroticomania: see **erotomania.**

erotism (er'ə·tiz·əm): *n.* **1.** sexual excitement. **2.** the tendency to experience sexual excitement more readily than average; or to be preoccupied with, or to exalt, sex in literature, art, or doctrine. **3.** sexual excitement aroused by stimulation of other bodily parts than the genitals. ➤In psychoanalysis all mucous membranes and organs of special sense are said to yield erotic excitement.—*Syn.* EROTICISM (i·rot'ə·siz·əm).—*adj.* **erotic.**

erotism/anal: see **anal erotism.**

erotism/genital: sexual excitement from stimulation of the external genitals. ➤The

term is used to characterize a narrow emphasis upon such local stimulation. Psychoanalysis postulates a stage of development in which genital stimulation is of primary importance.

erotism/lip: see **lip erotism.**

erotism/oral: see **oral erotism.**

erotization: *n.* (*psychoan.*) process whereby a bodily part, or a bodily or mental function, takes on sexual or **libidinal** importance.—*Syn.* **libidinization.**

eroto-: combining form meaning *pertaining to love* or *sex*.

erotogenic: *adj.* **1.** having an origin in sex. **2.** giving rise to **sexual, libidinal,** or **erotic** behavior or feeling.—*Syn.* **erogenous** (*prefd.*), EROTOGENETIC.

erotomania (er"ə·tō·mā'ni·ə): *n.* morbidly intense passion for the opposite sex; **nymphomania** or **satyriasis.** ➤It is not applied to passion for a person of the same sex, nor to absorbing passion for one person.—*Syn.* EROTICOMANIA (i·rot"i·kō·mā'ni·ə).

erratic: *adj.* **1.** freakish; subject to unexpected and unexplained or unexplainable change. **2.** (*stat.*) = **random.**

error: *n.* **1.** a mistake; a departure from correctness. **2.** belief in what is untrue. **3.** (*stat.*) departure from a **true score.**—*Syn.* **deviation** (2). **4.** (*exper.*) any variation in the dependent variable that is not caused by the independent variable; either a **chance** *****error (1) or a **constant** *****error. **5.** (*beh.*) any response that delays the correct response; any failure to conform to the conditions of the problem or to the arbitrary requirements of an experimenter.

error/absolute: 1. an error expressed in the units used in measuring. ➤This error is not considered to be either positive or negative.—*Distg. fr.* RELATIVE ERROR, which is expressed in terms of the size of the error relative to the magnitude of the obtained value. **2.** the observed or obtained value of a measurement minus the **true value** (or the mean considered as the most probable value of the true value), the difference taken without regard to sign.—*Syn.* **deviation, correction** (5). ➤The use of **error** (unqualified) to mean **absolute error** is not recommended unless the context leaves no doubt of the meaning.

error/accidental: see **accidental error** and **error/chance (1).**

error/anticipation: see **anticipation error.**

error/anticipatory = **anticipation error** (*prefd.*).

error/average: the average amount by which the separate judgments of a stimulus differ from those of a standard stimulus.—*Distg. fr.* average (or **mean**) *****deviation.

error/biased = **error/constant.**

error/chance: 1. that part of the **variability** of a set of observations or scores that can be attributed to **chance.** It will depart from the **true value** as much and as often in one direction as the other, so that the sum of chance errors for a large number of cases approaches zero. ➤*Syn.* ACCIDENTAL, COMPENSATING, FORTUITOUS, RANDOM, UNBIASED, VARIABLE ERROR, each of which has an implication of the *origin* or the *effect* of the error; but statistically they all are the same.—*Contr. w.* **error/constant, error/systematic,** mistake. **2.** the **mean *deviation** of a sample from the mean of a very large number of observed values. ➤In this usage the mean is taken as the true value, and it is assumed that the average deviation of the sample is due to chance.—*Syn.* **error/sampling** (much *prefd.*). **3.** the difference of a single measure from the mean of a large number of observed values when no cause is known. ➤This usage is incorrect.

error-choice technique: an attempt to detect attitudes by compelling the subject to choose in a situation where choice is rationally not justified: e.g., to choose between two equally unlikely alternatives. Often the respondent is informed that no *correct* choice is offered. Bias is revealed by a greater number of choices in one direction than would result from chance.—*Cp.* **forced-choice technique.**

error/compensating: an error, either positive or negative, of such magnitude that it cancels out one or more other errors, thus bringing the average of all such errors closer to zero; the kind of error that sometimes increases and sometimes decreases a measurement, exhibiting no consistent tendency in either direction; the kind of error that tends to balance or offset other such errors; an error that introduces no systematic bias into the measurement.—See **error/chance.**

error/constant: an error affecting all of a set of observations in the same manner; an error due to a factor that works consistently in the same direction. ➤E.g., some persons persistently judge larger the right-hand member of a pair of nearly equal objects (this is a constant **space error**). A constant error, if known, can be allowed for or corrected. It should be used strictly for something that is found in *all* the cases. —*Ant.* **compensating *error** or **chance *error.**—*Syn.* SYSTEMATIC ERROR, CUMULATIVE ERROR, BIASED ERROR. Neither **constant error** nor **chance *error** means the same as mistake.

error/cumulating or **/cumulative** = **error/constant.**

error/experience: see **experience error.**

error/experimental: 1. a **deviation** in the measured value due to any sort of inadequacy in the experimental procedure: e.g., **time error,** uncompensated **practice effects, space error, sampling *error,** use of a variable that combines two partially independent variables, inadequate measuring instrument, etc. **2.** more generally, a deviation due to failure to control the conditions under which observations are made.—*Cp.* **error of observation.**

error/fortuitous = **error/chance (1).**

error gradient: in a set of observations, the tendency for the error to decrease ci increase consistently.

error/instrumental: a **constant *error** due to a deviation of the instrument used in observation. If detected, it can be corrected for.

error/mean = **deviation/mean.**

error/median = **deviation/median.**

error method: obsolete designation for **adjustment procedure** or **constant stimulus method.**

error/motivated: an apparently accidental mistake that actually represents an underlying motivation.

error of estimate: 1. error involved in estimating the values of one variable from those of another by the use of a **regression equation. 2.** the margin of error to be expected in an individual's predicted score on a criterion variable as a result of the imperfect **validity** of the test. The formula is

$$\sigma_{est} = \sigma_y \sqrt{1 - r_{xy}{}^2}$$

where σ_y is the standard deviation of the criterion variable and r_{xy} is the coefficient of validity.—*Syn.* **standard error of estimate.**

error of expectation: see **expectation/ error of.**

error of measurement: 1. the deviation of an individual score or observation from its **true value** (ascertained or estimated) that is due to the unreliability of the measuring instrument and of the individual who is measuring.—*Syn.* **error of observation. 2.** the deviation due to the unreliability of the experimenter or tester. **3.** the deviation due to the unreliability of the instrument. (Not *recom.*).

error of observation: departure of a particular measure of anything from its **true value.** ➤In practice, departure of the measure from the average of a large number of measurements is accepted as representing the error of observation.—*Syn.* **error of measurement** (which see for other meanings).

error/perseverative: in learning a **behavior *chain,** making a response later in the series than its proper position.—*Ant.* **anticipation error.**

error/persistent = **error/constant.**

error/probable: see **probable error.**
error/process: see **process error.**
error quotient: a measure of how well a particular item has been learned, computed by dividing the frequencies of actual error by the number of opportunities to be in error.
error/random = **error/chance (1).**
error/refractive: see **refraction/error of.**
error/relative: the **absolute** *****error** divided by the **true value.**
error/sampling: 1. the error introduced when a group is described on the basis of an unrepresentative sample. ➤It is estimated by the deviation of the values or scores yielded by the sample from the scores of the population from which the sample was drawn.—*Distg. fr.* **error of measurement. 2.** any mistake in drawing a sample that keeps it from being **representative.** ➤If the sampling is supposed to be random, there may be a hidden constant factor causing selection to be biased; if the sampling is based on a rational plan, e.g., a stratified sample, any departure from the prescribed rules is a sampling error.
error/standard: see **standard error.**
error/subjective: any **error** in observation and/or calculation due to more or less permanent individual idiosyncrasy, whether known or not; the effect of prejudice, bias, a particular erroneous way of working, etc., in causing error. ➤*Distg. fr.* carelessness, mistake. **Subjective error** is preferably used only where it leads to a **constant** *****error.**
error/systematic: a regular and repeatable distortion, always in the same direction, in the summary of data or the conclusions based on them, and resulting from the manner of collection or statistical treatment of the data.—*Syn.* **error/constant.**
error/unbiased: see **error/chance (1), error/compensating.**
error/variable = **error/chance (1).**
error variance or *E*: that part of the total **variance** due to anything irrelevant to the investigation in hand that cannot be experimentally controlled, including **errors of measurement** and **sampling** *****error.**
eructation (i″ruk·tā′shən): *n.* belching.
erythr(o)- (e·rith′rō-): combining form meaning *red* or *reddened.*
erythrogenic: *adj.* of a stimulus giving rise to a sensation of red.
erythropsia (er″i·throp′si·ə): *n.* a condition of the retina (usually induced by overexposure to intense light) in which all objects appear tinged with red: e.g., in snow blindness.
Es (es): *n.* (*psychoan.*) *Ger.* for **id,** used occasionally in English without translation, generally with the article: *das Es.*
E **scale:** an opinion scale for estimating

readiness to accept or reject **ethnocentric** ideology.
escape from reality = **reality/retreat from.**
escape learning: a form of learning controlled by punishment. ➤Escape from punishment brings an end to the unpleasant or punishing situation and is therefore rewarding.—See **conditioned (instrumental) escape response.**
escape mechanism = **defense mechanism.**
escape/theorem of: (*H. S. Sullivan*) the principle that the self tends to avoid being influenced by an experience incongruent with the current organization of its functional activity.—*Cp.* **defense reaction.**
escape training: an experimental procedure in which an animal is exposed to a **noxious** stimulus at each trial.—See **conditioned (instrumental) escape response.** ➤*Distg. fr.* AVOIDANCE TRAINING, in which the noxious stimulus is administered only if the animal fails to make the prescribed avoiding response.
escapism: *n.* a tendency to retreat from the unpleasant, esp. when it should be dealt with realistically. ➤Many neurotic symptoms are interpreted as escapist devices. —*Cp.* **defense reaction.**—*adj.* and *pers. n.* **escapist.**
esophagus (i·sof′ə·gəs): *n.* the gullet; the tube that leads from the **pharynx** to the stomach.—*Var.* **oesophagus.**—*adj.* **esophageal** (ē″sō·faj′i·əl).
esophoria (es″ō·fô′ri·ə): *n.* see **heterophoria.**
esoteric (es″ə·ter′ik): *adj.* pertaining to a doctrine that is hidden from all but the initiated.
esotropia (es″ə·trō′pi·ə): *n.* a condition in which one eye fixes the object and the other deviates inward—a form of **strabismus.**
ESP = **extrasensory perception.**
essay examination: see **examination/essay.**
essential epilepsy = **epilepsy/idiopathic.**
EST = **electroshock therapy.**
establishment: *n.* (*H. Murray*) a division of the personality or self according to certain over-all functions carried on therein. ➤Murray adopts but modifies Freud's **id, ego,** and **superego** as establishments.
-esthesia, esthesio-, -esthesis: combining forms meaning *feeling, sensibility,* or *sensitivity*: e.g., **anesthesia,** lack of sensation; **hyperesthesia,** excessive sensitivity (esp. for pain, but see **hyperalgia**); HYPOESTHESIA, deficient sensitivity; **paresthesia,** mistaken sensitivity, e.g., the erroneous feeling of crawling insects on the skin; **synesthesia,** experiencing one kind of sensation as accompaniment of another, e.g., **chromesthesia.**—*Var.* -aesthesia.

esthesiometer (es·thē″zi·om′ə·tər): *n.* an instrument for measuring sensitivity of the skin to touch by determining the minimum spatial separation at which two points are perceived as two.

esthete: *n.* a person who is especially sensitive to art and beauty; sometimes, one who attaches overmuch importance to beauty. —*Var.* **aesthete.**

esthetics: *n.* the study of what constitutes the beautiful. ➤It may be empirical and factual (in which case it is a branch of psychology), or rational and a priori (in which case it is a branch of philosophy). —*Var.* **aesthetics.**

estimate: *v.* **1.** to arrive at a value or quantitative statement by inspection of the data, either without computation or by rough computation only. **2.** (*stat.*) to infer the whole from a measurement of the part. ➤In contrast to sense **(1),** such an estimate may require quite refined computations.

estral: *adj.* for **estrus.**

estrangement: *n.* increase in **social distance:** a stage beyond misunderstanding, but short of social conflict.

estrogen: *n.* any hormone that stimulates a female to **estrus.** Such hormones may also have other physiological functions.—*adj.* **estrogenic.**

estrus, estrum, or **estrous cycle** (es′trəs): *n.* **1.** periodic sex desire or **heat (3)** in female animals. **2.** the physiological changes in the reproductive organs of the female when in heat. ➤The word is usually applied only to subprimates.—*Syn.* **heat (3), rut (2).**—*Var.* oe-.—*adj.* **estral, estrous.**

eta or *η* (ā′tə; ē·tə) = **correlation ratio.**

ethereal: *adj.* of the class of smells resembling that of ether.

ethical judgment (or **knowledge**) **test:** see **character test.**

ethics: *n.* the study of the ideal in human character and conduct. ➤*Distg. fr.* **morality,** the code of good behavior accepted in a particular society.—*adj.* **ethical.**

ethnic: *adj.* **1.** pertaining to groups of people believed to be biologically related. **2.** pertaining to any important continuing group or division of mankind. ➤ETHNIC GROUP is an intentionally vague or general term used to avoid some of the difficulties of **race** (which see). The ethnic group may be a nation, a people (such as the Jews), a language group (the Dakota Indians), a sociologically defined so-called race (the American Negro), or a group bound together in a coherent cultural entity by a religion (the Amish).

ethnie (eth′ni): *n.* an **ethnic** group.

ethno-: combining form meaning *race, peoples.*

ethnocentrism: *n.* **1.** the tendency to exalt the superiority of the group (esp. the national or ethnic group) to which one belongs and to judge outsiders, often contemptuously, by the standards of one's own group. ➤It is the analog, for ethnic or national relations, of **egocentrism** in personal relations. **2.** a hypothesized syndrome of underlying attitudes that involve the following: division of the social world into **in-groups** with which one **identifies** and to which one submits, and **out-groups** to which one is hostile; positive **stereotypy** of the former and negative stereotypy of the latter; and the arrangement of the in-groups and out-groups into an evaluative hierarchy in which the former are always dominant and the latter always subordinate. —*adj.* **ethnocentric.**

ethnography or **ethnology:** *n.* (*anthrop.*) the study of **ethnic groups**—their origins, customs, occupations, and cultures—as related to their habitat and to other ethnic groups. ➤The distinction between **ethnography** as descriptive, and **ethnology** as explanatory, is not well observed.

ethnology: see **ethnography.**

ethnopsychology: *n.* the **comparative psychology** of races and peoples, esp. of nonliterate peoples.

ethology (ē·thol′ə·ji): *n.* **1.** the science of **ethics.** ➤It may be either a comparative study of ethical systems, or an attempt to found a system of ethics upon scientific principles. **2.** the empirical study of human **character (4). 3.** (*sociol.*) the study of manners, customs, and mores. **4.** (*psychol.* and *zool.*) the study of comparative behavior, or of the **ecology** of behavior. ➤Typically, the **ethologist** is trained in zoology and investigates the behavior of lower animal forms, but neither limitation is essential. The study of animal behaviors in the natural habitat, using every means to make observation complete, is essential. Ethology does not use **mentalistic** concepts, but it does employ **intervening** ***variables,*** including those of **instinct** or **species-specific behavior.** The term is a new designation for a very old discipline. ¶The above widely divergent meanings have in common a relation to the Greek *ethos,* meaning the essential nature or character of something.

ethos (ē′thos): *n.* **1.** the characteristic outlook on life of a given political, occupational, or cultural group. ➤*Distg. fr.* **ideology,** which is restricted to ideas and beliefs. Much of the ethos is unverbalized. **2.** the feeling tone associated with an outlook on life. (**Ethos** [1] is *prefd.*)

etiology (ē″ti·ol′ə·ji): *n.* the study of causes or origins, esp. of a disease. ➤Not to be used for the cause itself. An expression such as *the etiology of Harriet Brown's* *neurosis* is a mistaken attempt to substitute a prestigeful professional-sounding word for the simple word *cause* or *origin*. See **bogus erudition.**—*adj.* **etiological.**

ETS = **Educational Testing Service.**

eu-: prefix meaning *good, well, advantageous;* the opposite of **dys-.**

eudaemonism (ū·dē′mən·iz·əm; ū·dĭ′-): *n.* the ethical doctrine that the chief end of living is happiness or personal well-being.— *Cp.* **hedonism.**—*adj.* **eudaemonic** (ū″di·-mon′ik).

eugenics (ū·jen′iks): *n.* the attempt to improve the inborn qualities of a race or breed, esp. of men. ➤POSITIVE EUGENICS seeks to increase propagation of the specially fit, NEGATIVE EUGENICS to prevent propagation of the unfit. Though sometimes called a science, eugenics is properly an application of the science of **genetics.**—*adj.* **eugenic.**

eunoia (ū·noi′ə): *n.* soundness of mind. ➤An example of **bogus erudition.**

eunuch (ū′nək): *n.* a castrated male; occasionally, a woman who has lost the ovaries. —*adj.* **eunuchal; eunuchoid,** resembling a eunuch in bodily or psychological characteristics.

eunuchoidism: *n.* state or condition of having the psychological characteristics of a eunuch.—*adj.* **eunuchoid.**

eupareunia (ū″pə·rü′ni·ə): *n.* coitus accompanied by orgasm.—*Cp.* **dyspareunia.**

euphemism (ū′fə·miz·əm): *n.* the substitution of a mild or indirect word or phrase for one that is considered offensive, indelicate, or disagreeable: e.g., *pass away* for *die, gender* for *sex.*

euphoria (ū·fô′ri·ə): *n.* a mood or emotional attitude of invulnerability or "all-is-well": the individual has an intense sense-feeling of health and vigor, often despite real **somatic** disabilities (which are ignored). In pathological cases, unsystematized and transient **delusions** to fit the mood are generated: the person has a million dollars, the strength of an ox, or is ruler of the universe.—*adj.* **euphoric.**

eurymorph (yù′ri·morf): see **body build/ index of.**

Eustachian tube (yü·stā′ki·ən; -stā′shən): a small passageway that connects the middle ear with the **pharynx.**

euthanasia (ū″thə·nā′zhə): *n.* painless death; the practice of ending life painlessly. ➤It is advocated by some for persons suffering incurable disease.

euthenics (yü·then′iks): *n.* the applied science of improving man by regulating his environment.—*Cp.* **eugenics.**

euthymia (ū·thī′mi·ə): *n.* a joyful but tranquil mood; tendency to such a mood or feeling-state.—*Ant.* **dysthymia.**

evaluation: *n.* **1.** determining the relative importance of something in terms of a standard.—*Syn.* **appreciation,** but this word tends to suggest feeling tones and an approving attitude. **2.** (*educ.*) measurement of the attainment of educational goals, however defined. ➤Usually included is a study of the relative effectiveness of regulated conditions in furthering or hindering such attainment. **Evaluation** is *prefd.* to its synonym **educational** *measurement by those who object to the narrowness of merely measuring subject-matter learning, although such limitation on the latter is unnecessary. **Measurement** sounds cold, **evaluation** warm, but both assume a set of standards and involve the same kind of operations. If both are to be retained, **evaluation** may be used for **global** appraisal, **measurement** for more analytical appraisal. **3.** see *Kundgabe.*

evaluation/job: see **job evaluation.**

event: *n.* **1.** a part of reality that changes within space and time limits. ➤The limits may be great or small according to context: for the geologist a centuries-long emergence of a mountain chain may be a single event. But a definite beginning and end, both in time and space, are necessary; and to be one event the processes, activities, or happenings must be somehow related. A PHENOMENON is a relatively stable and generally less extensive grouping of data, so that several phenomena may be spoken of as taking part in one event. However, the two terms are often interchangeable. **2.** an occurrence or a temporally linked group of occurrences, with a beginning and an end, which form a unity because they are related to a person's need or purpose. **3.** (*H. A. Murray*) a portion of the narrative or description in a projective-test **protocol** that is related to a specific **press-need.**

event system: (*F. Allport*) a group of acts or behaviors created by the *inter*action of two or more persons committed to the same goal.

evidence: *n.* the facts or principles cited to support a conclusion. ➤To be counted as evidence, the relation of the data to the conclusion must be made clear.—*Distg. fr.* **proof** which, if accepted, makes logically *necessary* the acceptance of a conclusion.

evidence/anecdotal: see **anecdotal evidence.**

evident: *adj.* of that which easily and clearly leads to a conclusion.

eviration (ev″ə·rā′shən): *n.* **1.** loss of masculinity. **2.** delusional belief of a man that he has become a woman.

evoke: *v.* to call forth; esp., to call forth a **response** or an **act.**—*Syn.* **elicit; stimulate,** preferably restricted to the case of a relatively simple sensory process that evokes response.

evolution: *n.* 1. a process of orderly development and growth. 2. the theory that present animal and plant species have evolved or developed by descent, with modification, from other pre-existing species; organic evolution. ➤Modern psychology is thoroughly evolutionary: it holds man's behavior to be developmentally continuous with that of subhuman forms of life. 3. (*anthrop.*) see **diffusion theory.**—*v.* **evolve.**—*adj.* **evolutionary.**

ex-: prefix meaning *from, out of, away from, beyond.*

exaltation: *n.* a state in which mental processes are lively, the feeling tone pleasant, and the future tinged with joy; elation. It resembles **euphoria** but implies greater activity.

examination/essay: one in which the task is to write at some length upon an assigned topic.—*Contr. w.* **examination/short-answer.**

examination/mental: 1. a measurement, or a comprehensive set of measurements, of a person's psychological characteristics. 2. an unfortunate term for a test of intelligence.

examination/new-style = examination/ short-answer.

examination/objective: a written examination with answers so precisely prescribed that the score for any answer can be assigned by any competent person. ➤Most, but not all, objective examinations are of the **selective answer** or **completion** *test forms; examinations requiring free discussion, if carefully phrased and provided with exact but flexible scoring standards, are also objective. The essential character of the objective examination is that the same grade is always given.

examination/old-style: see **examination/ short-answer.**

examination/short-answer: any examination that does not require the composition of long or complex replies by the examinee. ➤It includes **completion** and **selective answer** *tests but also many examinations of traditional form.—*Syn.* NEW-STYLE EXAMINATION.—*Ant.* OLD-STYLE EXAMINATION, essay *examination.—*Cp.* **examination/ objective.**

examination/subjective: one marked or graded by the unaided judgment, opinion, or whim of an examiner. ➤Probably no examiner succeeds entirely in avoiding reference to an outside or objective standard; and no examination, even though styled *objective,* eliminates altogether a subjective element in marking.

exceptional: *adj.* differing to a marked degree in one or more characteristics from others of a given class.—*Syn.* **atypical.**

exceptional child: an inclusive term for children who deviate considerably from the average in physique, sensory acuity, intelligence, social conformity, emotional development, etc. ➤The term is correctly used for both extremes—gifted and feebleminded, giants and dwarfs, etc.—but the current tendency is to restrict it to the handicapped.

excess = (*stat.*) **kurtosis.**

excitable: *adj.* 1. (*physiol.*) of a living tissue that can be aroused. ➤The arousing force may come from outside the tissue or may consist of the chemical products of metabolism. The response may be a movement in the protoplasm (e.g., contraction in a fiber) or a chemical or electrical change (e.g., a **neural impulse**). 2. pertaining to an easily aroused and/or exaggerated emotional reaction. 3. prone to **excitement.**—*Syn.* irritable (*ambig.*); sensitive (which has question-begging theoretical implications).—*n.* (*concrete*) **excitation,** the fact of being excitable (usually in sense 1).—*n.* (*abstract*) **excitability,** the property of being excitable.—See also **excitement.**

excitant (ek·sī′tənt; ek′sə·tənt): *n.* an object, esp. a substance, that acts upon an organ and elicits activity therein; a **stimulant.**

excitation: *n.* 1. process whereby physical energy sets up changes in a **receptor.** 2. process whereby activity is set up in a nerve or in a muscle by nerve action; NEURAL EXCITATION. 3. = **neural impulse** (not *recom.*). 4. the hypothesized state of the organism or of the nervous system, induced by a stimulus (but influenced also by endogenous activity), that correlates with vigor of response.—*Cp.* **drive state,** which probably refers to the same phenomena. 5. (*P. Janet*) rapid increase in psychological tension as seen in joy, enthusiasm, inspiration.

excitation gradient: the drop in capacity of stimuli to elicit a conditioned response as the dissimilarity to the original conditioning stimulus increases. ➤The gradient is an expression of the limits of **stimulus** *generalization.

excitation/wave of: see **wave of excitation.**

excitatory agent = stimulus.

excitatory field: a region in the brain activated by a specific sensory process. ➤It is more properly an EXCITED FIELD. The term does not imply that the region is a permanent brain **area** for a given function; it is the area active at a particular time.

excitatory irradiation: the spreading of excitation from a strongly activated neural center to adjacent or functionally related mechanisms.

excitatory potential or $_sE_R$: (*C. Hull*) the hypothesized strength of the tendency to respond in a particular way; a **hypothet-**

ical *state variable combining the effects of drive and habit strength:

$$_sE_R = D \times V \times K \times _sH_R;$$

or for practical purposes:

$$_sE_R = D \times _sH_R.$$

EFFECTIVE EXCITATORY POTENTIAL, or $_s\bar{E}_R$, is excitatory potential minus inhibitory potential. MOMENTARY EFFECTIVE EXCITATORY POTENTIAL, or $_s\bar{E}_R$, goes a step farther by subtracting the oscillation factor.—Syn. reaction potential (which see).

excitatory tendency: the capacity of a given stimulus to arouse a particular response. ➤The term is usually employed with quantitative implication: a stimulus has a certain amount of capacity to elicit a response.

excitement: n. an emotional state in which there is strong pressure toward activity, expressed in quick, impulsive, usually inconsecutive movements.

exclusion/false or /valid: see false negative.

excretion: see secretion.

executive: n. a person or body of persons vested with authority to carry out, or order and direct others to carry out, certain actions.—Cp. administration.

exercise: n. 1. repeated performance of an act for the purpose of learning. 2. (pop.) performance of an already learned act. 3. (educ.) a task or problem assigned to a pupil to promote his learning. 4. physical activity engaged in for health or recreation.

exercise/law of: the generalization that, other things being equal, performance of an act tends to make subsequent performance of that act easier, more fluent, less subject to error. ➤It includes the sublaws of use and disuse.—See also association/laws of (1), frequency/law of.

exhaustion: n. 1. state of an organ or tissue when the catabolic rate is markedly reduced, with consequent impairment of function. 2. = sensory *adaptation. ➤An unfortunate usage implying that adaptation is due to tissue exhaustion, which is not known to be the case.—See exhaustion/procedure of. 3. a hypothetical state of an action system, consequent upon response, that results in heightened threshold for the stimuli of the system and reduced frequency and magnitude of the response thereafter. ➤This state is distinguished from fatigue by the enduring nature of the effects. ¶The construct is employed by ethologists in the study of lower organisms, and by psychoanalysts for instinctive (sometimes for other) action systems. (Cp. catharsis.) The action system is assumed to have a certain quantum of energy, some of which is drained off by each response and not, as a rule, replaced. Drive state is similarly conceived as being a

quantum of energy that is drained off by a response, but it is renewable after response.

exhaustion delirium: delirium reactions occurring under conditions of prolonged and intense physical effort, in toxic states, or with high fever.

exhaustion/procedure of: a method of studying sensory processes by testing sensitivity to various groups of stimuli after adaptation to another stimulus. ➤Used chiefly with smells.—Syn. METHOD OF EXHAUSTION (but this has another meaning in logic). Suggested syn.: METHOD or PROCEDURE of SENSORY ADAPTATION.

exhibitionism: n. 1. intentional exposure, usually compulsive, of sex organs under inappropriate conditions. 2. exaggerated or inappropriate efforts to call attention to oneself.

exhibition need: (H. A. Murray) the need to attract, excite, seduce, stir, amuse, entertain others; self-dramatization.

existential analysis: (existentialism) a method of psychotherapy designed to assist a person to react spontaneously to the world in the spirit of free will. The term is a translation of Daseinanalyse.

existentialism: n. a literary and philosophical doctrine, and a school of philosophical psychology based thereon. It holds that existence is incorrigibly evil, and that the only human good is a grim and hopeless but resolute struggle. The psychology is strongly voluntaristic.—Distg. fr. existential psychology (1).—See psychology/divisions and schools of, II, III, V.

existential judgment: a judgment that implies or directly asserts the actual presence of a datum in the universe. ➤"Mermaids have tails" is not existential, does not imply the existence of mermaids; "mermaids exist" is an existential judgment (probably false).

existential psychology: 1. view that the task of psychology is limited to the observation and description of the existent data or contents of experience, of mental contents. ➤It may be regarded as the logical outcome of structural psychology (1) with definite emphasis upon complete introspective description shorn of all interpretation, followed by analysis and classification of experiences as facts in and for themselves. The term was coined for the viewpoint of E. B. Titchener. 2. the psychological doctrines associated with existentialism, which holds that man must oppose his free will to a hostile, purposeless universe.—See psychology/divisions and schools of, III.

exit interview: see interview/exit.

exo-: prefix meaning outside, outer, outer part.

exocathection: see endocathection.

xocrine gland (ek'sō·krĭn; -krĭn): a gland that secretes through a duct, either into another organ (e.g., the liver into the small intestine) or to the outside of the body (e.g., the sweat glands).—*Ant.* **endocrine gland.** (But it is believed that some glands excrete both through ducts and by osmosis into the body fluids, i.e., have both endocrine and exocrine functions.)

xogamy (eks·og'ə·mi): *n.* see **endogamy.**

xogenous (eks·oj'ə·nəs): *adj.* of a condition or event that originates outside the body or outside the nervous system.— *Contr. w.* **endogenous, autochthonous.** ➤EXOGENOUS CHILD is technical slang for a handicapped child whose condition is not referable to heredity.—*Syn.* EXOGENETIC, EXOGENIC (ek"sō·jə·net'ik; -jen'ik).

xolinguistics: *n.* (*info. theory*) the study of the relations betwen the characteristics of a **message** and the characteristics of the individuals who produce and receive it. ➤Usually limited to verbal messages.—*Syn.* METALINGUISTICS.

xophoria: see **heterophoria.**

xophthalmic goiter (ek"sof·thal'mik): a disorder marked by protuberant eyes and an enlarged overactive thyroid. There is excessive and often incoordinated energy output, great emotionalism, ready fatigue, and incapacity for sustained effort.—*Syn.* BASEDOW'S, GRAVES', PARRY'S DISEASE.

xopsychic: *adj.* of mental activity achieving physical or social effects in the environment outside the person.—*Ant.* **endopsychic.**

xosomatic method: one utilizing the resistance of the skin to an electrical current or potential originating outside the organism. The Wheatstone bridge is usually used. —*Syn.* FÉRÉ'S METHOD.—*Distg. fr.* Tarchanoff's method (see **electrodermal response**).

xotropia (ek"sō·trō'pi·ə) = **divergence (2).**

Exp: (*Ror.*) *abbr.* for **experience-type** or **experience balance.**

exp.: *abbr.* for **experiment.**

expanded personality: the totality of environmental objects felt by a person to be irreplaceable parts of himself: his clothing (for an appearance-conscious person), his belongings, his loved ones, etc.

expansive: *adj.* free and unrestrained in feeling and imagination, and in verbal or bodily expressions thereof.

expansive delusion: a general term for delusions of wealth, power, importance, etc., accompanied by **euphoria.**

expansiveness: *n.* 1. a generalized tendency characterized by loquacity, high reactivity (esp. to social stimuli), optimistic big plans, friendliness—at least on the overt level. 2. (*K. Horney*) a neurotic condition

in which the patient thinks he really has achieved his **idealized** *self and manifests symptoms of perfectionism, arrogant vindictiveness, **narcissism,** and most of the behaviors of (1).

expectancy: *n.* 1. (*stat.*) = **expectation (3).** 2. an intervening **process variable** (e.g., an **attitude** or set) attributed to animals (or to other men) as a parallel to what is subjectively experienced as *expectation*; an acquired **disposition** whereby a *response* to a certain sign object or cue stimulus is expected to bring about a certain other *situation.* ➤The word *expected,* like **expectancy,** is not to be read subjectively; it is inferred from the animal's behavior. A dog running down a familiar street is inferred to have an expectancy when he begins to turn a corner before he can see it.—*Syn.* FIELD EXPECTANCY, SIGN-GESTALT-EXPECTATION, PRECOGNITIVE BEHAVIOR, MEANS-END EXPECTANCY, HYPOTHESIS BEHAVIOR.— *Cp.* **cognitive map.**

expectancy/generalized: the mean strength of the **expectancies** for a group of behaviors that are related because they have the same kind of reward or lead to the same goal.

expectancy/life: the calculated average number of years that a person in a given population is expected to live from birth or from a stipulated **life** *age. ➤The term is used for a group of persons as well as for an individual. It is arrived at by extrapolation from census figures and assumes (what is seldom the case) that essentially the same conditions will continue.

expectancy theory: (*E. C. Tolman*) the theory that what is acquired in learning is a disposition to react to certain objects as **signs** for certain further objects. ➤E.g., the animal learns to pull a loop as if this action would be followed by the appearance of food. It is not implied that the animal has "ideas" in the subjective sense; it is held merely that his behavior supports the inference that he has acquired the *equivalent* of a knowledge of relations.—*Cp.* **cognitive map.**—See **expectancy.**—*Syn.* EXPECTATION THEORY.

expectation: *n.* 1. a tense and somewhat emotional attitude toward the prospect of a certain event.—*Syn.* **anticipation,** which emphasizes motor preparation; **foresight** or **forethought,** which emphasize the intellectual aspect. 2. = **expectancy.** 3. (*stat.*) the probability of an occurrence multiplied by the amount to be gained by the occurrence. 4. = the **true** *mean.

expectation/error of: an error due to a preconceived idea of the nature of what is to be presented, or the time of its presentation.—*Cp.* **anticipatory response.**

experience: *n.* 1. actual living through an

event or events. →Many believe this is a better term to designate the subject matter of psychology than either **consciousness** or **behavior**. THE EXPERIENCED may then refer to the specific object to which one is responding or of which one is aware, AN EXPERIENCE to the fact of passing through and adjusting to a particular set of circumstances, THE EXPERIENCER to the self or organism that experiences. Semipopular usage is consistent with the above and generally clear in context. Experience is not static; it connotes activity, process, happening, doing. **2.** (*E. B. Titchener*) the totality of mental phenomena at a given moment as *directly* received, thus excluding inference. **3.** (*pop.*) knowledge derived from actual participation in events.—*adj.* **experiential,** pertaining to the process; **experienced,** pertaining to the data or object, or to the person who experiences.

experience balance or *Exp:* (*Ror.*) the ratio of **movement (M)** to **color (C)** responses (sometimes of movement to total responses) to the inkblots.—See **experience type.**

experience error: (*W. Kohler*) the error of supposing that the pattern of mental organization must parallel the pattern of the experience that causes it.

experiencer: *n.* he who experiences or has experiences, who reacts to environment. →This term is occasionally used by **behaviorists,** more often by **mentalists.**—See **experience.**

experience-type: (*Ror.*) the personality dimension of **introversiveness-extraten-siveness.** →A tendency to the former is said to be indicated by *M* responses, to the latter by *C* responses. The experience-type score is the **experience balance.**—*Syn.* *Erlebnistyp* (the original German term, *prefd.* by some writers in English).

experiment (eks·per′ə·mənt; not -pir-): *n.* a definite arrangement of conditions under which a phenomenon to be observed shall take place, with a view to determining for that phenomenon the respective causal influences of these conditions. →The phenomenon to be observed is called the DEPENDENT VARIABLE, being regarded as depending (at least possibly) on the conditions. The conditions themselves are the INDEPENDENT, TREATMENT, or EXPERIMENTAL VARIABLES. Any condition deemed to have no effect upon the independent variable is called an IRRELEVANT VARIABLE.

The use of **experiment** for a mere trial or tryout of a procedure without **experimental *controls** is deplorable, but the *adj.* **experimental** may be allowed in that wider (as well as in its proper) sense. **Observation** includes experiment but is also used in a restricted sense for careful attention without experimental arrangement.—See also **research, investigation, experimental psychology.**-*adj.* **experimental.**—*n.* **experimentation,** the art of experimenting.—*pers. n.* **experimenter.**

experimental coefficient: the difference between two means divided by 2.78 times the standard error of the difference. →The concept is no longer in common use.

experimental control = **control/scientific.**

experimental design: see **design/experimental.**

experimental extinction: see **extinction/experimental.**

experimental group: those subjects who are exposed to the **experimental** (or treatment) **variable** and whose performance will therefore reflect the influence, if any, of that variable. →*Contr. w.* the **control group** which, other factors being kept as equal as possible, is not exposed to the experimental variable.—See **control/scientific.**

experimentalism in education: see **education/experimental.**

experimental methodology: systematic statement of the working rules for designing and conducting experiments and interpreting results; or that portion of the whole set of rules used in a particular experiment.

experimental neurosis: see **neurosis/experimental.**

experimental psychology: 1. the investigation of psychological phenomena by experimental methods. **2.** the methods and the results obtained by experiment, systematically set forth. →Often arbitrarily limited to the psychology of the laboratory.

experimental series: those trials or observations made during the experiment proper (as distinguished from pilot or practice trials) and on the **experimental group** (as distinguished from **control groups**).

experimental treatment: a deliberate attempt to change a variable by alteration of some factor believed to have causal influence. →As compared with **experiment,** the term refers to a special and limited variation.

experimental variable: see **experiment.**

experiment/control: see **control/scientific.**

experiment/controlled: a redundant expression, since it is of the nature of **experiment** to be controlled. →In those circles where *experiment* is loosely used to mean merely a *tryout,* the redundant expression may be pardoned.

experiment/crucial: see **crucial.**

experiment/group: an experiment involving many subjects exposed to the experimental conditions at the same time.

experimentum crucis $=$ crucial experiment. —See **crucial.**

expert (eks′pėrt): *n.* one possessed of particular proficiency in some branch of science, art, or industry. ➤In the last, it denotes an artisan or workman of the highest class of competence. The other classes are in descending order of skill are JOURNEYMAN, APPRENTICE, NOVICE.—*adj.* expert (iks·pėrt′, eks′-pėrt). When the noun is used as adjective (as in *expert psychologist*), accent the first syllable; for the true adjective (he is *expert*), accent the last.

expiation (eks″pi·ā′shən): *n.* action performed to lessen sense of guilt.

expiration: *n.* the expulsion of breath from the lungs.—See **inspiration-expiration ratio.**

explanation: *n.* **1.** the simplification or clarification of what is said in a statement by showing its relationship to its context. **2.** any attempt to account for an event or for the character of an object. ➤HISTORICAL, GENETIC (ONTOGENETIC), or CAUSAL EXPLANATION is in terms of the previous events necessary to the occurrence of this event. The last emphasizes a particular series of previous events rather than the whole sequence, and generally attempts to account for only a particular aspect of an event or object. ¶Explanations are also classified as reductive or constructive. REDUCTIVE EXPLANATION describes the simpler processes that make up the event and evaluates their interrelationships. CONSTRUCTIVE (or CONSTRUCT) EXPLANATION sets forth the **constructs,** abstract principles, or laws involved in the event. All of these are distinguished from **description** by their emphasis upon evaluation of the relationships between the factors.

explicit: *adj.* **1.** directly stated or included in the data. **2.** an unfortunate synonym for **overt.**—*Ant.* **implicit.**

exploitation/parental: putting pressure upon a child to behave in ways that fulfill the parent's ambitions rather than the child's real needs.

exploitive attitude/direct $=$ **dependency/ passive.**

exploitive character: (*E. Fromm*) the kind of person who finds satisfaction in taking from others by force or by guile.

exploration/mental: any diagnostic technique that utilizes the client's responses to discover the psychological factors accountable for his present lack of **adjustment (2).** It includes **psychoanalysis, hypnotic** analysis, and **counseling.**

exploratory behavior: movements, or more generally a series of movements, that bring different portions or aspects of the surroundings into stimulus relation to the exploring organism; or the analog of such

movements in thinking, in which there is a shift from considering one aspect of a situation to considering another. The entire process is called EXPLORATION.

exponent: *n.* (*math.*) a number, written to the right and above (i.e., as a superscript) that shows the power to which a given number or expression is to be raised. ➤Positive whole-number exponents show how many times the number is to be *multiplied* by itself: e.g., $(x + y)^2$ signifies that $(x + y)$ is to be squared. Negative exponents indicate that the given power of the quantity is to be *divided* into 1: e.g., $a^{-2} = 1/a^2$. Fractional exponents indicate by the numerator the power to which the quantity is to be raised and by the denominator the root to be subsequently extracted: e.g., $N^{3/2} = \sqrt{N^3}$.—*Syn.* index.— *adj.* **exponential.**

exponential curve (eks″pō·nen′shəl): a curve for which the general formula is $y = e^{kx}$. It is often used to represent physical growth.

exposition need: (*H. A. Murray*) the need to relate facts, to explain, to judge, to interpret.

ex post facto: (*L.*) by virtue of something done after. ➤An EX POST FACTO CONTROL or EXPERIMENTAL DESIGN is one in which groups are matched on certain dimensions after the experimental variable has been administered. It is regarded as an imperfect design.

expression: *n.* **1.** anything an organism does, with the implication that the act is determined by the nature of the organism. ➤*Distg. fr.* **response,** which emphasizes somewhat more that the act is codetermined by environmental factors; and *fr.* **motor function,** which is (properly) restricted to muscular response.—*Syn.* EXPRESSIVE FUNCTION.—*Ant.* RECEPTIVE FUNCTION. **2.** a subsidiary accompaniment or relatively minor part of a response that is indicative of the total response when most of the latter is hidden or suppressed: e.g., blushing. ➤The phrase *expression of emotion* is misleading in suggesting that the responses denoted are not part of the emotion itself, but it is firmly entrenched in usage. **3.** changes in voice that indicate the emotional value of what is spoken or sung. **4.** (*rhet.*) a word, phrase, or other portion of discourse considered as a unit. **5.** (*math.*) an algebraic, numerical, or other mathematical statement or symbol for a quantity.

expression/method of: the measurement of **feeling** or **emotion** by recording the bodily changes involved. ➤The term is somewhat unfortunate in implying a certain theory about the relation of these changes to the feelings in question but is firmly fixed in technical vocabulary.

expressive babble or **jargon: babbling**

characterized by tones and inflections similar to those of speech.

expressive behavior: 1. a part or aspect of an act that is particularly revealing of the nature of the complex total. 2. relatively spontaneous or uninhibited behavior, esp. emotional behavior.

expressive function = expression (1).

expressive movements: movements distinctive enough to differentiate one individual from another, and hence useful in personality appraisal. Included are gross bodily movements and postures, gestures, facial expressions, manner of speech, etc.

extended family: see **family.**

extended source: (*vis.*) see **point source.**

extension: *n.* 1. (*phys.*) the property of a body of occupying space. 2. (*logic*) the aggregate of things to which a term applies; **denotation.**—*Contr. w.* **intension.**—*v.* **extend.**—*adj.* **extensive.**

extensionalization: *n.* the process of determining more accurately the objects really referred to by a term or statement. It requires becoming explicitly aware of the effect upon one's concepts of previous abstracting and identifying. ➤The process is sometimes used in **psychotherapy,** on the hypothesis that emotional problems are due to **semantic** confusion.

extension/concept: see **concept extension.**

extensity: *n.* a spatial **attribute** assigned to all or some sense data or sensations. It is not **extension** in space, which is a property of physical objects, but the raw material on which our perceiving of extension is said to be based.

extensor (eks·ten′sər): *n.* a muscle which by its contraction serves to straighten out a member, such as a finger or leg. ➤*Contr. w.* **flexor.** An extensor and a flexor form a pair of **antagonistic muscles.**

external: *adj.* 1. outside any system; esp., outside the body. 2. (*anat.*) on the surface of the body; away from the middle line of the body: e.g., the external rectus muscle, which attaches to the eyeball on the side nearest the temple.

externalization: *n.* 1. the process by which a **drive** comes to be aroused by an external stimulation rather than by an internal.—*Cp.* **reinforcement/secondary.** 2. the process by which a child gradually **differentiates** a world "out there" from his primal undifferentiated perception of body-environment. 3. the process of attributing certain parts or aspects of experience to an environment implicitly regarded as sharable with others or independent of one's experiencing. ➤The process raises important philosophical **(epistemological)** problems, but is a distinct (if ill-understood) psychological datum. 4. the attribut-

ing of one's own inner feelings, perceptions, or thoughts to the external environment. ➤E.g., a hallucinatory voice may be referred to the environment; an inner conflict may be projected upon the external scene so that one's own feelings of right and wrong seem to come from outside. K. Horney distinguishes an ACTIVE EXTERNALIZATION, in which feelings toward oneself are experienced as feelings toward others, and PASSIVE EXTERNALIZATION, in which feelings toward others are experienced as being directed by them toward oneself.—*Cp.* **projection.**

external rectus: one of the **eye muscles.**

external sense: a sensory mechanism that is stimulated only, or chiefly, by energy originating outside the body. ➤*Syn.* **exteroceptor,** although the latter refers only to the local sense organ and not to the whole system.—See **sense.**

external world: 1. the totality of physical phenomena outside the body of an organism. 2. the totality of objects other than the **self.** ➤This may be interpreted to include the body of the perceiver as external.

exteroceptor (ek′stər·ō·sep″tər): *n.* a sense organ stimulated directly by energy changes outside the body.—*Distg. fr.* **interoceptor** and **proprioceptor.**—*adj.* **exteroceptive.**

exterosystem: *n.* (*R. Munroe*) any complex inborn equipment that serves to relate the organism directly to the external world: a sensorimotor pattern, memory systems, phonation, etc.—*Near syn.* **ego functions.**

extinction or **extinction/experimental:** the progressive reduction in the **conditioned response** consequent upon either of two experimental procedures: (*a*) the repeated presentation of the CS without the US; or (*b*) the withholding of reward after the emission of a **conditioned instrumental response.** ➤Theorists differ on whether (*a*) and (*b*) are to be regarded as the same; they are operationally distinguishable.—*v.* **extinguish.**

extinction/differential: a procedure by which one conditioned response is **extinguished** and another of the same class is not.—*Syn.* DIFFERENTIATING EXTINCTION (*prefd.*).

extinction/latent: the process whereby an animal ceases to make approach responses to a formerly rewarding situation as a result of the withdrawal of the reward during a period in which the approach responses are not being made in that situation. ➤In ordinary **extinction** of approach or goal-seeking behavior, the approach behavior is followed by nonreward. In latent extinction, the approach behavior is absent from the nonrewarding situation.

extinction ratio: in periodic instrumental

reconditioning, the ratio of unreinforced to **reinforced** responses emitted by the animal: that is, the number of responses the animal makes which do not under the experimental conditions bring reward, divided by the number of times he makes the once-learned response which brings the reward.

extinction/secondary: the weakening of one **conditioned response** as a result of the experimental extinction of a similar **CR.**

extinguish: *v.* 1. to expose an animal to the experimental procedures of **extinction.** 2. to manifest response decrement: the CR *extinguished* rapidly. ➤This meaning is improper unless the procedure of extinction is at least the postulated cause.

extinguished: *adj.* said of a **CR** that has been subjected to **extinction.** ➤Only responses are extinguished; to speak of the animals as being extinguished is, at best, curious laboratory slang.

extirpation: *n.* complete removal or surgical destruction of a bodily part.

extra-: prefix meaning *outside of, beyond, besides*; sometimes (in hyphenated combinations) *more, larger, better: extra-large, extra-strong.*

extraception: see **intraception.**

extrachance: *adj.* significantly different from **chance** expectation.

extracurricular activity: one carried out by pupils, under the auspices of the school authorities, but not forming part of the regular schedule of studies.—*Syn.* COCURRICULAR ACTIVITY, implying that such activities are regarded as an important part of education.

extrajection: *n.* (*psychoan.*) the attributing of one's own mental characteristic or psychic process to another person; or transforming some psychic process into a symbolic representation, e.g., drawing a picture of a face full of hate.—*Syn.* **projection,** which see for other meanings.—*n.* **extraject,** the characteristic of oneself attributed to another.

extramural: *adj.* outside the walls of a given institution. Often used figuratively.

extraneous: *adj.* 1. of external origin; pertaining to an outside factor. 2. foreign to the matter in hand.

extrapolate (eks·trap′ə·lāt): *v.* to estimate the value of a variable, or to plot its curve beyond its known range, by inference from the variation of the variable within the known range. ➤If, throughout the known range, a variable doubles with every additional hour, it might be inferred that this rate of gain would continue. While often useful, extrapolated estimates are subject to tricky errors.—*n.* **extrapolation.**

extrapunitive: *adj.* (*S. Rosenzweig*) characterizing a reaction to frustration in which one is angry or indignant with those blamed for the frustration.—*Cp.* **impunitive** and **intropunitive.** All three terms are also used for **personality types.**

extrasensory perception or **ESP:** a response to an external event not presented to any known sense. ➤In a typical experiment, sets of ESP CARDS each bearing one of five symbols—star, circle, parallel wavy lines, square, and plus—are presented face down and the subject attempts to call what is on the face.—*Distg. fr.* **telepathy,** in which there is said to be perception not of an external event but of what is in another's mind.—See **cryptesthesia.**

extrasocial: *adj.* not involving human relationships.

extraspectral hue: a **hue** not found within the **spectrum;** the purplish hues that lie on the **color circle** between violet and a slightly crimson red.

extratensive: *adj.* (*Ror.*) characterized by a strong need for emotional contact with the environment, dependence upon conformity with others, and relative freedom from self-reference and self-interested motives. ➤*Ant.* **egocentric,** rather than **introversive,** though the latter contrasts somewhat with **extratensive.**—*n.* **extratensivity.**

extraversion: *n.* 1. literally, a turning outward. 2. an attitude of interest in things outside oneself, in the physical and social environment, rather than in one's own thoughts and feelings. 3. (*psychoan.*) the turning of the **libido** outward upon another person or object.—*Var.* **extroversion** (not *prefd.*).—*Ant.* **introversion.**—*pers. n.* **extravert.**

extraversion-introversion: a hypothesized **dimension** for the description and measurement of personality. ➤Three aspects are commonly distinguished: direction of interest and attention outward or inward, ease or difficulty of social adjustment, tendency to open or to secretive behavior. It is fairly certain that the dimension is not a unitary one but represents a collection of only loosely related variables. It is even probable that **extraversion** and **introversion** are not opposite: i.e., a person may become more introverted without thereby being less extraverted.

extravert: *n.* a person who tends strongly to the attitude of **extraversion** (2). ➤A number of personality characteristics, commonly alleged to be associated with the attitude, form an EXTRAVERT TYPE, and this is the usual implication of the term. Those who wish to avoid **type** implications should use the *adj.* **extraverted:** he is *extraverted,* rather than he is an *extravert.*—*Var.* **extrovert** (not *prefd.*).

extremity/phantom: see **phantom extremity.**

extrinsic: *adj.* characterizing that which does not form a real part of something (an object or a topic) but is related to it. ➤Originally **extrinsic** characterized a quantity or value assigned to something because of relation to external factors; e.g., a rating of *first* in one's class is **extrinsic.** For this the antonym is **intrinsic.** But extrinsic is also now used for a quality that is outside: one's reputation is *extrinsic.* Here the antonym is **inherent:** one's honesty is *inherent.*

extrinsic behavior: see **intrinsic behavior.**

extrinsic motivation: behavior controlled through the possibility of reward or punishment external to whatever satisfactions or annoyances reside in the behavior itself: e.g., working for a prize rather than for satisfactions in the task itself.—*Cp.* **motivation/intrinsic.**

extrinsic reward: see **reward/extraneous.**

extroversion = **extraversion** (*prefd.*).

extrovert = **extravert** (*prefd.*).

eye: *n.* the **receptor** for vision. ➤The human eye includes the EYEBALL and the OPTIC NERVE so far as it lies within the eye socket.

eye/compound: the form of eye characteristic of insects.

eye coordination: see **coordination/eye.**

eye/cyclopean: see **cyclopean eye.**

eyedness (īd'nəs) = **eye dominance.**

eye dominance: 1. a tendency to fixate objects with one eye rather than with both and to depend primarily upon the impressions of that one eye, though the nonpreferred eye is not blind. 2. the fact that one eye leads.—See **leading eye.**

eye ground: the picture presented to the examiner viewing the back of the eyeball through an ophthalmoscope.

eyelash sign: the normal reflex movement of the lid when the eyelash is touched. ➤The sign will be found in the unconscious epileptic or hysteric patient but not in one suffering from concussion or other organic lesion.

eye-mindedness: *n.* 1. tendency to apprehend ideas better when they are presented to the eye. 2. tendency to the predominating use of visual rather than other sorts of **imagery.**

eye movement/parallel: movement of the two eyeballs in which the lines of sight remain parallel: e.g., when looking from one distant object to another; eye movements without **convergence** (or **divergence**).

eye movements: rotary movements of the eyeball resulting from pull of the extrinsic eye muscles. ➤Does not include changes in the lens or iris muscle. Includes **convergence, divergence,** elevation, depression, **fixation (3),** pursuit, nystagmus (but not **focus,** which properly refers to convergence of light rays on the retina and not of the eyes on an object).

eye muscles: the six extrinsic muscles that rotate the eyeball. ➤There are three pairs for each eye: (*a*) INTERNAL RECTUS and EXTERNAL RECTUS, which rotate the eyeball inwardly and outwardly respectively; (*b*) SUPERIOR RECTUS and INFERIOR RECTUS, which rotate it upward and downward respectively; (*c*) SUPERIOR OBLIQUE and INFERIOR OBLIQUE, which rotate the eyeball upward and outward, and downward and outward, respectively. The *intrinsic* muscles —those of the **ciliary** body and of the **iris**—are not usually called eye muscles.

eye pause = **fixation pause.**

eye span: the amount grasped in one **fixation pause** of the eyes. Eye span is chiefly spoken of for the reading process and is measured by the number of letters or letter spaces apprehended.

eye-voice span: in oral reading, the distance, measured in letters, between the word being spoken and the word being looked at; the amount by which the eye leads the voice.

F

F: 1. (not *ital.*) Fahrenheit. 2. **face value** or midpoint of a class interval. 3. the sum of frequencies of all classes below this class. 4. (not *ital.*) **luminous flux.** 5. *F* **test.** 6. **surgency** or *F* **factor.** 7. (*Ror.*) scoring code for **form response.** 8. (*C. Hull*) the constant amount by which the potential habit strength is reduced by each reinforcement under any given conditions of learning.

F—: 1. (*Ror.*) = F-MINUS, scoring code for inaccurate or poor form response. 2. = **desurgency.**

F_1, F_2: the first and second **filial generations.**

f: 1. **frequency,** i.e., the number of cases in a class interval or other subdivision of a group.—*Cp. N,* the total number in the group. 2. an unstated functional relationship: e.g., *x is a function of y* is written $x = f(y)$. 3. (*C. Hull*) an incentive substance. 4. = **fluency** factor.

fables test: a test in which the task is to interpret certain fables. ➤It may be used as a **projective test** (when the fables are ambiguous), or as a test of intelligence.

fabrication: *n.* telling fantastic tales as true. —*Syn.* FABULATION.

fabulation = **fabrication.**

face sheet: the first page of a document (such as a case study report) which gives identifying data and sometimes a very brief summary of the data to follow.

facetious (fə·sē′shəs): *adj.* witty or lightly joking; exciting laughter, esp. in an inappropriate or unexpected situation.—*n.* **facetiousness.**

face-to-face group: see **group/face-to-face.**

face validity: see **validity/face.**

face value or **F**: (*stat.*) the **midpoint** of a class interval.—*Distg. fr.* **face** *validity.

facial angle: (*anthropom.*) the angle formed by the line drawn from the base of the nostrils to the base of the skull (or, roughly, from the base of the nostrils to the opening of the ear) with the line from the base of the nostrils to the most prominent part of the forehead.

facial nerve: the VIIth **cranial nerve,** which supplies **efferent** impulses to facial muscles and **afferent** impulses from taste organs in the front two-thirds of the tongue.

facial vision: perception of the approach of large objects without seeing them, chiefly through tactual sensations of air currents reaching the face. It is one way in which blind persons become aware of obstacles.

facilitation: *n.* 1. increased ease of performance, as measured by decrease in time or errors, increase of output, or decrease in sense of effort. 2. support of any act by another act, resulting in increased ease of performance. 3. (*neurol.*) greater ease in the transmission of nerve impulse in a specific **neuron** or **tract;** specif., 4. such ease in transmission as is believed to result from a prior excitation; = *Bahnung.* 5. (*neurol.*) an unfortunate synonym for **summation** (2, 3).—*v.* **facilitate.**

facilitation/law of: The strength of a reflex response may be increased through presentation of a second stimulus which does not itself elicit the response. E.g., the kinesthetic stimuli from firmly clasping the hands strengthens the knee-jerk response.

facilitation/reproductive: see **reproductive facilitation.**

facilitation/retroactive: the strengthening of a previously formed association by one formed later.—*Cp.* **retroactive** *inhibition.**

facilitation/social: see **social facilitation.**

fact: *n.* something that has happened; an event; an actual state of affairs; a thing or a phenomenon. ➤*Distg. fr.* statement, **opinion,** or **belief,** which refer to or are *about* facts or alleged facts. **Fact** may, however, refer to subjective phenomena: it may be a fact that Smith believes in a mermaid. (The mermaid is not fact, but Smith's believing is.) A QUESTION OF FACT refers to disputed phenomena, a QUESTION OF THEORY to the interpretation or explanation of phenomena.—*adj.* **factual.**—*abstr. n.* **factuality.**

factitious: *adj.* made by humans; artificial, not natural. ➤Used esp. where nonhuman origin is claimed or expected.

factor: *n.* 1. any one of several conditions which together cause an event; a part-cause, or anything that has an influence.—*Distg. fr.* component. 2. (*math.*) any one of the numbers which, when multiplied, give a stated product: 3 and 4 are **factors** of 12. 3. (*stat.*) any of the constructs that are the end products of **factor analysis** (which see). ➤Strictly speaking, these **factors** are simply the numbers which, multiplied together according to certain rules, reproduce the **factor matrix.** They are thus but a special case of meaning (2). But they are generally, if unwittingly, interpreted as representing the *cause* of the factor matrix, thus taking on the meaning of (1). This is particularly the case when the **factors** are given names: *number factor, verbal factor,* etc. 4. (*genet.*) the hypothetical element which codetermines, with appropriate environmental conditions, the appearance of a hereditary trait.—*Syn.* **gene.** 5. (*physiol.*) a substance produced by **metabolism,** e.g., a **hormone.**

factor analysis: a statistical method for interpreting scores and correlations of scores from a number of tests. ➤It consists of a search for the **factors (2)** which, under stated restrictions, can be multiplied to give all the **correlation coefficients** of each test with every other. The most usual restriction is that the factors be as few as possible and still reproduce all the correlations. ¶A factor when found represents the fact that for the persons tested there is an area or region of behavior within which individuals respond quantitatively in a consistent manner independently of the particular stimuli. E.g., it has been found that individuals score roughly the same for richness of vocabulary regardless of which random sample of words is used as a test. Hence, a vocabulary factor is hypothesized. ¶A factor describes the area within which such consistency can be found; a further inference is required if the consistency is to be explained as due to a **trait.** Hence, **factor** and **trait** should not be used synonymously, though they often are.—*Syn.* FACTORIAL ANALYSIS.—*v.* **factor analyze** or **factorize,** to carry out the operations of **factor analysis.**—*Distg. fr.* the verb *to factor,* which means to find two or more multipliers for a given product.

factor analysis/inverse = **Q** technique.

factor/areal: see **areal factor.**

factor axes: a set of coordinates representing the relationship of factors to each other and to the correlations in the **matrix.** The axes are located by factor **rotation** and are the solution regarded as best for a particular study.

factor/balancing: see **balancing factor.**

factor coefficient = **factor load.**

factor/common = **factor/group.**

factor configuration: (*factor anal.*) the positions and relations of the test **vectors** in space; a system fixed by and representing the correlation matrix. ➤*Distg. fr.* **factor structure,** which includes the **factor axes.**

factor covariance matrix: (*factor anal.*) a **matrix** in which the columns are the **loadings** of one factor on the several items and the rows are the loadings of another factor on those items. The cells contain the products of the two loadings for the given items.—*Distg. fr.* **factor matrix,** in which the cells contain the factor loadings.

factor efficiency: (*factor anal.*) the number of distinct situations in which a given factor acts as a **unit *trait** or **functional unit.**

factor/first-order: a factor derived from a **matrix** of *test* correlations.—*Contr. w.* **second-order *factor,** which is derived from a matrix of correlations between *factors.*

factor fixation: (*factor anal.*) defining the location of rotated factors by direction cosines in relation to a system of coordinates.

factor/general or **G** or **g: 1.** a factor found in all the tests being **factor analyzed. 2.** a factor believed to be common to all tests of ability. ➤By some methods of factor analysis, a common factor is found directly; Thurstone finds it as a second-order factor, i.e., by factor analysis of the **primary *factors.** The general factor is identified by most authorities, not as general intelligence, but as the common root of intelligent behaviors.—*Cp.* **factor/group** and **factor/unique.**

factor/group: (*factor anal.*) a **factor** present in more than one test in a set of tests being factorized, but not present in all; a factor that accounts for the high intercorrelation of the tests forming a group and their lower correlations with tests outside the group. ➤Thus, there is a higher intercorrelation between tests of memory for words than between those tests and others. Group factors are intermediate between a **specific *factor,** which accounts for variance in only one kind of performance, and a **general *factor,** which accounts for some of the variance in all kinds. There is a continuum of generality since some group factors are related to many, others to few, performances. The designation of a factor as specific or gen-

eral, however, is probably to be regarded as arbitrary, for no factor can be characterized as related to an absolutely unique performance, and almost none (if any) is related to any and all performances. A specific *factor** therefore means a group factor of narrow range, a **general *factor** means a group factor of very broad range. Or, preferably, *specific* and *general* are restricted to a particular **correlation *matrix:** the specific factor then is related to but one test in the matrix, the general factor to all, the group factor to two or more but not all.

In practice the above definition of a group factor is not strictly adhered to: one test may have a fairly high correlation with a test outside the group, yet on nonmathematical grounds it belongs with the others in the group. Group factors are often named by the initial letters of the "area" of performance in which the factor predominates: e.g., **V** factor (verbal), **w** factor (will), **c** factor (character).

factorial: *adj.* of a **factor.**—*Syn.,* in many combinations, **factor:** e.g., **factor** or **factorial analysis.**

factorial design: a plan for experiment in which the effect upon a **dependent *variable** of several experimental or **independent *variables,** caused or permitted to change together in a systematic way, is studied: e.g., the effect on work efficiency, not of temperature alone nor of humidity alone, but of different temperatures at different humidities. ➤This term derives from **factor (1)** and is distinct from **factor analysis.**

factorial invariance: the degree to which the **factor** pattern obtained from a given **matrix** remains unchanged when other tests are added to the matrix or when the same tests are given to different subjects.

factoring: *n.* **1.** finding **factors (2). 2.** the procedure of **factor analysis.**—*Syn.* **factorization** (for a concrete instance), **factor analyzing** (*prefd.*).

factorization/group method of: a method of **factoring** that uses only a portion of the **variance** of a **matrix** to determine the factor to be extracted.

factorize: *v.* to resolve into factors; specif., to make a **factor analysis.**—*Syn.* **factor.** —*n.* **factorization.**

factor loading: the amount that a given factor contributes to the **variability** of a particular test; the correlation of a factor with a test.—*Var.* **factor load.**

factor matrix: (*factor anal.*) a **matrix** whose elements are the **factor loadings** obtained from a factor analysis. ➤The columns represent the factors extracted, the rows the tests in the original battery. The **cell** formed by the intersection of column

and row contains the factor loading.—
Distg. fr. **factor covariance matrix.**
factor/primary: (*factor anal.*) **1.** a factor
that satisfies the requirement of **simple
structure. 2.** one of a group of factors
that divide up without substantial remainder and without overlapping the **covariance** of a **matrix.** ➤If the matrix is
extensive enough to represent a large division of behavior—e.g., all **cognitive** operations—the primary factors may be thought
of as the traits.—See **primary mental
*abilities.**
factor reflection: see **reflection (5).**
factor resolution: see **resolution/factor.**
factor rotation: see **rotation.**
factor saturation = **factor loading.**
factor/second-order: a factor that is common to factors rather than to the tested
variables. It is extracted by factoring a
matrix of factor correlations.—*Cp.* **oblique
(axes) solution.**
factor/simple = (*K. Holzinger*) **reference
vector.**
factor space: the region described by a set
of factors or within which a factor operates.
The dimensions of the region are not necessarily the three dimensions of Euclid or of
perception; they are defined by the empirically observed correlations among the
objects (tests, etc.) that lie in the space.
The number of dimensions is a function of
the correlations. The psychological significance of the dimensions is inferred from
the nature of the tests in the region.—
Distg. fr. **space factor.**
factor/specific or *s* **factor:** (*factor anal.*)
1. a factor found in only one test (or in
two or three tests believed to reflect the
selfsame variable) of the **matrix** being
analyzed. **2.** a factor found only in a very
narrow range of highly similar tests.—*Cp.*
factor/general, factor/group.—*Syn.* **fac-
tor/unique.**
factor-specification equation: an equation
of the form $X = aF_1 + bF_2 + cF_3$, where
X is any one test performance, a, b, and c
are **factor weights,** and F_1, F_2, and F_3 are
the several factors entering into the performance.
factor structure: (*L. Thurstone*) the positions and relations of the test **vectors** in
space upon which a system of coordinate
axes is imposed. ➤A certain position of
these axes is a **simple structure** (which
see). R. B. Cattell suggests **factor *resolution** as a substitute, to avoid confusion
with another meaning of **structure** in factor analysis.
factor theory: a description of mental organization in terms of **factors,** limited in
number, qualitatively the same from person
to person, but differing in strength. ➤A
factor is conceived as either (*a*) the ab-

stracted **communality** of a group of responses, or (*b*) the inferred personal or
organismic characteristics that account for
the communality. (See **factor** and **factor
analysis.**) In either case, there are differing theories on the relation of these factors.
The **TWO-FACTOR THEORY** originally hypothesized that each group of responses
could be described in terms of a general
factor, *g,* found in all cognitive processes,
and a specific factor, *s,* specific to each
small group of responses. Later this theory,
without change of name, accepted factors
of intermediate generality called **group
*factors. MULTIFACTOR** or **MULTIPLE GROUP
FACTOR THEORIES** hypothesize, not a general
factor, but many factors of varying degrees
of generality.—*Distg. fr.* **faculty psychology,** which is **a priori,** whereas factor
theory is based on empirical fact and **factor analysis.**
factor theory (of learning): see **learn-
ing/factor theory of.**
factor/unique: (*factor anal.*) a factor that
is found in only one variable or test of the
matrix in question; a factor defining that
part of the **variance** of a test which is not
shared with the other tests being factorized.
—*Cp.* **factor/group** and **factor/general.**
—*Syn.* **factor/specific.**
factor weight = **factor loading.**
factuality/levels of: a scheme for categorizing reports or **protocols** according to
the degree to which they depart from objective fact. ➤The steps suggested are:
bare **fact, context** or **meaning, interpretation, appraisal, generalization, evaluation.**
faculty/mental: obsolete term for one of
the supposed "powers of the mind" such as
cognition, will, memory, amativeness, pugnacity.—See **faculty psychology.**
faculty psychology: the doctrine that mind
is composed of a number of "powers" or
"agencies" (the **MENTAL FACULTIES,** such as
memory, will, attention) which produce the
various mental activities. ➤In its historical
form, the several faculties were speculatively
deduced from the assumption that acts
which superficially resemble each other
must have a common cause—an assumption
still popularly made. ¶Trait psychology and
certain interpretations of **factor analysis**
resemble faculty psychology in certain
formal aspects, but they differ so widely
in others that the term faculty psychology
should be reserved for the historic doctrine
and its popular descendants.—See **psy-
chology/divisions and schools of, VII.**
fad: *n.* a passing craze, hobby, fashion; a
custom or practice not directly useful, indulged in with immoderation.
f.a.g.r.: *abbr.* for **fractional *antedating
goal response.**

failure: *n.* **1.** not attaining the goal sought; in an experiment, not obtaining usable data. **2.** a person who does not meet acceptable standards of economic competence, esp. his own standards; more generally, a person who does not attain the major goals for which he is striving.

faintness: *n.* **1.** low intensity of stimulus. **2.** a usually brief condition of dizziness and muscular weakness, sometimes with partial loss of consciousness.

faith: *n.* firm (and usually emotional) acceptance of a belief upon admittedly non-rational grounds.

faith cure: healing, or aid in healing, of a pathological state in virtue of a firmly held belief by the patient. ➤The belief may attribute healing powers to the attendant healer, to medication or other physical therapy, to the Deity, to the patient himself, or to magical intervention.

fallacy: *n.* an error in reasoning, leading to an improper conclusion, i.e., one not justified by the considerations advanced. ➤The conclusion may actually be true, but not on the grounds given. A fallacy can be detected by careful attention without additional data. A MATERIAL FALLACY is not properly a fallacy; it is the drawing of a proper conclusion from either true or false premises, but not the conclusion required. —*adj.* **fallacious.**

fall chronometer: an instrument for measuring time by taking the fall of a relatively dense body through a constant distance as a unit.—*Syn.* GRAVITY CHRONOMETER, FALL APPARATUS.

fallectomy = **salpingectomy.**

false exclusion or **false inclusion:** suggested substitutions for **false positive** and **false negative,** respectively.—See **false negative.**

false negative: the number or proportion of cases wrongly excluded from a certain group by application of a certain standard or criterion. ➤E.g., if a certain test be used to select for college it will, unless it is a perfect test, exclude a certain number who would, if admitted, make a satisfactory record. These are the **false negatives.** Those who are chosen by the test and are unsatisfactory are FALSE POSITIVES. Those correctly chosen are VALID POSITIVES, those correctly excluded are VALID NEGATIVES. The term has come into psychology from medicine, where a positive test connotes presence of disease. But positive usually connotes presence of a *useful* quality, and false positive and valid positive suggest the opposite meaning from that intended. It is suggested that the four terms be FALSE EXCLUSION and FALSE INCLUSION, VALID EXCLUSION and VALID INCLUSION, all of which clearly suggest the meaning.

false positive = FALSE INCLUSION, under **false negative.**

falsification/retrospective: unintentional distortions in reporting or remembering past experiences, esp. by the addition of false elements.

falsity: *n.* lack of concordance with fact. ➤*Distg. fr.* **inaccuracy,** which stresses *degree* of nonconcordance.—*Cp.* **accuracy, precision, correctness.**

familial: *adj.* **1.** pertaining to the **family. 2.** occurring in members of the same family. ➤It may refer to either family **heredity** or **heritage,** or both.

familiarity: *n.* acquaintance with a situation or an act to be performed.—*adj* **familiar.**

family: *n.* **1.** a group of individuals related by blood or marriage. ➤The limits of **family** differ from culture to culture. Always included are the mother and her children, nearly always the father. This is the NUCLEAR FAMILY. The EXTENDED FAMILY may include all the descendants of a common great-grandparent with their wives and/or husbands. The FAMILY OF PROCREATION for a given individual is that of which he or she is a parent; the FAMILY OF ORIENTATION is that in which he is an offspring. Metaphorically, **family** may be used for any group considered to be bound by close ties. **2.** a group of persons living together in one household. **3.** (*biol.*) a group of related **genera,** a subdivision of an **order** in the classification of organisms. **4.** = HUMAN FAMILY: all men, including extinct species. Usually used when it is desired to emphasize a feeling of close relationship or brotherhood. **5.** any collection of closely related items: a *family* of curves, an attitude *family.*—*adj.* **familial.**

family/broken: in Occidental society, one which has lost father or mother by death, desertion, or divorce.

family constellation: the number and characteristics of the members of a family; esp., the pattern of their mutual relationships.

family limitation: any procedure designed to restrict the number of children. It includes infanticide, abortion, **contraception,** limitation of intercourse.—See **parenthood/voluntary.**

family/word: see **word family.**

fanaticism: *n.* excessive zeal for a cause, manifested by strong emotion and extreme, though often transient, efforts in its behalf. ➤Usually derogatory.—*adj.* **fanatic.**

fancy: *n.* whimsical imagination.—*adj.* and *v.* **fancy.**

fantasm: *n.* a vivid, seemingly real image of an absent person or form, or of what is assumed to be a disembodied spirit. ➤An image recognized as imaginary is a **fantasm;** when supposedly perceptual, it is an apparition.—*Var.* **phantasm.**

fantastic: *adj.* pertaining to, or of the nature of, **fantasy**; conceived by wild and unrestrained imagination.

fantasy: *n.* imagining a complex object or event in concrete symbols or images, whether or not the object or event exists; or the symbols or images themselves: e.g., a daydream. ➤Fantasy is usually pleasant and represents a sort of **wish fulfillment.** Originally synonymous with **imagination** (which see), it is now distinguished by the fact that, if it represents reality at all, it is whimsical or visionary, not primarily either constructive or reproductive. Yet it is not necessarily **delusive** or pathological. ¶Freud made distinction between dreams of fantasy and those showing **dream work.**—*adj.* **fantastical** (*prefd.*), as **fantastic** has acquired a wider meaning.—*Var.* **phantasy.**

fantasy/creative: (*C. Jung*) an **instinctual** process in which problems are subjectively solved by the uniting of opposites.

fantasy/forced: (*psychoan.*) an **affect-charged** fantasy provoked by the analyst. ➤It is resorted to in the case of patients who report few spontaneous fantasies. The supposition is that *any* fantasy the patient is able to produce will represent the unconscious.

fantasy formation: daydreaming, in contrast with logical and realistic thinking; autism.—*Syn.* FANTASY-MAKING, FANTASY THINKING.

fantasy/foster-child: see **foster-child fantasy.**

fantasy/rebirth: see **rebirth fantasy.**

fantom = **phantom.**

faradic (fə·rad′ik): *adj.* pertaining to the alternating electric current produced by the secondary winding of an induction coil. ➤The faradic current is much used to give an electric shock in laboratory experiments.

far point: the most distant point at which an eye can see an object distinctly under conditions of relaxed **accommodation.**—*Cp.* **near point.**

far-sight: *n.* either of two different conditions, **presbyopia** or **hyperopia** (which see), in which distant objects can be seen relatively more clearly than near ones; metaphorically, ability to estimate the future course of events.—*Syn.* FARSIGHTEDNESS.

fasciculus (fə·sik′ū·ləs): *n., pl.* **fasciculi** (-lī): (*neurol.*) a slender bundle or cluster of nerve fibers; esp., a subdivision of a **funiculus** of the spinal cord.—*adj.* **fascicular, fasciculate.**

fasciculus gracilis (gras′i·lis) = **Goll/ column of.**

fashion: *n.* a custom having but a brief life; more specif., a custom in clothing.

fatalism: *n.* **1.** the doctrine that the situation and acts of man are predetermined by Deity (or some substitute therefor) and are not subject to change, either by individual volition or by act of anyone else.

➤This view rules out any effect of environmental change. **2.** the doctrine that volition and effort cannot influence behavior.—*Ant.* **voluntarism.** ➤**Fatalism** is not quite the same as **determinism,** which may admit the role of volition and/or effort while explaining these as fully determined by past events. Its derogatory connotations are question-begging; it is no argument against a view to call it **fatalism.**

father complex = **Electra complex.**

father figure: *n.* **1.** the person who is put in the stead of one's real male parent, and who becomes the object of transferred attitudes or other habitual responses originally developed in relation to the parent. **2.** a mature person with whom one **identifies** and who comes to exercise such parental functions as advice, encouragement, or discipline.—See **figure (5).**—*Syn.* FATHER IMAGO (im·ā′gō).

father fixation: *n.* centering attention and feeling upon the father, somewhat to the exclusion of other persons, together with relative inability to shift attention to other persons.

father right or **mother right:** tracing of descent, hence of kinship, through the father or the mother respectively.—*Syn.* PATRILINY and MATRILINY. ➤There is no implication concerning the authority or power of the respective parents.

father surrogate: one who is reacted to as if he stood in place of a father.—See **surrogate.**

fatigue: *n.* **1.** (*pop.*) diminished ability to do work, either physical or mental, as a consequence of previous and recent work.—*Syn.* **work decrement** (*prefd.,* since it does not imply a single cause for the loss). **2.** impairment of function of sense organ, nerve, or muscle due to continued recent stimulation and activity.—*Syn.* PHYSIOLOGICAL EXHAUSTION (*prefd.*); for sense-organ fatigue, **sensory *adaptation (2). 3.** = weariness, a specific bodily feeling. **4.** the desire to quit performing a function after prolonged application to it. ➤The four meanings are often confounded.

fatigue/auditory: loss of sensitivity to sounds as a result of auditory stimulation. —*Syn.* AUDITORY ADAPTATION.—See **adaptation/sensory (2).**

fatigue/chromatic or **/color** = **adaptation/chromatic.**

fatigue/combat: see **combat fatigue.**

fatigue/nerve = **refractory phase (1).**

fatigue/retinal: depletion of capacity of the retina to respond to light and color stimuli. ➤Postulated to explain negative aftersensation, successive contrast, etc.—*Syn.* RETINAL ADAPTATION.—See **adaptation/sensory (2).**

fatigue/visual: decreased ability of visual performance and/or characteristic sensations or feelings resulting from prolonged visual work.—*Distg. fr.* **fatigue/retinal.**

FC: (*Ror.*) scoring code for a response that imputes to the inkblot a definite meaningful form made up in essential part by colored elements.

Fc: (*Ror.*) scoring code for a description of the inkblot primarily in terms of a form. The shading (or color) effects are described as giving texture or surface appearance to the form.

fc = foot-candle.

fear: *n.* an emotion of violent agitation or fright in the presence (actual or anticipated) of danger or pain. It is marked by extensive organic changes and behaviors of flight or concealment.—*Cp.* **phobia,** which refers to persistent and irrational specific fears.

feature profile test: a test wherein appropriately shaped blocks must be put together to form a human profile.

febrile (fē'bril; feb'-): *adj.* feverish.

Fechner's colors (feH'nərz): see **Charpentier's bands.**

Fechner's law: generalization that intensity of sensation increases as the logarithm of its stimulus. ➤Often incorrectly called **Weber's law** (which is a distinct formula), Fechner's formula has been subjected to varied interpretation and criticism. The formula is $S_I = k \log R$, where S_I = sensation intensity, $R = Reiz$ (*Ger.* for *stimulus*), k = a constant.—*Syn.* WEBER-FECHNER LAW.

Fechner's paradox: If stimuli differing in intensity are brought to the two eyes separately so that the two visual impressions fuse into one, the brightness of this **binocular** image is less than that of the brighter of the **uniocular** components.

Fechner's shadow experiment: a demonstration of Weber's law: the observer compares the brightness of the shadows cast by a single pole on a uniform surface from two independently variable light sources.

fecundity: *n.* capacity to have offspring. ➤While best usage distinguishes **fecundity** from **fertility** (the latter meaning the actual having of many offspring), the two are often confused and even reversed. While fecundity would seem to be primarily anatomic or physiological, INFECUNDITY may also be psychological. **Fertility** is a function of very many factors—physiological, psychological, economic, political, cultural, religious, etc. Both fecundity and fertility are also used figuratively of ideas, plans, projects, etc.—*adj.* **fecund** (which also means having many offspring).

feeble-mindedness: see **deficiency/mental.**

feeble-mindedness/high-grade: see **defective/high grade.**

feedback: *n.* **1.** in a machine, the automatic signaling of the degree of performance or nonperformance of an operation: e.g., the registration by a speedometer of the rate of rotation of the drive shaft.—*Cp.* **servomechanism, cybernetics. 2.** in an organism, the sensory report of the somatic result of a behavior: e.g., the kinesthetic report that indicates the speed and extent of a movement, or the pain that follows touching a hot object. **3.** (*social psychol.*) a direct perceptual report of the result of one's behavior upon other persons: e.g., the perception of the return smile that greets one's own. ➤**Feedback** in such cases involves implicit inferences and is thus not wholly the same as in (2). ¶It is only recently that the feedback principle has been isolated in mechanics and extensively made use of; in organisms the corresponding principle has long been recognized (*cp.* **knowledge of results, coenesthesia, proprioception, kinesthesia**); it is only the term which is new. And being new, its exact usage is not stabilized.

feeding problem: extreme difficulty in getting a child to eat an adequate amount of the right foods; or the child who makes such difficulty. ➤The term does not usually refer to physiological failure to absorb food but to refusal to eat.

feel: *v.* **1.** to touch and explore an object with the surface of the body, esp. with fingers. **2.** to receive sensory impressions from an object or situation. **3.** to experience a general bodily condition: to *feel* well, to *feel* fatigued, to *feel* cold. **4.** to experience pleasantness or unpleasantness; to have an emotion or **affect. 5.** to believe; to conclude, esp. when the person is not ready to defend his belief.—See **feeling.**

feeling: *n.* For the variety of popular usages, see an unabridged dictionary. Many are still current and considerably affect its technical use. We may distinguish four basic usages: **1.** in the broadest sense, any kind of **conscious** process or **experiencing.** ➤This old-fashioned usage is still current, esp. in contexts where it is not desired to emphasize the object of experiencing. **2.** the **sense impressions** from the skin and underlying tissues. ➤These are usually given special names (e.g., **pressure sensation**) or are lumped together as **cutaneous,** but the verb and gerund forms (e.g., *feeling of pressure*) are retained even in highly technical works, and extended to any general form of **sensing** (e.g., *feeling well*). **3.** = **affect** (3), or **affective** states or processes: **emotions, sentiments, passions, valences, desires, cravings, interests** are, or involve, feelings, though (at least in the last three) a strong **conative** aspect is also to be noted. —*Cp.* also **reinforcement,** a related term differently used. **4.** the elementary factors in the various affective states. ➤Traditional psychology generally distinguished two feeling elements, pleasure and unpleasure, or liking and disliking. Some added an elementary interest-feeling. Freudians hold to a **bipolar** theory of elementary feelings, usually called love and hate. Wundt distinguished three opposed pairs. **5.** a vague belief; or one not backed by clear evidence. ➤The difficulties of definition are nowhere greater than in stating the precise meaning of a term, such as **feeling,** which everyone understands—each in his own way. Metaphorically, we may speak of feeling as the overtone or as the coloring of experience, the evaluating aspect of our adjustments to environment.—*adj.* **feeling,** pertaining to the process or mental content; **felt,** pertaining to that which arouses feeling.—*Syn.* (for the *adj.*) **affective, hedonic.**

feeling/asthenic: see **asthenic feeling.**

feeling-into: *n.* a translation of *Ger.* **Einfühlung.**—*Syn.* **empathy.**

feeling of ——: see other noun: e.g., for *feeling of difference,* see **difference/feeling of;** for *feeling of inadequacy,* see **inadequacy/feeling of,** etc.

feeling tone: *n.* the **affective** component, the pleasingness or unpleasingness, of an **act** or object.

feeling type: (*C. Jung*) a **function type** belonging to the rational class: a person who is dominated habitually by **affects;** or a classification for such person. ➤The classification of feeling as *rational* is unusual, if not unique, to the school of Jung.—See **function type.**

fellatio (fə·lā'shi·ō): *n.* stimulation of the penis by friction in the mouth of another person, the FELLATOR (*m.*) or FELLATRIX (*f.*).

felt-need: *n.* a **need** of which one is explicitly aware; a recognition that there is something in the situation to which adjustment is needed. ➤In many educational contexts, the term has carried the implication that the felt-need is necessarily a sound guide to what a child should learn, and that a felt-need guarantees learning if only it can be found or activated. It is all too often used as *syn.* for **motive (1)** and **(2).**—*Syn.* **aware-need,** CONSCIOUS NEED.

female; *adj.* intrinsic to the female sex: *female* organs, *female* voice. ➤*Distg. fr.* FEMININE, commonly associated with females: *feminine* attire.

feminine: see **female.**

femininity: *n.* the usual characteristics, taken collectively, of women.

feminization: *n.* becoming more like the adult female of one's species. ➤Said of a male or of a young female.

fenestra (fə·nes'trə): *n.* (*L.*) a window; specif., the FENESTRA VESTIBULI or OVALIS (= **oval *window**) and the FENESTRA ROTUNDA (= **round *window**).

fenestration: *n.* an operation to relieve **conduction *deafness** by making a new permanent opening in the lateral semicircular canal as a substitute for the **oval *window.**

feral (fir'əl): *adj.* wild; undomesticated.

feral child: a human being who has been nurtured in complete social isolation from other human beings, either by animals or by only indirect contact with human caretakers.

Féré phenomenon or **method:** see **electrodermal response.**

Ferry-Porter law = **Porter's law.**

fertility: *n.* the having of many offspring; figuratively, the having of many ideas.—See **fecundity** for discussion.—*Ant.* **infertility,** the having of few offspring or none.—*adj.* **fertile.**

fertility/differential: **1.** the number of offspring that have been produced by an individual or a pair in a completed family, as compared with others. **2.** the predicted capacity of an individual or a pair to produce relatively many or few offspring. ➤Such prediction is at best of doubtful validity.

fertilization: *n.* (*biol.*) union of a male **gamete** or **sperm** with an **ovum** or egg.

fetal: *adj.* pertaining to the **fetus.**—*Var.* **foetal.**

fetishism (fē'tish·iz·əm; fet-): *n.* **1.** veneration of inanimate objects **(fetishes)** considered to possess magical powers; metaphorically, extravagant devotion to any object. **2.** an anomaly in which sexual excitement or gratification is habitually produced by an object other than sex organs or characteristics. ➤Fetishes are most often articles used by persons of the opposite sex (handkerchiefs, gloves, toilet articles, lingerie) or parts of the body, esp. the hair. The ardent feeling of the lover for the adored one's handkerchief as a token in her absence is only metaphorically called fetishism.—*Var.* **fetichism.**

fetus (fē'təs): *n.* an **embryo** in its more advanced stage of development; esp., the human embryo after the sixth to eighth week of pregnancy.—*adj.* **fetal, foetal.**—*Var.* **foetus.**

F factor: (*R. B. Cattell*) the factor defining the dimension of **surgency-desurgency,** found in tests of: speed of reaction time; speed in reversible perspective; ratio of speed to error in pursuitmeter, cancellation, etc.; ratio of vocabulary to general intelligence; alkalinity of saliva; concentration of cholinesterase in blood serum; etc.—*Cp.* **surgency.**

FFF = flicker fusion frequency (see **flicker**).

F-G = **figure-ground.**

fiat (fī'ət): *n.* (*L., let it be done*) a distinctive experience said to accompany certain acts of choice or volition.

fiber: *n.* **1.** a threadlike bit of living substance which, with others, makes up a tissue. **2.** = **nerve fiber.**—*adj.* **fibrous** (but this may also mean *of a tough thin layer*).—*Var.* **fibre.**

fibers/commissural: see **commissural fibers.**

fibre = **fiber.**

fibril (fī′bril): *n.* threadlike portion of a single **neuron.**—*Syn.* NEUROFIBRIL, NEUROFIBRILLA.

fibrillation: *n.* the division of a fiber into finer fibers or hairlike processes.

fiction: *n.* **1.** an imagined state of affairs not considered to be real. **2.** something taken *as if* true for the sake of argument, or as a basis for action in the hope that by such action it may be made true.—*Distg. fr.* **artifact,** and *fr.* **construct.**—*adj.* **fictitious.**

fiction/directive: (*A. Adler*) a fantasy of one's superiority which forms the basis of a life plan. ➤When too far out of line with reality, it is a NEUROTIC FICTION.

fiction/neurotic: see **fiction/directive.**

fiducial (fi·dü′shəl): *adj.* pertaining to, or based on, that which is trustworthy or reliable. ➤FIDUCIARY, pertaining to a trustee, is often but incorrectly used as a synonym.

fiducial interval: see **fiducial limit.**

fiducial limits: (*stat.*) the points or ordinates to the right or left of a representative statistic within which sampling variation may be expected to occur without loss of the **representative** character of the **statistic.** ➤The limits are set at such distance in sigma units from the statistic that a value of the statistic beyond these limits is

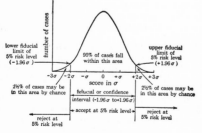

Fiducial Limits
and Confidence Level

not expected to occur by chance alone in more than a stated percentage of the samplings.

The distance between the limits (in sigma units) is called the FIDUCIAL, or CONFIDENCE, INTERVAL. Fiducial emphasizes the role of probability theory in determining the limits;

confidence emphasizes that the limits set, though based on probability, are a matter of choice. One decides, for nonstatistical reasons, to have confidence in a difference that happens as often as 95 per cent of the time (this is confusingly called the 5 per cent level of significance); or one elects to be more rigorous and to put confidence in a difference that happens by chance only once in a hundred samplings (this is called the 1 per cent level of significance). In practice, fiducial and confidence are interchangeable when used with LIMITS or INTERVAL. (Note that *fiduciary* does not mean the same as fiducial.)

CONFIDENCE LEVEL specifies the percentage of samples that may be expected to fall outside the confidence interval: one speaks of a statistic as stable or significant at the 5 per cent or 1 per cent confidence level. Although this meaning is rigorously definable, it is confusing: 5 per cent is not the per cent in which we are confident; it is the per cent that we must risk. It has therefore been suggested (by J. Royce) that **risk level** take the place of confidence level.

field: *n.* **1.** an area having boundaries. ➤As used in psychology, both **field** (area) and boundary may be used metaphorically. E.g., when we speak of rules setting boundaries to action, we refer not merely to a physical place but to the kind of action permitted. **2.** the entire space within which a set of forces operates. ➤In psychology, field is used to emphasize the complex totality of interdependent influences within which an organism functions, the constellation of interdependent factors that account for a psychological event. See **field theory.** In various combinations, the use of field emphasizes that the object to which the organism reacts is the product of interaction, within the field, of the organism with the non-organism.

field/behavior: see **behavior field.**

field cognition mode: (*E. C. Tolman*) a specific acquired way of apprehending or knowing some specific character of the field in which the organism behaves. It involves an interaction of perceiving, remembering, and thinking, and is manifested by specific reaction. ➤The term is employed to emphasize the contribution of the organism to the "stimulus" aspect of the stimulus-response sequence.

field/excitatory: see **excitatory field.**

field expectance = **expectancy.**

field force: (*K. Lewin*) a manifestation of energy by a person that must be defined in terms of the whole **field.** ➤For Lewin, strictly speaking all force is field force; the term is thus redundant for emphasis. It may be applied to forces that are field-determined in very marked degree and determined only slightly by less inclusive influences, such as a particular stimulus or particular trait.

field investigation: collection of data outside the laboratory, library, or clinic; the study of organisms in their usual habitats. ➤An inclusive term covering any kind of method from brief interview to carefully controlled experiment. Emphasis is upon the place, not the method.—*Syn.* FIELD OBSERVATION, FIELD RESEARCH, FIELD STUDY.—*Cp.* also **action research.**

field/mathematical: a region defined by any kind of mathematics, including (but not limited to) Euclidean geometry.—See **topology, field/scalar, field/vector.**

field observation: observation of events in their natural setting, without effort to control them for the purposes of the observation.

field/occupational: see **occupational field.**

field of ――――: see other noun: e.g., for *field of attention,* see **attention/field of.**

field/perceptual: see **perceptual field.**

field/phenomenal or **/phenomenological:** everything, including itself, experienced by an organism at any moment. ➤Emphasis is upon the external world *as experienced* by the reacting organism, not as it is in the abstractions of physical science. Objects physically present, but not perceived, are not part of the phenomenal field, and objects not physically present, but thought about, are.—See **field theory, phenomenology.**

field/psychological: (*topol.*) a region within which to order psychological facts according to the mathematical rules by which the **field** is determined. ➤In a very simple case, similarity may be represented as nearness in space and the facts about similarity shown graphically.—*Cp.* **field/mathematical.** The psychological field may include a limited set of psychological facts or all of them.—*Syn.* (*approx.*) **behavior field, behavioral environment** (both more limited), psychophysiological or **psychophysical** *field** (more inclusive).

field/psychophysical: (*K. Koffka*) an inclusive construct that brings into unified consideration the **behavioral environment** and the physiological field.

field research: see **field investigation.**

field/scalar: (*topol.*) a region where every point may have an associated set of magnitudes.

field/sensory: see **sensory field.**

field structure: 1. the pattern of relations between various parts of the **psychological** *field. 2. the arrangement in which psychological facts can be assigned precise positions in the field. ➤A field is said to be **structured** when the data of which it is composed find reasonably precise positions. It is INFINITELY STRUCTURED when every datum

is located. 3. the arrangement in which the psychological field is rigid and stable.

field study: see **field investigation.**

field-theoretical: *adj.* pertaining to **field theory;** according to the tenets of field theory.

field theory: any of several points of view that attempt to systematize psychological data by analogy with **fields of** *force in physics. ➤They postulate that the properties of related phenomena are derived from, or dependent on, the total **field** of which they are at that time a part. The theory substitutes *events* for *things* having fixed properties, and sees events as totalities in which parts of the event are what they are, qualitatively and quantitatively, only in terms of the rest of the event. ¶No brief characterization of **field theory** is at all adequate, and various writers differently state the case. With varying degrees of emphasis, a field theory may hold (*a*) that the organism and its surrounds form a unified interacting totality and can only arbitrarily be considered separately; (*b*) that the true instigator of behavior is always the totality of mutually influencing parts, and not an isolated stimulus (*cp.* **Gestalt**); (*c*) that objects are not independent physical forces but gain their object quality from the organism that reacts to them (i.e., that the property in an object of instigating response is never a correlate of its physical properties alone but depends also upon the organism); (*d*) and conversely, that the organism can only be described as an organism-in-a-field, its only properties being those of an organism-in-a-field.

At a *very* superficial level, the reader may take field theory to mean an emphasis upon the interrelatedness of a present event, upon the totality of influences that determine behavior.—See **psychology/divisions and schools of, V, VII.**—*adj.* **field-theoretical.**

field/vector: (*topol.*) a **region** where every point is characterized by both direction and magnitude.

field/visual: see **visual field.**

figural: *adj.* pertaining to, or showing the characteristics of, a **figure.**

figural aftereffect: the tendency to maintain the same kind of **figure-ground** relations in successive similar experiences. ➤If a straight line is tilted on a homogeneous ground, there is a tendency to continue to structure the visual field in the same direction. Hence, if a succeeding line actually tilts the same as the first, it is perceived as tilting less.

figural cohesion: the tendency of the parts of a figure to remain together as one figure. ➤E.g., once seen as forming a triangle, three dots tend to continue to be seen as a figure   208   finger spelling

triangle even when they are combined with other elements. **Camouflage** (which see) succeeds by destroying one figural cohesion in favor of another.

figure: *n.* **1.** the symbol for a digit(e.g., 8) or a number (e.g., 42.51). **2.** the outline or shape of anything, but esp. of a human body; or a likeness of such shape. **3.** a visual outline composed of solid lines, in comparison with a **pattern** in which space is outlined by dots or other discontinuous stimuli. **4.** a group of impressions from a single sense perceived as a whole and clearly marked off from adjacent impressions.—See **figure-ground. 5.** a person representing, in feeling and in idea, the essential (not necessarily the ideal) attributes of a certain role: a **father figure;** a **mother figure.** ➤The figure is not quite a **surrogate** or substitute; his relations with the other person may be too few for that. A teacher may be a mother surrogate without being very fully a mother figure; a purely fictitious character may become a mother figure. The figure is always the object of a marked and distinctive attitude.—See **father figure.**—*adj.* **figural, figured.**

figure/ambiguous: any of a large category of pictures which, when steadily regarded, are subject to changed interpretation without any actual change in the picture. ➤Thus, in a line drawing a staircase may

be so pictured that it may be alternatively interpreted as seen from below or from above. This is a **reversible (ambiguous) *figure.** In other cases, such as the "hidden man" type of puzzle picture (an **embedded *figure**), once the interpretation has changed it is difficult to see the original figure again.

figure-and-ground = **figure-ground.**

figure/composite: see **composite figure.**

figure/embedded: a form of **ambiguous *figure** in which a visual form or shape is so closely interwoven with other forms that it is difficult to perceive separately. ➤All **camouflage** involves embedding a figure into a background. When lines and colors forming part of the figure are seen as belonging to adjacent figures, the unity or gestalt of the embedded figure is destroyed. HIDDEN FIGURES are a special case of embedded figures.

figure-ground: *n.* a general property of a perceived field of being divided into at

least two parts or aspects, the **figure** and the **ground,** which mutually influence each other. ➤Derived from graphic art, where the distinction of figure and background is an old one, the concept is now generalized to all perception, or even to all awareness. The figure is perceived as having unity and as being segregated from the ground; the ground is relatively, though not entirely, homogeneous—i.e., the constituent impressions are not sharply marked off from each other. The figure is generally the part attended to, but the relationship is not necessarily static—figure and ground may be reversed by a shift in attention or intention. (It is possible, however, to shift attention to the ground without causing it to become figure.) More than one figure may be segregated on one ground, and what is figure for one ground may itself be ground for another figure. A number of properties have been experimentally ascribed to figure or to ground respectively.—*Syn.* FIGURE-AND-GROUND.

figure/hidden: see **figure/embedded.**

figure/reversible: one form of **ambiguous *figure** (which see). Most reversible figures are reversals of perspective.—See **perspective/alternating.**

filial: *adj.* pertaining to offspring or descendants.

filial generations: the successive generations from a single parent or pair. They are designated as FIRST FILIAL (or F_1), SECOND FILIAL (or F_2), etc.

filial regression: see **regression/filial.**

filiate: *v.* to establish a relationship like that of parent to child, as in a parent organization and its branches.

film color: one that lacks definite localization but seems to hover before an observer like a film or cloud. It is seen as soft, unsubstantial, nearly texture-free.

filter/acoustic: a device that screens out certain sound frequencies, allowing the rest to pass through: e.g., the ordinary loudspeaker filters out high frequencies.

final: *adj.* **1.** last of a series. **2.** purposive; pertaining to ends or goals.—*Syn.* (for **2**) **telic; teleological; FINALISTIC,** pertaining to a doctrine that exalts human purposes as of special significance.

final common path: a group of motor neurons upon which nerve impulses from afferent and connective neurons converge.

finalism = **teleology.**

finger painting: making pictures or designs by spreading pigments on a surface with the fingers. ➤Being less demanding of technique than brush or crayon, it is used to encourage graphic expression and in **projective tests.**

finger spelling: spelling by finger movements, each of which stands for a letter or phonic combination.—*Contr. w.* **sign language.**

finite (fī′nīt): *adj.* having measurable limits. ➤A FINITE DIFFERENCE is symbolized by Δ. *Contr. w.* **infinite,** having limits too great to be measurable; and *w.* **infinitesimal,** too small to be measurable.

firing: *n.* (*neurol.*) the process whereby activity in a receptor or in a neuron affects a neighboring nerve or muscle cell; the emission of a nervous impulse.—*v.* **fire.**

first-order correlation coefficient: a partial correlation coefficient in which the influence of only one **variable** is held constant.

first-order factor: see **factor/first-order.**

Fisher's test: a statistical test to determine the probability that a correlation coefficient of a given value could arise by random sampling from an uncorrelated population. ➤Tables show the *t* value for values of *r* at different **degrees of freedom** and number of variables.

fission: *n.* a method of reproduction wherein a cell divides into two parts, each of which grows into a full-sized cell like the original.

fission/group: by analogy with cell **fission,** the splitting of a social group into two separate groups.—*Contr. w.* **fusion/group.**

fissure: *n.* (*anat.*) any of the deep furrows or grooves on the surface of the brain. ➤The more shallow grooves are sometimes also called **fissures,** but are preferably termed **sulci.**—*adj.* **fissural.**

fissure/central: (*anat.*) a groove, at about the middle of the lateral surface of each cerebral hemisphere, which divides the **frontal** from the **parietal lobe.**—*Syn.* FISSURE OF ROLANDO, ROLANDIC SULCUS.

fissure/lateral: the cerebral fissure that separates the **temporal lobe** from the **parietal** and **frontal lobes.**—*Syn.* FISSURE OF SYLVIUS, SYLVIAN FISSURE.

fistula: *n.* a narrow tube or opening in some tissue resulting from surgery, incomplete healing, or abnormal incomplete growth.

fit: *n.* **1.** (*med.*) a sudden attack, or a convulsion. **2.** (*stat.*) conformity to a standard: e.g., conformity of the distribution actually found to that expected.—*v.* **3.** to adjust the representation of the actual data to conform to a standard. ➤Such adjustment is allowable only when made according to definite principles and rules.

fit/goodness of: the degree to which a set of empirical observations conforms to a standard or an expected (or theoretical) distribution, esp. when both empirical and theoretical are expressed as curves. ➤It is usually, but not necessarily, measured in terms of the mean of the squared deviations of the observations from the theoretical curve.—*Cp.* **least squares method, chi-square test of goodness of fit.**

fittingness/law of: (*Gestalt*) a generalization of **good continuation** and **closure** which holds that, during problem-solving or learning, **configurations** change so that their parts belong together according to their intrinsic relations, not according to an imposed relation.

five-track plan: see **ability grouping.**

fixated response: one that persists in spite of all attempts to modify it by ordinary reward and punishment.

fixation: *n.* **1.** strengthening a learned tendency, esp. a motor habit.—*Contr. w.* **acquisition. 2.** becoming set or rigid in a particular fashion, esp. in the form of **affective *fixation. 3.** = **fixation/visual.** —*v.* **fixate.**

fixation/abnormal: a persistent type of behavior without apparent motivation; rigidity; compulsive behavior. It is commonly attributed to **affective *fixation.**

fixation/affective: the establishment of a strong attachment for someone or something; or the manifestation of an excessive attachment. ➤The term usually refers to an attachment developed in infancy or early childhood which persists in an immature or neurotic form, with corollary inability to form normal attachments with other persons, objects, ideas, or ways of doing things. (Cp. **arrest of *development.**) Sexual **anomalies** and the **Oedipus complex** are so explained by many psychoanalysts. The object of attachment is sometimes called a **fixation.** The (AFFECTIVE) FIXATION POINT marks the level of development at which fixation occurs.

fixation/anxiety: see **anxiety fixation.**

fixation/binocular: see **fixation/visual.**

fixation/factor: see **factor fixation.**

fixation frequency: the number of **fixation pauses** made in reading a standard line.

fixation/law of: the generalization that if practice and study are carried far enough beyond the point of bare recall, the learning becomes permanent.—See **overlearning.**

fixation/libidinal = **fixation/affective.**

fixation line: see **fixation/visual.**

fixation movement and **moving fixation:** two different forms of **tension movement.**

fixation/negative: learning not to seek satisfaction in a class of activities because it is punished: e.g., a small child chided or repulsed for seeking food at the breast or bottle.—*Cp.* **fixation/positive.**

fixation of affect = **fixation/affective.**

fixation/parental: abnormally strong and persisting emotional attachment of offspring to a parent.

fixation pause: one of the brief moments during which the eyeball is at rest. ➤Only during these moments is it possible to make visual discriminations; during eye movements we see nothing or only a vague undifferentiated field.—*Cp.* **saccadic movement.**—*Syn.* PERCH, EYE PAUSE.

fixation point: see **fixation/affective** or **fixation/visual.**

fixation/positive: learning to prefer a means of obtaining a goal that is rewarded, generally by an added or extraneous incentive. ➤E.g., a small child, praised for eating solid food, learns to prefer it. In contrast, his attempts to satisfy hunger by breast or bottle may be punished, resulting in NEGATIVE FIXATION. Positive fixation (and perhaps negative) is a form of **canalization.**

fixation time: (*vis.*) duration of **fixation pause.**

fixation/visual: the turning or holding of the eyeball in such a position that the object of regard, or (VISUAL) FIXATION POINT, lies along the FIXATION LINE (the line drawn from the fovea through the pupil). In BINOCULAR FIXATION both eyes are held in this position (but it is now known that binocular fixation is not very common, one or other eye only being strictly fixated).— See **eye dominance.**

fixed-alternative: *adj.* pertaining to a question asked in a test, examination, or survey, requiring the answer to be selected from alternatives provided by the questioner.— *Ant.* FREE-ANSWER, **open-ended question.**— *Syn.* MULTIPLE-CHOICE, SELECTIVE-ANSWER. —See **test/selective answer.**

fixed-class society: one in which a person's class or caste is fixed by heredity, and mobility is not possible.—*Contr. w.* **open-class society.**

fixed idea: an idea, usually unfounded, firmly held despite evidence sufficient to convince normal persons. ➤The patient does not recognize its unreasonableness. An IMPERATIVE IDEA, on the other hand, he recognizes as unreasonable but cannot resist. An AUTOCHTHONOUS IDEA is an imperative idea which he attributes to some malevolent influence.

fixed interval reinforcement: see **reinforcement schedule** (PERIODIC REINFORCEMENT).

fixedness: *n.* lack of **flexibility** in solving problems; remaining set toward one method despite its inappropriateness.—*Cp.* **fixation, rigidity,** which are closely related concepts.

fixedness/functional: see **functional fixedness.**

fixed ratio reinforcement: see **reinforcement schedule.**

FK: (*Ror.*) scoring symbol for **vista response.**

flaccid (flak'sid): *adj.* relaxed; soft; flabby; low in muscular tone.

flagellation: *n.* whipping, esp. as a means of arousing various religiously oriented emotions (penitence, remorse, exaltation) and/

or sexual emotion. ➤Flagellants may invite flagellation from others or practice it on themselves. By extension, the term is used for the similar practice of cutting with knives.—*Cp.* **masochism** and **sadism.**

flagellomania: *n.* sexual excitement from whipping or being whipped.

flash device: any device for exposing something to be seen for a brief period: e.g., a **tachistoscope,** or merely a cardboard (FLASH CARD) on which words to be read or memorized are printed.

flashmeter: *n.* a commercial **flash device** permitting timing of exposure.

flattening of affect: incongruous absence of appropriate emotional response: e.g., when a psychotic person smiles pleasantly or has no expression at all while claiming to have some horrible experience or symptom.

flavor: *n.* the olfactory component of the combined experience, in eating food, of taste, smell, pressure, and temperature; or, the entire unitary experience as dominated by its smell. ➤It is often not recognized as smell, so tightly blended are the components.

Flesch formulas: formulas for computing (*a*) an index of how easy a passage of English prose is to read, and (*b*) an index of the "human interest" of the passage. ➤The latter term is admittedly not very descriptive and covers human interest only as a result of style, not content. The two indices are used together to measure the "difficulty" of the reading matter.

flexibilitas cerea: waxy flexibility.—See **catalepsy, catatonia.**

flexible: *adj.* 1. ready to make changes in behavior to meet the changing circumstances of the moment.—*Syn.* **adaptable.**—*Ant.* **rigid.** 2. ready to make enduring changes; teachable.—*Syn.* **modifiable** (*prefd.*). 3. of habits, sentiments, attitudes, or similar behavior patterns which have alternatives available for varying circumstances.—*n.* **flexibility.**

flexion: *n.* bending; esp., bending at a joint. ➤*Distg. fr.* FLEXURE, a permanent bending during growth.

flexor: *n.* a muscle that bends a limb or part. —*Contr. w.* **extensor.** See **antagonistic muscles.**

flicker: *n.* rapid periodic change in a visual perception conditioned by corresponding change in the intensity or other characteristic of the stimulus. ➤The CRITICAL FLICKER (FUSION) FREQUENCY (also called CRITICAL FLICKER, FLICKER FUSION POINT) is the rate of change at which the flicker is extinguished and a smooth **fusion** takes its place. This rate increases with increase either in absolute brightness or in difference between the two phases. This latter fact is utilized in FLICKER PHOTOMETRY in which brightnesses are compared by determining the critical flicker frequency of each when alternated on a reflecting surface having standard illumination.—*v.* **flicker.**

flicker/auditory: a periodically interrupted sound whose intermittency can be perceived by a listener.—*Syn.* AUDITORY FLUTTER, TONAL INTERMITTENCE, SOUND FLUTTER.

flicker/binocular: flicker evoked by a rapidly alternating presentation of stimuli to the right and left eyes, usually in such manner that the light cycle presented to one eye corresponds to the dark cycle of the other.

flicker/chromatic: visual pulsations, caused by differences either in dominant wave length, in purity, or both, between stimuli of equal **luminance** which are alternately applied in quick succession to the same retinal area.

flicker/contrast: see **contrast flicker.**

flicker frequency/critical: see **flicker.**

flicker photometry: see **flicker.**

flight from reality = **reality/retreat from.**

flight of colors: a succession of colors that may occur in the **aftersensation.**

flight of ideas: rapid succession of ideas, or of their overt verbal expression, which manifest only superficial relation to each other; failure to keep to any topic for more than a very brief time.

floating affect: (*psychoan.*) feeling set free from the object normally arousing it and attachable to almost anything.

floor of a test: the level beneath which a test ceases to distinguish between actual differences in the variable being tested. ➤Very low scores often represent chance success rather than actual differences; an easier test—i.e., one with a lower floor—may bring real differences to light.

flowery: *adj.* of a class of smells; = **fragrant.**

fluctuation/function: the nontrend variation of a series of observations or measures that results neither from chance variability in the stimulus circumstances nor from errors of measurement. It includes **oscillation** (2) and/or (3). This fluctuation is often added in with **error of measurement** but may be distinguished from it.

fluctuations: *n. pl.* **1.** (*biol.*) the relatively slight variations found within a species and normally distributed about the species **mean.**—*Distg. fr.* **mutation. 2.** (*stat.*) changes in the value of a statistic (e.g., the mean or the standard deviation) when calculated from successive and supposedly random samples. **3.** = ATTENTION FLUCTUATIONS, intermittent changes in the perceived character of an object when no change is made in the stimuli.—*Distg. fr.* sensory *adaptation.

fluency: *n.* **1.** a property of verbal com-

munications of flowing smoothly and easily; a characteristic of a person who thus speaks or writes. **2.** (*factor anal.*) a factor that characterizes the rapid giving of associative responses. ➤It has **loadings** in such tests as: the giving of as many words as possible in a short time, the number of responses to inkblots, productivity in completing stories. When limited to verbal associations, called **W** (*L. Thurstone*).

fluid: *adj.* **1.** (*psychol.*) of a situation that is unstable, that is changing or is easily open to change, that opposes few constraints to a person's actions. **2.** (*field theory*) permitting free action; characterizing the *organism-in-a-*field when there is easy connection or communication between the regions or tension systems of the field; or characterizing a tension system that is open to change, esp. one that permits relatively free action to the person in the field.—*Ant.* **rigid.**—*n.* **fluidity.**

flush: see **blushing.**

flutter/auditory = **flicker/auditory.**

flutter/sound = **flicker/auditory.**

flux/luminous: see **luminous flux.**

flux/radiant: see **radiant flux.**

flybar: *n.* aeronautical slang for "*fly*ing *by* auditory *r*eference"; hence, a complex of auditory signals or cues that can be substituted for visual cues in perceptual-motor tasks.

FM: (*Ror.*) coding symbol for the response of seeing animal movements in the **inkblot,** or movements that imply animal agency.

F-minus or **F—:** (*Ror.*) scoring code for inaccurate or poor form response.

F-minus-K index: an index to reveal whether the score on **MMPI** is honest or represents an effort to fake a "good" score.

focal: *adj.* of, or placed at, a **focus** (literal or metaphorical).

focal length: the distance required with a given lens to bring parallel rays of light to a **focus.**

focus (fō′kəs) *n., pl.* **focuses, foci** (fō′sī): **1.** the point upon which rays of light, heat, etc., from a given source are made to converge.—*v.* **2.** to adjust an optical system (including that of the eye) so that the **focus** (*n.*) falls upon the proper place, viz., on a photographic film, the retina, etc.

focusing: *n.* **1.** bringing to a **focus. 2.** the attitude or set which leads to careful meticulous effort to discriminate, to discover the exact nature of the stimulating circumstances, whether or not there is any objectively apparent demand for such accuracy. ➤The individual with such an attitude can usually point to good "reasons" for the behavior.—*Cp.* **rigidity, anal character.**

focus of attention: see **attention/focus of.**

foetal = **fetal.**

foetus (fē'təs) = **fetus.**

folie (fō"lē') : *n. Fr.* for **insanity.** ➤It is used with qualifying French words for a number of specific disorders, all of which can be named in English.—See *folie à deux.*

folie à deux (ä dœ) : *n.* (*Fr.*) the occurrence in two close associates of the same mental disorder at the same time. ➤Apparently the Greeks did *not* have a word for this; must we then resort to French? INSANITY IN PAIRS has exactly the same meaning. DOUBLE PSYCHOSIS would serve. (Or perhaps *gruesome twosome?*)

folium (fō'li·əm) *n., pl.* **folia:** a fold in the gray matter of the **cerebellum.**

folklore: *n.* legends, tales, songs, principles of behavior, technological rules, and other fragments of culture surviving into a later stage of society.

folk mind: the **group mind** of a people or nation.

folk psychology: 1. the psychology of nonliterate or less "advanced" peoples. **2.** a detailed study of the behavior of a particular race or people.

folkways: *n. pl.* traditional patterns of behavior, ingrained in persons of a given culture, which influence them without their explicit recognition of that fact. ➤*Distg. fr.* **mores,** which are consciously approved and enforced by the group.

fontanel (fon"tə·nel') : *n.* an area in the cranium of an infant which has not yet ossified; the "soft spot" found in most infants.

foot anesthesia: see **anesthesia/glove.**

foot-candle: *n.* a unit of **illuminance** or illumination equal to that produced by a uniform point source of one standard **candle** on a surface every point of which is one foot away from the source.

footedness: *n.* preferential use of one foot, e.g., in kicking.

foot-lambert: *n.* a unit of **luminance** or photometric brightness equal to the luminance of a perfectly diffusing, perfectly reflecting surface whose **illuminance** is one footcandle everywhere; = 1.076 **millilamberts.**

footrule correlation/Spearman's = **correlation/footrule.**

foramen (fô·rā'mən) *n., pl.* **foramina** (-ram'i·nə) : (*anat.*) a small perforation or opening, esp. in a bone. ➤The FORAMEN MAGNUM is the hole in the occipital bone through which the spinal cord passes into the brain case to become the **medulla.**

force: *n.* **1.** (*phys.*) that which causes motion or produces a change from a state of rest. The unit of force is the **dyne. 2.** (*psychol.*) a condition that produces change in behavior or experience.

forced-choice technique: a rating technique in which the rater is required to choose one item in each pair or triad of choices, even though none or all of the choices seems appropriate. ➤Typically the choices in each triad represent quite different, but not contradictory, characteristics: e.g., "Which best describes Mr. X: humorous, energetic, intelligent?" Each choice has a previously ascertained average "acceptability" or "attractiveness," and each variable to be rated is represented in many triads.

forced-cue situation: a simplification of the learning task in which the learner is compelled by the experimenter or teacher to observe that aspect of the environment to which a certain response is expected: e.g., the CS of classical *conditioning.

forced movements = **tropism.**

force/field of: (*phys.*) the region subject to influence of a given force. By analogy, PSYCHOLOGICAL FIELD OF FORCE means all the influences effective for a given behavior or behavior sequence.

forcing (of development): attempt to increase the rate of development. ➤It is usually implied that more is demanded of a child than he can do.

forebrain: *n.* that portion of the embryonic brain which subdivides into **telencephalon** and **diencephalon**; also, that part of the adult brain (telencephalon and diencephalon) which develops from it. ➤This uppermost portion of the brain—which includes the cerebral hemispheres, olfactory lobes, corpus striatum, and various parts of the thalamus—shows its most special development in the higher vertebrates.—*Syn.* PROSENCEPHALON.

forecasting efficiency/index of or *E*: a measure of the extent to which one can correctly predict one variable by knowing its relationship with another. The formula is

$$E = 100 \left[1 - \sqrt{\frac{N-1}{N-2}(1-r^2)} \right] ;$$

or more simply, $1 - \sqrt{1 - r^2}$.—*Syn.* PREDICTIVE INDEX, COEFFICIENT OF CORRESPONDENCE.

foreconscious = **preconscious.**

fore-exercise: *n.* a preliminary to the main experiment or test, designed to get the subject used to the situation, or to ascertain approximately the strength of the response that is to be measured.

foreign hull: (*topol.*) the facts or events that are not subject to psychological laws but may "surround" and influence the **life space,** e.g., a crash of thunder.

forensic (fô·ren'sik) : *adj.* **1.** argumentative, often, rhetorically argumentative. **2.** pertaining to the courts. ➤FORENSIC MEDICINE is the body of medical knowledge as it relates to legal questions, evidence in court, etc. FORENSIC PSYCHIATRY treats of legal questions in relation to disordered behavior, more particularly the questions of mental responsibility, committability, and the like. FORENSIC PSYCHOLOGY is sometimes unfortunately used for FORENSIC PSYCHIATRY, but should be reserved for the quite different body of knowledge relating to psychology of the law and the courts: e.g., the conditions determining whether certain evidence (offered by quite normal persons) is reliable.

foreperiod: *n.* the initial period in an experience; esp., in a reaction-time experiment, the interval between the *ready* signal and the stimulus.

forepleasure: *n.* (*psychoan.*) the pleasure accompanying increase in tension, esp. in the sex sphere; pleasure from stimulation of an **erogenous *zone.—Cp.* end pleasure.** ➤Note the contrast with the **drive-reduction hypothesis.**

forereference/principle of individuating: hypothesis that a behavior system can function before it is needed by the organism for life processes, e.g., erection in an infant.

foreshortening: *n.* **1.** the shortening of the apparent length of a line in proportion as it parallels the direction in which one is looking (the **line of *regard**), in contrast with a line transverse to that direction. **2.** in drawing, a similar shortening in the representation of lines according to the principles of **perspective.**

foresight or **forethought:** *n.* imagining, or symbolical representation, of events as likely to occur, in order to plan therefor.—*Cp.* **expectation, anticipation.**

forgetting: *n.* the loss or the losing, temporary or permanent, of something earlier learned; losing ability to recall, recognize, or do something.—*Syn.* **obliviscence.**—*Ant.* **reminiscence.**—*adj.* **forgetful,** of a person who forgets easily.—*n.* **forgetfulness,** the personal trait.—*v.* **forget.**

forgetting curve = **retention curve.**— See also **forgetting/rate of.**

forgetting/intentional: see **intentional forgetting.**

forgetting/rate of: the speed with which forgetting occurs, as measured by the **saving, recall,** or **recognition methods.** It is often represented by a CURVE OF FORGETTING or OF RETENTION.

form: *n.* shape or outline; an arrangement or pattern of elements or members, constituting a unitary whole, wherein the elements are in specific relationships with each other. ➤The pattern of the whole is at least relatively independent of the particular elements so that there may be considerable change in the latter without change in the former. E.g., the form of a triangle is independent of the lengths of the lines, but not of the lengths of each line relative

to the others. Similarly, the form of a melody is independent of the pitch at which it is sung. Form is the distinguishing property of a **figure.** It is a central concept in **Gestalt psychology.**—*Syn.* **structure** (*biol.*), **pattern, configuration, gestalt.** —*Ant.* **matter** or **content. 2.** = **test *form.**—See comparable *form. 3.** a class rank of students (chiefly in British public schools); a **standard** or **grade** in school advancement.

formal: *adj.* **1.** pertaining to **form. 2.** pertaining to general principles or rules: e.g., *formal logic,* dealing with the rules that define validity in thinking. **3.** insistent upon correct form; hence, stiff; pedantic. **4.** emphasizing form or rules at the expense of **matter** or **content.**

formal characteristic or **trait:** one that determines how other traits shall be manifested: e.g., "mental energy" determines how vigorously one's dominance, courage, or intelligence shall operate.

formal culture or **formal discipline:** the exercise of some activity, or the study of a subject, not so much for its own sake as because it acquaints one with forms or principles that will be useful in some other activity, or because it in some way (usually unspecified) helps one to learn another subject or skill. ➤Thus, the study of Latin is alleged to acquaint one with the "forms" of good taste in English or other literature better than, or as a useful supplement to, direct study of these literatures. When it is alleged that the study of such preferred subjects "trains the mind" in such forms, the doctrine is so closely allied to **faculty psychology** that even careful writers have confounded them. This, added to the disparaging connotations of **formal,** has tended to obscure the possibility that, with due precautions, training in "forms" (of thinking or of character, as well as of manners) may be fruitful. Whether certain subjects may provide particularly happy materials for such formal training needs special investigation.

formal exercises: 1. drill in abstract principles, rules, and forms. **2.** drill designed to strengthen a **faculty. 3.** drill in which teacher or pupils or both merely go through the forms of practice, without interest or intelligent appreciation of the value of the subject studied.—*Cp.* **formal (4), formal culture.**

formal identity: the relation between two objects of thought or perception of being subject to the same rules, of having the same form (in an extended sense), so that what is true of one in a formal sense is true of the other, despite differences in content or matter. ➤E.g., two sale contracts may be formally identical, though dealing with different properties; the relation of subject and predicate is the same (or nearly so) in English and French.

formalism: *n.* in systematizing a field of knowledge, emphasis upon a highly self-consistent and orderly organization. ➤The **hypothetico-deductive method** (which is a general program, not a mere method) and mathematical **models** for psychology are fully developed formalism. Formalism also tends to express itself in rival systems or schools, each striving for consistency within a framework. The framework is not necessarily a priori and philosophical—it generally attempts to base itself on observed fact. But it is a relatively rigid structure that determines and limits both theorizing and the direction in which facts are being sought. Formalism thus pays for its orderliness by some loss in richness and inclusiveness just as its opposite, eclecticism, gains richness and inclusiveness by loss in orderliness.—See **eclecticism** for discussion of both terms.

form/alternate: see **form/comparable.**

formant: *n.* (*speech*) the auditory factor that makes one vowel different from another.

formation/compromise: see **compromise formation.**

formboard test: any of a variety of **performance** *tests in which loose blocks of varied shapes are to be fitted into depressions in a base. ➤Sometimes each block fits one depression; sometimes several blocks must be fitted together to fill the space: e.g., a circular depression must be filled with a half-circle and two quarter-circle blocks.

form-color response: (*Ror.*) response category when definite meaningful form, made up in essential part of colored elements, is reported.

form/comparable: the generic term for a collection of test items so similar in content and structure to another collection that the two are regarded, not as different tests, but as versions or variant forms of the same test. Test forms are qualified as **comparable** if, as a minimum, they are substantially correlated. ➤To specify in what other respects tests are comparable, many terms have been technically employed, but usage differs greatly. The following usages are here suggested: (*a*) MATCHED FORMS, when the two forms are matched, item for item, in structure and content; (*b*) EQUIVALENT FORMS, when the raw scores of the two forms have the same statistical meaning; (*c*) ALTERNATE FORMS, when the two forms have unequal means and/or **variances**, but have been **standardized** so that their unequal raw scores can be transmuted by means of an equivalence table.

Besides these terms (which are not yet standardized but for which standardization may be hoped) the following have been used as at least partial synonyms: CORRELATED, DUPLICATE, EQUAL, PARALLEL, and SIMILAR FORMS. Almost any meaning that can reasonably be attached to the words seems to occur in technical writing. Let the reader beware!—See also **reliability coefficient (c)** for discussion of another aspect of equivalence of forms.

form/correlated: see **form/comparable.**

form determinant: (*Ror.*) the perceived form or shape that determines a response to the inkblot.—See **determinant/Rorschach.**

form/duplicate: see **form/comparable.**

form/equal: see **form/comparable.**

form/equivalent: see **form/comparable.**

formication: *n.* (fr. *L.* for *ant*) a sensation as of ants or other insects crawling on the skin.—*Distg. fr.* "ants in the pants."

form-level: *n.* (*Ror.*) the accuracy of the subject's percepts as measured by F and Ft responses to the inkblots.

form/matched: see **form/comparable.**

form/parallel: see **form/comparable.**

form psychology = **Gestalt psychology.**

form-quality = *Gestaltqualität.*

form response or F: (*Ror.*) a response that is determined exclusively or predominantly by the form of the **inkblot.**

form/similar: see **form/comparable.**

form/test: an assemblage, for administration at one trial or sitting, of test items designed to reflect a given function or trait. ➤It is not required that the function be unitary nor that the items reflect that function alone. When unqualified, **test** usually means a **test form.**—See **form/comparable.**

fornication: *n.* **1.** voluntary sexual intercourse involving an unmarried woman. **2.** more loosely, any sexual intercourse outside marriage. ➤Meaning **(2)** includes adultery as **(1)** does not.

fornix: *n.* a nerve fiber tract connecting the **hippocampus** with the **mammillary bodies.**

fortuitous: *adj.* **1.** happening by chance. **2.** not caused by the variable under examination.

foster: *adj.* of persons who give or receive sustenance or care as in a family, although not closely related by blood or marriage; or of the home of such a person: a *foster* parent, a *foster* home.—*Distg. fr.* **adoptive.**

foster-child fantasy: a secret belief, not uncommon in childhood, that one's parents are merely foster parents.

founded content: see *Gestaltqualität.*

four-color theory: see **color theories.**

fourfold table: (*stat.*) a table having two

columns and two rows; hence, one of four cells.

Fourier's law (fûr'yāz): (*phys.*) Any complex periodic vibratory movement (sound or light waves) may be represented as a particular sum of a number of simple vibratory movements having the form of sine curves. These sine curves or waves constitute FOURIER'S SERIES.

fovea centralis: a small pit in the **macula lutea**, usually the area of clearest vision.

F-plus or *F*+: (*Ror.*) scoring code for accurate or "good" form response.

fpm = feet per minute.

fps = feet per second.

fractional antedating goal response: see **antedating goal response/fractional.**

fractional anticipatory goal response = **antedating goal response/fractional.**

fragrant: *adj.* of a class of smells typified by the smell of hyacinths and violets.

frame of reference: a system of standards or values, usually merely **implicit**, underlying and to some extent controlling an action, or the expression of any attitude, belief, or idea. ➤A frame of reference is probably to be conceived as a highly generalized attitude that has only an ill-defined object, an object so vague that it seldom comes directly into view. Thus, within a "scientific" frame of reference certain considerations are accepted and others rejected, often with no thought of why. The term is unfortunately constructed, since the frame of reference is conceived as being far more than a *frame.*

frame/reference: (*stat.*) see **reference frame.**

fraternal twins: see **twins/fraternal.**

F **ratio:** (*stat.*) a value used in determining whether the difference between two **variances** is statistically significant or stable. The larger variance σ_1^2 is divided by the smaller, σ_2^2. (Some prefer the ratio $\dfrac{\sigma_1^2 - 1}{\sigma_2^2 - 2}$, esp. when samples are small.) This F is looked up in a table that shows the probability of a ratio of this size for N_1 and N_2 degrees of freedom.

free-answer question: 1. (*testing*) a question to which the respondent must frame his own reply. ➤*Contr. w.* **selective-answer *test,** in which he must choose among alternatives that are already phrased. **2.** in interviewing, an **open-ended question.**

free association or **free association test:** see **association/free.**

freedom/degrees of: see **degrees of freedom.**

freedom of movement: 1. absence of **barriers** in the psychological **field;** the comparative number of kinds and/or directions of action open to the person. **2.** (*J. Rotter*) the number of behaviors of differ-

ent kinds, related to a family of common goals, that the individual expects to be successful in leading toward those goals.

freedom/psychological: 1. absence of external constraint. **2.** experience or feeling that one can make his own decisions; consciousness of freedom. ➤Neither of these is contrary to **determinism. 3.** behavior not determined by previous conditions. ➤*Cp.* **determinism,** with which this meaning is incompatible.

free-floating anxiety or **fear:** see **anxiety/free-floating.**

free nerve ending: the finely branched ending of **afferent** neurons in the skin that are unconnected with any specific sense organ structure.

free-response test: see **test/free-response.**

free will: a philosophical doctrine that attributes causal efficacy in behavior to the volition or decisions of the person. ➤*Cp.* **determinism,** which holds that volition or decisions are themselves determined by prior influences.—*Syn.* **libertarianism.**

frequency: *n.* **1.** the number of cycles per second in a periodic vibration; = WAVE FREQUENCY. **2.** the number of times a given

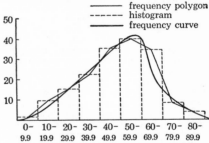

phenomenon occurs; esp., the number of times the several **values** of a **variable** are found. ➤Thus, if the variable be "age at death," the number of persons dying at each age is determined. This yields a FREQUENCY DISTRIBUTION.

When the numbers are systematically set forth, we have a FREQUENCY TABLE; when they are translated into graphic or spatial terms, we have various sorts of FREQUENCY GRAPHS or FREQUENCY DIAGRAMS. The three most common are the FREQUENCY POLYGON, the HISTOGRAM, and the FREQUENCY CURVE.

The FREQUENCY POLYGON is constructed by plotting each frequency above the midpoint of its **class interval** (laid out on the base line) and connecting the points so plotted by a straight line. The HISTOGRAM consists of a series of contiguous rectangles, of width proportional to the width of the class interval, and in height proportional to the frequencies in the several classes. *Distg. fr.* **frequency polygon/rectangular.**

When the blocks are separated on their base line we have a BAR DIAGRAM. The stepwise change from block to block makes the figure suitable for representing the actual measurements, which are always sensibly **discontinuous.**

If, however, it is desired to treat the variation as **continuous,** a frequency curve may be drawn by connecting the midpoints of such blocks with a continuous line. The area under the frequency curve (or of the sum of the blocks of the histogram) is called a FREQUENCY SURFACE. The **normal** *frequency curve is a regular bell-shaped curve (also called GAUSS' CURVE or a SINE-CURVE DISTRIBUTION).

Symbols: *N* for the number in a total group, *f* for the number in any division (such as a **class**) of the total.

frequency/cumulative: any entry (in a column) formed by adding the simple frequencies, and recording the total each time a new **class interval** is included.

frequency curve: see **frequency (2).**

frequency curve/cumulative: see **cumulative frequency curve.**

frequency-curve equation/normal:

$$Y = \frac{N}{\sigma\sqrt{2\pi}}e^{\frac{-x^2}{2\sigma^2}}$$

where *N* = number of measurements, *σ* = standard deviation of the distribution, *e* = the base of Naperian logarithms, and *x* = a deviation $(X - M)$.

frequency curve/normal: a curve representing the **frequency** with which the values of a variable are obtained or observed when the number is infinite and the variation is subject to **chance** or the laws of **probability.** ➤The curve is bell-shaped —that is, the highest frequency is in the middle, with a gradual and symmetrical

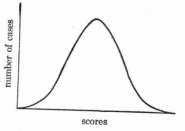

scores

tapering toward the extremes. Algebraically it is defined by the **frequency-curve equation.** ❡A close approximation to this curve is obtained with many distributions not determined by chance in the ordinary sense; it is the characteristic (but not invariable)

form for the distribution of **individual** *differences, of **variable error** (by definition), and of the deviations from a measure of **central tendency** when a very large number of measurements of the same thing is taken.—*Syn.* BELL-SHAPED CURVE, GAUSS' CURVE, CURVE OF ERROR, PROBABILITY CURVE, NORMAL CURVE, THEORETICAL FREQUENCY CURVE, and (*student slang*) THE CURVE.

frequency diagram: see **frequency (2).**

frequency distribution: see **frequency (2).**

frequency/fixation: see **fixation frequency.**

frequency graph: see **frequency (2).**

frequency/law of: the principle which asserts that the rate at which an **act** is acquired (or eliminated) is a function of the frequency with which it is (or is not) exercised. ➤It is now generally recognized that the principle is not acceptable without a number of qualifications of the meaning of exercise, etc.—*Cp.* **use/law of.**

frequency/marginal: see **marginal frequency.**

frequency polygon: see **frequency (2).**— *Distg. fr.* **frequency polygon/rectangular.**

frequency polygon/rectangular: a figure constructed by dropping a vertical from the ordinate representing the frequency above the midpoint of each class interval and connecting these verticals by horizontal lines.

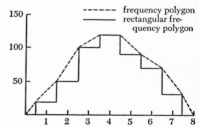

➤The result is a figure resembling the **histogram,** and it is frequently so called, but the base of each block extends from midpoint to midpoint of the class intervals, whereas in the histogram proper the base of the rectangles coincides with the class interval. The very fact that the histogram and the rectangular frequency polygon look alike but depict different quantities makes distinction in name necessary.

frequency surface: see **frequency (2).**

frequency table: see **frequency (2).**

frequency theories of hearing: see **hearing theories.**

frequency/wave: see **wave frequency.**

Freudianism (froid'i·ən·iz·əm): *n.* **1.** the doctrine set forth by Sigmund Freud and his close associates. ➤The term is often used to distinguish the founder's formulations from modifications and offshoots, but it is not clear where the line of allowable deviation is to be drawn. **Psychoanalysis,** as used generally (and in this dictionary), is a considerably broader term.—*Syn.* FREUDISM. —*adj.* **Freudian.**

friction: *n.* a relation between two or more persons characterized by diverse or conflicting purposes, mutual irritation, and constant (though generally weak) antagonism.

friendship: *n.* a relation between two persons that is characterized by mutual attraction and (generally) non**erotic** affection.

fright: *n.* acute fear with visible motor manifestations.

frigidity: *n.* **1.** abnormal lack of sexual feeling. **2.** the psychogenic blocking of normal manifestation of sexual desire. ➤Most often used with reference to women.—*adj.* **frigid.**

fringe of consciousness: that which is unattended to; or mental content that lies outside the **focus of *attention** (which see).—*Syn.* **margin of *attention.**

fringer: *n.* a person who, without being clearly rejected, is not genuinely accepted in a social group.

Froehlich's syndrome (Frœ'liHs sin'drə·-mē): a group of symptoms associated with insufficient pituitary activity: delay in skeletal development, obesity, infantilism, or childishness of body appearance.—*Syn.* ADIPOSOGENITAL DYSTROPHY, ADIPOSOGENITAL SYNDROME.

frontal: *adj.* **1.** (*anat.*) pertaining to the **anterior** aspect of a body or organ; or to a plane parallel to the longitudinal axis of the body (dividing it into front and back halves) at right angles to the **sagittal** axis. **2.** pertaining to the forehead.

frontal lobe: roughly, the upper or forward half of the cerebral hemisphere.

fruity: *adj.* of a class of smells, typified by that of fruits.

frustration: *n.* **1.** the blocking of, or interference with, an ongoing goal-directed activity. **2.** the **motivational** and/or **affective** state resulting from being blocked, thwarted, disappointed, or defeated.

frustration-aggression hypothesis: postulate that frustration *always* leads to aggression, sometimes of a concealed nature, and that aggression *always* is an indicator of some sort of frustration. ➤The postulate as stated is in effect a *theoretical* definition of **aggression,** not an empirical generalization.

frustration tolerance: the ability to accept frustrating circumstances without disruption and disordering of one's behavior.

F scale: (*Adorno* et al.) a questionary designed to measure attitudes toward democracy or fascism.

F score: a score designed to tell whether the testee has complied understandingly with the directions for the **MMPI.**

F test or **F:** a statistic used in estimating the chance probability of equaling or exceeding a given difference between the **variances** of two samples. ➤Dealing as it does with variance differences, *F* is an estimate of the probability of a stable difference between two samples taken as a whole. I.e., it involves both differences between means and differences between **standard *deviations.** In contrast, *t* is an estimate of the probability of a difference between two **representative** measures, not between two samples.

ft. L.: *abbr.* for **foot-lambert.**

fugue (fūg): *n.* (*L.* for *flight*) **1.** a long period in which a patient has almost complete **amnesia** for his past, although habits and skills are usually little affected. He usually leaves home and starts a new life, with sharply different modes of conduct. Upon recovery, earlier events are remembered but those of the period of fugue are forgotten. **2.** = epileptic **absence** (*prefd.* for this meaning).

Fullerton-Cattell law: a substitution for Weber's law: The error of observation tends to increase as the square root of the magnitude, the increase being subject to variation whose amount and cause must be determined for each special case. The formula is $\Delta R = k\sqrt{R}$.

"full organism" point of view: a point of view that emphasizes the differentiating and determining role of the organism in behavior events, in contrast with the point of view that tends to regard the organism as more nearly a passive registrant of external energy impacts. ➤The distinction is one of emphasis only.

Full-Range Picture Vocabulary Test: a test in which the testee indicates by word or gesture which of four pictures best illustrates the meaning of a given word. It is scaled for testing vocabulary from infancy to adulthood and is usable with persons having speech handicaps.—*Syn.* AMMON'S F-R TEST.

fumble-and-success = **learning/trial-and-error.**

function: *n.* **1.** (*math.*) a quantity that varies with the variation of another quantity, not necessarily proportionally. ➤The expression $y = f(x)$—sometimes also written $\phi(x)$—is read: *y is a function of x.* The **dependent *variable** is *y*; the **independent *variable** is *x*. **2.** that which is dependent upon something else. ➤This is the mathematical meaning without its quantification: prejudice is a *function* of ignorance. **3.** an ongoing process; activity rather than inactivity. ➤This idea is particularly evident in **functioning:** a *functioning* unit. **4.** the activity proper to or distinctive of a structure, or of an office or role: the *function* of the retina, the *function* of a leader. **5.** a useful activity; or a structure useful because of its activity: the *function* of maintaining balance. **6.** a distinctive process or activity; or a classificatory heading for activities: the principal psychological *functions*; thinking is composed of several *functions*. **7.** (*C. Jung*) any momentary manifestation of the **libido** or of the **psyche.** ➤This is a specialization of meanings (**4**) and (**6**).

The several meanings given above often combine in a given usage. Despite the range of ideas potentially referred to, **function** is usually clear in context.—*adj.* **functional.** —*v.* **function.**

functional: *adj.* pertaining to **function,** all meanings, but most commonly to (**3**) and (**5**).

functional cycle: (*Ger. Funktionskeis*) the sequence of behaviors which subserve a given biological function, whether or not the linkage of stimulus to response is innate.

functional defect: a disability due to lack of skill or some other psychological cause. —See **functional disorder.**

functional disorder: 1. a condition in which one or more of the normal activities of the organism cannot be properly performed, though there is no known pathological change in organic structure which can be related to the disorder. ➤Functional in this sense is merely an admission of present ignorance. **2.** a condition in which impaired performance is definitely known not to be correlated with pathological structural change in the organs or tissue *directly* involved, these structures being intact and their malfunction resulting from some pathological condition elsewhere in the organism.

➤The almost universally accepted postulate that all functioning is correlated with structure makes it difficult to interpret the common contrast between **functional** and **organic disorder.** The latter cannot mean *any* disorder that is correlated with structural change, for there are no disorders (i.e., functions) not so correlated. The above definitions of functional imply also permissible meanings of organic as an opposite: an organic disorder means either that the structural alteration as a cause is definitely known (a parallel to **1** above) or, more specifically, that a structural alteration has been found in the organ that directly controls the disordered function (a parallel to **2** above).

Paresis is a clear case of organic disorder in both senses: there is known structural impairment of the organ (the brain) that controls the disordered functions. **Hysteria,** by contrast, is functional in the first sense; we do not yet know what organic impairment is responsible. If and when such impairment is found, hysteria will be reclassified.

Glove *anesthesia illustrates the second meaning of functional. It is proved that this disorder is *not* due to structural impairment of the nerves and sense organs directly serving the affected part. When we find the structural impairment responsible, it will certainly be elsewhere in the body and glove anesthesia will remain a functional disorder in sense (**2**).

Contrast between functional and organic disorder tends to be confused by contrast between **organic** and **psychogenic.** A psychogenic disorder is one attributed to events in the person's psychological history. There is no known change in structure; hence, the psychogenic is functional rather than organic.

But **psychogenic** refers also to another aspect of the facts. That there are delusions in paresis is clearly due to structural brain impairment, but the particular content of the delusions is just as clearly referable to events in the psychological history. The fact of a *delusional state* would thus be called organic, the *delusional content,* psychogenic and functional.

The distinctions here made are by no means universally observed but they seem to represent that toward which careful usage tends. Complex as they may seem, they are doubtless an absurd oversimplification of the facts they represent.—*Cp.* also **constitutional, psychosomatic.**

functional experiment: an experimental design that seeks control by administering the **experimental variable** in many degrees, levels, or amounts, measuring the changes in the **dependent *variable** that are a function of these quantitative changes in the experimental variable. ➤It contrasts with what is called (somewhat unfortunately) the CRUCIAL EXPERIMENT, in which an experimental group is given the experimental variable and a control group is not.

functional fixedness: the degree to which an object cannot be perceived as functioning in, or belonging to, a context different from that in which it has just been perceived or employed: e.g., a stick just used as a ruler may not seem available for use as a weapon. ➤**Fixedness** is enough to convey this idea.

functionalism: *n.* **1.** = **functional psychology. 2.** the point of view that perception is an **instrumental** activity, closely related to, and dependent upon, other functions, esp. **need** or **affect.**

functionalism/probabilistic: (*E. Brunswik*) the point of view that stresses the importance of behavior defined as **distal** effects or **achievement.** It seeks functional relationships stated in terms of probability, rather than strict laws.

functionalistic: *adj.* pertaining to a functional point of view in psychology; emphasizing function rather than structure.

functional principle of neural organization: hypothesis that two systems of fibers closely related in function pursue spatially related pathways to the brain. ➤Thus, many fibers serving pain receptors in very different tissues or regions are grouped together in the spinal cord.—*Contr. w.* **topographical principle.**

functional psychology: a school which defines mental phenomena as processes or activities rather than as mental content, and which emphasizes the usefulness of these activities or **functions (5).** ➤In the *Funktion* psychology of Germany, the notion of utility is not prominent; in the American group it is central. Both **act psychology** and **dynamic psychology** are related.—*Syn.* FUNCTIONALISM. — See **psychology/divisions and schools of,** III.

functional psychosis: a **psychogenic** psychosis.—See **functional disorder.**

functional relation: a relation between variables such that a change in one produces a change in one or more of the others. —*Syn.* **causal** relation, **dynamic** relation.

functional type = function type.

functional unity: 1. the working together of a number of parts in executing a single action or purpose: e.g., the several parts of the heart working together to pump the blood. **2.** a relationship between various behaviors such that they must be considered as the activity of a single "organ" or **trait.** ➤Factor analysis is a means to *discovering* such trait or unity; *proof* lies in the fact that varied experimental conditions affect or fail to affect the behaviors in the same way.

function/behavior: see **mental function.**

function-engram: *n.* (*C. Jung*) the inherited structure **(archetype)** which invests a symbol with its real significance.

function fluctuation: see **fluctuation/ function.**

function/motor: see **motor functions.**

function/periodic: a relationship between two variables such that, at the regular recurrence of the one variable, the set of values for the other recurs: e.g., the tonal octave which recurs with the doubling of the sound-wave frequency.

function pleasure: (*K. Bühler*) the desire to exercise one's capacities and abilities and to enjoy doing so. ➤The original German, FUNKTIONSLUST (fŭnk'si·ōns·lŭst), is often used without translation.

function psychology: a term proposed for that branch of psychology which attempts to derive the general laws according to which psychological processes occur. It is coordinate with **differential psychology;** between them, these two include all of psychology.—*Distg. fr.* **functional psychology.**

function types: (*C. Jung*) those types which are distinguishable according to the way the person feels, thinks, senses, or intuits. ➤The function types are divided into the RATIONAL CLASS, which includes the **feeling type** and the **thinking** *type, and the IRRATIONAL CLASS, which includes the **intuitive type** and the **sensation type.**—*Cp.* with the **attitude types** of **introversion** or **extraversion,** which may be combined with the function types (e.g., an INTROVERTED THINKING TYPE) for a total of eight combinations.

fundament: *n.* **1.** one of the end items or terms between which a relation exists. E.g., two objects compared in size are **fundaments** for the relation "larger than." **2.** = **anlage. 3.** portion of the body on which one rests; the buttocks.

fundamental color = color fundamental.

fundamental response processes: (*color*) the several hypothetical physiological processes, sensitivities, or excitations which are believed to underlie the **fundamental** *colors.**

fundamentals/psychological: those parts of psychology which were traditional when an author began his professional study; anything that a given author holds to be of major importance.

fundamental (tone): the lowest partial of a compound tone, and the one by whose pitch the tone is identified.—See **partial tone.**

funded content = *Gestaltqualität.*

furor epileptica: a maniacal condition that follows *grand mal* or takes the place of the epileptic convulsion.—See **epilepsy.**

fusion: *n.* **1.** union of parts into a whole wherein the parts can only with difficulty, or not at all, be discriminated; or in which the whole functions as a unit. ➤This is the general meaning within which various authors give a special meaning.—*Cp.* **colligation, pattern, constellation. 2.** (*psychoan.*) the balanced union of the death and life instincts that characterizes normal persons.—*Ant.* **defusion,** the loss of such union.

fusion/binaural: the combination into a unitary impression of the sounds presented to the two ears.

fusion/binocular: the combination of two images, falling upon the two retinas, into a single visual impression. The images may be alike, or may differ slightly in form and color.—*Cp.* **disparity, stereoscopic vision.**

fusion frequency: see **flicker.**

fusion/group: an organized or unorganized merging of separate groups into a single group.—*Contr. w.* **group *fission.**

fusion/instinctual = **fusion** (2).

fusion/tonal: the blending of two or more tones; the degree to which a tonal combination is unified, smooth, and pleasing.

FV: (*Ror.*) see **vista response.**

FY: (*Ror.*) scoring code for form (*F*) as determined by flat gray (*Y*).

G

G: 1. (not *ital.*) = gravity. **2.** (*stat.*) a gain, or positive difference, in rank of an individual on the second of two tests. **3.** (*C. Hull*) **goal** or **goal object;** a need **reduction** or a stimulus that has been closely associated with need reduction; **primary *reinforcement;** also a primary goal reaction. **4.** (*Ror.*) response that includes the whole inkblot. (*Ger. Ganz* = whole.) **5.** (not *ital.;* sometimes written *g*) = (*factor anal.*) **general *factor.**

g: 1. (not *ital.*) = gram. **2.** = **mean** difference. **3.** = (*factor anal.*) **general *factor** (G *prefd.*). **4.** (*C. Hull*) a fractional part of a goal reaction that may be split off and carried forward in a behavior sequence as a **fractional *antedating goal reaction.**

gain: *n.* an increase in any variable; esp., the increment for an individual or group as a result of experimental treatment. →Sometimes used for both increment and decrement, the direction of change being indicated as POSITIVE GAIN and NEGATIVE GAIN.

gain from illness = **advantage by illness.**

gain/morbid: an advantage obtained by neurotic or other misbehavior, e.g., attention-getting.—See **advantage by illness.**

gait: *n.* manner of walking, running, or moving on foot.

Galilean method: (*field theory*) the way of thinking that explains in terms, not of the class to which an object belongs, but of the field of forces of which it is a part. →This is said to contrast with **Aristotelian method** and to have made itself effective first with Galileo's work. While disparaging dichotomies, the "Galileans" make a sharp dichotomy between **field theory** and **class theory.**—*Cp.* **Aristotelian classification.**—See **psychology/divisions and schools of,** VIII.

Galton bar: an instrument for determining the threshold for visual linear distance by means of the **method of *reproduction** or of **just noticeable differences.**

Galton's law: the principle that, on the average, a person inherits ¼ of his characters from each parent, ⅟₁₆ from each grandparent, etc. →While roughly true, this law has been largely superseded by **Mendelian ratio.**

Galton's questionary: an inquiry about mental **imagery.** Sent out in 1883, it is said to have been the first use of a questionary for psychological investigation.

Galton whistle: an instrument emitting very high tones. →Formerly used in determing the upper limit of hearing, it is now known to be not very accurate.

galvanic current: a steady direct current such as is obtainable from a battery.

galvanic (skin) response or **GSR** = **electrodermal response.**

galvanometer (gal″və·nom′ə·tər): *n.* an instrument for measuring the strength of an electric current.

galvanotropism: *n.* a simple orienting movement toward, or away from, electric stimulation.

game: *n.* organized play having definite rules and different roles for participants, and usually competitive.

gamete (gam′ēt; gə·mēt′): *n.* a cell of either sex that can combine with another to form a new organism.—*adj.* **gametic.**

game theory: a mathematical theory that deals with action in a conflict situation as if it were a game in which each player seeks to maximize his opponents' losses. The player is assumed to be a wholly rational being, utilizing calculations of risk.

GAMIN: *n.* (*Guilford-Martin*) a personality inventory intended to measure the traits of general activity (G), ascendance-submission (A), masculinity-femininity (M), inferiority feeling (I), nervousness (N).

gamma or **γ:** (*psychophys.*) the distance of any stimulus from the threshold, measured in terms of *h* (2).

gamma movement: see **motion/apparent.**

gam(o)-, -gamous, -gamy: combining forms meaning *marriage* or *sexual union.*

gang: *n.* a group, closely bound together by a self-imposed discipline, in pursuit of a common interest. →The concept of a GANG AGE is no longer accepted, since gangs occur from age 10 or 11 on into adult life. (*Cp. work gang.*) Nor is the gang necessarily antisocial, although the term often has this connotation.

ganglia/basal: see **basal ganglia.**

ganglion (gang′gli·ən) *n., pl.* **ganglia, ganglions: 1.** a group of nerve cells or cell bodies lying outside the brain and cord, and forming a sort of nerve center. **2.** a mass of gray matter in brain or spinal cord. ➤An unfortunate usage, but still current in the expression **basal ganglion.**—*adj.* **gangliar, ganglionic.**

gap/tonal: see **tonal gap.**

gargalesthesis (gär″gəl·es·thē′sis): *n.* tickle sensation.

gastric: *adj.* pertaining to the stomach.

gastro-: combining form meaning *stomach* or *belly.*

gastrocolic reflex: a wavelike constriction of the colon induced by introduction of food into the stomach.

GATB: General Aptitude Test Battery (of U.S. Employment Service).

Gaussian or **Gauss' curve** (gou′si·ən) = **frequency curve/normal.**

GED = **General Educational Development Tests.**

Gegenstandstheorie (gā′gən·shtänts·tā·ô′-rē′): *n.* (*Ger.*) "theory of objects"; a discipline, founded by Meinong, for the study of **objects,** conceived as distinct from physical stimuli, with properties dependent upon the general attributes of mental activity.—*Cp.* **phenomenology.**

Geisteswissenschaftliche   Psychologie: (*Ger., cultural science psychology*) the doctrine that psychology is the basic social science; that its goal and methods are fundamentally different from those of the natural sciences. ➤Cultural science psychology is **idiographic** rather than **nomothetic,** aims at understanding (*Verstehen*) rather than causal description, and holds that the individual experience is embedded in an articulated whole (*Strukturzusammenhang*) which is artistically or intuitively apprehended. "Natural science explains, culture science understands." *Verstehende Psychologie* (understanding psychology) and **structure psychology** (*distg. fr.* **structural psychology 1,** which is almost opposite) are varieties of the general school.—See **psychology/divisions and schools of, II.**

gender: *n.* **1.** a grammatical classification of nouns. **2.** a proposed synonym for **sex** wherever the sheer difference in physical structure between male and female is meant. ➤The contention is that **sex** is too heavily loaded with various associations to be used quite objectively. The concession to Victorianism seems as unnecessary as pantaloons on piano legs. Words have gender, persons have sex.—See **sex** (*adj.*) for discussion of terms.

gene: *n.* an inferred submicroscopic structure in the **chromosomes** which is the physical unit of heredity.—*adj.* **genic.**

gene/major: a single gene that produces a large effect on the variability of a trait.—*Cp.* **polygene.**

gene pair: in sexual reproduction, the combination of two genes (one from each parent) that determines a specific hereditary trait. If both determine the trait in the same way, the pair is **homozygous;** if the two genes tend to different effects, the pair is **heterozygous.**

genera: *pl.* of **genus.**

general: *adj.* applying to a class, or to all or nearly all of a group of items.—*Distg. fr.* **universal,** which applies to all without exception.

general ability: a loose expression for ability to cope with a wide range of problems; = **intelligence.**—*Contr. w.* special ability (see **ability**).

general ability test = general **intelligence** test.

general aptitude: see **aptitude.**

general attitude type = **attitude type.**

general concept: see **concept.**

General Educational Development Tests or **GED:** a group of tests in various scholastic subjects, designed to predict scholastic success.

general factor: see **factor/general.**

general intelligence = **intelligence.**

generality: *n.* a broad or general statement, lacking in particulars.—*Distg. fr.* **generalization.**

generality/attitude: the breadth or variety of situations or objects toward which, for a given individual, a particular attitude is taken: an attitude toward food is of higher generality than an attitude toward cheese.

generality/interorgan: see **interorgan generality.**

generalization: *n.* **1.** process whereby one reaches a judgment applicable to a whole class, often on the basis of experience with a limited number of the class; or the judgment itself. ➤The judgment may be merely implicit. The generalization often deals with abstract qualities: *crows are black* (ABSTRACT GENERALIZATION); or it may simply summarize observation: *these are all crows* (CONCRETE GENERALIZATION). The process is not necessarily a jump to a final conclusion: there is often a sort of preliminary generalization which is extended (or restricted) as further facts are perceived, and the generalization, as it expands, may cause distorted perception if the external facts are not too explicit and compelling. E.g., the generalization that crows are black may prevent perceiving the Australian white crow as a crow.—See **abstraction** and **concept. 2.** application of a general concept or idea to a relatively new object or situation. ➤The implication that the new situation belongs to a class need not be explicitly recognized.—See **transfer by generalization, stimulus *generaliza-**

tion, response *generalization. 3. an improper synonym for generality.

generalization/associative: either response *generalization or stimulus *generalization, usually the latter.

generalization/gradient of: see generalization/response and generalization/stimulus for the two forms of the gradient.

generalization/mediated: a stimulus *generalization to a stimulus that had not been used in the course of conditioning and is not similar physically to the conditioned stimulus. →E.g., a person conditioned to make a certain response to the word *ill* may make the response to the word *sick.—Syn.* semantic *conditioning (*prefd.*).

generalization/response: the principle that, after an animal learns to emit a certain response to a given stimulus, that stimulus becomes effective in eliciting "similar" responses. The greater the similarity of responses, the more frequently will the stimulus elicit the response: this is the GRADIENT OF RESPONSE GENERALIZATION.— See discussion under generalization/stimulus.

generalization/stimulus: the fact that after an animal learns to make a certain response to a certain stimulus, certain other previously ineffective stimuli will also elicit the conditioned response. →If the stimuli are perceptually "similar" it is said to be PRIMARY STIMULUS GENERALIZATION. The greater the similarity of the related stimulus to the conditioned stimulus, the more frequently it will elicit the response; this is the GRADIENT OF STIMULUS GENERALIZATION.—*Cp.* gradient. ¶MEDIATE STIMULUS GENERALIZATION refers to the case of stimuli, not perceptually similar, that participate in generalization because of the equivalence of the responses they evoke.— *Cp.* also semantic *conditioning, generalization/response.

Since neither stimulus nor response is ever exactly repeated, an element of generalization is involved in all learning. We call it by that name when the similarity is very great. When the similarity is less, we speak of equivalence (of stimuli or of responses). When it is still less we speak of transfer. The three terms form a continuum with no precise line between them. (But see transfer, which has other meanings.)—*Contr. w.* discrimination.

generalization/transfer by: see transfer by generalization.

generalization/verbal: 1. a statement in words of a general judgment. 2. in conditioning experiments, giving a conditioned response to words that are in some way related to the word which is the CS. If the

relationship is that the words have the same meaning, it is SEMANTIC CONDITIONED GENERALIZATION.

generalized: *adj.* 1. of a judgment that applies to all or most of a group of phenomena; of a verbal expression that can be used for all or most of a class. 2. of an object or sample or type instance that can stand for all or most of a class: it must have the qualities common to, and must lack the features that differentiate, the several examples or varieties.—*Cp.* schematic.

generalized curve: a graphic representation of growth or of learning as a function of time, other factors being kept constant by either experimental or statistical control. →It is a smoothed curve, adjusted to fit the actual observations.—Syn. GROWTH CURVE, LEARNING CURVE.

generalized-goal tension: state wherein the animal is oriented toward a broadly defined goal but not toward particulars: e.g., toward food, but not toward a particular kind of food.

generalized inhibitory potential or sI_R: (C. Hull) conditioned inhibition as a result of stimulus *generalization.

generalized other: see other/generalized.

generalized trait: see trait/generalized.

general paralysis = paresis.

general psychology: 1. the branch of psychology that studies what is true of individuals in general, in contrast with differential psychology, which studies what is true of particular individuals or special classes. 2. the synthesis or generalization of the facts and principles common to all branches of psychology, including general methodology. →Much of differential psychology is general in this sense, while much of general psychology (1) is too specialized to be included here. 3. those aspects of psychology which a given author believes to be of fundamental importance.—*Cp.* fundamentals/psychological.

generation: *n.* 1. the procreation or production of a new individual. 2. all the offspring of a pair of parents. 3. a single stage or rank in descent: a grandfather, his daughter, and his grandson make up three *generations*; hence, all those persons in a given population at the same stage: the older (or younger) *generation.* 4. the average time between the stages in descent—in man, conventionally about thirty-three years.

generations/filial: see filial generations.

generic (jə·nerʹik): *adj.* 1. pertaining to a genus. 2. having broad application; applying to all instances in a class or to all the subgroups in a class.

genesis: *n.* the origin of anything.—*adj* genetic.

genetic (jə·net′ik): *adj.* **1.** pertaining to the origin, history, and development of an organism or, by extension, of anything likened to an organism, e.g., a social institution. ➤It may mean ONTOGENETIC, pertaining to the development of an individual or one of its parts or organs; or it may mean **phylogenetic,** pertaining to the evolutionary origin of a race or species.—*Cp.* **genetic psychology. 2.** pertaining to the **genes.**—*Syn.* **genic** (*prefd.*). **3.** pertaining to **genetics.**

-genetic: a combining form meaning **genetic,** used esp. to form adjectives from nouns ending in *-genesis.*

genetic continuity theory: point of view that every stage of psychological development is an outgrowth of previous stages.—*Contr. w.* **preformism.**

genetic drift: a change from generation to generation in the frequency of certain **genes,** resulting from chance determination of exactly which genes are transferred to succeeding generations.—*Distg. fr.* changes due to **selection (2).**—*Syn.* GENIC DRIFT (*prefd.*).

genetic explanation: explanation in terms of how a phenomenon originated.—See **explanation (2).**

geneticism: *n.* the doctrine or attitude that phenomena that are inborn (e.g., **instincts** and **primary *drives**) or that occur very early in life (e.g., infantile **conflicts** and **fixations**) have a peculiar importance. ➤That the early event or activity is important, since it does (or at least may) influence what follows, is obvious. Usually however, it is implied that the early phenomena are peculiarly powerful, are peculiarly difficult to eradicate, or have some special quality. If emphasis is upon the importance of what is inherited, **hereditarianism** is a more explicit term; if emphasis is upon the primary role of early events in development, ONTOGENETICISM is more explicit.

genetic method: 1. attempting to understand a phenomenon by tracing its origin and development.—*Syn.* **historical method. 2.** tracing the influence of the **genes** in determining a structure or function. ➤Sometimes restricted to experimental breeding.

genetic psychology: 1. study of psychological phenomena (however conceived) in terms of their origin and development, whether in the individual (ONTOGENETIC) or in the species (PHYLOGENETIC). **2.** = **comparative psychology** conceived as concerned with the evolutionary origin of certain functions. ➤This meaning is obsolescent. If a special term is needed, EVOLUTIONARY PSYCHOLOGY is suggested.

genetics: *n.* the science of **heredity.** ➤PSYCHOLOGICAL GENETICS is concerned with the laws of inheritance of psychological phenomena, and with the influence of heredity on the occurrence and development of psychological functions.

genetic sequence: the order in which structures or functions appear in a developing organism, so far as this is determined by the **genes.**—*Syn.* GROWTH SEQUENCE.

genetic viewpoint: one that stresses development.

-genic (-jen′ik): **1.** combining form meaning *pertaining to* or *related to genes,* hence, to *heredity:* e.g., **eugenic. 2.** a combining form meaning *pertaining to origins,* particularly to *agent origin:* **pathogenic,** causing disease.

genic balance: the theory that the hereditary factor of any characteristic is not a single **gene,** but that gene interacting with all the other genes.

geniculate bodies (jə·nik′ū·lət): four oval-shaped masses on the underside of the **thalamus.**

genidentic: *adj.* having precisely the same origin or genesis; having the same **genes.**

genital: *adj.* pertaining to the organs of reproduction.

genital anomaly: see **sex anomaly.**

genital character: (*psychoan.*) the adult synthesis of psychosexual impulses, characterized by attainment of the **genital level.**

genitalize: *v.* (*psychoan.*) to treat an object as a symbol of the genitals.

genital level or **phase:** (*psychoan.*) the culminating phase of development in respect to sex in which the person has a genuinely affectionate relationship for the sex partner. ➤It does not mean, as the term might be interpreted, a phase with strong emphasis upon the genitals (i.e., **phallic stage**), nor a phase in which the interest lies primarily in coitus (i.e., **genital primacy**), though these distinctions are often not observed.

genital primacy: (*psychoan.*) state wherein the tendency toward **coition** predominates over such other psychosexual tendencies as **narcissism, sadism,** or **masturbation.** ➤Preferred to a term such as *sexual normality,* with its implications that all other types of sexual activity are pathological.—*Cp.* **genital level.**

genital-psychical development: psychosexual development measured, not by physiological potency, but by ability to love in an adult manner.

genitals (jen′ə·təlz): *n. pl.* the organs of reproduction, esp. the external organs.—*Syn.* GENITALIA (unnecessary).—*adj.* **genital.**

genital sensations: the specific sensations from the genital organs.—*Cp.* SEXUAL SENSATIONS, applied to the distinctive sensations of the two sexes and sometimes including those from other **erogenous** *zones.

genital zones: the external genitals and closely adjacent areas which give rise to **genital sensations.** ➤A narrower term than **erogenous** *zones.

genius: *n.* ability of the very highest order, esp. creative or inventive ability; a person exhibiting such ability. ➤*Cp.* **distinction, eminence, illustriousness.** The definition of genius as a person of IQ 140 or more is in disfavor.

gen(o)- (jen'ō-): a combining form meaning *race, kind, sex.*

genomotive: see **phenomotive.**

genotype (jen'ō·tīp): *n.* **1.** (*biol.*) the qualities or traits, shared by members of a biologically defined group, which form the basis for its classification; or a hypothetical animal or plant embodying those traits; a type organism. **2.** (*genet.*) the sum of all the traits that an individual is capable of **transmitting** biologically; or, a single such trait. ➤Sometimes the term is restricted to such transmissible traits as the individual does not himself manifest, whether suppressed by **dominance** or by environmental pressure. Thus, a **heterozygous** brown-eyed person is said to have the **genotype** for blue eyes, a rickety bandy-legged person to have the genotype for straight legs. If limited strictly to the context of **transmission,** the usage is unambiguous. But an expression such as gene pattern seems preferable, since genotype has other meanings. **3.** (*genet.* and *developmental psych.*) the sum total of those hereditary factors which have a causative effect on development. ➤In all discussions of **heredity,** terms tend to a subtle shift in meaning (not always explicit) when one turns from the problem of transmission to that of **development.** So with genotype. In (2) it refers to **traits;** in (3) it refers not to the traits themselves but to one kind of causal influence or factor that helps to form the traits. **4.** (*K. Lewin*) a phenomenon described in terms of its causes; the sum of the causes of a phenomenon: motives are *genotypical.* ➤This meaning omits entirely the reference to **heredity.** (But hereditary causes, so far as accepted, are *included* as **genotypical.**) Bandy legs exemplify the opposite of **genotype (2),** and an amputation causing one-leggedness exemplifies **genotype (3);** but, in meaning (4), either might be part of the genotype (i.e., of the cause) of an inferiority feeling.

The term PHENOTYPE contrasts with each of these meanings. In contrast with (1), it means traits appearing in a *group* as a result of a particular environment: e.g., the tanned complexion of outdoor workers. In contrast with (2), it means the actually ob-

servable trait found in an individual or group, regardless of the genetic origin. Thus, brown eyes as actually found are PHENO-TYPICAL, though clearly transmissible and hence also genotypical in sense (2). But bandy legs due to rickets are phenotypical and not genotypical. In contrast with **genotype (3),** phenotype means the sum of causative environmental factors. This is an uncomfortable meaning, since the phenotype in this sense is an abstraction, whereas in all the other meanings it is the actual. In contrast with **genotype (4),** phenotype means the actual, whatever its cause, and in contrast with what is causative.

The unhappy development of several confusingly related meanings for these two terms shows the folly of hoping to keep meanings clear by inventing a **neologism.** If it becomes current, it rapidly takes on diverse meanings; if it does not become current, it is useless. For psychology, moreover, the noun forms genotype and phenotype are disturbing in their implications of a **type,** and as collectives are not particularly useful. The adjective form PHENOTYPICAL, referring to structure or function as it actually is, seems a useful term which avoids *unnecessary* entanglement with the problem of heredity. In place of genotypical, however, **genetic** seems less pretentious and less ambiguous.

-genous (-jen·əs): suffix meaning *producing* or *produced by.*

gens (jenz): *n.* a division of an ethnic group defined by common descent through the male line. ➤*Distg. fr.* **clan,** in which descent is reckoned through the female line, although **clan** is often used for any tribal designation.

genus (jē'nəs) *n., pl.* **genera** (jen'ər·ə), **genuses:** (*L.*) a biological classification group made up of **species** and forming part of the larger classification group known as a **family;** by extension, the next higher category or class.

-gen(y): a suffix meaning *origin, generation, cause.*

geometric(al): *adj.* of a series that increases or decreases by a constant **ratio.**—*Syn.* **logarithmic.**—*Contr. w.* **arithmetic(al).**

geotropism (ji·ot'rə·piz·əm): *n.* a response, positive or negative, forced from an organism by a gravitational stress.—*Syn.* GEO-TAXIS.—*adj.* **geotropic** (-trop'ik).

geriatrics (jer″i·at'riks): *n.* (*med.*) the science and art of treating the old.

geri(o)- (jer'i·ō-): combining form meaning *old, old age.*

geriopsychosis = **senile psychosis.**

germ cell: a cell specialized for reproduction. ➤*Distg. fr.* **gamete,** such a germ cell in its mature state, ready for **conjugation.**

germinal period: in human beings, the first one or two weeks of prenatal life.

germ plasm: tissue that produces by fission the sperm cells (in males) or egg cells (in females), or both (in bisexual species).—*Contr. w.* **somaplasm.**

germ plasm/continuity of: see **continuity of the germ plasm.**

gerontology (jer″ən·tol′ō·ji): *n.* the study of old persons. It draws from anthropology, anthropometry, sociology, social work, medicine **(geriatrics),** and psychology.

Gesell developmental norms: a series of behaviors arranged in the order and approximate time of their appearance in infants.

gestalt. Gestalt (gə·shtält′, gä·shtält′) *n., pl.* **gestalts, Gestalten:** (originally *Ger.,* often *cap.*) **1.** a form, a configuration, or a totality that has, as a unified whole, properties which cannot be derived by summation from the parts and their relationships. ➤The term is now naturalized in English and often spelled without initial capital. It may refer to physical structures, to physiological and psychological functions, or to symbolic units. See **gestalt psychology** for illustration and discussion.—*Syn.* **configuration** (but this inadequately expresses the concept). **2.** (*ethology*) a set of responses elicited by a complex of stimuli not yet experimentally analyzed and defined. ➤This meaning is not recommended, since it is not consistently adhered to in ethology and is confusing in relation with (1), which has priority.

Gestalt completion test: a series of incomplete pictures so designed that the missing parts can be supplied correctly only if the picture is correctly perceived as a unified whole.

gestalt factor: a condition favorable to the experience of wholeness. ➤Thus, according to the PRINCIPLE OF PROXIMITY, closeness of the components in space or time is a gestalt factor—i.e., a condition favorable for an aggregate to be perceived as a whole.

gestalt/good: a stable configuration; one that does not tend to change as a result of its own inner dynamics. A good gestalt may be described as complete, a simple whole— stable, closed, coherent, regular, and symmetrical.—*Cp. Praegnanz,* **good shape/ law of.**

gestalt homology: the principle that parts of a whole may be compared with parts of another whole in terms only of their role or function in those wholes. ➤The keynote of a musical composition is **homologous** to the keynote of another, irrespective of pitch, timbre, loudness, etc. In both compositions it plays the same function. **Gestalts** are **homologous** only when all their parts are homologous in the above sense.

gestalting: *n.* the process of **sharpening** and intensifying the **wholeness** quality of a psychological phenomenon.

Gestaltism = **Gestalt psychology.**

Gestalt psychology or **theory:** the systematic position that psychological phenomena are organized, undivided, articulated wholes or **gestalts.** The properties of a gestalt are properties of the whole as such and are not derived by summation of its parts. Conversely, the parts derive their properties from their membership in the whole. The notion of "parts" with attributes of their own, independent of the whole, is held to be misleading. ➤The standard illustration is a melody, which has qualities *as a melody* that are not merely the sum of the component tones. It may be played by many instruments at different pitches so that the constituent tones are totally different, yet the melody is the same. Conversely, a given tone, say B flat, has different psychological (and musical) characteristics in different melodic settings—i.e., its qualities as a part of a whole depend on that whole. This is not to deny that B flat, heard in isolation, is a whole or gestalt in its own right. But such a B flat is not psychologically the same B flat that is heard in a melody.

As applied to behavior, Gestalt theory denies that response to a situation can be stated in terms of a combination of separate responses to a combination of separate stimuli; it is a whole response to the whole situation, with specific components serving as salient **figures** rather than as distinct elements. Learning is said to proceed, not by accretion, but by reorganization. ¶Many psychologists accept the reality of wholeness attributes, i.e., gestalts, without denying the existence of at least relatively autonomous elements.—*Cp.* **field theory,** which extends the gestalt principle; and **emergentism,** which states it in a very general form. (Gestalt is now often spelled without the capital.)—*Syn.* GESTALTISM, FORM PSYCHOLOGY.—See **psychology/divisions and schools of,** III, VII.

Gestaltqualität (gä·shtält′kä·li·tät″) *n., pl. Gestaltqualitäten:* (*Ger., form-quality*) the quality or character of a mental content as dependent on the way its constituents are put together; the mental quality founded upon the form or pattern of the combined elements.—*Syn.* FOUNDED (improperly, FUNDED) CONTENT. ➤The doctrine of *Gestaltqualität* is one form of **emergentism.**—*Distg. fr.* **Gestalt theory,** which denies that the elements of a combination have fixed qualities independent of the whole.

gestation (jes·tā′shən): *n.* **1.** the carrying of the embryo in the uterus. **2.** the period of development of the individual before birth.—*Syn.* **pregnancy.**—*adj.* **gestational.**

gesture: *n.* a movement of some part of the body for the purpose of communication. ➤As defined, speech is one kind of gesture.—*Distg. fr.* **posture,** which involves the whole body and is more static; and *fr.* **manipulation.**

geusis (gū'sis): *n.* an act of tasting.

***g* factor** = **factor/general.**

GG = **goal gradient.**

ghost: see **spirit** (2).

gibberish (jib'ər·ish, gib-): *n.* **1.** unintelligible, incoherent language. **2.** immature speech, marked by omission of final consonants and of difficult sound combinations. —*Syn.* **elision,** LEIPOLALIA.

gift: see **ability, gifted.**

gifted: *adj.* **1.** possessing a high degree of any special talent. **2.** possessing very high general intelligence, such as is attained by only 2 per cent of the population. ➤The idea of a gift as something passively received contaminates **gifted,** so that popularly giftedness is thought to be inherited, but technical use makes no such implication.—See **ability.**

gifted child: **1.** a child whose intelligence is in the upper 2 per cent of the total population of his age. **2.** a child having outstanding ability in any respect.—See also **gifted, ability.**

gigantism (jī·gan'tiz·əm): *n.* abnormal increase in stature due to the overfunctioning of the pituitary. ➤*Distg. fr.* **giant,** which is nontechnical.

given: *adj.* **1.** capable of being specified but left indefinite: a *given* individual means almost anyone who may be selected as an example, but that one person is to be specified.—*n.* **2.** that which is available at the start of an investigation or phase thereof: facts, accepted principles, or laws.—*Syn.* **datum** (*pl.* **data**), usually restricted to concrete phenomena or their symbolic representation.

gland: *n.* an organ for secreting or producing a substance to be used in or excreted from the body, or for producing cells. ➤The term has been loosely used, and certain structures with no known function of secretion are called **glands.** Anatomically, a distinction is made between DUCT and DUCTLESS GLANDS. Functionally, one may speak of GLANDS OF EXTERNAL SECRETION, which excrete through a duct to the outside of the body (e.g., kidneys, sweat glands), and of GLANDS OF INTERNAL SECRETION, which produce substances used in the body. Some internal secretions are passed to other bodily organs through a duct (e.g., bile); others are passed into the blood stream or lymph by osmosis. The latter are called **hormones,** and the glands producing them are ENDOCRINE GLANDS. (Some glands provided with ducts for other secretions also produce hormones.) Finally, CYTOGENIC GLANDS are those which produce new cells: gonads, spleen, lymph nodes, bone marrow. (Cytogenic glands may also produce hormones.) The anatomical and the functional classifications overlap rather than coincide, but ductless gland is often used when endocrine is meant, most of the latter being ductless.—*adj.* **glandular.**

gland/exocrine: see **exocrine gland.**

glandular response: the activity of a gland when elicited by stimulus from outside the gland. ➤The continuous production of blood cells is not a response; an *increase* set off by bacterial invasion would be. A glandular response may be mediated by the **autonomic** system, by **hormones** from other glands, or by other chemical conditions.

glandular theory: hypothesis that the function of the **endocrine glands** is a determining factor in behavior, particularly emotional behavior. ➤The hypothesis is too vague and general to be called a theory.

glans: *n.* (*L.*) the bulblike end of **penis** or **clitoris.**

glare: *n.* **1.** a property of a smooth glassy surface of reflecting an intense light. **2.** any intense light stimulus that reduces ability to make visual distinctions.

glassiness: *n.* the visual effect produced by a transparent solid.—*Cp.* **film color.**

glaucoma (glô·kō'mə): *n.* a condition of increased pressure within the eye leading to pain, to increasing visual impairment, and finally to blindness.

glia = **neuroglia.**

glioma (gli·ō'mə): *n.* a common kind of brain tumor.

glittering = **sparkling.**

global: *adj.* total; taken as a whole without attempt to distinguish separate parts or functions: his *global* fitness for this job.

globus hystericus (glō'bəs his·ter'i·kəs): (*L.*) the **illusion** or **hallucination** of having a lump in the throat.

glossal (glos'əl): *adj.* pertaining to the tongue.

-glossia: (*speech*) combining form meaning *anomaly of a speech organ.*

glossiness: *n.* a property of a perceived surface, correlated with the degree to which it reflects light, of forming mirror images. ➤Low glossiness is characteristic of rough diffusing surfaces, high glossiness of smooth surfaces.—*Cp.* **glare.**

glosso- (glos'ō-): combining form meaning *tongue* or *language.*

glossolalia (-lā'li·ə): *n.* fabricated speech "in a strange tongue," occurring chiefly in states of religious ecstasy but found also in psychopathic cases.

glossosynthesis: *n.* the making up of words: a symptom in certain pathological conditions. ➤It occurs also, occasionally legitimately, in scientific disciplines.—*Syn.* **neologism (2).**

glottal (glot'əl): *adj.* pertaining to the **glottis;** of sounds determined largely by the glottis.

glottis (glot'is): *n.* the opening between the free margins of the vocal cords.

glove anesthesia: see **anesthesia/glove.**

glow = color/illuminant.

-gnosia, -gnosis: combining form denoting *cognition* or *recognition:* **agnosia, psychognosis.** Corresponding adjectives end in **-gnostic.**

***G.O.* =** (*C. Hull*) **goal-orientation** index.

goal: *n.* **1.** the end result, immediate or remote, which an organism is seeking: e.g., to complete a term paper, to become a great actor, to find food, to be a good father. **2.** the end result of an action specified or required in advance by someone directing behavior. **3.** (*exper.*) the place or object toward which an animal's locomotion is directed, attainment of which brings the response sequence or action to a close; a place housing a lure (food, drink, protection, sex); or the lure itself. **4.** a consummatory act; or the stimuli that release the consummatory act.

➤The goal is often pursued without a specific goal idea, though such a picture of the end result is usually possible for humans and is, when present, a complication often ignored. But there can be no goal without an aroused **motive** or **drive.** ¶In much schoolwork, and in most animal experimentation, the animal does not know what the goal is—at least at first: **goal (2)** or **(3)** does not coincide with goal **(1).**

—*Syn.* **end. Purpose** is often a synonym but properly refers to that which makes a goal attractive: it is **subjective,** or at least **organismic,** whereas the goal is external.— See **motivation, teleology.**

goal behavior = goal-directed behavior.

goal/collective: a goal attainable only by **collective** effort.—*Distg. fr.* **goal/group.**

goal-directed behavior: responses whose objectively observable characteristics can be interpreted only as if they were intended for, or directed toward, attainment of a **goal.** ➤A **drive state** or **expectancy** is inferred, without necessarily attributing purpose to the animal.—*Syn.* GOAL BEHAVIOR. —*Cp.* **directed movement.**

goal-directed motivation: see **motivation/ goal-directed.**

goal gradient: in any kind of learning involving a series of performances (e.g., maze learning in which a series of motor choices

is made), the progressive increase in efficiency as the goal is approached. ➤The efficiency may be shown in increased speed or intensity of action, but is usually measured by decrease in error. The term is not always precisely used: e.g., the change is not always regular, as gradient (properly speaking) implies.

goal/group: any goal proposed for or accepted by a group. ➤*Distg. fr.* **collective *goal,** which is attainable only by collective effort, whereas a group goal may be attainable by individual effort of each member. —*Syn.* SOCIAL GOAL.

goal image: see **imagination.**

goal object = goal. ➤This term is used chiefly to contrast with MEANS OBJECT or MEANS ACTIVITY. A means object is a subordinate goal, a means needed to attain the goal.—*Syn.* GOAL SITUATION.

goal orientation: 1. a postural turning toward the **goal (1). 2.** tendency to make movements that are directed toward the goal. It is especially evident in anticipatory goal-directed movements that are in error: e.g., in a multiple-T **maze,** entering the alley that is toward the food box even though it is a **blind.**

goal process/directional: an intentionally noncommittal expression for any organismic activity that leads toward **goal behavior.** —*Approx. syn.* **preparatory response.**

goal response: 1. in instrumental conditioning, the response given to a rewarding stimulus. (Symbol: r_G) **2. = goal-directed behavior,** a sequence of response oriented to a goal.

goal response/fractional antedating or **anticipatory:** see **antedating goal response/fractional.**

goal set: *n.* an organismic determiner of behavior that is defined by the goal to be reached rather than by the responses necessary to reach it.

goal situation = goal.

goal stimulus: see **stimulus/goal.**

goiter/exophthalmic: see **exophthalmic goiter.**

golden mean: conduct more or less midway between opposite extremes. ➤According to Aristotle, it is the definition of virtue. —*Distg. fr.* **golden section.**

golden section: the supposedly most pleasing division of a line or an area into two parts x and y, proportioned so that x is to y as y is to the line or area.

Golgi-Mazzoni corpuscles (gôl'ji·mot·sō'-ni): a type of nerve ending, probably a **receptor,** found in the dermis.

Golgi tendon organ: a nerve ending found at the juncture of tendon and muscle, and believed to be a recorder of conditions of local tension.

Goll/columns of (gôl): nerve tracts on

both sides of the posterior median fissure of the spinal cord which carry **proprioceptive** impulses from legs and lower trunk. —*Syn*. FASCICULI GRACILES.

Gompertz curve: a curve defined by the equation $l_x = kg^{c^x}$, where *x, k, g,* and *c* are constants. ➤It was originally used as a life expectancy curve, l_x being the number of persons living at age *x,* but the curve has been found to fit other sets of empirical observations.

gonad (gō'nad): *n.* a sex gland: the generic term for **testis** (which produces the male **gamete** or **sperm**) and **ovary** (which produces the female **gamete** or **ovum**). In mammals, the gonads also produce certain **hormones.**—*adj.* **gonadal, gonadial, gonadic.**

gonadotrophic (gon″ə·dō·trof'ik): *adj.* of a substance that promotes growth or activity in the **gonads.**—*n.* **gonadotrophin.**

goniometer (gō·ni·om'ə·tər): *n.* an instrument for measuring the tendency to sway in a given direction.

-gonous, -gony: combining forms meaning *generation, descent, reproduction.*

good continuation/law of: (*Gestalt*) the generalization that a perceived element, such as a line, tends to continue in its established form: e.g., the arc of a circle tends to be perceived as continuing to finish the circle. ➤This law may be considered a corollary of the **law of *good shape** or the **law of *closure.**

Goodenough test (gŭd'i·nuf): a test of intelligence in which the subject is instructed to make the best picture of a man that he can. The drawing is scored according to the details represented, and the points are converted into **mental *age** norms.

good-me: *n.* that aspect or part of a child's total self that he recognizes as bringing him rewards (esp. approval or tenderness) from his parents; or the child's conception of his whole self as good.

goodness of fit: see **fit/goodness of.**

good shape/law of: (*Gestalt*) the generalization that figures, contours, or patterns are perceived in the most uniform, balanced, stable form possible.—See **precision/law of.**

Gottschaldt figures (gôt'shält): simple figures concealed in more complex figures, to test form perception.—*Syn.* HIDDEN FIGURES.

gp: *abbr.* for group.

GPA = grade-point average.—See **point-hour ratio.**

Grace Arthur Performance Scale: a number of performance tests arranged to yield an index of intelligence.

gradation: *n.* **1.** gradual change by steps or stages, usually by small steps. **2.** continuous change; change by imperceptible degrees. ➤This usage is etymologically incorrect but very common: the colors of the prism show a smooth *gradation.* **3.** a step in a series. **4.** arrangement of teaching material according to its difficulty.—*adj.* **gradated.**—*v.* **gradate.**

grade: *n.* **1.** a class constituted of things having the same relative standing; a position in a scale or series. **2.** in U.S. schools, a class or division normally representing the work of one academic year (= FORM or STANDARD in English schools). ➤The term is applied either to the pupils or to the tasks appropriate to a given year. **3.** a rating of excellence of performance, esp. in school; a **mark** (*prefd.*).—*v.* **4.** to assign an item to a position in a scale; to assign a number to something according to a scale of value or merit; to score or to mark.—*adj.* **graded.**

grade equivalent: a derived ***score** that states a person's achievement in terms of **grade norms.** ➤E.g., if a score of 87 falls within the limits of grade IV norms, its grade equivalent is IV. If the norms of two or more grades overlap, the grade-equivalent score is unsuitable.

grade norm: the score, or a narrow range of scores, that is typical of the actual performance of the school population for a given grade. ➤Usually the norm is taken as the range of scores from the 40th to the 59th percentile—i.e., it is the range of scores of the middle fifth of the pupils. A single score designated as the norm may be **mean, median,** or **mode.** It may be that of a given class or, more often, of the general population for a given grade (citywide, statewide, or nationwide).—*Distg. fr.* **standard.**

grade-point average or **GPA** = **point-hour ratio.**

grade scale: a scale for measuring level of development of an ability, in which the units of measurement are the successive school **grade norms.**—*Syn.* **grade-equivalent** scale.

grade skipping: the omission of one or more grades in progressing upward through a school.—*Syn.* DOUBLE PROMOTION.

gradient: *n.* **1.** a graded difference between two states or conditions that tends to be abolished by progressive lessening of the greater and increase of the smaller; or the differences between the two states at successive moments as equilibrium is being attained. ➤If two fluids under differing pressures are connected, the higher pressure lessens and the lower pressure increases until equality is reached. A continuous curve representing the differences at successive moments is the GRADIENT CURVE. ¶**Gradient** is sometimes used metaphorically of psychological or social differences, despite the fact that it is not known how far or under what accessory conditions the difference tends to be abolished by a change toward equality. (Differences in wealth, e.g., apparently do not tend to equalize under all conditions.)—*Syn.* DYNAMIC GRADIENT. **2.** any magnitude or variable which changes by progressive steps from high to low instead of remaining constant or varying irregularly. ➤A change from low to high is seldom called a gradient, which retains the notion of falling, even in this meaning. But a rise in the number of successes, converted into a fall in the number of failures, may then be called a gradient. Thus, the **goal gradient** in maze learning is computed as the decrease in errors as the goal is approached, although the empirical fact in experiments is often an *increase* in the number of correct choices, and this is generally considered a part of the goal-approaching effect to which goal gradient is applied. **3.** the rate of progressive change from high to low. **4.** a regular change in the strength of the tendency to respond as a function of systematic changes in stimulus conditions (distance, time-interval, intensity, etc.), usually named from the latter: e.g., stimulus-intensity *gradient*.

gradient/anterior-posterior: the metabolic pattern of the growing organism, which shows high activity in the head region compared with that of the posterior. ➤This is the major **axial gradient**, and is associated with **cephalocaudad development.**

gradient/avoidance: the curve showing the change, during training, in the avoidance response to a certain situation. ➤Typically, the curve shows a drop in the time between a warning signal and the avoiding reaction; or it may show an increasing frequency of the avoiding reaction to a **cue** stimulus.—See **gradient.**

gradient/axial: see **axial gradient.**

gradient/excitation: see **excitation gradient.**

gradient/growth: the progressive changes in magnitude of a bodily part or of some function.—See **cephalocaudad development.**

gradient/neural: a gradient measured in chronaxie.

gradient of effect: the generalization that if a certain stimulus-response sequence, in a series of such S-R sequences, is rewarded (or punished), the S-R sequences preceding or following have greater (or less) probability of occurrence. This effect falls off in a **gradient** according to temporal nearness to the primarily rewarded, or punished, sequence. ➤It is improbable that the gradient of effect, except under special circumstances, extends to wholly unrelated

sequences, even though they are temporally adjacent.—*Cp.* **gradient of *reinforcement.**

gradient of reinforcement: see **reinforcement/gradient of.**

gradient of response generalization: see **generalization/response.**

gradient of stimulus generalization: see **generalization/stimulus.**

gradient of texture: the gradual refinement in the grain of the visually perceived texture as the surface recedes from the viewing person—an important factor in judgments of distance.

gradualism: *n.* theory that development tends to proceed by fine, slight, even insensible steps or gradations rather than by sudden shifts.—*Contr. w.* **saltation.**

graduation = (*stat.*) **smoothing.**

-gram: combining form meaning *something written* or *drawn.*

Gram-Charlier series = **Poisson series.**

grandeur/delusion of: see **delusion of grandeur.**

grandiose: *adj.* **1.** magnificent; imposing (often with a derogatory connotation). **2.** characterizing unrealistically imposing plans, or unrealistic notions of one's own importance or ability.

grand mal: see **epilepsy.**

granular layer/internal: (*neurol.*) the fourth layer of the **cerebral cortex,** containing many small multipolar cells with short axons, as well as scattered small pyramidal cells; or a similar granular structure, such as the fifth and seventh of the ten layers of the retina.

graph: *n.* a line or spatial figure representing the results of measurement or statistics. ➤For a **continuous** variable, a curve or surface more truly represents the values than does a series of discrete numbers. For a **discontinuous** variable, a broken line should be used.—*Cp.* **diagram.**—*adj.* **graphic,** which also means *vivid, visually impressive.*

-graph: combining form that means something written or drawn, or something that writes or records: chronograph, telegraph.

graph/cumulative frequency = **ogive.**

graph/frequency: see **frequency.**

graphic alignment: the angle formed by letters or words with a base line.

graphic analysis: use of a graph to reveal relationships between the data so represented. ➤When the data conform to some well-known graphic form (e.g., the **normal *frequency curve**), deductions can be made from the geometric properties of the curve. Even irregular graphic forms may reveal relationships more clearly than do discrete numbers.

graphic individuality: the characteristics of a person's handwriting that make it unique, and thus make possible the identification of the writer.

graphic language: a communication recorded in visible symbols—written, printed, painted, incised, modeled.—*Syn.* WRITTEN LANGUAGE, *written* referring to any kind of visual symbol.

graphic method: 1. use of **graphs** or **diagrams** to present or to analyze data; = **graphic analysis. 2.** recording responses by means of a device that registers them in graphic form, usually on a moving paper.

graphic rating scale: see **rating scale/ graphic.**

grapho-: a combining form meaning *writing, drawing.*

graphodyne: *n.* a mechanism that transmits handwriting pressure to a recording device.

graphology: *n.* **1.** any investigation of handwriting. **2.** the analysis of handwriting characteristics for personal identification, for indications of specific psychological states at the time of writing, or for personality analysis. FORENSIC GRAPHOLOGY is the study of handwriting for purposes of legal evidence.

graphomania: *n.* obsessive desire to write, often degenerating into **graphorrhea.**

graphometry (graf·om'ə·tri): *n.* a projective procedure in which the subject is asked to describe what he has drawn while blindfolded, then, with blindfold removed, he says what the drawing looks like to him.

graphomotor projective technique: a diagnostic procedure in which the subject moves his pencil freely over a sheet of paper while blindfolded. The experimenter endeavors to interpret the drawings.—*Cp.* **graphometry.**

graphorrhea: *n.* **1.** impulse to write profusely. **2.** ungovernable impulse to write, resulting in a meaningless flow of words or word fragments.

graph/rectangular = histogram.

grasping reflex: the reflex response of clutching with the fingers (or toes) any small object that stimulates the palm (or sole). ➤This is broader than **Darwinian reflex,** which is limited to the grasping reflex in man, found only in very young infants.

gratification: *n.* state in which a previous desire is being satisfied; state in which one is aware of having just attained a desired end or condition; state in an animal following **drive reduction** or a **consummatory response.**—*Syn.* **satisfaction.**— *Ant.* DISAPPOINTMENT.

Graves' disease = exophthalmic goiter.

gray: *n.* an **achromatic color** of any lightness intermediate between the extremes of black and white. ➤Gray is peculiarly susceptible to influence by contrast: a lighter or darker color seen with gray in

the visual field influences its perception. —*Var.* **grey.**

gray-black shock: (*Ror.*) exaggerated response to the heavy shadings of the all-gray figures.

gray/cortical: see **cortical gray.**

gray matter or **substance: 1.** the part of the brain and spinal cord in which the nerve cells predominate over the myelinated nerve fibers, which are nearly white.—*Contr. w.* **white matter. 2.** (*colloq.*) brains; intelligence. ➤Based on the theory that the **cortex,** composed of gray matter, is the chief seat of the higher mental processes, the colloquialism is used by those quite ignorant of its true nature.

GRE = Graduate Record Examination.

great-man theory: point of view that social and historical events are largely due to the influence of outstanding individuals.

Greek love: homosexuality in males.

Greek neologisms: see **neologism.**

green: *n.* **1.** the hue attribute of visual sensations typically evoked by stimulation of the normal retina with radiation of wave length approximately 515 millimicrons. **2.** any hue predominantly similar to that of the typical green; the complement of red-purple or magenta.

gregariousness: *n.* **1.** tendency in certain animal species to live in herds or flocks. **2.** the human tendency to live in groups, to take satisfaction in the company of those with whom one feels kinship, and to be uneasy when deprived of association with one's kind. **3.** more loosely, all action that is actuated by a desire for fellowship with, or approbation from, one's fellows. While the tendency is held by some to be instinctive, the term does not imply such origin. —*adj.* **gregarious.**

grey = gray.

grief: *n.* an emotional state normally resulting from loss of something greatly cherished, manifested by sobbing, relaxed postural tone, etc.

grimace (grə·mās'; grim'əs): *n.* a distorted facial expression resulting from paralysis, muscular imbalance, or momentary emotional states such as pain or contempt, but sometimes also joy or amusement.

grooming: *n.* **1.** making one's person neat and tidy. **2.** in certain animals, the removal of dirt and parasitic insects from, and smoothing of, the fur.

gross motor coordinations: those in which the factor of strength is primary. ➤*Contr. w.* FINE MOTOR COORDINATIONS, in which strength is secondary to speed or precision.

gross score: (*stat.*) a score expressed in terms of the original units of measurement. ➤All **raw** *scores and certain **derived** *scores are gross scores. *Contr. w.* **stand-**

ard *score. Gross scores are usually symbolized by X and Y. A GROSS SCORE FORMULA is one expressed in gross scores: e.g.,

$$\sigma = \sqrt{\frac{\Sigma X^2}{N} - \left(\frac{\Sigma X}{N}\right)^2}$$

ground: n. 1. a rational basis for action or belief. (Usually plural.) 2. = background. —See figure-ground.

ground/eye: see eye ground.

group: n. 1. several items or cases, recognized as individually different but assembled, or thought about and treated, for some purpose or purposes as if alike.—Syn. class, category, classification, grouped *distribution. 2. = group/social (all meanings).—v. 3. to bring together any sort of items; to separate certain items from others by classification or emphasis.

group absolutism: tendency of members to believe that their group ways of acting are the only "correct" ways, that the ways of other groups range from "funny" or "absurd" to "immoral" or "pathological."— Cp. ethnocentrism.

group acceptance: the responses of group members to a single member, or candidate for membership, that establish his role and status in the group structure.

group analysis: the study of what is wrong with a group. ➤A confusing term formed by analogy with analysis (3) of an individual.—Distg. fr. group therapy, treatment of the individual by group means.

group/association: see association group.

group atmosphere: the feelings and attitudes manifested, often by minimal cues, in a face-to-face *group and influencing the activity of the group.

group behavior: 1. the behavior of an individual as influenced by being a member of a group. 2. the behavior of a number of persons acting together; teamwork: e.g., all pulling together on a rope.—Syn. COLLECTIVE BEHAVIOR. 3. the activity of a group as such, that activity being a joint product and not a mere summation of the acts of the members taken separately: e.g., the mutual stimulation of group thinking, the producing of ideas not possible for the individuals singly or alone.—Syn. (for 3) syntality.

group/coacting: see coacting group.

group consciousness: 1. that belonging to two or more persons as a group whole, generally with the implication that it is not a mere sum of individual consciousnesses. ➤Once much debated, the concept is now usually abandoned for that of group mind or group behavior (esp. 3). 2. an individual member's awareness of other members of the group.—Distg. fr. general consciousness, that knowledge common to all the group.

group contagion: the rapid spread of feeling—esp. fear, anger, amusement, or relief—through an assemblage, caused by perception of the feeling in others.

group/criterion: see criterion group.

group decision: 1. process of arriving by group discussion at a plan for action either by the group as a whole or by individuals in their role as group members. 2. a judgment or conclusion arrived at by group discussion and representing either a consensus or a majority vote of the members. ➤Often a mere group opinion is thus named, no plan for action binding on the members being involved.

group differences: see difference/group.

group dimension: a variable by means of which to characterize the group; a quantitative property or attribute of the group: e.g., cohesion.

group/direct-contact = face-to-face *group.

group dynamics: 1. the dynamic or cause-effect changes that take place within a social group; the way groups form and function. 2. the study of techniques and procedures for altering the structure and/or the behavior of a social group as a group. ➤In general, this study does not emphasize changing the group by bringing about more or less permanent changes in the members; it emphasizes eliciting from members some behavior (of which they are already capable) that will bring about the desired change in group structure or behavior (again, without primary concern for consequent change in the members as individuals).

grouped measures: measures or observations that are recorded merely as falling within a certain statistical class rather than recorded separately.

group/experimental: see experimental group.

group/face-to-face: two or more persons in such close physical proximity that each member may respond to sensory stimuli or signals emitted by each of the others, whether intentionally or not. ➤Contr. w. crowd, in which the perception of each of the others need not be so complete; and with primary *group, in which there are many bonds of association.—Syn. DIRECT-CONTACT GROUP.

group factor: see factor/group.

grouping: n. 1. (stat.) process of combining scores into classes, categories, or ranks. 2. classifying school pupils into classes or grades, or into subdivisions thereof.—See ability grouping.

grouping error: (stat.) the error that is introduced, when a continuous series of observations is divided into class intervals, by the assumption that all data of a given interval are concentrated at the midpoint of that class interval.

grouping/homogeneous: see **ability grouping.**

group interval = **class interval.**

group/marginal: a group incompletely assimilated into the culture within which it exists: e.g., an immigrant group.

group/matched: see **equivalent-groups procedure.**

group/membership: a group in which a person is an actual accepted member.— *Contr. w.* **group/reference.**

group mind: a **construct** to explain those behaviors of a group that cannot be accounted for by the sum of the characteristics of the individual members; the pattern of relationships accounting for **group behavior (3).**—*Syn.* syntality (*prefd.*).

group/minority: a stable subgroup within a nation or society that has particular interests different from those of the larger group and that is subject to some form of unfavorable treatment. ➤In the U. S., minority group refers chiefly to one of the following: a so-called racial or skin-color group, such as the Negro; a religious group with a strong in-group feeling and a sense of being not fully accepted by the majority; a national-origin group; the working class. *Distg. fr.* a *minority,* which need not be stable nor subject to unfavorable treatment: e.g., the dominant class in any society is always a minority but not a minority group.

group morale: see **morale.**

group/natural: a loosely used term for groups not requiring explicit pressure, esp. from outside, for their formation. ➤The term is appropriate for groups of adolescents, and avoids some of the associative implications of **gang** or **clique.**

group norm: see **norm/group.**

group/primary: a face-to-face organization of individuals who cooperate for certain common ends, who share many ideals and ways of behaving, who have confidence in, and at least some degree of affection for, each other, and who are aware of their similarity and bond of association: e.g., a family, a clan, a small club. ➤Freud makes the further restriction that a primary group is one in which all members accept the same person as leader and source of ideals.

group process: a general term referring to the procedures through which a group approaches, attacks, and solves a common problem.

group psychotherapy = **group therapy.**

group/reference: any group with which a person **identifies** and/or compares himself to such an extent that he tends to adopt its standards, attitudes, and behaviors as his own. ➤Such reference groups, to which people see themselves as belonging, may

or may not correspond to actual membership groups. For a particular person there may be—and usually are—several such groups.—*Cp.* **anchoring** (of attitudes).

group rigidity: the degree to which a group resists change in response to influences bearing on it.—*Distg. fr.* group exclusiveness.

groups/comparable: two or more sample groups, both representative of the total population from which they are drawn. ➤Such groups can be given contrasting treatment and the effects compared.

group/secondary: any group not having close or intimate ties, as in a **primary** ***group,** but possessing some common interest or similarity.

group/social: 1. a number of individuals regarded as having some quality in common.—*Syn.* **assemblage, aggregation, congeries. 2.** a number of individuals occupying an area so limited that there can be some direct communication between them by voice or gesture.—*Syn.* **assemblage, aggregation,** and (in some contexts) **crowd, face-to-face** ***group. 3.** two or more persons who interact and influence each other, and who are recognized in some special way because of the interaction. **4.** persons interacting with each other in such a way that some of their needs are, or seem to be, satisfied thereby. The mere feeling of group membership sometimes constitutes such satisfaction.— *Syn.* **coacting group.**—*Cp.* **reference** ***group.** ➤In all meanings but (1) there is an implication that the group possesses some unity or wholeness; but **group** is used for wholes varying from a loose mass to a compact unit.—*Distg.* the **group,** i.e., the persons, *fr.* the **organization.**

group/standardization: the group that is held to be representative of a population in determining **norms** and **standards.**

group structure: the relationships between the members of a social group (dominance, subordination, friendship, etc.) and its attributes as a group (size, group goals, cohesiveness, we-feeling, etc.) which define its relation to other groups or persons.

group superego: that portion of the **superego** derived, not from infantile and early childhood experiences and identifications (chiefly familial), but from the rules and purposes of peer groups. ➤Many psychoanalysts do not believe the superego can be thus modified after early childhood.

group test: see **test/group.**

group therapy: any form of **psychotherapy** in which several persons are treated simultaneously, though by no means always in the same way. ➤In psychotherapy, group treatment is sometimes considered more effective, not merely more economical of the therapist's time. The term should not be used to designate the mere use of social contacts as a means of treatment. Arranging that a boy have more playmates is not group therapy (it might be called social therapy), but the utilization of a group situation to facilitate therapeutic changes in several children may be.

group/vertical: one that draws members from two or more **social *classes.**

group/we-: any group with which the individual feels strongly identified. ➤*Contr. w.* THEY-GROUP, any other group than the one the individual belongs to.—*Syn.* **ingroup.**

group work = **social group work.**

growing pains: neuralgic pains experienced by a child or adolescent. ➤They are often attributed to the fact that the bones grow faster than the muscles but many so-called growing pains are of pathological origin. The term is often used metaphorically for any stress due to development.

growth: *n.* 1. the gradual increase in magnitude of an organism or its parts; or an analogous increase in the magnitude or range of a function: e.g., *growth* in arithmetical ability. ➤This meaning of growth as incremental distinguishes it from **development** (which see). Unfortunately, the distinction is not well observed, so that growth now often means 2. change toward a more developed or mature state.—*Syn.* (for 2) **development** (*prefd.*). ➤Since growth has no adjectival form, **developmental** is used for both (1) and (2).

growth/accretionary = **growth** (1).— *Distg. fr.* **growth/developmental.**

growth/anatomical: changes with age in size, shape, number, or pattern of bodily organs and structures.—*Distg. fr.* **growth/ physiological** or **growth/mental.**

growth/areal: see **areal growth.**

growth curve: a graphic representation of **growth,** showing successive time units on the horizontal axis and units of progressive change in the organism on the vertical axis. The curve may represent individuals or groups.

growth curve/mental: a graphic representation of the **growth** in any psychological function, usually in **intelligence.** It may represent the growth in a single individual or the average of many individuals. ➤In some cases the attempt is to represent the aspect of growth that is independent of learning; more often the over-all change in the function is recorded.

growth/developmental: an unnecessary synonym for **development.**—*Distg. fr.* **growth/accretionary.**

growth differential: a difference between two organisms due to different rates of growth. ➤Unless used in a mathematical sense (see **differential**), this term is unnecessary and an example of **bogus erudition.**—*Syn.* GROWTH DIFFERENCE, DIFFER-

ENCE IN GROWTH.—*Distg.* growth differential *fr.* **differential *growth.**

growth/differential: a growth marked by differences between the several parts in time of beginning or in rate of change. ➤*Distg. fr.* **dysplasia,** the *abnormal* difference in the end product of differential growth. Differences in rate of growth are the rule.— *Distg.* differential growth *fr.* **growth differential.**

growth/educational: any sort of changes that are the object or the result of education. ➤Some kinds of educational growth are the object of education but may not be attained; others are attained by learning in school without being the object of education.

growth/horizontal: an increase in the number of acts of the same level of difficulty that can be performed. ➤*Contr. w.* VERTICAL GROWTH, an increase in the difficulty of the acts that can be performed.

growth/lineal: changes with age in limb or stem length, in contrast with changes in volume or in breadth and thickness of the body.

growth/mental: properly, increase with age in any psychological performance, but often restricted to growth in **intelligence.**

growth motive: a motive that maintains tension directed toward distant goals.

growth/physiological: any enduring alteration in physiological activity as a function of age; sometimes a euphemism for sexual **maturation.**

growth principle: (*C. Rogers*) the belief that creative and integrative forces exist within the individual which, in an atmosphere free from censure and coercion, lead to improved insight and selection of better means of **adjustment.**

growth/skeletal: change with age toward a mature form in the bony structures. A common index is the **metacarpal** index.

growth/split: a pattern of growth, for a single individual, that manifests markedly different rates for different characteristics.

growth/vertical: see **growth/horizontal.**

G score = **score/grade.**

GSR = galvanic skin response (see **electrodermal response**).

guessing/correction for: in a test or examination, a greater penalty imposed for wrong answers than for failure to answer. It is supposed to discourage guesswork.

guessing sequence: a predictable pattern of choosing that does not reflect the person's knowledge or substantial preference. Since it is predictable, it reflects not chance but a bias toward some attribute of the sequence other than that upon which choice is supposed to be made. ➤Thus, there may be a constant tendency to choose a positive rather than a negative, or the right rather than the left, or to alternate choice, etc. The person is not necessarily aware of the bias.—*Cp.* **constant** ***error**, of which this is one form.

Guess-Who technique: a personality rating procedure that provides simple thumbnail word pictures of personality types, beneath which are to be written the names of associates who are thought to resemble the description.—*Cp.* **nominating technique.**

guidance: *n.* **1.** helping a person to find and select the opportunities and activities that will yield maximum satisfaction and profit, esp. in school (EDUCATIONAL GUIDANCE) and in his life work (VOCATIONAL GUIDANCE). ➤Instruction, counseling, and testing are methods of guidance. It usually includes both fact-giving and interpretation. Guidance involves consideration of available opportunities, of the qualities needed for the job (JOB ANALYSIS), and of the possession by the individual of the abilities, interests, and other personal characteristics desirable in the situation.—*Cp.* **counseling. 2.** a method of teaching in which the child is led to discover for himself the facts or responses required. ➤The assertion that "all teaching is guidance" is ambiguous: it may mean that the teaching process is a method of guidance in sense **(1)** (along with, or in place of, counseling or testing) ; or it may mean that teaching ought to use the method of sense **(2)**.—See also **child guidance** ***clinic.**

guidance clinic: see **clinic.**

guidance/vocational = **vocational counseling.**

guiding fictions: (*A. Adler*) a set of reference frames by means of which one can understand and categorize experience; guiding principles by which to evaluate one's experiences. ➤The principles are **abstractions** rather than *fictions.* In the normal person, they are flexible and lead to behavior oriented to reality.—*Cp.* **schema.**

Guilford-Martin Personnel Inventory I: a self-rating form for the traits of objectivity, cooperativeness, and agreeableness.

Guilford-Zimmerman Temperament Survey: a personality inventory concerning ten major personality traits identified through **factor analysis.**

guilt culture: a culture that relies largely on the individual conscience as a means of social control. ➤In such a culture, honor requires that one live up to one's own self-picture or **superego.**—*Distg. fr.* **shame culture.**

guilt/sense of: realization that one has violated ethical or moral or religious principles, together with a regretful feeling of lessened personal worth on that account. ➤UNCONSCIOUS GUILT is manifested by various indirect expressions, esp. lessened sense of worth, although the person denies the offenses. IMAGINED GUILT is believed to be a **screen** for some deeply repressed guilt. Thus, the person who has repressed incestuous desires, but not the guilty feeling connected therewith, is said to be likely to invent some lesser offense to explain the guilty feeling to himself and to protect himself against discovering the real cause.

guinea pig: 1. a small rodent much used in biological experiments; hence, **2.** humorously, any animal or person subjected to experiment.

gust: *n.* a unit of taste that equals the subjective strength of a 1 per cent solution of sucrose.

gustation: *n.* the sense of taste, receptors for which lie in the tongue and soft palate. —*Distg. fr.* esthetic taste.—*adj.* **gustatory, gustative.**

gustum *n., pl.* **gusta:** a single taste sensation or **sensum.**

Guttman analysis or **scaling** = **cumulative scale.**

guttural: *adj.* pertaining to the throat; specif., of speech sounds controlled in the throat.

gyn- (jin-; jīn-; gĭn-): combining form meaning *woman* or *female.* Before consonants, **gyneo-** or **gyno-.** The suffix **-gyny** is noun-forming, **-gynous** adjective-forming.

gynandrous (ji·nan′drəs; jī-): *adj.* **1.** of a woman who is markedly manlike in physical appearance. **2.** possessing a combination of male and female sex characters; **hermaphroditic** or pseudohermaphroditic.—*Cp.* **viraginity, androgyny.**—*n.* **gynandry.**

gyrus (jī′rəs) *n., pl.* **gyri** (-rī): (*anat.*) a fold of the surface of the **cerebral cortex,** bounded by **fissures** or **sulci.**—*Syn.* **convolution.**

H

H: **1.** = **harmonic** ***mean. 2.** (not *ital.*) = **heredity. 3.** = **habit strength** (also symbolized by $_sH_R$). **4.** (*Ror.*) scoring symbol for a report of human figures. **5.** (*info. theory*) = **entropy (3).**

$_sH_R$ = (*C. Hull*) **habit strength.**

$_s\overline{H}_R$: (*C. Hull*) effective **habit strength;** habit strength resulting from **stimulus** ***generalization.**

$_s'H_R$: (*C. Hull*) strength of a habit based on the same response conditioned to another stimulus.

$_{SS}H_R$ = (C. *Hull*) summation of the **habit strengths** associated with two or more stimulus elements that lead to a given **R.**

h: 1. = parameter of normal probability curve. 2. = **precision/index of.** 3. symbol for number of hours of food deprivation (in experiments with animals).

Haab's pupillary reflex: contraction of both pupils when a subject's gaze is turned toward a bright object in a darkened room.

hab: *n.* (C. *Hull*) a unit in which to express habit strength. It is taken arbitrarily as 1 per cent of the physiological maximum **(M)** of habit strength attainable by a standard organism under optimal conditions. ➤Hull seldom used this unit in his later writing.

habenula (hə·ben′ū·lə): *n.* (*neurol.*) an area of fibers in the **epithalamus,** closely connected with a stalk from the **pineal body.**—*adj.* **habenular.**

habit: *n.* 1. an acquired act, usually a relatively simple one, that is regularly or customarily manifested. ➤Although **habit** originally referred to coordinated muscular movements, it is now extended to other acts, e.g., *habit of thought.* 2. tendency toward an act that has become, by repeated performance, relatively fixed, consistent, easy, almost automatic; or the enduring structural basis for such behavior. A GENERALIZED HABIT is essentially the same as a trait. 3. the abstract characteristics of habitual acts. 4. = **habit formation.** 5. (*descriptive biol.*) any kind of action that characterizes a species (less often an individual): the *habits* of the wild duck. ➤In all usages except the last, the notion of *acquired* or *learned* behavior is clearly present. The notion of *characteristic* behavior, however, sometimes affects popular use of habit in its other meanings.—*Cp.* **habituation.**—*adj.* **habitual** (of the act), **habituated** (of the animal).

habitat: *n.* a geographical area suited to the life activities of a species, a group, or an individual. ➤*Contr. w.* **environment,** a collective term for all the influences impinging on an organism; and *w.* RANGE, that portion of the habitat actually occupied.

habit/complaint: see **complaint habit.**

habit contraction = **tic.**

habit deterioration: a symptom found in the **dementias** in which the habits appropriate to one's normal manner of living (such as cleanliness, control of excretion, social manners) are replaced by habits of a lower social level or by purely animal behavior.

habit family hierarchy: a grouping of possible routes or paths to the same goal point in the order of economy of effort needed to reach it (which is also generally the order of frequency of occurrence). ➤From a situation involving literal paths to a literal goal point, the concept is extended to include the "family" of all the means to any given end.

habit formation: 1. the process of establishing a **habit.** 2. **learning,** in general. ➤An example of **theory-begging: habit formation** clearly refers to an undeniable fact, but usage (2) implies a theory about learning. Thus, those who doubt the theory are deprived of a convenient term to refer to the fact.

habit-forming drug: one that leads to **drug addiction;** occasionally, one that leads to **drug habituation.**

habit hierarchy: 1. (C. *Hull*) all the responses that gain strength through **reinforcement** of one of them, arranged in the order of the amount of gain thus acquired. —*Cp.* **response *generalization.** 2. the organization of simpler habits into **habit patterns** of increasing complexity: e.g., the habits of writing the separate letters are organized into the writing of words, of words into phrases, etc. ➤The notion of inclusion is not necessary to the term **hierarchy** but is a special usage in the case of habits.—*Distg. fr.* **habit family.**

habit interference: the inhibition, weakening, or distortion of one or both responses when two responses to the same situation have been practiced.

habit/motor: see **motor habit.**

habit pattern: 1. = **habit** (2). ➤An unnecessary locution, since all habits are patterns. 2. nerve bonds assumed as the basis of **habit.** 3. several smaller **habits** combined in a unity: e.g., typewriting, which involves combining or unifying postural and eye-arm-finger habits. ➤These three meanings are often combined in a single vague use of the term. The last is the preferred meaning.

habit progression: the generalized tendency of old habits to give way to new as the organism matures.

habit/social: any acquired behavior that facilitates adjustment to social situations.

habit spasm: a **tic**-like mannerism.

habit strength or $_sH_R$: (C. *Hull*) an inferred part of the organism that is determined by variation in four empirical determinants: number of **reinforcements,** amount of reinforcing agent, time between stimulation and response, time between response and reinforcement.

habit training: intentional arrangement of the conditions for **habit formation.**

habitual: *adj.* pertaining to **habit,** or to the gradual acquisition of a mode of behaving.

habituation: *n.* 1. the gradual elimination of waste movement as a result of repeated reaction to a given situation. 2. the gradual increase in the certainty that the situation will elicit a given response.—*Syn.* **habit formation.**—*v.* **habituate.**

habitus: *n.* 1. the characteristic form of an organism, esp. its outward form.—*Syn.* body *type. 2. the form of an organism resulting from a mode of life. ➤Insofar as that mode influences evolution, such habitus may be **inherited:** e.g., the effect of divergent means of locomotion on the feet of man and ape. But there is no implication that habitus is in all cases permanent. 3. (*obsoles.*) a body form associated with liability to a particular disease.

hair cells: cells with cilia or hairlike protrusions; specif., such cells that act as **receptors** in the inner ear.

hallucination: *n.* a false perception which has a compulsive sense of the reality of objects although relevant and adequate stimuli for such perceiving are lacking; the acceptance of sense imagination as real. It is an abnormal phenomenon, though occasionally experienced by normal persons.— See **illusion.**—*adj.* **hallucinatory** (of the phenomenon); **hallucinated** (of the person).

hallucination/peripheral: one clearly suggested by a stimulus. ➤It seems likely that stimulation of a **receptor** is part of all hallucinations, but the stimulus is often not ascertainable.

hallucinosis: *n.* the condition of having hallucinations. ACUTE HALLUCINOSIS (lasting not more than a few weeks) is often marked also by great **anxiety.** It is usually of toxic origin, particularly alcoholic.

halo: *n.* 1. a ring of light around a bright object such as the sun or moon. 2. a bright ring about the dark negative **aftersensation** of a bright stimulus. 3. the glory or splendor attributed to a famous or beloved person.—See **halo effect.**

halo effect: the tendency, in making an estimate or rating of one characteristic of a person, to be influenced by another characteristic or by one's general impression of that person.

halving method: (*psychophys.*) a method for constructing a **ratio** *scale of sensory magnitude. A second stimulus is adjusted until it is exactly half of a standard on the dimension being scaled. The difference between the standard and the half is a unit step. The second stimulus in turn becomes a standard, and half of its magnitude is determined. The difference between the second and the third is another unit step, postulated as equal to the first unit step. The process is repeated indefinitely.

Hampton Court maze: a **maze** pattern which reproduces in smaller proportions the garden maze of Hampton Court.

hamster: *n.* a small ratlike animal used in experimentation.

handedness: *n.* preferential use of the right or left hand.—See **dextrality.**

handicapped: *n.* a person who has less than normal aptitude in performing the ordinary tasks of life, or of a particular vocation or avocation. ➤The usual reference is to a person PHYSICALLY HANDICAPPED, i.e., who has a specific anatomical or physiological deficiency (poor vision or hearing, spastic paralysis, etc.). But it may also apply to the **mentally** *deficient. It is less often used for the maladjusted or the educationally retarded individual.—*Contr. w.* CRIPPLE, a person *unable* by reason of physical deficiency to perform a certain kind of task. (This useful distinction is not always observed.)—*adj.* **handicapped.**—*n.* **handicap,** the reduced aptitude, or that which causes it.

haphalgesia (haf″al·jē′zi·ə): *n.* a sensation of pain when the skin is touched by a nonirritating substance.

haploid: *adj.* (*genet.*) of a cell having half the number of **chromosomes** found in the ordinary **somatic** cells.

haplology: *n.* (*speech*) the omission of syllables in pronouncing words because of excessive speed of utterance.—*Distg. fr.* **elision.**

haptics: *n.* the investigation of cutaneous sense data, of **touch** in its widest sense.— *adj.* **haptic.**

haptometer (hap·tom′ə·tər): *n.* an instrument for measuring sensitivity of touch.

hard colors: those colors that separate most easily from a gray field of equal **luminosity;** the long-wave (red, yellow) colors.

hard-of-hearing: *adj.* 1. having very inferior auditory acuity, not amounting to **deafness.** 2. able to make practical use of hearing only if a hearing aid is used.—See **hearing loss.**—*n.* the hard of hearing (without hyphen).—*Syn.* hypacusic.

harmavoidance need: (*H. A. Murray*) the need to avoid or flee from danger, to fear injury, illness, or death, to hide or take protective measures.

harmonic: *n.* 1. (*music, acoustics*) an **overtone** whose frequency of wave vibration multiplies that of the fundamental by whole numbers.—See **partial tone.**—*adj.* 2. pertaining to **harmony (3).**

harmonic analysis: resolution of a complex curve into the sine and cosine components of which, according to **Fourier's law,** it is composed.

harmonic mean: see **mean/harmonic.**

harmony: *n.* 1. the combining of parts into a well-proportioned whole; congruity; "fitting together well." 2. agreement in feeling, action, ideas, etc.; peaceable and friendly relations.—*Ant.* (for 1 and 2) disharmony, discord.—*adj.* (for 1 and 2) **harmonious.** 3. (*music*) the combination of simultaneous tones into chords, and the sequential arrangement of such chords into a well-proportioned and orderly whole; or the principles governing such combination. ➤*Contr. w.* MELODY, which has to do with the succession of single tones. **4.** (*music*) an inaccurate and obsolescent synonym for **consonance** as opposed to **dissonance.** ➤Dissonance, used in accord with current musical practice, is as much a part of **harmony** as is consonance.—*adj.* (for **3** and **4**) **harmonic.**

harp theory: see **hearing/theories of.**

harshness: *n.* **1.** a quality of sounds that have a markedly irregular wave form and/or abrupt changes in loudness. **2.** a quality of social behavior: a lack of sympathetic understanding of others, manifested in a harsh tone of voice and unkind actions.

hate: *n.* an enduring attitude or sentiment toward a person or personlike object, manifested by anger, aversion, and desire for the person's misfortune.—*Syn.* HATRED, **hostility.**—See **anger** for discussion.—*Ant.* **love.**

hatred: see **hate.**

H.C.: *abbr.* for **hypothetical *construct.**

Hd: (*Ror.*) a category for a report of parts of human figures.

head: *n.* (*sociol.*) a person whose authority over a group is conferred by outside power. —*n.* headship, the authority of such a person, or his relation to the group.

health/mental: see **mental health.**

Healy Picture-Completion Test: a test consisting of incomplete pictures which can be completed by inserting the missing parts.

hearing: *n.* perceiving sounds by means primarily of the sensory apparatus of the **cochlea** in the inner ear.

hearing aid: any mechanical device to assist in bringing sound vibrations to the sensory apparatus of the inner ear. ➤Characteristically, the aid is a device for magnifying the sound and for imposing the vibration on the bony structure surrounding the inner ear.

hearing/colored = **chromesthesia.**

hearing defect or **deficiency:** an impairment in auditory **acuity,** i.e., in the ability to perceive sounds and to discriminate between them.—See **deafness.**

hearing loss: a measure of an individual's hearing deficiency as compared with the so-called normal ear. It is measured, for different frequencies, in terms of just-perceptible stimuli and recorded (absolutely) in **decibels** or (relatively) as a percentage of normal **acuity.**—See **audiometer, audiogram, deafness.**

hearing theories: attempts to explain how physical sound vibrations give rise to the neural impulses of hearing. ➤The term is something of a misnomer since such theories include only a small part of the total problem of hearing.

The chief theories may be classified as (*a*) RESONANCE THEORIES (also called HARP, PIANO, or PLACE THEORIES), which suppose that the different portions of the **basilar membrane** are tuned to different frequencies corresponding with those of the sound wave. (*b*) FREQUENCY THEORIES (or TELEPHONE THEORIES), which suppose that the basilar membrane as a whole vibrates in tune with the sound wave and transmits the vibrations to the brain. (*c*) VOLLEY THEORIES, which suppose that the single nerve fibers need not respond to every successive wave of the stimulus but to every second, third, or fourth wave. (Each wave is thought to excite or fire a group of nerve fibers, the next wave to fire another group, etc. The pattern of neural impulse reaching the brain by the successive volleys represents the frequency of the sound wave.) (*d*) HYDRAULIC THEORIES, which stress the role of the amount of the basilar membrane involved in different wave forms. (*e*) SOUND-PATTERN THEORIES, which stress the kind of vibration pattern imposed on the basilar membrane. ¶These theories are not mutually exclusive, and concepts central to one may appear in another in a subordinate role.

hearing/visual = **speech reading.**

heat: *n.* **1.** a **sense datum** experienced when the skin is exposed to stimuli of considerably higher temperature than itself. ➤*Distg. fr.* **warmth.** It is believed that heat sensation is a fusion of warmth, cold, and possibly pain. It may be elicited by separate stimulation of receptors for warmth and cold. **2.** a general bodily experience of discomfort when the surrounding temperature is high, or a similar feeling set off by the autonomic system as in fever, etc. **3.** a state of sexual receptivity in female mammals; **estrus.**

hebephrenia (hē″bə·frē′ni·ə; heb″ə-): *n.* a disorder characterized by shallow and inappropriate **affect,** giggling silly behavior and **mannerisms, delusions** (usually unsystematic, and often of a **somatic** nature), **hallucinations,** and regressive behavior. ➤This disorder was formerly classed as one form of **dementia praecox;** it is now classed as a form of **schizophrenia.** —*Syn.* (*Stan. Psychiat.*) SCHIZOPHRENIC REACTION, HEBEPHRENIC TYPE.—*adj.* **hebephrenic** (-fren′ik).

hebetic (hə·bet′ik): *adj.* pertaining to youth, specif. to **puberty.** ➤Applied to mental disorders of adolescence.—*Syn.* HEBOID (hē′-boid).

hebetude (heb′ə·tüd): *n.* lethargy; emotional dullness; listlessness.

heboid = **hebetic.**

hecto-, hekto-: combining form which means *multiplication by 100* (or by a large

number): e.g., *hectogram,* 100 grams.—*Cp.*
centi-, which means *division by 100.*
hedonic (hē·don'ik): *adj.* pertaining to
pleasure, or to the **dimension** of pleasure-
unpleasure.
hedonic tone: the quality of a mental event
of being pleasant or unpleasant; an affective
"coloring" of an event. ➤*Syn.* **feeling tone,
affective tone.** Both are somewhat broader,
as they sometimes include **emotions,** whereas hedonic tone refers only to the simple
dimension of pleasure-unpleasure.
hedonism (hē'dən·iz·əm): *n.* 1. psychological doctrine that every act is motivated
by the desire for pleasure or the aversion
from unpleasure. 2. ethical doctrine that it is
a duty to seek pleasure and to avoid unpleasure or pain. ➤The two doctrines are
often confused.—*adj.* **hedonistic.**—*pers. n.*
hedonist.
hedonistic calculus: (*J. Bentham*) 1. the
measurement of **pleasure-pain** with the aid
of certain dimensions such as duration, intensity, the number of persons involved.
Qualitative differences in pleasure-pain are
ignored. 2. the view that a person makes,
for any experience, a sort of intuitive
global assessment of its net pleasure-pain,
and that motivation depends on such assessment.
Heilsweg (hīls'vāk): *n.* (*C. Jung*) (*Ger.,
healing way*) a method of therapy, characteristically concerned with helping the
patient to find more acceptable purposes.
Heinis constant (hī'nəs): a measure of rate
of mental growth offered as an improvement on the **intelligence quotient.**
Mental *age values are transmuted to
values on a scale having theoretically equal
mental growth units (mental age units are
not equal) and the transmuted values are
divided by chronological age to obtain the
Heinis constant.—*Syn.* PERSONAL CONSTANT
(not *recom.* as being **theory-begging**).
Heinis law of mental growth: a generalization and interpretation of the average increase of intelligence with age. The formula
is $y = 429(1 - e^{\frac{CA}{6.675}})$, where y = the attained intelligence at the age in question,
e = the base of the natural logarithm, and
CA = life age in years.
heliotropism (hē"li·ot'rō·piz·əm): *n.* an
automatic or forced orienting movement
toward a source of light.—*Syn.* HELIOTAXIS
(hē"li·ō·tak'sis), **phototropism** (*prefd.*).
helix (hē'liks): *n.* a spiral; specif., the in-
curved rim of the outer ear; by extension,
the whole of the outer ear.
Heller's disease = dementia infantilis.
Hellin's law: the generalization that, as the
number of babies in a multiple birth increases, the relative frequency of occurrence
compared to total births in a population

decreases in a geometric ratio: if the frequency of twins is $1/P$, that of triplets is
$1/P^2$, of quadruplets $1/P^3$, of quintuplets
$1/P^4$.
hemeralopsia (hem"ər·ə·lop'si·ə): *n.* 1. day
*blindness. 2. night *blindness. ➤Hope-
lessly confused in usage and to be avoided.
—*Var.* hemeralopia (-lō'pi·ə).
hemi- (hem'i-): prefix meaning *half.* ➤In
animals with bilateral symmetry, the division is nearly always into right and left
halves. Thus HEMIPLEGIA is paralysis of
right or left side of the body.
hemiballismus (hem"i·bəl·iz'məs): *n.* a
form of **hyperkinesis** resulting from brain
lesion and marked by repeated violent
movements on the opposite side of the
body from the seat of the lesion.—*Var.*
hemiballism (-bal'iz·əm).
hemiopia (-ō'pi·ə): *n.* blindness in one
lateral half of the visual field.—*Var.* **hemi-
anopia, hemianopsis.**
hemiplegia (-plē'ji·ə): *n.* paralysis of one
side of the body.—*adj.* **hemiplegic.**
hemispheres: *n. pl.* the two halves into
which the **cerebrum** or **cerebellum** is
divided.—*adj.* **hemispherical.**
hemispherical dominance: see **dominance (7).**
hemo- (hē'mō-): combining form meaning
blood.
hemoglobin (hē"mə·glō'bin; hem"ə-): *n.*
the red pigment of the red blood cells, a
protein that carries oxygen from lungs to
tissues and carbon dioxide from tissues to
lungs.—*adj.* **hemoglobic.**
hemophobia: *n.* pathological fear of blood.
hepatic (hi·pat'ik): pertaining to the liver.
Herbartianism (hər·bär'ti·ən·iz·əm): *n.*
1. an intellectualistic dynamic psychology,
put forward in 1825 by J. F. Herbart,
which stressed the competitive activity of
ideas. 2. a body of educational theory based
on Herbart, stressing particularly the need
to relate new ideas to the previously acquired body of ideas (the **apperceptive
mass**).
herd instinct: see **gregariousness.**
hereditarianism: *n.* the point of view that
stresses the influence of **heredity** in determining behavior. ➤In its older form of
nativism, the question was whether certain functions, e.g., space perceiving, are
innately determined. (Other functions were
admitted to be based on experience.) The
contemporary question is stated in quantitative terms: *to what extent* do genetic
factors influence behavior.—*Ant.* **environmentalism.**—See **psychology/divisions
and schools of, VI.**
heredity: *n.* (*biol.*) the totality of influences,
biologically transmitted from parents, that
determines the ways in which an individual
will make use of his environment; the trans-

mission from parents to offspring of that which tends toward the manifestation of certain characteristics in the latter. ➤The **chromosomes** (and perhaps other structures) in the germ cell contain factors called **genes** (or DETERMINERS). At **conjugation** the fertilized cell receives some genes from one parent, some from the other. These determine that the new organism, if permitted to develop in an environment reasonably normal for the species, will manifest a **trait** similar to that of the parent from whom the gene or genes were derived. (See **dominance**.) Hereditary determination is masked by the tendency to variability characteristic of all living beings, and by the fact that the nature of the environment also affects the traits manifested. ¶The actual trait manifested is called the **phenotype** and is regarded as determined by interaction, during the growth process, of the **genotype** (the genes involved in this trait) and the PARATYPE (the sum of related environmental conditions). The contrast between a hereditary trait and an acquired trait is at best one of degree, all traits being (phenotypically) both.

The adjectives **hereditary,** INHERITED, INNATE, INBORN, NATIVE, NATURAL, and ORIGINAL either qualify an *influence on development* rather than a manifested characteristic, or may be guardedly used for those characteristics which are modified little by ordinary changes in environment and are hence *chiefly* determined by heredity. (See also **species-specific**.) **Hereditary** and IN-HERITED sometimes refer to anything received from ancestors. (*Cp.* **inherit 2, 3; heritage**.) **Congenital** and **connate** (the latter to be distinguished from **conate**) specify that a trait is apparent at birth; it may or may not be chiefly due to **heredity**. (*Cp.* a **birth injury,** which is congenital but certainly not **hereditary.**) But **congenital** is often misused for **hereditary**.

heredity-predisposition theory: the view that some individuals are born with a hereditary tendency to a given disorder. Whether illness develops or not depends upon whether especially favorable or unfavorable circumstances are met. ➤The theory implies that the disorder rests upon a unitary combination of personal traits.

heredity/social = transmission (5).

heredity/species: all those characteristics of a **species** that are determined by the **germ plasm;** the **genotype** of a biological group such as a species.—*Cp.* discussion under **heredity.**—*Syn.* **species-specific** behavior.

Hering afterimage (hā′ring): the first positive **aftersensation** following a brief light stimulus. It is bright and of the same hue as the original sensation.

Hering grays: a set of 50 neutral-gray papers, graded from extreme white to extreme black in steps that approximate subjective equality. The set represents the **achromatic** series of colors.

Hering theory of vision: see **color theories.**

heritage: *n.* anything transmitted from one generation to another, whether by biological **heredity,** by social **transmission** of custom and tradition, or by the handing on of material possessions.

hermaphrodite (hər·maf′rō·dīt): *n.* an individual who has both male and female sexual organs. ➤It is believed that in man only one or the other set can be fully functional; but the individual may shift, naturally or by surgery, from one to the other. —*n.* **hermaphroditism,** the condition of having both kinds of sexual organs.—*adj.* **hermaphroditic** (hər·maf″rō·dit′ik), used also, by extension, of persons displaying psychological characteristics of both sexes.

hermaphrodite/psychosexual: one who has the psychological drives and other characteristics of both sexes.

heroin (her′ō·in): *n.* a white crystalline morphine derivative which is one of the most widely used of the habit-forming **narcotics.**

Herring-Binet test: an early **point-scale** modification, in English, of the Binet test.

hetero- (het′ər·ō-): combining form meaning *unlike, varied* or *various, other than: heterogeneous.*—*Contr. w.* **homo-** and **ortho-.**

heterocentric: *adj.* turned toward others than oneself.—*Contr. w.* **egocentric.**

heterodox: *adj.* pertaining to beliefs that are contrary to those generally accepted; or characterizing a person who holds such beliefs. ➤Used in science without disparagement, since **heterodoxy** is a condition of progress.—*Syn.* UNORTHODOX.—*Ant.* ortho-dox.—*n.* **heterodoxy.**

heteroerotic: *adj.* pertaining to sexual affection for others than oneself.—*Contr. w.* autoerotic.—See **heterosexuality.**—*n.* **heteroerotism, heteroeroticism.**

heterogamy (-og′ə·mi): *n.* dissimilarity between husband and wife in a specific trait. —*Ant.* **homogamy.**

heterogeneous (-jē′ni·əs): *adj.* characterizing any group of items that show marked dissimilarity.—*Ant.* **homogeneous.**—*n.* **heterogeneity** (-jen·ē′ə·ti).

heterogenital: see **sex** (*adj.*)

heterolalia (-lā′li·ə) = **heterophemy.**

heteronomy (-on′ə·mi): *n.* (*A.* Angyal) an activity that has its occasion outside the self rather than within. ➤The activity is not, however, environmentally determined except in minor degree; according to Angyal the self is not subservient to environment but uses it.—*adj.* **heteronomous** (not *heteronymous,* of words that are spelled the same but differ in sound and sense).

heterophemy (-fē'mi; -of'ə·mi): *n.* the saying or writing of something other than is intended.—*Syn.* HETEROLALIA, ALLOPHEMY, **slip of the tongue** or **pen, lapsus linguae** or **calami.**—*Var.* **heterophemia.**

heterophilic: *adj.* interested in achieving close personal relations with members of the other sex.

heterophoria (-fô'ri·ə): *n.* lack of balance between the muscles of the two eyes, so that one eye deviates abnormally from its position of fixation. ➤The deviation may be inward (ESOPHORIA), outward (EXOPHORIA), upward (HYPERPHORIA), downward (HYPOPHORIA), or rotated (CYCLOPHORIA). The condition tends to inhibit **fusion** of the two retinal images, thus causing eyestrain, **diplopia,** or the suppression of one image. —*Syn.* (*vis.*) **imbalance/muscular.**

heteroscedastic (-ski·das'tik): *adj.* of a double-entry table or matrix in which the arrays do not all have the same standard deviations.—See **scedasticity.**

heterosexuality: *n.* **1.** attraction to a person or persons of the opposite sex. **2.** the practice of sexual intercourse between individuals of opposite sex. **3.** a level of development characterized by such attraction or by such practice.—*Contr. w.* **homosexuality.**—*adj.* and *pers. n.* **heterosexual.**

➤Four distinctions have been proposed: ALTRIGENDRISM, nonerotic attraction to persons of the opposite sex; HETEROEROTISM, attraction having an **erotic** component but without overt sex behavior; HETEROSEXUALITY, attraction accompanied by overt sex behavior, such as courting and caressing but without genital contact; HETEROGENITALITY, sex behavior involving the genitals of both partners (including coitus). The first is etymologically unfortunate; and the distinction between heterosexuality and heterogenitality is probably as difficult to maintain at the verbal as at the overt behavior level.

heterosociality: *n.* social relationships between persons of opposite sex.

heterosuggestion: see **suggestion.**

heterotropia = **strabismus.**

heterozygous (-zī'gəs): *adj.* of an individual who has, with respect to a given trait, a **gene pair** containing both a **dominant** and a **recessive** gene; or of such a gene pair. Such an individual may transmit either of the two genes to offspring.—*Contr. w.* **homozygous.**—*n.* **heterozygote,** a heterozygous individual.

heuristic (hyü·ris'tik): *adj.* **1.** leading to discovery; esp., of an argument admittedly imperfect but designed to stimulate further thinking or investigation. **2.** (*educ.*) of a method of teaching that encourages pupils to seek the solution of problems, esp. by inductive procedures.

Heymans' law of inhibition (hī'mənz): $T_a = T_o + K_a$ where T_o is the simple **threshold** of a given **stimulus,** T_a is the threshold when it is raised by the presence of a second stimulus of intensity *A,* and K_a is a coefficient of inhibition which differs for different **modes** and different **subjects.** ➤Heymans regarded this as a general law of which **Weber's law** is a special case. The generality of the law is questioned though it holds in many cases.

hidden-cue situation: a task in which the learner must discover which feature of the stimulus situation will, if reacted to in a certain way, bring a reward: e.g., the turning of a knob permits a door to open, but the relation between the knob (**cue** stimulus) and escape is hidden.—*Cp.* **open-cue situation.**

hierarchy (hī'ər·är·ki): *n.* an arrangement of elements (persons, things, ideas) in rank order so that each rank is subordinate to the one above: e.g., the grades of an army from private to general form a hierarchy. ➤The term is a very general one and may refer to any kind of grading into successive levels of "high" and "low." ¶The basis of subordination must be the same at any one level, but may shift from one level to the other. Thus, the criteria for distinguishing the biological families from the genera are not the same as those for distinguishing species from varieties, yet the whole classification of organismic forms is a hierarchy. —*adj.* **hierarchic(al)** (-är'kik·əl).

hierarchy/correlation: a **matrix** in which the **correlation indices** fall off in size from one corner to the other three corners of the two-way table. ➤If this condition is fulfilled, the correlations can be accounted for in terms of a single **general *factor** and of **specific** and/or **group *factors.** But there is no way of knowing whether an imperfect hierarchy lies within the limits of chance deviation; and no empirical instances of perfect hierarchy are known.

hierarchy/dominance: the arrangement of behaviors or of behavior tendencies in an order such that each excludes behavior lower in the hierarchy and is excluded by behavior higher in the hierarchy. ➤If the stimuli to both behaviors A and B are present, and if A occurs but B does not, A is the higher in the dominance hierarchy.

hierarchy/habit: see **habit hierarchy.**

hierarchy/personality: an attempt to picture **personality** as composed of elements that are arranged in a hierarchy of inclusiveness or of superordination. ➤Thus, personality may be pictured as a hierarchy of motives. At the bottom are highly specific motives, each of which is subordinate to a higher motive, that to a still higher or more inclusive motive, and so on.—*Cp.* **lattice/dynamic.**

higher brain centers: 1. those lying in the **cerebrum. 2.** those concerned with more complex forms of mental activity.—See **brain centers.**

higher level skills: see **skills/higher level.**

higher mental processes: see **mental processes/higher.**

higher response unit: 1. a group of stimuli reacted to as if single. **2.** a complex but unitary response made up of simpler responses: in speaking, a phrase is a higher unit than a word.—*Cp.* **habit hierarchy.**

high-grade defective: see **defective/high-grade.**

hindbrain: *n.* the portion of the brain next to the spinal cord, including the **cerebellum, pons,** and **medulla.**

Hipp chronoscope: a clock recording in units of 1/1000 second, and formerly much used in **reaction-time** experiments.

hippocampus: *n.* (*neurol.*) a curved elevation, consisting largely of gray matter, in the floor of the inferior horn of the lateral ventricle.

hircine (hər′sīn; -sin): *adj.* characterizing a smell quality of which the odor of cheese is an example.

histamine (hist′ə·mēn; -min): *n.* an organic compound which stimulates visceral muscles and salivary, pancreatic, and gastric secretions, and dilates capillaries.

histogram: *n.* a graphic representation of a **frequency distribution,** consisting of a series of contiguous rectangles of width proportional to the class intervals (which should be equal if a histogram is to be used) and of height proportional to the number of cases in the several intervals. ➤In appearance it is similar to a **rectangular** **frequency polygon* but is based on a different plan.—*Distg. fr.* **historigram.**—*Syn.* COLUMN DIAGRAM, FREQUENCY HISTOGRAM.

histology: *n.* the study of the structure of bodily tissues.

historical approach: (*counseling*) a method in which the client is led to recount the whole cycle of events leading up to his problem.

historical explanation: see **explanation (2).**

historical method: the study of persons by tracing the events in their life history. ➤*Cp.* DEVELOPMENTAL METHOD, which has somewhat the same meaning but emphasizes much more the influence of **maturation,** whereas the historical method emphasizes learning and the causal influences of experience. Both are to be contrasted with

the **ahistorical** method.—See **psychology/ divisions and schools of, VIII.**

historigram (his·tô′ri·gram): *n.* (*stat.*) a graph, depicting the changes of a variable over a period of time, in which the **ordinates** are proportional to the values of the variable and the time intervals are plotted as **abscissas.**—*Distg. fr.* **histogram.**

hitch: *v.* to move forward or backward while in a sitting or prone position. ➤This is an infantile mode of locomotion much used prior to walking.

hodological space: see **hodology.**

hodology: *n.* a special geometry concerned with **paths** and **vectors** and the spaces in which they lie. ➤K. Lewin's SPECIAL HODOLOGICAL SPACE is a geometrical **model** or **construct** for which the vectors are defined in dynamic psychological terms. Direction from one hodological region to another is defined, not by the shortest distance (as in Euclid's space), but by the dynamic properties of the two regions, i.e., by their **valences.** The "shortest" distance is the one traversed with the least effort.—*Cp.* **topology.**

holergasia (hol″ər·gā′zhə): *n.* (*A. Meyer*) a psychosis involving the whole personality.

hole screen = reduction screen.

holism (hō′liz·əm): *n.* doctrine that a living being has properties which pertain to the whole rather than to its constituent parts, and that the dynamics of a living whole cannot be explained as resulting from *independent* elements.—*adj.* **holistic.**

holistic theory of intelligence: the doctrine that **intelligence** is an inseparable function of the entire **cerebrum,** that it is a property of the cerebrum which is continuously distributed throughout that organ.

Hollerith (hol′ər·ith): *n.* an electric sorting machine which facilitates many statistical analyses.

Holmgren test (hōlm′grən): a test of color blindness that involves the matching of skeins of different-colored yarn with three standard skeins.

holo-: combining form meaning *whole, complete.*

holograph (hol′ō·graf): *n.* a document in the handwriting of its author.

holoism (hō′lō·iz·əm): *n.* a philosophy of education that insists upon dealing with the whole individual, not with specific functions as if they were independent.—*Cp.* **holism.**

holophrastic (hol″ō·fras′tik): *adj.* characterizing the use of a word to refer to an entire situation rather than to some object, event, or abstract quality in the situation. ➤Some primitive languages require an entirely new word for every important alteration in the situation. A single word means "that man, my uncle, making fire"; a totally different word is required for "that man, my father, making fire," still another is needed for "that man, my uncle, fishing." By contrast, modern languages are highly analytical, a word referring not to the whole situation but to some aspect of it.

home/broken = family/broken.

home/foster: a private-family home that receives one or more children from outside the family for upbringing. ➤Not now used for a home in which the children are legally adopted, although FOSTER PARENT is sometimes so used.

homeo-, homoeo-: combining form meaning *similar, like.*

homeostasis (hō″mi·ō·stā′səs): *n.* the maintenance of constancy of relations or equilibrium in the bodily processes: e.g., the maintenance of a certain proportion of salt in the bodily fluids, no matter what the amount of fluid. Any departure from the equilibrium sets in motion activities that tend to restore it.—*adj.* **homeostatic** (-stat′ik).

homesickness: *n.* a yearning for the familiar home and persons that is so strong as to disrupt behavior and sometimes to give rise to **somatic** symptoms.

homicide: *n.* the illegal killing of one human being by another.

homing: *n.* tendency and ability to return to a former **habitat** when removed to a distance.

hominid (hom′ə·nid): *n.* the human race considered as a family of animals, a division of the order of **primates;** or an individual of that family. Included are all true men, the extinct *Pithecanthropus* as well as modern man.—*adj.* **hominid.**

homo: *n.* 1. man; a man. 2. (*cap.*) the genus of the human family. It includes all modern men as a single species, and several extinct species such as Neanderthal man.—*Cp.* **hominid, primate.**

homo-: combining form meaning *the same, like, of the same kind,* etc.

homoerotism: *n.* **erotism** for one's own sex. ➤The term is more general than **homosexuality** which, even in controlled form, has direct genital reference.

homogamy (hō·mog′ə·mi): *n.* 1. similarity of husband and wife in a specified trait or traits.—*Contr. w.* **heterogamy.** 2. inbreeding in an isolated or segregated group, resulting in the development of similar traits. —*adj.* **homogamous.**

homogeneity (hom″ō·jən·ē′ə·ti): *n.* 1. a characteristic of any group of items which show sameness or marked likeness in the quality or attribute under consideration. 2. a characteristic of a test wherein all the items measure only a single variable (which may be a composite, but in that case must

have unitary and consistent effect upon the test items). For the TEST OF HOMOGENEITY, see **independence/test of.**—*adj.* **homogeneous** (hō″mō·jē′ni·əs; hom″ō-).

homogeneity/coefficient of: (*J. Loevinger*) a measure of the extent to which the items of a test or attitude scale are measuring along the same **dimension.** It is the ratio of the average interitem **covariance** to the average covariance of a perfectly homogeneous set of items with marginals equal to those of the observed items.

homogeneous grouping: see **ability grouping.**

homogenitalism: see **homosexuality.**

homograph (hom′ō·graf): *n.* a word which, in its written form, has two or more different derivations and therefore two or more distinct meanings: e.g., **discipline,** which means a branch of learning, and also means control over the conduct of an inferior.

homolateral: *adj.* pertaining to the same side: e.g., a HOMOLATERAL REFLEX is one with stimulus and response on the same side of the body.

homologous (hō·mol′ə·gəs): *adj.* of bodily structures having essentially similar origin: e.g., the arm of man and the fin of fish.— *n.* **homolog(ue)** (hom′ə·log).—*abstr. n.* **homology** (hō·mol′ə·ji).

homology/behavioral: principle that specific behavior mechanisms form a continuity from the lower to the higher animals: e.g., aggressive attack in rats is **homologous to** aggressive attack in man.

homonomy drive: (*A. Angyal*) the tendency of human beings to participate in, to fit into, and to conform with, superindividual categories such as the family, the social group, a world order.—*Distg. fr.* **homonymy.**

homonym (hom′ō·nim): *n.* a word identical with another in sound but differing in origin, meaning, and often in spelling: e.g., *bear* and *bare.*—*abstr. n.* **homonymy** (hō·-mon′i·mi).—*adj.* **homonymous.**

Homo sapiens (hō′mō sā′pi·enz): *n.* (*L.*) the only extant species of genus **Homo;** man. ➤All men within historic time are regarded as forming this single species. *Sapiens* means intelligent.

homoscedastic (-skə·das′tik): *adj.* characterizing a **double-entry table** whose **arrays** have equal **variability.**—See **scedasticity.**

homosexuality: *n.* tendency to find sexual or erotic gratification with a person of the same sex. ➤When definite genital gratification is meant (pederasty, cunninlinctus, fellatio, mutual masturbation), the term HOMOGENITALISM is more precise; where the sexual element is highly sublimated, HOMOEROTISM is more precise.

Homosexuality is used for the entire range, with no necessary implication of genital practices. In professional usage, there is no implication of inherent pathology, hence **perversion** is not acceptable as a synonym.—*Syn.* GREEK LOVE (for men); **Lesbianism**, or SAPPHISM (for women); **inversion** and **sodomy** (with special meanings).—*adj.* and *pers. n.* **homosexual.**

homosociality: *n.* social relations between persons of the same sex.

homozygous: *adj.* of an individual who has, with respect to a given trait, a **gene pair** containing either two **dominant** or two **recessive** genes; or of such a gene pair. —*Contr. w.* **heterozygous.**—*n.* **homozygote.**

Honi phenomenon: failure of the expected illusion of shape and size, in the distorted room of the **Ames demonstration,** when the person observed is very well known to the observer.

horme (hôr′mi): *n.* purposive striving.—See **hormic theory.**—*Var.* **hormé** (-mā′).

hormic theory: a view which denies that behavior is completely explicable in purely mechanistic or physicochemical terms and asserts that it is always characterized by a striving or urge toward a goal or end which, even when not (consciously) purposeful, is yet **purposive.**—*Var.* **hormic psychology.** —See **psychology/divisions and schools of,** III.

hormone: *n.* a chemical substance produced by one organ and carried by the blood or lymph to another, where it produces a characteristic physiological effect. ➤Not all hormones come from the **endocrine glands.** Some authors restrict **hormone** to positively exciting substances, calling inhibiting substances CHALONES and both forms AUTACOIDS, but this distinction is now seldom observed.—*adj.* **hormonal.**

Horner's law: the generalization that the common forms of color blindness are transmitted from males to males through unaffected females.

horns/anterior: the ventral portions of **gray matter** in the spinal cord, especially connected with production of movement.

horopter (hô·rop′tər): *n.* (*optics*) the locus —with both eyes fixated on any one point— of points in external space whose images are formed on **identical retinal points** and are therefore seen as single.

hostility: *n.* tendency to feel anger toward, and to seek to inflict harm upon, a person or group.—See **anger.**—*adj.* **hostile.**

hostility/displaced = **aggression/displaced.**

House-Tree-Person Test or **H-T-P Test:** a test in which the task is to draw freehand a house, a tree, and a person. The drawings

are interpreted as **projections,** yielding an estimate of maturity.

Hoyt formula: a formula for computing reliability using **analysis of variance:**

$$r_{tt} = 1 - \frac{Vr}{Ve} = \frac{Ve - Vr}{Ve}$$

where Vr = variance for remainder sum of squares, Ve = variance for examinees.

$_sH_R$: Symbols of this general form are alphabetized H.

H scaling: a technique for enhancing the **reproducibility** of attitude scales. It uses several items of about equal frequency of acceptability as if they were one item in the construction of a scalogram.

H test: a test for the **statistical *stability,** or ***significance,** of differences when the observations are **ranked.**

H-T-P Test: see **House-Tree-Person Test.**

hue or **color hue:** *n.* that attribute of visual data, determined normally and chiefly by the dominant rate of light-wave vibration, by which a certain group of colors differ from the white-gray-black series and also from each other: blueness, redness, etc. **2.** any one of the colors possessing this attribute. ➤The very large number of such hues may be grouped as reds, yellows, greens, and blues with their intermediates, the oranges and purples.

hue/extraspectral: see **extraspectral hue.**

hues/invariable: see **invariable hues.**

hull/foreign: see **foreign hull.**

human: *adj.* **1.** pertaining to, or characterizing, man as a species; of that which differentiates man from lower animals. **2.** of weaknesses or faults that are excusable because common to all: anger is only *human.* —*n.* **human.**

human engineering: 1. an applied science, participated in jointly by psychologists and engineers, concerned with the design of equipment and the arranging of the physical conditions of work in relation to human sensory capacities, psychomotor abilities, learning capacities, body dimensions, comfort, safety, and satisfactions. **2.** the art of managing men as the engineer manages materials. ➤This usage is nearly obsolete, though the black art persists.

human family: see **family.**

human nature: the characteristics of all mankind; or those of the portion of mankind which a particular speaker has in mind. ➤It is usually implied that human nature is innate and unchangeable, even though the characteristics referred to clearly result from interaction of **innate** and **cultural** influences and are modifiable, even if not easily so.

humility: *n.* **1.** freedom from pride or arrogance. **2.** the attitude that others are superior. ➤Such attitude may be specific to some trait or individual, or may be quite general. For the latter, **inferiority feeling** is a preferred synonym.—*adj.* **humble.**

Humm-Wadsworth Temperament Scale: a personality questionary designed to reveal a person's status along five **dimensions: paranoid, hysteroid, manic, schizoid, depressive.**

humor (hū'mər): *n.* **1.** an expression, verbal or otherwise, that portrays a situation with a mixture of sympathy and amusement. **2.** a mood, emotional attitude, or tendency to respond favorably or unfavorably to other persons: catch him in a good *humor.* **3.** (*physiol.*) a liquid secretion: e.g., the bile, the **aqueous humor** of the eye. ➤The HUMORAL THEORY of Galen supposed that temperament depended on the proportion of four bodily **humors.**

Humphrey's paradox = arpeggio paradox.

hund: *v.* to oscillate back and forth about a prescribed value. ➤A characteristic of **feedback** systems to be minimized by good design.

hunger: *n.* **1.** (*animal exper.*) a hypothetical bodily state measured by duration of food deprivation. **2.** = HUNGER PANGS, a dull aching sensation, referred to what the person believes to be the stomach region. ➤They are due largely to HUNGER CONTRACTIONS, i.e., to the slow rhythmic contractions of the empty stomach and adjacent parts of the esophagus and small intestine under conditions of hormonal and neural control not well understood. **3.** = HUNGER DRIVE, the restless behavior oriented toward food. ➤Arising initially from need for food, it is often **conditioned** to times and places that have been associated with deprivation and satisfaction, in the absence of any organic need. **4.** a craving for anything one feels deprived of: *oxygen hunger, hunger for affection.*

hunger contraction: see **hunger (2).**

hunger drive: see **hunger (3).**

hunger pangs: see **hunger (2).**

Huntington's chorea: hereditary, chronic, progressive **chorea** with mental **deterioration.**—See **chorea.**

Hunt-Minnesota Test: a test designed to reveal intellectual deterioration that results from brain damage.

hybrid (hī'brid): *n.* **1.** offspring of parents belonging to two different species or varieties. **2.** offspring of parents, one of whom has, and one of whom lacks, a certain **unit *character.** ➤Every organism is thus hybrid in respect to some characters.—*adj.* **hybrid.**—*abstr. n.* **hybridity.**

hydraulic theory: 1. see **hearing theory. 2.** see **accommodation. 3.** (*personality*) belief that **motives** or **tensions** behave like a fluid under pressure, ready to break out through a weak spot when the pressure becomes too great. ➤Derisive: no one so names his own theory.

hydro- (hī'drō-): combining form meaning *water* or *liquid.*

hydrocephalus (-sef'ə·ləs): *n.* a condition of excessive amount and pressure of cerebrospinal fluid within the skull, characterized by marked enlargement of the head and an underdeveloped or atrophied brain. —*Var.* **hydrocephaly** (-li).—*pers. n.* **hydrocephalic.**—*adj.* **hydrocephalic** (-sə·-fal'ik), **hydrocephalous** (-sef'ə·ləs).

hydrophobophobia: *n.* morbid fear of hydrophobia. ➤How much farther shall we carry this agglutinizing process?

hydrotherapy: *n.* treatment by means of hot or cold water, externally applied in bottles, packs, or baths.

hygiene: *n.* the theory and practice of maintaining health in individual or community.—*adj.* **hygienic** (hī'ji·en'ik).

hyp- (hīp-): the form in which **hypo-** appears before a vowel.—See **hypo-.**

hypacusia (hip''ə·kū'zhə; hī''pə-): *n.* hardness of hearing; near-deafness.—See **hearing loss.**—*Var.* **hypacusis, hypoacusia. hypacousia.**—*adj.* and *pers. n.* **hypacusic.**

hypalgesia: *n.* diminished sensibility to pain.

hyper- (hī'pər-): prefix meaning *of high degree* or *excessive:* e.g., *hyperesthesia.* ➤Properly used only with words of Greek origin but often with others.

hyperacusia (-ə·kū'zhə): *n.* exceptionally good hearing.—*Var.* **hyperacusis** (-səs).

hyperalgesia (-al·jē'zi·ə) = **hyperalgia. hyperalgia** (-al'ji·ə): *n.* morbidly great sensitiveness to pain.—*Syn.* HYPERALGESIA.

hypercritical: *adj.* indulging in excessive or quibbling criticism.—*Distg. fr.* **hypocritical.**

hyperergastic: *adj.* pertaining to the overactive state characteristic of the manic phase of **manic-depressive psychosis.**

hyperesthesia: *n.* supersensitiveness to any sense impression, more specif. to touch.

hypergnosis (hī''pər·nō'səs): *n.* the **projection** of inner conflicts onto the environment.—*Var.* **hypergnosia** (-nō'zhə).

hyperkinesis: *n.* excessive mobility or motor restlessness. It includes **tremors, athetosis, choreoathetosis, hemiballismus.**

hyperkinesthesia: *n.* extreme sensitivity to kinesthetic sensations.

hyperlogia = hyperphrasia.

hypermetropia = hyperopia.

hypermnesia (hī''pərm·nē'zi·ə): *n.* unusual memory ability.

hyperopia: *n.* a condition in which light rays come to a focus behind the retina instead of directly upon it. ➤Commonly called FARSIGHTEDNESS (since distant objects can be seen with less strain upon the eye muscles of accommodation than near ones), which is a misnomer insofar as it implies what is not the case, namely, that the hyperope can see farther or more clearly at a given distance than a normal person.— *Var.* **hypermetropia.**—*pers. n.* **hyperope.** —*adj.* **hyperopic.**

hyperorexia (-ô·rek′si·ə): *n.* excessive appetite for food.

hyperosmia: *n.* heightened acuity or sensitivity to odors.

hyperphoria: see **heterophoria.**

hyperphrasia: *n.* abnormal volubility of speech, associated with morbid excitement in some psychoses.—*Syn.* HYPERLOGIA, POLYPHRASIA.

hyperphrenia: *n.* excessive degree of mental activity—a form of **mania.**

hyperplane: *n.* (*math., factor anal.*) the subspace of (*n* − 1) dimensions, defined by a reference vector perpendicular to it. In the case of three dimensions (*n* = 3), the hyperplane is a two-dimensional space (*n* − 1 = 2) defined by any two coordinate axes.

hyperplasia: *n.* excessive increase in the number of cells in a tissue or organ.—*adj.* **hyperplastic.**

hyperpnea (hī′pərp·nē′ə): *n.* panting; excessive breathing.

hyperprosexia: *n.* exaggerated attention to something, with inability to ignore it: e.g., to a flapping window shade at night.—*Cp.* **obsession.**

hypersomnia: *n.* uncontrollable sleepiness not due to sleep deprivation or to illness. It is usually accompanied by feelings of unreality.

hypertension: *n.* any high tension in a tissue; more specif., high blood pressure.

hypertension/essential: high blood pressure without known cause.

hyperthymia (-thī′mi·ə): *n.* heightened emotional response.

hyperthyroidism: *n.* a condition in which there is excessive secretion by the thyroid gland. Its most direct psychological correlate is great excitability and restlessness.

hypertonicity: *n.* excessive tension in the resting condition of a muscle.—*Var.* **hypertonia, hypertonus.**—*adj.* **hypertonic.**

hypertrophy (hī·pėr′trō·fi): *n.* excessive growth of a tissue or organ.

hypertropia: *n.* condition in which one eye fixes an object and the other deviates upward—a form of **strabismus.**

hypesthesia: *n.* undersensitivity (*prefd.*). ➤It is true that the English word does not specify the **sense** *modality, but neither does the Greek.—*Var.* **hypoesthesia.**

hypnagogic (hip″nə·goj′ik): *adj.* pertaining to drowsiness; bringing on sleep. ➤A HYPNAGOGIC HALLUCINATION or IMAGE is one that occurs while falling asleep or while awakening.—*Var.* **hypnogogic.**

hypn(o)- (hip′nō-): combining form meaning *sleep* or *trance.*

hypnoanalysis: *n.* psychoanalysis carried on while the patient is under hypnosis.

hypnogenic: *adj.* 1. producing sleep. 2. producing hypnosis.

hypnoidal (-noi′dəl): *adj.* resembling **hypnosis.**

hypnopompic: *adj.* of the drowsy state of awakening from deep sleep.

hypnosis: *n.* an artificially induced state characterized by greatly heightened suggestibility to the hypnotist. ➤Usually the person passes through a drowsy or sleeplike state, hence the name. The state is usually attained by bodily relaxation accompanied by attention, at the suggestion of the hypnotist, to a narrow range of objects or ideas. A person under hypnosis shows extreme responsiveness to any suggestion made by the hypnotist. Varying degrees or depths of hypnosis are distinguished.—*Distg.* **hypnosis,** the state, *fr.* **hypnotism,** the process. —*pers. n.* **hypnotist,** the person who induces hypnosis.—*v.* **hypnotize.**

hypnotherapy: *n.* the use of **hypnosis** either as an aid or as the primary means of treatment of bodily or mental disorder.

hypnotic (hip·not′ik): *adj.* 1. pertaining to **hypnosis** or **hypnotism.** 2. of a drug or other agency that induces sleep.

hypnotism: *n.* the theory and practice of hypnosis.—*Distg. fr.* the state of **hypnosis.**

hypnotize: *v.* to induce **hypnosis;** metaphorically, to influence another person, by strong persuasion or personal charm, to do what he would not otherwise have done.

hyp(o)- (hī′po-): prefix meaning *below, under, defective, lacking*: e.g., **hypothyroidism,** insufficiency of thyroid function.

hypochondria (-kon′dri·ə): *n.* morbid concern about one's health, with exaggeration of every trifling symptom.—*Var.* **hypochondriasis** (-kən·drī′ə·səs).—*pers. n.* **hypochondriac** (-kon′dri·ak).—*adj.* **hypochondriacal** (-kən·drī′ə·kəl).

hypocrisy (hi·pok′rə·si): *n.* a pretense to attitudes and beliefs one does not have.— *pers. n.* **hypocrite.**—*adj.* **hypocritical** (hip″ō-).

hypodermic: *adj.* pertaining to that which lies beneath the skin; specif., of a drug given by injection beneath the skin.

hypoergastic reaction (hī″pō·ər·gas′tik): the depressed state that characterizes the depressive phase of **manic-depressive psychosis.**

hypofunction: *n.* operation at less-than-normal rate or strength.

hypoglossal nerve (-glos′əl): the XIIth, or most **caudad, cranial** nerve.

hypoglycemia (-glī·sē′mi·ə): *n.* a deficiency of sugar in the blood.

hypoglycemic (shock) therapy: treatment of mental disorder by inducing **shock** due to severe shortage of blood sugar.

hypognathous (hī·pog′nəth·əs): *adj.* having an underjaw that projects beyond the upper.—*Cp.* **prognathous.**

hypokinesis (-kin·ē′səs): *n.* diminished motor function or activity.

hypologia: *n.* abnormal lack of ability for speech, resulting either from low intelligence level or from cerebral disorder.

hypomania: *n.* a mild state of **mania.** ➤There is excitement, energy, impatience, and flightiness; yet, in an otherwise normal person, the condition may be productive.—*pers. n.* and *adj.* **hypomanic.**

hypophoria: see **heterophoria.**

hypophrasia: *n.* the lack of speech, or slowness of speech, that characterizes the depressed phase of certain psychoses.

hypophrenia (-frē′ni·ə): *n.* (*E. Southard*) proposed synonym for **mental *deficiency.**

hypophysectomy (hī·pof″is·ec′tə·mi): *n.* surgical removal of the **hypophysis.**

hypophysis (hī·pof′i·səs): *n.* the **pituitary body.**

hypopituitarism (hī″pō·pi·tü′i·tə·riz·əm): *n.* deficient secretion of the **pituitary** gland.

hypoplastic: *adj.* structurally deficient; incomplete.—*n.* **hypoplasia.**

hypoprosexia (-prō·sek′si·ə): *n.* inadequacy of attention.

hypostatization (hī·pos′tə·tiz·ā″shən): *n.* attributing substantial existence to something; the postulation of **entities.** ➤Used especially of such attribution of distinct existence to **abstractions,** as is the case when truthfulness—the abstract quality of truth-telling acts—is regarded as existing as a **trait.**

hypothalamus (-thal′ə·məs): *n.* a group of **nuclei,** at the base of the brain, which constitutes the inferior portion of the **diencephalon.** It is involved in many visceral regulative processes.

hypothecate (hī·poth′ə·kāt): *v.* to loan; to pawn. ➤Since **hypothesis** had no good verb, **hypothecate** was seized on by those who did not know its meaning. The error was compounded when **hypothecation** was used for the formation of hypotheses. **Hypothesize** and **hypothesizing** (derived from hypothesis) are now, however, the accepted verbal forms.

hypothesis: *n.* 1. an explanation of a complex set of data, admittedly tentative and not yet proved. ➤*Cp.* **speculation,** for which supporting facts or arguments are very few and inadequate; and **theory,** which is a developed hypothesis supported by very substantial evidence. Formulation of a hypothesis is usually the first step in problem-solving. **2.** a process inferred to account for the fact that an animal will *repeat* a response to a certain stimulus many times, despite the fact that it often does not lead to satisfaction. ➤The animal is said to have the behaviorial equivalent of the hypothesis "If I make the response R′ to S′, I will reach my goal, G′."—See **expectancy.**—*adj.* **hypothetical.**—*v.* **hypothesize** (not **hypothecate,** which means to put in pawn).

hypothesis/and-summation: see **and-summation hypothesis.**

hypothesis/constancy: see **constancy hypothesis.**

hypothesis/null: see **null hypothesis.**

hypothetical: *adj.* of an idea or proposition tentatively accepted or proposed. ➤Hypothetical reasoning involves putting forward a **hypothesis** for examination of its logical and factual implications, as a step toward proof or disproof.—See **construct/hypothetical.**

hypothetical construct: see **construct/ hypothetical.**

hypothetical process variable: see **process variable/hypothetical.**

hypothetical proposition: a statement consisting of two parts: an ANTECEDENT clause introduced by *if* (or some equivalent) which states the condition under which a certain result will occur or under which a certain conclusion will be reached, and a CONSEQUENT which states the occurrence or the conclusion. E.g.: *If educational segregation does not provide equal facilities* (the antecedent), *it is unconstitutional* (the consequent).

hypothetical reasoning: a kind of formal reasoning that begins with a **hypothetical proposition** or premise: e.g., *if he reads the book, he will learn.* There are four possible premises to continue the argument: (*a*) *he does read the book* (= affirming the antecedent); (*b*) *he does not read the book* (denying the antecedent); (*c*) *he does learn* (affirming the consequent); (*d*) *he does not learn* (denying the consequent). Only (*a*) and (*d*) in combination with the hypothetical premise lead to logical conclusions; (*b*) and (*c*) are **fallacies.**

hypothetical state variable: see **state variable/hypothetical.**

hypothetico-deductive method: a general method that starts with a small number of empirically founded principles and definitions, subject to revision when new facts are found (hence, **hypothetical**), and that proceeds by rigorous **deduction** to experimentally testable theorems and corollaries —*Distg. fr.* **postulational method.**—*Syn* (*C. Hull*) MATHEMATICO-DEDUCTIVE METHOD (not *prefd.*).—See **psychology/divisions and schools of, I.**

hypothymia (-thī'mi·ə): *n.* condition of subnormal emotional response and depression.

hypothyroid: *adj.* deficient in thyroid secretion or activity.—*n.* **hypothyroidism.**

hypotonic: *adj.* of a muscle lacking tone or tension; relaxed.

hypoxemia (hī·pok·sē'mi·ə): *n.* a condition of deficient oxygen in the blood. ➤*Contr. w.* HYPOXIA, insufficiency of oxygen in the air inhaled.

hysteria: **1.** a disorder with a variety of symptoms: **hallucinations,** emotional upsets, **somnambulisms,** anesthesias, **paralyses,** etc. The essential feature is variously held to be emotional instability, weakness, or **dissociation.** ➤Where there are somatic symptoms (not merely disordered behavior), many authors refer to **conversion** *hysteria.—See **conversion** (2). **2.** (*pop.*) any unhealthy emotionalism. —*adj.* **hysterical** (-ter'ik·əl), **hysteric.**

hysteria/anxiety: see **anxiety hysteria.**

hysteria/conversion = **conversion (2).**

hysterical: *adj.* **1.** of symptoms due to a basic disorder of **hysteria;** or of a person who has hysteria. **2.** characterizing a functional disorder: *hysterical blindness, hysterical mutism, hysterical anesthesia, hysterical contracture.* ➤In all these cases, the local mechanism is structurally intact, yet the organism does not make use of it properly. In HYSTERICAL BLINDNESS, e.g., it can be proved that the eye transmits to the brain as usual but the patient does not see, or does not see certain kinds of objects.

hysterics (his·ter'iks): *n. pl.* **1.** an attack of **hysteria. 2.** (*pop.*) a fit of uncontrollable laughter and crying.

hysteriform (his·ter'i·form; -tir'-): *adj.* resembling **hysteria:** e.g., HYSTERIFORM SEIZURES, convulsions with partial loss of consciousness.

hysteroid (his'tər·oid): *adj.* simulating **hysteria;** of minor symptoms like those of **hysteria.**

I

I: 1. = index number. **2.** = **induction.**— See **abilities/primary mental. 3.** = **luminous intensity.**

I_R = (*C. Hull*) reactive *inhibition.

$_sI_R$ = (*C. Hull*) amount of conditioned **inhibitory potential.**—*Distg fr.* $_s\underline{I}_R$.

$_s\underline{I}_R$ = (*C. Hull*) generalized **inhibitory potential.**

$_s\underline{I}_R$: (*C. Hull*) aggregate **inhibitory potential.**

i: (*math.*) symbol for the **imaginary quantity** $\sqrt{-1}$ as a factor: e.g., $i\sqrt{9}$.

i. or **c.i.** = **class interval.**

-ia: noun suffix used with words of Greek origin, generally giving the root the meaning of *disease* or *disordered state*: e.g., **analgesia,** abnormal insensibility to pain.

-iatric, iatro-, -iatry: combining forms meaning *healing*; hence, *physician-healer* or *medicine.*

iatrogenic illness (ī·at″rō·jen'ik): a **functional disorder** caused by a physician's diagnosis or attitude. ➤It does not refer to the direct effects of medical treatment.—*Syn.* IATROGENIC NEUROSIS.

IBM = International Business Machine.

icebreaker: *n.* an easy practice exercise in a test or experiment, designed to put the subject at his ease.

iconic (ī·kon'ik): *adj.* pertaining to an idol, image, or representation of something; in logic, of a symbol that has many of the properties of that which it symbolizes: e.g., a motion picture.—*n.* **icon.**

ictus (ik'təs): *n.* **1.** the accentuation of a tone or syllable.—*Syn.* ACCENT. **2.** (*med.*) a seizure or stroke.

ICW Interest Record: the Institute of Child Welfare form for the cumulative record of a child's interests over a seven-year period. It includes athletic, social, mechanical, scientific, and intellectual-cultural interests.

id: *n.* (*L.* for *it*) (*psychoan.*) that division of the **psyche** from which come blind, impersonal, **instinctual** impulses that lead to immediate gratification of primitive needs. ➤The **id** is conceived as the true **unconscious,** or the deepest part of the **psyche.** It is in contact not with the world but only with the body, and in its relations with the body it is dominated by the **pleasure principle.** While descriptions of the id and its functions are couched in personalized terms, it is explicitly held that the id is not an entity but is merely a description of a system of actions. Some psychoanalysts now hold that the id is one aspect of the **id-ego,** and not a separate division.

idea: *n.* **1.** (*hist.*) any **mental content;** "whatever is the object of understanding when a man thinks." (*Locke*) **2.** any **cognitive** process not primarily and directly sensory: imagining and thinking. **3.** the object of any nonsensory cognitive process. **4.** (*pop.*) plan; project; general notion; central issue; fantasy; belief; opinion; something not actual or real; etc. ➤Nothing less than the complete *Oxford English Dic-*

tionary can give any idea of the many uses of **idea**. Such a term has no place in science, but this one is difficult to avoid since no substitutes have been generally agreed upon.—See **act/pure stimulus, covert response, symbolic process**.— *adj.* **ideational, ideal** (*hist.*).

idea/autochthonous: see **autochthonous** (3).

idea/controlling: see **controlling idea**.

idea/fixed: see **fixed idea**.

idea/imperative: see **fixed idea**.

ideal: *n.* 1. the representation of the essential characteristics of something, without details; the essence of something. 2. a condition regarded as desirable; a standard of perfection, often with the implication that it is unattainable. 3. a standard of behavior for oneself; a personal condition toward which one strives. ➤The SELF-IDEAL is the integration of the **values** one holds for oneself and which one seeks to realize; it is an important **sentiment** and an important unifying or integrating influence in personality.—*adj.* **ideal** (which is still sometimes also the adjective for **idea**); **idealized** for (1).

idealism: *n.* 1. philosophical doctrine that interprets the ultimate reality of the universe in terms of mind or self or spirit. ➤As it affects psychology, see **mind-body problem**. 2. practice of formulating lofty **ideals** (3) of personal conduct and of attempting to live by them. ➤Often there is the implication of being too much influenced by ideals and too little by practical considerations.—*Ant.* **realism** (which see for a variety of meanings).—*adj.* and *pers. n.* **idealistic**.

idealization: *n.* conceiving of something as **ideal** (2), perfect, or better than it is; an exaggeration of virtues and a minimizing of faults.—*Cp.* **autism**.

idealized: *adj.* 1. characterized by **idealization**. 2. pertaining to an **ideal** (1), or to an **ideal type**.

ideal type: a representation of all the essential characteristics of a certain category, although no one individual embodies all these characteristics: e.g., the *ideal flower* is a representation of all flower characteristics, but no flower has them all.

idea/overcharged: (*psychoan.*) an idea so strongly charged with feeling or **psychic energy** that it appears in a dream in more than one symbolic representation.

ideas/community of: see **community of ideas**.

ideation (ĭ″di·ā′shən): *n.* 1. the process of forming **ideas**. 2. the processes in a subhuman that enable it to react to an absent stimulus object.

ideational: *adj.* pertaining to **idea** or **ideation** (not to **ideal**).

ideational learning: see **learning/ideational**.

idée fixe (ē·dā″fēks′) = (*Fr.*) **fixed idea**.

idée-force (ē·dā·fors′): *n.* (*Fr.*) postulate that all ideas have a dynamic influence; that ideas inherently are directly related to action.

id-ego: *n.* (*psychoan.*) 1. the original matrix in the newborn out of which the **id** and **ego** develop. 2. that division of the **psyche** which performs the **id** and **ego** functions. ➤Formerly id and ego were conceived as separate entities; they are now considered by many to be merely names of contrasting functions.

identical: *adj.* 1. similar in every respect; sometimes, similar in every relevant respect. 2. interchangeable in every relevant respect under any conditions.—See **identity**.

identical elements theory: a theory of **transfer** of training which proposes that a new task is learned more easily to the extent that it contains the same components as tasks already mastered.—*Syn.* IDENTICAL COMPONENTS THEORY.

identical points: any pair of retinal points in the two eyes that, when the eyes are in the primary position, receive stimuli from the same objective point at infinite distance.—*Distg. fr.* **congruent points**.—*Syn.* IDENTICAL RETINAL POINTS, **corresponding points** (*ambig.*).

identical twins: see **twins/identical**.

identifiability principle: generalization that it is easier to learn to make responses to situations, or to elements in a situation, when those situations are readily identified separately or distinguished from others.

identification: *n.* ➤Three general meanings for this term are found: **A.** recognizing an **identity**; **B.** transferring response to an object considered as being identical with another; **C.** becoming identical through affiliation. Although the definitions are grouped according to these general meanings, any given usage may borrow something from each of the three general meanings.

A. 1. the process of recognizing that a given individual or specimen is in some important respect really the same as another; the perception of identity. **2.** the recognition in an individual of the attributes by which he (or it) can be classified or assigned to a place, role, or function: *identification* of a suspect, *identification* of a plant. **3.** the recognition of the unique pattern of a person; the recognition of the continuing identity of the self despite changes.—*Syn.* **individualization**, growth of self-awareness (both with a different emphasis but denoting the same process) ➤In meanings (1) and (2), there is recognition of common elements, leading to **classification**; in (3) of a unique totality, leading to **differentiation** from others. **4.** the typing of a person in terms of a group or a cause with which he is strongly affiliated: *identification* as a capitalist. ➤In (1) the attributes lead to classification; in (4) classification leads to the ascription of attributes.—*Cp.* **stereotyping.**

B. 5. reacting to a situation as if it were the same as one previously experienced—a behavioral recognition of identity in some respect. ➤All language involves this kind of identification. As compared with (1), emphasis here is upon the response *to,* rather than recognition *of,* identity. The recognition may be wholly implicit.—*Syn.* **transfer, transference, response *generalization. 6.** (*gen. semantics*) applying a class name, and thus implying a large degree of identity, though it does not in fact exist. ➤MISIDENTIFICATION or OVERIDENTIFICATION are more descriptive of this meaning.—*Cp.* (4). **7.** carrying over into relations with one person the response patterns that pertain to another: e.g., the child's reaction to the teacher as if she were his mother.—*Syn.* **transference.** ➤The shift may take place because of similarity in behavior, role, or appearance. Often the **cue** is minimal. ¶This kind of identification, especially when unconscious, is given much prominence in psychoanalysis. During treatment the **analysand** (usually unconsciously) identifies the analyst with the parent but also with himself. **8.** seeing another person as an extension of oneself, hence seeking satisfactions through that other, and sharing the other's griefs and triumphs. ➤This is the identification experienced in drama or literature, but it is also the mechanism at work when a parent insists that a child fulfill his own unfulfilled ambitions. This mechanism is a form of **wish fulfillment.**—*Syn.* **projection (2),** SECONDARY IDENTIFICATION.

C. 9. associating or affiliating oneself closely with a person or group. **10.** accepting as one's own the purposes and values of another person (or of a group); merging or submerging one's own purposes and values with the other. ➤**Imitation** of outward behavior, and **sympathy** or **empathy** with the other's feelings are frequent correlates. (Hence, **introjection** is a partial synonym.) Identification in this sense is sometimes a synonym for the sentiment of love (which it implies), but is better regarded as its correlate. According to psychoanalysis, the PRIMARY IDENTIFICATION is with parents and is the basis of the **superego.** ¶Identification in this sense is more active than that of meaning (8). It plays a large part in religious teaching and

in mysticism. It is a large factor in group cohesiveness.

The many meanings of **identification** are fairly congruous and do not create confusion when they blend, although they tend to lose precision.—*v.* **identify.**

identification/group: the process wherein the individual so strongly feels himself a member of a group that he adopts its ideas, beliefs, and habits.—*Cp.* **reference *group.**

identification/primary: see **identification** (10).

identification/secondary: see **identification** (8).

identification test: a test in which the examiner points to an object or part of a picture and requires the testee to name or otherwise identify it.

identification/transferred: see **identification** (7) or (8).

identify: *v.* **1.** to recognize in an individual or specimen the attributes by means of which it can be classified; esp. (in biology), to assign a specimen to its species.—*Syn.* **classify. 2.** to establish personal **identity;** to recognize the unique pattern of attributes of an individual; to distinguish an individual from everything else.—*Syn.* **individualize.** ➤Note that the same process of recognizing attributes leads to opposite effects in (1) and (2). **3.** to unite or combine as one; to treat as one for a certain purpose. ➤This is an extension of (1). **4.** to associate oneself with a person, interest, or group; to join a group.—*Cp.* **identification (9)** and **(10). 5.** to accept a person emotionally so completely that his purposes are more important than one's own.—See **identification (10).**

identity: *n.* **1.** sameness of essential character despite superficial differences. **2.** = PERSONAL IDENTITY, the unity of personality over a period of time. **3.** (*math., logic*) a relation between two or more objects, events, or symbols, such that one can always be substituted for the other; or the relation between two or more representations that, despite superficial differences, are known to refer to the same element of reality.—*Distg. fr.* **similarity.**

identity/formal: see **formal identity.**

identity/law of: the postulate of Aristotelian logic that A is A. ➤The postulate is useful as a test for verbal reasoning, but one of the important lessons of **empirical** experience is that A is not always A.

ideo- (id′i·ō-; ĭ′di·ō-): combining form meaning *idea.*—*Distg. fr.* **idio-.**

ideodynamics: see **idiodynamics.**

ideogram: *n.* an element in a system of writing wherein an object or an idea is directly represented by a single symbol (which may be complex): e.g., a picture of an eye meaning literally *the eye*; or a picture of two men and a woman meaning *trouble.—Syn.* IDEOGRAPH.

ideokinetic apraxia: see **apraxia/ideokinetic.**

ideology (ī″di·ol′ə·ji; id″i-): *n.* the complex system of ideas, beliefs, and attitudes that constitutes for an individual or a group a total (or at least very extensive) philosophy or world view.

ideomotor (id″i·ō·mō′tər; ī″di·ō-): *adj.* characterizing a sequence in which a motor response is elicited by an **idea,** as compared with **sensorimotor** in which it is elicited by a sense stimulus. ➤The IDEOMOTOR THEORY held that there is an inherent tendency in each idea to result in corresponding action, and especially that the idea or thought of a movement tends to bring it about.

ideomotor apraxia = apraxia/ideational.

idio- (id′i·ō-): combining form meaning *one's own, personal, private, distinct, invented*; hence, *unique, the only one of its kind.*

idiocy: see **deficiency/mental.**

idiocy/amaurotic: see **amaurotic idiocy.**

idiodynamics: *n.* a point of view in psychology emphasizing, as its central concept, the role of the personality or of the individual in selecting stimuli and organizing responses. ➤It contrasts with the view that makes its central concept the eliciting of responses by stimuli. It is not the same as IDEODYNAMICS, the emphasis upon the power of ideas.

idioglossia: *n.* speech that is defective in such degree that it seems to be another language. The same sounds may be used consistently for the same ideas but are unintelligible unless the hearer understands the key to the sound substitutions.*—Syn.* IDIOLALIA, INVENTED LANGUAGE.

idiographic: *adj.* pertaining to, or characterizing, an account of particular or individual cases or events.*—Ant.* **nomothetic.**

idiographic psychology: see **psychology/divisions and schools of, VII.**

idiolalia (-lā′li·ə) **= idioglossia.**

idiom (id′i·əm): *n.* **1.** the characteristic ways in which ideas are expressed in a language. **2.** a person's characteristic mode of behavior, esp. of socially noticeable behaviors.*—adj.* **idiomatic.**

idiopathic: *adj.* (*med.*) of a diseased condition or symptom whose origin is within the organ involved and not the result of something external to the organ; of a disease that is primary—i.e., does not result from another disease.*—n.* **idiopathy** (-op′-ə·thi).*—Distg. fr.* **idiosyncrasy.**

idiophrenic (-fren′ik): *adj.* **1.** pertaining to mental disorder caused by disease of the brain. **2. = psychogenic.** ➤It is often

argued that **neologisms** permit of precise and unambiguous terminology. Yet this term has almost exactly opposite meanings, the first of which is fortunately obsolescent, the second unnecessary.

idioretinal light = cortical gray.

idiosyncrasy (-sin′krə·si): *n.* **1.** a behavior or trait, or some pattern of behaviors or traits, peculiar to an individual or to a group; esp., such a characteristic as is readily noted and serves to distinguish the individual from others. ➤See discussion under **unique. 2.** an oddity. **3.** (*psychiat.*) hatred of a **fetish** object.*—adj.* **idiosyncratic** (-sin·krat′ik).

idiot (id′i·ət): see **deficiency/mental.**—*n.* (for the condition) **idiocy.**—*adj.* **idiotic.**

idiotropic (-trō′pik): *adj.* turning inward upon one's self; of a person content with isolation and deriving satisfaction from his own inner life.*—Syn.* **introspective.**

idiot savant (id′i·ō sə·vän′): *n.* (*Fr., idiotic scholar*) a feeble-minded person possessed of a high degree of some special ability, such as ability to calculate. ➤Where the special ability is of any degree of complexity, the appropriateness of the classification **feeble-minded** is questioned; but the idiot savant shows the same incapacities in other respects as those so classified, and frequently needs to be institutionalized.

idiotypic (-tip′ik): *adj.* pertaining to heredity.

idioverse: *n.* (*S. Rosenzweig*) a particular individual's universe of events.*—Syn.* **life space** (past and present).

idol: *n.* **1.** an effigy or natural object that is worshipped. **2.** a **prejudice** that obstructs scientific or logical thinking. ➤Bacon distinguished four kinds of idols (or IDOLA): the IDOLA TRIBUS (of the tribe), the prejudices common to mankind (or to a culture, as we should now say); IDOLA SPECUS (of the cave), the prejudices of specialization; IDOLA FORI (of the market place), the prejudices that come from association with other people; and IDOLA TEATRI (of the "theater"), the prejudices due to a received philosophical or religious doctrine.

I/E **ratio:** rate of **inspiration** divided by rate of **expiration.**

IER Tests: a **point scale** for intelligence developed by the Institute of Educational Research.

I. E. **scale:** a scoring procedure for the **MMPI** that yields scores on the dimension of social **introversion-extraversion.**

IFD: the initials of *idealism, frustration, demoralization,* the sequence which is said to characterize many maladjustments.

-iform: suffix meaning *in the form of, like,* or *similar to.*

I **fraction:** ratio of time of **inspiration** to the total time of **inspiration-expiration.**

I.J.S. Verbal Test: a test based on analysis of verbal associations. It attempts to measure creativity and organizational ability as qualities distinct from logical intelligence.

illata (il·ä′tə): *n. pl.* (*fr. L. inferre*) things inferred, such as molecules or other people's minds.—*Cp.* **construct.**

illegitimate: *adj.* **1.** of a child born out of wedlock. **2.** of that which violates laws, esp. laws concerning either sex relations or the canons of logic.—*Syn.* **illicit** (*prefd.* for logic).—*n.* **illegitimacy.**

illicit: *adj.* contrary to law, to custom having the force of law, or to logic.

illiteracy: *n.* **1.** inability to read or write. ➤The U.S. Census defines illiteracy as inability, after age 10, to read or write in any language. The usual criterion in the U.S. is inability to read or write at third- or fourth-grade standard, but sometimes the criterion is "unable to read anything." In psychological discussion, illiteracy does not include **alexia** and **agraphia. 2.** limited knowledge in a special field: e.g., musical *illiteracy.*—*adj.* and *pers. n.* **illiterate.**

illness/iatrogenic: see **iatrogenic illness.**

illness/mental: see **mental illness.**

illogical: *adj.* contrary to **logic.**—*Ant.* **logical** (which see).

illuminance: *n.* (*phys.*) the intensity of the light energy falling upon a surface; the density of light-flux incident to a surface. The most common unit of measurement is the **foot-candle.**—See **luminance, brightness.**—*adj.* **illuminant.**

illuminant color: see **color/illuminant.**

illumination: 1. = **illuminance** or *M*; roughly, the amount of light falling upon a surface. **2.** the supplying of light; or the study of light supply. **3.** a clarifying of a complex idea or problem. ➤Sometimes the term is restricted to sudden clarification or **insight,** or to the case where one returns to the essentials of the problem after a period of inattention, but these cases seem to denote the same process as the general one stated in definition **(3).** *Cp.* the stages of **preparation, incubation, illumination, verification.**

illumination flicker: flicker seen as belonging to the illuminated space rather than to the surfaces or objects seen in it.

illumination/law of: the principle that the **illuminance** of a surface varies directly as the **luminous** intensity of the light source, inversely as the square of its distance, and directly as the cosine of the angle made by the light rays with the perpendicular to the surface.—*Syn.* LAW OF ILLUMINANCE.

illusion: *n.* mistaken **perception.** ➤In some cases the laws of physics explain the error: e.g., the laws of **optics** account for the apparent bending of a stick thrust into

water (PHYSICAL ILLUSION). In others the explanation lies with the perceiver (PSYCHOLOGICAL ILLUSION). But in **illusion** there is always an object, though it is incorrectly perceived. In **hallucination,** the object is either lacking or has only a fantastic similarity to the object for which it is mistaken. In general, also, illusions are normal and subject to regular rule, whereas hallucinations, though not infrequently experienced by normal persons, are essentially abnormal phenomena. Both illusion and hallucination have a compulsive sense of their reality, usually even when one is assured of their unreality. Illusion is also loosely used for **delusion,** but this is to be avoided. (But the expression ILLUSION OF MEMORY is well established for a false memory in which the subject firmly believes.) In actual cases, however, it may be difficult to decide whether we have illusion, hallucination, or delusion.—*adj.*

illusory (i·lü′sə·ri), **illusive.**

illusion/assimilative: see **illusion/associative.**

illusion/associative: a visual illusion in which part of the field is misperceived because of the influence in the visual field of certain related objects or elements. ➤E.g., the length of a line is misperceived because of certain other lines seen as forming part of the same percept.—*Syn.* CONTRAST ILLUSION, which is somewhat more limited to contrasting related objects.—*Distg. fr.* ASSIMILATIVE ILLUSION, in which the whole percept is affected by the context or by the person's attitude. E.g., a bush seen as a crouching animal is misperceived as a whole, the perception of all its aspects or features being affected.

illusion/contrast = **illusion/associative.**

illusion/memory: 1. a **delusion** that the experience of another person is one's own. **2.** a false memory in which the subject firmly believes; a memory **delusion.**

illusion of movement: see **movement/ illusion of.**

illusory motion: see **motion/apparent.**

illustriousness: *n.* level of ability, as recognized by others, attained by one in a million. ➤See **eminence** for the gradation **distinction, eminence, illustriousness.**

image (im′ij): *n.* **1.** a likeness or copy. **2.** = OPTICAL IMAGE, a picture of an object produced by focusing with a mirror or lens; specif., the RETINAL IMAGE, a picture of an object on the retina when refracted through the optical system of the eye. ➤The **image,** subject to imperfections in the optical system, is a point-for-point duplication of the plane view of the object. The retinal image is to be clearly distinguished from all of the following meanings. **3.** (*traditional* and *pop.*) a mental copy of something not pres-

ent to the senses.—See **mental *image.**
4. a composite of a person's concepts, judgments, preferences, and attitudes toward some comprehensive object such as a nation or toward a cause such as pacifism. ➤The image in this sense emphasizes the cognitive content of a sentiment—which may sometimes be only loosely organized. **5.** = **imago** (which see). **6.** = **image/ memory** (which see).—*adj.* **imaginal.**—*v.* for (1) and (2), **image,** to reflect or refract onto a surface; for (3), **imagine,** to take account of the characters of an object not now present to the senses.

image/anticipation: see **imagination (2).**
image/body: see **body image.**
image/collective: (*C. Jung*) an image in the **unconscious** coming from racial experience; a **primordial *image.**
image/composite: 1. an **image** made up of parts of different **memory *images.**— See **imagination** (2). **2.** = **composite figure.**
image/eidetic: see **eidetic imagery.**
image/general: an **image** (3) regarded by the subject as standing for any one of a class of objects.
image/hallucinatory: an **image** (3) mistaken for reality.
image/hypnagogic: see **hypnagogic.**
image/idealized: *n.* **1.** (*psychoan.*) a false conception of one's virtues and assets developed as a **defense** against the demands of the **ego ideal. 2.** (*K. Horney*) the irrationally imagined unconscious image of oneself as he should be according to the dictates of neurotic pride. It is characterized by the glorified, aggrandized, and perfected qualities derived from a person's previous fantasies, experiences, needs, and capacities. —*Distg. fr.* **idealized *self.**
imageless thought: 1. (*structural psychol.*) an idea or thought which, upon careful introspective analysis, reveals no **sensations** or images. ➤Within the **structural psychology** school there is controversy concerning the existence of such thoughts. Apparently imageless thinking—e.g., the awareness of relationship—is explained by some as consisting of fleeting **kinesthetic** and **vocomotor** sensations and images. **2.** responding to the properties of an object other than those directly revealed by sensory process. ➤This is better called NON-SENSORY THINKING. In this meaning, the fact that sensory process may influence the thinking is not denied but the response nonetheless is primarily to nonsensory properties, such as relations.—*Cp.* **attitude, set.**
image/memory: a more or less complete representation of the attributes of an object or event once experienced but not now present to the senses, together with recognition of its "pastness"; a revival that re-

sembles but need not exactly copy a past experience. The image may be sensory or verbal or both.
image/mental: a mental representation of something not present to the senses. ➤It was the traditional view that, in **imagining,** the mind contemplated a sort of "mental stuff"—a copy or **image** of a not-present but objective reality. This view is metaphysical, but those who contend that this metaphysics has no place in psychology find it difficult, on the one hand, to say what the image is or, on the other, to dispense with the term altogether. No sharp line, moreover, can be drawn between the meaning of **image** and of **idea.**

Despite the fact that we cannot well say what an image is, we have many terms by which we distinguish different kinds. An image that is said to have the direct sensory quality of the original object is **concrete.** CONCRETE IMAGES are usually further distinguished according to their sensory quality as visual, auditory, olfactory, gustatory, tactual, or kinesthetic. They may also be called COMPOSITE when they combine more than one sensory **modality.**

Contrasted with concrete images are the VERBAL IMAGES representing either an object or a past speech experience in verbal terms. These also may be further classified as visual-verbal, auditory-verbal, kinesthetic-verbal (writing words), or vocomotor (speaking).

If an image carries a general meaning— *an image of a horse,* meaning *any* horse— it may be called a GENERAL IMAGE, although *general idea* better expresses this. Other distinctions according to the function served by the image are treated under **imagination.**—*adj.* **imaginal,** pertaining to an image; **imaginary,** pertaining to that which is not now actual but is mentally represented.—*v.* **imagine, image** (the latter more specific for the meaning *to have* or *to form a mental image*).
image/optical: see **image (2).**
image/personal: (*C. Jung*) a representation in the **unconscious** of a personal experience.—*Contr. w.* **image/primordial.**
image/primordial: (*C. Jung*) a representation in the **unconscious** of an experience of the human race; an inherited and unconscious idea or idea-feeling.—*Syn.* ARCHE-TYPE, **image/collective.**
image/recurrent: a visual, auditory, or other image that returns persistently.
image/retinal: the optical **image** of external objects formed upon the retina by the refracting surfaces of the eye.—See **image** (2).—*Distg. fr.* **image** (3).
imagery: *n.* **1.** the **imagining** processes taken collectively; or the process of imagining, in general. **2.** the kind of **mental**

*images (which see) characteristically used in a particular kind of task, or by an individual.—*Syn.* (for 2) TYPE OF IMAGERY, IMAGINAL TYPE, IDEATIONAL TYPE.

image/self-: see self-image.

image/tied: a mental *image attached to a perceptual object: e.g., the imagined feel of the rough texture of sandpaper when seeing it.

imaginal: *adj.* pertaining to an image, or to the process of imagining.

imaginary companion: see companion/imaginary.

imaginary quantity: a magnitude containing $\sqrt{-1}$ as a factor. ➤This factor is often written as i. Thus: $\sqrt{-4} = \sqrt{-1}\sqrt{4} = i\sqrt{4} = 2i$.

imagination: *n.* 1. a recombination into a new pattern of mental *images from past experiences. 2. the function of imagining. ➤The processes of imagining (or the mental images postulated as correlates of imagining) are variously classified according to their function or use: ANTICIPATORY IMAGINATION, the representation of future events, esp. of the goal sought (GOAL IMAGE), or of the movements (MOVEMENT IMAGE) needed to achieve the goal; CONSTRUCTIVE or CREATIVE IMAGINATION, an intentional recombining either for its own sake or as a plan for action; FANCIFUL IMAGINATION (IMAGES OF FANCY), in which the subject remains relatively passive and the recombining of portions from past experience seems to proceed without volition (dreams, daydreams, and the imaginings of delusion and hallucination are of this sort); REPRODUCTIVE or MEMORY IMAGINATION (MEMORY IMAGES), the more or less complete representation of a formerly experienced object or event, coupled with the recognition that it does represent a past actually experienced.—*adj.* imaginative, pertaining to the data, process, or person; imaginary, fictitious, produced by imagination.—*v.* imagine.

imagination/anticipatory: see imagination (2).

imagination/creative: see creative imagination, imagination (2).

imagine: *v.* 1. to respond to the properties of an object or event not present to the senses; esp., to respond to its sensory properties, though they are not present. 2. to form mental *images. 3. (*pop.*) to think or conceive.—*n.* imagination.

imago (i·mā′gō): *n.* (*biol.*) 1. the mature stage of certain insects during which they are winged and have functioning sex organs. 2. (*psychoan.*) a representation of a person, most often a parent, formed in the unconscious in early childhood and uncorrected by events in later reality, hence often idealized. ➤The imago may influence

personal relations at the conscious level, esp. by providing a pattern for the kind of person with whom to fall in love.—*Cp.* father figure.

imago/father = father figure.

imbalance/intellectual: the state of having sharp differences in various intellectual abilities.

imbalance/muscular: inequality in muscles of opposite function; specif., inequality of the eye muscles, which causes difficulty in fixating an object with both eyes.—*Syn* heterophoria (which see). ➤The condition may be functional or caused by structural defect.

imbecile: *n.* a person of very low intellectual ability.—See deficiency/mental.—*adj.* imbecile, imbecilic.—*n.* (for the condition) imbecility.

imbecility/moral: see moral imbecility.

imitation: *n.* action that copies the action of another more or less exactly, with or without intent to copy.—*Cp.* copy.—*adj.* imitative.—*n.* imitativeness, the tendency to imitate (in general or specifically).—*v.* imitate.

imitation/hysterical: manifestation by a patient of the symptoms of illness or behavior disorder shown by another patient.

immanent: *adj.* (chiefly *philos.*) indwelling; inherent; remaining within the subject considered. ➤Brentano postulated that within every conscious act there was a pointing to something outside: this is IMMANENT OBJECTIVITY. An IMMANENT DETERMINANT is a factor within the behavior itself that determines its course.—*Distg. fr.* IMMINENT, about to happen.

immature: *adj.* 1. of an organism or of its structures or functions which have not reached maximum development.—See maturity. 2. of behavior that would be more appropriate to an earlier age or stage of development.—*n.* immaturity.

immaturity/emotional: failure to display the emotional behavior usual and expected of one's age; or the display of emotional behavior suitable only to younger persons. ➤The term is of incredible vagueness.

immediate: *adj.* 1. without intervening phenomena.—See mediate. 2. following without delay.

immediate association: see association/immediate.

immediate experience: 1. a psychological process that seems to have no specific psychic antecedent; hence, esp., sheer sensing and various kinds of mystical or intuitive processes. ➤The usual expression is "given in immediate experience," and the usual implication is that it is not to be analyzed, argued about, or denied. 2. (*W. Wundt*) the realm of the psychological, in contrast with that of the physical, which is MEDIATE (i.e., derived) EXPERIENCE.

immediate knowledge: knowledge attained without any direct antecedent event, or without any process intervening between the external stimulus and the knowledge. ➤The former applies to divine inspiration and intuition, perhaps to insight; the latter to sensation, in contrast with perception or thought, both of which clearly have **mediate** processes.

immediate memory: see **memory/immediate.**

imminent: see **immanent.**

immobility: *n.* a condition in which there is no visible motion of an organism or of a specified part. ➤It is a true response to stimulation and involves quite definite muscular reaction, generally of both members of an antagonistic muscle pair.—*Cp.* **death feigning.**—*adj.* **immobile.**

immobility/social: condition in a society when individuals cannot change social class, role, status, or occupation, esp. when these social functions are hereditarily fixed.

immobility/tonic: see **tonic immobility.**

immoral: *adj.* characterizing persons or actions that violate the accepted social or religious standards of right and wrong. ➤*Distg. fr.* unconventional, violative of standards of propriety; illegal, violative of definite laws; **unmoral,** of a person who lacks understanding of morality; **nonmoral,** of that to which the criteria of right and wrong do not apply; **amoral,** of a doctrine that exalts the right of some persons to be outside moral prescription, or in weakened form, *syn.* with **nonmoral.**—See **ethics.**

immunize (im'yü·nīz): *v.* to protect an organism against a specific disease-causing germ by means of some change in the fluids or tissues.—*n.* **immunity** (the state); **immunization** (the process).

impairment: *n.* **1.** deterioration or loss of function: *impairment* of hearing in old age. **2.** a change in a tissue, identifiable only by physiological or biochemical methods, which limits its participation in the larger aspects of organic functioning. ➤It is doubtful, in view of the currency of meaning (1), that the arbitrary limitation of (2) can be maintained.

impairment index: a score on a battery of tests which are designed to distinguish brain-injured individuals from the normal.

impedance (im·pē'dəns): *n.* (*phys.*) that property of an electrical circuit which sets a limit upon the current that can be induced by a given electromotive force.

impediment/speech: (*pop.*) any of various disturbances to the free flow of speech, such as stuttering or lisping.

imperative idea: see **fixed idea.**

imperceptible: *adj.* characterizing that which is too weak to be perceived under the stated conditions.

imperception: *n.* **1.** insufficiency of **perceiving. 2.** = **visual** **agnosia.*

impersonal: *adj.* **1.** not concerned with persons. **2.** not influenced by one's own feelings or interests; **objective.**

impersonation: *n.* the active representation of one person by another. ➤*Distg. fr.* the behavior of the deluded person who acts like another because he believes he is.

impetus: *n.* (*psychoan.*) the force of an **impulse (2);** often, the force as measured by the motor element of the impulse. It varies from time to time.

implantation: *n.* the attachment of the fertilized ovum to the wall of the uterus.

implicit: *adj.* not directly stated, but understandable or deducible from what is stated.—See **implicit behavior.**—*Ant.* **explicit.**

implicit behavior: behavior not easily observable by another person, either because it lies within the body or is of minimal extent. ➤Such behavior can sometimes be reported by the subject (usually in unanalyzed form), and some parts of it may be detected by sensitive instruments. The movements of **internal speech** are an especially important class of implicit behavior.—*Syn.* IMPLICIT MOVEMENT, IMPLICIT RESPONSE, and esp. **covert behavior** (*prefd.*).—*Ant.* **overt behavior.** EXPLICIT RESPONSE, sometimes used as an antonym, is ambiguous.

implicit speech: see **internal speech.**

impossible: *adj.* characterizing that which cannot exist in nature. ➤*Distg. fr.* UNTRUE, not actually corresponding with the facts, and *fr.* INCONCEIVABLE, not capable of being seriously believed or even thought about.

impotence (im'pō·təns): *n.* **1.** a feeling of inability to control the course of events. **2.** inability in the male to **copulate,** generally an inability to have adequate **erection.** ➤It may be organic (caused by neural disorder or hormonal deficiency) or a **psychogenic** blocking of response to appropriate stimuli. It may be general, or specific to a certain situation or sex object. —*Cp.* **frigidity** in females. **3.** lack of **fertility** (an improper usage).—*Distg. fr.* **sterility.**

impotence/anal: (*psychoan.*) **1. psychogenic** constipation. **2.** inability to excrete except under conditions of privacy. ➤Both conditions are believed to be due to early training against giving offense.

impotence/orgastic: inability to achieve orgasm or complete psychological satisfaction in the sexual act.

impotence/psychic: 1. *psychogenic *impotence. 2. temporary and pathological inability to perform normal **psychic** activities.

impress (im'pres): *n.* the total effect of an individual upon his world.

impression: *n.* **1.** the neural effects of **stimulation.**—*Syn.* **excitation** (*prefd.*). **2.** the total and unanalyzed effect of a situation upon an observer.—See **sense impression. 3.** a judgment, admittedly not carefully analyzed nor firmly held; a belief: it is my *impression* that he has gone. **4.** (*hist.*) a **percept,** in contrast to an **idea.**

impression/absolute: see **absolute impression.**

impression method: a procedure in which the subject simply reports his pleasure, unpleasure, or other feeling when presented with a certain stimulus. The judgment may be relative or absolute.—*Cp.* **expression/method of.**

imprinting: *n.* a particular kind of learning characterized by occurrence in very early life, rapidity of acquisition, and relative insusceptibility to forgetting or extinction. ➤Imprinted behavior includes most (or all) behavior commonly called **instinctive,** but imprinting is used purely descriptively. It is not always **species-specific.**

improbable achievement technique: a technique in which deception or cheating by the testee is inferred if he attains a level of excellence that is highly improbable by honest means.

improvement: *n.* a betterment; a closer approximation to a standard; or the process of change that results in betterment. ➤May be applied to a single response, to a series, or to complex acts. While most improvement in behavior is due to learning, the term applies equally to **maturational** effects, and is sometimes used for betterments not learned but resulting from changes in stimulus or situation.

improvement over chance: (*stat.*) a measure of the effect of an **independent** *variable,** computed by subtracting from the observed average change in the **dependent** *variable** the amount of change that might be expected by chance.

impuberty: *n.* the state of not having reached **puberty.** ➤Said of children, but also of adolescents who show delayed development.—*Syn.* IMPUBERISM.—*adj.* **impubic, impuberal.**

impulse: *n.* **1.** an act performed without delay, reflection, voluntary direction, or obvious differential control by the stimulus. ➤Although the act is triggered by the stimulus, the determining factor is the person's state or condition. **2.** (*psychoan.*) an act determined by the **id;** an **instinctual** act. ➤Usually the properties of (1) are included. **3.** a tendency to act in a particular way; a readiness or impulsion to act: e.g., an *impulse* to scream. **4.** an awareness of one's readiness or impulsion. **5.** the hypothe-

sized physiological state or drive state that leads to the act or to the awareness.

impulse/nerve or **/nervous** = **neural impulse.**

impulse presentation: (*S. Freud*) the conscious process representing the physiological activity or state of **impulse.**

impulsion: *n.* an urge to perform a specific act. ➤There is an uneasy restlessness and a special susceptibility to those stimuli that trigger the response.—*Cp.* **compulsion,** in which the urge is to do something against one's inclination.

impulsive: *adj.* **1.** characterizing immediate action without reflection, or a person prone to act thus. **2.** characterizing action that cannot be suppressed, or a person who is habitually unable to suppress **impulse.**

impulsive act: an act performed without reflection or voluntary control.

impulsiveness: *n.* state or quality of being **impulsive;** hence, the tendency to act on **impulse (3).**—*Syn.* IMPULSIVITY.

impulsive obsession = **obsessive-compulsive reaction.**

impulsivity = **impulsiveness.**

impunitive: *adj.* (*S. Rosenzweig*) characterizing a reaction to frustration in which one does not blame either self or others but is more concerned with condoning what has occurred. The person may display embarrassment and shame but not anger.—*Cp.* **extrapunitive** and **intrapunitive.**

inaccessibility: *n.* a state of unresponsiveness to words and other social stimuli. It is a frequent symptom of schizophrenia.

inaccuracy: *n.* an error in a description or computation, or in a process of thinking, perceiving, or acting.—*Ant.* **accuracy.**

inadequacy/feeling of: a frequent symptom in **depressed** states, in which the subject does not feel himself competent to accomplish anything that requires effort or ability.

inadequacy/psychic: (*psychoan.*) the feeling of being unable to respond to sex promptings in a satisfactory way. ➤Held by many to be the basis of **anxiety neurosis.**

inadequate personality: (*Stan. Psychiat.*) a person who, without obvious mental disorder or deficiency, lacks judgment, initiative, and ambition, thus failing in almost everything attempted.

inadequate stimulus: see **stimulus/inadequate.**

inanition (in"ə·nish'ən): *n.* **1.** emptiness. **2.** exhaustion from starvation.—*adj.* **inane.**

inarticulate: *adj.* unable to express oneself in words; of a person who finds the expression of thoughts or attitudes difficult and so remains silent.

inattention/selective: not being guided in behavior by an aspect of the situation that is perceived. ➤While the phenomenon is probably very common, it can only be asserted when it is demonstrated that the person actually perceived the aspect or part of the situation. But if, e.g., a person is briefly shown various colors shaped as digits, he can often recall which digits were shown but cannot recall the colors. Color, then, is perceived but unattended to. The phenomenon may be produced by instructions; it is also believed to occur as a **defense mechanism** and is then called **perceptual *defense.**—*Cp.* abstraction.

Inbegriff (in'be·grif): *n.* (*Ger.*) an inclusive concept or totality.

inborn: *adj.* innate.—See **heredity.**

inbreeding: *n.* **1.** the breeding of close relatives. ➤The so-called **inbred** lines of genetics are established and maintained by unbroken brother-sister matings. **2.** the process by which a group or institution tends toward a static or retrogressive condition through absence of new biological or psychological elements, or new personalities.—*adj.* **inbred.**

incentive (in·sen'tiv): *n.* **1.** an object or external condition, perceived as capable of satisfying an aroused motive, that tends to elicit action to attain the object or condition. ➤Most incentives tend also to *arouse* a dormant motive or **drive state.** If an animal is already hungry (the motive already aroused), the perception of food arouses **expectancy** and tendencies to seek it. But the perception (or even the thought) of food may in addition arouse a dormant hunger motive. **2.** a supplementary goal object that elicits behavior tending toward attainment of the main goal; anything that increases the apparent satisfyingness of a goal: e.g., offering a child ㅋ prize for conscientious study.—*Approx. syn.* **extraneous** motive. **3.** any manipulatable aspect of the environment that can be used to energize and direct an animal's behavior.—*Ant.* DETERRENT. ➤It is probable that the three definitions relate to the same underlying phenomena.

incentive/secondary: an **incentive** that derives its value from its relationship with another incentive: e.g., money as a substitute for consumable goods.

incest: *n.* sexual intercourse between closely related persons of opposite sex. ➤The degree of relationship prohibited varies in different cultures, but apparently every culture does forbid what it defines as incest.—*adj.* **incestuous.**

incest barrier: (*psychoan.*) the group of conventional ideas and restrictions which intervene to loosen **libido** from **attachment** to the parent of opposite sex, and in general to loosen family ties in the adolescent.

incest dream: any dream having reference, direct or symbolic, to **incest.**

incest taboo: the prohibition (with penalties) of sexual intercourse between closely related individuals, esp. between those in the immediate family (parent-child, brother-sister).

incidence: *n.* frequency or range of occurrence of a condition.

incidence/angle of: (*optics*) the angle between the path of an oncoming ray of light and the line perpendicular to the surface at the point where the ray impinges.

incidental: *adj.* happening as an unintended accompaniment of something; of that which is not essential and not invariably found.

incidental learning: see **learning/incidental.**

incidental stimulus: see **stimulus continuum.**

incipient (in·sip'i·ənt): *adj.* initial; beginning to show; pertaining to an initial phase; esp. as in INCIPIENT MOVEMENT, an imperceptible or barely perceptible beginning of a movement that is not carried out. ➤Such movements often function as minimal cues to a person's intentions. **Internal speech** is said to consist partly of such movements in the speech organs.

inclusion/false or **/valid:** see **false negative.**

incoherence: *n.* lack of connectedness or organization of parts; more specif., disorder of verbal expression marked by disconnectedness, uses of unintelligible phrases, neologisms.

incommensurable (in"kə·men'shùr·ə·bəl): *adj.* of magnitudes or **variables** that cannot be exactly measured in units of the same scale. ➤The term is used for variables measured on the same dimension but requiring different scale units. Thus, the circumference and the diameter of a circle are both measured on the dimension of length but require different units if measurement is to be exact. But **incommensurable** also refers to magnitudes measured along qualitatively distinct dimensions: e.g., the duration and the intensity of a desire are incommensurable. This does not mean that they do not interact.

incompatible: *adj.* **1.** not capable of being together in the same system, or at least of being harmoniously together; esp. as in INCOMPATIBLE RESPONSES, those that cannot take place at the same time, though either may be elicitable by the same stimulus situation. **2.** of persons who cannot freely associate together without conflict or displeasure. **3.** of two judgments that cannot both be true (but both may be false). —*Syn.* (for 3) **contrary.**

incompetent: lacking the necessary capacity or skill for a particular task; more specif.

of a person (e.g., an insane or mentally deficient person) not legally capable of making choices and hence not legally responsible. —*Cp.* COMMITTABLE, which applies to a person who must be confined to an institution.

incomplete pictures test: a test making use of a series of incomplete drawings of common objects, each successive picture showing the object more completely. It is the subject's task to identify the object as early in the series as possible. ➤The test is believed to measure visual organization or visual **set** and is used also as an indicator of psychotic impairment.

incomplete sentence test: a type of **projective** test which consists of asking the subject to complete a prechosen list of half-completed sentences. ➤Often used are such sentences as: "I like ———"; "When I think of ———"; "I get angry when ———". Other incomplete sentences may direct the testee into associations connected with a particular desired topic, such as race relations, personal troubles, state of morale.—*Distg. fr.* **sentence completion test (1).**

incomprehensible: *adj.* characterizing anything which a person, after critical consideration, finds meaningless or self-contradictory. ➤It is implied that the fault is not in the critic.—*Cp.* **inconceivable.**

inconceivable: *adj.* characterizing a concept or statement which a person, after critical consideration, cannot find to correspond with anything actual or real.

incongruent = **incongruous.**

incongruity/problem of: the problem that arises when expectations set up in an individual are defeated by later environmental developments, necessitating prompt reorganization of expectations.

incongruous (in·kong′grü·əs): *adj.* characterized by lack of consistency, compatibility, or appropriateness; different from, or opposed to, what is expected.— *Syn.* INCONGRUENT (-ənt).—*n.* **incongruity** (-kən·grü′ə·ti).

inconsistent: *adj.* of a concept or judgment which, when analyzed, is found to be at least partly contradictory to what is known or accepted as true. ➤The INTERNALLY INCONSISTENT reveals contradictions within a complex concept or judgment. Thus, the notion of freedom of the will is held by some philosophers to imply contradictory ideas.

incontinence: *n.* **1.** inability to restrain within normal limits the natural evacuation of an organ. **2.** (*pop.*) failure or inability to restrain **lust.**

incoordination: *n.* **1.** failure of parts to work together to produce the effect for which the whole is designed. **2.** lack of balance in

the action of the different muscle groups necessary for complex movements; MUSCULAR or MOTOR INCOORDINATION. ➤The concept is essentially mechanical.—*Cp.* **cooperation.**

incorporation: *n.* the act of taking something into oneself, or the fact that one has done so. ➤The term is meant either literally, as when one eats and digests food, or figuratively for making knowledge or attitudes a part of oneself. According to psychoanalysis, in the **oral stage,** eating (i.e., incorporation) is not differentiated from sexual incorporation, and in certain regressions the two are confused or blended.

incorrigible: *adj.* characterizing behavior, esp. behavior violating accepted standards, that cannot be corrected or improved; or of a person manifesting such incorrigible behavior, general or specific: an *incorrigible* liar.

incredible: *adj.* unbelievable; so out of line with known facts or accepted beliefs as to arouse great disbelief.

increment (in′krə·mənt; ing-): *n.* the amount of increase in quantity; more generally, the amount of increase or decrease. The latter is NEGATIVE INCREMENT, or **decrement.**—*adj.* **incremental.**

incubation: *n.* **1.** a period of apparent quiet in a complex function during which unobservable development takes place, so that at the end of the period marked change in the function is found. **2.** in a complex act of thinking, a period during which knowledge and skill are integrated or coordinated. ➤The process is usually nonconscious.—*Cp.* G. Wallas' four stages of creative thought: **preparation, incubation, illumination, verification.**

incubus: *n.* a **nightmare.**

inculcation: *n.* teaching by repeated admonitions, with or without variation.

incus: *n.* one of the bones of the middle ear.—*Syn.* ANVIL.

ind. = *abbr.* for **individual.**

indecency: *n.* **1.** conduct greatly contrary to **mores,** esp. the mores concerning sexual relations. ➤What is **indecent** varies greatly from culture to culture and from occasion to occasion. **2.** a greater exposure of the body to public gaze than is acceptable to public opinion, or to the officers of the law who attempt to interpret that opinion.

indefinite: *adj.* without precise boundaries or limits. ➤Not to be confused with vague or unclear.

independence: *n.* **1.** a relation between two events, variables, or sets of data, such that neither is influenced by the other and change in one is possible without change in the other. ➤No event is independent of all other events; independence is relative to a stipulated or clearly implied set of events. **2.** (*logic*) a property of a proposition, the truth of which is not contingent upon the truth of certain other propositions. **3.** (*probability math*.) a property of two classes of events, *i* and *j*, such that the probability of an event's being in class *j* is unaffected by its being in class *i*. **4.** an attitude of self-reliance or of resistance to control by others.—*Ant.* **dependence.**—*adj.* **independent.**

independence/test of: (*stat*.) a test of the agreement between the actual and the expected frequency in the various cells when data are classified according to two or more variables.—*Syn.* TEST OF HOMOGENEITY.

independent variable: see **variable/independent.**

indeterminate: *adj.* **1.** (*math*.) of values not fixed, owing to lack of the necessary equation; or of values not capable of being fixed: e.g., 0/0, or 0×0. **2.** ambiguously, for either *undetermined* or *undeterminable,* though the two may be very different.

indeterminism: *n.* the doctrine that an event may not always be completely determined by its antecedents.—*Cp.* **voluntarism,** the view that a psychic event may be partly determined by a person's **volition.** The doctrine of FREE WILL is the chief form of indeterminism; few doubt that physical events are determined by their antecedent causes.—*Ant.* **determinism.**—See **psychology/divisions and schools of, V.**

index *n., pl.* **indexes, indices** (in'deks·əs; -də·sēz): **1.** a guide, pointer, or indicator. **2.** (*math*.) the ratio of one dimension of a thing to another dimension, e.g., cephalic *index*. **3.** (*math*.) an exponent showing the root or power of a quantity. **4.** (*stat*.) one of a series of numbers that express the changing magnitudes of a complex **variable.** ➤The term is almost synonymous with variable but is used where it is admitted that quantification is incomplete or imperfect, where the successive steps are of indeterminate size, or where the variable is complex and heterogeneous. Thus, the successive years of **mental *age** are indices of intellectual growth in which the differences from one year to another are unequal.

index/anatomical = ossification ratio.

indicant (in'di·kənt): *n.* any phenomenon that can be taken as a sign of the presence or operation of a given other phenomenon: a blush is an *indicant* of embarrassment. ➤If the two phenomena are in one-to-one relation, the indicant can be used as an index of the quantity of the other phenomenon. Thus, a testee's score on a properly constructed vocabulary test can be taken as an indicant of his total vocabulary. —*Syn.* symptom, INDICATOR.—*v.* **indicate.**

indicator/anxiety: see **anxiety indicator.**

indicator/complex: see **complex indicator.**

indicator/mechanical: an instrument in which motion of a mechanical part gives information about the state of some phenomenon: e.g., the pointers on dials (as on speedometers), the fluid columns of thermometers. Usually the moving part brings a reference point (the pointer or the top of the fluid column) into relation with a scale.

indices: *pl.* of **index.**

indifference point or **zone:** the transition stage between two opposing **continua:** e.g., the indifference zone between pleasantness and unpleasantness.

indifferent stimulus: a stimulus that has not yet elicited a particular response. ➤The expression is often used of the stimulus which is to become the conditioned stimulus. It is interesting to find it used by persons who object to such terms as **reward** as being **subjective.**—*Syn.* NEUTRAL STIMULUS, INEFFECTIVE STIMULUS.

indirect: *adj.* **1.** not proceeding by the shortest line. **2.** not proceeding toward a goal or purpose by the obvious or simple path. **3.** proceeding by means of intermediate steps. **4.** not the immediate result of a cause, yet linked to it by intermediate steps.

indissociation: *n.* (*J. Piaget*) the early stage in the child's development when perceived phenomena are not sharply distinguished from each other or from the self. ➤Older persons may in part recapture the indissociated state in revery or in extreme excitement.

individual: *n.* **1.** a single **organism,** as distinguished from aggregates or groups of organisms, or from the cells, tissues, and organs that compose the organism. ➤This meaning emphasizes distinctness, but is often used where no contrast with groups is implied and where **person** or animal would be more appropriate. See **person. 2.** any single case, instance, item, or event; any object measured or enumerated. ➤The emphasis here is upon singleness or oneness, but not upon **integration.** An individual is a unit of structure and/or behavior but need not be a highly integrated unit.—*adj.* **3.** characterizing one thing as set apart, or as functioning separately.—*Syn.* **unique.**

individual differences: see **difference/individual.**

individualism: *n.* **1.** personal attitudes or behavior that show independence of group standards. **2.** the practice of exalting the interests of the individual, of deliberately accenting personal peculiarities, or of being uncooperative in personal relations; or the theory that justifies such conduct.—*Distg. fr.* **individuality.**

individuality: *n.* that which differentiates one organism from all others, whether it be the organized sum total of its qualities (*syn.* **personality**), or its particular qualities or traits.—See **self**.—*v.* **individualize**.

individualization: *n.* **1.** the process by which an organism becomes different from all others, or becomes an **individual**.—*Cp.* **individuation. 2.** the process by which an observer takes note of the person as an individual. **3.** a method of teaching that stresses the adaptation of the educative process to the differing needs of individual pupils. The method does not imply teaching pupils one by one; individual needs may often be met in groups.

individualize: *v.* to perceive or think about some person or thing as a unit distinguishable from others; to pay attention to properties and attributes that distinguish one from others.

individual psychology: 1. (chiefly *hist.*) the descriptive psychological study of persons, utilizing the methods of the case study and of **differential psychology**. ➤This usage tends to be supplanted by **2.** the theory and practice of the school of Adler: it stresses the unique wholeness of the individual and finds in the individual's striving for superiority or power the source, often the unrecognized source, of most motivation. — See **psychology / divisions and schools of, III.**

individual response: giving an uncommon word as a response in an **association test**. ➤When the **Kent-Rosanoff** list is used, an individual response is a word not given in the **association-frequency table**. —*Distg. fr.* **egocentric response**, one making reference to oneself or one's own experience.

individual test: see **test/individual**.

individuation: *n.* **1.** the process whereby a part of a whole becomes progressively more distinct and independent; the **differentiation** of a whole into more and more independent parts. ➤The LAW OF INDIVIDUATION states that parts of wholes come into being and/or are recognized only by emergence from the whole: the whole is temporally prior to the parts. ¶Any kind of part-whole complex may show individuation: e.g., the details of a picture or a scene individuate; or an undifferentiated mass action becomes differentiated. ¶In a social group, **individuation** refers to the process whereby a person emerges as a distinct unit in the group, as a person with a distinct, even unique, role or status. Such individuation is a complex social process involving changes in the person **(individualization 1)** and in the way the person is perceived by others (which includes **individualization 2). 2.** = **individualization (2)** (*prefd.* for this more restricted meaning). **3.** (*C. Jung*) becoming

a distinct personality aware of his own individuality. ➤This definition is closer to **individualization (1)** than to **individuation (1).**

indoctrination: *n.* **1.** the effort to induce acceptance of a doctrine; teaching designed to gain acceptance rather than critical consideration. **2.** preliminary training designed to teach the particular policies, mores, and practices of a certain group.

induced color: a color or change in color that appears in a given portion of the subjective visual field, resulting not from direct stimulation of the corresponding portion of the retina but from concomitant stimulation of other portions.—*Cp.* **color contrast.**

induced emotion: see **induction/sympathetic.**

induced goal: a goal accepted, wittingly or unwittingly, under the influence of another person.—*Cp.* **internalization.**

induced tonus: a muscle **tonus** set up as a result of movement in another part of the body: e.g., the set jaw of the child trying to write.

inducing color: a color stimulus that induces a **contrast** effect. ➤*Distg. fr.* **induced color,** the color that constitutes the effect.

induction: *n.* **1.** (*logic*) "the process by which we conclude that what is true of certain individuals is true of a class, what is true of part is true of the whole class, or what is true at certain times will be true in similar circumstances at all times." (*J. S. Mill*)—*Cp.* **deduction. 2.** (*physiol.*) arousal of activity in an area, not by direct stimulation but by a spread of excitation from nearby areas. ➤See **induced color.** CORTICAL INDUCTION is a change in activity of an area in the brain, set up by activity in an adjacent area. **3.** = NEURAL INDUCTION, the process whereby a period of **inhibition** in one action system leads to heightened response in a related system (POSITIVE INDUCTION), or the process whereby a period of excitation of one action system leads to inhibition of a related system (NEGATIVE INDUCTION). **4.** the process by which a novice is prepared for, and introduced into, a social institution: e.g., military induction, orientation week for the induction of students.

induction/immediate spinal or **/direct spinal:** the summation of two or more **subliminal** stimuli upon the same functional area of the skin so that they elicit a response jointly.

induction/negative: (*I. P. Pavlov*) intensification of **inhibition** under the influence of preceding **excitation.**

induction/neural: see **induction (3).**

induction/perceptual: the process whereby

sensory processes arouse contributory elements in a total perception: e.g., a picture of a man pulling hard on a weight arouses **empathic** motor responses that contribute to one's total reaction to the picture.

induction/sympathetic: the arousal in a person of emotional response similar to that manifested by another in his presence.

induction test: one in which the task is to derive a principle from a number of particular instances.

induction/visual: see **visual induction.**

indulgence: *n.* the endeavor to see the desires, even the whims, of another gratified; excessive yielding to the demands of a child or subordinate, with failure to exercise needed constraint. SELF-INDULGENCE is the yielding to present desires without consideration of ultimate consequences.

industrial psychology: the scientific investigation of industrial problems by the methods, concepts, and principles of psychology and utilization of the findings to increase efficiency. ➤Industry is here used in a very comprehensive sense, to include both business and the executive activities of government. The range of activity of **industrial psychology** is equally great: **personnel** selection and training, employee **morale, human engineering,** psychology of advertising and salesmanship, consumerneed surveys, etc.—*Cp.* ECONOMIC PSYCHOLOGY, the study of the working of the economic system as a whole, which utilizes the findings of industrial psychology in that wider context.

ineffable: *adj.* incapable of expression in words or otherwise; esp., characterizing the **mystic** experience. ➤An ineffable experience is probably nearly pure feeling, with no detectable **cognitive** aspect.

inertia: *n.* (*neurol.*) property of the nervous system whereby the physiological effect lags behind stimulation, beginning later (INITIAL LAG) and also ceasing later (TERMINAL LAG). —*Cp.* **lag of sensation, latent period, perseveration.**—*adj.* **inert.**

inf.: 1. *abbr.* for **infinity.** 2. *abbr.* for **inferior.**

infancy: *n.* the period during which a human being or other mammal is almost wholly dependent upon parental care. ➤The root meaning of the word is *without speech.* The length of the period is variously defined: in law, from birth to legal majority at eighteen or twenty-one years; popularly, the first year or two; in **developmental psychology,** the first year.—See discussion, levels of *development.—adj.* **infant, infantile.**—*pers. n.* **infant.**

infantile (in'fən·tĭl, -tīl): *adj.* 1. pertaining to **infancy.** 2. pertaining to **infantilism.** 3. originating in infancy.

infantile amnesia: see **amnesia/infantile.**

infantile birth theories: see **birth theories/infantile.**

infantile paralysis: a popular name for **poliomyelitis.**

infantile sexuality: see **sexuality/infantile.**

infantile speech: see **speech/infantile.**

infantilism (in·fan'tə·liz·əm): *n.* 1. a condition of body or mind in an older child or adult that is characterized by failure of development or by a regression to an infantile condition. 2. a behavior, in one who is past infancy, that resembles infant behavior. ➤The term is strongly derogatory. A temper tantrum is a typical infantilism. —*Cp.* **development/arrest in** and **regression** (2).

infant psychology: the subdivision of psychology that treats of persons under one year of age.

infant test: a test of behavioral development for infants; a test to see whether the infant can perform certain tasks that are usual and expected at his chronological age: e.g., drinking from a cup, picking up a block. ➤While sometimes included under **intelligence tests,** it is known that infant tests do not reliably predict ability at later ages.

infatuation: *n.* an intensely **affective** (generally **erotic**) attachment of short duration. ➤It is usually implied that the attachment lacks reasonable basis.

infavoidance need: (*H. A. Murray*) the need to avoid shame, to escape failure or humiliation.

infecund: see **infertile.**

inference: *n.* 1. (*logic*) a judgment based on other judgments rather than on direct observation. 2. (*psychol.*) a mental process whereby, on the basis of one or more judgments, a person reaches another judgment regarded as proved or established by the former.—*v.* **infer.**

inferior: *adj.* 1. of lower degree, rank, worth, or size. 2. (*anat.*) of the lower part of the body in an upright animal such as man.—See **anterior.**—*Ant.* **superior.**

inferior/constitutional: see **constitutional inferior.**

inferiority complex: 1. (*A. Adler*) repressed fear and resentment of being inferior, esp. in some bodily feature or organ, leading to a variety of distorted behaviors. ➤*Distg. fr.* **inferiority feeling,** which is a conscious judgment or attitude. The popular statement: "I have an inferiority complex," is almost self-contradictory, since a complex is repressed and hence not known directly to him who has it. 2. (*psychoan.*) a **complex,** arising from the child's feeling of being unable to cope with the **Oedipus** situation, that leads to strivings not adjusted to reality. 3. (*pop. psychoan.*) belief in an inferiority that one has difficulty in accepting.—*Syn.* (for **3**) **inferiority feeling** (*prefd.*).

inferiority feeling: a tendency to unfavorable self-evaluation, whether or not justified by the facts, and toward depressed feeling or shame as a result.

inferiority/functional: (*A. Adler*) inability to do work that is adequate in quantity or quality.

inferiority/general: general lack of efficiency in work, play, and social relations. —*Distg. fr.* **deterioration.**

inferiority/morphologic: (*A. Adler*) deficiency or defect in shape, size, or strength of a particular organ.

inferiority/organ: see **organ inferiority.**

inferior oblique: see **eye muscles.**

inferior rectus: see **eye muscles.**

infertile: *adj.* **1.** having no offspring. **2.** not able to have offspring; sterile; = INFECUND. **3.** having few offspring; = RELATIVELY INFERTILE. ➤**Infertility** is often temporary; **sterility** usually means an enduring, but not necessarily incurable, condition.—See **fecundity.**—*n.* **infertility.**

infinite: *n.* **1.** (*philos., religion*) the unbounded totality of all there is; the Absolute, or God. (Usually capitalized.) **2.** (*math.*) that which is without bounds or limits.—*Syn.* **infinity** (*prefd.*).—*adj.* **3.** (*philos.*) subject to no limitation. **4.** (*math.*) greater than any assignable magnitude or quantity.

infinitesimal: *n.* **1.** (*math.*) a magnitude less than any magnitude that can be assigned to a variable; one that approaches zero as a limit. **2.** (*pop.*) something very small or negligible.—*adj.* **infinitesimal.**

infinite-valued logic: a logic based on the recognition that between completely true and completely false lie an indefinitely large number of truth values or truth descriptions.

infinity or ∞: *n.* an indefinitely large number, amount, or extension; the limit which **finite** magnitudes approach as they grow greater; a magnitude larger than any finite magnitude.

inflection: *n.* **1.** a bending; a change of direction. The POINT OF INFLECTION of a curve is where it changes from concave to convex, or vice versa. **2.** change in pitch; in speaking, modulation of the voice. **3.** alteration in the forms of a word to express grammatical distinctions.

influence: *n.* **1.** a part-cause of an event or condition; that which has effect on an event; a **factor.** ➤Used especially of a prior condition that plays a part in determining **behavior. 2.** an attribute of a person—whether due to status, role, or personality—whereby he produces an effect upon others.—*Cp.* **effect.**—*v.* **influence.**

influence/delusion of: the belief that others are exercising **occult** influence upon one.

informal test: see **test/informal.**

information: *n.* **1.** knowledge of facts gained through investigation, observation, study, or instruction. **2.** (*beh. theory*) that aspect of a stimulus situation which is a **cue** or a **clue;** the nonintensive aspect of the stimulus. **3.** (*info. theory*) a purely quantitative property of an **ensemble** of items that enables categorization or classification of some or all of them. ➤The AMOUNT OF INFORMATION in an ensemble (symbolized by H) is measured by the average number of operations (statements, decisions, tests, etc.) needed to effect categorization of the items. The greater the number of operations required, the less information is said to be contained in the ensemble of items. Information is the opposite of **uncertainty.**—*Cp.* **bit,** the unit of measurement for information. ¶In this theory, information is only a quantity. It does not specify content, usefulness, value, truthfulness, factual status, history, or purpose. The word is unhappily chosen for this meaning: the reader must remind himself that the author (probably?) did not mean by "information" what the reader, in talking with himself, means by that term. ¶Since, moreover, the nature of the operations needed to classify the items must be specified for each situation, it is important to note that the values of H in one situation will be incommensurable with those in another. One can, perhaps, compare the H of an English sentence with that of a German, but not the H of a sentence with that of a bushel of apples to be graded for quality.

—*adj.* **informational,** pertaining to information; **informative,** yielding information.—*v.* **inform.**

information/adapted: see **adapted information.**

information/amount of: see **information.**

information/average rate of: (*info. theory*) the average rate at which **signal** elements of a given set can be selected by **binary** choices.—*Syn.* SELECTIVE INFORMATION, used when the signals are regarded as equally probable.

information/status: information that does not change rapidly, that remains relatively fixed and up-to-date for long periods.— *Contr. w.* **information/transient.**

information test: a test that samples relatively superficial general knowledge of the sort likely to be learned more or less incidentally, rather than the knowledge obtained by study and instruction (for which **achievement test** is the term, although the distinction is not precise). An information test may be limited to a special field (sports, music, politics) or may range very widely. It forms part of many intelligence test batteries.

information theory: an interdisciplinary study (not a theory) dealing with the transmission of **messages** or **signals,** or the communication of **information (3).** ➤It draws upon **communications theory** (which includes much from physics and engineering), linguistics, psychology, and sociology. Three different aspects are treated. (*a*) SELECTIVE INFORMATION, the function of information or **signals** in reducing the unexpectedness of events, and the selection of information for this function. (The signals are treated as equally probable.) The unit of information for selection is the **bit** (which see). (*b*) STRUCTURAL INFORMATION, which deals with the influence of the complexity of form. The unit of structural information is the **logon.** (*c*) METRICAL INFORMATION, which deals with the reliability of the information. The unit is a **metron.**

Information theory does not directly deal with meaning or content, or with information as that term is commonly understood. It deals with physical representations that have meaning or content. It overlaps considerably with **communications theory** and **cybernetics.**—See **information (3).**

information/transient: (*human eng.*) information which may change rapidly and for which the operator requires a display capable of showing moment to moment changes.—*Contr. w.* **status *information.**

infra- (in′frə-): prefix meaning *below, beneath.*

infrahuman: *adj.* pertaining to, or characterizing, animals other than man; or of those characteristics shown by a human being that resemble those of lower animals. —*Syn.* **animal,** which often, however, is used to include the human being.

infrared ray or **wave:** a vibration frequency shorter than that of visible red and longer than that of radio waves.

infundibulum (in″fun·dib′ū·lum): *n.* a stalk by which the pituitary body is attached to the forebrain.

in-group: *n.* a group with a strong feeling of belonging together, to the exclusion of others. ➤*Syn.* WE-GROUP.—*Contr. w.* **outgroup** (or THEY-GROUP), composed of persons explicitly recognized as not belonging. While there is usually a strong positive **affect** toward members of the in-group, this may be lacking: the members of an "old" family may have a strong in-group feeling, yet detest each other as individuals.

inherence effect: a heightening of the qualities of a **figure** as a result of firm contour segregation.—See **segregation (1).**

inherent (in·hir′ənt): *adj.* existing in an object or person; permanently and inalienably forming a part of such object or person. ➤*Contr. w.* **external,** referring to what lies outside the object, even though related to it. Proponents of **field theory,** however, contend that if something is related to an object it is to that extent inherent—i.e., they deny external relations. *Syn.* **intrinsic** (which see).—*n.* **inherence, inherency.**—*v.* **inhere.**

inherit: *v.* **1.** (*biol.*) to receive from parents the capacity to develop traits like those of the ancestors.—See **heredity. 2.** to receive property from the estate of a deceased person. **3.** to receive from parents and elders the heritage of the society. ➤This usage is confusing.—See **transmission (5).**

inheritance: see **heredity.**

inheritance/intermediate: that in which the **dominant** trait does not fully exclude the **recessive** from expression in the first filial generation.

inheritance/multiple-factor: see **multiple-factor inheritance.**

inheritance/nulliplex: see **nulliplex inheritance.**

inheritance/social: a loose term for the process of transmitting culture.—*Syn.* **social *transmission** (*prefd.*).

inherited: see **heredity.**

inhibition: *n.* **1.** (*physiol., psychol.*) restraining or stopping a process from continuing, or preventing a process from starting although the usual stimulus is present; or the hypothetical nervous state or process that brings about the restraint. **2.** a mental condition in which the range and amount of behavior is curtailed, beginning or continuing a course of action is difficult, and there is a peculiar hesitancy as if restrained by external agency (though there need be no **delusion** of such restraints). **3.** (*psychoan.*) the process whereby an **instinctual** process is prevented from coming into consciousness by the activity of the **superego.** ➤This is not **suppression** or **repression**— though these are sometimes used as synonyms—but *prevention.* It is held that, if not inhibited, the instinctual process would have to be repressed by ego activity. In this view, inhibition causes no symptoms and is known only by inference.

—*adj.* **inhibited, inhibitory, inhibitive.** —*v.* **inhibit.**

inhibition/associative: see **associative inhibition.**

inhibition/central: inhibition of nerve impulses by a process or processes within the central nervous system.—*Cp.* **Wedensky effect, habit interference.**

inhibition/conditioned: see **conditioned inhibition.**

inhibition/conditioned reactive or sI_R: (*C. Hull*) a hypothetical state due to the conditioning of reactive *inhibition to whatever stimulus is present when a CR is extinguished. The stimulus thus acquires inhibitory power.

inhibition/connective: the increased difficulty in recalling separate parts that is experienced after the parts have been grouped into a connected whole. ➤If one group of subjects requires ten repetitions to learn items A-B-C, first presented separately, but another group requires twelve repetitions to recall the separate items after having first learned them as an organized and meaningful total, the difference is attributed to connective inhibition.—*Distg. fr.* **retroactive** and **proactive** *inhibition.

inhibition/cortical: inhibition of nerve impulse taking place in the cortex.

inhibition/differential: (*I. P. Pavlov*) the development of nonresponsiveness to stimuli that are somewhat similar to the conditioned stimulus. ➤It is the opposite of **stimulus** *generalization and occurs only under appropriate learning conditions.—*Cp.* **discriminative** *learning, of which this is one aspect.—*Syn.* DIFFERENTIATION (when used in the context of the **conditioning** experiment).

inhibition/external: (*I. P. Pavlov*) the reduction in a **conditioned response** sometimes found when an extraneous stimulus is presented simultaneously with the CS.—*Cp.* **conditioned inhibition, inhibition/ internal.** ➤Pavlov conceived the inhibition in terms of simultaneous excitations in the central nervous system; but the observable fact is a simultaneous *stimulus,* and the definition is better based on fact than on concept.

inhibition/extinctive: (*I. P. Pavlov*) = **extinction/experimental.**

inhibition/internal: (*I. P. Pavlov*) the hypothesis that an inhibitory process *I,* arising within the body, acts counter to the excitatory process *E,* which is established by conditioning. The resultant of the two processes at any time determines the strength of the tendency to respond. ➤Unless *E* is strengthened by reinforcement, it declines and *I* gains relative strength. The *I* process is a **hypothetical** *construct. The effects of internal inhibition include at least **extinction, inhibition of delay, differential** *inhibition, **conditioned inhibition.**

inhibition of delay: an inhibition that lessens the normal time interval between the stimulus and the response, esp. between a CS and CR.

inhibition/proactive: the state or process hypothesized to account for the lessened ease of learning of the later members of a series following learning of an earlier member.—*Cp.* **retroactive** *inhibition.

inhibition/reactive or I_R: (*C. Hull*) the hypothesized tendency to lessened response that is consequent upon effortful activity. It is independent of the effect of reward or reinforcement, and is a direct function of the interval since the last response and of the number of the preceding responses. ➤It applies particularly to short-time **decrements,** leaving no measurable long-time effects, and is abolished by rest.—See **conditioned inhibition.**—*Syn.* PRIMARY NEGATIVE DRIVE.—*Distg. fr.* **extinction.**—*Cp.* **fatigue.**

inhibition/reciprocal: see **reciprocal inhibition.**

inhibition/reflex: see **reflex inhibition.**

inhibition/reproductive: the **decrement** in retention following the connection of a common item with two or more different responses which follow in succession.

inhibition/retroactive: impairment of the normal effects of a learning activity when it is followed closely by another activity, esp. one somewhat similar to the first; or the hypothetical process accountable therefor.—*Ant.* RETROACTIVE FACILITATION.—*Syn.* NEGATIVE RETROACTION, **reproductive** *inhibition.—*Distg. fr.* **retrograde** *amnesia.

inhibition/social: a restraint upon behavior by group standards or by overt group action.

inhibition/vocational: a restriction of vocational effectiveness; esp., such restriction as a neurotic symptom.

inhibition/Wedensky: see **Wedensky effect.**

inhibitory potential or $_sI_R$: (*C. Hull*) the hypothesized temporary state of the organism that results from a response and that reduces the potential of recurrence of that response. The EFFECTIVE INHIBITORY POTENTIAL ($_sI_R$) is the strength of inhibition actually present at the given time.

inhibitory reflex: the decrement in the activity (**tonus**) of a muscle that reflexly follows the excitation of its **antagonist.**

initial spurt: a period of high effort or accomplishment near the beginning of an activity.—*Cp.* **end spurt.**

initiative: *n.* **1.** an introductory step or action, esp. one having a social aspect. **2.** the trait or tendency to start actions independently. Such independence may or may not involve originality.

injury: *n.* (*physiol.*) any damage to, or destruction of, tissue, resulting in impairment of organic **structure** or of **function.**

injury/current of: (*physiol.*) an electric current in tissue as a result of tissue or cell breakdown.

inkblot or **inkblot test:** see **Rorschach test.**

innate: *adj.* (*genet.*) pertaining to the differences in structure or behavior of two members of the same species that have been reared in the same environment. ➤Note that it is not a **characteristic** that is said to be **innate**, but only *differences* in characteristics. Walking is not an innate trait, but differences in ability to walk may (or may not) be wholly or partly innate. Innate does not mean the same as **unlearned** or as **species-specific.** (See both these terms, as well as **heredity.**) Though a clear meaning can be given to this term, it has been badly abused and is probably best avoided.

inner: *adj.* **1.** within the body. **2.** within the mind. ➤*Syn.* **internal.**—*Ant.* outer, external. Several contrasts are suggested. The contrasts of inner-outer and internal-external are open to some confusion. Intraorganic-extraorganic (or -environmental) makes one clear distinction; subjective-objective makes another distinction, though here there are other difficulties.

inner-directed: (*D. Riesman*) of a person whose general direction of reaction amidst shifting environmental pressures is determined by an early-instilled value system.—*Contr. w.* TRADITION-DIRECTED, **outer-directed.**

inner ear = **labyrinth (1).**

inner speech: see **internal speech.**

innervation: *n.* **1.** the supply of nerves to any organ or tissue. **2.** the excitation of a gland or muscle by a nerve. **3.** a confusing synonym for **excitation.** ➤Loosely, the stimulus is sometimes said to **innervate** the whole stimulus-response chain since it initiates the process.—*Distg. fr.* ENERVATION, which has almost the opposite meaning of deprivation of nerve energy; it is commonly used figuratively.—*Cp.* reciprocal **innervation.**—*v.* (for 2 or 3) **innervate.**

innervation ratio: (*neurol.*) the number of muscle fibers in a **motor unit** over the number 1 (representing the axon). It may be as high as 150:1 or as low as 3:1.

innervation/reciprocal: see **reciprocal innervation.**

input: *n.* the energy entering a system from without; in a communications system, that which acts on a receiver; in psychology, the **stimulus (1),** taken quite strictly.

inquiry (in·kwīr′i; in′kwǝ·ri): *n.* **1.** a search for truth or knowledge; investigation; research. **2.** interrogation; questioning. **3.** a particular question seeking for a subjective rather than an objective fact: e.g., an item in an opinion or attitude scale, a question in an introspective interrogation, a question concerning purposes and values, symptoms and troubles.—*Contr. w.* FACT-FINDING and **test item.**

insanity: *n.* any nontemporary mental disorder of sufficient gravity to bring a person under special legal custody and immunities.

➤The term is of such vague psychological meaning that it is now limited (except *pop.*) to the legal sphere. It is not a proper synonym for **psychosis.** Severe **mental** ***deficiency** is technically included as a special case, but intoxication and delirium are not.—*adj.* **insane.**

insecurity: *n.* an indefinite condition of feeling **anxious,** unsafe, threatened, or **apprehensive.** It is shown by withdrawing reactions, by severe limitations of responsiveness, and by inability to make friends because of lack of trust in self or in others.

insensible: *adj.* **1.** of a stimulus or object that cannot be sensed, either because it is below the **threshold** or is an **inadequate** ***stimulus.** **2.** incapable of sensing a particular class of **sense data,** or sense data from a given location. **3.** not responsive to any kind of sense stimulation; **unconscious;** in a **coma.** **4.** devoid of feeling or **affect.** ➤*Syn.* INSENSITIVE. The two are likely to be used interchangeably but, properly, INSENSITIVE means *relatively* insensible, lacking sensibility to some degree, whereas **insensible** means complete lack.—*Syn.* (for 3) **anesthetic.**—*n.* **insensibility,** INSENSITIVITY.

insensitive or **insensitivity:** see **insensible, sensitive.**

inside detail or **di:** (*Ror.*) a response in which the subject sees objects or images inside an **inkblot** area that to most subjects seems unbroken.

insight: *n.* **1.** reasonable understanding and evaluation of one's own mental processes, reactions, abilities; self-knowledge. **2.** the greater or less understanding of one's true condition when mentally ill; e.g., the ability to recognize the irrationality of some of one's impulses. **3.** the process by which the meaning, significance, pattern, or use of an object or situation becomes clear; or the understanding thus gained. ➤In Gestalt theory, insight was originally described as happening suddenly, and as a novel reaction not based on previous experience. The term still implies an all-or-none, or wholeness, reaction (one understands or one doesn't), but such understanding may appear gradually. (For the sudden insight, **illumination** or **inspiration** may be used.) —*Cp.* **continuity theory of learning. 4.** the apprehension of truths in direct unmediated fashion without reason, memory, or sensation; a mystical revelation. ➤It is a nice question how far the associations of this meaning have unwittingly caused many to reject it as a scientific construct—or, for that matter, to be attracted to it for the same reason.

insistence of a color: see **color insistence.**

insistent idea = **fixed idea.**

in situ (sĭ'tū): (*L.*) in place; in its natural or original place.

insomnia: *n.* inability to sleep, esp. when chronic.—*pers. n.* **insomniac.**

inspection: *n.* term proposed as a substitute for **introspection.**

inspection techniques/Monroe's: (*Ror.*) abbreviated evaluation procedures that do not attempt a complete personality description but emphasize those patterns of response to the **inkblots** that are deemed significant for a particular purpose.

inspiration: *n.* **1.** drawing in of the breath. **2.** a sudden grasp of the essentials of a problem (taken in the widest sense) that does not result from immediately preceding **reasoning** or **trial and error.** ➤*Cp.* **insight, intuition.** The term is a loose one, originally meaning that one drew in the new understanding as one draws in a breath from outside, perhaps from a supernatural source, e.g., from the Muses. It now means merely that one cannot trace the steps whereby one has attained to understanding.

inspiration-expiration ratio: the average quotient obtained by dividing the duration of **inspiration** by the duration of **expiration** in each respiratory cycle.

inspire: *v.* to increase the zeal of a person for a purpose or goal.

instability: *n.* **1.** the tendency to quick-changing emotions or moods; unreliability of emotional response.—*Syn.* EMOTIONAL INSTABILITY. **2.** lack of steadiness of purpose; lack of self-control.—*adj.* **unstable.**

instance: *n.* an example; one case out of many available possibilities which, for the purposes in hand, are equivalent.

instant: *n.* a moment; a time so brief that all events occurring therein seem to be, and are, treated as simultaneous.—*adj.* **instantaneous.**

instant *W*: (*Ror.*) an immediate response to the **inkblot** as a whole. ➤*Cp.* **additive** *W*, in which the details are perceived one by one and then synthesized into a whole.

instigate: *v.* to arouse; to incite; to stir up; to cause to happen.—*Syn.* **stimulate, excite.**—*n.* **instigation,** often better (though less usual) than **stimulus.**

instigator: *n.* in **group therapy,** a member who stimulates another to activity or verbalization.

instinct: *n.* **1.** an enduring **tendency** or **disposition** to act in an organized and biologically adaptive way that is characteristic of a given species. ➤While the behavior is usually (or always) unlearned, this criterion is difficult to apply. **2.** = INSTINCTIVE ACT, a particular behavior due to such tendency. **3.** (*ethology*) any set of responses, shown by a great majority of the members of a species, that are associated together in time under specified environ-mental conditions and specified **drive** conditions. ➤This definition accepts the impossibility of distinguishing between learned and unlearned behavior. **4.** (*psychoan.*) ➤Although he agreed in general with the above definitions, Freud added the requirement that an instinct be not reducible to simpler components. In his later writing, he postulated only two instincts, **Eros** or **love** or **life instinct,** and **Thanatos** or **death instinct.** But what others would call separate instincts (e.g., that of fear-flight) appear in psychoanalysis as distinct manifestations of Eros or Thanatos. In general, less stress is put on instinct, much on the **instinctual.** The instinctual refers to strongly motivational and emotional impulses—to that which is irrational and, in the first instance, unconscious or belonging to the **id.**

➤The concept of **instinct** has a long history and has been the subject of unbridled controversy. The following discussion is an attempt to consider the difficulties in defining the *term* so that it is acceptable to those who find the *concept* valuable. For those who deny the concept, no definition is needed.

(*a*) Some of the characteristics attributed to instinct can be ascribed only to the **tendency** (e.g., innateness), others only to the **act** (e.g., impulsiveness, affectivity).

(*b*) Some define the instinctive act in terms of **movements** and **overt behavior,** others in terms of **act** in its wider sense, while still others would include a specific **conscious** aspect or component. This difficulty, however, is not specific to instinct but is part of the general problem of defining any psychological unit.—See **act.**

(*c*) The instinctive act is conceived, not as rigidly determined, but rather as adaptable to circumstances. Varied response continues until **adjustment** is attained. The unity beneath the variety requires postulation of a **disposition,** which in this case is defined in terms of the goal to be attained. The **teleological** implication of this construct was formerly a serious difficulty but is now apparently accepted or explained away.

(*d*) To be characteristic of a species, behavior must be determined by heredity. The difficulties of the concept of **heredity** (which see) are multiplied when behavior rather than structure is in question, and when species heredity is assumed.

—*Syn.* **erg, species-specific behavior, propensity, primary *drive.** *Cp.* also **imprinting.**—*adj.* **instinctive** (which see), **instinctual** (which see).

instinct/aim of: see **aim (3).**

instinct/death: see **death instinct.**

instinct/delayed: one that does not operate until a considerable time after birth or hatching.

instinctive: *adj.* pertaining to **instinct;** characterizing an act originating in instinct rather than in learning.—See also **instinctual.**

instinctive behavior: see **instinct.**

instinct/object of: the person, or the state of affairs, which elicits instinctive action and to which that action is related: e.g., the object of fear-flight is the menacing wild animal.—*Cp.* **aim (3).**

instinct/partial: (*psychoan.*) a **libidinal** tendency associated with a particular **erogenous *zone:** e.g., the **oral** partial instinct, the **urethral** partial instinct, the **anal** partial instinct.—*Syn.* COMPONENT INSTINCT (of the sexual system).

instinct/passive: (*psychoan.*) an instinct with a passive aim. ➤**Masochism** is a passive instinct, since its aim is to *be* hurt. A passive instinct is not one characterized by inactivity (which would be self-contradictory).

instinct/possessive: (*psychoan.*) the infant's unconscious urge to conquer and retain the love object. ➤It is said to be shown by sucking, swallowing, fecal retention; later it is **socialized.**

instincts/complementary: (*psychoan.*) related impulses of opposite character; the two opposite expressions of one instinct. ➤E.g., in infancy all instincts tend to both active and passive expression.

instinctual: *adj.* **1.** of **species-specific** behavior that is impulsive and affective rather than rational; practically = **instinctive. 2.** (*psychoan.*) pertaining to behavior or psychic process that is strongly emotional, impulsive, and essentially irrational, and that is either a direct **id** function or derived from the id. ➤In earlier psychoanalytic writing, **instinctive** was used for *impulsive* behavior whether or not derived from id, **instinctual** for behavior having direct id motivation.—See **instinct (4).**

instinctual aim: see **aim (3).**

instinctual fusion = **fusion (2).**

institution: *n.* **1.** an enduring organization of some aspect of collective life (social, political, economic, religious) controlled by rules, customs, rituals, or laws. ➤The term is used abstractly (e.g., the *institution* of marriage), or very specifically for a particular local club, a world-wide religious order, a state or government, a prison, an orchestra. While the organization consists of persons, the pattern of their relationship is defined in such a way as to be relatively independent of the individual. **2.** the buildings housing an organization.

institutional behavior: action controlled chiefly by institutional rules and customs rather th‍ by the situation or by the personal qu‍ ies of the ac‍or.—See **J curve.**

institutionalization: *n.* such degree of habituation to the routine of an institution that one is uneasy or anxious about, even incapable of, living outside.

instruction: *n.* **1.** the systematic imparting of knowledge to others.—*Syn.* **teaching. 2.** (usually *pl.*) directions for procedure for oneself or, more usually, for others.—*adj.* **instructional,** pertaining to **instruction (1); instructive,** conducive to knowledge or to learning.

instructional test: a test to measure how much has been learned from a specified instructional unit. It is an **achievement test** over a relatively small unit and is usually teacher-made.

instruction/remedial: see **remedial instruction.**

instrument: *n.* **1.** that by means of which something is done; esp., a tool. **2.** a device for measuring the present value or magnitude of a variable. **3.** (*psych.*) a device for measuring or controlling the stimulus or the response. ➤The term refers to test blanks, inquiry schedules, or similar forms, as well as to tools and machinery.—*Cp.* **apparatus,** which is restricted to a machine or a complex mechanical tool.

instrumental: *adj.* **1.** pertaining to an **instrument. 2.** acting as an intermediary process in the accomplishment of something; acting as a means to attain an end. **3.** characterizing that which is valued as a means to an end, in contrast with that which is valued for itself.—See **instrumental act.** For instrumental conditioning, see **conditioning (2).**

instrumental act or **behavior:** behavior that effects a direct alteration in the environment. ➤Since **instrumental** directly suggests other meanings and does not clearly suggest the foregoing, the phrase is ill-designed.—*Syn.* **operant** behavior, **intervention** (behavior) (both *prefd.*).

instrumental communication: see **communication/instrumental.**

instrumental conditioning: see **conditioning (2).**

insula (in′syu·lə) = **island of *Reil.**

insulin (in′sə·lin): *n.* a **hormone** produced by the pancreas that enables the body to use sugar and other carbohydrates.

insulin coma: a state of **coma** induced by a large injection of insulin, either an overdose taken by accident or a carefully regulated amount administered for shock therapy.

insulin-shock therapy: the treatment of mental disorder by a dosage of insulin sufficient to induce **shock** and **convulsions.**—*Cp.* **electroshock therapy.**

intake: *n.* the number of persons admitted to a custodial institution.—*Distg. fr.* **input.**

integer (in′tə·jər): *n.* a whole number.

integral (in′tə·grəl): *adj.* pertaining to **in-**

tegers, or to the process of **integration.**— *n.* (esp. *math.*) the result of **integration.**

integral part: a part whose elimination would fundamentally alter the complex whole.

integrate: *v.* to bring parts together into a whole or totality; to bind firmly together into a functioning whole.

integrating remark or **response:** a counselor's remark that, without adding anything, reveals the fundamental unity of feelings and ideas expressed by a counselee. ➤The remark reflects the counselee's expressed feelings and restates clearly the relations between the feelings, or between the feelings and their causes, so far as these relations have been revealed by the counselee. The counselor clarifies relations by restatement and rearrangement, but uses only what is already explicit in the counselee's statements.

integration: 1. the process (or result) of bringing together and unifying parts into a whole; the production of units of a higher order. ➤It is a stronger term than **association, coordination,** or **organization.** In **integration,** though the parts may be distinguished, they lose their separate identity. 2. (*neurol.*) the bringing together and combining of neural impulses in a center in such a way as to produce coordinated activity. 3. the condition of an organism in which all its functions work together harmoniously or as a unit. ➤This is always an unattained condition, approximated as a limit.—*Syn.* adjustment, personality integration. 4. (*math.*) the process of summing up an infinite number of infinitesimals. 5. (*educ.*) the practice of presenting two or more school subjects as aspects of one unifying theme. ➤As a simple example, history and English may be combined. The **project method** combines subjects in relation with a project.—*Cp.* also **core curriculum.**—*adj.* **integrative,** producing integration; **integral,** of the process of integration, esp. in mathematics.

integration/educational: the policy of assigning children to schools and classes without discrimination because of race, color, or ethnic group membership.—*Ant.* EDUCATIONAL SEGREGATION.

integration/group: 1. a type of group thinking in which a **consensus** is created from differing contributions of members, welding the group into intellectual and emotional unity. 2. any group process of mutual **accommodation** that leads to an increased sense of **identification** with the group.—*Cp.* integration/social.

integration of behavior: the combining of two or more behavior units into a larger unit.

integration/personality: see **personality integration.**

integration/primary: (*psychoan.*) the conscious recognition by the small child that his body and its members are distinct from the environment, constituting a **somatic** unit which also possesses **psychic** qualities.

integration/secondary: (*psychoan.*) the gradual unification of psychic components, beginning about age 5 or 6; esp., the orderly combining of the pregenital discrete components of the sexual instinct into the psychosexual unity which is the adult, or mature, personality.

integration/social: 1. the process of firmly unifying the diverse elements of a society, individual, or group. 2. the process whereby the individual adjusts or accommodates himself harmoniously to group standards.

integrative attitude: the tendency to strive to perceive a field as having wholeness or unity. ➤It is related to the Rorschach **whole response** and to Wertheimer's striving for "structural survey-ability."

integrity: *n.* 1. the quality of being whole or undivided; hence, 2. moral consistency; honesty and truthfulness.

intellect: *n.* 1. (*hist.*) the **mental *faculty** by means of which man (and man alone) can think. 2. a class name for **cognitive** processes, esp. for those of thinking (i.e., relating, judging, conceiving). 3. ability, esp. high ability, to think.—*Cp.* **intelligence.**—*adj.* **intellective,** pertaining to intellect; **intellectual** (which see).

intellection: *n.* (*rare*) the process of thinking.—*adj.* **intellective.**

intellectual: *adj.* 1. pertaining to the **intellect;** = **intellective** (*prefd.*). 2. pertaining to ideas and to the "things of the mind." 3. pertaining to thinking or reasoning of high quality; dealing effectively with difficult problems; characterizing a person of high intellect. 4. pertaining to **intelligence.** ➤This is the most common meaning.—*n.* 5. a person interested in ideas, in contrast with the merely practical man. ➤The word is sometimes used for those who merely affect an interest in new or radical ideas, with the implication that the interest is a superficial pose, is more emotional than genuinely intellectual, and expresses attraction to novelty rather than to soundness. Or it may be applied to one whose interest in ideas is not balanced by practicality. But the tendency to these derogatory usages seems to be weakening.

intellectual deterioration: breakdown in the ability to think.

intellectualism: *n.* 1. (*metaph.*) the doctrine that ultimate reality is of the nature of **intellect** or **ideas.**—*Syn.* **idealism.** 2. (*epistemology*) the doctrine that knowledge is obtained from reasoning, or from reasoning alone.—*Syn.* **rationalism.** 3. (*psy-*

chol.) the doctrine that reduces all mental processes to **cognition. 4.** an emphasis upon the value of intelligence and of the higher mental processes.

intellectualization: *n.* analysis of a problem in purely **intellectual (2)** terms, to the neglect or exclusion of affective or practical considerations. ➤It is often a **defensive** reaction to avoid **affect.** A person will endeavor to name and define instead of avowing the feeling: "I have an Oedipus complex" instead of "I hate my father."

intelligence: *n.* ➤There is more agreement on the behaviors referred to by the term than there is on how to interpret or categorize them. Three concepts recur frequently in attempts to state its connotations: that of ability to deal effectively with tasks involving **abstractions**; that of ability to **learn**; and that of ability to deal with new situations. Popular opinion assumes that "real intelligence" is innate, but this is rejected from professional use of the term. ¶The first two of the following definitions limit themselves to stating operations by which intelligence is to be distinguished from other constructs; the third is a widely accepted description.

1. that hypothetical **construct** which is measured by a properly standardized **intelligence test.** ➤This definition sounds circular but is not: intelligence tests can be —and in fact have been—devised and standardized without having any particular or clear definition of **intelligence. 2.** (*H. English*) the individual's total repertory of those **problem-solving** and ***cognitive-*discrimination** responses that are usual and expected at a given age level and in the large population unit to which he belongs. ➤The "usual and expected" response has been defined, by implication of test standardization, as one of which 65 per cent to 75 per cent of the given population are capable. What is thus usual and expected changes qualitatively as well as quantitatively with age and with the population; intelligence tests, regarded as samplings of the total repertory, must reflect these changes. The **intelligence level** is measured by the proportion of the responses, usual and expected in the population, that an individual manifests in a **standardized** sample of task-demand situations. ¶This definition leaves open the question of the organization of these responses.—*Cp.* **factor/general** and **factor theory. 3.** (*G. Stoddard*) the ability to undertake activities that are characterized by difficulty, complexity, abstractness, economy, adaptiveness to a goal, social value, and the emergence of originals. **4.** (*pop.*) the rating a person obtains on an **intelligence test**; or, more loosely, the intelligence level. **5.** (*hist.*) =

intellect. 6. (*hist. and pop.*) the capacity to profit by experience.
—*Syn.* **general *intelligence.**— *adj.* **intelligent,** having or reflecting a high level of intelligence; **intellectual,** pertaining to intelligence (but see **intellectual** for other meanings).

intelligence/abstract: the ability to deal effectively with ***abstract *concepts** and **symbols.** ➤*Contr. w.* SOCIAL INTELLIGENCE (effectiveness in relations with persons), MECHANICAL INTELLIGENCE (effectiveness in dealing with concrete objects as **mechanisms**), and ESTHETIC INTELLIGENCE (ability to appreciate and/or to create beauty). These four manifestations of intelligence overlap, and the terms are passing out of technical usage.—*Contr.* also *w.* **concrete *intelligence** and **practical *intelligence.**

intelligence/academic: the ability to profit from study in books.—*Cp.* **intelligence/abstract.**

intelligence/adult: 1. general intellectual maturity. **2.** the measured **intelligence level** at which the annual average increase becomes small in comparison with interindividual differences. ➤On most tests, the annual average increase is small after age 13 or 14. **3.** the average intelligence level of the adults in a population. ➤This level is reached some time in the early twenties. Meanings **(2)** and **(3)** are commonly confused.

intelligence/biological: the abilities involved in **cognitive** activities, considered as a function of the physiological structure and functions of the brain.

intelligence/borderline: the level of development in intelligence of a person neither clearly feeble-minded nor yet quite normal. Persons at this level are capable of self-support, but only under somewhat favorable conditions.

intelligence/clinical theories of: those derived from observations of pathological forms of behavior.

intelligence/coefficient of: an index of relative intelligence obtained by dividing a person's score by the score that is the norm for his **life *age.** ➤This is the procedure of the **IQ** but also of such other scores as the **Heinis constant.**

intelligence/concrete: the ability to deal effectively with **concrete** situations or problems.—*Contr. w.* **abstract, academic,** and **verbal *intelligence.**

intelligence/esthetic: see **intelligence/abstract.**

intelligence/general = **intelligence.** ➤Unless the theory that intelligence is a unit function is implied, the adjective *general* is redundant.

intelligence/innate: a term reflecting a

concept of heredity now generally rejected. —See **innate**.

intelligence level: the degree to which a person can perform the tasks which collectively are called **intelligence;** a measure of intellectual ability relative to other persons. ➤In general, intelligence level is represented by a score on a test, but it may be informally rated or even guessed at. It is a gross error to suppose that the level of intelligence is expressed as **IQ;** in **age-grade scales**, it is the **MA**, not the IQ, which expresses the level.—*Syn.* **intelligence.**

intelligence level/functional: the habitual level on which intelligence functions. ➤It is contrasted with the tested level (or MEASURED INTELLIGENCE), which presupposes high motivation and freedom from emotional upset. In some cases, the tested level is not a good index of the functional level.—*Syn.* FUNCTIONAL INTELLECTUAL LEVEL.

intelligence/marginal: intelligence that is below average but not so low as that of the **mental *deficient.** ➤The term is not precisely used. It generally refers to persons with slightly better than **borderline *intelligence.**

intelligence/measured: intelligence expressed as a score on a test or series of tests.

intelligence/mechanical: see **intelligence/abstract.**

intelligence/multimodal theory of: see **multimodal theory of intelligence.**

intelligence/nonverbal: ability to perform tasks that are relatively little affected by differences in verbal ability: e.g., **performance *tests.** ➤The term does not imply that there is a kind of intelligence that functions without words.

intelligence/practical: the ability to do the right thing at the right time; the ability to size up a situation and respond effectively thereto.

intelligence/psychometric: the score on an intelligence test, or on a series of tests, taken under ideal conditions. ➤This term is used by those who do not wish to imply any **trait** of intelligence: they mean to say that psychometric intelligence is literally just the *score*.

intelligence quotient or **IQ** or **I.Q.**: a measure of a child's rate of development up to the age at which he is tested, computed by dividing the **mental *age (MA)** —as determined on a standardized test of intelligence—by the chronological or **life *age (CA)**. (To avoid decimals, this quotient is now multiplied by 100, but in older writings this was not always done.) ➤The basic assumption of the IQ is that there is a considerable average annual gain

in test performance; for most tests, however, there is little after ages 14 to 16. Hence, CA 16 (or less, according to the test) is used in computing the IQ of persons beyond that age.

A child whose test performance is normal for his CA receives the IQ rating of 100. The range of IQ from 90 to 110 is considered average or normal. IQ's above 120 are arbitrarily classified as "superior," below 80 as "inferior," but these categorizations should be used with great caution. They represent rate of development to date; conservative writers do not imply that this rate is primarily determined by heredity nor that the rate of development will necessarily continue to be the same. It should be noted, moreover, that IQ is not a measure of *level* of development; two children of the same IQ but different ages will perform very differently—both on test and in general. (For level of intelligence the **MA** is the measure.)

IQ's from different scales are not always equivalent, hence the name of the scale employed should always be given. In the U. S., if no scale is specified, the **Stanford-Binet** is usually referred to. ¶The popular phrase *IQ test* reveals misunderstanding of the IQ. —*Distg.* IQ *fr.* **deviation IQ.**

intelligence scale = **intelligence test.**

intelligence/social: see **intelligence/abstract.**

intelligence test: a series of tasks yielding a score indicative of the **intelligence** of the individual who attains that score. ➤The tasks require problem solving and/or various intellectual operations (such as conceiving, thinking, reasoning), or they reflect an earlier use of such intellectual functions (e.g., in information questions). (See **intelligence.**) They are standardized by finding the average performances of individuals who by independent criteria are of known degrees or levels of intelligence. The test is a **sample** of the cognitive-function tasks that are *usual and expected* in any large cultural group or subgroup.—*Syn.* INTELLIGENCE SCALE, INTELLIGENCE BATTERY. (N.B.: The term is not *intelligent test*.)

intelligence/verbal: the ability to work efficiently with problems that involve verbal symbols. ➤The term tempts to the assumption of a **unitary *trait,** but this interpretation is unnecessary. It may be used, as defined above, purely descriptively for the observed facts.

intelligibility: *n.* the quality of comprehensibility; a characteristic of communications, messages, or theories that can be understood, esp. that can be readily understood. ➤Absolute intelligibility is characterized by freedom from self-contradiction; relative intelligibility depends on the person receiving the communication, as well as on its form and content.

intend: *v.* **1.** to move toward a clearly apprehended goal with purpose to attain it. **2.** to be knowingly ready to strive for a goal when circumstances permit.—*n.* **intent,** said of the goal; **intention,** the process or fact of intending. **3.** (*archaic*) to mean, to refer to.—*Cp.* **intension.**

intension: *n.* (*logic*) all the qualities or properties comprised in a concept or meant by a term; **connotation.**—*Contr. w.* **extension.**—*Distg. fr.* **intention.**

intensity: *n.* **1.** (*phys.*) a measure of quantity of energy. **2.** a quantitative and unanalyzable attribute of sensory data, roughly correlative with the intensity of physical energy of the stimulus: brightness of colors, loudness of sounds, "strength" of a taste or smell. **3.** the strength of any behavior: *intensity* of emotion, *intensity* of motivation (but seldom, curiously enough, *intensity* of thinking).—*adj.* **intense,** of high intensity; **intensive,** pertaining to intensity; **intensitive,** of a dimension on which objects may be ranged according to intensity.

intensity/luminous: see **luminous intensity.**

intensity of sound: see **sound intensity.**

intent: *n.* **1.** a consciously sought **goal,** or one which is to be striven for when, or if, circumstances are favorable. **2.** a **meaning.**

intent analysis: a measure of social interaction in which verbal expressions are categorized according to their intent and direction of intent: e.g., as seeking support, conciliation, attempt at diagnosis of the situation, etc.

intention: *n.* **1.** aiming at an end or goal with clear awareness of what one does. **2.** a formulated purpose to follow a course of action when favorable opportunity arises. ➤It is often implied that the purpose is weak or wavering: The road to Hell is paved with good *intentions.* **3.** (*F. Brentano*) the property of pointing outside itself that is intrinsic or immanent in all conscious process.—See **objective *intentionality.** **4.** (*info. theory*) a decision in terms of which a person produces **output** signals.

intentional: *adj.* pertaining to **intent** or **intention;** purposeful; voluntary. ➤INTENTIONAL LEARNING is learning in which there is a conscious goal to learn a specific thing.

intentional accident: an accident brought about by an unconscious motive. ➤It is thus not truly an accident, but neither is it intentional, since that word implies conscious purpose.

intentional forgetting: forgetting due to **repression.** ➤The term is a misnomer, since **intentional** means *consciously purposed.*

intentionality/objective: (*F. Brentano*) the property, intrinsic to all psychic acts, of referring to objects, i.e., to something outside the act itself. The objects need not be physical. In fact, in Brentano's formulation, a world of "objects" interposes between the psychic act and the world of physical existence.—See **act psychology** (1).

intention movement: a movement that occurs early in a chain of movements, usually of low intensity and not followed immediately by the other movements, yet predicting to an observer that the rest of the chain will presently occur.

intention tremor: see **tremor.**

inter-: prefix meaning *between, among, with each other, mutual, reciprocal.*

interaction: *n.* mutual or reciprocal influence between two or more systems; esp. SOCIAL INTERACTION, that relation between animals in which the behavior of either one is stimulus to the behavior of the other. ➤A broader term than **communication.** Two animals may be in the same situation without significant interaction.

interaction/afferent: (*C. Hull*) a hypothesized relationship of mutual influence between the **peripheral** neural processes involved in perception.

interactionism: see **mind-body problem, psychology/divisions and schools of, IV.**

interaction principle: (*C. Hull*) All afferent neural impulses active in the nervous system at any given instant interact and change each other into something partially different, in a manner that varies with every concurrent afferent impulse or combination of such impulses.

interaction process analysis: a method of studying social groups wherein all the **explicit** person-to-person reactions in small face-to-face groups are carefully recorded according to a systematic classification and analyzed.

interaction recorder: a device for timing the different kinds of interaction in a small face-to-face group.

interaction variance: (*stat.*) that portion of the total variability which is not affected by **variance** in any one variable but is a function of changes in two or more variables occurring together, i.e., of the interaction of the changes of the variables. ➤It is conceivable, e.g., that increase in gonadal hormones would affect heterosexual behavior very little in the absence of certain social encouragement, and vice versa. If taken together, a very great change may be found: the difference is the interaction variance.

interactive episode: an incident in the course of therapy, beginning when the therapist notices distortion or incompleteness in the client's account, and ending when the client brings out new facts or makes new emotional responses dealing with the subject or topic in question.

interactive measurement: (*R. B. Cattell*) measurement that deals with the energy exchange between a person and his environment. ➤Raw scores—such as time, errors, repetitions—are interactive.

interbehavioral field: (*J. R. Kantor*) the postulate that a psychological event implies an interaction between the organism and the stimulus objects, both organism and stimulus having properties built up by previous interactions. The interbehavioral field is constituted by the interaction.

interbehavioral psychology: (*J. R. Kantor*) a point of view that defines psychology as the study of evolved events in which at least one of the interacting or interbehaving factors is an organism. The event consists in the interbehavior of an organism with other organisms, things, and relations which are structurally and existentially independent of the interbehaving organism. (That is, neither stimulus objects nor their properties are *created* in the interbehavioral act; but the characteristics of any particular psychological *event* are derived from previous interbehaviors.) The configurations or adjustments that constitute events called psychological are evolved—i.e., they are dependent upon or conditioned by previous interbehaviors.—*Syn.* INTERBEHAVIORALISM. —See **psychology/divisions and schools of, V.**

interbrain = diencephalon.

intercalation (in·tər″kə·lā′shən): *n.* **1.** the insertion of something among others; interpolation: the *intercalation* of leap day. **2.** (*speech pathol.*) the automatic and illogical insertion of an irrelevant sound or word between syllables or phrases in speaking.—*Syn.* EMBOLOLALIA, INTERPOLATION.— *v.* **intercalate** (in·ter′kə·lāt).

intercept: *n.* (*math.*) the distance from the origin to the point where some line crosses a reference **axis.** The *X* intercept is the distance along the *X* axis, the *Y* intercept along the *Y* axis.

intercorrelations: *n.* the correlations, generally arranged in tabular form, of each variable with every other variable in a group. A two-way TABLE OF INTERCORRELATIONS is a **correlation *matrix.**

intercourse: *n.* **1.** the give and take between two or more individuals or groups; social interchange. **2.** = **coitus.**

interest: *n.* ➤A term of elusive meanings. It is not clear how far the several meanings given below are distinct.

 1. the **attitude** or **set** of **attending.**
 2. the tendency to give *selective* attention

to something. **3.** an attitude or feeling that an object or event makes a difference or is of concern to oneself. ➤The feeling is generally characterized as being unique or unanalyzable. **4.** a striving to be fully aware of the character of an object.—*Cp.* **curiosity. 5.** the feeling without which a person is said to be unable to learn. ➤This feeling is usually not further defined. See **interest/ doctrine of. 6.** a pleasurable feeling that accompanies activity proceeding unhindered toward its goal. **7.** a tendency to engage in an activity solely for the gratifications of engaging therein; or the activity thus engaged in: a man of varied *interests.* ➤By a curious twist, this means that an interest is what one pursues when DISINTERESTED, i.e., when one has no ulterior purpose or stake in the activity.—See **interest inventory.**

interest/doctrine of: 1. (*educ.*) the view that learning cannot take place without a feeling of **interest.** ➤The feeling is usually not explicitly defined. Sometimes it seems to mean "pleasure in the prescribed activities designed to promote learning"; at other times, **interest (3)** or **(6).** Sometimes it means **motivation.** In spite of the difficulty in giving concrete meaning to this view, it is almost unanimously held, both popularly and in educational circles. **2.** the theory that all education should begin by an appeal to the present **interests (3)** or **(7)** of the individual. **3.** the view that the aim of education is to induce many-sided interests. ➤These doctrines have led to so much confusion, and to so much educational malpractice, that whatever can be shown to be good about them (apparently it is considerable) should be reanalyzed and renamed.

interest/extrinsic: see **interest/intrinsic.**

interest group: an organization of persons pursuing a common purpose or sharing an interest in the same thing.

interest/intrinsic: the attitude taken toward an object or activity that is valued in and for itself. ➤*Contr. w.* EXTRINSIC INTEREST, in which an object or activity is valued because of its relation to some other interest or to some goal.

interest inventory: a series of questions concerning the objects or activities which the individual likes, prefers, or in which he has an interest. ➤It is used in personality diagnosis, in vocational guidance, and in personnel selection.—See **interest (7).** The term INTEREST TEST for such a questionary is acceptable only when **test** is given its widest meaning.—*Syn.* INTEREST QUESTIONARY, INTEREST SCHEDULE.

interest situation: (*K. Lewin*) one in which an animal is attracted toward an object, with or without an intervening **barrier.**—*Contr. w.* **conflict situation.**

interest test: properly, a device for measuring **interests (7)**, but often used for **interest inventories** or questionaries, which do not measure the interests and are tests only in the widest interpretation of that term.

interference: *n.* **1.** diminution of **amplitude** of vibration when two physical waves in different **phase** come together. They may be two light waves or two sound waves. **2.** = **reciprocal inhibition** in learning. **3.** a conflict of competing or incompatible motives, percepts, acts. **4.** putting difficulties in the way of another person's activities, esp. when the other person regards this as unwarranted.

interference tube: a complex tube for the conduction of sound waves so arranged that waves of different length periodically cancel each other, the trough of one wave being opposed to the crest of the other.

intergrade/sex: an animal intermediate in its sex characteristics between the typical male and female of its species; an **intersexual** animal.—See **intersexuality.**

interiorization = **internalization.**

interjection theory: the theory that spoken language arose out of such automatic or forced interjections as "oof!" or "ow!"

intermarriage: *n.* **1.** the marriage of persons related by blood.—*Syn.* **consanguineous** marriage. **2.** the marriage of persons belonging to two different social groups, esp. of two different religious, ethnic, or so-called racial groups.—*Syn.* MIXED MARRIAGE, exogamy (see **endogamy**).

intermission: *n.* an interval of normal behavior between periods of mental disorder. ➤*Cp.* **remission,** the disappearance of symptoms that are expected not to return.

intermittence/tonal = **flicker/auditory.** —*Distg. fr.* **intermittence tone.**

intermittent tone = **interruption tone.**

intermittent reinforcement: see **reinforcement/intermittent.**

intermittent schedule = **reinforcement/intermittent.**

intern: *n.* a person who, having finished a prescribed course of formal instruction, practices a profession under the close supervision and informal instruction of persons experienced in the profession.—*Var.* **interne.**

internal: *adj.* **1.** inside a system or organization; esp., inside the body.—*Ant.* **external.** ➤These two terms are not properly used as synonyms for **subjective** and **objective,** although **internal** can mean *brought within the mind.*—See **internalization.** **2.** (*anat.*) toward the center, middle, or median line of an organism: e.g., IN-

TERNAL SQUINT is a turning of one eye toward the middle line.

internal capsule: a tract of nerve fibers passing through the **corpus striatum.**

internal consistency/coefficient of or r_{11}: a measure of the degree to which testees make comparable scores on different parts of a test taken at a single sitting. ➤The coefficient is usually computed either by the **Hoyt** or one of the **Kuder-Richardson formulas,** or by correlating **split-halves** of the test items and correcting by the **Spearman-Brown formula.** Other measures of internal consistency (see **cumulative scale**) are designed to determine whether the items are homogeneous in the sense that they measure the same function. The r_{11} seeks merely to determine whether a consistent *score* can be obtained from parts of the test. The coefficient has meaning only for the population sampled by the correlated tests.

internal ear = **labyrinth (1).**

internal environment: the total internal activities of the body considered as a set of influences acting upon any one activity. ➤E.g., the amount of oxygen in the blood is an internal influence analogous to an external influence such as the amount of noise in the environment.—*Syn.* INTERNAL MILIEU.

internalization: *n.* incorporating something within the **mind** or **personality;** adopting as one's own the ideas, practices, standards, or values of another person or of society. ➤When a child progresses from "mama believes" to "I believe," he has internalized that particular belief. A fully internalized process is not thought about as having been accepted from others. INTERNALIZED SOCIAL NORMS are the standards of conduct accepted from society or from a **reference *group.**—*Cp.* **superego,** which represents the internalization of the standards of parents.—*Syn.* INTERIORIZATION, INTROCEPTION.—*Cp.* **socialization,** often used as a synonym but properly meaning conformity in outward behavior without necessarily accepting the values.

internal rectus: see **eye muscles.**

internal secretion: see **gland.**

internal sense: general term for the **proprioceptor** and the **interoceptor** senses.

internal speech: 1. speech without vocalization; the framing of words silently "in the mind"; talking silently to oneself. E.g., in composition many persons first arrange the words mentally before writing them.—*Syn.* INNER SPEECH, ENDOPHASIA (not *prejd.*). **2.** soundless, invisible, reduced (i.e., incomplete or clipped) movements of the speech mechanism.—*Syn.* IMPLICIT SPEECH; COVERT SPEECH (*prejd.*). ➤*Distg.* both **(1)** and **(2)** *fr.* visible moving of tongue and lips, which is frequently present in silent reading. In

(1) we are dealing with a true language or speech function. It is almost certain that the movements of (2) (which can be observed by means of instruments) are *a part* of the process of (1), but it is not certain that they *constitute* it. The movements of (2) also play a part in thinking and in imagery. But the facts as now known do not permit the assertion that internal speech, in either sense, is the whole or even the central aspect of thinking and/or of imagery. Using internal speech as a synonym for thinking is **theory-begging.**

internuncial neurons: neurons that connect sensory and motor neurons within the **central nervous system.**

interoceptor: *n.* a sense organ or receptor inside the body, in contrast with one at or near the surface.—*Syn.* ENTEROCEPTOR, **visceroceptor** (somewhat more limited).— *Contr. w.* **exteroceptor** and **proprioceptor.**—*adj.* **interoceptive.**

interocular distance: the horizontal distance between the centers of the pupils of the two eyes when they are in the normal position for distance vision.

interorgan generality: (*G. Murphy*) a property of an organism as a unit, or of a system of related organs within one organism as a unit: e.g., the property of **irritability,** common to all the organs that together constitute the nervous system.

interosystem: *n.* (*R. Monroe*) any mechanism that functions essentially within the organism. The mechanism is controlled almost entirely by the autonomic system and by biochemical patterns and is only indirectly connected with external events.

interpersonal: *adj.* 1. occurring or existing between persons; pertaining to a relation between two or more persons. ➤An INTER-PERSONAL RELATION is one in which two or more persons are *reciprocally* related, or is the characteristic pattern of their behavior whenever either is in any way involved with the other. 2. characterizing qualities or properties generated by the interaction of persons. 3. = **social** (somewhat broader).

interpersonal theory: the view that personality development and mental disorder are determined primarily by social behavior and interpersonal situations and by the social order, rather than by **constitutional** factors and relatively impersonal experiences.

interpolation: *n.* inserting between two values in a series an estimated value or values of such magnitude as to conform to the plan of the series.—*Cp.* **extrapolation.**

interpolation/linear: (*math.*) estimating intermediate values of a mathematical function on the assumption that the function is linear.

interposition: *n.* in space perception, the partial obscuring of one object by another. It is a **cue** to the perception of relative distance.

interpretation: *n.* 1. describing, formulating, or reformulating something in familiar terms. 2. finding or explaining the meaning or significance of the raw data. ➤The process takes varied forms. It may consist of observing or stating the surrounding circumstances or context which give meaning to a datum, e.g., a child's scowling face interpreted as a response to a just-given rebuke. Or it may involve placing the datum in an intricate theoretical system: e.g., when a certain behavior is interpreted as expressing the Oedipus complex, full understanding of this interpretation requires an understanding of the entire Freudian theory. 3. (*psychoan.*) calling the patient's attention to the signs of his **resistances** in order to weaken them; also, explaining the **symbols** that have appeared during the **analysis.**—*Cp.* meaning (2). 4. (*introspective psychol.*) giving the meaning of an experience (*Ger., Kundgabung*) instead of merely describing it (*Ger., Beschreibung*).

interpretation/allegoric: assuming that a symbolic expression is *intended* by the speaker to be an allegory, parable, or figure of speech. ➤*Distg. fr.* psychoanalytic **dream analysis,** which assumes that certain expressions are *un*intentional symbols.

interpretation/anagogic: see **anagogic interpretation.**

interpretation/dream: see **dream analysis.**

interpretation/serial: (*psychoan.*) the interpretation of a series of dreams as a unit, rather than of each dream considered separately.

interpretive therapy: a form of **psychotherapy** in which the therapist helps the subject to put his conflicts into words, to understand their **symbolic** meanings, and, through this process, to learn to solve his problems.

interquartile range: (*stat.*) the distance between the end of the first **quartile** and the beginning of the third: it includes the middle 50 per cent of the values or cases in the distribution.

interrelate: *v.* to understand another person's psychological states and to communicate one's own particularly those which the other person needs to understand.

interruption tones and **beats:** tones and beats produced by successive interruptions of a tone of uniform pitch. When the interruptions are relatively slow, **beats** are heard; when they are rapid, a **tone** is heard whose pitch corresponds to the frequency of the interruptions.—*Syn.* INTER-MITTENCE TONE.

intersensory perception: perception in which more than one sense **modality** participates.

intersexuality: *n.* possessing qualities of both sexes, esp., the **secondary *sex characters.**—*Cp.* **hermaphroditism.**

intersocial: *adj.* of stimuli or of responses involving the relation of persons to persons.

interstimulation: *n.* the modification of behavior by the perceived presence of others, whether or not there is intentional communication.

intersubjective: of **subjective** phenomena believed to be shared by more than one observer. ➤The grounds for believing that others share a phenomenon are differently stated, but they generally involve reference to physical operations. Despite metaphysical difficulties in understanding it, intersubjective refers to a real class of events: e.g., perceiving, in contrast to illusion.

intertone: *n.* a tone of intermediate pitch, characterized also by **beats,** that is produced when two tones of nearly equal pitch are sounded together.—*Syn.* INTERMEDIATE TONE.

intertrial interval: the time between successive presentations of the stimulus or task-demand.

interv.: *abbr.* for **interview, interviewer.**

interval: *n.* **1.** the time between two instants or events, sometimes calculated from beginning to beginning, sometimes from the end of the first to the beginning of the second. **2.** the distance between two objects, areas, or boundaries, generally measured between the two edges closest to each other, but sometimes (without warning) between the centers of the two objects or areas. **3.** (*music*) the difference in **pitch** between two tones sounded either successively or simultaneously. **4.** = **class interval.**

interval/fiducial: see **fiducial limits.**

interval/median: (*stat.*) the group or class interval of a frequency distribution that contains the median.—*Syn.* MEDIAN GROUP, MEDIAN CLASS, MIDINTERVAL.

interval/modal: the group or **class interval** that contains the **mode.**

interval of uncertainty: the range between upper and lower **thresholds.**—*Abbr.* IU.

interval reinforcement: see **reinforcement/interval.**

interval scale: see **scale/interval,** also **scale interval.**

intervening process variable = **process variable/hypothetical.**

intervening variable: see **variable/intervening.**

intervention: *n.* **1.** action by an animal to alter the environment or its own relation to the environment.—*Syn.* **instrumental behavior. 2.** an action by a therapist that tends to direct or influence the client's behavior, during a therapy session or in general.

interview: *n.* **1.** a directed conversation with a person or persons that is designed to elicit certain predetermined kinds of information for purposes of research or to aid in guidance, diagnosis, or treatment. ➤In **nondirective** interviewing, much freedom is left to the interviewee, but the situation itself and the conventions of the relationship make the conversation a directed one **2.** = COUNSELING or TREATMENT INTERVIEW, a counseling session which starts from the information elicited and proceeds with guidance, counseling, or psychological treatment.—*pers. n.* **interviewer, interviewee.**

interview/counseling: see **interview (2).**

interview/depth: an interview that seeks to get below the superficial expressions of opinion and attitude to the motivations, conscious or unconscious, of the interviewee. ➤The questioning is more prolonged, and various methods are used to insure free expression from the interviewee. (*Cp.* the methods of **analysis, free *association, projection, nondirective** questioning.) The answers are analyzed and interpreted, either intuitively in terms of various theories, or by **content analysis.**

interview/diagnostic: see **interview** and **diagnosis.**

interviewee: *n.* in an **interview,** the person who responds.

interviewer bias: the effect upon the interviewing process and/or upon the record thereof of the personal knowledge, attitudes, and expectations of the interviewer; by extension, the effect also upon the interview of the personality characteristics and status of the interviewer, as apparent to the interviewee.

interview/exit: a conference with an employee or a pupil before termination of his connection with job or school, to determine his reasons for leaving, his plans for the future, etc.

interview/group: an interview in which there are several interviewees who may or may not have formed a social unit previously.

interview/sample: see **sample interview.**

interview/structured: an interview in which the asking of definite questions closely determines the subjects discussed, although (at least in theory) no suggestion is given concerning the interviewee's replies.—*Cp.* **interview/unstructured.**

interview/treatment: see **interview (2).**

interview/unstructured: an interview in which the interviewer does not determine the subjects discussed, or determines only the over-all subject, leaving decision about all subtopics to the interviewee. ➤The attainment of what seems the purely negative goal of *not* determining the flow of the interview has been found to require a very refined technique.

intimacy/principle of: the principle that a **gestalt** is not a mere aggregate from which members may be taken, or to which parts may be added, without changing both the whole and the other members. In a gestalt there is no independence of parts, but only the interdependence of members of the whole.

intolerance of ambiguity: see **ambiguity/ intolerance of.**

intoxicant: *n.* a substance that produces intoxication.

intoxication: *n.* **1.** a condition due to poisoning (esp. by alcohol), manifested in a great variety of behavioral effects ranging from exhilaration to stupefaction or coma. **2.** a state of elation due to personal success or some great happiness.

intra-, intro-: prefixes meaning *within, inside.* ➤**Intra-** means *being inside,* **intro-** *toward the inside,* but the two are often confused.—*Ant.* **extra-.**

intraception: *n.* (*H. A. Murray*) an imaginative, subjective, human outlook; romantic action.—*Ant.* EXTRACEPTION.

intracranial: *adj.* within the **cranium;** often, within the brain. ➤E.g., INTRACRANIAL PRESSURE is pressure on and within the brain. INTRACRANIAL ELECTRODES are actually in the brain or on the brain surface.

intramural: *adj.* taking place within an institution such as a school (e.g., INTRAMURAL ATHLETICS, sports between members of the same school) or a hospital (e.g., INTRAMURAL THERAPY, treatment within the hospital).—*Ant.* **extramural.**

intransitive relation: a relation such that, even though A has this relation to B and B has this relation to C, it still does not follow that A has this relation to C. "Like" and "disagree with" express intransitive relations.

intraocular modification: any change taking place in the visual signal, in its passage from the cornea to the ocular nerve, that results from either the general or the individual structure of the eye. ➤Besides **refractive** alterations, there are such factors as scattering of light, fluorescence, selective absorption.

intrapsychic: *adj.* arising, or taking place, within the **mind, psyche,** or **self:** e.g., an INTRAPSYCHIC CONFLICT, one between two impulses or motives in the same person. ➤Three related terms may be compared: **endogenous** means *originating* within the individual, not merely taking place there; **psychogenic** means *originating in previous experience* (while this is certainly "within the mind," the emphasis is bio-

graphical-historical); **autistic** refers to the distorting effect of one's needs or desires upon awareness of reality.—*Syn.* ENDO-PSYCHIC.

intrapunitive: a misspelling of **intro-punitive.**

intra-uterine: *adj.* within the uterus.

intraversion: *n.* a misspelling of **intro-version,** by analogy with **extraversion.** The contrasted terms are, properly, **intro-version** and **extraversion,** not *intraversion* and *extroversion.*

intrinsic: *adj.* of a property of something as it is, not as related to something else or as perceived. ➤The **luminosity** (physical strength) of a light may be called intrinsic, whereas its **brightness** depends on the surrounds and on the observer, and is therefore not intrinsic. A prize is not intrinsic to the goal-seeking activity.—*Ant.* **extrinsic. Inherent** is often used as a synonym, but it refers properly to a permanent or inalienable property. *Essential* refers to a property indispensable to the very nature of something: it is often used where the weaker *needed* or *needful* would be appropriate. Originally, intrinsic characterized the value of something, but this meaning has been weakened or lost.

intrinsic behavior: behavior that expresses itself through a specific organ or organs: e.g., winking. ➤*Contr. w.* EXTRINSIC BEHAVIOR, which has no specific response mechanism: e.g., leadership. The words **intrinsic** and **extrinsic** do not quickly suggest the behavioral distinction they represent.—*Cp.* the related distinction of **proximal** and **distal** behavior.

intrinsic eye muscles: see **eye muscles.**

intrinsic relation: a relation between the member parts of a whole.

introception = **internalization.**

introjection: *n.* a term of varied meanings: its general meaning is a *throwing in.* **1.** the absorption of the external world into oneself; hence, reacting to external events as if they were merely **subjective.** External events are viewed as one's own mental processes, or as a sort of dream. **2.** projecting one's own qualities into inanimate objects, or acting as if they were animate. ➤This attitude is explicit in **animism;** but it is often implicit, esp. in child behavior. —*Cp.* **projection, empathy, anthropomorphism. 3.** projecting oneself into the position of another person (or object) so that one shares his feelings. ➤It is a more complex process than mere **sympathy.**— *Syn.* **identification, empathy. 4.** a feeling that another's body has been substituted for one's own, that one's personality or mind is injected into an alien body. ➤This is an occasional symptom in **depression** psychoses. **5.** (*psychoan.*) investing **affect**

in the **image** of a person rather than in the real person: one may fall in love with an idealized image of someone and be unable to love the real person. **6.** (*C. Jung*) "the adjustment of the object to the subject."— *Cp.* **autism. 7.** an unfortunate synonym for **introception.**—*v.* **introject.**

intropunitive: *adj.* (*S. Rosenzweig*) characterizing a response to frustration in which one experiences humiliation and guilt and holds oneself to blame for the situation.— *Cp.* **impunitive** and **extrapunitive.**

introspection: 1. (*hist.*) the contemplation of one's own experiences. **2.** (*structural psychol.*) the report of what **mental content** or process is present, and the description thereof in terms of **elements** and **attributes. 3.** observation of one's own acts or behavior, and report on these in the descriptive categories of psychology; esp., report of **covert** acts or of the covert aspects of acts. **4.** (*pop.*) a morbid preoccupation and anxiety about health, status, ability, etc.—See **introspectionism.**—*adj.* **introspective.**

introspectionism: *n.* the school which holds that the basic method of psychology is **introspection (2)**, and that its basic data are the **mental contents** revealed by, or in, introspection.—*Syn.* INTROSPECTIVE PSYCHOLOGY, **structural psychology, content psychology.**—See **psychology/divisions and schools of, VIII.**

introversion: *n.* a turning inward upon oneself. ➤The following are listed among the chief manifestations of the turning inward: a tendency to shrink from social contacts, preoccupation with one's own thoughts (but note that thinking as such is not necessarily **introverted**—it may be outward-directed), sensitivity, proneness to **autism.** While introversion is not considered abnormal, it is closer to a number of pathological conditions than is **extraversion.**—See **extraversion-introversion.**

Introversion presents a difficult, though by no means unique, problem of terminology. It has been shown that a person may be "turned in upon himself" in one way and not in another—i.e., that the several modes of behavior denoted by this term have independent dynamics. But they all meet the formal conditions of the definition and have received a common name. To eliminate the term might seem to be denying the rather important behavior tendencies to which—however ambiguously—it refers. A given behavior may fairly safely be called **introverted** (but see the special **Rorschach** use of that term); but the noun **introvert** is peculiarly likely to be employed as a label implying a unified **trait**, if not a **type.** It is suggested that, pending clarification of factual and theoretical issues,

terms more descriptive of the specific behavior (averse to social relations, sensitive to criticism, etc.) be substituted.—*adj.* **introverted, introversive.**—*pers. n.* **introvert.**

introversion/active: (*analytic psych.*) a voluntary withdrawal from external reality.

introversion/passive: (*analytic psych.*) an involuntary inability to turn one's psychic activities outward upon reality.

introversive: *adj.* pertaining to, or characterizing, **introversion** or, more often, **introversiveness.**

introversiveness: *n.* (*Ror.*) the tendency to turn one's feelings inward upon subjective experience, and to inhibit outward manifestations of feeling. ➤The feelings may express themselves in fantasy and daydreams, in an **autistic** distortion of reality, or in esthetic imagining or reflective thinking of a wholly constructive character. Introversiveness is not to be taken, therefore, as either a good or a bad tendency in itself. The containment of feeling should not be confused with lack of feeling: introversiveness generally implies fairly strong feeling. ¶This term only partially overlaps in meaning with **introversion** (which see). *M* responses to the inkblots are taken to be signs of **introversiveness.**—*adj.* **introversive,** pertaining to introversiveness; **introverted** (in Ror. usage), markedly given to **introversiveness.**

introvert: *n.* a person who tends under stress to withdraw into himself and to avoid other people.—*Cp.* **extravert.** ➤Jung spoke of a distinct INTROVERT TYPE; that term has now become semipopular and refers either to a type (i.e., a classification of persons) or to a person who shows a strong unitary trait of introversion. Both **introvert** and INTROVERT TYPE, as usually used, ignore the evidence that introversion refers to several different and independent ways of acting.—See **introversion.**

introverted: *adj.* **1.** turned inward; tending toward **introversion** in any of its several manifestations. **2.** (*Ror.*) markedly **introversive.** ➤In this meaning the term takes on a semipathological connotation.

intrusion: *n.* in serial memory experiments, substituting a response that was not in the original list, or making a response from the original list but in the wrong place.

intuition: *n.* **1.** direct and apparently unmediated knowledge. ➤Said sometimes of sense knowledge, since no cogitation is involved; and of any other directly received knowledge: e.g., the mystic's uncommunicable knowledge of God, or a vague impression attributed to supranormal influence. **2.** a judgment, meaning, or idea that occurs to a person without any known process of cogitation or reflective thinking. ➤The judgment is often reached as a result of many **minimal cues** and of awareness of the similarity of the present instance to other experiences, though without awareness of the comparing or explicit recall of the other experiences. Most of our practical judgments of complex issues and of persons contain a large intuitive element. —*adj.* **intuitive,** by means of intuition, often also of a person believed to have a special gift of intuition; **intuitional,** pertaining to the process.

intuitive type: (*C. Jung*) a person who depends very largely on **intuition**—i.e., upon finely sharpened perception and the unconscious interpretation of faintly conscious stimuli. ➤This and the **sensation type** form Jung's *irrational* class of **function types** (which see).

invalid (in·val'id): *adj.* **1.** (*logic*) of an argument, conclusion, or method that violates the established rules of logic. **2.** of a test that does not measure what it is intended to measure.—See **validity.**

invalidate: *v.* to weaken or to overthrow an argument, conclusion, or agreement.

invariable color: see **color invariable.**

invariable hues: the three hues which are independent of the **Bezold-Brücke** phenomenon—i.e., which do not change with change in **luminance** of the stimulus. ➤Purdy's average values for the spectrum stimuli to the invariable hues are 474, 506, and 571 millimicrons, respectively.

invariance: *n.* **1.** the property of remaining constant while other conditions are changing: e.g., the distance between two points is the same even when referred to two different Cartesian coordinate systems.—*Syn.* INVARIABILITY. **2.** the tendency of a visual **aftersensation** to maintain its original size, regardless of the distance from the eye to the background upon which the image is projected.—*Cp.* **Emmert's Law.**—*n.* in**variate,** that which does not change.—*adj.* **invariant.**

invariant: *adj.* of a magnitude that does not change while certain other qualities do: the ratio of the diameter of a circle to its circumference is *invariant*—i.e., the ratio does not change, whatever may be the size of the circle.

inventory: *n.* a catalog or listing of all the items regarded as useful or relevant for a certain purpose. ➤Such an inventory is often used as a **check list** or as a rating **schedule.** Sometimes inventory refers to a representative *sampling of the total items. Thus, the **adjustment *inventory** is a sample of the behaviors regarded as signs of good or bad adjustment, although no complete inventory of these behaviors is conceivable.

inventory/adjustment: an inquiry form

listing behaviors known to be, or at least regarded as, diagnostic of good or bad **adjustment.** The rater indicates which of these behaviors the ratee has exhibited, or habitually or characteristically exhibits. ➤Strictly speaking, it is not an **inventory** but a **sample.**

inventory/horizontal: a listing of an individual's traits as observed at a single level of development. ➤*Contr. w.* VERTICAL INVENTORY, a listing that traces changes with the passage of time.

inventory/interest: see **interest inventory.**

inventory/occupational interest: see **occupational interest inventory.**

inventory/personality: see **personality inventory.**

inventory test: see **test/inventory.**

inverse correlation = negative *correlation.

inverse factor analysis = *Q* technique.

inverse square law: the principle that physical forces, emanating in straight lines from a center, decrease in intensity proportionately to the square of the distance from the source. The principle applies to light, sound, heat, and odor.

inversion: *n.* **1.** a turning upside down or in an opposite direction. **2.** (*math.*) a transposition of the order of members of a series **3.** a reversal—for a relatively short distance, and followed by a resumption—in the direction of a curve representing a **continuous variable.** ➤The rise of the curve is temporarily replaced by a fall, or vice versa. It is generally assumed that the change is an irregularity due to some factor extrinsic to the variable measured. **4.** = in**version of affect. 5.** = sexual *inversion.—*v.* **invert** (in·vèrt').

inversion/amphigenous: see **amphigenous inversion.**

inversion of affect: (*psychoan.*) a sudden change from love to hate, or vice versa; a manifestation of **ambivalence.**

inversion/sexual: *n.* **1.** condition of having some of the sex characters of the opposite sex; **hermaphroditism. 2.** assuming the characteristics or the role of the other sex.—*Cp.* **transvestism. 3.** assuming the role of the other sex in **homosexual** acts.—*Cp.* **perversion. 4.** sexual attraction to the same sex; **homosexuality.** ➤Freud distinguishes ABSOLUTE, OCCASIONAL, and AMPHIGENOUS INVERSION (this last meaning indifference to whether the sex object is male or female).—*pers. n.* **invert.**

invert (in'vèrt): *n.* a person whose erotic inclinations are mainly toward persons of his or her own sex.

inverted factor analysis = *Q* technique.

inverted Oedipus: a reversal of the **Oedipus complex** so that it is the parent of one's own sex with whom one wishes intimacy.

investigation: *n.* a systematic examination of phenomena in order to understand or explain them.—*Syn.* **research, experiment** (which see for its special meaning), **inquiry, examination.**

investment: *n.* (*psychoan.*) **1.** the actual expenditure of **psychic energy** upon an object; or the tendency so to expend it. **2.** the amount of psychic energy or **affect** with which an object is charged; the potential psychic energy of an object. ➤The **investment** changes rather easily from one object to another.—*Cp.* **displacement.**—*Syn.* **cathexis.**

invgt.: *abbr.* for **investigation.**

inviolacy need: (*H. A. Murray*) the need for **counteraction** plus the need for **defendance.**

involuntary: *adj.* characterizing a movement made despite effort not to make it; loosely, NONVOLUNTARY: made without intention or volition.

involuntary nervous system: obsolete term for **autonomic nervous system.**

involution: *n.* a decline; a period of retrograde change; specif., the period of life when physiological and psychological activities are manifestly deteriorating; presenile decline; sometimes used euphemistically for **menopause.** ➤The beginning of this period is conventionally dated from about age 45, but there are great individual differences.

involution(al) melancholia = **involutional psychotic reaction.**

involutional psychotic reaction: (*Stan. Psychiat.*) a mental disorder, developing at and related to the **climacteric,** characterized chiefly by depression. Frequent symptoms are insomnia, worry, guilt feeling, anxiety, agitation, delusional ideas, and hypochondria.—*Syn.* INVOLUTIONAL MELANCHOLIA.

ips(a)-, ipso-: (fr. *L.* reflexive pronoun: *himself, itself*) combining forms meaning *the same* or *of one's own.*

ipsative scaling: a method of assigning scale values that takes the individual's own characteristic behavior as the standard of comparison. ➤E.g., rating a response as better or worse than is usual for the given individual is simple ipsative scaling.

ipsilateral (ip"si·lat'ər·əl): *adj.* pertaining to the same side.—*Var.* **ipsolateral.**

IQ, I.Q. = **intelligence quotient.** ➤The locution "IQ test" is incorrect, since no test ever directly yields an IQ: the IQ is a *relation* between a test score and a person's life age. For the same reason IQ should not be used as an index of **intelligence level;** the IQ is the MA in relation to life age (or in the case of the Wechsler, in relation to statistical expectation).

iris: *n.* the pigmented disc surrounding the pupil of the eye.—*adj.* **iridal** (i'ri·dəl).

iris reflex = **pupillary reflex** (*prefd.*).

irradiance: *n.* a measure of the intensity of light per unit area that is emitted by a *radiant* source. ➤*Cp.* **illuminance,** a measure of the intensity of *reflected* light.

irradiation: *n.* **1.** (*optics*) a spreading, as of the rays from a light. **2.** an apparent increase in the size of a relatively small and bright figure seen on a darker background: e.g., a white square on a black field looks larger than a black square on white. ➤The term expresses a belief that there is a spreading of excitation in the retina. **3.** a spreading of an afferent neural impulse to neighboring fibers as it passes through the central nervous system. **4.** a spreading of excitation to a larger number of muscle fibers as intensity of stimulation is increased.—*Syn.* (*C. Sherrington*) REFLEX IRRADIATION.—See **induction. 5.** the eliciting of a conditioned response by stimulation of another receptor of the same general class but not the specific receptor of the original conditioned stimulus: e.g., a retraction of the right hand to a touch on the right may sometimes be elicited, without further training, by a touch on the left. If the touch on the left elicits a retraction of the right hand, we have **cross-conditioning,** or **transfer.** ¶The term **irradiation** is somewhat objectionable, since it seems to imply a hypothesis regarding the mechanism by which the effect arises. **Stimulus *generalization** is preferred by some as making no such implication; but it misnames the phenomenon, since the animal does not react to a more general class but to a different stimulus of the same class. **6.** the spread of excitation to neighboring or allied response structures when a response fails to adjust the organism to the situation, or when great effort is being put forth. **7.** exposure of a tissue to **radiation,** esp. to X rays and other ultra short radiation.

irradiation/excitatory: see **excitatory irradiation.**

irradiation pattern: a **field** property of the total learning situation (including the state of the learner) characterized by lack of interest or persistence and inability to perceive detail. The pattern is determined not by the task-situation nor by the learner but by the whole field.

irradiation theory of learning: the hypothesis that learning consists of selective **reinforcement** of one of the many responses that are elicited by **irradiation** (6).—*Cp.* the closely similar **trial and error.**

irrational: *adj.* contrary to reason or to the principles of logical thinking. ➤*Cp.* **nonrational,** not determined by reason. (But

Jung employs **irrational** where **nonrational** better expresses his meaning.)—*Syn.* **illogical.**—See **logical.**

irrational type: see **rational type.**

irreality level: (*K. Lewin*) a region in the person's psychological environment (his **life space**) in which actions, thoughts, and gestures are determined more by needs or desires than by recognition of the objective situation. ➤**Fantasy, daydreams,** distortions, fabrications, **prejudices** are typical behaviors on the irreality level. It is not implied that the person confuses this level with reality, though some (perhaps all) do to some extent. An infinite number of irreality levels may be conceived (*cp.* **irreality-reality dimension**); but it is also possible to speak of two levels, irreality and reality.—*Syn.* UNREALITY.

irreality-reality dimension: (*K. Lewin*) a dimension along which behaviors can be ordered according to the degree to which they are regulated by needs or desires, on the one hand, or by the objective situation on the other. It is permissible also to conceive of the dimension as divided into two zones or levels: the IRREALITY LEVEL and the REALITY LEVEL.

irregular replies: replies to a questionary or test that are not expected or provided for by the scoring or coding.

irrelevant: *adj.* not pertinent to the issue; unrelated.

irresistible impulse: a compulsion to an act that one knows to be wrong.—See **irresponsibility.**

irresponsibility: *n.* (*criminal law*) a basis for avoidance of criminal guilt. ➤It may be pleaded when, by reason of mental deficiency or disorder, a person cannot distinguish right from wrong. In some states the test for irresponsibility may include an **irresistible impulse.** The plea has little relation to psychological fact or principle.

irreversibility of conduction: (*neurol.*) the property of the **synapses** of **reflex arcs** or similar conduction structures of transmitting only in the direction from **receptors** toward the center and from centers toward **effector** organs.—*Syn.* FORWARD CONDUCTION.

irritability: *n.* 1. the characteristic property of living matter of responding by motion or change in form when subjected to **stimulation** or **excitation,** i.e., to change in external surroundings. 2. **contractility** of a muscle. 3. susceptibility to **irritation (2).** 4. oversensitivity to stimulation. Stimuli normally acceptable are reacted to emotionally, with rage or avoidance, occasionally with fright: e.g., the heightened reaction to ordinary sounds when one has a headache.—*adj.* **irritable.**

irritability/neural: see **neural irritability.**

irritation: *n.* 1. inflammation of a local tissue. 2. anger that is easily aroused but relatively mild, and expressed chiefly in verbal forms. 3. the act of exciting.—See **irritability (1).**—*n.* **irritant,** an agent of irritation.

ischemia (is·kē'mi·ə): *n.* a local diminution of arterial blood supply.

Ishihari color plates (ish"i·här'i): a test for **color blindness** consisting of squares, small circles, etc., printed in different hues and saturations in such a way that a given hue forms a pattern meaningful to the color-normal, but not to the color-blind or color-weak, eye.

island of Reil: see **Reil/island of.**

island/tonal: see **tonal island.**

-ism: noun-forming suffix meaning *act, action, process, state, doctrine, theory,* or *a practice dominated by a theory.*

iso- (ī'sō-): combining form meaning *equal, the same.*

isochron (ī'sō·kron): *n.* (*S. Courtis*) a unit of growth which is 1 per cent of the change on any dimension during the total period from zero development to complete maturity.

isochronal (ī·sok'rə·nəl): *adj.* equal in rate, frequency, or time of occurrence. ➤It does not mean equal in duration. 2. having the same **chronaxia.**—*Var.* **isochronous** (-nəs).—*n.* **isochronia, isochronism** (ī"sə·krō'ni·ə; ī·sok'rə·niz·əm).—*v.* **isochronize** (-sok'-).

isokurtic (ī"sō·kėr'tik): *adj.* (*stat.*) not showing **skewness.**

isolate: *v.* 1. to separate from all else; to put by itself; hence, to **abstract;** to think about a certain element or aspect of a problem in complete separation from other aspects. 2. (*psychoan.*) to separate an idea or a memory from its **affect.**—*Cp.* **undoing.** 3. to deprive of social contacts.—*n.* 4. a person who has no social contacts, or who has only meager and superficial relations with others.

isolates/breeding: groups of individuals delimited by social class, religious affiliation, habitat, or other cultural or geographical isolating influences so that mating occurs only within the group. ➤*Cp.* **endogamous group,** which emphasizes nonbreeding with other groups as a result of a particular marriage system.—*Distg. fr.* BIOLOGICAL ISOLATES, organisms that cannot interbreed.—*Cp.* **segregation.**

isolation: *n.* 1. the act of **isolating,** or the state of being **isolated,** esp. in the social sense. 2. a tendency to avoid social contacts. 3. (*psychoan.*) a process similar in effect to **repression,** but differing in that the underlying impulse or wish is consciously recognized, although its relation to present behavior is not. (In **repression,** the wish or impulse is not known to the in-

dividual.) **Isolation** is said to be common in **obsession-compulsion** neurosis, rare in normal persons. **4.** (*psychoan.*) the separation of an object from its **affect;** decathexis (see **cathexis**). ➤It is said to be a conscious process.—*Cp.* **undoing.**
5. = psychic *isolation (*C. Jung*), that sense of estrangement from one's fellows which results from the irruption into consciousness of materials from the **collective** *unconscious.

isolation amentia: mental deficiency due to very great lack of normal human contacts in early life.

isolation/artificial: see **artificial isolation.**

isolation defense: (*Ror.*) meandering comments about the **inkblots** that are interpreted by the examiner as an effort to avoid referring to those aspects of the inkblot which suggest the testee's conflicts or anxieties.

isolation effect: in the learning of a serial list, the effect of isolating or emphasizing a single item: e.g., printing one of the items in a distinctive type face.

isolation mechanism: (*psychoan.*) a symptom of **obsession-compulsion,** shown by a short period of complete inactivity after any word or deed that is linked with a distinctly unpleasant personal problem or **complex.**

isolation/psychic: (*analytic psychol.*) a tendency to withdraw from social contacts because one has a fearful secret which must not be divulged. ➤The fearful secret, according to Jung, may be unconscious material that has somehow broken into the consciousness.

isometric twitch: a slight muscular contraction to a new stimulus, made while the muscle group is pulling against a rigid spring and is thus incapable of much further shortening.

isomorphism: *n.* the doctrine that the **excitatory fields** in the brain have a formal, point-for-point correspondence with the experienced contents of consciousness. E.g., if there is a perceived difference in size, the excitatory fields in the brain have a corresponding size difference.—*adj.* **isomorphic.**

isomorphy (ī'só·môr″fi): *n.* (*logic*) a formal identity, point for point, between two conceptual systems. ➤*Contr.* w. HOMOLOGY, a point-for-point identity between two actual and real systems; and w. **model,** which often means a formal identity between a conceptual system and a real one.—See **isomorphism.**—*adj.* **isomorphic.**

isophilic: *adj.* (*H. S. Sullivan*) of affectionate behavior or feeling directed to one's own kind, specifically one's own sex. ➤It is distinguished from **homosexuality** by ab-

sence of genital lust which in the isophilic relation is neither expressed nor sublimated; it just is not there.

isophonic contour: a line showing the interdependence of two attributes of tone in their relation to the physical properties of the stimulus. ➤E.g., **loudness** depends chiefly upon intensity of the stimulus but also upon **frequency,** so that loudness and pitch are interrelated. The isophonic contour is a graphic representation of these relations.

isotropic: *adj.* of nonquantitative items or attributes placed in a consistent order on any nonquantitative basis: e.g., the ranks in the army (private, corporal, sergeant); the colors of a spectrum.—*Cp.* **hierarchy, rank order.**

-ist: noun-forming suffix meaning *agent,* or *one who professes an art or profession,* or *one who follows an -ism.*

It: (*psychoan.*) = **id.**

item (ī'təm): *n.* **1.** any single fact, part, or unit that is or can be isolated for examination or measurement. It need not be a natural or physically separable unit. **2.** a single unit of test or experimental materials: e.g., a single question in a test composed of many questions, or a single nonsense syllable in a list of syllables to be memorized.
➤As used in this dictionary, item has a very general reference. Anything whatever that can be thought of or reacted to separately is an item: the field of corn, the corn ear, the kernel of corn—each may be an item, as may also the fertility of the field, the farmer's gratification, and so on.

item analysis: 1. the determination of item difficulty, item discriminability, item internal consistency, item reliability, and other item characteristics of interest to test constructors or users; esp., **2.** the determination of the effectiveness of a test item for making the required discriminations between persons, i.e., of **item validity.** ➤The most commonly used methods compare the answers to the item of those scoring high and low (e.g., top and bottom 27 per cent) on the test as a whole, or on some criterion variable.

item difficulty: a measure representing the relative frequency with which a test item is passed or failed in a given testee population.

item operating characteristic: the probability that a subject will obtain a certain score on an item, as a function of a certain specified trait or attitude of the subject.

item scalability = scalability (2).

item scaling: the statistical procedure of assigning a test item to its place in a **dimension,** usually to its place on a scale of relative difficulty.

item selection: the process of determining the worth of an item as a part of a test or questionary. ➤A number of statistical methods have been developed for determining the **validity, reliability, scorability, scalability, unique** contribution, etc., of the item.

item validity: the extent to which an item measures what it is supposed to measure; the ability of an item to distinguish between those having much and those having little of some characteristic.

item weighting: process of determining the proportion of the total score of a test that is to be gained by passing a particular item. ➤Thus, correct response to some items may be given twice the score or weight given to others. Item weighting has not been found to increase materially the effectiveness of most tests.

iteration method: (*math.*) the use of successive approximations in solving equations.

-itis: noun-forming suffix meaning *inflammation* or, more generally, *pathological condition* in a (specified) tissue.

-ity: noun-forming suffix meaning *state, condition,* or *quality.*

IU = interval of uncertainty.

I.V.: 1. **= independent *variable.** 2. **= intervening *variable.**

J

J: (*C. Hull*) delay in **reinforcement.**

j = the number of **standard *deviation** units, counted from the mean as center.

Jacksonian epilepsy or **convulsion:** see **epilepsy.**

Jackson's law: the generalization that, when mental functions are lost through disease, those that developed late in the evolution of the species are the first to be lost: i.e., that deterioration retraces the order of evolutionary development but in reverse order.

jactation: *n.* (*med.*) a tossing about with jerking, irregular, convulsive movements of the body; excessive restlessness.—*Syn.* JACTITATION.

jamais vu (jə·mä′ vY): (*Fr., never seen*) applied to the phenomenon of feeling that one has never seen a place, though it is in fact familiar.—*Cp. déjà vu.*

James-Lange theory of emotions: the name commonly given to related but distinct theories as if they were one: **1.** (*C. Lange*) Emotions are identical with the changes in the circulatory system as these are induced by emotive situations. **2.** (*W. James*) Upon perception of certain emotive situations there follow marked organic "reverberations": changes in circulation, glandular action, contractions of both smooth and skeletal muscles. Concerning the relation of these to the emotion, James set forth three views without clearly distinguishing them: (*a*) the organic reverberation causes the emotion (the nature of the latter not stated); (*b*) through kinesthetic and organic sense organs, we perceive the organic reverberation, and the fused perception is the emotion; (*c*) the organic reaction is the emotion. Only the last of these is similar to Lange's independently stated view.

jargon: *n.* **1.** meaningless talk; specif., language peculiar to a particular trade, profession, or other group. **2.** (*speech pathol.*) unintelligible speech, manifested in some forms of idiocy, insanity, or brain lesion.— *Syn.* **paraphrasia, word salad** speech.

Jastrow illusion: an optical **illusion** in which the upper of two ring sectors, of equal size and placed one above the other, appears to be smaller.

Java man = Pithecanthropus erectus.

J coefficient: (*E. S. Primoff*) an estimate of the probable predictive usefulness of each of the subtests of a battery. It consists, for each subtest, of a correlation between the rated importance of a job element (e.g., lifting heavy weights) and the **beta weight** of that job element in the subtest. ➤The importance of the job element must be rated by those familiar with the job. Beta weights are at first estimated by test experts but can be improved statistically as actual validity data are accumulated on presumably similar populations.

J curve: (*F. H. Allport*) a representation of the frequency with which individuals comply in varying degree with a prescribed standard or rule that lies within the range of their capacity: e.g., the frequency of varying degrees of "stopping" at a red traffic light. The curve is shaped roughly like a capital letter J, or that letter reversed.

jealousy: *n.* an **attitude** or **sentiment** whose organizing principle is resentment that a beloved person shows affection to a third party.—*Cp.* **rivalry.**

jealousy/sibling: see **rivalry/sibling.**

Jendrassik's reinforcement of reflexes (jen·dras′iks): an increase in a reflex response, usually the **patellar reflex,** that results if the usual stimulus is given at the moment when the subject begins to pull hard on his interlocked hands.—*Cp.* **facilitation (3).**

jnd or **j.n.d. = just noticeable difference.**

jnnd = just not-noticeable difference.

job analysis: systematic study of the specific tasks required for a particular job, often also of conditions, pay, opportunities for advancement, etc. ➤More loosely, the term is applied to a statement of the personal qualities required for a given job, for which **job specification** is more appropriate.

job evaluation: the determination, usually by a joint committee of executives and workers, of the "worth" of a particular job, compounded of such variables as requisite skill and/or education, experience, hazards, discomforts, etc. Rate of pay is proportioned to the "worth" as thus estimated, with or without adjustment for seniority.

job placement: assignment of a person to a job, preferably on the basis of aptitude, personality, experience, and interest.

job specification: a concise description of a given job—its duties and opportunities—and especially of the qualities (physical, educational, intellectual, temperamental, etc.) required for competence in it.

Jocasta complex (jō·kas′tə): that part of the **Oedipus complex** which concerns the role of the mother as object of the infant's love and is shown by jealous resentment of the father. The term refers to Jocasta, mother and wife of Oedipus.

joie de vivre (zhwä də vē′vrə): (*Fr., joy of living*) zest; restless and flighty but pleasantly toned behavior without clear goal direction.

joint determination/coefficient of: (*stat.*) the proportional contribution (positive or negative) to the **variance** of the **dependent** *variable that results from correlated occurrence of two **independent** *variables. It is equal to twice the product of the two **path coefficients** of the independent variables and the correlation coefficient between them.

joint family = extended family (see **family**).

joint sense: see **kinesthesis.**

Jordan curve: (*topol.*) a closed curve that does not intersect itself, the shape of the curve being otherwise irrelevant. ➤In topological psychology, it is much used to define **regions** in **life space.**

Jost's law (yōsts): the generalization that, given two associations of the same manifest strength but of unequal age, (*a*) repetition increases the strength of the older more than of the younger, and (*b*) the older falls off less rapidly in a given length of time. ➤Sometimes spoken of as two laws.

joule (joul; jül): *n.* a unit of work equal to 10 million **ergs.**

journeyman: *n.* one who is able to carry on a craft or trade without supervision, but who lacks the highest degree of skill. ➤*Cp.* the trade hierarchy of **novice, apprentice, journeyman, expert.**

joy: *n.* an emotion, usually related to present experiences, highly pleasant and characterized by many outward signs of gratification. —*Ant.* **grief.**

judgment: *n.* **1.** (*logic*) the process of discovering or asserting an objective or intrinsic relation between two objects or concepts; or a statement of the relation in the form of a declarative sentence or proposition. **2.** (*hist.* and *pop.*) a **faculty** or power that enables a person to make judgments. **3.** the process of bringing to light and asserting the implicit meaning of a concept. **4.** a critical evaluation of a person or situation. It includes the processes of **appreciation,** comparison, and **appraisal** of values. **5.** (*attitude scaling*) the assignment of a statement of attitude to a position on an **attitude scale. 6.** (*psychophys.*) the verbal responses (such as *present, absent, greater, smaller, equal*) upon which computation of the **threshold** depends.

judgment/absolute: see **absolute judgment.**

judgment/comparative: see **comparative judgment.**

judgment/doubtful: see **doubtful judgment.**

judgment/existential: see **existential judgment.**

Jukes: the pseudonym for a celebrated family, most of whose members were social misfits, feeble-minded, and degenerate.

jumping apparatus: (*K. S. Lashley*) a device for testing visual discrimination and the learning of discrimination in small animals. The test animal is required to jump down onto a platform, sections of which are marked off by colors, visual forms, etc. If he jumps to the section arbitrarily designated correct by the *E,* he is rewarded; otherwise he is punished.

Jungian analysis (yung′i·ən): diagnosis (and usually treatment) of a patient according to the methods and concepts of C. G. Jung.—See **analytic psychology.**

Jungian psychology = analytical psychology.

just noticeable difference or **jnd:** a very small difference between two stimuli, one which under the experimental conditions is barely above the **threshold.** ➤The JUST NOT-NOTICEABLE DIFFERENCE (or JNND) is the largest difference between two stimuli which will just not be detected. In psychophysics it is assumed by some that the jnd's may be treated as equals throughout the range tested and, hence, may be the units of a **scale.**—See **just noticeable differences/method of.**

just noticeable differences/method of: a procedure for determining how small a difference of any sort in a stimulus or object, or between two stimuli, may be directly discriminated by an organism. ➤The difference between two discriminable stimuli is gradually decreased until discrimination is just lost; conversely, the difference between two stimuli that are not discriminable is gradually increased until discrimination is barely possible; the average of the two points thus determined yields the **difference *threshold.**—*Syn.* METHOD OF LEAST DIFFERENCES, METHOD OF MINIMAL CHANGES, METHOD OF LIMITS.

just not-noticeable difference or **jnnd:** see **just noticeable difference.**

juvenile: *adj.* youthful; immature; pertaining to a young person, an adolescent, or (occasionally) a child. ➤In most states a JUVENILE DELINQUENT is a **delinquent** younger than 18 years.

juvenile court: a court for the consideration of offenses against the law by persons of less than 18 years. ➤In general, there is no formal trial, its place being taken by **counseling** or by an informal hearing. The young offender is treated as a ward of the court and measures are taken for his improvement.

juvenile delinquency: see **delinquency.**

juvenilism: *n.* the carrying over into adult years of the characteristic appearance or behavior of the **adolescent.**

juxtaposition: *n.* 1. placing objects of any sort near, adjacent to, or touching each other; or the state of being so positioned. 2. the tendency to suppose that spatial or temporal nearness means causal or other intrinsic connection. ➤It is said by Piaget to be characteristic of children's thinking. —*v.* **juxtapose.**

K

K: 1. (*C. Hull*) **incentive** motivation, considered as a component of **reaction potential.**—*Distg. fr. K'.* 2. (*Ror.*) **diffusion response.**

K': (*C. Hull*) the physical **incentive** or **reward** in motivation.

k: 1. the **coefficient** of ***alienation,** $\sqrt{1-r^2}$. 2. (*Ror.*) scoring code for a response in which the subject tones down the shading effects, seeing the design in two dimensions as a topographical map or an X-ray picture. ➤For words beginning with *k,* see also *c.*

Kallikak: the pseudonym for a celebrated family with two lines of descendants, one of respectable citizens, the other of social misfits, criminals, and mental deficients.

kata-: variant of **cata-.**

katabolism (kə·tab'ə·liz·əm): see **metabolism.**

katasexual: *adj.* of sexual behavior in which the preferred partners are dead or infrahuman creatures.

Katz and Braly Questionnaire: an inquiry form for indicating preferences among **ethnic** groups.

K **complex:** the generalized cortical response evoked in man during sleep by auditory stimulation.

Keeler polygraph = lie detector.

Kelley's constant process: (*psychophys.*) a procedure for treating data from the **constant stimulus method,** in which the data are fitted to the best-fitting normal ogive by using σ.

Kelvin scale: a temperature scale based on absolute zero, or complete lack of heat (ap-

proximately −273° C.), as its starting point.—*Syn.* ABSOLUTE SCALE.

Kent EGY: a short intelligence test, used when a quick estimate of ability is desired. It contains ten questions given orally and is scored by points, the total possible being 36.—*Syn.* KENT SERIES OF EMERGENCY SCALES.

Kent-Rosanoff Series or **Test:** a standardized **free *association** test, consisting of a carefully chosen list of 100 words which have been given to 1000 normal subjects, under instructions to answer with another word as quickly as possible. The relative frequency of a given verbal response to each stimulus word has been tabulated and is used as a standard.

key: *n.* 1. information or concepts that open the way to understanding, as a literal key opens a lock; or a central concept upon which others depend, as the stones of an arch depend on the keystone. 2. = **answer key.** 3. the legend indicating the significance of the symbols used on a map, graph, or table. 4. a device whereby one system of symbols can be translated into another system: e.g., the code for a system of symbols indicating pronunciation.—See **coding key.** 5. (*music*) a family of tones, comprising a diatonic **scale,** having recognized relationships to the **tonic** (or keynote) of that scale; more specif., the particular **tonality** (2) of a particular musical passage or composition: the *key* of D major, or F minor.

key/answer: see **answer key.**

key/coding: see **coding key.**

kilo (kil'ō; kē'lō): *n.* a thousand grams; a kilogram.

kilo-: combining form meaning *multiplied by a thousand*: e.g., a kilometer = 1000 meters.

kinephantom (kin″ə·fan′təm): *n.* a misinterpretation of seen movement, esp. of silhouette shadows: e.g., the shadow of a windmill seen as turning in the reverse direction.—*Distg. fr.* the **illusion** of motion, interpreting a motionless datum as moving.

-kinesia: combining form meaning *movement*: e.g., AKINESIA, lack of movement; HYPOKINESIA, deficiency of movement; HYPERKINESIA, excess of movement.

kinesimeter (kin″ə·sim′ə·tər; kī·nə-): *n.* any instrument for measuring the **threshold** for sensation of movement.

kinesthesis (kin″es·thē′səs): *n.* the sense that yields knowledge of the movements of the body or of its several members. Its chief divisions are (*a*) MUSCLE SENSE, having sensors embedded in the muscles and stimulated by their contraction; (*b*) TENDON SENSE, having sensors in the tendons; (*c*) JOINT SENSE, having sensors on the surfaces of the joints and stimulated by their flexing; (*d*) STATIC SENSE, having sensors in the labyrinth of the inner ear. (Often not classified as kinesthetic.)—*Var.* **kinesthesia** (-zhə).—*adj.* **kinesthetic** (-thet′-ik).

kinesthetic method: 1. a method of correcting faulty speech by calling attention to the differing movement sensations of correct and faulty speech. **2.** a method of treating reading disability by having pupils trace the outlines of words.

kinesthetic response: (*Ror.*) a response that projects some kind of action or life into the **inkblot.**—*Cp. M.*

kinetic (ki·net′ik): *adj.* **1.** (*phys.*) pertaining to motion as a *physical* fact, not (properly) to movement as a biological fact or to behavior. **2.** of a very lively person.

kinetic energy: energy actually doing work. —*Contr. w.* *potential *energy.

kinetics/apparent visual: see **apparent visual kinetics.**

kinship: *n.* a relationship between two or more persons that is based upon common descent, but also usually including such close socially recognized relationships as those by marriage and by adoption. ➤The degree and kind of relationship that constitutes kinship in any society varies greatly, from that of common immediate ancestry ("blood relationship") through a variety of socially regulated relationships (called in our society "in-law relationships") by marriage, adoption, etc.—*Syn.* **consanguinity,** limited to relationship by common descent.

kinship system: (*anthrop.*) in any given society, the recognized kinds and degrees of **kinship.** the terms by which these are

called, and the status and behavior patterns associated with them.—*Syn.* RELATIONSHIP SYSTEM.

Kjersted-Robinson law: the generalization that the proportion of material learned during corresponding fractions of the total learning time is relatively constant for different lengths of material. The generalization is often stated thus: The form of the **Vincent curve** is independent of variations in the length of the list of items to be learned.

kleptolagnia (klep″tō·lag′ni·ə): *n.* sex excitement associated with theft.

kleptomania: *n.* obsessive impulse to steal, esp. in the absence of any economic motive or personal desire.—*adj.* and *pers. n.* **kleptomaniac.**

knee-jerk reflex: automatic forward extension of the lower leg produced by a sharp blow just below the knee cap.—*Syn.* PATELLAR REFLEX.

know: *v.* **1.** to have an idea or a cognition; to react to or to be aware of many features or properties of a complex situation, distinguishing them from other features. ➤To **know** is more complex than to **perceive** or to **apprehend,** less complex than to **understand** or to **comprehend.** To **know** usually means to know correctly and surely, although the noun **knowing** is sometimes qualified as *uncertain* or *incorrect*. **2.** to have memorized or learned something thoroughly; to have something firmly and clearly in mind; to be familiar with or to recognize something; to distinguish one thing from another.—*pers. n.* **knower.**

knower: *n.* one who knows. ➤In much philosophical writing the knower is the one who experiences or acts. The implied restriction to **cognition** makes the term only a limited synonym for **person.**

knowledge: *n.* **1.** the result of **knowing.** ➤Simple knowledge is called **apprehension** (which includes **perceiving**); more complex knowledge is called **comprehension** or **understanding** (which includes awareness of relations, meanings, etc.). **2.** the body of understood information possessed by an individual or by a culture. **3.** that part of a person's information which is in accord with established fact.—*adj.* **known.** —*pers. n.* **knower.**—*v.* **know.**

knowledge/functional: knowledge that can be applied and used. ➤Two contrasts are implied: with intrinsically useless knowledge, and with knowledge that for some reason the person cannot bring to bear in practical situations

knowledge of results: 1. the hypothesis that learning is facilitated when the learner is informed at each step about the progress he is making in his learning. **2.** the hypothesis that learning is facilitated when the learner is promptly informed whether a particular response is correct and, if incorrect, of the direction of error. ➤The two usages refer to distinguishable situations and probably to different psychological processes.

Knox Cube Test: a performance test in which the subject taps a series of four cubes in various prescribed sequences. The test is easily given with pantomime directions to those who do not speak the examiner's language.

Koenig cylinders (kœ'nig): a series of metal cylinders emitting tones of very high frequency, used for determining the upper **threshold** for pitch.

Kohler-Restorff phenomenon (kō'lĕr-res'-tôrf): in **right associates** experiments, the greater frequency of correct recall when the pair is presented in isolation, as compared with presentation as one pair in a series.

Kohs block designs: a test in which the task is to copy a geometric design by arranging small cubical multicolored blocks. It is usually employed as a test of intelligence.

kolytic (kō·lit'ik): *adj.* having an inhibitory action.

Korsakow's psychosis or syndrome (kôr'-sə·kôfs): extensive neural irritation, generally due to alcoholic excess, with unsystematic falsification of memory (**confabulation**) and loss of **orientation.**—*Var.* **Korsakoff.**—*Syn.* POLYNEURITIC PSYCHOSIS. —See also **alcoholic psychosis.**

Korte's laws (kôr'tiz): statements of the optimal conditions for apparent motion when two stationary visual stimuli are given in succession.

KPR = Kuder Preference Record.

Krause ending (krou'zə): a **receptor** appearing chiefly in the conjunctiva of the eye, the skin of the nipples, and the genitals. It is thought to be one kind of receptor for cold stimuli.—*Syn.* KRAUSE'S CORPUSCLE, KRAUSE'S END BULB.

Kretschmer type: see **body *type.**

K-R formulas: see **Kuder-Richardson coefficients.**

K scale: a special key for scoring the MMPI to correct for errors due to **malingering.**

kteis (kə·tīs'): *n.* representation of the female external genitals, esp. for use in decoration and as a symbol in cult worship. —*Cp.* **phallus.**

Ku = kurtosis.

Kuder Preference Record: a self-report form designed to disclose relative interest in broadly defined **interest** areas. ➤The vocational record deals with ten areas, such as the scientific, the musical, or that of social relations, that are related to occupations, but it does not inquire about occupations as such. The personal form has five sections inquiring about group and family situations, working with ideas, avoiding conflict, and directing others.

Kuder-Richardson coefficients of equivalence: any of several formulas for estimating from one administration of a test the correlation between comparable forms. The formulas are variations on the **chancehalves *correlation.**—*Syn.* K-R FORMULAS.

Kuhlmann-Anderson test: a series of test batteries for measuring intelligence from kindergarten age to maturity.

Kuhlmann-Binet test: a revision for the American culture of the Binet tests of intelligence. The test extends down to the four-months level. It is given individually. —*Distg. fr.* **Kuhlmann-Anderson test.**

Kundgabe (kŭnt'gä·be): *n.* (*Ger., giving information*) reporting what one was thinking about instead of describing the **contents** of the thinking in psychologically elementary terms. ➤Such report is not considered true **introspection** in **existential psychology.**—*Syn.* **evaluation,** but this does not give a good idea of the activity or of the German term to which it is supposed to be equivalent.

Kundt's rule (kŭnts): **1.** generalization that a distance divided by regular gradation marks appears greater than an unfilled distance. **2.** generalization that, in attempting to bisect a line in uniocular vision, one is likely to put the dividing point too far toward the nasal side.

kurtosis or **Ku** (kĕr·tō'səs): *n.* (*stat.*) the relative degree of flatness (PLATYKURTOSIS) or peakedness (LEPTOKURTOSIS) in the region about the mode of a **frequency curve,** as compared to the **normal *frequency curve** which is MESOKURTIC.

Kwint psychomotor test: an age inventory of **psychomotor** activities, for use with brain-damaged children, to indicate the extent to which motor development is retarded.

kymograph (kī'mō·graf): *n.* an instrument for making graphic records of temporal variations by tracing KYMOGRAMS upon a revolving drum.

kyphosis (kī·fō'səs): *n.* angular curvature of the spine, resembling a mild humpbacked condition.—*adj.* **kyphotic** (-fot'-).

L

L: 1. number of like signs. 2. (*Ror.*) scoring code for **lambda index.** 3. = **lumen.** 4. = limen (see **threshold**).

$_sL_R$ = (*C. Hull*) reaction threshold, the stimulus strength that will just barely evoke the response.

l = lower limit of the class in which the measure considered lies.

lab.: *abbr.* for **laboratory.**

labia (lā′bi·ə): *n. pl.* (*L., lips*) (*anat.*) the fleshy folds that surround an orifice of the body, esp. of the vagina.—*adj.* **labial.**

labile (lā′bil): *adj.* easily moved or changed; not stable; not rigid; free in the expression of emotion, or quickly shifting from one emotion to another.—*n.* **lability.**

laboratory: *n.* a place set aside for scientific research, esp., but not exclusively, for experiment. ➤Laboratory investigation contrasts with **field** investigation and with library research.

labyrinth: *n.* 1. the complicated membranous and bony structure in the inner ear that contains the sense organs of hearing and of the **static sense.**—*Syn.* INTERNAL EAR, INNER EAR. 2. a maze.—*adj.* **labyrinthine.**

labyrinth/auditory: a misleading term for the **labyrinth,** since it is not exclusively auditory in function.

labyrinthine sense = **static sense** (*prefd.*). ➤Since the **labyrinth** contains the organs for hearing, as well as for the static sense, the equating of labyrinthine sense with the latter only is confusing.

lacrimal (lak′rə·məl): *adj.* pertaining to tears.—*n.* **lacrimation.**

lactation: *n.* 1. production of milk by the mammary glands. 2. feeding an infant at the breast.

lacuna (lə·kū′nə) *n., pl.* **lacunae** (-nē): (*L.*) a gap, whether in evidence or data, in memory, or in consciousness.—*Cp.* **fugue, amnesia, petit mal.**—*adj.* **lacunal, lacunar, lacunary.**

ladder/counseling: see **counseling ladder.**

Ladd-Franklin theory of color vision: see **color theories.**

lag: *n.* time delay between the end of a process and the beginning of another related to it in some causal fashion: e.g., the interval between **input** and **output,** between **stimulus** and **response.**—*Cp.* **lag of sensation.**

lag/cultural: see **cultural lag.**

-lagnia: combining form meaning *lust* or *lustful desire,* or *pertaining to sexuality.*

lag (of sensation): the brief period following application of a stimulus during which it is not perceived (INITIAL LAG),

and after removal of the stimulus during which it is still perceived (TERMINAL LAG). ➤In vision, the fact that the terminal lag is the longer makes possible motion pictures and similar phenomena.

lag/social: the failure of social institutions and attitudes to keep abreast of the technology with which they are interrelated.— *Distg. fr.* **cultural lag.**

laissez faire (les″ā fâr): (*Fr., allow to do*) 1. (*soc. sci.*) the theory that government should interfere as little as possible with the free operation of "natural" economic laws; loosely, for any policy of "hands off." 2. a kind of leadership in which the leader exercises a minimum of control, or even of guidance or assistance. —*Var.* **laisser faire.**

laissez-faire atmosphere: a social situation in which the nominal leader gives little or no guidance, orders, or suggestions.—*Cp.* **authoritarian atmosphere, democratic atmosphere.**

-lalia, lalo- (-lā′li·ə, lal′o-): combining forms meaning *talk, talking, speech.* The form *-lalia* is used especially in combinations referring to **functional** speech disorders: e.g., **dyslalia,** any functional speech disorder; **bradylalia,** excessive slowness of speech (functional).

lallation (lə·lā′shən): *n.* 1. any unintelligible speech, such as infantile prattling or similar babble; or slovenly speech.—*Syn.* PSOPHOLALIA. 2. the substitution of *l* for more difficult consonants such as *r.*—*Syn.* (for both) LALLING.

lalopathy (lal·op′ə·thi): *n.* any disorder of speech.

lalophobia (lal″ō·fō′bi·ə): *n.* morbid fear of speaking. ➤Surprisingly enough, a not uncommon symptom.

laloplegia (-plē′ji·ə): *n.* inability to speak resulting from paralysis of speech muscles other than those of the tongue.

lalorrhea = **logorrhea.**

Lamarckianism: *n.* a theory of evolution which maintains the possibility that changes resulting from the use or disuse of an organ during an organism's life may be transmitted.—*Syn.* LAMARCKISM, THEORY OF INHERITED ACQUIRED CHARACTERISTICS.— *Contr. w.* **Darwinism.**

lambda or λ: *n.* wave length.

lambda index or *L*: (*Ror.*) the ratio of all scorings involving any **determinant** other than *F* to the total number of *F*+, *F*−, and *F* scorings; i.e., all non-*F*/all *F*.

lambert: *n.* a unit of **luminance** equal to $1/\pi$ candles per square centimeter, or to the uniform **luminance** of a perfectly diffusing surface emitting or reflecting light at the rate of one **lumen** per square centimeter, or to the average luminance of any surface emitting or reflecting light at the rate of one lumen per square centimeter. →The MILLILAMBERT, one thousandth of a lambert, is more often used.

Lambert's law: a law stating the relation between physical intensity of light and the angle of incidence with the illuminated or reflecting surface.

lamella: *n.* a thin metal plate, usually one set in vibration at a known rate.—See **Appunn's lamella.**

landmark: *n.* 1. a sensory cue, usually visual, facilitating **orientation.** 2. an indicator showing in words the magnitude of the rated trait that is symbolized by a mark on the rating line at that point. E.g., near one end of the rating line the landmark indicator might be "unusually good," in the middle "average," at the other end "unusually bad." Qualitative descriptions are also used.

Landolt circles or **rings:** incomplete circles with varying size of break, used to study visual acuity.

language: *n.* 1. any form of intercommunicative behavior, verbal or nonverbal. 2. the verbal behavior, oral or written, characteristic of an individual or a society. —*Syn.* LANGUAGE CODE. 3. the speech behavior (oral) of an individual or society.— *adj.* **linguistic.**

language/active: see **language/passive.**

language behavior: 1. any behavior in which language of any sort plays a principal part. →In man, this is practically all behavior. 2. any behavior serving as intentional communication; or any behavior that has a standardized meaning for one perceiving it; = **language.**

language/passive: verbal symbols seen or heard with understanding of their meaning. →*Contr. w.* ACTIVE LANGUAGE, words that a person can use intelligibly in speaking or writing. The ACTIVE and PASSIVE VOCABULARIES refer to the *number* of words that a person can, respectively, use or understand.

languor (lang'gər): *n.* neuromuscular relaxation and disinclination to motor activity, caused by weakness or exhaustion.—*Syn.* LASSITUDE.—*Distg. fr.* **listlessness.**—*adj.* **languid.**—*v.* **languish.**

Laplacian curve (lə·plas'i·ən) = **frequency curve/normal.**

lapse: *n.* 1. a slip or falling off; hence, a mistake or error: *lapse* of memory. 2. = *petit mal.*—See **epilepsy.**

lapsus calami = slip of the pen (see **slip of the tongue**).

lapsus linguae (lap'səs lin'gwē) = **slip of the tongue.**

lapsus memoriae (mə·môr'i·ē): (*L.*) a memory slip; a momentary failure in memory leading to an inappropriate response: e.g., failure to remember one's own telephone number is a *lapsus memoriae.*— *Syn.* MEMORY LAPSE (*prefd.*).

larva *n., pl.* **larvas, larvae:** (*zool.*) an animal in an immature but active stage of development, in which it is of radically different form from the mature stage. The caterpillar and the tadpole are larvas.— *adj.* **larval.**

larynx: *n.* the upper part of the windpipe; the organ of voice.—*adj.* **laryngeal** (lə·rin'ji·əl).

Lashley jumping stand: see **jumping apparatus.**

lassitude = **languor.**

lata (lä'tə): *n.* a disordered state characterized by hallucinations (often with sexual content), great excitement, and suggestibility.—*Var.* **latah, lattah.**

latency: *n.* 1. the condition of an organic mechanism between the beginning of stimulation or excitation and the beginning of the observable response. →The term is quite general and may apply to sense organs, nerves, muscles, or glands. 2. the interval between the onset of a stimulus and the onset of the associated reaction; = $_sT_R$ (*C. Hull's* notation).—*Syn.* REACTION LATENCY, RESPONSE LATENCY. 3. = SEX LATENCY or SEXUAL LATENCY (*prefd.*).—See **latency period.** 4. (*genet.*) an individual's potentiality for transmitting the genes for a trait he or she does not manifest.—*Cp.* **genotype** and **phenotype.**—*adj.* **latent** (which see).

latency period: (*psychoan.*) a period from about age 4 or 5 to about age 12 during which interest in sex is sublimated. →The latency period is evidently highly conditional upon the culture and is less universal than was originally supposed by Freud. But the term may be used to describe the facts when they are found, without implying that they are universal.—*Distg. fr.* **latent period.**—*Syn.* SEXUAL LATENCY.

latent: *adj.* 1. hidden; not apparent at the moment but potentially able to develop. 2. (*genet.*) pertaining to traits not manifest in the individual but for which the genes exist in his germ plasm.

latent class analysis: see **latent structure analysis.**

latent content: see **dream content.**

latent distance model: see **latent structure analysis.**

latent learning: see **learning/latent.**

latent period or **time:** that period intervening between the stimulus and the beginning of either (*a*) nerve conduction or (*b*) awareness.—See **latency (2).**—*Distg. fr.* **latency period.**

latent process: (*psychoan.*) a **structure** or **mechanism** in the **psyche** which lies dormant until, in the developmental process, the energy of the **id** is diverted into it. ➤The mechanisms for perception and thinking are said to be latent in infancy until the **ego** develops to the point where they are needed.

latent structure analysis: (*P. F. Lazarsfeld*) a method of **scaling** replies to an attitude questionary based on the assumption that contradictory or partially inconsistent replies can be explained in terms of the LATENT CLASS or LATENT DISTANCE found in deeper underlying attitudes. The logic of the analysis resembles that of **factor analysis.**

lateral: *adj.* pertaining to the side.—*adv.* **laterad,** toward the side.

lateral dominance: see **dominance (5).**

laterality: *n.* sidedness; the preferential use of one side of the body, esp. in tasks demanding the use of only one hand, one eye, or one foot.—*Cp.* **dominance (5).**

Latin square: an experimental design or pattern that provides as many different trials as there are experimental conditions, each subject being exposed to all the conditions but in a different serial order from other subjects. The conditions are represented by an arrangement of letters in rows and columns, each letter appearing once and only once in each row and column. Each subject is assigned to a row or to a column.

	trials		
	1	2	3
subjects 1	a	b	c
2	b	c	a
3	c	a	b

A SIMPLE LATIN SQUARE

lattah: see **lata.**

lattice/dynamic: (*R. B. Cattell*) a graphic representation of the causal interrelations of goal-seeking behaviors and tendencies. ➤It is a more adequate model than a **hierarchy,** exhibiting the fact that a given trend may be served by more than one preceding behavior and in turn may serve more than one succeeding purpose.—*Cp.* **hierarchy/personality.**

law: *n.* **1.** a verbal statement, supported by such ample evidence as not to be open to doubt unless much further evidence is obtained, of the way events of a certain class consistently and uniformly occur; NATURAL LAW. ➤A natural law is not conceived as *controlling* events; it describes them. Many writers use law where **generalization** or **principle** would be more appropriate. **2.** a rule of conduct imposed by government or by other duly constituted authority.

lay: *adj.* characterizing that which is *not* professional. ➤What is to be considered professional is much debated.—*n.* **layman.**

lay analyst: a person without a medical license who practices **analysis (3).** ➤The term is a misnomer; the lay analyst, if pro-fessionally trained in analysis, is not a layman despite lack of medical license.

layman: *n.* a person who is not professionally qualified for the kind of activity in question.

lazy W: (*Ror.*) scoring code for responses that require no synthesizing or analyzing effort on the part of the subject.

LDG = leaderless discussion group.

lead: *n.* **1.** the time by which one event precedes another; specif., the period by which changes in one time series precede corresponding changes in another related series. —*v.* **2.** to act first in a social situation. **3.** to act in such a way as to initiate, direct, and control the behavior of others. **4.** to ask a question in such a way as (at least partially) to determine the answer.—*adj.* **leading.**

leader: *n.* **1.** a person who at a given time and place by his actions modifies, directs, or controls the attitudes or actions of one or more followers; esp., that person in a group who most exhibits such influence. **2.** a person occupying an office or position that confers upon his suggestions or commands a certain authority or potential for controlling the behavior of a social group. ➤It is proposed by some to speak of a **leader** only when the authority is accorded him by his followers, of a **head** when the authority is externally imposed. **3.** a person possessing the traits supposed necessary for leadership. ➤These traits are variously defined; much research seems to indicate that there are no specific leadership traits. **4.** (*sociometry*) the person receiving the most **sociometric** choices. ➤This meaning is too special to be acceptable except in a narrow context.—*Syn.* **sociocenter** (*prefd.*). —See also **leader/status.**

leadership: *n.* **1.** the traits or skills characteristic of leaders or of the function of leading. ➤This meaning ignores the situation itself as a factor in determining who leads and how and, by implying that this is determined only (or chiefly) by the quality of the leader, is guilty of **theory-begging. 2.** the initiation, direction, or control of the actions or attitudes of another person or of a group, with the more or less willing acquiescence of the followers. ➤*Distg. fr.* **coercion,** in which unwilling acquiescence is obtained. This sense does not imply that there is a special class of persons who are leaders, nor that special qualities or kinds of action confer leadership. It is at least relatively theory-free.— *Syn.* LEADERSHIP FUNCTION, LEADING.—*Cp.* **headship,** leadership due to the authority conferred by outside power. **3.** action that influences the group in its pursuit of group goals. ➤This is an evaluative meaning: it seems to say that selfish leadership is not leadership.

leader/status: one who leads by virtue of

general public acceptance. ➤*Contr. w.* POSITIONAL LEADER, one who leads by virtue of his office or occupational position (e.g., a foreman, a teacher in reference to the children); and with SPECIALIST LEADER, one who leads by virtue of specialized knowledge or skill in the task.

leading eye: that eye which is the first to turn to the stimulus object to be examined. ➤In search or exploration of a visual field (e.g., in reading, where the search is normally very systematic), the two eyes do not turn from one object to another simultaneously. Usually they take turns in leading the way.—*Cp.* **dominant** *eye.

leading question or **remark:** a question or remark framed in such a way as to determine the nature of the answer, at least in part. ➤It may merely guide the respondent to an answer he could not make without help, or it may clearly indicate the expected answer. E.g., *Surely you don't believe that, do you?* is less a question than a form of persuasion.

leakage: *n.* 1. the dissipation of a psychic tension when succeeding conditions break down or supplant the conditions causing the tension. 2. any discussion by a client or patient with a third party concerning the details of his psychotherapy while it is in progress.

learn: *v.* 1. (*pop.*) to change one's way of acting, to acquire information, to memorize. 2. to become able to respond to a task-demand or an environmental pressure in a different way as a result of earlier response to the same task (practice), or as a result of other intervening relevant experience. 3. to undergo the change in psychophysiological structure which is the necessary condition of such difference in response, excluding such change as may be due to disease, surgery, fatigue, sensory adaptation. ➤The sign of learning is not a shift of response or performance as a consequence of change in stimulus-situation or in motivation, but rather a shift in performance when the stimulus-situation and the motivation are essentially the same. Such change in performance is said to require hypothesizing a change in the responding organism.

learnable drive or **reward:** any of a class of **drives** or **rewards** that can be **associated** to a previously ineffective **cue** as a result of learning.

learning: *n.* 1. scholarship; the possession of much knowledge and critical judgment, esp. in a particular field or discipline. 2. a highly general term for the relatively enduring change, in response to a task-demand, that is induced directly by experience; or the process or processes whereby such change is brought about. ➤Not included under learning are changes due to bodily injury or surgery, disease, fatigue, sensory adapta-

tion.—See **learn** *v.* ¶The distinction between learning, as a function of experience, and **maturation,** as a function of genetic factors, is difficult to carry through at the level of theory and all but impossible in practice.—See **maturation.** ¶Learning is manifested by performance, and all performance is dependent in part on learning, but the two are not identical. So-called **learning curves** are actually curves of performance. Learning is inferred from *performance and the conditions antecedent to performance.*

The word experience in the above definition is admittedly vague. Many authors therefore propose to substitute **practice** or **training** for **experience,** and to define these (implicitly if not explicitly) as the repetition of the response initially demanded by the task-situation. The experimental study of learning has been almost exclusively the study of learning as induced by practice in this sense. This, however, is to leave out of consideration certain part-phenomena which to many seem integral with the learning process. Moreover, it excludes certain kinds of behavior change, regarded by nearly everyone as learning, that do not quite seem a function of practice. To bring these phenomena under the definition of learning as practice requires a special explanatory theory. It is better, however, to adhere to the more general statement in the definition and to leave explanation to avowed theory.—See **theory-begging** and **learning theory.**—Partial synonyms, each referring to an aspect or a theoretical explanation: **memorizing; association;** the acquisition of **knowledge, insight,** or **skill; habit formation; character formation; socialization;** the acquisition of **attitudes, sentiments,** and other **affective** attachments; **conditioning; reorganization.**—*Cp.* also **retention, recall, recognition.**

learning activity: see **learning process** (2) and (3).

learning/associative: see **associative learning.**

learning/collateral or **/concomitant** = **learning/incidental.**

learning/conceptual: the process of modifying one's **concepts.** ➤It is sometimes defined as learning in which concepts are employed, but this inevitably means modifying one's concepts.

learning curve: a graphic representation of the measured changes at successive units of **practice.** ➤The units of practice (laid out on the horizontal axis) are usually in terms either of time spent in practice or of number of repetitions required; progress (recorded on the vertical axis) is gauged by amount recalled, time required for successful solution of a task. number of errors, number of partial solutions achieved, etc. Strictly speaking it is a curve of *performance*, not of learning. For the generalized learning curve, see **generalized curve.**

learning dilemma: a problem situation in which a response that formerly was effective no longer leads to the familiar goal.

learning/directed: learning guided and aided by the teacher or experimenter, generally by means of suggestions, outlines, or problems.

learning/discriminative: learning that is manifested in ability to make certain required perceptual discriminations, or to react differently to various objects or stimuli. ➤It does not denote a general increase in sensitivity, but rather the learning to note those particular cues or clues in a stimulus situation needed to evoke one response rather than another.—*Contr. w.* **generalization.**

learning/escape: see **escape learning.**

learning/expectancy: see **expectancy.**

learning/factor theory of: 1. (*W. Mc-Dougall*) the hypothesis that two subprocesses or factors are at work in all cases of learning: a "mechanical" process best exemplified in conditioning or rote learning, and a process of apprehending new meaning or relationships. 2. = BIFACTORAL THEORY OF CONDITIONING (*G. Razran*), which asserts that attitude determines the *incidence* of **conditioning (1)** and that stimulus properties determine the *magnitude.* 3. (*O. H. Mowrer*) the hypothesis that there are two kinds of learning: conditioning by stimulus substitution, involving the **autonomic** system; and problem-solving under conditions of reward, involving the **c.n.s.** ➤This theory would be more happily called a DUAL-LEARNING THEORY, since it postulates two different kinds of functions, rather than two factors of a single function. 4. (*O. H. Mowrer*) the hypothesis that learning is the process whereby a certain sign comes to evoke a certain response, the relationship being effected by two different kinds of **reinforcement**—drive reduction and drive induction.

learning/ideational: learning that involves meaningful material, either directly as that which is to be memorized, or as the chief means whereby a problem situation is solved. It is learning in which one "catches the idea," though not necessarily in an abrupt flash of inspiration. ➤It contrasts with rote *learning* and with much **motor learning** (although some motor learning is highly ideational). The term is descriptive, not explanatory, and therefore does not imply whether or not ideational learning is different in kind from rote learning or conditioning.

learning/incidental: learning that takes place without formal instruction or intent to learn and without ascertainable motive.

➤On theoretical grounds, many believe there is always a motive operative in learning; but so long as no specific motive is ascertainable the learning may be called incidental. Latent *learning is a kind of incidental learning that becomes manifest only when there is a change of motive. Incidental learning may happen *while* another learning takes place; **transfer is** learning as a *consequence* of another learning.—*Syn.* COLLATERAL LEARNING, CONCOMITANT LEARNING (both of which emphasize one aspect of the conditions under which learning occurs), PASSIVE LEARNING (which emphasizes lack of intent).

learning/insightful: 1. learning in which the animal acquires an awareness of the relation of many perceptual **cues** to a **goal,** or of the relation of the elements in a problem situation to each other. 2. learning guided by understanding of relations.—See **insight.**

learning/instrumental: learning to make a response that shortens in some way the distance between the animal and a goal. Either the animal or the goal may be moved, or barriers to locomotion toward the goal may be removed or surmounted.—*Syn.* instrumental **conditioning.**

learning/intraserial: the learning of the relationships that are presented *within* a series or serially presented list, in contrast with learnings that relate the components of the list to material outside it.

learning/latent: a change in the efficiency of a performance following a specified kind of intervening activity that does not involve attempting the performance in question or presenting a reward therefor, the change in performance being later manifested when a motive is supplied. ➤E.g., an animal fully fed and watered traverses a maze with apparent aimlessness; later, when hungry, he learns to reach the food box much sooner than do control subjects who have not explored the maze. However, many doubt that such learning occurs if conditions are adequately controlled.

learning/laws of: generalizations that state the empirically established functional relations between certain antecedent conditions and changes in performance of a task. ➤The definitions of "antecedent conditions" and of "task-performance" are explicitly, or often merely implicitly, derived from **learning theory** (which see). Since the empirical data are in nearly every case far from crucial, it would be more modestly accurate to speak of **generalizations or principles** of learning.

learning/logical = **learning/meaningful (1).**

learning/meaningful: 1. that variety of learning for which the evidence is the ability to recall or recognize the meaning of what was studied, regardless of whether one can reproduce what was studied in its exact original form.—*Syn.* SUBSTANCE LEARNING (*prefd.*), LOGICAL LEARNING (not *prefd.*), **rational learning.**—*Ant.* **rote** *learning, (in some situations) **verbatim** *learning. **2.** the learning of material that is highly meaningful for the learner. ➤This usage lacks specific reference.

learning/mechanical = **learning/rote.**

learning/modified whole method of: a modification of the whole learning method of memorizing in which difficult or important parts are given special attention as one goes along or are returned to for special practice.—See **learning/whole vs. part.**

learning/motor: see **motor learning.**

learning/movement: see **learning/place.**

learning/part-method of: breaking a comprehensive learning task into smaller fragments, each to be mastered separately and then combined into a whole. ➤The term is particularly appropriate for a common procedure in serial learning and memorizing.—See **learning/whole vs. part.**

learning/passive: learning in which no discernible effort or desire to learn is present. ➤*Prefd. syn.* for incidental *learning.

learning/perceptual: learning in which the principal change is that the learner *perceives* something differently. ➤The term sometimes includes, sometimes contrasts with, **conceptual** *learning. It contrasts with **motor learning** and learning of emotion.

learning/perceptual-motor: the learning to make an **overt** motor response that is not primarily verbal when a concrete, nonverbal, stimulus situation is presented. ➤Although verbal elements are almost certainly operative, this term refers to learning in which their influence is minimal. The contrast is with VERBAL LEARNING (stimulus and response both verbal) and with VERBAL-PERCEPTUAL LEARNING (stimulus verbal, response perceptual).—See also **learning/perceptual.**

learning/place: learning the location of a goal in space rather than the movements required to reach the goal. ➤Having learned the location, the animal can go there by different routes or by making different responses. The PLACE LEARNING EXPERIMENT is designed to test whether lower animals are capable of such learning. It is known that man sometimes is.—*Ant.* MOVEMENT LEARNING (*prefd.*), RESPONSE LEARNING (*ambig.*). —*Cp.* **sign learning.**

learning process: 1. a topic in psychology wherein learning is considered as an **event** rather than as a result or product (though it is͂ necessary to consider that product for the light it casts on the event). **2.** the activities, overt or verbal, engaged in during

learning, and designed (or believed) to promote learning: studying, thinking, practicing, attending, etc. ➤LEARNING ACTIVITIES seems a preferable term. **3.** the hypothesized **function** (or functions) by means of which an enduring change takes place in the organism during the learning activities. ➤This function is known as yet only by inference, and it is not established that there is any *one* learning process or function. Meanings (2) and (3) are often confused.

learning/relational: that form of **learning** in which the learner takes note of the relationships between items and thus learns a pattern, as well as (or even instead of) specific concrete items.—*Cp.* **learning/ meaningful (1).**

learning/response: learning to make certain responses rather than learning the topography in which the responses are made; the opposite of **place** *learning (which see). The animal proceeds by the route previously learned and makes the same movements when, under changed conditions, this no longer leads to the goal.— *Syn.* MOVEMENT LEARNING (*prefd.*).

learning/rote: memorizing in which the task as seen by the learner requires no understanding but merely the reproduction of words or other symbols in the exact form in which they were presented. ➤Frequent repetition is the commonly recognized means to memorizing. Unintentional understanding of the relationships involved is not precluded. **Conditioning** is equated with rote learning by some authors.—*Syn.* by-heart learning, MECHANICAL LEARNING, VERBATIM LEARNING (*prefd.*).—*adv.* **by rote.**

learning/selective: 1. the learning of those activities that bring satisfaction to the learner and the nonlearning of those that do not, even under adequate external opportunities to learn; the increased probability that one response among several will, as a result of learning activity, be more frequently elicited in a given situation. **2.** a theory that supposes all learning to consist in such a change in probability of response.

learning/serial: see **serial learning.**

learning set: 1. a generalized approach to problems as if the animal recognizes that they are to be solved by learning an **instrumental** response. ➤The animal, whether human or subhuman, reacts on the implicit hypothesis that a means to the end is to be discovered. The learning set is itself believed to be a result of **learning.**—*Syn.* **learning to learn,** SET TO LEARN. **2.** a specific selective or orienting factor which determines that, in a particular kind of problem situation, certain kinds of responses will be tried and others abstained from. ➤The animal has previously learned, not a particular solution to a problem, but a way of going at it. Thus, in memorizing non-sense syllables, most subjects soon fall into a certain rhythm in reciting them. A set may even cause perceptual distortion: e.g., in a series of color names, the inserted word *screen* is learned as *green*. Learning sets are probably among the most useful aspects of human learning but are found also in lower animals.

learning/social: a learning process in which social demands are the determining conditions. ➤A child's learning to be clean is chiefly determined by pressures from persons, even though the response concerns itself with dirt removal.

learning/solution: see **solution learning.**

learning/substance = **learning/meaningful (1).**

learning theory: an attempt to state the general nature of learning. ➤The first task of the learning theorist is to determine critically the kind of phenomena to which the word **learning** is to be applied, or, indeed, to determine whether there is an internally coherent body of fact to be so classified. It is true that the everyday meaning of learning *implies* such a theory (or several not too congruent theories); and an experiment on the conditions under which learning takes place implies by its very experimental design *what* learning is. ¶These implications, however, generally remain unargued and uncriticized even in sophisticated theoretical systems. Most learning theory, therefore, consists in providing a logical framework for the systematic ordering of the facts that have been thus traditionally or uncritically designated as the facts of learning. ¶The common expression "Learning theory states . . . ," when used to refer to the teachings of a particular theory of learning, is assumption bordering on presumption. It is an abuse no one defends but many practice.

learning to learn: learning any of the attitudes or skills that make learning more efficient. ➤The term does not include the learning of concepts and background information, though these also add to efficiency.—See **learning set.**

learning/trial-and-error: a complex event in which an animal, having no already established adjustive response to the requirements of a task-situation, responds at first to only its very general features with a wide variety of acts, then gradually eliminates the responses that prove unsatisfactory and repeats with increasing frequency those that prove satisfactory.—*Syn.* FUMBLE-AND-SUC-CESS. APPROXIMATION-AND-CORRECTION, TRIAL LEARNING.—*Cp.* insight, vicarious **trial and error, try/provisional.**

learning/verbal and /**verbal-perceptual:** see **learning/perceptual-motor.**

learning/verbatim: learning or memorizing word for word; by-heart learning.— *Syn.* **learning/rote.**—*Ant.* **learning/ meaningful.**

learning/whole vs. part: In the former, the entire learning material is worked through in successive repetitions from first to last; in the latter (also called PIECEMEAL LEARNING), the whole is broken into smaller sections to be separately learned, then combined into a whole. A **modified whole method of** *learning is also distinguished.

least action/law of: (*Gestalt*) the principle that the course of action taken is always that course which requires the least energy under the prevailing conditions; the theorem that an action always takes such form and direction that, under the given conditions, the product of the units of energy expended, multiplied by the units of time, is a minimum. ➤"Course of action" and "least energy" are to be understood in phenomenal *field terms. Thus, an *objectively* easy course of action may be imperceptible to a given person (i.e., it is not in the field for him), or it may be made difficult (require more energy) because of emotional blocking. ¶The term **law** is a misnomer: this is not an empirical generalization of fact but a theorem. In physics, the theorem of least action is one of the ways of telling what energy is; in psychology, it is now proposed to tell by a parallel theorem what organismic energy is. —*Syn.* PRINCIPLE OF LEAST ENERGY EXPENDI-TURE, PRINCIPLE OF MINIMAL EXPENDITURE OF ENERGY, **least effort principle,** PRIN-CIPLE OF LEAST ENERGY.

least differences/method of = **just noticeable differences/method of** (*prefd.*).

least effort principle: the hypothesis that an animal tends to select and to follow that route toward a goal which involves the least physical effort.—*Cp.* the law of *least action, which states that action *always* follows such a route; here a *tendency* is spoken of.

least energy (expenditure)/principle of = **least action/law of.**

least group size: a working principle that the optimal size of a learning group or class is the smallest group in which are represented all the abilities required for the learning activities involved.

least resistance/line of: the generalization or postulate that a person attempts to reach his goal in the easiest way, esp. with as little opposition as possible. ➤It is a variation of the **least action** postulate, emphasizing social rather than physical barriers.

least squares method: (*math.*) a procedure for finding the regular or smooth curve (or the mathematical **function**) which best represents or "fits" a series of plotted scores or similar values. The sum of the squares of the differences between the points to be fitted and the corresponding points on the fitted line is made to be a minimum. ➤Curves of known geometric characteristics (such as a parabola, a hyperbola, a growth curve, etc.) are fitted to the data by means of normal equations.—*Cp.* **smoothed** **curve, goodness of *fit.*

least squares principle: (*stat.*) the generalization that the most probable value to be obtained from a series of observations or measurements is that value about which the sum of the squares of the **deviations** is a minimum.

leaving the field: a metaphorical expression for any expedient that removes a person from a certain **psychological** **field,* esp. from a problem situation in which he faces frustration. ➤E.g., a child frustrated by a puzzle rejects it and plays with something else; a person changes the subject when bested in argument, or even when merely bored.—*Distg. fr.* efforts to alter the field, and from **rationalization.**

Leeraufreaktion (ler″ouf·re·äk′si·ōn′): *n.* (*Ger., reaction to emptiness*) reacting in the absence of a particular cue or signal when it is randomly omitted from a repeated series.

left-handedness = sinistrality.

legend: *n.* 1. a tradition, insupportable by adequate historical evidence, about a historical person or place. ➤*Distg. fr.* **myth,** which deals with imaginary persons or things. 2. a brief explanation appended to a drawing or chart.

legibility: *n.* the quality of a visual symbol, usually of a printed or written symbol, that makes it easy to read or to distinguish from other symbols.

legitimate: *adj.* 1. in accordance with law, with accepted standards, or with recognized principles; more specif., 2. (*logic*) of reasoning that accords with the rules of logic. —*Syn.* **logical.**—*Ant.* **illicit, fallacious.** 3. born of wedded parents.—*Ant.* **illegitimate.**—*n.* **legitimacy.**

leipo- (lī′pō-): combining form meaning *lacking, missing.* Used especially to denote some form of **elision** in speech abnormalities: e.g., LEIPOLOGIA, LEIPOLEXIA.

Leiter International Performance Scale: a series of intelligence tests designed to be free from influences peculiar to a particular culture or nation. ➤It consists of various wooden blocks, some with pictures on them. The tasks are matching of colors, pictures, and blocks of different forms; picture completion; discrimination of number of items; etc.—*Cp.* **test/culture-free.**

*emma (lem′ə): *n.* (*logic*) a preliminary proposition demonstrated or accepted for immediate use in the exposition or proof of another proposition. ➤*Cp.* **postulate,** which gains its claim to acceptance because it is a necessary element in a chain of reasoning which as a whole makes sense. The lemma is itself proved, or is supposed to be provable. It is a near-synonym for **premise** but is not limited to **syllogistic** reasoning.

length/focal: see **focal length.**

lens: in the eye, a transparent structure capable of changing its convexity in order to focus light rays directly on the retina. —*Syn.* CRYSTALLINE LENS.

-lepsia, -lepsy: combining forms meaning *seizure* or *attack: epilepsy, catalepsy.*

lepto-: combining form meaning *small, weak, fine.*

leptokurtic (lep″tō·kėr′tik): see **kurtosis.**

leptomorph: see **body build/index of.**

leptosome (-sōm): *n.* a person of slender, or **asthenic,** body build.—*adj.* **leptosomic, leptosomatic.**

lerema (lə·rē′mə): *n.* garrulousness of the insane or the senile.—*Syn.* LERESIS.

Lesbianism: *n.* homosexuality in women, esp. with **cunnilinctus.**—*pers. n.* **Lesbian.**

lesion: *n.* a change in a tissue from injury or disease.

lethal (lē′thəl): *adj.* causing death; fatal.

lethargy: *n.* 1. morbid drowsiness from which it is difficult to arouse a person. 2. inaction and apathy.—*adj.* **lethargic.**

leucocyte (lü′kō·sīt): *n.* one of the colorless cells of the blood.—*Syn.* WHITE BLOOD CELL, WHITE CORPUSCLE.—*Var.* **leukocyte.**

leucotomy (lü·kot′ə·mi) = **lobotomy.**

leukocyte = leucocyte.

leukotomy = lobotomy.

level: *n.* 1. an area or region—or figuratively, a position, rank, or degree—in which all things are equal in respect to the quality being considered: e.g., *level* of intelligence, the position or rank of persons who do equally well in tasks requiring intelligence, though not necessarily in the same tasks. 2. (*psychophys.*) the sensitivity of a **receptor** at a given time, compared with the established average **threshold** of that receptor. 3. a coordinating center for neural impulses named to show its position relative to the periphery or to the highest coordinating center. ➤Especially commonly named are SPINAL LEVEL, BRAIN STEM LEVEL, MIDBRAIN LEVEL, CORTICAL LEVEL. The several levels from spinal to cortical reflect increasing complexity of functions coordinated.

leveling: *n.* the tendency to perceive or to recall something as having greater symmetry, less irregularity, less incongruity than it objectively has. ➤E.g., the content of a rumor tends to become shorter, more concise, and thus more easily grasped. SHARPENING of the rumor—the process whereby certain elements are brought out more clearly and others are submerged, thus resulting in distortion—may go on simultaneously.

leveling and accentuation/rule of: the generalization that, where initial visual contrast is great, accentuation of contrast occurs; where it is small, leveling or reduction of contrast results.

leveling effect: the tendency, under certain conditions of measurement, for a second set of observations to cluster more closely about the mean than the first set. The range and/or the standard deviation of the second testing are less. ➤Leveling is not a statistical effect, but an effect in some way correlated with practice or repetition.—*Distg. fr.* **regression effect,** which is found in a restricted part of the distribution only, whereas the leveling effect is a phenomenon of the whole distribution.

level/occupational: 1. a class of occupations defined in terms of the amount of skill or ability required. **2.** a classification of occupations according to the prestige and socioeconomic status associated with them.

level of aspiration: see **aspiration/level of.**

level of confidence: see **fiducial limits.**

levels of factuality: see **factuality/levels of.**

levitation: *n.* rising in the air without material support. ➤The term is usually confined to the unreal experiences of dreams, or to the phenomena of **mediumistic** séances.

Levy Movement Scale: a series of blots made by finger painting, used as a **projective test** analogous to the Rorschach. ➤The pictures are particularly likely to elicit movement responses.—See *M.*

lewd: *adj.* lustful; excessively given to sexual thought or action, or provocative thereto. ➤The term originally meant *not clerical, unlettered.*

Lewinian (usually pron. lə·vin′i·ən): *adj.* characteristic of the point of view or work of Kurt Lewin.

-lexia (-lek′si·ə): combining form that denotes a (specific) *type of reading incapacity*: **bradylexia, alexia.**

lexicology: *n.* the branch of learning dealing with the derivation, meaning, and use of words. ➤Overattention to this discipline leads to sterile verbalism, its neglect to confusion and ambiguity.

lexis ratio: a statistic used to show whether a distribution of observations has hypernormal, normal, or subnormal **dispersion.**

$$L = \frac{\sigma}{\sigma_B}$$ where σ = obtained dispersion of percentage scores on a test, and σ_B = theoretically expected dispersion, calculated from the mean percentage of successes and the mean number of items attempted.

libertarianism: *n.* philosophical doctrine that man can influence the course of events by his choices and decisions.—*pers. n.* **libertarian.**

libertine: *n.* a person who is sexually unrestrained and promiscuous.

libidinal (lə·bid′ə·nəl): *adj.* pertaining to the **libido.**—*Distg. fr.* LIBIDINOUS (-nəs), highly active sexually; and *fr.* **licentious,** unrestrained by moral standards in sex activity.

libidinal object: (*psychoan.*) the person or thing with which **libido** is concerned, which provokes or excites **instinctual** activity related to it. ➤For psychoanalysis, LOVE OBJECT is a synonym, but this term can also be used in its ordinary sense for any person or object that regularly excites affection.

libidinization (li·bid″ən·i·zā′shən): *n.* process of becoming the object of **libido.**—*Syn.* **erotization.**

libidinous: see **libidinal.**

libido (li·bē′dō): *n.* (*psychoan.*) **1.** sexual craving. **2.** any **erotic** desire or pleasure. **3.** any **instinctual** manifestation that tends toward life rather than death, integration rather than disintegration.—*Syn.* **Eros, life instinct. 4.** any psychic energy, constructive or destructive.—*Syn.* **horme.**

➤Freud, who introduced the term, continually changed his usage as well as the concepts for which **libido** was proposed; and his followers have not in general been more consistent. Common to all uses is the idea of some sort of psychic dynamics or energy, an irrational and instinctual determiner of both conscious and unconscious processes. The sexual impulses are, at the least, the type to which other libidinal manifestations may be compared: in Freud's earlier treatment libido was quite simply a direct or indirect sexual expression; even in usage (4) the connection with sex cannot be severed. Freud later seemed inclined to drop the term libido altogether, but finally chose meaning (4), which is also Jung's usage. This is to introduce—or to increase—confusion between the professional use and the layman's understanding. The psychoanalytic movement has from the beginning suffered from an ambiguity about sex, if not in the writings of adherents, at least in the minds of those who follow from a distance. Libido is now firmly established as a semipopular term with a meaning somewhere between (1) and (2). Any other meaning is likely to be misinterpreted. If it is to mean *any* kind of psychic energy, why not use that phrase or the very closely akin **horme?** If it means any constructive instinctual activity, why not **life instinct?**—*adj.* **libidinal, libidinous.**

libido analog: a symbol that becomes a substitute for a **libidinal object.**

libido/bisexual: (*psychoan.*) attachment of the sexual impulse to persons of both sexes. —*Syn.* PSYCHOSEXUAL HERMAPHRODITISM.

libido fixation = **fixation/affective.**

libido/plasticity of: the tendency of libido to find indirect discharge routes when direct routes are blocked.

libido/vicissitudes of: the four major avenues of indirect gratification of libido: (*a*) **repression** with subsequent symptom- and dream-formation; (*b*) **sublimation;** (*c*) **transformation** into its opposite manifestation; (*d*) redirection of an instinctual aim from an external object onto the self.—*Syn.* PLASTICITY OF INSTINCT or OF LIBIDO.

license: *n.* **1.** permission, granted according to legal provisions, to practice a profession or occupation. ➤In general, the term is not used unless the occupation is forbidden to those without a license.—*Cp.* **certification.** —*n.* **licensure,** the granting of licenses. **2.** = **licentiousness.**

licentiate: *n.* a person having a professional **license.**

licentiousness: *n.* lack of restraint by moral standards, esp. in sexual activity.— *adj.* **licentious.**

L-I-D: symbols for *like, indifferent, dislike* as used in questionary forms.

Liebmann effect (lēp'män): the fact that differences of **luminosity** are more effective in maintaining contour lines between adjacent areas than are differences in **hue;** the fact that luminosity difference more sharply marks off an area than does hue difference.

lie detector: an apparatus for measuring blood pressure, pulse and respiration changes, and the **electrodermal response** when the subject is asked to answer questions. ➤The hypothesis is that if he is lying there will be emotional disturbance which will manifest itself in the above indices. But these indices reflect any kind of emotional change, even the puzzlement or bafflement of problem-solving.—*Syn.* **polygraph,** which can be used in other ways.

life: *n.* that property of plants and animals (and perhaps of viruses) whereby they maintain structural integrity by a constant interchange of elements with surrounding media. ➤There is no agreement about what that property is. Though there are ambiguous or difficult cases, a variety of criteria permit fairly reliable distinction of the living from the nonliving: metabolism, growth, response to stimulation or excitation, reproduction. None of these by itself is acknowledged as a necessary and sufficient defining quality.—*adj.* **living; vital,** pertaining to life.—*v.* **live.**

life/change of = **menopause.**

life cycle: the average time from birth to death of an **organism,** or of a **group, culture,** or **institution,** conceived as recurring in successive generations or epochs. ➤Certain crises, such as birth, puberty, and marriage, are said to divide the life cycle. —*Syn.* **life span,** which carries no implication of recurrence.—*Distg. fr.* **generation,** the average time from the birth of an organism to the median date of birth of its various offspring (in man, about 33 years).

life expectancy: see **expectancy/life.**

life goal: (*A. Adler*) the goal—implicit in all striving but seldom acknowledged even to oneself—of attaining a superiority that will compensate for the person's chief inferiority, real or imagined.

life history: the tracing of events, environmental and internal, in the development of a person or group, by accurate and detailed description of the entire life career or of a considerable portion thereof.

life instinct: (*psychoan.*) one of the two instincts (actually classes of instincts) in the **id.** It includes all the tendencies that strive toward the integration of living substance into larger wholes.—*Syn.* **Eros.**—*Contr. w.* **death instinct,** or Thanatos.—See also **libido.** ➤Individual development is conceived as the resultant of the opposed tendencies of construction and destruction, of life instinct and death instinct.

life lie: (*A. Adler*) the idea, sometimes included by a neurotic in his **life plan,** that he will fail because of circumstances beyond his control.

life-organization pattern: a more or less consistent mode of life, a role or group of roles, or a set of standards and practices for certain types of situations, that dominate or regulate the more important behaviors of a person during a considerable period of his life.

life plan: (*A. Adler*) the entire set of defensive behaviors by means of which a person prevents his supposed superiority from being disproved by the test of reality.—*Cp.* **defense mechanism.**

life space: (*K. Lewin*) **1.** the entire set of **phenomena (5)** constituting the world of actuality for a person or group of persons. **2.** the totality of facts that determine the behavior of a person or of a group. ➤A person's life space is conceived as composed of **regions** (which are states of affairs), objects (including persons), goals, and instrumentalities that affect his behavior at that moment; intraorganismic factors such as needs or motives, abilities, habits are also included. The emphasis is upon the interaction of organism and environment in an organized and unified **field.** While the construct is **ahistorical,** a given life space may have considerable duration unless it is characterized as MOMENTARY LIFE SPACE. The life space is often represented by **topological** diagrams.—*Syn.* TOTAL SITUATION (for a MOMENTARY LIFE SPACE), **psychological** *field.—For related terms, see **situation.**

life space/structure of: the interrelations of the **boundaries, barriers,** prescriptions, and proscriptions that make up the **life space.**—*Cp.* **support.**

life span: 1. the actual time from birth to death of an individual. **2.** the length of life characteristic of a given species. ➤*Distg. fr.* average length of life, or **life *expectancy.** The life span is essentially not a statistical concept. For the U.S., it would normally be thought of as at least 65 or 70 years, which is considerably more than the mean, median, or mode.

life table: a tabulation showing the **life *expectancy** of persons at each life age.

light: *adj.* **1.** of high **brightness** or **illumination. 2.** not heavy.—*n.* **3.** the stimulus to seeing; the radiant energy of those wave lengths which act as adequate stimuli to the visual sense.

light-adapted eye: an eye that has been exposed to light stimuli of relatively high intensity (ordinary daylight or higher) and has thereby become relatively insensitive to lower intensities.—*Cp.* **adaptation/sensory.**

light-determined response: (*Ror.*) see **shading** effect.

light-induction/simultaneous: the effect of stimulation of one part of the retina upon the activity of other parts; or upon the visual experience associated with other parts of the visual field.—*Cp.* **color contrast,** the most frequently noted instance.

lightness: *n.* attribute of an **object color** (in contrast with a **film color** or **illuminant *color**) by means of which it can be placed in the series between black and white. It applies to both hues and achromatic colors. —*Syn.* visual **intensity, brightness** (both of which also name an attribute of glowing colors).

light reflex: pupillary response, by dilation or contraction, to changes in light.

light sensation: that aspect of seeing which is functionally dependent upon radiant energy transmitted in waves from 390 to 760 micromillimeters—i.e., upon light—and upon the activities of the retina and its associated structures.

light wave: luminous radiant energy, regarded as an undulatory or wavelike phenomenon, i.e., as a transverse electromagnetic disturbance.

likelihood: *n.* **1.** a quantitative statement of one's rational belief about whether a certain event is to be expected to occur. ➤The quantitative statement may be in words

("very likely," "somewhat unlikely," etc.) or in terms of a proportion ("four chances in ten"). Strictly speaking, **probability** is a property of the event, likelihood a statement of a person's belief about the probability; but the two are often used interchangeably. **2.** (*stat.*) the relative chance that the **statistical constants** in a sample arose from a given set of **parameters** in the universe from which the sample was drawn.

likelihood ratio: the **probability** of the alternative hypothesis being considered, divided by that of the **null hypothesis.** ➤This is the basic quantity computed after each set of observations in a **sequential *analysis.**

like-mindedness: *n.* similarity in ideas and attitudes between two or more persons.

Likert procedure (lik'ərt): a method of constructing and scoring **attitude scales:** subjects are asked to indicate, on a three- or five-step scale, the degree of their agreement-disagreement with a statement. ➤*Cp.* **Thurstone scale,** which asks only for "agree-disagree" responses, but utilizes statements spaced at psychologically equal intervals.

limbic system: (*neurol.*) a group of structures, as yet poorly defined, generally including areas of the **transitional cortex** and ***subcortical *nuclei** formerly classified as part of the olfactory brain. ➤The limbic system is supposed to be related to the integration of emotional patterns. There is much controversy about just which structures should be included.

limen (lī'mən) = **threshold.**—*adj.* **liminal.**

liminal (lī'mə·nəl; lim'ə-): *adj.* at, or pertaining to, the limen, or **threshold.**

liminal sensitivity or **LS:** the sensory acuity of a person measured in terms of the average **liminal stimulus.**

liminal stimulus: a particular physical **stimulus (1)** that just barely evokes a sensory response, or that just barely brings a **sense datum** to awareness. ➤The liminal stimulus is the actual stimulus, the STIMULUS THRESHOLD or STIMULUS LIMEN is the magnitude of that stimulus, but the terms are often interchanged.—See **threshold.**

limit: *n.* **1.** the first or last value in a series. **2.** the end of a sensory continuum: e.g., the highest or lowest sound, the first or last color in the spectrum that seems to contain red, etc. **3.** the point beyond which further practice seems to effect no improvment.—See **limit/physiological.**

limit/physiological: the point beyon which, at a given level of maturity, n further gain in efficiency can be secured by practice. ➤The words imply that the limit is set by the physicochemical structure of the organs involved; actually, other factors may be more important.—*Syn.* PRACTICE LIMIT (*prefd.*).

limits/fiducial: see **fiducial limits.**

limits/method of = just noticeable differences/method of.

linear: *adj.* 1. pertaining to a line. 2. pertaining to a straight line; = RECTILINEAR. ➤This is the most common meaning. 3. pertaining to a **continuous variation.**

linear function: (*math.*) a relationship between two or more variables that can be represented by a straight line. The slope of the line is given by any *y* value divided by its corresponding *x* value.

linearity: *n.* the quality of being **linear;** capability of being represented by a straight line.—*Syn.* RECTILINEARITY.—*Contr. w.* **curvilinearity.**

linear-operator model: (*learning theory*) a schema for describing the relations between learning factors by means of a linear equation which states how the probability of a given alternative response increases or decreases with the occurrence of a certain positive or negative factor or operator.

linear perspective: see **perspective/linear.**

linear system: one in which the response to a complex **input** is the summation of the separate responses to the separate elements of the input. ➤This is essentially the opposite of the **gestalt** relation. Most organisms are *non*linear systems; most machines are approximately linear.

line/fixation: see **fixation/visual.**

line of direction: see **direction/line of.**

linga (ling′gə): *n.* a phallic symbol.—*Var.* **lingam** (-gəm).

lingual: *adj.* of, or pertaining to, the tongue.

linguistics: *n.* the scientific study of languages.

linkage: *n.* 1. the connection between stimulus and response, or, more generally, between any two psychological processes. 2. the tendency for certain **characters** of an organism to be inherited together, the offspring showing either both or neither. The linked traits are believed to be transmitted by genes located in the same chromosome.

link analysis: (*human eng.*) the attempt to design a system in which connections between parts shall be efficient; the study of successively used displays and/or controls, and of operating connections between all men and machines in a system, for purposes of achieving a system layout that will keep key links as short as possible.

linked characters: see **linkage (2).**

Link Instrument Trainer: a training apparatus that, without leaving the ground, closely simulates actual operating conditions for piloting a plane.

lip erotism: tendency to experience **erotic** satisfaction from stimulation of the lips, normally in kissing but sometimes by other stimuli. ➤According to one theory, much of the satisfaction of smoking, etc., comes from **lip erotism.**—*Syn.* **oral erotism** (which, however, has broader meaning).

lip key: an instrument for timing the beginning of lip movements in speech.

lip reading = **speech reading.**

lisp: *n.* (*speech*) imperfect pronunciation of the sibilants *s* and *z*, usually by substituting a *th* sound.—*Var.* **lisping.**

Lissajou's figures (lē″sə·zhüz′): the visible closed figures produced by reflection of a beam of light from two tuning forks which vibrate in perpendicular planes.

Listing's law: principle which states that the axis around which oblique movements of the eyes take place is in the same plane as the axes round which simple vertical and horizontal movements take place. This holds only when the visual axes are approximately parallel; otherwise swivel rotation may occur.

listless: *adj.* uninterested, indifferent, and making only slow feeble movements.—*Distg. fr.* **languid,** which implies muscular weakness or exhaustion.—*n.* **listlessness.**

literacy: *n.* ability to read and write, or to communicate by means of writing. ➤The acceptable level for a given purpose is arbitrarily and variously defined.—See **illiteracy.**—*adj.* **literate.**

literacy test: a test of ability to read or write. ➤Minimum standards for literacy are arbitrarily determined.

literal: *adj.* pertaining to letters: e.g., LITERAL AGNOSIA, loss of ability to recognize letters.

literature: *n.* (*tech.*) the published material of a given field of learning or part thereof.

little brain = **cerebellum.**

liveness: *n.* (*acoustics*) the characteristic of a room or auditorium that determines the naturalness of sounds heard therein.

living/standard of: see **standard of living.**

Lloyd Morgan's canon: see **Morgan's canon.**

L method: (*stat.*) a short-cut method for selecting a small number of items or of variables that, when weighted with equal gross score weights, will predict a **criterion** almost as well as or better than the entire pool of items or variables, similarly weighted, from which the sample is drawn.

load: *n.* 1. the number of clients or patients cared for by a therapist, counselor, or social caseworker. 2. (*stat.*) = **weight** or **factor loading.**—*v.* 3. (*stat.*) to multiply a set of values by a constant in order to make the set comparable to some other set.—See **weight.**

loading: *n.* (*stat.*) 1. = **weight.** 2. = **factor loading.**

lobe: *n.* a rounded or projecting part of an organ; specif., one of the five main divisions of the **cerebrum:** the **frontal, parietal, temporal,** and **occipital lobes,** and the CENTRAL LOBE or **island of *Reil.**

lobectomy (lō·bek′tɔ·mi): *n.* surgical excision of the prefrontal areas of the frontal lobes.—*Distg. fr.* **lobotomy.**

lobotomy (lō·bot′ɔ·mi): *n.* a surgical cutting of the white nerve fibers connecting the frontal lobes with the thalamus. ➤It is sometimes used in the treatment of mental disorders. Lobotomy is the commonest form of **psychosurgery.**—*Syn.* PREFRONTAL LEUKOTOMY, FRONTAL LEUKOTOMY, PREFRONTAL LOBOTOMY.—*Distg. fr.* **lobectomy.**

localization: *n.* 1. the perceptual reference of a sensory datum to a place in space: e.g., the reference of sounds to a place whence they seem to come, the reference of a tactile sensation to a place on the skin (both of which can be greatly in error). ➤Significantly, it is rare to speak of localization of visual sensations, though they are never localized on the retina but always referred to a place in space. 2. reference of mental and nervous functions to specific localities in the brain as their "seat." ➤This reference is not perceptual but rather a matter of inference.—*Syn.* BRAIN or CORTICAL LOCALIZATION.—See **brain center.**

local sign or **signature:** a character or attribute, said to be inherent in each distinct visual or tactual sensation, such that it can be distinguished from another sensation in respect to position in space, though in all other respects they may be alike.

location chart: (*Ror.*) an outline of the inkblot figure on which the examiner records the location of the subject's response.

locking/autonomic: see **autonomic locking.**

locomotion: *n.* 1. the transference of an organism from one place to another by its own movements. 2. figuratively, a change in the relationship of an organism to its environment or to its **life space.** ➤For K. Lewin, it may be a change in position or **valence** of **regions** in the life space, as well as a change of the individual's position in life space.—*adj.* **locomotor,** pertaining to locomotion; **locomotive,** causing locomotion.—*v.* **locomote.**

locomotion/ease of: (*K. Lewin*) a property of the **life space** at a given time, determined by the number and permeability of the **barriers.**

locomotion/psychological: (*K. Lewin*) action involving movement from one region to another in **life space.**—See **region.**

locomotion/social: a change from one socioeconomic class to another; more generally, any kind of change in social status or role.

locomotor ataxia: see **ataxia.**

locomotor behavior: movement that carries the whole body in one direction or another.—*Syn.* **locomotion.**

locus (lō′kɔs) *n.*, *pl.* **loci** (-sī): 1. a place, spot, or organ. 2. (*math.*) the total of all possible positions of a moving or generating element.

log = **logarithm.**

logagnosia = sensory **aphasia.**

logamnesia = sensory **aphasia.**

logarithm or **log:** *n.* (*math.*) the exponent indicating the power to which a number (the BASE) must be raised to yield a given number. ➤E.g., the base number 10 must be multiplied by itself, i.e., has the exponent 2, to yield 100: $\log_{10} 100 = 2$. Electronic calculators commonly employ logs with a base of 2. $\log_2 8 = 3$ means that the base number 2 must be multiplied by itself twice to produce 8.

logarithmic curve: (*math.*) the curve each point of which is determined by the natural value of one **coordinate** (usually y) and the logarithm of the value of the other coordinate. The equation is $y = \log x$.—*Syn.* LOGISTIC CURVE.

logarithmic mean = **mean/geometric.**

-logia: combining form denoting *speaking* or *saying*; or denoting *speech disorder associated with mental deficiency.*—*Cp.* **-logy.**

logic: *n.* that branch of philosophy which establishes the criteria by which, granting the correctness of the factual data employed, the worth or validity of arguments or reasoning may be judged. ➤It is concerned with whether reasoning is correct, not with the psychological conditions that lead to correct or incorrect reasoning. It is a normative, not an empirical, discipline.—*Cp.* **logic/formal, logic/symbolic.**

logic/affective: a sequence of judgments in which the connection between one judgment and another is chiefly emotional: e.g., "My mother is nice to me; she is good." ➤When the appearance of logical validity is maintained, although the judgments are made for emotional reasons, the affective logic takes the form of **rationalization.**

logical: *adj.* pertaining to, or characterized by, sound reasoning or **logic;** following the principles of logic. ➤The denotations of the adjective **logical** are somewhat broader than those of the noun logic; whereas the noun refers primarily to validity of *expression* of thinking in the form of propositions, the adjective refers also to arrangement and classification of data and to the actual processes of thinking that produce these expressions. Except that it carries no reference to concrete fact, logical means nearly the same as **valid** or **correct.** —*Contr. w.* ILLOGICAL, contrary to logic;

ALOGICAL or NONLOGICAL, of that to which considerations of logic do not apply; **intuitive**, not reached by *explicit* reasoning; **autistic**, determined by feeling and desire rather than by reasoning.

logical approach = (*educ.*) **logical method.**

logical deduction: a conclusion reached by proceeding from acceptable general principles according to the rules of logic. —*Contr. w.* empirical reasoning, which is based on facts and is usually **inductive.**

logical memory = **learning/meaningful (1).**

logical method: (*educ.*) the arrangement and presentation of instructional materials in a logical order and according to their own inherent relationships, with little or no regard to relative difficulties or to the needs and capabilities of the learners.—*Distg. fr.* **logical organization.**—*Syn.* LOGICAL APPROACH.

logical organization: an arrangement—of data, ideas, or anything to be communicated to others—in such a way as to display the inherent relations between the elements. ➤A logical organization does not necessarily follow a certain "logical order" in presenting material; it is designed to *make clear* the relations.—*Distg. fr.* **logical method.**

logic/formal: the body of rules or principles that deal with the acceptability of conclusions, as based upon the *form* of the propositions used in reaching a conclusion rather than upon their meaning.

logic/infinite-valued: see **infinite-valued logic.**

logic/symbolic: a treatment of **logic** that uses a formalized logical language and symbols especially designed for the purpose, in order to avoid the ambiguities of ordinary language.—*Syn.* MATHEMATICAL LOGIC, LOGISTIC.

logic-tight compartments: thinking that utilizes one set of premises when dealing with one situation, and an inconsistent set with another situation. ➤This is a **defense mechanism;** there is a faint realization that a comparison of premises might lead to uncomfortable conclusions.

logistic: *adj.* 1. pertaining to calculation; skilled in calculation.—*n.* 2. (*rare*) the art of calculation. ➤This use should remain rare, since confusion with military *logistics* is almost unavoidable. 3. = **logic/symbolic.**

logistic curve: 1. a curve, often used to describe growth, whose equation is $y = k/(1 + e^{a + bx})$, where x is time, y is the growth variable, and k, a, b are constants for the given population.—*Syn.* CURVE OF AUTOCATALYTIC GROWTH, PEARL-REED CURVE. 2. = LOGARITHMIC CURVE: $y = \log x$.

log(o)-: combining form meaning *word, thought, speech.*

logomania = **logorrhea.**

logopathy (log·op'ə·thi): *n.* any type of speech disorder.

logopedics (log"ō·pē'diks): *n.* the scientific study and treatment of speech disorders.—*Syn.* LOGOPEDIA (-pē'di·ə).—*pers. n.* **logopedist.**

logorrhea (log"ə·rē'ə): *n.* abnormal volubility, usually incoherent.—*Distg.* *fr.* **loquacity.**—*Syn.* POLYPHRASIA, HYPERLOGIA, LOGOMANIA, LALORRHEA.

-logy: combining form meaning *speech, discourse,* hence *knowledge* or *science.*—*Cp.* **-logia.**

longevity: *n.* long life; a span of life beyond the usual.

longitudinal: *adj.* 1. pertaining to length. 2. (*anat.*) in the direction of the long axis of the body.

longitudinal method: see **cross-section method.**

looking-glass self: see **self/looking-glass.**

loquacity: *n.* the tendency to speak often and at length. ➤*Distg. fr.* **logorrhea,** which is an abnormality. Loquacity is merely a fault.—*Syn.* LOQUACIOUSNESS.—*adj.* **loquacious.**

lordosis: *n.* exaggerated forward curvature of the spinal column; hollow back.—*adj.* **lordotic** (-dot'ik).

loudness: *n.* the heard attribute of a tone which corresponds to the physical attribute of **intensity.**—*Distg.* *fr.* **tonal *volume,*** which has a somewhat different but related meaning.—*Cp.* pitch, tonal attribute.

love: *n.* 1. a feeling, varied in its behavioral aspects and in mental content, but believed to have a specific and unique quality; affection; a feeling of attachment for a person (sometimes a thing); strong liking. ➤The feeling of love need not, though it often manifestly does, have an **erotic** element; and some theorists hold that all love feelings are erotic in essence.— *Syn.* **affection,** tender feeling. 2. a **sentiment** whose dominant feeling is affection, and whose goal is the close association of another person (or personified object) with oneself, and the happiness and welfare of that person. ➤The *feeling* of (1) is essentially a temporally limited *event.* The *sentiment* of (2) is an enduring *structure* (see **sentiment**). Yet the attributes of one of these are often ascribed to the other, probably because the feeling is seldom experienced except as an expression of the sentiment. 3. (*psychoan.*) the primitive and undifferentiated pleasure-seeking emotion (= **libido**), or a specialization thereof which contains a large element of (often-disguised) **lust.** 4. (*psychoan.*) the feeling expression of **Eros,** the instinct which accepts and constructs, or integrates.—See **libido,** usually a close synonym. ➤The psychoanalytic meaning of love has shifted as analytic doctrine has developed; the earlier view of (3) merged gradually (and incompletely) into that of (4). 5. a spiritual quality, possibly derived from sexuality but free of any sexual quality, which unites persons, giving them a sense of being interrelated. ➤See **agapism.** This meaning—religious, mystic, and literary, rather than scientific—nonetheless refers to a kind of relationship and of interpersonal behavior which it is important for psychology as science to consider.

love object: see **libidinal object.**

Lowenfeld test (lō′ən·felt) = **mosaic test.**

low-grade defective: see **defective/low-grade.**

loyalty: *n.* an attitude or sentiment of firm attachment to a person, group, institution, or ideal.—*adj.* **loyal.**

LQ: *abbr.* for lowest or first **quartile;** = Q_1, the value that is exceeded by three fourths of the measures.

LS = liminal sensitivity, the quantity of stimulation that barely reaches the **threshold.**

LSp: symbol for **life space.**

lucidity: *n.* 1. clarity of meaning or of perception. 2. an interval of sanity between periods of incoherent manifestations of insanity.—*adj.* **lucid.**

ludic (lü′dik): *adj.* playful; playfully pretending.

lues (lü′ēz): *n.* syphilis.—*adj.* **luetic** (-et′ik).

lumbar (lum′bər): *adj.* pertaining to the middle of the back.

lumbar puncture: the withdrawal, for diagnostic purposes, of a sample of **cerebrospinal fluid** by inserting a syringe needle between the lumbar vertebrae.

lumen: *n.* (*vis.*) the unit of **luminous flux.** It is equal to the flux through a unit solid angle from a uniform point source of one **candle,** or to the flux on a unit surface all points of which are at unit distance from a uniform point source of one candle. It is the strength of the light energy.—Symbol, *L.*

luminance: *n.* the light energy emitted, reflected, or transmitted; the **luminous flux** emitted per unit solid angle and unit projected area of source. This was formerly called photometric **brightness.** It may be measured in **lamberts** or **millilamberts.**

➤Four related terms may be compared: **luminance** is the strength of light in the whole three-dimensional space involved; its measurements are given in the units of solid geometry. **Illuminance** is the strength of light arriving at, or incident to, a *surface;* it is what the layman calls the illumination of the surface. Its measurements are in plane geometry terms. **Luminosity** is the strength of light as modified by prevailing physical conditions, such as translucence of medium, texture of surface, etc. **Brightness**

is the psychological attribute of color or light as perceived. Its physical correlate is **luminosity.**—See **illuminance, luminosity,** and **brightness** for further details.

luminosity: *n.* (*optics*) the **brightness**-producing capacity of light. Luminosity is not a function of the physical intensity of the light (i.e., of **luminance**) but of that light under all the prevailing *physical* conditions (distance, grain of the light surface, translucence of the medium, etc.). ➤It is **luminosity,** not **luminance,** which is the physical correlate of brightness. It is measured by the ratio of **photometric** quantity to **radiometric** quantity, e.g., **lumens** (photometric) per **watt** (radiometric).— *Syn.* **visibility.**

luminosity/absolute: luminosity expressed in absolute terms, such as lumens per watt, in contrast with luminosity as determined by distance and other such factors.

luminosity coefficients: the coefficients by which the color mixture data for any color need to be multiplied so that the sum of the three products is the **luminance** of the color sample to be specified.

luminosity curve: the curve of luminosity of spectral stimuli through the visible range, plotted as a function of wave length, with maximum luminosity as unity. ➤The curve is separately plotted for **photopic** and **scotopic vision;** unless specifically indicated otherwise, the former is always meant.

luminous: *adj.* having the appearance of emitting light; glowing; pertaining to a light source, in contrast with a reflected light.

luminous flux: rate of transfer of **luminous** or radiant energy, evaluated in terms of the experienced **brilliance** it produces. The usual unit is the lumen.

luminous intensity: luminous flux emitted per unit solid angle about a source. The usual unit is the candle or **candle power.**

lunacy: *n.* obsolescent legal term for a departure from normal mentality so grave as to bring a person under guardianship of the state. It includes the **insane** and the **mental defective.**—*adj.* and *pers. n.* **lunatic.**

Luria technique: a procedure for measuring emotional tensions. The subject responds to the words of a **free *association** test, simultaneously pressing down the fingers of one hand on a sensitive registration device and holding the fingers of the other hand as steady as possible.

lust: *n.* 1. craving for immoderate self-indulgence, esp. of the "lower" appetites; hence, 2. immoderate sexual craving. 3. the specific emotion associated with sex; sexual feeling.—*Distg. fr* (*Ger.*) *Lust,* which means pleasure.

luster: *n.* sheen or glossiness; perception in which shifty bright areas are seen upon the surface of an object. ➤Luster is characteristically experienced when observing a somewhat irregular and more or less polished metal object.—*Var.* **lustre.**—*adj.* **lustrous.**

lux: *n.* the **illuminance** of a surface one square meter in area receiving uniformly distributed flux of one **lumen;** or the **illuminance** produced at the surface of a sphere having a radius of one meter by a uniform point source of one international **candle** situated at its center.—*Syn.* METER-CANDLE LUX.

lying: *n.* communication to others of what one knows to be untrue or contrary to fact; attempt to deceive. ➤Any form of communication may be a **lie,** but verbal statements are meant unless the term is qualified. —*adj.* **lying.**—*n.* and *v.* **lie.**—*pers. n.* **liar.**

lying/pathological: 1. making absurdly untrue statements, only half believed by the person uttering them and often not expected to be believed by the hearer. ➤It is a symptom of mental disorder, though found in mild form in otherwise fairly normal people. **2.** falsification out of proportion to any purpose; extravagant untruths.

lymph: *n.* a body fluid, chiefly derived from the blood, containing certain white blood cells (LYMPHOCYTES). The lymph travels slowly in a series of lymphatic ducts to the large veins near the heart.—*adj.* **lymphatic.**

lymphatic temperament: see **phlegmatic.**

lymphocyte (lim'fō·sīt): see **lymph.**

lynching/bourbon: (*H. Cantril*) a lynching deliberately engineered by leading citizens to punish an individual for a specific offense.—*Distg. fr.* **lynching/proletariat.**

lynching/proletariat: (*H. Cantril*) a lynching, led by lower class members, which has as its main objective the persecution of an **out-group.**—*Distg. fr.* **lynching/bourbon.**

M

M: 1. (not *ital.*) = **mean/arithmetic. 2.** = **illumination. 3.** = (*C. Hull*) the learning maximum, 100 **habs. 4.** = associative memory factor (see **abilities/primary mental**). **5.** = (*Ror.*) **movement response.**

M^1 = arbitrary *origin.

M_G = geometric *mean.

$_wM$ = weighted **arithmetic** *mean.

m: 1. = any number. (Used in general formulas.) **2.** (not *ital.*) = meter. **3.** (*Ror.*) an inkblot response wherein movement is reported, although no live creature is the center of the activity. ➤The distinction between **movement** as organic and **motion** as nonorganic (physical) would permit us to speak of *M* as a movement response and *m* as a motion response, but this seems not to have been adopted by workers with Rorschach tests.

m_{AB}: observed frequency in cell at intersection of row A and column B.

MA or **M.A.** = mental *age.

Ma: (*psychophys.*) the mean transition point from A to not-A. Similarly *Mb,* from B to not-B.

machine theory: the view that mind or behavior is determined by relatively static factors, such as neural localization, rather than by the distribution of energy within a system. ➤The latter view is referred to as the **dynamic** or **field theory.**

Machover Test or **DAP:** a **projective test** requiring *S* to "draw a person."

macro- (mak'rō-): combining form meaning *large, extended* (in space).

macrobiotic (-bī·ot'ik): *adj.* long-lived; tending to prolong life.

macrocephaly (-sef'ə·li): *n.* abnormally large size of the head, usually accompanied by **mental *deficiency.**—*Cp.* **hydrocephaly,** a common form.—*adj.* **macrocephalous, macrocephalic** (-sef'ə·ləs; -sef·al'ik).

macrocosm: *n.* the great **cosmos,** i.e., either the physical universe or human society. ➤*Contr. w.* MICROCOSM, the small **cosmos,** e.g., the individual man as a unit.

macromania = **megalomania.**

macropsia: *n.* the illusion of seeing objects as larger than they are because of pathology of the retina or a spasm of the **accommodation** mechanism.—*Distg. fr.* **macroscopy.** —*Syn.* MACROPSY, MEGALOPSIA.

macroscopic: *adj.* **1.** looked at in the large or as a whole, without regard to details or to the component parts. **2.** large enough to be visible to the naked eye.—*Ant.* microscopic.

macroscopy (mə·kros'kə·pi): *n.* the viewing or study of objects with magnification.

macrosomatic: see **body size/general.**

macrosplanchnic build (-splank'nik): disproportionate size of the trunk in relation to the arms and legs.

macula acustica: a localized thickening of the wall of the **utricle** and of the **saccule** in the inner ear, containing receptor cells of unknown functions.

macula (lutea) (mak'ū·lə lü·tē'ə) *n., pl.* **maculas, maculae** (-ē): a yellowish area, roughly 2 millimeters in diameter, in the central region of the human retina, containing the **fovea centralis.**—*adj.* **macular.**

Maddox rod test: a measure of **muscular *imbalance.**—*Syn.* MADDOX PRISM TEST.

madness: *n.* nontechnical synonym for **insanity.**

MAF = minimum audible field (see **minimum audible pressure**).

magenta (mə·jen′tə): *n.* a purplish red hue (not in the spectrum), the complement of a green that has a wave length of 515 millimicrons.

magic: *n.* a practice designed to bring supernatural power to bear, not by prayer or request, but because the practice is believed to be the proper inducing cause of that power. ➤Many practices whose results are actually achieved by natural means are magic for their practitioners: e.g., it is good fertilizing to plant a fish with the maize or yams, although it may be done because the fish with its myriads of eggs symbolizes fertility. Many sociologists do not speak of magic if the practice is a regular part of organized religion, but in most cultures the line is difficult to draw. It is probable that most magic confuses **symbol** with **event,** insofar as manipulating the former is believed to affect the latter.

magic stage: a period during child development when merely imagining an object seems equivalent to having created it.—*Syn.* **omnipotence of thought.**

magnetism/animal: see **animal magnetism.**

magnetotropism: *n.* a simple response that orients an organism to a magnetic force. —See **tropism.**—*Syn.* MAGNETOTAXIS.

magnitude: *n.* **1.** a property of anything by means of which it is greater or less in some respect than something else. **2.** a quantity resulting either from counting the number of elements in an aggregate or from applying a measuring scale.

main-line shooter: (*slang*) one who takes narcotics by intravenous injection, thus obtaining fast results.

main score: (*Ror.*) a score based on the inkblot responses during the performance proper, in contrast to ADDITIONAL SCORES, those afterthought responses which come as additions or withdrawals. Responses that are needed for completion of a main response are also classed as ADDITIONAL if they occur later.

maintenance functions: those activities by which an organism preserves itself in a relatively constant state or condition.—*Syn.* homeostatic activities, **homeostasis.** ➤Usually restricted to physiological, but also applicable to psychological, activities. —*Distg. fr.* **maintenance level.**

maintenance level: 1. a relatively constant state of size, weight, or general physiological activity (in a mature animal); a steady state, secured by regulating diet and environmental conditions. ➤*Distg. fr.* **maintenance function (homeostasis),** which is an automatic regulation. **2.** a relatively constant ability to perform an act, maintained by **overlearning** or by a sufficient amount of review or repractice.

maintenance schedule: provision of food, water, practice, etc., in the quantity and at the times necessary to keep an animal at the **maintenance level.**

major solution: (*K. Horney*) a compulsive activity designed to eliminate a **basic *conflict** from awareness. It takes the form either of repression of that dynamic trend which conflicts with the **idealized *self** and acceptance of the other, or of withdrawal from the conflicting trends into resignation. —See **neurotic *solution.**

major work class: a special class, for pupils of superior intelligence, which provides an enriched curriculum without acceleration in grade progress.

Make-a-Picture-Story or **MAPS:** a **projective** test wherein the subject first selects a stagelike background and cardboard cutouts to go with it, then tells a story to go with the scene.

make-believe: *n.* behaving as if the present situation were something quite different from what it is, accompanied by varying degrees of recognizing the *as if* character of the process: e.g., the fantasies of young children.

mal-: combining form meaning *faulty* or *imperfect* in development or function: *malformation, maladjustment.*—*Syn.* (for words of Greek origin) **dys-.**

maladaptation: *n.* failure of an organism to have, or to develop, the characteristics biologically useful in interacting with the environment. ➤**Maladaptation** is more explicitly limited to biological change than is its antonym, **adaptation.**—*Cp.* **maladjustment.**—*adj.* **maladaptive.**

maladjustment: *n.* a more or less enduring failure of **adjustment,** esp. a failure greater than expected by others or oneself; failure to solve the problems posed by the everyday environment. ➤For a particular problem, **failure** or **frustration** is spoken of rather than maladjustment.—*adj.* **maladjusted.**

maladjustment/social: 1. inability to meet the demands of the social environment or to satisfy normal needs for companionship and social relations. ➤The maladjustment may stem from lack of social skills, inferior status, or inadequacy of the social environment (as, e.g., when the sex ratio is distorted). **2.** any relation between the components of an enduring social environment (personalities, groups, culture elements, etc.) that is unsatisfactory to the persons or groups therein.

maladjustment/vocational: a condition in which a person has either too much or too little ability for the pursuit of his occupation, or is dissatisfied with his job or with himself in the job.

malaise (ma·lāz'): *n.* (*F.*) **1.** a slight illness. **2.** a slight feeling of unwellness which precedes a more serious disease.

male: *adj.* of an organism that, in its mature state, produces spermatozoa or pollen, or has organs for such production. ➤**Male** refers to *male in contrast to female,* always having direct reference to sex difference. MASCULINE means *pertaining to a male,* hence is used of the qualities supposed to distinguish the sexes (also of grammatical gender). MANLY is evaluative, referring to the better qualities of a man, or distinguishing the man from the boy. MANNISH is used of a woman manifesting qualities like those of a man.—*n.* **male.**

malevolence: *n.* wishing ill to another.—*Cp.* **malice.**

malevolent transformation: (*H. S. Sullivan*) the change wherein a person comes to feel that he lives among enemies.

malformation: *n.* a structural defect in an organ.—*adj.* **malformed.**

malfunction: *n.* any organismic process not conducive to the biological survival of the organism or to the harmonious working together of its parts.

malice: *n.* the disposition to act so as to cause another ill.—*Var.* **maliciousness.**

malign (mə·līn): *adj.* **1.** = **malignant.**—*v.* **2.** to utter false and derogatory statements about another person; to regard with hatred or malice.

malignant: *adj.* (*med.*) of a disease with an unfavorable **prognosis.**—*Syn.* MALIGN. —*Ant.* **benign,** BENIGNANT.

malingering (mə·ling'gər·ing): *n.* feigning sickness or disability; by extension, feigning incompetence. ➤The deliberate deceit is, however, usually a cover for a real mental disorder or lack of competence.— *Distg. fr.* **hypochondria,** in which the patient believes in his imaginary illness.—*pers. n.* **malingerer.**—*v.* **malinger.**

malleus: *n.* the hammer-shaped small bone of the middle ear.

malobservation: *n.* failure to perceive or to record the essential or pertinent elements or aspects of an event.

malpractice: *n.* action that is contrary to the ethics of a profession, or that shows such culpable failure to observe the established procedures as to render one liable to legal action for damages, expulsion from professional associations, loss of license, etc.

Malthusianism: *n.* the doctrine that, in a given region, the population of a species tends to increase geometrically while the means of subsistence for that species increases only arithmetically, hence, that some method of population control is inevitable: war, pestilence, famine, or (in man) **family limitation.**

Mammalia (ma·mā'liə): *n. pl.* a class of **vertebrates,** characterized by embryonic development within the **uterus** and nourishment after birth by milk from the mammary glands of the mother.—*Syn.* MAMMALS.

mammillary bodies (mam'ə·ler"i): (*neurol.*) two small rounded bodies in the **hypothalamus.**

man: *n.* **1.** genus Homo of the **primate** order, of which *Homo sapiens* is the sole existing species. Man is distinguished from the apes by bodily structures, but chiefly by language, the use of tools, and a complex culture. **2.** any member of this genus. **3.** a male, esp. a mature male, of the genus.— *adj.* **human** (for 1 and 2); **male** (for 3).

management: *n.* the direction and manipulation of facilities of any sort, including persons, to accomplish a predetermined result; or the persons collectively vested with these functions. Both **administrative** and **executive** functions are included.

mandala (mun'də·lə): *n.* (*C. Jung*) the magic circle which represents symbolically the striving for total unity of self.

mand function: (*B. F. Skinner*) a speech utterance that makes demands upon the hearer and brings reward to the speaker when the hearer complies: e.g., the child's word "wah" (= "I want water"), which is rewarded when the mother gives him a drink.—*Cp.* **tact function.**

mania: *n.* **1.** popularly, any sort of violent abnormal conduct. **2.** technically but now infrequently, impulsive behavior characterized by violent and uncontrollable motor activity. **3.** an uncontrollable impulse to perform a certain kind of act. ➤For this meaning, the term is used in combination: a *mania* for stealing. **4.** as a distinct disease symptom, the hyperactive phase of **manic-depressive psychosis.**—*adj.* **manic, maniac, maniacal.**—*pers. n.* **manic, maniac** (chiefly *pop.*).

mania/anxious: see **anxious mania.**

maniac (mā'ni·ak): see **mania.**

maniacal: (mə·nī'ə·kəl): *adj.* pertaining to **mania.**

manic (man'ik; mā'-): *adj.* characterized by **mania.**—*n.* a person afflicted with, or manifesting the behavior of, mania.

manic-depressive psychosis (usually, man'ik): mental disorder characterized by marked emotional oscillation. ➤In the manic phase there is excitement, flight of ideas, overactivity, and occasionally destructive violence. In the depressive phase there is a feeling of inadequacy, retardation of ideas and of movement, anxiety or sadness, sometimes stupor or suicidal attempts. There is little or no **dementia** and not much tendency toward bodily deterioration. —*Syn.* (*Stan. Psychiat.*) MANIC-DEPRESSIVE REACTION.

manifest: *v.* **1.** to bring to attention; to bring to light; to display; specif., **2.** to disclose something to another by one's behavior. ➤A contrast to telling in words is often implied; but one's words may manifest more than intended.—*adj.* **manifest.** —*n.* **manifestation.**

manifest content: see **content/manifest.**

manifold: *n.* **1.** an assemblage of things of one kind, or having a property in common but not necessarily similar otherwise. **2.** a classification that includes two or more classes or divisions.—*Contr. w.* **dichotomy.** —*adj.* consisting of many objects.

manikin test: a test in which the task is to reassemble the parts (head, arms, legs, trunk) of a small wooden man.

manipulanda: *n. pl.* those characteristics of an object which, for a given organism (or species), make possible motor activity dealing with the object; those features of a situation which can be altered by the animal's motor activity, or by which the total situation can be altered.

manipulation: *n.* **1.** using the hands (or by extension, the feet or teeth) to alter the physical character of an object without destroying it: e.g., piling up blocks, untying a knot.—*Distg. fr.* **locomotion. 2.** control of a situation, esp. a social situation, by management of the factors involved. ➤Devious or covert activity is often implied.

mankind: *n.* all men collectively; man as contrasted with subhuman species, esp. in respect to behavior and to mental and social characteristics.—*Syn.* **man,** HUMANITY.

manly: see **male.**

mannerism: *n.* a characteristic oddity of speech or behavior. ➤In some cases of **schizophrenia** the mannerism is extreme and is regarded as a symbolic expression of underlying attitudes and ideas. As compared with the **stereotypy** of schizophrenia, the mannerism generally is less frequent and less complex.

manning table: a detailed statement of the personnel requirements of a given organization or unit.

mannish: see **male.**

manometer (mə·nom'ə·tər): *n.* an apparatus for measuring pressure in a gas or fluid. ➤The MANOMETRIC FLAME apparatus was formerly used in studying sound waves.— *adj.* **manometric** (man"ə·met'rik).

manoptoscope (mə·nop'tə·skōp): *n.* an instrument for measuring ocular **dominance.**

mantle layer: (*neurol.*) the middle layer of the walls of the embryonic **neural plate,**

which contains nucleated cells and develops into the **gray matter** of the central nervous system.—*Syn.* NUCLEAR LAYER.

man-to-man rating: see **rating/man-to-man.**

manual dominance: see **dominance.**

manual method: the method of communication by the deaf, among themselves and by them with others, that uses sign language, the manual alphabet, and other gestures. ➤*Contr. w.* ORAL METHOD, by which the deaf are taught to speak and to understand the speech of others visually; and with COMBINED METHOD, in which both oral and manual methods are used.—See **sign, sign language, manual *alphabet.**

Manus (mä'nüz): *n.* a tribe in the Admiralty Islands described by M. Mead as the type of an industrious, puritanical, nonliterate people. ➤The Manus, during World War II, were exposed to rapid **acculturation.**

manuscript writing: a form of handwriting that omits joining of the letters (as is done in the common CURSIVE WRITING). ➤*Syn.* UNCIAL SCRIPT. PRINT SCRIPT, often used as a synonym, should be reserved for writing that copies closely the printed forms of letters; it is thus a relatively uncommon form of manuscript writing.

MAP = minimum audible pressure.

map: *n.* a pattern of symbols that corresponds, point for point, with a physical state or a system of events or with a specified aspect thereof: verbal descriptions, geographical maps, statistical charts, mathematical equations applied to geometry, etc.

map/cognitive: see **cognitive map.**

MAPS = Make-a-Picture-Story.

marasmus (mə·raz'məs): *n.* a gradual withering of tissues, usually due to imperfect nutrition of the tissue involved.—*adj.* **marasmic.**

Marburg school: a group of students of **eidetic imagery,** advocates of a theory of types partly based thereon.

margin: *n.* the periphery of a two-dimensional figure; a border or edge.—*adj.* **marginal,** often used to mean *of uncertain classification* because the object or matter under discussion lies at the border between two classes.

marginal frequency: 1. (*stat.*) the sum of the frequencies in any one of the columns or of the rows of a double-entry table. The marginal frequencies are usually written in the lower or the right-hand margin. **2.** (*test* or *attitude scale construction*) the frequency of responses that lie outside the modal, or popular response, category. E.g., if 40 per cent choose the most popular alternative of a **selective answer *test,** the marginal frequency is 60 per cent.

marginal layer: (*neurol.*) the outer layer

of the walls of the embryonic **neural plate,** from which the nerve fibers develop.

marginal man: a person who is not a fully participating member of a group; esp., one who stands on the boundary between two groups, uncertain of his group membership. —*Cp.* **fringer.**

margin of attention or **of consciousness:** see **attention/margin of.**

marijuana (mar″i·wä′nə): *n.* a habit-forming drug derived from *cannabis indica.* It induces a feeling of well-being and a loss of self-criticism and inhibitions.

marital: *adj.* pertaining to marriage.

mark: *n.* **1.** a distinguishing quality or attribute of anything; a **characteristic. 2.** a conventional value or rating which indicates how a performance is to be socially valued; esp., a rating of schoolwork given by the teacher. ➤Unlike a **score,** it is not a multiple of some unit of measurement, hence it is essentially qualitative even though expressed in numbers or based on what seem to be quantitative scores. Thus, a teacher's mark of 90 for an essay is not 10 units greater than a mark of 80, despite the appearance of numerical exactitude. Mark is less ambiguous than with **grade** in this sense and is standard British usage. (But marks are used in Britain also for unit scores: he received 60 *marks.*)

marker test: (*factor anal.*) a test included in a factorial matrix, because of its *known* factorial structure, as an aid to **rotation** and identification of the factors in the present battery.—*Syn.* COMMON MARKER.

market research: 1. any systematic investigation of buying and selling. **2.** the investigation of volume of sales that may be expected under certain conditions.

Markov process: (*stat.*) a model for setting forth the **joint** *probabilities of the events in a sequence and the **conditional** *probabilities of each.

marriage: *n.* the social institution in which a man and woman unite in the establishment of a family unit. The accepted form for such union varies in different cultures: see **polygamy, monogamy, polyandry, polygyny,** etc. Sanction for forms of marriage may be customary, legal, religious, or any combination of these.

marriage/child: see **child marriage.**

marriage/group: a marriage system in which each of two or more persons of one sex is married to each of two or more persons of the other sex, the four or more marital partners forming the marriage group.

marriage/plural = polygamy.

masculine protest: 1. the desire of a female to be a male or to have masculine privileges; or of a male to avoid femininity. **2.** (*indiv. psychol.*) the struggle to become strong and to dominate. ➤Masculinity is

identified—confused, really—with superiority, femininity with inferiority. Both men and women exhibit some amount of masculine protest. In excess it is the core, according to A. Adler, of all neurosis.

masculinism: *n.* display by females of the male physical or mental **secondary** *sex characters.

masculinity: *n.* state or condition of an organism that manifests the characteristic appearance and behavior of a male.—*Distg. fr.* maleness, which connotes the possession of male **gonads.**—See **male.**—*adj.* **masculine.**

masculinity-femininity: a dimension, ranging between extreme **masculinity** and extreme **femininity,** by reference to which a trait or a person can be rated or described.

Mashburn apparatus: a mechanical device for measuring eye-hand and eye-foot coordination. The subject lines up corresponding pairs of red and green lights from a set of control levers.

mask: see **persona.**

masking: *n.* **1.** the partial or complete prevention of auditory perception by presenting a simultaneous sound of different pitch. ➤Masking may be an actual interference of one stimulus with another, or a lessening of perceptual effectiveness. **2.** the interfering effect of one sensory stimulus upon another simultaneous stimulus.

masochism (mas′ō·kiz·əm): *n.* **1.** a **sexual anomaly** characterized by erotic or sexual excitement and/or satisfaction from being subjected to pain, whether by oneself or another. ➤In many cases, orgasm ensues. The pain may become the sole condition of sexual satisfaction, or a necessary preliminary to other forms of sexual activity. **2.** the deriving of pleasure from being offended, mistreated, scolded, dominated, embarrassed, etc.; the tendency to court such mistreatment.—*Syn.* (*S. Freud*) IDEAL MASOCHISM; PSYCHIC MASOCHISM (*prefd.*). **3.** (*psychoan.*) the turning of any sort of destructive tendencies inward upon oneself.—*adj.* **masochist(ic).**

masochism/mass: (*Th. Reik*) the acceptance by the **masses** of hardship and sacrifices when imposed by a mass hero: e.g., the acceptance, by the Germans under Hitler, of guns rather than butter.

mass: 1. (*phys.*) the quantity of matter in a body as determined by the change in acceleration it effects upon another (standard) body. ➤For ordinary-sized objects, mass practically equals weight. **2.** an aggregate of organisms possessing only a minimum of social organization; a group of persons considered in terms of mere numbers, disregarding any tendency to social organization.

mass action: 1. uncoordinated and apparently random movements that involve large parts of the body musculature, often occurring without any specific external stimulation, and in any case lacking specific adaptive relation to the stimulus. ➤It is the characteristic behavior of the fetus and the newborn, but develops into, or is replaced by, more **adaptive** reactions. **2.** (*sociol.*) concerted overt action by a group of persons in the face of social opposition. **3.** see **mass action theory.**—*Syn.* MASS ACTIVITY.

mass action theory: (*K. S. Lashley*) the theory that large areas or masses of brain tissue function as a whole in learned or intelligent action. It contrasts with the view that the several functions are dependent on specific local areas. ➤The theory rests on the generalization that, when brain tissue is destroyed (as by surgery), the loss of effectiveness of a given learned behavior is dependent, not on the specific locality within the functional cortical area involved, but on the quantity of tissue therein destroyed. The term is sometimes incorrectly used to imply that there is no localization of function at all—which is contrary to the facts to which the term refers.—*Cp.* **equipotentiality.**

mass activity = **mass action.**

mass/apperceptive: see **apperception.**

mass contagion: see **contagion/mass.**

massed practice: see **practice/massed.**

masses/the: *n. pl.* the totality of those in the lower classes; the common people.

Massformel (mäs″fôr·mel′): *n.* (*Ger., measuring formula*) Fechner's final statement of the Weber principle in the form:

$$S = C \log R/R_o.$$

mass media: the instruments of communication that reach large numbers of people at once with a common message: books, press, radio, TV, motion pictures, etc.

mass methods: measurement of a considerable number of persons simultaneously. ➤The statistical treatment possible when the quantity of data is larger may compensate, or more than compensate, for the loss of experimental control usually (but not invariably) associated with mass methods.

mass movement: (*sociol.*) a concerted attempt by a considerable number of people to effect a direct and immediate change in society or its institutions. The members identify themselves with the movement and manifest crusading zeal.

mass observation: a technique of ascertaining the opinions or attitudes of a social entity. ➤Many observers listen, in a variety of strategically located places, to spontaneous remarks touching a certain subject. While the sampling problem is very great, the spontaneity gives many compensatory values. The recorded remarks may be **content analyzed.**

Masson disk: a white disk along one radius of which black squares are spaced. When rotated, a series of concentric rings of diminishing grayness is seen. If the ring that is just visibly gray is fixated, it will disappear and reappear somewhat irregularly.

mass polarization: the focusing of a large number of persons upon the same communication; the condition of a mass audience attentive to the same communication.—*Cp.* **polarization (4).**

mass psychology: the systematic study of relatively large aggregates of people which are not highly organized socially.—*Approx. syn.* CROWD PSYCHOLOGY.

mass reflex: undiscriminating response by a large group of **effectors** to a single stimulus. ➤E.g., when the spinal cord is cut, any stimulus whatever to the leg results in a defensive withdrawal, sweating, voiding of the bladder, etc.

master attitude scales: see **generalized *attitude scales.**

mastery: *n.* **1.** ability to control the actions of others. **2.** such proficiency in some discipline or complex task that one can meet perfectly certain defined (or commonly accepted) standards of accomplishment.—See **test/mastery.**

mastery motive: the motive to achieve, to attain excellence.—*Syn.* MASTERY NEED.

masturbation: *n.* the induction of erection and the obtaining of sexual satisfaction, in either sex, from manual or other artificial mechanical stimulation of the genitals. ➤It is usually self-induced. Imaginative stimulation of erection is PSYCHIC MASTURBATION.—*adj.* **masturbatory, masturbational.**

MAT = MILLER ANALOGIES TEST, a difficult **analogies test** used to predict success in graduate study.

matched-dependent behavior = **imitation** (*prefd.*).

matched groups: see **equivalent-groups procedure.**

matching test: see **test/matching.**

mate: *v.* **1.** to copulate. **2.** to marry or otherwise enter into an enduring relation with a person of opposite sex.—*n.* **mating.**—*pers. n.* **mate** (also slang for a close companion of the same sex).

material: *adj.* **1.** having to do with **matter. 2.** too important to be neglected.

materialism: *n.* **1.** a philosophic view, now nearly obsolete, that **matter** is the only kind of reality.—See **mechanism, mind-body problem. 2.** the pursuit of creature comforts; or a value system that exalts the means to such comforts at the expense of intellectual and spiritual activities.—See **psychology/divisions and schools of, III, IV.**

materialization: *n.* alleged production of

physical phenomena by a **spirit** which more or less temporarily assumes material form: e.g., the spirit leaves (so it is said) an impression of a hand in wax.

maternal behavior: the behavior of caring for the young and helpless. ➤Many species exhibit **species-specific** forms of such behavior. In humans, except for nursing behavior, it is not established which maternal behaviors are species-specific.

maternal drive: the tendency of a female animal to care for the young: to feed, shelter, protect, and otherwise mother them. ➤The **drive** may have many learned components.

maternal impressions/influence of: the discredited doctrine that the mother's experiences, feelings, or ideas *directly* influence the fetus.—*Cp.* **prenatal influence.**

mathematical model psychology: an attempt to systematize the data of psychology by means of mathematical and statistical **models;** the derivation from such models of concepts for the ordering of psychological data. ➤Mathematical (and statistical) concepts are used not merely in deriving a particular empirical conclusion, as in traditional experimentation, but in deriving the **constructs.** E.g., the construct of the **s-population** substitutes for **object** or thing in many contexts (but not in all) and is regarded as a superior way of categorizing certain data.

The idea of a mathematical framework for psychology is not new; it was proposed by Leibnitz. Fechner's modification of Weber's law was a mathematical model, and there have been many others at different levels of generality. The contemporary movement proposes a consistent substitution of mathematico-statistical concepts of the traditional; it is still in the program stage. It has affiliations with **hypothetico-deductive method, information theory, cybernetics.** Hodology and **topological psychology** represent the attempt to use a specific kind of mathematics in building the model.—See **psychology/divisions and schools of, I, VIII.**

mathematico-deductive method: 1. = **postulational method. 2.** = (*C. Hull*) **hypothetico-deductive method** (*prefd.*).

mating/assortative: selection of a mate who shows characteristics similar to one's own.

mating behavior: the complex of behaviors closely associated with mating: those of courtship, of the preliminaries to **coitus,** and of coitus.

natriarchy (mā'tri·är"ki): *n.* **1.** a social unit ruled by a woman. **2.** a society in which descent is reckoned through the female line, the children belonging to the mother's clan. Property is usually, but not always, inherited through the female line. ➤The term is a misnomer for **(2),** since sociologists do not believe this social system is a vestige of a society *ruled* by women. MATRILINEAL SOCIETY is more descriptive.

matrices: *n. pl.* of **matrix.**

matrilineal (mā"tri·lin'i·əl; mat"ri-): *adj.* pertaining to descent or inheritance through the female line.

matriliny (mat'rə·lī"ni): see **father right.** —*adj.* **matrilineal.**

matrix (mā'triks; mat-) *n., pl.* **matrixes, matrices** (-sēz): **1.** an enclosure that gives form to what lies within it; figuratively, the verbal or thought context that gives form or meaning to a term, or the psychological conditions that favor certain developments. **2.** (*math.*) a rectangular arrangement of numbers or symbols which, in MATRIX ALGEBRA, is submitted to certain mathematical operations such as inversion, transposition, etc.—See **matrix/correlation.**

matrix/conceptual: see **conceptual matrix.**

matrix/correlation: a table showing the **correlation coefficient** of every variable with every other variable in a set. ➤The matrix displays each variable at the head of a row and of a column; hence, each coefficient occurs once in the portion of the table above the upper-left to lower-right diagonal, and once below that diagonal.

matrix/factor: see **factor matrix.**

matrix/factor structure: 1. (*L. Thurstone*) see **factor structure. 2.** = (*R. B. Cattell*) **factor matrix.**

matrix/lambda: (*R. B. Cattell*) the matrix of cosines which is used in rotating a **factor matrix** to a new position in the search for **simple structure.**

matrix/product: (*factor anal.*) the result of multiplying together **factor loadings** of variables.

matrix/residual: the matrix that remains when the **variance** due to a factor is extracted.

matter: *n.* **1.** any part of the physical universe; a body capable of imparting acceleration to another body; that which is composed of molecules, atoms, electrons, etc. ➤An older definition postulated that **matter** was that which was extended in space, but this concept is difficult to apply to subatomic physics. **2.** those parts of the universe capable of eliciting reactions in organisms; a collection of stimuli; that which gives rise to the qualities (visual, auditory, tactual, etc.) attributed to objects. ➤As usually held, the concept of matter is flagrantly metaphysical. The foregoing definitions are not entirely free of such criticism, but they represent current usage by philosophically sophisticated scientists of a term too firmly entrenched in vocabulary to be dislodged.—See **materialism, mind-body problem.**—*adj.* **material.**

maturation: *n.* 1. **development;** the attainment, or the process of attaining, **maturity.** ➤This is the nuclear meaning, common to all the following. As stated, the concept is too broad, but authorities differ in the limitations they propose. The resulting definitions probably refer to somewhat, but not exactly, the same facts. 2. those developmental changes that are due to heredity. ➤In its strict form, this is probably not held by anyone, but it influences other definitions. 3. the **variance** in developmental changes due to heredity. ➤All developmental changes are conceived as having a **maturational** aspect interacting with an environmental aspect. In this meaning, maturation is neither a change nor a process of change but an abstracted *aspect* of change. 4. those developmental changes that take place more or less inevitably in all normal members of the species so long as they are provided with an environment suitable to the species. ➤In this concept, the normal environment is conceived as playing a supportive, or permissive, rather than a determining role in development. Special environmental factors, including educational factors, are modifying influences that deflect maturation. 5. that development in which the observed differences between individuals are correlated with previous differences in the *organisms* rather than in the environment. ➤This divorces the concept of maturation from that of heredity, since the "previous differences in the organism" may have been largely determined by past environment.

In the development of behavior, maturation and **learning** are closely intertwined, though logically distinct. For a given learning, a certain amount of maturation is a prerequisite; but that learning may in turn make further maturation possible.—See **growth, development, maturity.**—*adj.* **maturational,** pertaining to the process; **maturing,** pertaining to the function or to the organism that is changing; (*not* **mature,** which pertains to **maturity.)**—*v.* **mature.**

maturation/anticipatory: the hypothesized development of a structure or a function before the organism has need of it in its interaction with environment. ➤Such development is questioned by some of those who emphasize the role of environment.

maturation-degeneration hypothesis: the hypothesis that from birth onward an organism changes first toward an optimal state **(maturity)** and thereafter declines. ➤What constitutes the optimal state is variously defined. The fact of a rise and de-

cline is genetically determined, but the details are influenced by environmental factors.

maturation hypothesis: the doctrine that some modes of behavior are determined by heredity, but are not manifested until certain organic structures have matured.

maturation/principle of: (*educ.*) doctrine that learning is ineffective unless both the intellectual and the emotional maturity level of the child are considered in arranging tasks.

maturation/stimulus-induced: a developmental process that does not begin until elicited by some environmental demand but, once initiated, is controlled in direction and quality by the **intrinsic** character of the organism. ➤Such a process is often mistaken for, and may in fact be combined with, learning.

maturity: *n.* 1. the state or condition of complete or adult form, structure, and function of an organism, whether in respect to a single trait or, more often, all traits. ➤*Distg. fr.* **maturation,** which refers to *changes* leading toward maturity. Maturity of behavior is nearly always given a commendatory connotation as in 2. a vaguely defined condition which may refer to (*a*) practical wisdom (**intellectual *maturity**) in contrast with intelligence; (*b*) steady and socially acceptable emotional behavior (**emotional *maturity**); or (*c*) mastery of effective social techniques (**social maturity**). The term may be used relative to chronological age: a child is judged emotionally mature for his years. 3. the arbitrarily set period between ages 21 and 65.—See **development/levels of.**—*adj., v.* **mature.**

maturity/emotional: the degree to which a person has departed from the emotional behavior appropriate to childhood and manifests that of adulthood. ➤A complete catalog of emotional behaviors typical for various ages has not been made. Even if available, it is doubtful that it would be used as a reference point for this concept. Each writer seems to prefer his own list of "childish" emotional behaviors. Definition of adult emotional maturity is even more subjective.—See **maturity (2).**

maturity/intellectual: 1. attainment of adult intelligence, or of intelligence commensurate with one's age. This meaning is apt to be confounded with 2. practical wisdom; skill in dealing with personal problems; in general, that aspect of ability which is attained through actual experience rather than by study or instruction.

maturity/psychological: maturity **(1)** in all, or in most, psychological traits. ➤Despite the central role of **intelligence** in acquiring other manifestations of maturity, this term is often arbitrarily limited to the nonintellectual.

maturity rating: a judgment of the degree to which a person's activities fall below or above the norm for his age or other group in which he is to be classified. Most maturity ratings are made on a complex dimension of social adjustment.

maturity/social: see **maturity (2)** and **social maturity.**

maxim: *n.* a practical guiding principle, generally not supposed to be directly based on a scientific law. ➤Rules for procedure in experimentation are maxims. When a maxim is thoroughly tested and of wide applicability it is called a **canon.**

maximal (or **maximum**) **sensation:** the intensity of sensation that is not increased by increase of stimulus.

maximation/reciprocal: in interpersonal relations, a behavior that arouses in another person the sort of behavior which confirms and reinforces one's original expectation. E.g., if a child is treated as stupid he may so act as to confirm the judgment.

maximum *n., pl.* **maximums, maxima: 1.** the greatest quantity or value actually attained by a variable; or the greatest deemed logically, or permissibly, attainable. **2.** a value greater than those immediately preceding and following it in a series; a high point on a curve. ➤In this sense a function, series, or curve can have several maximums. —*Ant.* minimum.—*adj.* **maximal, maximum.**—*v.* **maximize,** to make as great as possible.

maximum likelihood/method of: (*factor anal.*) a method that finds the best-fitting **factor matrix** for a given number of factors and compares, by a **chi-square** statistic, this matrix with the empirical **correlation *matrix.**

maximum performance test = test of maximum performance.

Max T = channel capacity.

Maxwell disks: two or more colored disks that are split along a radius and mounted on a rotating spindle in such fashion that they overlap in any required amount. When the rotation is above the **critical *flicker frequency,** a **color mixture** is produced, the hue and brightness of which is proportional to the amount of color exposed in the several disks.

Maxwell's demons: a fanciful representation of physical forces as if they were minute humanlike agents. ➤**Interactionist** theorists are sometimes accused of thinking in such terms.

Maxwell triangle: see **color triangle.**

maze: *n.* a network or labyrinth of pathways, some of them blind alleys, but with one or more leading to an outlet or other goal. ➤A maze may be of any degree of size or complexity. It is always so arranged that the true path to the goal cannot be immediately perceived by the test animal. The commonest form, the MULTIPLE-T MAZE, consists of a number of T-shaped sections, the correct choice at the intersection leading to a new T-shaped section, and so on until the goal (feedbox or exit) is reached. In a PAPER MAZE the paths are drawn, and *S* traverses them with pencil. In a WATER MAZE the paths are marked by walls in the water, and *S* must swim to the goal. In an ELEVATED MAZE the pathways are narrow tracks placed on trestles. ¶Mazes are much used in studies of animal learning. Paper mazes are common as tests of intelligence.

maze/alley: a **maze** constructed with walled runways.

maze/stylus: a maze pattern, cut into a block, through which the subject traces his way with stylus or pencil and without visual guidance.

maze/temporal: a maze in which certain elements must be traversed more than once and in a certain sequence. E.g., the animal may be required to enter the blind alley at the left, then at the right, then at the left again before the path straight ahead (which leads to the goal) is open. Thus the task—a relatively abstract one—is to respond to temporal order as such.

M-C = multiple-choice (test or **experiment).**

McNaughten rule or **test:** a legal principle defining criminal responsibility in the case of the insane or mentally deficient. It holds that a person is not excused from criminal liability except upon proof that he was under such defect of reason as not to know the nature and quality of his act, or that the act was wrong. This 100-year-old legal doctrine, though quite out of line with contemporary understanding of abnormal behavior, is still the main test in most states.—*Var.* **M'Naughten.**

MD: 1. = manic-depressive. 2. = mental *deficiency.

Md, Mdn = median.

m.d., m.v. = mean *deviation.

Md D = median *deviation.

mean: *n.* (*stat.*) **1.** any **measure of *central tendency** except a position average. Unless qualified, it always refers to **2.** the **arithmetic *mean.**—See also **mean/geometric** and **mean/harmonic.**—*Syn.* (less precisely defined) **average.**

mean: *v.* **1.** to intend; to purpose; to affirm an intention: what do you *mean* to do? **2.** to use a **symbol** or symbolic act to refer to something: by tipping his hat he *means* respect. ➤A person is often unaware that his action means what it does: by compulsive handwashing he unwittingly *means* that he wants to be cleansed of guilt.

3. to intend to convey a meaning or significance to someone else: do you *mean* what you say? **4.** (with an impersonal subject) to refer to something; to denote or connote; to have a specific significance: e.g., the symbol of the circle *means* perfection, or (illustrating both **3** and **4**) that word does not *mean* what you *mean* it to.—*Syn.* **symbolize. 5.** to have a certain level of significance: the lecture *meant* nothing to the child.—*adj.* **meaningful. 6.** to imply.

mean/arithmetic or **M** or **X**: a **measure of *central tendency** calculated by dividing the sum of all the values by the number of cases in a statistical series.—*Syn.* ARITHMETICAL AVERAGE, **mean.** (If unqualified, **mean** always refers to the **arithmetic mean.**)—*adj.* **mean.**

mean/assumed: any arbitrary value in a series, usually one near the middle, from which **deviations** are calculated in a short cut to determining the mean. The algebraic sum of the deviations divided by the number of cases is added, positively or negatively, to the assumed mean. The resulting value is the actual mean of the series, not an approximation.—*Syn.* GUESSED AVERAGE, GUESSED MEAN, WORKING MEAN.

mean deviation: see **deviation/mean.**

mean error procedure = **adjustment procedure.**

mean/geometric: the *n*th root of the product of *n* values or numbers: e.g., $\sqrt[n]{a \cdot b \cdot c}$ is the geometric mean of *a*, *b*, and *c*. The geometric mean is used in averaging rates of change, ratios, etc.

mean gradation/method of = **equal sense differences method.**

mean/guessed or **GM** = **mean/assumed.**

mean/harmonic or **H** or M_H: the **reciprocal** of the **arithmetic *mean** of the reciprocals of a series of quantities. ➤The formula for *H* is $1/H = (1/N)\Sigma(1/x)$, where N = number of cases and x = any score.

meaning: 1. that which is purposed or intended: the *meaning* of the maneuver. **2.** that which a **symbolic** act refers to or signifies: hat-tipping has the *meaning* of respect. ➤When there is clear intent, this usage coincides with **(1).** Sometimes, however, the actor may not know to what the symbol refers, in which case the symbol is overtly meaningless but has a hidden or unconscious meaning. In other cases the notion of intent is weakened, and a meaning is merely a pointing to something. **3.** the apprehended relations within a class referred to by a concept; the conventional or socially agreed-upon sense or significance of a symbol, esp. of a language symbol: the *meaning* of a concrete noun is essentially the object referred to. In this sense, either the **connotation** or the **denotation** of a word constitutes its **meaning. 4.** (*pop., philos. of educ.*) an attribute of an object or idea that makes it of emotional value or concern.—*Cp.* **meaningful.**

➤These are the definitions of meaning proper. Other statements are overt theories about meaning (see **meaning/context theory of**) or are attempts to smuggle in a theory under guise of a definition. (*Cp.* **theory-begging.**) Thus, the "definition" of meaning as "the response elicited by a stimulus" either proposes a wholly useless usage (there are already many synonyms for response) or is an assertion of the *nature* of what is called meaning. Or again, the assertion that meaning is "what one is directly aware of" attempts to state the nature of awareness, not of meaning.

—*Syn.* **sense (7),** SIGNIFICATION, **significance,** PURPORT, IMPORT. **Sense** refers to a particular meaning; SIGNIFICATION is accepted meaning (see **3**); **significance** and IMPORT stress the importance of the meaning; PURPORT is the general drift. B. R. Buckingham suggests that, for concepts, meaning consists of relations within the class, **significance** of relations external to it.—*Cp.* **significance, mean** (*v.*).

meaning/context theory of: 1. (*structural psychol.*) doctrine that **meaning** consists of the **images** habitually associated with the sensory presentation or sensation ➤These images are often fused so that analysis is difficult. The meaning of the red spot amidst green in the June garden is "strawberry," and this meaning consists of the word imagery plus fragments of other imagery—gustatory, olfactory, tactile. **2** doctrine that the meaning of any object consists of (*a*) certain conscious processes that are related to the object and (*b*) the relations between the object and those processes. **3.** doctrine that meaning consists of **covert** movements and motor sets or motor readiness—i.e., of the tendencies toward action that are partially aroused by an object. ➤Thus, the meaning of the red object amidst the green is its naming in internal speech as "strawberry," plus the readiness to pluck and eat.

meaningful: *adj.* **1.** pertaining to what has meaning, esp. much meaning. **2.** pertaining to what arouses in a particular person a variety of ideas or associations. **3.** understandable. **4.** (*educ.*) characterizing something as being important to a person, as exciting his interest.

meaning/motor theory of = **meaning/context theory of (3).**

mean/logarithmic = **mean/geometric.**

mean/obtained: a mean calculated from actual observations.—*Contr. w.* **mean/true.**

means: *n. s.* or *pl.* any object, device, procedure, or activity that intervenes between a problem situation and its final adjustment and is directed by the organism toward such adjustment: a *means* to an end.

means activity: an activity that brings an organism closer to a goal, often merely by bringing a **means object** into view. ➤*Distg. fr.* GOAL ACTIVITY. Cutting one's meat is a means activity, chewing and swallowing is a goal activity.—See **consummatory response.**

means-end capacity: (*E. C. Tolman*) a hypothesized ability, innate or acquired, to react to relationships between **means objects** and **goal objects.** ➤FORMAL MEANS-END CAPACITY is the ability to react to such formal properties as distance, sequence, difference, similarity, etc.: e.g., a rat's ability to perceive one route to the food box as shorter.

means-end expectancy = **expectancy (1).**

means-end readiness: (*E. C. Tolman*) a state of selective readiness, innate or acquired, such that the organism will acquire certain **expectancies** more readily than others.

means-end relations: (*E. C. Tolman*) all the intervening objects and relations between a means and an end that are real to the organism in terms of its previous commerce with them. ➤Tolman speaks of the distance in time or space from means to end, and the direction one lies from the other; but other relations may be involved, e.g., the means may be contingent on some other factor.

means object: any object, response to which brings an organism closer to the goal. It may be merely a **cue** to the proper course of action—e.g., the activity of entering a correct alley in a maze brings into view some **cue** that the goal is being approached. The means object can be thought of as a subordinate goal but, unlike the **goal** (or **goal object**), it does not bring the action to a conclusion. The means object instigates an expectancy.

mean square: the square root of the mean of the squares of all the values in a set.

mean-square contingency coefficient or ϕ^2: a function to aid in determining whether or not the entries in a given contingency table could have been produced by chance factors only.—*Distg. fr.* **contingency coefficient** (which see).

mean-square error = **variance.**—*Syn.* MEAN-SQUARE DEVIATION.

mean-stimuli method = **equal sense differences method.**

mean/true: a purely theoretical value consisting of the mean of *all* the items in the universe concerned, assuming that they have been perfectly measured. Any single **obtained** *mean is taken as an imperfect representative or estimate of the true mean,

the value of which is estimated by averaging all the obtained means.—*Cp.* **score/true (2.)**

mean/working = **mean/assumed.**

measure: *n.* **1.** a result obtained by **measurement;** any quantification of a variable, including determination of presence or absence; a **value** or **score.**—See **score. 2.** a unit or standard used in measurement. **3.** a statistic.—*v.* **4.** to determine the magnitude, quantity, or value of anything; to make a measurement: to determine how many times a unit quantity is contained in a given quantity; or to determine whether a phenomenon is present or absent.

measure/derived = **score/derived.**

measure/discrete: the number of objects or events in a given aggregation when the objects are not related to each other by intermediate objects: e.g., the number of children in a classroom; the number of trials in an experiment. ➤The number of errors actually made is also a discrete measure, though the distinctly separated errors are believed to be in most cases points on a continuum.—*Syn.* POINT MEASURE.

measurement: *n.* **1.** the comparison of something with a unit or standard amount or quantity of that same thing, in order to discover how many times the unit amount is contained in the first item. **2.** any process by which a quantity is attributed to something; the assignment of numerals to things, in accordance with certain conventional rules, so as to represent their **magnitude. 3.** assignment to a position on a **scale** of more or less. ➤In this wider sense, it is **measurement** to determine presence or absence of a property, without further quantification. Even assignment to a **qualitative** series can be interpreted as a measurement in this sense: e.g., to say that a color is red, not green, is to assert the existence of a determinable quantity of red and the nonexistence of green. This is QUALITATIVE MEASUREMENT. ¶**Measurement** is preferably distinguished from **enumeration,** the counting of discrete items. **4.** the use of tests or other more or less objective measures in a school or similar practical situation; **educational** *measurement. ➤Measurement is the preferred term when tests are used, **evaluation** when more subjective judgments are employed.—*Cp.* **mental** *measurement, **educational** *measurement, appraisal, rating, evaluation.—See **standard, scale.**—*v.* measure.

measurement/absolute: see **absolute measurement.**

measurement/direct: measurement in which the observer perceives on a scale the quantitative statement of the value. ➤*Contr. w.* INDIRECT MEASUREMENT, in which the perceived indication must be transformed to another scale. Time read from a clock is direct measurement. Measurement of a rectangular area is indirect, being calculated from the direct measures of length and breadth.

measurement/educational: the study and practice of applying measurement to educational processes or outcomes. It includes the age-old practice of marking or grading of pupil performance, the rating of pupil personality and character, testing of all sorts in the schools; and the scientific study of the foregoing.

measurement/indirect: see **measurement/direct.**

measurement/mental: 1. the assignment of an act or response to a place on a psychological **scale.** ➤The primary datum, the **response,** may be taken to represent or to reflect phenomena or events that are otherwise categorized. The response, "The left one is brighter," may be ordered to a scale of color brightness, which is not a scale of responses (as response is ordinarily conceived) even though the scale can only be established from a study of responses. The measurements of both **psychophysics** and **differential psychology** come under this definition. **2.** the quantitative determination or estimation of any psychological **function, trait,** or **disposition:** the determination of the response strength of a habit, of the strength of a person's attitude (temporary or enduring), of ability, etc. ➤**Mental testing** in its broadest sense is synonymous; but the term **mental measurement** is often employed by those who use **testing** in a more restricted sense.

measure of precision: see **precision/index of.**

measures/comparable: see **comparable measures.**

measure/true: see **score/true;** also **mean/true.**

meatus/external auditory (mi·ā′təs): the passage leading from the external ear to the middle ear.

mechanical: *adj.* **1.** pertaining to **mechanics. 2.** pertaining to, or resembling, a machine. **3.** lacking life or lifelike qualities: *mechanical* thinking, *mechanical* association. **4.** characterizing a person able to deal with machines, tools, etc.

mechanical ability: ability to deal with concrete objects, or, more specifically, to manipulate objects as **mechanisms.**—*Syn.* MECHANICAL APTITUDE; MECHANICAL INTELLIGENCE, which lays somewhat less stress upon the motor skills involved, more upon effective understanding (often nonverbal) of mechanical relationships. The term does not imply that a **unitary *trait** underlies the ability.

mechanical-aptitude test: a test designed to predict how well a person can learn to perform tasks involving the understanding and manipulation of mechanical devices.

mechanical causality: an assigned explanation of events, namely, that things affect each other through contact. E.g., the door opens because a material object or force presses against it.—*Cp.* **phenomenistic causality, logical deduction.**—See also **mechanistic theory.**

mechanical intelligence: see **mechanical ability; intelligence/abstract.**

mechanical stimulation: stimulation of a receptor by pressure. ➤It contrasts with chemical stimulation (as in taste and smell) and with radiant stimulation (as in vision or heat). Stimulation by sound waves is sometimes classed as mechanical, sometimes as undulatory.

mechanics: *n.* **1.** the branch of physics that investigates the motion of particles and of masses. ➤**Mechanics** and **dynamics (1)** are very closely related. The former studies the motions, the latter the forces that cause the motion. **2.** (*educ., arts*) the details that make for correctness in a performance, in contrast with those aspects which require thinking and/or esthetic feeling and judgment. In language, e.g., it includes correct grammar, spelling, and punctuation; in arithmetic, computation; in music, adherence to standard pitch and tempo, etc.

mechanism: *n.* **1.** a machine; or a system operating like a machine; a systematic combination of parts working together and performing specific functions; a structure in which changes in one part produce predictable changes in another part. **2.** the way in which a machinelike system operates: the *mechanism* of oxygen interchange in the lung. **3.** the means used to secure an end or carry on a function: the conditioning *mechanism.* ➤In psychology, the term usually refers to the bodily parts that are conceived as means to a psychological function. **4.** a more or less permanent way of acting to secure an end: **habit** mechanism, **attention-getting** mechanism, **adjustment** mechanism. ➤This meaning is often combined with **(2)** or **(3)**. E.g., **conditioning** mechanism sometimes means the neural arrangements (meaning 3), sometimes that a given result is attained by the method of conditioning (meaning 4). **5.** (*psychoan.*) = MENTAL MECHANISM, a mental structure determining behavior and typically operating unconsciously: e.g., **defense mechanism.** ➤These mechanisms are essentially **motivations,** but the individual usually cannot refer his behaviors to these motivations until they have been revealed by analysis.—*Syn.* dynamism. **6.** = **mechanistic theory.**

➤Confusion results from the fact that definitions (1) through (5) may be used with or without any implication of **mechanistic theory**. Indeed, (3), (4), and (5) are often used with **teleological** implications that are contrary to that theory. We have, so to speak, nonmechanistic mechanisms.—*adj.* **mechanical**, like a machine; **mechanistic**, pertaining to **mechanics**, or to **mechanistic theory**.

mechanistic theory: the philosophical doctrine that all the activities of living beings are completely explicable in terms of the laws of physical mechanics—i.e., in terms of the motions of particles in space-time, or in terms of the kinds of energy interchange known to physics. ➤According to this view, no new or distinctive principles beyond those of physics are required for the explanation of **vital** and psychological phenomena. **Mechanism** should be, but often is not, distinguished from **determinism** (which see).—*Syn.* **mechanism** (but note the many other uses of the term); **materialism**, a somewhat obsolescent name for this doctrine. Opposed doctrines are **idealism, dualism, teleology, vitalism, mentalism.**—See **psychology/divisions and schools of, II, V.**—*adj.* **mechanistic.**

mechanization: *n.* 1. the process of rendering an activity machinelike, i.e., automatic, smooth-working, effortless. 2. the introduction of machines to perform all or part of the functions previously performed by organisms.

mechanomorphism: *n.* the practice of describing psychic activities in exclusively nonpsychic and mechanistic terms, of rigorously refraining from any expression that has any **mentalistic** connotations. ➤The word names a practice rather than a doctrine. Just as some persons are overly inclined to ascribe human modes of behavior to animals **(anthropomorphism)**, others are inclined to deny to animals and man alike any attributes not strictly those of a machine. When this denial is explicit and rationalized, it is the doctrine of **mechanism;** when it is primarily on a descriptive and terminological level, it is **mechanomorphism.**

medial: *adj.* in or toward the middle; toward the midline of the body.—*Syn.* **median** (*prefd.* for *stat.*), MESIAL (*obsoles.*).

medial plane: a plane that longitudinally bisects a symmetrical body.—*Syn.* MEDIAN PLANE, MESIAL PLANE (*obsoles.*). Sagittal plane is slightly broader.

media/mass: see **mass media.**

median or **Md(n).:** *n.* 1. the value (attained by calculation) that separates all the cases in a ranked distribution into halves. 2. that score in a ranked distribution which has exactly half of the cases below it and half (or half minus one, when *N* is an even number) above it.—*Syn.* **quartile** two (Q_2), fiftieth **percentile.** ➤The two meanings are often confused, but the magnitudes of the two forms of the median seldom differ materially.

median/crude = **median/rough.**

median gray: an intermediate gray that is characterized as neither whitish nor blackish. ➤It could be determined experimentally by finding a gray with an equal number of **jnd's** on each side of it; usually it is located by taking the gray that, to direct inspection, is midway between black and white.

median plane = **medial plane.**

median/rough: the midpoint of the interval in which the median occurs.—*Syn.* CRUDE MEDIAN.

mediate (mē'di·ət): *adj.* 1. interposed between two items or terms. 2. dependent upon an intervening object or process. ➤In a chain of events, any event is mediate between those before and after it. ¶In discussion of **cognition**, it is generally held that all knowledge is mediate: perception depends on intervening psychological processes following stimulation; other cognition depends on intervening associations and thinking processes. But sensation is sometimes classed as **immediate knowledge,** it being held that no *psychological* process intervenes between stimulus and sensation.—See also **association/immediate** and **/mediate.**—*adj.* **mediating,** which implies a relating function.

mediate (mē'di·āt): *v.* 1. to interpose between disputants; to settle a dispute by bringing the parties to agreement.—*Distg. fr.* arbitrate. 2. to be an intermediary in bringing something to pass; hence, to cause; more specif., to be a link in a thought process.—*n.* **mediation** (for the process), **mediacy** (for the abstract quality).

mediate association: see **association/ immediate.**

mediation theory: the theory that certain stimuli (usually called **signs** in this theory) do not directly initiate **instrumental behavior** but activate an intervening process that is connected in a complex systematic way with many **action systems.** ➤The mediation theory is thinking described in S-R terms.—*Cp.* **pure-stimulus *act, expectancy, sign gestalt.**

mediator: *n.* (*commun. theor.*) the system that intervenes between the **receiver** and the **transmitter.** It combines the function of **destination** and **source.** ➤An organism, in its function of receiving and transmitting information, is a **mediator.**

medical practice: traditionally, the diagnosis and treatment of disease by a professionally qualified person. ➤Although such practice has been defined in many statutes and regulations, the limits of medical practice are far from clear. No logically tenable definition of mental treatment can be drawn without including many procedures that cannot be limited to medical practice; the counseling of priest or minister, of lawyer, of psychologist, of psychoanalyst, or of just plain friend constitutes "mental" treatment but not medical practice. An analogous difficulty affects the definition of psychological practice. Falling back on merely traditional ideas of what constitutes such practice is not helpful in the light of the many changes in procedures and basic conceptions that are taking place.

medical psychology: see **psychiatry.**

meditation: *n.* **1.** serious and sustained reflection or contemplation. **2.** a quiet and relaxed state in which a person attempts to achieve an integration of feelings, emotions, attitudes, and ideas, often (but not necessarily) with the belief that this is achieved with the cooperation of a "divine spirit" or principle.

medium *n., pl.* **mediums, media: 1.** that through which something is accomplished. **2.** anything that fills space; specif., anything in space through which a wave passes. **3.** (*parapsych.*) a person who claims to be at times subject to the control of a disembodied spirit, during which paranatural phenomena occur.—*adj.* (for 3) **mediumistic.**

mediumship: see **medium (3).**

medulla (oblongata) (mi·dul′ə ob″lông·-gä′tə; -gä′tə): the bulblike prolongation upwards of the spinal cord, forming the lowest part of the brain and containing nerve centers to control breathing, circulation, etc.—*Syn.* AFTERBRAIN.

medullary sheath (med′ə·ler″i): the white substance surrounding the **axis cylinder** of most nerves.—*Syn.* MYELIN SHEATH.

medullated (med′ə·lāt″əd): *adj.* covered with a **medullary** (or myelin) **sheath.**

me/empirical = **me/psychological.**

mega-, megalo-: combining form meaning *large, extended, powerful.*

megalocephaly = **macrocephaly.**

megalomania: *n.* morbid overvaluation of oneself.

megalopsia = **macropsia.**

megrim (mē′grəm) = **migraine.**

Meissner corpuscles: *n. pl.* small elliptical bodies in the hairless portions of the skin, containing nerve endings believed to be pressure or touch **end organs.**

mel: *n.* the unit of a **ratio *scale** for pitch. ➤The pitch of a tone of 1000 cps is arbitrarily set at 1000 mels. Steps are measured by fractionation: i.e., the listener adjusts an auditory stimulus until its tone is judged just one half as high in pitch as a comparison tone, and this subjective interval is postulated as equal to any other such interval. The number of mels to a given musical interval increases as the pitch goes from bass to treble.

melancholia: *n.* a pathological state in which the individual is depressed, inaccessible to most stimuli, and seems sad without apparent or adequate cause.—*Distg. fr.* **melancholy,** which may be normal.

melancholia/involutional = **involutional psychotic reaction.**

melancholic: *adj.* **1.** pertaining to **melancholy.** **2.** characterizing persons given to "black" or depressed moods; or pertaining to the **temperament** so characterized.

melancholy: *n.* a mood characterized by persistent sadness and loss of interest.—*Distg. fr.* **melancholia.**

melioristic: *adj.* tending to make things better; aiming at improvement rather than perfection; willing to accept improvement that is short of perfection.—*n.* **meliorism.**

melody: *n.* (*music*) an organized succession of single tones, in a rhythmic pattern, that expresses a musical idea.

member: *n.* (*Gestalt theory*) any constituent having a specific function in a whole. ➤The term is preferred to **part,** which tends to imply a separateness that is denied in **Gestalt theory.**

membership: *n.* a relationship between an individual and an enduring structured social group in which the individual has a position and a role. The members have certain goals in common, advance toward these goals being recognized as advance for all, though not always equally. When a member does not so recognize a group goal, he is to that extent losing membership.

membership character: 1. any quality or attribute by means of which an object is recognized as belonging to a total. **2.** the attributes of any element of a **gestalt** that are direct functions of being part of a totality. ➤In Gestalt psychology *all* attributes are, strictly speaking, dependent upon the whole; but some change little with changes in the gestalt, while others change greatly. The latter attributes constitute the membership characters.

membership group: see **group/membership.**

memorandum *n., pl.* **memoranda:** that which is to be learned, memorized, or remembered. ➤It is a suggested term for the task set in learning and memory experiments.

memoric (mə·môr′ik): *adj.* pertaining to **memory.**

memoriter (mə·môr′ə·tər): *adj., adv.* by rote; by heart. ➤The MEMORITER METHOD neglects the meaning and seeks learning of exact words by sheer repetition. No one advocates such a method, but it is practiced.

memorization/anticipation procedure of = prompting method.

memorize: *v.* to learn, esp. by repetition, so that one can repeat a verbal passage or can reproduce a perceptual presentation (as, e.g., by rearranging a set of colors or figures in the order in which they were seen).—*Syn.* COMMIT TO MEMORY.—*n.* **memorization, memorizing.**

memorizing: *n.* a learning activity that results in the ability to reproduce fairly definite images or ideas, or in the ability to repeat words or phrases.—See **learning,** the more general term.—*adj.* **memory, mnemonic** (which see).—*n.* **memorization,** for the abstract process, whereas memorizing refers to the particular instance or activity.

memory: *n.* **1.** the general **function** of reviving or reliving past experience, with more or less definite realization that the present experience is a revival. Four distinct phases of memory have been recognized: (*a*) **memorizing** or **learning,** (*b*) **retention,** (*c*) **recall,** (*d*) **recognition. 2.** the total scope of things one can remember; the memory "store." **3.** any past experience that is recalled: He lived on past *memories.* ➤Modern psychology does not assume a single or unitary **faculty** of memory.—*Cp.* **rote** *learning,* **logical memory, mneme, recollection, reminiscence.**—*adj.* **memorial, memory,** pertaining to memory; **mnemonic,** concerned with memorizing.—*v.* **remember, memorize, learn.**

memory afterimage: a peculiarly vivid revival of an experience a brief moment after it has ceased. ➤E.g., after making a stupid verbal blunder, one seems to hear the words ringing in one's ears. Yet, for all the vividness of the experience, it is clearly in the field of **memory** and not of **perception,** as is the case with the **afterimage** or **aftersensation** (which see).—*Syn.* PRIMARY MEMORY IMAGE.

memory/associative: see **associative memory.**

memory/collective: the memories (or ideas), or the **memory traces,** supposed by some to be inherited by all members of a group who share a common heredity. ➤The memories are generally supposed to be latent or unconscious; they are activated by certain kinds of experience and act to modify conscious behavior. See **unconscious/collective.**

memory color: the remembered color of an object which, in conjunction with the direct sensory impression, determines the perceived color. ➤The memory color often almost completely outweighs the present sensory quality so that the object is seen as it is remembered, not colored as it actually is under present conditions of lighting. E.g., an orange seen in blue light is usually seen as orange.—*Cp.* **color constancy.**

memory/cover: see **cover memory.**

memory curve: a graphic representation of the effectiveness of **memorizing** or of **memory.**—See **learning curve.**

memory drum: a mechanical device for the serial presentation of **memoranda** for regulated periods and at regulated intervals.

memory experiments: any experiments designed to study the general laws of **learning** or **memorizing,** of forgetting, of **recall** or **reproduction,** of **recognition;** or of **individual *differences** in any of these respects. ➤The material may be verbal (including letters and digits), or nonverbal and concrete; it may be presented to the subject in any possible manner for perceiving during the PRESENTATION or LEARNING PERIOD. Evidence that learning has taken place may be gained by RECOGNITION PROCEDURES or REPRODUCTION PROCEDURES. The latter includes PROCEDURES OF FREE RECALL (**association test** and **cursory enumeration**) and procedures in which a series is memorized. To this last belong the **reconstruction procedure** and the procedures of **complete learning** or memorizing, of **right associates** (or Treffer method), of **prompting,** of **retained members,** and of **memory span.**

memory image: see **image/memory.**

memory/immediate: memory for what has been presented within the past few seconds. —*Cp.* **memory span, memory *image.**

memory/inaccessible: a memory not subject to recall but not permanently lost, being recoverable without new learning. ➤The term is not usually employed for a highly temporary blocking of recall.—*Cp.* **amnesia, repression.**

memory/logical = learning/meaningful (1).

memory/musical: the ability to recall or recognize a sequence of tones.—*Syn.* TONAL MEMORY.

memory/organic: see **organic memory.**

memory/productive: the putting together of items or portions of past memories, recognized as such, into new patterns: e.g., remembering what a cow's head looks like and combining it with a memory of a pig's body. Productive memory may include "remembered" events that did not occur and other distortions.—*Cp.* **reproductive *memory.**

memory/racial: that part of a person's mental equipment that is supposed by some to be derived from remote ancestry. Not only structures but mental processes are included: feelings, ideas, impulses.—*Syn.* BIOLOGICAL MEMORY, COLLECTIVE MEMORY.— See also **collective *unconscious,** often a synonym but with added implications.

memory/reproductive: a memory that preserves both the form and content of the past, without addition or distortion (but often with much omission).—*Cp.* **memory/ productive.**

memory span: the number of items that can be correctly reproduced immediately upon conclusion of a single presentation. ➤Usually the correct order is required. The MEMORY-SPAN TEST is the same as the **attention-span** test or RANGE OF APPREHENSION TEST.—*Cp.* **memory/immediate.**

memory system: an elaborate and artificial device to assist memory, generally by forming associative connections between the already learned system and the to-be-remembered fact.—*Syn.* MNEMONIC SYSTEM.

memory trace: the inferred change in the nervous system that persists between the time that something is learned and the time that it is recalled.—*Syn.* MNEMONIC TRACE, **engram.**

memory/unconscious: 1. the enduring changes in the organism, due to experiences, which are hypothesized to account for remembering or recalling those experiences. ➤These changes cannot be directly observed; it is only in this sense that they are unconscious. They give rise to ordinary conscious remembering.—*Syn.* **mneme** (*prefd.*). **2.** (*psychoan.*) the store of ideas and **affects** that have been repressed. They have not been entirely deprived, however, of **psychic** effect: they appear in various disguised forms as conscious activities.

menacme (mə·nak′mē): *n.* the period in a woman's life between puberty and menopause.

menarche (mə·när′kē): *n.* the first menstruation in the human female.—*adj.* **menarchal.**

mendacity/pathologic: untruthfulness in exaggerated degree; **pathological** *lying.

Mendelian ratio: the frequency ratio (in the offspring of a particular kind of mating) between those manifesting a **dominant** and those manifesting a **recessive** character in respect to a given **phenotypical** trait. ➤The 3:1 ratio obtained from the crossing of *purebred lines,* often thought of as *the* Mendelian ratio, is only a special case; other crosses yield different ratios. Note that the Mendelian ratio is not that prevailing in the **genotypical** characters resulting from a particular kind of mating.

Mendelism: *n.* a general type of heredity based on three general principles: the existence in the germ plasm of elements called **genes** that are transmitted as **unit characters** relatively independent of other unit characters; the **segregation (2)** of the genes in the reproduction process; genic **dominance.**—*Syn.* MENDELIANISM, MENDELIAN INHERITANCE.—*adj.* **Mendelian.**

meninges (mə·nin′jēz): *n. pl., s.* **meninx** (mē′ningks) the three membranes **(dura,**

pia, arachnoid) that cover the brain and spinal cord.—*adj.* **meningeal.**

meningitis: *n.* inflammation of the **meninges.**

meniscus: *n.* a lens concave on one side, convex on the other.

menopause: *n.* the period of natural cessation of the menstrual cycle; "change of life." ➤It may or may not be accompanied by various uncomfortable symptoms, such as "hot flashes" and disturbances of psychological adjustment. Contrary to a popular opinion, there is often no diminution of erotic excitability.—*Syn.* **climacteric** (also applied to analogous phenomena in the male).—*adj.* **menopausic, menopausal.**

menses (men′sēz): *n. pl.* the material discharged during menstruation. ➤Often applied to the period itself, for which **menstruation** is preferred.

menstruation: *n.* the monthly discharge of blood from the uterus of a sexually mature woman.—*Syn.* MENSTRUAL CYCLE, THE PERIOD (*pop.*), and a variety of slang terms. —*adj.* **menstrual.**—*pers. n.* **menstruant.**

mensuration (men″shù·rā′shən): *n.* measurement.—*v.* **mensurate.**

mental: *adj.* **1.** in general, pertaining to **mind, psyche,** or **self.** ➤In this general use, **mental** may be applied to **content** (see **2** below), to **act** (see **3** below), to **structure** (see **4** below), or to all of these, and whether they are conceived of as **conscious** or **unconscious.** How the mental in this sense is to be distinguished from other personal or psychobiological phenomena is usually left unstated or unexamined. See discussion under **mind** for the variety of viewpoints. **2.** (*structural psychol.*) pertaining to the content of mind; pertaining to the **introspectible** or conscious: to colors, tones, noises, feels, emotions, thoughts, volitions, etc. **3.** (*act* or *functional psychol.*) pertaining to the acts or functions of mind, or of a self, or of a psychobiological **organism**—to looking or seeing, hearing, feeling, emoting, thinking, deciding, learning, communicating, etc. ➤This usage is most nearly consonant with contemporary viewpoints in psychology but is not consistently adhered to. **4.** pertaining to the structure of mind: to habits, sentiments, attitudes, sets, expectations, mental mechanisms, mental blocks, etc. ➤This usage also is consonant with much contemporary investigation.—*Cp.* **hypothetical** *construct. **5.** pertaining to internal or **covert** activity rather than to **overt:** e.g., *mental* work, *mental* arithmetic. **6.** pertaining to the **intellectual** or **cognitive** rather than to the **affective** or **conative:** e.g., **mental tests** (unfortunately so named). **7.** originating in mind.—*Syn.* **psychogenic** (much to be *prefd.*). **8.** (*pop.*) imaginary or unreal:

illusions are merely *mental.* ➤This embodies a mixed-up metaphysics.

Mental is so confusingly used that one would gladly dispense with it. Undoubtedly, moreover, its continued use tends to thinking in **mentalistic** or **dualistic** terms and is thus an example of **theory-begging.** Yet it seems almost impossible to rule it out of even severely technical discussions. *Cp.* traditional terminology.—*Syn.* **psychic, psychological, personal, conscious, organismic, behavioral,** and (in special contexts) **psychogenic, intelligent.** The mental is variously contrasted with the **physical, physiological, somatic, spiritual, social, emotional, sensory.**

mental abilities/primary: see **abilities/ primary mental.**

mental ability = (*semipop.*) **intelligence.**

mental age: see **age/mental.**

mental analysis: 1. distinct attention to the attributes, parts, or qualities of an object without physically separating it into component parts. **2.** the attempted listing of the mental qualities of a person. **3.** = **psychoanalysis.**

mental chemistry viewpoint: the doctrine that, by **association,** mental elements are fused and transformed into compounds unlike their elements, as atoms are formed into qualitatively different molecules.—*Syn.* (*J. S. Mill*) MENTAL SYNTHESIS.

mental conflict = **conflict (1).**

mental content: see **content/conscious.**

mental defective: an individual who is academically, vocationally, and socially incapacitated by his mental limitations. He is unable to function adequately except in a sheltered environment.—See **deficiency/ mental.**

mental deficiency: see **deficiency/mental.**

mental deterioration: the irreversible loss of mental organization, general or specific, found in some but not all mental diseases, and in some but not all aged persons. ➤*Distg. fr.* MENTAL DISORGANIZATION, a more general term covering also temporary breakdowns in behavior coordination as a result of emotional stress, drugs, fever, etc.

mental development: the progressive changes in mental organization from conception to death of an individual; esp., the progressive changes between birth and maturity, or during any specified part of the life span. ➤Sometimes only those changes attributable to heredity are regarded as developmental, but more often changes due to learning are included. See **maturation.** Degenerative changes may or may not be excluded.—*Syn.* **ontogenesis.**—*Distg. fr.* **mental evolution.**

mental discipline: see **formal culture.**

mental disease: a general term for any disabling disorder, whether **psychogenic**

or **somatogenic,** characterized by grave failure of **adjustment.** ➤Though well established, the term is unfortunate: "mental" tends to imply a radical difference from "bodily," and "disease" to imply that the departure from normal functioning, whether called bodily or mental, is essentially of the same order. Both implications are debatable. —*Syn.* **mental disorder** (*prefd.*), **psychosis** and **neurosis** (mental disease includes both), **insanity** (a legal or layman's term).

mental disorder: any grave or disabling failure of **adjustment,** whether relatively temporary or chronic, **psychogenic** or **somatogenic, functional** or **organic.** ➤This term is preferred, for psychological use, to **mental illness** or **mental disease.** It does not usually include **mental *deficiency;** it does include both **psychosis** and **neurosis.**

mental disorganization: see **mental deterioration.**

mental element: a psychological datum that resists analysis into simpler components. The traditionally accepted elements are **sensations, images,** and simple **feelings.** ➤This term is nearly always (but not necessarily) restricted to the components of **mental content,** i.e., to the end products of **introspective** analysis.

mental energy: see **energy/mental.**

mental evolution: the attainment, in the scale of zoological evolution, of progressively higher levels of mental functioning. ➤*Distg. fr.* **mental development,** the progressive change in the individual with age.

mental faculties/theory of: see **faculty psychology.**

mental function: 1. any activity or operation having a mental character, as distinguished from **mental *structure** on the one hand or **mental content** on the other. ➤E.g., thinking is a mental function or activity. The *structure* or mechanism of thinking, although not known in any detail, is usually believed to be primarily **cortical.** The mental *content* of thinking is the thought or idea. ¶The word *function,* in this expression, emphasizes the adjustive or useful property of the operation and treats it as a whole; thus, an **act** is a closer synonym than a **behavior.** BEHAVIOR FUNCTION, preferred by those who dislike mentalistic terms, nonetheless refers to the same kinds of operations. **2.** a particular kind of capacity or ability: e.g., the intelligence function, the speech function are called mental functions.

mental growth: see **growth/mental.**

mental healing: the use of **suggestion** or **faith** in the attempt to cure disease. ➤*Distg. fr.* **psychotherapy,** which makes use of any psychological means but does not include, as mental healing does, the attempt to cure **somatic** disease.—*Syn.* MIND CURE, FAITH CURE, DIVINE HEALING.

mental health: a relatively enduring state wherein the person is well **adjusted,** has a zest for living, and is attaining **self-actualization** or **self-realization.** It is a positive state, and not mere absence of mental disorder.

mental hygiene: the science and art of preserving and maximizing **mental health.** ➤It includes all measures aimed at preventing mental disorder and at improving the psychological adjustment of individuals and their capacity for harmonious relationship in groups.

mental illness: 1. a disorder of behavior; a breakdown of adjustment so severe that professional psychotherapy is indicated. ➤Mental illness is more general (and vague) than **mental disease.** In most cases **behavior disorder** or *behavior *maladjustment would better communicate what is meant. **2.** a disorder due to psychic causes, whether the symptoms are somatic, psychic, or behavioral; **psychogenic** illness.

mental imagery: see **image/mental.**— *Distg. fr.* **aftersensation** and **image/ memory.**

mentalism: *n.* **1.** the doctrine that there is a distinct group of conscious or mental phenomena not reducible without remainder to physical phenomena. ➤*Cp.* **mechanism (1),** which is very nearly the contradictory doctrine. Traditionally, all mental phenomena were supposed to be conscious; but many authorities recognize as distinctly mental (i.e., distinguishable from purely physiological processes) a class of phenomena which are not conscious. ¶Mentalism in one form or another is a central doctrine of **dualism** and of **emergentism. 2.** attributing mental function to animals below man and to inanimate objects.—*Syn.* **animism.** —See **psychology/divisions and schools of,** III.—*adj.* **mentalistic.**

mentality: *n.* **1.** the quality that characterizes **mind. 2.** the varied manifestations of mind in a single person; almost a synonym for **personality. 3.** the degree of mental activity or of potential activity; esp., the degree of intellectual activity.

mental level: 1. the **level** of intellectual functioning or of ability. ➤In children, it is often measured in **MA** (not in **IQ). 2.** (*C. Jung*) any of the three divisions of the **psyche: consciousness,** the **personal *unconscious,** the **collective *unconscious.**

mentally handicapped: of a person who is socially, vocationally, and academically hampered, but not incapacitated, by his mental limitations. ➤The mentally handi-

capped person is distinguished from a **mental defective** by the fact that he does not require a sheltered environment.

mental maturity: 1. an adult level of functioning in all important abilities, or in all behavior functions. ➤Despite its widespread use, it is practically impossible to render this meaning explicit. **2.** the average adult level of ability; esp., the average adult level of intelligence. ➤Usage (2) is as much too restricted as usage (1) is too vague: to equate intellectual maturity with mental maturity is to claim too much for the former.

mental measurement: see **measurement/ mental.**

mental mechanism: an unfortunate synonym for **defense mechanism.**—See **mechanism (5).**

mental organization: 1. the pattern or system of interrelations among the mental operations or the **mental *structures** of an individual; esp., **2.** the enduring relationships of **dominance,** or of superordination-subordination, among behavior tendencies. ➤Often used valuatively: a high level of *mental organization.*

mental phenomena: see **mental.**—*Syn.* **psychic** or **psychological** phenomena (*prefd.*).

mental philosophy: the study of the ultimate or metaphysical nature of **mind** and its place in nature. ➤Because of its primarily deductive character, it is also called RATIONAL PSYCHOLOGY. In modern times, efforts to separate it from scientific psychology have been fairly successful.

mental process: 1. a progressive action or series of actions having a **mental** character; the living through, and responding to, an event. ➤The term implies a more-than-momentary time interval.—*Syn.* **act, behavior, mental function. 2.** (*structural psychol.*) the streamlike flow in time of that which is experienced, of **mental *content.** ➤This usage has been misleading.

mental processes/higher: thinking in all its forms (including constructive imagination), in contrast with **sensation** and **imaging.** ➤Whether **perception** or **fantasy** are to be included with the higher processes is not clear.

mental ratio: a proposed substitute for **intelligence quotient.** ➤It has the advantage of being as yet unspoiled by many misinterpretations. But **mental** in this context is unfortunate.

mental retardation: a genteelism for **mental *deficiency.**

mental scale: a device for assigning numerical scores to different levels of mental performance, either in general or (more often) in intelligence.—*Syn.* **mental test.**

mental set: see **set/mental.**

mental structure: see **structure/mental.**
mental synthesis: see **mental chemistry viewpoint.**
mental test: 1. any measure of individual differences in behavior.—See **test** (3). 2. = **intelligence test** (*prefd.*).
mental work: see **work/mental.**
mentation: *n.* (*obsoles.*) a collective term for mental processes as actually going on.
menticide: *n.* the murder of mind: a metaphorical term for the systematic attempt to break down a person's mental organization, to destroy his standards of values and ideals, and to induce radically different behavior patterns.—*Approx. syn.* BRAINWASHING.
me/psychological: 1. a set of qualities and attributes associated with the words *me* or *mine*; whatever a person perceives, or believes to be true, about the organism that he calls *me*. 2. a complex object, composed at first of the BODILY ME—i.e., the kinesthetic, tactual, and other experiences related *directly* (as experience) to the body—and later greatly enriched by a wide variety of ideational and affective elements associated with this perceptual core (the EXTENDED ME, or **ego extension**). ➤The body-oriented experiences, at first not differentiated from external-object experiences, are held to **segregate** in infancy from other experiences and to combine into a new and distinct perceptual unity in the same way as the experiences that constitute the percept of any other object. The ME-PERCEPT is not merely a percept of how the body appears (visually or otherwise); it includes such experiences as that of the close conjunction of kinesthesis and the seen motion of the hand (which differs from the seen motion of independent objects), or the complex feeling of effort. It is a body percept, not a percept of the body. The expansion (and sometimes the contraction) of the boundaries of the me to include those feelings and ideas that seem peculiarly oriented toward oneself is greatly influenced by physiological, linguistic, and social factors. Successive me-experiences have a strong quality of belonging with each other. --*Syn.* SELF-PERCEPT, **self-concept, perceived *self,** EMPIRICAL ME.—See **self.**
merit ranking: arranging any kind of data in respect to any specified characteristic in an order of magnitude or of more or less. ➤The notion of value implied in "merit" is often discarded: e.g., an arrangement of color-sample papers in order of redness is called a **merit ranking.** The steps or intervals between items in a merit ranking may be very unequal.—*Syn.* ORDER OF MERIT RANKING.
merit rating: an appraisal of an individual's work record for a stated period, often in-

cluding evaluatory statements about his personality, his adjustment to the job and to his associates, his capacity for growth, etc.—*Syn.* PROGRESS REPORT, EFFICIENCY RATING, FITNESS REPORT, PERFORMANCE APPRAISAL, SERVICE REPORT, etc.—*Cp.* **quality *scale.**
Merkel's law: the hypothesis that equal supraliminal differences between sensations correspond to equal stimulus differences.— *Cp.* **Weber's law.**
Merrill-Palmer scale: thirty-eight tests of ability, including both performance and verbal tests, suitable for children between 24 and 63 months. ➤It is administered as an **age scale** but scored as a **point scale.** The directions permit greater discretion in making allowance for **negativism,** special handicaps, etc., than most scales.
mesaticephalic (mes″ə·ti·sə·fal'ik) = **mesocephalic.**—*Var.* **mesaticephalous** (-sef'-ə·ləs).
mescal (mes·kal'): *n.* a narcotic drug that produces, among other symptoms, brilliant-colored hallucinations.
mesencephalon (mes″en·sef'ə·lon): *n.* the midbrain; that part of the brain, developed from the middle portion of the primitive brain, lying beneath and surrounded by the **cerebrum.** It consists of the **corpora quadrigemina,** lamina, and cerebral **peduncles,** and is traversed by the **cerebral aqueduct.**—*adj.* **mesencephalic** (-sə·fal'ik).
mesial = **medial.**
mesmerism (mez'mər·iz·əm; mes-): *n.* an early name for **hypnotism.**
mes(o)-: combining form meaning *in the middle, intermediate* in size, place, or degree.
mesocephalic (mes″ō·sə·fal'ik; mē″sō-): *adj.* of a head with median relationship between its greatest length and breadth; having a cephalic index between 76 and 80.9.— See **cephalic index.**—*Syn.* MESATICEPHALIC, MESATICEPHALOUS.—*n.* **mesocephaly** (-sef'-ə·li).
mesoderm: *n.* the middle of the three cellular layers of the embryo, which develops into the bones and muscles.—*Contr. w.* **ectoderm, endoderm.**—See **ectomorphic.** —*adj.* **mesodermal.**
mesokurtosis: see **kurtosis.**—*adj.* **mesokurtic.**
mesomorphic: see **ectomorphic** and **body build/index of.**
mesopic vision: (mə·sop'ik): vision intermediate between **photopic** and **scotopic** vision, and consequently attributed to the combined functioning of the rods and cones.
mesosomatic: see **body size/general.**
message: *n.* 1. that part of one person's behavior which is perceived by another as having implications or meaning for him. ➤It is not necessary that the person emitting the behavior intend it as a message: a

blush conveys a *message*. But the term is usually restricted to cases where the receiver recognizes the perceived behavior as significant. **2.** (*language*) a sequence of **symbols** strung together in time according to a pattern and with intent to communicate. **3.** (*commun. theor.*) that part of the **output** of a **communication unit** which forms part of the **input** of another unit; a meaning selected and **encoded** by a **source** and **decoded** by a **destination**; a **signal** or event in a **channel** relating a source to a destination. ➤Where the communication units, or the source and destination units respectively, are persons, these definitions mean exactly the same as **(1).** Their value is in emphasizing the similarity, and the *formal* identity, of communication between persons and between physical units such as telephone stations, etc. (But the limits of merely formal similarity must be recognized.)

A message may be IMMEDIATE, as in face-to-face communication; or MEDIATE, as in writing, musical recording, art objects.

meta-: combining form meaning *between, by means of, over and above, beyond, next to.* ➤This Greek prefix has so many meanings that each combination must be separately considered.

metabolic gradient = **physiological gradient.**

metabolism (mǝ·tab'ǝ·liz·ǝm): *n.* the sum of the processes concerned in building up (ANABOLISM) and breaking down (CATABOLISM) of protoplasm, i.e., of living cells or tissues. ➤The **basal metabolic rate (BMR)** is the rate of catabolism of an organism when awake but as quiescent as possible.—*adj.* **metabolic** (met"ǝ·bol'ik).

metacarpal: *adj.* pertaining to the five elongated bones between the wrist and fingers. The rate of development of these bones, as judged by X ray, is a common index of anatomical development.

metagenital: *adj.* (*H. S. Sullivan*) characterizing a sexual situation in which one's own genitals need not be involved, but any other person's are.

metagnosis (met"ag·nō'sǝs): *n.* changing one's mind. ➤METAGNOSIOMETRY is proposed by B. Bass for the measurement of changes in attitudes or preferences, esp. of groups.

metalanguage: *n.* **1.** that part of any language system which deals with the rules and regulations for the proper use of that language. It includes grammar, syntax, semantics, much of logic, etc. **2.** a terminology that rises above the distinguishing features of two or more terminologies; a language that expresses in common terms the concepts that are common to two or more disciplines. ➤E.g., the neologisms of informa-

tion theory are said to provide a common language for certain concepts common to engineering and psychology.

metalinguistics = **exolinguistics.**

metallic color: the color typically evoked by selective reflection from certain metallic and other surfaces which possess the physical feature known as metallic reflection, and which exhibit chromatic high lights similar in hue to the surfaces as a whole.

metamers (met'ǝ·mǝrz): color stimuli that have different spectrophotometric characteristics but are seen as identical colors under favorable conditions of comparison.—*Syn.* METAMERIC COLORS (-mer'ik).

metamorphosis (-môr'fǝ·sǝs; -môr·fō'-): *n.* marked and relatively abrupt change of form, such as the change from tadpole into frog; transformation; metaphorically and loosely, an abrupt change of personality.—*v.* **metamorphose** (-môr'fōz).

metanerg (met'ǝ·nǝrg): *n.* (*R. B. Cattell*) a dynamic or *motivational source *trait that results from environmental influences.—*Cp.* **erg.**—*adj.* **metanergic** (-nêr'jik).

metaphrenia (-frē'niǝ): *n.* (*G. Staercke*) the mental state of one whose **libido** has withdrawn—at least temporarily—from emotional participation in the family or group and is directed to practical gainful interests, or to the concerns of politics and the state. Metaphrenia is said to be the mental condition of the individual in Western society.

metaphysics: *n.* that branch of philosophy concerned with the ultimate nature of existence. ➤In psychology, the term is nearly always one of reproach since the metaphysical has no place in the science of psychology; but there is no imputation that metaphysics as such is not perfectly legitimate and even necessary.—*adj.* **metaphysical,** which has also the popular meaning of *abstruse.*

metapsychics (-sī'kiks): *n.* **1.** = **parapsychology. 2.** a body of doctrine that accepts the reality of spirits, spiritualistic phenomena, cryptesthesia, etc. ➤**Parapsychology** is an attempt to apply scientific methods to the study of these "unusual" phenomena; **metapsychics (2)** is a belief not based on scientific method.

metapsychoanalysis: *n.* (*O. Rank*) an **analysis (3)** that goes beyond **psychoanalysis.**

metapsychology: *n.* **1.** a systematic attempt to deal with what lies beyond the empirical facts and laws of psychology: the problems of relation of mind and body, of the place of mind and behavior in the cosmos, etc. ➤Metapsychology is, thus, related to psychology as metaphysics was to physics in Aristotle's system. The problems dealt with are philosophical. **2.** a systematic attempt to state the empirical facts and laws of psychology in the language of physiology. ➤This is not so much a branch of philosophy (in contrast with **1**) as a psychology dominated by a philosophical thesis. **3.** a systematic attempt, usually speculative, to state the completely general laws of psychology. ➤Here **meta-** means *going beyond present knowledge,* but does not imply a philosophy.—*Syn.* **nomothetic** psychology. **4.** = **parapsychology** (*prefd.*). **5.** (*S. Freud*) a comprehensive system that treats of every mental process under three aspects: its cause-and-effect relations (MENTAL DYNAMICS); its position in the total structure of mind—i.e., whether it belongs to superego, ego, or id (MENTAL TOPOGRAPHY); and its functional value—the aspects of libido it is designed to satisfy (MENTAL ECONOMY). Freud never quite finished his system from this standpoint.

metascience: *n.* the scientific study of science; scientific **empiricism.**

metempiric(al) (met″em·pir′i·kəl): *adj.* pertaining to concepts or constructs that lie beyond **empirical** verification, though they are clearly related to experience. ➤*Distg. fr.* **metapsychic,** which applies to matters of alleged experience not *explainable* in ordinary scientific terms. Most authorities hold that **values**—or rather value claims—are metempirical: i.e., we cannot justify the choice of one set of values over another on empirical grounds, though such value claims are developed in individual and social experience.

metempsychosis (mə·temp″si·kō′sis): *n.* the doctrine of transmigration of the soul after death.

metencephalon (met″en·sef′ə·lon): *n.* that part of the developing nervous system which becomes the **medulla oblongata.**

meter-candle = **lux.**

method: *n.* **1.** a systematic way of dealing with facts and concepts. ➤This is the broad usage which includes four different kinds of operation. It is suggested that these operations be distinguished by separate terms: (*a*) **rational principie,** the form of reasoning utilized: e.g., **hypothetico-deductive** principle, **inductive** principle (both more often called methods); (*b*) **point of view,** a way of looking at the data, or the intention assumed in an investigation: e.g., the **nomothetic** point of view, the **mechanistic** point of view; (*c*) **method** in the restricted sense of (**2**) below; (*d*) **procedure,** a specific type of operation or order of attack in an investigation, a bringing into relationship of the variables that bear on the problem at hand: e.g., the procedure of **limits** (more often called the *method* of limits), the **nondirective** (or **client-centered**) **procedure.** **2.** a mode of

attack that orients a science in its investigations and is applicable generally therein: e.g., the method of **introspection,** the **historical** (or **ahistorical**) method, the method of **experiment,** of **case history,** of **testing.** ➤Specific ways of pursuing an investigation (see *d*), though often called methods, are better called **procedures.**— *Cp.* also **techniques.**

method / analytical: see **analytical method.**

methodology: *n.* **1.** the systematic and logical study and formulation of the principles and **methods (1)** used in the search for fact or truth. **Methodology** may be general or restricted to a particular science, or even to a specific investigation. **2.** the procedures actually used in a particular research: the *methodology* of the investigation was sound.

methodology/experimental: see **experimental methodology.**

meticulous: *adj.* characterizing a tendency to rigid and undiscriminating precision, order, neatness, etc.—*n.* **meticulosity, meticulousness.**

metrazol (met′rə·zōl): *n.* a convulsion-producing drug sometimes used in **shock therapy.**

metric (met′rik): *adj.* **1.** pertaining to **measurement. 2.** pertaining to the system of measurement based on the meter and the gram.—*Cp.* **C.G.S. system.**

-metric: suffix meaning *pertaining to measurement.*

metric assumption: an **assumption** that justifies using a particular measuring operation; or, slightly more generally, one that justifies a particular mathematical and/or statistical operation. ➤E.g., the operation of averaging makes the assumption that the data summed are homogeneous, or all of one kind in respect to the property for which the mean is being computed.

metric methods: 1. psychophysical methods. **2.** those methods that involve assigning numbers to represent quantity.

metron: *n.* the unit of metrical information. It is a measure of the degree of confidence merited by a descriptive statement. —See **information theory.**

metronoscope (mə·tron′ə·skōp): *n.* a mechanical device that exposes, for appropriately timed intervals, short bits of print for reading. The interval may be varied so that the device can be used either to test or to practice reading speed.

-metry: combining form meaning *measurement.*

M-F index = **masculinity-femininity** index.

mg = milligram: one thousandth of a gram.
μg: = microgram: one millionth of a gram.
MG-age: maximum growth age; age at the

end of the year of maximum growth in standing height.

micro- (mī'krō-): combining form meaning *small, very small, diminished.—Ant.* **macro-, mega-.**

microcephalic (-sə·fal'ik): *adj.* having an abnormally small head. ➤Usually applied only when the smallness is so grave as to be associated with marked mental deficiency, or in an adult when the cranium is of less than 1350 cubic centimeters capacity.—*Syn.* MICROCEPHALOUS (-sef'ə·ləs).

microcosm: *n.* a small system that images or reflects the universe; the human being as a mirror of the universe, or **macrocosm.**

microgram: *n.* one millionth of a gram. —Symbol μg.

micromillimeter: *n.* one thousandth of a **micron;** one millionth of a millimeter.— Symbol mμ.—*Syn.* MILLIMICRON.

micron (mī'kron): *n.* a unit of length equal to one-thousandth of a millimeter.—Symbol μ.

microphonia: *n.* marked weakness of voice.

microphonic/aural: see **aural microphonic.**

micropsia (mī·krop'si·ə): *n.* visual abnormality, either **functional** or **retinal,** characterized by decrease in the apparent size of seen objects.—*Var.* **micropsy** (mī'-krop·si).—*Ant.* **macropsia.**—*adj.* **microptic.**

microsecond: *n.* one-millionth of a second.

microsomatic: see **body size/general.**

microsplanchnic (-splank'nik): *adj.* characterizing an individual with small trunk and relatively long limbs.—*Cp.* **asthenic type.**—*Ant.* **macrosplanchnic.**

microstructure: *n.* the microscopic texture or grain of the surface of an object, which often affords effective clues to its recognition.

microtome (mī'krō·tōm): *n.* an instrument for cutting thin sections of tissue for microscopic examination.—*adj.* **microtomic** (-tom'ik).—*n.* **microtomy** (mī·krot'ə·mi).

micturition (mik"chù·rish'ən): *n.* urination.—*v.* **micturate.**

midbrain = **mesencephalon.**

middle ear: the air-filled space containing the three auditory bones (hammer, anvil, and stirrup). It lies between the eardrum and the inner ear, or **labyrinth.**

mid-interval = **median *interval.**

midparent: *adj.* of the mean of the measurements (or the weighted measurements) for any given characteristic in both parents: e.g., the averaged height of the parents, with or without a weighting for sex differences. For many characteristics the midparent value is useful in predicting hereditary development.

midpoint: *n.* the point halfway between the limits of a given interval or range.

midrange value: a crude **measure of *central tendency,** obtained by taking the **mean** of the highest and lowest values of a series of observations.

midscore = **median (2).**

Mignon delusion (min'yon): the **delusion** that one's parents are not really one's own and that one is actually the child of some distinguished family.

migraine: *n.* a nervous disorder marked chiefly by severe recurrent headaches, usually on one side only, with nausea.—*Syn.* MEGRIM (*obsoles.*).

milieu (mē·lyœ'): *n.* the immediate environment, physical or social or both, sometimes including also the internal state of the organism.—For related terms, see **situation.**

milieu therapy: the treatment of mental disorder or maladjustment by making definite and (usually) substantial changes in the person's immediate environment or life circumstances.—*Syn.* SITUATION(AL) THERAPY.

militarism: *n.* **1.** a highly complex pattern of attitudes that leads a person to approve a national policy of military preparedness and military action as the court of appeal for settlement of international differences. **2.** a complex of attitudes that exalts military behavior and ideals, and that makes for acceptance and enjoyment of the conditions of service in the Armed Forces. ➤Though there is much overlap, (1) and (2) are not identical.—*Distg. fr.* **military psychology.**

military psychology: 1. the form of **applied psychology** (which see) that treats of the psychological problems of the Armed Forces. ➤It deals with selection, assignment, training, equipment, motivation, and morale, each of which, though having a nonpsychological aspect, presents many psychological problems.—*Distg. fr.* the psychology of war and peace, and from **militarism. 2.** (*pop.*) the characteristic attitudes and modes of thinking and acting found in military establishments.

Miller Analogies Test: see **MAT.**

Mill Hill Tests: vocabulary tests for schoolage children (ages 4 to 14) and for adults (age 14 and over). Each test consists of two sets of 44 words arranged in ascending order of difficulty. The subject gives definitions for the words in the first set, and synonyms for those in the second. ➤Since the standardization is based on British subjects, the order of difficulty for other English-speaking groups must be expected to vary somewhat.

milli- (mil'i-): combining form meaning *divided by a thousand;* a thousandth.

millilambert: *n.* the most commonly used unit of **luminance,** equal to one thousandth of a **lambert.**

millimicron: *n.* one thousandth of a micron, or one millionth of a millimeter. It is a unit of length for light waves and similar very short wave lengths.—Symbol **mμ**.—*Syn.* MICROMILLIMETER.

milliphot (-fot): *n.* a unit of **illuminance** equal to 1/1000 of a **lumen** per square centimeter, or of a centimeter-candle, or of a **phot**.

millisecond: one thousandth of a second.

Mill's canons: the **rational principles** that guide the use of **induction**, consisting of the **canons of *agreement, of *differences, of *agreement and difference, of *residues**, and of **concomitant variation**.

mimetic (mi·met′ik): *adj.* 1. imitative; responding to the perception of another animal's behavior by very similar behavior.—*n.* **mimicry**. 2. responding to **species-specific** behavior with similar behavior and without any previous learning to do so; **instinctively** imitative.—*n.* **mimesis** (mi·-mē′səs).

mimetic response: imitation; copying the behavior or appearance of other organisms.

mimicry: *n.* see **mimetic (1)**.

mind: *n.* 1. the organized totality or system of all **mental** processes or **psychic** activities, usually of an individual organism. ➤The emphasis is upon the relatedness of the phenomena. Mind in this sense does not commit the user to a metaphysical position about the nature of these processes. Hence, it may be used by those who define psychology in terms of **acts** or **behaviors**, but who recognize that acts or behaviors have a quality (mental) that distinguishes them in some fashion from physiological processes. It is, however, more congenial to those who recognize a category of processes, such as feelings and cognitions, which, though related to behavior, are still distinct. In sum, while the term may be, and sometimes is, used by any psychologist except strict **behaviorists**, it tends to have a **mentalistic** flavor. 2. the sum total of the enduring structures that are hypothesized to explain behavior or mental processes. ➤These structures are **hypothetical *constructs**, having the properties that must be ascribed to them to account for the observed phenomena. No assumption need be made about how these relate to **somatic** structures. The term is preferred, however, by those who deal with **molar** phenomena, for which no specific or detailed correlation with anatomical structures is known. ¶Thus, many psychologists hold that a sentiment, e.g., is an **organismic** structure; but since its characteristics are wholly those inferred from behavior, it is called a mental structure (a part of a mind) to distinguish it from those structures open to anatomical observation or inferred from physiologically described process. But this usage, like (1),

tends to incline the scale to the acceptance of **mentalism** and is generally avoided by those who are committed to the opposite metaphysics of **monism**. 3. = **self, psyche,** or **soul**. ➤Mind as a synonym for any or all of these three is at best not needed; at worst it tends to be misleading. 4. = **intellect**. ➤Compare the popular or literary contrast of *mind and heart*. 5. a characteristic way of thinking and feeling: an inquiring *mind*, the Greek *mind*.

The term **mind** has such a battered history that it can hardly be used clearly in technical writing; yet it is almost unavoidable.—See **mental, mind-body problem, person**.

mind blindness = **agnosia/visual** (*prefd.*). —*Distg. fr.* **blindness/mental**.

mind-body problem: the **metaphysical** issue concerning the relation of mind, or that which is **mental**, to the body. ➤The chief theories are: (*a*) INTERACTIONISM: mind influences body, and body mind; (*b*) PARALLELISM: mental processes and bodily processes run strictly parallel courses without influencing each other; (*c*) DOUBLE ASPECT THEORY: mind is body seen from a certain viewpoint, body is mind seen from another; (*d*) TWO (or DOUBLE) LANGUAGE THEORY: mental terms and bodily terms are but two different "languages" describing the same phenomena; (*e*) ORGANISMIC RESPONSE THEORY: mental processes are a distinctive kind of response made by an organism in interacting with its environment; (*f*) EPIPHENOMENALISM: mental processes are a by-product of bodily activity and of no causal (or other?) importance; (*g*) MATERIALISM: only body is real; (*h*) IDEALISM: body and bodily processes are manifestations of mind (with many types of suggestion concerning the relation of a particular "mind" to a particular "body").—See also **emergentism**.

If it be granted that there is in any sense at all a distinctive set of phenomena called **mental**, there are empirical correlations to be established between these facts and the facts of physiological functioning. This is the broad area of **physiological psychology**. The mind-body problem seeks to go beyond or behind such correlation to the ultimate relationship. This inquiry is essentially metaphysical and of no greater pertinence to the science of psychology than to the science of physics, except that it uses many of the same terms. But because some of the terms are the same, the metaphysical issues are often unwittingly introduced into the scientific context of psychology. In the view of some philosophers, the whole problem is unreal, the result of starting from false assumptions.

mind/collective: 1. a **consensus**. 2. the common mental processes in a group which result in concerted action.—*Syn.* **group mind. 3.** an organized system of behavior tendencies that belongs to a group, over and above the behavior of the individuals therein.—*Syn.* **group mind, syntality.**

mind-deafness = auditory **agnosia** (*prefd.*).

mind dust (or **mind stuff**) **theory:** a somewhat derogatory name for **monadism.**

mind/folk: see **folk mind.**

mind/group: see **group mind.**

mind-twist hypothesis: the view that mental disorders are **functional** rather than **organic.**—*Contr. w.* **brain-spot hypothesis,** which holds that they result from **brain lesions.**

miniature life situation: a procedure for the study of natural behavior under controlled conditions.—*Cp.* **assessment program.**

miniature situation test: one in which the test situation and the test performance are closely similar to their real-life counterparts, concerning which the test is therefore hoped to be more highly predictive.

miniature system: a set of interconnected laws and principles designed to explain a few closely related psychological facts: e.g., a theory to explain rote learning, a theory to explain the facts of audition.—*Cp.* **model.**

minimal: *adj.* pertaining to a **minimum** (which see).

Minimaländerungen (min″i·mäl·en'dər·-ûng·ən): *n. pl.* (*Ger.*) minimal changes.

minimal changes procedure: (*psychophys.*) the procedure in which the experimenter varies the stimulus upward and/or downward by very small amounts. The subject reports the apparent relation (greater or less) to a standard or criterion stimulus. From a number of such comparative judgments, a threshold is calculated.—*Cp.* **just noticeable differences.**

minimal cue: 1. the smallest aspect of a situation that can elicit or modify a response. **2.** a greatly **reduced cue** that elicits at least the major portion of the original response. ➤Such a reduced cue is apparently more effective when it is not specifically attended to. The response elicited may be, or may include, a verbal or subverbal interpretation. E.g., a very slight movement of a person's face immediately elicits the interpretation that "he is bored." Attempts to report the **cue** that led to the interpretation are generally unsuccessful— the analytic attitude is unfavorable to being sensitive to minimal cues.

minimal essentials: those items of instruction in a given field or topic which cannot be dispensed with if what is learned is to have any practical or functional value.

minimum *n., pl.* **minimums, -ma:** (*stat.*) **1.** the lowest value a variable can have. **2.** a value that is less than the values imme-

diately preceding and following it in a series; a low point on a curve. ➤In this sense a series or curve can have several minimums.—*Ant.* **maximum.**—*adj.* **minimal, minimum** (often interchanged).—*v.*

minimize, to reduce a variable to its lowest term.

minimum audible field: see **minimum audible pressure.**

minimum audible pressure: the least pressure *at the eardrum* that can be heard. ➤*Cp.* MINIMUM AUDIBLE FIELD, the least pressure of a sound wave that can be heard, measured at the center of the region occupied by the observer's head (after his withdrawal). The two **thresholds** are not the same.

minimum separable: the minimum distance on the retina two images must be to be seen as two.—*Cp.* **two-point threshold** (on the skin).

Minnesota Multiphasic Inventory or **MMPI:** a personality inventory consisting of a series of 550 statements to be asserted or denied of an individual, usually by himself. The patterns of response characteristic of persons having certain personality qualites (esp. of those tending to certain **neuroses** or **psychoses**) have been empirically determined. Scoring keys are used to detect presence or absence of these patterns.

Minnesota Paper Form Board: a test in which the task is to identify the pictured shapes that will fit into certain pictured outlines. ➤It thus parallels on paper the task of the **formboard,** at least for persons used to working with visual designs.

minor: *adj.* **1.** lesser; smaller; less important.—*n.* **2.** a person below the age of full civil rights and responsibility. **3.** a secondary field of study.

minority group: see **group/minority.**

miosis = **myosis.**

miotic = **myotic.**

mirror drawing: drawing while viewing the hand (and usually the design to be copied or traced) only in a mirror. ➤A common laboratory task is the tracing of a star seen only in a mirror. The task is a test of skill and is suitable for investigating the displacement of an old sensorimotor coordination by a new one.

mirror perception: see **strephosymbolia.**

mirror reversal: the symmetrical right-left shift in apparent position perceived when an object is viewed in a mirror; or any parallel change in position: e.g., one curve may be a **mirror reversal** of another. In reading there may be mirror reversal of single letters (*p* for *q*), of the order of letters within a word (*yam* for *may*), or of the order of a whole line.

mirror self = **self/looking-glass.**

mirror tracing: see **mirror drawing.**

mirror writing or **mirror script**: writing that presents the appearance of ordinary writing when seen in a mirror, i.e., with the left-right relations reversed.—*Syn.* PALINGRAPHIA (not *recom.*).

misanthropy (mis·an′thrə·pi): *n.* hatred of man; aversion to other persons.—*Ant.* philanthropy.—*adj.* **misanthropic** (-throp′-ik).—*pers. n.* **misanthrope** (mis′ən·-thrŏp).

miscegenation (mis″ə·jə·nā′shən): *n.* the marriage or breeding of two different genetic stocks or varieties; in human beings, the physical union of persons of different racial descent. ➤The term is essentially biological. But racial stocks in humans are defined by a mixture of sociological and biological criteria, hence **miscegenation** has no precise reference. In popular use, the term has taken on a condemnatory implication as if it were essentially a "bad" process—in part because the structure of the word vaguely suggests sex or illicit sex—but it has, properly, no valuative implication, and empirical evidence does not indicate that the biological effects of racial mixture are bad.

mischievousness: *n.* **1.** childish behavior that causes annoyance or displeasure to others. **2.** a tendency to violate rules merely for the sake of violating them, or to tease a person in authority, but without serious antisocial intent or revolutionary design.

misdemeanor: *n.* a minor infraction of the law, or of any rule.

mis(o)-: combining form meaning *hating, hatred*.—*Ant.* **philo-**.

misogamy (mi·sog′ə·mi): *n.* hatred of marriage.

misogyny (mi·soj′ə·ni): hatred of women.—*adj.* **misogynous**.—*pers. n.* **mysogynist**.

misperception test: a test that requires a subject to report what he perceives when shown relatively unstructured or ambiguous material. ➤The report is taken to reveal the testee's cognitive background or his inner needs or drives. For the latter, **projective test** (though somewhat ambiguous) is an established usage. Misperception, however, implies incorrectness; and there is no incorrectness in thinking an inkblot looks like two dancing dinosaurs, even though such a report be rare. APPERCEPTION TEST is suggested as better than either **misperception** or **projective test**.

missing-parts test: a test in which the testee must perceive and report what is missing from a picture.

mitosis (mī·tō′səs): *n.* the formation of **gametes** by a cell division in which the chromosomes split, half of each going to the daughter cells.—*Cp.* **reduction division**, in which the chromosomes do not split but segregate, half the number going to each daughter cell.

mixed cerebral dominance: see **dominance/mixed cerebral**.

mixed sampling = **sampling/double**.

mixoscopia (miks″ō·skō′pi·ə): *n.* association of sex excitement with spectatorship of sexual acts.—*adj.* **mixoscopic**.

mixture/color: see **color mixture**.

ml. = **millilambert**.

mm. = **millimeter**.

mμ = **millimicron**.

MMPI = **Minnesota Multiphasic Personality Inventory**.

mneme (nē′mē): *n.* **1.** the enduring basis in a **mind** or in an organism that accounts for the facts of **memory**—i.e., of **recall** or **recognition**.—*Syn.* memory trace. **2.** (*R. Semon*) the fact that any organism—protista, plant, or animal—is enduringly modified by stimulation. ➤The specific effect present when the organism returns to the secondary indifference state is the ENGRAPHIC EFFECT; the change effected in the organic substance is the **engram** of the specific experience. Phenomena that result from engrams are called MNEMIC.—*adj.* **mnemic** (nē′mik; nem-): see above, but note that **mnemic** may also mean merely *related to memory*.

mnemonic (ni·mon′ik): *adj.* pertaining to **memory**, or to the art of **memorizing**; more specif., pertaining to the art of improving memory.—*n.* **mnemonics** (see **mnemotechnics**).

mnemonic trace = **memory trace**.

mnemotechnics (nē″mō·tek′niks): *n.* the art of improving memory. ➤The term has dubious connotations reflecting **faculty psychology**, but there are genuine techniques whereby recall can be made more effective.—*Syn.* MNEMONICS.

-mnesia (-nē′zhə): combining form meaning *memory*: HYPERMNESIA, abnormally complete memory; HYPOMNESIA, abnormally deficient memory; AMNESIA, loss of memory.

Mo = **mode** (1).

mob: *n.* a crowd in which the participants' normal control of their actions gives way to highly emotionalized and violent action, often toward an illegal or antisocial end.

mobility: *n.* **1.** capacity for movement or contraction. ➤*Cp.* MOTILITY, the capacity for those complex coordinated movements which enable the organism to move from place to place or to effect a change in the external world: a face is **mobile**, a person MOTILE. **2.** ability to make a relatively rapid change in one's geographic, social, or occupational location or status. ➤Unless qualified, **social mobility** means motion upward. Note that in (2) the distinction made in (1) between mobility and motility has been lost.—*adj.* **mobile**.

mobility/horizontal: a change from one social position or role to another within the same social stratum or class.

mobility/social: see **social mobility.**

mobility/vertical: movement of persons or groups up or down in social or occupational strata.

modal (mō′dəl): *adj.* pertaining to a **mode.**

modality or **modality/sense** (mō·dal′ə·ti): a sense department, more inclusive than **sense quality,** of data that qualitatively resemble each other more than they resemble other sense data. ➤The sense data of a modality are generally, but not always, mediated by a single type of receptor. The generally accepted list of modalities is: vision, hearing, smell, taste, warmth, coolth, pain, and pressure (the classification of the last two being still unsettled). Certain others are problematic.

The several qualities of one modality form a continuum (yellow grades into green), whereas a continuum from one modality to another (yellow grading into sour or into pain) seems artificial and contrived.—*Syn.* sense (1), SENSE MODE, SENSORY MODALITY (not *recom.*), SENSORY MODE (not *recom.*).

mode: 1. (*stat.*) the most common value or class of values in a series; the peak or peaks in a **frequency curve.** ➤When there is more than one peak, the frequency curve is spoken of as **multimodal,** each such peak being a mode. 2. = sense *modality. 3. (*H. A. Murray*) an action pattern whereby a need is regularly satisfied. 4. a prevailing fashion. 5. (*music*) an arrangement of tones and intervals within the octave according to one of several fixed patterns of relationship: major *mode,* Dorian *mode.*—See **scale/diatonic.**—*adj.* modal.

mode/apparent = **mode/crude.**

mode/computed = **mode/refined.**

mode/crude: the midpoint of the **class interval** containing the greatest number of observations; the midpoint of the modal class.—*Syn.* APPARENT MODE, EMPIRICAL MODE, INSPECTIONAL MODE.—*Ant.* THEORETICAL MODE, **mode/refined.**

mode/empirical = (*stat.*) **mode/crude.**

mode/estimated = **mode/refined.**

mode/inspection = **mode/crude.**

model (mod′əl): *n.* 1. a small copy of the real thing. 2. that which is to be copied, esp. an ideal or perfect form of something.—*Syn.* pattern. 3. a physical device that shows how something works (a working model), or that displays the relationships of parts of a whole (e.g., a model of the solar system).—*Approx. syn.* DISPLAY. 4. a description of a set of data in terms of a system of symbols, and the manipulation of the symbols according to the rules of the system. The resulting transformations are translated back into the language of the data, and the relationships discovered by the manipulations are compared with the empirical facts. ➤The model may be a system of relations

and transformations defined by a particular kind of mathematics. Or it may consist of the set of relations and operating principles of a given empirical theory which are copied for a different set of data. ¶E.g., a preliminary survey indicated that the fibers of the **organ of** *Corti in the ear might resonate like the strings of a harp. It was therefore at one time suggested that the theory of resonance as developed in physics might be a model for a theory of hearing. If this model were applicable, then the relationships and operations of resonating bodies must apply to the organ of Corti, with certain resultant relationships among auditory data. Some of these relations were found not to hold and the model, at least in its simple form, has been abandoned. ¶A model is only a very careful analogy; and the logic of models applies also to very simple analogies. Models are useful for *discovery* of hypotheses, not for verification of theories.

model/conceptual: a diagrammatic representation (usually very complex) of a concept.—See **model** (3).

mode/crude (*stat.*) the midpoint of the class interval containing the greatest number of instances or cases.—*Syn.* APPARENT MODE, EMPIRICAL MODE, INSPECTIONAL MODE.—*Contr. w.* true *mode, refined *mode, theoretical *mode.

mode of appearance: *n.* (*color*) the characteristic way a light or a color appears, depending on how it is perceived as being a light source, a reflected or surface light or color, a film color, an aperture color, or the like.

mode pleasure: the satisfaction that is independent of attaining a goal and that results purely from the way an activity is performed; the satisfaction attained in **play.**

mode/refined: (*stat.*) an estimate of the value of the **mode** in the **universe** from which a given sample is drawn.—*Syn.* ESTIMATED MODE, COMPUTED MODE.—*Ant.* crude *mode, true *mode.

modesty: *n.* 1. unpretentiousness; self-effacement or self-depreciation. 2. conformity with convention regarding display of the body. ➤A degree of display permitted on the beach would be highly immodest in a drawing room. 3. conformity with convention in the display of courtship activities and love-making.

mode/theoretical: (*stat.*) an estimate of the **true** *mode; the abscissa corresponding to the maximum ordinate of the theoretical frequency curve fitted to a given set of observations.

mode/true: the mode in the universe from which a given sample is drawn. In any infinite universe, it is necessarily unknown. It is estimated by the **theoretical** *mode.

modification: *n.* 1. any change in structure or behavior. 2. (*genet.*) variations in the phenotype due to environmental influences. —*v.* **modify.**

modulator/visual: (*R. Granit*) a hypothesized specific receptor yielding a specific or unique sensation of **hue.** ➤How many kinds of modulators are in the retina is not determined. **Brightness** is attributed to a different receptor mechanism.

mogi-: (moj'i-): combining form meaning *difficult, painful.*

mogigraphia (-graf'i·ə): *n.* writer's cramp.

mogilalia (-lā'li·ə): *n.* difficult speech, such as stuttering or stammering.—*Syn.* MOLILALIA.

mogiphonia (-fō'ni·ə): *n.* difficulty in speaking because of overuse of the voice or of the effort to speak loudly.

molar (mō'lər): *adj.* 1. pertaining to a **mass** or masses. 2. pertaining to that which is relatively large and unanalyzed.—See **molar behavior.**

molar behavior: 1. a large-unit segment of the total behavior stream that possesses essential unity. 2. a unit of the behavior stream whose unity and distinctness derive from the ends it serves or the effects it produces in the external world. ➤It is not implied that all behaviors leading to the same goal belong in the same unit; the molar unit is a unit of actually occurring behavior, not a class. Thus, the varied ways a person behaves in getting to his office—by motoring, walking, or bicycling—are equivalent, but the molar unit consists in the particular way in which he actually did get there. 3. a behavior unit considered as an **emergent** phenomenon, having qualities not statable as a sum of the parts. 4. (*E. C. Tolman*) any behavior that shows **docility** —i.e., that has been learned and may be further modified by learning. 5. behavior described in nonphysiological, psychological constructs.

➤To assert that these five definitions refer to the same data is to take a theoretical position, though they undoubtedly do to some extent. ¶**Molar behavior** is contrasted with **molecular behavior,** a small unit, generally defined in terms of specific movements, or of specific movements elicited by specific stimuli, or in physiological terms. As the opposite of (3), **molecular** means the behavior unit reached by **reductive *analysis.** ¶The distinction between molar and molecular is not absolute in practice—it is often difficult to say whether a unit is molar or molecular; probably the distinction is not absolute in theory. The terms characterize not so much two classes of behavior as two ways of describing or conceiving the same behavior event. *Going to class* would probably be called molar behavior in all five senses; but the same phenomenon can also

be described as a sequence of molecular units, i.e., as a series of stepping movements or even as a succession of neuromuscular processes. (But some writers would characterize the last as not molecular but **atomistic.**)

molarism: *n.* a preference for the study of **molar behavior** as the best (or only) subject matter of psychology.—See **psychology/divisions and schools of, VII.**

molar stimulus trace = stimulus trace.

molecular (mō·lek'ū·lər): *adj.* 1. pertaining to molecules. 2. characterizing the relatively small, or that which is the product of detailed analysis.—See **molecular behavior.** —*Contr. w.* **molar.**

molecular behavior: 1. behavior described in units of isolated muscular movements or glandular activities. 2. behavior described as composed of physiological-neurological activities, whether observed or (more often) inferred or postulated. 3. behavior described in relatively small units.—*Contr. w.* **molar behavior,** which see for discussion of both.

molecularism: *n.* an emphasis upon **molecular behavior** as preferred subject matter in psychology.—See **psychology/divisions and schools of, VII.**

molilalia = mogilalia.

molimina/premenstrual (mō·lim'ə·nə): physiological or psychic symptoms, differing from woman to woman, in the three or four days preceding the menstrual period.—*Syn.* PREMENSTRUAL TENSION.

moment: *n.* 1. a minute time interval; an instant. 2. (*stat.*) the average of the deviations from a mean (or from some other reference point) after each deviation has been raised to a certain power: $\Sigma x^m/N$ wherein x is any deviation, m is the power to which each x is raised, and N is the number of cases. ➤The ORDER of the moment is given by the power: if the deviations are squared (x^2), we have the SECOND-ORDER MOMENT. PRODUCT MOMENTS are those in which the deviations of two (or more) variables from their respective means are raised to a certain power and multiplied before summation: $\Sigma x^m y^n/N$. The Pearson formula for correlation utilizes the second-order product moment.

momism: *n.* (*pop.*) excessive dependence upon one's mother or mother substitute.

monadism (mon'əd·iz·əm; mō-): *n.* Leibnitz's doctrine that reality is composed of ultimate units of being, or MONADS, each pursuing its development according to an inward law. These units are combined in systems of increasing complexity of organization, each of which is also a monad. **Self** or **soul** is a very complex monad, but the material world is also made up of monads. —See **psychology/divisions and schools of, IV.**

monaural (mon·ô′rəl): *adj.* **uniaural;** pertaining to hearing with one ear.

mongolism: *n.* a congenital condition characterized by a flat skull, oblique eye slit, stubby fingers and thumbs, and a fissured tongue. Severe **mental *deficiency** at **imbecile** or **idiot** level is an invariable accompaniment.—*Syn.* MONGOLIAN IMBECILITY, MONGOLIAN IDIOCY.—*pers. n.* **mongol(ian).**

monism: *n.* 1. the view that ultimate reality is of only one kind or quality.—*Ant.* **dualism** or (from one point of view) **pluralism.** 2. the view that the phenomena of psychology are of the same kind as, or are completely reducible to, those of the physical sciences; practically = **mechanism (1).**—*Ant.* **mentalism.** ➤The assumption that monism is scientific is false; both monism and dualism are **metaphysical** doctrines concerning which science is neutral. —See **psychology/divisions and schools of, IV.**

monitor: *v.* to attend to any activity or operation, whether of machine or organism, giving warning when the operation is not proceeding properly. ➤Machines can be built to monitor other machines or organisms, and in **feedback** to monitor themselves. Persons also can monitor.—*n.* **monitoring.**

mon(o)-: prefix meaning *single, only, alone, one.*

monochorionic twins: see **twins/monochorionic.**

monochromatic vision: an abnormality of vision in which all colors are perceived as matching a single primary color of varying degrees of **brightness** and **saturation.**—*Syn.* MONOCHROMATISM.

monocular: *adj.* pertaining to one eye; or to vision with only one eye.—*Syn.* **uniocular.**

monogamy: *n.* the marriage system in which each partner has but a single mate; the durable pairing of two persons of opposite sex.—*Cp.* **polygamy, polygyny, polyandry, promiscuity.**—*adj.* **monogamous.**

mono-ideism (mon″ō-ī·dē′iz·əm): *n.* obsession with a single idea; inability to think of anything else but one idea. The singleness is seldom quite complete.

monomania: *n.* obsolete term formerly applied to **paranoid** conditions.

monoplegia (-plē′ji·ə): *n.* paralysis of one limb or other single muscle group.

monorhinic (-rin′ik): *adj.* smelling with one nostril only.

monotic (mon·ō′tik): *adj.* affecting a single ear; esp. as in MONOTIC STIMULUS, one presented to a single ear.

monotone: *n.* a person who sings or speaks with very little change of pitch.

monotonic: *adj.* 1. of that which has but one quality or **tone.** 2. pertaining to two variables so related that, for each value or magnitude of one, there is one and only one value for the other. ➤A continuously rising or falling curve can represent two such variables.

monotony: *n.* 1. speaking or singing upon a single tone; lack of inflection, change of tone, or cadence in speech. 2. the continuance of a situation with little or no change; or the repetition of the same response over and over.—*adj.* **monotonous.**

monozygotic (mon″ō·zī·got′ik): *adj.* (*genet.*) developed from a single **zygote** or fertilized ovum; esp. as in MONOZYGOTIC TWINS, those developing from a single egg **(identical *twins).**—*Var.* **monozygous** (-zī′gəs).—*n.* **monozygosity.**

monster: *n.* 1. an organism deviating very greatly from the type of the species, generally in an unfavorable or maladaptive direction. ➤*Cp.* **sport,** a lesser deviation; and **malformation,** a deviation confined to an organ or part. 2. a person whose antisocial or immoral behavior is so grave that normal persons recoil from him.

mood: *n.* 1. a relatively mild emotional state, enduring or recurrent; an echo of an emotional reaction with or without remembrance of the original stimulus.—*Cp.* **temperament.** 2. an internal state of readiness for a specific kind of emotional response: excited, joyful, depressed, etc.

Mooney Problem Check List: a questionary for high school or college students concerning their persisting difficulties or problems.

moot: *adj.* debatable.

moral: *adj.* 1. pertaining to **morals** or **morality.** 2. characterizing a person or conduct as being in accord with the individual's own code of morals or with the code of the group with which he identifies himself. ➤For the several antonyms, see **immoral.**

moral code: a set of rules accepted in a given society or large social group as binding upon everyone in the group. Violations are punished by strong group disapproval, sometimes also by legal process.

morale (môr·al′): *n.* a prevailing temper or spirit, in the individuals forming a group, which is marked by confidence in the group, self-confidence with respect to one's role in the group, group loyalty, and readiness to strive for group goals. ➤GROUP MORALE is the composite of the individuals' morale.—*Syn.* group **cohesiveness.**

moral imbecility or **insanity:** obsolescent term denoting inability to understand moral principles and values and to act accordingly, though in some cases no other mental deficiency is discoverable.

morality: *n.* 1. that quality of conduct which

makes it right or wrong. **2.** = **morals.**
➤Standards of right and wrong may be
worked out by the individual or (more
often) may result from social evolution. In
either case, morality accepted by the individual is INTERNAL MORALITY, that imposed
by coercive sanctions is EXTERNAL MORAL-
ITY. But issues of right and wrong are
regarded as having a special urgency, a
peculiar sanctity.—See **morals, mores,
ethics.**—*adj.* **moral.**

moral realism: (*J. Piaget*) an attitude
found in small children (occasionally in
others) that rightness and wrongness inhere
in certain conducts and are *objectively* perceptible and self-evident. ➤The child is apt
to believe that anyone can *perceive* the badness—not merely judge it—when someone
takes what does not belong to him. The badness is considered to be as objectively real
as the speed with which the act is performed.

morals: *n. pl.* **1.** an individual's personal
standards of conduct as right or wrong; or,
more often, the standards of the group with
which he identifies himself. **2.** actual conduct in reference to standards of right and
wrong. ➤**Morality** is the abstract character of behavior as right or wrong; **morals**
are the concrete standards or the concrete
behavior. To ask about morality is to raise
a question of whether the conduct is of such
nature that it is to be judged right or
wrong; to ask about morals is to raise the
question of how well the moral standards
are observed, or of what they are. The
distinction, however, is not always observed.—*Cp.* also **ethics, mores.**—*adj.*
moral.

morbid, morbidity: see **pathology.**

nores (môr′ēz) *n. pl., s.* (*rare*) **mos** (mōs):
those customs of a social group that are
egarded as having a peculiar sanction
o that violation brings condemnation upon
the offender. ➤The term is much used to
emphasize the social origin of **morals,** in
contrast to a divine injunction or a rational
ethical design.—*adj.* **moretic** (môr·ē′tik)
(*rare*).

Morgan's canon or **principle:** a maxim
formulated by Lloyd Morgan in 1894: "In
no case may we interpret an action as the
outcome of the exercise of a higher psychical
faculty if it can be interpreted as the outcome of one which stands lower in the
psychological scale." ➤Thus, an act should
not be described as **thinking** if it can be
described as **memory;** or as memory if it
can be described as **reflex.** The maxim is
often misquoted and made the basis for inferences it cannot bear. It is related to the
principle of *parsimony (which see).

moron: *n.* a person with the least degree of
mental *deficiency that is recognized

definitely as such. ➤The popular or newspaper usage of **moron** for a sex offender of
low intelligence is without warrant.—*adj.*
moronic.

Moro reflex: a response of the newborn infant, elicited by a forcible blow to the surface on which he is lying, which consists of
general clutching movements of the arms
and legs. The response gradually evolves into
a fine quick body jerk.

morpheme: *n.* the smallest linguistic unit
with a meaning of its own. ➤It is composed
of one or more **phonemes.** *Hat* is a morpheme with only one phoneme. *Hats,* a
morpheme because of its distinctive meaning, is made up of two phonemes, *hat* and *s.*
The morpheme may mean a thing (LEXICAL
MORPHEME), or a relation (RELATIONAL
MORPHEME).

morphogenesis: *n.* the origin and development of form or structure in an organism.

morphological index: a combination of
various measures of bodily proportions
which yields a single figure to describe a
person's physique.—See **body build.**

morphology: *n.* the biological science that
deals with bodily forms and structures.—
Syn. **anatomy.**

mortality: *n.* **1.** the proportion of deaths to
a population or to a specific population
group; the death rate. **2.** metaphorically, the
proportion of those who fail to meet some
prescribed test: e.g., academic *mortality,* the
proportion dismissed or resigning from
school or college.

mortido (môr·tē′dō): *n.* the **death instinct.**

mosaic: *n.* a design made of many small
pieces, separately perceptible upon close
examination; any combination of parts resembling such a design.

mosaic hypothesis = **bundle hypothesis.**

mosaic test: a **projective test** in which
the task is to "make anything you like out
of the pieces," the pieces being 465 small
wooden bits of different colors and shapes.
—*Syn.* LOWENFELD TEST.

mother complex = **Oedipus complex.**

mother figure: the analogue of **father
figure.**—See also **figure** (5).

mother right: see **father right.**

mother surrogate: see **surrogate.**

motif (mō·tēf′): *n.* a dominating feature or
theme.

motile: *n.* a person whose preferred sensory
imagery is of his own movements.—*Distg.
fr.* **motile,** the adjective of **motility.**

motility: *n.* **1.** see **mobility. 2.** the style
and speed with which a person moves.—
adj. **motile.**

motion: *n.* any displacement of a **mass.**
➤*Cp.* **movement,** which is motion by an
organism or one of its parts.

motion/apparent or **movement/apparent:**

an illusion of motion elicited by certain patterns of nonmoving stimuli (or of stimuli not moving in the manner perceived). ➤In vision, several kinds of apparent motion studied tachistoscopically have received distinctive names: the ALPHA MOVEMENT, in which otherwise similar objects of different size are rapidly presented and the viewer sees one object as shrinking or expanding; the BETA MOVEMENT, in which there is a similar shift in position; the GAMMA MOVEMENT, in which a single object presented successively seems to expand or shrink if the illumination is altered from one presentation to the next; the DELTA MOVEMENT, in which the objective position is the same but seems to shift with change in illumination; the BOW MOVEMENT, in which under certain conditions the perceived motion is curved; the SPLIT MOVEMENT, in which an object (generally a line) seems to divide—one part moving in one direction, the other in another—to form a new figure which is that of a second exposed object. *Cp.* **phi phenomenon.** Motion pictures are a familiar form of apparent motion. ¶In all these terms, **motion** would be a better word than **movement** (see **movement**), but the latter is more frequently used.—*Syn.* **phi phenomenon,** best reserved for another meaning; ILLUSORY MOTION (*ambig.*); PHENOMENAL MOTION.

motion/phenomenal = motion/apparent.

motion study: systematic observation of the repetitive movements involved in a certain task in order to discover the most efficient sequence of each element of the cycle.

motivate: *v.* **1.** to rouse an organism to action by activating a **motivation (2);** to provide an **incentive. 2.** (of an object) to serve as an incentive or goal.

motivation: *n.* **1.** the nonstimulus variables controlling behavior; the general name for the fact that an organism's acts are partly determined in direction and strength by its own nature (or enduring structure) and/or internal state. ➤When the term is thus used, it contrasts with two other determinants of action: **ability,** and the **stimulus** or **situation.** But since the stimulus is conceived as touching off the motivation, it is sometimes half included under that term. **2.** a specific hypothesized process that energizes differentially certain responses, thus making them dominant over other possible responses to the same situation; a specific hypothesized personal or organismic determiner of the direction and/or strength of action or of a line of action: his *motivation* was easily inferred.—*Syn.* **motive** (which see). *Cp.* **drive,** often used as a synonym. Hull's momentary effective **excitatory potential** attempts to give a

quantitative statement of this concept.—*v.* **to be motivated. 3.** an activity by a second person designed to arouse motivation (in sense 2) in the first person: the teacher's *motivation* of the pupils was efficient, so that their *motivation* to study was high.—See **extrinsic motivation, incentive.**—*v.* **motivate.** ➤It is interesting that only this meaning of **motivation** has found its way into general dictionaries, despite the fact that professional usage has emphasized sense (2) for at least thirty years.

An extraordinary number of terms name various aspects or classes of motivation. The following list (each term is defined in its proper place) is undoubtedly incomplete: ambition, **appet, appetite, attitude, complex, craving, desire, determining tendency, disposition, drive, emotion, end, goal, habit, homeostasis, horme, impulse, incentive, instinct, interest, libido, motive, need, preference, purpose, sentiment, set, temperament,** tendency to action, **urge, valence, value,** want, **wish.**

While many authors carefully define some terms relating to motivation, there is much loose usage. Two anchor points are **need** and **goal.** Need refers to a lack in the organism or person, a deficiency. There may or may not be awareness of the need, and it may or may not be defined in terms of physiological process or tissue state. The goal is an end result, a state or condition which, when attained, brings to an end a directed course of behavior or action. ¶Between the need and the goal lies the behavior leading to the goal; but most psychologists hypothesize also a **personal** or **organic** determiner of the behavior that is not wholly a function of the need. For this need-instigated, goal-oriented determiner, **motivation (2)** or **motive (3)** are the most general terms. **Drive,** while often given very specific definition, is frequently used interchangeably with motivation, as are desire, wish, urge, craving, and even purpose. But need itself, without postulating an intervening motive, is considered by many to be directly determinant of action; hence, need takes its place less as a synonymous *term* than as a substitute *construct* for **motive (3).** (But those who thus stress need may use **motive** in sense 1 or 2 of that term.)

Somewhat similarly, while a goal does not unambiguously identify the motive, the relation is close; hence, goal and motive are often equated or even used interchangeably.

motivation/conjunctive: (*H. S. Sullivan*) striving for a real or permanent satisfaction of needs.—*Ant.* **motivation/disjunctive.**

motivation/disjunctive: (*H. S .Sullivan*) a motivation displaced from satisfaction of a real need toward a substitute that offers some measure of immediate, but not long-run, satisfaction.—*Cp.* **motivation/conjunctive.**

motivation/extrinsic: see **extrinsic motivation.**

motivation/goal-directed: motivation (2) directed toward a specific outside object. ➤The term is a condensed expression for "that behavior of the animal on a number of occasions which leads to the inference of a specific characteristic determining whether and how the animal seeks or avoids a certain goal."

motivation/internal: one derived from changes within the organism: e.g., sleep, hunger, thirst.—*Cp.* **need, appetite.**

motivation/intrinsic or **motive/intrinsic:** a motivation in which the satisfaction or **incentive** conditions are obtained within the activity itself. ➤*Distg. fr.* EXTRINSIC MOTIVATION, in which the satisfaction is artificially related to the activity, e.g., by giving a prize. The distinction is by no means as absolute as it sounds. Any complex situation affords both extrinsic and intrinsic motivational elements. Moreover, a motivation, at first extrinsic, may come to be intrinsic: i.e., an activity at first engaged in for outside satisfactions becomes itself satisfying.

motivation/primary: **1.** motivation that seeks to meet a need without being directed toward a specific outside object: e.g., a hunger motive not directed toward a particular food. ➤It is almost a synonym for **internal *motivation. 2.** an unlearned motivation.—*Syn.* **primary *drive, primary *need.**

motivation research: (*advertising*) a study of consumer motivation; the attempt to discover motives, esp. hidden motives, that may be appealed to in order to induce persons to buy, or motives that must be circumvented lest they refuse to buy. ➤There is no attempt to relate goods to real needs but only to relate sales appeal to favorable attitudes and motives. Psychoanalytic concepts are extensively employed: e.g., a certain appeal is rejected because it is supposed to meet resistance generated by the Oedipus complex.

motivation/secondary: a learned motivation; one that is not directly related to the satisfaction of a **primary *need.**—*Cp.* **primary *motivation (2).**

motivation/unconscious: a motivation inferred from the person's prevailing pattern of behavior but of which he himself is not aware.

motive: *n.* **1.** that which one consciously assigns as the basis of his behavior. **2.** the consciously sought goal which is considered to determine behavior. **3.** a specific personal or organismic factor controlling behavior; any state or event within the organism that (under appropriate circumstances) initiates or regulates behavior in relation to a goal; = **motivation (2).** ➤Originally, **motive** strongly carried the meaning of a **conscious** factor, something of which one was aware. The psychoanalytic schools preserve the distinction but postulate conscious and **unconscious** motives. Currently, **motive** tends to lose all connotation of that which can be known by the actor: it is much employed even in animal experimentation and by behaviorists, competing with **motivation (2)** as the most general term. Partial synonyms, often used interchangeably, are **drive,** want, **need, incentive,** each of which has specific meanings.

motive/avoidance: see **avoidance motive.**

motive/extrinsic or **/intrinsic:** see **motivation/intrinsic.**

motive/physiological: a motive based on a demonstrable body need, as for food or water.—*Syn.* ORGANIC MOTIVE.—*Contr. w.* **social motive.**

motoneuron: *n.* a nerve cell in direct connection with an **effector.**

motor: *adj.* pertaining to muscular movement (or by extension, to muscular movement and/or glandular activity), or to that which causes movement; pertaining to the executive aspect of organismic activity.

motor aphasia: see **aphasia.**

motor apraxia = ideokinetic *apraxia.

motor area: that portion of the brain wherein pointlike electrical stimulation produces contraction of specific circumscribed muscles. It includes the ascending pre-Rolandic convolution and certain neighboring areas. In general, the motor area coincides with the **motor *cortex** and with the **motorium.**

motor cell = **motor nerve.**

motor cortex: see **cortex/motor.**

motor diffusion: the tendency, found in the early developmental stages, to make widespread and nonspecific responses.

motor equivalence: the fact that a single result is brought about by any of a number of different muscular movements: e.g., a child can spell his own name orally or can print or write it; or a rat can depress the escape lever with his paw or with his teeth.

motor functions: **1.** a general term for any movement classified according to what it accomplishes; = distal response (see **distal vs. proximal variables**). **2.** a general term for **efferent** neural processes and the end-organ activities excited thereby.

motor habit: a habit defined specifically in terms of the movements made, rather than in terms of the sensory discriminations made (sometimes called SENSORY HABITS), or of the end adjustment which the response secures. ➤The distinction is only a loose one.

motor incoordination = incoordination (2).

motorium (mō·tôr'i·əm): *n.* the brain centers directly involved in the **innervation** of skeletal muscles.—*Syn.* **motor area.**

motor learning: learning in which the task is described in **motor** terms. ➤*Contr. w.* **ideational** ***learning,** in which the task is to understand certain ideas or relations. The distinction is not basic; motor learning generally involves ideational elements, and vice versa.

motor nerve: an **efferent** nerve terminating in a muscle; by extension, an efferent nerve terminating in a muscle or gland.

motor point: the junction of a motor nerve with muscles.

motor primacy theory: the hypothesis 'hat the bodily mechanisms for movement develop before the sensory mechanisms are fully ready for functioning.

motor reaction type: see **reaction type.**

motor sense: a sense dependent upon **proprioceptors; kinesthesis.**

motor theory of consciousness: the theory that **consciousness** is the **subjective** correlate of motor activity. ➤The theory displaces emphasis upon the **sensory** or **afferent** with emphasis upon the **efferent;** or perhaps it may be said to emphasize that an entire neural circuit from stimulation to motor response is necessary to consciousness. More specifically, it holds that the particular quality of consciousness is due to the motor response: that how one perceives an object depends on how one reacts to it muscularly, either overtly or in muscular set.

motor theory of meaning: see **meaning/ context theory of (3).**

motor unit (*anat.*) the nerve cell, its axon, and the muscle fibers supplied by it.

mouches volantes (müsh vō·länt'): *n. pl.* (*Fr., flying flies*) flylike specks, in the transparent substances of the eye, which are occasionally seen to dance in the field of vision. They are always present but are normally unobserved.—*Syn.* MUSCAE VOLITANTES.

movement: *n.* **1.** any **motion.** ➤This usage is to be discouraged in psychology. **2.** a change in position of an organism or of one or more of its parts. ➤When the change results from the organism's own muscular contraction, it is called ACTIVE MOVEMENT; when from external force, it is PASSIVE MOVEMENT. (But note that passive movement almost always involves some muscular activity.)

movement/apparent: see **motion/apparent.**

movement/ballistic: a movement in which a bodily member (hand, leg, eyeball, head) is "thrown" in a certain direction by a muscular contraction that ceases before the excursion is completed, the full excursion being completed by momentum. ➤Ballistic movement is necessarily rapid. *Cp.* **movement/tension.**

movement determinant: see **determinant/ Rorschach.**

movement/freedom of: see **freedom of movement.**

movement/illusion of: the illusion that one's body or some bodily part is in motion although it is not. ➤*Distg. fr.* **apparent** ***motion,** in which some part of the external world is falsely perceived to be in motion.

movement image: see **imagination (2).**

movement/involuntary: see **involuntary.**

movement/phi: see **phi phenomenon.**

movement/random: see **random activity.**

movement response or *M*: (*Ror.*) a response imputing human movement, or movement of an animal acting like a human, to the **inkblot** pattern. ➤*M* is an important **Rorschach** ***determinant.**—*Cp. m,* a **motion** response.

movements/associated: see **associated movements.**

movement/tension: slow movement of a bodily part (arm, foot, head) in which the **agonist** and **antagonist** muscles are in continuous opposition to each other. ➤Two kinds are distinguished. In FIXATION MOVEMENT, the motion may be practically null: this is the movement of holding still, with the opposed muscles pulling equally. In MOVING FIXATION, the tension is maintained, but one set of muscles pulls more strongly on the bodily part. *Cp.* **movement/ballistic.**

movement/voluntary: 1. a movement made as a result of **intent** or **volition. 2.** (*anat.*) a movement controlled by the **cerebrospinal nervous system,** in contrast to one controlled by the **autonomic nervous system.**—See **nervous system.** ➤This meaning represents a confused mixture of anatomic considerations with an obsolescent psychology.

moving average: see **moving total.**

moving fixation: see **movement/tension.**

moving total: a method of smoothing a succession of items by replacing each item by the sum of that item and a fixed number of adjacent items. E.g., a three-month moving total would enter for Feb. the sum of data for Jan., Feb., and Mar.; for Mar. the sum of Feb., Mar., and Apr.; etc. For a MOVING AVERAGE, successive totals are divided by *N*.—*Syn.* MOVING SUM.

ms., msec. = millisecond: .001 second.

μ-test (mū-): *n.* a test of the unusualness of the size of a mean or other sampling statistic.

MU = the equal mental units of growth postulated by Heinis.—See **Heinis constant.**

Müller-Lyer illusion (mY'lər-lir″): the distorted perception of length when a line has arrowheads, or reversed arrowheads or "feathers," as in the figure. The former

looks shorter, the latter longer, than an unadorned straight line.

Müller-Schumann law: When any two items, A and B, have been associated, it is more difficult to form an association between either and a third item, K.

Müller-Urban method: (*psychophys.*) a procedure, for treating data from the **constant stimulus method**, that assumes that the best measure of the **threshold** is the median of the best-fitting ogive curve for the observed distribution.

Müller-Urban weighting: (*psychophys.*) a procedure in fitting observations to the normal curve for determining the best value of *h*, the measure of precision. At $p = .50$, the weight is a maximum of 1.00; at $p = .01$ or .99 the weights are at a minimum.

multi-: Latin prefix meaning *many* or *various*: *multilateral*, many-sided. ➤For words of Greek origin, **poly-** should be used.

multicellular: *adj.* composed of many cells.

multidimensional scaling: a method for ascertaining the number of factors required to describe a large set of judgments of the form "*i* is more like *j* than it is like *k*," repeating this form of judgment for all possible triplets of the items of the classes represented by *i, j, k.*

multigroup method: (*R. B. Cattell*) a factor analysis that extracts all factors simultaneously instead of successively.—Also called **multiple-group method,** which however may extract fewer than *all* factors.

multimodal: *adj.* of a **distribution** that has at least two modes or peaks.—*Cp.* **bimodal,** having two modes.

multimodal theory of intelligence: the theory that intelligence is a composite of a very large number of specific abilities.

multiordinal terms: terms that can represent several levels of abstraction, depending on the context in which they are used: e.g., *hate of hate* is different from *hate.*

multiphasic test: see **Minnesota Multiphasic Inventory.**

multiple birth: the bearing and delivery of more than one offspring in a single pregnancy. ➤The offspring—twins, triplets, etc. —may be fraternal or identical or any combination thereof.

multiple-choice experiment: a type of test for perceptual discrimination or for learning. ➤In the Yerkes MULTIPLE-CHOICE BOX, the person or animal obtains a reward if he opens the correct door of several. The correct door is shifted from trial to trial but is identified either by a perceptual cue, such as a certain color, or by its position in a temporal series, e.g., successively the second, fourth, sixth doors.

multiple-choice test: see **test/selective answer.**

multiple correlation: see **correlation/ multiple.**

multiple determination/coefficient of or **R^2:** in **multiple *correlation,** that percentage of the correlation between two variables which can be accounted for by the effects of other variables when it is assumed that all the factors in the independent variables are included within the determining factors of the dependent variable. It is the square of the multiple *R*. The COEFFICIENT OF MULTIPLE NONDETERMINATION is $1 - {_c}R^2$ or K^2.

multiple-discriminant technique: (*stat.*) a generalization of Fisher's **discriminant function** technique in a design where a score is used to assign an individual to more than one classification.—*Syn.* MULTIPLE-REGRESSION PATTERN ANALYSIS.

multiple-factor: an adjective phrase applied especially to a theory or to an analytic method that postulates the possibility of more than one common factor in a battery of tests.—See **factor analysis.**

multiple-factor inheritance: control of the genetic portion of variability of a trait by the combined action of several pairs of **genes:** e.g., in man, many genes control body size or skin color.

multiple-group method: a **factor analysis** that extracts several factors simultaneously instead of successively.—See also **multigroup method.**

multiple personality: see **personality/ multiple.**

multiple R = correlation/multiple.

multiple-regression equation: see **regression equation/multiple-.**

multiple response/principle of: An animal reacts to a novel situation with a varied repertory of plausible responses.—*Syn.* PRINCIPLE OF VARIED REACTION.

multiple-response test: see **test/multiple-response.**

multiple sclerosis: a diseased condition characterized by hardening of many spots in the brain and cord, with resulting impairment of behavior.

multiple scoring = **scoring/differential.**

multiplicity: *n.* the quality of being made up of many components.

multipolar nerve cell: one having many prolongations from the cell body.

multitrait measurement: measurement using a scale that is sensitive to the joint effect of many traits. ➤All measurements to some extent reflect the functioning of several traits or of the whole individual. In multitrait measurement, no attempt is made to single out the variation of a single trait. Instead, full effect is allowed to the interaction of traits upon each other.—See **causation/principle of multiple.**

multivariate: *adj.* characterizing a measure that reflects several variables.

multivariate test: a statistical test for detecting differences between groups, not in respect to each variable taken separately, but in respect to all available variables.

mumbled speech or **mumbling:** indistinct and sluggish articulation of speech, regardless of origin.—*Syn.* ASAPHOLALIA.

Mundugumor: *n.* a primitive people of New Guinea studied by M. Mead and widely cited as typical of a society dominated by competitive aggression. ➤This is an oversimplification deplored by Mead.

Munsell color system (mun·sel'): an atlas of about 1000 standard **surface *color** samples by means of which to specify the **hue, color value,** and **chroma** of any other surface color. The standard colors of the atlas are arranged in what purport to be equal visual intervals along each of the three dimensions, and each sample is specified by a letter-number notation. A comparison color can be specified by assigning it the notation of the standard color it most resembles or by interpolation between two standards. ➤The MUNSELL BOOK NOTATION refers to the original *Book of Color* (1929) ; MUNSELL RENOTATION refers to a revised notation giving different scale values to the standard color samples.

muscae volitantes (mus'sē vol"i·tan'tēz): *n. pl.* (*L., flying flies*) = *mouches volantes.*

muscle: *n.* a bundle of many fibers of **contractile** tissue. ➤Each muscle has been given a name. In addition, they are classified as **antagonistic muscles, skeletal** or **striate *muscles, smooth** or **unstriped *muscles.**

muscle action potential: see **action potential.**

muscle/antagonistic: see **antagonistic muscles.**

muscle balance: (*ophthal.*) the tendency to maintain a position of fixation with either eye when **fusion** is prevented.—See **imbalance/muscular.**

muscle reading: the interpretation, usually through contact, of slight involuntary movements and the "reading" thereby of a person's mind, i.e., of the direction of his thoughts.

muscle sensation: 1. the particular quality of pressure felt when the sense organs in the muscles are stimulated. **2.** awareness of such quality; loosely, awareness of a muscular movement, i.e., movement perceiving.— *Syn.* (for 2) **kinesthesis.**

muscle sense: see **kinesthesis.**

muscle/skeletal: see **muscle/striate.**

muscle/smooth: see **muscle/striate.**

muscle spindle: see **spindle/muscle.**

muscle/striate or **/striped:** a muscle having a striped appearance under the microscope. ➤SKELETAL MUSCLE (attached to a part of the skeleton) is used as a synonym, although technically the heart (which is not so attached) is also a striate muscle.— *Contr. w.* UNSTRIPED or SMOOTH MUSCLES, which present a smooth appearance under the microscope, and which line the walls of the gastrointestinal tract and of the blood vessels. The anatomical division corresponds roughly with function: the skeletal muscles move the organism in its environment, the smooth muscles chiefly promote internal adjustment. The former are innervated by the **somatic** section of the central nervous system, and most of them can be brought under voluntary control. The latter are innervated by the **autonomic nervous system** and are involuntary.

muscle tonus = **tonus.**

muscle twitch: a derogatory term for the ultimate analytic unit of response as conceived by behaviorists. ➤The term is inaccurate: a twitch is a larger complex than the single-fiber contraction of behaviorist theory; and neither the convulsiveness nor the suddenness of the true twitch is applicable. Muscle twitch was chosen by opponents because for some subtle reason it sounded ridiculous.

muscle/unstriped: see **muscle/striate.**

muscle/voluntary: see **voluntary muscle.**

muscular type: see **reaction type.**

musculature (mus'kū·lə·chər): *n.* collective term for all the muscles; often, = SKELETAL MUSCULATURE, all the skeletal muscles.

mussitation: *n.* **1.** = **mumbling. 2.** speechless moving of the lips.

mutation: *n.* an abrupt change in the nature of a gene so that it thenceforth reduplicates itself in a new form. It may or may not be immediately observable as a change in **phenotype.**—*adj.* **mutant, mutating.**

mute: see **mutism.**

muteness: see **mutism.**

mutism (mū'tiz·əm): *n.* **1.** lack of speech development resulting from congenital or early deafness; deaf-mutism. **2.** inhibition, voluntary or involuntary, of speech; refusal to speak.—*Syn.* MUTITAS, DUMBNESS. —*adj.* and *pers. n.* **mute.**—*abstr. n.* **muteness,** the quality of being mute.

mutitas (mū′ti·təs): *n.* (*obs.*) = **mutism.**

mutual: *adj.* 1. of two things having the same relationship each with the other. 2. shared alike and reciprocally by each member of a (pair or) group.

m.v. = mean variation = **mean *deviation.**

*μ*v. = microvolt.

myasthenia (mī″as·thē′ni·ə): *n.* muscular weakness resulting from disease.

mydriasis (mi·drī′ə·səs): *n.* extreme or abnormal dilation of the pupil of the eye.— *Ant.* **myosis.**—*adj.* **mydriatic** (mid″ri·-at′ik).

myelencephalon (mī″ə·len·sef′ə·lon): *n.* (*neurol.*) the lower part of the embryonic **hindbrain,** which develops into the **medulla oblongata.**—*adj.* **myelencephalic** (-sef·al′ik).

myelin (mī′ə·lən): *n.* the white fatty material that surrounds the **medullated** nerve fibers, forming the MYELIN SHEATH (= **medullary sheath).**

myelinization (mī″ə·lin·ə·zā′shən): *n.* the formation of the **myelin** sheath. ➤A much-used but indirect index of the nerve's readiness to function.—*Var.* **myelination.**

myelinogenetic law: the principle that a nerve is usually not ready to function until the **myelin** sheath has developed.

myelitis (mī″ə·lī′təs): *n.* inflammation of the spinal cord.

myelon (mī′ə·lon): *n.* the **spinal cord.**

my(o)- (mī′ō-): prefix meaning *muscle* or *muscular.*

myoclonus (-klō′nəs): *n.* muscular spasms of alternating rigidity and relaxation.

myoesthesis (-es·thē′səs): *n.* the sensation of muscle activity.—*Syn.* **kinesthesis.**

myogenic: *adj.* originating in muscle tissue.

myograph: *n.* an instrument for measuring the vigor of muscular movement. ➤The ISOTONIC MYOGRAPH measures contraction against a negligible constant external resistance. The ISOMETRIC MYOGRAPH measures contraction against a strong resistance so that only a small change in muscle length can be made.

myokinetic: *adj.* pertaining to muscular movement.

myokinetic test: (*Mira-y-Lopez*) one in which the subject copies previously-seen simple line drawings with both hands simultaneously and without vision. The kinds of deviations from the original drawings are taken as indices of personality tendencies.

myoneural junction = **neuromuscular junction.**

myopia (mī·ō′pi·ə): *n.* a condition of the eye in which, with relaxed accommodation, the light rays come to a focus in front of the retina instead of directly upon it. ➤It is popularly called NEARSIGHTEDNESS be-

cause near objects can be approximately properly focused by accommodation; hence, the loss of visual acuity is chiefly apparent with distant objects.—*Ant.* **hyperopia,** or farsightedness.—*adj.* **myopic.**—*pers. n.* **myope.**

myosis (mī·ō′səs): *n.* extreme or abnormal contraction of the pupil of the eye.—*Var.* **miosis.**—*Ant.* **mydriasis.**—*adj.* **myotic, miotic.**

myotactic reflex: contraction of a muscle produced by suddenly stretching it longitudinally. ➤It is believed to be effected by a two-neuron arc, afferent neurons in the muscle connecting directly with the motor neurons.

myotonia: *n.* muscle rigidity or spasm.— *adj.* **myotonic.**

mysophobia (mī″sō·fō′bi·ə): *n.* morbid fear of dirt or contamination. Its most usual symptom is overfrequent or **compulsive** hand washing.

mysticism: *n.* the doctrine that there is a kind of knowledge in addition to that received through the senses or by thinking. ➤The mystic revelation seems, for the experiencer, to have a peculiar and compelling value. It is unstatable in words—that would be to receive knowledge through the eyes or ears. **Mystic** should not be used as a synonym for *mysterious, occult,* or *supernatural.* "Visions" (as of heaven and hell) are usually not mystical since one *sees* and *hears* the glory one reports—these are **hallucinations** or revelations, whether **veridical** or not. Nor should **mystic** be used for judgments arrived at by processes which the subject cannot state—these are **intuitive. Mystic** as a term of reproach is usually applied to a scientist using nonscientific method, or flourishing a resounding phrase or label without being able to state what it really means. This metaphoric usage is not recommended. ¶The mystic trance is evidently very similar to **feeling (3):** one may question whether it is not merely a strongly emotional state that almost entirely lacks, somehow, awareness of any objects or tendency to any kind of external activity.—*adj.* **mystic(al).**—*pers. n.* **mystic.**

myth: *n.* 1. a story that has sacred or cult-lore associations, but lacks actual historical basis. ➤*Distg. fr.* **legend,** which has some historical basis and less (or no) religious association. 2. a false but persistent idea or theory that is widely accepted.—*adj.* **mythical.**

mythology: *n.* the body of **myths** current in a given culture.—*Cp.* **folklore.**

mythomania: *n.* a tendency to report extraordinary imaginary adventures as if true.

myxedema (mik″sə·dē′mə): *n.* a disorder of adults and older children in which there is reduced thyroid secretion, low basal metabolism, apathy, and lethargy.

N

N: **1.** (*stat.*) the number of instances of whatever sort in the total **population**; the number of cases or of observations. **2.** (*C. Hull*) the number of **reinforcements. 3.** code symbol for a **need** attributed to one of the characters of **TAT. 4.** (not *ital.*) = **number factor** (see **abilities/primary mental**).

N': the total number of cases or observations in a second group.

n: **1.** (*stat.*) the number of items in a limited portion (e.g., in a class or centile) of a total group. **2.** the number of variables. **3.** the number of unreinforced elicitations of a response required to produce experimental **extinction. 4.** (often not *ital.*) = **need,** or amount of need.

nadir (nā′dər): *n.* the lowest point in a distribution, or (more properly) in a **system** of phenomena.—*Ant.* ZENITH, the highest point.

naevus = nevus.

nail biting: a nervous habit of biting the fingernails down to the quick. It develops in childhood or adolescence but often persists into adulthood.—*Syn.* (for those who must have it in Greek) ONYCHOPHAGIA.

naive, naïve (nä·ēv′): *adj.* **1.** unsophisticated; inexperienced in the complexities of a wider society than that of home and neighborhood. **2.** characterized by a fresh approach to scientific problems. ➤Frequently used derogatorily for an approach that ignores the history of the problem. **3.** in experiments, of subjects inexperienced in anything deemed helpful to performance of the experimental task.—*n.* **naiveness, naiveté** (nä·ēv·tā′).

Nancy school: a group of psychiatrists, under the leadership of H. Bernheim, who utilized hypnosis, which they held to be a normal phenomenon of **suggestion.**

nanism (nā′niz·əm; nan-) = dwarfism.— *adj.* **nanoid.**

narcism = narcissism.

narcissism (när·sis′iz·əm): *n.* **1.** self-love, ➤The term is applied to high valuation of one's own bodily qualities and, by extension, of one's deeds and personal qualities. It is sometimes erroneously used for **autoerotism.** In psychoanalysis, **narcissism** is said to be an early stage in human development, or a neurotically arrested stage.— See **primary *narcissism. 2.** (*K. Horney*) identification with the **idealized *image** of self, and loving the unrealistically glorified attributes of self seen therein. It is a **comprehensive solution** for basic ***conflict.** ➤The variant **narcism** (när′siz·əm) is etymologically incorrect but now accepted.

—*adj.* **narcissistic** (när″sə·sis′tik).—*pers. n.* **narcissist.**

narcissism/negative: underestimation of oneself.

narcissism/primary or **/primal:** (*psychoan.*) the early stage when the infant's **libido** is turned toward his own body. ➤The partial persistence of this stage, or return thereto, is a major factor in some neuroses. The use of **autoerotism** for this stage lessens the usefulness of that term for a more specific meaning.

narcissism/secondary: (*psychoan.*) the withdrawing of **libido** from objects and investing it in the **ego;** esp., investing it in the image of one's ego built up in childhood by identification with parents.—See **ego ideal/narcissistic.**

narcissistic object choice: (*psychoan.*) the taking of the self, rather than the mother, as a love object; the investment of **libido** in objects similar to oneself.—*Cp.* **anaclitic object choice.**

narco-: combining form meaning *torpor, stupor, numbness.*

narcoanalysis: *n.* treatment of behavior adjustment while the individual is in a stage of sleeplike torpor or relaxation induced by a drug. ➤Treatment may be by **suggestion** (NARCOSUGGESTION) or by talking out problems (NARCOCATHARSIS) while under the effect of the drug. NARCOSYNTHESIS utilizes the material, obtained while the patient is drugged, for *later* interpretation of the difficulty. The drugs used have been dubbed "truth serums," but they cannot be used to extract truth from an unwilling respondent.

narcodiagnosis: *n.* diagnosis of mental disorder while the patient is under narcosis.

narcolepsy: *n.* excessive inclination to sleep, manifested in periodic attacks.

narcomania: *n.* a morbid desire for relief from bodily pain, generally by means of narcotics.

narcosis: *n.* a condition in which automatic activities and normal responsiveness to stimuli are greatly reduced as a result of narcotic drugs.—*adj.* **narcotic.**

narcosynthesis: see **narcoanalysis.**

narcotherapy: *n.* the use of **narcosis** in the treatment of mental disorder.

narcotic: *n.* a drug, usually of opium or its derivatives, that produces deep sleep or stupor.—*adj.* **narcotic.**—*pers. n.* **narcotic.**

narcotism (när′kə·tiz·əm): *n.* **1.** state of being under the influence of a narcotic. **2.** addiction to narcotic drugs.

nares (nā′rēz): *n. pl.* the nasal passages.— *Syn.* NOSTRILS.

narrative method: a procedure in which

the subject is encouraged to relate facts in his own way without interruption or suggestions.

nascent (nas'ənt; nā'-): *adj.* pertaining to birth or beginning; characterizing the earliest phase of development.—*Syn.* **incipient,** which implies at least the possibility that the development will be checked.

national character: the relatively enduring personality characteristics most frequently found in a given nation, esp. the most frequent values.

native: *adj.* inborn; hereditary.—See **heredity.**

native behavior: behavior determined by factors present from the beginning of the organism.—See **heredity.**

native trait: an inherited structure of the organism; or the behavior pattern which the structure makes possible.

nativism (nā'tiv·iz·əm): *n.* **1.** the doctrine that stresses the influence of **heredity,** in contrast with that of experience, in the development of the structures or functions of an organism. **2.** the doctrine that the capacity to perceive space and time is inborn and can function without having been developed by prior stimulation or experience. ➤According to this view, a person born blind and later restored to sight would be able to perceive objects as localized in space.—*Cp.* **empiricism (1).**—See **psychology/divisions and schools of, VI.**— *adj.* **nativistic.**

natural: *adj.* **1.** pertaining to **nature. 2.** subject to **natural law.** ➤The adjective shares with the noun **nature** its variety of meanings. The **natural** may be opposed to the acquired, the reflective, the constrained, the artificial, the affected, the humane, the divine, the spiritual, the revealed, the regenerated, the supernatural, the surprising, the monstrous (both biological and moral), the legitimate, and to that which would exist without man.

naturalism: 1. the philosophic point of view that considers mental phenomena, and particularly moral values, as **natural** phenomena, to be interpreted in the same way as the phenomena of **natural science. 2.** the educational point of view that stresses, as the goal of education, the development and expansion of what is natural in man, as opposed to **discipline** and the cultivation of an imposed set of standards and values. ➤The point of view is expressed in many specific doctrines from Rousseau to Dewey. The general philosophic position of **(1)** is **rationalistic** and **positivistic;** the educational point of view is **romantic.** Yet the two are often held together.

naturalistic observation: observation of events as they occur in nature, without ex-

perimental control of the behavior: e.g., nest building, children at play, the voting behavior of congressmen.

natural law: 1. a general statement of the uniformities and regularities discovered in the sequence of events, or of a coherent set of events of a particular sort: e.g., *the law of falling bodies.*—*Syn.* LAW OF NATURE. **2.** a regulation of human behavior based on long-established custom or divine sanction rather than on legislation. ➤The two kinds of natural law are quite different, but the prestige of **(1)** has often been invoked to support **(2),** and vice versa. It is suggested that **(1)** be called SCIENTIFIC LAW, and that **(2)** be called either CUSTOMARY LAW (or **mores)** or DIVINE LAW.

natural sciences: those dealing with natural objects, generally taken to include physics, chemistry, and biology and to exclude mathematics, philosophy, and the social sciences. ➤The question of whether psychology is a natural science is essentially terminological. Because of its uncertain boundaries, the term is of doubtful value. *Cp.* the series *physical sciences, biological sciences, social sciences,* in which psychology bridges the gap between biological and social, though belonging primarily (according to most authorities) with the former. —*Contr. w.* **normative sciences, social sciences.**

natural selection: the theory that the inheritance of certain structures is explained by their utility to the organism in the struggle for survival.

nature: *n.* The varied meanings of this word may be best understood in terms of their evolution. The word is derived from the Latin root meaning *birth.* Hence, **1.** the innate or hereditary characters of a person or organism. ➤This meaning often carries the implication of the impulsive or instinctual, as contrasted with the reasoned or rational, which cannot be conceived as inborn. Here belongs the phrase, *a child of nature.* ORIGINAL NATURE emphasizes the hereditary, referring both to innate capacities and innate dispositions to act (the **instincts). 2.** the peculiar qualities that mark off one individual (or one species) from another. ➤At first, these peculiar qualities were conceived as inborn; later the connotation was broadened to include any distinguishing character: *every man has his own nature.* By still further extension, the notion of the inborn gives way to that of the intrinsic or essential, so that it is possible to speak of *the nature* (or essential properties) of inanimate objects. **3.** that which regulates one's behavior: one can act only *according to one's nature.* ➤Here belongs, however, the notion that under exceptional circumstances one may act *un-*

naturally, i.e., contrary to one's nature. The contrast is with the artificial, the constrained, or the abnormal. The phrase HUMAN NATURE also belongs in this meaning; it refers to that which is possible, normal, or befitting man as opposed to other beings (beasts or gods), or to that which man can be expected to do under ordinary circumstances. (But here the notion of the inborn enters once more; human nature is generally conceived as determined or *fixed* by heredity: *you can't change human nature.* This conception is challenged in the dictum: *It is human nature to change.*) **4.** the established order of events: that which happens according to law, in contrast with the supernatural. **5.** that which is; the state of the environment, even of the whole universe. ➤In this meaning, nature is often personified: *Nature's wonders to extol.* **6.** that in the external world which is not due to man or man's intelligence: *the beauties of nature.*

Thus, by a paradoxical development the same word means what a person is, in contrast to the forces acting on him; yet it also means those very forces. So too we have the paradox that one may act "unnaturally," yet strictly in accord with one's nature. ¶**Nature** and **natural,** having gained the connotation of something good or at least excusable, are often used as a cover for a writer's favorite whimsies and partialities, or as a bulwark of whatever is.

nature/law of = **natural law (1).**

nature-nurture problem: the problem of the relative influence of heredity and of environment in the development of organisms.

nature/second: 1. the habitual; behavior that takes place promptly, without premeditation or intent. **2.** (*psychoan.*) the **superego.**

nausea (nô′shə): *n.* a complex and unpleasant sensory and motor state characterized by gastric contractions, a tendency to vomit, salivation, sweating, dizziness, dull pain in throat and gullet.—*adj.* **nauseous.** —*v.* **nauseate.**

Neanderthal man (ni·an′dər·täl): a species of extinct human that flourished in middle Paleolithic times in Europe.

near effect: (*K. Goldstein*) **1.** = LOCAL NEAR EFFECT, the degree of excitation of a neural component as a function of its distance from the point where the stimulus is applied. **2.** = FUNCTIONAL NEAR EFFECT, the degree of excitation as a function of the greater or less appropriateness of the stimulus for the neural component in question.

near point (of accommodation): the nearest point to the eye at which an object can be seen clearly. This varies according to the **accommodation** power of the individual eye.—*Cp.* **far point.**

near point (of convergence): the nearest point at which the two eyes can simultaneously look directly and still maintain **fusion.** An object brought closer is seen as double.—*Distg. fr.* **near point (of accommodation).**

nearsightedness = **myopia.**

necessary: *adj.* **1.** of that part of the antecedent state of affairs without which a certain event does not take place; or of an event considered as depending on certain antecedents. **2.** of a judgment or conclusion that is logical; or of the kind of thinking process forced upon a person by logical principles.—*Ant.* **contingent. 3.** of something forced upon a person by compelling considerations, esp. by moral considerations; morally necessary.

necessity: *n.* **1.** that which is unavoidable. **2.** a powerful **need. 3.** = moral necessity. —See **necessary (3).**

Necker cube: an ambiguous *figure that consists of a line drawing of a cube showing all twelve edges as if the cube were transparent.

necro-: combining form meaning *dead.*

necrophilia: *n.* sexual attraction to corpses. —*Var.* **necrophilism** (nə·krof′ə·liz·əm).— *adj.* **necrophilic.**—*pers. n.* **necrophile.**

necrosis (ne·krō′səs): *n.* the disintegration of cells that are in contact with other still-living cells.—*adj.* **necrotic** (-krot′ik).

need: *n.* **1.** the lack of something which, if present, would tend to further the welfare of the organism or of the species, or to facilitate its usual behavior; or the thing, activity, or condition (internal or external) that is lacking.—*Syn.* (with special implication) **motive. 2.** a **tension** induced in the organism by such a lack, either internal or external.—*Syn.* **drive** (*prefd.*). **3.** an unsatisfied motive. **4.** = **felt need. 5.** (*exper.*) a tissue deficiency defined in terms of controllable deprivations: e.g., a need for food as defined by a 24-hour deprivation, on the assumption that deprivation and tissue deficiency are closely correlated.

➤When **need** in sense (1) is equated with **motive,** it is implied (or should be) that the need or lack in question directly evokes action—a conception that renders the construct of **drive** unnecessary. The usage of (2), on the other hand, so far from dispensing with the drive construct, equates **need** with **drive,** giving us two terms for the latter construct and leaving no good term for the lack. In many cases, however, writers use **need, drive, motive,** and **motivation** synonymously; when it is desired to make a distinction, it is recommended that **need** be used as in (1). ¶The concept of **need** runs through the terms **want, craving, desire,** and **wish,** but each has specific connotations.

For the several specific needs, see the qualifying expression: e.g., **blamavoidance need**. For qualification of **need** in general, see the terms following: e.g., **need/basic**, **need/manifest**.

need/affiliative: see **affiliative need**.

need/basic: one from which other needs are derived; a **primary *need**.

need cathexis: *n.* the attachment of a need to a specific object, or class of objects, as a means to its satisfaction. ➤*Cp.* **canalization (2)**. This is a modification of the psychoanalytic use of **cathexis**, one that substitutes **tissue *needs** for **libido**.

need/conscious: one of which the person is explicitly aware.—*Syn.* **felt need**.

need/derived: a need growing out of the operation of **primary *needs** but constituting a distinct motive in its own right. ➤This term is noncommittal as to whether the need thus derived becomes autonomous (see **autonomy/functional**) or must be periodically strengthened.—*Approx. syn.* **acquired *drive**.

need-drive-incentive pattern: a hypothesis about motivation which asserts that physiological **needs** are created by **deprivation**, that these give rise to **drives** which stir to, and may guide, activity until a related goal object **(incentive)** is attained, and that the response to the goal object **(consummatory response)** reduces the drive.

need/external: the lack of some object or condition in the environment that would, if present, promote the biological or psychological efficiency of the organism. ➤Only if the lack in the environment creates a lack in the organism does it become a genuine need. But the term is convenient to designate a condition clearly correlated with an **internal *need**.

need/felt: see **felt need**.

need gratification: 1. making good a deficit; supplying a lack; satisfying a need. 2. reducing a condition of **tension**; reducing a **motivational** condition.

need-integrate: *n.* (*H. A. Murray*) a representation of movements, pathways, agencies, or goal objects which may be analyzed **thematically** to reveal the needs of the individual.

need/internal: a need that arises from changes within the organism, relatively independently of direct external stimulation. —*Syn.* SOMAGENIC or SOMATOGENIC NEED, **need/tissue**.—*Ant.* **need/external**.

need/manifest: 1. a need that is easily inferrible from behavior. 2. a need that has erupted into overt behavior.

need/neurotic: (*K. Horney*) an **anxiety**-driven or **compulsive** desire or demand for a certain behavior on the part of others. ➤The behavior desired from others varies

according to the kind of **neurotic *solution** adopted: e.g., if the solution is **self-efface-ment**, the neurotic requires a person who will accept his affection.

need pattern: the total organization of a person's needs.

need/press: see **press-need (pattern)**.

need/primary: 1. an **internal *need**.— *Ant.* **external *need**. 2. a need determined by genetic factors; an **innate** need.—*Ant.* DERIVED, SECONDARY, or ACQUIRED NEED. ➤The contrast between an innate and an acquired need is usually made in terms of the external objects needed, but it may also be made in terms of internal needs.

need reduction: anything that lessens the deficiency constituting a need; satisfaction of a need, complete or partial.

need/somagenic or **/somatogenic = need/internal**.

needs/pupil: the conditions necessary for the optimal development of the pupil—intellectually, physically, socially. ➤Such needs are determined both by the pupil's present state and by the probable future demands that will be made upon him. The latter qualification is often ignored. Meeting pupil needs is generally considered the goal of education.

need state: the condition of an organism as the result of some deprivation. ➤What the word *state* adds to *need* is not apparent, but the phrase is common.—*Distg. fr.* **drive state**.

need tension: a tension that develops within the organism when a need is not relieved.

need/tissue: an **internal *need** with special emphasis upon a physiochemical lack in a specific tissue. ➤The term is often restricted to needs originating in the viscera, but this is arbitrary. Any kind of tissue may lack something.

neencephalon (nē″en·sef′ə·lon): *n.* the "new brain," i.e., the cortex and parts of the brain developed in close relation to it.—*Ant.* PALEENCEPHALON, the old brain, which is all the rest.

negation: *n.* 1. denial, dispute, or disproof of a statement. 2. refusal of a suggestion; objection to a suggested action.—*Syn.* (for 2) **negativism** (*prefd.*). 3. (*Ror.*) rejection by a subject of an inkblot response immediately after he has made it.

negation/delusion of: the denial that obvious conditions or objects exist.

negative: *adj.* 1. of a quantity less than zero. 2. of a direction defined by change from more to less; or of a reversed direction. 3. pertaining to denial, dispute, objection, repulsion, or hostility. 4. characterizing an attitude that tends toward **negation** or **negativism**. 5. of an interpersonal relation characterized by dislike or hostility. ➤**Negative** is much used undiscriminatingly to characterize anything disliked or disapproved by the writer. ¶For most terms beginning with **negative,** see the noun thus qualified.

negative/false or **/valid:** see **false negative.**

negative-negative conflict = **avoidance-avoidance conflict.**

negative phase or **stage: 1.** a short period preceding adolescence during which children in Western culture commonly (but not universally) tend to withdraw from social companionship, to daydream, to mope, and to be disorderly and disobedient. **2.** a period marked by **negativism** (*prefd.*).

negative retroaction = **inhibition/retroactive.**

negative self-feeling: see **self-feeling/positive** and **/negative.**

negative sensation: (*G. Fechner*) a sensation below the **threshold.**

negative transference: (*psychoan.*) the development of a hostile attitude toward the analyst. ➤The term is unfortunate; it refers to the transference of a negative attitude, not to a transference in a negative direction.—See **transference.**

negativism: *n.* the tendency to resist suggestions from another person; persistent refusal, without apparent or objective reason, to do as suggested. ➤The resistance to suggestion is often accompanied by characteristic expressions of stubbornness: scowling, head shaking, verbal refusal, etc. ACTIVE NEGATISM is doing the opposite of what is suggested or commanded. PASSIVE or INTERNAL NEGATIVISM is not doing the usual, normal, or expected: e.g., the patient does not eat unless prompted. In mild form, negativism is found in many otherwise normal persons. It is often found in children at ages 2 to 4, and as a symptom in **catatonia.** —*Syn.* **contrasuggestibility,** CONTRARINESS, **resistance (4).**—*adj.* **negativistic.**

ne(o)-: combining form meaning *new, recent, latest.*

neo-analyst: *n.* a psychoanalyst who rejects the **instinctual** or biological emphasis of orthodox psychoanalysis and finds the source of neuroses in conflicts having a social origin.

neobehaviorism: *n.* a general point of view that emphasizes the central position of **response** in the definition of psychology. ➤Neobehaviorism is not a close-knit school with well-defined doctrines. In contrast with the older **behaviorism,** there is less antipathy to traditional terms (though attempt to avoid the dualism those terms seem to imply is usual), and **self-report** is guardedly used. There is much use of *molar *constructs, and some neobehaviorists utilize **purposive** and **gestalt** concepts. A position essentially like that of contempo-

rary neobehaviorism was explicitly announced (by W. McDougall and by W. E Pillsbury) before the birth of behaviorisr as such; and a very large part of scientifi psychology has always been response oriented. Almost any psychology that turn from analysis of consciousness to investiga tion of what organisms do, and to the con ditions under which they perform effec tively, may be called neobehavioristic. *Near syn.* **behavior theory,** which tends t be closer to behaviorism as originally se forth.—See **psychology/divisions an schools of, III.**

neocerebellum: *n.* the portion of the cere bellum lying between the prepyramid fissure and the fissura prima. It is that por tion of the cerebellum which has shown th greatest expansion in the phylogenetic se ries.

neo-Freudian: *n.* a follower of Freud wh departs in material ways from the latter doctrines. ➤The term is not used for thos psychoanalysts who early broke away fro Freud and formed schools of their own, e.g Adler, Jung. But very many contemporar psychoanalysts consider their position to b a considerable modification of the orthodo Freudian position.—*Cp.* **neo-analyst,** whic is slightly more comprehensive.—Se **psychology/divisions and schools o III.**

neolalia (-lā′li·ə): *n.* speech containin many words devised by the speaker; tendency to **neologism.**

neologism (nē·ol′ə·jiz·əm): *n.* **1.** a new coined word; or, an old word used in a ne and different sense. **2.** the behavior or a of coining words.—*Syn.* (for 2) NEOLOG ➤Coining new and bizarre words is a com mon symptom among psychotics, but i only slightly different form it infects scier tists and scholars. One should particularly b wary of Greek neologisms when they be the gifts of apparent—but only apparent precision. (See **adiadochokinesis** an **phobia.**) Such neologisms are too ofte merely manifestations of **bogus erudition.**

Forcing a new meaning upon an estab lished word, and joining words to form phrase with a highly special meaning n suggested by the words themselves, a equally neologistic and may be equally mor strous. Outright manufactured terms, suc as **watt** or **troland,** are much to be pre ferred to a clumsy Teutonic piling of word on another—as in "discriminal proce continuum." ¶Neither elegance nor etymc logical purity, however, is the main cri terion. **Photon** is bad Greek (a third de clension noun is given a second declensio ending). Nevertheless, it is good solid Eng lish. We get **photon** by easy analogy wit *ergon,* a term already established. Som grammarians may wince; but they have more important work to do than to struggle vainly against a term which, however literally barbarous, is a soundly conceived neologism. It immediately suggests by associative analogy part of the meaning it is to carry, and it does not suggest the wrong meaning.

A new object or a new idea requires a new term, i.e., a neologism. Any such neologism should, however, be challenged above all by its parents) to show that it is legitimate, i.e., necessary and convenient.—See **rational coinage, arbitrary definition.**

eonate: *n.* a newborn infant.—See **development/levels of.**—*Syn.* NEONATUS.—*adj.* **neonatal.**

eopallium (-pal'i·əm): *n.* the **cortex cerebri** exclusive of the olfactory **pallium.** —*adj.* **neopallial.**

eophenomenology: *n.* (*D. Snygg* and *A. Combs*) a psychological school whose basic postulate is that behavior is continuously determined by the behaver's **phenomenological** (or **phenomenal**) *field* at each instant of action. ➤The field is organized and tends to as little change as external events impinging on it permit. The perceived **self** is a major part of the field. A major advantage claimed for this point of view is that it becomes theoretically possible to predict which of the potential stimuli will actually affect an individual's behavior, whereas stimulus-response systems, interpreted strictly, cannot.—See **psychology/divisions and schools of,** III, II.

eoplasm/brain: a brain tumor.

eopsychoanalysis: *n.* any of several departures from the strict doctrines of Freud which nonetheless remain within the general framework.—*Syn.* **neo-Freudianism.**

erve: *adj.* pertaining to a bundle of **neurons** (a **nerve**) and, by extension, to organs made up of neuron bundles.—See **nerve tissue.** ➤By preference, **nerve** is an anatomical term. NEURAL, in contrast, is primarily a functional or physiological term referring to the activities of nerves. NERVOUS refers to pathological conditions. But these distinctions are not consistently adhered to. *Nervous* is entrenched in the expressions **nervous system** and **nervous arc,** where nerve would be preferable; *nerve impulse* and *nervous impulse* (the latter clearly ambiguous) are used where **neural impulse** would be better. Moreover, largely for euphony, *neural* tends also to displace **nerve.** The confusion is probably too firmly entrenched to be remedied and seldom leads to error. For compound terms beginning with one of the three, therefore, search may be made under either of the others.

nerve: *n.* a bundle of **neurons,** generally with a sheath.—*Syn.* **nerve fiber** (more precise). ➤The several nerves, if defined in this dictionary, are listed under the distinguishing adjectival element: e.g., **trochlear nerve.**

nerve block: local and temporary inability, produced by anesthesia or similar means, of a nerve to transmit excitation.

nerve cell: 1. a neuron considered as a complete cell.—*Syn.* **neuron** (*prefd.*). **2.** the central portion of a neuron, including the nucleus, and exclusive of the **axon** and **dendrite** prolongations.—*Syn.* cell body, NERVE CELL BODY (*prefd.*).

nerve center: see **center/nerve.**

nerve/centrifugal = **efferent** nerve.

nerve/centripetal = **afferent** nerve.

nerve current: see **neural current.**

nerve ending: the end of a neuron fiber elsewhere than in a **synapse**—i.e., in an **effector** organ such as a muscle or gland.

nerve excitation: see **excitation.**

nerve/facial: see **facial nerve.**

nerve fiber: 1. a threadlike bundle of **neurons** enclosed in a white covering or sheath.—*Syn.* **nerve. 2.** a hairlike projection from the more compact portion of a neuron: an **axon** or **dendrite.**—See **neuron.**

nerve impulse = **neural impulse.**

nervelessness: *n.* **1.** lack of vigor or spirit. **2.** a condition characterized by lack of firm muscular tone and consequent weakness of voluntary control of movement.

nerve/motor: see **motor nerve.**

nerve-muscle preparation: a muscle, and the nerves attached to it, surgically removed from the body of an experimental animal and used in physiological investigation. ➤It was formerly believed to reveal the nature of the local neuromuscular function, but this is now known to be an oversimplification.

nerve pathway: the route followed by the nerve impulse in a particular **stimulus-response** sequence.

nerve pattern: the relationships, either in space or functionally, of the nerve cells involved in a given bit or kind of behavior. ➤The pattern is nearly always a part of the **conceptual nervous system** (which see). —*Syn.* NEURAL PATTERN.

nerve plexus: a netlike grouping of nerves, esp. of nerve cell bodies with relatively short axons and dendrites. Such a plexus permits complex interconnections.

nerve process: see **neural process.**

nerve root: a group of **axons** connected directly with the brain or spinal cord.

nerve tissue: the totality of those cells, the **neurons,** having a common developmental history and the specialized functions (*a*) of being affected by certain forms of physical energy or stimuli (RECEPTIVE or SENSORY FUNCTION), (b) of transmitting the energy transformation to other parts of the body (TRANSMISSIVE and INTEGRATIVE FUNCTION), and (c) of thus exciting changes in the internal or external relations of the body through muscular and glandular activity (EXCITATORY FUNCTION). ➤These functions may be regarded as a development of the **irritability** characteristic of all living cells. This is the basic definition to which are related, directly or indirectly, all terms employing **nerve, nervous, neural,** and **neuron.**—*Syn.* NERVOUS TISSUE.

nerve trunk: a relatively large bundle of peripheral axons (see **neuron**), excluding their terminations or nerve endings.

nervism: *n.* the hypothesis that all functions of the body are controlled by the nervous system. ➤The term is Pavlov's new name for an old idea.

nervous: *adj.* **1.** pertaining to a **nerve** or nerves, or to their activity. ➤See **nerve** (*adj.*) for distinctions of **nerve, nervous,** and **neural.** For phrases beginning with **nervous,** see also entries under **nerve** and **neural. 2.** of a person easily excited emotionally and exhibiting twitchy and unsustained activity. **3.** pertaining to diseased conditions of the nervous system.

nervous arc or **circuit:** the path taken by **neural impulse** from a **receptor,** through one or more connector neurons, to an **effector** or executive organ; the anatomical-functional unit of behavior.—*Syn.* (*prefd.* but less common) NERVE ARC, NEURAL ARC, **reflex arc** (not *recom.*).

nervous breakdown or **prostration:** see **breakdown/nervous.**

nervous disease or **disorder:** properly, an **organic** disorder of the **nervous system;** often, loosely, any relatively mild mental disorder, including the **neuroses.**

nervous energy: (*pop.*) vigorous, but often unsustained, activity. ➤The frequent implication is that of uneconomical activity.

nervous habit: a tendency to make relatively useless but fairly well-coordinated movements that indicate **tension,** restlessness, or **nervousness:** bodily twisting, rubbing of hands on other body surfaces, rapping, strained postures, pursing of lips, manneristic vocalizings, etc.

nervousness: *n.* **1.** restless, impulsive, or purposeless activity. **2.** a state in which one responds readily and with excessive or nonadaptive emotional responses, esp. of fear. **3.** mental ill-health: a layman's diagnosis that may mean anything.—See **neurosis.**

nervous system or **N.S.** or **n.s.:** all the organs in the body that are composed of **nerve** tissue. The nervous system is sub-

divided according to either a **structural** or a **functional** scheme.

I. Structural or anatomic scheme:
   A. CENTRAL NERVOUS SYSTEM or C.N.S.: the brain and spinal cord.
   B. PERIPHERAL NERVOUS SYSTEM: all outlying nerve structures. (The word *peripheral* means outer, or **distal,** to the central nervous system, not necessarily to the body as a whole; hence, the peripheral system supplies organs inside the body also.)
II. Functional scheme:
   A. AUTONOMIC DIVISION: the nerve supply of the viscera in the broad sense, including esp. **smooth *muscles, exocrine glands,** and some **endocrine glands.**
      1. Structural subdivision of the autonomic:
         a. CRANIOSACRAL division
         b. THORACOLUMBAR division
      2. Functional subdivision:
         a. PARASYMPATHETIC
         b. SYMPATHETIC
   B. SOMATIC DIVISION: all the nerve structures not in the autonomic, including esp. the general and special sensory nerves and the nerve supply of skeletal muscles.

Somatic does not clearly describe the denotation of SOMATIC DIVISION, but no acceptable term is current. The distinction between AUTONOMIC and SOMATIC is primarily for the PERIPHERAL subdivision (I, B), but distinct central connections for the two are recognized. Such brain structures as the **thalamus,** however, have both autonomic and somatic functions.

A number of confusions and overlappings in terminology represent chiefly the residual effect of older thinking about the nervous system. SYMPATHETIC is still occasionally used as a synonym for the whole AUTONOMIC. Often also the function description SYMPATHETIC, is substituted for the anatomical, THORACOLUMBAR. The two are nearly but not quite the same. (Parasympathetic and craniosacral are similarly equated.) —See **autonomic nervous system.**

The term CEREBROSPINAL NERVOUS SYSTEM is sometimes used for the brain, cord and the afferent and efferent nerves, excluding the autonomic. This represents an out-of-date classification made when the autonomic was regarded as far more independent of the brain than is now supposed. CENTRAL DIVISION sometimes means the brain only sometimes brain and cord. PERIPHERAL DIVISION (I, B) is sometimes equated with the SOMATIC subdivision (II, B) instead of including also the autonomic peripheral nerves (as in current usage). SKELETAL NERVES are those serving skeletal *muscles.

The close relation between psychological phenomena (however conceived) and the nervous system is recognized by practically everyone (see **mind-body problem, person**). But many theoretical explanations of behavior are in terms of the **conceptual nervous system** (which see) rather than of the actual nervous system.

nervous system/conceptual: see **conceptual nervous system.**

nervous tissue = **nerve tissue.**

net table = **abac.**

network/social: a set of relationships between persons such that one of them can influence others with whom he is in contact only through those that are intermediate in the net.

neural: 1. pertaining to the function of nerves. 2. pertaining to nerve structure. ➤See **nerve** (*adj.*) for distinction between **nerve, nervous, neural.** Compound terms beginning with **neural** may sometimes be found under **nerve** or **nervous.**

neural arc = **nervous arc.**

neural bond: a hypothetical relation between the hypothetical elements in the **conceptual nervous system.** ➤*Distg. fr.* synapse, an observable structure uniting neurons. Certain behaviors are regularly associated, hence a sort of physical bond is inferred between the portions of the conceptual nervous system that underlie these behaviors. Practically no actual observations of neural functions give any substance to this harmless but empty hypothesis.—*Syn.* **associative bond, habit,** STIMULUS-RESPONSE SEQUENCE, all preferred as being stated in terms of the data.

neural circuit: 1. = **nervous arc.** 2. the passage along a **neural impulse** from a receptor to an effector, or from one center to another.

neural conduction: transmission of excitation or **neural impulse** along nerve fibers and from neuron to neuron.

neural crest: see **neural plate.**

neural current: energy change that passes from one neuron to another. ➤The name is metaphoric, the exact nature of the change being unknown. Much evidence that it is electrochemical has accumulated.—*Syn.* NEURAL IMPULSE.

neural discharge: the propagated **excitation** or disturbance in a nerve. ➤The emphasis is upon the passage from one neuron into others, or into an **effector,** so that the first element returns to an unexcited state unless re-excited.—*Syn.* FIRING (OF A NEURON).

neural equivalence: the capacity of one part of the nervous system to perform the function of another part.—See **equipotentiality.**

neural excitation = **excitation (2).**

neural facilitation = **facilitation (3).**

neural fold: see **neural plate.**

neuralgia: *n.* a nervous disorder, usually sharply localized, giving rise to a sharp, intermittent, localized pain.

neural groove: see **neural plate.**

neural impulse: 1. = **neural current.** 2. a single pulsation along a neuron.

neural irritability: the property of nerve tissue of being affected by specific environmental changes, and of responding by a change in itself which may be transmitted to other tissues, neural or otherwise.

neural linkage: a change, of unknown character but probably taking place largely at the **synapse,** whereby two or more neurons are connected.

neural pattern = **nerve pattern.**

neural plate: (*neurol.*) in vertebrate embryos, a thickening of ectodermal cells along the dorsal midline, from which the central nervous system later develops. The cells develop into a pair of folds (NEURAL FOLDS) which grow up and around the NEURAL GROOVE, finally coming together at the top to make up the embryonic NEURAL TUBE. The walls of this tube develop into the brain and spinal cord. The ridgelike NEURAL CREST on the dorsal aspect gives rise to the spinal **ganglions** and the sympathetic nervous system (see **nervous system**).

neural process: 1. any change in **nerve tissue.** 2. any slender terminal branch of a neuron; a terminal fibril. ➤The first should be called a **neural process,** the second a **nerve process,** but actual usage is confused.

neural reverberation: (*D. O. Hebb*) the brief continuation of brain activity after a stimulus has ceased. ➤The phenomena of the **memory afterimage** are believed to correlate with it, and many other phenomena give indirect evidence of it.

neural rivalry: state when two or more opposed **neural impulses** are simultaneously active. ➤Apparently it is the muscular or glandular responses which are set against each other. RESPONSE RIVALRY would be more descriptive.

neural transit: neural discharge from **receptor** to **effector.**

neural tube: see **neural plate.**

neurasthenia (nū″rəs·thē′ni·ə): *n.* a **functional disorder** characterized by feelings of weakness and a general lowering of bodily and mental tone. ➤The term is passing out of technical use. But the adjective *neurasthenic* is still applied to a **neurotic** general fatigability. It is a misnomer, since the disorder is neither an organic weakness nor a deficiency of the nerves.—*adj.* and *pers. n.* **neurasthenic** (-then′ik; -thē′nik).

neuraxis (nù·rak′səs): *n.* the brain and spinal cord.—*Syn.* CEREBROSPINAL AXIS.

neurilemma (-ri·lem'ə): *n.* (*neurol.*) the thin membranous outer covering of a nerve fiber. In medullated fibers it surrounds the **medullary sheath.**

neurin: *n.* 1. an extract of nerve tissue. 2. (*W. McDougall*) the specific energy involved in nerve excitation and conduction. —*Var.* **neurine.**

neurite = axon (see **neuron**).

neuritis: *n.* a painful inflammation of a peripheral nerve.—*adj.* **neuritic.**

neuroanatomy: *n.* the **anatomy** of the nervous system.

neurobiotaxis/law of: (*A. Kappers*) **Dendrites** of developing nerve cells are stimulated to grow toward the **axons** of neighboring and simultaneously active **neurons,** probably because of electrical influences.

neuroblast: *n.* an embryonic nerve cell.

neurocyte: *n.* 1. = **neuron.** 2. = **nerve cell** body.

neurofibril or **neurofibrilla** = **fibril.**

neurogenic: *adj.* 1. forming **nerve tissue;** giving rise to **neural impulse.** 2. originating in a **neural** or **nervous** condition.— *Syn.* NEUROGENETIC.

neuroglia (nú·rog'li·ə): *n.* tissue, composed of a special type of cell, that acts as supporting tissue for the **cerebrospinal axis.** —*Syn.* GLIA.

neurogram: *n.* 1. the hypothesized alteration in the brain as a result of experience. —*Cp.* **engram.** 2. a schematic representation of activity of the nervous system and its parts.

neurohumors: *n. pl.* collectively, the chemical agents that **mediate** the activity induced by stimulation of nerves.—*adj.* **neurohumoral.**

neurolinguistic: *adj.* (*general semantics*) characterizing the fact that human beings react not simply to events, but to events as they have been named and talked about in our language systems.

neurological examination: an examination of sensory and motor responses, esp. of the reflexes, to ascertain whether there are localized impairments of the nervous system.

neurologist: *n.* 1. a professional student of **neurology.** 2. a physician specializing in **organic** diseases of the nervous system.

neurology: *n.* the science of the structure and function, normal and abnormal, of the nervous system.—*Cp.* **neuropsychiatry.**

neuromuscular: *adj.* pertaining to both nerve and muscle.

neuromuscular junction: the surface where a motor nerve comes into contact with the muscle it **innervates.**—*Syn.* MYONEURAL JUNCTION, **motor point.**

neuromuscular spindle = **spindle/muscle.**

neuron (nú'ron): *n.* the single cell which is the fundamental unit of structure of **nerve**

tissue. ➤Each neuron consists of a central portion, the CELL BODY, from which extend two fibers, the DENDRITE and the AXON(E) or NEURITE. The dendrite is usually very short and ends in a complicated branching effect, the END BRUSH. Axons are usually longer, often have branches called COLLATERALS, and end in a much smaller end brush. **Excitation** starts with the end brush of the dendrite and is transmitted to the ends of the axon. The latter may act directly on muscle or gland—an **effector**— or may transmit the excitation to the dendrite of another neuron. The meeting place of axon and dendrite is the **synapse** (which see).

Neurons are classified as SENSORY NEURONS, those which are in contact with receptor or which initiate the neural impulse at the dendrite end; CONNECTING, or COMMISSURAL, NEURONS; and MOTOR NEURONS, those which terminate in an effector organ. According to the NEURON THEORY, the neuron is the histologic and metabolic unit of nervous tissue; but modern thinking holds that the functional unit is not the neuron but the **nervous arc** or circuit.— *Var.* **neurone** (-rōn).

neuronic: *adj.* pertaining to a neuron.— *Distg. fr.* **neurotic.**

neuropathic: *adj.* 1. characterizing an **organic** disease of the nervous system. 2. pertaining to, or similar to, **functional nervous** disease. ➤Since **neurotic** is available as a synonym for (2), usage now tends to restrict **neuropathic** to (1).—*n.* **neuropathy** (nú-rop'ə·thi).—*pers. n.* **neuropath.**

neuropathology: *n.* 1. the science that deals with diseases of the nervous system.—*Distg fr.* psychiatry.—*pers. n.* **neuropathologist** 2. the presence of disease affecting any part of the nervous system.

neurophrenia: *n.* (*rare*) a general term for behavior disorder attributed to central nervous system impairment.

neurophysiology: *n.* the branch of physiology dealing with the activities of **nerve tissue.**

neuropil(e) (-pil; -pīl): *n.* a network of delicate non**medullated** nerve fibrils found anywhere in the nervous system; esp., such fibrils found at the junction point, or **synapse,** between two or more **neurons.** —*Var.* **neuropilem** (-pī'ləm).

neuroplexus: *n.* a network of peripheral nerve fibers.—*Syn.* **plexus.**

neuropsychiatry: *n.* a combination specialty in medicine that deals with both **organic** and **functional** nervous and mental disorders.—*adj.* **neuropsychiatric.**

neurosis (nú·rō'səs) *n., pl.* **neuroses** (-sēz): 1. obsolescent term for the activity of the nervous system or of some of its specific parts. 2. a mental disorder ill-defined in character but milder than psychosis.

➤**Functional disorder** is usually meant, though **somatic** conditions play a part in neuroses both as factors in the cause and as symptoms. The term is no longer used for a specific, local, organic nerve disorder, which is called **neuropathy**. (But see **actual *neurosis,** in which some of the older meaning lingers.) ¶The widely held theory that neurosis is always derived from **anxiety** should not be incorporated in the definition.

The manifestations of neurosis are varied: **hysteria, obsessions, fugues, phobias, anxiety,** and many minor behavior symptoms. Professional treatment is needed; institutionalization is seldom indicated.—*Syn.* **psychoneurosis, nervousness, nervous *breakdown** (the last two being lay terms of indefinite meaning).—*adj.* and *pers. n.* **neurotic.**

neurosis/actual: a neurosis in which the personality is disordered as a consequence of an **organic** difficulty. ➤E.g., a person with rapid heart beat or angina may become extremely anxious and the whole personality may be overwhelmed by the fear induced by the organic disease.—*Syn.* **pathoneurosis.**

neurosis/analytic: *n.* a neurosis induced by a too-prolonged **analysis:** the patient loses his natural attitude toward life and becomes permanently dependent upon **analysts.**

neurosis/anxiety: see **anxiety neurosis.**

neurosis/arrangement of the: (*A. Adler*) the unconscious **schema**—the pattern of character traits, sentiments, and neurotic symptoms—which serves to hold the patient within the limits of a **life plan** set by early experience and by the striving for superiority.

neurosis/benign: (*E. J. Kempf*) a serious disturbance of personality in which the individual accepts the source within himself of the wishes or cravings that cause the distress, and thus is likely to recover.

neurosis/biological: a **neurosis** resulting directly from some failure of the brain to function in the normal physiological manner.

neurosis/combat: the **traumatic *neurosis** of front-line troops, popularly called **shell shock** in World War I, sometimes euphemistically called **combat fatigue** in World War II.

neurosis/compensation: 1. (*E. J. Kempf*) excessive and neurotic striving for status or achievement, initiated by fear of impotence or fear of losing control over asocial cravings.—*Cp.* **compensation. 2.** a **traumatic *neurosis** in which desire for monetary compensation (or its equivalent, e.g., discharge from military service) plays a part.

neurosis/compulsion = **obsessive-compulsive reaction.**

neurosis/compulsive-obsessive = **obses-sive-compulsive reaction.**

neurosis/experimental: compulsive, stereotyped, and chaotic behavior or inhibition of behavior, induced when an experimental animal is compelled by severe punishment to attempt discriminative responses that are too difficult. ➤E.g., in conditioning experiments, the animal is presented with two very similar stimuli, reaction to one of which avoids severe punishment; failing to discriminate between the two, the animal sometimes "goes to pieces," makes wild, random responses, or reduces all its observable responses to a state of near-coma. The equating of this behavior in experimental animals with **neurosis** in man has been questioned.

neurosis/mixed: a combination of symptoms of the **hysterical** and **obsessive-compulsive** types.

neurosis/narcissistic: (*psychoan.*) one in which the libido regresses to a pregenital phase, failing to become properly invested in an object or person. ➤Some analysts use the term for all neuroses of functional character, with the implication that all neurosis is a failure to cope with **narcissism.**—*Cp.* **transference *neurosis.**

neurosis/obsessional: a neurosis characterized by many **obsessive** ideas and actions. ➤It is now common to join this syndrome with that of **compulsive** actions and to speak of an **obsessive-compulsive reaction.**

neurosis/pension: neurotic behavior induced or exaggerated by an intense desire to obtain a pension or compensation.

neurosis/transference: (*psychoan.*) **1.** a neurosis in which the **libido** is invested in highly inappropriate or socially handicapping ways: e.g., in **anxiety hysteria. 2.** an artificial neurosis, occurring at a certain stage of **analysis,** when the analysand begins to regard the analyst as if he were one or both of his parents in the **Oedipus** situation, and re-enacts the old attitudes.

neurosis/traumatic: a **neurosis** precipitated by a severe accident, injury, or fright. ➤The individual presents physical signs that are related emotionally to the **traumatic** episode.—*Cp.* **conversion** hysteria.

neurosis / vegetative: (*psychoan.*) the effect of unconscious conflict in disturbance of the **vegetative** functions. ➤*Distg. fr.* **conversion** hysteria, which affects the **sensorimotor** functions. Hypertension and duodenal ulcer are believed to be often symptoms of vegetative neurosis. The disturbed vegetative function is not conceived as the *expression* of a conflict but as a response of the body to the persistent or recurring conflict.

neurosyphilis: *n.* syphilis that attacks the nervous system. Its two chief syndromes are locomotor **ataxia** and **paresis.**

neurotic: *adj.* **1.** pertaining to, or affected by, **neurosis. 2.** characterizing behavior that resembles that of neurosis; erratic and excessively emotional behavior. **3.** tending toward neurosis.—*pers. n.* **neurotic.**

neurotic character: 1. the basic quality, or complex of qualities or traits, that leads to the overt manifestations of **neurosis.** ➤The neurotic character may be conceived as a matter of degree. **2.** a person having the kind of personality likely to develop into neurosis; a person predisposed to **neuroticism. 3.** a person manifesting a neurosis; a neurotic. ➤Confusion between the three meanings seems inevitable.

neurotic inventory: a series of questions about a person, designed to reveal any tendency toward **neurosis.**

neuroticism: *n.* **1.** the abstract quality characterizing **neuroses.** ➤In contrast, the neurosis is the actual disorder or the concrete state of the afflicted person. **2.** a mild condition of neurosis.

neurotic process: (*K. Horney*) the characteristic activities, conscious and unconscious, by which the neurotic identifies with his **idealized *self,** is alienated from his **real *self,** and hates his **actual *self,** but thereby avoids an intolerable amount of inner conflict.

neurot(o)-: combining form meaning *neurosis, neurotic*: e.g., NEUROTOGENIC, producing or favoring neurosis.

neurovegetative system: that portion of the nervous system involved in the control of **vegetative** processes. It is chiefly the **autonomic nervous system.**

neutral: *adj.* not belonging to either of two classes or categories; in between; lying between positive and negative sides at the zero point, or in a zone closely surrounding the zero.

neutral color = **achromatic color.**

neutral environment: (*S. R. Slavson*) a physical and social environment (including the therapist) that is designed to impose no specific or rigid limitations on the persons undergoing **group therapy,** so that each member can take from the environment whatever he needs.

neutralizer: *n.* (*S. R. Slavson*) in **group therapy,** a member who counteracts the aggressions and destructive behaviors of other members.

neutral stimulus: see **stimulus/neutral.**

nevus (nē′vəs) *n., pl.* **nevi** (-vī): a pigmented birthmark.—*Var.* **naevus.**

newborn: *n.* an infant of age less than one month.—*Syn.* **neonate.**—See **development/levels of.**

nexus (nek′səs): *n.* **1.** a connection or link between members of a group or items in a series. **2.** = CAUSAL NEXUS, that element in a complex whole which makes two things or

events mutually dependent: the causal *nexus* was their desire to cooperate.

night blindness: see **blindness/night.**

night fantasy: (*psychoan.*) **fantasies** experienced in sleep, differing from those of dreams in not being subject to **dream work.**

nightmare: *n.* a dream full of fear and anxiety, depicting fearful events.

night terrors: a nightmare from which the dreamer (usually a child) awakes but the terror continues. Often the dream is not recalled and the cause of the terror is not known.—*Syn.* PAVOR NOCTURNUS.

night vision: seeing under sharply reduced illumination; or the degree of vision of which an organism is capable under reduced illumination.

nihil ex nihilo fit: (*L., nothing comes from nothing*) a Scholastic statement of the law of universal causation.

nihilistic delusion: (nī″i·lis′tik): a **delusion** that the existing order of things has disappeared.

nirvana (nir·vä′nə): *n.* **1.** the goal of life, according to Buddhist teaching, in which all desires are extinguished and individuality is merged with the cosmos. ➤Psychoanalysts equate the NIRVANA PRINCIPLE, based on the loss of individuality, with Freud's **death instinct. 2.** a blissful state of existence in which all needs are satisfied.

nirvanism (nir·vä′niz·əm): *n.* the feeling of loss of personality or of loss of desire.

Nissl bodies: large granules found in the **dendrites** and **nerve cell** body.

nisus (nī′səs): *n.* Leibnitz's term for **drive.**

NIT = National Intelligence Test.

nociceptor (nō″si·sep′tər): *n.* a **receptor** for hurtful stimuli; a pain receptor.— *Contr. w.* **beneceptor.**—*adj.* **nociceptive.**

noctambulation (nok·tam″bū·lā′shən): *n.* sleepwalking at night.—*Syn.* **somnambulism.**—*adj.* **noctambulant.**—*pers. n.* **noctambulist.**

nocturnal: *adj.* pertaining to or occurring at night.

nocturnal emission: loss of **semen** during sleep.

nodal: *adj.* having the nature of a **node.**

nodal behavior: in **group therapy,** a peak period of great activity, generally aggressive or disorderly. It is followed by a period of quietude called the ANTINODE.

nodal point: (*optics*) either of two points located on the **axis** of a lens system so that a ray passing through one point emerges from the other on a parallel course. ➤The two points in the human eye are close together and about 7 millimeters behind the cornea. From every point in the visual field a ray of light may be conceived to pass through the nodal points to the points on the retina where the stimulus takes effect.

no data: a tabulating category used when

no answer is given or when the data returned cannot be tabulated under any accepted heading.

node: *n.* **1.** the point in a wave where it has zero **amplitude.**—*Ant.* crest. **2.** a point in a psychological **field** around which the field is organized. **3.** (*anat.*) a protuberance or knotty swelling.

noegenetic (nō″ə·jə·net′ik): *adj.* (*C. Spearman*) pertaining to the creation or generation of new items of knowledge on the basis of **sentience.**—*Cp.* **eduction.**—*n.* **noegenesis.**

noesis (nō·ē′səs): *n.* **1.** a **cognitive** or **intellective** process. **2.** (*C. Spearman*) the property of yielding or being knowledge.—*adj.* **noetic** (-et′ik).

noise: *n.* **1.** the sensory effect of irregular (aperiodic) sound waves; a sound that lacks tone, that is composed of conflicting pitches. ➤Such conflict is only relative—the gradation from pure tone to noise is a continuum. **2.** undesired sound: e.g., a beautiful song may be mere noise if it interferes with a task. **3.** (*commun. theory*) anything that introduces extraneous variability into a communication process, or that raises the **entropy (3)** or reduces the **information** —i.e., difference between **input** and **output** generated by random error in the communication system itself. ➤Although based upon a proper analogy with (2), this usage can be confusing unless the author makes clear that he is using the word in an unusual or extended sense. A confounding of the *data* of audition with the data of vision would be condemned by all; should we then adopt a terminology that confounds auditory with visual? The prime purpose of names is to show differences, not similarities. It is suggested that the word **clutter** would create fewer confusions.—*Cp.* **noise/white.**—See **rational coinage. 4.** in radar readings, a lighted area on the tube face that does not represent reflecting objects in space. ➤This is a specialization of meaning **(3).**

noise/white: random fluctuation noise; the noise that is heard when very many sound waves of different lengths are combined so that they reinforce or cancel one another in haphazard fashion. ➤The phrasing of this term (unlike **noise 3**) clearly indicates its analogical nature, hence no confusion results. But the analogy with white light must not be pressed too far; there are many differences.

nomadism (nō′mad·iz·əm; nom′əd-): *n.* (*psychopathol.*) a pathological tendency to change residence frequently.

Nomenclature/Standard (Psychiatric): see **Standard (Psychiatric) Nomenclature.**

nominal: *adj.* **1.** of, consisting of, or pertaining to, a name or names; or to a noun or nouns; pertaining to distinctions based on words, not on factual differences; hence, **2.** not of great importance: a *nominal* expense.

nominal aphasia: see aphasia/nominal.

nominalism: *n.* **1.** (*philos.*) the doctrine that holds that concepts, abstractions, or universals are but words, and that only concrete particulars are real. **2.** a tendency to be overimpressed with verbal formulations, to believe that what is named must be real. ➤Paradoxically, modern believers in **nominalism (1)** (who call themselves, not by that name, but rather **empiricists** or **positivists**) now use **nominalism (2)** as a derogatory term.

nominal weight = **weight (2).**

nominating technique: a rating technique in which the rater selects or names the person in a small population who seems best (or least) to conform to a certain criterion: e.g., *the most popular in the group, my best friend in the group, the one I'd least like to live with,* etc. ➤The combination of many such ratings is used to characterize both the group structure and the personality of the individuals.

nomogram: *n.* a chart to facilitate the finding of the value of a third variable when the respective values of two correlative variables are given. ➤It consists typically of three parallel lines representing the values of the three related variables in such a way that a straight line through points on the first two will intercept the third line at a point representing the related value. E.g., let one line represent the values of **Pearsonian** *r,* a second the number of cases; the third line can be read to show the value of the **standard error** of any value of *r* for any given number of cases.—*Var.* **nomograph.** —*Distg.* **nomograph** *fr.* monograph.

nomological: *adj.* pertaining to the formulation of general scientific laws.—*Prefd.* to its *syn.* **nomothetic.**—See **psychology/ divisions and schools of, VII, IX.**—*n.* **nomology.**

nomothetic: (-thet′ik): *adj.* characterizing procedures and methods designed to discover general laws. ➤*Contr. w.* **idiographic,** which pertains to the attempt to understand a particular event or individual. (The spellings *nomathetic* and *ideographic* are erroneous.)—*Syn.* **nomological** (*prefd.* as having a noun form).

non-: prefix meaning *not, lacking, without.* ➤*Syn.* un-, in- or im-, a- or an-, anti-. *Un-* is more appropriate for Germanic roots, *in-* or *im-* for Latin roots. *Non-* and *anti-,* although Latin prefixes, and *a-,* although Greek, are used for words of any origin. (But, for all the above, etymology is often violated.) *In-* and *anti-* tend to be stronger than *un-* or *non-.* Compare, for **example,**

*non*moral with *un*moral and *im*moral, *non*social with *anti*social.

nonacademic: *adj.* **1.** pertaining to school subjects that do not, or do not seem to, involve much verbal ability: athletics, music, arts, crafts, etc. **2.** pertaining to abilities such as are needed in working directly with things or with people, or to ability shown otherwise than in schoolwork or related tasks.

nonadditive: adj. **1.** characterizing a **gestalt**, i.e., a whole having properties that cannot be derived by adding the properties of the several parts. **2.** of an aggregate whose components are too heterogeneous to permit of adding: potatoes, triangles, and the Declaration of Independence make a nonadditive aggregate. ➤Note that meanings (1) and (2) are strikingly contrary.

nonadjustive behavior: action that does not help the individual to meet the practical requirements of his life but may, at least temporarily, bring satisfaction or release from tension. PERSISTENT NONADJUSTIVE BEHAVIOR, though temporarily satisfactory, leads to increasing tension.—*Cp.* **adjustment, maladjustment.**

non compos mentis (non kom′pəs men′təs): *adj.* mentally incapable of regulating one's affairs in normal fashion; mentally defective or deranged.

nonconscious: *adj.* of that which does not display any degree of consciousness; esp., of lifeless substance. ➤*Distg. fr.* **unconscious,** which refers to a special condition or activity of a living organism.

noncontinuity learning theory = **discontinuity theory of learning.**

noncontradiction/law of = **contradiction/law of.**

nondetermination/coefficient of: the proportion of the variance in the **dependent** *variable which is not accounted for by the independent *variable or variables. It is the complement of **coefficient of *determination.**—*Distg. fr.* coefficient of *multiple* nondetermination, for which see **multiple determination/coefficient of.**

nondirective procedure: a procedure in psychotherapy or counseling in which the therapist (or counselor), after establishing an atmosphere of **acceptance** of the client (or counselee), carefully refrains from directing the communication of the client. (Hence the adjective *nondirective.*) Instead, he attempts to reflect back to the client what the latter has said, sometimes restating the client's remarks (see **clarification remark**), but never attempting to correlate them with facts or other statements and trying never to evaluate them. Responsibility for discovering the nature of his problem and planning its solution rests with the client.—*Syn.* **therapeutic *coun-**

seling, client-centered *therapy,** the latter preferred when both the underlying doctrine and the procedure are meant. For nondirective interviewing, see **open-ended question.**

nondirective therapy = **therapy/client centered.**

noneducable: *adj.* a term applied loosely to persons who do not, in a given time and with given effort, learn enough to be worth the effort.

nonlinear: *adj.* **1.** not capable of being represented by a straight line. **2.** = **curvilinear.** (A poor but common usage.)

nonliterate: *adj.* pertaining to a culture or a people who lack written language: a *non literate* society. ➤*Prefd.* to **primitive** and PRELITERATE, since it does not imply a position on a ladder of progress.—*Distg. fr.* **illiterate.**

nonmetric: *adj.* **1.** pertaining to that which lacks quantity or magnitude. ➤It is a fundamental postulate of science that all *actual* things have quantity; but there are concepts, or at least words put forward as concepts, which do not have quantity. **2.** pertaining to that which is described in non-quantitative terms; nonmetricized. ➤It is not implied that it *cannot* be quantified.

nonmoral: *adj.* characterizing that to which **moral** considerations do not apply. ➤*Distg. fr.* **immoral,** contravening or violating moral injunctions; **amoral,** characterizing a person indifferent to morality or pretending to be above moral considerations; **unmoral,** lacking moral perceptions (but also used as synonym for **nonmoral**).

nonparametric: *adj.* of a method or test used in analyzing data that do not assume any particular **parameter;** specif., of methods that do not assume that the **true** distribution is **normal.**—*Syn.* **distribution-free.**

nonparametric statistics: see **statistics, nonparametric.**

nonrational: *adj.* characterizing that to which **reasoning** and **rational** considerations do not apply. ➤*Distg. fr.* **irrational,** contrary to reasoning or **rationality** or lacking rationality where it could be expected or hoped for.

nonreader: *n.* a person who, after extended instruction, is unable to read well enough to be able to use the skill. ➤It is implied not that the failure is incurable, but that it will not be remedied by ordinary instruction.

nonresponse: *n.* a category, in tabulating data, in which are recorded all failures to respond to a particular item. Various statistical methods of handling such a category are in use, but all assume that **nonresponse** is significant.

nonsense figure: a figure that neither

closely resembles any familiar thing nor conforms exactly to any simple geometric or regular form.

nonsense syllable: a pronounceable combination of letters, used chiefly in memory experiments, that has no meaning in the language of the person using it.

non sequitur (sek′wi·tər): a conclusion that does not logically follow from the premises; by extension, the argument that leads to such a conclusion.

nonsocial: *adj.* **1.** lying outside the **social** sphere; not pertaining to a plurality of individuals or to groups. **2.** of a person who is indifferent to the group, does not consciously identify with it, or concern himself with its welfare.—*Distg. fr.* **unsocial** or **unsociable,** lacking social qualities; and from **antisocial,** working against society or its rules.—*Syn.* **asocial,** which has a stronger connotation of turning away from society.

nonspecific response: one that cannot be attributed to a given stimulus.—*Syn.* **emitted** response (see **emission 2**), **spontaneous** response (see **spontaneous behavior**).

nonverbal test: see **test/nonverbal.**

nonvoluntary: see **involuntary.**

Nordic race: one of the three hypothetical races from which modern Europeans are said to be descended. ➤The Nordics were tall, blond, and **dolicocephalic:** they are best represented in Scandinavia. The ALPINES were of medium stature, semibrunet or colorless blond, and **brachycephalic.** The MEDITERRANEANS were short, brunet, and **dolicocephalic.** All European nations today are composite in respect to these three racial stocks, and others (Mongolian, Semitic, Negro) are also represented. Individuals may correspond to the theoretical physical **types;** large groups do not.

norm: *n.* **1.** (*stat.*) a single **value,** or a **range** of values, constituting the usual performance of a given group; any measure of **central tendency,** or a range of values on each side of that measure. ➤The range to be included in the norm is arbitrary but is usually no greater than twice the standard deviation.—*Distg. fr.* **standard. 2.** the usual in quality, form, size, or function. ➤In a term such as SOCIAL NORM, it is often impossible to tell whether meaning **(1), (2),** or **(3)** is intended. **3.** = **standard.** ➤This usage is unfortunate, since it deprives **norm** of its quantitative reference merely to provide *standard* with an unnecessary synonym. **4.** that which functions in accord with its design; the biologically typical. ➤This meaning is seldom overtly accepted, but it probably infects all but the most severely quantitative usage.—*Ant.* non-normal.

normal: *adj.* **1.** conforming to, or not deviating from, the usual or the average or the type or the **norm;** hence, **2.** neither **abnormal** nor **subnormal;** not suffering from **mental disorder** or **mental *deficiency.** —See **abnormality. 3.** (*stat.*) characterizing a distribution that may be represented by a **mesokurtic** bell-shaped curve. ➤This was called the normal **frequency** because it was formerly believed to be the "usual," but it is now known that the conditions for such a distribution are far from universally fulfilled.—See **frequency. 4.** not caused by, or influenced by, special conditions or treatment.—*Syn.* **regular. 5.** constituting a standard worthy of emulation and possible of attainment for most persons.—*Cp.* **ideal.** —*Syn.* **standard** (*prefd.*). **6.** forming a right angle; perpendicular (of a line); esp. (*optics*), of a perpendicular to the surface at the point where a ray of light strikes it.

normal curve, normal distribution, normal equation, normal frequency: see **frequency curve/normal** and **frequency.**

normality: *n.* the state or quality of being **normal** in any of the meanings given; esp., the state of being free from **mental disorder.**

normalize: *v.* **1.** to adjust a set of measures so that they conform to a normal **frequency. 2.** to alter something in such a way as to make it **normal,** or in accord with an accepted **norm.**

normal law of error: (*K. Gauss, P. Laplace*) the generalization that errors of measurement are distributed in a normal **frequency.**

normal probability: see **frequency curve/ normal** and **frequency.**

normative: *adj.* pertaining to **norms, standards,** or **values.** ➤A NORMATIVE SCIENCE is a discipline that systematically studies man's attempts to determine what is correct, valuable, good, or beautiful: **logic, ethics, esthetics.**—*Ant.* EMPIRICAL SCIENCE. There are many normative elements in psychology (*cp.* **mental hygiene**), and a full-blown NORMATIVE PSYCHOLOGY, based in part on empirical scientific psychology, is emerging.—*Distg.* NORMATIVE SCIENCE *fr.* NORMATIVE STUDY or INVESTIGATION, which usually refers to an attempt to set up statistical norms.

norm/composite: a **norm (1)** for the distribution obtained when scores from two or more measurements are combined. The scores must be reduced to a common basis (*cp.* **derived *score**) and appropriately weighted.

norm/developmental = age norm.

norm/grade: see **grade norm.**

norm/group: 1. the **norm (1)** representing the achievement of a given group. **2.** = social ***norm** (*prefd.*).

norm line: a smoothed ***curve** drawn to

represent the mean or median scores of successive age or grade groups.

norm/local: the **norm** determined by the performance of the population of a given locality. ➤*Contr. w.* NATIONAL NORM, STATE-WIDE NORM, the norm determined by the performance of such specified larger populations. A local norm is valueless unless based on a sufficient number of cases.

norm/national: a **norm** (1) based on a nationwide **sampling.**

norm/occupational: the representative range of scores on a particular variable made by successful workers in a given occupation.

norm/percentile: a point on a scale defined by the percentage of scores in the population that lie below this point. It is merely a **percentile** score of a standard population.

norm/social: 1. any socially sanctioned mode of behavior. 2. social behavior occurring sufficiently often to be accepted without criticism or special notice. ➤Since the latter tends to become the former, the two meanings are not always distinguished; and neither is distinguished from 3. a **frame of reference** or a **standard** by which behavior is judged in a given social group.—*Syn.* GROUP NORM (not *recom.*).

nos(o)-: combining form meaning *disease.*

nosology (nō·sol′ə·ji): *n.* the classification of diseases; the branch of medicine that treats of the classification of diseases, and of distinctions between them.—*adj.* **noso-logical.**—*pers. n.* **nosologist.**

nosophobia (nos″ō·fō′bi·ə): *n.* morbid fear of disease, or of a specific disease.

nostalgia: *n.* homesickness.—*adj.* **nostalgic.**

notation: *n.* the representation of any system by a system of symbols.—*Syn.* CODI-FICATION, **code.** ➤The most familiar notations are the alphabet and the number system.

notation/color: see **Munsell color system.**

notice: *v.* to observe attentively enough to be able to report.

noticeable: *adj.* characterizing something that can be perceived; specif., of a stimulus intense enough, or a stimulus difference of any sort great enough, to be perceived and reported.—See **just noticeable differences/method of.**

notion: *n.* an idea; esp., a vague idea, or one not well supported by fact or reasoning.

notochord (nō′tə·kôrd): *n.* the embryonic forerunner of the brain and spinal cord.

nous (nous, nüs): *n.* (*Gk., mind*) in philosophy, the reason (generally conceived as a **faculty**).

novice: *n.* a person with practically no training or experience in a particular trade or profession. ➤*Cp.* the trade hierarchy: **novice, apprentice, journeyman, expert.**

noxa (nok′sə) *n., pl.* **noxae** (nok′sē):

anything, physical or mental, that is injurious to health.—*Cp.* **trauma.**—*adj.* **noxal.**

noxious (nok′shəs): *adj.* injurious, harmful.

NP: *abbr.* for **neuropsychiatry.**

N.S. or **n.s.** = **nervous system.**

nuclear: *adj.* pertaining to a **nucleus.**

nuclear complex = **nuclear problem.**

nuclear family: see **family.**

nuclear layer = **mantle layer.**

nuclear problem: a core or central problem, a central conflict, which has its roots in infancy, and plays a part in the entire development of the personality, esp. of later conflicts and complexes. ➤For A. Adler, the nuclear problem is the feeling of **inferiority,** for Freudians it is the **Oedipus** situation, for neopsychoanalysts any early conflict may become for a particular person the nuclear problem.—*Contr. w.* **conflict/actual.**—*Syn.* ROOT CONFLICT, NUCLEAR CONFLICT, NUCLEAR COMPLEX.

nucleus *n., pl.* **nuclei, nucleuses:** 1. a central mass or point about which matter is gathered; a focal point. 2. the most important portion of every living cell, having a definite structure separated from the rest of the cell, or **cytoplasm.** 3. a cluster of cells within the cerebrum.—*adj.* **nuclear.**

nucleus/amygdaloid: see **amygdaloid nucleus.**

nucleus/red: either of two large oval nuclei situated in the **mesencephalon,** one on each side of the **middle line.**

nuisance/attractive: see **attractive nuisance.**

null hypothesis: the logical **contradictory** of the hypothesis that one seeks to test. ➤If the null hypothesis can be proved false, its contradictory is thereby proved true. (See **opposition** 1.) Since one exception can overthrow a generalization, it is usually easier to disprove the null than to prove the original hypothesis directly. Hence, a common research design calls for a testing to see whether the null hypothesis can be denied or disproved. There are two cautions: only the strictest logical contradictory can be used as a null hypothesis (a contrary hypothesis does not serve); and, *failure* to disprove the null hypothesis does not permit of any inference. ¶In a typical experimental design, the hypothesis is that two variables show a greater-than-chance difference. The null hypothesis is that there is no difference greater than could be expected by chance; this is tested by appropriate examination of obtained differences.

nulliplex inheritance: inheritance determined by a **recessive** factor from each parent.

number blindness = sensory **acalculia.**

number combination = **number fact.**

number completion test: one in which the task is to complete a series of numbers that are arranged according to some plan or pattern: e.g., 3, 6, 12, ——, ——.

number concept: 1. the **idea** one has about the number system. **2.** (*educ.*) the correctness and extent of a pupil's grasp of the idea of number and of the number system.

number fact or **combination:** an arithmetic statement of the result of computation between two numbers: $2 + 6 = 8$, $4 \times 3 = 12$, $9 \div 3 = 3$ are number facts. The BASIC FUNDAMENTAL NUMBER FACTS are those employing in the computation only the numbers 1 to 9.

number factor or **N:** a factor, found in the analysis of many ability tests, manifested in facility for manipulation of numbers and for closely related operations.—See **abilities/primary mental.**

number form: an imaginal representation of the number series in which the person "sees" each number as having a position in

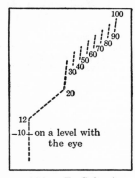

(After F. Galton)

space. ➤Often a vivid image of such spatial representation is evoked when hearing or seeing numerals. A fairly common form has the numbers from 0 to 9 on one line, those from 10 to 19 on a line at an angle to it, etc. to 100.—See **synesthesia.**

number/rational: a number expressible as the quotient of two whole numbers or integers. An IRRATIONAL NUMBER is a perfectly definite number, but it cannot be expressed as a quotient between two integers: e.g. π, the ratio between circumference and diameter of a circle; the square root of 2.

numerical value = absolute *value.

nurturance: *n.* the tendency that leads one to provide nurture—i.e., food, shelter, and other care—to the young or to the weak and incapable.

nurture: *n.* **1.** the environmental factors collectively—whether those of education and training, or those directly influencing physical growth and metabolism—that affect an individual from conception onward. **2.** those environmental factors provided by parents and by social agency; rearing; upbringing. —*Contr. w.* **nature (1).**

nutriance need: (*H. A. Murray*) the need to seek food and drink.

nutrient: *n.* a substance taken into the body and transformed into living tissue or stored.

nyctalopia (nik″tə·lō′pi·ə): *n.* **1.** = **day *blindness. 2.** = **night *blindness.** ➤The term is too ambiguous for any use.

nyctophobia: *n.* morbid fear of the dark.

nymphomania: *n.* abnormally strong sex desire in females.—*Syn.* ANDROMANIA.—*Ant.* **frigidity.**—*Cp.* **satyriasis,** abnormal sex desire in males; **erotomania,** the general term.

nystagmus (nis·tag′məs): *n.* a quick, jerky movement of the eyes, followed by a slower return. ➤In most cases the movement is lateral; but ROTATORY NYSTAGMUS, in which the eye moves about the visual axis, and VERTICAL NYSTAGMUS, in which the eye moves up and down, also occur. It is a normal phenomenon in pursuit movements of the eye (e.g., watching the landscape from a moving vehicle), but may also be symptomatic of visual defect or of brain lesion. Its presence or absence under varied stimulation (**caloric *nystagmus, rotational *nystagmus, galvanic *nystagmus**) is used in neurological diagnosis.—*adj.* **nystagmic.**

nystagmus/caloric: induction of nystagmus by irrigation of one or both ears with hot or cold water.

nystagmus/galvanic: nystagmus induced by passing an electric current through the auditory **labyrinth.**

nystagmus/rotational: nystagmus induced by rapid rotation of the body, the quick phase of the eye movement being in the direction of rotation, the slower drift in the opposite direction. In POSTROTATIONAL NYSTAGMUS, the directions of the nystagmic movement are reversed.

O

O: 1. = observer. (*pl. Os.* Usually *ital.*) **2.** = organism. ➤In either (1) or (2), *O* can be used for the individual experimented on.—*Syn. S* (1). **3.** = (*Ror.*) original response. **4.** = oscillation.

$_8O_R$ = (*C. Hull*) behavioral *oscillation. —*Distg. fr.* S-O-R, stimulus→organism→response.

obedience: *n.* conformity to rules and commands. ➤As compared with **compliance,**

there is often an implication that obedience is unwilling or unpleasant.

object: *n.* **1.** anything whatever. **2.** that of which a **subject** or a **person** may be aware, toward which he takes any sort of attitude, or to which he responds; any phase, aspect, or part of the environment in the widest sense: a unit of the situation which has a relatively constant meaning for a person. ➤Objects may be material (more accurately, **physical**), **social**, or **abstract** (i.e., **conceptual**).—*Cp.* perspective (2). In terms of inclusiveness we have a series: **stimulus, object, situation, field. 3.** that which one seeks or strives for; aim; purpose; **objective** (*n.*). **4.** the **conscious** *content, in contrast both to the **act** or **process** of knowing or being aware, and to the actual environment or **stimulus. 5.** that which, presented to our perception, has a fixed and stable character, independent of the desires or opinions of the perceiver. **6.** that which has an existence independent of any **subject** or knower. **7.** = **object of** *instinct. ➤These meanings are often confounded so that two or more are implied in any given usage. In this dictionary, usage (2) is nearly always intended.

object assembly test: 1. a test requiring the subject to put together simple objects that have been disassembled. **2.** a jigsaw puzzle used as a test.

object assimilation: the tendency of the **memory** *image of a particular object to be altered toward a type form, to become with time more and more typical of the class to which it belongs: e.g., the memory of a particular ear of corn more and more approaches the image of the typical ear. ➤The object may logically be classifiable into several classes; the memory image assimilates to the type image of that class most functional for the individual.

object attitude: (*structural psychol.*) the attitude in which the observer is set to attend to the meaning or context of an experience. ➤It contrasts both with the **stimulus attitude (2)** and with the **process attitude.**

object/behavior: an object toward which there is a socially standardized kind of behavior: e.g., a fountain pen, a chair, chopsticks. ➤A given individual may not know, or may elect to ignore, the socially recognized behavior.

object blindness: a disorder in which, though able to see, the person cannot recognize objects as such.—*Syn.* agnosia/visual.

object cathexis: (*psychoan.*) **1.** diversion of the **libido** from its primary sexual aim and its investment in an object not directly sexual. **2.** more generally, investment of libido in an object.—*Syn.* (for **2**) **object choice.**

object choice: (*psychoan.*) selection of an object or person as the love object.—*Syn.*

object cathexis. ➤The choice may b narcissistic or anaclitic, the object may be real or merely imaginary.

object color: color seen as belonging to ar object. ➤This includes **surface** an **volume** *colors to the extent that surface and volumes are perceived as objects o. parts of objects. Object colors are relatively insensitive to changes in viewing conditions i.e., they exhibit the phenomenon of **con stancy.**

object constancy: see **constancy/object.**

object finding: (*psychoan.*) the process o transferring **libido** from **erogenous zone.** to objects in the environment.—*Cp.* **object libido, object cathexis.**

objectification: see **sublimation.**

objectify: *v.* to make a phenomenon apparent to the senses; to make **objective.**

objectifying attitude: (*K. Goldstein*) ar attitude wherein the subject is reacting t the properties of an external object, disregarding his personal reactions to it. ➤Ob jectivity, or objectivity attitude, are mor suitable for this meaning.

objectifying function: the process by which the *Gestaltqualität* is created.

object/instinctual or **object of instinct** see **instinct/object of.**

objectivation: *n.* (*psychoan.*) that specia form of defensive **projection** in which one's own feelings are ascribed to anothe who, as it happens, actually has them ➤E.g., an unsympathetic person covers up by a sensitive detection of the lack of sympathy manifested by others. When the projection is to an inanimate object, the actua possession of corresponding feelings car only be symbolic. For the latter, defensive **empathy (1)** seems a better term.

objective: *adj.* **1.** (*philos.* prior to Kant) existing in idea; of that which is the object of a subject's awareness. ➤This meaning is almost the direct opposite of **2.** (*philos.*) existing in fact in the world, not merely in idea; not **subjective. 3.** = **physical;** open to observation by physical instruments. **4.** not dependent upon the judgment or accuracy of the individual observer; free from personal and emotional bias; hence, **5.** open to observation by any competent observer. **6.** localized by the observer outside his own body: visual data are localized as objective, whereas **kinesthetic** data are not. **7.** pertaining to an **object.**

➤Meanings (2), (3), (4), (5) are often not clearly distinguished; OBJECTIVE DATA, e.g., may imply any of them.—See **objective psychology, test/objective.**

objective: *n.* that at which one aims.—*Syn.* **goal, purpose, aim.**

objective psychology: a point of view or school of psychology which restricts itself to that which is open to observation by any competent observer, i.e., to data subject to measurement in physical terms. ➤In a broad sense, virtually all contemporary psychology is objective; its data are the data of response or performance. But objective psychology, as so named, rejects introspective data and introspective interpretations of data.—*Contr. w.* **phenomenology, subjective psychology, content psychology.**—*Approx. syn.* **behaviorism, objectivism.**

objective type: see **subjective type.**

objectivism: *n.* **1.** = **objective psychology. 2.** (*educ.*) a point of view that stresses impersonal standards in education.

objectivity: *n.* freedom from bias; impersonality; judgment unaffected by feeling. ➤The OBJECTIVITY OF A TEST applies to the test form and to its scoring, not to the attitude of the testee.

object libido: (*psychoan.*) **libido** bestowed upon persons, objects, causes, etc., external to the self. It is said to be the work of the **ego.**—*Contr. w.* **ego libido.**—*Syn.* OBJECT LOVE.

object loss: (*psychoan.*) loss of the love coming to one from a certain person.

object love = **object libido.**

object of instinct: see **instinct/object of.**

object size: the size of an object as determined from measurement at its surface. ➤When **size constancy** holds, a person perceives a not too distant object as near its object size.

oblique: *adj.* of a line or a plane meeting another line or plane at some angle other than 90°.

oblique (axes) solution: (*factor anal.*) a solution wherein the axes representing factors are not at right angles, i.e., they are OBLIQUE FACTORS. ➤Such factors are correlated with each other; the matrix of the correlations between factors (FACTOR MATRIX) can be factored to yield **second-order *factors.**—*Contr. w.* **orthogonal solution.**

oblique muscles: a pair of **eye muscles** (which see).

obliviscence (ob″li·vis′ǝns): *n.* **1.** forgetfulness. **2.** the tendency of material that has been learned to disappear or to become unrecallable. ➤*Contr. w.* **reminiscence,** the tendency of material learned to recur later.

oblongata = **medulla oblongata.**

obnubilation: *n.* clouding of consciousness; partial stupor.

obscenity: *n.* gestures, language, or pictures that violate the established conventions of what may properly be expressed under certain conditions in respect to sex and the excretory functions. ➤**Obscenity** obviously varies with the circumstances and with the culture; the effort to define it by legislation meets grave difficulties.—*Distg. fr.* **indecency.**—*adj.* **obscene.**

obscurantism (ob·skyûr′ǝn·tiz·ǝm): *n.* **1.** deliberate attempt to keep others from understanding. **2.** opposition to public enlightenment, to science and education.—*adj.* **obscurant.**

observation: *n.* **1.** directed or intentional awareness or scrutiny of particulars or facts. ➤It is sometimes opposed to **experiment;** more commonly the latter is taken to be a particular form of observation. **2.** a numerical value or score by which an observed fact is represented. **3.** remarks, esp. informal remarks, stating what has been observed.

observational methods: techniques and procedures for assisting the observer to make more complete and accurate observation. ➤Included are mechanical aids to observation, charts and check lists for prompt and inclusive records, motion picture photography and sound recording, special training of the observer.

observation/error of: see **error of observation.**

observation/naturalistic: see **naturalistic observation.**

observation/random: see **random observation.**

observer or *O:* *n.* **1.** one who attends closely to an object or event with a view to noting and reporting about it. **2.** one who makes **introspective** observations; = **subject (3)** (which see).—*Contr. w.* **experimenter.**

observer/participant: a person who observes a social process while himself taking part in it.

obsession: *n.* an idea that haunts one and cannot be shaken off. It is usually associated with dread or anxiety.—See **obsessive-compulsive reaction.**—*adj.* and *pers. n.* **obsessive.**

obsessional neurosis: see **neurosis/obsessional.**

obsession/masked: (*psychoan.*) an obsession that manifests itself in a disguised form, esp. in the form of a psychogenic alleged pain. ➤The pain is said either to be the means whereby a pleasurable obsessive idea is kept from consciousness, or to be the representative in consciousness of the repressed idea.

obsession/somatic: one that centers upon a bodily feature: e.g., Cyrano's *obsession* with his nose.

obsessive-compulsive reaction: (*Stan. Psychiat.*) a psychoneurotic behavior in which **anxiety** is associated with preoccupation with unwanted ideas (OBSESSION) and with persistent impulses to repeat certain acts over and over (COMPULSION): e.g., the compulsion to count every step, to touch every tree one passes in walking, to wash the hands constantly, etc. ➤OBSESSIONS and COMPULSIONS were formerly distinguished, but it is now recognized that they form only a single syndrome or behavior pattern. See **compulsiveness.** The obsessive-compulsive reaction is classified as a **psychoneurosis**, and **compulsive personality** as a **personality disorder**, but the overlap is great.—*Syn.* COMPULSION NEUROSIS, OBSESSIVE-COMPULSIVE NEUROSIS. The simple term **compulsiveness** is often used for the whole syndrome.

obstacle sense: the ability, often found in the blind and in some others, to avoid obstacles without visual warning.—*Cp.* **facial vision.**

obstruction method or **technique:** a means of measuring the relative strength of an animal's motivation by determining to what extent it will endure a negatively rewarding stimulus in order to reach a goal. ➤In the COLUMBIA OBSTRUCTION BOX the animal is separated from the goal or incentive by an electrically charged grid. The strength of the motivation to seek the goal provided—food, mate, offspring—is measured by the number of approaches, contacts, or crossings in a given period.

obtained score = **raw *score.**

Occam's razor (ok'əmz): a general canon of thinking stated in the form that "entities" (= explanatory principles) should not be needlessly multiplied. ➤See **parsimony/principle of.** The application of Occam's razor to the concepts, constructs, and terms of psychology would have made this dictionary a smaller book.

occasionalism: *n.* (*philos.*) a form of parallelism holding that God directly causes the bodily processes that correspond to or are parallel to psychic processes (or vice versa) on the occasion of a change in either.

occipital lobe (ok·sip'ə·təl): a major division of either cerebral **hemisphere:** in man it is situated in the dorsal portion.

occlusion: *n.* a closing; a stopping of a passageway.—*v.* **occlude.**

occultism: *n.* the attempt to control natural processes by secret and magical procedures; or belief in the possibility of such control.—*adj.* **occult.**

occupation: *n.* 1. an activity in which a person regularly engages for pay. 2. whatever one is doing.

occupational ability pattern: the average test scores on a variety of tests made by workers in the several occupations.

occupational family: a group of occupations that require similar ability and training.

occupational field: a broad area of occupations that require, for their successful pursuit, similar abilities, aptitudes, and vocational-interest patterns.—*Cp.* **occupational family,** which is somewhat narrower.

occupational hierarchy: 1. the ordering of occupations according to the severity of requirements, or of a particular requirement, for competence: e.g., the ordering of jobs according to the average intelligence found

necessary. **2.** the ordering or rating of occupational groups according to the social esteem in which they are held. ➤The rating depends upon a variety of ill-defined criteria and differs according to the phrasing of the inquiry.

occupational interest inventory: an inquiry form listing a considerable number of **interests** that have been found to correlate with the interests manifested by persons of demonstrated success in a variety of occupations.

occupational level: see **level/occupational.**

occupational prestige: see **occupational hierarchy.**

occupational test: a test of ability in a given vocation.—*Distg. fr.* **vocational aptitude test.**—*Cp.* **trade *test.**

occupational therapy: treatment of disorders by giving the patient purposeful work to do. In certain surgical cases, the work is designed to exercise certain muscles, but the more usual purpose is to induce a healthier "frame of mind."

ochlophobia (ok"lə·fō'bi·ə): *n.* morbid fear of crowds.

octave: *n.* a pitch interval between two tones, one of which has twice the vibration frequency of the other; or the higher of the two tones so related.

ocular: *adj.* having to do with the eye.—*Syn.* **ophthalmic.**—*Distg. fr.* **optic** (which see).

ocular dominance: see **dominance (5).**

oculo- (ok'ū·lō-): combining form meaning *the eye* or *pertaining to the eye.*

oculogyral illusion or **movement** (-jī'rəl): the apparent movement of a very faint light in a darkened room which occurs as a result of **rotational *nystagmus.**

oculomotor: *adj.* pertaining to eye movements of three sorts: of the extrinsic muscles which turn the eyeball (**eye-muscle** movements); of **accommodation,** chiefly effecting changes in the lens; of the **iris,** effecting change in the pupil.

oculomotoric (-mō·tôr'ik): *adj.* properly, pertaining to the neuromuscular *system* that moves the eyeballs. ➤It is often employed as a fancy term for **oculomotor,** i.e., as pertaining to eye movements.

oculomotor nerve: (*neurol.*) the IIIrd cranial nerve, which innervates all the extrinsic **eye muscles** except the external rectus and superior oblique.

odd-even technique: see **correlation/chance-halves.**

odor: *n.* that which is smelled. ➤Odor may refer either to the stimulus or to the **mental *content.**—*Syn.* **smell,** scent.—*adj.* **odorous.**

odorimetry (ō"dər·im'ə·tri): *n.* the measurement of odors.

odor prism: (*H. Henning*) a schematic representation of relations between the supposed basic six classes of odors and of the transitional or mixed odors.

oe-: for words beginning with **oe-** see **e-.** (Exception, **Oedipus.**)

Oedipus (ed′i·pəs; ē′di-): *n.* a mythical character best known as the hero of two of Sophocles' tragedies. Unwittingly he killed his father and married his mother. ➤According to Freud, this myth represents a universal infantile experience which is later repressed. See **Oedipus complex.**—*Var.* **Edipus.**—*adj.* **Oedipal.**

Oedipus/complete: (*psychoan.*) the simultaneous presence of a tendency to display **object love** for the mother and **identification** with the father, and of a tendency to display object love for the father and identification with the mother. ➤The strength of the respective loves of mother and of father is determined chiefly by experience and may vary from person to person.

Oedipus (or **Edipus**) **complex:** (*psychoan.*) the repressed desire of a person for sex relations with the parent of opposite sex. ➤The Oedipus complex specifically refers to the desire of the boy for his mother; but in theoretical discussions it is broadened to include the analogous desire of the girl for her father, specifically called the **Electra complex.** The Oedipus complex is held by psychoanalysts to be practically universal. The repression is effected very early and its manifestations are extremely numerous and varied. In early childhood, the repression is relatively weak and the complex manifests itself in less disguised forms as hostility toward the like-sex parent and as rivalry for the affection of the opposite-sex parent. In adult life the manifestations are subtly disguised. The Oedipus complex is the **nuclear complex** of all **neuroses.** ¶**Oedipus** alone is often used for **Oedipus complex.**—*Syn.* MOTHER COMPLEX.—*adj.* **Oedipal, Edipal** (also without capitals).

Oedipus/inverted: see **inverted Oedipus.**

oesophagus: see **esophagus.**

oestrogen: see **estrogen.**

oestrum, oestrus or **oestrous cycle** = **estrus.**

offense: *n.* **1.** action contrary to law, morals, or social convention. **2.** a hostile act, one designed to damage an enemy.—*Var.* **offence.**—*adj.* **offensive.**—*v.* **offend.**

Office of Strategic Services or **OSS:** an organization of the U.S. Government during World War II that obtained military information in enemy countries and carried on various forms of psychological warfare. The OSS developed a number of psychological procedures for the assessment of personality.

official optimism: the denial of "negative things" in the self.

ogive (ō′jiv; ō·jīv′): *n.* **1.** a curve with a double bend, as in the letter *S.* **2.** (*stat.*) a graphic representation of a cumulative frequency distribution. ➤This curve is a special form of **ogive (1);** it has a double

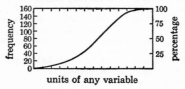

units of any variable

An ogive curve representing cumulative frequency.

bend (roughly like an *S* tilted forward) but rises continuously. The cumulative frequencies may be plotted so that each ordinate of the ogive expresses either the percentage or the number of observations that are "more than" the corresponding abscissa.—*Syn.* CUMULATIVE FREQUENCY GRAPH.—*adj.* **ogival** (ō·jī′vəl).

ohm (ōm): *n.* the unit of electrical resistance.

Ohm's law: (*audition*) a generalization that the hearer perceives a complex tone not as a single sound but as a compound of the simple tones of which it is composed, so that with careful attention (and some training) the separate components can be distinguished. ➤It is thought that the analysis takes place in the ear itself by a physical separation of the complex acoustic wave. The irregular wave forms that give rise to noises are not so analyzed, but nearly all noises incorporate some tones which can also be analyzed out.—*Distg. fr.* **Fourier's** analysis of the complex physical wave into a series of simple (sinusoidal) wave forms. Since Ohm's law deals with the perceived sounds, not with the stimulus, it is improperly (though usually) called Ohm's **acoustic** law.—*Syn.* OHM'S AUDITORY LAW (*pref'd.*).

-oid: suffix meaning *similar, like,* or *apparently like.*

old age: see **development/levels of.**

olfactie (ol·fak′tē): *n.* a unit of intensity of smell.

olfaction (ol·fak′shən): *n.* the sense of smell.—*adj.* **olfactory,** pertaining to smelling or to the sense of smell, or characterizing a stimulus as belonging to that sense; **olfactible,** of intensity great enough to be smelled; **olfactive** (*rare*), creating a smell.

olfactometer (ol″fak·tom′ə·tər): *n.* an instrument that regulates the amount and intensity of a smell stimulus.

olfactory: see **olfaction.**

olfactory brain = **rhinencephalon.**

olfactory bulb: either of two oval masses of gray matter lying on the floor of the cranium just above the nasal cavity, one on each side. The bulbs are an extension of the cerebrum and are centers for smell.—*Syn.* OLFACTORY LOBE, **rhinencephalon** (somewhat more inclusive).

olfactory lobe = **olfactory bulb.**

oligergasia (ol″i·gǝr·gā′zhǝ): *n.* (*A. Meyer*) any of the more or less static disorders that comprise all types of **mental *deficiency.**

olig(o)-: combining form meaning *few, little, scanty.*

oligoencephaly = **mental *deficiency** that is **constitutional** in origin.

oligologia (ol″i·gō·lŏ′ji·ǝ): *n.* fewness of words; lack of terms wherewith to make fine distinctions. ➤This disorder is most uncommon in several of the subfields covered by this dictionary.—*Syn.* OLIGOPHASIA, OLIGOLALIA, OLIGOGRAPHIA.

oligophrenia (-frē′ni·ǝ) = **mental *deficiency.**—*adj.* **oligophrenic** (-fren′ik), of feeble intellect.

oligophrenic detail or **Do:** (*Ror.*) a kind of response to the **inkblot** that is judged to be impoverished and indicative of low mental level.

omnibus test: see **test/omnibus.**

omnipotence/infantile: (*psychoan.*) the implicit expectation or expectancy of the very young child that his wishes fulfill themselves. No conscious generalization is involved.—See **omnipotence of the id, omnipotence of thought.**

omnipotence of the id: (*psychoan.*) a figurative expression for the view that the **id,** not being restricted by reality, can always find satisfaction through **wish fulfillment.** For the id, an image of something is as good as the thing itself—i.e., it is immediately satisfying.

omnipotence of thought: acting as if mere wishes or thoughts were realities, or as if they must have results in the external world. It is a sort of magic belief: whatever you think, happens.

omnipotency/theory of: the hypothesis that in late infancy and early childhood the individual literally regards himself as able to control all the persons around him. **Negativism** results when he is disabused of this idea.

onanism (ō′nǝn·iz·ǝm): *n.* **1.** properly, COITUS INTERRUPTUS (withdrawal before ejaculation). **2.** = **masturbation.** ➤This usage is common but incorrect.

oneiric (ō·nī′rik): *adj.* pertaining to, or resembling, a dream; of a dreamlike waking state.

oneir(o)-: combining form meaning *a dream.*

one-tailed test: see **two-tailed test.**

one-trial learning: 1. (*E. R. Guthrie*) the acquisition by a stimulus pattern of its full associative strength on the first occasion of its pairing with a response. **2.** (*B. F. Skinner*) the increase to a maximum of the probability that a given **R** will follow a given **S** as the result of one rewarded pairing. ➤*Cp.* the **continuity theory,** which postulates that an increment of stimulus-response strength is accumulated at each rewarded pairing until a maximum is reached.

one-way screen: a screen or window permitting vision through it in only one direction, so that from one side an observer can watch unobserved.

onliness: *n.* the state of being an only child.

onomatopoetic (on″ǝ·mat″ǝ·pō·et′ik): *adj.* of words that imitate the sounds of nature: e.g., crack, meow. ➤The ONOMATOPOETIC THEORY (sometimes called the DING-DONG THEORY) attributes the origin of language to the imitation of natural sounds. **Neologisms** which thus mimic natural sounds are a common symptom in schizophrenia.—*Var.* **onomatopoeic** (-pē′ik).—*n.* **onomatopoeia, -poesis.**

onset: *n.* **1.** the moment when a stimulus reaches **threshold** value; or the period from first application of a stimulus of given strength until a threshold value of sensory response is reached. **2.** the beginning of a disease or disorder.

onto-: combining form that denotes *being, existence;* specif. (*biol.*), *an individual living being.*

ontogenesis or **ontogeny** (on″tō·jen′ǝ·sǝs; on·toj′ǝ·ni): *n.* the origin, or origin and development, of an individual organism or of one of its organs or functions. ➤*Contr. w.* PHYLOGENESIS, PHYLOGENY, the origin, or origin and development, of a biological group (a variety, species, or phylum) or, metaphorically, of a group taken as analogous to a species. **Ontogeny** denotes the abstract general problem of origin and development within the organism's life history: e.g., the problem of the adequacy of ontogeny to explain individual differences. **Ontogenesis** deals with the particular: e.g., the ontogenesis of John Doe's particular skillfulness. A similar distinction holds for PHYLOGENY and PHYLOGENESIS.—*adj.* **ontogenetic.**

ontogeny: see **ontogenesis.**

ontology: the metaphysical study of the ultimate nature of being.

open-class society: one in which **social mobility** up and down the scale is possible. —*Contr. w.* **fixed-class society.**

open-cue situation: a learning task in which all the means necessary to reach a desired goal are visible to the animal. The task is to grasp the relations of these means to each other and to the goal.—*Cp.* **hidden-cue situation.**

open-ended question: a question that defines the general topic inquired about but leaves to the option of the person replying both the form and the substance of the reply. The answer may be a gesture, a single word, or an extended comment. ➤An OPEN-ENDED or NONDIRECTIVE INTERVIEW asks several questions related to a general topic, questions that are broadly phrased and leave much scope to the interviewee to determine what shall be talked about: e.g., "How goes it with you?"; "Are things better or worse than they used to be?"—*Cp*. **client-centered** (or nondirective) *****therapy,** which uses such questioning.—*Syn*. FREE-ANSWER QUESTION, esp. for academic examination questions.—*Contr. w*. **fixed-alternative** question.

open group: one to which new members can be added. ➤Said especially of a **therapy** group.

open-mindedness: *n*. readiness to consider different points of view; the attitude with which we greet ideas that conform to our prejudices.

openness/figural: (*Gestalt*) the degree to which the total area of a shape is not enclosed within the **figure.** ➤Shapes are usually experienced as "possessing" an area around them approximately equal to the area of the circle within which the shape could be inscribed. Of this total area, part is open (without a boundary line) to the surrounding space, the rest is enclosed by the boundary lines of the figure. Thus, a Maltese cross includes in its area the space between the arms; this space is open. A circle is generally experienced as completely enclosing all the area that "belongs" to that figure, hence has zero figural openness.

open question = **open-ended question.**

operant (op'ər·ənt): *adj*. characterizing, or pertaining to, a response or a behavior that is identified by its consequences in the environment. ➤Usually there is no known specific stimulus, though the behavior takes place in a definable situation: e.g., an animal in a puzzle box emits operant behavior that is certainly relevant to the whole situation but not at first to any identifiable aspect or cue—the essential fact is that the animal opens the door. Some authors include in their definition the lack of identifiable stimulus, but it is undesirable to make ignorance a criterion of meaning if it can be avoided. —See **respondent.**—*Cp*. also **instrumental behavior, vacuum response.**

operant conditioning = instrumental conditioning (see **conditioning** 2).

operant learning: the form of learning wherein the organism becomes progressively more likely to respond in a given situation with that response which, in previous similar situations, has brought about a rewarding or satisfying state of affairs; or wherein a stimulus, having evoked a re-

sponse that brings into view a rewarding stimulus or that prevents or removes an obnoxious stimulus, thereafter is more likely to evoke that response.—*Syn*. OPERANT CONDITIONING, INSTRUMENTAL CONDITIONING, TYPE-R CONDITIONING, REINFORCEMENT CONDITIONING.—See **conditioning** (2) and discussion.

operant level: 1. the rate of occurrence of an **operant** response before the response has been experimentally **reinforced. 2.** the rate of such occurrence after the response has been **extinguished.** ➤It is not known whether (1) and (2) are identical within the limits of error.

operant reserve = **reflex reserve.**

operate: *v*. to do work; to act; to produce an effect. ➤Properly, *operate* is distinguished from **function,** which means to operate in a context or system, or to serve an end or purpose; but the two are often interchangeable.

operating characteristic: 1. a quantitative statement of the effects to be expected when using a procedure or object. **2.** (of a test of significance) the probability of accepting the **null hypothesis** for each possible, statistically defined, situation.—*Cp*. **power function of a test, item operating characteristic.**

operation: *n*. a doing; a performing; or what is done or performed. ➤An EMPIRICAL OPERATION alters the nature or relations among facts; a LOGICAL or MATHEMATICAL OPERATION changes the relations between symbols according to the rules of logic or mathematics.

operational: *adj*. pertaining to an operation or procedure. ➤The word has acquired a halo of profundity of which it should be divested. Esp., **operational** does not imply truth, correctness, or scientific validity, but simply that one is talking about a procedure. —*Distg. fr*. **operational analysis** or **research.**—See **operationalism, operational definition.**

operational analysis: (*commun. theory*) the determination of the relation between **input** and **output** in a transmission system. ➤Under certain conditions the animal organism may be treated as a transmission system. Both input and output must be measured in units that can be added.

operational definition: defining a term by stating the operations or procedures employed in distinguishing the object referred to from others.

➤According to the doctrine of **operationalism** all the meaning of any term rests ultimately upon facts of direct observation, but it may be several degrees removed from the observation. The meaning of **IQ** is the division of mental age by chronological age, neither of which is an observed fact; but each of the latter two terms reaches back to direct observations. Sometimes, however, the linkage with empirical fact is lacking and the definition lacks meaningful reference.

The duty of the editor of a dictionary is not to decide whether a term has operational meaning, though when one is current it is given. For dictionary purposes it is enough that we find ordinarily used words that can regularly be substituted for the term defined. Thus, **pyrophobia** is defined as a "morbid fear of fire"; many doubt that either *fear* or *morbid* can be operationally defined. When we do have an operational definition, it does not guarantee the actual existence of the object or event named, but only that it has meaning.

operationalism: *n.* the doctrine that terms, propositions, concepts, constructs, and theories are given all their meaning—in the last analysis—by the methods of observation or investigation used to arrive at them, that they have no other meaning than is yielded by the procedures or operations by which the things or processes to which they refer are known. ➤Thus, a given **mental *age** means merely that under certain standard conditions the child can perform such tasks as counting backward, fitting blocks into appropriate slots, reproducing a design from memory. A **threshold** means just that the individual has made certain judgments when certain prescribed psychophysical procedures have been followed. It follows that a threshold obtained by one psychophysical procedure does not mean the same as one obtained by another procedure, unless the equivalence is proved by other procedures. In the same way **classical** and **instrumental *conditioning**, being defined by distinct operations, must be considered distinct concepts until linked (as some think they have been) by common operations.

On the other hand, many terms that are given apparently different verbal definitions turn out to have reference to the same operations—in which case there is only one concept.

Operationalism is related to but distinguishable from **physicalism** and from **positivism.**—*Cp.* **operational definition.**—*Syn.* OPERATIONISM.—See **psychology/divisions and schools of, VIII.**

operational research: a fact-finding procedure for the control of any system in operation. ➤It includes a clear statement of the results to be aimed at, identification of the relevant **variables** and their statement in quantitative terms, measurement of their fluctuations in the given situation, and discovery of how these variables interact. The system may be a machine, a social organization, or a combination of machine

and person. The aim of operational research is to discover how, under the necessary over-all conditions, rules, and limits, the system can best accomplish what it is designed or expected to do.—*Cp.* **action research.**—*Syn.* OPERATIONS RESEARCH.

operationism = **operationalism.**

operator: *n.* (*math.*) a symbol indicating an operation to be performed upon other symbols. E.g., in the expression X^2, the 2 is an operator.

ophthalmia (of·thal'mi·ə): *n.* an inflammation of the outer tissues of the eye, especially of the conjunctiva. OPHTHALMIA NEONATORUM is a contagious inflammation of the eye contracted during birth.

ophthalmic (of·thal'mik): *adj.* pertaining to the eye.—*Syn.* ocular.—*Distg. fr.* **optic.**

ophthalm(o)- (of·thal'mō-): combining form meaning *eye* or *eyes.*

ophthalmology: *n.* that branch of medicine which treats of the eye. It includes surgery, medication, and the prescription of glasses.—*pers. n.* **ophthalmologist** or **oculist,** a physician or surgeon specializing in this field.

ophthalmometer (-mom'ə·tər): **1.** an instrument to measure the curvature of the front surface of the **cornea. 2.** any **ophthalmic** instrument.—*adj.* **ophthalmometric.**—*n.* **ophthalmometry.**

ophthalmoscope: *n.* an instrument permitting inspection of the inside of the eye, esp. of the **retina.**

ophthalmotrope (-mə·trōp): *n.* an instrument for demonstrating the movements of the eyeball by means of a model of the six pairs of extrinsic **eye muscles.**

-opia, -opy: combining forms meaning *defect of sight.*

opiate (ō'pi·it; -āt): *n.* **1.** any drug containing opium or a derivative. **2.** anything tending to quiet or soothe a person: his speech was an *opiate.*—*adj.* **opiatic** (-at'ik).

opinion: *n.* **1.** a belief that one holds to be without emotional commitment or desire, and to be open to revaluation since the evidence is not affirmed to be convincing. It is capable of verbal expression under appropriate circumstances, at least to oneself. ➤The presumed objectivity of opinion distinguishes it from other attitudes, even though the objectivity may be self-deception (most opinions being, in fact, truer expressions of desire and of personality structure than the holder supposes). But even though influenced thus by motive or desire, **opinion** is addressed to a matter involving some knowledge and a measurable amount of factual evidence. Otherwise it would be pure fancy. **2.** that which is thus believed, stated in words for oneself. ➤Public statements may or may not represent the "true" opinion. **Opinion-poll** takers record public (i.e., overt) statements under conditions as favorable as possible to correspondence between the overt statement and the covert (inner) statement. If the belief cannot be verbalized, set is a more suitable term. **3.** = **attitude.** ➤Since verbal statements of opinion are often sought as a revelation of attitude, *opinion* and *attitude* are often used interchangeably. This blurs a useful distinction between the ostensibly intellectual *opinion* and the ostensibly valuative *attitude.*—See **attitude.**

opinionaire: *n.* a questionary seeking **opinions** on a wide variety of topics.

opinion poll: a survey of opinions arrived at by questioning on specific issues.—See **opinion/public.**

opinion/public. the general trend of **opinion, attitude, sentiment,** or **judgment** that is held by a large social group or **public (2).** ➤In this phrase, distinctions between attitude, opinion, and sentiment are usually ignored. Unanimity is not implied, but some sort of consensus is. ¶A PUBLIC OPINION POLL or SURVEY appraises feeling-action readiness (attitude or sentiment) by collecting, from a representative sample of a large social group or public, overt expressions of opinion, of interest, of approval-disapproval or other dimension of feeling, concerning a particular issue. Appraisals may be made by interview or by written questionary.—See **opinion (2).**

opium: *n.* a **narcotic** drug, produced from one species of poppy, which depresses the higher nerve centers and creates a feeling of **euphoria.**—*adj.* **opiate** (which see).

opportunistic: *adj.* **1.** of behavior dependent upon circumstances for direction and satisfaction. ➤It is contrasted by G. Allport with **propriate** (which see). Since satisfactions frequently experienced come to be preferred, the opportunist finds satisfaction in what is common in the environment. **2.** adapting to the circumstances of the moment, often to the neglect of principle; hence, expedient.

opportunity class: a class for pupils of any age or grade who do not adapt readily to ordinary school procedures or in an ordinary class grade. ➤Theoretically, such a class is not primarily for the mentally deficient, and its members are expected to return as soon as possible to regular classes. But the term is often a euphemism for vocational and prevocational training of those deemed unsuited for further academic study. The term should (and sometimes does) include classes for pupils making extra progress as well as for those who are retarded. —*Cp.* **special class.**

opposite/reversal into: (*psychoan.*) a **defense** procedure by means of which gratification is obtained by inverting the instinctual **aim,** when the direct aim is blocked. E.g., a child whose instinctual aim is to beat somebody is said to find gratification in being naughty and thus being himself beaten.

opposites test: a test in which the task is to give the opposite or contrary of a given word.

opposition: *n.* **1.** (*logic*) a relation between concepts or propositions such that the truth of one implies a limitation on the truth of the other. Two important principles of opposition are the PRINCIPLE OF CONTRADICTION (to be distinguished from the fundamental law of thought sometimes called the **law of *contradiction**) and the PRINCIPLE OF CONTRARIETY. If the falsity of one proposition implies the truth of the other, and vice versa, they are mutually CONTRADICTORY. (See **null hypothesis,** based on this principle.) If the truth of one proposition implies the falsity of the other, but the falsity of one does not imply the truth of the other, they are CONTRARY. **2.** resistance to ideas or efforts of another person or group, not necessarily accompanied by anger or wish to injure. ➤*Cp.* **conflict,** which usually implies anger and desire to hurt. At the verbal level, opposition may be thought of as impersonal, conflict as personal; but the distinction is probably only relative and not great.

optic(al): *adj.* **1.** pertaining to the science of **optics. 2.** pertaining to the eye, or to vision. ➤For this meaning **ocular** or **visual** (respectively) are more accurate, but a given phenomenon may be **optic(al) (1),** ocular, and visual. Moreover, **optic** occurs in many neurological expressions: e.g., **optic nerve.**

optical axis: the central line of vision; the straight line through the centers of curvature of both **lens** and **cornea.**

optical illusion: an **illusion,** whether physical or psychological, that affects vision.

optic disc: the area in the **retina** where the fibers of the optic nerve are gathered before leaving the retina. The area, nearly but not wholly insensitive to light, is also known as the **blind spot.**

optician: *n.* one who makes lenses.—*Distg. fr.* **optometrist, oculist, ophthalmologist.**

optic lobe: either of the superior pair of the **corpora quadrigemina.**

optic nerve: the IInd cranial nerve, which connects the retina with the visual centers.

optic representation: the spatial relations of an object as these are presented to the retina, not as they are perceived. ➤A photograph is an optic representation, but it is generally subjected to a sort of **object *constancy** of perception.

optics: *n.* the branch of physics that studies light or radiant energy.

optic thalamus: *obsoles.* for **thalamus.**

optimal stimulation principle: (*C. Leuba*) the postulate that the organism tends to learn those reactions that produce an optimal level of total stimulation or excitation. ➤According to this view, either **drive reduction** or **drive arousal** may lead to an *optimal* level of stimulation.

optimism: *n.* a highly general **attitude** or personality **trait** that sees good in most objects and events and expects outcomes to be favorable.

optimize: *v.* to cause a **variable** to be at the best level for the purpose in hand.

optimum: *n.* the best value in a given series for the purpose in hand. ➤It need not be the greatest or the least: the optimal illumination is that at which one sees best, even though one can still see at vastly higher or lower levels of illumination.—*adj.* **optimal** or **optimum.**

optional transmission: (*Lorente de Nó*) the hypothesis that the **firing** or **excitation** of a given neuron by another given neuron depends not only on their immediate connection, but also on other events in the **cell assembly** or larger system.

opto-: combining form denoting *vision,* or *the eye* in relation to vision.

optogram: *n.* an image of a light-reflecting object formed on the retina.

optokinetic reactions: movements of the eye caused by visual stimulation; sometimes, the perceived motion in the visual field that results.—See **autokinetic.**

optometry (op·tom'ə·tri): *n.* **1.** the measurement of the eye and of visual functions. **2.** the art and practice of increasing the efficiency of visual perception. ➤The **optometrist** may prescribe visual training, corrective exercises, and spectacles, but he may not use surgery or medication. **Optometry (2)** is a profession overlapping with, but distinct from, the medical specialty **ophthalmology.**—*adj.* **optometrical.** —*pers. n.* **optometrist.**

-opy: see **-opia.**

oral: *adj.* **1.** pertaining to the mouth or analogous opening. **2.** pertaining to speaking, or to the spoken word.—*Syn.* **verbal,** which is ambiguous.—*Distg. fr.* **aural.**

oral-aggressive: *adj.* (*psychoan.*) pertaining to character traits that represent **sublimation** of the oral biting phase: aggressiveness, envy, ambition, exploiting others.

oral anxiety: (*psychoan.*) anxiety aroused in the **oral (libido) stage.** ➤It is said to be represented later by fantasies of an immense object in small pieces inside the body.

oral cavity: the cavity extending from the lips to the **pharvnx.**

oral character: (*psychoan.*) **1.** a characteristic of a person that reflects his experience during the **oral (libido) stage.** ➤E.g., optimism is said to result from a largely pleasurable experience in suckling. **2.** a personality that is unduly influenced by **oral erotism;** a person who has regressed or been arrested at the level of a slightly transformed oral erotism.—*Syn.* ORAL PERSONALITY.

oral dependence: (*psychoan.*) the desire to recover the security felt when safe in the mother's arms with the mouth anchored to the nipple as a source of intense gratification.

oral drive: a **drive** leading to oral satisfactions, i.e., to those resulting from stimulation of the inner membranes of the mouth, as in sucking and mouthing.

oral erotism: a tendency to derive pleasure or satisfaction from stimulation of the lips and inner membranes of the mouth, as in sucking or mouthing objects. ➤In psychoanalysis, this tendency marks one of the pregenital stages of development, the **oral (libido) stage.** Persons who show an overdeveloped oral erotism have regressed to, or been arrested at, this stage.—See **erotism** and **oral (libido) stage.**—*Distg. fr.* sexual anomalies such as **cunnilinctus** or **fellatio.**—*Var.* **oral eroticism.**—*adj.* **oral-erotic.**

oral-incorporative: *adj.* (*psychoan.*) of tendencies to possessiveness, voracity, greed, and envy that are rooted in the early infantile effort to incorporate part of the mother (finger, nipple, etc.) into oneself. They are said to represent the ultimate in the effort to maintain the security of closeness to the mother. An ORAL-INCORPORATIVE PHASE (better, STAGE) is said by some psychoanalysts to be found in early infancy.

orality: *n.* **1.** = **oral erotism. 2.** the oral component in a variety of neurotic disorders.—*Cp.* **oral character (1).**

oral (libido) stage: (*psychoan.*) the infantile period in which **desire** has not been differentiated into desire for nourishment and desire for sexual activity, and, hence, taking food has something of a sexual nature. ➤In later sexual anomalies concerned with the mouth, this primitive sexual character of oral activity is developed at the expense of normal genital satisfactions.

oral method: the employment by the deaf of oral speech and of **speech reading** (also called **lip reading** or **visual hearing**) as the chief way of communicating with other persons, whether deaf or hearing.—*Contr. w.* **manual method.**

oral neurosis: (*I. Coriat*) term used to imply the theory that the functional speech disorders such as stuttering (generally held to be **neurotic**) are specific disorders of the **oral libido**.

oral optimism: (*psychoan.*) a tendency to optimism attributed to the infant's having been easily and abundantly satisfied in suckling.

oral-passive character = receptive character.

oral personality = oral character.

oral primacy: (*psychoan.*) the concentration of **libido** mainly on the oral zone so that satisfaction is chiefly derived from mouth contacts. ➤In earliest infancy oral primacy is normal, and mouth contacts therefore play a major part in building up the child's knowledge of reality. **Fixation** on, or **regression** to, the ORAL PRIMACY STAGE are hypothesized as causing neurotic symptoms.

oral reading habit: moving the lips and tongue when engaged in "silent" reading.

oral regression: (*psychoan.*) a tendency to return to the earlier stage of development in which **oral erotism** was dominant, or to manifest anomalous behaviors which symbolically represent that stage.

oral sadism: (*psychoan.*) the unconscious desire to bite, to injure or destroy by biting.

oral stage = oral (libido) stage.

oral test: see **test/oral.**

orangutan (ə·rang'ü·tan″): *n.* one of the **anthropoid** apes, the other two being the gorilla and the chimpanzee.—*Syn.* ORANG (ō'rang).

orbital (or'bit·əl): *adj.* of any orbit; esp., of the bony cavity surrounding the eye.

orchido-: combining form meaning *testis.*

order: *n.* 1. a temporal or spatial arrangement of things. 2. (*scientific method*) any system of relations such that one can pass from one item to another according to definite rules or in definite directions without missing any. ➤In a LINEAR ORDER all the items are strung out as if on a line; to proceed from the 1st to the 6th, e.g., it is necessary to traverse the 2nd, 3rd, 4th, and 5th in that sequence. 3. a command; a rule issued by authority. 4. (*biol.*) a category for classification: a group of organisms above the **family,** below the biological **class.** 5. an approximate place in an **order of magnitude.** ➤This meaning was originally mathematical. *The second or third order* means the squared or cubed degree of the original magnitude. But the term is often loosely used to place a datum approximately: it is of the *order* of the tens, the thousands, the billions; or it is of the *order* of a light year, meaning a *very* long time.—*v.* 6. to put things or ideas in order; to arrange data or objects systematically; to put a particular datum in its determinate place in a certain system. 7. to command; to manage persons by directions which they are con-

strained to obey.—*adj.* **orderly,** in order, each item in place; **ordinal,** pertaining to order or indicating succession: an *ordinal* number.

order/cyclic: an arrangement whereby a certain pattern or sequence of items regularly recurs: e.g., the order of the symbols *adxadxadx.*

order/linear: see **order (2).**

order of a matrix: (*stat.*) the size of a **matrix** stated as the number of rows and columns it contains. It is written: *a matrix of the order of* m *by* n.

order of magnitude: the arrangement of objects or data in a sequence so that, for each item in the sequence, the preceding item is always less and the following is always more.

order of merit (ranking): see **merit ranking.**

ordinal: *adj.* indicating order or succession; esp., as in ORDINAL NUMBERS: first, second, etc.—*Distg. fr.* **cardinal** numbers.

ordinal position: one indicating place in a succession. ➤Ordinal position is usually indicated by the number series: first, second, third, etc.

ordinate: (ôr'din·ət): *n.* (*math.*) 1. the vertical reference axis of a two-dimensional chart.—*Syn.* Y AXIS. 2. the shortest distance from a point *P* along a line parallel with the *Y* axis to the horizontal or *X* axis of a two-dimensional chart.—See **axis.**—*Syn.* Y DISTANCE, Y VALUE.—*Ant.* **abscissa.**

orectic: see **orexis.**

Orestes complex (ô·res'tēz): (*psychoan.*) the repressed desire of a son to kill his mother. ➤*Cp.* **Oedipus complex,** of which the Orestes complex is said to be an outgrowth.

orexis (ô·rek'səs): *n.* the **affective** and **conative** aspect of an act, in contrast with the **cognitive.**—*adj.* **orectic** (ô·rek'tik).

organ: *n.* a structural part of an organism adapted for the performance of some specific **function** or functions. ➤A **somatic** structure is ordinarily referred to, but **psychic** or **psychosomatic** structures or organs have been postulated.—*adj.* **organic** (which see for other usages).

organ-erotic: *adj.* pertaining to the attachment of **erotic** feeling to a special bodily organ.

organ erotism = organ libido.

organic: *adj.* 1. pertaining to an **organ. 2.** pertaining to an **organism,** or to that which has organs.—*Syn.* **organismic** (*prefd.*). **3.** resulting from the organization of something, or related in fundamental fashion to its constitution. 4. **vital,** not merely **mechanical.** 5. bodily, as contrasted with mental.—*Syn.* **somatic** (*prefd.*).—See **organic disorder,** in contrast with **functional disorder.**

organic analogy: a description of society in the terms of a biological organism.—*Syn.* ORGANISMIC ANALOGY, **organic concept of society.**

organic child: (*tech. slang*) a **brain-damaged** child.

organic concept of society: 1. a point of view that compares society to a biological **organism,** or regards society as really being an organism. **2.** a description of society that emphasizes the mutual dependence of its components and the high degree of organization therein.—*Syn.* **organic analogy.**

organic disorder: impairment of function attributed to specifically known or hypothesized pathological lack or impairment of organic structure.—See discussion under **functional disorder.**—*Syn.* **constitutional** disorder, but this often implies that the condition is congenital or at least of long standing.

organic evolution: see **evolution (2).**

organicism: *n.* **1.** the view, opposed to both **vitalism** and **mechanism,** which holds that life is the result of organization. **2.** the view that social groups are organisms analogous to living beings. **3.** the view that all disorders, physical or mental, are organic. —See **organic disorders.**

organicity: *n.* **1.** the condition or property of being **organic;** having organic origin. **2.** (*med.*) dysfunction due to structural changes in the **central nervous system.**

organic memory: a persistent change, resulting from **excitation,** in living tissue.— See **mneme.**

organic psychosis: a serious mental disease attributed to structural impairment of the brain. ➤It is held by many, on general grounds, that all mental disorders are due to structural brain changes; but **organic psychosis** should be reserved for those disorders for which specific empirical evidence of structural brain change is known, e.g., **paresis.**

organic sensations: those coming from inside the body, in contrast to those peripherally located. ➤Since the eye or the ear is no less an organ than the bowels, organic is illogical in this usage.—*Syn.* (both *prefd.*) **interoceptive** sensations, **visceral** sensations.

organic trait: one attributed, on the ground of specific empirical evidence, to the activity of living tissue. ➤On general grounds, perhaps all traits are **somatogenic; organic trait** is restricted to cases where at least partial empirical fact is in evidence.

organic variable or **O variable:** a state or a process within the organism or person that is regarded as a codeterminer (along with the stimulus) of the response: e.g., a stomach-ache, a habit, an attitude, a visceral tension, all of which influence how one acts in a given situation. ➤The term is more often used for those states or processes known only from verbal report or by inference from behavior. The **hypothetical** *****state variable** and the **hypothetical** *****process variable** are subdivisions. Since the term does not usually emphasize the variations of the state or process, but rather its function in determining action, ORGANISMIC FACTOR would be more appropriate.—*Syn.* (both *prefd.*) ORGANISMIC or PERSONAL FACTOR (or VARIABLE).

organ inferiority: (*A. Adler*) the doctrine that real or imaginary defect or inferiority of any organ may cause a painful feeling of inferiority and efforts to **compensate** therefor.—See **inferiority complex** for a fuller statement of Adler's view.

organism: *n.* a living being capable of maintaining itself as a system and composed of parts capable of performing certain coordinated functions; any plant or animal, including the protista. (The status of viruses is uncertain.) ➤In effect, this defines organism as that which performs the **functions** of an organism. No agreement on what constitutes organismic functions has been reached; we can only enumerate them. It is customary, however, to define organism by pointing to the physiological functions only. This is either arbitrary, or it represents the imposition of a metaphysical bias by mere act of defining. (See **theory-begging.**) Organism should be defined in terms of *all* the functions it is empirically found to perform, including those which, in our present state of knowledge, are called psychological as well as those called physiological. The organism should therefore be conceived as *psychophysiological,* as that system which performs both psychological and physiological functions.—*Syn.* **psychobiological organism, psychophysiological organism, psychophysical organism** (*ambig.*), **person** (which see).—*adj.* **organismic** (*prefd.*), **organic** (not *recom.;* it is *ambig.* when thus used).

organism /constancy of: see **constancy of organism.**

organismic (ôr″gən·iz′mik): *adj.* **1.** pertaining to the **organism** (which see). ➤Organismic is used by **positivistic** and **behavioristic** writers to point up an opposition to **mentalistic** notions, but also by some extreme antibehaviorists (chiefly educationists) to emphasize a **holistic** attitude. Thus, a certain kind of emotional fervor (on both sides) has made strange terminological bedfellows. But the denotation of the term is quite clear: it just means *pertaining to an organism.* **2.** characterizing the doctrine or point of view of

organismic psychology. 3. = (*J. R. Kantor*) **interbehavioral. 4.** characterizing the qualities of an individual as interrelated and interactive because they are qualities of an integrated organism.—*Cp.* **age/organismic.**

organismic analogy = **organic analogy.**

organismic behavior: behavior that depends upon the organism as a whole, rather than upon particular parts. ➤This is a difficult distinction, since all behavior is probably a function to some degree of the whole organism. See **organismic.**

organismic concept of development: the concept that evolutionary change proceeds by change in organisms as wholes, not by change in particular organs as if independent.

organismic psychology: any of several fairly distinct points of view, all of which reject *mind-body *dualism and hold that physiological studies certain of the functions or activities of an **organism.** ➤One form of organismic psychology is **holistic;** a second is **behavioristic;** and many are **functionalistic.** See **organism** for discussion of organismic functions.—See **interbehavioral psychology** and **psychology/divisions and schools of, III.**

organismic quotient: organismic ***age** divided by **life** ***age.**

organism/social: a social group or a society conceived to function or develop in ways so closely similar to those of an organism as to suggest (at the least) that the same dynamic principles are at work—i.e., that the same laws describe both.

organization: *n.* **1.** an ensemble composed of different parts which perform distinct but interrelated and coordinated functions, so that the parts form a unity or whole; or the process whereby such a systematic arrangement is brought into being.—*Syn.* **group, system, gestalt, organism** (restricted to living beings), **organization/social. 2.** the process whereby psychophysical excitations distribute themselves into a perceptual **gestalt. 3.** the degree of unity, of interdependence, found in any complex whole: a high degree of *organization.*

organization/logical: see **logical organization.**

organization/principle of: the generalization that the members of a **gestalt** are not equally influential in determining the **phenomenal pattern.**

organization/social: 1. the pattern of relationships found in a society; esp., the pattern between subdivisions based on differences in age, sex, kinship, occupation, privilege, authority, etc. **2.** the system of **expectations** and personal interactions that affect the role and status of the members of

a social group. **3.** an association of individuals bound together by rules and by definition of their respective roles within the association. The purpose may be of any sort, from economic survival to social conviviality to propagation of African violets.

organization/visual: see **visual organization.**

organize: *v.* **1.** to arrange parts so that they work together in a coordinated way. **2.** to arrange data for ready reference, or in such way as to display their relations (logical, chronological, etc.) with each other.

organ libido: erotic feeling associated with a bodily organ.—*Syn.* ORGAN EROTISM.

organogenetic period: the first 6 to 8 weeks of human pregnancy, during which time the structural patterns are laid and the embryo develops from the fertilized cell to a human organism.

organogenic: *adj.* originating in a particular organ.—*Cp.* **somatogenic,** which is more general.

organokinetic period: the last 7 months of human pregnancy.—*Cp.* **organogenetic period.**

organon (ôr′gə·non): *n.* a body of principles setting forth how knowledge is to be acquired or increased. ➤*Syn.* **scientific method.** Aristotle's organon was a compendium of **logic,** but modern forms include all rules or principles for dealing with **empirical** fact.

organ pleasure: (*psychoan.*) **erotic** pleasure, derived from stimulation or activity of a particular organ, which is not yet integrated with the activity of other organs to constitute the race-preservation instincts.—*Syn.* ORGAN LIBIDO.

organs/vocal: see **vocal organs.**

orgasm: *n.* a group of involuntary movements in the genital organs, accompanied by pleasure and strong sex feeling. In the male, the chief components are the movements which eject the semen; in the female, somewhat analogous rhythmic contractions take place. The orgasm is the releasing climax of **coition,** but it may be experienced under other conditions.—*adj.* **orgastic** (*distg. fr.* **orgiastic**).

orgiastic (ôr″ji·as′tik): *adj.* characterized by ecstasy, frenzy, revelry, or excessive indulgence.—*n.* **orgy** (ôr′ji).

orgone theory (ôr′gōn): (*W. Reich*) the doctrine that there is a specific, identifiable energy (ORGONE ENERGY) which accounts for life.

orientation: *n.* **1.** the discovery or knowledge of where one is and where one is going, either literally in space and time, or figuratively in relation to a confusing situation or a puzzling problem, or to people and personal relations. ➤The orientation is COGNITIVE when it consists chiefly in knowing the situation; POSITIVELY or NEGATIVELY CATHECTIVE when it consists primarily in feelings; EVALUATIVE when comparisons are made and the relation of the situation to personal goals is brought out.—Partial *syn.* **insight. 2.** the discovery of what or who one is; = SELF-ORIENTATION.—*Syn.* AUTO-PSYCHIC ORIENTATION (*rare*), SELF-INSIGHT. **3.** turning toward a source of stimulation (*cp.* **tropism**) or in a prescribed direction, literally or figuratively. **4.** a **set** toward a certain stimulus, or a predisposition toward certain behavior patterns. **5.** the direction taken by something. **6.** a very general point of view, not necessarily verbalized, which helps to determine acceptance or rejection of scientific postulates, hypotheses, and methodologies. **7.** the process of helping a person to an orientation in any of the above senses: an *orientation* program.—*v.* **orient** (not *orientate*).—*adj.* **oriented** (not *orientated*).

orientation/family of: see **family (1).**

orientation needs: those needs that tend to oppose **adience** by turning the organism into new paths.

orientation/social: 1. the general direction taken by the behavior of a social group. **2.** the attitude taken by an individual toward the customs and ideology of a social group.

oriented: *adj.* **1.** pointed in a certain direction. **2.** having the knowledge of position or course that is expected in a given situation.—See **orientation.**

orienting response: a response that alters the position of the animal's entire body with reference to the location of a particular stimulus condition.—*Syn.* **tropism.**

origin: *n.* (*math.*) **1.** the reference or starting point for a mathematical operation; specif., **2.** the point where the **abscissa** and the **ordinate** intersect.

original nature: see **nature (1).**

original response or *O*: (*Ror.*) an **inkblot** response that appears not oftener than once in a hundred records.

original score = raw *score.

origin/arbitrary or *M'*: (*stat.*) any point used as a zero point, and from which all values on the scale are measured as deviations. ➤An arbitrary origin is often selected as a reference point for convenience in computation.

ortho- (ôr'thō-): combining form meaning (literally) *straight,* or (figuratively) *correct, proper.*

orthodox: *adj.* said of whatever is officially accepted by any particular social grouping; or of persons who adhere to the officially accepted.—*Ant.* heterodox, HERETICAL.—*n.* **orthodoxy.**

orthogenesis: *n.* **1.** the doctrine that the germ plasm of a species tends to be gradually modified by its own internal conditions. **2.** the doctrine that organic **evolution (2)** as a whole has a determined direction. **3.** the doctrine that an organism has a normal course of development which it follows unless prevented by a severe distortion of environmental conditions. (Variation of environment within a wide range does not alter the normal development.) **4.** name here proposed for the view that the human personality has intrinsic resources for normal and wholesome growth and behavior unless subjected to distorting forces from without. ➤This view underlies **Progressive Education, client-centered *therapy,** **neo-Freudianism,** and many other trends in contemporary psychology.—See **psychology/divisions and schools of,** V.

orthogenic: *adj.* concerned with proper or good development. ➤An ORTHOGENIC CLASS provides corrective treatment for mentally handicapped or seriously maladjusted pupils.

orthogenital: *adj.* of sexual situations or satisfactions that are biologically normal—i.e., (in man) closely related to **coition.**

orthognathic (ôr″thog·nath′ik): *adj.* of a skull having a facial profile angle of 85° to 93°—i.e., with the forehead and upper and lower jaws forming an approximately vertical line.—*Cp.* **prognathous.**—*Var.* **orthognathous** (ôr·thog′na·thəs).— *n.* **orthognathism, orthognathy.**

orthogonal (ôr·thog′ə·nəl): *adj.* rectangular; forming right angles.

orthogonal solution: (*factor anal.*) a solution in which the axes representing factors are at right angles to each other. Such factors are uncorrelated or independent.— *Contr. w.* **oblique (axes) solution,** in which the factors are correlated.

orthopsychiatry: *n.* the study of mental disorder with emphasis upon early treatment and prevention, and based on the combined resources of psychiatry, pediatrics, psychology, and social work.

orthoptics: *n.* training designed to increase the capacity of the two eyes to work together, esp. in the case of muscular interbalance, **amblyopia,** etc.

Orthorater: *n.* trade name for an instrument for testing visual **acuity, phoria, stereopsis,** and color vision.

os (os) *n., pl.* **ora** (ō′rə): (*L.*) the mouth, or any mouthlike opening in the body.— *adj.* **oral.**

os (os) *n., pl.* **ossa** (os′ə): (*L.*) a bone.— *adj.* **osseous** (os′i·əs).

oscillation or *O*: *n.* **1.** a swinging back and forth; or any change showing similar reversal of direction. **2.** (*C. Hull*) the degree of nontrend variability in response strength of a particular response system. **3.** (*factor anal.*) the degree of nontrend variability characterizing an individual's responses to the same test or task on different occasions; an OSCILLATION FACTOR or TRAIT.—*Cp.* **function *fluctuation,** which is a nontrend characteristic of a series of observations, as distinguished from that of a response system (see **2**) or that of a person (see **3**).

oscillation/behavioral or sO_R: (*C. Hull*) the change from moment to moment of the **reaction potential,** sE_R; the standard deviation of the reaction potential.

oscillograph (os'ə·lō·graf): *n.* an instrument that produces a visual record of the wave form of an electric current.

oscillometer (os″ə·lom'ə·tər): *n.* an instrument for recording mechanical oscillations, as of a ship at sea.

Oseretsky Scale: a scale for measuring a child's maturity of motor proficiency.

osmo-: combining form meaning *smell.*

osmosis (os·mō'səs; oz-): *n.* the passage of fluids through a membrane or porous substance.—*adj.* **osmotic.**

OSPE = Ohio State Psychological Examination, a widely used test of academic aptitude.

osphresis (os·frē'səs): *n.* the sense of smell.

OSRD = OFFICE OF SCIENTIFIC RESEARCH AND DEVELOPMENT, U.S. Government.

OSS = **Office of Strategic Services.**

osseous (os'i·əs): *adj.* pertaining to bones.

ossicles/auditory (os'i·kəlz): a chain of small bones in the middle ear that transmit the movements of the eardrum to the fluids of the inner ear.

ossification ratio = ANATOMICAL INDEX: the ratio of the ossified area of the wrist bones, as shown by X-ray photographs, to the area of a certain "carpal quadrilateral." It is a measure of skeletal growth. The ratio is often converted into an **age equivalent** scale, the **carpal *age.**

ossification/social: the hardening of social behavior patterns so that they resist changes, even when they no longer meet social needs.

ossify (os'ə·fī): *v.* to change into, or to form, bone. →Often used figuratively for any hardening or stiffening: his attitudes had gradually *ossified.*

ostracism: *n.* treatment of a person by a social group with indifference, contempt, and the denial of all but the most necessary social contacts.—*v.* **ostracize.**

Ostwald colors (ost'vält): a series of several hundred **chromatic** and **achromatic** samples, each corresponding to a certain theoretical pigment combination of "full color content, white content, and black content," and designated in an arbitrary letter-number system of notation.

O technique: see *R* **correlation.**

other/generalized: the concept an indi-

vidual has of others, of *otherness* in contrast to *selfness.* In mature persons it includes attribution to others of selfhood analogous in general form to one's own.

other/the: **1.** everything not the **self;** the psychological environment. **2.** a person, not oneself.—*Syn.* ALTER.

otic (ō'tik; ot'ik): *adj.* pertaining to the ear.

otitis media (ō·tī'təs mē'di·ə): inflammation of the middle ear.

ot(o)- (ō'tō-): combining form meaning *the ear.*

otogenic tone (ō″tō·jen'ik): see **tone/otogenic.**

otoliths: *n. pl.* small crystals in the **endolymph** of the **labyrinth** of the inner ear. They strike the nerve endings when the endolymph is set in motion, thus giving rise to a neural impulse which assists in maintaining balance.

otology (ō·tol'ə·ji): *n.* the science of the ear: its anatomy, functions, and diseases.—*pers. n.* **otologist,** nearly always limited to a specialist in diseases of the ear.

otosclerosis (ō″tō·sklə·rō'səs): *n.* an impairment of hearing, generally progressive, resulting from bony deposits interfering with the movable parts concerned in **acoustic** reception.

ouija board (wē'jə; often mispronounced wē'jē): a simplified **planchette,** sometimes used by **mediums** to obtain "messages."

outbreeding: *n.* mating outside one's own group. The term is sometimes used figuratively for the introduction of new ideas, customs, etc., into a social group.—*Syn.* exogamy (see **endogamy**).—*Ant.* **inbreeding, endogamy.**

outcome: *n.* **1.** a change in the external world as a result of behavior. **2.** a change in an organism's behavior or behavior potential as a result of experience or taking part in some event; the result of learning, broadly conceived.

outer: *adj.* **1.** external; beyond the enclosing boundaries of any system; esp., beyond the boundaries of a body. **2.** away from the center; toward, or forming, the enclosing boundary.—*Ant.* **inner.**

outer-directed: *adj.* (*D. Riesman*) of a person who responds primarily in conformity with other persons, who seeks approval and popularity as his chief goals.—*Contr. w.* **inner-directed.**

out-group: *n.* any group of persons other than that to which the person in question belongs; or any persons, whether in a social grouping or not, who are not members of one's own group.—*Syn.* THEY-GROUP.—*Ant.* **in-group, we-group.**

outlet: *n.* **1.** any activity, or any object closely associated with the activity, leading to the satisfaction of a **drive** or **need. 2.**

(*A. Kinsey*) any means whereby a sexual **orgasm** is elicited.

outpatient: *n.* an ambulatory patient receiving treatment from a hospital or clinic.

output: *n.* **1.** that which, or the amount of that which, a man or a machine produces in a given length of time. **2.** (*commun. theory*) the **signal** emitted by a **source;** in the case of an animal, overt behavior which acts as a signal for another animal or which acts upon a nonliving communication system. ➤Sometimes the signal is said to be put into a **channel** by a **transmitter,** but the actual meaning is the same.

O variable = organic variable.

ovarian (ō·văr'i·ən): *adj.* pertaining to an ovary.

ovariotomy (ō·ver"i·ot'ə·mi): *n.* surgical removal of the ovaries.—*Syn.* OVARIECTOMY (-ek'tə·mi).

ovary: *n.* one of a pair of glandular organs producing the **ovum** or egg cell; the primary female organ of reproduction.

over-: combining form meaning *more than expected* or *more than is needed* (usually without hyphen).

overachievement: *n.* better performance than predicted from a measure of **aptitude;** specif., receiving higher marks in school, or making better scores on school **achievement tests,** than predicted from a test of general *intelligence* or of **academic *aptitude.**—*Ant.* UNDERACHIEVEMENT.—*pers. n.* **overachiever.**

overage: *adj.* older chronologically than the average for the school grade in which one is placed.

overcompensation: *n.* making an effort that results in more than merely redressing a balance or in more than removing a defect. ➤The result may be to turn a defect into a strength—in which case overcompensation is beneficial; or it may be to overreact, to "lean over backward"—in which case the overcompensation is excessive and usually harmful. But the term itself implies only the greater-than-immediately-needed effort. It is, however, often used where **compensation** (which see) would be more accurate and appropriate.

overconforming: *adj.* of a person who is overresponsive to the demands of persons in authority or of the group, and whose behavior consequently lacks spontaneity.

overdetermined: *adj.* having many causes: applied esp. to a behavior disorder or a dream process that has many causes or determining factors. ➤Psychoanalysts hold that most (or all) dreams and neurotic symptoms are overdetermined, thus making it necessary to carry analysis beyond the first unconscious **determiner** found.—*n.* **overdetermination.**

overexclusion: see **overinclusion.**

overinclusion: *n.* (*N. Cameron*) a defect of personality organization such that the person cannot quickly eliminate from the repertory of responses associated with a certain object those that are inappropriate in a given circumstance. ➤*Contr. w.* OVER-EXCLUSION, in which the person so quickly and rigidly eliminates competing responses as to lose flexibility or adaptability to changing circumstances.—*Cp.* **rigidity.**

overindividual: *adj.* of behavior or customs originating in a social group, and not explicable merely in terms of individuals. ➤The term need not assume a **group mind.**

overinhibited: *adj.* (*R. L. Jenkins*) characterizing a person who finds it difficult to give spontaneous expression to his own ideas and/or feelings and impulses. ➤*Cp.* **overconforming,** which implies an explanation for overinhibition.—*Syn.* **inhibited.**—*n.* **overinhibition.**

overlap/criterion: see **criterion overlap.**

overlapping element or **factor:** a factor common to two or more tests.

overlapping of groups: the extent to which the scores of individuals in two groups fall within the same limits.

overlapping of response: the beginning of the succeeding response in a series before the preceding has ceased.

overlearning: *n.* learning in which practice proceeds beyond the point where the act can just be performed with the required degree of excellence. There is no implication that the practice has been carried to injudicious lengths.

overorganization: *n.* that condition of a system or organization in which there are more ways provided to accomplish ends than are needed, esp. where there are too many rules and red tape.

overproduction: *n.* excess movement.

overprotection: *n.* providing greater care for an infant or child than is necessary. ➤The term has a very inclusive reference: pampering, indulgence, excessive physical contact, prevention of independent behavior, oversolicitude, shielding from competition, etc.

overreaction/emotional: an emotional response that is greater than would be expected from the nature of the situation or from the subject's own evaluation of it.

oversatiation: see **satiation.**

oversoul: see **transmission theory.**

overt (ō'vərt; ō·vĕrt'): *adj.* open to view; public; unconcealed: an *overt* act.—See **overt behavior.**

overt behavior or **response:** an act that can easily be observed by an outsider; a visible, audible, or tangible muscular or glandular activity. Overt behavior may be symbolic (see **symbolic process**) or **oper-**

ant.—See **covert behavior** for discussion.
overtone: *n.* (*music*) any partial tone except the **fundamental.**—See **partial tone.**
ovum (ō'vəm) *n., pl.* **ova:** (*L.*) the female germ cell or egg.—*Contr. w.* **sperm** cell.

oximetry (ok·sim'ə·tri): *n.* measurement of the amount of oxygen in the hemoglobin.
oxycephaly (ok''si·sef'ə·li): *n.* the condition of having a cone-shaped or sugar-loaf head.

P

P: 1. = **person.** 2. = **percept.** 3. perceptual speed (see **abilities/primary mental**). 4. = **probability ratio.** 5. = preference score. 6. (*H. J. Eysenck*) a symbol for the degree or level of personality organization. **➤P—** refers to the less stable, less well organized; **P+** to the stable, better organized, less neurotic. 7. (*Ror.*) scoring code for **popular response.** 8. = physiological **drive state.** 9. see **P technique.**
p: 1. the proportion of a population possessing a given characteristic. **➤**Since *q* is the proportion not possessing it, $p + q = 1$. 2. = **probability** of a given event, or probability of success. 3. = **percentile.** 4. the difficulty of a test item. **➤**It varies inversely with the percentage of cases in a sample who get the item right. 5. the percentage of cases in a given group.
pacing: *n.* 1. provision of tasks that correspond in difficulty to the natural developmental rate of the learner.—*Cp.* **maturation, readiness, forcing.** 2. controlling the speed at which an extended act is performed; esp., controlling the speed of reading.
paedicatio (ped''i·kā'shi·ō) = **pederasty.**
paed(o)- = ped(o)-.
paidicatio = pedication.
paid(o)- = ped(o)-.
paidophilia = pedophilia.—*Var.* **paedophilia.**
pain: *n.* 1. unpleasure; the opposite of **pleasure.** **➤**This older usage, which is still common, is occasionally confusing. Either **pain (1)** is asserted to be the same as **pain (2)**, or the distinction is ignored. In psychoanalysis, pain is said to result when too much **affect** accumulates. 2. = SENSORY PAIN, the sensation that results when the skin is stimulated by a sharp point; or similar sensation from other organs and/or stimulation; or the sensation that results when any sense organ is too intensely stimulated. **➤**The qualitative identity of **(1)** and **(2)** is debated. SENSORY PAIN is not always painful in sense **(1)**.—See **pain sense.**—*adj.* **painful.**—*v.* **pain.**
pain principle: the unconscious striving for death or nirvana; the desire for pain and destruction. **➤**The earliest formulations of psychoanalysis stressed the pleasure principle. Later its twin, the pain principle (only

implicit in Freud's earlier writings), was added.—See **death instinct.**
pain/psychic: a **functional** pain; one for which no ascertainable stimulus is present.
pain/referred: pain experienced as coming from some other area than that stimulated.—*Cp.* **referred sensation.**
pain sense: a specific sense yielding **pain (2)** and believed to have free nerve endings as its **receptors.** The pain sense is distributed over the entire periphery and over many internal bodily surfaces.
paired associates = right associates procedure.
paired comparison: a procedure in which objects are compared with each other in pairs, each with each, till all combinations are given. It is often used for the study of emotional and esthetic values.
palatability: *n.* the acceptability of a foodstuff as dependent upon the **receptors** of the head, esp. those of taste, touch, and smell, but also in part of seeing and hearing.—*adj.* **palatable.**
paleo-, palaeo- (pā'li·o-): combining form meaning *ancient, prehistoric, primitive.*
paleopsychology: *n.* the investigation of psychological processes that are believed to be vestiges held over from an earlier evolutionary period. **➤**C. Jung postulates many such vestiges in the **collective** *unconscious.*
palilalia (pal''ə·lā'li·ə): *n.* the pathological repetition of words and phrases.
pali(n)- (pal'in-): combining form meaning *backward, again, repetitive,* esp., *pathologically repetitive.*
palingraphia = mirror writing (*prefd.*).
palinlexia (-lek'si·ə): *n.* **backward reading.**
palinphrasia (-frā'zhə): *n.* frequent or habitual repetition of words or phrases in otherwise coherent speech.—*Var.* **paliphrasia.**
pallesthesia (pal''es·thē'zhə) = **palmesthesia.**
palliative (pal'i·ā''tiv; -ə·tiv): *adj.* easing or reducing pain or discomfort without removing the cause.
pallium: *n.* old term for the cerebral cortex or for the superficial **white matter** of a cerebral hemisphere.
palmar response (pal'mər): the handgrasp response occurring in the newborn.

Light pressure on the palm produces closure of the hand, and attempts to pull away the grasped object result in gripping or clinging.

palmar scoop: the method by which infants at 3 or 4 months grasp a small object: the thumb is ineffective and the object is scooped up by the four fingers and the side of the palm.

palmesthesis (pal"mes·thē'səs): *n.* sensitivity to vibrations.—*Var.* **palmesthesia, pallesthesia.**—*Ant.* PALMANESTHESIA.

palmistry: *n.* the attempt to read a person's character, and sometimes his past and possible future, from the lines on the palm of the hand.

palp (palp): *v.* **1.** to touch or explore with the fingers. **2.** to feel a touch.—*Syn.* PALPATE (pal'pāt).—*n.* **palpation.**

palpable (pal'pə·bəl): *adj.* **1.** touchable. **2.** directly observable by the senses. **3.** obvious: *palpable* falsehood.

palpate = **palp.**

palpation: see **touch (1).**

palpebral (pal'pə·brəl): *adj.* pertaining to the eyelid.

palpitation: *n.* very rapid beating of the heart.

palsy (pôl'zi): *n.* paralysis; esp., **paralysis agitans,** in which there is a continuous coarse tremor in the hands.

palsy/cerebral: a condition resulting from injury to the **motor areas** of the brain, usually characterized by **spasticity** of one or more limbs and often accompanied by spastic paralysis of speech musculature, sometimes by **athetosis.** ➤The brain injury is seldom restricted to the motor area and other symptoms occur. About 20 per cent of those with cerebral palsy are mentally deficient.

pan-, panto-: combining forms meaning *all, every.*

panel: *n.* **1.** a group from whom representatives are chosen for a specific activity: the *panel* from which jurors are selected. **2.** a group of persons discussing an issue somewhat informally before an audience. ➤Originally they were drawn as representatives from the audience, but the term has been corrupted to include highly unrepresentative outside experts.

panel design or **study:** a technique in which a single sample of informants is interviewed, usually about the same variable (e.g., income, voting preference, a certain attitude) and recurrently over an extended period of time, for the purpose of studying the processes of change in response.

panic: *n.* sudden overpowering fear.

panophobia: *n.* fear of everything.—See **phobia.**—*Var.* **pantophobia.**

panpsychism: *n.* the doctrine that the only reality is mental or psychic, that everything that exists is mindlike.—See **psychology/ divisions and schools of. IV.**

pansexualism: *n.* the view, ascribed to Freudians by their opponents, that everything is to be explained by the sex **motif.**

pantheism (pan'thē·iz·əm): *n.* the doctrine that God and the universe are one.

pantophobia = **panophobia.**

panum phenomenon: If two parallel lines near together are presented to one eye, and one line to the other so that it is stereoscopically combined with either of the other two, the combined line is seen as nearer.

papilla (pə·pil'ə) *n., pl.* **papillas, papillae** (-ē): a nipple-shaped prominence or elevation.—*adj.* **papillary** (pap'ə·ler"i; pə·- pil'ə·ri).

par(a)-: prefix meaning *at the side of*; hence, *unusual, abnormal,* or *slightly abnormal*; in speech pathology, referring to *sound substitutions.*

parabiosis (par"ə·bī·ō'səs): *n.* temporary loss of conductivity in a nerve.—*adj.* **parabiotic.**

paracentral gyrus: (*neuroanat.*) a convolution on the middle surface of the hemispheres and round the upper end of the central fissure.

paracentral vision: see **vision/paracentral.**

parachromatopsia = partial **color blindness.**—*Var.* **parachromopsia.**

paracusia (-ə·kū'si·ə): *n.* **1.** selective deafness to deep tones. **2.** the alleged ability of partially deaf persons to hear better in the presence of noise. **3.** any disorder of hearing except deafness.—*Var.* **paracusis** (-səs).

paradic (pə·rad'ik): *adj.* of that which follows a **paradigm,** or which functions in accord with its pattern or design.—*Syn.* **normal (3).**

paradigm (par'ə·dim; -dīm): *n.* a model, pattern, or example that exhibits all the variable forms of something: e.g., the pattern showing all the grammatical forms of a word.

paradox: *n.* a statement that involves self-contradiction; a state of affairs which, as observed or described, includes seemingly incongruous or contradictory elements. It is usually implied that the paradox dissolves with fuller understanding.—*adj.* **paradoxic(al).**

paradoxical cold: cold felt when an actually warm object (roughly 45° C. or above) stimulates the **receptor** for cold. ➤It is believed that paradoxical cold fuses with warmth to yield the perception of hotness.—*Syn.* PARADOXICAL COOLTH (*prefd.* but less common).

paradoxical warmth: a feeling of warmth when the stimulus lies between 29–31° C., which is typically a cool stimulus.

paraesthesia = **paresthesia.**

paragenital: *adj.* pertaining to sex intercourse in which procreation is prevented.— See **contraception.**

parageusia (par″ə·gū′si·ə): *n.* abnormal taste; a taste **hallucination.**—*adj.* **parageusic** (-gū′sik).

paragrammatism: *n.* speech showing disturbances in grammatical and/or syntactical relationships.

paragraphia: *n.* the habitual insertion of wrong and unintended words in what one writes. ➤The word is usually, though not always, applied to a pathological condition and parallels the phenomenon of **paraphasia** (which see) in speech.—*Distg. fr.* **paragrammatism.**

paragraph-meaning test: a test of ability to grasp the central thought of a paragraph.

paralalia (-lā′li·ə): *n.* the habitual substitution, in speech, of wrong sounds for the proper ones.—See **paraphasia.**

paralexia (-lek′si·ə): *n.* a form of **dyslexia** in which the disturbance in reading takes the form of substitution or transposition of letters, syllables, or words.

parallax (par′ə·laks): *n.* the apparent movement of objects in the field of vision as the point of view is shifted laterally. Objects nearer to the observer than the point fixated seem to move against the direction of the shift, objects beyond the point fixated move with the shift. ➤The phenomenon is explained in terms of the geometry of the lines of sight. It makes no difference whether the observer moves with respect to the environment or the environment with respect to the observer.—*Syn.* MONOCULAR MOVEMENT PARALLAX.—See also **parallax/binocular.**—*adj.* **parallactic.**

parallax/binocular: the difference in the point of view or optic angle of the two eyes due to their lateral separation; or the resulting inequality of separation of the retinal images of unequally distant objects. ➤If a pencil be lined up by the favored eye with a vertical line in the background and then viewed by the other eye, it will be seen to shift apparent position in respect to the background reference line. This shift is greater when the pencil is nearer the eye. In binocular vision, such a difference in lateral displacement of objects results in different **retinal *disparity** for near and far objects; this is one factor that makes perception of relative distance possible.

parallax threshold: (*vision*) If two points are separated by x distance, and the remoter point is y distant from the plane through the nodal points of the two eyes, and a is the interocular distance or stereo base, then the parallax difference (in radians) or threshold P will be given by

$$P = \left(\frac{a}{y-x} - \frac{a}{y} \right) = \frac{ax}{y(y-x)}$$
$$= \text{(approximately) } \frac{ax}{y^2}$$

parallel (eye) movement: see **eye movement/parallel.**

parallel form: see **form/comparable.**

parallelism: see **mind-body problem.**

parallelism/cultural: the independent development of similar culture traits and patterns in different societies.—*Cp.* **diffusion theory.**

parallelism/psychoneural: the doctrine that for every conscious or mental event there is a corresponding neural activity. ➤The reverse relation is not usually asserted.—*Cp.* the broader concept, **parallelism/psychophysical.**

parallelism/psychophysical: the doctrine that for every conscious process there is a corresponding or parallel process in the body. ➤The doctrine makes no assumption about causal relation, nor does it assert an ultimate or metaphysical difference between the parallel systems of events.—See **mind-body problem.**

parallel law: a **psychophysical** principle stated by Fechner: If two stimuli of different intensity are presented to a receptor for a stated duration, the absolute sensory intensities diminish (because of **sensory *adaptation** or fatigue) but the ratio of difference remains the same.

parallel play: see **play/parallel.**

parallel proportional profiles/method of: (*R. B. Cattell*) a **factor analysis** procedure that employs several **matrices** at a time and applies the principle of **parsimony** to the whole set instead of to the analysis of each matrix in turn. ➤A **factor** derived parsimoniously from one matrix may result in an unparsimonious multiplication of factors if it is introduced into a second matrix.

paralog: *n.* a two-syllable nonsense word: e.g., defig, latak, nigot, tarup.

paralogism: *n.* unintentional fallacy.

paralysis *n., pl.* **-ses:** loss or impairment of a function. ➤Unless qualified, a motor function is usually referred to, but SENSORY PARALYSES are also spoken of.—*Syn.* **palsy.** Various kinds of paralysis are named by using the combining form **-plegia:** MONOPLEGIA, paralysis of one limb or muscle group; PARAPLEGIA, of the lower limbs; HEMIPLEGIA, of one side; DIPLEGIA, of both sides. Other kinds are named by symptoms (e.g., **spastic *paralysis**), by location (e.g., FACIAL PARALYSIS), or by cause (e.g., OCCUPATIONAL PARALYSIS).—*adj.* **paralytic.**

paralysis agitans: a paralytic disorder characterized by continuous coarse tremor of the hands; the condition commonly called **palsy.**—*Syn.* PARKINSONISM, PARKINSON'S DISEASE.

paralysis of the insane/general = **paresis.**

paralysis/spastic: a condition marked by spasmodic jerky muscle contractions (esp. in voluntary movements), and by a steady increased tone in certain muscle groups.— *Syn.* BIRTH PALSY, LITTLE'S DISEASE.

paralytic dementia = **paresis.**

parameter (pǝ·ram'ǝ·tǝr): *n.* **1.** (*math.*) a constant in an equation of two or more variables each of whose values characterizes a particular form of the equation or a particular curve of the family of curves defined by the equation. **2.** (*psychol.*) any constant that defines the curve of the equation for some psychological **function** (e.g., learning, growth). ➤Such a constant is the mathematical expression of the change induced in the curve by a change in the materials, subjects, experimental procedures, etc. A parameter may be **rational** (based on a particular theory) or **empirical** (i.e., a generalization and smoothing of actual data); but even when empirical, the parameter is a property of a hypothetical infinite population or set of causes. Hence, it is always an estimate. Where a particular **sample** or particular method of estimate is in question, the proper term is a **statistic.**—See **nonparametric. 3.** (*tech. slang*) the curve representing performance under specified experimental conditions. ➤E.g., the learning curve for a group of rats in a T maze is sometimes called the learning parameter for the experiment. This usage is not recommended. **4.** (*psychoan.*) the differentiating character of a technique of **analysis** used for a particular disorder, or for a particular client. ➤Some of Freud's followers, although holding closely to his underlying theory, depart widely from the model of therapy which he set forth. That which makes the difference is the parameter.—*adj.* **parametric.**

paramimia (-mim'i·ǝ): *n.* a form of **apraxia** in which gesture language is distorted so that it does not appropriately express feeling.

paramnesia (par″am·nē'zhǝ): *n.* **1.** properly, false memory. **2.** usually, false recognition: e.g., the *déjà vu* (or "seen-this-before") illusion. ➤Extensive paramnesia is much more often responsible for false testimony than mere forgetting.

paranoia (par″ǝ·noi'ǝ): *n.* (*Stan. Psychiat.*) a (rare) **psychosis** characterized by systematized **delusions** with little or no **dementia.** ➤Delusions of grandeur and of persecution, one or both, are most typical, and are defended by the patient with much appearance of logic and reason. The paranoid system, though extensive, is relatively isolated and thus leaves the rest of the personality largely unaffected, in which respect it is distinguished from **paranoid *schizophrenia.**— *Syn.* PARANOID REACTIONS.—*adj.*

and *pers. n.* **paranoid, paranoiac** (both with other meaning).

paranoiac (-noi'ak): *n.* a person suffering from **paranoia** or **paranoid *schizophrenia.**—*Distg. fr.* paranoid.—*adj.* paranoiac.

paranoid: *adj.* **1.** pertaining to, or resembling, **paranoia** or paranoid ***schizophrenia;** having **delusions** of grandeur and/or of persecution. **2.** of a person whose behavior resembles that of paranoia or paranoid schizophrenia; or of a person manifesting a **paranoid trend.** ➤The resemblance may be so close that psychosis is suspected; or it may be so slight as to be figurative. ("Don't be so paranoid" may mean "Don't have such grandiose ideas," or even "Don't be so sensitive to criticism.") **Paranoid** for **paranoiac** loses a useful distinction.—*pers. n.* **paranoid.**

paranoid character: 1. (*obsoles.*) the kind of personality likely to regress into **paranoia. 2.** = paranoid personality (*prefd.*).

paranoid dementia (precox) = **schizophrenia/paranoid.**

paranoid personality: 1. (*Stan. Phychiat.*) a **personality disorder** somewhat similar to **paranoid *schizophrenia** but without the deterioration or systematized delusions. The individual is suspicious, envious, jealous, stubborn, extremely sensitive to what seem to be slights or injuries, much inclined to **projection. 2.** loosely, any person with grandiose ideas and a tendency to believe that only a hostile combination of circumstances (including people) prevents his true ability from being realized.

paranoid trend: a tendency to grandiose ideas and/or sensitivity to real or apparent criticism. ➤The grandiose ideas or the delusions of persecution may be as extreme or as irrational as those of either **paranoia** or **paranoid *schizophrenia,** but they are less central in the organization of personality and do not control an important part of the person's daily life; hence, the paranoid trend is not a psychosis.

paranormal: *adj.* of phenomena that, as far as can be seen, are not explainable in terms of generally accepted scientific principles. ➤It is implied that, if the phenomena are confirmed, the scientific principles must be drastically revised.—See **parapsychology.**

paranosic (-nō'sik): see **advantage by illness.**

paraphasia (-fā'zhǝ): *n.* the habitual introduction of very inappropriate words into one's speech. ➤At least half a dozen other **neologisms** refer to speech impairments of this general character: PARAPHRASIA, a misuse of words or phrases; PARAPHEMIA, the use of wrong sounds or words; **parapraxis,** a broader term but inclusive of paraphasia; **acataphasia,** inability to connect words properly in a sentence; ABOIEMENT, involuntary production of inappropriate sounds; **paralalia,** the habitual substitution of one letter sound for another; and so on. ¶No doubt each of these terms was introduced to emphasize some fine distinction. But not every empirically observed difference in behavior, not every possible conception, requires a separate name. The many shifts in meaning in the actual usage of many of these terms shows that the fine distinctions are not taken seriously by others than the coiners of the terms.

paraphemia: see **paraphasia.**

paraphilia: *n.* a distortion or anomaly of sexuality.—*Syn.* **sexual anomaly** (which see).

paraphonia: *n.* any abnormal condition of the voice.

paraphrasia: see **paraphasia.**

paraphrenia: *n.* a general, but obsolescent, term for **dementia praecox** and/or **paranoia.**

paraplegia (-plē'ji·ə): *n.* paralysis of the lower limbs or lower section of the body. —*adj.* **paraplegic** (-plej'ik; -plē'jik), **paraplectic.**

parapraxis: *n.* a generic term for such minor errors in behavior as a slip of the tongue or pen, misplacing articles, memory blockings, small accidents, etc. ➤In psychoanalysis, attributed to ***unconscious** ***conflict.**—*Var.* **parapraxia.**

paraprosexia: *n.* fixation of attention upon an object or idea without progress in developing the idea, as in **fixed ideas.**

parapsychology: *n.* a division of psychology dealing with psychological phenomena that appear not to fall within the range of what is at present covered by **natural law.** ➤It deals with the irregular, the fantastic, the allegedly supranormal; with trances, clairvoyance, telepathy, mediumistic possession, etc. Parapsychology aims to bring these phenomena within the scope of natural law, if necessary by expanding the boundaries of the latter.—*Distg. fr.* **pseudopsychology.** —*Syn.* PSYCHISM, **metapsychics, psychic research.** Parapsychology is the preferred term.

parasagittal (par"ə·saj'i·təl): *adj.* of a plane parallel to the **sagittal** plane.

parasexuality: *n.* anomalous or perverted sexuality (see **sexual anomaly**).

parasympathetic division of the nervous system: the cranial and the sacral parts of the **autonomic nervous system.** ➤This division is more often active in relaxed or quiescent states; it thus contrasts with, and is to some extent functionally opposite to, the sympathetic division.—See **nervous system.**

parataxic: *adj.* **1.** characterized by malad-

justment in respect to emotions and desires. **2.** (*H. S. Sullivan*) of the development of skills, attitudes, and ideas without bringing these adequately into relationship with other aspects of one's personality; living in water-tight compartments.—*Cp.* **prototaxic** and **syntaxic.**—*n.* **parataxis.**

parathyroid glands: four small bodies in the neck which produce a specific **hormone,** the main function of which is to maintain the calcium and phosphorus balance in the blood. Deficiency in this hormone causes **tetany.**

paratypic (-tip'ik): *adj.* pertaining to environmental influences.—See **heredity.**— *Ant.* **genotypic.**—*n.* **paratype.**

parent: *n.* **1.** an organism that has produced offspring; a father or mother. **2.** figuratively, one who creates or produces something, esp. something novel.

parental behavior: the care and nurture, physically and psychologically, of a young organism. ➤In some species the behavior is very largely **instinctive;** in man, it is disputed to what extent this is true.

parental rejection: see **rejection.**

parenthood/voluntary: the voluntary regulation of the number and spacing of children to be borne by a given mother.—*Syn.* PLANNED PARENTHOOD, **birth control.**— *Distg. fr.* **contraception,** which is only one of several means of preventing involuntary parenthood. Voluntary parenthood also includes positive measures such as are needed to correct sterility, etc.

parent image: 1. the way the child or adult remembers his parents to have been at an earlier stage. **2.** a parent **surrogate.**

parents/dethronement of: the process whereby a child ceases to regard his parents as omnipotent and omniscient rulers, entitled to his submission, and begins to find other persons to whom he turns. ➤The concept, like the expression, is a deliberate exaggeration.

parergastic reactions (par"ər·gas'tik): (*A. Meyer*) symptoms typical of **schizophrenia.**

paresis (pə·rē'səs): *n.* psychosis with progressive **dementia** and paralyses, resulting from prior syphilitic infection of the brain. —*Syn.* GENERAL PARALYSIS (OF THE INSANE), DEMENTIA PARALYTICA, PARETIC PSYCHOSIS. —*adj.* and *pers. n.* **paretic** (pə·rē'tik).

paresthesia (par"es·thē'zhə): *n.* wrong or imaginary localization of such cutaneous sensations as pricking, tickling, burning.— *Cp.* **formication.**—*Var.* **paraesthesia.**

parietal (pə·rī'ə·təl): *adj.* of the middle region of the top of the skull and extending downward on each side behind the temples; or of the brain areas beneath that skull area.

parietal lobe: a major division of either

cerebral hemisphere, lying between the **frontal** and **occipital lobes** and above the **temporal lobe.**

Parkinsonism = **paralysis agitans.**—*Syn.* PARKINSON'S DISEASE.

parole: *n.* release from restraint, conditional upon "good behavior." ➤Originally it meant the release of prisoners of war upon giving their word not to engage further in military action. It is now generally applied to the release of prisoners from penal or correctional institutions, subject to supervision by a PAROLE OFFICER.—*pers. n.* **parolee.**

parorexia: *n.* abnormal desire to eat unusual substances.

parosmia: *n.* 1. any disorder of the sense of smell. 2. olfactory **hallucination.**—*adj.* **parosmic.**

parosphresia: *n.* 1. partial **anosmia.** 2. = **parosmia.**

parotid gland (pə·rot'id): the large salivary gland in the cheek in front of, and just below, the external ear.

paroxysm: *n.* 1. spasm; fit; convulsion. 2. a sudden recurrence or intensification in the symptoms of a disease.—*adj.* **paroxysmal.**

parsimony/principle of: the general principle of scientific thinking that the simpler of two hypotheses is to be preferred. ➤It is variously stated. Occam taught that explanatory principles ("entities") should not be needlessly multiplied; this is **Occam's razor.** Lloyd **Morgan's canon,** applying the principle to comparative psychology, warned that actions should be interpreted, whenever possible, as manifestations of the psychologically "lower" of two or more processes. But the explanation of an action in terms of the lower process of memory rather than the higher process of thinking is not genuinely simpler if many additional assumptions must be made to support the memory explanation.—*Syn.* PRINCIPLE OF ECONOMY, **Occam's razor, Morgan's canon.**

part: *n.* something that is less than the whole of any object, whether physical or ideational; the result of dividing something. —*Ant.* **whole,** total, totality.—*adj.* **partial,** preferred for a functional division; **part,** preferred for a structural division.

parthenogenesis (pär"thə·nō·jen'ə·səs): *n.* reproduction from an unfertilized egg. ➤It is a modification of sexual reproduction and is not to be confused with the asexual multiplication of lower organisms. The drone, or male honey bee, is developed by parthenogenesis.

partial: *n.* a **partial tone.**

partial activity/law of = reduced cues/ **principle of.**

partial aim: (*psychoan.*) any of the **pregenital** means of gratifying the sexual instinct.

partial color blindness: see **color blindness.**

partial correlation: see **correlation/ partial.**

partial insanity: a medicolegal term for a condition of limited responsibility by reason of mental disorder.

partialization: *n.* (*O. Rank*) the breaking down of the original undifferentiated awareness of the outer world.—*Syn.* **differentiation (3).**

partial love: (*psychoan.*) love focused upon a **part-object** rather than upon a whole person.

partial regression equation = **regression equation/multiple.**

partial sight: seriously defective vision ➤It is usually defined as less than 20/70 acuity (see **acuity/visual**) in the better eye after correction; or as a progressive eye disorder that will probably reduce vision below 20/70; or as some other serious visual malfunction, such as **tunnel vision** (but not **color blindness**).—*Cf.* **blindness, sight conservation class.**— *Syn.* PARTIAL BLINDNESS (not *prefd.*).—*adj.* **partially seeing, partial-sighted, partially blind** (not *prefd.*).

partial (tone): (*music, acoustics*) any on of the component pitches that make up musical tone emitted by a single sounding body. ➤A sounding or vibrating body, with a few exceptions, vibrates not only over it whole extent, but in fractional parts. Each such part sets up a **pure *tone** whose pitch corresponds to its vibration frequency a frequency that is an integral multiple o the vibration rate of the sound-producing body as a whole. These tones, or partials fuse to form a compound tone. The par tials are numbered in series from the lowest The FIRST PARTIAL, which is lowest an loudest, is alternatively called the FUNDA MENTAL; all the others are UPPER PARTIAL or OVERTONES. (Note that the *second par tial* is the *first overtone.*) Upper partial are also called HARMONICS, and the entir series of partial tones forms the HARMONI (or OVERTONE) SERIES. ¶The pitch of th compound tone is heard as that of its fun damental, although its component part may be analyzed out by the trained listene or with the help of an instrument. The pro portion of the various partials present in given tone chiefly determines its characte istic **timbre.**

participant: *n.* one who takes part in group situation or activity. ➤A PARTIC PANT OBSERVER gathers observational dat while taking part in the activities.

participation: *n.* 1. a dynamic interpla between two or more **systems** where each is influenced by, and influences, th others, the interchange constituting a cha acteristic event. ➤While **participation**

more commonly applied to the interaction of organismic systems, any system may be a participant in an event. In the batting of a home run, the bat and the ball each constitute a participating system no less real and no less crucial than the batter. See **transaction. 2.** sharing directly or indirectly in a social activity. ➤**Identification** with the group is often implied. **3.** (*J. Piaget*) a childish way of thinking in which outer events are not distinguished from inner; acting as if whatever is thought about has as much reality as any objective thing or event. **4.** acting on the belief that one can be a particular individual, yet can also be other persons, or at least a part of other persons. ➤Thus, in some nonliterate societies an individual is clearly himself; yet he may, on occasion, be thought not merely to represent or impersonate but to *be* the rain god. A similar belief is sometimes found in **schizophrenia.**

participation/law of: (*L. Levy-Bruhl*) the tendency in primitive thinking to act (or to think) as if things that are perceived as similar are not merely similar but the same. ➤The tendency plays a large role in magic.

participation/mystical: (*L. Levy-Bruhl*) a condition in which the person does not distinguish between himself and the object of his awareness but feels himself to be one with whatever he perceives or thinks about.

participation schedule: a **check list** upon which to record the degree and kind of an individual's participation in group activities.

particular complex: (*psychoan.*) a **complex** based upon the special events in a particular life history, rather than upon some universal trait or tendency.

particularism: see **universalism.**

partile: *n.* the generic name for one of the set of points that divide a serially ordered or **ranked distribution** into a number of divisions, each of which contains the same number of scores. Each point is located as coinciding with the obtained score in the distribution *below which* the required fraction of the scores is found. ➤If there are 100 such divisions (each containing $\frac{1}{100}$ of the scores), the division points are called **percentiles** (sometimes **centiles**, but this usage, though logical, conflicts with another established usage). Other partile points are named by adding *-ile* to the root of the Latin ordinal number: e.g., DECILE (setting off divisions of $\frac{1}{10}$ of the cases), OCTILE ($\frac{1}{8}$), SEXTILE ($\frac{1}{6}$), QUINTILE ($\frac{1}{5}$), QUARTILE ($\frac{1}{4}$), TERTILE ($\frac{1}{3}$).

The several partiles are numbered from the bottom up; thus, the first percentile (better named *percentile 1*) is the point score below which $\frac{1}{100}$ of the cases lie, *tertile 1* is the score below which $\frac{1}{3}$ of the cases lie, *percentile 99* is the score below which $\frac{99}{100}$ cases lie. The unit score next

above the highest obtained is sometimes called the 100th percentile, but this is not recommended. Any highest partile should be designated by a number that is 1 less than the number of divisions: for the sextile, 5; for the octile, 7; for the decile, 9, etc. The lowest score in a distribution is sometimes given a zero rank—e.g., a zero quartile or Q_0. But a partile is a dividing point and a zero quartile (if allowed) would be a limiting, not a dividing, point. The lowest partile is therefore of rank 1.

The several partile terms are sometimes used, not only for the dividing *point* score, but also for the divisions set apart by such points. This can be confusing. If both division and point be called by the same partile name, we have such difficulties as that the top quartile as a point is quartile 3, as a division is quartile 4. Further, with such usage the expression "He is in the 3rd quartile" means that the person is *below* the 3rd quartile (defined as a point), which sounds like nonsense. To avoid confusion, a partile term standing alone should refer exclusively to the *point divider* of ranked distribution. The respective divisions may be called THIRDS, FOURTHS, TENTHS; or TERTILE DIVISIONS, QUARTILE DIVISIONS, etc. It would help also if the points were referred to by cardinal numerals (*cp.* Q_1, Q_3) and the divisions by ordinals. (See **percentile** for exception in the case of hundredths. See also **centile** for comparison of these divisions with statistical **class.**)

The partile terms are also used to indicate the **rank** of an individual score or person. The individual is given the rank of the PARTILE DIVISION in which he belongs. Such expressions as QUARTILE RANK may be accepted as an ellipsis for QUARTILE DIVISION RANK. In the case of hundredths, it is CENTILE RANK, not percentile rank.

part-instinct: *n.* (*psychoan.*) an instinct component; a specific manifestation in conscious experience of either the **life instinct** or the **death instinct.**

partition: *n.* in cognizing, the point or plane of separation between object and subject. ➤If one explores a rough surface with a pliant stick, the rough surface is the object. The stick is regarded as an extension of the hand and thus part of the subject in exploring the object. The partition lies between surface and stick. But if one turns one's attention to how the stick feels tactually, the partition shifts to the point of separation between stick and skin.

partition measure: any statistic that sets off one part of a **frequency** distribution from another. ➤It refers primarily to **partile** measures such as the median, upper quartile, third decile, etc.

partitive behavior: (*T. Burrow*) behavior in which one reacts to the symbolic **or**

linguistically analyzed aspect of an event, and primarily in terms of its intellectual implications, with (at least) relative neglect of its emotional or motivational values.

partitive thinking: thinking that breaks down a previously perceived total content into parts.—See **analysis (1)**.—*Syn.* ANALYTICAL THINKING.

part method of learning: see **learning/part method of.**

part-object: *n.* (*psychoan.*) an anatomical part of a person as the object of love (or hate) without reference to the person as a whole. ➤E.g., the baby loves the breast or nipple (a part-object) without necessarily loving his mother as a **whole-object.** The persistence of this tendency into adult life is said to be a measure of various **affective *fixations.**

parturition (pär"chü·rish'ən; pär"tü-): *n.* the act of giving birth to offspring.—*adj.* **parturient** (pär·tü'ri·ənt).

passion: *n.* 1. strong emotion. 2. emotion so strong as to override judgment and will. 3. (*pop.*) sexual emotion or tendency. (An unnecessary usage.)

passive: *adj.* 1. of a state of rest or inactivity. 2. of an attitude in which the person, being acted upon, makes no effort to control the course of events.—*Ant.* **active.**

passive-aggressive personality: (*Stan. Psychiat.*) a person, lacking genuine independence, who reacts to difficulties either by indecisiveness and a clinging to others for help, or by irritability, temper tantrums, and misdirected destructiveness or obstructionism.

passive vocabulary: see **language/passive.**

passivism: *n.* submission to the will of another in anomalous (so-called **perverted**) sex practices.

passivity need: the need to be relaxed and inactive, to receive benefits without effort, to allow others their way.

past pointing: When a person has been rotated he will, if his ***vestibular *receptors** are in order, point past a given target in the direction in which he was rotated.

patella (pə·tel'ə): *n.* the kneecap.—*adj.* **patellar.**

patellar reflex (pə·tel'ər) = **knee-jerk reflex.**

paternalism: *n.* 1. protection and control of adults—by government, employers, etc.—as if they were children. 2. the attitude which denies to adults who are in a subordinate position the right to control their personal affairs.

path: *n.* (*topol. psychol.*) the line or linelike region connecting two points or point **regions;** the route over which psychological locomotion takes place; a geometrical model for any psychological activity; the locus of all the regions repre-

senting a psychological activity. ➤E.g., the path to a lunch includes not only the geographical space traversed but any other activity necessary to it, such as paying for it. Or, paying alone might be regarded as a path. In this case it is a linelike region, rather than a point region, since there are alternative ways of paying—by coins, bills, check, chit, or washing the dishes.

path coefficient: (*stat.*) in a criterion variable, the ratio of the variability that is due to one of the independent variables to the total variability. The SIMPLE PATH COEFFICIENT is the partial regression coefficient using standard deviations as the unit of measurement.

pathergasia: *n.* (*A. Meyer*) a physiological or anatomical malfunction that limits the person's capacity for psychological adjustment: e.g., having one leg short which, for some individuals, causes a variety of maladjustments.

pathetic fallacy: attributing human emotions to all of nature.—*Syn.* **anthropomorphism.**

pathetic nerve = **trochlear nerve.**

pathic: *adj.* pertaining to, or affected by disease.

path(o)-: combining form meaning *feeling, suffering, disease.*

pathogenesis: *n.* the origin or development of a disease or disorder.—*adj.* **pathogenic,** causing disease.

pathognomy (pə·thog'nə·mi): *n.* 1. the recognition of feelings and emotions. 2. the recognition of disease; diagnosis. ➤In **Rorschach testing,** responses held to be distinctive of a certain disorder are called PATHOGNOMIC SIGNS.—*adj.* **pathognomic** (path"əg·nom'ik), **pathognomonic.**

pathological fallacy: depicting the psychological nature of man in the image of the patient; conceiving of psychological processes in terms of the abnormal. ➤That the normal may be illumined by a study of the pathological is not denied; the fallacy consists in supposing that an abnormal process or quality is typical when, in fact it is exceptional. Thus, the existence of an **Oedipus complex** at the heart of all neuroses, as asserted by psychoanalysts, cannot be taken as proof that all normal persons pass through an Oedipal conflict. For this, other evidence is needed.

pathology: *n.* 1. a condition of the organism such that a cell or other organ is prevented from performing its usual function a diseased, disordered, or abnormal condition of the organism or its parts. 2. the scientific discipline which studies such conditions. ➤In medicine, pathology usually refers to **organic** conditions in distinction from **functional;** but there is clearly also a pathology of function, including behavior functions. MORBIDITY is a close synonym but sounds harsher. **Abnormality** (which see) has a quantitative reference, connoting some or considerable deviation from the usual structure or function. Pathology is also used as a combining form: *psychopathology, neuropathology.—adj.* **pathological.—***pers. n.* **pathologist** (usually restricted to the specialist who studies destructive change in tissues).

pathomimesus (path″ō-mi·mē′səs): *n.* the feigning of disease symptoms. ➤It may be deliberate (see **malingering**), or it may be a more subtle process in the course of which certain uncomfortable tensions are relieved by the pretense of illness. E.g., guilty feelings for failure to accomplish something may be relieved if one can believe he was too ill.—*Syn.* PATHOMIMICRY.

pathoneurosis: *n.* a neurotic preoccupation with a real organic impairment or illness.

pathopsychology: *n.* a term proposed for the *psychological* study of abnormal psychic data, in contrast with **psychopathology,** which (it is proposed) should be restricted to the *medical* approach to these data. ➤The proposal is etymologically sound, but implies a rigid distinction that has not found acceptance.

pathos: *n.* **1.** suffering; great unhappiness of psychic, rather than physiological, origin. **2.** that quality of a person's experience (or of a work of art representing it) which arouses sympathetic sorrow or pity. **3.** (*esth.*) the emotional, and therefore personal, quality of a work of art, in contrast with its universal elements. **4.** (*sociol.*) the attitude, toward a cherished idea or custom or institution, that it is not to be discussed or criticized.

patriliny (pat′rə·lĭ″ni) = **father right.—***adj.* **patrilineal** (-lin′i·əl).

patriotism: *n.* a **sentiment** whose object is one's fatherland and whose central emotion is love or tenderness.

pattern: *n.* **1.** a sample or model to be copied. **2.** a number of perceived parts forming a design; a whole in which the parts are separately distinguishable but together constitute a unity; a grouping in which the relationship between the parts is emphasized. ➤The elements of a pattern may be simultaneous or successive. See **pattern/sensory, pattern/behavioral.** The use of **pattern** is often redundant: e.g., *habit pattern* (all habits are patterns). —*Syn.* **gestalt,** configuration; (for sensory patterns) **colligation, complication.** —*v.* **3.** to impose a **pattern,** design, or meaning upon sensory or conceptual data; to arrange data in a pattern.—*Syn.* **structure** (*v.*).

pattern/action = **pattern/behavioral.**

pattern analysis: 1. a method for finding, in an assemblage of test items, **clusters** that belong together according to some significant principle. ➤E.g., one might seek test items that, despite superficial dissimilarities, require similar ability to answer correctly. The procedure is to group the items in tentative clusters according to a systematic plan, and to test whether the same kind of answer is given significantly more often to the items in the cluster than would be true by chance. **2.** the attempt to find a pattern or configuration of scores that is more predictive of some **criterion** than each of the scores taken separately. ➤*Distg. fr.* **multiple** **correlation* analysis, which seeks for the best combinations of *variables* to predict a criterion, whereas pattern analysis seeks the best pattern of *scores* for a given set of variables. Thus, by multiple correlation we determine whether the addition of a test of athletic performance to a test of verbal ability improves prediction of scholastic success. Pattern analysis asks whether the score pattern in which athletic ability is lower than average and verbal ability is high is more likely to predict academic success than the score pattern of high athletic ability and below-average verbal ability. Pattern analysis implies that the variables not only correlate but interact.—*Syn.* PROFILE ANALYSIS, CONFIGURAL ANALYSIS.

pattern/behavior(al): a complex act made up of distinguishable lesser acts, simultaneous or successive, that from some standpoint or other are regarded as a functional unit. ➤E.g., the sequence of behaviors—cutting the meat on the plate, conveying it to the mouth, chewing and swallowing it—is a unit of easily distinguished parts but, when considered as "the act of eating meat," it forms a single whole, a behavioral pattern. ¶A NERVE PATTERN is the set of nerves believed to be involved in a particular behavioral pattern, with particular reference to the relationships between these nerves. This nerve pattern belongs to the **conceptual nervous system** (which see).

pattern/constitutional: the pattern, or set of relationships between organs or between functions, laid down by **species** **heredity.—Cp.* constitutional (2).

pattern discrimination: reacting to the **pattern** as such rather than to the components of which it is made up; reacting to the complex of relations: e.g., reacting to letters as shapes (i.e., to certain spatial relationships) rather than to the particular size or colors used in printing them. ➤Pattern discrimination rests upon ignoring certain aspects of the stimulus situation. It is generally believed that all **perceiving** is pattern discrimination, but the latter term emphasizes the aspects of perceiving referred to in the definition.

pattern/growth: the sequence, in a life history, in which various characteristics appear or assume a certain relative strength.

patterning: *n.* **1.** the imposition of a **pattern** or system upon a group of data. ➤*Cp.* **ordering,** which is the imposition of a predetermined system, whereas in patterning the data may suggest the pattern or system. **2.** the learning to respond to a whole pattern of stimuli as such; = POSITIVE PATTERNING.—*Ant.* NEGATIVE PATTERNING, learning to respond to certain parts of a pattern, not to the whole.

pattern/instinctive releasing: a grouping of stimuli (whether the grouping is innate or acquired) that elicits **instinctive** behavior.

pattern/neural = nerve pattern (see **pattern/behavioral**).

pattern/sensory or **/perceptual:** sensory data that manifest a unity within which are included such relationships as **figure-ground,** contrast, similarity, and various spatial and temporal relations. ➤Emphasis is upon the design or upon the relationships rather than upon the sensory properties taken by themselves. Where the parts are so integrated that they are not separately apprehended, **fusion** or **blend** results. —*Syn.* **configuration, colligation, complication** (*obsoles.*), **gestalt.**

pattern similarity/coefficient of: (*R. B. Cattell*) a statistic measuring the degree to which two variables have the same profile or pattern of relation with other variables. —Symbol r_p.

pattern/stimulus: see **stimulus pattern.**

pattern variable: (*T. Parsons* and *E. Shils*) a term given to each of the five dimensions by which it is proposed to categorize any action. Any action may be described as tending toward (*a*) specificity or diffuseness; (*b*) affectivity or affective neutrality; (*c*) universalism or particularism; (*d*) quality or quantity of performance; (*e*) self-orientation or collectivity orientation. ➤In choice situations, a choice of one side of *each* of these dichotomies is necessary if the meaning of the situation is to be fully clear to the actor.

pause/eye = **fixation pause.**

pause/fixation: see **fixation pause.**

Pavlovian conditioning = **conditioning** (1).

Pavlovianism: *n.* the experimental procedures and the point of view of the physiologist I. P. Pavlov. The procedures were those of classical **conditioning** (1); the point of view was that psychic processes are identical with the physiological processes by means of which they are studied.

pavor (pä'vor, pā'vər): *n.* (*L.*) terror; esp. as in PAVOR NOCTURNUS (nok·tèr'nəs), a night terror, a terrifying dream.

Pcs.: (*psychoan.*) *abbr.* for **preconscious.**

PE, P.E., or **p.e.** = **probable error.**

peak clipping: (*speech*) elimination of the

high-**amplitude** portion of a speech wave. ➤Peak clipping causes loss in naturalness but little loss in intelligibility. CENTER CLIP-PING, which eliminates the central part of the amplitude, reduces intelligibility.

peak top diagram = frequency polygon (see **frequency 2**).

Pearsonian (or **Pearson's**) **correlation** = correlation/product-moment.

peccatophobia: *n.* a morbid fear of sinning.

pecking order: a graded and accepted order of privilege, priority, and **dominance** established in a small **face-to-face** *group by aggression and intimidation. ➤So called from the description of the behavior of barnyard fowl: A pecks B, B pecks C, C pecks D, and D runs from any of them.

PEC scale: an opinion scale for estimating a person's position on the variable of politicoeconomic conservatism.

pectoral: *adj.* pertaining to the breast region.

pedagogy: *n.* the study of educational goals and processes; the theory (less often, the art) of teaching.—*adj.* **pedagogic.**—*pers. n.* **pedagog(ue).**

pedal: *adj.* pertaining to the foot: the *peda* extremities.

pedantry: *n.* ostentatious flourishing of knowledge or of what one fondly assumes to be knowledge; the making of finer distinctions than is needed; the use of unusual and highly technical terms where simpler ones are available. ➤This view contributes to making technical dictionaries necessary; it also makes their editors unhappy.—*Approx. syn.* **bogus erudition.**—*adj.* **pedantic.**—*pers. n.* **pedant.**

pederasty (ped'ər·as"ti; pē'də-): *n.* anal **coitus** with a boy or young man.—*Distg. fr.* **sodomy.**—*pers. n.* **pederast.**

pederosis (ped"ər·ō'səs): *n.* (*A. Forel*) the use of children by adults as sexual objects; **pedophilia.**

pediatrics: *n.* the branch of medicine that deals with the health and diseases of children.—*adj.* **pediatric.**—*pers. n.* **pediatrician.**

pedication (ped'ə·kā'shən): *n.* **1.** = **pederasty. 2.** = **sodomy.**—*Var.* **paidication** (-kā'shi·ō).

ped(o)-, paid(o)-, paed(o)-: combining forms meaning *child* or *infant.* First spelling *prefd.*—*Distg. fr.* PED(I)-, combining form (from a different root) meaning *foot.*

pedologia = **speech/infantile.**

pedomorphism (pē"dō·môrf'iz·əm): *n.* the attributing of childish limitations to the adult human; describing adult behavior in terms appropriate to child behavior. ➤*Contr. w.* ENELICOMORPHISM, an uncommon term for the common error of attributing adult characteristics to the child

●edophilia (pē″dō·fil′i·ə): *n.* an adult's sexual attraction to children.—*Var.* **paidophilia** (pā″dō-).—*adj.* **pedophilic.**

●eduncle (pi·dung′kəl): *n.* any stalklike bundle of nerve fibers on the surface of the brain, connecting various parts.—*adj.* **peduncular, pedunculate.**

●eduncle/cerebellar: one of the bands of nerve fiber by which the **cerebellum** attaches to the brain stem. There are three on each side, the SUPERIOR CEREBELLAR PEDUNCLE, the MIDDLE CEREBELLAR PEDUNCLE, and the INFERIOR CEREBELLAR PEDUNCLE.

eduncle/cerebral: either of the two **peduncles** that pass from the **pons** to the cerebral hemispheres, forming the main connection with the spinal cord.—*Syn.* CRUS CEREBRI.

eer: *n.* **1.** a person deemed an equal for the purpose in hand. **2.** a companion or associate on roughly the same level of age or endowment. **3.** an **age-mate.** ➤Meaning (3) would be defensible if adhered to. But to use **peer** to denote the age-mate, while also connoting that the age-mate is the equal or the normal associate in other respects than age, has led to false reasoning and unfortunate social and educational policy. Since **peer** can scarcely be divested of its more general meaning of *equal,* it should not be used for the merely *age-equal.*

eer group: the group with whom a child associates on terms of approximate equality. ➤It is necessary to stress that the equality is only approximate; the peer group is usually very heterogeneous in nearly every respect. And the idea that the group of **age-mates** is actually the best (or the only) peer group for a child is so obviously false that some strong bias must be assumed as the explanation for the frequency with which this is implied or even explicitly asserted.

eer rating: a rating by one's **peers** (which ee).

●gboard: *n.* a performance test consisting of a number of holes into which small pegs are to be inserted at top speed.

●jorism (pē′jə·riz·əm; pej′ə-): *n.* the doctrine that things are getting worse all the time.—*Ant.* **optimism.**—*adj.* **pejorative.**

●llet: *n.* **1.** in tests of infant development, a small round object to be picked up. **2.** a standardized morsel of food used as a lure in experiments with small animals.

●nalty: *n.* any unpleasant consequence imposed (or suffered) for violation of a law, order, or custom.

●nile (pē′nil; -nīl): *adj.* pertaining to the **●enis.**

●nilingus (pē″ni·ling′gəs) = **fellatio.**

●nis: *n.* the male external organ of copulation and urination.—*Cp.* **phallus.**

penis envy: (*psychoan.*) the **repressed wish** to possess a penis. This wish is part of the female form of the **castration complex.**

penology: *n.* the study or art of treating those convicted of crime. The treatment may be conceived as deterrent or as reformative.—*adj.* **penological.**—*pers.* *n.* **penologist.**

pension neurosis: see **neurosis/pension.**

pentatonic: *adj.* (*music*) of a **scale** having only five tones within its octave.

pentothal: *n.* a sodium salt that is used as a general anesthetic by intravenous injection.

peptic: *adj.* pertaining to digestion; hence, pertaining to the stomach.

perceive: *v.* to be aware of objects primarily through one's senses. ➤Although perceiving is predominantly sensory, the influence of past experience is embodied as an (often) indistinguishable component so that, e.g., what is for the eye an orange-colored disk is perceived as a succulent fruit. The use of *perceive* as a synonym for *see* is to be discouraged.—*Cp.* **sensation.** —*adj.* **perceptual.**—*n.* **perception, percept.** (See both these terms.)

percentile: *n.* **1.** one of the 99 point scores that divide a ranked distribution into groups or parts, each of which contains $\frac{1}{100}$ of the scores or persons. The points are located to coincide with the obtained score below which in each division $\frac{1}{100}$ of the cases fall. They are numbered from the bottom up, 1 to 99. ➤Analogy with other partile terms would logically name this a **centile,** but percentile is now firmly established and centile has acquired a different meaning. Inconsistencies abound, however. See **partile** for discussion of rationale. **2.** = CENTILE DIVISION or **centile.** ➤Poor usage. **3.** = CENTILE RANK. ➤A poor usage but quite common. See **centile.**

percentile curve or **graph:** a **cumulative frequency curve** in which the cumulated frequencies are stated as percentages of the total number of cases or measures. The curve is of the **ogive** form.

percentile norm: see **norm/percentile.**

percentile score: a score representing the percentage of persons in a given sample who fall below a given **raw *score.** ➤Percentile scores are usually not well suited to the computation of means, correlations, and the like.

percept (pėr′sept): *n.* **1.** the object of **perceiving;** what one perceives. ➤**Percept** is not used when the object is described in physical (or **physicalistic**) terms; for this, **stimulus, stimulus object,** or *physical object* is used. The picture as seen on the wall is the percept; the pattern of light waves (or the picture described as that which reflects such light waves) is the stimulus or physical object. ¶Different systems offer different interpretations of the relation of the object as perceived to the physical object. The issue is philosophical, but psychologists almost inevitably take sides, though often only implicitly. The percept as the *object* of perceiving is also distinguished from the act or process of perceiving. (But see 2.) 2. a single perceiving; a unit of the perceiving response. —*adj.* **perceptual.**—*n.* **perception** (which see).—*v.* **perceive.**

perception: *n.* 1. an event in the person or organism, primarily controlled by the excitation of sensory receptors, yet also influenced by other factors of a kind that can be shown to have originated in the life history of the organism. ➤The event is primarily **cognitive** rather than **affective** or **conative,** though it usually (or always) manifests all three aspects. It is an organized complex, though its several components can sometimes be separately recognized. It is usually very difficult to distinguish the integrated whole which constitutes the perception event from the associations, memories, and feelings that ensue. The above seems to be the common denominator in the following more specialized definitions (2–6). 2. the awareness, or the process of becoming aware, of extraorganic or intraorganic objects or relations or qualities, by means of sensory processes and under the influence of **set** and of prior experiences. ➤In some usages the awareness of intraorganic objects or processes is excluded. 3. (*structural psychol.*) a fusion of **mental contents** that has sensory data as its core. 4. a **sensation,** together with a context of other experiences that give it meaning. 5. the process of discriminating the qualitative or quantitative differences between objects or processes, extraorganic or intraorganic. 6. (*beh.*) a hypothetical internal event controlled primarily by stimulation of sense **receptors** but influenced also by habit and **drive state.** ➤Perception is inferred from the nature of the physical stimulus and from the behavior the stimulus apparently elicits. It is taken to be the direct or indirect controller of all behavior. 7. an immediate or **intuitive** awareness of the truth about something, analogous to sensory perception: *perception* of mathematical truth, moral *perception.*

➤While **perception** is probably employed more often by more psychologists than any other term, a few have doubted that it refers to a class of events having scientific unity or coherence. ¶—*adj.* **perceptual,** pertaining to the process or the data of perception; **perceptive,** pertaining to a particular process, or characterizing the perceiving as being highly effective or discriminating; **perceptional,** pertaining to

the study of perception.—See also **percept, perceive, transaction theory.**

perception/binocular: seeing with two eyes acting together and in such way that only one visual field is apprehended—i.e., so that the images on the two retinas are fused. ➤Binocular perception is the primary, but not the only, condition under which objects may be seen as having three-dimensionality, and as being located in space with reference to the viewer.

perception/enriched: the perception of signs, signals, symbols, or ambiguous stimuli in which what is perceived goes far beyond what is presented to the senses and is greatly influenced by the needs and values of the perceiver.—*Cp.* autism, **perception/impoverished, perception/literal.**

perception/extrasensory: see **extrasensory perception.**

perception/impoverished: perception under experimental conditions in which the environment is greatly simplified. ➤E.g., in measuring the audibility of a tone, a single pure tone is presented in a soundproof room, with the usual attendant noises and most of the sights eliminated. Such impoverished perception helps in the study of more complex forms, but great care must be taken in drawing conclusions from one to the other.

perception/intersensory: see **intersensory perception.**

perception/literal: the true-to-fact recognition of the color, size, shape, or distance of objects in their normal surroundings without the artificial restrictions imposed in impoverished *perception or the bias introduced by the subject in enriched *perception.

perception/obstacle = **facial vision.**

perception/physiognomic: see **physiognomic (2).**

perception set = **set/perceptual.**

perception/social: 1. the perceiving of social objects, whether persons or social groups. 2. the perceiving of those behaviors of another person that reveal his attitudes, feelings, or intentions. ➤Very often the behaviors thus perceived are **minimal cues** to which only slight direct attention is given.

perception/span of = **span of *attention.**

perception time: 1. (*obsoles.*) the time required for the brain processes involved in perception. ➤It was formerly thought possible to compute this by subtracting the times needed for other parts of the perceptual process from the total **reaction time.** 2. the sum of the durations of the **fixation pauses** in reading.—*Distg. fr.* **time perception.**

perceptive: *adj.* capable of perceiving; esp. capable of sensitive and discriminating perceiving in social situations.—See also **perception.**

perceptual: see **perception** (at end).

perceptual anchoring: see **anchoring/perceptual.**

perceptual-conceptual repertory: the stable recognized patterns of perceptions into which sensory complexes are organized. ➤Species differ radically in their capacity to organize sensory complexes into such patterns. The confirmed city dweller does not see the browning wheat field as ready for harvest; the country dweller may find the directions in the subway confusing rather than patterned.

perceptual defense: see **defense/perceptual.**

perceptual field: all those aspects of the external world to which at a given time an animal makes a discriminating response. ➤The perceptual field may include distorted or illusory elements: it consists of what the animal perceives, not what is there. The term does not imply **field theory.**

perceptual illusion: see **illusion.**

perceptualization: *n.* the process of combining or organizing sensory elements into a meaningful whole; or the emergence of a new meaning for a **percept.**

perceptual-motor learning: see **learning/perceptual-motor.**

perceptual restructuring: a change in the pattern of a **percept:** e.g., the process whereby what seemed a crouching animal is reperceived as a low bush.

perceptual schema: the **cognitive schema** that helps to determine the organism's reaction to an external **stimulus situation.**

perceptual segregation: the separation of part of a **perceptual field** from effective relation to other parts, either by physical means or by attention to dissimilarities, boundary lines, etc. ➤E.g., two colors next to each other show color contrast, but a sharp boundary line segregates them from each other so that the mutual influence is reduced or eliminated.

perceptual speed: see **abilities/primary mental.**

perceptual transformation: the change induced in the **percept** of an object or situation by a change in **context:** e.g., the change in the percept of an object when a new use is suggested.

perceptual unity: the fact that an object is perceived as a unified whole and not as a combination of details or of abstract qualities; or that several related objects are perceived as a whole, not as separate things. ➤There is normally a strong **set** toward such unity but it may be increased or diminished.

perch: *n.* (*reading*) a brief resting point for the eye; any of the points at which the

eye stops in its movement across a line of reading material. ➤The eye moves along the line in a series of short, jerky movements interrupted by brief rests. Little or nothing is seen while the eye is in motion. —*Syn.* **fixation pause,** EYE PAUSE.—*Cp.* **saccadic movement.**

percipient: *n.* 1. the person who perceives. 2. (*parapsychol.*) the receiver in telepathic communication.

perfectionism: *n.* the practice of demanding of oneself or others a higher quality of performance than is required by the situation.

performance: *n.* what a person does when faced with a task (whether self- or other-imposed); a personal activity considered as producing a result; more abstractly, a class or set of responses that alter the environment in a way that is defined by the class, the class itself being discovered and specified only by observing responses in two or more situations. ➤Examples are approach, avoidance, escape, going to class, answering a test item (but see **test/performance** for a specialized meaning). Single movements are not performance but the means thereto. In some learning theories, the making of a response to a task-demand (performance) is distinguished from the enduring modification of ability to respond to a task-demand (learning). An **operant** response is a response defined by its membership in a performance class of responses. **Achievement** is performance evaluated with respect to its adequacy.

performance curve: a graphic representation of **performance (1 or 2)** as a function of another variable, such as incentive, number of trials, time interval, etc.—See **learning curve,** a more usual but less accurate term for this curve.

performance test: see **test/performance.**

pericardial: *adj.* located in the region around the heart.—*n.* **pericardium.**

perimacular vision: see **vision/perimacular.**

perimeter: *n.* (*vision*) an instrument for mapping what can be seen when different parts of the **retina** are stimulated—i.e., for mapping the sensitivity of the retinal field. ➤The stimuli are presented on a semicircular arm which rotates about its middle radius, the eye being fixed on the center of rotation. The resulting map is projected onto a spherical surface.—*Cp.* **campimeter.**

perimetry: *n.* the operating of a **perimeter,** or the body of facts obtained from its use.

period: *n.* 1. (*phys.*) the interval of time for one complete phase or cycle of a regularly recurring event; the time required to return to the original state. 2. (*physiol., pop.*) the days of the **menstrual** flow; the MENSTRUAL PERIOD.

periodic: *adj.* regularly recurring; of that which regularly returns to an original state after a given time.—*n.* **periodicity,** the quality of being periodic.

peripheral (pə·rif′ər·əl): *adj.* **1.** pertaining to an external boundary or surface, esp. to the boundary of a bodily organ or of the whole body. **2.** (*neurol.*) pertaining to those nerves or parts of nerves that are farthest from the brain and spinal cord. ➤The usage is not very precise: it may be restricted to nerves that reach the tissues of the body near or at the surface; or it may be extended to include nerves terminating or originating in an internal organ (such as the liver). **3.** (*psychol.*) of any process that is directly related to the external world—sensory, muscular, and even glandular processes; anything that is not *central,* i.e., not directly a function of the **higher brain centers** or of the **personality.** ➤As in meaning (2), it is arbitrary whether processes in the internal organs are to be included; in this meaning they usually are. Hence, *visceral *drives or emotions are often said to be peripheral. But a motivation (or an emotion, for some authorities) as a function of personality would be considered central. **Peripheralists,** in order to make their point of view workable, generally include as many processes as they can under the concept **peripheral; centralists** for parallel reasons reverse the process.—*Distg. fr.* PERIPHERAD, toward the periphery.— *n.* **periphery.**

peripheral cell: (*K. Lewin*) a differentiated portion of the inner-personal region of the person, lying between the innermost or central cells and the perceptual-motor region. ➤Most of the peripheral cells are said to be needs or similar contemporary facts, not **dispositions.**

peripheralism: a point of view that emphasizes, for psychological explanation, the events that take place at the periphery or boundaries of the body rather than events in the central nervous system. ➤The difference is in emphasis and concerns chiefly the nature of explanatory variables.—*Syn.* PERIPHERALIST PSYCHOLOGY.—See **centralist psychology; psychology/divisions and schools of, V.**

peripheral nerve: 1. a nerve, whether **afferent** or **efferent,** whose major distribution is to a peripheral region.—See **peripheral** (2). **2.** a nerve from the **cerebrospinal system** to the periphery. ➤This usage reflects an obsolete conception of the **autonomic system,** which today is regarded as also peripheral.

peripheral nervous system: see **nervous system.**

peripheral regions: 1. those parts of the body close to the surface. **2.** those regions that lie farthest from the center of the per-

sonality structure. ➤The specific properties of a peripheral region have not been described in terms gaining common consent. For some authors the expression is metaphorical. Others define the peripheral regions in terms of certain factual differences, such as that the **behavioral *patterns** of these regions are more readily altered.

peripheral vision: see **vision/peripheral.**

periphery of the retina: the area of the **retina** farthest from the center of vision. ➤It is not precisely delimited. In general it refers to the area devoid of cones wherein only achromatic distinctions may be made. —See **color zones.**

peristalsis (per″i·stal′səs): *n.* the wormlike movement by which the contents of the **alimentary canal** are propelled.—*adj.* **peristaltic.**

peritoneum (per″i·tō·nē′əm): *n.* the membrane lining the inner wall of the abdomen and some of the organs therein.—*adj.* **peritoneal** (-nē′əl).

permeable: *adj.* **1.** of that which can be penetrated by something without being ruptured: a membrane *permeable* to alcohol. **2.** of a **boundary** that can be pierced or pushed through. **3.** (*topol.*) of the degree to which the structures or activities of a **region** of the **life space** can be reached by influences or forces from outside the region. ➤Modification depends upon the stability or rigidity of the structures and their accessibility to influence. The forces that penetrate a region despite resistance at the boundary are conceived of as **field forces** within the life space of the particular organism. **4.** (*G. A. Kelly*) characterizing a **construct** that admits new **elements** (2) to its field of ordinary application.—*n.* **permeability.**—*v.* **permeate.**

permissiveness: *n.* the attitude that grants freedom of choice and expression to another person out of respect for his personality. ➤The term has been used with a fairly wide connotation for the opposite of regimentation, **authoritarianism, dominance,** or **punitiveness.** The **permissive** attitude differs sharply from indulgence (though the overt behavior may show much similarity) and from neglect. Approval of the permitted actions or expressions is not implied. *Cp.* **acceptance,** which perhaps denotes the same underlying attitude with a different emphasis.

permutation: *n.* (*math.*) any arrangement or ordering of a number of items. ➤Items *abc* have six threefold permutations: *abc, acb, bac, bca, cab, cba.*—*Cp.* **combination.** —*v.* **permute, permutate.**

pernicious trend: marked behavior **regression.**

persecution/delusion of: see **delusion of persecution.**

perseverance (pėr″sə·vir′əns): *n.* a tendency to continue with an activity despite difficulties or opposition.—See **perseveration (2)**, which is more general.

perseveration (pər·sev″ər·ā′shən): *n.* **1.** tendency of organismic activity to recur without apparent **associative** stimulus.— *Cp.* **reminiscence. 2.** the tendency to continue in any activity, once it is begun, until it is finished; or, relative difficulty in shifting from one task to another, or in changing methods to suit a change in conditions.—*Cp.* **rigidity, stereotypy. 3.** = (*speech pathol.*) **cataphasia.**—*v.* **perseverate.**

perseveration theory of learning = **consolidation theory.**

persistence: *n.* **1.** continuance of an effect after its cause has ceased to operate. **2.** maintaining a course of action despite obstacles or opposition. ➤**Persistence** is the actual continuance, **perseverance** the psychological tendency to continue. **3.** continuance in time.

persistence/academic: the continuance of enrollees on the roll of a school or college. It is measured by the ratio of the number of entering pupils to the number of those continuing over a stated period.—*Ant.* **attrition.**

persistence of vision: see **vision/persistence of.**

persistent resignation: see **resignation/neurotic.**

person: *n.* a single living being, esp. (but not necessarily) a human being; a creature who performs both physiological and psychological functions; (*W. Stern*) "a living whole, individual, unique, striving toward goals, self-contained and yet open to the world around him, capable of having experience."

➤The phenomena of psychology always have reference to someone who **acts** or **behaves** or who has a **mental content.** Better than any other, the term **person** (although not extensively so used) seems to the editor to reflect the way in which the majority of psychologists today conceive of this "center of reference," this performer of biopsychological functions. PSYCHO-BIOLOGICAL (or PSYCHOPHYSIOLOGICAL) ORGANISM has practically identical meaning.

Organism, by far the commonest term today, carries for most readers a strongly metaphysical implication—that psychological activities are caused by a material body. If this connotation is not intended— and it is generally agreed that metaphysics should be excluded from science—organism needs to be more carefully defined or more sparingly employed.

On the other hand, to ascribe physiological activities to a body or **soma,** and psychological activities to a **self, psyche,** or **personality,** is to suggest a greater separateness of the two classes of phe-

nomena than is generally believed to be true. While self or psyche do not actually imply a metaphysical **dualism,** they so strongly suggest it that their employment in scientific psychology has been restricted.

Without committing the user to any of the competing metaphysical views about the body-mind relation, **person** refers both physiological and psychological activities to the same performer. This seems a great terminological advantage. All the terms discussed in this article refer to a complex organization or whole that interacts with an environment.

The following refer to the psychological performer in special contexts or with special implications. Each is defined in its own place: **actor, agent, animal, consciousness, ego, experiencer, individual, knower, mind, nature, nervous system, organism, personality, proprium, psyche, psychobiological organism, reactor, self, subject.**

persona (pər·sō′nə): *n.* (*L., theatrical mask*) the role which a person plays; the mask he puts on not only for others but for himself. It represents his conscious intentions and the requirements of the real situation, not the more deeply rooted components of personality. ➤Jung calls the man who tends to identify himself with the mask the PERSONAL MAN, in contrast to the INDIVIDUAL MAN who tends to identify with his own true personality elements.

personal: *adj.* **1.** pertaining to, or having the quality of, a **person. 2.** pertaining to only one person. **3.** characterizing one's private affairs; not public: that question is too *personal.* **4.** pertaining to the **persona. 5.** carried on directly between individuals. ➤The PERSONAL APPROACH (e.g., in social work or counseling) concerns person-to-person relations, in contrast to relations to groups or to the physical environment. **Impersonal** (which see) is not a direct opposite.

personal ascendancy: see **ascendance.**

personal audit: a questionary or inquiry form that lists possible personal assets and liabilities and asks an individual which are to be attributed or not attributed to himself.

personal constant/(Heinis) = **Heinis constant.**

personal data sheet: a questionary listing any sort of facts concerning the individual. ➤It may cover the more or less objective data of age, sex, occupation, residence, etc.; or it may have questions concerning the person's usual behaviors in a variety of social situations. It usually does not include ratings of **traits,** since these are **not** data but inferences from data.

personal document: any self-revealing record that intentionally or unintentionally yields information about the subject's personality or psychic life.

personal documents method: (*G. Allport*) a method of studying the individual through the use of diaries, systematic self-study guides and inventories, personal correspondence, and thematic writing.

personal equation: 1. any difference in performance due to difference between the individuals.—*Syn.* **individual** *difference. 2. difference between individuals in simple **reaction time.** ➤The term was originated by astronomers for the differences in recording stellar transits by different observers. 3. (*pop., psychiat.*) personal peculiarities that influence some outcome and must be allowed for if the true **dynamics** of the situation are to be discovered.

personal identity: 1. the fact that an individual remains himself, different and distinct from others, despite all changes in his activities and **psychobiological** structure. 2. the subjective sense of continuous personal existence. ➤Note that personal identity in sense (2) may be lost despite the persistence of (1).

personal idiom: the socially visible behavior characteristics that distinguish one person from another, esp. those qualities not otherwise of great adaptive value: manners, mannerisms, postures, tricks and styles of speech, etc.

personalism: *n.* 1. = PERSONALISTIC PSYCHOLOGY, i.e., psychology considered as the study of the reactions or activities of a **person.**—*See* **psychology/divisions and schools of,** III. 2. the philosophic doctrine which holds that the person or **personality** is the fundamental fact of existence. 3. the ethical doctrine which makes the value of persons the source of all other values. ➤This doctrine may or may not conceive of Deity as personal.

personalistic psychology: 1. = **personalism** (1). 2. a point of view that emphasizes the fact that every psychological activity or function is the act of a **person** or is embedded in a personal life, and deprecates treating these functions in abstraction from the person. ➤To study **skill** rather than *the skillful John Brown* is regarded as legitimate only if the abstraction involved is clearly recognized and ultimately transcended.—*Syn.* PERSONALISTICS.—*Distg.*

personalistic psychology, which is all of psychology studied from a certain point of view, *fr.* the *psychology of personality,* which usually refers to a certain part of psychology (see **personality 3, 4, 5, 6**).

personalistics = **personalistic psychology** (2).

personality: *n.* ➤G. Allport lists 50 meanings of personality and of its parent terms **persona** and **person,** and no doubt he missed a few. Several root ideas appear in various combinations in modern usage.

In ancient Rome the **persona** was a theatrical mask, whence came the notion of *appearance,* of the individual as socially perceived. (See 3 and esp. 5 below; but the idea infects other meanings, including those embodied in PERSONALITY TESTING and PERSONALITY ADJUSTMENT.) A second sense was that of **role,** the part played in the drama. (*Cp. dramatis personae,* the persons of the play.) A third meaning was that of *the player* himself. (See 2 below.) Thus, the **personality** came to mean the outward appearance (even the false appearance), and also the true inner being or self. Either or both ideas are likely to be found in a given author.

The meaning of **personality** is influenced also by the way it is studied. It may be studied as it is, distinct from other entities. In that case, it is conceived as having certain properties. Or personality may be studied in terms of how individuals differ. It is then conceived as a collection of traits. These two approaches are complementary, each actually implying the other, but emphasis on one or the other affects the connotations of the term.

These root ideas contribute in varying ways to the following definitions: 1. the quality or state of being a **person,** rather than a thing or an abstraction. 2. a person studied psychologically or as a unique whole; the **self,** the **psyche,** the psychological individual; the psychological aspect of the ***psychophysiological** ***organism;** "the dynamic organization within the individual of those psychophysical systems that determine his unique adjustment to his environment." (*G. Allport*)—See **person** for discussion. 3. the distinguishing qualities of an individual taken as a unitary being, esp. those that distinguish the individual in social relations. ➤This is the popular use, but it affects scientific usages. Valuation is often implied, as in the expression: a strong *personality.* 4. the pattern of **motivation** and of temperamental or emotional **traits** of the individual (in contrast to cognitive traits and ability). ➤While very common, the limitation thus imposed is regarded by most psychologists as somewhat arbitrary. But it is the meaning incorporated in the terms **personality disorder** and **personality tests.** 5. those characteristics of the individual that give rise to his reputation, or that are perceived by others; a man's social-stimulus value. ➤Note that this view says that personality is *only* what affects others, what they perceive. This usage, once quite common, is now obsolescent. 6. the social aspects of individual human nature; those aspects of one's nature that have developed in social interaction and have other persons or social values as their object. This is a common sociological usage.

See **person,** where related meanings are discussed.

personality/alternating = dual personality (see **personality/multiple**).

personality/amputation of: the gradual reduction of spontaneity and of richness of personal behavior during the processes of **socialization** and education.

personality/anal: see **anal character.**

personality/authoritarian: see **authoritarian personality.**

personality/common: (*H. A. Murray*) the most commonly repeated patterns of **regnancies,** or behavior units, during any period of life.

personality/compulsive: see **compulsive personality.**

personality continuity: see **continuity/ personality.**

personality disorder: 1. a disorder of behavior that is manifested chiefly in **motivation** and by social **maladjustment,** rather than primarily in emotional or intellectual disturbances. ➤The term is extraordinarily inclusive, covering many aspects of neurotic and psychotic behavior as well as lesser difficulties (even the disorders of disapproved ideology, if they are not primarily due to faulty intelligence). Since this meaning is in any case vague, it should be abandoned in favor of **(2).** **2.** (*Stan. Psychiat.*) a classification that excludes neuroses and psychoses: it refers to pathological development in personality structure, with little or no **anxiety** or sense of distress. ➤It includes **inadequate, schizoid, paranoid,** and **cyclothymic personalities, emotionally unstable personalities, passive-aggressive personality, compulsive personality,** and the **sociopathic personality disturbances.** The whole personal history rather than any particular symptom is the test for these disorders.

personality/dual: see **personality/multiple.**

personality dynamics: see **dynamics.**

personality/expanded: see **expanded personality.**

personality formation: a **structure** or **mechanism** that causes a person to display a persistent behavior tendency, esp. one that is individually characteristic, or that tends to color a number of other behavior tendencies.—*Syn.* CHARACTER FORMATION, **trait,** PERSONALITY STRUCTURE.

personality function: an activity or function related to personality. ➤The term's chief usefulness is to be an erudite ornament. One may, of course, believe in a function

of the whole personality, or that personality manifests several functions; but neither of these possible meanings of personality function seems to be usual. In the expression, "one of two factors in *personality function* that determine behavior," the omission of "in *personality function*" would leave the meaning entirely unaltered.

personality hierarchy: see **hierarchy/ personality.**

personality/inadequate: see **inadequate personality.**

personality integration: the organization and unification of a person's motives and dynamic tendencies, resulting in harmonious coaction of these tendencies and the minimizing of inner conflict; or the process whereby the organization is attained.— *Syn.* PERSONALITY ORGANIZATION, which lays more stress upon the relationship between parts, less upon a final unification.

personality/intraconscious: a **coconscious** personality that knows the thoughts and feelings of the other personality.

personality inventory: a check list, usually to be filled out by a person about himself, consisting (*a*) of many statements about personal characteristics which the subject checks as applying or not to the ratee, or (*b*) of questions to be answered *Yes, No,* or *Doubtful.* ➤Usually, **norms** based upon large representative populations, or upon samples with specific personality characteristics, are provided to assist interpretation of individual scores.

personality/lifetime: (*H. A. Murray*) the temporal configuration formed by the successive patterns of **regnancies** from birth to death.

personality/momentary: (*H. A. Murray*) the pattern of **regnancies** during one event in a person's life.

personality/multiple: a condition in which the normal organization of mental life is disintegrated or split up into distinct parts or subpersonalities, each with a fairly complicated organization of its own comparable with that of a normal individual or personality. ➤Even in extreme cases of multiple personality, however, we do not have completely independent personalities united only by a common physique. There seems always to be an underlying personal unity, despite much disintegration. DUAL PERSONALITY is a special case of multiple personality.—See also **coconsciousness, dissociation.**

personality organization = **personality integration.**

personality pattern disturbance: (*Stan. Psychiat.*) a broad classification for relatively enduring maladjustive or psychopathological patterns of behavior or personality. Under conditions of stress, persons suffering from such disorder are likely to graduate into psychosis. It includes **inadequate personality, schizoid personality, cyclothymic personality,** and **paranoid personality.**

personality/primary and **/secondary:** respectively, the original (or fundamental) phase, and the organized but split-off (or dissociated) phase, of a **multiple *personality.**—See also **dissociation.**

personality problem: a persisting personal difficulty that restricts or interferes with personality adjustment. ➤The term is vague and inclusive: shyness, excessive talkativeness, jealousy, rudeness are typical personality problems. Lack of money is not a personality problem, but feeling inferior because of it is.—*Distg. fr.* **problem personality.**

personality reorganization: a fundamental change in the enduring tendencies to action, esp. in the **value system.**

personality sphere: 1. a means of representing personality traits as lying on the surface of a sphere with connections both on the surface and through the interior. **2.** (*R. B. Cattell*) the whole area of personal behavior, as described by a somewhat condensed list of descriptive terms from an unabridged dictionary. ➤The assumption is that every important aspect of behavior has been symbolized in language, though not without overlapping.

personality structure/basic: the unity that underlies individual ways of behaving, giving consistency to otherwise contradictory-seeming traits or behaviors, and giving meaning to otherwise inexplicable mannerisms and eccentricities.

personality syndrome: the acquired pattern of personality characteristics which, though unique in its individual expression, bears resemblance to the personality structures of others who have shared similar problems and made similar adaptations to those problems.

personality test: a loosely used expression for any instrument facilitating the evaluation of personality. Many are properly **ratings** rather than **tests.**

personality trait: an enduring disposition or quality of a person that accounts for his relative consistency in emotional, temperamental, and social behavior; a **trait** that accounts for differences in **personality** (4). ➤**Abilities** are arbitrarily but commonly excluded.

personality trait disturbance: (*Stan. Psychiat.*) a broad category for persons unable to maintain emotional equilibrium and independence because of disturbed emotional development. It includes the **emotionally unstable,** the **passive-aggressive personality,** the **compulsive personality.**

personality type: a classification of an individual according to the pattern of his behavior tendencies. ➤There are many divergent systems of classification. See **type, constitutional type.**

personal-social behavior: all individual actions that are determined by other persons or by socially modified objects. ➤It includes reactions to culture patterns, customs and mores, social institutions, the adjustments to domestic life and social groups, and to community requirements.—See **social behavior.**

personal-social motive = social motive.

personate: *adj.* belonging to the person; of behavior that is determined by the whole person, not by some segment thereof.—*Contr. w.* **propriate,** of behavior regarded as *basic* to personality.

personation = impersonation.

person/composite: see **composite figure.**

personification: *n.* **1.** attributing personal qualities to an abstraction or to a representation of a person. **2.** a variety of **projection** wherein a person attributes favorable or unfavorable qualities to another person as a result of frustration of his own wishes.—*v.* **personify.**

personnel: *n.* **1.** the body of persons in any group, taken collectively; the persons who compose a given group, esp., the employees of an industry. **2.** the human factor in an industry, in contrast with the material factor.—*adj.* **personnel.**

personnel psychology: that subdivision of **applied psychology** which treats of the psychological qualities of the individual in relation to his tasks in industry, the armed forces, or any other institution. It deals with employment procedures, selection, placement, promotion, supervision, morale problems, and other aspects of the human problem in work, or with the analogous problems of pupil and student personnel. In schools and colleges it usually, and in industry it sometimes, includes **counseling** and vocational **guidance.**

personology: *n.* **1.** the study of **personality** as a distinct branch of psychology. **2.** the study of all psychological events in terms of the variables of personality, or of those events as related to a **person.**—See **psychology/divisions and schools of, V.**

perspective: *n.* **1.** the delineation of objects on a plane surface in such a way as to give the same impression of relative position, size, etc., as if the objects represented were in three dimensions. **2.** the interrelationships or proportions of the parts of a whole, as seen or thought about from a particular vantage point; esp., the capacity to view a situation in its true proportions and interrelationships. TIME (or TEMPORAL) PERSPECTIVE is the improved perspective that comes when events are viewed from a certain distance in time.

perspective/aerial: the diminished distinctness, resulting from atmospheric conditions, with which a more distant object is seen. It acts as a **cue** to perception of distance.

perspective/alternating or **/reversible**: a drawing that suggests the third dimension but is capable of alternative interpretation, one part of the figure seeming now closer, now farther from the viewer than the other parts; a form of **reversible *figure**. ➤ILLUSION OF REVERSIBLE PERSPECTIVE is sometimes spoken of, but there is no illusion unless all graphic representation be called illusion.

perspective/angular: see **angular perspective**.

perspective/linear: the relative sizes of the visual images of objects at different distances from the eye; or the principles according to which the relative size of the visual image is determined by distance.

perspective size: the size of the image of an object at a given distance from a viewing point as determined by the geometry of **perspective**. ➤It differs slightly from the retinal image due to the properties of the eye as an optical system, and from the apparent size of the object due to the phenomena of **size constancy** or other conditions affecting perception.—*Contr. w.* **object size**.

persuasion: *n.* the process of obtaining another's adoption of a course of action, or his assent to a proposition, by an appeal to both feeling and intellect.—*v.* **persuade**.

perturbation: *n.* (*info. theory*) a disturbance superimposed on, or added to, the information needed by the recipient of a message. The greater the perturbation, the less is the probability that the course of action chosen will be the desired one.—*Prefd.* to **noise** (3).

perversion: *n.* a socially condemned departure from ordinary conduct, esp. in the sexual sphere. ➤What is condemned in one society is not condemned in another, and acts permitted under certain circumstances are condemned in others. Most commonly referred to as perversions are **exhibitionism, fetishism, homosexuality** (sometimes separately classified as **inversion**), and **masturbation**; but there are many others. Perversion, however, does not include **incest**, rape, and unchastity or normal sex relations with forbidden persons. Since the term has accumulated vast emotional overtones, it is suggested that **sexual anomaly** or ANOMALOUS SEXUAL BEHAVIOR be substituted.

perversion/infantile polymorphous: (*psychoan.*) the theory that the sex instinct in the child has no predetermined outlet but

leads to various behaviors that would be called **perversions** if present in an adult.

perverted: *adj.* turned away from, or against, the right course of action; misdirected or misapplied.—*n.* **perversion**, which see.

petit mal (pə·tē″ mal′): see **epilepsy**.

p.f. = **phenomenal *field**.

p **factor**: a tendency to persevere in an activity once it is started; a factor of behavioral inertia or **perseveration**.

P-F Study = **Picture-Frustration Study/ Rosenzweig**.

PGR = psychogalvanic response (see **electrodermal response**).

*p***H**: *abbr.* for potential of hydrogen; a symbol for the hydrogen ion concentration, or acidity-alkalinity balance, in a liquid.

$$pH = \log_{10} \frac{1}{[H\cdot]}$$ where $[H\cdot]$ is the effective H-ion concentration in normality. Pure water is pH 7; any higher value than 7 is alkaline, any lesser is acid.

phacoscope: *n.* an instrument for observing the size changes that take place in the **Purkinje-Sanson images** during **accommodation**—i.e., those reflected from the front and back surfaces of the lens of the eye.—*Var.* **phakoscope**.

-phagia, -phagy: combining form meaning *eating*.

phagocyte: *n.* (literally, *a cell eater*) a white blood cell that attacks foreign microorganisms.

-phagy = **-phagia**.

phallic (fal′ik): *adj.* **1.** pertaining to the **phallus**. **2.** (*psychoan.*) pertaining to the **penis**.

phallicism (fal′ə·siz·əm) = **phallic worship**.

phallic love: (*psychoan.*) narcissistic love of the penis (for girls, of the penis equivalent), normal in the **phallic stage**. ➤It is manifested in pride in the penis, great curiosity about it in oneself and others, and particularly in masturbation. (But masturbation at a later stage of development may have other motivation.)

phallic primacy: see **primacy/phallic**.

phallic stage: (*psychoan.*) the period in the development of **infantile *sexuality** marked by interest and feeling attached to the penis (among girls, to whatever is the symbolic equivalent for the penis). ➤The period is said normally to follow the **oral** and **anal stages** and to occur about age 3 to 7.—See **phallic love, phallic *primacy**.—*Syn.* PHALLIC PHASE (less accurate).

phallic symbol: (*psychoan.*) any pointed or upright object that may represent the **phallus**: e.g., a dagger, a spire, a closed umbrella, a pen, a cigarette, a walking stick, etc.

phallic worship: religious reverence for the

creative forces of nature as symbolized by the **phallus**.—*Syn.* **phallicism, phallism.** —*Cp.* **kteis.**

phallism (fal'iz·əm) = **phallic worship.**

phallus (fal'əs): *n.* **1.** a representation of the penis, or of penis and testes, especially for use in decoration and as a symbol in cult-worship. ➤In the Dionysian ceremonies in ancient Greece, as well as in certain (East) Indian cults and in many religions of nonliterate peoples, the sculptured representation of the penis (or penis and testes) was (is) the object of veneration as a symbol of fertility and of creative and death-defying forces.—*Cp.* **kteis. 2.** (*psychoan.*) the penis as the object of libido during the stage of **infantile *sexuality,** i.e., before genital primacy has developed. ➤Since it properly means a stylized representation, the use of **phallus** when the actual organ is meant is an unexpected delicacy of expression.—*adj.* **phallic.**

phantasm: see **fantasm.**

phantasy: see **fantasy.**

phantom: *n.* **1.** a semblance of something; a faint image of an object; a ghostlike appearance. **2.** (*psychoan.*) anything in the unconscious representing a person.—*Var.* **fantom.**

phantom extremity or **limb:** the persistent or recurrent feeling, experienced by many amputees, of sensations as if from the missing member.

phantom sound: an indefinitely localized single sound heard when two qualitatively similar sounds with slight differences in intensity or **phase** are brought to the two ears separately.

pharmacopsychosis: *n.* a psychosis causally associated with taking a drug.

pharyngo-: combining form meaning *pharynx:* e.g., *pharyngology.*

pharynx (far'ingks): *n.* that part of the throat that leads from mouth and nose to the **larynx** and **esophagus.**—*adj.* **pharyngeal** (fə·rin'jē·əl; far″in·jē'əl).

phase: 1. a recurrent state in something that exhibits a series of changes: e.g., the several phases of the moon, the rhythmic alternations of pressure and release in air waves (any moment of which is a phase that is later repeated). ➤Two **periodic** waves (sound, light, electric) are IN PHASE when their maximum magnitudes occur together. They are in OPPOSITE PHASE when the peak of one coincides with the trough of the other. If one wave is attaining its maximum before the other, it is the PHASE LEADER. **2.** (*chem.*) the state of a substance as being solid, liquid, or gaseous. **3.** a passing state of affairs in a person's life: the puppy-love *phase.* ➤**Stage** is preferred for (3), unless it be implied that the state of affairs is recurrent (which is often not the case).—*adj.* **phasic** (fāz'ik).

For combination terms with **phase,** see also **stage,** or the modifying word.

phase/anal: see **anal stage.**

phase angle: the part of a **sinusoidal** wave cycle at which a point on the wave is to be found at a particular instant. ➤The phase angle is measured in degrees, or the 360th part of the cycle.

phase difference: (*aud.*) any difference in the phase relations of two sound waves, esp., the difference in phase of the sound wave as received by the two ears. ➤The slight difference in audible intensity due to the phase difference helps in sound localization.

phase/oral-incorporative: see **oral-incorporative.**

phase rule: (*phys.*) $P + F = C + 2$, where P is the number of phases, C the number of components, and F the **degrees of freedom.** ➤The rule, discovered by Gibbs for heterogeneous systems with respect to such intensive variables as pressure and temperature when the system is in equilibrium, is believed by some to apply to behavior.

phase sequence theory: (*D. O. Hebb*) a theory that conceives of the neural correlates of behavior and/or conscious process as consisting of a number of **cell assemblies** joined serially in PHASE SEQUENCES.

phase space: a system of **coordinates** representing the several dimensions of an object or event.

-phasia: combining form meaning *speech disorder due to cortical lesion*: e.g., **aphasia, dysphasia.**

phatic: *adj.* pertaining to communication of a friendly feeling by word, gesture, or facial expression, regardless of the intellectual content of the words used.

-phemia: combining form referring to speech disorder of psychogenic origin: e.g., BRADYPHEMIA, slow speech from psychological causes.

phenobarbital: *n.* a sedative or **hypnotic** drug.

phenomenal: *adj.* **1.** (*pop.*) unusual; extraordinary. **2.** pertaining to, or having the character of, a **phenomenon** or phenomena. ➤The word shares the ambiguity of the noun **phenomenon.**

phenomenal field: see **field/phenomenal.**

phenomenalism: *n.* **1.** a philosophical doctrine teaching that human knowledge is limited to appearances, never reaching to the true nature of reality. **2.** = **phenomenology.**

phenomenalistic introspection: a simple report of one's **phenomenal *field,** including what one is doing. ➤While the field may be divided into functional parts for convenience of report, the report is not systematically analytical. A person may report he sees a spirited horse; he attempts to analyze neither the particular cues that mean "spirited," nor indeed those that mean "horse."

phenomenal motion: perceived motion; motion as experienced, in contrast to motion as known to physical science. ➤*Perceived motion* (or *perceived movement,* when one's own bodily movement is in question) is less ambiguous.—See **phenomenal pattern, motion/apparent.**

phenomenal pattern: that which is perceived, in contrast to the physical or objective stimulus. ➤While the phenomenal pattern and the stimulus may be distinguished in all cases, the distinction becomes necessary when changes in the phenomenal pattern occur without change in the stimulus pattern (as in the case of ambiguous figures).

phenomenal regression: the principle that what one perceives is intermediate between what would be expected from the nature of the physical stimulus and what would be expected from the **object** *constancy, and that the percept tends with more careful observation to shift toward the former. ➤An automobile seen at some distance is perceived as larger than would be inferred from the geometrical-perspective relations, and smaller than if it were perceived as an object of constant size.

phenomenal report: a verbal statement of what one experiences on receiving an experimental stimulus.—*Contr. w.* **introspection.**—*Syn.* **Kundgabe.**

phenomenal self: see **self/phenomenal.**

phenomenistic causality: a method of reaching a conclusion about events, commonly used by young children, in which appearance is given the status of cause: e.g., "the sun rises because it is so bright."

phenomenology: *n.* a theoretical point of view that advocates the study of **phenomena (4)** or direct experience taken naïvely or at face value; the view that behavior is determined by the phenomena of experience rather than by external, objective, physically described reality.

➤Data are necessarily the product of the methods used in observing. For **introspection** (or perhaps one should say for **introspectionism**), a table is an arrangement of lights and colors (or of tactual qualities, even of smells); for physical science (or for **physicalism**), it is a mass occupying space. **Phenomenology,** in contrast with both, would take the table as just what the subject perceives it to be, i.e., as a table (or, it might be, as a place to park one's feet). Cows, busses, a threatening voice, a delightful aroma, a remembered event of long ago, are to be studied just as they are for the experiencer, not as modified by any observational rules.

Physicalism contends that all the data of experience can be translated into the language of physical science; phenomenalism, admitting the possibility, contends that the translation involves an abstraction from reality, a loss of part of what is real. Many contemporary psychologists, without espousing the doctrine, employ phenomenalistic descriptions extensively.—See **psychology/ divisions and schools of, III, VIII.**

phenomenon *n., pl.* **phenomena: 1.** literally, that which appears. **2.** mere appearance in contrast with reality, esp. with an inferred underlying reality. ➤This established philosophical usage contrasts sharply with the others. **3.** that which is open to observation, in contrast with what is known only by inference. **4.** an occurrence or happening itself, in contrast with its causes. **5.** a datum of experience, or a group of data; something of which we are aware and on which we can report; esp., unanalyzed experience.—See **phenomenology. 6.** a fact; that which is known in connection with a certain object or topic: the *phenomena* of chemical solutions. **7.** astounding or surprising fact.—*adj.* **phenomenal** (not phe*nom*inal). (Note also that **phenomena** is a plural, not a singular, noun.)

phenomotive (fē′nō·mō″tiv): *n.* (*W. Stern*) the motive that is apparent to introspection. ➤*Ant.* GENOMOTIVE, the underlying need that actually brings about both the phenomotive and the action.

phenotype (fē′nō·tīp): *n.* (*genet., psychol.*) that which actually makes its appearance in a living being; a *manifested* structure, condition, or function. ➤Depending on context, any or all of three contrasts are implied by the term: (*a*) with the hereditary predisposition to develop the phenotype; (*b*) with the causative factors that bring the phenotype into being; (*c*) with the underlying but not observed structure that is inferred to account for an observed function (or phenotype). See discussion under **genotype.**—*adj.* **phenotypic(al).**

phenylketonuria = **phenylpyruvic amentia.**

phenylpyruvic amentia (fen″il·pī·rü′vik): a severe mental deficiency caused by the lack of the enzyme necessary for oxydizing phenylalanine, causing an accumulation of phenylpyruvic acid. The condition is usually considered hereditary.—*Syn.* PHENYL-PYRUVIC OLIGOPHRENIA.

ϕ^2 (fī) = **mean-square contingency.**

phi coefficient, ϕ **coefficient:** a measure of relationship when both variables are divided into two qualitatively discrete groups: e.g., fathers and sons, five-fingered and six-fingered.

phi-gamma function or $\phi(\gamma)$: the integral of a normal distribution of **psychophysical** judgments stated in terms of *h;* a **cumu-**

lative frequency **curve** or **ogive** stated in terms of h for which the formula is—

$$p = \int_{-\infty}^{\gamma} \frac{1}{\sqrt{\pi}} e^{-\gamma^2} d\gamma$$

➤The assumption that data obtained by the **constant stimulus method** will fit the phi-gamma function is the PHI-GAMMA HYPOTHESIS.

philander: *v.* to perform some of the courtship acts without serious intention, with or without deception of the other person.—*n.* **philanderer.**

-philia, -phily: combining form meaning *love, affinity for.*

phil(o)-: combining form meaning *loving:* *philosophy, philogyny.*

philosophical psychology = **rational psychology.**

philosophy: *n.* the effort to formulate a unified and consistent conception of the universe with the aim of understanding its ultimate nature. ➤Its two major branches are **metaphysics** and **epistemology. Logic,** although historically a branch of philosophy, is now more often grouped with mathematics. The derogatory overtones of the phrase *merely philosophical* in some psychological writing do not imply objection to philosophy as such but to philosophy improperly introduced into a scientific discipline.—See also **rational psychology.**

philosophy of psychology: see **psychology** (2).

-phily = **-philia.**

phi-phenomenon: 1. the perception of motion as such; an experience of something in motion. ➤This experience was described by M. Wertheimer as irreducible to any other attribute. It could stand either alone in the PURE PHI-PHENOMENON (no other attribute such as color, place in space, or size being present) or as an aspect of a perceptual **colligation** or complex. **2.** the appearance of motion generated by stationary stimuli, as when two lights flashed in brief succession are perceived as motion from one to the other. ➤*Syn.* APPARENT MOVEMENT, **apparent *motion** (*prefd.*), which see.

phlegmatic (fleg·mat'ik): *adj.* sluggish; apathetic; not easily stirred to emotion. ➤The phlegmatic was one of the four basic **temperaments** described in antiquity. It was supposed to result from predominance of phlegm or lymph over other bodily fluids.

-phob-: combining form meaning *fear* or *aversion:* e.g., GYNOPHOBIA, fear or dislike of women; **photophobe,** one who is oversensitive to bright light. ➤The usual implication of *morbid* fear or aversion is sometimes weakened so that only an unusual

or distinctive dislike is meant: e.g., **xenophobia,** aversion to strangers.

phobia: *n.* **fear;** nearly always, excessive fear of some particular type of object or situation; fear that is persistent and without sound grounds, or without grounds accepted as reasonable by the sufferer. ➤The term is compounded, usually without hyphen, with other words of Greek origin to designate the specific object of fear.— *Syn.* (*Stan. Psychiat.*) PHOBIC REACTIONS.— *adj.* **phobic.**—*pers. n.* **phobiac, phobist.**

➤**Phobia** has some convenience as meaning *morbid fear,* although (as **photophobia** shows) it does not uniformly have that meaning. But the editor fails to find a single case among over 180 listed terms where the compound with phobia is clearer, more convenient, more euphonious, or less ambiguous, than if the morbid fear had been characterized in English. Thus, OPEN-SPACE PHOBIA is in every respect superior to the familiar **agoraphobia** (the Greek would mean *fear of the marketplace,* which was anything but "open"), except that it does not evince the "erudition" of its user. **Acrophobia,** from its etymology, could mean fear of the extremities, of the crown of the head, of the peak of anything, of the crest of a wave, of the end of time, even of the end of the evening—so versatile is the Greek *akros.* Is not the simple English "fear of high places" better? The case is even clearer with less well-known compounds such as ASTRAPHOBIA (which means fear of lightning, not of stars), and HEMATOPHOBIA (fear of sight of blood, not fear of blood).—See **bogus erudition, neologism.**

phobiac (fō'bi·ak): *n.* a person having a **phobia.**

phobophobia: *n.* fear of fearing.

phon (fōn) *n., pl.* **phons:** a measure of the psychological intensity (loudness) of a tone. ➤It is equal to the number of **decibels** (a measure of physical pressure) of the 1000 c.p.s. tone that sounds equally loud. This will vary slightly for different persons.— *Distg. fr.* **phone.**

phonation: *n.* the production of speech sounds; vocal production, as distinguished from **articulation.**

phonautograph: *n.* an instrument for the graphic recording of sound waves.

phone: *n.* (*linguistics*) an elementary speech sound; a single speech sound represented by a single symbol in a phonetic system.—*Syn.* SOUND UNIT, PHONETIC UNIT.—*Distg. fr.* **phon.**

phoneidoscope (fō·nī'də·skōp): *n.* an instrument making possible visual observation of sound waves.

phonelescope (fō·nel'ə·skōp): *n.* a **phonoscope** for observation, measurement, and photographic recording, of sound waves.

phoneme (fō'nēm): *n.* **1.** (*linguistics*) a group of closely similar speech sounds commonly regarded in a given language as being the same sound and having a distinct function in determining meaning. ➤E.g., in Korean, the sounds *r* and *l* both occur but they are regarded as variants of the same sound—whether one or the other sound is used depends on the other sounds with which it occurs, not upon the meaning the sound helps to convey. In English, *r* and *l* have different roles in conveying meaning. Hence, in Korean these sounds are **allophones** of the same phoneme; in English they are distinct **phones** and do not constitute a single **phoneme**. But the various ways *r* is pronounced in English are one phoneme. There are said to be 35 phonemes in English.—*Distg. fr.* visual symbols such as letters: the phoneme is the *sound* heard. **2.** an auditory verbal **hallucination**; hallucinatory "voices."—*adj.* **phonemic** (fō·nē'mik; -nem'ik).

phonetic: *adj.* **1.** pertaining to **phonetics.** **2.** of a system of writing in which each symbol stands for one sound, and each sound has one symbol.

phonetic method: 1. a method of speech correction by showing the positions of tongue, lips, jaw, etc., to produce each sound. **2.** a method of teaching foreign languages that emphasizes phonetics. ➤*Distg. fr.* **phonic method,** which is sometimes mistakenly called **phonetic method.**

phonetics: *n.* the study of the production of vocal sounds, esp. in relation to language. It includes physiological, physical, and psychological data.

-phonia: combining form meaning *functional disorder of voice*: e.g., **dysphonia, aphonia.**

phonic: *adj.* of sounds; esp. of voice sounds.

phonic method: the teaching of reading by emphasizing from the start the sounds that are represented by the letters and letter combinations.—*Syn.* PHONICS.

phonism: *n.* the sound indirectly induced in auditory **synesthesia.**

phon(o)- (fō'nō-): combining form meaning *sound, voice.*

phonodeik (-dīk): *n.* an instrument for photographic recording and projection of sound waves in air. ➤It is more sensitive and accurate than the **phonautograph** or **phonelescope.**

phonogram: *n.* **1.** a symbol that represents a speech sound. **2.** a diagram showing the positions of the speech organs in producing various sounds.—*adj.* **phonogrammic, -gramic.**

phonopathy (fō·nop'ə·thi): *n.* any disease or disorder of the voice.

phonophobia: *n.* morbid dread of hearing one's own voice. (Unfortunately rare.)

phonoscope: *n.* a generic name for any device rendering sound waves visible.

phoria: *n.* the way the eyeballs are turned or oriented in sighting an object; esp., an anomalous turning so that the two eyes are not coordinated.—See **heterophoria.**

phorometry (fō·rom'ə·tri): *n.* measurement of the balance or imbalance of the muscles turning the eyeball.

phosphene: *n.* a bright form seen in the dark, produced by distortion of the eyeball either during the normal process of **accommodation** and **convergence** or by an external pressure.

phot (fot; fōt): *n.* a unit of **illuminance** equal to that produced at a surface all points of which are at a distance of 1 centimeter from a uniform point source of 1 candle.—*Syn.* CENTIMETER-CANDLE; **lumen** per square centimeter.

photerythrous (fō"tə·rith'rəs): *adj.* of heightened sensitivity to the red end of the **spectrum.**

photic: (fō'tik): *adj.* pertaining to light.

photism (fō'tiz·əm): *n.* **1.** hallucinatory impression of bright light. **2.** that form of **synesthesia** in which a visual impression invariably accompanies a sensation from another **modality:** e.g., colored hearing **(chromesthesia).**

photistic visualization: the production of vivid visual images in regular association with certain experiences. ➤The term is proposed as a substitute for **synesthesia,** which has been limited to the production of an image from another **modality.** The association of a color image with a seen number is photistic visualization; so also is the association of colors with music.

phot(o)-: combining form meaning *of or produced by light*; or *of a photograph* or *photography.*

photochromatic interval: the interval or range of stimulus intensity within which a chromatic stimulus can be perceived as light **(absolute *threshold** for light) but cannot yet be perceived as **hue** (threshold for hue).—*Syn.* COLORLESS INTERVAL.

photokinesis: *n.* the effect of light in stimulating activity other than direct response to the light.—*adj.* **photokinetic.**

photoma (fō·tō'mə) *n., pl.* **photomata:** a flash of light or color without external stimulus; a simple **hallucination** of light. —*Cp.* **photism.**

photometer (fō·tom'ə·tər): *n.* any optical device that utilizes equations of **brightness** to permit the measurement of **candle-power, illuminance,** or **luminance.** ➤The EQUALITY-OF-BRIGHTNESS PHOTOMETER employs simultaneous comparison of juxtaposed visual areas; in the FLICKER PHOTOM-

ETER the stimuli to be compared are presented successively in the same visual area. See **flicker.**—*adj.* **photometric** (-met'-rik).—*n.* **photometry.**

photometric brightness = luminance.

photometric measure: a measure of *luminous *radiant energy in photometric terms **(candlepower, illuminance, luminance)** rather than in terms of sensation magnitude on the one hand, or of physical energy on the other.

photometry/visual: the measurement of **luminous** radiation or light on the basis of its effect upon the visual **receptors,** under standard conditions, and usually involving an adjustment of two contiguous parts of the visual field, either to identity or to a minimal difference. HETEROCHROMATIC PHOTOMETRY involves the measurement of the relative intensity of differently colored radiations.—*Cp.* **flicker.**

photon (fō'ton): *n.* a measure of brightness or of retinal **illuminance** defined as that illumination upon the retina which results when a surface brightness of 1 candle per square meter is seen through a pupil of 1 square millimeter area.—*Syn.* **troland** (now *prefd.,* since **photon** has been given another meaning in physics).

photophobia: *n.* extreme sensitivity to light; the tendency to shun light. ➤Note that **phobia** here does not mean **fear.**

photopic adaptation (fō·top'ik; -tō'pik) = **adaptation/brightness.**

photopic vision: vision as it occurs under illumination sufficient to permit the full discrimination of colors. It is believed to depend upon the functioning of the retinal **cones.**—*Syn.* DAYLIGHT VISION.—*Contr. w.* **twilight** or scotopic vision.

photoreceptor: *n.* a **receptor** that can be stimulated by light waves, giving rise to visual experience. ➤The photoreceptors are the **rods** and **cones** of the retina; sometimes the accessory structures (the eye muscles for accommodation, e.g.) are included.

phototaxis = phototropism.

phototropism: (fō"tə·trō'piz·əm; fō·tot'-rō-): an orienting movement by an organism away from (negative), or toward (positive), a light: e.g., the sunflower's turning toward the sun. ➤The term is usually restricted to a forced movement. See **tropism.** —*Syn.* PHOTOTAXIS.—*adj.* **phototropic.**

PHR = point-hour ratio.

-phrasia: combining form referring to speech disorder associated with psychosis or grave mental disorder.

phrenasthenia (fren"as·thē'ni·ə) = **mental *deficiency.**

-phrenia, phreno-: combining forms meaning *mind, mentality.*

phrenic nerve (fren'ik): the nerve that actuates the diaphragm, with branches to the pericardium and the lungs.

phreno- = -phrenia.

phrenology: *n.* a doctrine that the excellence of **mental faculties or traits** is determined by the size of the brain area upon which they depend and that this can be judged by the development of the skull overlying the area. ➤Modern psychology rejects entirely the **faculty psychology;** and modern neurology has entirely disproved the kind of brain localization asserted in phrenology. The practice today is a form of quackery.

phrictopathic sensations (frik"tō·path'ik): indefinitely localized, unpleasant, and foreign-seeming tingling sensations of touch.

phyletic (fī·let'ik): *adj.* pertaining to a **phylum,** or to a line of descent; **phylogenetic.**—*n.* **phylesis** (fī·lē'səs).

phyl(o)- combining form meaning *tribe, people, race,* or *biologically defined group.*

phyloanalysis: *n.* (*T. Burrow*) a method of treating behavior disorders based on the hypothesis that all symptoms reflect an impaired tensional balance which affects the person's relation with the basic governing principle of the species.—See **phylobiology.**

phylobiology: *n.* (*T. Burrow*) a proposed behavior science that emphasizes the **phyletic** motivation of the organism's reactions. It postulates a biological unity as a central governing principle in both the individual and the species.

phylogenesis = phylogeny.

phylogenetic: *adj.* **1.** pertaining to the origin and development of a characteristic in the race or other biological division. **2.** pertaining to that which is hereditary in a species or variety.—*Syn.* **species-specific.**

phylogenetic memory: a vague idea or tendency that is found in most or all contemporary men and that represents a stage in the history of mankind. ➤Freud, e.g., once postulated a sort of memory of the "father of the primal horde." The concept of such memories is little accepted.

phylogenetic principle: the principle that the individual tends in his own life to manifest behaviors that rehearse the prehistory of man or even of man's animal ancestry: *ontogeny recapitulates phylogeny.* ➤The principle is no longer accepted as having general validity, but Jung has taken over part of it in his doctrine of **archetypes.**—*Syn.* **recapitulation theory.**

phylogeny (fī·loj'ə·ni): *n.* the origin and evolution of a species or other biologically defined population unit.—*Syn.* **ontogenesis.** —*Syn.* PHYLOGENESIS (fī"lō·jen'ə·səs).— *adj.* **phylogenic, phylogenetic.**

phylum *n., pl.* **phyla, phylums:** the most inclusive division in the biological classification system for plants and animals.

physical: *adj.* **1.** pertaining to physics or physical science: i.e., concerned with the movements of particles. ➤Considerable confusion in psychology would be avoided if this meaning alone were preserved. **2.** characterizing a **material** thing.—*Syn.* **external** (*prefd.* in most contexts). **3.** pertaining to or characterizing the body or the **physique.**—*Syn.* **somatic** (*prefd.*). ➤The last two meanings are very apt to imply respectively the existence of matter and the existence of a body which in some way contrast with mind; both implications are metaphysical, none the less so for being unhesitatingly acceptable to common sense.

physical gestalt: an object in the external world having a unity among its components that is independent of the observer: e.g., an umbrella, a relief map, a table lamp, or even a mere collection, such as a bowl of grapes.

physicalism: *n.* a philosophical or logical view that all meaningful propositions can be expressed without distortion in the language of physical science. ➤The doctrine does not assert superior metaphysical reality for physical science, nor deny the existence of a set of problems to be dealt with by the methods of psychology. **Operational definitions** usually lead to statements in physical language. It would be possible, if less convenient, to reverse the process and to define all physical propositions in psychological language.—*Syn.* LOGICAL BEHAVIORISM.—See **empiricism/ scientific, operationalism, psychology/ divisions and schools of, II, III.**—*adj.* **physicalistic.**

physicalistic interactive score: see **score/ interactive.**

physical medicine or **therapy** = **physiotherapy.**

physical science: see **physics (2).**

physical stimulus: see **stimulus (1).**

physical therapy = **physiotherapy.**

physicochemical: *adj.* pertaining to the realm of physics and chemistry.

physics: *n. pl.* construed as *sing.* **1.** the science dealing with matter and energy. **2.** = PHYSICAL SCIENCE, the general science that studies matter as nonliving. It includes physics, chemistry, physical geology, physical geography, astronomy.

physiogenetic: *adj.* characterizing that which originates in the functioning of the body or of some organ or tissue.

physiognomic (fiz″i·og·nom′ik): *adj.* **1.** pertaining to **physiognomy. 2.** of a type of experience, esp. perceptual, in which **cognition** is suffused with **affective** or **conative** elements: a rundown house looks tired; a tripod, proud. ➤**Empathy (1)** is physiognomic, as is much of what Piaget calls **egocentric (2).**

physiognomy (fiz″i·og′nə·mi): *n.* **1.** art of judging mental traits or attitudes from the outward appearance of the face and, by extension, of other visible bodily structures. ➤Actual systems of physiognomy belong to quackery, since scientific studies reveal insignificant or unstable relationships. (But *cp.* **constitutional type.**) **2.** the cast or expression of the face.

physiological age: see **age/physiological.**

physiological gradient: a **gradient** of **metabolic** action; a continuous gradation from high metabolism in an area decreasing toward adjacent areas.

physiological limit: see **limit/physiological.**

physiological motive: see **motive/physiological.**

physiological psychology: 1. the study of the correlations of physiological processes or activities with **behavior** or **act.** ➤The discipline need not concern itself in any way with the philosophical **mind-body problem** (though its findings clearly bear on that). Accepting that there is an event called *seeing,* for example, it endeavors to trace all the interrelations between variation in seeing and variation in the activities of the retina and its associated structures of the eye, nerve tracts, and brain centers.—*Syn.* PSYCHOPHYSIOLOGY, PHYSIOPSYCHOLOGY. **2.** an unfortunate synonym for **experimental psychology.**

physiological state: the general **metabolic** condition of the organism.

physiological zero: the temperature at which an object does not give rise to **thermal** sensations. It varies according to the area stimulated, but averages about 33°C. ➤CUTANEOUS ZERO is suggested as more accurate.

physiology: *n.* the study of certain of the functions of a living organism. ➤The relation of physiology to psychology is a close one, and one that is perplexing to define in view of rival theories. Those who make psychology a biological science dealing with **responses** cannot satisfactorily state how to divide the field of responses between the two. Those who define psychology in terms of **consciousness** face the **mind-body problem** in critical form. However, growth, digestion, respiration, reproduction, excretion—considered as such— are examples of phenomena that are primarily physiological.—*Contr. w.* **anatomy, morphology.**—*adj.* **physiological.**

physiotherapy: *n.* the branch of medicine dealing with treatment by physical means, excluding drugs and surgical cutting and including massage, hydrotherapy, heat treatment, **electrotherapy** (but not **electroshock therapy**). Many of these procedures are licensed for limited medical practice.—

Contr. w. **psychotherapy.**—*Syn.* PHYSICAL THERAPY, PHYSICAL MEDICINE.

physique: *n.* the structural organization of an animal body, esp. of a human body.— *adj.* **physical** (often *ambig.*).

PI = **proactive *inhibition.**

pia (mater) (pī'ə mā'tər): *n.* (*L.*) a highly vascular, thin membrane covering the brain and spinal cord.

piano theory: see **hearing theories.**

pica (pī'kə): *n.* a craving to eat unsuitable objects.

Pick's disease: circumscribed atrophy of the cerebral **cortex,** with resultant **aphasia** and progressive **dementia.**

pictograph: a representation of an object, action, or idea by a picture or symbol suggestive or imitative thereof.—*Distg. fr.* **ideogram,** which is part of a formalized writing system.—*Var.* **pictogram.**

pictorial display: the utilization of pictures or graphs to convey information. ➤The pictures or graphs must utilize the same continuum as that on which the information is scaled and must not distort critical relations.

pictorial test: a test in which the task is related to pictured material used as a substitute for, or supplement to, verbal material.

picture arrangement test: a series of individual scenes which, when correctly arranged, tells a simple comic-strip story. The subject arranges the several disarranged pictures in each set.

picture completion test: a set of simple line drawings of common objects with an important detail omitted from each. The subject must correctly identify the missing part of the picture.

Picture-Frustration Study/Rosenzweig: a **projective** test in which a mildly frustrating situation is pictured and the subject is asked what the frustrated person would probably say. ➤The frustrations are either ego-blocking or superego-blocking. Responses are classified as showing "obstacle-dominance," "ego-defense," and "need persistence"; or as extrapunitive, intropunitive, and impunitive.—*Abbr.* **P-F Study.**

picture interpretation test: a test in which the subject must make a brief interpretation of a pictured scene. ➤In the **Binet scales,** the subject is asked to "tell about" the picture: interpretation is a more mature response than description or mere enumeration.

picture/retinal: *prefd. syn.* for **retinal *image.**

Piderit drawings: a series of ultrasimplified drawings of a male face, to illustrate how change of outline of any part of the face affects the emotional expression: e.g., the effect of upturned or downturned cor-

ners of the lips. Boring and Titchener prepared a cutout profile with interchangeable parts yielding 360 compounds for the basic face.

piecemeal activity/law of: A part or element of a situation may be **prepotent** in causing response.—*Cp.* **reduced cues/ principle of.**

piecemeal learning: see **learning/whole vs. part.**

pie chart: a circle divided by radii into sectors of different sizes, used as a graphic representation of proportional magnitudes. ➤As the relative areas of such sectors are hard to judge by eye, this device is misleading.

pillars of Corti = **rods of Corti.**

pilomotor response (pī"lō·mō'tər): the technical name for goose-pimples.

pilot study: a brief and simplified experiment or survey to try out methods or to discover whether a proposed project seems likely to yield valuable data.

Piltdown man: skeletal remains alleged to be those of a primitive man similar to **Neanderthal man,** but later proved to be a hoax.*—*Syn.* *Eoanthropus dawsoni,* SUSSEX MAN.

pincer technique: grasping a small object between finger and thumb. The age of its appearance is a measure of motor development in infants.

pineal gland or **body** (pin'i·əl): a small structure, lying just above the thalamic region, very nearly at the geometric center of the brain. ➤Its function is unknown. Because of its central location, Descartes suggested that it was the organ by which the soul influenced the brain and the brain the soul.—*Syn.* CONARIUM, EPIPHYSIS CEREBRI, CORPUS PINEALE.

P IQ: an intelligence quotient computed from performance test scores.

pitch: *n.* the character of a tone as high or low. It is determined chiefly by the vibration frequency.

pitch/absolute: ability to recognize the pitch of a single tone and name it without a comparison tone being given; or to produce a named tone vocally. ➤*Absolute* does not here mean *absolutely precise* but means *not based on direct comparison.* The capacity for absolute pitch is affected by training.

pitch brightness: see **density/tonal.**

pitchfork: *n.* a small tuning fork of **standard *pitch.**

pitch/relative: 1. the pitch of a sound as higher or lower than some other with which it is compared; hence, **2.** given a standard tone, the ability to recognize or reproduce pitch intervals.—*Contr. w.* **pitch/absolute.**

pitch/standard: a tone of fixed vibration rate used as standard in tuning musical instruments. ➤A number of different pitches have been proposed; in the U.S. most instruments and orchestras are tuned to $a' = 440$ d.v., but for work in acoustics $c' = 256$ d.v. is often used.

pithecanthropus erectus (pith″ə·kan·-thrō′pəs i·rek′təs; pith″ə·kan′-): an extinct **primate** related to modern man (*homo sapiens*), probably to be classified as the lowest human in the evolutionary scale yet discovered.—*Syn.* JAVA MAN.

pithecoid (pi·thē′koid; pith′ə-): *adj.* apelike or monkeylike.

pituitary gland or **body:** a very important compound **endocrine** gland, about the size of a pea, lying at the base of the brain. It has many functions and is sometimes called the master gland because of its influence on the other endocrines.—*Syn.* HYPOPHYSIS.

pity: *n.* an emotion of sadness or solicitude aroused by the distress or misfortune of another.—*Distg. fr.* **sympathy,** which means sharing the other's feelings.

pivotal condensation method: (*Aitkin*) a method for obtaining the **regression coefficients** and **multiple *correlation** by employing a series of **matrices.**

Pk = psychokinesis.

placebo (plə·sē′bō): *n.* a preparation containing no medicine (or no medicine related to the complaint) and administered to cause the patient to believe he is receiving treatment.

place learning: see **learning/place.**

placement: *n.* (*personnel*) the assigning of a worker to the job for which he is judged best fitted. ➤Fitness includes the individual's satisfaction as well as his abilities in relation to the job.

placement test: a test that enables a pupil to be assigned to the appropriate class level for instruction, either in general or in a particular subject.

placenta (plə·sen′tə): *n.* in mammals, the vascular structure within the uterus to which the fetus is attached by the umbilical cord and through which it is nourished.—*adj.* **placental.**

place principle of hearing: a theory (with several variants) that supposes the heard pitch to be determined primarily by the place in the **basilar membrane** that is excited.—*Contr. w.* frequency theory (see **hearing theories**).

plan: *n.* **1.** a scheme of action; a way, proposed to oneself or others, of carrying out some intention. **2.** a representation of certain spatial relations: the *plan* of a house. **3.** the **hypothetical *construct** designed to explain animal behavior that seems to be directed by foresight of circumstances and anticipation of a goal. ➤It is not implied that the mechanism is the same as in the

plans of humans.—*v.* **4.** to consider and decide upon a relatively complex set of activities that seem likely, in the light of all the foreseeable circumstances, to lead to a goal.

planchette (plan·shet′): *n.* a small tripod "table," with a pencil for one leg, used for automatic writing.

planned parenthood = parenthood/voluntary.

planophrasia = flight of ideas.

plantar reflex: flexion of the toes when the sole is lightly stroked. ➤In certain organic disorders of the nervous system, this reflex is lost and the **Babinski sign** reappears.

plantigrade: *adj.* pertaining to a position for standing or a mode of walking in which the foot touches the ground with the entire sole, including the heel. ➤It is illustrated by the bears and man. The plantigrade position is assumed by human infants at about 7 months, but the age variability is great.

plasticity: *n.* **1.** the capacity that permits an animal to change as a result of taking part in an event.—*Syn.* **docility,** learning capacity, modifiability, **educability.**—*Ant.* **rigidity. 2.** in studies of **eidetic imagery,** the tendency for the image to be influenced by the conditions immediately preceding its appearance. **3. = adaptability.** —*adj.* **plastic.**

plasticity of libido: see **libido/plasticity of.**

plateau: *n.* an intermediate period of no apparent progress in learning. ➤It is so

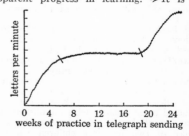

weeks of practice in telegraph sending

called from the graph of performance, where such a period appears as a flat stretch.—*Cp.* **physiological *limit.**

plateau test: (*factor anal.*) a criterion of whether further **rotations** are necessary.

Platonic friendship or **love:** comradeship in which there is no overt sexual behavior and which the participants believe to be without **erotic** components. ➤Modern usage usually confines the term to heterosexual relations, but Plato clearly included homosexual relations as well. Psychoanalysts (and cynical popular opinion) consider that the denial of an erotic component is self-deception.—*Distg. fr.* PLATONISM, the general philosophy of Plato.

platonization: *n.* 1. maintenance of a relationship between two persons of opposite sex on a nonerotic basis. 2. converting the energy generated by **erotic** feeling into nonerotic activities—a form of **sublimation.** 3. the substitution of thinking about a desired action for actually performing it. ➤It is regarded in psychoanalysis as a defense against impulse to do what is contrary to the superego. Platonization sometimes comes close to implying the magical **omnipotence of thought.**

platoon-volley theory: (*aud.*) a theory of hearing which holds that a given vibration frequency causes discharge of the auditory nerve in a rapid succession of **volleys,** each in a distinct set of fibers (platoons). ➤The theory is posited to avoid the difficulty that, because of the **refractory period,** the same fibers cannot respond by successive firings fast enough to keep up with the higher frequencies; hence, it is the frequency of firing in different fibers that corresponds with the frequency of vibration.—See **hearing theories.**—*Syn.* VOLLEY THEORY.

platycephaly (plat″i·sef′ə·li): *n.* flatness of the crown of the head.—*Var.* **platycephalism** (-izm).—*adj.* **platycephalic** (-sə·-fal′ik), **platycephalous** (-sef′ə·ləs).

platykurtic (-kėr′tik): see **kurtosis.**—*n.* **platykurtosis.**

play: *n.* voluntary activity pursued without ulterior purpose and, on the whole, with enjoyment or expectation of enjoyment. (Certain elements of play may not be enjoyed.)

playback: *n.* playing over a recorded interview for the interviewee so that he may add to or correct what he had said.

play/free: play undirected by a supervisor. —*Contr. w.* organized *play.

play/organized: 1. play, or a program of play, that is planned in advance, governed by rules, and supervised. 2. any game conducted in accordance with established rules.

play/parallel: the side-by-side independent play of two or more children (or occasionally adults) doing much the same things but without active cooperation and yet with heightened interest because of each other's presence and activity: e.g., golf, the play of two children each building a house.

play projection: the process whereby a testee (usually a child), playing freely with certain materials, unself-consciously reveals his outlooks and attitudes. ➤The materials most often used are household toys and doll figures that can easily represent family persons. But any play is a projection, and *may* be a *revealing* projection.—See **projection** (**2, 3, 4**) and **projective technique.**

play therapy: the utilization of play, in the presence of the therapist, as a means of helping a child to rid himself of certain maladjusting tensions. ➤The child is encouraged in one way or another to re-enact the situations in which he has emotional difficulty and to display the feelings which in the real situation are inhibited. E.g., he may swear at a doll representing the father. Play therapy was elaborated upon the basis of **catharsis** theory but may be otherwise explained. It is a specific *procedure,* not just any child playing. The presence of the therapist is essential.

pleasantness: *n.* 1. = **pleasure (1)** or **(2)** (*prefd.*). 2. the abstract quality of external objects or events (esp., of social events) that arouses agreeable feeling or **pleasure (1)** or **(2).**—*Syn.* agreeableness.

pleasure: *n.* 1. an elementary—hence, undefinable—feeling, at one end of a **continuum** that passes through a neutral point to the other end, which is UNPLEASURE (sometimes called **pain**).—*Syn.* **pleasantness.** 2. a vaguely defined emotional condition characterized by desire for its continuance. 3. an unlocalized specific kind of sensation (or fusion of sensations) from internal bodily organs, perhaps with contribution from the external genitals. 4. the state of the organism when a tension is being reduced. ➤Both **(3)** and **(4)** are couched in definition form, but they go beyond definition to theory. They do not so much describe pleasure as attempt to explain it.

pleasure-ego: *n.* (*psychoan.*) that portion of the **ego** made up of processes congruent with instinctual impulses.

pleasure/function: see **function pleasure.**

pleasure-pain principle: (*psychoan.*) the postulate that man's life is controlled by two opposed principles, the **pleasure principle** (or its modification by the **reality principle**) and the **pain principle.** The pleasure principle is manifested in **libido** or the **life instinct,** the pain principle in the **death instinct.**—*Syn.* NIRVANA PRINCIPLE, which B. Low and Freud held to include both life and death instincts.

pleasure principle: (*psychoan.*) the demand that an **instinctual** need be immediately gratified, either directly (e.g., by food to satisfy hunger) or by **fantasy or wish fulfillment.** ➤According to the earliest formulation of psychoanalysis, **unconscious** or **id** activities are completely dominated by this principle: fantasy is not distinguished from reality; hence, fulfillment can be immediate. But with development of the **ego,** the person becomes aware of the demands of reality (the **reality principle**); and with development of the **superego,** he becomes aware of **ideal** demands. Pleasure is still sought, but not in the primitive fashion of the id. However, the pleasure principle, operating unconsciously in the id, incites to many activities that deform the ego processes.—See also **pain principle.**

-plectic: an adj. form of **-plegia.**

-plegia, -plegy: combining form meaning *paralysis, paralytic stroke* or *attack:* HEMIPLEGIA, paralysis of the right or left half of the body; PARAPLEGIA, paralysis of the lower half of the body.

plethysmograph (pli·thiz′mə·graf): *n.* an instrument for recording changes in volume of a part of the body. The changes measured are usually due directly to variations in blood supply.

plexus: *n.* a network of nerves or veins; esp., a network of nerves outside the central nervous system: e.g., the SOLAR PLEXUS, which lies behind the stomach.

plosive: *adj.* (*phonetics*) explosive: used of any of the six consonants *p, b, t, d, k,* or *g.*

plot: *v.* (*stat.*) to enter scores individually in a **frequency** table or a **scatter diagram,** or to locate scores on a surface as a means of graphing.

plot/treatment: in agricultural experimentation, one of the portions of a field that is subjected to special experimental treatment—e.g., to a certain kind of fertilizer; by generalization to any experiment, a division or grouping of the **dependent *variable** that receives a different amount or kind of treatment.

pluralism: *n.* **1.** a metaphysical doctrine which holds that ultimate reality consists of more than two kinds of entity, that reality is composed of several kinds of distinct, discontinuous, and irreducible elements.—*Cp.* **dualism, monism. 2.** any explanation that emphasizes many elements; a tendency to see many things where others might see only one or two: e.g., finding many explanations of the relation of somatic activities to the development of personality. **3.** divergence and separatism; a tendency for a group to break up into smaller distinct units.

pluralistic behavior: (*F. H. Giddings*) any type of action performed by nearly every person in a given group or region: e.g., covering exposed parts of the body in cold weather.—*Syn.* MULTI-INDIVIDUAL BEHAVIOR.

pluralistic ignorance: what everyone believes that "everyone else" believes, though he himself does not.

plurel (plů·rel′): *n.* (*sociol.*) any number, greater than one, of human beings who have at least one attribute in common.—*Syn.* **class, category.**

plus gesture: (*A. Adler*) overt behavior intended to demonstrate some sort of superiority as compensation for a feeling of inferiority.

PMA = primary mental *abilities.

p-n = (*H. A. Murray*) **press-need.**

PNAvQ = positive-negative ambivalent quotient.

pneumat(o)-: combining form meaning *breath,* hence, more generally, *air.* ➤It is used especially of instruments employing air pressure. **Pneumo-** occasionally occurs where *pneumato-* would be more accurate.

pneum(o)-: combining form meaning *lung.*

pneumocardiograph: *n.* a pneumatic device for recording heart action.

pneumogastric nerve = vagus nerve. ➤The Germans call this the "lung-stomach" nerve, which exactly describes it. Why need English use Greek?

pneumograph: *n.* an instrument for recording the strength and duration of respiratory expiration and inspiration. A PNEUMATOGRAPH is that form of pneumograph which directly measures and records the breath. Other forms record the movements of breathing.

Po: 1. = position response. 2. a brief attitude scale for the study of anti-Semitism.

Poggendorff illusion: a spatial illusion in which a straight line, interrupted as it

crosses a pair of parallel lines (or a thin rectangle), seems not to be the same line, the exit line seeming lower than the extension of the entry line.

point/anchoring: see **anchoring point.**

point biserial: see **correlation/point biserial.**

point/critical: (*S. R. Slavson*) a stage or point in therapy at which the problems are clearly envisioned and the client mobilizes his resources to solve them.

point-hour ratio or **PHR:** a weighted index of the grades or marks received for academic work in an American high school or college. Letter grades are transmuted into numbers: e.g., A = 4, B = 3, etc. Each number is multiplied by the hours of credit assigned the course in which the grade is gained. The resulting products are summed and divided by the total number of credit hours.—*Syn.* GRADE-POINT AVERAGE or GPA.

point of regard = fixation point (see **fixation/visual**).

point of subjective equality: see **subjective equality/point of.**

point of symmetry or **PS** = **point of** *subjective equality.*

point of view: (*C. Ruckmick*) a term proposed as substitute for one of the several current meanings of **method.** The point of view indicates "the purpose which prompts the investigation, the attitude assumed in the scientific study." Examples: behavioral, statistical, quantitative or qualitative, explanatory or descriptive, comparative, and genetic *points of view.*

point scale: a group of test items or problems for each of which a numerical credit is given for success. The standing of the person tested is based on the total points amassed.—*Cp.* **age-equivalent scale.**—*Distg. fr.* **scale points.**

points/congruent: see **congruent points.**

point score = **raw *score.***

point source: (*vis.*) a light source so small, as compared with the distance from the observer, that it may be considered a point. ➤The stimulating properties of a point source may be expressed in terms of its radiant intensity in the direction of the pupil. The stimulating properties of an EXTENDED SOURCE may be expressed in terms of the areal density of point sources of unit radiant intensity to which the extended source is equivalent.

point system: 1. the scoring used in a **point scale.** 2. academic rating using the **point-hour ratio.** 3. a system of assigning different point scores to various extracurricular activities according to their importance, time-consumingness, etc. ➤This is a basis for limiting the amount of participation of an individual or for judging the "activeness" of members of different clubs.

point-to-point correspondence: a relationship, spatial or logical, such that for every point or item in one variable, another similarly located point or item occurs in the other variable.

Poisson distribution (pwǝ·soN'): (*stat.*) a special case of the **binomial** distribution where the probability of a defined event is extremely small. ➤It is sometimes applied to accident data.

Poisson series: a **frequency** distribution for which the successive frequencies are given by

$$e^{-m}\left(1, m, \frac{m^2}{2!}, \frac{m^3}{3!}, \frac{m^4}{4!} \cdots \frac{m^n}{n!}\right)$$

when m is the mean value of the distribution. Such a series is found by noting the frequencies of occurrence of an event which has a relatively small probability of occurrence.

polar continuum: a **continuum** defined by ends that are completely opposite, i.e., by **polar opposites** (which see).—*Cp.* **bipolar.**

polar coordinate: either of two quantities by which to locate in space a point P: the LENGTH COORDINATE OP, and the ANGULAR

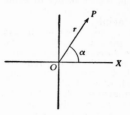

COORDINATE α, which is the angle between a line OX and the line OP.

polarity: *n.* 1. the quality of having two poles or opposite ends, or of acting with respect to two poles: a magnet has *polarity.* 2. the fact that neural impulse always passes from one pole of the neuron (the **dendritic** end) to the other (the **axon** end). 3. the manifestation of opposite behaviors or personal traits; **bipolarity.** ➤E.g., it is believed that all children show polarity of affection toward parents (i.e., love and hatred).—*Cp.* **ambivalence,** often used as a synonym but also possessing other meanings. 4. the state of a social group when one person is the center of attention or otherwise dominates it: e.g., most audiences exhibit a considerable degree of *polarity.*—*adj.* **polar.**—*v.* **polarize.**

polarization: *n.* the process of inducing **polarity;** the degree of polarity. 1. (*optics*) treatment of a beam of light so that the waves all oscillate parallel to a single axis. This is accomplished by screening out other waves. 2. (*elec.*) concentration of higher electric potential at one pole. ➤The bodily organs and tissues exhibit electrical polarization. 3. causing a person to adjust behavior to two poles (instead of adjusting to many points of reference); = BIPOLARIZATION. ➤E.g., the goal of moral instruction usually is to get the pupil to orient his behavior to the **polar continuum** of goodness-badness.—See **bipolar.** 4. causing a person to adjust to one pole of a bipolar relation: e.g., causing a person to accept a submissive role. ➤This includes the case where a group is made to adjust primarily to one person, as at a lecture. *Cp.* **mass polarization.** See **polarity** (4).

polar opposites: objects or behaviors or traits that are not merely opposite but at opposite poles; the extremes of opposition. ➤It is not implied that there are no intermediates: polar opposites often define a continuum. E.g., absolute goodness and absolute badness are polar opposites on a continuum that has innumerable gradations between.

poliomyelitis: *n.* inflammation of the gray matter of the spinal cord, resulting in extensive neural symptoms. ACUTE ANTERIOR POLIOMYELITIS is the familiar INFANTILE PARALYSIS.

poll: *n.* **1.** literally, the head, or the top of the head. **2.** a counting of heads, i.e., of persons. **3.** a counting of the number of persons favoring or disfavoring a given person or issue, as in voting. **4.** an **opinion** (or attitude) poll.—*pers. n.* **pollster,** one who takes a poll, esp. an opinion poll.—*v.* **poll.**

Pollyanna mechanism: the attempt to believe that "all is well" despite one's actual dissatisfaction.

poly-: combining form meaning *many* or *excessive:* POLYGLOT, one who speaks many languages; POLYDACTYLISM, having too many (i.e., extra) fingers.—*Syn.* (for words of Latin origin) **multi-.**

polyandry: *n.* a marriage system in which a woman may have several husbands at the same time.—*Cp.* **polygyny.**—*adj.* **polyandrous.**

polychromatic theory: hypothesis that there are many kinds of retinal **cones,** each kind sensitive to a particular band of light-wave frequencies.

polydactyl (pol″i·dak′til): *adj.* having more fingers than normal.—*n.* **polydactylism.**

polydiurnal (-dī·ėr′nəl): *adj.* many times daily.

polygamy: *n.* a marriage system in which a person of either sex may have more than one mate at the same time. ➤The term is commonly used where **polygyny** would be more specific, since polygamy also includes **polyandry** and **group *marriage.**—*Syn.* PLURAL MARRIAGE.—*adj.* **polygamous.**

polygenes: *n. pl.* genes having such small quantitative effect on the variability of a trait that they are known only collectively. They cannot be isolated by genetic techniques.—See **gene/major.**

polyglot: *n.* a person speaking several languages.—*adj.* **polyglot.**

polygon/frequency: see **frequency (2).**

polygraph: *n.* apparatus for simultaneously recording on a revolving drum a number of activities or reactions.

polygyny (pō·lij′ə·ni): *n.* a marriage system in which a man may have several wives at the same time. ➤*Cp.* **polyandry.** Polygamy (which see) is often used where polygyny is meant.—*adj.* **polygynous.**

polylogia (pol″i·lō′ji·ə): *n.* much or continual talking, usually incoherently.—*Syn.* **logorrhea.**

polymorphous perversity: see **perversion/infantile polymorphous.**

polyneuritic psychosis = **Korsakow's psychosis.**

polyneuropathy/alcoholic: a condition involving deterioration in many peripheral and central nervous structures.

polyopia (-ō′pi·ə): *n.* abnormality of the refractive apparatus of the eye whereby more than one image is formed on the retina. ➤*Distg. fr.* **diplopia,** in which the normal single images on each retina are not fused normally. A HYSTERICAL POLYOPIA is seeing double in the absence of local organic difficulty.—*Var.* **polyopsia** (-op′si·ə).—*adj.* **polyopic** (-op′ik).

polyphony (pō·lif′ə·ni): *n.* music in which two or more melodies, independent but related in varying ways, proceed simultaneously.

polyphrasia = **logorrhea.**

polyuria (pol″i·ū′ri·ə): *n.* profuse urination.—*adj.* **polyuric.**

ponderal growth (pon′dər·əl): growth in weight, either of a single organ or of the whole body.

pons (Varolii) (pons və·rō′li·ī): a convex white eminence at the base of the brain. Its nerve fibers connect the cerebrum with the contralateral side of the cerebellum.

pooling procedure: combining the values obtained by different measures and treating the result as one variable. ➤E.g., measures of different school achievements may be combined to measure academic achievement as a whole. The several measures may be assigned varying **weights;** if the different scores are merely added, this means that each is weighted 1, the assumption being that one kind of achievement is equal to each of the others.

popular response: 1. a kind of response to a stimulus, esp. a verbal or other symbolic response, that is made by very many people. ➤E. g., the response *white* to the word *black* in an **association test** is a highly popular response. **2.** (*Ror.*) a frequently occurring response to a given inkblot. It is symbolized by *P.*

population: *n.* **1.** all the organisms, or all of a stated kind, occupying a certain geographical area at a given time. ➤Sometimes specified as a GEOGRAPHICAL POPULATION. **2.** all the instances about which a statement is to be made. ➤*Distg. fr.* **sample,** which refers to those cases actually observed, measured, or experimentally treated, which are regarded as *representative* of the whole. Some authors speak of POPULATION UNIVERSE, **statistical *universe,** or REFERENCE POPULATION for the entire group, and of SAMPLE POPULATION for the representative group in the sample. But confusion arises when SAMPLE POPULATION is then abbreviated to *population* instead of to **sample.**

pornography: *n.* originally, the depiction of harlotry; by extension, the depiction of whatever the user of the term regards as

obscenity (which see).—*adj.* **pornographic.**

porropsia: *n.* (*vis.*) a condition in which objects, without size distortion, look more distant than they are.

Porter's law: the generalization that the critical *flicker frequency increases with the log of the brightness of the stimulus and is independent of the wave length.— *Syn.* FERRY-PORTER LAW.

posit (poz'it): *v.* to assume or to take for granted what is necessary for the immediate action or argument. ➤*Contr. w.* **infer.** Posit was formerly often used for **hypothesize** by those who hesitated to use that verb (which has only recently been accepted as standard English). But the two have somewhat different meanings that may now be kept distinct.—*Cp.* **postulate.**

position: *n.* 1. (*sociol.*) in a social structure, a small area that plays a part in determining the activity of the individual who occupies it. ➤Position partly determines who will bring influence to bear on the occupant and what the nature of that influence will be; and it greatly affects the influence the occupant will have on others. (E.g., consider the influence of the occupant of a pulpit or of the presidential office.) Since position so largely determines **role,** the two are sometimes used interchangeably, but they are not the same. OFFICE is more nearly synonymous. 2. (*topol.*) a **region** or subregion of a **life space** within which any fact, event, or characteristic lies; a locus in a life space of a number of forces of given magnitude and direction acting upon the occupant (of the position) and of a number of forces potentially elicitable by the occupant by virtue of that fact. ➤The occupant is usually a person, but **position** is general and the occupant can be a thing: a ribbon around a woman's neck has position, not only in the geometry of Euclid but in topological psychology.

positional leader: see **leader/status.**

position factor: the influence of the spatial or temporal placement of the stimulus upon the response; or a tendency to select a certain direction of response: e.g., a preference for the first of a multiple-choice test alternative, a tendency to turn left rather than right in a maze.—*Cp.* **sequence preference.**—*Syn.* POSITION PREFERENCE.

position habit: a tendency to prefer going to an accustomed place: e.g., going to one's accustomed place at the dinner table even though it is not set for eating. It is shown also by animals.

positioning reaction: moving a physical object until it occupies a prescribed position in space. ➤Many practical situations require that the object be maintained in position by intermittent positioning reactions: e.g., keeping a moving vehicle on course.

position (in the family): 1. see **position** (1). 2. see **birth order.**

position preference = **position factor.**

position response or *Po:* (*Ror.*) a response determined by the accident that the position of a feature in a given inkblot figure recalls or suggests a similar position that pertains to the association reported: e.g., an area is called "North Pole" because it is at the top.

positive: *adj.* 1. (*math.*) numerically greater than zero; having a plus (+) sign; not **negative.** 2. definite; expressed unqualifiedly; admitting of no condition: a *positive* command. 3. confident; overconfident. 4. like a model or standard; esp., having the same quantitative sign as the model: a *positive* afterimage. 5. oriented toward a certain reference point, literally (in space) or figuratively: a *positive* tropism; a *positive* attitude toward socialism (i.e., tending to agreement); a *positive* (i.e., friendly) attitude to a person. 6. concerned with the verifiable; **empirical,** not speculative or theoretical.

positive and negative cases method = **constant stimulus method.**

positive/false or /**valid:** see **false negative.**

positive-negative ambivalent quotient: (*V. C. Raimy*) the ratio of remarks showing a positive or favorable self-evaluation to negative and ambivalent remarks in a given statement by a counselee.—Symbol **PNAvQ.**

positive-negative conflict = **approach-avoidance conflict.**

positive-positive conflict = **approach-approach conflict.**

positive self-feeling: see **self-feeling/ positive.**

positivism: *n.* 1. (*hist.*) the philosophical point of view, formulated by Comte, which sought to dispense with all theological and metaphysical concepts. It holds that knowledge consists of observation of sensory phenomena and the classification of these data according to the categories of necessary succession (= causality, but Comte scorned that term as having metaphysical implications), coexistence, and resemblance. 2. the doctrine that science is limited to observed facts and to what can be rigorously deduced from facts, that all concepts and conclusions refer to facts and derive all their meaning from facts. ➤See **scientific** *empiricism and **operationalism,** which are specific forms of positivism. No one questions that science is concerned with facts, but some believe that science has other concerns as well. As a basic attitude in psychology, positivism tends to be: **analytic** rather than **synthetic, elementaristic** or **reductionist** rather than **molar** or **Gestaltist, empiricist** rather than **nativist, environmentalist** rather than **geneticist, peripheralist** rather than **centralist, associationist** rather than **creative synthesist, reactivist** rather than **activist, nomological** rather than **idiographic,** and usually **monistic** rather than **dualistic.** Yet it is conceptually possible to take the positivist position in combination with the other member of each of these dichotomies. **3.** loosely, the attitude of scorning speculation and of exalting the role of **empirical** fact, esp. in science.

positivism/logical = **scientific** *empiricism (1).

possession: *n.* the condition of being under the control of an alien spirit: an old theory to explain insanity, and a not infrequent delusion in psychosis.

possessiveness: *n.* a tendency to maintain exclusive ownership or control over something, to be unwilling to share what one has with others. ➤The objects of possessiveness may be most varied: from worthless playthings (such as a shiny stone) to a beloved mate. There is no necessary implication that the same dynamic influences cause all kinds of possessiveness.

possible: *adj.* characterizing an assumption or hypothesis as supported by a slight, but only a slight, preponderance of evidence. ➤It is one of a series of quasi-quantitative terms: impossible, improbable, possible, probable, proved or demonstrated. All these refer to the *weight* of evidence and not to the logical status of a proposition as **self-evident** or self-**contradictory.**—*n.* **possibility,** which is also used abstractly for position anywhere in the above series.

post-: prefix meaning *after, behind, later.*

post.: *abbr.* for **posterior.**

posterior: *adj.* situated at the rear of a part. ➤This term and its antonym **anterior** are ambiguous in anatomy: **cephalocaudal** or **dorsoventral** are preferred.

posterior root: see **spinal root.**

post hoc, ergo propter hoc (pŏst hok ėr′go prop′tər): (*L.*) after this, therefore because of it: the fallacy of inferring that because one thing followed another it was caused by the other.

posthypnotic suggestion: a suggestion made to a hypnotized subject that he will perform in a prescribed way later in a waking state. The subject usually carries out the activity without knowing why.

postmature infant: one born considerably after the normal 40 weeks of gestation.

postnatal: *adj.* occurring after birth.—*Ant.* **prenatal, congenital.**

post partum: (*L.*) after childbirth.

postpuberal phase: a one- to two-year period in adolescent development beyond the **puberal phase** during which most of the skeletal growth is completed.

postremity: *n.* (*V. W. Voeks*) the generalization that the last thing an organism does in a situation is the most probable thing it will do when the situation next recurs.

post-test: *n.* a test to determine performance after the administration of an **experimental variable.**—See **pretest** and **before-after design.**

postulate: *n.* an underlying principle whose acceptance is sought or assumed, in the absence of direct crucial evidence, because it is a necessary link in a chain of reasoning which as a whole is thought to be logically sound or to lead to a factually verifiable conclusion. ➤Examples are Hull's postulate that the greater the delay in reinforcement, the weaker will be the resulting reaction potential; or Euclid's postulate that two parallel lines do not intersect. A postulate is not self-evident (for which the term is **axiom**), nor a logical derivative of an accepted principle (a **corollary**), nor a conclusion to be established directly by factual evidence (a **hypothesis**). **Assumption** is often used as a synonym but is properly a more general term that includes **hypothesis.** SUPPOSITION is still more general for any tentative statement or belief. PRESUPPOSITION is a near-synonym. —*adj.* **postulated; postulational,** of a system clearly based on a postulate, and therefore not empirical.—*v.* **postulate.**

postulational method: (*logic*) the use of a formal language system based on a set of relations, called postulates or implicit definitions, between otherwise undefined terms. Manipulation of the terms according to the laws of the system brings out relationships not previously known. ➤Modern geometry uses such postulation, and it plays a part in theoretical physics. In mathematics **hypothetico-deductive** means the same as postulational, but in psychology and in most empirical sciences the former is differently conceived.

postural: *adj.* pertaining to **posture** or to the maintenance of posture.—*Syn.* **tonic (1).**—*Contr. w.* **kinetic, phasic.**

postural reflexes: the totality of those reflexes or reflexlike responses which maintain the body in relatively static positions.

postural set: see **set/postural.**

postural substrate: the total set of **kinesthetic** messages whereby a person is aware of his posture.

posture: *n.* the position of the body as a whole with respect to the pull of gravity, or of its members in relation to one another.— *adj.* **postural.**

potency: *n.* **1.** power, esp. in high degree. **2.** latent or undeveloped power.—*Syn.* **potentiality** (more usual). **3.** relative ability, esp. of a male, to perform the sexual act. **4.** (*topol.*) the relative degree to which one part of the **life space** determines behavior —*adj.* **potential, potent** (usually referring to a high degree of potency).

potential: *adj.* **1.** characterized by **potency.** **2.** pertaining to **potentiality.**—*Ant.* (for **2**) **actual.**—*n.* **3.** the degree of electrical charge. —See **electromotive force.**

potential/excitatory: see **excitatory potential.**

potentiality: *n.* a present property of something by means of which it may in future exhibit a quality it does not now exhibit; that present property, often known only by inference, which makes possible the acquisition or development of a certain quality.—*Cp.* **aptitude, capacity.**

potential/reaction: see **reaction potential.**

potential/response: the range of possible behaviors permitted by conditions within the learner.

potential/specific action = **reaction potential.**

potlatch: *n.* an Amerind ceremonial in which prestige is gained by giving away or destroying one's property.

poverty: *n.* a condition of relative lack of material goods. ➤The base for comparison depends on the culture and on the individual's level of expectation and aspiration.

power: *n.* **1.** (*math.*) the product of a number multiplied by itself one or more times. **2.** (*math.*) the index number that is written as a superscript to show how many times a number is to be multiplied by itself: e.g., the 2 in 4^2, the 3 in x^3. **3.** (*phys.*) the rate of doing work. The units are erg per second, watt, or horsepower. **4.** muscular strength. **5.** (*optics*) the degree to which a lens magnifies. **6.** = **ability.**—See also **test/power.**

power factor: (*W. C. Halstead*) that aspect of intelligence which indirectly energizes other factors, and reflects the over-all efficiency level of the functioning brain.

power fields: that part of the **life space** (which may include other persons) over which the person has control.

power figure: the person who, for a given individual, represents social power.

power function (of a test of significance): (*stat.*) an index of the probability of rejecting a specified hypothesis at a given **risk level** when alternative hypotheses are assumed to be true; the equation showing the probability of rejecting or failing to reject a false **null hypothesis.** The POWER OF A STATISTICAL TEST OF SIGNIFICANCE increases in proportion as the number of failures to reject the false hypothesis decreases.—*Cp.* **operating characteristic.**

power of a test: see **power function.**

power/social: the ability or authority to control other persons, to obtain their obedience, to compel their actions.

power spectrum: (*aud.*) the graph of mean-square amplitude (see **amplitude 3**) against frequency of a sound wave. ➤This is especially useful in evaluating the intensity of a mixed sound or noise.

power test: see **test/power.**

p, q: (*stat.*) the relative frequencies of two complementary classes, so that $p + q = 1$.

PR = percentile rank (see **percentile**).

practical: *adj.* **1.** pertaining to that which works, to that which serves social, utilitarian, or ethical values. **2.** manifested in the actual performance of something. **3.** not merely theoretical; closely related to tangible fact. ➤*Distg. fr.* PRACTICABLE, which means capable of being performed or carried through: a scheme may be *practical* (related to tangible fact) but not PRACTICABLE (not possible of execution).

practice: *n.* **1.** the occurrence of a specifiable response or group of responses in the presence of a specifiable stimulus situation. The greater the number of occurrences, the greater the practice. ➤This definition equates practice with **behavior** or **act,** on the grounds that no operational difference can be found. **2.** performance of an act one or more times, with a view to its fixation or improvement. ➤This is the usual usage. It does not specify who wants the improvement (the learner or the experimenter) or in what the improvement consists. **3.** any performance of an act or behavior that leads to learning. ➤This usage is logically unavailable to those who define **learning** as the correlate of practice. **4.** (*pop.*) a habitual act: it is my *practice* to rise early. —*Cp.* **repetition.**—*v.* practice, practise, to perform repeatedly with a view to improvement.—*Cp.* **exercise.**

practice curve: a graphic representation of improvement in a function with successive practice periods. ➤The abscissa should represent time, the spacing of the practice periods being marked by points on the curve.—*Syn.* **learning curve, performance curve** (*prefd.*).

practice/distributed: in learning, an arrangement whereby the periods of practice are spaced out as widely as the total available time permits. ➤In PROGRESSIVE DISTRIBUTION, the separation is at first short and becomes increasingly long. *Cp.* spaced *practice, a similar but not the same design.—*Syn.* DISTRIBUTED REPETITION, DISTRIBUTED LEARNING.—*Ant.* massed *practice.

practice effect: the change that follows

practice. ➤The term is usually employed when the practice effect is not itself what is at issue, but is something to be eliminated or allowed for. E.g., different amounts of practice effect may invalidate a test.

practice limit: the point beyond which further practice brings no further change in performance. ➤The limit is not temporary, as in the **plateau**, though it may be passed when the organism has developed to a higher capacity. This term avoids theoretical implications and is more descriptive than the more usual **physiological** *limit; it is therefore preferred.

practice/massed: the arrangement of periods for learning with little or no interval between the successive presentations or practices.—*Cp.* distributed *practice, spaced *practice.

practice material: preliminary task problems set in order to orient the subject to the nature of a test or experiment. ➤Usually the problems are easy and the solution fairly obvious. The purpose is to demonstrate how to proceed, or to put the subject at ease.—*Cp.* **icebreaker.**

practice/negative: the learning of correct performance by stressing practice of errors. —See **Alpha, Beta, Gamma hypotheses.**

practice period: 1. an opportunity for preliminary rehearsal of a performance, so that the subject knows what is expected of him. **2.** a period for learning or for **practice (2)** in a learning experiment.

practice/spaced: practice in which there is a considerable time interval between successive performances.—*Ant.* massed *practice. ➤Spaced practice is not quite the same as **distributed** *practice, which properly refers to a spacing as wide as the total available time permits.—*Syn.* SPACED LEARNING, SPACED REPETITION.

practice theory of play: 1. the doctrine that play is an innately provided rehearsal for important adult actions. ➤This doctrine is no longer taken seriously but it affects the acceptance of the following: **2.** the generalization that a young animal has opportunity in play for the practice of skills and abilities that will later be of **adaptive** value. ➤This generalization avoids saying that this is *why* the child plays; it may be why adults approve and facilitate certain kinds of play.

prae-: *var.* of **pre-,** as in *dementia praecox.* **praecox** = **precox.**

Praegnanz/law of = **precision/law of.**

pragmatic: *adj.* **1.** interested in practical outcomes, rather than in processes; disinclined to dogmatism or elaborate theorizing. **2.** (*info. theory*) pertaining to aspects of **messages** that concern the sender or recipient.—*Cp.* **pragmatics.**

pragmatics: *n.* (*C. Morris*) the study of the relation of **signs** to the users of signs, both receivers and senders. ➤E.g., the study of propaganda is very largely a study of the different kinds of effects produced by different verbal signs (i.e., language): the word *comrade* formerly produced a favorable response but in recent years has been degraded to a political vilification. In DESCRIPTIVE PRAGMATICS the signs a person uses are studied as a clue to his character.

pragmatism: *n.* **1.** the philosophical doctrine that the meaning of anything derives from its practical consequences, that action is the test of truth. **2.** the tendency to be **pragmatic (1).**

Prägnanz (präg'näns): *n.* (*Ger.*) pregnance (see **precision/law of**).

praise: *n.* the expression of sincere approval of a person or of his deed or product. ➤*Contr. w.* FLATTERY, insincere expression of approval.—*Ant.* blame.

-praxia: combining form meaning *action* or *doing.*

praxiology: *n.* **1.** psychology considered as the scientific study of **acts, behaviors,** or deeds. ➤It does not, like behaviorism (at least in its earlier form), deny or entirely exclude consideration of **mental processes:** it considers them as among the antecedent conditions of acts or behavior. But, unlike **mentalism,** it does not make these processes the defining subject matter of psychology.—*Near syn.* neobehaviorism. **2.** that portion of psychology devoted to the study of behavior in relation to values (moral, religious, logical, social, esthetic); the study of **conduct.**

praxis: *n.* a system of procedures adopted and made conventional for the accomplishment of practical results.

prayer: *n.* any action designed to bring the individual into effective relation with deity: petition, communion, adoration, and thanksgiving.

pre-: prefix meaning *before,* with reference to time, location, or rank: *preadolescence.*—*Var.* prae- (esp. *Brit.*).

preadolescence: *n.* **1.** the arbitrarily distinguished period of age 10 to 12.—*Syn.* LATE CHILDHOOD. **2.** the two years before puberty. ➤This is a variable period and can be determined for a given child only after it is over.—See **development/levels of.**

precenter: *v.* to provide the subject with a point of fixation near the center of the field of regard in which a stimulus object is to be presented.

précis (prä·sē'): *n.* a brief summary of the leading ideas of a book or article, utilizing the words of the author so far as possible.

precise: *adj.* sharply and definitely delimited; cut off exactly at the places intended; not vague; strictly conforming to a rule or definition.—*n.* **precision, preciseness.**

preciseness: see **precision (1).**

precision: *n.* **1.** making precise; or the state or quality of being precise. ➤Properly, precision is *making precise,* PRECISENESS is the quality of *being precise,* but the distinction is often not observed. **2.** fineness of measurement; measurement using very small units of measurement: an instrument of *precision.*—See **accuracy** for comparison with **reliability, correctness,** and **accuracy.**—See also **precision/index of. 3.** (*Gestalt*) the extent to which a pattern of experience or behavior (i.e., a **gestalt**) shows clearness and definiteness, directedness and economy, stability and strength.— See **precision/law of.**

precision alternative: (*Ror.*) an alternative response to inkblots, offered by the subject, as though he considers it more precise than the one he has just given.

precision/index of or *h*: a measure of the closeness with which a series of measures

clusters about the **mean:** $h = \dfrac{1}{\sigma\sqrt{2}}$ · ➤The

name derives from the fact that if the mean is taken as the true value, *h* measures the precision with which the several measures approach this true value. 'When *h* is large, the σ is small and the frequency curve is tall and narrow; when *h* is small, the curve is low and broad.

precision/law of: (*Gestalt*) the most general law of the organization of experience or behavior. It holds that a **gestalt** tends, to the extent that conditions permit, to become sharply defined or precise, stable, strong, regular, symmetrical, simple, meaningful, and parsimonious. ➤The different adjectives are conceived as only so many ways of depicting one basic property of a gestalt, that of PREGNANCE (often spelled as in *Ger.* PRAEGNANZ or PRÄGNANZ).—*Syn.* LAW OF PREGNANCE (or of PRAEGNANZ).

precocity: *n.* unusually early or rapid development or maturation.—*adj.* **precocious, precox.**

precoding: *n.* the advance assignment of code symbols, usually numbers, to the different kinds of expected response that are to be analyzed. ➤E.g., the numbers 1, 2, or 3 might arbitrarily be assigned to the reported ages on an inquiry form, 1 meaning a child (less than age 13), 2 an adolescent, 3 an adult.

precognition: *n.* (*parapsych.*) **cognition** of a future event that could not be known through rational inference.

preconception: *n.* a notion, view, or theory formulated in advance of gathering facts. ➤It is usually implied that the preconception is not given up when the facts are in,

or that it influences the gathering or interpretation of the facts. It is more general than **prejudice,** which implies valuation.— *adj.* **preconceived.**—*v.* **preconceive.**

preconditioning/sensory: an experimental design in which two stimuli (between which there is no **stimulus *generalization**) are repeatedly presented consecutively, after which the animal is conditioned to respond in some specific way to the second. Sensory preconditioning is shown if the first *S* now elicits the **CR.**— *Cp.* **pseudoconditioning.**

preconscious: *adj.* (*psychoan.*) not present in consciousness at a given moment, but recallable more or less readily when wanted. —*Syn.* FORECONSCIOUS.—*Cp.* **unconscious.**

precox (prē'koks): *adj.* **1.** (*L., undercooked, parboiled*) precocious; developing early.— *Var.* **praecox.**—*n.* **2.** = **dementia praecox.**

predelay reinforcement or **reward:** a variation of the **delayed-response** experiment in which the animal is rewarded (e.g., by food) in a certain place, then is prevented for varying periods from returning to that place. The test of learning is whether the animal will return to that place after the delay. ➤The original delayed-response experiment might be called POSTDELAY REWARD DESIGN.

predelinquent: *n.* one whose present behavior is somewhat antisocial so that a prediction of **delinquency** is reasonable unless something is done to head it off.

predetermine: *v.* **1.** to take steps to assure a certain outcome, not leaving it to chance. **2.** to formulate what a result is to be, in advance and on the basis of little or no evidence but with some guidance from analogous instances.—*Syn.* (for **2**) PRECONCEIVE.—*Distg. fr.* FORECAST or PREDICT, which imply the possession of more evidence.

predicate thinking: acting as if objects were identical because they resemble each other in some important respect—i.e., because they share the same predicate. ➤It is as if a person were to say: "I can eat *this* red fruit. *That* fruit is red; I can eat it too." Psychoanalysts hold that the **id** thinks predicatively; for the id, any object that *resembles* a **phallus** *is* a phallus. Predicate thinking is thus the basis for symbolism; a **symbol** may escape the **censorship** and be accepted in consciousness while also satisfying the id's instinctual demands.

predication: *n.* **1.** (*logic, gram.*) the linking of a predicate with a subject; the ascribing of a certain attribute to the subject of a proposition. E.g., the assertion that "imitation is a learned phenomenon" links *imitation* (the subject) with *learned phenomenon* (the predicate). **2.** (*psychol.*) all the processes entering into the making of a predication in the logical sense. ➤There is no implication that these are the same from one proposition to another. The processes by which one comes to the predication "this is heavier" may be totally different from those which lead to "this is morally excellent."—*Distg. fr.* **prediction.** —*Syn.* **judgment, conception;** but **predication** is somewhat more general, since it may include **implicit** judging processes. —*adj.* **predicate** (pred'i·kit), **predicative** (-kā"tiv).—*v.* **predicate** (-kāt).

predictability: see **predictive efficiency.**

prediction: *n.* a statement about an event not yet observed, detailing what will be found when it is observed. ➤Prediction presumes a considerable amount of factual knowledge relevant to the unobserved event, and of the general principles of nature that bear upon the case. Correct prediction is generally considered to be the test of validity of a scientific conclusion or law. *Contr. w.* **preconceive** and **predetermine.** See also **forecasting efficiency/index of.**— *Syn.* FORECAST.—*v.* **predict.**

prediction/differential: prediction, on the basis of **empirical** evidence, of a certain outcome rather than one or more other stipulated outcomes; esp., such a prediction based on a set of test scores: e.g., prediction of B-level academic work rather than A- or C-level; prediction that a certain person will be diagnosed manic rather than schizoid.

predictive efficiency: a measure of the proportion of correct predictions that a test, a general rule, or a law makes possible. ➤E.g., a certain test for college admission may make possible 60 per cent of correct predictions of academic success.—*Distg. fr.* PREDICTABILITY, which is a property of a particular *event.* Thus, the predictability of John Doe's academic success may be held to be high or low, depending on how much we know about him and the college.—See **false negative, forecasting efficiency/ index of.**

predictive index = forecasting efficiency/ index of.

predictive value = validity.

predisposing cause: a factor not strictly necessary to the occurrence of an event but one that (*a*) makes it occur more frequently, (*b*) makes it occur more intensely or energetically, or (*c*) acts as a substitute for some other factor in the usual causal pattern.

predisposition: *n.* 1. = **disposition.** 2. a gene-determined characteristic favoring the development or acquisition of a certain trait or quality, esp. a disease.—*Syn.* **genotype,** slightly different in meaning, but more in line with scientific knowledge of heredity.

pre-established harmony: the doctrine that mental and physiological events run independent courses, neither affecting the other, but maintaining parallel courses because Providence has ordained it so.—*Cp.* **mind-body problem.**

preference: *n.* 1. the turning toward, or accepting, one **stimulus object** rather than another. ➤Preference is shown by doing the one thing sooner, more often, or with more vigor or zeal (but not always better). 2. a liking for one person or thing over another.—*v.* **prefer.**

preference method: a procedure in which two stimuli differing in only one character (e.g., in intensity, size, or sensory quality) are presented in such a way that the animal (without preceding differential training) is allowed to choose one or the other.—*Syn.* PREFERENCE PROCEDURE (*prefd.*).

preference test: see **Kuder Preference Record.**

preformism: *n.* the doctrine that organismic development is but the unfolding of certain patterns or powers, present in rudimentary and latent form from the start. ➤In its earlier form, the doctrine (sometimes called PREFORMATION) supposed that all structures of the mature organism were present in the seed: the acorn literally contained the oak in little.—*Contr. w.* **genetic continuity, epigenesis.**

prefrontal: *adj.* pertaining to the anterior portion of the frontal lobes of the cerebrum.

prefrontal leucotomy or **lobotomy:** see **lobotomy.**

prefrontal lobectomy: see **lobectomy.**

pregenital phase or **stage:** (*psychoan.*) a period in infancy, preceding the dominance of the **genital zone,** when **libido** is turned to oral and anal satisfactions. An adult may regress to this stage, or its remnants may affect adult behavior.—*Cp.* **perversion/infantile polymorphous.**—*Syn.* PREGENITALITY.

pregnance: see **precision/law of.**

pregnancy: *n.* the sheltering of an embryo in the uterus of a vertebrate female.—*adj.* **pregnant.**

pregnant: *adj.* 1. pertaining to **pregnancy.** 2. characterizing a **gestalt** that shows **pregnance.**

prehensile: *adj.* capable of grasping an object: the monkey's *prehensile* tail; the ape's *prehensile* foot.—*n.* **prehension.**—*v.* **prehend.**

prehension: *n.* 1. the act of taking hold of an object or grasping it. ➤In the human infant the gradual refinement of prehension is considered one of the most significant signs of development. 2. (*rare*) a simple grasping of a sensory quality, percept, or idea; the simplest or most primitive mode of cognition; simple **apprehension.**

prehension/pincer (pin'sər): grasping a small object with thumb and fingers opposed.

prejudice: *n.* **1.** a favorable or unfavorable belief or judgment, made without adequate evidence and not easily alterable by the presentation of contrary evidence. **2.** a particular **attitude** or **sentiment** that inclines or predisposes the individual to act, think, perceive, and feel in ways that are congruent with a favorable or (more often) an unfavorable judgment about another person or object. **3.** failure or refusal to consider a person's own individual qualities, reacting to him instead as if he possessed the qualities (esp. the unfavorable ones) that rightly or wrongly are attributed to his social group: race *prejudice,* ethnic *prejudice,* class *prejudice,* etc. ➤*Cp.* PRECONCEPTION, which lacks the emotional connotation of **prejudice** and need not be a valuative judgment.—*Syn.* BIAS, which emphasizes the distortion of **cognition** rather than of feeling but is otherwise interchangeable with **prejudice (1)** or **(2).** Because prejudice is so emotionally loaded a term, it is suggested that FAVORABLE or UNFAVORABLE ATTITUDE be substituted, with other adjectives such as *fixed* or *rigid* if needed.

preliterate culture or **society** = **nonliterate** culture or society (*prefd.*).

prelogical thinking: a mode of thinking that does not follow the standard rules of logic but has a sort of logic of its own. ➤It is said to characterize the thinking of children, so-called primitive peoples, and certain psychotics. It seems probable that what is called prelogical is merely ignorant or *non*logical thinking (consisting, e.g., of **associational** processes).

premature: *n.* a vertebrate animal born before the end of the normal period of pregnancy; in human beings, a viable fetus delivered before the end of the normal gestation period. ➤An infant weighing less than five pounds or delivered earlier than 270 days after the presumed date of conception is judged premature.

premenstrual tension = **molimina/premenstrual.**

premise (prem'əs): *n.* (*logic*) a proposition that forms part of the basis upon which a conclusion rests.—See **syllogism.**—*Var.* **premiss.**—*v.* premise (pri·mīz').

prenatal: *adj.* prior to birth.—*Ant.* **postnatal.**

prenatal behavior: **1.** movements of the fetus. **2.** fetal responses to specified stimuli.

prenatal influence: any factor that affects the development of the fetus. ➤To be *distg. fr.,* but often confused with, INFLUENCE OF MATERNAL IMPRESSIONS, the discredited doctrine that a mother's experiences, ideas, or feelings *directly* influence the fetus.

prenubile: *adj.* **1.** of the whole period of life before **puberty.**—*Distg. fr.* **prepuberal,** which refers to the two or three years immediately prior. **2.** nonmarriageable because of immaturity.

pre-Oedipal (prē·ed'ə·pəl; -ē'də-): *adj.* of behavior that antedates the **Oedipus** conflict.

pre-Oedipal stage: the period in early infancy when the child's love is given almost exclusively to the mother.—See **Oedipus.**

preparation: *n.* **1.** the first part of a complex action; making ready. **2.** (*G. Wallas*) the stage in creative thinking during which the thinker obtains information, skills, and techniques that later come to fruition in what he creates or invents. ➤*Cp.* the other stages described by Wallas: **incubation, illumination, verification.**

preparatory interval: the time between a "ready" or warning signal and the presentation of a stimulus.

preparatory response: any response, related to a goal activity, that does not directly bring satisfaction.—*Contr. w.* **consummatory response.**

preparatory set: see **set/preparatory.**

prepercept: *n.* that of which one is aware in **preperception** (usually in sense **2**).

preperception: *n.* **1.** (*W. McDougall*) perceptual *set* (*prefd.*). **2.** an anticipatory image or idea of what is to be perceived. ➤Such an idea functions as one form of **perceptual *set,*** but the latter is more general. **3.** the beginning stage in the unfolding of a perceptual process, when details are vague and not yet ordered. ➤It is difficult to report directly what is taking place in this stage. But by making the field ambiguous or difficult, preperception may be prolonged and the elicited responses may yield clues to what is being perceived. This is taken advantage of in the study of **perceptual *defense.***—*v.* **preperceive.**

prepotent response: a response that takes precedence over another when the appropriate stimuli to both are present. E.g., a protective response, such as flinching from pain, generally takes precedence over an ordinary voluntary movement.

prepotent stimulus: see **stimulus/prepotent.**

prepsychotic: *adj.* characterizing behavior that is symptomatic of a threatened **psychosis;** or, a person whose behavior leads one to believe that he is likely to become psychotic.

prepuberal stage: the transitional period between childhood and adolescence; the one or two years preceding the **puberal** stage. ➤Phase is often incorrectly used for **stage**

—*Syn.* **preadolescence,** PREPUBESCENCE, PREPUBERTY, PREPUBERTAL STAGE.

prerecognition hypothesis: an unverbalized expectation of what is about to be perceived. ➤The hypothesis or **expectancy** is supposed to be generated by previous experiences in similar situations. Its existence is inferred from differences in behavior.

presby-: combining form denoting *old age.*

presbyophrenia (prez″bi·ō·frē'ni·ə): *n.* a form of **senile psychosis** in which apparent mental alertness combines with grave memory defects.—*adj.* **presbyophrenic** (-fren'ik).

presbyopia (-ō'pi·ə): *n.* a defect of vision with advancing age, due chiefly to hardening of the lens of the eye. ➤Near vision is affected much more than far vision, thus often making bifocal lenses advisable. But it is a misunderstanding to believe that distance vision is better: it, too, is worse. Hence, *distg. fr.* **hyperopia.**

preschizophrenia / coarctated or **/ inhibited:** a mode of behavior characterized by **blocking, withdrawal,** marked **anxiety,** feelings of strangeness, incompetence, extreme **inhibition** of **affect,** and some kinds of sexual preoccupation. It is regarded as symptomatic of a beginning **schizophrenia.**

preschool: *n.* an institution for the education of young children deemed not yet ready for the formalized program of the first grade. Almost no attention is given to **tool subjects:** emphasis is upon personal and social development and health habits. It includes nursery school and kindergarten.

presentation: *n.* 1. any form of placing something before a person for understanding: the teacher's *presentation* of the theory of gravitation. ➤**Presentation** was the second of Herbart's Five Formal Steps in Teaching. 2. the act of bringing a stimulus into effective relation with the subject in a psychological experiment; exposing a stimulus object so that the subject senses, perceives, or otherwise reacts psychologically. 3. the material used as stimuli in an experiment: e.g., the pattern of dots being shown in a tachistoscope, the salts being tasted, the sequence of three tones being listened to. 4. = **object** (2). 5. the aspects of a thing as known. 6. the particular thing or object known in **perceiving.** 7. (*psychoan.*) the way in which an instinctual drive expresses itself: it is the instinct plus some vehicle of expression. ➤E.g., a person dreads sharp instruments. The instruments are the presentation by which a dread (which may actually have nothing to do with ordinary cutting) expresses itself.

presentiment: *n.* a vague expectation or foreboding of a coming event.

present/psychological: a brief interval, a single or undivided "now" of experience;

the duration of a single experience. ➤The *present* of objective time—the time measured by clocks—is a line between past and present and has no "thickness," i.e., duration. The psychological present has duration, though brief.—*Syn.* (*philos.*) SPECIOUS PRESENT.

press: *n., pl.* **press** or **presses:** (*H. A. Murray*) stimuli or stimulus objects that (for a given person) more or less regularly constitute a unit because the separate parts mean the same thing or are aspects of the same thing, and are reacted to as a unified object. ➤A given press may, under other circumstances, be made up of less inclusive presses. Thus, for a child, "school" constitutes a unified set of experiences and is called "press-school." But part of the school press may be "arithmetic" as a distinct subpress. ¶The originator of the term prefers *press* for the plural, but this has led to some difficulty.

press-need (pattern): (*H. A. Murray*) the pattern of the **S-R** connections that are subsidiary to a given relation between a **press** and a **need.** ➤E.g., a child may "need" to surpass in schoolwork (the press). He may, according to circumstances, study hard, try to get help from the teacher, bluff, or cheat. These form the press-need pattern.

pressor nerve: one that stimulates a **vasomotor** center to heighten blood pressure.

pressure: *n.* 1. a pushing upon, or against, something; exertion of force while in contact. 2. a sensation normally resulting from force applied to the surfaces of the body, esp. to the skin; also, certain other sensations from muscular movement which have the same quality as skin-pressure sensation.—See **pressure sensation.** 3. a complex idea and feeling of being compelled to act, whether or not one wishes to; a tension due to **coercion,** whether by persons or by circumstances.—*Syn.* (for 3) **tension.**

pressure/acoustic: the average force per square centimeter exerted upon an area by a succession of sound waves, usually as measured in **dynes.** ➤For the study of hearing, the acoustic pressure is taken at the eardrum or at the **basilar membrane.**

pressure balance: 1. an instrument for controlling the amount and rate of application of pressure to the skin. 2. an instrument for testing judgments of lifted weights.

pressure gradient: (*psychophysiol.*) the gradual tapering away in all directions from the center that results when an elastic membrane (e.g., the skin) is deformed by a point pressure.

pressure of thought: ideas coming so fast that they crowd upon each other and cannot be verbalized. ➤It is an occasional symptom in **manic** conditions: an idea **is**

barely begun before it is pushed out by another.

pressure sensation: a specific mode of sensing, characteristically experienced when a force is applied to the skin, but also elicited from pressures exerted upon certain specific receptors in the internal organs, the muscles, and the joint surfaces. ➤It is sometimes held that strong and light pressures are qualitatively different. There are a number of different receptors for pressure, but they are believed to yield sensations belonging to the same sensory or qualitative mode. **Kinesthetic** sensations are pressure sensations. It may be noted that sound and light, both measured physically as pressures, are not considered to yield pressure sensations.

pressure spot: any one of a very large number of small areas on the surface of the body that are more sensitive to pressure— i.e., yield pressure sensations at lower stimulus intensity—than neighboring areas.

prestige: *n.* the attribute of being highly regarded by associates so that one's actions strongly influence others. Many factors contribute to prestige—**position, role,** personal relationships, or personal qualities and traits. It may be temporary. It may be general, or specific to certain areas. A successful businessman has prestige in business affairs but should not on that account have it in other matters; but prestige normally tends toward considerable generality.

prestige suggestion: the process by which an opinion is more acceptable, or an incentive more powerful, or a command more readily obeyed, when coming from a person who has **prestige**—i.e., is regarded as trustworthy.

prestriate: *adj.* anterior to the **corpus striatum.**

presumption: *n.* 1. a partially proved conclusion. ➤*Contr. w.* **assumption,** a conclusion held in the absence of proof to the contrary. The distinction is often ignored. 2. arrogance; expecting others to defer to one's opinions or rank.—*adj.* **presumptive** (for 1); **presumptuous** (for 2).

presupposition: *n.* an informal synonym for **postulate.**

pretend: *v.* to act in such a way as to give a false impression about oneself or one's action: to *pretend* to be the person named.— *Syn.* **make believe,** which implies that the false impression is not to be taken seriously. —*n.* **pretense, pretence.**

pretest: *n.* 1. a **practice** test. 2. a test given to determine some kind of performance (individual or group) in advance of administration of training or of some experimental condition. ➤The pretest scores subtracted from the postexperiment (or

ENDTEST) scores yield a measure—if certain conditions are met—of the effect of the experimental condition.

priapism (prī'ə·piz·əm): *n.* persistent abnormal erection of the penis, usually without accompanying sex desire.

pride: *n.* a sentiment of high esteem for one's own ability or status; a sense of one's own worth.—*Distg. fr.* **vanity** and conceit. —See also **egoistic.**

pride/neurotic: (*K. Horney*) irrational and exaggerated pride in one's supposed personal characteristics.—See **pride system.**

pride system: (*K. Horney*) the totality of the neurotically valued and the neurotically hated attributes of the self. ➤The valued attributes may be either nonexistent or exaggerated. The hated attributes are generally real: they are neurotically hated because the hatred is excessive.—*Cp.* **self/idealized.**

primacy: *n.* the condition or fact of being first in any respect.—*adj.* **primary** (which see for distinctions), **prime, primitive, primordial.**

primacy/law of: the hypothesized principle that the first acts in a series tend to be better learned and to show especial resistance to forgetting.

primacy/oral: see **oral primacy.**

primacy/phallic: (*psychoan.*) the concentration of **erotic** interest during one stage of the **pregenital** period upon the **phallus** (for boys, upon the penis; for girls, upon whatever for them is the penis equivalent).

prima facie (prī'mə fā'shi·ē): (*L., at first appearance*) characterizing evidence that seems sound when superficially examined, but about which one desires to reserve judgment.

primal: *adj.* first in time.—See **primary.**

primal horde stage: a hypothetical stage of family organization before the primitive clan stage. It consisted of the dominant male, his females, and his subordinate younger males. ➤The stage is inferred primarily from psychoanalytic, rather than anthropological, evidence.

primal scene: (*psychoan.*) a recollection from childhood, relating to an early sexual experience; or the child's fantasy of intercourse between parents, whether based on observation plus childish misinterpretation or wholly created imaginatively from fragments of observation.

primaries/color: see **color primaries.**

primary: *adj.* first; esp., first in logical rank. ➤From the *L. primus* (first) come several adjectives in common use. Each is likely in certain contexts to steal the distinctive meaning of one of the others. **Primary** is the work-horse or general-duty word meaning *first:* its specific meaning is *first in logical rank.* **Primary** also means *that with which we start,* hence, the simple, the innate, or the basic. PRIMAL means *first in time.* PRIME means *first in importance or quality.* (But see **prime numbers**.) **Primitive** means *simple,* or early in evolution or development. PRIMORDIAL means *first in order,* or of the first eras of the world (the latter also called PRIMEVAL).

primary abilities: the basic units that make up **general ability** or **intelligence.** ➤*Primary,* here, does not mean **innate.**— See **abilities/primary mental.**

primary amentia = **primary feeblemindedness**

primary arithmetical facts = **arithmetic/fundamentals of.**

primary attention: that given without effort, and apparently without having been learned.

primary attitudes: (*sociol.*) those attitudes acquired because of one's membership in a particular **primary *group.**

primary color: see **color primaries.**

primary data: 1. the data as originally collected during an investigation, before being sorted, classified, or summarized. **2.** the data in possession of the original investigator.

primary drive: see **drive/primary.**

primary factor: see **factor/primary.**

primary feeble-mindedness: mental *deficiency for which no cause in the life history of the individual can plausibly be assigned. It is therefore deemed hereditary.— *Syn.* PRIMARY AMENTIA, CONSTITUTIONAL or FAMILIAL or ENDOGENOUS MENTAL DEFICIENCY.

primary hue: see **color primaries.**

primary memory = **memory afterimage** (*prefd.*).

primary mental abilities: see **abilities/primary mental.**

primary position: (*vis.*) the position which the eyes assume when the head and body are erect and the eyes fixate an infinitely distant point in the median and horizontal planes.

primary process: see **process/primary.**

primary qualities: (*hist.*) those properties or attributes of any kind of object without which it does not exist. ➤*Contr. w.* SECONDARY QUALITIES, which are dispensable. E.g., it was said that an apple can be an apple without its *redness* but cannot be an apple without the property of *extension* or space-filling. The distinction has proved both metaphysically and psychologically difficult and is no longer often made.

primary stimulus generalization: see **generalization/stimulus.**

primate: *n.* the highest order of mammals, which includes the Lemuridae (a suborder of monkeylike animals) and the Anthropoidea (a suborder including monkeys, apes, and man).

prime: *adj.* **1.** first in importance or quality. **2.** designating the stroke used to distinguish a symbolic letter: *a',* read *a prime.*—*n.* **3.** = **prime number. 4.** the **fundamental tone,** or first **partial,** of a **clang.**

prime number: a number divisible only by itself or by the number one.

primipara (prī·mip′ə·rə): *n.* a female who has borne offspring only once.—*adj.* **primiparous.**—*n.* **primiparity** (prī″mə·par′-ə·ti).

primitive: *adj.* characterizing the earliest stage of development or evolution; ancient; rude; simple; undeveloped. ➤See **primary** for distinctions from **prime, primordial.** PRIMITIVE PEOPLES are without written history, or without writing. Current usage prefers *preliterate* or, better yet, **nonliterate** peoples, since such peoples are frequently not rude, simple, or undeveloped.

primitive behavior: 1. the actions (if any) peculiar to **nonliterate** peoples. **2.** behavior that resembles man's presumed behavior at earlier stages in his evolution. **3.** that part of man's behavior which has not been subjected to cultural or rational restraint—often equated with the **instinctual.**

primitivization = **regression (2).**

primordial (prī·môr′di·əl): see **primary.**

primordium (prī·môr′di·um): *n.* (*biol.*) the embryonic basis for an organ or bodily part.

principal: *adj.* **1.** outstanding; chief; leading; most important. **2.** characterizing a datum or fact by reference to which other facts are classified or put in order.—*Distg. fr.* **principle.**

principal axis: see **principal component method.**

principal color: see **color principals.**

principal component method: (*factor anal.*) a factor method which locates one axis (the MAJOR PRINCIPAL AXIS) so that it defines a factor which accounts for the maximum possible **variance** of the correlation matrix, and another axis (the MINOR PRINCIPAL AXIS, **orthogonal** to the first) which accounts for the maximum possible of the remaining variance. The term PRINCIPAL COMPONENT is used either for the factor or for the **factor loadings.**

principals/color: see **color principals.**

principle: *n.* **1.** a guiding maxim of conduct. **2.** a **canon** of scientific procedure. **3.** a statement of a uniformity in nature. ➤**Principle** is often used where the uniformity discovered seems for some reason not quite fundamental or not fully enough established to be called a **law.** Psychology has more principles than laws. **4.** the essential constituent of a substance that produces its characteristic effect: the *principle* of a drug.—*Distg. fr.* **principal.**

principle/descriptive: a generalization that is not sufficiently complete to make it acceptable as a scientific explanation but is useful as a guide to further study or to choice of action.

principle of inertia = (*psychoan.*) **repetition-compulsion.**

prior entry/law of: the generalization that of two presentations, both perceived, one attentively and the other inattentively, the former will seem to have been presented measurably sooner. ➤Thus, in the COMPLICATION EXPERIMENT the task is to determine the location of a revolving clock hand (or a pendulum) at the moment a bell is sounded. If the hand (or pendulum) be attended to, the bell relatively attended from, the subject reports the bell sound as occurring later than it does; or vice versa.

priority: *n.* the property of being earlier in time; or, loosely, of being logically more fundamental, or more important.—*Cp.* **primacy.**—*adj.* **prior.**

prism: *n.* (*optics*) a wedge-shaped **lens.** ➤As light passes through the lens it is bent, the short waves more than the long, so that mixed light waves are dispersed or spread out to form a **spectrum.** Prisms of low strength do not cause noticeable dispersion and are used in spectacles to offset the turning away of one eye from normal fixation; the lens bends the rays from the object viewed so that they fall more nearly on the area of optimal vision.—*adj.* **prismal, prismatic.**

prism diopter: (*optics*) the strength of a prism measured by 100 times the tangent of the angle through which the light rays are bent by the lens.

private: *adj.* **1.** of an individual, not of a group. **2.** of that which is peculiar to a given person; belonging to a person. **3.** not open to observation by anyone else. ➤This is one meaning of **subjective. 4.** not governmental; unofficial.

privation: *n.* lack, esp. involuntary lack, of the means to satisfaction of a need. ➤*Cp.* **deprivation,** the loss or taking away of such means; and **frustration,** the blocking (usually by another person) of a goal-directed activity that has begun.

privilege: *n.* **1.** access to the means of satisfying motives or desires. **2.** = SPECIAL PRIVILEGE, an unfair advantage obtained by exploitation or fraud, or sanctioned because of one's status, role, or power.

proactive: *adj.* characterizing a stimulus or a process that affects a subsequent related process. ➤*Cp.* **retroactive,** characterizing a process that modifies the effect of an earlier one. In the sequence ABC, the effect of B upon C is proactive, its effect upon the results of A is retroactive. In the literal sense, every stimulus and every process must be considered proactive, but the term is reserved for future effects upon *related* (or presumably related) processes.—*Cp.* **inhibition/proactive.**

probabilism: *n.* the doctrine that it is possible with some degree of probability to predict certain sequences of events on the basis of past experience and by means of logical operations. ➤Probabilism is the general statement of a principle of which **determinism** is a highly special case. The latter is the belief in perfect predictability when all relevant facts are known, the former a belief in the possibility of degrees of predictability depending on the degree of relevant information.—See **psychology/divisions and schools of,** V.—*adj.* **probabilistic.**

probabilistic cue learning: (*E. Brunswik*) the view that during learning a given stimulus or **cue** becomes capable of evoking not one response but a set of responses, each having its own probability of being evoked by that cue.

probabilistic hypothesis: (*E. Brunswik*) the postulate that correctness of perceiving does not mean that action in accord with the perception will be adaptive, but only that it will *probably* be so. ➤In the long run, a correct (or veridical) percept can be relied on. In general, e.g., what looks straight can safely be treated as straight, and vice versa. Not so the illusory or incorrect. The straight stick in the water producing the bent-stick illusion cannot safely be reacted to as it appears. Illusion is the exception to a statistical probability.

probabilities/complementary: the probability of a given event's happening and the probability of that event's not happening. —Symbolized by $p + q = 1$.

probability: *n.* **1.** (*math.*) the likelihood of the occurrence of an event, estimated as a ratio between the number of ways in which the event may occur and the number of ways in which alternative events may occur. ➤E.g., a die may fall equally well with any of the six faces up. Thus, the total number of ways in which it can fall is 6. The ace can turn up in only 1 way. Its probability is 1 in 6.—*Distg. fr.* **likelihood,** which is the degree to which a hypothesis is confirmable by facts. **2.** the quality of being **probable;** or the degree to which something is probable: some degree of *probability* attaches to any estimate of a future event. ➤A rough scale of *probability* extends from *impossibility,* through bare *possibility, high improbability, probability,* to *certainty.* **3.** a measure of the reasonableness of a belief. **4.** = **probability theory.** ➤The relationship of mathematical **probability** to psychological probability is very intricate. In general, psychologists are more interested in mathematical probability, which they use in calculations.—*adj.* **probable.**

probability chart or **table:** a table setting forth the frequency with which the several values of a variable occur.—See **frequency.**

probability/compound = joint *probability.**

probability/conditional: the relative frequency with which one event occurs when a certain other event occurs.—*Syn.* CONTINGENT PROBABILITY.

probability/contingent = **probability/conditional.**

probability curve: when not qualified = **normal *frequency curve.**

probability distribution = **frequency** distribution.

probability function: the relation that is graphed in the **normal *frequency curve.** —See **frequency curve equation.**

probability integral: 1. (*math.*) the **integral** of the **probability function.** 2. the area under the **normal *frequency curve** between any two given abscissa values. ➤This includes the case where the two abscissa values are the ends of the distribution so that the whole area is measured.

probability/joint: the relative frequency of a joint event that includes an event from class i and an event from class j, both classes forming part of a **probability space.** —*Syn.* COMPOUND PROBABILITY.

probability measure: (*info. theory*) a statement of the frequency with which a given element in an **ensemble** will be found in state x_i of classification x. The probability measure is variously symbolized: $p(x_i)$ or $p(i)$ or p_i.

probability/normal: see **frequency curve/normal** and **frequency.**

probability of a test/discriminating: the proportion of correct to incorrect discriminations or decisions made by using a test: e.g., the proportion of persons correctly categorized for admission or rejection to college on the basis of an **aptitude test.**—See **false negative; power of a *test.**

probability of response: the average frequency of occurrence of instances of a class of responses, relative to the maximum possible frequency of any response under a specified set of stimulus conditions.

probability ratio: the number of circumstances under which a given event will occur, divided by the total number of circumstances in a certain defined set: written p/q.

probability space or Ω: a system of events, defined, and divided into a finite number of subclasses, S, with each defined and its probability of occurrence, $p(i)$, estimated.

probability theory: 1. the mathematical treatment of **probability**; the science of measuring or predicting chances. ➤The theory is based on the postulate of the uniformity of nature, the mutual cancellation of opposite errors of observation if enough cases are taken, etc. 2. an ellipsis for PROBABILITY THEORY OF LEARNING: any theory using the mathematical theory of probability to explain learning.

probable: *adj.* 1. worthy of belief; of a proposition or belief having (or seeming to have) a preponderance of evidence for its truth. 2. of an event more likely to happen than not.—See **probability.**

probable error or **P.E., PE, p.e.:** a measure of the **variability** of a measure; the extent to which the obtained values deviate from the measure in question; a measure of the error of **sampling.** ➤The P.E. is .6745 of the **standard error,** and is less often used than the latter. In a normal distribution, half of the **deviations** from a measure fall within the range of that measure plus or minus P.E.; thus, an error of measurement or sampling within the range of ±P.E. is as likely to occur as not.—*Syn.* PROBABLE DISCREPANCY, PROBABLE DEVIATION.

probation: *n.* giving a person a chance to prove his ability to meet certain requirements, whether of achievement or of conformity to social regulation. ➤Probation usually follows a failure and implies a suspension of the normal penalties for failure.

probit analysis: (*stat.*) a method that uses **probability theory** to analyze all-or-nothing responses.

problem: *n.* a situation in which, knowing certain of the elements, it is desired or required that the others be ascertained. ➤The situation may be a "practical" one, the unknown elements the necessary **adaptive** responses. For this, **task** is a synonym. A true solution to a problem implies more than ready-made or automatic responses or the operation of rote memory. *Distg. fr.* PUZZLE, in which almost none of the elements required for solution are at first known to the respondent.—*adj.* **problematic(al).**

problematic(al): *adj.* of uncertain or doubtful validity or outcome; pertaining to a **problem.**

problem behavior: 1. behavior that perplexes the observer (sometimes also the person behaving). 2. behavior that is at least somewhat antisocial or abnormal and, hence, creates a problem either for the actor or for those about him. ➤*Distg. fr.* BEHAVIOR PROBLEM, a *person* who persistently displays problem behavior.—See **problem child.**

problem box: a box that must be opened to obtain a certain reward. Its fastenings are such as to present a **problem,** if not a complete puzzle, to the animal working on it.

The SKINNER BOX is a problem box standardized for use with small mammals.

problem check list: a self-report form on which a person is presented with brief characterizations of the kinds of situations or problems that often give rise to concern (spending money, appearance, adjustment to opposite sex, academic or vocational achievement, etc.) and is asked to check those items he feels to be especially pressing for him.

problem child: one whose conduct differs from socially acceptable standards so greatly that he cannot be dealt with by "common sense" or the usual techniques. ➤Misbehavior is usually, but not always, implied. All children manifest problem behavior at times and are problems to those who deal with them; but not all children are problem children.—*Syn.* PROBLEM PERSONALITY, which includes adults.

problem method: an instructional procedure in which learning is provoked by supplying challenging problems.

problem personality: an individual who does not adjust well to his social circumstances, who gives trouble to his associates. —*Distg. fr.* **personality problem.**—*Cp.* **problem child.**

problem-solving: the process of selecting from a number of alternatives those that lead to a desired goal.

procedure: *n.* the manner of controlling all the relevant conditions in order to elicit a given phenomenon or to elicit it in varying strengths or frequencies. ➤The term, though general, is especially used for the experimental control of conditions. It is restricted to control related to a particular class of phenomena.—*Cp.* **method.**

proceeding: *n.* (*H. A. Murray*) a single (but usually complex) subject-object or subject-subject interaction of sufficient duration to include the significant elements of a given sequence of behaviors; a dynamically significant pattern of behavior having a determinable beginning and end. ➤In a given case it may be difficult to determine beginning and end, and one proceeding may overlap another. Murray contends it is the basic datum for psychology.—*Approx. syn.* **act.**

process: *n.* **1.** a change or a changing in an object or organism in which a consistent quality or direction can be discerned. ➤A process is always in some sense active; something is happening. It contrasts with the **structure** or form of organization of what changes, which structure is conceived to be relatively static despite process change. Both physiology and psychology are primarily sciences of process.—*Syn.* **activity, behavior. 2.** the manner in which a change is effected; specif., a change in re-

sponse strength as a result of a particular experimental operation: e.g., extinction *process.*—*Syn.* **function. 3.** (*E. B. Titchener*) a **conscious** *content (which see) observed as an occurrence without reference to its context, meaning, or value. **4.** the physiological activities involved, or believed to be involved, in a particular behavior. ➤Sometimes called the UNDERLYING PROCESS. —*Syn.* PHYSIOLOGICAL ACTIVITY (*prefd.*) or PHYSIOLOGICAL PROCESS. **5.** (*anat.*) a relatively slender projection from an organ. **6.** (*K. Lewin*) any psychological means whereby tensions in distinct parts of a system become equalized. A process may be a perceiving, a thinking, a feeling or an acting.

process attitude: (*structural psychol.*) the attitude in which the **introspective** observer gives attention to and describes **processes** in sense **(3).**—*Contr. w.* **object attitude.**

process/constant: see **constant process.**

process error: an error introduced into data in the process of producing, measuring, recording, or computing.—*Contr. w.* **sampling** *error.**

process/learning: see **learning process.**

process/primary: (*psychoan.*) the process, located in the **id,** by which there is immediate and direct satisfaction of an **instinctual** wish; or that aspect of conscious activity which represents it. ➤It is supposed that the id does not discriminate between **image** and reality; hence, in the absence of an immediately satisfying object or situation, an imaginary satisfaction is produced. Not being oriented toward reality, the satisfaction is only temporary. The laws governing the primary process are different from those of consciousness. They are known chiefly from the study of dreams, which are wish-fulfilling primary processes—or, rather, they are the reflection of such processes in consciousness.— See **condensation, displacement, secondary** *process.*—*Syn.* PRIMAL PROCESS (*prefd.*).

process/secondary: (*psychoan.*) conscious activity; action guided by objective realities; activity in the **preconscious** or **ego;** or such activities taken collectively. ➤*Contr. w.* **process/primary,** PRIMAL PROCESS (*prefd.*). Secondary the process may be, yet civilization is its product. The related term, **reality principle,** has more accurate implications.

process variable/hypothetical: a **hypothetical** *construct referring to an actual, though presently unobservable, inferred activity or process that is conceived to have properties and/or effects other than those leading to its being inferred. ➤E.g., the **censorship** of psychoanalysis is conceived as a process or activity that accounts for certain behaviors (or lack of behavior). But this censorship process, if it truly exists as inferred, must be supposed to have other, predictable effects than those which lead to its being inferred. **Drive** is also an example.—*Contr. w.* **state variable/hypothetical,** which is conceived as a relatively stable intervening condition.—See **construct/hypothetical.**—*Syn.* INTERVENING PROCESS VARIABLE (not *recom.*).

procreation: *n.* the biological processes of sexual reproduction.

procreation/family of: see **family.**

prodigy: *n.* a person who manifests any spectacular trait or quality, esp. an outstanding ability either special or general. Popularly, the term has come to mean almost exclusively a person showing exceptional ability at an early age: i.e., a precocious prodigy.

prodrome (prō'drōm): *n.* an early or warning symptom of a disease or disorder.—*adj.* **prodromal** (prod'rō·məl).

production procedure: an experimental procedure in which the *O* operates certain controls to modify the stimulus to accord with a prescribed standard. ➤E.g., *O* may move an object forward or back till it is judged equidistant to a certain standard.

production process = objectifying function.

productive memory: see **memory/productive.**

productiveness: *n.* **1.** = **productivity. 2.** that quality of a person's behavior that conduces to his own development and happiness and/or to that of social groups and persons with which he is identified.

productive orientation: in a mentally healthy person, the outlook that permits him to be creative in work and social relations and to use well whatever potentialities he has.

productivity: *n.* a measure of the amount accomplished, esp. of work requiring some originality or adaptability.

product matrix: see **matrix/product.**

product moment: *n.* the sum, or the mean, of the products of paired observations scored as **deviations** from the mean of all the observations of each variable, or from some other measure as origin. ➤The individual's score on one test, taken as the amount his *raw score* departs from the mean of that test, is multiplied by the similarly calculated score for the other test. The products thus obtained for all those tested are summed, or more often averaged, to give the **product moment,** also called **covariance.** For the product-moment correlation coefficient, see **correlation/product-moment.**

product scale: see **scale/product.**

profession: *n.* **1.** an occupation that requires an extensive general and specialized education, that involves many intellectual elements, that has a code of ethics defining certain obligations to society in its practice, that confers considerable social status and power upon those who practice it, and that utilizes all this to effect practical changes in the physical or social world. **2.** the body of practitioners of a **profession** (1).

proficiency: *n.* ability of acceptable degree, generally of high degree, for a kind of task or for a vocation.—See **ability** for many partial synonyms, of which **competence** is the closest.

profile: *n.* a representation of something in outline by a curved or irregular line; esp., a **profile chart** (which see).

profile analysis: a method for appraising individual uniqueness and trait organization, consisting in a search for characteristic patterns in the trait profiles of an individual. —*Cp.* **trait organization, trait profile, pattern analysis.**

profile chart: a curve uniting the points representing an individual's scores or relative position in each of several types of performance, with all scores rendered comparable by statistical treatment. ➤An EDUCATIONAL PROFILE compares the pupil's achievements in several school subjects; a PSYCHIC PROFILE or PSYCHOGRAPH displays his standings in a number of traits.

progeria (prō·jir'i·ə): *n.* a form of dwarfism combining infantile and premature-senility traits.

prognathous (prog'nə·thəs): *adj.* of a skull in which the upper jaw protrudes beyond the plane of the forehead.—*Contr. w.* **orthognathous.**—*n.* **prognathism, prognathy.**

prognosis *n., pl.* **prognoses:** prediction of the duration, course, and outcome of a certain process or activity, esp. of a disease, but also of an individual's academic career (EDUCATIONAL PROGNOSIS), job success (VOCATIONAL PROGNOSIS), etc.—*adj.* **prognostic.** —*v.* **prognose, prognosticate.**

prognostic test: one designed to enable prediction of the kind of achievement attainable under stated conditions.

program: *n.* a plan for action, or for carrying out a task or investigation.

programmatic: *adj.* characterizing a program or **schema,** with detail or elaboration intentionally postponed but with the places for such elaboration indicated.—*Syn.* **schematic.**

programming: *n.* the preparation of a computing machine to perform certain prescribed operations upon the data that are fed into it. ➤Punching the "multiply" key on an ordinary computing machine is a

very simple kind of programming. In more
elaborate electronic computers, each kind
of operation has a numerical code and "instructions" detailing the operations to be
performed on the data are put on tape and
stored in the machine.—*v.* **program.**

progress: *n.* **1.** motion or movement in a
given direction, esp. in the direction of a
desired goal. **2.** change in a structure, organization, institution, or organism that is
considered an improvement.—*Ant.* **regression.**—*adj.* **progressive.**—*v.* **progress.**

progress/age-grade: advancement in school
measured by the ratio of grade attained to
grade expected at the child's age.

progress/grade: the rate of pupils' advance through school grades.—*Cp.* **ac-
celeration/educational.**

progression: *n.* **1.** the act of advancing,
including walking and running. **2.** (*math.*)
a series of terms each of which bears a
constant relation to the preceding. ➤In
ARITHMETIC(AL) PROGRESSION each term is
derived by adding or subtracting a certain
amount from the preceding, in GEO-
METRIC(AL) PROGRESSION by multiplying or
dividing by a certain number (e.g., each
successive number is three times the preceding).

progression/law of: (*J. Delboeuf*) the
generalization that successive increments in
sensation are in an arithmetical **progression** while stimulus increments are in a
geometrical **progression.**➤ This is a re-
formulation of the Weber-Fechner principle (see **Fechner's law**).

progressive: *adj.* **1.** moving forward; advancing. **2.** pertaining to **progress,** to
steady improvement. **3.** increasing in extent or severity, esp. of a disease or disorder. ➤Note that a PROGRESSIVE DISEASE is
opposite in meaning to (**2**).

Progressive Education: when spelled with
capitals, a term for a broadly conceived reform movement, advocating one or more
of the following: the development in pupils of an experimental attitude rather
than indoctrination of them; the acceptance
of subject matter as means rather than as
ends in human development; the recognition of individuality; motivation in school
by relating the school closely with everyday living; the rejection of such culture as
is mere ornament as a proper educational
goal; the development of every aspect of
the pupil's personality as the goal of
education.

Progressive Matrices Test: a test, designed to measure general intelligence, consisting of 60 abstract designs from each of
which a part has been removed. The *S*
chooses the missing insert from six or
eight presented alternatives.

progressive total: a total based on all the

data up to a given time or position in a
series.—*Syn.* **cumulative** total.

project: *n.* a planned undertaking, with a
fairly well-defined field but often without a
fully defined goal.—See **project method.**

projection: *n.* **1.** = **eccentric *projection**
(which see). **2.** the process of unwittingly
attributing one's own traits, attitudes, or
subjective processes to others: e.g., the
child's naïve assumption that adults feel as
he does.—*Syn.* ASSIMILATIVE PROJECTION.—
Cp. **animism. 3.** the process of ascribing
to others one's own unacknowledged desires or faults. ➤This is presumed to be a
defense against a sense of guilt or inadequacy.—*Syn.* DISOWNING PROJECTION. **4.** the
process of perceiving objective stimuli in
line with personal interests, desires, fears,
or expectations. ➤This is most usually displayed when the stimulus or situation is
not clear, and hence personal factors rather
than external reality determine the response.
See **projective test, projective technique. 5.** the reception in spatially separated areas of the cortex (PROJECTION AREAS)
of nerve impulses from the several sense
organs and lower centers.

projection area or **center** = **sensory
area.**

projection/assimilative: see **projection**
(**2**).

projection/disowning: see **projection (3).**

projection/eccentric: localization of a
sense datum at the position in space of the
stimulating object, rather than at the point
of stimulation on the body. ➤Visual sense
data are habitually projected: the pink is
seen as on the rose petal, not as on the
retina. Sounds also are usually projected.
Smells, however, have an indefinite localization. With the sense of touch, the stimulating
object is usually at the point of bodily stimulation so there can be no projection; but
when an object is explored with a pliant
rod, the resulting data are usually projected
to the object at the end of the rod instead
of being perceived in the hand.—*Cp.*
stimulus error.

projection fibers: nerves leading into and
away from **sensory areas.**

projection/optical: 1. forming an image of
an object by means of an optical instrument, e.g., a motion picture projector. **2.**
the locus of the localizations in outer space
corresponding with the image on the retina
as determined by the refractive apparatus
of the eye—i.e., the places in space which
would produce the image, given the kind of
refraction of the particular eye.—*Distg. fr.*
projection/visual.

projection/play: see **play projection.**

projection/visual: the process of attributing a spatial location to a viewed object.
➤This location usually is not exactly the

same as the **optical** *projection and sometimes differs markedly.—*Syn.* **localization.**
Projective-Movement-Sequences Test: a
projective test using motion pictures of
various bodily movements, to be described
or interpreted by the subject.
projective technique: a procedure for discovering a person's characteristic modes of
behavior (his attitudes, motivations, or
dynamic traits) by observing his behavior in
response to a situation that does not elicit
or compel a particular response—i.e., to a
relatively unstructured, ambiguous, or vague
situation. ➤Thus, a child's response to an
empty sheet of paper and colored crayons
may reveal his emotional mood or his more
enduring sentiments. The man reminded by
a glorious sunset to tell his wife to have
bacon for breakfast is presumably revealing certain aspects of personality. If the
situation is a standard one, **projective tests**
are spoken of. See also **play projection.**
projective test: a relatively unstructured,
yet **standard,** situation to which a testee is
asked to respond, but with as few restrictions as possible upon the mode of response. ➤E.g., a picture of clouds may be
shown with the request: "Tell me about
this." It is postulated that, since the situation and directions do not specify the response, one's enduring propensities, or one's
current mood, will determine the response.
Inkblots, cloud pictures, cartoons, vaguely
defined pictures, incomplete sentences, play
materials, drawing tasks have been used as
materials. Test responses are usually
analyzed for **personality** characteristics,
but they may also reveal certain modes of
cognition. Interpretation of the responses
requires much training.—See also **play
projection.**
projectivity: *n.* (*H. A. Murray*) the tendency to project unconsciously one's own sentiments, emotions, and needs into others;
maintaining wish-engendered beliefs.—*Ant.*
objectivity.
project method: a procedure wherein the
pupil organizes his schoolwork, under guidance, about a relatively complex activity of
immediate interest to himself. Learning the
standard school subjects is, for the most
part, incidental to carrying on this activity. (E.g., arithmetic may be learned by
playing store or by planning a picnic menu
and buying food therefor.) Both group
and individual activities are included.
projicient (prō·jish'ənt): *adj.* serving to
relate the organism to the external world.
➤It is said of the nerves that serve the
skeletal muscles (motor nerves) and the
sense organs (sensory nerves), i.e., of all
peripheral nerves except those of the autonomic system.

prolactin: *n.* a pituitary hormone associated with the secretion of milk.
prolegomena (prō"lə·gom'ə·nə): *n. pl.*
(often construed as *sing.*) an extended and
detailed introduction to a scholarly work
or to a course of study. ➤*Distg. fr.*
orientation, which is relatively superficial; and *fr. preface* or *introduction,* which
are usually less extended.
proliferation: *n.* the multiplication of cells
in a living body, esp. by cell division.
promiscuous: *adj.* mixed haphazardly; esp.,
of social or sexual intercourse in which
there is little or no selectivity. The noun
promiscuity has come to mean, almost exclusively, nonselective sexual intercourse.
prompting method: a procedure in
memory experimentation wherein the number of promptings required to bring the *S*
to an errorless reproduction of a series is
the measure of learning.—*Syn.* RETAINED
MEMBERS PROCEDURE, ANTICIPATION METHOD.
pronation: *n.* movement to a prone position; esp., a movement that brings the
hand to a prone position—i.e., with palm
down.—*Ant.* SUPINATION, movement to a
position with palm, belly, or other part
upward.
pronouncedness: *n.* the quality or degree
of goodness of a color, such as the whiteness of a white or the greenness of a green.
➤It tends to correlate with psychophysical
expectation; thus, increasing **illuminance**
tends to increase the pronouncedness of a
white or chromatic surface color but to decrease the pronouncedness of a black.
proof: *n.* facts or supposedly valid generalizations, in support of a proposition or
hypothesis, of such cogency as to convince
any reasonable person. ➤DEMONSTRATION
sometimes means proof that one believes
can never be shaken (e.g., the theorems of
geometry); but it also means the process
or act of presenting proof. Proof may be
inductive, deductive, or both.—*Cp.* **authority** (4) and **persuasion.**—*adj.* **proved.**
—*v.* **prove.**
proofreader's illusion: a misreading because of overlooking a misspelling of a
familiar word; more generally, any similar
misperception.
propaganda: *n.* actions or expressions of
opinion, by individuals or groups, that are
deliberately designed to influence the
opinions or actions of other individuals or
groups. ➤When its purpose is clearly
avowed, it is called WHITE PROPAGANDA;
when concealed, it is BLACK PROPAGANDA.
propaganda analysis: see **analysis/
propaganda.**
propagation: *n.* **1.** reproduction of organisms. **2.** transmission or conduction of a
neural impulse. 3. spreading or disseminat-
ing news, rumors, ideas.—*Cp.* **propaganda.**

propensity: *n.* a hypothesized enduring characteristic of the person or organism that leads or inclines to a certain goal-seeking behavior. ➤McDougall proposed to substitute INNATE PROPENSITY for **instinct** (at least in man) to avoid certain difficulties with the latter term. R. Cattell proposes **erg** for innate, **metanerg** for acquired, propensity. Tendency, **disposition (2),** and **drive (1)** are close synonyms.

property: *n.* a quality, characteristic, or attribute found in all examples of a group or class of objects or events; an intrinsic characteristic: change is a *property* of all learning.

prophecy formula: (*stat.*) any formula for estimating the scores to be expected on some future measurement.—See **Spearman-Brown formula.**

prophylaxis: *n.* the prevention of disease or disorder.—*adj.* **prophylactic.**

propinquity: *n.* nearness in any specific respect; esp., nearness of blood relationship or nearness in space.—*Syn.* PROXIMITY.

proportion: *n.* 1. the ratio of the magnitude of one part to another or to the whole. **2.** an agreeable or pleasing size relation between the parts of a whole.—*adj.* **proportional,** relating to proportion; **proportionate,** in a proper or designated ratio.

proportionality: *n.* (*factor anal.*) the criterion that any two columns of correlation coefficients must be in direct proportion if the two-factor pattern in a set of tests is to be assumed.

propose: *v.* to formulate in words (or equivalent symbols) a plan or procedure to be acted upon. ➤**Propose** is stronger than *suggest* (as well as more explicit) but somewhat weaker than *direct* or *order.* It usually involves less detail than does **plan.**—*n.* **proposal.**

proposition: *n.* (*logic*) a verbal (or equivalent **symbolic**) statement put forward as true, or as something to be tested for truth; the verbal statement of a judgment. ➤FORMAL PROPOSITIONS are statements without reference to observable events; their truth consists in being related according to the laws of logic to a system of rules. E.g., the "truth" of a theorem in geometry is simply that the symbols have been put together according to the principles of geometry (or of a particular geometry). EMPIRICAL PROPOSITIONS are arrays of symbols corresponding with observable events.

propositional speech: speech in which the relations of the words to each other yield a new meaning not given by mere addition of the distinct words. ➤All true sentences are propositional, but many phrases also qualify: e.g., *a right turn,* but not *a beautiful tree* (the latter probably being merely additive).

propriate: *adj.* (*G. Allport*) pertaining to the **proprium;** characterizing a pattern of behavior in which one seeks the goals of his own developing self, not waiting on circumstance but seeking or creating the conditions favorable to his purposes.—*Cp.* **inner-directed.**—*Contr. w.* **opportunistic.**

propriety: *n.* conformity to the conventional standards of a society, with emphasis on the minor standards; observance of etiquette in social and professional relations. ➤E.g., it is a violation of propriety to pick one's teeth in public, or to graph time along the *Y* axis.—*Ant.* IMPROPRIETY. —*adj.* **proper.**

proprio-: combining form meaning *one's own, belonging to oneself.*

proprioceptive reflex: a reflex mediated by **receptors** in tendons or deep in the muscles and by a simple arc through the spinal cord.

proprioceptor: *n.* any **receptor** sensitive to the position and movement of the body and its members, including (*a*) receptors (in the vestibule of the inner ear and in the semicircular canals) sensitive to the orientation of the body in space, and to bodily rotation, and (*b*) receptors (in the muscles, tendons, and joints) sensitive to the position and movement of bodily members, and giving rise to **kinesthetic** sensations.—*Distg. fr.* **exteroceptor, interoceptor.**—*adj.* **proprioceptive.**—*n.* **proprioception,** perceiving mediated by proprioceptors.

proprium: *n.* (*G. Allport*) those aspects of personality, collectively, that seem peculiarly one's own, that make for individuality and inward unity.—*Syn.* **self, ego** (both of which have other meanings).—*adj.* **propriate** (which see).

prosencephalon (pros″en·sef′ə·lon) = **forebrain.**

prosthetic: *adj.* characterizing an artificial device replacing a missing bodily part: e.g., a denture.—*n.* **prosthesis.**

prostitution: *n.* promiscuous sexual intercourse for financial gain; figuratively, compromising ideals in order to gain an advantage.

prostration: *n.* lying prone; extreme exhaustion such that **postural reflexes** are largely abolished. ➤It is usually applied to cases of shock or disease rather than of extreme fatigue.

prostructural change: a **common fate** or change, in a group of objects, which conforms to their natural groupings or structure.

protanomaly (pro″tə·nom′ə·li): *n.* a form of anomalous color vision characterized chiefly by relative insensitivity to the red end of the spectrum.—*adj.* **protanomalous.**

protanopia (-nō′pi·ə): *n.* a form of **color blindness** in which red and blue-green stimuli are confused and the luminosity is abnormally low at the long-wave end, but a normal proportion of red and green stimuli suffices to match a given yellow.—*Syn.* RED BLINDNESS.—*adj.* **protanopic** (-nop'ik).— *Syn.* SCOTERYTHROUS.—*pers. n.* **protanope** (prō'ta·nōp).

protective response: a movement designed to rid the animal of a noxious stimulus. ➤Preferred to **defense reflex**, since **defense** has taken on a different meaning.

protensity: *n.* 1. (*structural psychol.*) the **attribute** of a mental process of occupying time. ➤According to this usage, protensity is not measured physical time, nor is it a judgment by the observer of how long a mental process has lasted. It is a directly perceived aspect of the experience, just as is **extensity**. Titchener restricted the term to **sensation**.—See **attribute.** 2. the time taken for a response.—*Syn.* RESPONSE DURATION (*prefd.*).—*adj.* **protensive.**

protest child: a child who is rather consistently "difficult" and **negativistic.**

protest/masculine: see **masculine protest.**

proto-: combining form meaning *first, original, primitive.*

protocol: *n.* the original record of the results of an experiment or investigation, properly limited to record made during or immediately following the event.

protocol sentences: (*S. S. Stevens*) those sentences that relate to the simplest elements of experience.

protopathic: see **epicritic sensibility.**

protoplasm: *n.* the semifluid substance of which all living cells are composed. ➤It includes both NUCLEOPLASM (the substance of the nucleus) and **cytoplasm.**—*adj.* **protoplasmic.**

prototaxic: *adj.* (*H. S. Sullivan*) characterizing a mode of experience in which momentary states are **undifferentiated** and unrelated. ➤This is the primary experience of the newborn. It is only approximated, and then under unusual conditions, in adult life.—*Cp.* **parataxic, syntaxic.**

prototype: *n.* an early (or the earliest) form found in an evolutionary series with which later forms are compared; by extension, the earliest form of a response pattern regarded as evolving.

proverbs test: one in which the task is to explain the meaning of proverbs.

provisional try: see **try/provisional.**

prox.: *abbr.* for **proximal.**

proximal: *adj.* 1. (*anat.*) of that portion of a bodily member which lies closest to center: the thigh is *proximal*, the foot is distal. 2. contiguous or touching; near. ➤A PROXI-MAL DESIRE is a desire for something near or immediate as a means to a more distant

goal. 3. see **distal vs. proximal variables.** —*Ant.* **distal.**

proximity/principle of: see **gestalt factor.**

proximo-distad direction of development: the generalization that controlled movements **proximal** to the body axis mature before the more **distal.**—*Cp.* **cephalocaudad development principle,** with which this generalization is often combined.

Pr scale: a personality scale that measures racial prejudice without overt reference to questions of racial or ethnic bias.

prudery: *n.* exaggerated and superficially motivated regard for the moral code; esp., excessive shrinking from minor violations of the sex code. It is sometimes used as the equivalent of PRUDISH SEX MODESTY, an excessive shrinking from display of the body. —*Syn.* PRUDISHNESS.

PSE = point of *subjective equality.*

pseudesthesia (sü"des·thē'zhə): *n.* an illusion of sensation, esp. a false localization. It is especially noteworthy in the illusion of touch or pain in a **phantom limb.**

pseud(o)-: combining form meaning *false, pretended, spurious, counterfeit, similar but not genuine.*

pseudochromesthesia = **chromesthesia.**

pseudoconditioning: *n.* the eliciting of a response to a previously neutral stimulus by presenting the neutral stimulus after a series of effective stimuli. The neutral stimulus is not paired, as in true **conditioning,** with the unconditioned stimulus or unconditioned response.—*Syn.* REFLEX SENSITIZA-TION (which implies an explanation).—*Cp.* **preconditioning/sensory.**

pseudodementia: *n.* a temporary condition in which the individual is unable, by reason of apathy or other emotional conditions, to act with his normal intelligence.

pseudofovea: *n.* a new area of maximum distinctness of vision which sometimes develops in **hemiopia.**

pseudo-isochromatic charts: charts for testing color vision, composed of color spots that yield a recognizable pattern (number, letter, irregular line) to a normal observer, but yield a different or not recognizable pattern to an abnormal observer. The **Ishihari color plates** are an example.

pseudolalia (-lā'li·ə): *n.* the utterance of meaningless sounds.—*Syn.* PSEUDOLANGUAGE.

pseudologia (fantastica) = **pathological** *lying.*—*adj.* **pseudological.**

pseudomemory: *n.* a false memory of something one has not experienced.—*Cp. déjà vu.*—*Syn.* **paramnesia,** for a normal instance; **pseudomnesia,** for a pathological condition.

pseudomnesia (sü"dom·nē'zhə): *n.* a pathological form of **pseudomemory.** ➤The term PSEUDAMNESIA for a transitory

amnesia has also been suggested. Confusion between such similar sounds is almost certain. Neither seems greatly needed.

pseudophone: *n.* an instrument for transposing the sounds that would normally enter the right ear to the left, and vice versa, resulting in illusions of sound localization.

pseudopsychology: *n.* any clearly unscientific or fallacious system claiming to be psychology. ➤*Distg. fr.* **parapsychology.** The term is not to be lightly hurled at serious opponents; it should be reserved for demonstrable quackery.

pseudoscope: *n.* an instrument that transposes the right and left images from an object so that the right eye sees what the left eye normally sees and vice versa. Distance relations are inverted, so that a hollow sphere looks solid, a solid looks hollow, etc. —*adj.* **pseudoscopic.**

pseudosensibility = pseudesthesia.

pseudosocial child: a child whose primary loyalty is to a group that is predatory or parasitic upon the larger society. ➤The term is somewhat misleading, since the child's reactions are adaptive and social.

pseudosolution = solution/neurotic.

Ψ: the Greek letter *psi,* often used as a symbol for **psychology.**

psi (process) (sī; psī): *n.* (*parapsychol.*) an intra-individual process that cannot be described in terms of presently accepted natural laws. ➤The term is somewhat narrower than **parapsychological,** since the latter may refer to the extra-individual outcome. The psi process consists in whatever it is that enables the individual to "send" or receive **telepathic** messages, etc. (provided, i.e., the process turns out to be not conformable to accepted scientific descriptions).

Psi system: (*S. Freud*) any one of the parts constituting the psychic mechanism: the perceptual system, the memory system, the preconscious system, the unconscious system, etc.

psopholalia (sō″fō·lā′li·ə) = **lallation (1).**

psychanalysis: *n.* 1. **psychoanalysis.** 2. **Jungian analysis.**

psychasthenia: *n.* an obsolescent term, used by Janet, for a neurosis marked by morbid anxiety, fixed ideas, obsessions. It most nearly corresponds with the **anxiety reaction** or with the **obsessive-compulsive reaction** of the **Standard (Psychiatric) Nomenclature.**—*adj.* **psychasthenic.**

psyche (sī′ki): *n.* 1. historically, the personification (by the Greeks) of the life principle. It is thus broader than **mind.** 2. the performer of psychological functions or acts. ➤The term is favored in psychoanalysis. It suggests, though it need not rigorously imply, a **dualism.** If a separate

term is desired for the performer of specifically psychological activities, **psyche** seems preferable to **mind** or **self,** which are near synonyms. (But see **person.**)—*adj.* **psychic(al).**

psychergograph = serial discrimeter.

psychiat.: *abbr.* for **psychiatry, psychiatric.**

psychiatric social worker: a social worker trained to work with patients and their families on problems of mental health and illness, usually in close association with psychiatrists and clinical psychologists.

psychiatrist: *n.* a person, licensed to practice medicine, who is engaged professionally in the prevention, diagnosis, treatment, and care of **psychic (1)** or mental illness. ➤Under existing laws in most states, the medical license is the only *legally* necessary qualification. Most psychiatrists, however, have extensive specialization in psychiatry as well, but few have background preparation in the science of normal behavior.

psychiatry: *n.* a medical specialty dealing with the prevention, diagnosis, treatment, and care of mental illness and defect and, by extension, of many problems of personal adjustment. ➤Historically, psychiatry grew up within the framework of medicine and dealt with the *medical* care of the mentally *ill.* As the science and art developed, much of its treatment was not specifically medical, and many of those treated were not (in any ordinary sense of the word) ill, either somatically or mentally. (See, e.g., **personality trait disturbance.**) The practice of psychiatry is thus often indistinguishable from that of other specialties that deal with problems of psychological adjustment. The term MEDICAL PSYCHOLOGY (most often used in Britain) is fairly descriptive of the practice of psychiatry but not of the curriculum for training in that field, which seldom includes any background in psychology of normal people.—*adj.* **psychiatric.**

psychiatry/forensic: that part of psychiatry dealing with legal issues concerning the mentally ill or defective.

psychiatry/social: a point of view in psychiatry that emphasizes the role of social interaction in the cause, prevention, and cure of mental disorders. ➤It does not connote an attempt to cure the mental ills of society.

psychic: *adj.* 1. a general term for all the phenomena constituting the subject matter of psychology; pertaining to **mind, person, self, psyche.** ➤This usage, a revival of an older meaning, is finding increasing acceptance in recent years.—*Syn.* **psychological, mental.** 2. pertaining to the phenomena of **spiritism,** or **mediumship.**—*Syn.* **metapsychic, parapsychological.** ➤A PSYCHIC is a person claiming supernatural or "metapsychic" powers. **3.** pertaining to **sublimated,** or "higher" and more spiritual, expressions of natural tendencies, esp. the sex tendencies; divorced from (the ordinary) physical manifestations. ➤Not a good usage. **4.** an ambiguous synonym for **psychogenic (2),** or for **functional** (contrasted with **organic**) ; e.g., **psychic *pain, psychic *blindness.** ➤One should speak of *psychogenic pain* or *functional pain,* whichever is meant.—*Syn.* PSYCHICAL (esp. for **2**).

psychic determinism: 1. the postulate that psychic or mental processes are never fortuitous, but are completely explicable in terms of their antecedents.—See **determinism. 2.** the postulate that all actions have antecedent motives, conscious or unconscious. ➤Many psychoanalytic writers use **psychic determinism** only in connection with **unconscious** motives, but apparently would accept determination of action by conscious motives as possible, though uninteresting.—*Cp.* **psychic energy hypothesis.**

psychic distance: see **distance/psychic.**

psychic energy hypothesis: the doctrine or postulate that mental or psychic process or activity has dynamic or causal efficiency. ➤The doctrine may assert that psychic energy has ultimate metaphysical reality. Often there is merely a pragmatic recognition that such events as *desiring to achieve,* whatever their metaphysical status, may be the necessary antecedents of certain behaviors.—*Cp.* **psychic determinism (2),** which says the same thing but emphasizes the outcome; also **mind-body problem, dynamic psychology.**

psychic profile = **psychogram (1).**

psychic reality: an ambiguous name for the fantasy world when reacted to as if it were actual.

psychic research: the study of those mental or behavioral phenomena which are apparently inexplicable by natural laws as these are now known.—*Syn.* **parapsychology** (which see).

psychic science = **psychic research.**

psychic secretion: (*I. P. Pavlov*) a secretion elicited by a hitherto neutral stimulus: e.g., a **conditioned** salivation.

psychic stress reaction: a maladjustive response to excessive stimulation or to a situation making excessive demands on a person. ➤It is considered to be a normal, not a **psychotic,** reaction, but it is not easy to state differentiating characteristics.

psychic structure: see **structure.**

psychic system: any organized portion of the total personality having distinct dynamic properties; a disposition to respond in particular ways to relatively large and internally coherent aspects of the psychic field.

psychic trauma: a highly stressful or damaging experience that causes a lasting psychopathological change in the person. —*Cp.* **psychogenesis.**—*Syn.* PSYCHOGENIC TRAUMA (*prefd.*).

psychic vaginismus: painful spasm of the vagina, caused by repugnance to the sexual act, which prevents coitus.

psychism = **parapsychology.**

psych(o)-: combining form meaning *pertaining to mind, psyche,* or *psychology.*

psychoacoustics: *n.* an intermediate discipline dealing with the physics of sound as related to **audition** and with the physiology and psychology of sound-**receptor** processes.

psychoan.: *abbr.* for **psychoanalysis.** ➤In this dictionary, a term has been designated *psychoan.* when it clearly derives from Freud and his close disciples and has not acquired a different usage. Many terms, however, have become part of the public domain, though they still retain the marks of a Freudian origin. **Conflict** and **repression,** e.g., cannot be restricted to the Freudian usage, however much the concepts owe to Freud; but such terms as **id, death instinct, libido** must be designated as psychoanalytic even when used by persons who are not close followers of Freud.

When the designation *psychoan.* is used, the definition is formulated in the terms of psychoanalytic doctrine and—for the most part—in psychoanalytic terminology. This may be to condone some **theory-begging.** To define **id** as **unconscious** is certainly to imply at least provisional acceptance of a doctrine. But id is a term whose whole meaning is to be found within the boundaries of the psychoanalytic doctrine. To attempt restatement in other terms is not to redefine but to theorize.

psychoanalysis: *n.* **1.** a body of doctrine set forth by Freud, with modifications by his close disciples. The doctrine is based on the concepts of **unconscious *motivation, conflict,** and **symbolism.** ➤The boundaries of psychoanalysis are not sharply defined. In America it is applied to positions that deviate in many ways from Freud's. (But where the deviation is considerable, **neopsychoanalysis** is preferable.) **Depth psychology** often designates the group of psychological positions based on the importance of the **unconscious** (thus including **analytical psychology, individual psychology,** and **neopsychoanalysis**). **Dynamic psychology** is used still more inclusively for a position emphasizing motivation, whether conscious or unconscious.—See also the abbreviation **psychoan.** for a discussion of when a *term* is said, in this dictionary, to be psychoanalytic. **2.** the psychoanalytic movement as a cultural phenomenon: a movement of thought that has developed from the Freudian doctrine. ⮞In contrast to (1), the psychoanalytic movement cannot be confined to Freud and his immediate disciples. It includes not only analytic psychology, individual psychology, and other departures from Freudian orthodoxy, but also the literary, political, and social ideologies more or less consciously influenced by the antirationalistic psychology of Freud and his followers. 3. a special technique for the investigation of human motivation; = analysis (3, 4) (which see).—*adj.* psychoanalytic.—*pers. n.* psychoanalyst. Note: Freud opposed the shorter form *psychanalysis,* but it is occasionally used.

psychoasthenics: *n.* the investigation of mental *deficiency.

psychobiological organism: the integrated whole living being, capable of both psychic and physiological activity.—See organism.

psychobiology: *n.* 1. the study of the reactions of the psychobiological organism. 2. the psychological system of A. Meyer, which stresses the functional value of psychic processes in adaptation to environment.

psychoceramic: *n.* slang for a crackpot, or for a person with a mental illness.

psychodiagnosis: *n.* any procedure designed to discover the underlying factors that account for behavior, esp. for disordered behavior.

psychodiagnostics: *n.* 1. the interpretation of behavior signs (such as gait, posture, gestures, facial and vocal expressions) and of physiognomy and other anatomical signs as indicators of personality and character. ⮞*Syn.* characterology (2). While much of this is quackery, there are also scientific investigations in this field. 2. the use of the Rorschach test.

psychodometer (-dom′ə·tər): *n.* a mechanical device for measuring response time; more generally, a device for measuring the rapidity of psychological processes.

psychodrama: *n.* the improvised enactment by a client of certain roles and dramatic incidents, prescribed by the therapist and designed to reveal what certain kinds of social relations really mean to the client. Often the same role is enacted "as you would usually act," "as your wife thinks you act," "as you would like to act," etc. An audience, and usually other actors, are part of the procedure.—*Cp.* role-playing.—*Syn.* drama therapy (which has other meanings).

psychodynamic: *adj.* 1. characterizing any psychological system that strives for explanation of behavior in terms of motives or drives; of a system that attributes causal efficiency to certain (or to all) psychological processes. 2. pertaining to psychoanalysis. ⮞This usage is unduly restrictive and unnecessary. 3. of a psychological

process that is changing, or is causing change.—*n.* psychodynamics, the study of mind in action.

psychoeducational: *adj.* pertaining to the psychological aspects of the learning process in general, or of progress and adjustment in school.

psychoeducational clinic: see clinic.

psychogalvanic reflex or response = electrodermal response.

psychogalvanometer (-gal″və·nom′ə·tər): *n.* a device for measuring electrodermal response.

psychogenesis: *n.* 1. the origin and development of the psychic, however defined: of behavior, of mental or psychological processes, of mind, or of personality. 2. the origin of a psychic event in a previous psychological activity or experience. ⮞*Cp.*

psychogenic disorder. PSYCHOGENETICS is the study of psychogenesis, but the two terms are sometimes interchanged.—*adj.* psychogenetic for both (1) and (2); psychogenic (*prefd.* for 2).

psychogenetic: *adj.* pertaining to psychogenetics or psychogenesis.—See psychogenesis, psychogenic.

psychogenetics: *n.* 1. the study of psychogenesis. 2. the study of the inheritance of psychological attributes.

psychogenic: *adj.* 1. pertaining to psychogenesis (1), i.e., to the origin of psychic or psychological processes or attributes.—*Syn.* psychogenetic (*prefd.*). 2. pertaining to psychogenesis (2); having a psychic origin; originating in experience. ⮞Much preferred to psychogenetic for this meaning, but usage vacillates.—See functional disorder.

psychogenic disorder: impairment in psychological functioning with no known pathological change in organic structure and with assertion of a causal antecedent in the psychological history.—See functional disorder for discussion.

psychognosis (sī·kog′nə·sis): *n.* 1. the science and art of understanding the individual person. 2. (*B. Sidis*) the study of the person by means of hypnosis. 3. the study of the person from anatomic signs.—*Syn.* (for 3) characterology (2).—*adj.* psychognostic (sī″kog·nos′tik).

psychogram: *n.* 1. a profile representation of an individual's psychological traits.—*Var.* psychograph.—*Syn.* PSYCHIC PROFILE. 2. (*H. A. Murray*) a representation of the themas predominant at various stages in an individual's biography.

psychography (sī·kog′rə·fi): *n.* art of literary characterization of an individual, real or fictional, making free use of psychological or psychoanalytic categories and theories; a psychological biography or character description.

psychoid: *adj.* **1.** resembling the **psychic.** —*n.* **2.** (*H. Driesch*) that special form of the hypothesized vital process which is found in human bodily activity. ➤The term has broader reference than the **psychic.**

psychokinesis or **PK:** *n.* **1.** (*parapsych.*) the hypothesized direct influence exerted by a subject on a physical system, without any known intermediate physical energy or instrumentation: e.g., the supposed determination by will alone of how the dice shall fall. **2.** (*psychiat.*) maniacal, uninhibited motor responses.

psycholagny: *n.* sexual excitement that begins, continues, and ends in imagination.— *Syn.* MENTAL MASTURBATION.

psycholepsy: *n.* a sudden decrease from the normal level of mental tension, esp. a decrease so severe as to amount to **depression.**—*adj.* **psycholeptic.**

psycholinguistics: *n.* the study of the relations between communications or messages and the characteristics of the persons who communicate; specif., the study of language as related to the general or individual characteristics of the users of language. ➤It includes the processes by which a speaker or writer emits **signals** or **symbols** (see **encoding**) and the processes by which these signals are interpreted (see **decoding**).—*Cp.* **exolinguistics.**

psychological: *adj.* **1.** pertaining to **psychology.** **2.** characterizing the subject matter—the activities or events—studied by psychology. ➤This usage is favored by those averse to the terms **mental** or **psychic(al).** —*Syn.* **behavioral** (more limited). **3.** (*pop.*) nicely timed, or otherwise well adapted to influence others: the *psychological* moment.

psychological clinic: see **clinic.**

psychological deficit: the state of a person whose performance, in some special respect or in general, falls clearly below what is reasonably to be expected of him.

psychological environment: those aspects of the external world which are presently affecting the individual. This includes those portions of the world brought into the present by imaginative or verbal representation, and for some writers (e.g., Lewin) those aspects of the world of unreality (e.g., the attainment of a certain skill not yet realized) believed in by the individual.

psychological me: see **me/psychological.**

psychological primaries = **color primaries** (1).

psychological scale: see **scale/psychological.**

psychological space: see **life space.**

psychological statistics: see **psychometrics.**

psychological structure: see **structure/mental.**

psychological test: see **test** (3) and **scale/psychological.**

psychological warfare: a vague term for the manipulation of psychological influences to strengthen the ability of one's own country to wage war and to weaken that of the enemy. It is primarily concerned with **morale** and does not usually extend to training methods.

psychologism: *n.* **1.** the view that psychology is the basis of all the sciences, or that greatly emphasizes the importance of psychological principles for the social sciences and philosophy. **2.** the view that the normative sciences of logic, ethics, and esthetics rest on facts of experience. **3.** the doctrine that the data of psychology possess metaphysical reality, that sensations, thoughts, and imagination are real.—*Cp.* **mentalism,** which may stop short of asserting ultimate reality for such processes.

psychologist: *n.* a person who has made an extensive study of psychology under professional guidance. ➤In some states the use of this term is restricted to persons meeting certain professional standards. The standard for associate membership in the American Psychological Association (two years of graduate study and one year of professional work in psychology, or three years of graduate study) may be taken as defining the minimum qualification of a psychologist.— *Distg. fr.* **psychiatrist.**

psychologist/analytical: see **analytical psychologist.**

psychologistic: *adj.* a derogatory epithet for another person's method of psychological thinking. It is most often used by **positivists** to characterize **subjective psychology.**

psychologist's fallacy: 1. reading into the mind the **psychologist** is examining what is true of his own; **projection** (2). **2.** attributing to a specific behavior the properties, esp. the motivations, that seem "logically necessary" to it, rather than examining the behavior: e.g., attributing to a child the motives that an adult in the same situation would have had. ➤The fallacy is ill-named; it is very *un*psychological.

psychology: *n.* **1.** a branch of science dealing with **behavior, acts,** or **mental processes,** and with the **mind, self,** or **person** who behaves or acts or has the mental processes. ➤The subject matter of psychology is variously conceived and described (see **psychology/divisions and schools of**). Nonetheless, the problems attacked and the scientific activities of psychologists have considerable unity. **2.** a branch of philosophy, generally regarded as a part of **metaphysics.** ➤Originally psychology was both a science dealing with empirical facts and their relations, and a philosophical interpretation of such facts. A fairly definite separation between philosophical and scientific psychology has now been effected and **psychology,** unless specially designated as philosophical, now practically always refers to the empirical science. Relationships remain. A philosophic discipline deals with the basic assumptions of science in general and of psychology in particular; and there are implications for philosophy of the findings of psychological science which constitute a PHILOSOPHY OF PSYCHOLOGY. **3.** (*pop.*) the psychological activities or **mentality** involved in a situation, or characteristic of a person: the *psychology* of the farmer (i.e., his attitudes and motives); the *psychology* of spectatorship.—*adj.* **psychologic(al).**—*pers. n.* **psychologist.**

For the various categories of psychology, see under the qualifying word: **functional psychology, self psychology,** etc.

psychology/divisions and schools of: The several divisions of psychology may be based on differences in basic point of view and postulates, on differences in methods of study and investigation, on differences in the subject matter considered, and on differences in the fields of activity. The first set of differences gives rise to schools (sometimes spelled with a capital when naming a particular school), the third and fourth to the branches or fields. The second set—based on differences concerning methodology—may be elevated to the status of a basic point of view, thus becoming a school (as when the denial of **introspection** became a basic postulate in **behaviorism**), or may remain simply descriptive of a means of data gathering.

A school is, properly speaking, a group of adherents of a doctrine or set of doctrines, occasionally of a set of doctrines set forth by a single person (e.g., the school of **individual psychology** based on the teachings of A. Adler), but is also extended to name the doctrines or teachings themselves. It is usually more sharply set off by doctrines rejected than by doctrines advocated: a school is known by the company it does *not* keep. Enthusiastic commitment, if not fanaticism, is usually implied.

In contemporary psychology there is a tendency to minimize the controversy over schools. As Dewey once remarked, there are many problems we cannot solve; sometimes we just get over them. If this means decline in partisanship, it should be wholesome. If, however, it means an unwitting acceptance of one view without critical evaluation of alternatives—as too often it does—one may question the trend. To say that a question has been wrongly stated, and thus should never have been raised, is

no excuse for bland acceptance of one answer to it.

In actual fact, most of the more general theories that are at the forefront of discussion in contemporary psychology explicitly avow, or simply imply, a position on the issues or dimensions leading to the schools herein distinguished. But a theory of vision, of hearing, or of transfer is *relatively* independent of other such theories and of the more inclusive points of view and schools. Nonetheless, the distinction between a general school (discussed here) and some of the major theories (discussed elsewhere in their proper alphabetical place) is hard to draw.

In the accompanying outline (see p. 423 ff.) we have tried to set forth certain major issues or dimensions about which there is difference of opinion, and certain major divisions that define professional activity. The many subgroups within a division and the shifts of orientation (often unannounced) make for greater complexity than can fairly be represented.

A school frequently takes a position on several, even on most, of the issues or dimensions; but it is entered in the outline only for those dimensions that seem to be central or defining. Thus **behaviorism** is not entered on the dimension of **environmentalism,** despite an overwhelming preference of behaviorists for it, on the ground that this is independent of their central thesis.

Terms in bold face type are specifically defined in their alphabetic positions in this dictionary; and since many have other meanings distinct from those implied here, each such term should be consulted. Alternative names are often not entered in the outline. *The following comments are to be read in close coordination with the outline.*

I. The issues in this section concern one's view of the general nature of psychology and of how it is to be developed. Most psychology is now **empirical** in the widest sense of being based on, or regulated by, observation; but there are still psychologies based upon philosophical or theological premises as the regulative principle throughout. (This is to be distinguished from the way particular philosophical tenets influence a particular school.) ¶The divisions discussed in C and D reflect a quite different dimension—whether, in systematizing the facts of psychology, to strive for the maximum rational order and over-all consistency, or for the maximum understanding of subordinate issues with some loss in tightness of organization. For the former approach, **formalism** is suggested as the most descriptive name; for the latter, **eclecticism** is the established term. But, as we have defined the dimension, all psychologists are more or less eclectic and more or less formalistic—most of them, indeed, occupy different positions on the continuum at different times.

II. A few psychologists envisage psychology as distinct in kind from all other sciences, whether in its subject matter, in its methods, or both. Here belong the German schools of *Geisteswissenschaftliche Psychologie* ("social science psychology," often misleadingly translated "cultural psychology") and *Struktur Psychologie,* and probably most **rational psychology** (see section I) and **existentialism.** Perhaps this position is implied in the more extreme form of American **structuralism** or **existential psychology.**

Most other psychologists seek to place their discipline in relation to some classification of all sciences. The chief contemporary issue is whether the most fruitful alliance is with biology or with the social sciences.

III. The issues in this section, while currently little debated, still divide psychologists, and decisions taken on some of these issues are reflected in many of the other sections and in most psychological thinking. Does psychology study only externally and objectively observed events? Or does it study a subjectively defined object of awareness, or a special kind of event or act? Or does it study persons or selves?

One group of psychologists recognize as *data* for their science only what can be objectively or publicly observed. **Materialism** is an obsolescent (and chiefly metaphysical) statement of this view. **Behaviorism** is perhaps the commonest term for this position. Some forms of **neobehaviorism** or of **stimulus-response psychology,** while accepting psychic phenomena as intervening variables, hold that only what can be objectively observed is a *datum* of psychology.

In contrast, **mentalism** holds that there are data *peculiar* or distinctive to psychology, though not necessarily different in an ultimate or metaphysical sense from those of physics. These distinctive data may be conceived either as contents of mind (or objects of awareness), or as events. While the several schools dealing with events prefer different ways of characterizing them, the characterizations are not necessarily mutually exclusive: a given author may conceive of the event in terms of **act, function, purpose,** and **organism** all at once. But it is also possible to have an **act psychology** that is not **functional psychology** or **purposive psychology.** The psychology of event or process is often combined with the psychology of content.

Personalistic psychologies usually believe that selves or persons (see **person**) are aware of mental contents or emit psychic acts—i.e., they are also mentalistic. But it is possible to hold to a strictly objectivist personalism.

IV. Distinctions in this section are formulated to answer the traditional metaphysical question: what sorts of ultimate reality are there? **Monism** (of both kinds) with its assertion that there is but one reality—at least for science—is almost inevitably metaphysical. (Ironically, many monists profess scorn of metaphysics.) But **dualism** sometimes stops short of metaphysics: it may hold that there are two kinds of observable phenomena without asserting their ultimate distinction. **Double-aspectism** and **emergentism** are attempts to rise above the monism-dualism opposition.

The several schools listed in III nearly all state (or at least imply) positions on the divisions of IV. Thus, **objectivists** are nearly always **monists,** but some **stimulus-response** theorists and **neobehaviorists** have a view close to **double-aspectism.** **Mentalists** are divided. Some are *spiritistic *monists,** some are **emergentists,** probably most are **dualists. Personalism** may be **dualistic** or **spiritistic,** but is more often **emergentist.**

V. The first grouping in this section reflects another ancient philosophical question: whether or not psychic occurrences are causally determined and predictable. In dealing with any particular phenomenon, psychologists are almost inevitably **deterministic,** or at least **probabilistic,** even when—on general philosophical or theological grounds—they leave room for some **indeterminism.** The issue of **teleology** or finalism is less sharp for psychology than for physics, since an organism, but not a physical object, can be conceived as influenced by the future in the form of a present anticipation or expectancy.

The contrast **mechanism-purposivism** is often confused with **determinism-indeterminism.** It is true that mechanism is deterministic; but purposivism may be so as well (and in actual thinking about particular events, generally is).

Peripheralism and **situationalism** find the determination of behavior chiefly in the impact of specific features in the environment (i.e., stimuli and stimulus complexes or situations) on the **receptor** (hence, peripheral) organs. **Centralists** stress the contribution of the brain, and **personologists** describe the central determiner as an organized personality.

A new grouping, as yet without a distinctive name, consists of those who stress the tendency of the organism to normal and wholesome growth and behavior unless subjected to severely distorting environmental conditions. The relative independence of the organism arises not solely from striving (as in **voluntarism**) but from all its powers and capacities. This optimistic view of human potentialities underlies Progressive Education, **client-centered *therapy**, the **neo-Freudian** movement (perhaps also orthodox **psychoanalysis**), and many other trends in psychology. We propose that it be named **orthogenesis (4)**. ¶In contrast, **field theory** finds psychological events or data constituted by the totality of participating components—the organism as a part of an environmental field. In most forms of field theory, the environment is described in **phenomenological** terms. A specific form of field theory insists that stimulus and response must both be defined in terms of the organism-field interaction— the stimulus or the response as such being abstractions.

A new grouping, without a name or clearly defined boundaries but related to **cybernetics** and **information theory**, envisages psychological activities as messages. Since a message cannot exist by itself, the resulting view somewhat resembles field theory; but the message is related to the objective physical world rather than to the **phenomenal** world as in the older field theory.

VI. The dichotomy of **nativism** versus **empiricism** has been largely replaced by the controversy of **hereditarianism** versus **environmentalism**. The older question was: "Which psychic process must be attributed to experience and which to the inherited character of the organism?" The newer question is: "What are the relative contributions of **genetic** and of environmental factors in the *development* of abilities and traits?" A special form of environmentalism puts stress on cultural factors as determining personality.

VII. The divisions logically distinguished in this section are often associated with those of previous sections. Thus, the analytic approach is characteristic of **objectivist** psychology, though logically the two can be separated (as they were, e.g., in **structural psychology**, which was both mentalistic and highly analytic).

The several divisions are not mutually exclusive. Thus, the study of the general laws of behavior functions is complementary, not antagonistic, to the study of how individuals and classes of individuals differ. **General psychology,** as the traditional

designation for the study of the general laws of behavior function, creates confusion, since nearly all psychology seeks to be general. But **nomological** or **nomothetic** psychology, proposed as a substitute, is also an unfortunate term since most of differential psychology is also law-seeking (therefore, nomological). Since **functional psychology** is now little advocated under that name, FUNCTION PSYCHOLOGY is herewith suggested for the attempt to set forth the general laws according to which psychological processes take place.

Elementarism and **associationism** are generally found together. **Gestalt** and **field theory** are by definition opposed to elementarism and in general also to associationism.

VIII. The choice of method does not necessarily or properly lead to mutually exclusive divisions. It is true that most **objective psychology** completely rejects **introspection,** but the reverse is not true The advocates of **ahistorical** methods and interpretation generally concede that the historical method yields psychological understanding. The contrast between the **Aristotelian** and the **Galilean,** while sometimes sharply drawn, does not prevent use of both methods by the same person.

Only the major special methods are listed under E. They often overlap: e.g., the **clinical** method may be both **statistical** and **experimental.**

IX. The kind of organism studied leads to divisions often differing greatly in content, and to some extent in special methods. These divisions are sometimes included with those of the next two sections under the classification of fields of psychology.

X. Any distinguishable group of psychological data (events, processes), or of constructs (inferred dispositions, psychological structures), may form a field of study; hence, only examples are listed. The fields often overlap: e.g., perception and learning overlap in a very complex way.

XI. In **psychotechnology,** since its effort is to solve any large-scale human problem by utilizing the resources of psychology, the number and diversity of divisions is limited only by the number of human purposes and problems. The several technologies overlap: e.g., educational psychology, concerned with the problem of inducing people to learn, is a large part of industrial psychology as well as being independent. Only major divisions are outlined here.

Divisions and Schools of Psychology

I. Divisions reflecting conceptions of bases for systematization:

    A. Psychology based on fact or observation
        { 1. **Empìricism** (in widest sense)
          2. **Scientific psychology**

    B. Psychology based on philosophical postulates
        Rational or **philosophical psychology**

    C. Systematization regulated by maximizing orderly consistency
        { 1. **Formalism**
          2. **Hypothetico-deductive method**
          3. **Mathematical model psychology**

    D. Systematization regulated by maximizing inclusiveness of facts and concepts
        Eclecticism

II. Divisions (schools) reflecting conceptions of the position of psychology in the system of sciences:

    A.   As distinct and independent science
        { 1. **Geisteswissenschaftliche Psychologie, Struktur Psychologie**
          2. **Existentialism**
          3. **Structuralism**

    B.   As branch of physics   **Mechanism, Physicalism**

    C.   As branch of biology

    D.   As coordinate with biology

    E.   As basic science in sociology

    F.   As one of the social sciences

III. Divisions (schools) reflecting conceptions of the nature of psychological data:

    A. Objective psychologies: the study of   Objective behaviors or activities
        { 1. **Materialism**
          2. **Behaviorism**
          3. **Physicalism**
          4. **Neobehaviorism**
          5. **Stimulus-response psychology**

Divisions and Schools of Psychology—*continued*

B. Subjective
psychologies:
mentalism, the
study of

    Contents or
    objects of
    awareness

1. **Structural** or
    existential psychology
2. **Phenomenology**
    (Gestalt)
3. **Neophenomenology**

    Psychic events,
    acts, or
    processes

1. **Act psychology,**
    Representationalism
2. **Functional psychology**
3. **Organismic psychology**
4. **Purposive** or **hormic**
    psychology (incl.
    dynamic psychologies,
    Freudian and **neo-**
    Freudian psycho-
    analysis, analytical
    psychology, individual
    psychology, existen-
    tialism, voluntarism)

C. Personalistic
psychologies:
the study of

    Persons or
    selves

1. **Self psychology**
2. **Personalism**
3. **Organismic**
    psychologies
    (certain forms)
4. **Freudian** and **neo-**
    Freudian psycho-
    analysis, Individual
    psychology

IV. Divisions (schools) reflecting conceptions of the relation of psychic data to the non-psychic—i.e., of the **mind-body** problem and its contemporary variants:

A. **Monism**
    (materialistic)

1. **Materialism**
2. **Behaviorism**
3. **Epiphenomenalism**

B. **Monism**
    (spiritistic)

1. **Idealism** (including
    some forms of **self**
    psychology)
2. **Monadism**
3. **Panpsychism**

C. **Dualism**

1. **Interactionism**
2. **Parallelism**

D. **Dualism**
    (heuristic)

1. **Double-aspectism**
2. **Emergentism**

V. Divisions (schools) reflecting conceptions of how psychic occurrences are brought about:

A. Psychic occurrences   Unpredictable   **Indeterminism**
                                Causally determined   **Determinism**

B. Psychic occurrences   Determined by   **Determinism,**
                                  preceding events   **Probabilism**
                                  Determined by goals   **Teleology, Finalism,**
                                  lying ahead   **Vitalism**

C. Psychic occurrences   Determined by   **Mechanism**
                                  mechanical laws

Divisions and Schools of Psychology—*continued*

D. Psychic occurrences   Determined chiefly
by stimulation

- 1. **Peripheralism**
- 2. **Situationalism**
- 3. **Reactivism**

Determined chiefly
by nature of
organism

- 1. **Centralism**
- 2. **Personology**
- 3. **Activism**
- 4. **Orthogenesis**

Determined
interactively

- 1. **Field theory**
- 2. **Interbehavioralism**
- 3. **Cultural-personal
interaction**
- 4. **Cybernetics**

E. Psychic occurrences   Determined in part
by personal or
organismic striving

- 1. **Purposivism**
- 2. **Voluntarism**
- 3. **Existentialism**
- 4. Most forms of **dynamic**
or **depth psychology**

VI. Divisions (schools) based on conceptions about the origin of psychic phenomena:

A.

- 1. **Nativism**
- 2. **Hereditarianism,
Geneticism (2)**

B.

- 1. **Empiricism**
- 2. **Environmentalism** (incl.
cultural determinism)

VII. Divisions based on conceptions of the purpose or goal of psychology:

A.

- Descriptive
- Explanatory
and predictive

B.

- Ascertainment of
general laws of
psychological
functions

    **Nomothetic,
nomological,
general,** or
function psychology

- **Differential
psychology**

- 1. Individual and group
differences
- 2. **Typology**
- 3. **Faculty psychology,
factor theories**
- 4. **Idiographic psychology**

C.

- Analytic approach

- 1. **Elementarism**
- 2. **Reductionism**
- 3. **Sensationalism**
- 4. **Atomism**
- 5. **Molecularism**

- Synthetic approach

- 1. **Associationism**
- 2. **Connectionism**
- 3. **Creative synthesis**

- Molar approach

    Molarism

- Totality approach

- 1. **Gestalt, configurationism**
- 2. **Field theory**
- 3. **Neophenomenology**

Divisions and Schools of Psychology—*continued*

VIII. Divisions based on methods:

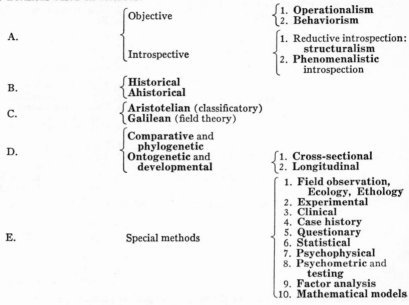

A.
- Objective
  - 1. **Operationalism**
  - 2. **Behaviorism**
- Introspective
  - 1. Reductive introspection: **structuralism**
  - 2. **Phenomenalistic** introspection

B.
- **Historical**
- **Ahistorical**

C.
- **Aristotelian** (classificatory)
- **Galilean** (field theory)

D.
- **Comparative** and **phylogenetic**
- **Ontogenetic** and **developmental**
  - 1. **Cross-sectional**
  - 2. **Longitudinal**

E.   Special methods
1. **Field observation, Ecology, Ethology**
2. **Experimental**
3. **Clinical**
4. **Case history**
5. **Questionary**
6. **Statistical**
7. **Psychophysical**
8. **Psychometric** and **testing**
9. **Factor analysis**
10. **Mathematical models**

IX. Divisions (fields or branches) based on the organism studied:

A. Subhuman   Animal psychology

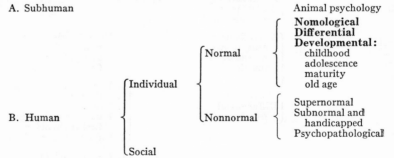

B. Human
- Individual
  - Normal
    - **Nomological**
    - **Differential**
    - **Developmental:** childhood, adolescence, maturity, old age
  - Nonnormal
    - Supernormal
    - Subnormal and handicapped
    - Psychopathological
- Social

X. Divisions (fields or branches) according to the specific kind of data studied:

     A. Processes or events—e.g., **sensation, perception, feeling** and **emotion, thinking, response** process, **learning,** etc.

     B. Structures or **dispositions**—e.g., **attitudes, habits, sentiments, temperament, abilities, response** tendencies, **needs, drives,** etc.

XI. Psychotechnologies or applied psychologies (fields or branches):

     A. Civic and political
     B. Economic (incl. business)
     C. Educational
     D. Esthetic
     E. Family relations
     F. Human engineering

     G. Legal
     H. Personal adjustment
     I. Psychotherapeutic
     J. Recreational
     K. Vocational

psychology/new: a vague term for the "latest thing" in psychology. ➤In the last half of the nineteenth century, it was **experimental** and **physiological psychology**; in the first quarter of the twentieth, it was **psychoanalysis**, then **behaviorism**, then **Gestalt**. Fortunately, no "new" psychology has enough current vogue to enjoy this dubious title.

psychometric: *adj.* **1.** pertaining to mental testing and to any quantitative assessment of an individual's psychological traits or attributes. **2.** pertaining to experiment, esp. to **psychophysical** experiment. **3.** pertaining to the mathematical and statistical treatment of psychological data.—*n.* **psychometrics.**

psychometric constant delta or Δ: a constant in the method of **constant stimuli,** the product of *h* times *I*. It is a function of the individual observer, and is independent of the standard stimulus used.

psychometric function: a mathematical formula expressing the relation between the quantitative variation in a given stimulus and the judgments of a subject who, under specific instructions, is reporting about the stimulus.—*Syn.* PSYCHOLOGICAL FUNCTION.

psychometrician (-mə·trish'ən): *n.* **1.** a mental tester; a person skilled in administering and interpreting mental tests. ➤The term designates a psychologist who specializes in this work. The suggestion that it be the designation for a test technician or **psychotechnician**—i.e., for a person, not a professional psychologist, who is trained in the giving of tests—has met with fierce opposition. **2.** a specialist in the mathematical and statistical treatment of psychological data.—*Syn.* PSYCHOMETRIST (sī·kom'ə·trist).

psychometrics (-met'riks): *n.* **1.** the study of mental testing. **2.** the branch of psychology dealing with the development and application of mathematical procedures to psychology.—*Syn.* PSYCHOLOGICAL STATISTICS (somewhat less inclusive).

psychometrist (sī·kom'ə·trist) = **psychometrician.**

psychometrizing (sī·kom'ə·trīz'ing): *n.* (*parapsych.*) the alleged process of deriving information about a human event by touching an object related to that event.

psychometry (sī·kom'ə·tri): *n.* **1. mental testing. 2. psychometrizing.**

psychomotor: *adj.* pertaining to motor effects of psychical processes. ➤Although the term has obvious (and unfortunate) **dualistic** implications, it is used by many behaviorists.

psychomotor tests: tests of motor skill; tests in which the score depends upon the precise coordination of a sensory or idea-tional process and a motor activity: e.g., aiming at a target.

psychoneural parallelism: see **parallelism/psychoneural.**

psychoneurosis: *n.* **1.** a disorder of behavior, without gross disorganization, in which **functional** or **psychogenic** factors predominate and for which psychotherapy seems indicated. ➤How to distinguish between psychoneurosis and psychosis is controversial. **2.** (*Stan. Psychiat.*) a disorder characterized by **anxiety** which may be directly felt or may be controlled by **defense mechanisms.** There is no gross distortion of reality perception nor any gross disorganization of personality. ➤It includes **anxiety reaction, conversion (2), phobia, obsessive-compulsive reaction, depressive reaction** (but not **manic-depressive psychosis**).—*Syn.* PSYCHONEUROTIC DISORDER; **neurosis** (much more commonly used). **3.** (*psychoan.*) disorder of behavior resulting from conflict and not manifesting pathological somatic symptoms. ➤A sharp distinction from **actual** *neurosis was formerly made but has now been abandoned.—*adj.* and *pers. n.* **psychoneurotic.**

psychoneurotic inventory: a series of questions about attitudes, feelings, and behaviors, the answers to which have been found significantly related to neurotic difficulties.

psychonomic (-nom'ik): *adj.* **1.** having to do with **psychic** law. ➤The term is general and may be given special meaning by the writer. **2.** (*rare*) pertaining to the relation of psychological development to environmental factors.—*Cp.* **nomothetic.**— *n.* **psychonomics.**

psychopath: *n.* **1.** a person suffering from any mental, or mental and nervous, disorder. **2.** (*pop.*) an eccentric or queer person, one near the border of mental disorder. **3.** a person with a **personality disorder.**—*Syn.* PSYCHOPATHIC PERSONALITY. ➤**Psychopath** is now little used technically, but see **psychopathic** and **psychopathy.**

psychopathic: *adj.* pertaining to any mental disorder, but esp. to one not yet profound or not yet diagnosed.—See **psychopathy.**

psychopathic hospital: one for early diagnosis and treatment of mental disorders. The patients need not be subject to commitment as insane. Compared with insane hospitals, with their emphasis still largely (though not exclusively) upon custodial care, the psychopathic hospital emphasizes study of the individual patient. The term is sometimes used for a **receiving hospital** for mental patients.

psychopathic personality = **psychopath.**

psychopathology: *n.* the systematic investigation of morbid mental conditions.—*Cp.*

pathology. ➤Strictly speaking, psychopathology is a branch of psychological science and is to be contrasted with **clinical psychology** and **psychiatry,** which are technology.—*adj.* **psychopathological,** pertaining to such investigation (not to be used as synonym for **psychopathic).**— *pers. n.* **psychopathologist.**

psychopathy (sī·kop'ə·thi): *n.* **1.** any specific mental disorder. **2.** a mental disorder, particular type not known. ➤The use of **psychopathy** for **personality disorder** is illogical and frowned upon, though fairly common. Personality disorder is a specific characterization; **psychopathy (2)** is an admission that one does not know, specifically, how to classify the condition.

psychopedics (-pē'diks): *n.* the art or technology of psychological treatment of children; professional guidance to foster wholesome behavior in children; child guidance and child **clinical psychology.**

psychopharmacology: *n.* the study of the effects of drugs and poisons on psychological functions.

psychophysical: *adj.* **1.** pertaining to **psychophysics. 2.** having a spiritual and a material, or a mental and a bodily, nature conjoined. ➤This usage, though common, is not recommended. **Psychophysiological** or **psychosomatic** are more exact.

psychophysical dualism: see **dualism.**

psychophysical function: see **psychometric function.**

psychophysical measurement: 1. the quantification of psychological **attributes** or **dimensions.** ➤To quantify a *psychological* attribute—e.g., auditory intensity, visual hue—it is necessary not only to refer to a physical dimension such as intensity, size, or force but to specify the procedures used to elicit a certain class of responses from a certain class of observers.—See **attribute. 2.** specif., the determination of **thresholds** and **scale** values for stimuli that can be arranged along a physical **continuum.** ➤The statistical procedures and basic logic used in such measurement have been extended to stimuli that cannot be correlated with a physical continuum— e.g., in measuring attitudes—but these measurements should be called **psychological,** not psychophysical.

psychophysical parallelism: see **parallelism/psychophysical.**

psychophysics: *n.* **1.** study of the relation between the physical attributes of the **stimulus** and the quantitative attributes of sensation: e.g., the relation of the energy of the stimulus to the intensity of sensation.—See **Weber's Law. 2.** study of the general relation between external stimuli and **mental processes** or **behavior.** ➤This comes close to defining psychological ex-

periment in general and seems a needless usage. **3.** experimental study of the **mindbody problem.** ➤The above three meanings were combined by Fechner, who coined the term. **4.** (*logical positivism*) the use of a human being as an instrument of observation of a variable that can be arranged along a physical continuum, under a set of strictly specified conditions. ➤See **psychophysical measurement, attribute.** This is somewhat more inclusive than meaning (1).—*adj.* **psychophysical.**

psychophysiological: *adj.* pertaining to both the psychological and the physiological; describable by the concepts of both psychology and physiology. ➤The term does not imply how the two components are related.

psychophysiologic autonomic and visceral disorders: Standard (Psychiatric) Nomenclature for what are more commonly called **psychosomatic disorders.**

psychophysiology: see **physiological psychology.**

psychosensory: *adj.* ➤This word is redundant: the **sensory** is always **psychic** or **psychological.** It has been used for experiences whose sensory quality does not originate in sense organs: for this the term is **imaginal** (or, in a special case, **hallucinatory**). It has also been used for **perceptual,** which is preferred.

psychosexual: *adj.* **1.** pertaining to the mental aspects of sex.—*Cp.* **erotic. 2.** characterizing a manifestation of sex as having both a directly physiological (or **somatic**) and a psychic aspect. **3.** characterizing a psychic process as having its origin or cause in a somatic sexual process.—*n.* **psychosexuality.**

psychosis: *n.* **1.** (*hist.*) the total mental state at any particular moment; or any specific mental process. ➤This meaning, though now rare, is still available. **2.** any severe, specific mental disorder or disease process that has a characteristic origin, course, and symptoms.—*Syn.* (*Stan. Psychiat.*) **psychotic disorder** (which see, for more explicit characterization).

For specific psychotic disorders, see the qualifying expression: e.g., **manic-depressive psychosis.**—*adj.* **psychotic.**

psychosis/alternating: see **alternating psychosis.**

psychosis/deteriorative: a severe mental disorder marked by progressive impairment of mental functions, esp. those of personality integration.

psychosis/functional: see **functional disorder.**

psychosis/senile: see **senile psychosis.**

psychosis/toxic: a chronic or acute psychosis resulting from impairment of brain function by poisons.

psychosocial: *adj.* a general term for whatever is both **psychic** and **social.** It may be given various special meanings.
psychosoma (-sō'mə) = **psychosome.**
psychosomatic: *adj.* **1.** pertaining to or characterizing a phenomenon that is, in some sense or other, both **psychic** and **somatic.** ➤Sometimes it means that the phenomenon is inherently both psychic and somatic **(dualism);** sometimes it means that the traditional distinction of psychic and somatic is false, that the phenomenon displays a unity of psychic and somatic **(monism);** sometimes it means that the writer declines to take a position. But see **psychosomatic disorder. 2.** pertaining to the relation of the tangible organic structure or body to mental or psychic phenomena.—*Cp.* **mind-body problem.**
psychosomatic disorder: a **psychogenic** (or partly psychogenic) disorder having **somatic** or physiological symptoms and (potentially) producing harmful structural somatic alterations. ➤As distinct from what may happen in **neurosis,** the physiological symptoms do not relieve anxiety; as distinct from **hysteria,** the symptoms do not symbolize a repressed cause. Thus, it is held that worry or anxiety may be a major factor in causing gastric ulcer. The hyperacidity and other gastric activities (the physiological symptoms) do not relieve the anxiety nor do they symbolize the cause thereof. PSYCHOSOMATIC MEDICINE emphasizes the role of psychic factors in many (or all) diseases, or in maintaining health.
psychosome (-sōm): *n.* the organism regarded as emitting both psychic and somatic behavior, or as emitting behavior that partakes of the nature of both.—*Cp.* **psychosomatic (1).**—See **person.**
psychosophy (sī·kos'ə·fi) = **mental philosophy.**
psychostatics: *n.* a little-used but useful term for the study of psychological **structure.**—*Ant.* **psychodynamics.**
psychosurgery: *n.* brain surgery performed as treatment for certain mental disorders.
psychosynthesis: *n.* (*S. Potter*) the opposite of psychoanalysis; a form of COUNTERPSYCHIATRY aimed at restoring useful inhibitions and at putting the **id** back where it belongs. ➤This is a lay movement. In treatment sessions (synthesis), patients are encouraged *not* to give free rein to their associations; rather they are to refrain from saying anything till they have considered whether it ought to be said. By curious paradox, whereas psychoanalysis really seeks the synthesis of ego and id, psychosynthesis would keep them apart (with the reality-related ego dominant).
psychotechnician: *n.* a person skilled in certain psychological procedures, esp. in

mental testing or experimentation. ➤It is usually implied that the person does not have the over-all preparation of the professional psychologist and should work under direction.
psychotechnics: *n.* application of psychological principles to the control of behavior, esp. for practical purposes.—*Distg. fr.* **psychotechnology.**—*adj.* **psychotechnical.**
psychotechnology: *n.* the body of psychological facts, methods, concepts, and principles developed in the attempt to direct and control behavior for practical ends. ➤This term is preferred to **applied psychology** (which see). There are as many divisions or branches of psychotechnology as there are comprehensive human purposes. E.g., **educational psychology, industrial psychology, human engineering, psychotherapy.**—*Distg. fr.,* **psychotechnics,** the actual practice based on psychotechnology.—*adj.* **psychotechnological.**
psychotherapeutic: *adj.* **1.** having curative value for mental disorders. **2.** pertaining to **psychotherapy.**
psychotherapist: *n.* a person professionally engaged in **psychotherapy.** ➤The term usually includes psychiatrists, clinical psychologists, and psychiatric social workers. It is not usually applied to teachers, physicians, clergymen, or lawyers, although their professional activity often has therapeutic value.
psychotherapy: *n.* the use of any psychological technique in the treatment of mental disorder or maladjustment. ➤The term is very general. It includes "faith cure," suggestion, hypnosis, psychoanalysis, provision of rest, assurance, advice, consultation designed to relieve anxiety, psychodrama, etc. Nearly always personal consultation is a part of the technique, sometimes the whole of it. The term carries no implication about the seriousness of the disorder (there can be psychotherapy for psychosis or for thumbsucking), the duration or intensity of treatment, or the theoretical orientation of the therapist. But the term should be reserved for treatment by a professionally trained person—i.e., by clinical psychologist, psychiatrist, or psychiatric social worker.—*Distg. fr.* **clinical psychology, psychiatry.**—*adj.* **psychotherapeutic.**
psychotherapy/ambulatory: see **ambulatory psychotherapy.**
psychotic (sī·kot'ik): *adj.* pertaining to a **psychotic disorder** or **psychosis;** characterizing a certain behavior pattern as symptomatic of psychotic disorder or (at least) as strongly resembling the behavior of such a disorder.—*pers. n.* **psychotic,** one who exhibits such behavior.
psychotic disorder: (*Stan. Psychiat.*) a

general term for a disorder characterized by some "degree of personality disintegration and failure to test and evaluate correctly external reality in various spheres." Individuals with such disorders fail to relate themselves effectively to other people. The chief forms are **manic-depressive, schizophrenic,** and **paranoid** disorders.

psychro- (sī'krō-): combining form meaning *cold*: e.g., PSYCHROESTHESIA, a condition wherein a part of the body, though warm, is perceived by the subject as cold.

***P* technique:** a statistical test of the **functional unity** of several behaviors by measuring their temporal **covariance.** ➤Behaviors are said to belong to the same unity if, for a given individual, they vary together at different times and under different conditions. The *P* technique is a correlation of occasions with behaviors of a given kind.—See *R* **correlation.**

ptosis (tō'sis): *n.* a falling, or paralytic drooping, of the eyelid.—*adj.* **ptotic.**

puberal: *adj.* pertaining to **puberty.**—*Var.* **pubertal.**

puberal growth stage: a period, associated with puberty and lasting from 2 to 4 years, during which growth exceeds the average rate over the 5-year period centered at the peak of maximum growth.—*Syn.* PUBERTAL SPURT, ADOLESCENT SPURT.

pubertal = puberal.

pubertas praecox = precocious *puberty.

puberty: *n.* the period during which the generative organs become capable of functioning and the person develops **secondary *sex characters.** ➤In the female, its onset is marked by the beginning of menstruation; in males, one fairly reliable sign is the pigmenting of underarm hair. The end is conventionally given as age 14 in males, age 13 in females, but variation is wide. Subtle mental, especially emotional, changes are associated with puberty.—*Cp.* **levels of *development.** Puberty is usually reckoned as the first subphase of **adolescence,** though a few writers make it a distinct preceding stage.—*adj.* **puberal, pubertal.**

puberty/precocious: excessively rapid maturation in children, before the usual age of puberty, as a result of disorder of the **pituitary gland.** The sex glands attain adult maturity in size and function, the **secondary *sex characters** appear early, and there is usually considerable development of sex interest.—*Syn.* PUBERTAS PRAECOX.

puberty rites: a course in tribal lore taught by precept and ritual to those arriving at the age of puberty; an initiation into the adult life of the community.—*Cp.* **pubic rites.**—*Syn.* PUBERAL RITES.

pubes (pū'bēz): *n. s.* the hair, or the hairy region, of the lower abdomen and crotch. ➤The growth and pigmenting of this hair is one sign, not too reliable, of puberty.—*Distg. fr.* PUBES (a plural noun), the pubic bones which are part of the pelvis.—*adj.* **pubic.**

pubescence: *n.* the process of attaining puberty; the early stage of puberty. ➤Often improperly used for **puberty.**—*adj.* **pubescent,** of one just reaching puberty.

pubic: *adj.* pertaining to the region occupied by the external genitals.

pubic rites: (*anthrop.*) ceremonies involving the genitals, esp., scarification or mutilation ceremonies. ➤Such pubic rites often play a major part in **puberty rites;** but circumcision, a pubic rite, often takes place in infancy.

public: *adj.* **1.** pertaining to the people or to the state. **2.** open, not private or restricted; objective, not subjective.—*n.* **3.** a more or less ephemeral group of persons, not necessarily physically assembled, but united by one or more common interests and some means of communication. **4.** = the GENERAL PUBLIC, the general body or total aggregate of a nation or community.

public opinion: see **opinion/public.**

public relations: 1. the attitudes and judgments of the public, or of distinct segments of the public, toward an organization or an individual. **2.** the art or profession of maintaining good public relations. ➤The chief means are those of publicity, though there is much consideration of whether a given activity will injuriously affect the opinion of important sections of the public, or whether it can be presented in a favorable light.

public school: 1. (*U.S.*) a school, usually one below the college level, supported and controlled by an agency of the state. **2.** (*Brit.*) an endowed school, highly selective of its pupils, called **public** because its ancient charter did not restrict it to a certain class. ➤In the U.S. such schools are called *private* or *preparatory* (preparatory for college), but in Britain a preparatory school is a lower school that prepares for the public school.

pudenda: *n. pl., s.* **pudendum,** the external genitals.

puerile (pū'ər·il): *adj.* boylike; childlike; of immature behavior by an adult (usually derogatory).—*Cp.* **regression, fixation.**—*n.* **puerility, puerilism.**—*Syn.* CHILDISHNESS.

puerperal (pū·ėr'pər·əl): *adj.* pertaining to childbirth.

pugnacity: *n.* the tendency to fight, to resist by attack any hampering of one's actions. ➤It is often implied that the tendency is innate.—*adj.* **pugnacious.**

Pulfrich effect or **phenonomenon:** An object oscillating in simple **harmonic** motion in the frontal plane will, when viewed monocularly through a filter of medium density, be seen as moving in an ellipse whose plane is perpendicular to the frontal plane and parallel to the floor.

pulmonary (pul'mə·ner"i): *adj.* pertaining to the lungs.

pulsation: *n.* a rhythmic throbbing, moving, or vibrating; a rising and falling of intensity.

pulse: *n.* the rhythmic rise and fall of pressure at a given point in the arteries, resulting from heart action.

pulse/anacrotic: see **anacrotic pulse.**

punch-drunk: *adj.* of the pattern of symptoms consequent upon many brain concussions. There is disturbance of gait and mental confusion or cloudiness. ➤This syndrome is often observed among pugilists.

punched card method: a technique for recording data by punching a hole in a particular place on a card, so that the data can be rapidly tabulated by mechanical or electronic means.

punctate: *adj.* applied to a point: a *punctate* stimulus.

punctiform: *adj.* pointlike.

punishment: *n.* **1.** the infliction of a penalty by one animal upon another because the second has done something disapproved by the first or has failed to do something. The penalty may be any kind of dissatisfaction: a painful stimulus (physical or social), or denial or removal of a satisfaction. ➤A human being may be said to punish himself; it is doubtful that other animals do. Punishment may be inflicted as retaliation, as deterrent, and/or as motivation to learning. **2.** any **incentive** with negative **valence,** i.e., capable of producing pain or annoyance or dissatisfaction. ➤In this usage the social implication of the original meaning is watered down. **3.** In psychological experiments, any dissatisfaction imposed on the animal for nonperformance of the response chosen by the experimenter as correct. ➤The correct response is often entirely arbitrary, and the dissatisfaction is usually nonpersonally administered. Often it is a mere signal to the animal that the response is inacceptable—with human animals it may be the signal "wrong."—*Cp.* **reinforcement/negative.** ¶The situation referred to in (1) obviously contains elements missing from (3), and inferences drawn from either may be inapplicable to the other—a fact easily granted but often forgotten in discussions of the role of punishment in learning.—*Ant.* **reward.**—*adj.* **punitive** (usually only for 1).—*v.* **punish.**

punishment/corporal: the infliction of bodily pain as punishment (usually **punishment 1**).

punishment fantasy: imagining or reflecting how unpleasant the consequences would be if a certain wish were to be fulfilled: e.g., "If I threw my food on the floor (as I want to), I'd be spanked."

punishment/natural: **1.** directly experiencing the ill effects of one's own behavior, esp. of one's misbehavior. **2.** a point of view that considers such experience particularly valuable for learning or for moral guidance.

punitive: *adj.* **1.** pertaining to **punishment (1). 2.** characterizing the tendency to enforce obedience by means of **punishment (1).**—*Cp.* **impunitive, intropunitive, extrapunitive.**—*Ant.* **permissive.**—*n.* **punitiveness,** the trait of being punitive.

pupa (pū'pə): *n.* (*zool.*) an insect in the stage of development that follows the **larval** stage and precedes the **imago:** e.g., the chrysalis stage of butterflies in which the insect is encased in a cocoon and is highly immobile.—*adj.* **pupal.**—*v.* **pupate.**

pupil: *n.* **1.** the variable aperture of the iris through which light passes on its way to the retina of the eye.—*adj.* **pupillary. 2.** a child attending a lower-level school. ➤While persons in secondary schools are occasionally called pupils, STUDENT is more usual at this level. **3.** any person studying under the close personal instruction of a teacher.

pupil/Argyll-Robertson: see **Argyll-Robertson pupil.**

pupil/artificial: a small screen with a very small aperture that is attached to the cornea as a means of controlling the visual stimulus.

pupillary reflex: change in the size of the pupil as the iris muscle contracts or relaxes, in response either to change in light intensity or to change in point of fixation for near or far. ➤The term is a misnomer; IRIS REFLEX is more descriptive but less usual.

puppy love: a highly romantic and intense form of love in the adolescent period, taken very seriously by the affected party but believed (or hoped) by others to be transient.

pure: *adj.* **1.** free from any heterogeneous or extraneous material; free from mixture or combination. **2.** morally upright; uncontaminated.

pure number: (*stat.*) a number that is independent of the units of measurement of the quantities used in its determination.—*Syn.* ABSTRACT NUMBER.

pure-stimulus act: see **act/pure-stimulus.**

pure tone: see **tone/pure.**

Purkinje afterimage (pêr'kin·yā): the second positive visual **aftersensation**

which appears most plainly in the hue complementary to that of the primary sensation.

Purkinje cell: a large cell, with many dendrites, in the middle layer of the **cerebellar** cortex.

Purkinje effect or **phenomenon:** the fact that the red-yellow end of the spectrum decreases in brilliance, with decreased illumination, more rapidly than does the red-blue end.

Purkinje figures: the shadowy images on the retina of its network of blood vessels.

Purkinje-Sanson images: the three images of an object which can be seen by an observer of the eye: one from the corneal surface, one from the front and the other from the back surface of the lens.

purples: *n. pl.* a series of related hues, ranging between blue and red, normally evoked by combinations or mixtures of long- and short-wave radiation within the visible spectrum. They are the complements of the greens and yellow-greens.

purple/visual: see **visual purple.**

purpose: *n.* 1. that which a person sets before himself as the end to be attained by action. 2. (*beh.*) a determiner of behavior inferred when the organism persists in a series of acts (often of quite varied character) until it reaches some specific environmental situation or physiological state. ➤*Syn.* **aim, end, goal.** While purpose can be objectively defined as in (2), it more often implies a conscious process. *Distg. fr.* **purposiveness,** which does not so imply. See also **motive.**—*adj.* **purposeful.**

purposiveness: *n.* the property of an organismic activity of being directed toward a goal, of being persistent and adaptable (**docile**) relative to some end; the property of a behavior of being influenced in its course by the result to be attained. ➤It does not imply definite and conscious **purpose.** Some theorists regard purposiveness as an inadmissable concept in science. Others make it the central concept of psychology, the defining character of behavior. (See **purposive psychology.**) A third group distinguish between purposive behavior, in which persistent striving is clearly evident, and nonpurposive behavior in which the striving, if present, is not so evident.—*adj.* **purposive.**

purposive psychology: the doctrine that behavior is distinguished from purely mechanical change or from physiological activity by **purposiveness.**—*Distg. fr.* **purposivism.**—*Syn.* **hormic psychology.** ➤Several schools are basically purposive, sometimes without emphasizing the fact: **dynamic** and **depth** psychologies, **existentialism** (but not **existential psy-**chology), **voluntarism,** and some varieties of **neobehaviorism.**—See **psychology/ divisions and schools of, III, V.**

purposivism: *n.* any psychological point of view which holds that **purposes** are in some sense effective determiners of behavior.—*Distg. fr.* **purposiveness, purposive psychology.**—See **psychology/ divisions and schools of, V.**

pursuitmeter: *n.* an instrument for measuring the ability to adjust a series of responses to accord with the changes in a continuously moving stimulus.—See **pursuit reaction.**

pursuit/ocular: the following of a moving object by successive **fixations** of the eyes. When the eye reaches the limit of its turn, there is a RETURN SWEEP and, following readjustment of the bodily or head position if necessary, a renewed series of pursuit movements.

pursuit pendulum: a form of **pursuitmeter** in which the moving object is a pendulum.—See **pursuit reaction.**

pursuit reaction: movements designed to correspond in a specified fashion with position changes of a continuously moving stimulus: e.g., keeping a pointer continuously aimed at the weight on the end of a swinging pendulum.—*Syn.* PURSUIT TEST.

putting through: a training procedure in which the subject's limbs are mechanically manipulated for him so as to accomplish a given end.

puzzle: see **problem.**

puzzle box: an enclosure that prevents an animal from reaching a goal or lure until he has manipulated a special device that opens the enclosure. ➤Either animal or lure may be in the enclosure.—*Syn.* **problem box** (when the opening is relatively simple). The THORNDIKE PUZZLE BOX was an early form; the **Skinner box** is much used now.

pyknik type (pik′nik): (*E. Kretschmer*) a classification of human body structure characterized by large body cavities, considerable subcutaneous fat, and general roundness of contour. ➤Kretschmer and others believe that this physical type is associated with a tendency to **cyclothymia.**

pylorus (pī·lôr′əs): *n.* the opening from the stomach into the **duodenum.**—*adj.* **pyloric.**

pyramidal tract (pi·ram′ə·dəl): 1. those nerve fibers passing through the medullary **pyramids** to form the **efferent** path from the precentral gyrus of the cerebral cortex to the motor centers in the brain stem and cord. 2. by extension, other fibers which do not pass through the pyramids but have similar function.

pyramid/color: see **color pyramid.**

pyramids: *n. pl.* elevated regions on the

front of the **medulla,** one on each side of the anterior median fissure.

pyro- (pī′rō-): combining form meaning *fire* or *heat.*

pyromania: *n.* uncontrollable impulse to set things afire.

pyrophobia: *n.* morbid fear of fire.

pyrosis: *n.* heartburn.

Q

Q: 1. = (*stat.*) **quartile deviation. 2.** = **questionary** or **questionnaire. 3.** (*ital.*) = (*vis.*) **luminous** energy. **4.** (*ital.*) (*Ror.*) a general symbol used for the examiner in recording **inkblot** responses: it indicates qualification, restriction, or self-doubting expression by the subject.

Q₁, Q₂, Q₃: first, second, third **quartile** points.

q: that proportion of a sample which lacks the attribute in question. ➤*Cp.* **p,** the proportion having the attribute: $p + q = 1$.

Q data: data derived from **questionnaires.**

Q method = **questionnaire** method.

Q sort: a personality inventory in which the subject (or someone making judgments about him) sorts a considerable number of statements into piles that represent the degrees to which the statements apply to him. Each statement thus gets a score indicating relative strength within the individual of the quality or trait it represents. ➤*Distg. fr.* **Q technique** (but Q-sort scores can be correlated by the *Q* technique).

Q technique: a procedure for correlating persons: the scores of each person on a series of tests are correlated with the scores of another person on the same tests. It yields a measure of the similarity of the two persons in the traits tested.—See **R** **correlation.**—*Syn.* INVERSE (or INVERTED) FACTOR ANALYSIS.

quadrant: *n.* **1.** any one of the four parts of a plane formed by the intersection of two perpendicular lines or axes. **2.** (*stat.*) one of the four **cells** of a 2 × 2 **table.**—*adj.* **quadrantal.**

quadrigemina = **corpora quadrigemina.**

quadriplegia (kwod″ri·plē′ji·ə): *n.* paralysis affecting both arms and both legs.

quadrupedal (kwod·rü′pəd·əl; kwod″rü·-ped′əl): *adj.* having, or using, four feet or limbs.—*n.* **quadruped.**

quale (kwā′lē) *n., pl.* **qualia:** any bit of experience as it is, without any reference to its context, relations, or meaning. ➤The description of elementary qualia may be said to be the primary task of **structural psychology;** and the denial that such qualia exist is the basic thesis of **Gestalt psychology** and **field theory.**

qualifier: *n.* **1.** a characteristic or property

by which things belonging in the same superordinate classification are distinguished: e.g., a *hunting* vs. a *herding* dog. **2.** (*sociol.*) a distinguishing characteristic of certain individuals in a group that leads them to split off into subgroups: e.g., the complex set of characteristics which led certain individuals of the Christian faith to form Protestant sects while others remained Catholic.

qualitative measurement: see **measurement.**

quality: *n.* **1.** an aspect of experience differing in *kind* from all other aspects, hence, serving to distinguish or identify the experience. ➤Quality in this sense is not capable of variation in amount, intensity, extensity, or degree, and cannot be expressed numerically.—*Contr. w.* **quantity. 2.** specif., the distinguishing mark of sensation: e.g., the quality by which a pain differs from any other sensation. ➤Note that a sensation named from its quality (e.g., pain) can have intensity, which varies in quantity. But if there is a change in the *kind* of pain (i.e., in quality) we have a new sensation. The distinction of quality from quantity is often difficult, however. **3.** the relative goodness of anything; degree of excellence, esp. the excellence due to being of pure composition. ➤Note that this is a quantitative meaning and in this respect is opposite to (1).—*adj.* **qualitative.**

quality complex: a mixture of ideas and fragments of ideas compressed together without apparent logical or reality-related connection. It is found in some dreams and in the language of some schizophrenics.

quality scale: see **scale/quality.**

quanta: see **quantum.**

quantal: *adj.* of a variable that changes by discrete quantitative steps or **quanta.** ➤The QUANTAL METHOD of psychophysics consists of adding fixed increments to a standard stimulus with no time interval between them. The observer reports apparent presence or absence of increment.

quantal hypothesis: the hypothesis that changes in sensation or sensory response take place by discrete and separable steps; the view that sensory experience does not form a **continuum.**

quantity: *n.* that property of a phenomenon by virtue of which it can be counted or measured; that aspect of a phenomenon which can be described in terms of the numerical system: e.g., amount, extent, degree, intensity, duration, are quantities.—*Contr. w.* **quality.**—*adj.* **quantitative.**—*v.* **quantify,** to assign a number that shows amount, extent, etc.

quantum *n., pl.* **quanta: 1.** a specific, discrete amount. **2.** (*phys.*) the elemental unit of energy according to the quantum theory. **3.** (*psychophys.*) see *quantal method* under **quantal.**

quarrelsome: *adj.* tending to indulge in more or less angry dispute or controversy; easily provoked to the expression of angry differences of opinion.

quartile (kwôr′tĭl, -til): *n.* **1.** one of the three points that divide a serially **ranked** distribution into four parts, each of which contains one fourth of the scores. ➤This is the usage of careful writers. **Quartile** without a qualifying expression should be reserved strictly for a point. **2.** one of the four parts or sections of the distribution thus divided. ➤This is a confusing usage. Quartile division or fourth should be used for this meaning. **3.** the range of scores from lowest to highest in any one of the four divisions or fourths. ➤This is better called quartile interval. **4.** an elliptical expression for quartile division rank, the rank order of an individual, stated in terms of the rank of the quartile division in which he falls.

➤See **partile** for discussion of the rationale of quartile and allied terms. The three quartiles are symbolized by Q_1, Q_2, Q_3, but the use of these symbols for the quartile divisions leads to numerical error.

Both quartiles and quartile divisions (or fourths) are numbered from the bottom up. Note that the top point (quartile) is three, the top division is fourth. Use of cardinal numbers for the quartiles and of ordinals for the quartile divisions is recommended as a help in distinguishing them.

quartile deviation or **Q:** the semi-interquartile range or interval; half of the distance between **quartiles** one and three. ➤It is a rough measure of **variability** or scatter. In a normal distribution it is equal to the **probable error.**

quartile interval or **range:** see **quartile** (3).—*Distg. fr.* **semi-interquartile range,** or **Q** (see **quartile deviation**).

quasi (kwā′sī; -zī; kwä′si): *adj., adv., prefix* meaning *as if; as it were; resembling; seemingly.*

quasi measurement: the assignment of a numerical value to a datum although not all the rules for measurement proposed by a particular theorist have been followed.

➤E.g., some theorists hold that ratings do not meet the requirements for "true" measurement; yet they permit of numerical treatment.

quasi need: a tension state that determines a goal and goal-directed activity but has its origin, not in a biological deficit, but in an intention or purpose. ➤*Ant.* biological need. One has a biological **need** for food but a quasi need for more information. The term is unfortunate, seeming to imply something not quite genuine, whereas a quasi need has the same motivating properties as a biological need.

quasi scale: see **scale** (7).

questionary: *n.* the English form of the French word **questionnaire** (which see).

questionnaire (kwes″chən·âr′): *n.* (Fr.) a more or less elaborate set of questions on a given subject. ➤The questions are not designed to test the individual's ability to answer the question, but to find out what his answer is. They may seek subjective opinion or objective fact: *What is your age? Who do you think will win the World Series? Are you generally stubborn?* The answers are usually subjected to statistical treatment.—*Cp.* **self-inventory.**

Despite its widespread use, **questionnaire** is a foreign term, to the layman a fancy foreignism. In the U.S. its pronunciation (given above) is hybrid. Why should not *questionnaire* follow the example of *vocabulaire* and *dictionnaire* (both once standard forms in English) and put on honest English garb? **Questionary** has been in our language for three centuries; it is immediately spellable, pronounceable, and nearly self-evident in meaning.

Quincke tube (kwing′ki): **1.** (*acoustics*) one of a set of glass tubes, sounded by blowing across the open end and used to obtain high pitches in studies of **difference tones** and the like. **2.** a type of **interference tube.**

quintile: see **partile.**

quota control: *n.* a method of population sampling in which the number of elements (e.g., persons or business firms) from each stratum (e.g., social class) in the sample is proportionate to the number of elements from each stratum in the population as a whole.

quota sampling: see **sampling/quota.**

quotidian (kwō·tid′i·ən): *adj.* daily.

quotient: *n.* the number resulting from the division of one number (the dividend) by another number (the divisor). ➤Much muddled thinking would be avoided if it were remembered that the **IQ** is just such a number, not a quantity of intelligence. ¶For kinds of **quotient,** see under the several qualifying terms: **intelligence quotient, achievement quotient,** etc.

R

R: 1. = (*Ger., Reiz*) **stimulus.** ➤This is the use in older psychophysical writings, now rare because of confusion with **R** for **response. 2.** = **response.** ➤Note that (1) and (2) are nearly opposite. **3.** (*ital.*) = multiple *correlation coefficient. **4.** = (*ital.*) **footrule *correlation** (now little used). **5.** = general reasoning factor (see **abilities/primary mental**). **6.** (*Ror., ital.*) symbol for the total number of responses to the **inkblots**—an index said to have little significance.

R_G: (*C. Hull*) a goal-attaining response; a **consummatory response.**

$R_{1\cdot 23\cdots n}$ = multiple *correlation coefficient.

R_p = **response probability.**

R_u or **UR:** the response regularly made to a given stimulus prior to **conditioning**, or prior to a particular conditioning procedure; the **unconditioned response.**

r: 1. = **product-moment *correlation** coefficient. ➤Subscripts symbolize the variables correlated: thus r_{Ba} means the correlation of variable B with variable a. **2.** = **pure-stimulus *act.**

r_{bis} = **biserial *correlation** coefficient.

r_G: (*C. Hull*) a **fractional *antedating goal response**; an instance of a **pure-stimulus *act.**

$r_{(\infty x)(\infty y)}$ = correlation coefficient corrected for **attenuation.**

$r_{11}, r_{2II}, r_{3III}$ = **reliability coefficients** of tests 1, 2, 3, etc.

r_{12}, r_{xy} = **product-moment *correlation** coefficients. The subscripts indicate the variables entering into the correlation.

$r_{12\cdot 34\cdots n}$ = **partial *correlation**, the correlation between variables 1 and 2 when the influence of variables 3, 4 · · · n is removed.

r_t or r_{tet} = **tetrachoric *correlation** coefficient.

r_v: correlation by the percentage of unlike signed pairs.

abdomancy (rab'dō·man"si): *n.* finding water, lost objects, etc., allegedly by the divining rod.—*Syn.* RHABDOMANCY, DIVINATION, DOWSING.

race: *n.* (*physical anthrop.*) a large subdivision of mankind distinguished by a common ancestry and by the greater frequency of occurrence within the group of a considerable number of inherited bodily characteristics (usually visible ones). ➤It is necessary to specify frequency of occurrence, rather than presence or absence, since all traits occur in all populations: a few Dutch have frizzy hair and there are some red-haired Negroes. No one character constitutes a criterion of race. Peoples of different skin color may be greatly alike in other (and more important) physical traits, and peoples of the same skin pigmentation may differ greatly in other features. It is almost certain that no people, tribe, or nation is today a *pure* race—even the small and geographically isolated peoples are racially mixed. And no *large* population is sufficiently homogeneous in physical features or in common ancestry to conform to the definition. Thus, many authorities would abandon the term as suggesting meanings contrary to fact. They speak instead of peoples, **ethnic** groups (which see), or (in many contexts) simply populations. The term **race** is occasionally used for subhumans, but *breed* or *variety* is preferred.

race differences: differences in either physical or mental characters associated with what is called a **race.** ➤Psychological race differences have been difficult to establish.

race prejudice: the unreasoned attitude or belief that especially good or bad qualities (more often the latter) are associated with a given so-called **race** or **ethnic** group.— See **prejudice.**

racial memory: see **memory/racial.**

racism: *n.* the doctrine that stresses the importance of what is called **race** as a basis for group and intergroup action, esp. for segregation and for superior rights for one group. ➤*Cp.* ethnocentrism, which may be largely unwitting, whereas racism is a definite argued-for doctrine.

radiance: *n.* a measure of radiant energy in terms of the rate of emission and the area of the source. It is the analog of **luminance**, which measures the radiant energy in terms of the light produced.— *Syn.* RADIANT INTENSITY.

radiant energy: (*phys.*) **1.** the energy associated with waves produced in some medium such as air or water; specif., **2.** the electromagnetic commotion sometimes conceived as waves in the hypothetical medium, ether. ➤Radiant energy of wave length 400 to 760 micromillimeters is known as light. If the energy is composed of equal wave lengths, it is HOMOGENEOUS RADIANT ENERGY; if of mixed wave lengths, it is HETEROGENEOUS.

radiant flux: (*phys.*) the rate of emission of radiant energy, expressed in ergs per second or in watts.

radiant intensity = **radiance.**

radiation: *n.* **1.** diffusion in all directions from a source or center: *radiation* of heat from a stove. **2.** the spreading of neural **excitation** to adjacent nerve elements. **3.** = **radiant energy.**—*Distg. fr.* **irradiation.**

radical: *adj.* **1.** pertaining to a root. **2.** of persons or proposals that seek rapid and fundamental change; or of such changes. ⇒*Contr. w.* SUPERFICIAL, characterizing slight or nonfundamental change; and *w.* CONSERVATIVE, characterizing slow or nonexistent change.—*n.* **3.** (*math.*) the radical sign, $\sqrt{}$, indicating that the quantity beneath the sign is to be factored into its roots; also, one of the roots: three is a *radical* (or root) of nine.

radiograph: *n.* an X-ray photograph, esp. of a bodily part.

radiometer (rā″di·om′ə·tər): *n.* an instrument for measuring **radiant energy.**—*Distg. fr.* **photometer.**—*n.* **radiometry.**

radix (rā′diks) *n., pl.* **radixes, radices** (-sēz): a bundle of nerve fibers at their point of entry or departure from the central nervous system.—*Syn.* **nerve root.**

rage: *n.* a violent or intense anger, marked by contorted facial expressions and by threatened or actual attack.—See **anger.**

rami communicantes (rā′mī kə·mū″ni·-kan′tēz): *n. pl.* the bundles of nerve fibers that connect the **sympathetic ganglions** with the spinal nerves.

ramus (rā′məs) *n., pl.* **rami** (-mī): (*anat.*) **1.** a branch of a vein or a nerve. **2.** one of the nerve tracts connecting the sympathetic with the central **nervous system.**

random: *adj.* **1.** occurring without voluntary control; occurring by chance; haphazard. ⇒Often used as a synonym for **chance** to avoid the popular misunderstanding of the latter. See **random sample.**—*adv.* **randomly, at random.**—*n.* **randomness.**—*v.* **randomize** (which see).

random activity or **movement:** movement made without purpose or foresight, not determined by instinct or habit, and not obviously elicited by any specific **cue** in the situation. ⇒It is a basic postulate that no movement is entirely chance or random. Random movement, therefore, means *relatively* undetermined movement. The term often signifies merely that the observer cannot tell what determines it.—*Cp.* **learning/trial-and-error.**—*Syn.* VARIED RESPONSE (*prefd.*).

random error = **error/chance (1).**

random group = **random sample.**

randomize: *v.* to select by chance or at **random;** to treat a population (of persons or of things) in such a way as to eliminate any selective factor: e.g., to arrange stimuli for presentation in an order known to be a chance order; to distribute items in relation to certain classes or categories in a purely random fashion: e.g., to distribute

randomly the experimental subjects to certain parts **(treatment *plots)** of the experiment.—*n.* **randomization.**

random movement: see **random activity.**

random observation: unplanned observation in which the situation is not controlled so as to bring about systematic variations in the observed phenomenon, nor is the observer prepared for a specific kind of phenomenon.

random sample: a number of items of any sort drawn from a larger group or population in such a manner that every individual item has the same (and independent) chance to be chosen as every other. ⇒It is usually hoped that the random sample will be representative of the larger, but this is not safe unless the sample is large.—*Syn.* RANDOM GROUP.—*Cp.* **sampling/representative, sampling/random.**

range: *n.* **1.** (*stat., measurement*) distance from the highest to the lowest score or **value (4)** in a distribution. ⇒Sometimes the range is taken as the distance from highest to lowest, plus one unit. This is a crude measure of **dispersion. 2.** (*sociol.*) a geographical area actually occupied by a species, group, or individual. ⇒*Contr. w.* **habitat,** the area *suited* to the life activities; and *w.* **environment,** a collective term for all the influences impinging on an organism.

range/audibility or **/audio-frequency:** see **audibility limit (2).**

range/discriminating: that range of scores at which a test or scale yields reliably discriminating scores for a given population. ⇒E.g., very low scores on a test are likely to reflect various kinds of chance factors in which case the difference between one low score and another has no real significance. Such low scores lie outside the discriminating range.

range effect: in **tracking** or **pursuit reactions,** the tendency to make too large a movement when the target motion is small, too small a movement when the target motion is large.

range scale: see **scale/range.**

rank: *n.* **1.** the position of an item or datum relative to others that have been arranged in order according to any defined character (size, importance, social status, value to the firm, etc.). The highest position is rank 1, the next highest rank 2, etc.—See **rank order. 2.** (*math.*) a number describing a property of **determinants** or **matrices.**—*v.* **3.** to arrange any kind of items in order of magnitude, importance, amount of chroma, strength of valence, etc.—*n.* **ranking,** the process of assigning rank.

rank (difference) correlation: see **correlation/rank difference.**

ranked distribution: a distribution o

scores or items arranged in order of magnitude or merit. The scores are then said to be in **rank order,** and the number showing the position of a score in the order is called its **rank.**

Rankian psychoanalysis (ränk'i·ən): a relatively independent offshoot from Freudian psychoanalysis, founded by Otto Rank.

rank order: arrangement of a series in such a way that each successive member will represent a value larger (or smaller) than the preceding. ➤It is not necessary that the *amount* of difference between successive members be measured, nor is it implied that successive differences are even approximately equal.

rank order correlation: a method of computing the relationship between two variables when scores on these variables are stated in **ranks** rather than in magnitudes. Two methods are in use: the **rank difference** *correlation (ρ or **rho**) and Spearman's footrule method of gains (*R*) (see **correlation/footrule**).

rank order method = **merit ranking.**

rapport (rə·pôr'; ra·pôrt'): *n.* **1.** a comfortable and unconstrained relationship of mutual confidence between two or more persons, esp. between tester and testee, counselor and client, teacher and class. **2.** the special relationship between the hypnotist and the hypnotized which makes the latter peculiarly sensitive to stimuli emanating from the former. **3.** (*parapsych.*) the relation between a medium and his supposed spirit *control. **4.** = EMOTIONAL RAPPORT, a condition in which the person is likely to respond in an emotionally appropriate manner to his environment. ➤This meaning is present chiefly when speaking of *lack* of rapport, e.g., as in **hebephrenia.**

rapture: *n.* **1.** a state, said to be very rare, beyond or above mystic **ecstasy. 2.** extravagant pleasure, joy, or love.

rare detail or *dr:* (*Ror.*) a scoring category for a carefully organized report of details not often reported.

rate: *n.* **1.** a ratio between two quantities, stated in numerical terms. ➤An unusual usage in psychology. **2.** a numerical statement of magnitude or frequency, divided by the number of units of time: e.g., annual death *rate,* the number of deaths divided by the number of years. **3.** = **rate of change.** —*v.* **4.** to assign to a given person or datum a rank, score, or mark that implies some quantity. **5.** to assign such a mark by a subjective process or upon the basis of judgment.—*n.* **rating** (which see).—*pers. n.* **rater, ratee.**

ratee: *n.* the person being rated.—See **rate** (4) or (5).

rate of change: the amount of change in a variable in a given time divided by the

value of the variable *before* the change: e.g., an increase in weight, in one month, from 130 to 140 pounds represents a rate of change of 10/130.

rate score: see **score/rate.**

rate test: see **test/rate.**

rating: *n.* an estimate—made under rules which prescribe systematic procedures for accuracy, completeness, and freedom from bias—of the characteristics or qualities of a person, process, or thing. ➤The estimate may merely assert presence or absence of a quality (sometimes called QUALITATIVE RATING), or it may assign a place on a quantitative scale. A person may also rate himself (SELF-RATING). ¶It is difficult to distinguish rating from **measurement.** A direct perceptual comparison of a datum with a set of similar data arranged in a **scale**—e.g., the comparison of a length with a series of lengths, of a light intensity with a set of standard light intensities—is called measurement. But a comparison of John Doe's "soldierliness" with that of a set of individuals to each of whom a scale value has been assigned is called **rating.**—*pers. n.* **rater, ratee.**—*v.* **rate.**

rating/behavior: 1. assigning to a specific observed behavior or class of behaviors a score, mark, or rank. **2.** observing and recording the presence or absence of a given class of behaviors. ➤Behavior rating refers to report about actual behaviors, in contrast with ratings that involve generalization and inference (TRAIT RATING).

rating/man-to-man: a comparison of the **ratee** with a group of individuals who have been chosen to exemplify different degrees of a particular trait. The ratee receives the score or rank of the person he most resembles in the trait in question.

rating scale: a device by which a rater can record, for the case in question, the estimated magnitude of the trait or quality rated. ➤Most such scales provide procedures designed to make the estimate more careful and objective.—See **rate** (4) and (5).

rating scale/graphic: a form for recording a rating according to the strength of some quality or trait. ➤It consists of a straight line (usually 4 to 14 centimeters in length) representing the entire range from a conceivable maximum to a conceivable minimum strength of the variable in question. The relative strength of the specimen being rated is indicated by a check mark at a proportionate distance from the ends. Descriptive phrases at intervals along the line guide location of the mark. E.g., in rating a parent on a dimension of "severity of regimentation," a point near the minimum end might be characterized as "just enough to keep the child out of hospital or jail"; a point near the middle might be marked "restrictions moderate and practical," etc.

ratio: *n.* **1.** a relation—in number, quantity, or degree—between two things: the *ratio* of births to deaths. **2.** more specif., a **quotient.**

For compound terms in which ratio = **quotient,** see the qualifier: **achievement quotient, intelligence quotient,** etc.— See also **point-hour ratio.**

ratio/association-sensation: see **association-sensation ratio.**

ratiocination (rash″i·os″in·ā′shən): *n.* the act of reasoning, or of drawing deductive conclusions.

ratio/critical: see **critical ratio.**

ratio/extinction: see **extinction ratio.**

rational: *adj.* **1.** pertaining to **reasoning** or, more broadly, to the higher thought processes. **2.** based on, or justifiable by, reasoning, esp. by correct reasoning. **3.** having reasoning ability; or having and using reasoning ability. **4.** influenced by reasoning rather than by emotion.—*Cp.* **objective.**

rational coinage: ➔New things and new concepts require new terms. The chief problem in coining new terms arises when assigning a new meaning to a familiar word. The governing principle is clear: the new meaning must be readily perceived as an appropriate extension of the old by virtue of analogy between them in some carefully stated particular.

The word "readily" in the above principle must not be overlooked. Some new meanings require such complex comparison that analogy scarcely helps their use or understanding. We do not recall, when we see the word, the truly rational basis of its new significance. On the contrary, we are more likely to be reminded of the old meaning and the associations built up around it over the years. If these conflict with the new meaning, confusion and ambiguity will overtake the unwary, and irritation will fill the heart of the careful reader at having to do a "double-take" each time he meets the term.

Noise as used in **communication theory** is an example. Any extraneous or irregular sound is ordinarily called noise—it interferes with getting a message. It is only a slight extension to think of anything irregular in a telephone circuit as a noise, hence to define noise as "any random variation in a communication system." From there it is only a short step to say that a random variation in the communication system between the retina and the occipital center is also a noise. The word *noise,* however, has ineradicably *auditory* associations, and the communication system from eye to occiput is not auditory. When an author inquires,

as one recently did, how much the efficiency of the visual communication system (neural) is lowered by noise, every normal user of English thinks at once of the distracting effects of random and irrelevant sounds. It is no less than infuriating to discover, sentences later, that the author was talking about something quite different.

It is not metaphor that we condemn. "Visual noise," e.g., has freshness and vigor. But the use by some writers of *noise,* without any qualifier, for something that is not auditory is (in their own terminology) itself a "noise"—i.e., an unnecessary obstruction to communication. By the same token, "acoustic noise" is redundant, not redundant as used in the lingo of **information theory,** but in the time-honored English sense of "exceeding what is necessary." **Redundancy** and **entropy,** as used in information theory, are other examples of inept coinage which, one predicts, will never become truly current.—See **arbitrary definition.**

When the principle of analogy is intelligently used, however, new terms are easily accepted. **White** ***noise** immediately suggests the proper analogy with white light. **Signal** for the neural impulse is so close to its original meaning as hardly to need explanation. And from the same circle as redundancy come **input, feedback, channel**—all terms whose new meanings are consistent with what the words themselves suggest.

rationale (rash″ən·al′; -ā′li): *n.* the underlying reason or ground for an opinion or action.

rational equation: one embodying a hypothesis that can be tested by seeing how closely the equation can be made to fit the data. ➔The general nature of the **parameters** is dictated by the theory, and their exact values must be determined to fit the data.—*Cp.* **empirical equation.**

rationalism: *n.* one of various philosophical positions that exalt the value or function of reason in the search for truth.

rationality: *n.* the quality of being reasonable or **rational,** or of being acceptable to **reason.**

rationalization: *n.* **1.** the process of giving rational order or interpretation to what was previously merely a vague **intuition,** or was chaotic and confused; or the result of that process. **2.** the process of concocting plausible reasons to account for one's practices or beliefs when these are challenged by oneself or others; or the tissue of justifications thus produced. ➔No conscious criterion warns us that we are thus rallying to the defense with reasons unconnected with the true **motivations;** we appear to ourselves to believe that we are giving real grounds.—See **defense.**—*v.* **rationalize** (both meanings).

rational learning: 1. learning that includes adequate understanding of the facts in their relationships, e.g. the reason for each step in a mathematical proof.—*Contr. w.* **blind learning. 2.** the learning of material which, for the individual learner, is meaningful and rational.—*Contr. w.* **rote *learning, nonsense-syllable** learning.

rational number: see **number/rational.**

rational principle: (*C. Ruckmick*) a general type of reasoning that characterizes an investigation: e.g., **hypothetico-deductive; inductive** or **deductive; analytic** or **synthetic;** or mixed.—See **method** for discussion.

rational problem-solving: arriving at a solution by sound reasoning on the basis of the best available evidence; realistic problem-solving.—*Contr. w.* **defense mechanism.**

rational psychology: a system in which the framework for the systematizing of empirical facts consists of philosophical (or theological) assumptions.—*Syn.* PHILOSOPHICAL PSYCHOLOGY.—*Ant.* **empirical psychology, scientific psychology.** ➤A psychology based throughout upon the assumption that all psychological phenomena are manifestations of an immortal immaterial soul is a rational or philosophical psychology. It is not always recognized that a psychology based on the assumption that all psychological phenomena are manifestations of a material body is equally a philosophical psychology, no matter how much factual material may be amassed. Empirical or scientific psychology is neutral to such assumptions. ¶A **hypothetico-deductive** system appears similar to rational psychology, since both employ rational deductive procedures. But the basic postulates of rational psychology arise outside psychology and are for that discipline a priori; the basic postulates of a hypothetico-deductive system arise within psychology from a survey of facts, and are subject to revision in the light of facts.—See **psychology/divisions and schools of, I.**

rational type: (*C. G. Jung*) a classification of individuals who regulate their conduct chiefly by thinking and feeling, in contrast with the IRRATIONAL TYPE for whom sensation and intuition are predominant.—See **function types.** ➤Note the assignment of *feeling* to the rational side of the dichotomy, a usage peculiar to the school of Jung.

ratio reinforcement: see **reinforcement/ratio.**

ratio scaling: see **scale/ratio.**

raw: *adj.* in its natural state, or nearly so.

raw score: see **score/raw.**

ray: *n.* representation by a line of the direction of travel of light or radiant energy.

Rayleigh equation: a statement of the proportion of red and green stimuli required to match a given yellow. ➤Usually a spectrum red (670 mμ) is mixed with a spectrum green (535 mμ) to match a spectrum yellow (589 mμ). Persons who are anomalous **trichromates**—i.e., either red-weak or green-weak—require either more red or more green for a match.

RB: *abbr.* for **reactional biography.**

Rc = **CR,** the response that is conditioned. —See **conditioned response,** note on symbols.

R class = **response class.**

R correlation or **R technique:** a technique to determine (under constant conditions and for a given population of persons) how closely two tasks or functions are related. ➤When **correlation** is spoken of without qualifier, the *R* correlation is usually meant. It is to be contrasted with the *Q, O,* and *P* techniques. (We follow here the terminology, and to a large extent the analysis, of R. B. Cattell.) The *Q* TECHNIQUE, which is the same as the INVERSE FACTOR TECHNIQUE, correlates persons rather than functions: it asks, essentially, how similar two persons are (under constant conditions and in respect to a population of tasks). The *P* TECHNIQUE is a **factor** method that requires the measurement of one person on many tasks and on many occasions. The task functions characteristic of the person are not influenced in consistent fashion by variations in occasion and hence emerge as clusters. The *O* TECHNIQUE is a factor method that determines the effect upon **variance** of types or classes of occasions, thus permitting the inference that certain occasions are dynamically similar despite superficial differences. The method correlates occasions for the same person on two tests at a time.

In each of the four techniques, a pair of variables is compared and is conventionally entered in the vertical columns. The *R* technique compares *tasks,* with different persons for the horizontal rows. The *Q* technique compares two *persons,* with tasks for the rows. In the *P* technique the columns are the same person on different task functions (compared two at a time) and the rows are occasions. In the *O* technique the columns are the same person on different occasions (compared two at a time) and the rows are task functions. It is to be noted that the *P* and the *O* techniques yield, not a single correlation, but a correlation **matrix.**

RdA = **reading *age.**

RdQ = **reading quotient.**

reaction: *n.* **1.** (*psychol.*) what an organism

does when stimulated; a relatively simple way of acting when an outside stimulus impinges on the organism. ➤It is usually defined in terms of the muscular and glandular activities elicited by the stimulus, but occasionally in terms of the effect produced in the external world. The term may also cover the entire sensorimotor process, even including affective components.—See under **act** for the relation to kindred terms. **2.** (*psychiat.*) = REACTION PATTERN, a combination of behaviors forming a cluster or syndrome and constituting a distinct kind of disorder or disease. **3.** (*sociol.*) a social movement opposite to the prevailing tendency; or one judged to be contrary to human progress. **4.** (*pop.*) a social response indicating attitude or feeling: what was his *reaction?*—*adj.* (for **1** and **2**) **reactive,** which see; (for **3**) **reactionary.**

In phrases, **reaction** is often interchangeable with **act, behavior, movement, process, response.** Most phrases with *reaction* are entered under the qualifying adjective: e.g., *abient reaction* is entered as **abient response.**

reactional biography: the history of an individual with emphasis upon his actions rather than upon the situations to which he has been exposed. ➤The term is used instead of **experience,** to avoid **mentalistic** connotations.

reaction arc: see **nervous arc.**

reaction chain: see **chain/behavior.**

reaction/circular: see **circular behavior.**

reaction-evocation potentiality = **reaction potential.**

reaction/false: reacting in an experiment to a stimulus other than the one prescribed; or a similar reaction in nonlaboratory situations: e.g., the runner who leaves the mark before the gun, having *seen* a movement.

reaction formation: *n.* (*psychoan.*) establishment of a trait or a regular pattern of behavior that is directly opposed to a strong unconscious trend; or the pattern itself. ➤Reaction formation is more permanent and covers a greater area of personality than a **defense reaction.** Development of aggressive behavior as a means of repressing or denying fear, or of great sympathy as a means of repressing sadistic impulses, are examples. The original impulses are, however, likely to break through at times.—*Cp.* **reactive reinforcement.**

reaction key: a circuit interrupter, resembling a telegraph key, often used in the measurement of **reaction time.**

reaction latency or $_sT_R$: see **latency (2).**

reaction levels: a conception or **model** of the working of the nervous system according to which simple functions are carried out by the lower levels of the nervous

system, more complex functions by intermediate levels, and still more complex functions at the highest level. Four *anatomical* levels roughly correspond with functional levels: the spinal, the hindbrain, the midbrain, and the forebrain. The **autonomic nervous system** does not quite fit into this model but perhaps belongs with the spinal level.

reaction potential or $_sE_R$: (*C. Hull*) the possibility that a particular response will occur. It is a function of **habit strength** ($_sH_R$) multiplied by a function of the relevant drive **(D).** The unit for measuring $_sE_R$ is called the **wat.**—*Syn.* REACTION TENDENCY (less precise), REACTION-EVOCATION POTENTIALITY, SPECIFIC ACTION POTENTIAL.

reaction psychology: a point of view that emphasizes the motor activity of the organism. ➤Without necessarily denying mental content or introspection, certainly without denying that the permanent or temporary organization of the animal influences the response, action is primarily conceived as reaction-to-stimulus. Reaction psychology has a somewhat less **molecular** connotation than **stimulus-response psychology.** *Distg. fr.* **reactivist psychology,** which emphasizes the stimulus.

reaction system = **action system.**

reaction time: the interval between application of a stimulus and the beginning of the subject's response. ➤It is necessary to specify how the beginning of the response is to be demonstrated. In the traditional experiment, it is such a movement of the hand on a telegraph key as would make (or better, break) an electric current. Occasionally the **reaction time** is taken to extend to the completion of a response, in which case that fact should be explicitly stated.

In SIMPLE REACTION TIME, a predetermined response is made as quickly as possible to a prearranged signal. In DISCRIMINATION REACTION TIME, response is made to one, but not to others, of two or more expected signals. In COGNITIVE REACTION TIME, response is not to be made until the stimulus is recognized. In CHOICE REACTION TIME, a different response is specified for each kind of stimulus. All of these except the first are called COMPLEX or COMPOUND REACTION TIMES.

If, from the total of the reaction time, there is subtracted the time required for the passage of **afferent** and **efferent** impulses to and from the cortex, and for the conversion of the efferent impulse into muscular contraction, the difference is the CENTRAL, ABBREVIATED, or REDUCED REACTION TIME. (But this so-called SUBTRACTION PROCEDURE is now generally regarded as invalid.)

Since the stimulus to be expected is in some way stipulated and the response to be made is agreed upon in advance, INTENTIONAL RESPONSE TIME would be more accurate than **reaction time.** The reaction time of popular thinking is the time required for an adaptive response to an *unexpected* stimulus. The correlation between this and the intentional response time of the classical reaction time experiment is not high.

—See also **reaction type, association test.**

reaction type: 1. in **reaction time** experiments and related situations, those persons or that group of reactions that are controlled by a particular **set.** In the MUSCULAR (or MOTOR) REACTION TYPE, the subject is set to respond as quickly as possible and attention is on the movement he is to make; in the SENSORY REACTION TYPE, he is set to apprehend the coming stimulus. The MOTOR TYPE gives lower average reaction times and a greater number of false reactions. **2.** (*psychiat.*) a syndrome described in terms of the preponderating symptom; or the person exhibiting such a syndrome. ➤E.g., a PARANOID REACTION TYPE is a group of symptoms (or a person exhibiting them) characterized by **paranoid** behavior.

reactive: *adj.* **1.** capable of responding; or easily aroused to response. **2.** characterizing that which functions only when an external source of energy impinges; or of behavior that is primarily determined by the external situation. ➤*Contr. w.* **active,** characterizing a system that functions as a result of changes within itself. (The changes may consist of further internal changes or may affect things outside the system.) ¶ A REACTIVIST PSYCHOLOGY (REACTIVISM) stresses the part played by external stimulus in determining behavior, an ACTIVE (or ACTIVIST) PSYCHOLOGY stresses the role of the person or organism. This contrast, though it is only of emphasis (since all psychologists concede that all behavior is to some degree both reactivist and activist), tends as much as any other to dichotomize contemporary psychology.—See **psychology/divisions and schools of, V. 3.** = counteracting (see **reactive reinforcement**).

reactive depression = **depressive reaction.**

reactive psychosis: psychosis primarily attributable to very strong environmental pressures.—*Syn.* SITUATION PSYCHOSIS.

reactive reinforcement: (*psychoan.*) the hypothesized tendency of a conscious process to stir up an unconscious process in the opposite direction: e.g., conscious hate activates unconscious love. ➤COUNTERACTING REINFORCEMENT would better express the meaning intended, since what is supposed to be reinforced is reaction *against,* not re-

action *to.*—*Cp.* **reaction formation; bipolarity.**

reactive type: a person whose behavior is not primarily determined by his own nature and condition, but is instead strongly contingent upon external conditions.—*Cp.* **other-directed.**—*Distg. fr.* **reaction type.**

reactivist psychology: see **reactive.**

reactor: *n.* the one who reacts to a stimulus or stimulus situation. ➤This is one of the many partial synonyms for **person.** As contrasted with **actor** or **agent,** the term stresses relative passivity.—*Cp.* **reactive.**

readability: *n.* the quality of a written or printed communication that makes it easy for any of a given class of persons to understand its meaning, or that induces them to continue reading. ➤The criteria brought forward for determining readability suggest that it is not a single variable but a combination of at least three or four.

readiness: *n.* **1.** preparedness to respond or react. **2.** a state or condition of the person that makes it possible for him to engage profitably in a given learning activity. It depends on (*a*) maturity, (*b*) relevant preparatory training, and (*c*) an aroused interest or motive. ➤While readiness is sometimes spoken of as if it were a trait or entity, there is no single condition of readiness: it is a composite of many personal qualities and conditions and differs from one learning task to another. See **reading *readiness.**

readiness and unreadiness/laws of: (*E. L. Thorndike*) three postulates intended to help state the meaning of **satisfaction** and **annoyance** without using subjective terms: (*a*) when a **conduction unit** is ready to conduct, conduction by it is satisfying, provided nothing is done to alter its action; (*b*) for a conduction unit ready to conduct, not to conduct is annoying; (*c*) when a conduction unit unready for conduction is forced to conduct, conduction by it is annoying.

readiness grouping = **ability grouping** (which see).

readiness/maturational: that part of the necessary ability or motivation to respond to a learning situation which is due to having attained sufficient **maturity.**

readiness/reading: the totality of **personal** factors conductive to satisfactory progress in learning to read under given conditions of instruction. ➤The readiness is not an absolute but a matter of more or less. The relevant factors may be intellectual, emotional and motivational, or physiological. Both general **maturation** and effective specific previous experiences play a part. A child may be ready for one kind of reading method and not for another.

reading: *n.* **1.** the perception of written,

printed, or engraved symbols constituting a communication, and the (at least partial) understanding of the conventional meaning of the symbols. ➤WORD-NAMING (pronouncing the word), while sometimes mistaken for reading, is neither necessary nor sufficient. The ability to read single or isolated symbols is an improper and partial criterion of **reading** in the full sense, which involves understanding a message of greater complexity. **2.** the perception of gestures, lip movements, etc., and the understanding of their conventional meanings. ➤Reading is seldom applied to auditory perception of messages: **hearing** and *listening* are the nearest (but inadequate) words for the process of "sound-reading."

reading age: see **age/reading.**

reading/backward: see **backward reading.**

reading disability: a marked inability to read as well as expected, relative to mental age and amount of instruction received. ➤The term is relative. The reading ability that is normal for a fourth-grader is a disability in a high-school student.—*Distg. fr.* **illiteracy.**—*Syn.* **dyslexia** (pathological).

reading ladder: a classification of reading materials for difficulty, so that the learner can be given material just one step more difficult than his present level.

reading/mirror: reading from right to left when the convention of the language is from left to right.

reading quotient or **RdQ:** a measure of a child's rate of learning to read, computed by dividing his reading age—as determined on a standardized reading test—by his chronological age. ➤Mental age is sometimes used as the divisor, but this is confusing.

reading readiness: see **readiness/reading.**

reading/remedial: individual or group instruction pointed directly at correcting specific ascertained faulty reading habits.

reading span: the number of words perceived in a single **fixation** pause.—*Syn.* RECOGNITION SPAN. ➤The usual procedure is to present only one line and to count the number of words grasped per fixation. This is inaccurate, since good readers, while perceiving a third of one line, will often perceive words in the next two or three lines.

real: *adj.* **1.** existing in fact; not imaginary or theoretical. **2.** existing as a physical object, not merely as an object of awareness. ➤The second meaning, especially, is heavily loaded with metaphysical implications, many of them rather old-fashioned.—See **realism.**—*Syn.* **actual,** which is somewhat more emphatic and is sometimes influenced by its meaning. in other European lan-

guages, of being present here and now.— *Distg. fr.* **true,** which applies to propositions and conclusions.—*n.* **reality.**

realism: *n.* **1.** any of a number of philosophical doctrines which assert that objects have an independent existence—i.e., are not dependent for their existence upon the knower. **2.** an attitude of being sensitive to, and guided by, things as they are, rather than as one wishes they were. **3.** an attitude of scorning elaborate and idealistic efforts to alter the *status quo*; a willingness to do what seems to need doing, even if it falls short of the desirable or the ethical. **4.** (*J. Piaget*) the tendency in naïve persons, esp. children, to accept one's own personal perception as being a correct apprehension of the way things truly are. ➤E.g., the child who sees a picture on the back of father's newspaper may think father sees it too; or he believes that his dream really happened and may implicitly expect others to have experienced it too. This usage is confusing, since the tendency so named is related to **illusion,** whereas **realism** is at the other end of a continuum from illusion. **5.** (*educ.*) any of several movements that advocate orientation of pupils to the contemporary and the concrete world rather than to the classic, literary, and verbal worlds.—*Ant.* (for **1, 2, 3**) **idealism.**—*adj* **realistic.**—*pers. n.* **realist.**

realism/moral: see **moral realism.**

reality: *n.* **1.** the totality of material objects—i.e., of objects having mass, of things directly measurable in seconds, centimeters or grams. **2.** the totality of all conditions imposed by the external world upon an organism's activity; the totality of existing objects, including such constructs as gravity; the totality of that which cannot be merely wished or thought away. ➤If one considers the question of whether a ghost firmly believed in is or is not real, the near impossibility of avoiding metaphysical implications is apparent. Yet there is no simple synonym.—*Cp.* **irreality level.**

reality adaptation: the ability of a person to adjust himself to things as they are without **rationalization** or **autistic** perception

reality awareness: the perception of external objects as different from the self and from each other.

reality/contact with: perceiving the **milieu** substantially as do most persons in one's culture. ➤Contact with reality requires more than correct sense perception. For a Hindu child, a cow must be perceived as sacred; for an American, swimming trunks on a man at the beach are perceived as adequate covering. Some individuality of perception is compatible with being in contact with reality.

reality ego: (*psychoan.*) the pleasure-yielding objects of the external world that are absorbed by the **ego.**

reality feeling: an unreflective and immediate attitude that an object is actually there, that the world is substantial and enduring. ➤It is to be contrasted with **belief** in the reality of the world. Occasional loss of reality feeling is nearly universal, but prolonged loss is indicative of serious mental disturbance.

reality/flight from: see **reality/retreat from.**

reality-irreality: see **irreality-reality dimension.**

reality level/objective: (*gen. semantics*) that level of reality which is reachable through sense observation, with or without the aid of instruments. ➤New developments in science make it difficult to draw a strict line between such direct observation and inference.—See **irreality-reality dimension.**

reality principle: (*psychoan.*) awareness of the demands of the environment and adjustment of behavior to these demands in such a way that the individual ultimately secures satisfaction of instinctual needs. ➤The reality principle is thus a modifier of the **pleasure principle.** It is part of the **ego** structure.

reality/retreat from: 1. the substitution of imaginary satisfactions for those that involve facing facts. **2.** more generally, any behavior that enables one to evade facing facts: e.g., **rationalization, daydreaming,** the resort to alcohol, a fatiguing whirl of gaiety, a neurotic "illness" that prevents one's taking an examination one fears but will not admit one fears, etc. **Fugue** is an extreme retreat from reality.—*Syn.* FLIGHT FROM REALITY.

reality situation: the actual environment objectively considered: the physical, the economic, and the interpersonal factors (including the *real* attitudes and emotions of others).

reality testing: 1. tentative action to see whether something will work. ➤It differs from **trial and error** in being guided by hypothesis or implicit hypothesis. In psychoanalysis, it is a function of the **ego. 2.** active experimenting and checking by the child to determine how far he can modify an event or process and how far it resists modification. ➤Through such trial the child gradually learns to distinguish between himself and external reality.

rearrangement test: see **test/rearrangement.**

reason: *n.* **1.** the totality of those activities or functions that enable man to think logically. ➤Historically, the totality was ascribed to a faculty, the Reason; but many different processes are now known to be involved in logical thinking. **2.** a statement

offered as explanation or justification of a belief or act. **3.** a statement of one's **motivation. 4.** a cause. **5.** the intelligible or understandable aspect of a phenomenon. **6.** a sound mind.—*v.* **7.** to think; esp., to infer; to think correctly or logically.—*adj.* **rational.**

reasonable result: (*math.*) a value, obtained by calculation and/or substitution, that lies within the range of practicable possibility. ➤E.g., if one calculated a business profit of 800 per cent, one would suspect error.

reasoning: *n.* **1.** that form of thinking which finds its completest expression in logical forms (whether the conclusions reached are valid or not). The reasoner is usually aware that a **judgment** (the conclusion) is dependent upon other judgments (the **premises**). **2.** problem-solving by means of general principles.—*Syn.* RATIOCINATION.

reassurance: *n.* a procedure in psychotherapy that seeks to give the client confidence in a favorable outcome. It makes use of suggestion, of the prestige of the therapist, of persuasive arguments, and of the citation of parallel cases.

rebelliousness/neurotic: a form of **neurotic *resignation** (which see) in which there is persistent active resistance to the acceptance of "**shoulds.**" ➤The resistance may be directed outwardly against rules and regulations or significant authority figures, or inwardly as discontent with oneself.

rebirth fantasy: (*psychoan.*) the symbolic representation of being born, generally in a dream or other fantasy: e.g., a dream of emerging from water.

rebreather technique: a method of experimentally inducing **anoxia** through inhalation of dilute mixtures of oxygen and nitrogen, simulating the oxygen deficiency of rebreathed air.

recall: *n.* **1.** the process whereby a representation of past experience is elicited; specif., evoking or experiencing an **image.** ➤The term, so innocent-appearing, implies a complex theory, and undoubtedly influences the thinking of people who would reject the theory if explicitly stated. **2.** the repetition of words or similar material previously learned.—See **redintegration, recognition, recollection, remembering.**

recall method or **procedure:** a means of measuring **retention** or **forgetting** by determining the percentage of once-learned items the subject can recall or otherwise reproduce after a given interval.

recall score method = **retained members method.**

recall test: see **test/recall.**

recapitulation theory: the doctrine that

the individual, in his personal development, passes through a series of stages that represent stages in the evolutionary development of the species. ➤Formerly, the principle was thought to hold with much exactness and was made the basis of educational objectives; it is now believed no more than roughly true (esp. of behavior tendencies) although of some value in embryology. The theory was stated in the famous sentence: *ontogeny recapitulates phylogeny.*

receiver: *n.* (*commun. theory*) that which transforms a **signal** into a **message:** in an animal, the sense organ and its connections in the brain.

receiving hospital: an institution that receives for diagnosis and early treatment individuals suspected of mental disorder. Legal commitment as insane is not necessary. If short treatment is not deemed sufficient, the patients are recommended for treatment in other institutions.

recency/law of: the principle or postulate that a given item is more likely to remind a person of some recent **associate** than of one more remote in time; that, other things being equal, what is learned is remembered in proportion to its recency.—*Cp.* **Jost's law.**

recenter: *v.* to replace an inadequate **figure-ground** relation with a better; to anchor the perceptual field to a different part thereof. ➤E.g., if the correct choice of a path to a goal has been the middle of three, and that middle has always been red, the animal (or person) may react to red as the cue to the right path (is said to be **centered** on red). If the first (and still wrong) path is now made red, and if the animal chooses that path, he is said to be **decentered.** When he learns to react to middleness as the cue to the right path, he is **recentering.** The whole perceptual field is reorganized: the figure at first was *the red,* is now *the middle.*

recept (rē'sept): *n.* **1.** (*neurol.*) the process or change taking place in the **afferent** side of a **neural transit.** ➤The term avoids implying anything about sensation or perception. **2.** (*hist.*) the mental image of that which is common to a series of perceptions that have been repeated with variation.

receptive character: (*E. Fromm*) a person who requires support from other persons, is passive in relation to them, and finds gratification in what is given him. Fromm also speaks of RECEPTIVE ORIENTATION.—*Syn.* ORAL-PASSIVE TYPE.

receptivity: *n.* **1.** openness to influence by sensation or by ideas; inclination to accept readily. **2.** an attitude in which one puts forth no effort.—*Syn.* PASSIVITY (*prefd.*).

receptor: *n.* in an animal body, a specialized structure that is sensitive to specific

forms of physical energy and initiates a **neural impulse;** one of the sensitive parts of the body by which we detect changes in the environment or in the position or movement of the body. ➤*Syn.* **sense organ** (which is sometimes restricted to a highly complex structure that includes nonneural parts, whereas **receptor** may refer also to an afferent nerve ending that receives stimuli). Receptors are classified according to the **sense** *modality (vision, audition, smell, taste, pressure, coolth, warmth, pain); or as **exteroceptors, interoceptors,** and **proprioceptors.**—*adj.* **receptor.**

receptor/distance: see **distance receptor.**

recess: *n.* a period of rest, recreation, or other radically altered activity interposed between periods of work or prescribed behavior.

recessive: *adj.* **1.** tending to recede or go back; failing to come to expression. **2.** (*genet.*) characterizing a **gene** that does not express itself (i.e., does not produce an observable effect in the offspring) unless both members of a **gene pair** are recessive; of a gene that remains latent or subordinate if the other member of the gene pair is **dominant. 3.** (*genet.*) characterizing the observable trait that develops when both genes are recessive.—See **recessive character** and **dominant (3).**—*n.* **recessiveness,** the quality of being recessive; **recessive,** a RECESSIVE GENE or RECESSIVE TRAIT.

recessive character or **trait:** a trait, controlled by heredity, that remains latent or subordinate to a **dominant character** (see **dominant 3)** unless both members of the gene pair are recessive.

recessive gene: see **dominant (3).**

recidivism (ri·sid'ə·viz·əm): *n.* the repetition or recurrence of delinquent or criminal conduct, or of a mental disorder. ➤Some authorities limit the term to cases in which recurrence leads to a second conviction or commitment.—*Syn.* RECIDIVATION.—*adj.* **recidivous.**—*pers. n.* **recidivist.**

recipathy (ri·sip'ə·thi): *n.* a term formed by combining *reciprocal* and *sympathy* to mean an interaction at the level of feeling such that two persons, from sharing each other's feelings, come to a common feeling.

reciprocal: *n.* **1.** (*math.*) the number required to multiply a given number to make unity: 6 and 1/6, or *n* and 1/*n*, are reciprocals.—*adj.* **2.** done or given in return; mutual; corresponding, but reversed or inverted.

reciprocal inhibition: inability to recall either of two **associated** items, because of their interference with each other.—*Syn.* INTERFERENCE.

reciprocal innervation: the arrangement whereby the contraction of one of a pair of **antagonistic muscles** is accompanied by relaxation of the other. When this is followed by a reversal, alternating movements of the member result.

reciprocity principle: the generalization that response is influenced by the product of duration and intensity of the stimulation, independently of the magnitude of either one alone. ➤E.g., a very brief hot stimulus equals a longer moderately hot stimulus. The principle holds only within narrow limits.—*Syn.* BUNSEN-ROSCOE LAW.

recitation: *n.* **1.** a teaching procedure in which pupils orally demonstrate, by **recall** and by answers to questions, what they have learned (or, more often, what they have memorized). **2.** that aspect of an instructional unit given over to questioning back and forth between pupils and teacher, as contrasted with laboratory, lecture, pupil reports, or study. SOCIALIZED RECITATION includes pupil participation in group activities (usually small groups), pupil leadership, and considerable emphasis upon spontaneity of discussion.

recitation procedure: a technique of memorizing wherein the subject tries (at stated intervals or at every trial) to recall as much as possible before reviewing or studying further. ➤An experimental procedure, but usable also in study.

recognition: *n.* **1.** awareness of an **object (2)** as one that has been previously experienced; a form of remembering. **2.** awareness of the meaning of a symbol: word *recognition.* **3.** acknowledgment of a person's merit.—*adj.* **recognitional, recognitive.**—*v.* **recognize.**

recognition method, procedure, test: a procedure in which the subject is required to say whether a presented item has been previously presented, or to indicate which of a group of items has been previously presented.

recognition span: see **reading span.**

recognition vocabulary: see **vocabulary/ recognition.**

recollection: *n.* the form of remembering that follows desire or effort to remember, and that places what is remembered in its past context: i.e., events are more or less dated and associated with their past attendant circumstances.

reconditioning: *n.* **1.** strengthening a conditioned response by reintroducing the unconditioned stimulus. ➤The term is more purely descriptive than **reinforcement. 2.** bringing about discontinuance of a conditioned response by associating a new response with the stimulus. ➤An unfortunate usage: DECONDITIONING is more descriptive.

reconstruction: *n.* interpretation of biographical and autobiographical data (including psychoanalytic **protocols**) to find what they mean in the life of the subject:

e.g., correlation of a child's loss of mother at age 3 with his present excessive striving for teacher's attention. ➤The term is usually used only when the data are extensive. A theoretical point of view, implicit or explicit, governs the process.

reconstruction method or **procedure:** a procedure for testing **retention** in which the subject is asked to restore a disordered series to its previously studied order.

record/anecdotal: see **anecdotal record.**

record/behavior: see **behavior record.**

record/cumulative: 1. a continuous and continuing record, in which new material is added to the old. **2.** a student's **point-hour ratio** from matriculation to date.—*Syn.* ACCUMULATIVE RECORD.

recovery: *n.* the return of an organism or an organ to its normal state after impairment of function; or, such return after stimulation.—*Cp.* **homeostasis, refractory period.**

recovery quotient: the ratio between the **arousal** and the **discharge indices** of behavior. It is a measure of **homeostatic** balance.

recovery/spontaneous: When a conditioned response has been **extinguished,** it can often be elicited again after several days of rest, though response strength is diminished.

recovery time: the brief interval following response when that response cannot be repeated.—*Syn.* **refractory period.**

recreation: *n.* any activity, voluntarily (at least semivoluntarily) engaged in, designed to give pleasure and to refresh the participant mentally or physically.—*Cp.* **play.**

recruitment: *n.* (*neurol.*) a widening of the effect when stimulation is prolonged. In EXCITATORY RECRUITMENT, more and more **effectors** are excited; in INHIBITORY RECRUITMENT, an inhibitory stimulus inhibits response in more and more effectors.

recruitment of loudness: (*aud.*) the phenomenon that, as intensity of a tone increases, perceived loudness increases more rapidly for the partially nerve-deaf ear than for the normal ear. Hence, nerve-deaf persons hear better at high intensity than would be expected from their intensity threshold.—*Syn.* AUDITORY REGRESSION.

rectilinear: *adj.* capable of being represented graphically by a straight line.—*Cp.* **curvilinear.**—*Syn.* **linear.**—*n.* **rectilinearity.**

recurrent: *adj.* repeated after a time interval.—*Cp.* **periodic** or **rhythmic,** which are more specific.

red: *n.* **1.** the **hue** attribute of visual sensations typically evoked by stimulation of the normal human eye by long-wave radiation, from around 650 millimicrons to the end of the visible spectrum. **2.** any hue predominantly similar to that of the typical red; the complement of blue-green or **cyan.**

red-green blindness: a common form of partial **color blindness,** or **dichromatism,** in which red and green stimuli are confused because they are seen as various saturations and brightnesses of yellow, blue, or gray.—*Cp.* **protanopia, deuteranopia.**

redintegration: *n.* **1.** the re-establishing of a whole; putting together again.—*Syn.* REINTEGRATION. **2.** (*hist.*) the principle that the presence in consciousness of one element of a whole tends to the **imaginal** revival of others, or of the whole. TOTAL REDINTEGRATION is complete recall of every detail. **3.** (*H. Hollingworth*) the principle that presence of a single element of a former event tends to bring about the psychological consequence of the event as a whole. ➤The simple case is that wherein part of the former stimulus situation elicits the response. But the "element of the former event" may be a response (with its proprioceptive sensations), may be a feeling tone, or may be the imaginal or ideational content. Any of these may act as **cue.** The consequent is equally broadly conceived as motor, glandular, feeling, or imaginal and ideational response. **4.** the principle that any sensory process occurring simultaneously with a response elicited by some other stimulus tends to become capable of independently eliciting the response. ➤This is essentially the principle of classical **conditioning (1)** or the **law of *contiguity.** Note that the operation of redintegration as in meaning (4)—i.e., the repeated elicitation of the response by the conditioned stimulus without the original stimulus—leads to **extinction,** whereas the operation of redintegration as in meaning (3)—i.e., of responding to the reduced cue—generally strengthens the tendency to react to that cue.

redirection activity: (*ethology*) an activity elicited by two very different simultaneous stimuli but oriented toward only one. ➤E.g., in some territory-claiming birds, intruders are fought off by the male only after the acquisition of a mate. The addition of the mate is an essential condition for a nonmating behavior. This has been said to be the analogue, perhaps the basis, of **displacement;** but the two processes seem quite different.

red-sighted: *adj.* displaying a heightened color sensitivity for red, or a tendency to see all objects tinged with red. ➤It results from (*a*) some unknown variation in the eye or nervous system, or (*b*) prolonged exposure to the complementary green, or (*c*) overexposure to intensive light and possible hemorrhage. The last form is called **erythropsia.**

reduced cues/principle of: With repetition, a progressively smaller part of the original situation is needed to elicit the response.—*Syn.* LAW OF PARTIAL ACTIVITY.

reduced eye: a simplified schematic system or model designed to have the same optical properties as the average unaccommodated human eye.—*Syn.* SCHEMATIC EYE, LISTING'S REDUCED EYE.

reductio ad absurdum (ri·duk′shi·ō ad ab·sėr′dəm): a method of disproving a proposition by showing that it leads logically to an absurd conclusion—i.e., one contrary to accepted truth. ➤"The less you eat, the healthier you will be" leads to the absurd conclusion that eating nothing is healthiest of all.

reduction: *n.* a lessening of a state or activity; specif., in psychology, the hypothesized lessening of a **drive,** a **need,** or a **tension.** ➤The empirical data leading to inference of a reduction in drive, need, or tension are often so vaguely stated that it cannot be told whether we have three different processes or only one. Reduction (in one or all of the three activities or states) is theorized as constituting **reinforcement** or **motive.** See **drive-reduction hypothesis.**—*v.* **reduce.**

reduction division: (*biol.*) the formation of **gametes** by so dividing the cell that only half of the chromosomes go to each daughter cell. ➤*Contr. w.* **mitosis,** a kind of division in which each chromosome splits and the daughter cells have a full number.

reductionism: *n.* a general point of view which holds that complex phenomena are to be understood and explained by analyzing them into ever simpler, and ultimately into strictly **elementary,** components. ➤Analysis, even reductive analysis (see **analysis 1**), is a method of investigation employed by everyone. Reductionism is a point of view about the results of analysis: it holds that the analyzed parts are real and that the whole can be completely explained as made up *only* of the analyzed parts. It is thus the opposite of **emergentism** and **Gestalt,** which hold that the whole is more than the sum of its parts. The reductionism of **structural psychology** attempted to reduce all psychological phenomena to the most elementary *psychological* processes. Contemporary reductionism generally seeks to phrase psychological problems in stimulus-response terms and to reduce these further to physiological or even physicochemical terms. (The term **reductionism** is more likely to be used by its opponents than by its advocates.)—See **molar, molecular, explanation;** also **psychology/ divisions and schools of, VII.**

reduction screen: an opaque screen (typically of cardboard) with two small clean-edged holes in the center placed so that the holes viewed binocularly at a comfortable distance do not fuse. The two visual fields are seen in good approximation to the objective light intensities.—*Syn.* HOLE SCREEN.

reductive explanation or **analysis**: see **reductionism, explanation (2), analysis (1).**

reductive interpretation: (*C. Jung*) an interpretation of behavior, not in terms of its function as a **symbol** for the individual, but as a **sign** of some unconscious process. ➤It is reductive interpretation when a **tic** is interpreted as a sign of unconscious conflict or tension. It is symbolic interpretation when the tic of wrinkling the nose is taken to symbolize a conflict-charged effort to avoid bad smells.

redundancy or *T* **function:** *n.* (*info. theory*) that property of a message which reduces the error of prediction for a given event to less than chance by virtue of the fact that the message contains information about what will come next. ➤If a message begins "Hurry h———", it contains some information about what will (probably) follow, hence the error of prediction is less than a chance level. Such a message contains **redundancy.** The message "Hurry h———" is redundant not only about its own continuation but about the event it may lead to—e.g., there is an above-chance probability that the recipient will *go* home.

This new meaning for redundancy does violence to its ordinary established meaning of *excess*. "Hurry h———" may have more information than none at all, but it does not have too much; rather, it still has too little. To say it is redundant is confusing. Is a communication redundant? "That's bad," according to the old meaning, "pare it down." "That's good," says the new meaning, "make it more so."—See **neologism, rational coinage.**

re-education: *n.* 1. restoration of a lost function by appropriate training. 2. getting rid of certain habits or attitudes and gaining new ones in their place. 3. the whole process of learning and teaching involved in restoring a person to a functioning place in society after incapacitating injury or illness, or after a period of delinquency or crime. ➤A person must relearn to walk after being fitted with an artificial leg; a businessman needs to learn to delegate more responsibility and to save himself after a certain kind of neurotic illness; a juvenile delinquent needs to learn a new system of values and perhaps certain vocational skills.

reefer: *n.* (*slang*) a marihuana cigarette.

re-enactment/emotional = **abreaction (1).**

re-enforcement = **reinforcement.**

refer: *v.* 1. to assign a sense impression to its source or to a place in space: to *refer* the toot to the distant train. 2. to send a client to another agency or professional colleague for help.—*n.* **reference, referral.**

reference axes: (*factor anal.*) the axes of two independent (or **orthogonal**) common factors, in relation to which the other factor axes are located.

reference frame: 1. = **frame of reference.** 2. (*stat.*) the final position after **rotation** of the **vectors** that represent the **factors.**

reference group: see **group/reference.**

reference/objective: a quality, inherent in certain perceptual processes, of pointing to the objective world. ➤Sounds, except for a ringing in the head and similar so-called subjective phenomena, seem to be inherently external; most visual experiences are of something "out there."

reference vector: (*factor anal.*) the set of coordinates or axes in relation to which **test *vectors** are located. They provide anchoring lines or planes by reference to which the mathematical relations found in the **correlation *matrix** can be expressed geometrically and trigonometrically. In **rotation** these axes must retain the same origin as the test vectors but may be rotated about the origin.

referent: *n.* the object, event, or abstraction that is pointed to by a word or other symbol. ➤Note that the referent may be abstract as well as concrete, though some contend that the abstract referent is meaningless unless it *rests* on concrete referents. *Cp.* the analogous requirement of **operational definition.**

referral (rē·fêr'əl): *n.* the act of sending a person to another person or agency for help; or the person so sent.

referred sensation: a sensory experience localized elsewhere than at the point stimulated. ➤Most sounds and sights, but only some tactual experiences, are regularly so referred.—*Cp.* **projection/eccentric, reference/objective, pain/referred.**

refixation: *n.* fixating the eye again after a brief period when **fixation** is lost; more specif., the fixation that follows a regressive movement in reading.

reflected color: color seen as reflected from a perceived object. It is contrasted with **film color** and **illuminant *color,** and generally coincides with **surface *color.**

reflection: *n.* 1. = (*hist.*) **introspection.** 2. thinking about the significance, meaning, or value of certain experiences or facts; reflective thinking. 3. (*phys.*) the turning back of particles or waves striking a surface.—*Cp.* **refraction.** 4. production of an image by a mirror, or as in a mirror:

SPECULAR or MIRROR REFLECTION. **5.** (*factor anal.*) changing the algebraic signs throughout of some of the columns (and throughout the corresponding rows). It may be done to maximize the number of plus signs in the new correlation matrix, or to keep all the variables in the same "direction." ➤E.g., if a certain personality test is scored for unsociableness, and if the other tests are all of "positive" traits, reflection of the unsociable correlations may be desirable so that the entries are the correlations for sociableness. **6.** a manifestation of the influence of a certain variable: delinquency as a *reflection* of poor environment.

reflection/angle of: (*optics*) the angle between the path of a ray of light and the line perpendicular to the surface at the point from which the light is reflected.—*Distg. fr.* **refraction.**

reflection/corneal: see **corneal reflection.**

reflection of feeling: a technique in counseling or psychotherapy in which the counselor restates what the client has said in such a way as to bring out not so much the intellectual as the emotional meaning of the client's remark.

reflection response: (*Ror.*) one half of an **inkblot** card reported as the mirror reflection of the other.

reflection/specular = **reflection (4).**

reflex: *n.* **1.** (*hist.* and *gen.*) a very simple act in which there is no element of choice or premeditation and no variability save in intensity or time. ➤Unless qualified (as in ACQUIRED REFLEX), a **species-specific** or **innate** behavior is usually meant. **2.** a stimulus-response correlation, demonstrably unlearned, that is observable in all members of a species, and whose response strength is not influenced appreciably by changes in **drive. 3.** = **reflex arc.**—See discussion under (4) following. **4.** a relationship such that a given stimulus is followed by a given response. ➤Neither **(3)** nor **(4)** implies innateness, but the influence of **(1)** and **(2)** is so strong that this implication is often read into them; **(3)** and **(4)** are therefore not recommended.

Specific (or local) reflexes are listed in this dictionary under their differentiating names: e.g., **iris reflex, Babinski reflex.** Descriptive characterizations of kinds of reflexes follow after **reflex:** e.g., **reflex/compensatory.**

reflex arc: the theoretical unit of function in the nervous system (as the **neuron** is the unit of structure). At its simplest, the arc consists of a **receptor** nerve which, excited by a stimulus, transmits this excitation to an **effector** nerve via an intermediate neuron. ➤No such simple arc has been observed; all actual reflex arcs have more than the minimum of three neurons.—*Syn.* REFLEX

CIRCUIT, **nervous arc** (less common, but preferred as avoiding the innateness connotation of **reflex**). *Cp.* **sensorimotor arc,** which is slightly different.

reflex/association: = (*V. M. Bekhterev*) **conditioned response (1).**

reflex circle: the tendency of a muscle contraction to stimulate **proprioceptors,** which in turn restimulate the muscle.

reflex circuit = **reflex arc.**

reflex/compensatory: an automatic corrective movement made when the body, or a major part of it, loses equilibrium.

reflex/conditional or **/conditioned:** see **conditioned response (1).**

reflex/delayed: see **response/delayed.**

reflex/galvanic: see **electrodermal response.**

reflex inhibition: the reduction or complete inhibition of responsiveness of one reflex by action of another, or more generally, of one reaction by another.

reflexivity: *n.* (*logic*) the attribute of a dyadic (or two-termed) relation of "bending back." A relation R is **reflexive** if xRx holds for all x's. Equality, class inclusion, and formal equivalence are reflexive relations.

reflex latency = **reflex time.**—*Cp.* **latency.**

reflex/mass: see **mass reflex.**

reflexogenous zone (rē″fleks·oj′ə·nəs): a specific area on the body surface in which all points are roughly equivalent for the stimulation of a given reflex.

reflexology: *n.* the doctrine that all behavior can be explained in terms of reflexes and combinations of reflexes, esp. of **conditioned reflexes.**

reflex/prepotent: a **species-specific** reaction of such high survival value that it tends to take precedence over others: e.g., startle, avoidance, struggle, sensitive-zone, and sex reactions. The term is now seldom used.

reflex reserve: (*B. F. Skinner*) the total number of responses made after a reinforcing or rewarding stimulus is withdrawn: e.g., in the Skinner box, the number of times the animal tries the movement that earlier brought food. ➤It is a measure of resistance to **extinction.** The author of the construct now deems it unnecessary, but others do not.—*Syn.* OPERANT RESERVE.

reflex sensitization: the fact that, after repeated elicitation of an **R** by an **S,** the R may sometimes be elicited by a previously less effective or neutral stimulus.—*Cp.* **pseudoconditioning.**

reflex/spinal: 1. a complete reflex circuit passing through the spinal cord but not directly through a higher center. **2.** the reflex response that is manifested when the control of brain centers is removed.

reflex time: the **reaction time** of a reflex.—*Syn.* REFLEX LATENCY.—See **latency.**

refraction: *n.* a change in direction of propagation of a wave (light, sound, etc.) in passing from one medium to another of different density or elasticity.—*Distg. fr.* **reflection.**

refraction/error of: (*vis.*) the failure to focus the optical image normally upon the retina, either because of irregularities in the shape of the eyeball or in the optical characteristics of the cornea, aqueous humor, lens, or vitreous humor. These errors may be partly corrected by lenses.

refraction/index of: a number expressing how much a ray of light is bent in passing from one transparent medium to another. It depends on the nature of the two media and on the curvature of the bounding surface. ➤*Distg. fr.* ANGLE OF REFRACTION, the angle between the path of the ray through a medium and the line perpendicular to the surface at which the ray entered the medium.

refractory: *adj.* not subject to discipline; stubborn; disobedient; hard to cure.

refractory period or **phase: 1.** a brief period following stimulation of a nerve or muscle during which it is unresponsive to a second stimulus. The refractoriness may be ABSOLUTE (no response) or RELATIVE (response only if the stimulus is very strong). **2.** a brief period following the first movement of a movement system or set of related movements when a second movement cannot be initiated even though it is not **antagonistic** to the first. ➤This phenomenon is not found when the movements are a series or where the two stimuli are reacted to as a pair.

refrangible: *adj.* capable of being refracted, as rays of light.

refutation: *n.* overthrowing an argument by counterargument, either by proving the contradictory to the conclusion, or by showing the logical error of the argument.—*v.* **refute.**

regard/field of: the total space within which objects can be seen by moving the eye, with head stationary.—*Distg. fr.* **visual field.**

regard/line of: (*vis.*) the line from the fixation point on the object being viewed to the center of rotation of the eyeball. ➤*Distg. fr.* **line of** *direction,* which runs from the fixation point to the fovea.

regard/point of = fixation point (see **fixation/visual**).

regeneration: *n.* **1.** (*biol.*) replacement by growth of a lost part of the body. **2.** restoration of physical or intellectual vitality or of moral strength.

regimen (rej'ə·men): *n.* a systematic regulation of diet, exercise, rest, and general hygiene, designed to maintain or improve general health or to fulfill some more specific purpose.—*adj.* **regiminal** (rə·jim'ə·nəl).

region: *n.* **1.** a general area or space. **2.** (*topol.*) any distinguishable part of the **life space.** ➤Psychological regions are defined by present or contemplated *activities* rather than by the objective spatial areas in which activities occur. E.g., a child using a porch as a stage is in the region of "play acting" rather than in the region of the "porch." Regions are separated by **boundaries.** When a person changes activity, he moves from one region to another across a boundary.

regional-localization theory: (*neurol.*) the theory that specific areas of the brain are set aside as the **brain centers** (which see) for specific kinds of acts.

region/connected: (*topol.*) a realm of activities in which any special activity (or point) may be connected with any other activity without going outside the **region.** ➤In such a region, e.g., one activity may facilitate or depress another without (important) effect outside the region.

region/incident: (*topol.*) a realm of activities that can be reached from a given **region** without entering a third; a psychologically adjacent region. ➤If hard work leads directly to promotion, then work and promotion are incident regions; but if one must play politics as well, then locomotion from work to promotion must pass through the politics region and work and promotion are not incident. Whether the two regions are incident depends (as in this illustration) more upon the momentary **life space** than upon the nature of the activities.

region/motoric (mō·tôr'ik): (*K. Lewin*) that aspect of the person which manifests itself directly in outward appearance and overt response; the executive aspect of personality. It is the region that lies between the inner-personal **life space** and the psychological environment.

region/motor - perceptual: (*topol.*) a **boundary** between the environment and the inner-personal region; a region that must be traversed in going from the environment to the inner-personal region or vice versa.

region/neighboring: (*topol.*) a region having a common boundary with another.

region/psychological: (*topol.*) any division of the **life space** having attributes distinguishing it from other divisions. ➤The region may lie within the person or within the environment, or may straddle the boundary between person and environment.

regions of personality/private: (*K. Lewin*) the more central regions of personality, which are regarded in a given culture as of less public concern or interest. ➤It is explicitly held that the degree of privateness is culturally determined, but a given individual may resist invasion of privacy more or less than is common. The greater or lesser **accessibility** of the private region is thus subject to personal and social control.

register/vocal: see **vocal register.**

regnancy: *n.* (*H. A. Murray*) the briefest unit of experience; the shortest single **gestalt.** ➤*Distg. fr.* such abstract aspects of experience as sensory **intensity (2)** or sensory **quality.** The regnancy is a complex whole, however brief. The term is usually used in the plural since a single regnancy cannot be observed.

regression: *n.* **1.** moving backward.—*Ant.* **progress** or **progression. 2.** (*psychol.*) a return to earlier and less mature behavior; or, manifestation of more primitive behaviors after having learned mature forms, whether or not the immature or primitive behavior had actually formed part of the person's earlier behavior. ➤*Cp.* **dedifferentiation.** A great variety of behavior has been interpreted as regression; almost anything disapproved may be so called. It is explained as a reaction to stress, difficulty, and failure. In psychoanalysis, regression means relapse into infantile behavior (but note that infantile behavior has special connotations here: see **infantilism**).—*Distg. fr.* arrest (see **development/arrest in**) or **fixation. 3.** (*psychol.*) the tendency, during a general weakening of **retention** (as in senility), for memories to be lost in the inverse order of their acquisition: i.e., new memories are lost before old ones.—*Cp.* **Jost's law. 4.** (*stat.*) the fact that the predicted score or value of a dependent variable (when stated in standard scores) is closer to the mean of the sample than is the predictor score or value of the independent variable (also stated in standard scores). The mean of the predicted variable of those individuals who have a given predictor score tends to be closer to the mean of the whole sample than the predictor score. ➤Thus, if we predict school marks from an intelligence test, the mean school performance for children of any intelligence level will tend to be closer to the average of the class than is the intelligence level. Children of +2 units of standard score in intelligence will not, if enough cases be taken, average +2 units of standard score in school marks but will average somewhere between +2 and 0 units.—*Cp.* **regression effect. 5.** (*stat.*) = **regression coefficient. 6.** = (*genet.*) **regression/filial** or **segregation (3). 7.** (*vis.*) right-to-left eye movements in reading, for the purpose of examin-

ing words already passed over. **8.** (*conditioning*) the fact that during **extinction** of R_2 to S, a previously extinguished R_1 to the same S occasionally reappears. **9.** (*conditioning*) the fact that after punishment the subject frequently reverts to a **CR** that had previously been acquired. ➤This may be the analogue of **regression (2)**.—*adj.* **regressive, regressed.**—*n.* **regress** (rē′gres), seldom used, but emphasizing the act rather than the fact of going back.—*v.* **regress** (rē·gres′).

regression/act: see **act regression.**

regression analysis: (*stat.*) a method, adapted from the least square **multiple *regression equation,** for predicting the values of a quantitative variable from the nonquantitative or **category** scores of a correlated variable: e.g., predicting the number of pieces produced per hour from qualitative ratings of the worker as *Excel., Good, Fair, Poor, V. Poor.*

regression coefficient: (*stat.*) the constant in a **linear *regression** equation that measures the slope of the **regression line;** the number that represents the number of units change (increase or decrease) in one variable on the regression line associated with a unit change in the other; the multiplier of the independent variable term in the linear regression equation. ➤When two or more predictive variables are employed, the multipliers of these variables are **multiple *regression** coefficients; in this case the regression coefficient measures the slope of the fitted plane or hyperplane.

regression curve: any smooth curve (including a straight line) fitted to the means of one set of arrays in a double-entry table.—*Syn.* CURVE OF MEANS, **regression line** (restricted to the rectilinear form).

regression/curvilinear: see **regression line/curvilinear.**

regression effect: the tendency for a group, selected as being any given amount above or below the mean on one test, to be closer to the mean on a second test unless the two tests are perfectly correlated. ➤This is a special case of **regression (4).** It is independent of the order in which the two measurements are made, and is a function solely of the lack of correlation. It results from the fact that a certain number of individuals are found in the specified narrow range partly by reason of **errors of measurement** which do not respectively help or hinder all of them on another testing. The regression effect does not affect the range, mean, or standard deviation of the entire distribution but only that of a selected sample.

regression equation: a formula for computing the most probable value of one variable, Y, from the known value of another variable, X; an equation for computing the amount of change in one variable for a unit change in another. It is spoken of as the regression of X on Y.

regression equation/multiple: an equation for computing, for each individual, a score on a **criterion** variable (the PRE-DICTED SCORE) from his scores on each of several other variables. It is based on the correlation of each of the variables with the criterion and on their inter-correlations. ➤E.g., the equation enables a statement of the probability that any given freshman will have a **PHR** of 2.7 if we know his scores on certain placement tests that have known correlations with the criterion of PHR and with each other.—*Syn.* PARTIAL REGRESSION EQUATION, MULTIPLE REGRESSION.

regression/eye: see **regression (7).**

regression/filial: the tendency for offspring of parents departing widely from the central or standard type of the species to depart less widely than their parents: e.g., the offspring of two very tall parents are likely to be nearer the mean.—*Distg. fr.* **atavism.**

regression line: 1. the line that describes the relationship between two variables. **2.** the curved or straight line that, according to some theorem (usually that of **least squares**), best fits the relationships actually found. ➤In most psychological statistics, the regression line is the best fit to the means of the rows or columns of a **double-entry table.**

regression/linear: the regression that obtains when the line that best fits the means of the rows, or columns, in a correlation table is approximately straight.—*Syn.* REC-TILINEAR REGRESSION.

regression line/curvilinear: a regression line, adjusted for chance fluctuations, that manifests a regular curve and is not even approximately a straight line. ➤Chance fluctuations from **rectilinearity,** which always occur and are of greater magnitude when the number of cases is small, do not entitle the regression to be dubbed curvilinear. With an infinite number of cases, a true curvilinear regression line would always be curved, and a linear regression line would be straight, with no deviations therefrom.

regression/multiple: see **regression equation/multiple.**

regression neurosis: a neurosis characterized by a return to more primitive and essentially inadequate, but temporarily or apparently more comfortable, modes of adjustment.

regression/nonlinear: a **regression line** that is not a regular straight line (or a sufficient approximation). It includes **curvilinear** *regression lines.**

regression of X on Y: the regression equation showing the most probable values of X for given values of Y. ➤The dependent or predicted value, X, is said to regress on the independent or predictor value, Y.

regression/partial: see **regression equation/multiple.**

regression/phenomenal: see **phenomenal regression.**

regression/rectilinear = **regression/linear.**

regression/skew = **regression/nonlinear.**

regression/spontaneous: spontaneous reliving in the present tense of a specific previous episode in an individual's life when, under hypnosis, it is suggested that he is now of the age when the episode occurred. ➤E.g., a person told he is 6 years old may talk about the button shoes he wore at that age.

regression/temporal: see **regression (1, 2).**

regression time: the time spent in **regression (7)** during reading. The time spent to readjust **fixation** at the beginning of a new line is sometimes also included.

regression weight = **regression coefficient.**

regressive transmission: see **segregation (2).**

regret: *n.* an emotional response to one's remembrance of a past experience that one wishes might have been different.

regular: *adj.* following a definite pattern, formula, law, or principle; repeating at predictable intervals.—*n.* **regularity.**—*v.* **regularize.**

rehabilitation: *n.* restoration to a satisfactory physical, mental, vocational, or social status after injury or illness, including mental illness. ➤The status need not be the same as that preceding the injury or illness. Rehabilitation may be concurrent with, and may play a part in, therapy (physical or psychological), yet it has a distinct goal.

rehearsal: *n.* **1.** performing an act prior to the time when it will be needed; hence, **2.** going over in one's mind previously studied data; repetition with a view to later recall. It may be involuntary, self-imposed, or other-imposed.

reification (rē″ə·fi·kā′shən): *n.* supposing, or acting as if one supposed, that an abstract quality has concrete actuality or existence; treating an abstract concept or construct as if it referred to a thing. ➤The error is most insidious in psychology. No one is likely to think that, because some objects are *thick,* there is an actual *thick-*

ness apart from thick books, thick papers, or thick boards; but because there are *"thick" heads,* it is all too easy to suppose that *"thickness"* is what makes them *"thick."*—*v.* reify (rē'ə·fī).

Reil/island of (rīl): a part of the cortex lying at the bottom of the Sylvian fissure, and covered over by folds of the cortex. ➤The structure is not developed in subprimate brains.—*Syn.* INSULA (*L.*).

reinforce: *v.* to strengthen by addition; esp., to strengthen a learned way of behaving by some external or internal influence. ➤The term itself does not specify what "addition" it is that strengthens learning, and there are many theories about its nature.—See **reinforcement.**

reinforcement: *n.* **1.** the strengthening of something by adding to it; or that which strengthens, when added. ➤This is the basic idea running through all the special usages. Besides the following meanings of **reinforcement** as used alone, see also combinations: e.g., **reinforcement/secondary. 2.** (*neurol.*) the strengthening of a response to a stimulus by the simultaneous activity of another excitatory process: e.g., the more vigorous knee-jerk reflex when the hands are tightly clasped at the time of the tap on the knee.—*Syn.* **facilitation** (*prefd.*). **3.** the natural occurrence or the experimental presentation of the **unconditioned stimulus** along with the **conditioned stimulus;** or the strengthening of the **conditioned response** relationship thereby. ➤The term thus denotes either the strengthening or the condition for strengthening. By extension, some speak of the original *establishment* of the **CR** also as reinforcement. It is always a positive process even though the conditioned response is avoidance or escape. Thus, it is the direct opposite of **extinction,** which is the weakening of the CR when the **CS** occurs without the concurrence of the **US. Reward** is an inappropriate synonym for this meaning. ¶This is the original usage in learning theory; it is a direct denoting of the experimental fact and need imply no theory. (Thus, in using this definition no decision need be made as to whether it is the contiguity of US and CS, or of the CS with the response elicited by US, that is causally effective; in either case reinforcement refers to the same experimentally defined conditions.) It is recommended that reinforcement be restricted to this meaning, but currently it certainly is not. **4.** the strengthening of an **instrumental** or **operant** ***conditioned response** when that response leads to a satisfying state of affairs; or that satisfying state. ➤For difficulties in defining *satisfying state,* see **satisfaction.** Note that the **reinforcement** of meaning

(3) precedes, and the **reinforcement** of this meaning follows, the performance. Moreover, for this meaning, distinction must be made between nonreinforcement, which leads to **extinction,** and **negative** ***reinforcement,** which is the administration of a dissatisfying state of affairs and leads to an escape response.—*Syn.* **reward,** objected to by many but recommended as clearly distinguishing this phenomenon from that of (3).—*Ant.* **negative** ***reward** (*prefd.*) or **punishment. 5.** anything that reduces a **drive** or a **tension.** ➤It is an admissable theory that the only reinforcement is a reduction of drive, but the statement of this theory too often masquerades as a definition: see **theory-begging.**—*Syn.* **drive-reduction, tension-reduction** (either *prefd.*). **6.** any condition, or the total circumstances, that strengthen a stimulus-response correlation; any circumstance or event that increases the probability that a response will recur in a situation like that in which the reinforcing condition originally occurred; or, quite generally, any condition strengthening learning. ➤This extremely vague usage is prevalent but not recommended. It almost always reflects circular thinking: learning occurs when there is a reinforcement, and it is reinforcement if learning occurs. **7.** the hypothetical organismic processes within the organism caused by the circumstances of **(6).** ➤The circularity is not lessened by postulating an unknown. **8.** the recognition by the subject of the correctness of a response.—*Syn.* **confirming reaction** (*prefd.*). **9.** = GOAL ATTAINMENT (*prefd.*).

➤It is not uncommon to find several of these meanings united in the same usage of the term. Reinforcement sometimes means a stimulus, sometimes a response, sometimes any of several organic effects of either stimulus or response, or any combination of these. So versatile a term is rapidly losing scientific usefulness. It is strongly recommended that the vague and circular meanings of **(6)** and **(7)** be entirely abandoned, that reinforcement be restricted to meanings **(1)** and **(3),** and that, for the operationally distinct meanings of **(2), (4), (5), (8),** and **(9),** the listed synonyms be substituted.—*Var.* **re-enforcement.**—*v.* **reinforce.**

reinforcement/aperiodic: see **reinforcement schedule.**

reinforcement/autogenic: see **autogenic reinforcement.**

reinforcement/conditioned: see **reinforcement/secondary.**

reinforcement/delayed: in operant ***conditioning,** a **reward** or **negative** ***reward** which is not administered until several seconds after the response.

reinforcement/differential: 1. of a stimulus, the procedure used in discrimination training wherein a response is rewarded when made to one stimulus and is negatively rewarded when made to other stimuli. **2.** of a response, the procedure that rewards a particular (generally quite specific) response and negatively rewards any other or similar responses to a specified stimulus. ➤This procedure produces stereotyped response.

reinforcement/external: a form of reinforcement that is predictably effective for a given group or culture.—*Syn.* DEPENDABLE REINFORCEMENT (*prefd.*).

reinforcement/fixed interval: see **reinforcement schedule.**

reinforcement/gradient of: the generalization that, in a series of acts, the closer an act is to the **reward,** the more it is strengthened.

reinforcement/heterogeneous: the presentation, following a response A, of a reward which elicits another response B of dissimilar character. ➤This is the pattern in instrumental conditioning (see **conditioning 2**).

reinforcement/homogeneous: the presentation of a stimulus X simultaneously with another stimulus Y that evokes the same, or closely similar, response as X. ➤This is the pattern of classical conditioning (see **conditioning 1**).

reinforcement hypothesis: 1. (*I. P. Pavlov*) the generalization that the temporal contiguity of a stimulus with an **unconditioned** or **reflex** stimulus-response activity strengthens the tendency of the former to elicit the response.—*Cp.* **reinforcement (3). 2.** (*C. Hull*) the generalization that the concomitance or near-concomitance of **drive reduction** with the activity of a stimulus-response linkage strengthens the tendency of the S to elicit the R.—*Cp.* **reinforcement (4). 3.** a theory that learning depends upon reinforcement. ➤In view of the many meanings of **reinforcement,** it is ambiguous to refer to *the* reinforcement theory of learning.

reinforcement/intermittent: an experimental design in which a nonreinforcing or nonrewarding situation is irregularly interspersed with reinforcing situations during the conditioning period, resulting in slower conditioning and in slower extinction.—See **reinforcement schedule.**—*Syn.* **reinforcement/partial** (not *prefd.*); INTERMITTENT SCHEDULE.—*Ant.* CONTINUOUS REINFORCEMENT or REWARD.

reinforcement/internal: 1. any intraorganismic process that modifies a learned response. **2. drive reduction. 3.** the subject's awareness that a pleasant or unpleasant event has occurred. ➤It is assumed that this awareness modifies response. All three usages belong to the excessively vague meanings of **reinforcement (6, 7).**

reinforcement/interval: an experimental design in which the reward is presented at fixed time intervals.—*Contr. w.* **reinforcement/ratio.**

reinforcement/irrelevant: the presentation of a stimulus not related to the **drive** state: e.g., the presentation of water as a reward to a hungry animal. ➤But the advice to reach for a cigarette instead of a sweet was based on the fact that a considerable number of stimuli may be related to a single drive state.

reinforcement/law of: see **reinforcement hypothesis.**

reinforcement/negative: a way of training a subject not to make a response by giving him a dissatisfying or punishing or tension-increasing stimulus. ➤*Distg. fr.* **extinction,** which is the weakening of a **CR** by withholding the reward.—*Cp.* the terms **conditioned (instrumental) escape** and **conditioned (instrumental) avoidance response,** which are appropriate to classical conditioning, whereas negative reinforcement or negative reward is appropriate to **operant *conditioning** and to **reinforcement (4).**

reinforcement/neural: see **reinforcement (2).**

reinforcement/partial: 1. maintenance (or restoration) of a **CR** by presentation of a part only of the original rewarding or reinforcing conditions. **2.** = **intermittent *reinforcement** (*prefd.*).

reinforcement/pre-delay: see **pre-delay reinforcement.**

reinforcement/primary: 1. the presentation of a stimulus situation that reinforces or rewards any animal of a given species without need of prior training; or the state of affairs that so reinforces. ➤In early classical **conditioning (1)** experiments, the **unconditioned stimulus** was supposed always to be the innate stimulus to a reflex, and hence primary. As the **paradigm** was expanded, learned **S-R** associations often took the place of reflexes. The S is designated the unconditioned S but is not primary. In **operant *conditioning,** a primary reward or reinforcement is one that is satisfying in the absence of prior learning. The concept of *the primary* is subject to all the difficulties of the **innate.** —*Syn.* **primary *reward. 2.** any strengthening of response strength resulting from reduction of a **primary *drive.** ➤This statement combines two theories and an assertion about fact; it is therefore a pseudo definition.

reinforcement/ratio: in **operant *conditioning,** the delivery of a reward or reinforcement after the animal has made a standard number of responses. ➤*Contr. w.* INTERVAL REINFORCEMENT, in which the reinforcement is delivered at standard intervals.

reinforcement/reproductive: an increase in the probability that an idea will be recalled or a response repeated by virtue of the fact that it has associative connections with many other items, each of which may instigate the reproduction.

reinforcement retroaction paradox: the problem of how reinforcement can strengthen a response tendency after the response has ceased.

reinforcement schedule or **reward schedule:** a schedule prescribing when the subject is to be reinforced or rewarded, either in terms of temporal interval or of the succession of responses—e.g., every fifth response to be reinforced. ➤Reinforcement may be CONTINUOUS (every response in operant conditioning rewarded), or INTERMITTENT (partial). For the latter there are many variations: PERIODIC or APERIODIC (= VARIABLE INTERVALS), FIXED or VARIABLE RATIO of rewarded to nonrewarded responses, etc. While applicable to classical conditioning, the variable or intermittent schedule is more likely to be found in operant conditioning.

reinforcement/secondary: any reinforcing or rewarding event or state that derives its effectiveness from a previous process of learning or conditioning; or the operation of bringing about that event or state. ➤Some of those who assert that **primary *reinforcement** is drive-reduction hold that secondary reinforcement does not lead directly to reduction of drive.—*Syn.* CONDITIONED REINFORCEMENT, SECONDARY (or CONDITIONED) REWARD.

reinforcement/serial: a **reward** or **confirming reaction** that is obtained after each act in a series provided the act is performed in the prescribed order.

reinforcement/terminal: a **reward** or **confirming reaction** obtained at the end of a series of acts performed in a prescribed order.

reinforcement value: the degree to which a given situation affects the probability of occurrence of those responses with which it is associated as a reinforcement or reward. ➤The total or average reinforcement value is unmeasurable; the term can refer only to the value for a specified range of responses.

reinforcement/variable interval: see **reinforcement schedule.**

reinforcement/variable ratio: see **reinforcement schedule.**

reinforcing stimulus: 1. the rewarding stimulus experimentally administered or naturally experienced after the subject has made the prescribed **operant** response. ➤The term appropriately belongs to the **instrumental *conditioning** situation; it is not a good synonym for the **unconditioned stimulus** of classical conditioning, though it is sometimes so used.

reinstatement: *n.* general term for any manifestation of learning and remembering in which the subject repeats, recalls, or re-enacts what was earlier learned.

reintegration: see **redintegration (1).**

rejection: *n.* the process or the fact of regarding something as worthless, of throwing something away, or of refusing to admit it to a certain category. ➤In interpersonal relations rejection is seldom absolute or complete, and usually it manifests itself in indirect ways: by excessive criticism of the person rejected, by invidious comparisons, by signs of hostility, crossness, or refusal to pay attention to the other person. PARENTAL REJECTION means rejection of the child by the parent. It is usually not admitted, even to oneself. (The reverse relation may be called REJECTION OF THE PARENT.)

rejection/region of = **critical region.**

rejuvenation: *n.* the restoration of a person to youthfulness. ➤A number of surgical and mental procedures have been tried as modern equivalents of the fabled "Fountain of Youth."

relapse: *n.* the recurrence of a disorder after a period of improvement or **remission.**

relata (ri·lā′tə): *n. pl.* (*L.*) two or more things that are related. ➤The word is used to contrast with the relationship itself.

relation: *n.* **1.** the bearing or influence one object may have upon another. **2.** that which forms a connection between two things, of such nature that what is true of one has some relevance to the other; relationship. The relation is conceived to exist in at least partial independence of the *relata* or things related. ➤There is a very complex LOGIC OF RELATIONS of which mathematics is a special form. One analysis finds that every particular relation, such as *in front of,* may be characterized by presence or absence of one of the four basic ATTRIBUTES OF RELATION: **reflexivity, symmetry, transitivity,** and connectedness. **3.** a specific kind of conscious **object (2).** ➤We may be aware of the relations between two things in some sense independently of the two things: vividly aware of the difference, e.g., while only unclearly aware of the two things, and vice versa. The difference is a relation or CONSCIOUS RELATION. The analytic nature of conscious relations is unsettled.—*v.* **relate** (*psychiat. slang*), to interact with others, esp. to interact easily with others.

relation/functional: see **functional relation.**

relation/measure of: (*stat.*) any mathematical formulation showing the kind of change in one variable that is paralleled by change in another.—See **correlation.**

relationship: *n.* (*sociol.*) 1. the fact of any kind of **relation** between persons. 2. = kinship.

relationship system = kinship system.

relative: *adj.* 1. having **relation** to something. 2. not **absolute** or **intrinsic** but dependent upon comparison with certain other data for meaning, size, importance, or relation to other variables. 3. not complete; small or moderate in comparison with what could be. ➤E.g., *relative* contraction of a muscle does not stretch the muscle to its limit.—*n.* 4. a person having a **kinship** relation to a given person.

relative measurement: see **absolute measurement.**

relativism or **relativity:** *n.* 1. the general principle or hypothesis that any experience is so related to, or dependent upon, other experiences that its nature can only be understood by taking these other experiences into account; or, more broadly, that any aspect of experience is related to all other aspects. ➤**Gestalt theory** is a particular form of relativism. The **Weber-Fechner law** is sometimes called the PRINCIPLE OF RELATIVITY, though it is only a highly special case. 2. (*sociol.*) the view that social phenomena, whether institutions or mores, must be understood in relation to the particular society of which they are part; esp., the view that ethical precepts and practices are related to the prevailing ways of making a livelihood, of making war, of family, of scientific knowledge.

relativistic: *adj.* pertaining to **relativity** or the **relativity attitude.**

relativity attitude: 1. the attitude or belief that the truth about anything is always dependent upon the context, that standards of conduct are not absolute but relative to time, place, culture, and historical circumstances.—*Contr. w.* **absolutism** (2). 2. See the antonym, **constancy attitude.** ➤Neither meaning is closely related to the physical theory of relativity.

relaxation: *n.* 1. the return of a muscle, after **contraction,** to its normal or usual length. 2. the easing up or lowering of "mental tension"; reducing the tendency to anxiety, fear, anger, or any emotional response deemed too violent or too easily aroused; also, the means to this end. 3. the technique used in psychotherapy to keep the client at ease, esp. by harmonizing the therapist's behavior with the moods and motivations of the client.

relaxation/progressive: (*E. Jacobson*) a training technique in which the person learns to relax muscle groups, one by one, beginning with those easiest to control.

relearning: *n.* the process of learning again what had once been learned and is now forgotten or partly forgotten.—*Cp.* **re-education,** a broader term.

relearning procedure: in memory experiments, measuring **retention** by the ease with which the **memoranda** can be relearned. ➤Either the number of repetitions or the time required for relearning is compared with the original learning period. The procedure may be employed even after forgetting has proceeded so far that no recall or recognition of the memorized material is possible.

release phenomenon: (*neurol.*) the activity of a **lower *center** when a higher controlling center does not function; the uninhibited motor discharge consequent upon damage to a **higher brain center.**

releaser: *n.* (*ethology*) an aspect of one animal or person (structural or behavioral) that releases a particular **species-specific** response in another animal or person; a primary social stimulus.

release therapy: a form of psychotherapy in which improved adjustment is obtained when opportunity is provided, under the eye of the therapist, for free expression of hostile and destructive impulses. ➤*Cp.* **catharsis.** The presence of the therapist and his **acceptance** of the client's expression seem to be essential; ACCEPTANCE THERAPY is, therefore, more descriptive. **Play therapy** is the most usual form of acceptance therapy.

releasing (or **releaser**) **mechanism:** (*ethol.*) a hypothetical structure in a **conceptual nervous system** invoked to explain the fact that a particular stimulus complex releases automatically one of a certain restricted class of responses. ➤An INNATE RELEASER is a **reflex.**

relevance: *n.* 1. close relationship, esp. close logical relationship, to the matter in hand. 2. (*stat.*) an index that reflects the closeness of agreement between what the test measures—other than **chance**—and the function it is designed to measure. ➤This definition is very similar to the usual one for **validity.** But validity as commonly measured includes the factor of **reliability** (or unreliability), which is a measure of the extent to which the test is responsive to chance influences. 3. (*H. English*) such relation between an act and a person's ability to meet a task-demand that performance of the act alters the ability. ➤**Practice** of the act required by the task-demand usually (but perhaps not always) alters the ability; hence, practiced acts are relevant. But, as studies in **transfer** show, acts other than those which meet the task-demand may have relevance. Thorndike's **belongingness** is either a synonym or a special form of relevance in this sense.

reliability: *n.* **1.** accuracy; dependability; trustworthiness; the quality or qualities of a person or thing in virtue of which it can be counted on.—*Cp.* **accuracy. 2.** (*measurement*) the complex property of a series of observations, of a measuring instrument, or of the entire measuring process, that makes possible the obtaining of similar results upon repetition; the degree to which such similar results may be predicted; the degree to which measurement is free from random influence. ➤Reliability is a generic term referring to several types of evidence. When repeated performance of the same act by the same individual is in question, reliability is the opposite of **variability,** and the **standard error of measurement** (or one of its equivalents) is an appropriate index. For testing, there are several distinct correlation measures of reliability, all misleadingly given the one name of **reliability coefficient** (which see).

reliability coefficient: a misleading general term for any measure of reliability employing **correlation coefficients.** ➤Several different coefficients are computed, each an answer to a distinct question. (The terminology has not stabilized; we follow in the main that of the Joint Committee on Technical Standards in Testing. See *Psychol. Bull.,* 1954, **51,** Supplement.) (*a*) If the same test is given again, after a suitable interval to minimize differential practice effects, will comparable scores be obtained? This TEST-RETEST CORRELATION is called a **stability coefficient.** A statement of the interval between tests is essential to its interpretation. (*b*) Do the several parts of the test yield the same scores, so that they can with some assurance be substituted for each other? By internal analysis of the scores obtained from testing at a single sitting (usually by **chance-halves *correlation**) an **internal consistency coefficient** (which see) is obtained. (*c*) If **comparable *forms** of the test (i.e., duplicate, equivalent, or alternate forms) are given at essentially the same time, will comparable results be obtained? Correlation between two forms given at the same time is essentially the same as a chance-halves correlation, and the information is the same as in (*b*). But the correlation of comparable forms is more often called the **coefficient of *equivalence (1).** (*d*) If comparable forms are administered at different times, the correlation coefficient may be called the **coefficient of *stability and equivalence.** This is one of the commonest and most practical of the measures of reliability; for theoretical analysis it is less serviceable,

since it is composite. All the coefficients of reliability have application only to the population sampled by the correlated tests.

reliability coefficient/random halves = correlation/chance-halves.—See also **internal consistency/coefficient of** and **reliability coefficient** (*b*).

reliability/index of: an estimate of the correlation between actual scores on a given test and the corresponding (theoretical) true scores. It is obtained by taking the square root of the **reliability coefficient.**

reliability/random-halves method of: see **correlation/chance-halves, reliability coefficient.**

reliability/sampling: a measure of the agreement between two or more samples from the same population.—See **stability/statistical.**

reliability/split-half method of: see **correlation/chance-halves** and **reliability coefficient** (*b*).

religion: *n.* a system of attitudes, practices, rites, ceremonies, and beliefs by means of which individuals or a community put themselves in relation to God or to a supernatural world and often to each other, and from which the religious person derives a set of values by which to judge events in the natural world.

remark/acceptance: see **acceptance.**

remedial instruction: teaching that is designed to remove, where possible, *specific* causes of lack or deficiency. ➤In the total process, specific diagnosis plays an important part. E.g., failure in arithmetic may result from misunderstanding "carrying"; special teaching to correct the misunderstanding is given. REMEDIAL READING may include **orthoptic** training, teaching for basic vocabulary, **phonics,** teaching to skim, etc.

remember: *v.* to reinstate some part, or all, of a previous experience so that it may function in present behavior; to recall; to call images to mind; to repeat what was earlier learned. ➤Remember is usually restricted to a process that is conscious or that has directly conscious results. Thus, repeating a phrase exactly as one heard it is not remembering unless one knows that it was the reinstatement of a particular experience.—*Syn.* **recollect.**—*Cp.* **reminiscence.**

reminiscence: *n.* **1.** (*hist.*) the return, unbidden and without associative cues, of memories from past experience. ➤Some philosophers have even supposed that the memories may come from a previous incarnation. **2.** recall of previous experience without realizing that it is recall: e.g., unconscious plagiarism, the use of scholarly or artistic material from a predecessor without realizing its derivation. **3.** relatively complete and unselective recall of past experience without specific purpose of guiding present behavior; recall for enjoyment thereof. **4.** recall or recognition, without intervening overt practice, of items previously not recallable; an increment in a practiced act after a period of nonpractice. ➤This is the usual technical meaning in psychology.—See **retention.**

remission: *n.* temporary abatement or cessation of the symptoms of disease. SPONTANEOUS REMISSION is the cessation of symptoms without known relation to any curative agency.—*v.* **remit.**

remote: *adj.* **1.** distant; esp., distant in a series of items to be learned. A REMOTE ASSOCIATION is a learned tendency for an item to call to mind an item not close to it in the learning period. **2.** of a percept referred to an object explored by means of a probe object: e.g., the roughness of a ribbed object explored by means of a pliant stick. ➤The contrast is with RESIDENT sensations, the sense data referred to the skin surface.

renal (rē′nəl): *adj.* pertaining to the kidney.

renifleur (ren′i·flər): *n.* (*Fr.*) a sniffer; one who associates full sex excitement with smells.

renunciation: *n.* **1.** (*religion*) surrender of personal desires to the will of God as the individual understands or. **2.** (*psychoan.*) the **ego**'s refusal to seek the satisfactions demanded by the **id,** because they are out of line either with the demands of reality (the id might demand the pleasure of floating through the air by jumping off a cliff, but the ego recognizes the reality consequences), or with the demands of the **superego** (the superego might demand an utterly unrealistic perfection of conduct which the ego must reject).

reorganization theory: (*learning*) the theory that learning consists not of acquiring independent new parts but of altering the structure of a whole or **gestalt.** ➤The view contrasts with **associationism,** either in its classical form in which the mind is supposed to receive new ideas, or in its modern form in which the organism is supposed to acquire a **bond** between a particular S and a particular R (or family of S's and R's). According to the reorganization view, reaction to the learning problem causes a change in how the learner cognizes a meaningful part of the environment, or a greater or lesser change in the learner himself—a change that is not merely the *addition* of a new and independent S-R unit, but a restructuring of personality in relation to the problem.

repertoire/behavior (rep′ər·twär): all the behaviors possible for a given individual, or for a species; or, all behaviors available under specified stimulus conditions.

repetition: *n.* **1.** making, doing, or saying something highly similar to what one made, did, or said before. ➤Identical repetition is impossible, yet it is seldom specified how great the similarity must be to constitute repetition. **2.** doing or saying something over and over with intent to learn. ➤Combined in this meaning (which is very common) are two different operations: repeating with the hope of being able to repeat later without change (as in rote memorizing and much else like it); and repeating with intent to change and improve one's performance.—*Syn.* **rehearsal, practice. 3.** answering a teacher's questions by stating the contents of a lesson, whether or not in the original words.—*Syn.* RECITAL (more often used for a public performance); **recitation** (which see). **4.** (*exper., stat.*) one instance of an experimental procedure; a trial. ➤In this usage the notion of doing *again* is lost. When one does something for the second time, that is considered to be the second repetition, not the first.

The term in all its usages is probably too firmly entrenched to be dispensed with entirely, but its ambiguity should be recognized.—*v.* **repeat.**

repetition compulsion: an irrational need to repeat some behavior pattern over and over in an effort to allay anxiety: e.g., Lady Macbeth's hand washing.

repetition/law of = law of **use* or **law of *frequency.**

replacement: *n.* (*psychother.*) the substitution of normal activities and thoughts for unwholesome or neurosis-determined activities and thoughts.

replicate: *v.* to reproduce or copy an original in all essentials; esp., to repeat an experiment with all essentials unchanged; to produce a REPLICA.

replication: *n.* the subdividing of an experiment into a number of parts—the REPLICAS—each of which contains all the essential elements with which the experiment is concerned. Comparison of the several replicas enables discrimination between the effects of the essential conditions and those of irregular or irrelevant variables.

report: *n.* an account of what took place, whether by an actor or by an observer.—*Cp.* **protocol.**

represent: *v.* to stand for; to substitute for something by being a symbol; to take part in certain operations in place of something else without distorting the operation.—*Distg. fr.* REPRODUCE, which implies similarity.—*adj.* **representative.**—*n.* **representative,** that which represents; **representation,** the act of representing.

re-present (rē″pri·zent′): *v.* to present

again.—*Distg. fr.* **represent,** to stand for something.

representation: *n.* standing for, or in the place of, something else; specif. for psychology, an experience, a psychic activity, or a mental content that in some essential way re-presents an earlier experience. ➤E.g., the concept *horse* is a representation of many direct or indirect experiences of horses. Traditionally, representation meant having a mental content (an **image** or an **idea**) that stood for something else, but it is now used quite abstractly for the representative *function* by many who disbelieve in mental content.

representationalism: *n.* the view that psychic process (esp., perceiving) is a representation of the external world. ➤The view takes many forms. See **copy theory, isomorphism, psychology/divisions and schools of,** III.

representation/double: see **double representation.**

representative: *adj.* capable of being substituted for something, of taking its place without causing substantial error: e.g., a *representative* score.

representative design: see **design/representative.**

representative factors: the hypothesized activities that enable the organism to continue or to renew response after the original stimulus is withdrawn. ➤In man, **images** and verbal symbols are the chief, but may not be the only, representative factors. The term is not applied to the lag of response immediately following cessation of stimulus. *Cp.* **delayed response.**

representative measure = **representative score.**

representativeness/test: the extent to which a test contains items measuring every outcome it is desired to test: e.g., in a test of fundamental operations in arithmetic, the extent to which there are items covering *all* operations that are deemed fundamental.

representative sample: see **sampling/representative.**

representative score or **value:** a number or magnitude that can be thought about or employed in calculations, instead of using all the scores in a set; esp., a **measure of *central tendency:** a **mean, median,** or **mode.** (But a magnitude such as $M \pm SD$ is also a representative value, and a better one than M alone.)

representative theory: the doctrine that reality is known only through **ideas,** which are the signs or copies of real objects. ➤This philosophic doctrine is almost universally repudiated, but it still influences the thinking of both lay and professional persons because much psychological terminology was formulated under its influence.

repress: *v.* **1.** to keep under or to put down; not to allow to happen; to inhibit an ongoing activity. **2.** (*psychoan.*) to banish from consciousness; to maintain a barrier against the return, or even the first entry, into consciousness of a certain psychic activity.—*Cp.* **censorship.**

repressed complex: see **complex (2).**

repressed wish: a desire or wish that is systematically (though not necessarily invariably or completely) repressed.

repression: *n.* the exclusion of specific psychological activities or contents from conscious awareness by a process of which the individual is not directly aware. Exclusion includes preventing entry into, forcing out of, or continuously preventing return to, consciousness. ➤The definition states, with a minimum of theoretical implication, the fact to which the term refers. Since the concept is central in all **depth psychology,** the term as commonly used carries many other implications: that repression is a **defense mechanism** against anxiety or guilt; that it is performed by the **censorship;** that repressed activities, though excluded from consciousness, carry on in the **unconscious** and project various symbolic representations of themselves into consciousness. ¶For those who desire to refer to the fact without the accretion of theory, EXCLUSION or **blocking** may be used as a synonym.

PRIMAL REPRESSION is denial of *first entry* into consciousness of **id** activities. It is the mechanism whereby certain instinctual processes are permanently forbidden ingress to consciousness. PRIMARY REPRESSION is denial of *re-entry* into consciousness of contents that would cause guilt or anxiety. **Repression** (without qualifier) is often used for this meaning. SECONDARY REPRESSION is repression of contents that would remind the person of the excluded contents of primal and/or primary repression. (But sometimes SECONDARY REPRESSION is used for any repression not primal. This is not recommended.) If the exclusion is voluntary, **suppression** is the correct term, but repression is often extended to cover such cases. Repression is to be contrasted both with the expression of a motive or activity and with its simple disappearance.—*adj.* **repressed.**—*v.* **repress.**

repression/organic: inability, associated with severe head injury, to remember certain events. ➤Since the forgotten events appear to have no relation to personal motives or to psychic conflict, the assumption is that they are associated with a frightening organic trauma. The synonym **anterograde *amnesia** makes fewer assumptions.

repression/primal: see **repression.**

repression/primary: see **repression.**

repression-resistance: see **resistance (5).**

repression/secondary: see **repression.**

reproducibility coefficient: (*L. Guttman*) an index of the proportion of responses to a test which can be "reproduced"—i.e., predicted—from knowledge of item difficulty and total scores.—See **scalability.**

reproduction: *n.* **1.** making or bringing forth a close copy of something; specif., for psychology, having an **image** that copies something, or executing a previously learned response or pattern of responses (e.g., repeating a series of words). **2.** (*biol.*) the production of a new organism by parent organism(s). Both ASEXUAL and SEXUAL REPRODUCTION are included.

reproduction procedure or **method: 1.** (*psychophys.*) = **adjustment procedure. 2.** (*memory*) the attempt to reproduce material, learned as completely as possible, as a measure of **retention.** The reproduction may be verbal (oral or written), pictorial, or rearranging objects in their original order or pattern.

reproductive facilitation: (*learning*) an increase in **reproduction** as a result of some other activity interposed between the learning and the reproduction periods.—*Cp.* **reproductive interference, retroactive *inhibition,** its opposites.—*Cp.* **transfer.**

reproductive function: any activity or operation involved in bringing a new organism into existence; or the total of such activities. ➤*Distg. fr.* **sexual function,** which is limited to those functions that differ in the two sexes.—*Syn.* GENERATIVE FUNCTION.

reproductive imagination: see **imagination (2).**

reproductive interference: (*learning*) the decrease in **reproduction** due to an activity intervening between the learning and the reproduction periods. ➤*Syn.* **retroactive *inhibition,** which usually refers to an immediately intervening activity; reproductive interference is more general and more descriptive but less common.

reproductive memory: see **memory/reproductive.**

reproductive strength or **tendency:** the expression of all the summated factors that increase the probability that a given response will be made. It includes **associative, impressional,** and **perseverative** tendencies, and other factors.—*Approx. syn.* **response strength.**

reproof: *n.* reprimand; censure for failure or fault. ➤In experiments with human beings, often used as a form of **negative *reward.**

repugnance: *n.* an emotional attitude marked by dislike and opposition.—*Syn.* **antipathy.**

repulsion: *n.* an emotional attitude marked by dislike and avoidance.—*Syn.* **aversion,** negative **valence.**—*Ant.* **attraction.**—*v.* **repulse, repel.**

reputation: *n.* an evaluation by contemporaries of an individual's qualities or worth; what a person is believed to be like (as opposed to what he may really be). ➤**Prestige** is high reputation; FAME is lofty and widespread reputation.—*Syn.* REPUTE.

reputation rating or **test:** any method of obtaining from respondents a quantitative statement of how a person is viewed by his associates or peers.—See **Guess-Who technique, sociometric tests.**

required behavior: any behavior that, in a culture or smaller established social group, is demanded of individuals. The demands may or may not be enforced by overt penalties, but there is always some disapproval of noncompliance. ➤Many required behaviors are related to age; as the child grows older, a few demands are relaxed but many others are added.—*Syn.* (for the larger cultural group) **folkways.**

requiredness: *n.* the property of a **gestalt** that is manifestly incomplete or distorted of "requiring" a change in order to be itself: e.g., a circle with a small gap exhibits requiredness.—*Cp.* **closure/law of.**

rereading procedure: a technique in memorizing in which learning is tested after a prescribed number of readings of the **memoranda.**—*Contr. w.* **recitation** procedure.

research: *n.* systematic, detailed, and relatively prolonged attempt to discover or confirm the facts that bear upon a certain problem or problems and the laws or principles that govern it. ➤Originally limited to first-hand observation, the term now extends to other kinds of data: e.g., historical *research,* based on documents.—*Syn.* **investigation,** more usually limited to a specific problem.—*v.* **investigate** (*prefd.* to *v.* **research**).

research/field: see **field investigation.**

resemblance: *n.* likeness; similarity; esp., outward, visible, or observable similarity.—*v.* **resemble.**

resemblance/law of: see **similarity/law of.**

resentment: *n.* mild or controlled anger because one's sense of justice or fairness has been violated.

reserve: *n.* **1.** disinclination to take the initiative or to speak freely in social intercourse; a tendency to keep one's ideas and feelings to oneself. **2.** see **reflex reserve.**

resident (sensations): see **remote (2).**

residual: *adj.* **1.** remaining after certain events, or after certain operations have been performed: e.g., RESIDUAL HEARING, that which remains after being partially deafened.—*n.* **2.** the difference between an observed and a computed value. **3.** (*factor anal.*) that portion of the **variance** of a **factor matrix** that is left after the variance attributed to all the factors described has been extracted.

residual matrix: see **matrix/residual.**

residue: *n.* (*V. Pareto*) a real motive; a manifestation of the basic sentiments. ➤*Contr. w.* derivation, a fictitious motive (**rationalizations** and similar mechanisms).

residues/canon of or **/method of:** one of Mill's working principles of **induction:** the unexplained remainder of an effect can be assumed to result from the unexplained remainder in the antecedent situation.—See **agreement and differences/canon of, concomitant variations method.**

residuum: *n.* **1.** a remainder left over; a **residual. 2.** a trace or **engram** left as the result of every experience.

resignation: *n.* **1.** an emotionally tinged attitude expressed in cessation of active response to a situation one has previously tried to alter; a state of submission or acquiescence. **2.** voluntary renunciation of an office, privilege, or status that one has held.—*v.* **resign.**

resignation/dynamic: (*K. Horney*) resignation to an unfavorable situation, coupled with alertness to opportunities for changing it.

resignation/neurotic: (*K. Horney*) a **major solution** for inner conflicts consisting of withdrawal from anything that involves awareness of the conflict. ➤There are three forms: PERSISTENT RESIGNATION, characterized chiefly by inertia; **shallow living,** characterized by compulsive hyperactivity in ways that avoid meeting the conflict; and **neurotic *rebelliousness.**

resistance: *n.* **1.** (*phys.*) the action of a body against an opposing force; specif., **2.** the opposition offered by a body to the passage of an electric current. It is measured in **ohms. 3.** sensation or perception experienced when moving a part of the body against a force or a resting mass. **4.** opposition offered by one person to the orders, suggestions, or actions of another.— *Syn.* RESISTIVE BEHAVIOR.—*Cp.* **negativism.** —*adj.* **resistive. 5.** (*psychoan.*) opposition to any attempt to lay bare the content of the **unconscious.** ➤The strength of **resistance** is a measure of the repressing force. **Resistance** is always found in **analysis (3).**

resistance/conscious: intentional withholding of information by a client or patient in psychotherapy because of shame, fear of rejection, distrust of the therapist, etc. ➤Unconscious **resistance (5)** is often to

be suspected as lying behind the conscious motives.

resistance/passive: refusal to yield to commands or coercion, but without expressing aggression (verbal or otherwise) against the person attempting coercion.—*Syn.* NONVIOLENT NONCOOPERATION, NONVIOLENT RESISTANCE.

resocialization: *n.* the attainment by a maladjusted person of those attitudes and skills that will facilitate his becoming again an accepted member of the community.

resoluteness: *n.* firm adherence to a line of action duly chosen. ➤**Resoluteness** is preferred to its synonyms **determination, decision, resolution,** all of which have additional related, but distinct, meanings.

resolution: *n.* **1.** solution of a problem by analyzing into its elements; or such solution because of new data or a new way of looking at the problem. **2.** = **resoluteness** (*prefd.*). **3.** a decision concerning a line of action. **4.** analysis of a compound into its constituents: e.g., analysis of a compound tone into its constituent pure or simple tones.—*v.* **resolve.**

resolution/factor: (*R. B. Cattell*) the statistical interpretation that results from a particular **rotation** of **factor axes,** esp. the one finally accepted; the particular position, after rotation, of the factor axes in relation to the positions and relations of the test **vectors.**—*Syn.* (*L. Thurstone*) **factor structure.**

resolving power: the capacity of the eye to see two objects viewed simultaneously as two distinct objects; the capacity to perceive as distinct two objects casting images on the retina in close proximity.

resonance: *n.* **1.** a vibration imposed on an object by a force applied with periodic frequency: e.g., the vibration of a piano string when a loud tone is sung nearby. ➤If the resonating body has a natural vibration frequency close to that of the inducing force, TUNED RESONANCE or SYMPATHETIC VIBRATION results. If the resonating object has a quite different frequency, it is FORCED RESONANCE or FORCED VIBRATION. **2.** a rich, vibrant quality of voice.—*adj.* **resonant.—** *v.* **resonate.**

resonance-place theory: see **hearing theories.**

resonance theory: 1. see **hearing theories. 2.** (*learning*) the generalization that items fitting a certain **set** are more likely than others to be recalled during the time when that set is operative. ➤The hypothesis is that the whole set is subexcited.

resonance-volley theory: (*aud.*) a theory that combines the resonance and the frequency theories.—See **hearing theories.**

resonator: *n.* a device making use of the principle of resonance to intensify a tone.

respect: *n.* a sentiment of appreciation of the worth of another person or of a cause, institution, work of art, etc.

respiration: *n.* breathing.—*adj.* **respiratory.**—*v.* **respire.**

respirograph (res'pir·ō·graf): *n.* a graphic record of the strength, rapidity, and regularity of breathing.

respondent: *adj.* 1. characterizing behavior that is identified by the specific eliciting stimulus. ➤It is contrasted with **operant** behavior, which is identified by its effect on the environment. This contrast is clear if the word *identified* is kept in mind. It is true that respondent behavior always does affect the environment, directly or indirectly; but it is *identified* by its stimulus. Operant behavior is always in a sense influenced by stimuli, hence is to some extent identified; but it is *identified* by its effect.—*Cp.* also **random activity, trial-and-error *learning, autochthonous behavior.**—*n.* 2. the organism that reacts to any stimulus; specif., the person who replies to a question in an interview, questionary, survey, etc. ➤For statistical treatment, persons to whom questions are addressed, but who do not reply, are sometimes categorized as nonresponding respondents.

response or **R:** *n.* 1. an answer, esp. a fairly formal answer. 2. any organic process consequent upon stimulation. 3. any muscular or glandular process that depends upon stimulation. 4. any psychic process consequent upon previous psychic process, whether sensory or imaginal. 5. the unit of the executing processes of the organism or person.—*Syn.* R CLASS. ➤The criterion of what constitutes such a unit is that the activities which form it vary, in the same way and to the same extent, with variation in the environmental conditions. Application of this criterion is by no means simple, but many responses are immediately and almost universally recognizable as unitary: e.g., walking, despite very great differences in the activities that constitute the walking response.

Response is one of the most widely used terms in psychology. It is generally agreed that the task of psychology is the study of the conditions that determine response—i.e., it is agreed that the response is the dependent variable that is to be determined as a function of other variables. But the several meanings of the term given above are by no means always equivalent. Commonly, the term is *defined* as in (3), but in use a writer gravitates toward meanings (4) or (5), occasionally pulling back to (2) or (3). Further ambiguity is introduced by failure to realize that experimental procedures and practical life alike deal with

response classes, not with **response occurrences.** (See those terms.) ❧**Reaction** can nearly always be substituted for response with no change of meaning; **behavior** (or *a* behavior) in most usages has also exactly the same denotation, but may have slightly different connotations (usually not spelled out). (See also **act** and **stimulus-response psychology.**)

Because, in compounds, one of the close synonyms—**act, behavior, movement, process, reaction**—is often substituted, most phrases containing *response* are defined under the qualifying word: e.g., **abient response,** which may also be called *abient reaction* or *abient behavior.* But see also the following entries, which are about response and not about particular responses.

response adequacy: the degree to which a response makes a change in the stimulating situation that serves the need or motive pattern of the organism. ➤An adequate response restores an old, or creates a new, equilibrium and is therefore (in terms of the immediate moment) psychologically satisfactory, though its biological or its long-term personal effects may not be.

response amplitude: 1. the quantitative measure of one dimension of a response. ➤The dimension chosen is usually the one for which the response is named—e.g., the amplitude of a salivary response may be measured by the number of drops of saliva. (Other measures are possible.) 2. an ambiguous term for **response magnitude.**

response/approach: see **abient behavior.**

response attitude: in reaction time experiments, the **set** to respond as soon as the stimulus is given; an orientation primarily toward the coming movement rather than toward the coming stimulus.—See **stimulus attitude (1).**

response circuit: the arrangement of neurons from a **receptor** to an **effector.** ➤The term is deliberately noncommittal concerning the complexity of the neural arrangement.

response class, R class: a class of behaviors or parts of behavior all of which produce essentially the same change in the organism's relation to environment. ➤The changed relation may be made by direct alteration in the environment (the lever is depressed, the food is taken into the mouth), or by muscular or glandular rearrangements within the organism (the head is turned toward the object). An **R class** may be brief or long-lasting, relatively simple or very complex. The movements or other parts may be qualitatively very different: for certain purposes of locomotion, e.g., creeping or rolling belong in the same R class. Moreover, a particular behavior may on one occasion belong in the same class with another behavior, on other occasions in a different class; or a given response class may form part of a larger class. It is the animal's whole behavior by which identification of a response class is made possible (but not always easy). ¶Nearly all psychological laws or dynamic principles actually deal with the R class rather than with the **R occurrence,** but this fact is generally ignored. The term **response,** used alone, nearly always actually denotes a response class.

response/conditioned: see **conditioned response.**

response/covert: see **covert behavior.**

response/delayed: see **delayed response.**

response/differential: a response that is elicited by only one stimulus from among several similar stimuli. ➤DIFFERENTIATED RESPONSE would be more accurate, since the response is nearly always one that had earlier been elicited by the other stimuli and is now, as a result of learning, restricted to one.—*Syn.* SELECTIVE RESPONSE.

response dispersion: see **dispersion/response.**

response/distal: see **distal vs. proximal variables.**

response duration: see **protensity.**

response equivalence: see **equivalence (3)** and **generalization.**

response/explicit = **overt response** (*prefd.*).

response function: (*J. R. Kantor*) an organismic adaptive action developed in correspondence with the **stimulus function** in previous interbehavioral events.

response generalization: see **generalization/response.**

response hierarchy: the arrangement of a class of behaviors in the order of probability in which they will be elicited in a certain situation.

response/implicit = **covert response** (*prefd.*).

response/incompatible: see **incompatible.**

response instance: a single occurrence of a section of the behavior stream that has unity and can be repeated. ➤See **response occurrence.** While (strictly speaking) no behavior part is ever repeated, there are identifiable part-behaviors so like others as to be regarded as instances of each other or of some **response class** that is narrowly defined to include only very similar behaviors. E.g., each wink of the eyelid may be regarded as one instance of the eyelid response. A continuous series runs from the unique response occurrence through the repeatable but narrowly limited response instance to the response class. Perhaps by **response** most psychologists mean a class of response instances, but there is a tendency to slip over into meaning a response

class in the broader sense, especially when dealing with the **dynamics** of response.

response intensity: the dimension reflected by change in the magnitude of muscular and glandular activities that normally parallels a change in stimulus strength (motivation being constant) or in motivation (stimulation being constant); or such changes in kind of activity as are equivalent to the change of magnitude. ➤Thus, a person may blink for a short time at a moderately bright light; at a very bright light he may blink harder and longer, and may add other aversive behaviors such as screening the eyes or turning the head. Response intensity is a useful dimension for a **response class.**

response latency or $_sT_R$: the duration of the interval between a stimulus and the onset of a response.—*Syn.* **reaction time** (which see, for several ways of defining the time limits.)—See also **latency (1)** and **(2).**

response learning: see **learning/response.**

response magnitude: a somewhat general term for several quantitative dimensions used to describe a **response instance:** amplitude, duration, intensity, frequency, rapidity.—*Syn.* **response strength** (often, however, arbitrarily restricted).

response measurement: the assignment of numbers to response or **response instances** according to the rules of measurement. ➤Measures include resistance to **extinction, response amplitude, response intensity, response latency, response magnitude, response probability, response rate, response strength.**

response/negative = **abient response.**

response occurrence, R occurrence: a particular and unrepeatable behavioral event. ➤Strictly speaking, all responses are unrepeatable, i.e., one can never do anything exactly as before. Thus all responses are R occurrences. But there are **response classes** in which one R occurrence is interchangeable for any other in the class. Nearly all psychological laws actually concern the R class, not the R occurrence.—*Syn.* **response,** SIMPLE RESPONSE, RESPONSE UNIT.—*Cp.* **response instance.**

response-oriented psychologies: all psychological points of view that make the response the primary datum or **dependent *variable.** ➤Included are **stimulus-response psychology, behaviorism, reaction psychology, act psychology, functional psychology,** and most forms of **personalism** or **self psychology.**—*Contr. w.* **content psychology, structural psychology.**

response pattern: a qualitatively and quantitatively distinct grouping of responses; an

act or action. ➤Both **overt** and **covert** responses may be included.—See **pattern.**

response probability or R_p: **1.** relative frequency with which a response occurs compared to number of opportunities offered for its occurrence. ➤This implies that a given stimulus or stimulus situation sometimes elicits alternative responses (including "no response"). **2.** strength of conditioning (presumably measured as in **1**). **3.** the dependent variable in **probability theory** of behavior.

response/proximal: see **distal vs. proximal variables.**

response rate: the number of **response instances** occurring in unit time.

response-reference: *n.* (*E. Brunswik*) the position of a response on the dimension from **distal** to **proximal.**—See **distal vs. proximal variables.**

response schema: see **schema (4).**

response/selective = **response/differential.**

response/serial: one of a set of responses, having at least a loose unity, that follow each other in a definite order.

response set: see **set/response.**

response/startle: see **starting reflex pattern.**

response strength: 1. = **response magnitude. 2.** the magnitude of response as a function of the number of times the response has been elicited or emitted. ➤This is an arbitrary definition or else begs a theoretical question.

response system: 1. the sensory, neural, muscular, and glandular structures that are coordinated to effect any specific response (or **R class**); the complex of organic circuits active in a response. **2.** all the organic structures involved in response in general. ➤This is an unnecessary usage; it merely means the whole organism or body. **3.** a complex of bodily processes organized to effect a given type of change in the organism-environment relationship. ➤Many specific responses, or even R classes, are interchangeable in such a system: e.g., if unable to move the eyes far enough to see a certain object, one may turn the head.— *Syn.* **action system,** and a very large number of other terms (e.g., **habit**) that refer to specific kinds of response systems.—See **system.**

response threshold: the minimum value of **state variable** that will evoke a response—i.e., of all the conditions, internal and external, codetermining the response.

response time: the time required to make a stipulated response. ➤The term is loosely used. Sometimes response time is calculated from the time of application of the stimulus to the end of the response, sometimes from the observable beginning to the observable

end of the motor or glandular response.— See **reaction time.**

response/trial: see **trial response.**

response variable or **R variable:** the dependent variable in all psychological observation; that which changes as a result of any sort of change in the environmental or organismic variables. The R variable may be, and generally is, extremely complex.— *Cp.* **response occurrence, response instance.**

responsibility: *n.* **1.** accountability for actions and their consequences; the status of the normal adult who is assumed able to conform to laws, customs, and standards, and who may justly be punished if he does not. **2.** the attitude of accepting such a status. **3.** the character trait of carrying out one's agreements or one's duties.—*adj.* **responsible.**

responsive: *adj.* of an organism that emits a **response** to a certain stimulus; or of an organism ready to respond to any stimulus.

rest: *n.* **1.** (*phys.*) the state of a body not moving in relation to its surroundings.— *Ant.* **motion. 2.** the condition of an organism not overtly responding. ➤Only relative rest is possible to the living organism.—*Ant.* **movement. 3.** a period of recuperation and nonactivity in a particular action system.—*Ant.* **activity, work.**

restlessness: *n.* a tendency to aimless and constantly changing movements.—*Syn.* JACTITATION (included here to show how far one can go in an effort to avoid plain speech).

restraining forces: (*Gestalt*) those psychic tendencies that tend to keep psychic phenomena separate or apart, that tend to prevent the formation of a **gestalt.** ➤In perception, sensory processes seem to be restraining.—*Contr. w.* **cohesive forces.**

restraint: *n.* the prevention of an organism's actions by physical bonds, barriers, or counteractions directed against it.—*Syn.* see **constraint.**

restructure: *v.* **1.** (*topol.*) to change the relative position of part-**regions** without changing their number. **2.** to make a fundamental change in the relationships of parts of a **field,** chiefly as a result of change within the person rather than in the external circumstances.

restructuring/perceptual: see **perceptual restructuring.**

result: *n.* **1.** a phenomenon that follows whenever a certain other phenomenon occurs, and that does not otherwise occur.— *Cp.* **cause.**—*Syn.* **consequence. 2.** (*pl.*) the data obtained from an experiment or investigation.—*Contr. w.* **conclusions.**

resultant: *n.* the force exerted when two or more forces are combined.

retained members method: a scoring procedure in which **retention** is measured by what proportion of the whole can be reproduced at the time of testing. This method of scoring is usually employed with the **right associates procedure.**—*Syn.* RECALL SCORE METHOD, TREFFERMETHODE.

retardation: *n.* 1. the slowing up of mental development, esp. in the intelligence or in school achievements; backwardness. ➤No assumption is made about the cause.—*pers. n.* **retardate,** a person who is retarded. 2. a marked slowing up of responses, esp. of verbal responses; excessively slow reaction time.

etardation/educational: slower progress in school than is normal or expected.—See discussion under **acceleration/educational.**

retention: *n.* 1. (*physiol.*) inability, or refusal, to evacuate bladder or rectum. 2. (*learning*) the fact that an organism continues able to perform a certain learned act after an interval in which the performance has not taken place; or the degree to which parts of a complex performance can be manifested after an interval; the fact that the aftereffects of an experience, as manifested in changed performance of a related act, persist. ➤The word **retention** suggests a static holding-on, whereas the facts referred to are those of performance and change of performance. Although the definition is very broad, any attempt to restrict its meaning or to distinguish different basic kinds of retention implies controversial theory. ¶Decrease in retention is **forgetting;** increase is **reminiscence (4).** ¶Learning is measured after a very brief interval, retention after a somewhat longer one, but the measuring operations are essentially the same. In learning, emphasis is upon the conditions for establishing a certain result; in retention, it is upon maintenance of that result. There are many methods of measuring retention: see esp. **prompting method, recall method, recognition method, reconstruction method, retained members method, saving method.**—*Syn.* **mneme, habit.**—*Ant.* **forgetting; attrition** (rare and special). —*adj.* **retentive.**—*abstr. n.* **retentiveness,** the ability to be retentive; **retentivity,** the general property (or properties) hypothesized as the basis for retention.—*v.* **retain.**

retention curve: a curve having a measure of remembering on the vertical axis and elapsed time since learning on the horizontal axis. The curve may take many forms.—*Syn.* FORGETTING CURVE.

retention/selective: ability to remember ideas or events of a certain class better than others.

retentiveness: *n.* the ability or capacity of an individual for retention. ➤Implicitly,

at least, this term is quantitative: one speaks of great *retentiveness.*

retentivity: *n.* the hypothesized property or properties of organisms that make retention possible.

retest consistency/index of: see **reliability coefficient (a).**

reticular: *adj.* netlike. ➤The RETICULAR SUBSTANCE or FORMATION of the brain consists of small clumps of cell bodies or **gray matter** embedded in fibers.—*Var.* **reticulate.**—*n.* **reticulum.**—*v.* **reticulate.**

retina: *n.* the innermost membrane or coat of the eyeball, having a complex but chiefly neural structure. ➤It receives the optical image formed by refraction by the cornea and lens. This image acts upon the **rods** and **cones,** which comprise (in man) one of the ten layers of which the retina is composed. These are the specific **receptors** for vision, but the retina (or the eye as a whole, with all its appendages) is also spoken of as the receptor (or **sense organ**) for vision.

retinal elements: the **rods** and **cones** of the retina, or the nerve fibers leading from them.

retinal field: the particular pattern of rods and cones that is affected by a particular stimulus field.

retinal horizon: the imaginary horizontal line across the retina that corresponds with the terrestrial horizon when the eye is in the **primary position.**

retinal illuminance: the **illuminance** of the retina, the usual units being the **troland** and the **lux.**

retinal image: see **image/retinal.**

retinal light = cortical gray.

retinal oscillations: variations in the state of excitation of the visual neural apparatus, following a single momentary stimulation. They are experienced as a brief succession of alternating bright and dark phases, such as **Charpentier's bands** or recurrent afterimages.

retinal picture = retinal *image.

retinal rivalry: irregular alternation of colors or figures when the two eyes gaze upon different fields that cannot be given unitary interpretation.—*Syn.* BINOCULAR RIVALRY.—*Ant.* **binocular *fusion.**

retinal rods: see **rods.**

retinal zones = color zones.

retinene: *n.* a pigment of the retina, related to carotene, from which **visual purple** is formed. Its deficiency causes **night *blindness.**

retinitis: *n.* inflammation of the retina.

retinitis pigmentosa: a pathological condition of the pigmentary layers of the retina, accompanied by diminished color sensitivity (esp. for blue), retracted color fields, and lowered power of dark adaptation.

retinoscope: *n.* a mirror with a small hole at its center for observing the interior of the eyeball. The observer peeps through the hole while projecting a beam of light into the eye.

retraction: *n.* 1. the drawing back of a limb or similar bodily appendage. 2. the withdrawal or disavowal of a statement previously made as unwarranted or in error.

retreat from reality: see **reality/retreat from.**

retroactive: *adj.* having effect in backward direction; working backward; affecting the past.—For examples, see **retroactive *amnesia, retroactive *facilitation, retroactive *inhibition.**—*n.* **retroaction.**

retroactive association: a connection between an item and any item that preceded it in the learning series or pattern: e.g., in a series *x-y-z,* the association between *z* and either *x* or *y.* The term is restricted to temporal series.

retroactive facilitation: see **facilitation/ retroactive.**—*Syn.* POSITIVE RETROACTION. REPRODUCTIVE FACILITATION.

retroactive inhibition: see **inhibition/ retroactive.**

retrobulbar: *adj.* 1. of the dorsal side of the medulla. 2. behind the eyeball.

retroflex: *adj.* 1. bent abruptly backward. 2. (*psychol.*) pertaining to beneficial conditions (*rare*).

retrogenesis: *n.* a hypothesis that a new growth process does not develop out of a fully developed structure but out of undifferentiated structure: e.g., further growth does not begin at the end of a plant stem in leaf or fruit, but from buds that originate on the stem lower down. ➤It is hypothesized that this rule holds also for **behavioral** development.

retrograde: *adj.* 1. moving backward or in a reverse direction. 2. degenerating.

retrogression: *n.* meeting a presently unsatisfactory situation by behavior found satisfying at an earlier period in development. ➤Preferred by some as avoiding the psychoanalytic implications of **regression.**

retrospection: *n.* systematically reviewing an experience as soon after its occurrence as possible and making verbal report thereon, at least to oneself. ➤By some it is held to be the only possible kind of **introspection.**

retrospective falsification: see **falsification/retrospective.**

return sweep: the movement of the eyes in reading from the end of one line to the beginning of another.

reverberation: *n.* the back-and-forth **reflection** of a wave form in a confined space.

reverie: *n.* a state in which the train of thought or of images is little directed purposively, and in which one is relatively insensible to external happenings. ➤Reverie

may have a single coherent object but does not have a theme: e.g., one may think about the old homestead, its discomforts, the joys one experienced there, how it has fared, etc. without these "thoughts" having a "theme." In a **daydream,** there is said to be a theme, even when the objects change and even though the theme may be difficult to discern.—*Var.* **revery.**

reversal/cue: see **cue reversal.**

reversal formation = **reaction formation.**

reversal/(mirror): see **mirror reversal.**

reversibility: *n.* the property of a sequence that can be followed in backward order. A thinking sequence is distinguished from a stimulus-response chain by this property.

reversible figure: see **figure/reversible.**

reversible perspective: see **perspective/ alternating.**

reversion: *n.* 1. inheritance, or manifestation, of a **recessive** trait that was not manifest in the immediate parents. 2. = **atavism** (not *recom.*). 3. = **regression** (2) or (3).—*v.* **revert.**

review: *n.* a re-examination or study of material previously studied, whether teacher-led or self-directed.

revival = **recall** or **reproduction.**

reward: *n.* a satisfaction-yielding stimulus or stimulus object that is obtained upon the successful performance of a task (which may be self- or other-imposed): e.g., a food pellet delivered when the animal depresses a certain lever; a scholarship for the best academic record. ➤It is established that the rewarded act or response has a statistical likelihood of being repeated and learned (*cp.* **law of *effect**), but this is not a necessary part of its definition.

The term **satisfaction** formerly had mentalistic overtones but is now often employed as in the above definition for an objectively describable fact. (See **satisfaction.**) Some authors prefer the term **reinforcement** to **reward** because the latter seems to have **anthropomorphic** or **mentalistic** connotation. But neither its etymology nor its common usage has such a connotation. Moreover, there seems need for both terms, reinforcement and reward, the former in its original meaning in classical **conditioning (1),** the latter as above defined for instrumental **conditioning (2).** To use reinforcement for the two operationally distinct procedures is a flagrant case of **theory-begging.**

But reinforcement is a neologism, is longer and therefore more impressive, hence, has been used instead of **reward** in most discussions and in most combination terms. *Primary reward,* e.g., is so much more frequently called **primary *reinforcement** that it must be so listed in this dictionary, though every criterion except frequency cries out against it.

Unless qualified, reward means POSITIVE REWARD. But see **reward/negative.**

reward/conditioned = **reward/secondary.**

reward/delayed: see DELAYED REWARD REACTION under **delayed response.**

reward expectancy: (*E. C. Tolman*) the hypothesized process aroused in an animal when it perceives the circumstances that have regularly been associated with a **reward.** The **expectancy** manifests itself in searching behavior when the reward is withheld.

reward/extraneous: a reward that has, for the subject, no intrinsic or logical relation with the performance rewarded. ➤*Syn.* EXTRINSIC REWARD.—*Contr. w.* **intrinsic *reward.** There is no clear way of determining whether a given reward is extraneous, and rewards at first extraneous often become intrinsic for a given learner.

reward/intrinsic: a reward so closely associated with the successful performance of a task that, for a given subject, it cannot be separated or distinguished from the end state. ➤The intrinsic reward seems to coincide or overlap with the **goal,** though the connotation of the term is not the same. No clear criterion distinguishes an intrinsic from an **extraneous *reward.**

reward/negative: the unsatisfactory stimulus or stimulus situation that is experienced when the performance of a task is unsuccessful. ➤The negative reward may be either **extraneous** or **intrinsic.**—*Syn.* **punishment** (but negative reward has more specific connotations and is preferred for experimental descriptions); **reinforcement/negative** (common but not recom.).

reward/positive: a term used to emphasize sharply a contrast with **negative *reward.** **Reward,** if not qualified as *negative,* is considered to be positive.—See **reward.**

reward/primary: a stimulus object that is satisfying to an animal without its having to learn to like it; an innately satisfying stimulus. ➤In experimental work with animals, food, drink, and sex objects are most often employed as primary rewards. Various escape responses seem unlearned, but whether *escape* is a primary reward is disputed.—*Syn.* **reinforcement/primary** (which see).

reward/secondary: a reward that has become a source of satisfaction through learning, usually (perhaps always) from association with another object or stimulus situation that is satisfactory.—*Syn.* **reinforcement/secondary.**

reward/sedative: a reward that brings to an end a cycle of goal-seeking activity and does not stimulate the individual to begin another.—*Ant.* STIMULATING REWARD.

reward situation: one in which satisfaction can be attained only after performing a task which in itself is not sufficiently attractive to be undertaken.—*Syn.* **extraneous *reward** situation.

reward/token: an object or state of affairs that has no intrinsic rewarding value but serves as a rewarding or reinforcing stimulus: e.g., a poker chip for a chimpanzee who has learned that he can exchange it for food.

r_G = (*C. Hull*) **fractional *antedating goal response.**

rhathymia (rə·thī'mi·ə): *n.* a factor, found by factor analysis of **extraversion-introversion** questionaries, that correlates with carefree happy-go-lucky behavior.

Rh (blood) factor: an agglutinating factor (so named because first found in the red cells of the rhesus monkey) present in the blood of about 85 per cent of humans. It causes antibody formation if introduced into blood lacking it, i.e., into RH NEGATIVE blood. ➤An RH POSITIVE fetus causes antibody formation in an Rh negative mother. This generally produces transfusion reactions in later Rh positive fetuses, with resulting pathology in the offspring (specif., abortions, stillbirths, and possibly mental deficiency).

rheo-: combining forming meaning *a flow, a current.*

rheobase: *n.* the strength of direct current just sufficient to excite a nerve or muscle.—See **chronaxie.**—*Var.* **rheobasis.**

rheoscopic: *adj.* pertaining to methods of observing the rapidly moving, as by slow-motion photography, etc.

rheostat: *n.* a sliding resistance in an electrical current regulating its strength.

rheotropism or **rheotaxis:** *n.* a **tropistic** response to the flow of water; a turning in line with the direction of flow.

rhinencephalon (rī″nen·sef'ə·lon): *n.* the **olfactory bulb** and a portion of the **forebrain** in the lateral ***fissure.**—*Syn.* OLFACTORY BRAIN.—*adj.* **rhinencephalic** (-sef·al'ik).

rhino-: combining form meaning *nose, nasal.*

rho or ρ: coefficient of correlation for squared rank differences:

$$\rho = 1 - \frac{6\Sigma D^2}{N(N^2 - 1)}$$

rhodopsin (rō·dop'sin) = **visual purple.**

rhombencephalon (rom″ben·sef'ə·lon): *n.* the **hindbrain.**

rhythm: *n.* the periodic recurrence of groups within a series. ➤The smaller groups constitute **gestalts** or wholes, each filling a determinate interval, so that a perceived rhythm may also be characterized as a repetition of intervals. The grouped items may be stimuli, percepts, or movements. In many rhythms, the groups are composed of a stressed (or accented) and one or more unstressed items, and what is repeated is the pattern of stresses, all else being subject to change.—*adj.* **rhythmic(al)**.

rhythm/subjective = **accent/subjective**.

RI = retroactive *inhibition.

rickets: *n.* a deficiency disease in children, marked by faulty bone development.—*adj.* **rickety**.

riddance reflex: any of the reflex or reflex-like movements that eliminate a painful stimulus.

Ridgway colors: an outmoded system of color names originally designed for identifying the plumage colors of birds.

right: *adj.* **1.** correct; conforming to any prescribed standard, but esp. to esthetic or moral prescription. **2.** pertaining to that side of an animal which lies to the south when it faces the rising sun.—*Syn.* **dextral**, pertaining to the right side; **dextrad**, toward or placed on the right side.

right-and-wrong cases/method of = **constant-stimulus method**.

right-and-wrong test: see **McNaughten test**.

right associates procedure: a much-used procedure in the study of **learning** and **retention**. Items (usually verbal) are presented in pairs for learning; then the first of each pair (usually not in the original series order) is presented for a brief time and the subject endeavors to reproduce the second. The score is the number of successes or of **retained members**.—*Syn.* (*Ger.*) Treffermethode, paired associates.

righting reflex or **response:** see **static reflex**.

righting reflex/visual: see **visual righting reflex**.

rigid: *adj.* **1.** stiff; unyielding; inflexible. **2.** logically precise; of a proposition that does not permit of variation. **3.** (of muscles) tense.—See **rigidity**.

rigidity: *n.* **1.** (*physiol.*) a state of strong and continued muscular contraction. **2.** relative inability to change one's action or attitude when the objective conditions demand it; clinging to a no-longer-appropriate way of acting or feeling. ➤Rigidity may be **cognitive**, esp. **perceptual**—i.e., it may be an inability to perceive things differently even when the objective conditions have changed. Rigidity may also be **affective**, or it may show itself in **overt** action. Lewin makes rigidity a property of the **barriers** in **life space**, but the observable fact is the lack of change in behavior.—*Distg. fr.* **perseveration**, which is the continua-

tion of a response actually going on, whereas rigidity is resistance to undertaking a new kind of response. The existence of a generalized **trait** of rigidity is questioned.

rigidity/decerebrate: a condition, resulting from surgical removal of the cerebrum, in which all or nearly all the skeletal muscles are contracted.

rigidity/hypnotic: a hypnosis-induced state of more or less general muscular contraction, so that the person's body is stiff.—*Cp.* **catalepsy**.

riot: *n.* a disorderly outbreak in which three or more persons assembled together respond in common to some occurrence.—*adj.* **riotous.**—*pers. n.* **riotist, rioter.**

ripen: *v.* to mature.

risk level: the percentage of samples that may be expected by chance to fall outside the **fiducial limits;** a measure of the risk that the value of a statistic is affected by chance. ➤A 5 per cent level of risk means that in 5 cases in 100 a statistic greater or less than the limits may be expected by chance. The term is proposed (by Joseph Royce) as a substitute for CONFIDENCE LEVEL, which is confusing. The risk level increases as the percentage of chance cases increases, whereas the confidence level decreases as the percentage increases.—See **fiducial limits.**

rite: *n.* a prescribed form for conducting a ceremony, esp. a religious ceremony. ➤Not a good synonym for **stereotyped** behavior (but **ritual** is so used).

ritual: *n.* **1.** a code or system of **rites** and ceremonies to be performed at intervals and regarded as having religious or other special significance: e.g., the rituals of initiation in primitive societies or in secret societies. **2.** the order and manner of carrying out a child's training when regarded by the parent as almost inviolate; or the activities demanded by a child as a "necessary" part of the daily routine. **3.** the senseless, repeated behaviors (other than **tics**) that are part of **obsessive-compulsive reactions**. **4.** any stereotyped behavior that is not directly **adjustive** but that protects (or seems to protect) the individual against internal conflict; or stereotyped behavior that serves (or seems to serve) a *social* purpose: e.g., the preening of birds in courtship; the elaborate cleaning, filling, and lighting of a pipe under mild stress conditions.

rivalry: *n.* the attempt to get or to do the same thing as well as others, but without direct conflict.—*Distg. fr.* **competition, jealousy.**

rivalry/envious: a struggle to obtain something possessed by another, or to obtain one as good or better.—*Distg. fr.* **rivalry/jealous.**

rivalry/jealous: an attempt to equal or surpass another person, motivated by fear of losing the affection or respect of a third person.—See **jealousy.**

rivalry/neural: see **neural rivalry.**

rivalry/retinal or **/visual:** see **retinal rivalry.**

rivalry/sibling: rivalry between **sibs.** ➤The apparent rivalry for excellence being often merely a rather transparent cover for jealous desire to usurp a sib's place in the affection of a parent, the two terms **sibling rivalry** and sibling **jealousy** are unfortunately often confounded.—See **rivalry/ jealous.**

RL = *Reiz-Limen, Ger.* for stimulus **threshold.**

RMS = **root-mean-square.**

Ro: symbol for the original response that was made to the **indifferent stimulus** before it was conditioned.

robot (rō′bət): *n.* **1.** a machine capable of performing most human functions. **2.** a person acting like a machine; or one reduced to carrying out only machine functions.

R occurrence = **response occurrence.**

rods or **retinal rods:** rod-shaped structures in the retina, which are believed to be the specific **receptors** for gray or achromatic visual qualities at low intensities. ➤*Cp.* retinal **cones,** which are believed to be the specific receptors for daylight intensities, both colored and achromatic. There are no rods in the **fovea.**

rods of Corti: minute rodlike structures forming the arches in the **organ of** *Corti in the inner ear.—Syn.* PILLARS OF CORTI.

rod vision: vision in which only the **rods** function, the **cones** of the retina not participating.—*Syn.* **twilight vision,** SCOTOPIC VISION.

Rolandic fissure = **fissure/central.**

role: *n.* **1.** the part played by an actor. ➤The part as actually played (hence, depending on the actor), and the part as written down (in ancient times, literally on a roll), lead to two distinct extensions of the idea in (2) and (3). **2.** the function played by an individual in a group; the individual's characteristic kind of contribution to a group: it is the *role* of the most intelligent person to correct errors. **3.** the behavior that is characteristic and expected of the occupant of a defined position in the group: the *role* of the chairman or of the secretary. ➤Undoubtedly, role (2) is affected by role (3), and vice versa; but the two represent distinct concepts. The one depends on the personality in relation to the group, the other on social or cultural expectations.— *Var.* **rôle.**

role conflict: the situation in which a person is expected to play two **roles** which it seems to him, cannot be harmonized: e.g. it is a common adolescent predicament that it is impossible to play the part of the almost-adult person he is, and yet be obedient to parental injunctions.

role-playing: *n.* **1.** performing a role (2 or (3). **2.** acting according to a role that is not one's own; imitating a role. **3.** a method of studying the nature of a certain role by acting out its concrete details in a contrived situation that permits of better and more objective observation. ➤E.g., one may "act out" the role of a mother punishing her child, spontaneously supplying the cause of punishment and the manner thereof. The role may be suggested by oneself or by another. In psychotherapy, role-playing is used in a variety of ways: to discover how the client conceives of certain important social roles and how he believes he functions therein, to help the individual gain insight into the conduct of others who have a certain role to play in real life, to give practice in more adequate ways of fulfilling a role, and (in play therapy) to effect catharsis. It is also used as an educational device, e.g., in leadership training.

romanticism: *n.* a highly general attitude toward life and toward artistic expression that emphasizes freedom, spontaneity, the value of feeling and of fantasy. ➤The romantic attitude is generally contrasted with the CLASSIC, with its emphasis on formal symmetry, and the due expression of feeling under rules. It is by no means clear that the general attitude is psychologically unitary—that, e.g., there is a correlation between a romantic attitude toward marriage and appreciation of Brahms. The contrast between **Dionysian** and **Apollonian** attitudes perhaps better expresses the distinction.

Romberg sign or **symptom:** falling or excessive swaying when trying to stand with feet together and eyes shut. ➤It is a sign of extensive damage to the nervous system esp. in the posterior column of the spinal cord. (See locomotor **ataxia.**) But it may also be hysterical or **functional.**

root: *n.* **1.** (*math.*) a number which, multiplied by itself the indicated number of times, gives a certain other number. ➤Thus 4 is the third root of 64. When no ordinary number is indicated, the second or square root is meant. **2.** (*neurol.*) a bundle of fibers leaving or joining a central portion of the nervous system.

root conflict = **nuclear problem.**

rooting reflex: head-turning and mouth opening movements in an infant when his cheek is stroked.

root-mean-square or **RMS:** the square root of the sum of the several value squared, divided by the number of values:

$$\sqrt{\frac{\Sigma X^2}{N}}$$

When the values are deviations from the mean, the **RMS** equals the **standard *deviation.**

oot/spinal: see **spinal root.**

Rorschach = Rorschach test.

Rorschach category: a phrase used in this dictionary to avoid repeating the longer expression: a category used in the Rorschach test to classify the **content** reported by the subject when instructed to tell what he "sees on each card, or anything that might be presented there."

Rorschach ranking test: a modification of the Rorschach test in which the subject is asked, for each of the inkblot cards, to rank nine possible responses in an order from "best"—i.e., most descriptive of the card—to "worst."

Rorschach test: a **projective test** utilizing 10 cards, printed with bilaterally symmetrical inkblots, to which the subject responds by telling what he "sees on each card, or anything that might be presented there." ➤He is later systematically questioned, in a loosely prescribed fashion, about his responses. In interpretation, no single element or category of response is given a fixed significance apart from its relation to the whole response; and the test is said to be diagnostic of personality as a whole. Each category of response, nonetheless, is taken to reflect—other things being equal— the operation of certain personality traits.

Rosanoff test: see **Kent-Rosanoff Test.**

Rosenzweig P-F Study = **Picture-Frustration Study/Rosenzweig.**

rostral: *adj.* pertaining to the beak, hence, to the head end of an animal.

rotary-pursuit task: a **pursuit-reaction** test in which the task is to move an indicator to conform to the motion of an irregularly rotating object.

rotation: *n.* **1.** motion about a center or axis. **2.** (*factor anal.*) the process of moving the **factor axes** in such a way that a larger number of points will fall on the **hyperplanes;** a change in the position of the factor axes such that they more closely represent the correlation coefficients of the **matrix.**

rotation/oblique: (*factor anal.*) a rotation of the **factor axes** such that they meet at acute angles. In this case, the factors correlate with each other and a **second-order** *factor can be extracted.—Cp.* **rotation/orthogonal.**

rotation/orthogonal: (*factor anal.*) a rotation of the factor axes so that they meet at right angles. The correlation between such factors is zero.

rotation perception: the experience induced when the rate or direction of rotation of a person's body is altered. Any marked change in the rate causes movement in the fluids of the **semicircular *canals** and thus excites the receptors therein. Slowing of the rate induces an illusion of rotation in the opposite direction.

rote learning: see **learning/rote.**

Rotter board (rō′tər): a device used in the study of **level of *aspiration.** It imposes a perceptual-motor task insusceptible to any considerable modification by learning or incentive and in which the subject's "success" is controlled by the experimenter.

roughness: *n.* **1.** the percept resulting when tactual stimuli are of contrasting intensity and the several sensations fuse only incompletely. **2.** = TONAL ROUGHNESS, the percept when there is rapid and irregular alternation of intensity in a tone.

rounding off: (*stat.*) discarding one or more digits to the right of a specified digit. The specified digit is then increased by one or left unchanged according to a rule. ➤A common rule is to increase the last-place digit by one if the dropped number is more than 5, to keep it unchanged if the dropped number is less than 5; if the dropped figure is exactly 5, the last-place number is increased if odd, left unchanged if even.

round window: see **window/round.**

row: see **column.**

rpm = revolutions per minute. (Also RPM.)

rps = revolutions per second.

RQ = recovery quotient.

RS = reinforcing stimulus (see **reinforcement).**

R/S ratio: (*B. F. Skinner*) the ratio between the magnitude of the response (R) and the intensity of the stimulus (S).

RT = reaction time.

R_t or r_t: symbol for **tetrachoric *correlation** coefficient.

R **technique:** see *R* **correlation.**

Rubin's (goblet) figure: an **ambiguous *figure** that can be seen either as a goblet or as two facial profiles.

rubric (rü′brik): *n.* a heading; hence, a division or classification: it does not belong under this *rubric.*

rudiment: *n.* **1.** the unfinished; the undeveloped; hence, **2.** the simple beginnings of a subject of study; the elements: the *rudiments* of psychology. **3.** (*biol.*) an organ arrested at an early stage of its development.—*Cp.* **vestige.—***adj.* **rudimentary.**

Ruffini corpuscle: a branched-nerve **end organ** found chiefly in subcutaneous tissue. It is believed to mediate warmth sensations. —*Syn.* RUFFINI CYLINDER.

Ruffini papillary endings: nerve endings,

in the papillary layer of the skin, which are believed to mediate pressure sensations. —*Syn.* RUFFINI PLUMES.

rule: *n.* a guide for action; a standing order covering many specific cases but of relatively limited range. ➤In science, rule is to be distinguished from **law** and from **canon.** It is usually a comparatively rough working principle, lacking complete rational or empirical support, but useful as a tentative guide to action.

rumor: *n.* an unverified report or account of an event that circulates chiefly by word of mouth.

run: *n.* **1.** (*exper.*) a single presentation of a series of stimuli or tasks; or the single performance of a prescribed task; a trial. **2.** (*stat.*) one performance of an operation or series of operations that is capable of repetition: e.g., examining the data for the

highest and lowest value and casting them out, then repeating.—*v.* **3.** (*animal psychol.*) to expose an animal repeatedly to an experimental situation (esp., to a maze); hence, to train an animal: the rats were *run* ten days in a T maze.

runway: *n.* (*animal psychol.*) a pathway leading from a starting box to a goal box. ➤Detours or **blind alleys** may lead off from the runway. It may be elevated or enclosed, in both cases restricting the animal. Locomotion may be of any sort, including swimming.

rut: *n.* **1.** copulation, esp. of infrahuman animals. **2.** the breeding season. **3.** a narrow groove or furrow in the ground; hence, a fixed and narrow routine; confinement of ideas, feelings, or actions to a narrow range. —*Cp.* **stereotype.**

R **variable** = **response variable.**

S

S: 1. = (*ital.*) **subject** (in an experiment). (*pl. Ss*) **2.** = **stimulus. 3.** = sensory **intensity** (2), when R = stimulus. **4.** = space factor (see **abilities/primary mental**). **5.** = (*Ror., ital.*) white space response. **6.** = (*psychophys.*) **standard stimulus.**

S_D or D = **drive stimulus.**

S_G = (*C. Hull*) goal *stimulus.

s: 1. = **sensation.** (*pl. ss*) **2.** (*stat.*) the **standard *deviation** from any point in the distribution, or from any point except the mean. **3.** (*psychophys.*) the **variable stimulus**, any value of the variable stimulus. (Also written **V**). **4.** (*C. Hull*) the neurophysiological afferent impulse evoked by the stimulus, esp. when that impulse continues after the cessation of the stimulus (= PERSEVERATIVE STIMULUS TRACE). **5.** (*C. Spearman*) special ability (see **ability**).

s' = (*C. Hull*) **stimulus trace.**

s_G = (*C. Hull*) FRACTIONAL GOAL STIMULUS, a proprioceptive stimulus resulting from a **fractional *antedating goal response,** r_G.

sabotage: *n.* malicious destruction of machinery by those using it; hence, any underhanded or deliberate attempt by a participant to obstruct an operation or enterprise.

sabotage/masochistic: (*psychoan.*) any kind of openly destructive or deliberately obstructive behavior, the underlying motive of which is to bring punishment upon oneself.

saccadic movement (sə·kad′ik): a quick jump of the eye from one **fixation point**

to another, as in reading. ➤*Contr. w.* the slower pursuit movement in following a moving object, and with the **perch** during which the eye is at rest. During saccadic movement, the eye is nearly or quite blind.

saccadic time: the sum, for a given reading unit, of the time intervals during which the eye is in movement, as contrasted with the sum of **fixation times.**

saccule (sak′ūl): *n.* (*anat.*) the smaller of the two sacs in the **vestibule** of the inner ear.—*Var.* **sacculus** (-yə·ləs).—*adj.* **sacculate.**

sacral (sā′krəl): *adj.* pertaining to the **sacrum,** or to the region of the sacrum.

sacral division: an anatomic division of the autonomic nervous system. ➤Functionally, the sacral and the cranial divisions are often grouped together and contrasted with the thoracolumbar (or sympathetic) division.—See **autonomic nervous system.**

sacred: *adj.* **1.** pertaining, or belonging, to the divine or to worship of the divine; hence, **2.** not to be lightly or frivolously dealt with. ➤The SACRED DISEASE is an old term for the *grand mal* form of **epilepsy.**

sacrum (sā′krəm): *n.* (*anat.*) the thick triangular bone, composed of five fused vertebrae, at the lower end of the spinal column. It joins with the hipbones to form the back of the pelvis.—*adj.* **sacral.**

sadism: *n.* **1.** the tendency to associate sexual satisfaction with the infliction of pain upon another. ➤In some cases the infliction of pain itself yields satisfaction; in others it is a necessary preliminary to other forms of sexual activity.—*Syn.* active **al-**

golagnia.—*Ant.* masochism. 2. loosely and generally, love of being cruel; the **compulsive** tendency to vent aggression and destructiveness upon another person. ➤Vindictiveness, exploitation, humiliation, or frustration of another may substitute for, or be added to, the infliction of physical pain on another. Overt sexual satisfaction may or may not accompany these behaviors. —*adj.* sadistic.—*pers. n.* sadist.

sadism/anal: (*psychoan.*) proneness to cruelty that has its origin in the infant's resentment of punishment inflicted during toilet training.

sadism/inverted: the active repression of strong sadistic tendencies. It manifests itself as the fear and shunning of any conscious expression of hostility or aggressiveness, or as inertia or hopelessness.

sadism/oral: see **oral sadism.**

sado-masochism: *n.* the tendency to both **sadism** and **masochism.**

safety device: (*K. Horney*) an expedient whereby a neurotic attempts to cope with the hostility of his environment; more generally, an indirect way of protecting oneself from threat. ➤Many normal tendencies carried to excess (e.g., assertiveness) are interpreted as safety devices.—*Cp.* **defense mechanism** (more specific) and **style of life.**

sagittal (saj′i·təl): *adj.* (fr. *L., arrow*) (*anat.*) **1.** pertaining to the arrow-shaped suture between the two parietal bones of the skull. **2.** pertaining to the plane which, passing through the sagittal suture, divides the body into right and left halves; or to any plane parallel to this plane.

sagittal axis: (*optics*) the line that runs from the center of the retina through the center of the lens and pupil and projects into the field of vision.

sagittal fissure: the large fissure separating the two cerebral hemispheres.

St. Vitus' dance = chorea/Sydenham's.

salience: *n.* **1.** (*W. Stern*) the degree to which an experience stands out sharply and is relatively disconnected from the rest of experience.—*Ant.* embeddedness. **2.** the relative prominence of certain parts of the psychological field in relation to other parts. ➤Salience is not intensity or strength; it is distinctiveness and a sort of immediately perceived importance.—*adj.* salient.

salivary: *adj.* pertaining to saliva or its production.

Salpetrière school (sal·pet″ri·ār′): an early school of psychopathology founded by Charcot. It was especially interested in hypnosis.

salpingectomy (sal″pin·jek′tə·mi): *n.* cutting or tying off the Fallopian tubes, the ducts that carry the egg cell into the uterus. ➤This is the simplest *surgical* method of

contraception in women. It corresponds with **vasectomy** for men.—*Syn.* TUBECTOMY, FALLECTOMY.

saltatory (sal′tə·tôr·i): *adj.* pertaining to leaping or dancing. ➤SALTATORY GROWTH or DEVELOPMENT proceeds by sudden "leaps," rather than by many small changes which summate. SALTATORY SPASMS are **clonic** contractions that cause the patient to leap or jump.—*n.* saltation.

same-group procedure: an experimental plan or design in which a group acts as its own **control.** ➤A common example is the ABBA pattern in which one notes changes in the dependent variable after periods in which the treatment variable is applied (condition A) or not applied (condition B).

sameness/trait of: (*H. A. Murray*) adherence to certain places, people, and modes of conduct; persistence of purpose; consistency of conduct; rigidity of habits.

sample: *n.* a part of a **population** which, for the purpose in hand, is taken as **representative** of the whole population, so that certain conclusions based on the sample will be valid for the whole population. ➤**Population** is construed very broadly; it may be persons, objects, operations, events, scores or values of a variable, which for the purpose are considered as a group or set. The kinds of conclusions that can validly be drawn depend upon the nature of the population (which is itself always a sample of some larger population) and upon the way the sample is drawn; this is the province of SAMPLING THEORY.—*Distg. fr.* selection, which is a choice according to a known property or attribute.—*v.* sample.

Sampling is interchangeable with **sample** in many compounds.

sample/adequate: a sample large enough for the accuracy required, although not necessarily **representative** or free from bias.

sample bias: any factor in the method of drawing a sample that lessens its **representative** character. ➤E.g., in a sample of the offspring of a group of white rats, one rat might be taken from each litter. Since litters differ in size, the offspring of relatively infertile parents will be (for most purposes) OVERREPRESENTED, and **bias** is present. Or if the experimenter always takes the rat nearest at hand, he will have overrepresentation of those rats who most often approach the front of the cage. **Bias** does not here have the connotation of emotional prejudice, though such prejudice is one form of sample bias.

sample group = sample.

sample interview: an interview with an individual who forms part of a sample. ➤It is not an interview regarded as typical.

sample/matched: a sample so drawn as to have the same characteristics, in every respect believed to affect **representativeness**, as another sample. It will commonly have, as a minimum, the same **range, mean**, and **standard *deviation** in respect to any variable believed to affect the representativeness.

sample overlap: the range of values or scores common to two or more samples of the same population.

sample/random: see **random sample**.

sample/representative: see **sampling/representative**.

sample/selected = selected group (2, 3).

sample space: a geometrical representation in which the criteria used in defining a sample constitute the dimensions of a "space." Any item "within this space" may represent the space. Thus, if the sample space is constituted by "women who wear jodhpurs," the sample item may wear either wool or silk jodhpurs.

sample/stratified: see **sampling/stratified**.

sample/time: a sample, drawn by taking all the observable data that fall within a given time (or a number of times), and chosen to represent the variable in question: e.g., the number of times a speaker says "er-aw" during the first, the middle, and the last 5 minutes of a 2-hour speech.

sample/work: see **work sample**.

sampling: *n*. the process of drawing a sample. ➤SAMPLE THEORY is a consideration of the principles involved in drawing such a sample as permits valid inference to be made. It rests primarily upon **probability theory**, since all sampling (as contrasted with **selection**) involves **chance**.—See **sampling/representative** and **sampling/random**.

sampling/area: see **area sampling**.

sampling/behavior: recording precisely what a subject is doing at prescribed times, so chosen as to yield a **representative *sample** of the occasions and circumstances of the subject's life.

sampling/block: 1. grouping the units to be investigated into certain important categories (which must together include all the **population**), then taking a sample from each category or "block." ➤This general meaning includes **area sampling** and **stratified *sampling**. 2. taking a sample from each contiguous geographical area that contains the population.—*Syn*. **area sampling**.

sampling/controlled: sampling in which some control other than chance is exercised over the inclusion of items in the sample: e.g., **area sampling** or **stratified *sampling**.—*Syn*. DIRECT SAMPLING.

sampling/direct = **sampling/controlled**.

sampling/disproportional: sampling in which the number of cases drawn from each of the various strata (see **sampling/stratified**) is not proportional to the number of units in the strata.

sampling/domal: see **domal sampling**.

sampling/double: use of two or more methods of sample selection at different levels of an investigation.—*Syn*. MIXED SAMPLING.

sampling error: see **error/sampling**.

sampling/extensive: in achievement testing, the use of a wide variety of items covering many subtopics. ➤*Contr. w*. INTENSIVE SAMPLING, in which fewer subtopics are covered with many items devoted to each.

sampling/intensive: see **sampling/extensive**.

sampling population: the **population** (which see) from which a sample is to be drawn. ➤The population consists of individual items each of which has a chance to be drawn for the sample. The **universe** consists of all those individual items which conform to the criterion by which the population is marked off or defined. E.g., the population might be all sophomores in X College, but conclusions might be sought concerning the **universe** of all college sophomores. This is in effect to say that a population is itself an areal or stratified sample of a universe from which a smaller sample is operationally drawn.

sampling/proportional: drawing a sample in which all significant elements are represented in the same proportion in which they occur in the **statistical *universe**.

sampling/purposive: selection of a portion of the population that has, in respect to one or more characteristics already statistically known, the same average (or other measures) as the whole population.

sampling/quota: drawing a certain proportion of items from a set of subgroups constituting the **population**.—*Cp*. **area sampling, stratified *sampling**. ➤Unless the subgroups are constituted by a criterion that is independent of the variable being tested (which is seldom true), the sample loses in representativeness.

sampling/random: drawing a sample by chance: i.e., in such a way that every item in the population has an equal and independent chance of being included in the sample. ➤The term comes close to being redundant since **sample** usually means a part taken at **random**, as contrasted with a **selection**. But some sampling methods combine selection and randomness (see, e.g., **controlled *sampling, area sampling, stratified *sampling**). Random sampling may be restricted to sampling that involves *only* random choice (*syn*. SIMPLE

SAMPLING), or may be used (with quantifying expression) for the degree to which only random choice prevails in a sampling procedure.

sampling/representative: taking a sample that accurately depicts what is true of the population from which the sample is drawn; taking a sample that includes in due proportion or frequency every relevant or required characteristic of the whole; drawing a sample that has the same distribution of scores as the entire population. ➤All samples are by definition *designed* to be representative. If it is not to be redundant, **representative sampling** must refer to the extent to which a sample is *truly* representative.

sampling servo: a mechanism that measures error in a process at regular intervals and applies a correction proportional to the error.—*Syn.* DEFINITE CORRECTION SERVO.

sampling/situational: see **situational sampling.**

sampling stability: When successive samples drawn according to a consistent plan give the same result, the sampling is regarded as having stability.—*Cp.* **sample/ adequate.**

sampling/stratified: dividing the **population** to be surveyed into a number of nonoverlapping classes or categories which together include all cases, followed by taking cases at random from within the categories, the number from each category being proportional to the total number therein.

sampling theory: see **sample** and **sampling.**

sampling variability: the extent to which a series of samples differs by chance from a truly **random *sample.** It is estimated from the standard deviation of the series.

sanction: *n.* **1.** permission for, or social approval of, a proposed act. **2.** (usually in the plural) penalties for violation of legal and social imperatives (or rewards for conformity).

sanguine temperament: a very ancient classification for a personality characterized by warmth, ardor, and hopefulness or optimism. It was originally supposed that the blood (*L. sanguis*) was the cause of this type of behavior.

sanity: *n.* a prescientific term for the normal mental condition of the human individual.—*Ant.* **insanity** (which see).—*adj.* **sane.**

Sanson images = **Purkinje-Sanson images.**

sapid (sap'id): *adj.* capable of exciting the sense of taste.

sapphism = **Lesbianism.**

sarcasm: *n.* the use of bitter, caustic, contemptuous, or stinging remarks, often in the form of ironical statements.

S-A-T (es·ā·tē): **1.** = **School Ability**

Tests. **2.** = Scholastic Aptitude Test (of CEEB).

satiation (sā″shi·ā′shən): *n.* **1.** full gratification of an **appetite** or, more generally, of a **need** or **desire**; the providing of a needed object so completely that appetite or desire is extinguished; or the state of the organism when such gratification has been attained. **2.** a state of relative insensitivity to stimulation that follows exposure to a succession of closely related stimuli.—*Syn.* SATIETY (sə·tī′ə·ti); (for 2) SATIATION EFFECT (*prefd.*).—*v.* **satiate.**

satisfaction: *n.* **1.** the state of an organism when the currently dominant motivation tendencies have attained their **goal;** or the attaining of such a state. **2.** the feeling state of a person who has gratified his appetites and desires. ➤The word is difficult to define without circularity: what is a goal except a satisfaction? E. L. Thorndike, using the term SATISFIER, spoke of a state or condition "which the animal does nothing to avoid, often doing things which maintain or renew it."—*Ant.* **annoyance.**—*Cp.* **reward, reinforcement, valence.**—*v.* **satisfy.**

satisfier: *n.* an external state leading to **satisfaction,** which see.—*Ant.* **annoyer.**

saturated test: a test that has a high **factor loading** (i.e., that correlates highly) with a certain **factor.**

saturation: *n.* **1.** = **color saturation. 2.** (*factor anal.*) the degree to which a test is loaded with a given factor.—See **factor loading. 3.** (*chem.*) the degree to which a liquid has absorbed or dissolved a chemical substance.

satyriasis (sat″i·rī′ə·sis): *n.* abnormally strong sex desire in men.—*Cp.* **nymphomania.**—*pers. n.* SATYROMANIAC.

saving method or **procedure:** an experimental procedure that measures strength of **retention** by decrease in time, in errors, or in number of trials needed for relearning, as compared with the original learning.—*Distg. fr.* **retained members method.**

S-B: *abbr.* for **Stanford-Binet** intelligence test.

Sc: 1. = **CS, the conditioned stimulus. 2.** = stimulus component.

scalability: *n.* **1.** capability of being represented as a regular progression of quantities, or of being assigned a place on such a progression. ➤It is almost an axiom that everything that exists can be scaled, i.e., measured, if enough effort is given to it. Hence, this meaning gives way to the following highly specialized meaning. **2.** a characteristic of the items of a test or test battery that makes it possible, knowing the scores individuals make on the test as a whole, to predict their response to any single item. This characteristic can only be determined for a given population; a battery possessing scalability for college students might not have it for high-school freshmen or for the general population. ➤Scalability is found when all the items under consideration reflect the same (and only the same) variability in the persons being tested: the items then differ only in their difficulty, or in something that parallels difficulty. Thus, if a series of problems that differ in computation difficulty for fourth-graders are completely uninfluenced by differences in reading difficulty, motivation, understanding of the task, etc., and if "computation" is for these pupils a single-variable task, then knowing that a pupil answered a total of 14 right enables us to say just *which* items (with an allowance for chance) were right or wrong. To the extent that this is not true, the test or the item is not scalable.—*Syn.* **unidimensionality.**—*adj.* **scalable.**

scala media (skā′lə mē′di·ə): the smallest tube of the **cochlea,** containing the **organ of *Corti.**—*Syn.* COCHLEAR CANAL.

scalar analysis: the procedure that emphasizes finding the place on a scale occupied by a given variable. ➤Specifically applied to motivation, it seeks to determine the strength of a particular motive in a particular person. It contrasts with **vector** analysis, which seeks to discover the direction of effect, and what the motivating force accomplishes.

scalar product or **value:** (*stat.*) the product of the length of **vector** *a,* multiplied by the length of **vector** *b,* multiplied by the cosine of the angular separation of the vectors. If the two vectors are of unit length, the scalar value is the cosine of the angle. If the vectors are **test *vectors,** the scalar value represents the correlation between the two tests.

scala tympani (tim′pə·ni): a spiral tube in the **cochlea,** filled with a fluid and connecting with the **scala vestibuli.**—*Syn.* **tympanic *canal.**

scala vestibuli (ves·tib′ū·lī): a spiral tube in the **cochlea** filled with the fluid that receives the acoustic vibrations from the **stapes** and communicates them to the **organ** of ***Corti.**—*Syn.* VESTIBULAR CANAL.

scale: *n.* **1.** any device for determining the magnitude or quantity of an object or event of any sort; a device for assigning a number or numeral that will indicate how much of something there is; a measuring device that provides a set of standards (numbered according to certain working rules) with which to compare the object to be measured, in order to assign to it a number or mathematical value that represents its magnitude. ➤The term is of wide applicability:

a **scale** of some sort is involved in every measurement or estimate. Implicit in every case is a set of rules for assigning the numbers or values: it is these rules that give meaning to the numbers. The objects may be perceptual or conceptual. The following definitions are specializations of the general concept. **2.** a representation of magnitude or quantity by a series of numbered spatial intervals: e.g., a yardstick, a thermometer. **3.** a physical device that performs some or all of the operations called for by the rule, and displays the numbers to be assigned to the object: e.g., a voltmeter, a clock, a Geiger counter. ➤Such a device is properly an **instrument** embodying a scale. **4.** a series of objects numbered to show the magnitude of each, the object to be measured being assigned the same number as the standard object to which it is closest in magnitude. ➤The standard objects may be conceptual, as may be the objects to be compared. E.g., a list of legal offenses, arranged and numbered in order of the severity with which they are punished, is a scale of legal seriousness. **5.** a series of test items, tasks, or questions, each of which has been given a number or score value on the basis of empirical evidence of their average difficulty for a certain group of individuals. ➤Here belong intelligence, personality, and attitude scales, but not those questionaries which have no empirical scoring system. **6.** the rules for assigning a number: e.g., the rules determining the classification of an employee as belonging in class I, II, or III. **7.** (*L. Guttman*) a test or attitude-measuring device that meets the criterion of **scalability** (which see). ➤This imposes a severe restriction on what is to be called a scale; nearly everything hitherto so named would have to be called a QUASI SCALE. It is doubtful that such restriction on an established term is the best way to make the distinction Guttman emphasizes.

—*Adj.* **scalable** (often restricted to meaning (7).—*n.* **scaling** (which see).—*v.* **scale (9)** (which see).

Compounds of **scale** descriptive of the scaling process or rationale are entered under *scale* with a qualifying word: **scale/additive,** etc. Compounds referring to measuring devices for a particular variable are entered under the qualifying word: **attitude scale,** etc.

scale: *n.* **8.** (*music*) a stepwise succession of tones ascending or descending in pitch by intervals that are conventionally determined in any particular musical tradition or system. ➤Most scales are based on the octave, the same interval relationships being repeated in higher or lower octaves. A vast number of scales are in use throughout the world. The bulk of Western music

is based on seven-tone **diatonic *scales.**
—*Cp.* also **scale/chromatic.**

scale: *v.* **9.** to assign numbers to objects (perceptual or conceptual) or to events according to a system or a working rule. ➤This operation is basic to measurement and hence to all science.

scale/absolute: a scale that starts from **absolute *zero** and increases by units that are equal at all points on the scale.—See **scale/additive.**

scale/additive: a scale whose subdivisions or scale units are equal at all points on the scale; a scale with EQUAL SCALE UNITS which can therefore be directly added. ➤A meter stick is an additive scale: a centimeter in the middle has the same magnitude as one at either end. But an **MA** scale is not additive, since the difference between MA 3 and MA 4, a difference of one year of mental age, is not known to be equal to the difference between MA 10 and MA 11, also one year of mental age. Although few psychological scales are truly additive, in many the adding of scores does not greatly distort the facts. In other instances it does. **Standard *scores** are considered to be additive by some authorities, **ratio *scale** scores by most.—*Cp.* **scale/absolute.**

scale analysis: (*L. Guttman*) determining the degree of **scalability (2)** of a test or attitude scale.

scale/analytical = **diagnostic test.**

scale/a priori: a scale in which numbers are assigned to the steps of the scale on the basis of expert judgment rather than on the application of rational rules to empirical data. E.g., the **Bogardus *Social Distance Scale** arbitrarily makes "close kinship by marriage" one step above "membership in a club."

scale caption: the verbal description or the numerical value assigned to division points on a scale.

scale/chromatic: (*music*) the succession of twelve equal semitones which forms the pitch basis of present Western music. ➤*Cp.* **diatonic *scale,** the usual seven-toned scale (major, minor, or modal) of Occidental music, in which whole tones and semitones are arranged in varying combinations. The chromatic scale consists of these seven, plus five intermediate tones, the latter being conceived of as inflections or colorations (hence, the word *chromatic*) of the basic diatonic scale on which any particular composition is built.

scale/classificatory = **scale/nominal.**

scale/continuous: a scale that assumes **continuous variation** in the *underlying* variable. ➤It may have division numbers at intermediate points representing how far proportionally the points are from a minimum in the direction of a maximum, but

these dividing points are regarded as arbitrary. E.g., the division points on the centigrade thermometer (degrees) represent 1/100 of the difference between the freezing and boiling points for water, although temperature change is continuous. **Graphic *rating scales** permit the rater's judgment to be *expressed* on a continuum when the underlying variable is assumed to be continuous. Both the centigrade scale and the graphic rating scale are continuous.

scale/cumulative: see **cumulative scale.**

scale/derived: a scale whose units are **derived *scores.**

scale/designatory = **scale/nominal.**

scale/diatonic: (*music*) a scale made up of the particular related tones that form a **key.** ➤In Western music, the traditional major and minor scales and the church modes, each of which has its characteristic interval pattern, comprise the (seven-tone) diatonic scales. The difference in these patterns is chiefly in the position of the **semitones.** In a MAJOR SCALE, semitones occur between the third and fourth, and between the seventh and eighth, tones (all other intervals being **whole tones**). The MINOR SCALE is variable in its sixth and seventh tones: in its so-called "natural" form (that most closely approximating the church mode from which it is descended), the semitones fall between the second and third, and between the fifth and sixth, tones. Major and minor scales are transposable—i.e., they may begin at any of the twelve pitches of our octave, although the major or minor pitch pattern is the same for all—and hence we speak of twelve major and twelve minor keys (C sharp minor, A major, etc.). —*Cp.* **scale/chromatic.**

scale/difficulty: a test or scale whose scoring units are tasks graded in order of difficulty. ➤The tasks may be given unit scores in proportion to their difficulty for the population concerned, an individual's score being the sum of such weighted scores for items passed. Or the individual may be given the rank score of the most difficult item passed, or of the least difficult item failed. —*Cp.* **point scale.**

scale/fundamental: a scale in which a value is expressed as a proportional part or ratio of the standard amount of one of the three dimensions: length, weight, electrical resistance. ➤The term implies the acceptance of a philosophical position that only such dimensions are fundamental. A fundamental scale is a **ratio *scale.**

scale/graphic = **rating scale/graphic.**

scale interval: the quantity separating one division of a scale from the next. ➤The quantity may be of any sort, and may be arbitrary for any given measuring operation —e.g., either an inch or a yard may be

the scale interval.—*Distg. fr.* **interval
*scale.**

scale/interval: a scale that uses differences between two items or reference points as the equal units of the scale. ➤If the distance or interval between points *a* and *b* is taken as the unit for a scale, measurement consists in determining how many such units are contained in a given magnitude: e.g., the Fahrenheit temperature scale, the meter stick, the yardstick. On an ordinary test, intervals between successive scores (number of items correct, etc.) are not equivalent—i.e., score 55 to score 56 may not represent an interval equivalent with score 100 to 101. Hence such a test is not an interval scale. But **standard
*scores** derived from such tests are generally held to form an interval scale.

scale/isochron: see **isochron.**

scale/logarithmic: a scale in which the spatial interval between its successive divisions is proportional to the difference between the **logarithms** of the two numbers.

scale/major: see **scale/diatonic.**

scale/mental: see **mental scale.**

scale/merit = **scale/quality.**

scale/minor: see **scale/diatonic.**

scale/nominal: a schema for labeling persons, objects, processes, or properties by letters or numbers that serve only to identify them, either as individuals or as members of a class. No quantitative relationships are implied except the equivalence, for a specific purpose, of all those given the same label.—*Syn.* DESIGNATORY SCALE, CLASSIFICATORY SCALE.

scale/ordinal: a device to determine whether an object or quality is greater or less, and assigning numbers accordingly: e.g., a set of rules for determining order of merit. The numbers assigned are **ordinal** numbers or their equivalent (such as highest, middle, or lowest rank).

scale points: the points dividing a continuum to be used as a scale into intervals, usually equal intervals, numbered to indicate magnitude. ➤The points are often symbolized by a line, as in the case of ordinary footrules where the point is the intersection of the divisional line with the edge of the ruler.—*Distg. fr.* **point scale.**

scale/product: a scale consisting of a series of standard products or performances to which have been assigned numbers representing an order of merit, the subject's performance being given the scale value of that standard performance it most resembles: e.g., a handwriting scale consisting of a series of samples, each numbered to indicate its relative excellence. Product scales are one kind of **ordinal *scale.**—*Cp.* **quality *scale.**

scale/psychological: a device for meas-

uring something that is described in psychological terms. ➤Popularly (and correctly) the term applies to such devices as intelligence tests, but in technical writing it is employed to emphasize measurement along a dimension whose units are psychological rather than physical. Indeed, some writers restrict its use to a scale that is not paralleled by any physical scale: e.g., a scale of aggressiveness. The limitation is arbitrary; the degrees of redness of lights directly perceived and estimated form a psychological scale, even though it parallels (to some extent) a physical scale in terms of wave length.

scale/quality: 1. a scale in which the successive steps or units are qualities rather than quantities. **2.** a scale in which the successive units reflect progressively greater worth or value as determined by some empirical criterion: e.g., a **product *scale,** a **merit** rating.—*Syn.* MERIT SCALE. ➤Note that in (2) greater worth or value is a quantity as well as a quality. See **quality (3).**

scale/range: a test series designed to measure primarily the number and variety of tasks, related to some underlying variable, in which the testee has ability.—*Cp.* **altitude of intelligence.**

scale/ratio: a scale whose unit of measurement is a given fraction of a certain standard difference; specif., for psychology, a scale whose unit of measurement is a fraction of a perceptual difference. ➤One can determine that a certain color is halfway between two reds in redness. Halving again the distances between that color and the two original colors, four perceived differences are obtained which can be regarded as equal and used as units of measurement to determine how many such units are included in a given magnitude. Ratio units of this sort are generally considered to constitute an **additive *scale.**

scale reproducibility: (*L. Guttman*) the property of a test whereby it is possible to predict the subject's response to any item if his total score is known. ➤Perfect reproducibility is as rare as perfect correlation and depends on it.—*Syn.* **scalability (2).**

scale/Snellen: see **Snellen chart.**

scale/tempered or **/equal-tempered:** (*music*) a **scale (8)** whose tones are contained in those produced by tempered tuning. ➤A scale is described as PURE when its tones follow the mathematically prescribed intervals of their vibration ratios. It is *tempered* when some adjustment is made, for practical purposes, in the tuning. A series of pure scales on different keynotes have relatively few of their tones coinciding in pitch: e.g., the D sharp of the

E major scale is perceptibly different from the E flat of the B flat scale. TEMPERAMENT (or TEMPERED TUNING) effects a compromise in which neither tone is strictly accurate but both are sufficiently close to be acceptable to the ear. EQUAL TEMPERAMENT, the now universal tuning system for keyboard instruments, divides the octave into twelve equal parts (semitones).

scale/test: see test scale.

scale/tonal: see tonal scale.

scale value: 1. the number assigned an object (perceptual or conceptual) or an event in accordance with a working rule—i.e., according to a scale. **2.** the number assigned to one of the distinct divisions or reference points of a scale.

scaling: *n.* **1.** the construction of a scale (in any of its senses).—*Cp.* **standardizing. 2.** the employment of a scale in order to assign any object to its proper position; measuring.

scaling/ipsative: see ipsative scaling.

scaling/multidimensional: see multidimensional scaling.

scalogram = cumulative scale.

scalogram board: a mechanical device to facilitate selection of items for a scalogram.

scan: *v.* **1.** to run the eye quickly over something; to skim. **2.** to scrutinize closely for certain particulars. **3.** to traverse a given area with a light, a radar beam, or a motion picture camera, to illuminate or photograph what is there.

scapegoat: *n.* **1.** among the ancient Israelites, a pure white goat upon whom the priest ceremonially heaped all the sins of the people. The goat was then driven into the wilderness to die. **2.** figuratively, any person or group that becomes the object of displaced *aggression. ➤The scapegoat is blamed for frustrations and disappointments having other origin. Often there is deliberate effort to induce people to accept a scapegoat.—See **displacement**.—*n.* **scapegoating,** for the process.

SCAT (es·sē·ā·tē) = School and College Ability Tests.

scatological: *adj.* pertaining to dung or excrement; characterized by interest in excrement. ➤The word is occasionally used figuratively for **obscene**.

scatter: *n.* **1.** the extent to which items in a statistical series are closely grouped about the **mean** or are dispersed over a wide **range**.—*Syn.* **variability, dispersion** (*prefd.*). **2.** the extent to which the test items passed or failed by a testee come from widely different levels of difficulty: e.g., when the testee both passes and fails some of the tests assigned to Year VI of a **Binet scale,** and also both passes and fails some in Year XII. **3.** by analogy, the extent to which relative success and failure are divergently manifested in qualitatively different tests: e.g., doing excellently in verbal tests, poorly in numerical tests, etc.; the pattern of the subtest scores.—*Syn.* INTRAINDIVIDUAL VARIABILITY. **4.** discontinuity in thinking or in verbal expression. ➤*Cp.* the common expression *scatterbrained*.

scatter analysis: the attempt to find significant relationships or patterns among various **subtest** scores. Analysis may deal either with amount or qualitative pattern of the scatter.

scatter diagram: a chart or table that enables comparison of scores on one test or variable with scores on another. ➤It shows the scatter, or distribution of scores, on variable Y for all the individuals attaining a given score on variable X. The scores (or classes of scores) on X are represented by horizontal rows, the scores on Y by vertical columns. In the boxes or cells formed by the intersection of the rows and columns is entered a check mark for each individual receiving the corresponding X and Y scores. Thus, if a person scores 10 on one test, 20 on the other, a check is made in the cell formed by the intersection of row 10 with column 20.—*Syn.* BIVARIATE FREQUENCY TABLE, CORRELATION CHART, CORRELATION GRAPH, CORRELATION TABLE, DOUBLE-ENTRY TABLE, DOUBLE-FREQUENCY TABLE, **scattergram** (which see for another meaning), SCATTERPLOT, TWO-WAY TABLE. **Scatter diagram** or SCATTERPLOT are sometimes restricted to the working tables in which the entries are tallies, the other terms being used when the entry in each cell is the number representing the sums of tallies.

scattergram: *n.* **1.** a graph showing a given person's scores on the **subtests** of a test battery; a graphic presentation of an individual's **scatter (2** or **3)**. **2.** = scatter diagram.

scatterplot = scatter diagram.

scedasticity (ski″das·tis′ə·ti): *n.* the relative variability of the rows and columns of a double-entry table or **scatter diagram**. HOMOSCEDASTICITY is the property of the scatter diagram whose rows and columns have the same **standard *deviation** within the limits of chance variability. HETEROSCEDASTICITY is the property of a scatter diagram wherein the column and/or row standard deviation exceeds chance variability.—*adj.* **scedastic**.

scene/traumatic: an experience that a person wants to forget because remembrance of his part therein is too wounding to his self-esteem or too contrary to his value system.

schedule: *n.* **1.** a written or printed list; specif., a detailed written plan for future procedure, indicating when each operation is to be carried out; or an outline of regularly recurring events. **2.** a form or outline used to guide data gathering: it lists things to be noted or operations to be performed. **3.** a blank form, such as a questionary, with questions and space for answers. **4.** a memorized procedure to guide an interview or an experiment.

schedule/intermittent: see **reinforcement/intermittent.**

schedule of reinforcement or **of reward:** see **reinforcement schedule.**

schema (skē'mə): *n., pl.* **schemas, schemata** (-mə·tə): **1.** a number of ideas or concepts combined into a coherent plan or outline; a plan or model that displays the essential or important relations between concepts; a **model. 2.** a framework for the systematic recording of data; an outline showing the interrelationships of data, esp., one that subordinates detail. **3.** = **perceptual** or **cognitive schema. 4.** (*H. Head*) = RE-SPONSE SCHEMA, the hypothetical organismic state which determines that the next movement shall be part of the same action pattern as the preceding movements. ➤Whether, from a given bodily position, movement A or movement B follows, depends on the whole series of preceding movements. Having reached the letterspace after *and,* one's hand is in position to write almost any other word; but if the previous word was *ham,* the word *eggs* is likely to be written automatically. One step follows another, not merely because one knows by **feedback** that the body is in position for such a move, but because the whole series has established or activated a pattern or schema. The schema is more elaborate than a **set** or **determining tendency. 5.** a pre-representative drawing; a child's drawing manifesting no obvious sign of being representative of anything.—*adj.* **schematic** (which see).

schematic: *adj.* **1.** pertaining to a **scheme** or a **schema. 2.** pertaining to a **schematization;** diagrammatic; stripped of detail; expressed in outline only.

schematic eye = **reduced eye.**

schematization (skē"mə·ti·zā'shən): *n.* the reduction of a complex of data or of concepts, with suppression of details, to a simplified and comprehensible outline of essentials, esp. of formal relationships.—*v.* **schematize.**

scheme: *n.* a project; an orderly plan or outline of what is to be done; a program. ➤The term emphasizes action more than does **schema.** Used as a verb, **scheme** has acquired the connotation of underhanded planning.

schism (siz'əm): *n.* a division or separation; esp., a division into discordant groups or parts.—*adj.* **schismatic.**

schismogenesis (siz"mō·jen'ə·sis): *n.* the

processes of creating a schism; the processes whereby a cleavage in a social group is brought about and intensified.

schizo-: combining term meaning *division, cleavage, splitting.*

schizoid (skiz'oid): *adj.* **1.** pertaining to **schizophrenia.**—*Syn.* **schizophrenic** (*preferred*).—See **schizoid personality. 2.** resembling schizophrenia; of a persistent pattern of behavior, or of a personality, that is somewhat withdrawn from the outer world and directed inwards. ➤*Syn.* **schizothymic,** which, however, is restricted to behavior that, while qualitatively similar to schizophrenia, is definitely within normal limits. **Schizoid** leaves that question open: it frequently means behavior close to the border of abnormality, perhaps an antecedent or early form. Verbal descriptions of schizothymic or schizoid behavior show great variety, but they probably refer to the same underlying trends.

schizoid personality: (*Stan. Psychiat.*) an enduring and maladjustive pattern of behavior manifesting avoidance of close relations with others, inability to express hostility and aggressive feelings directly, **autistic** thinking. The person is seclusive, shut-in, and unsociable. ➤Under stress or prolonged unfavorable conditions, the individual may graduate into **schizophrenia;** but many remain indefinitely at the **psychoneurotic** level—queer, eccentric, relatively inefficient (esp. as social beings) but able to carry on.

schizophrene (skiz'ō·frēn): *n.* a sufferer from **schizophrenia;** a schizophrenic.

schizophrenia or **schizophrenic reaction** (skiz"ō·frē'ni·ə, -fren'ik): *n.* (*Stan. Psychiat.*) a group of psychotic reactions characterized by fundamental disturbances in reality relationships, by a conceptual world determined excessively by feeling **(autism),** and by marked affective, intellectual, and overt behavioral disturbances. In many cases there is progressive **deterioration.** Many varieties are distinguished clinically. —*Syn.* DEMENTIA PRAECOX (*obsoles.*).—*adj.* **schizophrenic.**—*pers. n.* **schizophrene, schizophrenic.**

schizophrenia/catatonic: a psychosis marked by conspicuous motor symptoms— either generalized inhibition **(stupor, mutism, negativism, catalepsy 2)** or excessive motor activity and excitement. The individual often regresses to a state in which only the **vegetative** activities are maintained.—*Syn.* CATATONIC DEMENTIA PRAECOX, **catatonia.**

schizophrenia/hebephrenic = **hebephrenia.**

schizophrenia/paranoid: a psychosis characterized chiefly by **autistic** and unrealistic thinking, hallucinations, and many often highly elaborate and systematized delusions, particularly of persecution and of grandeur. The whole personality is affected and there is apt to be deterioration; hence the delusions tend to be, and especially to become with the passage of time, less systematized. In these respects this psychosis differs from **paranoia.** There is likely to be a constant attitude of resentment, hostility, and aggression. Excessive religiosity is often present, as in other forms of schizophrenia.—*Syn.* PARANOID DEMENTIA (PRAECOX) (*obsoles.*) ; PARANOID FORM OF SCHIZOPHRENIC REACTION (*Stan. Psychiat.*).

schizophrenia/process: a chronic form of schizophrenia.—*Distg. fr.* **reactive *schizophrenia.**

schizophrenia/reactive: an acute attack showing most of the characteristic symptoms of schizophrenia from which, however, rapid recovery may be expected under favorable circumstances.

schizophrenia/schizo-affective: a psychosis in which both the ideational system and the feelings are affected. Delusional or bizarre thinking is combined with elation or depression.

schizophrenia/simple: a psychosis marked chiefly by a reduced relatedness to the external world and an impoverishment of human relationships. There is apathy and indifference, usually a slow **deterioration,** seldom delusions.—*Syn.* DEMENTIA (PRAECOX) SIMPLEX (*obsoles.*) ; SCHIZOPHRENIC REACTION, SIMPLE TYPE (*Stan. Psychiat.*).

schizophrenic reaction/simple type: see **schizophrenia/simple.**

schizothymia (-thī'mi·ə): *n.* a tendency to schizoid behavior within the limits of normality. It is not to be considered even potentially morbid.—See **schizoid.**—*adj.* **schizothymic.**

scholaptitude = scholastic aptitude (see **aptitude/academic**).

scholar: *n.* **1.** one who is enrolled in a regular course of instruction; a pupil or student. **2.** the recipient of a scholarship. **3.** a person who by long study has acquired high competence in some field of knowledge. ➤Possession of skill, however great it may be, does not make the scholar.

scholarship: *n.* **1.** mastery in some field of knowledge; knowledge of the facts, and understanding of their relationships, in a comprehensive **discipline** or subject of study. **2.** a stipend, recognized by public agency, for the support or partial support of a student. **3.** level of academic proficiency; the average marks or grades in schoolwork.

scholastic: *adj.* **1.** pertaining to the school. —*Syn.* **academic. 2.** (*usually cap.*) pertaining to the medieval philosophy based on Aristotle.—*n.* (for 2) **Scholasticism.**

scholastic aptitude: see **aptitude/academic.**—*Syn.* SCHOLAPTITUDE.

scholastic test: a test of ability in a school subject or subjects.—*Cp.* **achievement test.**

school: *n.* **1.** an institution specifically devoted to education and consisting, as a minimum, of a teacher and pupils or students, with or without buildings and equipment. **2.** (*often cap.*) the followers of a certain scholar who promulgate his doctrine; or any group of thinkers whose theories are in accord and who join forces to further their doctrines. ➤A **school** is known by the company it does *not* keep; it is set off by the rejection of certain doctrines more sharply than by its positive concepts and theories. The term generally carries the implication of enthusiasm if not of fanaticism.—See **psychology/divisions and schools of. 3.** a major division of a university, usually a division that prepares students for a particular profession: *a School of Social Administration.* ➤A school is usually less extensive than a college (in the American sense of these terms) and may be administered within a college.

School Ability Tests or **S-A-T** (es·ā·tē): tests for intermediate and secondary schools. —See **School and College Ability Tests.**

School and College Ability Tests or **SCAT** (es·sē·ā·tē): a series of test batteries, designed for use in schools and colleges, to assess the capacity of the pupil for successful study at the next-higher educational level. Each battery has four subtests: *sentence completion, vocabulary, computational skill, quantitative reasoning.*

school psychologist: a person with extensive professional training in psychology who utilizes psychological concepts and procedures in studying school problems and attempting to improve conditions. ➤Traditionally, much of his time has been spent in diagnosing scholastic and behavior problems of individual children, but this limitation is arbitrary. The school psychologist counsels concerning psychologically sound classroom atmosphere, problems of curriculum, and classroom assignment of pupils. He may also do psychotherapy with individual pupils who show behavior difficulties.

sciascope (sī'ə·skōp) = **skiascope.**

science: *n.* **1.** the study of natural phenomena by the methods of the physical and biological sciences; **natural science** (which see). ➤This usage, while common, arbitrarily excludes most investigations and systematizations of knowledge in the psychological and social disciplines. Such division is not warranted either by historical development or by the contemporary state of affairs, and it gives to **science** in English a narrower connotation than that of related expressions in other European languages. **2.** organized and systematic knowledge. ➤This usage, though occasionally useful, is as much too broad as the first is too narrow. **3.** a particular body of knowledge—e.g., physics, physiology, psychology—distinguished by the special set of operations employed in gathering **empirical** facts and by a distinctive set of **constructs** employed in interpreting the data. ➤E.g., although physiology and psychology deal with the same object—viz., the organism—they utilize different methods and constructs (with some overlapping) and thus develop distinct systems of knowledge.

scientific: *adj.* pertaining to, or having the character of, science. ➤Though, for most people, scientific is a term of approval, it does not mean *true, valid,* or *correct*; it denotes adherence to the temper and method of science.

scientific attitude: the attitude of searching for, and being guided by, facts rather than by what one wishes the facts to be; objectivity.

scientific management: 1. (*F. W. Taylor*) a system for improving worker efficiency through time-and-motion study and wage incentives. **2.** more broadly, the application of scientific procedures to the problems of worker efficiency.—*Syn.* EFFICIENCY ENGINEERING. ➤The term does not usually cover other aspects of management.

scientific method: the systematic statement of the general principles and precepts (found in all the sciences and in all sound investigation and thinking, whether or not specifically called scientific) that deal with the systematic, accurate observation of facts and their permissible interpretation; = SCIENTIFIC METHODOLOGY. **2.** in any particular investigation, a rule for procedure that yields factual data and knowledge about the functional relations of the data. —See **method.**

scientific psychology: any psychological system that rests on the search for facts or that utilizes scientific methods. ➤Scientific psychology is often contrasted with speculative psychology; but all science (not only psychology) necessarily includes speculation. Scientific and *philosophical* psychology (see **psychology 2**) can be properly contrasted; but the latter is so little discussed that this is seldom the contrast implied. Since virtually all present-day psychology is scientific in orientation, the term has little value.—See **psychology/divisions and schools of, I.**

sciosophy (sī·os′ə·fi): *n.* any elaborate system of beliefs dealing with what claims to be fact but not supported by contemporary science: e.g., astrology, phrenology. ➤Para-

psychology, as the objective-minded investigation of such phenomena as those of alleged telepathy, is not sciosophy; but **metapsychics** as a body of belief in the reality of these same phenomena is. Today's sciosophy may be tomorrow's science; but the chance of this in any particular case is small.

sclerosis (skli·rō′səs): *n.* hardening.—*adj.* **sclerotic** (-rot′ik).

sclerotic (coat): the tough white outer coating of the eyeball.

scoliosis (skō″li·ō′səs; skol″i-): *n.* abnormal lateral curvature of the spine.—*adj.* **scoliotic.**

scope: *n.* the extent, range, area, or limits of an action, an investigation, or a mental activity: the *scope* of a child's understanding.

-scope: combining form meaning *an instrument for seeing*: telescope, microscope.

-scopia, -scopy: combining forms meaning *looking at, examination, scrutiny.*

scopic (skop′ik): *adj.* of a procedure or instrument requiring that the quantitative values or scores be directly observed visually. ➤*Cp.* **graphic method,** a procedure in which they are recorded by the instrument.

scopophilia (skō″pō·fil′i·ə): *n.* sexual pleasure derived from peeping in order to observe disrobed human figures or sexual acts.—*Var.* **scopophilia, scotophilia** (neither *prefd.*).—*Syn.* VOYEURISM.

scorable: *adj.* characterizing a test or test item that can be scored, or scored reliably.

score: *n.* **1.** a number or credit assigned to a psychological datum, usually to a response but sometimes to a stimulus situation; esp., a credit assigned to a particular test response, indicating the position of the datum —its quality or its quantity—on a **dimension** or **scale.** ➤Adjacent scores, say scores 5 and 6, are not necessarily the same distance apart on the dimension or scale as other adjacent scores, say scores 7 and 8. **2.** the sum of the credits obtained by a testee on a given test or test battery.—*n.* **scoring,** the obtaining of a **score.**—*v.* **score,** to obtain or to assign a score.

➤**Value, measure, magnitude, score** are often used interchangeably. A **value is,** properly, a specific quantity of a variable, the amount existing at a given time and place. The same variable is conceived as manifesting several values, depending on circumstances (including those of how the value is measured or estimated). **Measure** is the number (or equivalent symbol) assigned something as the result of measuring. Unlike value, which assumes variation, measure may be the quantity of something that does not vary (though there may be errors of measurement). A measure always has a magnitude, but **measure** calls attention to the measuring process. **Magnitude,** on the other hand, calls attention not to the process but to the size discovered by the process. A **score** is a value or measure assigned for a particular phenomenon. Scores are specific and discontinuous even when they are believed to *represent* continuous variation. It is more natural to think of the score as being attained by the performer (though someone has to measure the performance).

For combination phrases, see either **score(s)** or **scoring.**

score/age: see **age score.**

score/composite: see **composite score.**

score/crude: 1. = raw *score. **2.** an approximation of the **true** *score.

score/derived: a score derived from another score or scores by a statistical manipulation of the original data or measures; a score that has been converted from a qualitative or quantitative mark on one scale into the units of another scale: e.g., the number of problems correctly solved in an arithmetic test (raw score) converted into A-B-C-D marks (derived score).—*Cp.* also **age score, standard** *score.—*Syn.* DERIVED MEASURE.

score/difficulty: a score that represents the highest level of difficulty attained by the testee on a given variable.

score/grade or *G* **score:** a **derived** *score that expresses ability or achievement in terms of the grade level for which that achievement is average: e.g., a grade score of 4-4 in spelling means spelling at the level usually attained in the 4th month of the 4th grade.

score/graphic: a score represented graphically: by a line, bar, diagrammatic figure, etc.

score/gross: see **gross score.**

score/interactive: (*R. B. Cattell*) a score that describes the subject's interaction with the environment, expressed in physical units. ➤Restriction to physical units of measurement is not suggested by the wording of the term, which could easily refer to measuring in other units (e.g., number of persons offended by a given TV program). PHYSICALISTIC INTERACTIVE SCORE is suggested as more accurate.

score/obtained or **/original** = **score/raw.**

score/operant: (*H. B. English*) a score describing the alteration in the physical or social environment effected by a subject's behavior. ➤Most **raw** *scores are operant; most derived scores are not.—*Cp.* **score/interactive.**

score/percentile: see **percentile score.**

score/rate: the number of test items completed in a specified time.—*Syn.* SPEED

SCORE.—See **test/rate** and **comprehension test.**

score/raw: the score as originally obtained from the test or measuring instrument; a value or magnitude of an observation that has not been submitted to any statistical treatment: e.g., the number of problems solved in an arithmetic test, the number of seconds needed to run 50 yards. A group of raw scores constitute the RAW or CRUDE DATA.—*Syn.* CRUDE SCORE, ORIGINAL SCORE, OBTAINED SCORE.—*Contr. w.* **score/derived.**

score/reduced: 1. a score from which a constant such as the mean has been subtracted. **2.** a score expressed in units based on a measure of **central tendency.**

score/sigma = **score/standard.**

score/speed = **score/rate.**

score/standard: 1. any **derived** *score using as its unit the **standard** *deviation (or some fraction thereof) of the **population** that is regarded as the criterion group. —See *T* scale, stanine. **2.** = *z* score or *z*, the difference between the **obtained** *score and the mean, divided by the standard deviation:

$$z = \frac{x - M_x}{\sigma_x}$$

—*Syn.* SIGMA SCORE, SIGMA VALUE, STANDARD MEASURE. ➤Standard scores, when based on normal distributions, are for most purposes comparable even though the raw scores are incomparable. Thus, by standard scores it is possible to show that a person can jump better than he can run (even though feet jumped is incommensurable with yards per second) or that he is more intelligent than he is emotionally stable.

score/standard gross: a **gross** or **raw** *score divided by the standard deviation of the distribution.—*Distg. fr.* **score/standard.**

scores/ungrouped: a tabulation of scores without grouping contiguous scores in classes; scores in which the unit of tabulation is the unit of measurement.

score/transmuted: a score derived from another score or set of scores and expressed in units of another scale: e.g., Fahrenheit temperatures converted into centigrade.

score/true: 1. the value or magnitude of an observation, or the score on a test, that is entirely free from error. **2.** the mean of an infinite number of observations of a given thing or event. ➤This mean is estimated to coincide with the mean of a sufficiently large number of observations so that it is a stable value. In practice, the mean of a large number of observations is regarded as the true score within the limits of its own standard error.—*Syn.* TRUE VALUE, TRUE MEASURE.—*Cp.* **mean/true.**

score/z = **score/standard (2).**

scoring/differential: scoring a test battery in more than one way to obtain measures along more than one dimension or variable. ➤E.g., in scoring an interest test, answers correlating with "music interest" are given positive credits for music; the same answers may receive zero or negative credits for salesmanship.—*Syn.* MULTIPLE SCORING.

scoring/multiple: see **scoring/differential.**

scoring/objective: scoring according to a code or rule so that all competent scorers arrive at the same score for a given response: e.g., in a verbal completion test, scoring as correct only those words that appear in a criterion list.—*Cp.* **test/objective.**

scoring/subjective: scoring that requires complex judgments by the scorer, as in grading essay examinations.—*Cp.* **test/subjective.**

scoterythrous (skō″tə·rith′rəs): *adj.* pertaining to color vision in which the red end of the spectrum loses **chroma** and may be darkened.—See **protanopia.**

scoto-: combining form meaning *dark, darkness.*

scotoma (skō·tō′mə) *n., pl.* **scotomata** (-mə·tə): a blind or partially blind area on the retina. ➤A POSITIVE SCOTOMA results in seeing a black spot; a NEGATIVE SCOTOMA is not ordinarily noticed. The **blind spot** normal to every eye is sometimes (inappropriately) called the PHYSIOLOGICAL SCOTOMA.—*adj.* **scotomatous.**

scotoma/scintillating: the appearance of bright flashes or sparks before the eyes, usually temporary.

scotomization (skō″tə·mə·zā′shən): *n.* the formation of a scotoma; metaphorically, the formation of "mental blind spots"—i.e., of areas wherein one cannot appreciate anything that conflicts with the **egoistic** pattern.

scotopic adaptation = **dark adaptation.**

scotopic vision (skō·top′ik) = **twilight vision.**—*Syn.* SCOTOPIA (-tō′pi·ə).—*Ant.* **photopic vision.**

screen: *n.* (*psychoan.*) whatever acts as a concealment: e.g., a person in a dream who symbolizes another, keeping the dreamer from realizing the real object of his dream feelings.

screening: *n.* 1. selecting persons or items for inclusion or exclusion. 2. preliminary selection; a rough choice that eliminates certain persons and includes others for more careful consideration later.—*v.* **screen.**

screen memory = **cover memory.**

screen/one-way: a device that permits persons on one side of a screen to see what is happening on the other side without themselves being seen.

script/mirror: see **mirror writing.**

scruple: *n.* a relatively minor ethical consideration or ground for hesitating to do something.—*adj.* **scrupulous,** sensitive to even minor ethical considerations.—*v.* **scruple.**

scrying: *n.* **crystal gazing.**

S curve: *n.* 1. a general term including all curves that are more or less S-shaped, such as the ogive and the **logistic curve.** 2. ≔ ogive.

SD, S.D., or *σ* = **standard *deviation.**

SE = **standard error.**

séance (sā′äns): *n.* (*parapsych.*) a group sitting, usually in darkness, for the purpose of obtaining **parapsychic** phenomena.

search model: a brief summary of the facts to be searched for, which will enable confirmation or rejection of a hypothesis.

Seashore tests: a series of phonographic records presenting the stimuli or tasks for the measurement of some relatively elemental auditory and musical abilities.

seat of mind or **of consciousness:** (*hist.*) a place in the brain believed to be the controlling point for conscious process. ➤A confused metaphysical concept.

sec. = second or seconds, the 60th part of a minute of time or the 60th part of a degree.

seclusion need: (*H. A. Murray*) the need to be alone or inconspicuous, to maintain privacy.

seclusiveness: *n.* the tendency to cut oneself off from human contacts.—*v.* **seclude.**

secondary: *adj.* 1. next below the first in class, rank, importance, or significance; hence, inferior. 2. dependent upon something else; derived from an original: *secondary* source (a source based on the original account), *secondary* reinforcement (**reinforcement** derived from the primary or original reinforcement). 3. auxiliary or supplemental; of that which is resorted to in the second place. 4. second in time sequence. —*Ant.* **primary.**

For most phrases with **secondary,** see the principal word.

secondary advantage or **gain:** see **advantage by illness.**

secondary automatic: *adj.* characterizing a thoroughly habitual response that runs off smoothly, without attention. ➤The contrast is with **reflex,** an innately automatic response.

secondary function: (*O. Gross*) hypothesized continuance of a brain activity for a brief time after its proper function has been fulfilled.

secondary inferiority feelings: those that develop when a newly fashioned style of life fails as a previous one did, giving rise to defeatism.

secondary position: (*vis.*) 1. the position

assumed by the eyes when they have rotated from the **primary position** about either the vertical or the horizontal axis, but not both. 2. loosely, any position of the eyes other than the primary position. ➤Those who hold to the stricter definition of (1) also speak of a TERTIARY POSITION, which is any position other than the primary or secondary.

secondary qualities: see **primary qualities.**

secondary sensation: the image that is concomitant with a sensory process in **synesthesia.**

secondary sex character: see **sex character/secondary.**

second moment: (*stat.*) 1. the sum of the products of the separate frequencies times the squares of their separate deviations from the point used as origin (usually the mean): $\Sigma(X - M)^2$. 2. that sum divided by the number of cases: $\dfrac{\Sigma(X - M)^2}{N}$.—*Syn.* (for 2) **variance.** The square root of this second moment is the **standard *deviation.**

second order: see **order (5).**

second-order factor: see **factor/second-order.**

secretion: *n.* 1. the production and discharge by an organ or tissue of a physiologically active substance; or the substance thus produced.—*Distg. fr.* EXCRETION, the collection and discharge of waste products.—*adj.* **secretory.**—*v.* **secrete.**

sect: *n.* an **in-group** or **we-group** of persons who adhere to special doctrines or practices, or follow a certain leader (or all three combined). Members have a sense of special worth because of belonging and because of following creed and practice; outsiders are kept at some **social distance.** ➤Etymologically, the word means *a group divided off.* Hence, sect refers to a special group within a larger whole: e.g., the Methodists within the larger Christian body. A scientist may admit he belongs to a **school,** never to a sect; the latter term is reserved for the schools to which others belong.—*adj.* and *pers. n.* **sectarian.**

section: *n.* (*anat.*) 1. a thin slice cut from a tissue or organ. 2. a surgical cutting through of a tissue—e.g., of a muscle or nerve.

sectioning: *n.* (*educ.*) division of the pupils of a single class or grade into smaller groups for separate instruction. ➤Ideally, sectioning is designed to bring pupils together for educative experiences in such a way as to maximize their development. There are great differences in theory and practice on how to accomplish this.—See **ability grouping.**

secular: *adj.* 1. pertaining to change that takes place over successive generations; hence, pertaining to that which takes place in finite time. ➤SECULAR CHANGES are slow, require years to accomplish, or occur only after intervals of years.—See **secular trend.** 2. pertaining to this world rather than to the hereafter; hence, not religious.—*n.*

secularization, elimination of religious significance or influence: e.g., substituting non-religious for religious control of schools, or eliminating religious instruction.

secular trend: the direction of change manifested by some variable over a long period. It may be graphically displayed as a straight line or a regular curve.

security: *n.* 1. a state in which satisfaction of needs and desires is guaranteed. ➤Sometimes it is implied that satisfaction comes without effort, more often that reasonable striving will obtain satisfaction. 2. a complex attitude of self-possession, self-confidence, and certitude that one belongs in valued social groups.—*Contr. w.* **insecurity.**

security/emotional: a state in which the person feels assured of satisfaction of his emotional needs, esp. of his need to be loved.

seduction: *n.* inducing another person, without force or threat, into unlawful sexual relations.

segmental behavior: 1. movements controlled *primarily* by a single region of the spinal cord. 2. behavior related to a single goal and inadequately related to broader purposes.

segregation: *n.* 1. (*psychol.*) the detachment of a group of psychological phenomena from adjacent phenomena and their formation into a coherent, distinct group. ➤The concept comes from **Gestalt** and the study of figure-ground relations, but is generalized to any psychological phenomena. 2. (*genet.*) in sexual reproduction, the breaking up of **gene pairs** so that only one gene from each pair appears in the **gamete** (i.e., sperm or ovum). ➤When two gametes combine to form a new organism, gene pairs are re-formed, one gene of each pair being derived from each parent. If one gene of a pair is **dominant,** the other **recessive,** the trait determined by the recessive gene will not appear in the organism. But the recessive gene may be transmitted and, if combined with another recessive, may reappear in subsequent generations. This is properly called REGRESSIVE TRANSMISSION or REGRESSION; but **segregation,** which is the mechanism, is sometimes used for the outcome. 3. (*sociol.*) the separation or setting apart of one or more categories of a population, either geographically (as in ghettos, separate districts for residence) or by provision of separate facilities (schools, theaters, playgrounds, churches, railroads, restaurants).

Segregation may rest on law, on consciously maintained custom, or on unconscious selective action of prejudices. ➤*Distg.* *fr.* **prejudice** and *fr.* **discrimination (3).** A labor union that does not practise segregation (members work and meet together) may show discrimination by in fact excluding members of an ethnic group from holding office, and workers may show prejudice by reacting to fellow workers according to ethnic group membership.—*Syn.* **isolation,** an extreme form of segregation.—*Ant.* **social *integration.**

seizure: *n.* **1.** a sudden attack of any disorder. **2.** a **convulsion** or **fit.**—*v.* **seize.**

seizure/audiogenic: see **audiogenic.**

selected group: 1. a social group with standards of eligibility for membership.— *Ant.* OPEN GROUP. **2.** a grouping for scientific research of persons, objects, or events that resemble each other in certain specified respects more than they resemble a **random sample** drawn from the population. **3.** a smaller group drawn from a population in such fashion that it reproduces certain specified characteristics of the total: e.g., a group selected to have the same distribution in respect to age, sex, education, and earned income as the total population. Such a group may be more representative than a **random sample** with the same *N.* Meanings **(2)** and **(3)** are thus nearly opposite.—*Syn.* (for **2** and **3**) SELECTED SAMPLE.—*Ant.* **random sample.**

selection: *n.* **1.** (*stat.*, *exper.*) the choice of an item for inclusion in some group, class, or category; or the emergence of certain items, following the application of a working principle, as belonging to a distinct group. ➤*Distg. fr.* **classification,** which properly deals with the assignment of a whole set of items to their appropriate places in a classificatory system; selection may deal with only a single item or a single category. **2.** (*genet.*) the process by which certain **genes** or gene combinations change in frequency from generation to generation because of reproductive advantages. POSITIVE SELECTION leads to increased frequency of the gene, NEGATIVE SELECTION to decreased frequency.—*Syn.* NATURAL SELECTION, usually reserved for Darwin's particular account of selection or for some variant of Darwin's theory.

selection/artificial: the process whereby plants or animals possessing especially desirable traits are intentionally chosen either for homogeneous breeding or hybridizing.

selection index or ***D*:** (*H. J. Eysenck*) a formula for determining the discriminatory usefulness of a test: $D = \dfrac{P}{P + P_m + P_f}$ when P = proportion of persons actually belonging in a category and whose score so indicates, P_m = proportion of persons belonging in a category and whose score does not so place them, and P_f = proportion of persons not belonging in the category whose score places them there.—*Cp.* **false negative.**

selection method: 1. = **recognition method. 2.** a method in which the subject selects from a collection of stimuli that one which he judges equal to a standard stimulus.

selection/natural: see **natural selection.**

selection/proportional: taking from each of the divisions into which a total is divided a number of instances equal to the proportion of that division to the total. The result is a **stratified *sampling.**

selection/random = **random sample** (much *prefd.*, since the meanings of **selection** and of **random** are contrary).

selection ratio: the ratio of the number chosen by a certain criterion to the number available for choice.

selection/social: see **social selection.**

selection test = **selective answer *test.**

selection/vocational: choice from among applicants of those most likely to succeed in a given job. ➤One speaks of VOCATIONAL CHOICE (by the prospective employee), **vocational counseling** (by a presumably disinterested professional person), and **vocational selection** (on behalf of the employer).

selective answer test: see **test/selective answer.**

selective inattention: see **inattention/ selective.**

selective information: see **information theory.**

selective learning: see **learning/selective.**

selective response = **response/differential.**

selective silence: a brief period—in an association reaction experiment, in a counseling session, or in conversation—during which a person withholds response. ➤It is regarded as possibly indicating that an anxiety-provoking factor has been broached.

selectivity: *n.* the perceptual response to aspects of stimuli together with the ignoring of others.—*Cp.* **attention, abstraction, selective *inattention.**

self: *n.* ➤Extensive employment in everyday speech greatly affects technical usage of **self.** Thus, while *self* as a reflexive pronoun has no obvious connection with the psychological definitions, it makes more readily acceptable the concept of **self** as an object. The nearly 1000 combination forms (e.g., *self-interest, self-adjustment, self-control, self-contradiction*) and certain literary usages (such as *selfsame material, better self, to thine own self be true*) are all subtle influences pervading the explicitly stated meanings.

In technical discussion two distinct concepts appear and reappear (and are too often confounded): (A) the self as the subject, the agent, the individual person, the living being; or as a specific part or aspect of that being; and (B) the self as the individual that is somehow revealed or known to himself. These two concepts seem distinct enough, but those who stress the second concept usually attribute to the self certain dynamic characteristics which at least seem to borrow from the first concept.

1. (*W. James*) all that a person is tempted to call by the name *me* or *mine*. **2.** the living being. ➤Except where contrast between the self and other beings is being made, **person** is preferred for this meaning. (See **person** for reasons.) A variant takes **self** to be the BODILY SELF, one's own body (*cp*. self-mutilation).—*Syn*. **ego, individual, organism, person, proprium, subject. 3.** that aspect or part of the person or organism which carries out psychic, mental, or psychological acts; the agent for **behavior** (as distinguished from physiological activities). ➤The **self psychology** of M. Calkins is based on this meaning. This is also C. Jung's usage. The definition implies a greater separateness of the data of psychology and physiology than is acceptable to most psychologists; but if it is deemed necessary to refer to a separate agent for psychological phenomena, **self** seems an appropriate term. **4.** the complex organization of characteristics making up the individual.—*Syn*. **personality** (*prefd.* for this meaning). ➤With this usage, the influence of concept (B) begins to be felt. The personality is indeed the actor or agent but it is also that which is known by oneself or by others. **5.** the individual subject revealed to his own observation as the identical and persistent center of psychological processes. ➤Here concepts (A) and (B) are thoroughly combined. **6.** the ideas, feelings, and strivings that are recognized, interpreted, and valued by the individual as his own. ➤This seems to be essentially the **self percept** or **self concept** of V. Raimy and many clinicians. In actual use, this self is assigned many of the attributes of the self as subject-agent. **7.** (*H. B. English*) a **sentiment** composed not only of a special object of experience, the **psychological *me** (which see), but of the feelings and strivings organized about that object; an organization of personal activity oriented with reference to a complex object called *the me*. ➤This definition refers to many of the data generally included under **(6)** or **self percept** or **self concept,** but gives fuller recognition to the role of noncog-

nitive elements. The self concept includes *knowledge about* one's feelings; the self of this usage refers also to the actual feeling-striving that is instigated by what is known, but is not necessarily itself known. The sentiment of **self-regard** (*W. McDougall*) probably denotes many of the same facts. It is believed to be the central meaning of self in much untechnical discussion and in many of the combination terms.—*Syn.* **proprium.**—*adj.* **self, propriate.**

self-abasement: *n.* extreme submission or yielding to another, together with strong feelings of inferiority.—*Cp.* **self-feeling,** positive and /negative and subjection.

self-absorption: *n.* extreme, but not necessarily pathological, withdrawal of attention from what is going on about one. ➤It does not usually refer to absorption with self so much as with problems and ideas.—*Distg. fr.* **introspection, introversion.**

self-abuse: *n.* (*pop.*) a euphemism for masturbation. ➤The expression reveals complete misunderstanding both of **self** and of **masturbation.**

self-acceptance: *n.* an attitude toward one's own self and one's personal qualities that finds them of unique worth. There is an objective and unemotional recognition of one's abilities and limitations, one's virtues and faults, without undue sense of pride, guilt, or self-blame. It does not imply passivity; rather, self-acceptance generally leads to constructive efforts. It is believed by many to be essential to healthy personality.

self-accusation: *n.* blaming oneself, usually falsely or to unwarranted degree.—*Syn.* **intropunitiveness.**

self-activity: *n.* **1.** a behavior regarded by the person as initiated primarily by or within himself (though objective stimuli may provide a releasing cue). **2.** behavior directed at changing one's own behavior patterns.

self/actual: (*K. Horney*) the total psychophysical being at a given moment, including both conscious and unconscious mechanisms.—*Cp.* **self/idealized** and **self/real.**

self-actualization: *n.* **1.** (*A. Maslow*) the processes of developing one's capacities and talents, of understanding and accepting oneself, of harmonizing or integrating one's motives; or the state resulting from these processes. ➤The term represents a variety of data better understood when taken globally than when analyzed; it points to problems for the psychologist to study rather than to a problem solved.—*Approx. syns.* SELF-DEVELOPMENT (emphasizing the temporal evolution of inner unity), **self-realization, autonomy, individuation, productiveness.** POSITIVE PSYCHOLOGICAL

HEALTH. **2.** (*K. Horney*) the delusory acceptance of the **idealized** *image as actual. ➤The term is confusing. It does not mean that one actually becomes what one envisages as ideal, but rather that one believes in the actuality of one's idealized image.

self-administering test: see **test/self-administering.**

self-alienation: *n.* **1.** a state in which the person feels that his self is unreal. **2.** (*K. Horney*) a shift in a person's energies and consciousness away from his **real** *self, with resultant loss of awareness of **intrapsychic** processes.

self-analysis: *n.* an attempt to understand one's own behavior—one's abilities and disabilities, and one's motivations. ➤The term is not, as a rule, technically used for the attempt to psychoanalyze oneself, partly because psychoanalysts generally disapprove of the practice despite the fact that Freud himself proved it possible.

self-appraisal: see **self concept, self-assessment.**

self-assertion: *n.* the tendency, in social situations, to press for the achievement of one's own goals, even at the expense of others. ➤*Distg. fr.* **leadership,** which may concern itself with the clarification and achievement of goals of the group or of the followers.—*Cp.* **ascendance.**

self-assessment: *n.* an evaluation or appraisal of one's personal qualities or traits. ➤*Distg.* the SELF-ASSESSMENT QUESTIONARY *fr.* one that calls for a descriptive report of actual behavior without evaluation (e.g., a **behavior check list**).

self-attitude: *n.* an evaluation (generally only implicit) of one's own self or **personality;** an attitude of acceptance-approval or of rejection-disapproval of what one is, in general or in some particular respect, usually one regarded as central.

self-awareness: *n.* knowledge of one's own traits or qualities; insight into, and understanding of, one's own behavior and motives.

self-comprehension = **self-awareness.**

self concept: 1. a person's view of himself; the fullest description of himself of which a person is capable at any given time. ➤Emphasis is upon the person as object of his own self-knowledge, but his feeling about what he conceives himself to be is usually included.—*Distg. fr.* SELF-APPRAISAL, which emphasizes an explicit valuing of one's good and bad points.—See **self** (6) and **me/psychological. 2.** = **self-attitude.**

self-consciousness: *n.* **1.** (*pop.*) an emotional condition of heightened attention to the impression one is making on others and, hence, to such parts of one's own behavior as are thought to be the basis for that impression. **2.** awareness of the **self. 3.** awareness of one's own existence as an identical person.—*adj.* **self-conscious** (also applied to the special case where one is explicitly aware of what he is doing and why).

self-consistency: *n.* **1.** behavior that manifests relatively high conformity with the central pattern of behavior and motivation of the personality; behavior that is determined, not primarily by the situation, but rather by long-term goals. **2.** (*P. Lecky*) the theory that the growth of personality consists in the development of a self-picture and the progressively greater harmonizing of behavior therewith. **3.** (*logic*) the quality in any communication (a theory, argument, description) or line of thinking of being composed of parts that are compatible with each other.

self-control: *n.* the ability to inhibit either impulsive or goal-seeking behavior for the sake of a more inclusive goal.

self-correlation: *n.* correlation between two administrations of the same test, or between a test and a **comparable** *form regarded as equivalent, or between random halves of the test.—See **reliability coefficient.**

self-criticism: *n.* **1.** the recognition that certain of one's behaviors do not conform to the standards one has adopted. **2.** ability to recognize realistically the strengths and weaknesses of one's character or behavior. ➤In certain maladjustments, lack of this ability is an outstanding symptom.

self-deception: *n.* failure to recognize the true state of affairs in something that closely concerns oneself. The deception is always at least partially unwitting.—*Cp.* **rationalization.**

self-demand schedule: a flexible arrangement whereby the infant is fed when he gives signs that he is hungry. ➤The normal infant usually settles gradually upon a fairly regular schedule of his own. The term may logically be extended to other **appetites** or acquired **drives.**—*Syn.* DEMAND FEEDING.

self-denial: *n.* deliberate forgoing of satisfactions. ➤Self-denial for the sake of the effect on one's character is **asceticism.**

self-determination: *n.* the regulation of behavior, not primarily by immediate circumstances nor by direct pressure of **social** *norms, but by personal initiative and for the sake of individual goals. ➤This does not commit one to the doctrine of freedom of the will.—*Cp.* **cultural determinism.**

self-development: see **self-actualization** and **productiveness.**

self-direction: *n.* judging for oneself what needs to be done, making plans for doing it, and executing the plans.

self-discipline: *n.* regulation of one's own conduct; control of impulse by motives related to the ideal that the individual has adopted for himself; or control of present behavior for the sake of more inclusive satisfactions.—*Syn.* **self-control.**

self-display: *n.* the tendency to exhibit one's excellences of any sort, esp., to do so conspicuously or even inappropriately. ➤*Distg. fr.* **exhibitionism,** which tends to be restricted to socially inappropriate display of sex organs.

self-distribution: *n.* a nonvoluntary shift in the dynamic relations of a **phenomenal** ***field*** that results in a higher degree of organization. ➤Thus, if one listens to a perfectly even metronome, the beats come to have a rhythm that is not intentionally imposed by the listener.

self-divided: a personality subject to strong inner conflict.—*Cp.* **personality/ multiple.**

self-dynamisms: *n. pl.* (*H. S. Sullivan*) the pattern of the enduring motivations that form the **self-system:** the more inclusive motives toward biological satisfactions and the motives that lead to security in social relations.

self-effacement: *n.* (*K. Horney*) a major **neurotic ***solution*** of inner conflicts that is characterized by identification with the despised self and subsequent unconscious idealization of dependency, compliancy, and love.

self-evaluation: *n.* making a judgment about oneself or about some characteristic of oneself.—*Syn.* **self-rating.**

self-evident: *adj.* (*logic*) of a proposition which no one can doubt, which immediately elicits acceptance from anyone who understands it.—*Syn.* **axiomatic** (which is stronger).

self-expression: *n.* **1.** acts that reveal and help to develop the individual's personality. **2.** activity enjoyed for the direct satisfaction it yields.

self-extinction: *n.* (*K. Horney*) a form of neurotic behavior in which the person has no sense of his own personality as a self-experiencing, self-directive entity. He endeavors to live through the lives of others, seeing himself only as a reflection of others.

self-feeling/positive and **/negative:** (*W. McDougall*) the contrasted simple feelings that together are the nucleus of the sentiment of **self-regard.** ➤Positive self-feeling is the central feeling resulting from triumphant achievement or praise; negative self-feeling is central when one feels that he has fallen short or is criticized. But McDougall distinguishes positive self-feeling from self-love or egoism, negative self-feeling from inferiority feeling.

self-fulfilling prophecy: the principle that an expectation, belief, or prediction by a participant in any event is a factor working toward fulfillment of the prediction.

self/glorified = **self/idealized.**

self-gratification: *n.* the satisfaction of one's own nonutilitarian needs, esp. of those needs associated with enhancement of self: the need to belong, to be praised, to feel oneself successful, etc.

self-gratification mores: (*G. Murphy*) those **mores** that prescribe the ways for obtaining nonutilitarian satisfactions: e.g., the gleaming silver of the table, the measured cadence of a dance.—*Contr. w.* **self-maintenance mores.**

selfhood: *n.* that by which one is oneself; the integration of motives. ➤The term is fluid enough to take on more specific meanings according to context.

self-ideal: see **ideal (3).**

self-idealized: (*K. Horney*) the perfected and glorified self which the neurotic believes himself to be after he unconsciously identifies with his previously imagined **idealized ***image.*** ➤According to Horney, neurotic pride leads to an almost impossible idealization of what one ought to be. Since the reality falls too far short of this ideal, solution of the conflict is sought in the belief that one *is* what his pride-regulated ideal says he *should be.* SELF-IDEALIZATION is the process by which this idealized self is developed and maintained.—*Distg. fr.* self-ideal (see **ideal 3**).

self-identification: *n.* **1.** a giving of self to another; a kind of yielding of self to the purposes of another: **identification (9 and 10). 2.** loving another who is like oneself; admiration and love of one's own qualities when manifested by another. ➤No confusion of the other with oneself is implied; one's own qualities merely seem admirable even in someone else.

self-image: the self one *thinks* oneself to be. ➤This is not a directly observed self-object but a complex concept: of one's personality, character, status, body and bodily appearance, etc. It may differ greatly from objective fact.—*Distg. fr.* **self/perceived** (which see).

self-inventory: *n.* a list whereon a subject checks the traits he believes himself to have.

selfish: *adj.* seeking one's own benefit without regard to others. ➤The word has completely lost its general meaning of *pertaining to the self.*—*n.* **selfishness.**

self/looking-glass: that part or quality of a person's **self-image** which is formed on the basis of perceiving how others react toward him. ➤The behaviors of others are intuitively interpreted as reflecting what kind of self others consider him to be. **Social ***self*** is sometimes used as a synonym but is better reserved for the behavior arising from one's social relations.—*Syn.* MIRROR SELF.

self-love: *n.* an individual's love or affection directed at or upon himself or upon whatever seems a central part of his **self.** ➤It may be love of one's own body **(narcissism)** or of one's personality. Egocentrism, egoism, and egotism are all related to self-love but are not quite the same. See **ego (3).**

self-maintenance mores: (*G. Murphy*) **mores** that prescribe the ways to be followed in those activities which sustain and preserve the life of the individual and the group.—*Contr. w.* **self-gratification mores.**

self-marking test: see **test/self-marking.**

self-maximation: *n.* becoming the kind of person one wants to become. ➤The varied descriptions of what this term means reflect cultural and personal ideals.

self-observation: *n.* **1.** = introspection. **2.** literally, observing one's own self. **3.** observing one's own behavior.

self-other system: the perceived relationship of self to other persons.

self/perceived: a particular totality of experiences, unique for each individual, having a peculiar quality of intimacy and a strong quality of belonging together, as a result of which the totality is segregated from other experiences of the individual. ➤At a later stage this segregated whole is named "me" or "mine," but it is probable that the segregation begins before the verbalization. The experiences involved are segregated because they are different—because they have different consequences for the organism—just as the several experiences connected with a book or a violin are segregated. Included in the perceived self are bodily feelings and sensations, the perception or imagination of one's bodily appearance or manners, and certain of one's attitudes, beliefs, and ideas. As a matter of direct unreflective experience, these differ from other experiences that have a more external reference and are not so intimately "mine."—*Distg.* the **perceived self** *fr.* the **self-image** (the self one thinks oneself to be).

self percept = **self/perceived.**

self/phenomenal: 1. the self directly experienced as one pole or focus in the person-environment interaction. ➤Self is held to be implied and revealed in every psychological event. **2.** the self directly known in self-perception; the image, notion, concept, or percept of oneself; = **self/perceived.** ➤While the perceived self of (**2**) probably grows out of the self of (**1**), the two meanings are distinct. But in both, self is a matter of direct awareness, not of inference. It may include one's perception of his roles, status, or aspirations.

self-preservation: *n.* collective noun for the behaviors that conduce to the continuance of an organism as a living system. ➤The term SELF-PRESERVATIVE INSTINCT overemphasizes the innateness of the activities that maintain life; and it falsely implies a unity when in fact there is a diversity of such activities having nothing in common except that, under certain circumstances, they do maintain life.

self psychology: the view that psychology must be defined by reference to the **self** or **person,** and that mental activity or behavior can only be understood in terms of the varying attitudes or changes in the self. ➤It accepts the occasional legitimacy of studying an act in abstraction from the fact that it is *someone's* act, the act of a self or person; but it insists that this act cannot be fully understood until the abstracted fact is brought back into the context. **Personalism,** as a synonym, is a somewhat broader term.—See **psychology/divisions and schools of, III.**

self-rating: *n.* a systematic plan for enumerating one's own performances or traits and appraising their strength.

self/real: (*K. Horney*) the source of the energy that, in each individual, can be mobilized in the direction of constructive, healthy growth. ➤While all persons have such a growth potential, it varies individually in attributes and strength.—*Cp.* **self/actual** and **self/idealized.**

self-realization: *n.* balanced and harmonious development of all aspects of a personality; fulfillment of generic and personal potentialities.

self-recitation: *n.* the method of spending some fraction of the study time in attempted recall with the material hidden.

self-regard: *n.* (*W. McDougall*) the sentiment that seeks the enchancement of the **self.** ➤See **sentiment.** Self-regard is described as a highly complex structure; its central component is the feeling of satisfaction when the situation (physical or social) is favorable to the individual (**positive *self feeling**), of dissatisfaction (**negative *self feeling**) when it is not. —*Syn.* SELF-REGARDING SENTIMENT, **self-sentiment.**

self-report: *n.* information furnished about oneself. ➤The report may be a simple statement of elementary personal facts (age, marital status, occupation, etc.), an elaborate personality rating, a questionary, an autobiography.

self-report inventory: a device used in personality measurement in which the subject marks a list to indicate whether certain kinds of behavior describe him or not, how he would react to certain imaginary situations, and the like.—*Distg. fr.* **self-inven-**

tory, which is usually a list of traits, not of behaviors.

self-salience: *n.* the distinctiveness of self in relation to the not-self, whether of physical or social environment; the degree to which the self stands out sharply from its surrounds.

self-sentiment: *n.* (*W. McDougall*) the complex sentiment having the **self** as object.—See **sentiment** and **self-regard.**—*Syn.* SELF-REGARDING SENTIMENT.

self/social: 1. that aspect of the individual which is perceived by others in social intercourse. 2. those characteristics of a person which are especially important in determining social interaction. 3. that part of one's personality which is determined by social influences. 4. the picture of himself that depends on how a person believes others see him. ➤The term is fluid and may carry any meaning consistent with its two components.

self-system: *n.* (*H. S. Sullivan*) the final (or near final) choice of potentialities that the individual seeks to develop and to integrate; an **ideal** of self. ➤Not all the incorporated tendencies are consciously recognized and most of the rejected alternatives are **repressed** rather than consciously **suppressed**. The self-system is the result of interpersonal experience.

sella turcica (sel'ə tĕr'si·kə): the bony depression, located at the base of the brain, that contains the **pituitary gland.**

semantic approach: a method of teaching correct usage of words by emphasizing meanings rather than formal grammar.

semantic count: tabulation of the frequency with which a particular and distinctive meaning of a specific word occurs in written or printed communication. ➤Separate tabulation would be made for *game* as a form of play, for *game* as an animal hunted, and for *game* as an adjective meaning *lame.*—See **word count.**

semantic image: any image that points to or is indicative of a meaning. ➤It contrasts with the concrete image which just represents the concrete object. Given a picture of an apple, one may have a tactual image of the texture with no reference to a meaning. Most semantic images are verbal: e.g., the verbal image "food" when seeing the apple. But nonverbal images can also be carriers of meaning: e.g., the image of a red light signifying "danger."

semantics: *n.* (usually construed as *sing.*) 1. the science of **meanings** of words or other signs; the rules that describe the way signs relate to objects (interpreting *object* in a very broad sense). 2. = GENERAL SEMANTICS, the study of human responses to signs and symbols. ➤While GENERAL SEMANTICS referred originally to the par-

ticular school led by Korzybski, the term has broadened to cover what might be called applied semantics, the consideration of right and wrong ways of reacting to symbols. See **semantic therapy,** a special branch. —*adj.* **semantic,** pertaining to meaning, to the process of communicating meaning, or to reacting to meaning. (The *adj.* is thus somewhat broader than the *n.*)

semantic therapy: the effort to improve personal adjustment by correcting the faulty interpretation of emotionally charged words: e.g., a reinterpretation of what is meant by *femininity* on the part of a young woman who thinks herself "unfeminine."

semantic unit: a language unit having a distinct function as a carrier of meaning.—*Cp.* **phoneme, morpheme, word, utterance.**

semantogenic disorder: maladjustment resulting from persistent faulty understanding of the meaning of emotionally charged words.—*Cp.* **semantic therapy.**

semasiology (si·mā″si·ol'ə·ji): *n.* the study of the development and changes in meanings of words; historical **semantics.**

semeiology (sē″mī·ol'ə·ji): *n.* 1. the science of **signs,** or of the language of signs. ➤Included by some under this term is the study of the language of science. 2. (*med.*) the systematic study of the signs of specific diseases; symptomology.—*Syn.* SEMEIOTICS (-ot'iks).

semen: *n.* the male germ cells; or the fluid containing the cells.—*adj.* **seminal,** often applied figuratively to a small idea destined to grow big.

semicircular canals: see **canals/semicircular.**

semi-interquartile range or *Q* = quartile deviation.

semilogarithmic graph: a chart with one axis scaled arithmetically and the other logarithmically.—See **scale/logarithmic.**

semiology = semeiology.

semiopathic: *adj.* (*T. Burrow*) disordered or pathological use of symbols.—*Cp.* **semantic therapy.**

semiotics = semeiology.

semitone: *n.* the smallest interval normally used in music of the Western world; half of a **whole tone;** the distance between adjacent keys on a keyboard instrument: e.g., B—C, C—C sharp.—*Syn.* HALF STEP, HALF TONE.

senescence: *n.* becoming old; or the period in which one becomes old. ➤The word **senility** having acquired disparaging connotations, **senescence** tends to replace it for the period when one *is* old.—*adj.* **senescent.**

senile (sē'nīl; -nil): *adj.* pertaining to old age; manifesting the behavior characteristic of old age.

senile psychosis: a chronic disorder in the aged, with impairment of brain tissue, marked by **dementia** (sometimes extreme), loss of memory, stubbornness, and irritability (often extreme).—*Syn.* GERIOPSYCHOSIS; (*Stan. Psychiat.*) CHRONIC BRAIN SYNDROME WITH SENILE BRAIN DISEASE.

senilism (sē′nĭl·iz·əm; -nil-): *n.* manifestation of signs of senility, somatic or behavioral, either in old age or prematurely.

senility (sə·nil′ə·ti): *n.* 1. old age. 2. loss of mental, or mental and physical, functions in old age.—*adj.* **senile.**

senium (sē′ni·um): *n.* old age.

sensa: *pl.* of **sensum.**

sensation: *n.* 1. the elementary unanalyzable and uninterpreted item or unit of that which one apprehends when certain **receptors** are excited. ➤Colors, sounds, odors, tastes, warmth, coolth, and pressures are familiar and relatively unquestioned examples of such items.—*Syn.* **sense datum,** SENSUM, SENTIENDUM, **sense impression.** 2. = **sensing;** the process or activity of apprehending colors, sounds, tastes, etc. 3. the topic in psychology, dealing with (1) and/or (2).

➤Nowhere has the intrusion of philosophic viewpoints worked more havoc with psychological terminology than here; it is virtually impossible to state a meaning for **sensation** that will be acceptable and not subject to confusion. Traditionally, **sensation** (1) has been interpreted as a kind of "mental stuff," a correlate of the excitation of parts of the nervous system. As defined above it is held to be part of the *object of awareness.* Redness is simply what a person sees when his eye is affected by vibrations of a given frequency. This statement leaves many questions unanswered; but they are philosophical, not psychological. ¶But further, (1) and (2) are frequently confused, a confusion increased by the fact that in **structural psychology** sensation as a form of **conscious *content** is called a *process,* while sensation as the activity of (2) above is—at least theoretically—not considered. ¶It is proposed that, as far as linguistic propriety and old habits will permit, sensation be used exclusively for (3); sense datum, sentiendum, sensum, or sense impression for (1); sensing for (2). However, in reporting the view of others, and in combinations, the word *sensation* must sometimes be retained.—*Cp.* **perception.**

sensation(al)ism: *n.* 1. the doctrine that all experience *consists* of sensations (or sense data) and their copies (**images**) and combinations. 2. the doctrine that all knowledge is *derived* from sensations.—See **psychology/divisions and schools of, VII.**—*adj.* **sensationist.**

sensation difference: any difference between sense data that can be demonstrated or thought about.—*Distg. fr.* **sensed difference.**

sensation increment: (*psychophys.*) an increase in intensity of a **sense datum.**

sensation level/auditory: for a sound, the intensity level in **decibels** above a given reference level, usually above the **threshold.**

sensation/negative: see **negative sensation.**

sensation type: (*C. Jung*) a person whose behavior is dominated by sensation.—See **function types.**

sensation unit: 1. any one of the total of discriminable bits of experience of sensory origin that may exist in any sense **modality;** a sense distance equal to a **just-noticeable-difference** interval. 2. = SU or AUDITORY SENSATION UNIT, a logarithmic unit of loudness corresponding to the energy unit, the **decibel.** ➤When the decibel is one j.n.d. of loudness (as it is under certain conditions), the auditory sensation unit is a special case of **sensation unit (1).**

sense: *n.* 1. a classification of sense data resembling each other more than they resemble other sense data; = sense **modality:** all sounds belong to the auditory *sense.* 2. a classification of sense data according to the kind of **receptor** that mediates them: the muscle *sense,* the joint *sense.* ➤The classificatory categories of (1) and (2) do not always correspond. The receptor for pressure in the muscles differs anatomically from that in the skin, but the pressures seem qualitatively the same. Achromatic colors are qualitatively the same whether mediated by rods or by cones. 3. (in the *pl.*) all the sense data or all the distinct receptor mechanisms; hence, the capacity for receiving impressions from the external world and impressions of the bodily state; the sphere of sensation as contrasted with feeling, thinking, or conation. 4. a **receptor** or **sensor.** ➤Either of these is better for this meaning. 5. a special kind of awareness: *sense* of time, *sense* of humor. 6. = **sensibility.** 7. meaning or significance: it makes *sense.* 8. good judgment. 9. an aggregate opinion or decision of a group; a **consensus:** the *sense* of the meeting. 10. (with prep. *in* or *out of*) sane and normal: in one's *senses.*—*adj.* **sense** or **sensory,** often used interchangeably, esp. in compounds.

sense: *v.* 1. to apprehend by means of sensory receptors. 2. to have an activity in a sense organ and its neural connections. 3. to feel; to form an intuitive judgment; to apprehend what is not specifically communicated: to *sense* the child's shyness.—*n.* **sensing.**

sense datum, *pl.* **data:** 1. the elementary

unanalyzable, and uninterpreted unit of that which is experienced when a sense **receptor** is stimulated.—*Syn.* **sensation (1)**, SENSUM, **sense impression**, SENTIENDUM. —See **sensation. 2.** a particular instance of **(1).** ➤It is believed that this term has fewer philosophical or nonempirical associations than any synonym except SENSUM. Although it lacks an adjective form, it can usually borrow **sensory.**

sensed difference: immediately experienced difference in the simultaneous or successive presentation of two stimuli. ➤*Distg. fr.* **sensation difference** or **sense distance,** which is a difference in two sense data that can be demonstrated or thought about but need not be immediately given or experienced directly. The red seen yesterday differs from the green seen today (sensation difference) but is not a sensed difference.

sense discrimination: the process by which one is aware of difference between two sense data, or of change in a **sense datum.** —*Cp.* **sensory discrimination.**

sense distance: the interval, along any dimension of sensation, that separates two **sense data.** It may express quality, intensity, duration, extensity, time order, or place as directly apprehended.—*Syn.* SENSIBLE DISTANCE or INTERVAL.

sense experience: awareness derived from sensory stimulation; one or more **sense data.** ➤Sense experience is not necessarily a single bit of experience, nor unanalyzable. The term merely emphasizes the sensory origin of the awareness.

sense/external: see **external sense.**

sense feeling: the blend of pleasure or unpleasure with **proprioceptive *sense data:* e.g., hunger, headache, a feeling of joyful excitement.

sense illusion: misapprehension of an object that is due directly to the sensory mechanism or to relations inherent in the objective situation.—*Syn.* perceptual **illusion** (*prefd.*).

sense impression: 1. = **sense datum. 2.** the inferred fact that the **sensorium** has been activated by a specific receptor process. ➤The term is used by some behaviorists as a substitute for **sensation,** the latter being deemed metaphysically objectionable.

sense intuition: (*hist.*) the synthesizing of sense data that occurs in perception, resulting in apprehending external objects.

sense limen: see **threshold.**

sense modality: see **modality.**

sense mode: see **modality.**

sense/motor: see **motor sense.**

sense/muscle: see **kinesthesis.**

sense organ: 1. any organ the stimulation of which initiates the process of being aware of sense data. It consists of the endings of afferent nerves and of cells asso-

ciated with these endings that are specialized for the reception of a special form of energy. **2.** somewhat loosely, the relatively simple afferent nerve endings that receive a special form of energy. **3.** any receptor, whether or not it gives rise to sense data. —*Syn.* **receptor** (*prefd.* for 3), **sensor.**

sense perception: the process of perceiving as determined primarily by action of sense organs. ➤Except that **perception** (which see) is used by some with extraordinarily extended meaning, this term would have to be judged redundant.

sense process = **sensory process.**

sense quality: 1. that elementary attribute of a **sense datum** by which it most characteristically differs from others. ➤It contrasts especially with quantitative attributes such as **intensity, extensity,** and **protensity.** In general, it persists through any quantitative change. Redness, sourness, sensory pain, tonal pitch, are qualities. **2.** a particular bit of experience; a **sense datum.**—*Syn.* SENSORY QUALITY.

sense ratios method: a general term for methods of scaling sensory magnitude by adjusting or selecting a stimulus to equal a given fraction of a standard stimulus and using the ratio as a scale unit.—See **halving method,** the commonest example.

senses/higher: the sense modalities of vision and hearing, sometimes also including smell and taste.

sense/special: one of the four senses (vision, audition, smell, taste) whose receptors are in the head.

sense/systemic: a sensory mode of experience based on **interoceptors**—i.e., on receptors found in the internal organs.— *Syn.* **visceral sense.**

sense threshold: see **threshold.**

sense/vibration: see **vibratory sensitivity.**

sensibilia: *n. pl.* (*L.*) those things or qualities that can be apprehended by the senses. —*Syn.* SENSIBILES.

sensibility: *n.* **1.** capacity for sensing, either in general or in some particular mode: e.g., visual *sensibility.*—*Syn.* **receptivity. 2.** susceptibility to feeling and emotion.—*Syn.* **sensitivity** (*prefd.*) **3.** (*pop.* and *obsoles.*) capacity for good judgment. ➤While a useful distinction between sensibility and **sensitivity** has been maintained in careful writing (see **sensitivity 1**), it is often lost and the terms are interchanged. This is true also of the antonyms **insensibility** and **insensitivity** (see **insensible**).—*adj.* **sensible.**

sensibility/common: see **common sensibility.**

sensibility/subcutaneous: see **subcutaneous.**

sensible: *adj.* **1.** characterizing an object

that can, at least in part, be apprehended by the senses. 2. of sufficient amount or intensity to be perceptible; above the **threshold**. 3. meaningful. 4. showing good judgment or good sense. 5. (*obsoles.*) keenly aware. 6. = (*obsoles.*) **sensitive** (*prefd.*).

sensible distance or **interval**: see **sense distance**.

sensing: *n.* the psychological process, initiated at a sense organ, of being aware of **sense data**. ➤It is generally agreed that sensing does not occur apart from other psychological events. It is essentially an abstraction.—*v.* **sense** (which see).

sensitive: *adj.* 1. pertaining to **sensitivity** or to **sensitiveness**.—*n.* 2. a person supposed to be able to receive **paranormal** impressions or communications.

sensitiveness: *n.* having a low response threshold, esp. to pleasantness or unpleasantness; the tendency, not merely to detect, but to be easily moved by sense stimuli or emotive situations. ➤*Distg. fr.* **irritability**, which means reacting crossly; and *fr.* **sensitivity**. Sensitivity (1) or (2) refers to arousal of the sense organs. **Sensitivity (4)** emphasizes fineness of *perception* of others' behavior, whereas **sensitiveness** stresses easy reactivity. When such reactivity is emotional, **affectivity** is more precise. But **sensitive** is the adjective for both sensitiveness and sensitivity, and often for sensibility as well.

sensitive zone: 1. any region on the body surface whose stimulation arouses strong response. 2. = **erogenous *zone**.

sensitivity: *n.* 1. the condition or state of being susceptible to stimulation. ➤*Distg. fr.* **sensibility**, which refers to abstract capacity, whereas sensitivity refers to a particular state: a person has cutaneous sensibility but loses cutaneous sensitivity under local anesthesia. 2. the degree to which a person can be stimulated by stimuli of low intensity; **absolute sensitivity**. ➤*Distg. fr.* sensory **acuity**, the ability to *distinguish* simple stimuli. 3. the degree to which an instrument responds to changes in the phenomena it measures: the *sensitivity* of a chemical balance. 4. capacity to perceive, or to perceive and interpret, the behavior of others, esp. from **minimal cues**. 5. (*pop.*) the tendency to be easily hurt or offended. —*adj.* **sensitive** (also used for **sensitiveness**).

sensitivity/absolute: see **absolute sensitivity**.

sensitization: *n.* the process of becoming, or the state of being, sensitive or oversensitive to a definite stimulus.

sensor: *n.* 1. a simple **receptor**, generally merely a free nerve ending, whose activity initiates the process of sensing. 2. = the whole **sense organ**, complex or simple.

sensorial: *adj.* pertaining to the **sensorium**. —*Distg. fr.* **sensory**.

sensorial response: see **reaction type**.

sensorimotor: *adj.* 1. pertaining to the **neural transit** from a sense organ to a muscle. ➤Some authors use the form SENSORY-MOTOR and restrict it to this meaning. 2. of any act whose nature is *primarily* dependent upon the combined or integrated functioning of sense organs and motor mechanisms. ➤The word *primarily* is crucial; all activity—even the vegetative functions—depends to some extent on sense organs and motor mechanisms, and all activity depends on more than that.—*Distg. fr.* **ideomotor**, which refers to action primarily dependent upon thought processes; and *fr.* the semi-autonomous **vegetative** functions.

sensorimotor arc: the pathway followed by neural impulse from **sensor** to **effector**. ➤As compared with **reflex arc**, it may include higher-level pathways, but does not properly include such pathways as are not associated with **sensation**.—*Syn.* neural (or **nervous**) arc, slightly more comprehensive.

sensorium: *n.* 1. the **sensory areas** in the brain; loosely, the brain considered as the center to which sensory processes go. 2. the entire sensory mechanism: receptors, afferent nerves, and sensory or projection areas in the brain.—*Cp.* **motorium**.

sensory: *adj.* 1. pertaining to the activity of a **sense organ**. 2. pertaining to directly observed objective data, i.e., to **sense data**. 3. pertaining to a **sense** (1) or (2).—*Syn.* sense (*prefd.*). 4. pertaining to **sensation** (1) or (2).—*Ant.* (in many contexts) **motor**: see, e.g., **aphasia**. ¶For combination terms with **sensory** not listed below, see the noun: e.g., **acuity/sensory**.

sensory areas: those regions of the cerebral cortex in which the **afferent** tracts from sense organs terminate.—See **brain center**.—*Syn.* PROJECTION AREAS, SENSORY CORTEX.

sensory circle = **tactile circle**.

sensory cohesion: (*K. Goldstein*) the unreflecting experience of two objects as belonging together because they are sensorily similar. ➤Two or more red objects in a jumble of varicolored ones need not be separately apprehended and then judged to be similar; they may be immediately apprehended as "the reds," a totality to which the distinct pieces contribute.

sensory cortex = **sensory areas**.

sensory discrimination: responding to differences in sense data or in stimuli; the degree to which one can respond to small differences. ➤The response may be verbal. Those who are troubled by the mentalistic implications of **sensation** or **perception** often use sensory discrimination as a synonym.—See **acuity/sensory**.

sensory drive: a **drive** oriented toward, and dispelled by the attainment of, a specific form of sensory experience: e.g., a drive for sweetness or bitterness (not merely for food in general), for tactile stimulation, for vivid colors.

sensory field: 1. all the stimuli affecting a **receptor** at a given time; or all those affecting the whole organism at a given time. **2.** all the things a person experiences through the senses at a given time; the PERCEPTUAL FIELD.

sensory habit: a learned pattern of behavior in which emphasis is upon discrimination between stimuli, as contrasted with MOTOR HABIT in which emphasis is upon new combinations of motor response. ➤It is a sensory habit when a person learns that one sound indicates the rear doorbell, another the front doorbell. It is a motor habit when a person learns the coordinated movements of typewriting. The distinction is merely of emphasis; sensory habits involve motor responses, and motor habits involve sensory discriminations.

sensory integration postulate: (*H. Birch* and *M. Bitterman*) "When two afferent centers are contiguously activated, a functional relation is established between them such that the subsequent innervation of one will arouse the other." ➤*Cp.* **law of *contiguity,*** which is not restricted to afferent centers.

sensory intensity: see **intensity (2).**

sensory interaction: the mutual effect upon each other of sensing processes that are simultaneous: e.g., the **size-weight illusion.** ➤In theory, every process affects every other simultaneous process in the same organism. This term should be reserved for differences empirically demonstrated to be functions of specified simultaneous processes.

sensory modality: see **modality.**

sensory-motor = **sensorimotor (1).**

sensory nerve: a nerve from the **receptor** organ to the cord or brain. ➤In some cases the peripheral end of the sensory nerve is itself the receptor; in others there is a distinct sense organ from which the nerve starts.—*Syn.* **afferent** nerve.

sensory organization: 1. the process by which sensory processes or experiences are related and coordinated; or the resulting system of relationship; = **perceiving** or **percept.** ➤It is a report of sensory organization when a subject says, "A deep red was surrounded by a pale green." **2.** (*Gestalt*) the form of organization found when the perceptual field is **isomorphic** with the stimulus field: e.g., physical stimuli in the form of a square perceived as "square."

sensory process: 1. a neural process or activity directly originating in a **receptor. 2.** a **sensing;** the activity whereby an organism becomes aware of **sense data. 3.** = (*structuralism*) **sensation (1),** the process observed in introspection as a function of sense organ activity. ➤The word *process* in this usage means only that change occurs.

sensory projection areas = **sensory areas.**

sensory quality: see **sense quality.**

sensory reaction: see **reaction type.**

sensory stimulus: a tautological expression, justified to emphasize use of the word **stimulus** in its strict sense, i.e., as a form of physical energy affecting a sense organ.—See **stimulus (1).**

sensory system: the **afferent** nerves and the appended sense organs, usually including also the **sensory areas,** but sometimes limited to peripheral afferent nerves.

sensory type: obsolete term for a particular bodily conformation (similar to the **asthenic**).—*Distg. fr.* sensory **reaction type.**

sensual: *adj.* **1.** pertaining to gratification obtained from stimulation of the senses, esp. of the "lower" senses; hence, **2.** lustful; pertaining to sexual gratification. **3. sensuous** (an unfortunate use).—*n.* **sensuality.**

sensum *n., pl.* **sensa:** a **sense datum.**

sensuous: *adj.* pertaining to the senses or to the sensory aspect of experience; capable of arousing the senses. ➤*Syn.* **sensual,** VOLUPTUOUS. In contrast with **sensual,** which is usually derogatory, **sensuous** has no necessarily unfavorable connotations. VOLUPTUOUS implies luxurious indulgence in the sensuous.—*n.* **sensuousness.**

sensus communis (sen′səs kə·mū′nis): (*L.*) **common sense.**

sentence-completion test: 1. a test of ability in which the testee must supply an appropriate word or phrase to complete a meaningful sentence. **2.** = **incomplete sentence test** (which see).

sentence repetition test: a standard set of sentences of increasing length to be read one by one to the testee, with instruction to repeat each sentence verbatim.

sentence/word: see **word sentence.**

sentience (sen′shəns; -shi·əns): *n.* **1.** abstract term for the fact of **sensing. 2.** the simplest and most primitive form of cognition; mere apprehension of a sensory quality with no concomitant associations or meaning; pure **sensation.** ➤Sentience is a never actually attained limit on a continuum, with fully meaningful perception at the other end; but it is approximated in passive sensing.

sentience need: (*H. A. Murray*) the need

to enjoy sensuous pleasures, sights, and sounds.

sentiendum (sen"shi·en'dəm) *n., pl.* **sentienda: sensation, sense datum.**

sentiment: *n.* a complex **disposition** or organization of a person with reference to a given object (whether a person, thing, or abstract idea) that makes the object what it is for him. The sentiment is identified both by the object and by certain *central* affective relations between the person and that object, other related emotions and actions being congruent with the central emotion. ➤Thus, if the sentiment is that of a mother's love for her child, anger or fear is provoked when the child's welfare is threatened. While the organization of a **sentiment** is primarily affective and conative, there is also considerable elaboration of ideas relevant to the object. ¶Sentiment differs from **attitude** in being more personal and much more complex. (*Cp. a favorable attitude toward Great Britain* with *the Briton's sentiment of patriotism.*) A **complex** may be regarded as a repressed sentiment. Sentiment is sometimes infected with some of the connotations of **sentimentality** from which, however, it is to be distinguished.—*Syn.* MENTAL or PSYCHIC SYSTEM, **metanerg, derivation, canalization.** There are many terms for special forms of sentiment: **prejudice, belief, means-end readiness,** and **habit** (the last with emotional aspect unemphasized, but present). The *adj.* **sentimental** belongs to **sentimentality,** not to **sentiment.**

sentimentality: *n.* **1.** weak and shallow emotion. **2.** overindulgence in emotion or **sentiment;** emotion without due cause. **3.** enjoyment of emotion for its own sake. ➤The three meanings are often combined. —*adj.* **sentimental.**

separation anxiety: (*psychoan.*) the infant's fear of losing the mother object. ➤For Freud, this is based not merely on the birth trauma, but on many incidents of the infant's early experience.

septum *n., pl.* **septa:** (*biol.*) a partition or dividing wall between two spaces or cavities in an organism: e.g., the nasal *septum.*

sequela (si·kwē'lə) *n., pl.* **sequelae** (-lē): (*med.*) a pathological result or sequel of disease.

sequence: *n.* **1.** the following of one thing by another. **2.** the order in which events or objects occur. **3.** (*Ror.*) the order in which the testee responds to wholes, details, and rare details in the inkblots. **4.** a temporal series of phenomena. **5.** (*math.*) a succession of quantities, each derived from the preceding quantity by the same operation.—*adj.* **sequential.**

sequence preference: a tendency to make

responses in a certain order: e.g., rats usually tend to make alternate right-left turns in a maze.—See **position factor.**

sequential analysis: see **analysis/sequential.**

sequential test: (*stat.*) a test to determine the effect of further data upon the level of **statistical *significance** in order to determine when the point has been reached where the addition of further data is probably unnecessary for a given level of statistical significance; or, alternatively, that even though additional data are added the required level is unlikely to be reached. The test is used in **sequential *analysis.**

sE̲ᴿ: ➤This group of symbols is entered as if written *E.*

serendipity: *n.* the process, art, or fact of finding one thing while looking for another.

serial action = **serial behavior.**

serial-anticipation method: see **prompting method.**

serial association: see **serial learning.**

serial behavior: activity in which the temporal order of the several responses is the important feature. ➤The responses are not independent; they are functions of the whole series.

serial correlation: (*stat.*) a measure of relationship between successive values of a variable in time or space.

serial discrimeter (dis·krim'ə·tər): an apparatus that presents a new stimulus for a discrimination response as soon as a prescribed response to the preceding stimulus is made.—*Syn.* PSYCHERGOGRAPH.

serial exploration/method of = **just noticeable differences/method of.**

serial learning: learning to make certain responses in an exact prescribed order. In SERIAL MEMORIZING the response is verbal: a set of words must be recalled in the order of first presentation. In other cases, certain overt motor responses must follow in prescribed order.—*Syn.* SERIAL METHOD, SERIAL ASSOCIATION, **behavior *chain** learning.

serial memorization: a form of **serial learning.**

serial method: see **serial learning.**

serial position effect: the influence of the position of an item on the learning of a series of items.

serial response: see **response/serial.**

seriatim (sir"i·ā'tim; ser"i-): *adv.* in series; one after the other.

seriation: *n.* the process by which unorganized data are put into the form of a statistical series.

series *n. s.* and *pl.:* a group of items that form, or are arranged in, an order, each leading to the next according to some definite principle, temporal, spatial, or logical. All series can be represented by the number series. ➤The alphabet is a series arbitrarily arranged in temporal or spatial order. Father, son, and grandson constitute a series; but the group Father, Son, and Holy Ghost is a trinity, not a series (except as a series of words). Series may represent **continuous** or **discontinuous** variation. —*adj.* **serial.**

series/experimental: see **experimental series.**

servo or **servomechanism:** *n.* a control system for maintaining the operation of another system at prescribed rates and strengths: e.g., a thermostat. ➤The servo-mechanism receives a signal showing the amount of energy (the **input**) supplied to the operation system and a **feedback** signal showing the rate, strength, and/or direction of the operation (the **output**). The response of the servo to these signals regulates the input so that a prescribed output is maintained. **Homeostasis** in living bodies is a special case of servo functioning, but there are many others: e.g., the regulation of the angle of a bottle from which one is drinking to maintain an even flow.—See **feedback, cybernetics.**—*Syn.* SLAVE SYSTEM.

set: *n.* ➤The more than 100 meanings of **set** in the unabridged dictionary include six concepts pertinent for psychology: those of aggregation; of tendency or disposition; of orientation, guidance, or determination; of preparation, expectation, or readiness; of facilitation; and of fixity or rigidity. The first and last give rise to distinct definitions (1 and 3 below); the remaining four are merged in definition (2), but various authors emphasize one or another of the four.
1. a group, lot, aggregate, or series of items of any sort: a *set* of pictures, the country club *set*, the *set* (or totality) of points which satisfy a certain mathematical condition. 2. a temporary, but often recurrent, condition of the person or organism that (*a*) orients him (it) toward certain environmental stimuli or events rather than toward others, selectively sensitizing him (it) for apprehending them; (*b*) facilitates certain activities or responses rather than others. ➤In its earlier psychological usage, set was a more or less temporary facilitating condition produced by instructions or by some manipulation of the experimental conditions. It was thus separable from the enduring dispositions—**habits, instincts, canalizations, sentiments, attitudes**—and from **habit strength** or associative bond strength. Somewhat like a **drive,** it worked upon a particular action system from outside that system. But a temporary set can become an enduring disposition or habit, a simple **attitude;** and the term now often includes that meaning.—*Syn.* **Ein-**

stellung, **determining tendency,** and (in special contexts) **disposition, adjustment, expectation.** 3. the establishment of a fixed form of behaving; **habituation; stereo-typing.**

Set is often (but not always) qualified to show the kind of effect produced by an organic or personal condition: e.g., attitudinal *set,* affective *set,* **motor** *set (but for this, set* alone may be used).—*adj.* and *v.* **set.**

set/abstract: the tendency to apprehend things in terms of abstractions.

set/culture: (*sociol.*) a relatively enduring attitude that predisposes an individual to accept cultural forms congruent with those he is accustomed to, and to reject others.

set/hypnotic: a set induced by instructions of the hypnotist and carried over into the posthypnotic period.—*Syn.* POSTHYPNOTIC SUGGESTION.

set/learning: see **learning set.**

set/mental: a preparatory adjustment or readiness for a particular kind of action or experience, usually as a result of instructions; = **set (2).** ➤It is difficult to see what the qualifying word **mental** adds to **set,** except to insure that it is taken in a psychological sense. But see **neural** *set and **organic** *set.

set/motor: 1. a readiness for a given muscular movement. 2. a group of movements that prepare for a given muscular reaction. ➤The preparatory movements may be in another group of muscles or may be **tonic** innervations of the muscle group being prepared, or both. Note that (2) restricts motor set to readiness dependent on a certain kind of mechanism, whereas (1) leaves the nature of the mechanism unspecified. Many authors shift back and forth between these meanings, without warning.

set/neural: 1. a temporary state of subexcitation of a **response circuit.** ➤*Syn. Bahnung,* **facilitation,** or (in some older writings) **reinforcement.** This usage is now uncommon. 2. a hypothetical condition in the nervous system that accounts for the sensitizing and facilitating effects of **set (2).** ➤In most cases the qualifier **neural** is not to be taken literally; the writer is merely proclaiming that he is not a **mentalist.** If **neural** is seriously meant, meaning (1) may be intended; or the writer may mean the **tonic** innervation of a response mechanism (for which **motor** *set 2 is preferred).

set/objective: the determination of an experience, esp. of a perception, by an overriding principle that reflects objective facts. ➤If drawings are presented in this order—square, triangle, circle; square, triangle, ellipse—the ellipse (if not too obviously different) will be seen as a circle. Note that the set could as well be called subjective, depending on the point of view.—*Approx. syn.* expectancy.

set/organic = set (2). ➤The qualifying word **organic** adds nothing to the meaning of **set**; it merely notifies the reader that the author is not thinking in mentalistic terms. Organic set and **mental** *set refer to precisely the same effects on behavior. But some authors apparently use **organic** set for **motor** *set (2).

set/perceptual: a readiness to perceive the environment in a certain way, generally in accord with a pattern. ➤E.g., in a "hidden figure" picture, a set to perceive a tree inhibits seeing the outline of a face. In this instance the set has both a positive effect (seeing the tree) and a negative effect (not seeing something else that is objectively in the picture). It may also distort the total perceptual process, causing illusion. **Perceptual** in this phrase is often given very extended meaning where COGNITIVE SET would be more correct. **Determining tendency** and *Aufgabe* refer to the same phenomena but with emphasis upon the motor elements of the response.—*Syn.* PERCEPTION SET, **preperception** (1). **Perceptual *defense** is conceived as a negative perceptual set against perceiving what one does not want to perceive.

set/perseverative: a set induced by previous experience and held over in a succeeding situation for which it may or may not be appropriate.

set/postural: a **tonic** contraction of the muscles that predisposes a person toward a specific action: e.g., a runner poised to start.

set/preparatory: a bodily attitude or posture that prepares the person for some other response.—*Cp.* set/postural, set/ motor, both nearly synonymous.

set/response: 1. in a reaction time experiment or similar situation, the readiness to *respond,* in contrast to STIMULUS SET, the readiness to apprehend the expected signal. ➤The response set results in quicker reactions but also in more errors. 2. a set to follow a certain pattern in responding: e.g., to alternate responses of *True* and *False* in a True-False test, or to give not more than three consecutive *True* or *False* responses. ➤This combines concepts from set (2) and set (3).

set/situation: a more or less temporary orientation toward the observation of outward circumstances and an intent to adapt one's behavior thereto.—*Contr. w.* **motor** *set, a predisposition to a particular group of movements; and *w.* inner determination, a predisposition toward attaining certain values or goals.

set/situational = stimulus set (see set/ response).—*Distg. fr.* situation *set.

set/stimulus: see set/response.

setting: *n.* 1. the process of moving a **mechanical** *indicator to a desired position, esp. to a particular value as read on the indicator scale; or of moving the indicator to match another indicator. ➤The indicator may be moved directly, as when a trip meter is set at zero for a trip; or it may be moved by altering the operation of which it is the indicator, as when the speedometer is brought down to 50 mph by adjusting the speed of the car. 2. the point to which the indicator is (or should be) moved. 3. the arrangement of the elements of a situation: e.g., managing so that two opponents meet in the presence of a superior.

setup: *n.* the spatial arrangement and the interconnections of instruments for an experiment; more loosely, any arrangement.

set/unconscious: a set of which the person concerned is unaware, either directly or indirectly. ➤A set is in all cases an *inferred* condition; but the individual may not make the inference, and may be unaware that his behavior is guided by set.

sex: *adj.* 1. pertaining to, or characterized by, anything related to the distinction between those organisms bearing egg cells (females) and those bearing sperm cells (males). 2. specif., pertaining to the organs of reproduction and the anatomical differences between male and female.

➤While usage is far from consistent, the following distinctions are prevalent and are recommended: **Sex** is the general term, and also the term when there is specific reference to anatomical or morphological distinctions: *sex* organs, *sex* differentiation, *sex* characteristics, *sex* chromosomes. This includes the use of sex to refer to the differences between male and female. **Genital** is the closest *syn.,* esp. for (2).

Sexual, also having a general meaning, specifically refers to the functions relating to reproduction, and, in certain contexts, to functions preliminary to reproduction (courting, etc.). **Erotic** refers to sensations, feelings, and motives, the latter especially when the person is aware of the motive. (But when the motive is called **drive,** *sex* or *sexual* are the usual adjectives.) **Psychosexual** means **erotic,** or the combination of sexual behavior or activity (including caressing) with erotic feelings. **Amorous** refers to lovemaking in which sexual behavior is involved. **Libidinal** refers both to behavior functions and to experience; in psychoanalysis it has a very extended usage. (See **libido.**) **Gender** refers to grammatical distinctions; its use as a synonym for *sex* or *sexual* is a timorous

euphemism. **Sensual,** in one of its meanings, refers to sexual gratification, or to the
tendency to be overoccupied therewith.

Altrigendristic has been suggested for
the nonerotic activity between persons of
opposite sex. Etymologically the term is ill-
constructed and has not gained wide use,
but it fills a terminological need. When the
interest and activity become amorous,
heteroerotic is used. **Heterosexual** is a
general term for any sort of relation between the sexes but it also refers specifically
to overtly sexual behavior, such as courting
and caressing, and to sexual intercourse.
HETEROGENITAL refers specifically to genital
contact. **Homosexual** is a general term
for sexual behavior oriented to persons of
one's own sex. **Homoerotic** refers to sexual
interest in one's own sex without overt
sexual behavior.—See also **heterosexuality,
homosexuality.**

sex: *n.* **1.** either of the two divisions or categories of organisms, female or male, that
are based on the distinction of producing,
respectively, egg cells or sperm cells; the
category of females or the category of males.
2. the sum of the characters that make male
and female different, esp. the physical characters. **3.** the behavior domain closely related to the organs of reproduction.—*Syn.*
(for **3**) **sexuality** (*prefd.*).

sex-: **1.** combining form meaning *six.* **2.**
combining form meaning *sex.*

sex aim: see **sexual aim.**

sex anomaly: **1.** a wide deviation from the
normal in the structure or form of the
organs of reproduction.—*Syn.* GENITAL
ANOMALY. **2.** = **sexual anomaly** (much
prefd. for a functional deviation).

sex character: any characteristic or trait,
whether structural or functional, that is
found much more frequently in one sex
than in the other. ➤Manifestation of a
trait strongly characteristic of the other sex
is regarded as a **sex** (or **sexual**) **anomaly.**
PRIMARY SEX CHARACTERS are those of the
reproductive organs.—See also **sex char-
acter/secondary.**

sex character/secondary: a genetically
transmitted anatomical or behavioral trait,
typical for either sex but not for both, and
not necessary to reproduction: e.g., the
greater amount of facial hair and the bass
voice in males. ➤Which behavioral traits,
if any, conform to the definition is a matter
of dispute.—*Distg. fr.* **sex-linked character,** a trait found much more often, or
only, in one sex but not in all members.

sex chromosome: a **chromosome** that
plays the major part in determining the sex
of the offspring. ➤In most species, sex is
determined by a special pair: the female
offspring receives two like (or X) chromosomes; the male receives one X and one Y

chromosome which is smaller. Some species
lack the odd sex chromosomes: in that case
males are Xo instead of XY. In some
species, the female receives the odd chromosome. The sex chromosome carries determiners for other traits than sex; these
are called **sex-linked characters.**

sex delinquency: any violation of established legal or moral codes in respect to
sexual behavior. ➤While the term is very
vague, emphasis is upon breaking rules.
Sexual anomaly may or may not be
deemed sex delinquency. In the U.S., **delinquency** has almost become equated with
juvenile delinquency, and sex delinquency
is often similarly limited to juvenile behavior.

sex determination: the biological mechanism that determines whether the new
organism will be male or female.—See **sex
chromosome.**

sex differences: any significant difference
between males as a group and females as a
group, e.g., in mathematical abilities. ➤The
term does not imply that the differences are
genetically determined, though that implication is often made. It seldom applies to
differences in the primary **sex characters,**
and is improperly equated with differences
in sexual behavior.—*Cp.* **difference/group,
difference/individual.**

sex differentiation: the interacting processes during development, some biological
and some social, that bring about the
typical sex differences. ➤E.g., the greater
muscular development of the male is caused
partly by genetic determinants, partly by
training that is socially motivated.

sex distribution: the relative proportion
of males and females in a given population.
—*Syn.* SEX RATIO.

sex education: **1.** instruction dealing with
the organs and processes of reproduction.
➤An unfortunately restrictive usage. **2.** any
educative process designed to help the individual to healthy and/or socially approved sexual adjustment. ➤It deals not
only with sex but with **sexuality,** and
may include not only instruction but such
activities (not necessarily overtly sexual
or erotic) as seem likely to promote sexual
adjustment. The contemporary tendency is
away from a purely negative consideration
of sexual control toward constructive sexual
expression. For this meaning, SEXUAL EDU-
CATION is more descriptive but it is uncommon.

sex feeling = **erotic** feeling (*prefd.*).

sex hygiene: **1.** the study of the health of
the reproductive organs. **2.** the study of
healthy sexual adjustment; the psychophysiological and moral expression and control of sexual impulses. ➤More exactly (but
seldom) called SEXUAL HYGIENE. Its limita-

tion to methods of preventing and curing venereal disease is arbitrary and unfortunate.

sex-influenced character: a trait transmitted as **dominant** in one sex, **recessive** in the other. ➤E.g., baldness may be transmitted by either parent to a male, but must be transmitted by both parents if it is to appear in the female.

sex intergrade: see **intergrade/sex.**

sex latency: see **sexual latency.**

sex-limited character: a trait that can be suppressed by one kind of sex **hormone; a** trait manifesting variation in only one sex. ➤E.g., in chickens the female sex hormones permit hens to develop only hen feathers but the male sex hormone permits the growth of either hen or cock feathers. (Which the cock will have depends on other factors in his gene pattern.) Sex limitation is one factor in **secondary *sex characters.**

sex-linked character: a trait transmitted by genes located on the sex chromosomes and found more frequently in one sex than the other; e.g., red-green color blindness. —*Distg. fr.* **sex-influenced** and **sex-limited characters,** and *fr.* **sex characters/secondary.**

sex object: see **sexual aim.**

sex offenses: see **sex delinquency.**

sex perversion = **sexual anomaly** (which see).

sex ratio: the ratio, at any specified time, of the number of males in a given population per one hundred females.

sex reversal: a transformation in an adult organism wherein the sex organs of one sex are surgically removed, or deteriorate, and the rudimentary sex organs characteristic of the other sex develop, so that the female becomes a male or vice versa.

sex rivalry: 1. behavior intended to exalt the achievements and status of one sex over the other. **2.** competition between the child and the parent of the same sex for the attention and affection of the parent of opposite sex.

sex role: the pattern of attitudes and behavior that in any society is deemed appropriate to one sex rather than the other. ➤The role is taught by precept and example. There is no act except childbearing and suckling that is not, in some society, part of the male role; none that is not, in some society, part of the female role. Even symbolic childbearing is a part of the male role in some cultures.

sex sensations: the **sense data** resulting from stimulation of receptors in the genitals or, more generally, in the **erogenous *zones.**—*Distg. fr.* **sex feeling.**—*Syn.* SEXUAL SENSATIONS (*prefd.*).

sextile: see **partile.**

sexual: *adj.* **1.** (*biol.*) pertaining to reproduction by union of two sex cells, in contrast to **asexual** reproduction. **2.** a very general term applied to feelings or behavior related to the **functions** of reproduction and of its preliminaries.—See **sex** (*adj.*) for distinctions between **sex, sexual,** and **erotic.**

sexual aim: the relief of specific physiological tensions by sexual action. ➤It is contrasted with SEXUAL OBJECT, the person or thing toward which the activity is directed.—*Syn.* SEX AIM, common but not *recom.*—*Cp.* **aim** (3).

sexual anesthesia = **frigidity.**

sexual anomaly: behavior in the sexual sphere that deviates rather sharply from the normal but is not considered to be necessarily pathological. ➤The term is proposed as a substitute for sexual **perversion,** on the grounds that evidence is lacking that perversions are intrinsically pathological and that a less condemnatory term is socially desirable.—*Distg. fr.* **sex anomaly,** which refers properly to anatomical deviation.— *Cp.* **deviation/sexual, perversion.**

sexual congress = **coition.**

sexual deviation: see **deviation/sexual.**

sexual function: any physiological activity performed exclusively by one sex.—*Cp.* **reproductive function.**

sexual infantilism: 1. failure to develop fully the anatomical characters of adult sex.—*Syn.* SEX INFANTILISM or INFANTILE SEX (*prefd.*). **2.** regression to, or arrested development at the level of, **infantile *sexuality** (which see).

sexual instinct: 1. the tendency, largely but not wholly innate, toward the courtship behavior and the sexual congress that is characteristic of the species. **2.** (*psychoan.*) a term for almost every pleasure-seeking tendency.—See **libido.**

sexual intercourse = **coition.**

sexualism: *n.* emphasis upon sex: e.g., **pansexualism.**

sexuality: *n.* **1.** the sum of a person's sexual behaviors and sexual tendencies; the strength of sexual tendency. **2.** the quality of being sexual, or of having sexual functions or implications. **3.** excessive preoccupation with sex and sex behavior.—*Cp.* **pansexualism, sexuality/infantile.**—See **sex** (*adj.*) for distinctions in sex-related terms. —*adj.* **sexual** (not **sex**).—*v.* **sexualize,** to bring something within the sexual sphere.

sexuality/infantile: (*psychoan.*) the capacity of the infant and young child to have experiences that are essentially sexual; the sum total of the infant's sexual behavior and experience, whether conscious or unconscious. ➤No brief statement of the psychoanalytic definition of this term is possible. Infantile sexuality is and is not sexual in the usual sense. See **libido.** Neopsychoanalysts do not emphasize, to the degree that Freudians do, the role of infantile sexuality in the genesis of neurosis.

exual latency: (*S. Freud*) a hypothesized lull in the development of sexual functions and impulses beginning at about age 5 and lasting till puberty. It involves extensive repression of the earlier **infantile *sexuality*** postulated by psychoanalysis. ➤The phenomenon is believed to be in part determined by the **culture.**

exual maturation: the development of the organs of reproduction to a fully functioning level. ➤*Distg.* the actual maturing of the reproductive system *fr.* its many more or less reliable overt *signs* (such as facial hair in males).

exual object: see **sexual aim.**

exual reflex: erection, or erection and **orgasm.**

exual reproduction: (*biol.*) the production of a new organism by the union of two sex cells.—*Ant.* ASEXUAL REPRODUCTION, which includes reproduction by fission of one cell, and by means of spores.

exual selection: preference in mating for organisms having certain physical or mental traits, resulting in the gradual preponderance of those traits in the population.

exual soliloquy: talking to oneself at some length about one's sexual desires, as a means of relieving tension.

exual trauma: a severely disturbing or anxiety-arousing experience, usually in infancy or early childhood, related in some way to sex.

   factor = **specific *factor.**

s_G, s_G: see under *S* or *s*.

hade: *n.* any color darker (i.e., of lower lightness) than median gray.—See **color shade.**

hading: *n.* (*Ror.*) one of the major determinants of response to the inkblot: it is the perceived density of color (chromatic or achromatic) of the inkblot. The SHADING EFFECT or LIGHT-DETERMINED RESPONSE is the subject's description of such shadings.—See **determinant/Rorschach.**

hading shock: (*Ror.*) manifesting emotion in response to the shading effect of the inkblot pattern.

hadow: *n.* (*C. Jung*) the converse in the unconscious of whatever the person has emphasized in his ego consciousness. Its strength is proportional to the strength of the ego trends.

hadow/acoustic or **/sound:** see **sound shadow.**

hallow living: (*K. Horney*) a form of **neurotic *resignation*** (which see) characterized by compulsive seeking of superficial and disinterested activity, with em-

phasis on distracting pleasure, opportunistic success, or automatic conformism.

shaman: (shä'mən; sham'ən): *n.* (*anthrop.*) a person who practices magic or communicates with supernatural powers iɔ trances, etc.

shame: *n.* an emotional attitude excited by realization of a shortcoming or impropriety, of having acted in an unworthy manner, or esp., of having improperly exposed the body.—*Distg. fr.* **modesty** (which see) and *fr.* **sense of *guilt.**

shame culture: *n.* that form of social control in which a person's behavior is regulated by the ridicule or criticism of others. —*Distg. fr.* **guilt culture.**

sham feeding: allowing an animal to swallow food taken into the mouth but removing it through an opening in the esophagus before it reaches the stomach.

shamming: *n.* counterfeiting a posture or activity in order to deceive another animal. e.g., the feigned broken wing of a bird seeking to draw an intruder away from the nest.

sham rage: prompt, poorly organized, brief responses (similar to those of normal rage behavior) elicited in decerebrate and decorticate animals by almost any stimulus. The sham rage response is suppressed in the normal animal by cortical action.

shape: *n.* **1.** a spatial form or figure; a **space** having definite contour or boundary. **2.** a **gestalt;** a perceived figure; a unit segregated from its surroundings.

shape constancy: the tendency to see an object as of the same shape regardless of the viewing angle.—*Cp.* **constancy/object.**

shaping = **approximation *conditioning.**

shared field: a psychological **field** or a unitary part of a total field held consciously in common by two or more persons. ➤*Cp.* COMMON FIELD, in which the field is the same but the persons do not recognize the communality.

sharp: *adj.* (*music*) **1.** raised in pitch by a semitone: e.g., C sharp, which is a semitone higher than C.—*Ant.* FLAT. **2.** of a tone slightly higher than it is supposed to be.

sharpening: *n.* **1.** the process of accentuating differences in perceived objects. **2.** a memory distortion that overemphasizes distinguishing characteristics so that events recalled are better defined and more distinct than the originals.—*Ant.* **leveling.**

sheath/medullary: see **medullary sheath.**

sheath/myelin: see **medullary sheath.**

Sheldon type: see **constitutional type** and **ectomorphic.**

shell shock: a term used in World War I for the neurosis associated with being under gunfire, esp. of heavy guns. ➤It was at first thought to result from concussion caused by the force of high explosives but was soon recognized as a **functional disorder.** In World War II, the term **combat fatigue** largely replaced **shell shock.**—*Cp.* **commotional shock.**

Sheppard's correction: a correction to be applied to the **variance** or **standard** *deviation obtained from grouped measures. ➤The coarser the grouping, the more effective is this correction.

shibboleth: *n.* originally, a password to be pronounced as a test of one's group membership; hence, any arbitrary test of orthodoxy or of belonging; or more generally, any catchword used to impress people.

shifting/law of: the generalization that a response quickly loses its initial advantage over other similar responses to the same situation unless some sort of pressure to continue is present.

shift of level principle: (*K. Koffka*) the generalization that, when surrounding circumstances alter the position of two stimuli on a continuum, the two tend to keep the same relation to each other. ➤E.g., two shades of the same color may both seem lighter or darker under changed illumination, but they maintain their sensed difference from each other.

shock: *n.* **1.** a complex of symptoms resulting from accidental injury, surgery, drugs, or strong emotion. Most bodily functions are deranged, perhaps as a result of sharply curtailed circulation or of chemical change in the blood. **2.** the sudden effect of a powerful electric current passing through the body. ➤Only if very powerful does this shock result in **shock (1). 3.** a condition of lowered excitability in nerve centers that have been surgically severed from other centers. When the cord is cut anterior to the point of motor outflow, SPINAL SHOCK results: the spinal reflex centers are depressed, and the muscles exhibit flaccid paralysis. **4.** = **shock therapy.**

shock/color: (*Ror.*) see **color shock.**

shock/commotional: see **commotional shock.**

shock therapy: the treatment of mentally ill persons by inducing shock, with or without convulsions, by means of drugs or by passing an electric current through the brain. ➤It is not known by what means the shock effects improvement (as it does in many cases), nor what permanent changes it may or may not cause.

short-answer examination or **test:** see **examination/short answer.**

short-circuit appeal: an attempt to secure action by directly arousing some strong **drive** or impulse, bypassing or omitting factual or rational considerations: e.g., advertising a product as the choice of men of distinction (the snob appeal) instead of describing its virtues.

short-circuiting: *n.* **1.** the simplification c an act as it becomes habitual; the elimina tion of unnecessary movements.—*C* **short-circuiting law. 2.** the hypothetica functional elimination of alternate and sup plemental neural pathways with repetitio of a stimulus-response association. ➤This merely a restatement of the observed fac of (1) in terms of unobserved, inferre neural phenomena—an example of **neur** *tautology. **3.** the elimination of factu or rational considerations and the dire arousal of a drive or incentive.—See **shor circuit appeal.**

short-circuiting law: (*R. B. Cattell*) t generalization that learned traits tend be modified in the direction of behavi demanding less **deflection strain** (whic see) and less **cognitive-dynamic inves ment strain** (which see).

short-circuiting theory: (*M. Wertheime* the hypothesis that when two points point-areas on the skin or retina are stim lated at such an interval as to give rise **phenomenal** (or **apparent**) *motion, t cells lying between the two brain cente corresponding to the point-areas are al fired by spread of excitation from t stimulated brain centers.

short-sample technique: a method systematizing observations in which the o server reports behavior for brief samp periods dispersed at intervals in such a w that the behavior is thought to be rep sentative. ➤More details but less cont can thus be reported.

short tone: the tone heard when the au tory stimulus is very brief—approximat 0.1 second and less. ➤Such tones seld occur in nature but may be electronica produced.

"shoulds" (shùdz): *n. pl.* (*K. Horney*) ir tional, excessive demands and standards by the **idealized** *image of the neuro self. These "shoulds" act as internali authority, pressing the neurotic to comp sive and exaggerated behavior. When f fillment fails, they produce self-hate.

$_sH_R$: Symbols in this group are listed as written *H.*

shrinkage: *n.* **1.** a reduction in size. (*stat.*) the reduction in the **multiple *c relation** when the test battery is appl to a group other than the criterion gro Shrinkage increases as the number of t in the battery increases.

shut-in personality: a person seriou lacking in expressiveness, either of feeli or thought, and in sociability. This i common antecedent of **schizophrenia.**

shyness: *n.* discomfort and partial inh tion of the usual forms of behavior wher the presence of others, esp. when the ject of attention.

sib: *n.* **1.** (*genet., psychol.*) one of two

more offspring of either sex from the same mother or the same father. ➤Some authors classify these as sibs only when both parents are the same.—*Syn.* SIBLING.—*collective n.* **sibship,** all the sibs of one family. **2.** (*anthrop.*) all persons descended from a single ancestor in either male or female line, according to the system of reckoning kinship in a given society.—*Syn.* SIBSHIP.

ibling rivalry: see **rivalry/sibling.**

ibship: see **sib.**

ide comparison: (*psychophys.*) the influence exerted on a subject's judgment by preceding stimuli. ➤The term is somewhat misleading as no explicit comparison need be made.

dedness = **laterality.**

ght: *n.* the sense whose receptor is the eye (more specif., the retina) and whose stimulus is light—i.e., radiant energy of wave length from about 400 to 760 millimicrons.—*Syn.* **vision.**—*adj.* **sighted.**—*v.* see.

ght conservation class: a special class for partial-sighted pupils.—*Syn.* SIGHT-SAVING CLASS.

ght(ing) line = **visual axis.**

ght/line of = **direction/line of.**

ght method: a method of teaching reading by having pupils recognize whole words or phrases without specific **phonic** or word analysis.

ght-saving class: see **sight conservation class.**

: a symbol for **summation.** It is placed before the symbol for a variable all of whose measured values or scores are to be summed algebraically. ➤E.g., ΣX means that all the values of X are to be summed. Sometimes limits are indicated by symbols written above and below: e.g., $\sum_{1}^{N} Y^2$ means that all the values of Y^2 between 1 and N (inclusive) are to be added. Σ is the Greek capital letter *Sigma.* It is read "sum of," not "sigma," since the latter is the reading of σ (lower case sigma).

gma or σ: **1.** = **millisecond,** one-thousandth of a second. **2.** = **standard *deviation.** ➤σ is often used with qualifying subscripts; without such qualification it has one of the two meanings given above.—*Distg.* σ (read "sigma") *fr.* Σ (read "sum f").

= **standard error of mean.**—*Distg. fr.* σ_M.

σ = **standard error of measurement.** -*Distg. fr.* σ_M.

= **variance.**

gma measure = **standard *score.**

gma/partial = **standard error of stimate.**

gma score = **standard *score.**

sigma value = **standard *score.**

sign: *n.* **1.** in general, an indicator.—See **signal, symbol. 2.** any object or event—esp. an action, or the direct result of an action—perceived as having a significance beyond itself: e.g., the blush of embarrassment, the slouched posture of fatigue or boredom. ➤In this sense, **sign** contrasts with **symbol,** which is an action (or the result of an action) *intended* by the performer to have significance beyond itself. Thus, a slouched posture becomes a symbol only when it is intended to reveal to others that one is tired or bored. Words are primarily symbols, though the intent to communicate in some cases may be so weakened that they are mere signs: e.g., the exclamation "ouch!"—*Syn.* **symptom,** best restricted to a sign of disorder.—See **expectancy,** the state resulting from a **sign. 3.** a stimulus that substitutes for another in evoking a response—e.g., the conditioned stimulus in classical **conditioning (1). 4.** a conventional gesture standing for a word or words, or for an idea: e.g., nodding for "yes," the sign language of the deaf. **5.** (*math.*) the positive or negative quantity of a mathematical expression; or, the printed or written marks ($+$ or $-$) for positive or negative; or, more generally, any mark having a fixed conventional meaning: e.g., Σ, the sign for algebraic summation.—*v.* **sign,** to communicate by making signs; **signify,** to show by sign, to be a sign of, to have meaning.

signal: *n.* **1.** a **sign** communicated by one person to another in order to indicate that the time and place for a certain action are at hand.—*Cp.* **symbol. 2.** any perceptible or measurable event capable of being transmitted, i.e., of happening in one place as a consequence of happening at another: e.g., a radio or radar signal. ➤Any number of intermediary events (which may or may not resemble either the antecedent or the consequent signals) may intervene and be the means of transmitting the signal. Ideally, the consequent event should be identical in all relevant respects to the antecedent, but signal transmission is never perfect. Usually, a signal is so related to a code that a message can be sent by means of the signals. Since all stimuli applied to the periphery of the body are transmitted to the brain, it has become fashionable to call them signals; but this usage suggests, if it does not rigorously imply, the theory that the stimulus is **isomorphic** with the events in the brain. It has also become fashionable to call the **neural impulse** a signal—a usage that is consistent if each neuron is considered a transmission *unit.* **3.** a pattern of stimuli to which an animal responds. ➤This meaning is so close to the other two as to be confusing, and is unnecessary. **Colligation,**

stimulus pattern, object, and situation are all available for this meaning.—*v.* signal.

signature: see local sign.

sign/eyelash: see eyelash sign.

sign gestalt: (*E. C. Tolman*) a complex object that is reacted to by the expectation that certain kinds of behavior will lead to a goal.—See expectancy.—*Syn.* SIGN OBJECT.

significance: *n.* 1. a meaning; that which is signified. 2. importance; value; that which makes a difference; that property of a communication whereby it yields knowledge and/or leads to action on the part of the person to whom it is addressed.—*Syn.* sense (7), meaning, PURPORT, IMPORT. (See meaning at end.)—*adj.* significant. —*v.* signify.

significance ratio = critical ratio.

significance/statistical: (*stat.*) the degree of probability that, in an infinite series of measurements of the kind in question, the value or score actually obtained will not by chance alone occur with significant frequency, hence can be attributed to something other than chance. ➤There are many TESTS OF STATISTICAL SIGNIFICANCE: see critical ratio, *t* (3), *F* test. ¶Statistical *stability* has been suggested as a preferred synonym, since it seems almost impossible to divorce the term statistical significance from the idea that the *score* is important or of significant magnitude, though neither is meant. If significance is to continue in use, authors are advised to employ the full expression, statistical significance, even when the context seems to make clear that the general meaning of significance is not intended.

significant difference: a difference between two statistics, computed from separate samples, which is of such magnitude that the probability that the samples were drawn from different universes is less than some defined limit.—*Syn.* STABLE DIFFERENCE.— See stability/statistical.

significant figure: (*math.*) 1. a figure or digit that expresses a certain magnitude. ➤In the number .206, 2, 0, and 6 are all significant; but in .026 the 0 is not an expression of magnitude but only a means of placing the decimal point. 2. a figure or digit expressing a magnitude large enough, under stated conditions, to have meaning or importance and hence to be included in future operations. ➤If the average number of persons employed is calculated to be 304.27, it would be better for most purposes to regard the fraction .27 as not significant.

significant gesture or symbol: (*G. H. Mead*) a gesture that has the same meaning for others that it has for its maker.

significate: *n.* (*E. C. Tolman*) that which is signified; any remembered or imagined object pointed to by present stimuli. ➤In classical *conditioning, the unconditioned stimulus is the significate of the conditioned stimulus. In maze problems and the like the food in the food box is the significate of the perceptual cues which lead to that goal. The significate is the object of expectancy.

significs = semantics.

signified object = significate.

sign language: 1. a means of communication by the use of gesture. 2. more specif. a highly developed system of conventionalized gestures used as a substitute for speech in communication with the deaf, or among the deaf themselves. It does not include finger spelling.

sign learning: 1. (*E. C. Tolman*) a theory of learning maintaining that the organism learns relations between signs and what they stand for, rather than sequences of movements. ➤A rat is said to learn that the red light over one maze alley signifies food, as opposed to the view that the rat learns the series of movements that carries him into the red-labeled alley.—*Cp.* place *learning, response *learning. 2. (*O. H. Mowrer*) simple conditioning in which one stimulus comes to be a substitute for another in eliciting a response.—*Cp.* solution learning.

sign/local: see local sign.

sign object: see sign gestalt.

sign-significate relation = expectancy.

silent: *adj.* (*W. Kohler*) a proposed synonym for unconscious. ➤In many contexts, unconscious is at least verbally inconsistent: e.g., *unconscious* desire, *desire* being by definition a conscious process. Many psychic structures may be said to operate silently part of the time.

similar form: see form/comparable.

similarities test: 1. a test requiring statement of the similarities between two objects or ideas. 2. a test in which objects are to be grouped according to their similarities.

similarity: *n.* 1. correspondence between data in some determinable respect. 2. the property of two or more data of having some, but not all, their characteristics exactly the same; = partial identity. ➤This statement directly contradicts the holistic, and implies an elementaristic position. (For the former, an identical part in two different wholes is a self-contradiction.) It is therefore somewhat theory begging, a theory in the guise of a definition. 3. the property of stimulus objects whereby they elicit identical responses. ➤This also is an explanation in the guise of a definition. For the fact referred to

EQUIVALENCE OF STIMULI is correct.—*Syn.* LIKENESS, **resemblance** (generally restricted to perceived similarity).—*adj.* **similar.**

similarity/coefficient of: (*stat.*) a measure of relationship based on the difference of the average deviations of observations measured from the two diagonals of a correlation table.

similarity/law of: the **associationist** principle that a thought, idea, or feeling tends to recall to mind another that resembles it in some respect.—*Syn.* LAW OF RESEMBLANCE, since it is only observed similarity that is effective. The law was reinterpreted in later associationism as a special case of **contiguity.**

similarity paradox: the paradox that similarity in the materials to be learned may have opposite effects when they are presented for learning in close sequence: on the one hand, as similarity of tasks increases, the amount learned per presentation tends to decrease; on the other hand, when the two tasks are of maximum similarity—i.e., are practically identical—performance of either task is **practice** of the other, a condition favorable to learning. ➤In certain specific experiments, amount learned plotted against the degree of similarity takes the form of a spread-out fishhook. This is the SKAGGS-ROBINSON PHENOMENON.

similarity/pattern: see **pattern similarity/coefficient of.**

simple: *adj.* 1. elementary; not further analyzable.—*Ant.* **complex.** 2. easy to understand or do.—*Ant.* SUBTLE or DIFFICULT. —*n.* **simplicity.**

simple sampling: see **sampling/random.**

simplest path/law of: (*Gestalt*) the principle that behavior always follows the simplest path open to the organism at the time. This is a variant of the **law of *least action.**

simple structure: (*stat.*) the stage (usually the final stage) in factor analysis in which such mathematical simplicity is achieved that no further mathematical operations are indicated—at least not for mathematical reasons. In this stage, the **factors** are so defined or located (by **rotation**) that the sum of the number of factors required to describe each test is a minimum, the **factor axes** having been rotated so as to maximize the number of zero correlations of tests with factors. ➤The requirement is that *each* test is to be explained as the product of as few factors as possible without increasing the *total* number of factors required for the correlational data being analyzed. Some authorities rotate the axes further, if necessary, to obtain a definition of the factor that can be psychologically interpreted, though usually with care not to disturb the mathematical simplicity of simple structure.

simulation: *n.* resemblance, esp. false resemblance; shamming; deception; pretense; **malingering.**—*Cp.* imitation.

simulator: *n.* a training situation or, more often, a training device that employs, in the learning period, conditions and equipment obviously like those in which the learner is to perform later.

simultaneity (sī″məl·tə·nē′ə·ti): *n.* the occurrence of two or more phenomena at the same time.—*adj.* **simultaneous.**

sin: *n.* conduct that violates what the offender believes to be a supernaturally ordained moral code.—*adj.* **sinful.**—*abstr. n.* **sinfulness,** the quality of action that is sinful.

sine wave: (*phys.*) a wave, made up of the vibrations of the particles in the transmitting medium, that rises to its maximum and falls to its minimum in equal time and by smooth gradation. ➤Both sound and light

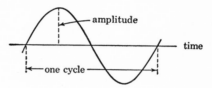

Sine curve graph of a pure tone.

have sine waves as physical stimuli. The conventional graphic (not the pictorial) representation of a sine wave is a curve with the formula $y = A \sin px$, or $y = \cos px$, where A is amplitude and p is 2π times the frequency.—*Syn.* SINUSOIDAL WAVE.

single action: a type of motor activity in which a single coordinated response follows a given stimulus pattern.—*Contr. w.* **serial behavior,** in which the stimulus initiates a sequence of responses.

single factor inheritance: (*genet.*) the control of the genetic portion of variability of a trait predominantly by **genes** at a single position on a particular **chromosome.**

singleton: *n.* a mammal born without litter mates; a singly born individual.—*Contr. w.* **twin, triplet, multiple birth.**

single variable/law of: the rule of experimentation that, if the treatments applied to equivalent groups or individuals differ in only one respect, any resulting differences in effects may be attributed to the single respect in which the treatments differ.

sinistrad (sin′is·trad): *adj., adv.* toward the left. ➤SINISTRAD WRITING is from right to left, as in Arabic or Urdu and in mirror writing.

sinistral (sin′is·trəl): *adj.* pertaining to the left side of the body.—*n.* a person who prefers the left side of the body in motor performances; a left-handed or a left-eyed person.—*Contr. w.* **dextral.**

sinistrality (-tral′ə·ti): *n.* preference for using the left side of the body in motor activity, esp. the left hand.—*Contr. w.* **dextrality, ambidextrality.**—*adj.* **sinistral.**

sinusoid (sī′nus·oid): *n.* any of the class of simple harmonic, vibratory motions, such as the **sine wave.** Any such wave can be described by its **frequency, amplitude,** and **phase angle.**—*adj.* **sinusoidal.**

$_sI_R$: This group of symbols is entered as if written *I.*

sitophobia (sī″tō·fō′bi·ə): *n.* morbid aversion to eating.—See **bogus erudition.**

situ: see **in situ.**

situation: *n.* **1.** a place or position. **2.** a combination of circumstances affecting a person; a complex or **gestalt** of stimuli. **3.** (*topol.*) a part (or all) of a **life space** described in terms of its content or meaning. The situation may endure over long periods or be momentary.

➤It is possible to order the determiners of organismic action along a continuum of relative complexity: stimulus, object, surround, situation, environment, field. **Stimulus** is least complex. **Object,** in its usual meaning, comes next: it is a particular thing, having mass and spatial limits. (But note that another meaning of object is that to which the subject reacts—anything, including unreal things or objects of thought and imagination.) **Surround** includes *all* the things currently affecting the organism; it does not usually refer to relations or events. **Situation** includes both things and events, and is thus broader than surround, although it need not include all the things. **Environment** is very inclusive and has something of the notion of permanence, whereas surround and situation are temporary. Environment also may include those physical circumstances that surround but do not palpably affect behavior, though potentially capable of doing so. (See also **milieu.**) **Field** is most inclusive, since it denotes (or in a context may denote) the past and the present, the inner and the outer, the real and the imaginary determinants of action. It emphasizes a dynamic interaction rather than the influence of one aspect upon the organism.

situational analysis: study of the behavior characteristically associated with natural or lifelike situations, as contrasted with contrived or laboratory situations.

situational index: an aspect or property of an object or situation that defines its **valence** and its qualitative relation to a particular trait or drive. E.g., the cry ᴏ "Fire!" in a theater defines the comple situation as fearful.

situationalism: *n.* a point of view tha stresses the influence of the present situa tion in determining behavior. It contras with emphasis upon the past, and with em phasis upon factors in the personality.—Se **psychology/divisions and schools of, V**

situational personality syndrome: (*M Mead*) a pattern of social behaviors, be lieved by the individual (usually implicitly to be possible for him, which he tries ou to see how they fit a new kind of cultur or social situation: e.g., the behavior of young immigrant trying to adapt to a ne country.

situational sampling: the observation an recording of a person's behavior in certa recurring real-life situations that are re garded as being representative and cruci in respect to certain traits or behavic trends.

situational stress test: see **stress test.**

situational test: a measure of a person's r action to a situation that requires an actu adaptive response, rather than a mere "test response. The situation may be contrived b the examiner but must be recognized ɑ posing a real problem to be solved, inde pendent of its status as a test. E.g., will a applicant for a position scramble to pic up the prospective employer's pencil?

situational therapy = **milieu therapy.**

situational unit: (*K. Lewin*) an elemeɴ of a psychological **field** that serves to dᴇ termine the direction and velocity of bᴇ havior, i.e., the meaning of a psychologic event. ➤The unit is relatively compleɺ being extended in time (not momentary and including many objects. Less inclɯ sive units may form part of more inclɯ sive units, yet the smallest has its ow quasi-independent meaning.

situation/analytic: see **analytic situatioɴ**

situation/conflict: see **conflict situatioɴ**

situation/forced-cue: see **forced-cue tecɦ nique.**

situationism = **situationalism.**

situation/overlapping: (*topol.*) a situa tion that shares a part of the **life spac** with another situation. ➤The person generally located in the common part. Sᴇ **psychologists** would postulate that tɦ person is a part of every situation; henc all situations are, at least to that exteɴ overlapping.

situation-process: *n.* a phrase that, b hyphenation, draws attention to the faᴄ that what is described as if it were a relativeɩ stable pattern of stimuli or objects actually always in process of change.

situation psychosis = **reactive psychosi**

16 D scale: (*N. Bayley*) a derived score fᴇ

intelligence. The scoring unit is a multiple of the standard deviation from the mean score at age 16 on several standardized tests. ➤The scale permits comparison of growth at different ages, using tests having different age ranges and different raw scoring systems. Age 16 was taken as the reference point for convenience only.

six-three-three plan: the division of the school years into elementary, junior high, and senior high school.—*Cp. w.* division into eight years of elementary plus four of high school, and with the six-two-four plan.

size-age confusion: the tendency to judge age by size, hence, to expect behavior appropriate to size rather than to age.

size constancy: the tendency to perceive a familiar object as of a certain standard size, despite moderate variation in its distance from the observer or in other viewing conditions.—See object *constancy.

size-weight illusion: the perception of a visually large object as heavier, when hefted, than a visually smaller object of objectively equal weight.

Skaggs-Robinson phenomenon = similarity paradox.

skeletal: *adj.* pertaining to bones, or to all the bones collectively (the skeleton). ➤A SKELETAL MUSCLE is one that is attached, at least at one end, to a bone.—See **muscle/striate.**

skeletal age: see **age/carpal.**

skelic index (skel'ik): (*anthropom.*) the ratio between the length of the legs and the trunk.

skepticism: *n.* the attitude of unbelief, of doubt. ➤Strictly speaking, it should be distinguished from **agnosticism** (the attitude that one does not know) and from the attitude of *denial*; but these distinctions are logical and it is doubtful that the underlying psychological attitude is different.—*adj.* **skeptical.**—*pers. n.* **skeptic.**

skewness or *sk*: *n.* the extent to which a **frequency curve** is twisted to one side or other, so that it extends farther to one side of the mode than the other. ➤Skewness is said to be toward the longer tail; it is POSITIVE when the longer tail of the curve is of cases greater than the mode, NEGATIVE when the longer tail is less than the mode.—*ant.* **symmetry.**—*adj., v.* **skew.**

skiascope (skī'ə·skōp): *n.* an instrument for determining the refractive condition of the eye.—*Syn.* **retinoscope.**

skill: *n.* ability to perform complex motor acts with ease, precision, and adaptability to changing conditions. Skill is evaluated in terms of end results.—*Cp.* **skills/higher level.**

skill/basic: see **basic skills.**

skill/fundamental: a skill that is required for further progress; esp., one of the FUNDAMENTAL EDUCATIONAL SKILLS: adding, subtracting, reading, writing. ➤Ironically, thinking is not classed as a fundamental educational skill.—*Cp.* **basic skills, skills/higher level.**

skill sequence: a performance in which waste motion has been eliminated and the separate component responses have been integrated into units: e.g., the sequence of movements in serving a tennis ball.

skills/higher level: (*R. H. Seashore*) work methods or behavior patterns applicable to a variety of concrete tasks, in contrast with the particular skills embodied in one task. The higher level skills include **set, attitude,** "tricks of the trade," **learning to learn,** and other qualitative variations in ways of reacting. ➤E.g., in reading, grouping words into meaningful phrases is a higher level skill. It is not necessary that such skills be preceded by lower level skills: they are "higher" because more general in application.

skills/higher level study: (*F. P. Robinson*) an application of the concept of **higher level *skills** to problems of academic learning or study methods. The skills are habitualized general methods empirically proved useful, such as preview of headings before reading, immediate review, effective note-taking, use of the library, etc. The SQ3R method embodies five higher level skills.

skill/study: any technique used in studying, such as outlining, skimming, note-taking.—See **higher level study *skills.**

skimming: *n.* a method of rapid reading in which the reader does not attempt to read the complete text but either (*a*) looks for certain special items (SEARCH SKIMMING), or (*b*) attempts to get the general idea of the passage.

skin: *n.* the external covering of many animals. It consists of two main layers, the **epidermis** on the outside and the DERMA beneath it.—*adj.* **skin** (*syn.* **dermal, cutaneous**).

skin erotism: erotic pleasure derived from scratching or stroking the skin.

Skinner box: an enclosure provided with one or more devices whose correct operation brings the animal either escape from the enclosure or some other reward. The escape mechanism may be a bar to be depressed, a key or button to be pecked, a loop to be pulled, or a panel to be pushed, depending on the anatomic conformation and the habits of the animal to be tested.

skin potential: the electric potential of the skin.—See **electrodermal response.**

skipping = grade skipping.

slang: *n.* **1.** the jargon of a particular calling. ➤A fair proportion of this dictionary must be adjudged slang in this sense. **2.**

language that is widely current but not (yet) embodied in conventional and sober use: (among others) neologisms, extravagant or forced figures of speech, or grotesque distortions of accepted speech.

slave system = servomechanism.

sleep: *n.* a special state of the organism characterized by relative inactivity, reduced consciousness, and reduced responsiveness to external stimuli. ➤All these characteristics are found also in other states, but sleep is nonetheless a distinct, if as yet (psychologically) ill-described, condition.

sleep center: a portion of the brain (in the hypothalamus): if it is surgically removed or electrically stimulated, the animal goes to sleep.

sleeper effect: a change in public opinion taking place after an opinion survey has been made. The result is to make the survey look more inaccurate than it was.

sleeping sickness: see **encephalitis.**

sleepwalking = somnambulism.

slip comparison: in **paired comparison** experiments, comparison of the second term with a member of the preceding pair.

slip of the tongue or **of the pen:** the inadvertent introduction of an incorrect or irrelevant word or phrase that changes the intended meaning of the sentence. ➤It is interpreted in psychoanalysis, and now quite generally, as representing a "true" but repressed meaning or wish of the writer or speaker. (But what one intends to say may be a more genuine expression of what one really means or feels than what "slips out," even though the latter is significant.)—*Syn.* (*L.*) LAPSUS LINGUAE or LAPSUS CALAMI, respectively.

slope: *n.* (*math.*) **1.** the inclination of a line from any base line; esp., the angle of a line with an **abscissa. 2.** the tangent of the angle between the line and the abscissa.

slope of a curve: (*math.*) the slope of a line tangent to the curve at any given point. It is a value that constantly changes.

slow: *adj.* often applied, rather untechnically, to a person of slightly retarded development.—See **slow-learning.**

slow-learning: *adj.* of a child who is definitely handicapped if kept in school with his age-mates but who is capable of profiting from academic instruction that permits him to advance more slowly. ➤There is no implication that the slowness is irremediable. The term is probably a misnomer. The children in question are slow in developing, not necessarily slower to learn at the level of development attained. They are slow because unready.—*Syn.* **dull normal, retarded,** both denoting approximately the same kind of individuals but emphasizing somewhat different characteristics.

slow motion: the projection of a motion picture at reduced speed so that the motions pictured can be more easily analyzed.

ₛLₑ: (*C. Hull*) reaction threshold, the stimulus strength that will just barely evoke the response.

slychology: *n.* a coined term for a prostitution of psychology by slyness, ingratiation and managing people for the manager's profit. ➤The term denotes one popular concept of psychology, not without its obvious exemplifications.

small sample technique: a group of statistical procedures and/or experimental designs that permit guarded but dependable conclusions from a small number of cases.

smell: *n.* **1.** the sense or sense modality of **olfaction. 2.** a particular sense datum or sense quality mediated by stimulation of the olfactory membrane.

smooth curve: a curve that does not change direction suddenly or erratically.—*Distg. fr* **smoothed *curve.**

smoothed curve: see **curve/smoothed.**

smoothing: *n.* (*stat.*) any method of fitting a **smooth curve** to a curve that is irregular because of sampling error, without falsifying the characteristics that belong to the phenomenon being investigated ➤There are several mathematical techniques for smoothing, and it may often be done freehand to a reasonable approximation.—*Syn.* GRADUATION.

smooth muscle: see **muscle/striate.**

smoothness: *n.* **1.** the complex tactual sense datum or percept elicited when pressure stimuli are very small and very close together. **2.** a characteristic of tonal impressions that fuse evenly.

Snellen chart or **test:** a rough test for acuity of vision consisting of specially designed letters of standardized sizes to be read at a specified distance. ➤The test seems deceptively easy to use but readily leads to false conclusions when interpreted by untrained persons.

snow: *n.* (*slang*) cocaine. A SNOWBIRD is a cocaine addict.

snow blindness: a temporary impairment of vision in which some objects are blacked out and all other objects are tinged with red. It is caused by long exposure to very bright light, such as that of glaciers or snow fields, welding operations, etc.

sociability: *n.* inclination to seek the company of others and to be friendly and agreeable toward them.—*adj.* **sociable.**

sociability rating: an index of the proportion of a person's time given to activities directly involving others.

social: *adj.* of whatever relates to the interaction of two or more persons or to the influence of one upon another. ➤The term is designedly very broad; comparatively few psychological phenomena are nonsocial. In phrases, it is employed when the social aspect is to be emphasized. Thus, **adjustment** (in man) inevitably involves many social interactions; **social *adjustment** refers to changes in behavior that specifically and importantly alter one's relations with other persons.—See also **social object, social phenomenon, societal.**

social action: 1. action by a group of persons as a group; collective endeavor. **2.** organized effort to change institutions, customs, or group relationships. ➤*Distg. fr.* **social work,** which has its focus on the individual or small groups. Social action might endeavor to alter or restore certain kinds of family relationship in the whole society, social work to improve the pattern in a particular family.—*Syn.* SOCIAL or POLITICAL REFORM.

social adaptation: see **adaptation/social.**

social adaptiveness: a complex of the characteristics enabling a person to "get along." ➤It thus includes social adjustment techniques, social intelligence, ability to plan ahead, and certain dynamic or motivational qualities. Convenient as it may seem to have a single term for the net outcome, it is doubtful that such diverse components should be included under one term.

social adjustment: see **adjustment/social.**

social age: see **age/social.**

social aggregate: all the persons occupying a geographical area defined by the observer; a group of persons in propinquity, no other relation being necessarily involved.—*Syn.* **aggregation** (*prefd.*).

social anthropology: the behavioral or social science dealing chiefly with the culture of nonliterate societies.—*Syn.* **cultural *anthropology.**

social ascendancy: mobility upward, esp. in respect to power, prestige, and influence. ➤*Distg. fr.* **ascendance,** the tendency to control the behavior of associates.

social assimilation: the process whereby cultures or subcultures are merged into a homogeneous unit, generally by the disappearance or transformation of cultural elements of the less dominant group. Complete uniformity of individual behavior is not necessary.—*Syn.* **cultural *assimilation.**—*Cp.* **acculturation.**

social atom: see **atom/social.**

social attitude: see **attitude/social.**

social behavior: 1. behavior influenced by the presence and behavior of other persons. **2.** behavior controlled by organized society. **3.** behavior that is directed at or seeks to influence others. **4.** = **group behavior.**—*Distg. fr.* socialized behavior (see **socialization**).

social being: 1. one who can live normally only as a member of society. **2.** a person who enjoys the company of others and who usually so acts as to further the welfare, and esp. the sociability, of the group.

social casework: see **social work.**

social class: see **class/social.**

social climate: 1. see **climate/psychological. 2.** collectively, those folkways and mores of a community or larger unit that seem to the social scientist to be characteristic of the society.

social climbing: a conscious effort to rise from one **social *class** to another.—*Cp.* **social mobility.**

social code: a system of regulations having group sanctions.

social cohesion: that property of a group which holds it together; a condition of a group whose members feel more inclined to remain within it than to leave it.

social consciousness: 1. awareness that certain experiences involve persons. **2.** awareness that experiences are shared with others. **3.** = **collective consciousness. 4.** sensitivity to the needs of people in society; interest in social issues.

social control: 1. regulation of behavior of individuals by the group, community, or social institutions. **2.** the effort to regulate social institutions in the interests of the whole social group.

social convention: see **convention.**

social decrement: see **social increment.**

social distance: 1. the relative accessibility of one person or group to association with another person or group; the degree of intimacy with which a person is willing to associate with another person or group.—*Cp.* **Social Distance Scale. 2.** the amount of difference between two persons or two groups in **mores** and **ideals.**—*Syn.* social (or group) difference (*prefd.*). **3.** = **distance/psychic (2).**

Social Distance Scale/Bogardus: a rating scheme in which the rater indicates the degree of intimacy to which he would be willing to accept a designated person or a representative of a social group. ➤The scale has seven levels of acceptance: as close relation by marriage, as member in a club or as a chum, as a neighbor, as employee in one's place of work, as citizen, as a visitor to one's country, nonacceptance on any terms.

social drive: a **drive** to satisfy social needs; a drive that impels to the attainment of certain kinds of relations with persons rather than to the acquisition of physical objects.

social dynamics: the causation of changes in culture, institutions, or societies. ➤*Cp.* SOCIAL EVOLUTION, a descriptive account of such changes.

social facilitation: enhancement of a motivated behavior by social stimulation.

➤There is a tendency to restrict the term to enhancement by incidental social stimuli, such as the mere presence of others; but it is difficult to deny to such social stimuli as encouragement, urging, prodding, or even threats, a role in social facilitation.—*Distg. fr.* **rivalry** or **competition.**

social fact: 1. any direct interaction or relation between persons. **2.** any result of social interaction. ➤This meaning needs more careful restriction than it usually gets. *All* behavior is directly or indirectly the result of social interaction. See **social factor. 3.** a form of behavior acquired from the culture.—*Syn.* (for **3**) CULTURAL FACT (*prefd.*).

social factor: any determinant of behavior attributable to a relationship between persons. It refers either to a present social stimulus or to the influence of earlier social behavior. ➤This term is preferred to **social fact,** first, because it does not imply any nonsocial behavior and, second, because it recognizes that nonsocial factors codetermine behavior.

social group: see **group/social.**

social group work: the guidance of leisure-time activities of persons in groups to further their development through group experience.—*Cp.* **social work.**

social growth: the development of the individual in those traits that facilitate social interaction. ➤Social growth is not limited to growth in conformity; much social growth lies quite outside the range of what is expected by the culture.

social heritage: the totality of social institutions and culture traits transmitted from one generation to the next; the influence upon present-day society of the accumulated experience and material achievements of past generations.—*Syn.* social transmission (see **transmission 5**) (*prefd.*).

social hygiene: properly, any effort to promote healthy social relations; more often, a euphemism for **sex hygiene.** ➤Social hygiene often means merely the effort to control prostitution and venereal disease.

social image: (*T. Burrow*) the deeply ingrained and affectively toned ideas and beliefs current in a given society but nonetheless lacking demonstrable objective basis.

social imperative: a rigidly binding custom.

social incentive: a person, object, or state of affairs that can (*a*) satisfy a **social need,** (*b*) incite to activity by arousing a **social drive** otherwise latent, or (*c*) provide occasions for satisfying social activities.

social increment: the increase in performance when a person is in the presence of others as compared with when he is alone. ➤*Contr. w.* SOCIAL DECREMENT, the loss in

performance. A gain in quality is a SOCIAL SUPERVALENT.—*Cp.* **social facilitation.**

social inheritance = social transmission (see **transmission 5**).

social instinct = **gregariousness.**

social intelligence: see **intelligence, abstract.**

social interaction: the mutual stimulation of one person by another and the response that result; the mutual modification of the behavior of individuals.

sociality: *n.* **1.** that characteristic of a person which leads to cooperation with others —*Syn.* **sociability,** somewhat broader in meaning. **2.** = **gregariousness. 3.** (*A Gesell*) a certain outgoing responsiveness to other persons that makes a person, particularly a child, attractive. **4.** the quality of being **socialized.**

socialization: *n.* **1.** the processes whereby person (esp., a child) acquires sensitivity to social stimuli (esp., the pressures and obligations of group life) and learns to get along with, and to behave like, others in his group or culture; the process of becoming social being; or the result of those processes. ➤Although it is a major part of the acquisition of **personality,** socialization should not be treated as a synonym for that term.—*Cp.* **acculturation. 2.** bringing industry or any other institution under social control for the benefit of all.—*v.* **socialize** (which see for other meanings).

socialize: *v.* **1.** to make social. **2.** to promote **socialization. 3.** to **sublimate** an impulse. **4.** to mingle freely with others, esp. in playful activities. **5.** (*educ.*) to promote personal interaction (between teacher and pupils, and esp. among pupils) as a mean of education.—See **socialized instruction.**

socialized delinquent = **pseudosocial child.**

socialized instruction: a method of instruction that maximizes the interaction of student with student, the teacher serving chiefly to keep the process going and within bounds.

socialized speech: speech in which a person, in addressing himself to another, considers the other's point of view, tries in some way to influence him, or exchange ideas with him.—*Contr. w.* egocentric speech.

social maladjustment: see **maladjustment/social.**

social maturity: the degree to which an individual has acquired the social and socialized behaviors that are usual and expected for his age, or for his age and status or the social behavior characteristic of the supposedly typical adult. ➤It is by no means clear just what behaviors should be included and the term has a vague reference.

social mind: 1. the characteristic level of

thinking and acting of a given community. —*Approx. syn.* public *opinion. 2. = group mind.

social-mindedness: *n.* sensitivity to socioeconomic problems, awareness of their complexity, and belief that improvement is possible.

social mobility: movement within a given culture from one class to another, esp., movement upward from a class of lower to one of higher status; or the degree to which a society or community permits such movement.—See class/social.

social motive: a motive that is stimulated, and in part satisfied, by other persons: e.g. the desire for approval. ➤*Contr. w.* physiological *motives, which are satisfied by a change in physiological functioning. But social and physiological motives often, or usually, fuse: e.g., eating in the company of friends.—*Syn.* PERSONAL-SOCIAL MOTIVE.

social need: in man, a need whose satisfaction requires the responses of a person, usually another person, but occasionally oneself.—*Cp.* social motive, affiliative need, status need.

social network: see network/social.

social neuter: a group member who for any reason (including his own indifference) has an insignificant influence on group activity.—*Cp.* instigator, isolate.

social norm: see norm/social.

social object: a person or persons, or a group of persons. ➤Person here includes any animal that seems to the reactor to be a fellow creature. It also includes imaginary or supernatural persons and personifications.

social organism: see organism/social.

social organization: see organization/social.

social phenomenon: any datum, object, or event, the nature or existence of which depends upon persons other than the observer. ➤All persons are themselves social phenomena, as well as everything they are perceived as doing, or as having done or made.

social pressure: coercion exerted by the generalized social atmosphere. ➤*Distg. fr.* customs, taboos, laws, or commands, all of which are more formalized and explicit.

social process: any social change distinctive enough to have a name.

social psychology: the branch of psychology that studies the phenomena of social behavior; the study of the behavior of individuals and of groups in a social environment, esp. as that behavior is affected by the presence or influence of other individuals. ➤The chief difficulty is in distinguishing it from sociology. Many writers hold that social psychology restricts itself to the individual in interaction with others,

in contrast with the group taken as such. But the same writers often include consideration of how the individual group member affects the group. (Thus, so-called racial differences are generally treated as part of social psychology.) ¶A clear formal distinction may be made in terms of the explanatory concepts utilized. Social psychology utilizes the concepts that are derived from the study of the behavior of individuals, sociology the concepts derived from the study of institutions and of social groups as such. This distinction is not universally accepted; and, even if it were, it would be difficult to apply concretely. Hence, social psychology is actually a hybrid discipline that inherits problems, data, and concepts from both parents.—See psychology/divisions and schools of, II.

social quotient: the ratio between social *age and chronological *age.

social reality: 1. everything that exists, viewed as affecting social phenomena. 2. the opinions and beliefs that are held in common by members of a collectivity and that furnish a basis for validation of individual beliefs; "what everybody knows."

social reinforcement: the strengthening of a response or response tendency by social *stimuli; strengthening the tendency to make a given response by insuring that it wins a social reward such as approval, a parent's love, attention.

social repression: the control by collective action of conduct that deviates from the usual, expected, or approved.—*Syn.* SOCIAL RESTRAINT (*prefd.*), SOCIAL SUPPRESSION.

social restraint = social repression.

social role = role (2) or (3). ➤Since all roles (even that of an actor) are social, the term is redundant, but it is frequently encountered. Perhaps it is felt that a four-letter word such as role cannot by itself carry the necessary professional prestige.

social sanction: see sanction.

social scale: the hierarchy of social classes, and the standards for assigning persons to their places in the hierarchy.

social sciences: the sciences concerned with man living in relation to other men in a social environment, esp. social anthropology, sociology, and social psychology; more generally, the fields of study concerned with social organization and institutions: (in addition to the above) economics, history, political science, economic geography, law. —*Cp.* behavioral science.

social selection: the differential survival and reproduction of those individuals in a species who best meet certain (vaguely defined) social criteria. ➤Its best defined form is sexual selection, the differential reproduction of those who can best attract and hold a mate or mates. But other social factors influence survival and/or reproduction: e.g., certain beliefs, or certain class or group memberships.

social self: see **self/social.**

social sensitivity: ready awareness of the less obvious clues that show how another person feels. ➤Properly speaking, it does not imply a sympathetic response; but since sensitivity and **sympathy** so often go together, one term may be used for the other.

social situation: that part of the psychological environment or **psychological** *field at any given time which consists of persons and their relationships; the totality of all the directly perceived social influences impinging on a person at a given time.

social space: (*K. Lewin*) a **region** having certain geometrical properties that represent social data. ➤The social space is not conceived as being metaphorical; it is said to be a real empirical space. See **space.** A **sociogram,** though derived from a different psychological theory, represents a social space.—*Cp.* **hodology, topological psychology.**

social status: a person's position and special function, esp. his **class** membership, as seen and accepted by other members of the social group.—*Cp.* **role.**

social stimulus: see **stimulus/social.**

social stratification: the division of a society into relatively rigid social *classes.

social structure: 1. the pattern of relationships, formal and otherwise, by which any social group is organized. 2. that which makes a social unit a distinct whole, different from others. ➤The differentiation may be in the component parts (subgroups and individuals) and their interrelations; or it may be in the beliefs, folkways, institutions, and other cultural factors.

social studies: those parts of the social sciences that are studied in elementary and high school, usually as integrated subject matter rather than as the separate disciplines of economics, geography, sociology, politics, etc. ➤The term does not include studies (such as English) that merely have a social *aim.*

social supervalent: see **social increment.**

social technique: a social practice engaged in to satisfy either physiological or social needs: e.g., cooperation or competition.

social transmission: see **transmission (5).**

social type: 1. a person who is representative of many others forming a distinct social category. 2. a person whose personality characteristics are primarily molded by social, rather than **somatic,** influences. —*Ant.* body *type. 3. (*pop.*) a person whose interests and activities are mostly social.

social work: activities and services for the improvement of social conditions in a community. It includes **casework** and **social group work.** ➤The definition is too broad

and vague for the actual activities of the social work profession; yet apparently every logical restriction would eliminate activities that do form part of the profession. Examples of social work are district nursing organizations, settlement houses, aid for the needy, recreation. SOCIAL CASEWORKERS deal with individuals or families, usually in connection with a social work institution or service. See also **psychiatric social worker.**

societal: *adj.* pertaining to a **society** or to social groups; derived from social groups; having the character of a society.

society: *n.* 1. mankind as a whole. 2. the social order, in contrast with the individual; the network of social groups within which the person lives. ➤A social order usually has a distinctive **culture (1);** society emphasizes the organization and structure of the network, **culture** the customs, roles, behaviors. 3. a relatively permanent or continuously existent group of persons (organisms). ➤To be permanent implies some degree of organization, interaction, cooperation. Some relatively lowly organisms form societies. **Society** is usually restricted to groups formed of one species only (but *cp.* **symbiosis 2).**

sociocenter: *n.* the person most frequently chosen in a **sociometric test.**

sociocentrism: *n.* taking one's own immediate social group as the standard of excellence, morality, and virtue. ➤Logically, it is a step away from **egocentrism;** but psychologically it merely substitutes the group for the individual self at the center leaving intact most of the attitudes. While the term would seem to include cases where the attitude toward the group is generous sympathetic, and altruistic, it usually connotes a harder and more selfish group-centered behavior.—*Cp.* **ethnocentrism** which is sociocentrism on a larger scale.

sociodrama: *n.* dramatization and **role-playing** used to teach which kinds of behavior are socially desirable.

socioeconomic-free test: see **test/culture-free.**

socioeconomic status: an individual's position in a given society, as determined by wealth, occupation, and social class.

sociogenesis: *n.* the origination of a mode of behavior in social experience, i.e., as a result of past interpersonal behaviors.

sociogenetic: *adj.* 1. (*sociol.*) having to do with the origin of a society. 2. characterizing behavior as determined by social experience.

sociogenous = **sociogenetic (2).**

sociogram: *n.* a map or diagram showing actual interactions, or certain desired or acceptable kinds of interactions, between individual members of a group. ➤Originally the term referred to a diagram that showed the relations of attraction and antagonism revealed by a **sociometric test,** but it has been extended to cover other sorts of relationships. Individuals are represented as circles or squares; lines with arrows show the direction of specified interaction. E.g., A ⟷ B, a very simple sociogram, might represent the fact that A and B are attracted to each other.

sociology: *n.* the behavioral or social science dealing with group life and social organization, chiefly in literate societies.—*Cp.* **anthropology/cultural** and **social psychology.**

sociology/psychological: a branch of sociology that makes extensive use of psychological data and concepts.—*Distg. fr.* **social psychology** (which see).

sociometric test: (*J. L. Moreno*) a variety of rating in which the rater names those in his group who possess certain specified qualifications. ➤Originally the rating was limited to naming those liked or disliked. The rater is usually informed that his rating may be used in the formation of smaller groups such as committees.—*Syn.* **nominating technique,** SOCIOPREFERENCE TECHNIQUE (both *prefd.*).

sociometry (sō″shi·om′ə·tri): *n.* the quantitative study of the psychological properties of populations; specif., the experimental technique of the **sociometric test** and the results obtained from its use. ➤As conceived by J. L. Moreno (who coined the term and developed the sociometric technique), the psychological properties consist of what the group members perceive, think, and feel about the other members. But the term is gradually spreading to quantitative studies of other aspects of group relationships.—*adj.* **sociometric** (sō″shi·ō·met′rik; sō·si-).

socionomics: *n.* the study of the influence of nonsocial factors on the social order or on particular social groups: e.g., the effect of climate.

sociopathic personality disturbance: (*Stan. Psychiat.*) a broad category for disorders in one's relationship with society and with the cultural milieu. It includes **antisocial** and **dyssocial reactions,** sexual *deviations and sexual anomalies.

sociopathy (sō″si·op′ə·thi): *n.* **1.** a vague term covering any kind or complex of abnormal attitudes toward the social environment. **2.** any abnormality manifested by a social group.

sociotype: *n.* a **stereotype** that has a definitely collective origin and is widely or nearly universally held by a group.

socius (sō′shi·us) *n., pl.* **socii** (-ī): (*sociol.*) the individual human organism or person, regarded as a participant in social relationships or social behavior; the elementary unit of sociological analysis.

sodomy (sod′ə·mi): *n.* **1.** (*pop.*, sometimes *legal*) any "unnatural" sexual relations. ➤Since it is almost impossible to define "unnatural" in this context, this usage should be abandoned.—*Syn.* **sexual anomaly. 2.** = anal **coitus.** ➤This is the original and preferred meaning, based on the Biblical story of the city of Sodom. (See Gen. 19.)—*Cp.* **pederasty. 3.** = zooerasty, sexual intercourse between a human and an animal. ➤This historically incorrect usage has become widespread so that it is the only meaning given by one authoritative psychiatric dictionary (which misquotes the Biblical source).—See **homosexuality.**

softening of the brain = **paresis.**

softness: *n.* the tactually perceived quality of a surface that can be easily depressed by the moving member (e.g., the finger) containing the tactual receptors.

soldier's heart = **effort syndrome.**

solipsism (sol′ip·siz″əm): *n.* philosophical view that one can be certain of nothing except one's own experience, thus, that only experiences exist. This is an extreme form of **idealism.**—*adj.* **solipsistic.**

solution: *n.* **1.** resolving the difficulties posed by a problem; finding the answer to a relatively complex question; or the answer thus found. **2.** (*math.*) the determination of the values that fulfill the conditions imposed by an equation.—*v.* **solve.**

solution/auxiliary: see **auxiliary solution.**

solution/comprehensive: see **comprehensive solution.**

solution learning: (*O. H. Mowrer*) *overt *instrumental habit formation; trial-and-error learning under **reinforcement.**—*Cp.* **sign learning (2).**

solution/major: see **major solution.**

solution/neurotic: (*K. Horney*) an unconscious dynamic intrapsychic movement which attempts to neutralize, minimize, avoid, or exclude from awareness an inner conflict, thus relieving tensions and producing partial psychic integration and harmony. **Comprehensive solutions, major solutions,** and **auxiliary solutions** are the forms of neurotic solution.

soma (sō′mə) *n., pl.* **somas, somata: 1.** the body; the body as a whole. **2.** (*genet.*) the SOMAPLASM or SOMATOPLASM, all the cells of the body except the germ cells.—*Cp.* **germ plasm.**

somaesthesia = **somesthesia.**—*Var.* **somaesthesia.**

somaplasm = **soma (2).**

somatic (sō·mat′ik): *adj.* **1.** pertaining to the body rather than to the environment; = **organismic** (*prefd.*). **2.** bodily, not mental. ➤This usage is flagrantly metaphysical unless *bodily* and *mental* are most carefully defined. But **somatic** has acquired fewer metaphysical associations than *bodily,* hence, is preferred.—*Cp.* **psychosomatic,**

mind-body problem. 3. pertaining to the body as a whole in contrast with a particular part; more specif., **4.** pertaining to the rest of the body other than the nervous system. **5.** pertaining to the peripheral **nervous system,** in contrast to the **autonomic.** (A confused usage.) **6.** pertaining to the bodily wall, in contrast either with head and limbs or with the viscera and internal organs. **7.** pertaining to the SOMAPLASM, all the cells of the body except those specialized as germ cells.

somatic compliance: (*psychoan.*) the participation of the soma (or body) with the **psyche** in the production of hysterical symptoms. ➤The term is a recognition that all functional disorders are **psychosomatic,** or a denial that the distinction between **functional** and **organic** is absolute.

somatic disorder: 1. a disorder of the body exclusive of the nervous system. **2.** a disorder of **organic** origin, as *distg. fr.* one of **functional, psychogenic,** or **psychosomatic** origin.—See **functional disorder.**

somatic motor system: the special set of neurons that control the activity of the striate muscles.

somatic nerves: the nerves serving the sense receptors and skeletal muscles, in contrast with visceral nerves, which serve the internal organs. ➤Since **somatic** has other meanings than here implied, the usage is confusing.—*Syn.* **peripheral nerve** (*prefd.*).

somatist (sō′mə·tist): *n.* (*psychiat.*) one who attributes mental disorders to physical causes.

somato- (sō′mə·tō-): combining form meaning *somatic.*

somatogenesis: *n.* **1.** (*embryol.*) the transformation of germ-cell protoplasm into somatic or body-cell protoplasm. **2.** genesis of any **organismic** phenomenon within the tissues of the body; specif., the development of certain behavior patterns because of metabolic changes in tissues.—*Contr. w.* **psychogenesis.**—See **functional disorder.** —*adj.* **somatogenic.**

somatoplasm = **soma (2).**

somatopsychic = **psychosomatic.**

somatopsychosis: *n.* a psychosis in which the chief symptom is a delusion about the patient's own body.

somatosexuality: *n.* **sexuality** expressed in a bodily activity.

somatotonia: *n.* (*W. H. Sheldon*) a personality type marked by a predominance of muscular activity and vigorous bodily assertiveness. It is the correlate of the mesomorphic bodily type (see **ectomorphic**).

somatotype = **type/body.**

somatotypology: *n.* the classification of persons according to body form, generally

with the implication that important physiological and psychological characteristic are correlated with the body forms. ➤Ther are many pseudoscientific, and a few scien tific, somatic typologies.—See **constitu tional type, body *type, ectomorphic.**- *Syn.* SOMATOTYPY.

-some: combining form meaning *bodily o a body.*

somesthesia: *n.* the sense yielding direc impression of bodily condition. It mediated by data from skin, muscles an joints (**kinesthesis**), and from **receptor** within the body. Once called the COMMO SENSE, it contrasts with the special senses c sight, hearing, taste, and smell.—*Va* **somaesthesia, -sis.**—*adj.* **somesthetic.**

somnambulism (som·nam′bū·liz·əm): **1.** walking in one's sleep. **2.** by extensior performing any other fairly complex ac while in a sleeplike condition. ➤No memor of such acts remains in the waking stat but in certain chronic somnambulists the is memory from one trance to another.- *adj.* **somnambulistic.**

somniferous = **soporific.**

somniloquy (som·nil′ə·kwi): *n.* talking i sleep or in hypnotic trance.

somnolence (som′nō·lens): *n.* **1.** (*pop.* sleepiness. **2.** (*med.*) prolonged drowsines a trancelike state that may persist for day threshold.

somnolent detachment: general lack reactivity; drowsiness and lack of interest i the external world, believed to be the re sult of prolonged severe anxiety.—*C apathy.*

som(o)-: combining form meaning *som relating to the soma or body.*

sonant: *n.* a voiced speech sound.—*An* SURD. ➤The sonant-surd distinction is n the same as that of vowel-consonant.

sone (sōn): *n.* the unit of the **ratio *scal** of loudness. It is the loudness of a 100 cycle tone 40 **decibels** above the mea threshold.

sonometer (sō·nom′ə·tər): *n.* an instru ment, used in auditory demonstrations, cor sisting of two or three strings of variab length and adjustable tension stretche above a resonator.

sophism (sof′iz·əm): *n.* **1.** a subtly fals argument, one difficult to refute logicall **2.** = SOPHISTRY, an intentionally deceptiv argument, esp., one in **syllogistic** form; c the intent to deceive by such argument.- *adj.* **sophistic** (sə·fis′tik).

soporific (sō″pə·rif′ik; sop″ə-): *adj.* sleep-inducing agent, such as a barbiturat drug, a dull lecture.—*Syn.* SOMNIFEROU **hypnotic** (*ambig.*).—*n.* **soporific.**

S-O-R = stimulus→organism→response.

sO_R: = (*C. Hull*) **behavioral *oscillatio** —*Distg. fr.* **S-O-R.**

sorting test: a test designed to measu

conceptualization (and aberrations thereof) by presenting the subject with different concrete objects and requiring him to put them into categories of his own choice. ➤In CHAIN SORTING the category changes from moment to moment: a red object is associated with a red object but the latter, being square, is next associated with a square block, which in turn is associated with a wooden tool. LOOSE SORTING uses vague and overgeneralized categories such as "anything small."

-O scale: a way of scoring the MMPI to distinguish between subtle and obvious indicators of personality.

oul: n. 1. (Aristotle) the vital or life principle, that which makes alive. 2. (metaph., theol.) a permanent entity or substance hypothesized as the permanent reality behind mental life.—Syn. spirit.—Ant. body. —See mind-body problem. 3. formerly, but now seldom, = mind, self, or psyche. 4. (pop.) the opposite of the intellect (esp. in the contrast of the soulful versus the mental). ➤The term is so heavily freighted with metaphysical connotations as to be wholly unsuited to scientific discourse. The soul is a proper subject of religious belief or unbelief, but not of empirical investigation.

oul-image: (C. Jung) a part of the psyche that is deep in the unconscious, made up of the animus (or male component) and the anima (or female component).

ound: n. 1. (phys.) energy propagated in longitudinal waves in an elastic medium. ➤See sound wave. If the sound waves are of appropriate frequency and intensity for a given species, they constitute the physical stimulus for hearing. 2. (psychol.) a sense datum or sensory experience dependent upon the impact of such waves at an appropriate rate and intensity upon a functioning auditory mechanism.—Syn. AUDITORY SENSATION, SOUND SENSATION, SOUND SENSE DATA. ➤There are two classes of sound, tones and noises.

ound cage: an apparatus for determining how well sounds can be localized.—See sound perimetry.

ound energy flux: the average in ergs per second (over one full cycle) of the rate at which an acoustic stimulus is delivered through a given area.

ound flutter = flicker/auditory.

ound hammer: a device (used in reaction-time experiments) consisting of a heavy piece of metal whose fall upon a metal plate simultaneously produces a sound signal and closes an electric circuit that starts a recording apparatus.

ound intensity: 1. (phys.) the sound energy flux per unit area, perpendicular to the direction of propagation. ➤For psy-

chological purposes, this is measured at the eardrum. The unit is ergs per second per square centimeter. 2. (psychol.) the quantitative attribute of sound; the loudness. ➤It is a function primarily of the physical intensity, but also of frequency and of the properties of the total perceptual field.

sound perimetry: the determination of the precision with which a subject can localize a sound coming from different positions in space. ➤Sounds of equal loudness are presented at equal distances from different positions in front, in back, and from both sides, the subject being required to indicate where the sound came from.

sound pressure level: the intensity of a sound stated in decibels based on a reference intensity or "zero" point of 0.0002 dynes pressure per cm^2. ➤The reference intensity is set at this point because it corresponds with the modal absolute *threshold.

sound/sensation level of: the intensity of a sound expressed in decibels above its absolute *threshold level.

sound shadow: the area from which a sound is blocked off when an object opaque to sound and many times the dimensions of the sound wave is interposed.—Syn. ACOUSTIC SHADOW.

sound spectrograph: an electric device that indicates the changes in the intensity-frequency pattern of sounds as a function of time.

sound substitution: any replacement of one speech sound by another: e.g., wun for run.

sound unit = phone.

sound wave: a progressive longitudinal vibratory disturbance made up of alternating areas of condensation and rarefaction in an elastic medium, propagated from an oscillating source of energy in cycles between about 20 and 50,000 per second. If the successive waves form a regular or periodic pattern, they give rise to a tone, if an aperiodic pattern, to noise. In the SIMPLE SOUND WAVE, the periodic pattern that repeats itself is a sine (or sinusoidal) wave; it is the stimulus to a pure *tone. COMPLEX or COMPOUND SOUND WAVES, if periodic, can be analyzed, according to Fourier's law, into a series of simple waves. Complex periodic waves are the stimuli to compound *tones.

sour: n. a quality of taste, generally regarded as one of four or five such elementary qualities.

source: n. (commun. theory) the system that emits the signals which influence another system. ➤For psychology, it may be an organism that emits perceptible behavior influencing another organism. 2. (psychoan.) the organic or tissue condition, or the somatic process, that stimulates an instinctual activity.—*Syn.* **tissue** ***need.**

source/extended: see **point source.**

source/primary and **/secondary:** respectively, an original report giving actual data (occasionally, the original presentation of an author's ideas) and a later report, generally by another person, based on the primary source.

source trait: see **trait/source.**

sour grapes mechanism: a form of **rationalization** in which a person, when impeded or frustrated, rids himself of regret or anger by convincing himself that the goal was not worth reaching anyway.

space: *n.* an abstract geometrical construct of a system of positions, directions, and magnitudes, considered entirely without regard to what it is that has these dimensions. ➤The traditional **space** of physics (= **extension**) is not the **space** of orthodox perception-description (= **extensity**), though both are three-dimensional. Recent physics and psychology alike have utilized more than Euclid's three dimensions. The **space,** in such a term as **life space,** must be regarded as being as fully and as literally a **space** as is that of the living room. Life space also has positions, directions, magnitudes. Likewise, in factor analysis, the **factor space** is not a metaphor or figure of speech. The space is not the same kind as that occupied by a bumblebee but it is just as genuinely space. The limitation in popular thinking of space to that which can be filled by material objects represents adherence to a sixteenth-century philosophy now abandoned by all careful students.—*Cp.* **topology, hodology.**—*adj.* **spatial.**

space/auditory: see **auditory space.**

space/common factor: see **common factor space.**

space/conceptual: see **conceptual space.**

spaced learning or **repetition:** see **practice/spaced.**

space error: a tendency to be biased in discriminations, judgments, or responses by the spatial position of stimuli in relation to the observer. E.g., some observers tend to overestimate the stimulus on the left (arbitrarily called a POSITIVE ERROR), others that on the right (NEGATIVE ERROR); some animals tend to turn right rather than left in mazes, etc.

space factor: a **unit factor** of ability, isolated by factor analysis, which accounts for individual differences in ability to perceive spatial relations, or which explains the variance in test responses requiring such perception of space relations.—*Distg. fr.* **factor space.**

space/hodological: see **hodology.**

space/life: see **life space.**

space of free movement: (*topol.*) **regions** accessible to the person from his present position; that part of the **life space** in which goal seeking is unhampered. The limits are determined chiefly by (*a*) what is prohibited by social and institutional constraints, (*b*) what is beyond the person's abilities (which in turn is partly determined by physical factors).

space orientation: 1. a position in space. 2. adjusting the position of the body (esp., the direction it faces), or of a bodily member, to the stimulus objects impinging on it: e.g., turning the head toward a source of sound. 3. awareness of one's location in physical space.

space perception: the direct awareness (*primarily* through sensory processes but probably never exclusively) of the spatial properties of an object, esp. in relation to the observer; the perception of position, direction, size, form, distance, by means of any of the senses.

space/psychological = **life space.**

space relations: the relationships between objects in respect to their three-dimensional space attributes. ➤These relationships may be judged or more directly perceived. A **unit factor** of ability to perceive space relations is believed established.

space time: a construct that regards time as a fourth dimension along with the traditional length, breadth, and thickness of Euclid's geometry.

space/visual: see **visual space, visual field** (2).

span/auditory: see **auditory span.**

span/eye: see **eye span.**

span/eye-voice: see **eye-voice span.**

span of attention: 1. the number of objects presented for a very brief moment that can be correctly reported immediately thereafter. ➤The span can be ascertained for any sense modality. The assumption apparently implied by the term and the operational definition, that it makes no difference what kind of object or what the attitude of the subject, has been proved false. There is no single span of attention; further specifications are necessary. The same holds true of the synonyms: ATTENTION RANGE, SPAN OF APPREHENSION, SPAN OF DISCRIMINATION, RECOGNITION SPAN, PERCEPTUAL SPAN. 2. an ambiguous term for the length of time a person can (or will) attend to a single object. ➤When "single object" is taken to mean some complex object, INTEREST SPAN is less ambiguous.

span of consciousness: (*obsoles.*) the total number of different **objects** (2) of which one can be simultaneously aware. ➤The term is misleading.

sparkling: *adj.* characterizing the appearance of a surface whereon there are many changes, in color or brightness of limited area and duration, so that there seems to be constant movement on the surface.—*Syn.* GLITTERING.

spasm: *n.* a localized, energetic, involuntary muscular contraction.—*adj.* **spasmodic.**

spasm/nodding: a disorder of infancy in which the head shakes or nods repeatedly. —*Syn.* SPASMUS NUTANS.

spasmoarthria = **spastic *speech.**

spasmophemia = **stuttering.**

spastic: *adj.* pertaining to, or afflicted with, **spasticity.**—*pers. n.* **spastic,** a person so afflicted.

spasticity: *n.* **1.** heightened resistance to flexion or extension of a joint. ➤The stretch of the muscle group involved in either movement sets up a **proprioceptive** reflex of resistance. Spasticity is attributed to a lesion in the central nervous system that disturbs the normal balance between facilitation and inhibition of the motor neurons. **2.** loosely, = **spastic *paralysis.**

spastic paralysis: see **paralysis/spastic.**

spatial: *adj.* pertaining to space. ➤For phrase combinations see **space.**

spatial summation: (*neurol.*) a more than additive increase in motor activity in a limited area when **volleys** from two or more **afferent** nerve fiber groups reach the area together. ➤I.e., if afferent group *a* elicits *x* response, and group *b* elicits *y*, *a* + *b* elicits more than *x* + *y*. The term means summation in a given space, not summation of spaces.

spatial threshold = **two-point threshold.**

spay: *v.* to remove the ovaries of an animal. —*adj.* **spayed.**

speaking/automatic: see **automatic speaking.**

Spearman-Brown formula: a means of estimating the reliability of a test when altered by adding or subtracting items of the same kind:

$$R_n = \frac{nr_m}{1 + (n-1)r_m}$$

where R_n is the estimated reliability coefficient of a test of n items, r_m is the obtained reliability coefficient of the test of m items.—See **reliability.**—*Syn.* PROPHECY FORMULA.

Spearman footrule: see **correlation/footrule.**

special ability: see **ability.**

special aptitude: see **aptitude.**

special case: any instance of a general class or rule that differs so much from the others that it is misleading if taken as representative of its class: e.g., a right triangle is a special case of the *triangle* class. ➤Every instance of a general class probably has some nontypical properties and is to that extent special.

special class or **school:** organized provision for the special educational needs of mentally or physically defective children. ➤Unlike pupils in an **opportunity class,** those in a special class are not as a rule expected to return to regular classes, and the curriculum may differ considerably from the standard (e.g., by including lip reading for the hard of hearing). But **special class** is also used generically for any nonregular class; and, on the other hand, opportunity class is euphemistically used where special class is more appropriate.

special education: see **education/special.**

specialist leader: see **leader/status.**

special sense: see **sense/special.**

species: *n. s.* and *pl.* **1.** (*logic*) a named subgroup or subdivision differing from other subdivisions of the more inclusive group (the **genus**) in stated qualitative characteristics. **2.** (*biol.*) a subdivision of living beings that is more inclusive than a **variety,** less inclusive than a genus; a subdivision of a genus. ➤Most animal or plant groups that have common names (dog, man, pig, wheat, elm) are species. N.B.: the singular is **species,** not *specie* (which means coined money).

species heredity: see **heredity/species.**

species-specific: *adj.* of behavior shown by a great majority of the members of a **species** under the same or highly similar circumstances. ➤The behavior is thus part of the defining characteristics of the species, just as is a certain structure, say a wing or a toe. Absence of the behavior constitutes a deficiency abnormality—again like absence of a wing or toe. The term is coming into frequent use as a substitute for **instinctive;** it avoids many of the controversial implications of the latter.

specific: *adj.* **1.** pertaining to a **species. 2.** distinctive; of any datum clearly distinct from others for any reason.—See **specificity.**

specific ability: a personal trait corresponding to a **specific *factor.**—*Cp.* special ability (see **ability**).

specific action potential: see **reaction potential.**

specific-assignment sampling: in **public *opinion** surveying, a method in which the interviewer is instructed exactly where to go and whom to interview.—*Cp.* **area sampling, quota control.**

specification equation: a variety of **multiple *regression equation** for predicting a test score, knowing a person's strength on a given trait (or **factor**) and the **loading** of the factor on the test.

specific determiner: in an examination, a word or phrase that suggests the correct answer to a person who would not otherwise know. ➤Thus, "always" in a True-

False test is so often associated with a false statement that clever students, in the absence of knowledge, tend to mark *false* a statement containing the word.

specific energy of nerves or **of sensation:** the theory that sensory quality is a function primarily of the sensory mechanism and is relatively independent of the stimulus. ➤Thus, a hot stimulus applied to a receptor for cold evokes coolth, not warmth. Originally, the determination of sensory quality was attributed to the receptor organ only; the theory was later broadened to include the influence of the brain areas to which the neural impulse travels.

specific hunger: a drive toward specific food incentives, such as a craving for sweets.

specificity: *n.* **1.** the fact or quality of being characteristic of a particular phenomenon or type of phenomenon; or of limitation to just one phenomenon. ➤In learning, a stimulus is said to show specificity when it becomes specialized so that it elicits only one response class. **2.** (*factor anal.*) that part of the **variance** not in the **communality.**

specious present: an unfortunate synonym for **psychological *present.**

spectator: *n.* one who looks on; a person viewing a spectacle and not actively participating therein. ➤Before television, spectators were physically congregated. A new terminology is needed for solitary versus congregated viewers.—*Cp.* **audience.**

spectral: *adj.* pertaining to, or produced by, a **spectrum;** esp. as in SPECTRAL COLORS, those seen when white light is dispersed by a prism.

spectrograph/sound: see **sound spectrograph.**

spectrometer (spek·trom′ə·tər): *n.* a **spectroscope** fitted with a divided circle or wave-length drum for isolating or identifying wave lengths or regions of the spectrum.

spectrophotometer (spek″trō·fō·tom′ə·tər): *n.* a **photometer** for measuring the intensities of a light of approximately a single wave length.

spectroscope: *n.* (*phys.*) an instrument for making a spectrum visible. The usual prism spectroscope consists of a slit, collimator, prism, and a second lens.—*adj.* **spectroscopic.**

spectrum *n., pl.* **spectra, -trums: 1.** a band of radiant energy in which, after passing through a prism or being otherwise dispersed, energy of each wave length is segregated and all components lie spread out in regular order. **2.** the series of colors obtained when white light is dispersed by a prism: it is a continuously changing band ranging from a scarlet red through orange, yellow, green, blue, to blue-green. (The

corresponding wave lengths are from about 760 to 400 millimicrons.)—See also **spectrum/acoustic.**—*adj.* **spectral.**

spectrum/acoustic or /**auditory:** the range of sound audible to the normal human ear —from about 20 to upwards of 20,000 cycles per second.

spectrum colors: see **spectrum (2).**

spectrum line: (*phys.*) any one of the narrow lines, each representing light of a definite wave length, that are observed in the solar and other spectra, certain groups of lines being characteristic of specific chemical elements in the gaseous state. They appear bright when caused by emission, dark when caused by absorption.

spectrum locus: a curve on which all spectral colors can be so located as to show their relations to each other. ➤*Cp.* **color triangle, color circle.** The spectrum locus is roughly horseshoe in shape. When the curve is closed by a straight line across the open end, the enclosed surface is the locus of all physically realizable colors.

spectrum/power: (*aud.*) a plot showing the mean square amplitude for each frequency of a sound. For **white *noise** the plot is a straight line.

specular: *adj.* pertaining to, or resembling, a mirror.

speculation: *n.* thinking in which the factual basis for the hypotheses propounded is slight. ➤Although often used derogatorily, speculation has an important place in discovery and even in verification.

speech: *n.* **1.** any communication through a system of conventional vocal symbols. **2.** that which is spoken; esp., a public address.

speech/articulate: a vocal communication in which sounds are joined together to produce meaningful sound combinations.

speech/automatic: see **automatic speech.**

speech block: momentary inability to continue speaking, usually accompanied by anxiety and tension: a form of **stuttering.**

speech center: the region in the brain governing utterance of articulate speech (**Broca's convolution**). For right-handed persons, it is in the left hemisphere. ➤The concept suggested by this term, of a definite brain region controlling speech, is now known to be oversimple.

speech/contamination of: see **contamination of speech.**

speech/defective: speech that deviates so far from that of other people in the group that it calls attention to itself, interferes with communication, or causes maladjustment to the speaker's social environment. The difficulty may be organic or functional. —*Syn.* **speech disorder.**

speech disorder: any long-term disorder in speaking or in perception of speech (sometimes also of writing or of gesture) so grave as to interfere seriously with communication. ➤Some authorities restrict the term to disorder of functional origin, usually to one symptomatic of morbidity. Others divide it into functional and organic speech disorders. Disorders of voice only—harshness, squeakiness, hoarseness, monotone, etc.—are usually put into a separate category of VOICE DISORDER. The terminology of speech disorders is extraordinarily luxuriant and confused.

speech/egocentric: see **egocentric speech.**

speech/infantile: a manner of speaking in which all but principal words are omitted, and easily enunciated sounds are substituted for the more difficult.—*Syn.* BABY TALK, PEDOLALIA, PEDOLOGIA.

speech/inner or **/internal:** see **internal speech.**

speech/pantomimic: 1. communication by means of gestures, movements, and facial expressions without using words. 2. the execution of the movements for articulated speech without voicing or whispering the sounds. It is sometimes used as a device in speech therapy.

speech reading: the comprehension of another's speech, without the use of hearing, by observing his facial movements and other visual cues.—*Syn.* VISUAL HEARING (somewhat *ambig.*); LIP READING (common, but inadequately descriptive).

speech/scanning: halting, deliberate speech, delivered in a monotonous drawl with each syllable accented and normal phrase intonations absent.—*Syn.* ATAXIC SPEECH, ATAXIARTHRIA.

speech sounds test: a test of ability to discriminate spoken sounds. ➤One such test consists of sixty spoken nonsense syllables that are variants of the *ee* **digraph.**

speech/spastic: the manner of speech often found in victims of **spastic *paralysis.** It is very labored, with defective articulation and overexerted facial muscles.

speech/synthetic: speechlike sounds produced by a machine. Simple sounds are put together, one by one, till the desired effect is obtained.

speed: *n.* rate of movement, change, or accomplishment; amount of change per unit of time.

speed score = score/rate.

speed test: see **test/speed.**

speed-up: *n.* pressure on workers to increase output.

spelling demon: a particular letter combination or word that a given pupil persistently misspells; or such a word persistently misspelled by many persons.

sperm: *n.* 1. the developed male cell of reproduction. 2. the liquid secretion containing such cells; the **semen.**—*adj.* **spermatic.**

spermatozoon (spėr″mə·tō·zō′ən): *n.* a mature sperm cell ready to fertilize an egg. —*adj.* **spermatozoal.**

sphere: *n.* in an extended sense, the locus of certain properties or events defined by three or more **dimensions.** ➤Its usage is often merely metaphorical—only some of the geometrical properties of a sphere are implied, and nothing is to be inferred from the geometrical description that is not *explicitly* asserted. **Field, area, domain,** and **space** itself are similarly used in a metaphorical way. But sphere may also be a strictly geometrical **construct** in which, although the dimensions are not spatial, all the relationships set forth in geometry are rigorously maintained. This is its use in factor analysis.—*Cp.* also topology, hodology, field theory.—*adj.* spherical.

spherical aberration: see **aberration/ spherical.**

sphincter: *n.* a muscle that wholly or partly closes an orifice or passage by drawing together the edges or walls.

sphincter morality: (*psychoan.*) the kind of behavior supposed to result from excessive and too early attempts to teach the child control of defecation.—See **anal character.**

sphygmo- (sfig′mō-): combining form meaning *pulse.*

sphygmograph (-graf): *n.* an instrument for recording the pattern of strength and rapidity of the pulse.—*Syn.* SPHYGMOMETER (-mom′ə·tər).

sphygmomanometer (-mə·nom′ə·tər): *n.* an instrument for measuring (arterial) blood pressure.

spike: *n.* in an **electroencephalogram,** a component of the graph of the **action potential** that comes in the initial phase and represents a large and sudden change in potential superimposed on a slower wave rhythm.

spinal: *adj.* pertaining to the backbone or spine, or to the **spinal cord.**

spinal animal: an animal in which all connections between the spinal cord and the brain have been cut, so that the activities of trunk and limbs are controlled by the spinal cord.

spinal canal: the canal or tube, formed by the vertebrae of the backbone, which contains the **spinal cord.**

spinal column: the backbone; the series of vertebrae that form the supporting axis of the body and protection for the spinal cord.

spinal cord: the long thick cord of nerve tissue that extends along the back, enclosed in the **spinal canal.** ➤Note that the spelling is not *chord.*—*Syn.* MYELON; CORD.

spinal fluid = cerebrospinal fluid.

spinal ganglia: groups of nerve cells forming an enlargement of the neurons of the dorsal **root** of each spinal nerve. The fibers from these cells are **afferent.**

spinal nerves: (*neurol.*) thirty-one pairs (in man) of nerves that leave the spinal cord at various points. Each typically contains both **afferent** and **efferent** fibers from both **autonomic** and **cerebrospinal** subsystems.

spinal reflex: see **reflex/spinal.**

spinal root: the beginning portion of the pairs of nerves that leave the spinal column and join to form a nerve trunk. The ANTERIOR (or MOTOR or VENTRAL) ROOT emerges from the anterior part of the cord and is efferent. The POSTERIOR ROOT is the portion of the **afferent** nerve between the **spinal ganglion** and the cord.

spinal tonus: the **tonus** maintained by the spinal cord when connections with the brain are severed. ➤It must not be assumed to be identical with the contribution of the spinal cord to behavior regulation in the intact animal.

spindle/muscle: a group of muscle fibers, supplied with sensory nerve endings, all enclosed in a tissue fluid and a capsule of connective tissue.—*Syn.* SPINDLE, NEUROMUSCULAR SPINDLE.

spindle tendon: a specialized **muscle** *spindle found at the junction of a tendon with muscular tissue.—Syn. NEUROTENDINAL SPINDLE, GOLGI'S CORPUSCLE.

spiral (omnibus) test: see **test/omnibus.**

spirit: *n.* 1. (*metaph., theol.*) = **soul;** an immaterial being, possessed of some permanence, to which are ascribed many or most of the activities of a living person, esp. those called **mental.** ➤Such a being may or may not be embodied or incarnate—i.e., associated (in ways variously stated) with a visible body—but is itself essentially immaterial. 2. a ghost; a being, as in (1) divested of its body, yet retaining certain bodily characteristics such as visibility and extendedness. 3. a supernatural being; a deity or semideity. 4. the life or vital principle; that which differentiates the living from the nonliving. 5. the temper, mood, or disposition that temporarily or permanently characterizes a person: a brave *spirit,* in good *spirits.* 6. = loyalty or morale: college *spirit.* 7. the essential principle; hence, the real intent: the *spirit,* not the letter, of the law. 8. an alcoholic solution.

spiritism: *n.* 1. a philosophical belief that there is associated with human organisms, or more generally with all natural objects, a principle of organization, a **spirit,** that has properties other than those of physical science. ➤The term is general, comprehending many different conceptions of spirit. 2. = **spiritualism,** *prefd.* for a cer-

tain cult or religious belief.—*adj.* (for 1} **spiritistic.**

spiritual: *adj.* 1. having to do with **spirit.** 2. **mental,** in contrast with bodily or material. (A poor usage.) 3. concerned with the finer, nobler, or more elevating aspects of life. ➤**Materialistic,** often used as *ant.,* has too many other meanings to be a clear opposite.—*n.* (for 3) **spirituality.**

spiritualism: *n.* 1. the philosophic doctrine which asserts that the reality of the universe is fundamentally that of **spirit** (1). (A better but less common term than **idealism.**) 2. = **spiritism** (1). 3. a cult or religious belief in the activities of **spirits** in the affairs of this world.

spirograph (spī′rō·graf): *n.* an instrument to measure the rate and amount of breathing. The SPIROGRAM is the graphic record obtained.

spirometer: (spī·rom′ə·tər): *n.* an instrument for measuring the volume of air one can expire at one breath. ➤Note that it does not measure the volume of air contained in the lungs.

splanchnic (splangk′nik) = **visceral** (1).

split-half correlation = **correlation/chance halves** and **reliability coefficient** (*c*).

split movement: see **motion/apparent.**

split-off consciousness: (*W. James*) a partly organized set of experiences that are relatively autonomous or independent of the main body of experience.

spoiled: *adj.* 1. of a person whose childhood and life experience lead him to expect to have his own way and to be catered to by those around him. 2. (*exper.*) of a response that should not be included with the rest in calculations. ➤There is a variety of legitimate grounds for exclusion: the subject may have violated instructions, there were unintended cues (but these must be specified and known to have been used), etc. It is to be noted that a spoiled response cannot be regarded as if it had not occurred: it inevitably influences later responses. The remedy for spoiled responses is prevention, not statistical exclusion, of bad data.

spongioblast (spon′ji·ō·blast″): *n.* (*neurol.*) one of the ectodermal cells of the embryonic **neural tube** which later form the **neuroglia.**

spontaneity: *n.* the quality of behavior that is self-initiated. ➤While outside stimulation acts as a **cue,** the behavior reflects the inner state of the person rather than the demands of the environment (i.e., is expressive) and tends to disregard restrictive social controls or remote consequences. **Spontaneous behavior** probably denotes the same quality defined negatively.—*Syn.* (*approx.*) **impulsiveness.**—*Contr.* w. **rigidity, self-control,** ANXIETY CONTROL (none fully opposite to spontaneity). In

spontaneity test, spontaneity therapy, spontaneity training, Moreno uses the term in a restricted sense.—*adj.* **spontaneous.**

spontaneity test: (*J. L. Moreno*) putting the subject into a standard lifelike situation in which he improvises his behavior freely vis-à-vis certain persons to whom he is known to be emotionally related. Attention is given to the emotions expressed and to the **roles** assumed.

spontaneity therapy: (*J. L. Moreno*) **sociodrama** and **spontaneity training** adapted to the person's needs. Special attention is given to acting out the problems that have been troubling him, with encouragement toward formulating a different set of values as he becomes convinced of the inadequacy of his own attitudes.

spontaneity training: (*J. L. Moreno*) enacting a variety of lifelike social situations, under encouragement to act freely and spontaneously but within certain specified limits: e.g., to try to calm down an excited child, to hurry up a clerk, to express concern over another's troubles.

spontaneous behavior: behavior that cannot be shown to be elicited by any particular stimulus: it may be elicited by sheer metabolic change or by unidentifiable stimuli.—*Syn.* emitted behavior (see **emit** 2).—See also **spontaneity.**

spontaneous discharge: a neural impulse that apparently originates in the individual neuron itself as a result of metabolism.

spontaneous recovery: see **recovery/spontaneous.**

spoon-feeding: *n.* **1.** conveying food to a person's mouth for him when he is unable or refuses to do so for himself. **2.** metaphorically, an educative process that makes everything easy for the learner, permitting him a maximally passive role.

s-population: *n.* a finite number of small independent environmental events, of which only one instance or sample is effective at any one time. →The events need not be equivalent stimuli (see **equivalence 2**) or belong to the same stimulus family, but for any given occasion if any *one* is presented the others are not. The several appearances of a thing viewed from different positions form an *s*-population. The concept is used in a statistical interpretation of behavior. The number of "elements" effective in a given sample (or the average number over a given period) is symbolized by **s**.—*Syn.* STIMULUS POPULATION.

sport: *n.* (*biol.*) an organism innately and markedly different from its parents and from the general type of the species; a **mutation** that makes a striking difference in the **phenotype.**

spots/sensory: points of relatively high sensitivity on the skin, as disclosed by pointlike stimulation by pressure or thermal stimuli. →It is unnecessary to assume that these points correspond with any exactness to the location of distinct cutaneous receptors.

spot/warm: see **warm spot.**

spouse: *n.* a marriage partner of either sex.

spread/associative: see **associative spread.**

spread of effect: see **effect/spread of.**

spurious: *adj.* deceptively similar; not genuine; having considerable error arising from identifiable sources. →In a SPURIOUS CORRELATION COEFFICIENT something other than the tendency of the two variables to vary concomitantly affects the value obtained: e.g., the correlation obtained when one of the variables actually includes the other with which it is correlated.

spurt: *n.* **1.** a suddenly increased display of the energy brought to bear on a task, generally with a gain in effectiveness. →Both INITIAL and END SPURTS are found. **2.** a sharp increase in rate of growth; a GROWTH SPURT. →Here the idea of energy output is subordinated to the outcome, reversing the emphasis in (**1**).

SQ3R: (*F. P. Robinson*) a descriptive formula of a method empirically found conducive to effective study: *Survey, Question, Read, Recite, Review.*

square contingency = chi square.

squint = strabismus.

SR = stimulus response, or the stimulus-response relationship. Also written S-R and S→R, the latter being read "S leads to R."

S⟷R: (*J. R. Kantor*) symbol for stimulus-response interaction, or interbehavior.—See **interbehavioral psychology.**

SRA: *abbr.* used to identify a number of tests published by Science Research Associates.

S-R-S sequence: a stimulus leading to a response that leads to another stimulus.

SS = standard *score.

S **score:** a score which is the sum of all the scores of an individual on all the variables. →*S* scores are useful in checking computations.

SSCQT = Selective Service College Qualification Test.

$_{ss}H_R$**:** (*C. Hull*) summation of the habit strengths associated with two or more stimulus elements that lead to a given R.

St. = stimulus.

stabilimeter (stā″bi·lim′ə·tər): *n.* an instrument for measuring the amount of bodily sway when the subject (usually blindfolded) stands erect and endeavors to hold perfectly still.

stability: *n.* **1.** (*phys.*) absence of motion in a physical mass in relation to surroundings. **2.** (*biol.*) the property of species of not varying from generation to generation.

3. (*psychol.*) a characteristic of a person not given to swings in mood or marked changes in emotional attitude; EMOTIONAL STABILITY.—*adj.* **stable.**

stability and equivalence/coefficient of: see **equivalence/coefficient of (2).**

stability/coefficient of: the correlation between the two administrations of a test with a suitable interval between them to minimize the differential effects of practice. ➤The interval and the population sampled must always be specified. Some would restrict this term to the case where the same test form is given at both testings. Where a **comparable *form** is used, the more exact name is the coefficient of stability and equivalence (see **equivalence/coefficient of, 2**). Although not in common use, the symbol r_{st} is suggested for this coefficient.

stability/emotional: see **stability (3).**

stability/functional: maintenance of a **function (4)** at a reasonably constant level.—*Syn.* STABILITY OF FUNCTION.

stability/occupational: remaining in the same occupation (not necessarily for the same employer) over a stated period of years; or the proportion of a given group who so remain.—*Cp.* **turnover/labor.**

stability/statistical: the degree of probability that a given value is not merely the result of chance. ➤*Syn.* **statistical *significance,** more common but ambiguous, since it is sometimes taken to mean *of appreciable amount.* **Stability** here refers to the fact that the value will remain the same (within determined limits) whenever the relevant conditions are repeated. A STATISTICALLY STABLE DIFFERENCE (or STATISTICALLY SIGNIFICANT DIFFERENCE) is a difference between two values that is unlikely to be merely the result of chance.

stable (.01): *adj.* statistically stable or significant at the 1 per cent level; of a statistic that will not vary more than a determined amount, by chance alone, more frequently than once in 100 times.—*Syn.* SIGNIFICANT (.01).—See **stability/statistical.**

stadiometer (stā″di·om′ə·tər): *n.* an instrument for measuring standing or sitting height.

stage: *n.* a presumably natural or non-arbitrary division of a changing process. ➤To use **stage** (as some do) for an arbitrary division may mislead those accustomed to the correct meaning. LEVEL, which is appropriate when one means a point on a continuum (whether arbitrary or not), is suggested for cases where no implication of natural division is intended. *Cp.:* the *level* of the river reaches flood *stage* when it spills over the banks.—*Distg. fr.* **class** or **category,** which apply to static groupings.—*Cp.* **phase.**

stage/anal: see **anal stage.**

stage/anal-sadistic: see **anal-sadistic stage.**

staircase illusion: a reversible visual illusion in which a drawing of a stairway is seen either as from above or from below.—See **figure/ambiguous.**

staircase phenomenon: the stepwise increase in response to a muscle to a series of single induction shocks of equal strength.—*Syn.* TREPPE (*Ger., step*) PHENOMENON.

stammering: see **stuttering.**

stance reflex: see **static reflex.**

standard: *n.* **1.** that which is expected; a socially or practically desirable quality or level of performance. ➤*Distg. fr.* **norm,** which is the average of *actual* performance; from the **ideal,** which may represent a level scarcely worth attainment; and from perfection. Thus, business standards for handwriting are well below the norm for eighth grade. **2.** a fixed and durable unit of any sort used for comparison and in construction of **scales.**—See also **standard stimulus. 3.** in some English schools, = **grade (2).**

standard deviation: see **deviation/standard.**

standard difference: the difference between two means divided by the standard error of that difference.—*Syn.* STANDARD RATIO. Also called **critical ratio,** which is slightly more general.

standard error or **SE:** a measure or an estimate of the sampling errors affecting a statistic; a measure of the amount the statistic may be expected to differ by chance from the true value of the statistic. It is the root-mean-square deviation of the obtained values of the statistic on successive samples—i.e., it is the **standard *deviation,** not of the distribution of the primary measurements, but of the distribution of the statistic in question. When the statistic i the mean, its standard error is often esti mated.—See **standard error of mean.**

standard error of estimate or σ_{est} or σ_{xy} the **standard *deviation** of the difference between the actual values of the **dependen *variable** and those estimated from the re gression equation. It is estimated by tak ing the standard deviation of the dependen variable, σ_o, multiplied by the square root of the quantity 1, minus the square of the correlation coefficient: $\sigma_{est} = \sigma_o \sqrt{1 - r^2}$. (The formula may be generalized for multiple correlation.) Where the differences ar known the formula is

$$\sigma_{est} = \sqrt{\frac{\Sigma(X - X')^2}{N - 1}}.$$

standard error of mean or SD_M or σ_M: an estimate of the amount that an obtained mean may be expected to differ by chance from the true mean:

$$SD_M = \frac{SD_{dist}}{\sqrt{N-1}}.$$

—*Syn.* **standard error (SE).**

standard error of measurement or $\sigma_{(M)}$: an estimate of the root-mean-square departure of a series of observed scores from their corresponding true scores.—*Distg. fr.* σ_M (without parentheses around the subscript).

standard error of sampling: a measure of the discrepancies of the observed frequencies of a distribution from the frequencies of a theoretical curve or of a curve fitted to the observed frequency distribution.

standardization group: the group (believed to be representative of a population) that is used in determining the **norms** for a test. ➔Note that it is *not* the group used in trying out procedures for practicality, etc., though that is necessary for standardizing. The norms can be determined only after procedures have been stabilized.

standardize: *v.* **1.** to bring something into line with established standards; or to establish standards of performance or product. **2.** (*testing*) to determine (presumably on the basis of empirical investigation) the exact procedures to be used in testing, the permitted variations in environmental conditions, the method of scoring.—*n.* **standardization,** the outcome of standardizing.

standardized test: see **test/standardized.**

standard measure = standard *score.

standard observer: the hypothetical human being whose sense receptors (or any particular sense receptor) are completely normal. ➔For color vision, the discriminatory capacity of this hypothetical creature has been defined.

standard of living: a more or less realistic standard level of consumption toward which a social group strives.

Standard (Psychiatric) Nomenclature: the nomenclature adopted in 1950 by the Council of the American Psychiatric Association as that officially proposed by the association for the classification of mental disorders. ➔Extensive use (including much verbatim or near-verbatim quotation) of the official nomenclature has been made in this dictionary. It must be recognized, however, that many terms not included in the Standard Nomenclature are in use and must be defined. The nomenclature, moreover, was designed more as a framework for classification than as a set of terms suitable for the description of disordered behavior.—*Abbr.* (in this dictionary) **Stan. Psychiat.**

standard ratio = standard difference.

standard score: see **score/standard.**

standard stimulus: in an experiment, that one of the pair or group of stimuli which is treated as a basis of comparison with the others.

standard test: see **test/standardized.**

Stanford-Binet or **Stanford Revision of the Binet Scale: 1.** a revision, made in 1916 to fit American conditions, of the **Binet-Simon scale** for intelligence. It involved so many changes as to be virtually a new scale. **2.** a further revision, with new norms, in 1937. Often called the TERMAN-MERRILL REVISION, though officially still the Stanford-Binet, or **S-B.**

stanine (stā'nīn): *n.* (*stat.*) a unit consisting of 1/9 of the total range of the standard scores of a normal distribution. ➔The term is a condensation of *standard nine.* The mean falls at 5, the SD at ±2. The unit, which was developed by the U.S. Air Force, has computational advantages.

Stan. Psychiat.: *abbr.* for **Standard (Psychiatric) Nomenclature.**

stapes (stā'pēz): *n.* one of the **auditory *ossicles** in the middle ear.—*adj.* **stapedial** (stə·pē'di·əl).

starting (or **startle**) **reflex pattern:** a complex involuntary response to an unexpected strong auditory stimulus. It is predominantly a flexion response, but there are also visceral components. ➔The response is too complex, and involves too large a cortical component, to be a true reflex. It is rather to be regarded as a primitive emotional response.—*Syn.* STARTLE RESPONSE (*prefd.*).

stasis (stā'sis; stas'əs): *n.* (*Gk., standing still*) a state in which there is no movement or change.—*adj.* **static** (stat'ik).

state: *n.* a condition not manifesting any marked change in respect to the qualities or properties that define it: e.g., quiet *state*; but also excited *state*, in which there is much change but not in respect to the excitement, which remains relatively constant.

state/conscious: 1. the totality of conscious process at any given moment, or for a brief period. ➔It is usually described in terms of reportable objects or content of which the person is aware. **2.** a condition during which the person is aware, or aware of a certain situation or problem.—*Syn.* STATE OF CONSCIOUSNESS.

state variable/hypothetical: (*K. Spence*) a relatively unanalyzed, more-or-less enduring condition of an organism that is hypothesized to have resulted from, and is defined by, a past interaction of the organism and the environment: e.g., a **drive state.** State variable refers to a condition that is related to a particular class of stimuli and/or responses; it rarely refers to the total state of the organism.

static: *adj.* not moving or changing; not exerting force.—*Ant.* **dynamic.**

static reflex or **response:** a response that

modifies the orientation of the body with respect to gravity. There are two types: STANCE REFLEXES, in which the body is kept in a relatively fixed posture, and RIGHTING REFLEXES or RESPONSES, which restore the body to a normal or prescribed posture.

static sense: the sense whereby one perceives the orientation of the head with respect to gravity, or its movements in space; hence, the sense whereby passive bodily motion is perceived. ➤Its sense organ lies in the vestibule of the inner ear, adjacent to that of hearing.—*Syn.* VESTIBULAR SENSE, EQUILIBRIUM SENSE. **Labyrinthine sense** as a synonym is confusing.

stationary state: the condition of a **system** (1 or 2) that does not change its condition or state *as a system* with the passage of time; the state of a system that is neither absorbing nor emitting appreciable energy, although within the system itself there may be a complex energy interchange.—*Syn.* STEADY STATE. ➤A waterfall remains in a stationary state over a considerable period. A nonradioactive atom is in a stationary state. Many systems considered in psychology are said to be in a stationary state.

statistic: *n.* 1. any value that expresses the end result of statistical manipulation of other values. 2. = **statistical constant.**

statistical constant: a value or number that describes a series of quantitative observations or measures; or a value, calculated from a **sample,** that is supposed to describe the population from which the sample is drawn: e.g., a **mean, standard *deviation, correlation coefficient.**—*Distg. fr.* **parameter.**—*Syn.* **statistic, constant** (both with other meanings).

statistical error: any error that vitiates the conclusion to be drawn from a **statistic.**

statistical psychology: the use of statistical principles to derive the explanatory or systematic **constructs** by means of which to order the data of psychology. ➤Distinguish from the use of statistics in order to derive a conclusion from empirical data. Statistical psychology is a **mathematical model psychology,** the latter preferred for a systematic attempt to substitute a mathematical model for traditional constructs, the former for less inclusive and **heuristic** attempts.

statistical significance: see **significance/ statistical.**

statistical stability: see **stability/statistical.**

statistic/ancillary: see **ancillary statistic.**

statistic/consistent: a **statistic** which more and more approaches a correct or true value as the size of the sample is increased.—*Ant.* INCONSISTENT STATISTIC.

statistic/efficient: a statistic which, as the size of the sample is increased, has a normal distribution of **error** and a smaller **standard error** than any other measure that could be used to estimate the true value of a particular **statistical constant.**

statistics: *n.* 1. the science and art that gathers and coordinates numerous facts within a determinate field, treating these mathematically so that the numerical relations between these facts may be displayed clearly and freed from anomalies due to **chance** factors. It thus brings to light the operation of regular causes whose action is otherwise obscured. 2. a set of numbers expressing the end result of statistical manipulation of values that represent classified facts and data; or loosely, the classified facts themselves: e.g., the *statistics* of rate of death.

statistics/descriptive: those statistics used only for the purpose of describing the sample from which they are derived.—*Contr. w.* INFERENCE STATISTICS, used to infer characteristics of the population from which the sample is drawn.

statistics/inference: see **statistics/descriptive.**

statistics/nonparametric: the statistical operations that are available when it is not possible to assert that the **frequency distribution** is normal (as is the assumption of the statistics most commonly used). ➤ *Syn.* DISTRIBUTION-FREE STATISTICS, but this is misleading since nearly all statistics make some assumption about the distribution.

statistics/psychological: see **psychometrics.**

statistics/vital: the collection, presentation, analysis, and interpretation of numerical data concerned with human beings, esp. births and deaths.

statokinetic: *adj.* of those adjustments made by the body while in motion that nonetheless maintain a relatively stable posture and orientation.

statue of Condillac: the philosopher Condillac's parable in explanation of a **sensationist** account of mental life, wherein he imagined a statue to be endowed with one sensation after another until it should be fully conscious.—See **sensationalism.**

status (stā′təs; stat′-): *n.* 1. a state or condition of affairs, or of a person. 2. (*med.*) an abnormal state: e.g., *status lymphaticus,* overdevelopment of lymphatic tissue. 3. the position accorded, formally or informally, to a person in his own group; the acceptance and honor accorded to a person. ➤While office or class usually confer status, they do not always do so. Status is always dependent upon the others in group or community, and is partly a matter of how others directly perceive an individual.—*Cp.* **class, role.**

status epilepticus: a succession of epileptic

attacks without intervening recovery of consciousness.

status grouping: a grouping, recognized by the community, of persons who have equivalent status.

status leader: see **leader/status.**

status need: the need for an established and respected relationship with others, manifested by striving for prestige, power, domination, or popularity. ➤It differs from, but may be an alternative for, the need for affection.

STDCR: a **personality inventory** developed from factors found in the analysis of **extraversion-introversion** questionaries. The factors are S = social **introversion,** T = thinking introversion, D = **depression,** C = **cycloid** tendency, R = **rhathymia** (tendency to carefree and happy-go-lucky behavior). This inventory is incorporated, with changes, in the Guilford-Zimmerman Temperament Survey.

stem = **brain stem.**

stem length: a measure of body size, practically the same as sitting height.

stencil: *n.* a device for facilitating scoring objective tests. It is a transparent or perforated sheet to be laid over the answer sheet so that correct or incorrect answers may be quickly identified and checked.— *Syn.* SCORING KEY.

sten scale: a scale having ten unit-steps, or ten scores, each being one-half **standard *deviation.** ➤The term is a contraction of "standard scale of ten units."

step (interval) = **class interval.**

stepwise phenomenon: (*Gestalt*) the experience that a series has a direction and proceeds by finite steps: e.g., the experience when one hears ascending or descending pitches of a musical scale. They are heard as a *whole series,* not as this tone, that tone.

steradian (stə·rā'di·ən): *n.* (*geom.*) the unit of solid angle; the angle subtended by the spherical surface of area equivalent to the square of the radius of the sphere.

stereo- (ster'i·ō-; stir-): combining form meaning *solid, three-dimensional.*

stereoagnosis (-ag·nō'səs) = **astereognosis.**

stereognosis (ster"i·og·nō'səs): *n.* perception of objects or forms by touch.—*adj.* **stereognostic.**

stereogram: see **stereoscope.**

stereopathy (-op'ə·thi): *n.* the abnormality constituted by persistent and long-continued **stereotyped** thinking.

stereopsis: *n.* **1.** stereoscopic vision—i.e., perceiving objects as in three dimensions. **2.** the displacement of two objects in the third dimension (or of two views of an object), measured in angle seconds. The displacement correlates with **disparity** of retinal images when viewing the objects. **3.**

the acuity with which a person is able to make discriminations of depth or of third-dimension position.

stereoscope: *n.* an instrument for viewing two flat pictures (STEREOGRAMS) so presented, one to each eye, that they fuse into a single impression, usually of solid objects seen in relief.—*adj.* **stereoscopic.**—*n.* **stereoscopy** (-os'kə·pi), the perception of depth or solidity; the having of **stereoscopic vision.**

stereoscopic vision (-skop'ik): **1.** perception of depth or solidity, esp. when based on the fusion of two slightly disparate images, but also when based on other sensory cues such as intervention, perspective, etc. **2.** perception of the third dimension in flat pictures viewed in a stereoscope.

stereotropism (-trō'piz·əm): *n.* a simple orienting response made to contact with a solid object.—*Cp.* **tropism.**—*Syn.* STEREOTAXIS (-tak'səs).

stereotype: *n.* **1.** a relatively rigid and oversimplified or biased perception or conception of an aspect of reality, esp. of persons or social groups: e.g., the perception of "bankers"—in general and without discrimination (except possibly for a particular banker)—as invariably cold-hearted in business dealings. ➤The stereotype need not be verbalize. The term comes from printing —it is difficult to make changes once the metal *stereotype* is cast. **2.** = **stereotyped behavior.**—*adj.* **stereotyped, stereotypic(al).**

stereotyped behavior or **response: 1.** a behavior that is rather uniformly elicited in a particular problem situation and alterable very little by attendant circumstances or motivation, or by the outcome. **2.** a relatively invariant mode of behavior determined by a particular motive. The responses may be of any sort—verbal, expressive, postural, or operant.

stereotyped movement: an abnormal, recurrent, or persistent movement, posture, or spoken word or phrase, having little relation with stimulus or situation. ➤A larger complex of movements than a **tic,** it is essentially an **operant** behavior that loses its adaptive quality by reason of repetitive and inappropriate employment. It is a frequent symptom in several psychoses.

stereotype/personality: a specific personality description ready at hand for attribution to an individual (or any individual of a class) perceived to manifest a few traits thought to be typical. Thus, being "fat" is taken to imply a whole complex of traits amounting to the "fat person's personality." If an Italian is vivacious, he is perceived as a "typical Latin," endowed with the complex of traits that form—for the perceiver—the "Latin" stereotype.

stereotypy (ster″i·ō·tī′pi): *n.* a condition in which the individual persistently manifests stereotyped movements or thinks in stereotypes. ➤Many psychoses manifest manneristic, stereotyped movements; and **delusions** are one form of extreme stereotyped thinking. But otherwise normal persons may also display rather marked stereotyped behavior or thinking.

sterility: *n.* inability to serve as one partner in the union of **gametes** (mature germ cells) to start a new life. ➤Sterility can result from lack of gametes, from failure of the mechanisms that bring the gametes together, or from unfavorable physiological conditions that destroy the gametes or the newly fertilized ovum. It may also be psychological—i.e., it may be due to any psychological cause that interferes with bringing the gametes together. The mechanism of interference is for the greater part unknown, but the fact is established. Neither **sterility** nor **infertility** is properly used for voluntary limitation of offspring. Sterility usually implies an enduring but not necessarily uncurable condition.—*Cp.* **infertile.**—*adj.* **sterile.**

sterilization: *n.* rendering an individual (of either sex) incapable of reproduction or of having offspring. ➤The simplest means at present are **vasectomy** in males and **salpingectomy** in females (neither of which unsexes the individual); but castration and removal either of uterus or of both ovaries prevent reproduction, and massive shortwave radiation of the sex glands may destroy the germ-producing tissue.

-sthen-: combining form meaning *strong, strength*: e.g., **asthenia** (a- = *no*, -sthenia = *strength*), meaning weakness; **neurasthenia**, originally meaning nerve weakness.

sthenia (sthə·nī′ə; sthē′ni·ə): *n.* strength; vigor.—*Ant.* **asthenia.**—*adj.* **sthenic** (sthen′ik).

stigma *n., pl.* **stigmas, stigmata** (stig′mə·tə): **1.** any peculiar marking or conformation of the body, not necessarily limiting to physiological functioning but thought to be a sign of somewhat general degeneration. ➤E.g., many (not all) feebleminded have a variety of anatomical markings of unesthetic character, some of which (such as cross eyes) are also directly handicapping. **2.** figuratively, a stain on a person's reputation.—*Cp.* **stigmatize. 3.** *pl.* (**stigmata** only) certain markings, supposedly of supernatural origin, impressed on the bodies of saints: e.g., marks resembling the wounds of Christ.—*adj.* **stigmatic** (-mat′ik).

stigmatize: *v.* to mark a person with a stigma. ➤Used esp. in a metaphorical sense: to *stigmatize* as a liar.

Stiles-Crawford effect: Light rays passing through the edge of the pupil have less stimulating effect than those that pass through the center.

Stilling test: a test for color weakness consisting of a chart showing many colored dots some of which, differing in color from the surrounding dots, form numerals. These numerals are easily read by color-normal persons, but are imperceptible to the color blind or the color weak.

stim = **stimulus.**

Stimmung (shtim′ŭng): *n.* (*Ger., mood*) an affective mood or set sensitizing the organism to the external stimulating situation; a central motive state.

stimulant: *n.* a drug that increases a physiological activity. ➤It is possible for a drug to increase one activity and depress another.

stimulation: *n.* **1.** the application to a **receptor** of an appropriate form of physical energy. ➤Each receptor is adapted to receive (to be activated by) certain kinds and strengths of energy. The energy may come from within the body, but it is external to the receptor system. *Cp.* **excitation,** which is the activity or arousal of nerve tissue. If the nervous mechanism is intact, stimulation always leads to excitation; hence, the term commonly includes the excitation that immediately follows. **2.** the whole process by which a form of physical energy or stimulus evokes a response. **3.** the arousal of an organism by any means—almost = **motivation.** (Not a good usage but prevalent.)—*adj.* **stimulating.**—*v.* **stimulate.**

stimulation/accessory: a stimulation of one sense organ that indirectly produces change in the activity of another sense organ while it is also being stimulated.—*Cp.* **sensory interaction.**

stimulogenous fibrillation: (*morph.*) (*S. T. Bok*) the hypothesis that the growth of nerve fibers is toward areas of electrical irradiation, proceeding from stimulated receptors, muscles, or other nerve fibers.

stimulus or **S** *n., pl.* **stimuli:** Three basic concepts appear in various combinations in definitions (1) to (7): a **stimulus** is something that (A) stirs or prods the organism, (B) is external to the organism or to a definitely organized part of an organism, and (C) is associated with sensory processes. (Sense 8 below does not manifestly utilize these concepts.)

1. a physical event, or a change in physical energy, that causes physiological activity in a sense organ.—See **stimulation (1).** ➤This is the traditional technical meaning. It is not required that the stimulus be described in ultimate physical units—i.e., in strictly **physicalist** language—but the possibility of such description is implied.

(Thus, the expression "the *stimulus* was a heavy cube" implies a description in the language of physical energy.) Nor is purely verbal consistency required—red is not a physical term, but when the stimulus is said to be a red light, a certain form of physical energy is clearly referred to. The stimulus may be intraorganic, as when a muscle movement causes pressure on certain end organs. Yet even in the case of such intraorganic stimuli the energy is external to the sensory mechanism upon which it acts. A physical event impinging on a receptor but not initiating its normal receptor function is often, but improperly, called a stimulus. (And the expression **inadequate *stimulus** is unhappy for this event.) ¶The chief trouble with this definition is that it seems impossible to adhere to. Physical energy as stimulus is an initiator of behavior; but not all initiators can be described, even in schematic fashion, in terms of physical energy. (Thus, a father's anger as stimulus to a child's fear is not describable, at least at present, in physicalist language.) Yet many who formally accept definition of stimulus in terms of energy slip into locutions, such as "social stimulus," inconsistent with it. In psychophysics and in experimental study of sensation, however, stimulus usually retains consistently the traditional meaning. It is sometimes symbolized R (for *Ger., Reiz*).

2. a **signal**, a particular part of the environment, that initiates a response in an organism. ➤*Syn.* SIGN STIMULUS. The difficulty here is much the same as in **(1).** A dinner bell signal can indeed be described in physical-energy terms; but it is doubtful that the analysis of the bell sound *as an initiator of response* can be carried through without talking about something more than the energy of the air waves. **3.** = INTERNAL STIMULUS, an event inside the organism that affects a receptor; or any event inside the organism that plays an important part in the initiation of a response. ➤This thoroughly confused usage fails to distinguish between the ***afferent *feedback** from an internal event and the event itself. —See **drive stimulus. 4.** a **sense datum** or **sensation**; or an object of **perception.** ➤Probably no one formally defines stimulus in this way; but many writers, including some behaviorists, use it this way on occasion. It is, however, an unfortunate usage, alike for behaviorist and for mentalist. The former has no place in his system for sense data or perceptual objects but only for external energy and the organismic activities the energy elicits. The latter distinguishes physical energy from the percept, but the term stimulus then belongs on the side of physical energy (sense 1). **5.** an **incentive**;

something that prods the organism to greater effort. ➤This is essentially a layman's meaning, but it influences professional use of the term. **6.** any mental activity that leads to another. ➤Again, an important lay usage that finds its way into professional writing.—*Cp.* **(3)** above. **7.** any phenomenon, object, aspect of an object, or event, however conceived or described, which modifies behavior by eliciting activity in a sense organ. ➤This deliberately inclusive and nondiscriminating meaning is distilled from the loose usage that is by far the most prevalent.

It seems clear that *stimulus* cannot, in actual use, be effectively restricted either to a physicalistic or a mentalistic meaning. Much as one would like to see stimulus restricted to its traditional meaning, it is probably too late, no delinquency being so incorrigible as a semantic one. Insistence upon the restricted meaning in formal definition has not kept the usage consistent; it has merely led to the fallacy of the ambiguous middle term: "A stimulus is a form of physical energy; the father's anger is the stimulus to the child's fear; therefore, the father's anger is a form of physical energy." Perhaps, however, stimulus can be held to a useful meaning as in **(7)**, which combines the three basic ideas set forth at the beginning of the entry: the ideas of (A) incitement, (B) external agent, (C) relation to sensory process.

8. (*J. R. Kantor*) that act of a **stimulus object**, or distinguishable aspect of an interbehavioral event, which corresponds with a reciprocal response of an organism. ➤Though distinguishable, stimulus and response are held to be inseparable. (See **stimulus function, interbehavioral psychology.**) Stimulus is not conceived as eliciting response in an organism: rather, stimulus and responding organism participate in an interbehavior. Though differently conceptualized, stimulus in this sense probably refers to very much the same data as in **(7)**.
—See **situation** for the relation of stimulus to allied terms.

stimulus/adequate: a form of energy that normally excites a given type of **receptor.** —*Cp.* **stimulus/inadequate, stimulus/ineffective.**

stimulus/ambiguous: see **ambiguous stimulus.**

stimulus/anomalous: a more descriptive but less common term for **inadequate *stimulus.**

stimulus attitude: 1. in reaction time experiments, the **set** to observe the coming stimulus, the response being allowed to follow low automatically. ➤It contrasts with **motor *set** or RESPONSE ATTITUDE, in which the observer is set to make a certain response as soon as the stimulus is presented. **2.** the set to attend to the qualities directly given by the stimulus (or by the **proximal** *stimulus). ➤According to **structural psychology,** this procedure is necessary for the introspective analysis of sensation. It contrasts with the OBJECT ATTITUDE, the set to attend to the context or meaning or to the perceptual object.—*Cp.* **stimulus error.**

stimulus/aversive: a stimulus which, if applied following a response, decreases the tendency to that response on later similar occasions.

stimulus-bound: *adj.* **1.** characterizing perceiving in which variations in the stimulus situation almost totally determine the process, to the exclusion of the more normal joint determination of perceiving by the stimulus and by the perceiver. ➤Stimulus-bound perception is the logical opposite of both **illusion** and **hallucination,** but is not on that account to be deemed normal; it is frequently **maladjustive. 2.** of a person whose responses are excessively dependent upon the details of the stimulus situation.—*Syn.* **rigid** (not *prefd.*). **3.** characterizing perception in which elements of low attention value have almost no effect, the perceiving being almost wholly determined by that which is at the focus of attention.

stimulus/conditional or **/conditioned:** see **conditioned stimulus.**

stimulus/constant: see **constant stimulus method.**

stimulus/consummatory: 1. the stimulus for a **consummatory response. 2.** a stimulus that terminates response to a set of stimuli. ➤No observable consummatory response is the corollary of this stimulus.

stimulus continuum: a series of stimuli that may, under certain circumstances, be substituted one for the other: e.g., a series of colors of the same hue, or (in conditioning) the stimuli very like the US or CS which can by **stimulus *generalization** elicit the **CR.** ➤*Distg.* the latter *fr.* IN-CIDENTAL (better, COINCIDENTAL) STIMULI, those stimuli, not forming a series with the experimental stimulus (either CS or US), which become conditioned because they are consistently present during conditioning: e.g., a click from the apparatus when the experimental stimulus is presented. Such a coincidental stimulus is as much a conditioned stimulus as any other; it is merely not the one the experimenter bargains for.

stimulus control: the regulation of variation in organismic response by variation in the stimulus, the **central** process being regarded as a constant. ➤That *both* stimulus and central process influence behavior is denied by no one; this term asserts for some

behaviors a *relative* freedom from control by central process. **Field theorists** tend to deny that even relative freedom may safely be held to.

stimulus differentiation: 1. (*Gestalt*) the process whereby what is at first perceived as relatively homogeneous comes to be seen as composed of distinct but interrelated parts of a whole; or the result of such process. **2.** the process by which an organism gradually learns to respond differently to two stimuli which originally elicited the same response.

stimulus/discriminative: a cue stimulus that releases the **operant** response; the stimulus that is learned in operant learning.

stimulus/distal: see **distal vs. proximal variables.**

stimulus/drive: see **drive stimulus.**

stimulus/effective: one that produces a response when applied to a given **receptor.** —*Cp.* **stimulus/inadequate.**—*Syn.* **stimulus/adequate** (more common but less descriptive).

stimulus equivalence: see **equivalence (2),** and **generalization/stimulus.**

stimulus error: (*E. B. Titchener*) a report "not in terms of sensation, but in terms of stimulus"; allowing one's perception or judgment of a simple sense object to be influenced by former association, the general context in which it lies, and unreflective interpretations. ➤A distant sound may be declared "loud," though it is actually so low when it reaches the ear that it won't wake the baby, whereas a softer sound near by is called "low," yet does wake the baby, who does not yet commit the "stimulus error." This kind of report is an "error" only when the subject is under instruction to report in terms of **sensation,** or of the **proximal *stimulus.**

stimulus field: the totality of stimuli that act on the organism at any moment; or the totality of stimuli of any given **modality.**

stimulus function: (*J. R. Kantor*) those characteristics of the interbehavioral field which are ascribable to a **stimulus object.** ➤Any number of stimulus functions may inhere in a complex stimulus object. The stimulus object may be thought of as independent of a particular interbehavioral event; but the stimulus *function* is a property of a complete unique event, not merely of the object taken in isolation.

stimulus generalization: see **generalization/stimulus.**

stimulus/goal or S_G: a **proprioceptive** stimulus resulting from **goal-directed behavior,** R_G.

stimulus/inadequate: a form of energy that excites a receptor for which it is not the normal or ADEQUATE STIMULUS. ➤E.g., a warm object applied to a receptor for coolth is sensed as cold, not warm. Since the inadequate stimulus is not *ineffective,* ANOMALOUS STIMULUS would be more descriptive.—*Cp.* **stimulus/ineffective.**

stimulus/incidental: see **stimulus continuum.**

stimulus-induced maturation: see **maturation/stimulus-induced.**

stimulus/ineffective: a form of energy that does not arouse sensory activity when applied to the receptor. ➤It may be insufficiently intense, or the receptor may not be adapted to the form of energy. A light from the visible range may lack enough intensity to be seen; and ultra-violet rays (short wave lengths) do not excite any receptors.—*Cp.* **stimulus/inadequate.**

stimulus-intensity dynamism: (*C. Hull*) the principle that, other things being constant, the magnitude of the stimulus-intensity component (V) of the reaction potential (sE_R) is a monotonic increasing logarithmic function of S.

stimulus/liminal: see **liminal stimulus.**

stimulus/maintaining: a stimulus that, provided a certain response tendency or **drive** state continues, continues to elicit response until a certain consummatory response is made. E.g., a hole in her nest maintains the repair responses of a wasp until it is filled.

stimulus method: a technique for correction of articulatory defects of speech involving repeatedly hearing and discriminating sounds, then trying to reproduce them.

stimulus/neutral: any stimulus that does not produce the response one is looking for. ➤This is the state of the conditioned stimulus before conditioning begins.—*Cp.* **inadequate *stimulus.**

stimulus object: *n.* **1.** a stimulus that is made up of many smaller stimuli. ➤The component stimuli may be defined in any of the ways given under **stimulus.** Often it is implied that the combination is **nonadditive.**—*Syn.* **stimulus situation,** somewhat more inclusive. **2.** (*J. R. Kantor*) anything that has developed a unique or individual function in an interbehavioral field and that reciprocally corresponds with an organism's specific response. ➤An organism may be a stimulus object for another organism.

stimulus pattern: a more or less stable grouping of stimuli; a complex stimulus considered as including the qualitative and the spatial, temporal, and other quantitative relations of the component stimuli; or the relations of stimuli, abstracted from specific concrete details. E.g., in considering the alternating red and white stripes of the American flag, the pattern may be taken to include the specific color qualities, or may

be thought of as that of "alternating stripes," color ignored.

stimulus population: see **s-population.**

stimulus/prepotent: a stimulus that has the ascendency over all simultaneously competing stimuli in controlling the response of the organism.

stimulus/private: a change inferred to occur inside an animal but observable by another only with special instrumentation or not at all. ➤It is intended as a behaviorist term for that which is introspected.—*Cp.* **covert behavior.**

stimulus/proximal: see **distal vs. proximal variables.**

stimulus/reinforcing: any stimulus that alters the probability or strength of the later occurrence of a response with which it occurs simultaneously.—See **reinforcement.**

stimulus-response correlation: the observable fact that a certain specified energy change (= **stimulus**) tends to be followed by a specified movement in a given organism. E.g., an increase in light reaching the eye is followed by contraction of the pupil; change from warm to cold in an object touching the skin will be followed by retreat or aversive movements if the animal has had a certain training.

stimulus-response psychology: the viewpoint that the task of psychology is to determine the correlations between explicit stimuli and explicit responses—i.e., to discover what an organism does when stimulated in this way or that. ➤**Mental process** is not necessarily denied nor **introspection** necessarily discarded, but emphasis shifts to the dynamic relation between environment and the resulting reaction. Stimulus-response psychology tends to be relatively **reactive** and **peripheralistic,** finding the control of behavior *chiefly* in the stimulus and in the sensory mechanisms affected by stimulus. Yet modern **associationism,** though it postulates certain **central** processes, is essentially a stimulus-response psychology, dealing with the conditions under which a given stimulus-response correlation is established. The tendency is to explain complex behavior in terms of relatively small and distinct units (*cp.* **atomism, reductionism**), thus contrasting with **Gestalt, field theory,** and self psychology.—See **psychology/divisions and schools of, III.**

stimulus/sign: a stimulus, originally neutral, that comes to elicit a **species-specific** response. ➤The acquisition of sign stimulus is similar to **canalization** except that in the latter the stimuli that gain power to evoke a consummatory response are not conceived as originally neutral.

stimulus situation: a complex of conditions and events acting as a stimulus for **a**

person's behavior. ➤The expression is only formally redundant: it emphasizes that the several stimuli are taken globally or as a complex, not as separate units. Listening to a concert is a stimulus situation: the music —either a particular sonata or a single phrase—is the stimulus object, the air waves or the individual tones are the stimuli.

stimulus/social: any **stimulus (7)** that in any sense can be called social: e.g., a person or persons, a group as a group, an object thought of as essentially a social product; a stimulus that evokes a social response. ➤The term is very fluid. Social seems to be added chiefly to make clear that one does not mean a *physical* **stimulus (1)**.

stimulus/subliminal: a stimulus below the **threshold**. ➤See **liminal stimulus**. A subliminal stimulus may sometimes have an indirect effect.

stimulus trace or *s'*: (*C. Hull*) the hypothetical **molar** aftereffects following termination of a brief stimulus; an afferent process rising quickly to a maximum and gradually diminishing to zero as a time function of strength when stimulus energy ceases to act. ➤*Cp*. **mneme, trace.** While the facts are probably the same, the stimulus trace is differently conceived by Hull from the **trace** of earlier theorizing.—*Syn*. MOLAR STIMULUS TRACE.

stimulus/unconditioned or US = **unconditioned stimulus.**

stimulus value: *n*. any quantitative statement of a stimulus, most often an intensity description.

stimulus variable or **S variable**: the stimulus as a measurable variable among a complex of (possibly) interrelated variables, such as the subject's ability, age, life history, drive state or motivation, etc. ➤STIMULUS FACTOR more neatly summarizes this meaning but is less often used.

stimulus/variable: see **variable stimulus.**

stimulus word: in association tests or experiments, the presented word designed to elicit either the word having the strongest associative link at the moment with the stimulus word or a prescribed associate learned previously during the experiment.

stirp(s): *n*. the sum total of the **genes** or determiners of biological heredity in a given fertilized ovum.

stochastic (stō·kas'tik): *adj.* characterizing a process or series of events for which the estimate of the probability of a certain outcome approaches the true probability as the number of events increases. ➤A succession of throws of dice is stochastic. A STOCHASTIC NETWORK is a system of events bound to each other in causal dependence; at each critical point the next event is not invariably determined (as in the classical con-

cept of **causation**) but has a certain probability of occurrence.

stocking anesthesia: see **anesthesia/ glove.**

stoic: *adj*. (*pop*.) of an attitude of resigned endurance of pain or adversity.—*n*. **stoicism.**

storm-and-stress period: a period in early adolescence of great emotional turmoil. ➤Once believed to be a necessary accompaniment of growth, it is now recognized as an avoidable corollary of certain cultural influences.

story recall test: a test of memory for meaningful materials: the subject is required to reproduce the essential ideas, but not the exact words, of a brief passage or story.

$sT_R = (C. Hull)$ reaction **latency (2)**; re-**action time.**

strabismus (strə·biz'məs): *n*. cross-eyedness; either divergent or convergent SQUINT; lack of coordination of eye muscles so that the two eyes do not focus on the same point. —*Syn*. HETEROTROPIA.—*Distg. fr.* **heterophoria.**—*adj.* **strabismal.**

strain: *n*. 1. the state of a system when it is exposed to a **stress**. ➤Although a system is not destroyed or put out of action by strain, it is deformed, various parts being forced out of their normal relation with other parts. 2. extreme muscular **tension.** 3. injury resulting from excessive tension, muscular or psychological. 4. a special kind of sensation stimulated by muscular tension. 5. a species subdivision, of individuals having common lineage, but not having sufficiently marked common characters to constitute a named breed.

strain/cognitive - dynamic investment: (*R. B. Cattell*) the strain that comes with increase in the number and fineness of discriminations to be made and with increase in amount of delay to action necessary in proceeding toward a goal.

stratification: *n*. (*sociol*.) a horizontal or layerlike division of a society or social group —e.g., into **classes** or **castes.**—*adj*. **stratified.**—*v*. **stratify.**

stratified sample: see **sampling/stratified.**

Stratton's experiment: inverting the retinal image by wearing prisms that turn the entire visual field through 180°.

streaming: *n*. British term for placement of pupils in an educational group that is proceeding toward appropriate educational goals at a rate appropriate for the pupils assigned.—*Cp*. **acceleration/educational** and **ability grouping.**

stream of consciousness: see **consciousness/stream of.**

strength/associative: see **associative strength.**

strephosymbolia (stref"ō·sim·bō′li·ə): *n.* reversal in perception of left-right order, esp. in letter or word order: *bat* read as *tab.* ➤*Distg. fr.* MIRROR PERCEPTION, in which not only the order of the letters but the letters themselves are reversed. In strephosymbolia, reversal of the individual letters is rare. The reversed words need not be meaningful, and reversal for a given word does not invariably occur.

stress: *n.* **1.** a force, applied to a **system,** sufficient to cause **strain** or distortion in the system, or, when very great, to alter it into a new form. ➤The term may be restricted to physical force and physical systems, or extended to psychological forces and systems. **2.** emphasis on certain words or syllables in spoken language.

stress interview: a species of **stress test** in which a person is interviewed while under intentionally induced emotional strain.

stress test: a test in which the task itself, together with the prescribed conditions of testing, puts the subject under great emotional strain, esp. by giving him tasks impossible of achievement. ➤The tasks are generally of lifelike nature and the purpose of the test is partially or wholly disguised.

striate body = **corpus striatum.**

striate muscle: see **muscle/striate.**

striatum = **corpus striatum.**

striped muscle = **muscle/striate.**

strip key: a scoring key for tests, with answers so arranged in a column on a strip that they can be aligned with the testee's responses on the test blank.

strith: see **ulstrith.**

striving: *n.* vigorous or energetic exertion or effort.

stroboscopic effect or **illusion** (strō"bō·-skop′ik): **1.** the apparent motion of slightly different visual objects when seen in rapid succession, as in motion pictures. **2.** more specif., the effect for visual perception when a moving object is illuminated by a rapidly intermittent light. ➤If, e.g., a set of evenly spaced black bars in motion is illuminated by flashes of light so distributed that the bars move forward one step for each flash, the bars will seem to stand still; if the flashes come somewhat less frequently than the bars, the bars will seem to move in the direction of their actual movement but more slowly; if the flashes come more frequently, the bars will seem to move slowly backward. The STROBOSCOPE is an instrument for producing and observing this effect; it can be used for measuring speed of motion in instruments or machines. Tactual stroboscopic effects are also found.—*Cp.* **apparent *motion.**

stroke: *n.* **1.** (*med.*) a sudden and severe seizure. **2.** (*pop.*) an apoplectic seizure.

strong color: a color of high **saturation.**

Strong Vocational Interest Blank: a self-inventory, covering a wide variety of interests and likes-dislikes, which can be scored for similarity to the interest patterns of persons pursuing various vocations.—*Abbr.* SVIB.

structural: *adj.* pertaining to, or having the characteristics of, a **structure.** ➤When contrasted with the ambiguous term **dynamic,** structural also becomes somewhat ambiguous, tending toward the meaning of **static.** In contrast with **functional** or **behavioral,** it tends to mean the potential or the substantive basis for behavior, the **dispositional.** In a biological context, it means **organic, constitutional,** or **morphological.**

structural information: see **information theory.**

structuralism = **structural psychology.**

structuralization: *n.* the process of imposing form or structure upon a formless or heterogeneous mass of phenomena; or the result of the process.—*v.* **structure** (not *structuralize*).

structural psychology: 1. a point of view or school of psychology that analyzes mental states or contents into elementary constituents by the method of introspection aided by experiment.—*Syn.* **content psychology, existential psychology.**—See **psychology/divisions and schools of,** III. **2.** = **structure psychology.** ➤To maintain the distinction between (1) and (2), it is recommended that the German *Struktur Psychologie* be retained for this school.

structure: *n.* **1.** something made; any enduring arrangement, grouping, pattern, or articulation of parts to form a relatively stable system or whole. ➤The term has proved adaptable to many uses—one speaks of the *structure* of the atom, the *structure* of a sentence, the *structure* of a bodily organ, mental *structures,* the *structure* of society. The use of structure in connection with buildings and the like gives the term an overtone of strength. ¶Structure is contrasted with **function** or **process** (though these may themselves have structure), with the formless, and with the temporary or rapidly changing. Structure usually implies stability of the component parts, whereas the parts of a **gestalt** or a system may alter so long as the interrelationships remain the same. Gestalt emphasizes wholeness; **system** emphasizes rationality of arrangement; **organization,** an arrangement of parts according to their role or function. But these distinctions are not rigid and the four terms are often interchangeable. (In Gestalt circles, **structure** and **gestalt** are close synonyms.) ¶Structure is often redundantly added to terms that essentially imply it: e.g., personality *structure*—by any definition, **personality** *is* a structure.—*adj.* **structural**, pertaining to a structure; **structured**, having a firm structure.

—See also the phrase terms embodying **structural** and **structure**, esp. **structure/mental.**

structure: *v.* **2.** to impose a **structure** on a situation or an event that lacks it; to put parts together so that they form a unified or organized whole; or to increase the unity and articulation of the parts of a whole. ➤Parts previously distinct may be physically joined, or parts actually unified may be newly seen as forming a whole. **3.** to define and describe the relationships present in a situation, so that another person will be aware of them; to set forth data so that relationships can be seen. ➤The verb *structuralize* is an unnecessary form.

structure/biological: the spatial arrangements and connections of the constituents of an organism (or any of its parts). ➤*Syn.* ORGANIC STRUCTURE, **constitution, morphology, anatomy.** (Properly speaking, morphology and anatomy are the sciences dealing with structure, but both are used also for the structure itself.) Biological structure is generally used to contrast with **function.** For contrast with **mental** *structure, see that term.

structured stimulus: a complex stimulus in which the parts are closely **articulated.**

structure/factor: see **factor structure.**

structure-function reaction: (*Gestalt*) a unified reaction to a situation that has been perceived as a whole; a **global** reaction.

structure/mental or **/psychological: 1.** personality viewed as stable and organized, with parts related to each other and to the whole as are the parts of a building. **2.** any component of such a whole that is hypothesized to account for recurrent similarities of behavior under varying conditions; a relatively distinct, enduring part of a person inferred as the basis for specific function. ➤These structures are **constructs.** While few psychologists question that they are related to the visible body or **soma** in some fashion (see **mind-body problem**), the psychological subdivisions of the structure of the person seldom parallel closely the subdivisions described by anatomy. Psychological structures are constructs and have only such properties as must be assigned them to account for the behaviors for which they are the basis. If the error of **faculty psychology** is to be avoided, it must be recognized that not every named variety of behavior has its own specific structural basis. ¶A large number of terms in psychology are essentially terms

of structure rather than directly of **function**, though all are inferred from function: e.g., **ability, attitude, sentiment, disposition, tendency, trait.** Many others refer both to the function and to its inferred structure: e.g., **emotion.** Such usage is dangerous since it suggests (even if it does not imply) that the underlying structure has a one-to-one relation with the function —which is seldom the case. **3.** the interrelations of the describable parts of a complex psychological phenomenon, such as a **conscious *content,** or an **act** or **action.** ➤In this meaning, structure does not contrast with function but is a description of a function. Such structure is not enduring, but it may be recurrent.

structure of a region: (*topol.*) the number, arrangement, and dynamic interactions between component parts or subregions.

structure/perceptual: the interrelations of the parts of what is perceived. ➤The term shares the ambiguities of the term **perception.** Reference is usually to **phenomenological *structure;** but sometimes it is to **stimulus *structure,** and sometimes (no doubt) to a bit of both.

structure/personality: a redundant expression, since **personality** itself connotes a complex structure.

structure/phenomenological: the interrelations that prevail in the **phenomenal *field.** ➤E.g., when one looks toward the window, a house plant is seen standing out against a gray sky. The relationships of the plant as figure to the rest of the field as background constitute the major characteristic of the field structure. But in the field are other structural relations such as the nearness of the plant, the farness of the sky, and—since the plant was a gift—affective and memory components as well.

structure psychology: a school of German psychologists who seek to describe the theoretical types of man and the theoretical relationships between the traits within each type. ➤No actual person is presumed to conform to a theoretical or "ideal" type, but it is considered possible to understand actual behavior by comparison with the theoretical or ideal.—*Distg. fr.* **structural psychology (1),** almost the direct opposite.—*Syn.* STRUKTUR PSYCHOLOGIE (*prefd.* in order to keep this distinction).— See *Geisteswissenschaftliche Psychologie* and **psychology/divisions and schools of, II.**

structure/simple: see **simple structure.**

structure/stimulus: the particular way in which **stimuli** are joined in forming complex stimuli; the pattern of stimuli.

Struktur Psychologie (shtrŭk·tûr′) = **structure psychology.**

stub: *n.* the phrase, at the left of a row in a

statistical table, that defines or names the variable.

student: *n.* a person enrolled in a secondary or higher educational institution; or one engaged in serious independent study.—*Distg. fr.* **pupil,** though often used as a synonym.

student personnel work: 1. the encouragement and direction of all student activities, other than class or laboratory instruction, designed to promote the development of personality and character. **2.** analyzing the student's personality (in the widest sense of the term) and helping him to discover how he may best develop himself.

Student's test = *t* (3).

study: *n.* **1.** relatively protracted application to a topic or problem for the purpose of learning about the topic, solving the problem, or memorizing part or all of the presented material. **2.** a branch of learning; a science or discipline. **3.** a research or investigation; or a report of an investigation. —*v.* **study,** to attend to something with intent to understand it and to improve oneself in relation to it.

study of values: see **Allport-Vernon Study of Values.**

stupor: *n.* **1.** a condition allied to **coma** but less severe. The patient is inaccessible to stimuli (though not unconscious), shows loss of orientation and minimum activity.— See **stupor/catatonic. 2.** = **mutism** (*prefd.*).

stupor/catatonic: a symptom common in **catatonia:** impressions of the external world are normally received but there is **negativism** and **stereotypy,** or (alternatively) extreme **suggestibility.**

stupor/epileptic: see **epileptic stupor.**

stuttering: *n.* a speech impediment in which the even flow of words is interrupted by hesitations, rapid repetition of speech elements, and spasms of breathing or vocalization muscles. ➤*Syn.* SPASMOPHEMIA; also STAMMERING, limited by some to speech stoppages or blocking, reserving stuttering for speech repetitions.

stuttering scale/Iowa: a scale composed of 33 nine-second samples of phonographically recorded stuttered speech, ranked by the **equal-appearing intervals method** according to the degree of stuttering deemed to be manifested in the samples. The speech of a stutterer is compared with the samples and assigned the scale value of the sample it most resembles.

tyle: *n.* the sum total of the details of behavior that influence the attainment of a goal comparatively little but that give to an individual or to a particular performance a characteristic, almost an identifying, manner. ➤Two golfers drive equally straight and far but with recognizable differences in manner; the same sentence is pronounced with equal clarity but with distinctive details of intonation, etc. A. Adler, hypothesizing a style pervasive of *all* one's behavior, called it a STYLE OF LIFE and conceived it as a technique for dealing with (or living with) one's inadequacies and inferiorities and for gaining status.—*adj.* **stylized,** of behavior that has a formal and traditional style; **stylistic,** having marked and unusual characteristics obviously constituting a special style; mannered or manneristic. (**Stylish** is pre-empted by a popular usage.)

style of life: see **style.**

stylistic tests: tests designed to reveal the **style** in which one performs certain standard actions. ➤The assumption is that aspects of style revealed in the standard sample are common to wide areas of behavior: e.g., that the style manifested in rapid wide-sweeping movements in handwriting will be found in other aspects of a person's behavior.

SU = auditory **sensation unit (2).**

Su = **unconditioned stimulus.**

sub-: combining form meaning *under, beneath, less than.*

subacute: see **acute.**

subception: *n.* reaction to a stimulus object that is not fully enough perceived to be reportable. ➤Indirect evidence of subception is obtained from effects on the simultaneous perception of other objects, from certain nonverbal responses, or from effects on memory.—*Cp.* **perceptual *defense.**

subconscious: *adj.* **1.** not clearly conscious but capable of being made so. ➤The term is subject to all the ambiguities of **conscious** and a few of its own. It may be said to imply that there exist phenomena that are (*a*) **mental** in nature, (*b*) influential for, or basic to, personal consciousness, but (*c*) not actually apprehended by the personal consciousness. Many hold that (*a*) and (*c*) are irreconcilable concepts. **2.** (*psychoan.*) pertaining to phenomena of either the **preconscious** or the **coconscious.**—*Distg. fr.* **unconscious,** in which repression is said to be always operative. But in popular psychoanalysis the unconscious and the subconscious are thoroughly confused. **3.** (*obsoles.*) = **subliminal.** ➤Not now good usage. **4.** pertaining to what is in the margin of attention. ➤Not good usage.—*Syn.* MARGINAL.

subcortical: *adj.* **1.** pertaining to the neural structures lying beneath the cortex, whether in the cerebrum itself or in those portions of the nervous system lying beneath (**caudad** to) the **hemispheres. 2.** pertaining to the functions of the nervous system that are not directly dependent upon cortical control.

subculture: *n.* a division of a cultural group

or population consisting of persons who share special cultural characteristics at the same time that they share the major characteristics of the whole culture. ➤Most religious denominations in America do not differ enough in anything but Sunday services (if that) to be deemed subcultures; but those with special food taboos, initiatory rites, and prohibition of outmarriage are subcultures. So is "high society."

subcutaneous: *adj.* beneath the skin or the surface of the skin. ➤SUBCUTANEOUS SENSIBILITY is sensitivity to pressures arising from **receptors** in the deeper layers of the true skin or in the tissues beneath.

subject: *n.* **1.** a topic; that which one observes or studies, of which one thinks, speaks, or makes assertions. ➤In this (primarily logical) sense, subject is nearly the same as a complex **object (2)**. **2.** the being who thinks, feels, acts; the center of reference for **mental** phenomena.—See **person**. **3.** the person or other animal to whom stimuli are applied for the purpose of evoking responses; or, more generally, the person whose reactions are observed.—*Abbr.* **S.** ➤Senses (1) and (2) seem diametrically opposed, yet in (3) they are united: the person observed is at the same time the being to whom the phenomena must be referred. **4.** in general, an individual exposed to any kind of experimental treatment: e.g., a person given a new drug for testing.

subjectify: *v.* to make **subjective**; to impose on phenomena one's subjective **frame of reference** or evaluation, sometimes to the point of distorting an observation or report about the external world.

subjection: *n.* the state of being under the control of another person.

subjective: *adj.* **1.** pertaining to a **subject (2)** or **person.** ➤This is the basic meaning from which the others are derived as presumed corollaries. These fall into three groups, but a given employment of the word may imply some element of any or all three: (A) confined to a subject or experiencer, therefore private, not public (senses **2, 3, 4**); (B) pertaining to a subject or person, therefore mental or psychic (senses **5, 6, 7**); (C) pertaining to *one* subject, therefore individual (sense 8). In nearly all cases, some synonym is to be preferred to this thoroughly ambiguous term. **2.** intrinsically inaccessible to the observation of more than one person; characterizing experience as necessarily appertaining to the experiencer alone. ➤A widespread philosophical tradition held that a person's mental processes were intrinsically private. Behaviorism was a revolt against accepting such a private world as the object of scientific consideration. But the whole postulate is philosophical rather than psychological, and modern logic seems to show

that it is self-contradictory.—*Syn.* **private;** INTROSPECTIBLE (though some writers speak of nonintrospectible subjective experience). —*Ant.* **public; objective. 3.** not open to verification by others; not utilizing public or communicable standards. ➤This is the commonest use. An observation is subjective when the conditions under which it took place are not described or describable; a test is graded subjectively when the grader cannot state his criteria; an opinion is subjective when the person cannot tell upon what it is based. **Subjective** in this sense is often equated with *untrustworthy* or *unreliable*; but the judgments of a teataster, e.g., are predictable and trustworthy even though based on criteria he cannot describe. —*Syn.* unverifiable, **intuitive.**—*Ant.* **objective,** verifiable. **4.** pertaining to observation made without the aid of instruments. ➤This is an extension of (3) and apparently assumes that only instrumental observation is verifiable—which is false. **5.** = **mental** or **psychic.** ➤Subjective is often merely interchanged with these terms. This usage generally occurs in a context implying a **dualism** between the external world and the psychic world. **6.** characterizing sensations or sense data which the experiencer does not refer to the external world. ➤In general, such sense data yield information about the bodily state. Pain (usually), fatigue, organic sensations, and the so-called bodily feelings are called subjective. The phenomena referred to under this usage are, however, miscellaneous. Even visual sensations are sometimes not referred to the external world; and kinesthetic and tactual sensations may or may not be so referred, almost at will. (One speaks of roughness as one's own tactual sensation, or of the roughness of sandpaper.) Since the data are miscellaneous, no single synonym is available or needed: more specific designations are preferred. **7.** imaginary; hallucinatory; not correspondent with reality: his troubles are *subjective*. **8.** belonging to or related to a *single* subject or person; dependent upon the individual's method of observing or judging, or on his frame of reference and values. ➤Individual differences in **overt** behavior are not characterized as subjective, but differences depending upon personal standards or upon merely inferred personal traits are said to be subjective. In sharp contrast with (2) or (3), such differences may be verifiable and dependable.—*Cp.* **point of *subjective equality.**—*Syn.* **individual, personal.**—*Ant.* **impersonal.**—*n.* **subjectivity.**

subjective accent or **rhythm:** see **accent/subjective.**

subjective attributes: those characteristics of an experience which are inseparable from the experiencer: e.g., the quality or intensity of a color or sound. ➤*Contr. w.* the physical dimensions of the physical stimulus.—See **stimulus, subjective** (2 and 3).

subjective equality/point of: 1. the point along a continuum at which, for a given observer, two stimuli or two sense data are judged or perceived to be equal. 2. a point more exactly determined for psychophysics in any of the following ways: (*a*) the most frequently occurring value of the comparison stimulus that is judged equal to the standard; (*b*) the point where the two **psychometric functions** of the "greater" and "less" judgments intersect; (*c*) a point halfway between the upper and lower **thresholds.** If the distribution is symmetrical, these three determinations yield identical values. 3. (*comp. psychol.*) the point at which no relevant differences in the animal's responses to two stimuli can be detected by the experimenter. ➤The point is an objective datum, even though it is subjectively located—i.e., located by the observer's individual discrimination or lack of it.—*Syn.* POINT OF NONDISCRIMINATION (*prefd.*).

subjective error: see **error/subjective.**

subjective psychology: 1. any psychology that holds that there is a distinct kind of datum to be studied by psychology. 2. a psychology that studies private data—i.e., the data of **introspection.**—See **subjective.**

subjective rhythm: see **accent/subjective.**

subjective sensations: 1. actual **sense data** (not **images**) that correlate with activity of a sense organ but not directly with any stimulus outside the organism: e.g., **entoptic** phenomena, ringing in the ears, the feeling of reversed rotation after rotation stops. 2. any sense data not referred to the external world.—See **subjective (6).**

subjective test: see **test/subjective.**

subjective type: a person who tends to judge events in relation to himself and his own values.—*Syn.* **autistic** type. ➤*Contr. w.* OBJECTIVE TYPE, a person who tends to observe and evaluate events as they are in themselves, without reference to his own desires.

subjectivism: *n.* 1. the tendency to be strongly influenced in perception and thinking by one's personal **frame of reference.** E.g., a city of 10,000 is considered huge because one was brought up in a village, etc. —*Syn.* **subjectivity.** 2. the philosophical doctrine that makes personal and individual experience the test of reality, truth, goodness, or beauty.

sublimation: *n.* refinement or redirection of the energy belonging to a primitive tendency into new, noninherited channels; somewhat more broadly, such alteration in instinctive behavior as will bring it within

the boundaries of conventional approval and yet allow partial satisfaction. ➤In Freudian theory, the sublimated tendency is the **libido;** it is the **sexual aim** which is altered. ¶The following forms have been distinguished. (*a*) CANALIZATION—the tendency, essentially unaltered, is restricted within narrow boundaries: e.g., fighting is restricted by boxing rules. (But see **canalization** for another meaning.) (*b*) DEFLECTION or VICARIOUS COMPENSATION—the tendency is deflected toward other objects than the stimulating one: e.g., fighting is directed against an unoffending person. (*c*) PLATONIZATION—the natural manifestations are altered to purely "mental" substitutes: e.g., fighting finds outlet in chess. (*d*) OBJECTIFICATION—one gets vicarious satisfaction from watching a spectacle, as at a theater or in a novel (*cp.* **identification**). (*e*) SUBJECTIFICATION—the tendency is turned inward upon oneself, as in the self-flagellation of hermits and ascetics. (*f*) FANTASY and DAYDREAMING—one gets satisfaction for a thwarted drive in all manner of imaginary ways. Sometimes called **retreat from *reality.**

subliminal (sub·lim′i·nəl; -lī′mə-): *adj.* 1. below the **threshold;** of stimuli that cannot be discriminated under the conditions of the experiment. 2. of stimuli that are too weak to be specifically apprehended and reported but not too weak to be influential on conscious processes or behavior; or of the effects of such stimuli.—See **subception.**

subliminal learning: learning that has not proceeded far enough to enable recall.

submental: *adj.* beneath the chin. ➤It does *not* pertain to inferior mentality.

submission: *n.* yielding to the commands or leadership of another; conforming one's behavior to that of another.—*adj.* **submissive.**—*v.* **submit.**

submissiveness: *n.* tendency to **submission;** a personal trait leading one to accept the domination of others.

subnormal: *adj.* below, or less than, **normal** (which see).

subordination: *n.* 1. placing a given item or datum in a lower category or class.— *Cp.* **coordination, superordination.** 2. accepting the domination of one's behavior by another person or persons.

subservience: *n.* subordinating one's own interests or purposes to those of another.

subshock therapy: a mild form of **shock therapy.**

subsidiation: *n.* the relationship of means to end; the relationship that prevails when an act is performed in order to attain an intermediate state that brings the person closer to a goal.

subsidiation/dynamic: see **dynamic subsidiation.**

substance: *n.* 1. (*philos.*) the essential nature of anything, physical or psychical; that which makes a phenomenon what it is. **2.** the essential meaning of a communication, as distinguished from its form of expression.

substance memorization or **learning** = learning/meaningful (1).

substantia nigra (sub·stan′shi·ə nī′grə): a broad thick mass of pigmented nerve cells separating the dorsal and ventral parts of the **cerebral *peduncle.**

substantive state: (*W. James*) a part of the **stream** of *consciousness that is definite and enduring enough to be denoted by a noun. ⇒*Contr. w.* TRANSITIVE STATES, which elude separate observation and are referred to by prepositions and conjunctions. The experience of "motion" is substantive, but "toward" is transitive and exists only in relation with two substantive states: e.g., *motion toward home.*

substitute: *adj.* in certain phrases, a synonym for **conditioned.** ⇒SUBSTITUTE STIMULUS, esp., is more descriptive than **conditioned stimulus,** though less common.

substitute formation: (*psychoan.*) the substitute cognitive content or complex of ideas to which an **affect** attaches itself when repression banishes the former cognitive content but fails to banish the affect. —*Cp.* **affect/displacement of.**

substitute/regressive: (*psychoan.*) **displacement of *affect** to an aim or object appropriate only to an earlier phase of development.

substitution: *n.* **1.** any response resorted to when the more direct route to a goal is impeded or blocked. **2.** an unintentional replacement of one behavior by another: e.g., an error in oral reading consisting of saying a word not in the text in place of one that is. **3.** a defense mechanism whereby a person maintains his self-esteem by substituting approved goals for unapproved ones, and by substituting activities that can be carried out successfully for activities doomed to failure.—*Cp.* **sublimation, compensation, overcompensation.**

substitution neurosis: (*psychoan.*) a neurosis in which the anxiety of repression brings about psychic changes rather than the physical changes of **conversion** neurosis.

substitution test = **code test.**

subsume: *v.* to classify any datum or phenomenon as an instance of some more general class or law; to include under.

subtest: *n.* a division of a test designed to measure a particular aspect of that which the test as a whole measures.

subtraction method: obtaining a value for a certain variable by subtracting the value of one observation from that of another observation: e.g., subtracting a simple reaction time from a complex reaction time

to get a measure of the factor of choice. ⇒The method at its best is somewhat unreliable and in many cases makes invalid assumptions, yet it cannot be wholly dispensed with.

subvariable: *n.* one of two or more variables that are components of a larger variable.

subvocal speech: slight movements of lips, tongue, and larynx as in speech, but producing no audible sound. ⇒Such movements occur in thinking and are supposed by some to be the sole vehicle of thinking in its broadest sense.—*Syn.* IMPLICIT SPEECH, COVERT SPEECH.—*Cp.* **internal speech** (which is probably subvocal, but may have other elements).

succession: *n.* **1.** the following of one datum or item by another, esp. in a series. **2.** (*structural psychol.*) the following of one experience by another; or the experience of change. ⇒*Distg. fr.* **duration,** an attribute of an experience of lasting an appreciable time.—*Ant.* **simultaneity.**

successive contrast: see **color contrast.**

successive intervals/method of: a modification of the method of **equal-appearing intervals** in which intervals are defined by descriptive phrases or by sample specimens.

successive practice/method of: a method that employs the saving in the learning of B as a result of having practiced A as the measure of **transfer** from A to B. The control group learns B without having learned A.

successive reproductions method: a procedure in the study of forgetting wherein the subject is asked, at relatively long intervals, to reproduce the material previously learned. ⇒The changes found seem to follow a pattern inconsistent with the hypothesis that forgetting is a simple decay or loss.

succorance: *n.* **1.** the act of giving protection, aid, or assistance to someone. **2.** the tendency to solve one's problems by seeking aid or protection from someone. ⇒This usage is etymologically inverted: succorance should be the tendency to extend, not to seek, aid. But in context there is little confusion.

sucking: *n.* **1.** the reflex process whereby the mammalian infant grasps the nipple and draws milk into its mouth by suction. **2.** any suction exerted by the mouth. **3.** = **suckling** (1).—*v.* suck, *prefd.* to **suckle,** which has the meaning *to give to suck.*

suckling: *n.* **1.** the chain of reflexes involved in infant feeding: the grasp of the nipple, the suction, the swallowing. **2.** the act of giving the breast to an infant. **3.** a nursing infant; an infant in the nursing stage.—*v.* **suckle.**

suffer: *v.* **1.** to experience pain or bodily

discomfort; to experience grief or great anxiety. 2. to accept without resistance.— *n.* **suffering.**

sufficient reason/principle of: (*Leibnitz*) the postulate that, given sufficient facts, it is always possible to discern how and why any event is what it is. ➤*Syn.* PRINCIPLE OF UNIVERSAL RATIONALITY. The principle is the assertion of the reign of law and of the adequacy of human understanding; it is taken for granted by most scientists.

suggestibility: *n.* the state of being suggestible; or the hypothetical general trait of being susceptible to suggestion.

suggestible: *adj.* ready to accept suggestion from another and to modify one's behavior in at least partial accord therewith.

suggestion: *n.* 1. the process by which one person, without argument, command, or coercion, directly induces another to act in a given way or to accept a certain belief, opinion, or plan of action. 2. the verbal or other communication by means of which one person induces such action in another. ➤There is often an implication that suggestion is devious and designed to circumvent critical consideration.—*Syn.* HETEROSUGGESTION when contrasted with **autosuggestion.**

suggestion/negative: suggestion aimed to prevent or inhibit a particular behavior (including ideas, etc.). ➤*Cp.* **counter-suggestion,** which aims to remove an earlier suggestion.

suggestion/therapeutic: the abatement of anxiety by means of suggestion.

suigenderism (sū″i·jen′dər·iz·əm): *n.* (*rare*) nonerotic association with persons of one's own sex.—*Contr. w.* **homoerotism** and **homosexuality.**

sui generis (sū′ī jen′ər·is): (*L., of its own genus or class*) the only example of its kind; a unique instance.

sulcus (sul′kəs) *n., pl.* **sulci** (-sī): (*anat.*) a furrow or groove; esp., one of the shallow furrows on the surface of the brain separating the convolutions or **gyri.**—*Cp.* **fissure,** sometimes used as *syn.*—*adj.* **sulcal, sulcate.**

sum/algebraic: the aggregate of a number of quantities connected by the signs + or −; the sum of a number of quantities when their signs are taken into consideration; the sum of all the positive quantities diminished by the sum of all the negative quantities.

summation: *n.* 1. (*stat.*) a total or aggregate; or the act of finding a total by adding. The symbol for **summation** is Σ (which see, alphabetized *sigma*). 2. = SENSORY SUMMATION EFFECT, the increase in sensory intensity (or other quantitative attribute) when two or more stimuli are presented in rapid succession to the same **receptor** (TEMPORAL SUMMATION), or when

two or more stimuli of the same **mode** are presented to closely adjacent areas (SPATIAL SUMMATION). 3. = RESPONSE SUMMATION EFFECT, the increase in response when the **efferent** impulses arrive at the motor cells in rapid succession (TEMPORAL SUMMATION), or simultaneously from different **afferent** tracts (SPATIAL SUMMATION). 4. a joint effect produced by two or more factors or causes. 5. the production of a different kind of response when successive faint stimuli are applied: e.g., the tickle response to a succession of light touches. 6. (*advert.* and *propaganda*) the increased effect obtained (or hoped for) from the repetition of the same slogan or other appeal.—*Syn.* SUMMATION EFFECT, CUMULATIVE EFFECT.
➤Summation should be (but often is not) distinguished from **cumulation,** which is the formation of an aggregate by adding at different times; and from **integration,** the unification of parts into a pattern or organization.—*v.* **summate,** to make a summary or summation.

summation curve = ogive.

summation effect: see **summation** (3 and 6).

summation method: (*stat.*) any method of computing moments or product moments by the addition of class frequencies.—*Syn.* CUMULATIVE SUMMATION METHOD, **cumulative *frequency** method.

summation of stimuli: the adding of one stimulus to another to enhance or increase its effect.—See **summation** (2).

summation time: the longest interval between stimuli that will permit a joint effect, or summation.

summation tone: a very faint third tone that may sometimes be heard when two tones are sounded together. The pitch has a vibration frequency equal to the sum of the frequencies of the two tones.—*Contr. w.* **difference tone.**

sum total: 1. an emphatic synonym for sum. **2.** a group of data considered as having an influence corresponding to their sum rather than to each datum taken separately. —*Distg. fr.* **gestalt,** which is a whole that is more than the sum of its parts. (But **sum total** is often said when **gestalt** is the more accurate.)

superego: *n.* (*psychoan.*) a system within the total **psyche** developed by incorporating the parental standards as perceived by the ego; or, somewhat more broadly, by incorporating the moral standards of society as perceived by the ego. The **superego** has two parts: **ego ideal** and **conscience.** (It has been quipped to be that part of the psyche most readily soluble in alcohol.)

superego motivation: conscious and unconscious motivations that derive from parental and social standards and injunctions.

superficial: *adj.* 1. (*anat.*) pertaining to, or

located on, the surface of the body or of an organ. **2.** dealing with the trivial and obvious aspects of a topic, to the neglect of fundamentals. **3.** of an aspect of personality not closely related to, or central in its relations with, other aspects; of an aspect that can be dispensed with without essential change.

superficial reflex: a muscular contraction elicited by scratching or pinching the skin. —*Syn.* SKIN REFLEX.

superior: *adj.* higher or better. For its use in anatomy, see **anterior.**

superior adult level: the three groups of tests (Superior Adult I, II, III) that are more difficult than the Average Adult tests (MA XV) of the 1937 Stanford Revision; or any equivalent level of test difficulty on another test scale.—See **superior intelligence.**

superior colliculus: either of the anterior **corpora quadrigemina.**

superior intelligence: that level of general ability arbitrarily defined for adults as that attained by only 15 per cent of the total population; and for children as that indicated by a **Stanford-Binet** IQ of 120. (On the 1937 S-B revision, 12.63 per cent of the standardization group attained IQ 120 or higher.)

superiority feeling: an attitude that one is better in some or all ways than the general run of persons. ➤Although some persons genuinely feel superior, a disproportionate display of superiority feeling is commonly held to be a **defense** against feeling inferior.—*Cp.* **inferiority feeling.**

supermoronity: *n.* a term proposed for **borderline defect.** ➤*Ambig.,* since it may be taken to mean **normal.**

supernatural: *adj.* beyond or transcending nature and natural laws, or ordinary human experience.

supernormal: *adj.* exceeding greatly the average or norm, yet believed to be consistent with natural law.—*Contr. w.* **supernatural.**

supernormal recovery phase: a brief phase in the recovery of conductivity in a nerve fiber during which excitability of the nerve is above normal.

superordination: *n.* placing an item or datum in a higher category or class.—*Ant.* **subordination.**

supersonic: *adj.* having a speed beyond that at which sound travels; esp., of waves in a sensible or material medium having a vibration frequency beyond the limit of hearing (for human beings, about 20,000 per second).

superstition: *n.* **1.** a quasi-religious belief or practice, generally a survival or corruption of an earlier religious belief, now lacking adequate support either in the prevailing religious system or in the current body of established fact. ➤The word carries a strongly derogatory connotation. Hence, it is tempting to apply it to any belief or practice one wishes to condemn ("All this talk of reinforcement is just superstition"); but to use it so is to rob **superstition** of its specific meaning or, worse yet, to make it the vehicle of emotional question-begging. Beliefs having no reference to the magical or the supernatural, even though scientifically unsupportable, are better called misbeliefs and errors, or (when stubbornly held in the face of evidence) prejudice. Thus, the assertion of a natural cause–effect relation between a maternal fright and a birthmark is better described as unscientific than as superstitious. Beliefs forming part of a regular religious system (e.g., the Hindu worship of the cow) are not superstition, however like it they may seem to outsiders. **2.** (*B. F. Skinner*) in instrumental conditioning, any response conditioned either to the total situation or to some cue that does not lead to the goal. ➤These useless or hindering responses must be unlearned if the animal is to make the instrumental responses promptly and without lost motion. The analogy with human superstition is more amusing than illuminating. When such responses are persisted in, **stereotypy** is the word.

supination: *n.* a movement of hand or arm that brings the palm upward; or a corresponding movement of the foot.—*Ant.* pronation.—*adj.* **supine.**

support: *n.* **1.** providing for the needs of another person, esp., of a dependent. **2.** giving comfort, encouragement, approval, or acceptance to a person. ➤In psychotherapy, support is generally limited to **(2).** But the concept is much broadened in **supportive therapy.**

supportive ego: (*S. R. Slavson*) the person in group psychotherapy who helps a fellow member to gain status or to work out his intrapsychic problems.

supportive therapy: a form of psychotherapy in which the therapist gives direct help. ➤He may participate in analyzing the problem, in planning corrective measures, in taking follow-up steps (e.g., by joining a conference with a spouse in an effort to improve the couple's interbehavior); and, above all, he provides encouragement. The last aspect is most often emphasized.

supposition: see **postulate.**

suppression: *n.* **1.** (*physiol.*) complete stoppage or inhibition of an activity.—*Distg. fr.* **extinction. 2.** a form of self-control by which impulses or tendencies to action are kept from overt expression. **3.** (*psychoan.*) a conscious exclusion of disapproved desires. ➤*Contr. w.* **repression,** in which the process of exclusion is not conscious (although this generally accepted distinction is not always adhered to). For Freud, the suppressing force comes from the **ego ideal,** and the conflict between that force and the disapproved ideas takes place in the **ego.**

suppression areas: restricted regions of the cortex whose stimulation leads either to (a) suppression of certain motor activities specific to the area, or (b) momentary suppression of the spontaneous electrical activity of the entire cortex. ➤The experimental evidence for such areas has been questioned.

suppression/conditioned: the experimental procedure of presenting a **neutral *stimulus** during the performance of a given behavior, followed by an **aversive *stimulus,** neither being contingent on the animal's behavior. Conditioned suppression is said to occur if response strength decreases during presentation of the originally neutral stimulus.

suppression/monocular: the nonuse of the impressions or signals from one eye, although the visual mechanism is intact. ➤While complete suppression is probably rare, there is failure of binocular fusion and the signal from one eye is the primary basis for perception.

suppressor variable: a variable in a prediction battery that correlates zero with the criterion but highly with another predictor in the battery. It has the effect of subtracting from the predictor variable that part of its **variance** which does not correlate with the criterion, and hence increases the predictive value of the battery. ➤E.g., although "shop mathematics" has a high *r* with the criterion of work success, in selection it lets through some poor workers who are merely good in mathematics. A general mathematics test, which has a low *r* with the criterion and a high *r* with shop mathematics, can be so negatively weighted in combination with the shop math test that those who are merely good in mathematics will not have a good enough combined score to be selected. The general mathematics test is a **suppressor variable.**

supra-: prefix meaning *above,* or *higher in position or rank.*

supraliminal: *adj.* above the **threshold**—either **absolute *threshold** or **difference *threshold.**

supraliminal differences: those above the **difference *threshold.**—See **equal sense differences method.**

suprarenal glands = **adrenal glands.**

sUR: see under *U.*

surdimute: *adj., n.* **deaf-mute.**

surdity = **deafness.**

sure-thing principle: (*L. J. Savage*) If act A is at least as good as act B for *all* pos-

sible states of the world, and better than B in at least one, then A should be preferred over B. ➤The principle is regarded as a foundation for statistics.

surface color: see **color/surface.**

surgency: *n.* a trait inferred to account for behaviors that are cheerful, lively, responsive, sociable, trustful. ➤The pattern is not quite that of **mania** nor of **extraversion,** though it resembles both.—*Ant.* DESURGENCY, which connotes depression and anxiety, and is related to **agitated *depression.**—*Syn.* **F factor,** which see.

surrender/psychotic: the breakdown of the effort to face reality. It is a **regression** found in fullest form in **hebephrenia.**

surreptitious: *adj.* done secretly, by stealth, or fraudulently; esp., of the insertion into a discussion of something that is easily overlooked and tends to deceive the discussants.

surrogate: *n.* a person who functions in another's life as a substitute for some third person: e.g., for the child, the teacher is often a parent surrogate. ➤The surrogate need not be consciously recognized as a substitute. The child does not often realize the nature of his relation to the teacher; but he acts, in relevant ways, as if the teacher were the parent. According to psychoanalysis, since in dreams the surrogate figure is not recognized for what it is, **id**-originated feelings toward this figure that would otherwise be inacceptable may be expressed.

surround: *n.* the immediately effective and present portion of the environment. ➤The term has elastic limits. It may mean all the momentary physical and social stimuli for a given person; or it may be restricted, e.g. to an adjacent visible area such as the wall on which a picture hangs.—See **situation** for discussion of related terms.

sursumvergence: *n.* turning one eye upward in comparison with the other.

survey (sėr'vā): *n.* **1.** a critical inspection or examination. **2.** a comprehensive study or examination; hence (usually) one less detailed; a bird's-eye view.—*v.* **survey** (sər·vā').

survey/attitude: see **attitude survey.**

survey/normative: an investigation designed to determine the norms of performance for certain variables in a given population—i.e., to discover the **frequency** distribution in the population of the levels of ability in certain kinds of tasks.

survey research: the investigation of public opinion, using scientific **sampling** methods and carefully planned methods of questioning.

survey tests: tests designed to yield reasonably accurate information concerning the general level of accomplishment of a whole class or group. ➤Emphasis is upon breadth of coverage and actual state of affairs, rather than upon details or upon discovery of causal factors.

survival value: that quality of a given physical trait or behavior pattern which affects the probability of survival of the individual or the species.

survivor: *n.* (*stat.*) a person who remains available for a second or later test or examination after a time lapse, with or without intervening experimental treatment. ➤It is not implied that nonsurvivors are dead: they are only nonavailable, for whatever reason.

susceptibility: *n.* relative likelihood of being affected by a given influence or factor.

suspicion: *n.* 1. an inkling, hint, or intimation; esp. (and originally), an attitude of doubt of another person's sincerity. 2. = SUSPICIOUSNESS, a hypothetical trait characterized by such an attitude.—*v.* **suspect.**

S variable = **stimulus variable.**

SVIB = **Strong Vocational Interest Blank.**

Swindle's ghost: a prolonged positive aftersensation.

Sydenham's chorea: see **chorea/Sydenham's.**

syllogism: *n.* a formalized kind of reasoning in which acceptance of two judgments (the PREMISES) as true seems to the reasoner to compel him to accept a third judgment (the CONCLUSION). E.g.: "Religious beliefs are not properly called superstitions. This is a religious belief. Therefore, it is not properly called a superstition." Any syllogism may also be written in the form of a hypothetical syllogism. E.g.: "If A is B, it is not C. But A is B. Therefore, A is not C." Formal logic embodies a set of rules for testing whether the syllogism is valid—i.e., whether one is justified in accepting the conclusion.—*adj.* **syllogistic.**—*v.* **syllogize.**

Sylvian fissure = **fissure/lateral.**

sym- = **syn-.**

symbiosis (sim″bi·ō′səs): *n.* 1. literally, living together. 2. (*biol.*) a relationship between two species such that neither can survive without the other: e.g., a certain butterfly is needed to convey the pollen from male to female yucca plant, the larva of the butterfly later feeding on the resulting seed. 3. figuratively, of any close, mutual-aid relationship between individuals, as (e.g.) within the family. 4. (*psychoan.*) the incorporation of a symptom into the **ego,** so that it becomes a part of the personality: e.g., a delusion of grandeur. 5. (*E. Fromm*) a condition in which a person depends upon others, not for cooperative mutual support and affection but for exploitation and the satisfaction of neurotic needs: e.g., the sadistic wit dependent upon his stooge. The stooge equally depends upon the wit—perhaps financially. Both "profit,"

but the "profit" is neurotic.—*adj.* **symbiotic.**

symbol: *n.* 1. in the broadest sense, anything that stands for something else. 2. in writing or printing, any arbitrary or conventional mark (a character, diagram, letter, or abbreviation) that takes the place of a word or words: e.g., *n.* for *noun*; marks used in logic and mathematics to indicate operations or relations, such as $+$, $\div$, $\sqrt{}$, $\gtrless$. (In terms of sense **5,** these are symbols of symbols.) 3. a mental process that represents external reality; an **image** or an **idea.** 4. anything that is apprehended as standing for something else.—*Syn.* **sign** (*prefd.*), **symptom** (the latter best restricted to a special sense). 5. any conventional action designed by the performer to have significance beyond itself; or any object so used as to have such a conventional significance: e.g., a soldier's salute. ➤**Sign** and **symbol** are often used interchangeably, but many logicians seek to restrict symbol to sense **(5),** sign to sense **(4).** Certainly distinction should be maintained between that which stands for something else because of natural similarity or associative relation (smoke as a *sign* of fire), and that which stands for something else because it has been given a conventional or contrived significance (smoke of a burnt sacrifice as *symbol* of a religious ritual). ¶Any act may be employed as a symbol, but the chief instances are intentional gestures and words, spoken or written. Not all gestures are intentional, however; nor does speech always have meaningful intent. Hence, gesture and speech cannot quite be equated to symbol. A symbol may be intended only for the performer himself—a string tied around the finger as a reminder, a secret naming of oneself as "Superman" or "Don Juan." ¶Most (perhaps all) animals apprehend signs; it is debated whether any employ symbols.—*Syn.* (for 5) **signal, message,** both with rather special meanings.

➤Meanings **6–9** below are primarily psychoanalytical but have gained great currency. All carry the notion, not of intentional representation (as in **5**), but of *disguised* representation—one might almost say of intentional (albeit unwitting) *mis*-representation. Failure to distinguish between meaning **(5)** and these meanings has led to great confusion. For all schools of psychoanalysis, the doctrine of the symbol is central; psychoanalysis is essentially symbol analysis. (See **dream analysis.**)

The following relatively distinct but related meanings are current, usually without being explicitly distinguished: 6. (*psychoan.*) an idea in the conscious area of the **psyche** (i.e., an idea of which the person is aware) that takes the place of a mental process in the unconscious. The conscious idea becomes the object of the unconscious idea's instinctual motivation, the individual being unaware of the displacement or substitution. ➤When described as a **wish** or **desire,** the symbol includes not only the idea but the instinctual motive that goes with it. In Freudian psychoanalysis, the instinctual motive is a manifestation of **libido.** The fact that substitution of symbol for reality is necessary is ascribed to **conflict** or **repression;** the form taken by the symbol results partly from **censorship.** Some analysts believe that there are **universal** *symbols. Jung supposed them to be innately provided. **7.** (*psychoan.*) any overt behavior or physiological activity that represents an unconscious conflict and/or that serves as a partial satisfaction for repressed instinctual motives. ➤The mechanism is the same as in **(6),** but the symbol is objectified in overt behavior or bodily symptoms. **8.** an external object that, because of similarity or other association with an object of instinctual desire, thereby becomes a substitute or representative of the primary object: e.g., a pencil as a phallic symbol. **9.** an **affect** or feeling, usually anxiety, representing a conflict in the unconscious. ➤The mechanism is substantially that of **(6);** but here the feeling, rather than the object to which it is attached, is the symbol.—*adj.* **symbolic.**—*v.* **symbolize.**

symbol/anticipatory: a **sign;** something perceived as indicating the coming of something else.—*Cp.* **symbol/expressive** and **symbol (4).**

symbol-digit test = **code test.**

symbol/expressive: a behavior perceived as the **sign** of the internal state of an animal: e.g., a sigh.—*Cp.* **symbol/anticipatory** and **symbol (4).**

symbolic construct: a **symbol,** generally a word, that stands for a set of relationships among empirical data: e.g., the word *dog* (or *dogginess*) stands for the abstract similarities among actual dogs.

symbolic display: a display that portrays information in terms of intermediate or transformed scales: e.g., any representation by means of graphs.—*Contr. w.* PICTORIAL DISPLAY, in which the representation is direct.

symbolic process: the organismic activity or behavior of utilizing **symbols** (esp. in sense 5); that aspect of behavior that involves a symbol. ➤This term comes from behavioral investigations. It is recommended for general use in place of **symbolization,** which should be restricted to the psychoanalytic use.

symbolism: *n.* **1.** the theory of **symbols. 2.** the practice of making extensive use of symbols. ➤All communication, including the

esthetic, depends on symbols—i.e., on using a product of behavior to mean something beyond itself (as in speech). The term **symbolism** sometimes emphasizes this characteristic of language. More often it means the use of symbols having an *added* meaning. Thus, a figurative expression such as James' **stream of** *consciousness refers directly to a concrete experience but also evokes an abstract meaning. Symbolism in visual art may use traditional symbols (such as the halo to mean holiness) or more subtle suggestive symbols. **3.** (*psychoan.*) the processes involved in the disguised representation in consciousness of unconscious or repressed contents or events. ➤Myth, dream, and humor are said to be full of such unwitting symbolism; and psychoanalysts often find evidence that a conscious **symbol** (sense 2) has an unconscious symbolism as well.—*Syn.* SYMBOLIZATION (*prefd.* for 3).

symbolization: *n.* (*psychoan.*) the process of utilizing **symbols (6, 7, 8, 9).** ➤It is suggested that **symbolization,** now widely used in psychoanalysis, be restricted to this meaning. For the process of using symbols **(1, 2, 3, 4, 5),** see **symbolic process.**—*Syn.* **symbolism (3),** which tends to be more abstract and general.

symbol of a construct: (*G. A. Kelly*) an **element (2)** that represents not only itself but also the **construct** by which it is abstracted.

symbol/propositional: a **sign** of a sign.

symbol-substitution test = **code test.**

symbol/universal: (*psychoan.*) an object or a mental content (an **idea,** a dream **image**) that for all men represents the object of a primal or unconscious desire.

symmetrical relation: (*logic*) a relation that holds when the terms are inverted: black is different from white; $x = y$.—*Ant.* **asymmetrical relation.**

symmetry: *n.* the property of having similar, equal, or parallel form or character on both sides of a dividing line (BILATERAL SYMMETRY); or, by extension, at regular intervals about a center (RADIAL SYMMETRY). ➤Used literally for spatial distributions, or metaphorically for any kind of relationship: e.g., the equality relation ($x = y$) in mathematics is symmetrical.—*Ant.* **asymmetry;** (*stat.*) **skewness.**—*adj.* **symmetrical.**

sympathectomy: *n.* surgical cutting of part of the **autonomic nervous system.**

sympathetic ganglion: any of the nerve centers of the sympathetic division of the **nervous system.**

sympathetic nerve = **vagus (nerve).**

sympathetic nervous system: see **nervous system.**

sympathetic vibration: see **resonance.**

sympathin (sim′pə·thin): *n.* a hormone

similar to adrenin in action, probably secreted at the **effector** ends of the nerves of the sympathetic **nervous system.**

sympathy: *n.* **1.** feeling *with* another person: feeling joy with his joy, sorrow with his sorrow. ➤Usually only the painful or unpleasant kind of shared feeling is denoted.—*Cp.* **empathy.**—*adj.* **sympathetic.** —*v.* **sympathize.**

symptom: *n.* any event or appearance that occurs with something else (or, by extension, just before it) and indicates its existence or occurrence; specif., something that indicates presence of a pathological condition.—*Syn.* **sign, index.**—*adj.* **symptomatic.**

symptomatic act: (*S. Freud*) a normal or everyday sort of act that, in a particular instance, represents an unconscious factor: e.g., **slips of the tongue.**—*Syn.* symbolic act (see **symbol** 6–9).

symptom cluster: a group of symptoms that tend with high frequency to occur together, having relatively high intercorrelations.—*Syn.* **cluster, surface *trait,** SYMPTOM CONSTELLATION; also **syndrome** (which see).

symptom formation: (*psychoan.*) the process by which a substitute object is found for an **instinctual** or **id** impulse, esp. when the substitute, though permitting some satisfaction, is a form of behavior not generally acceptable.

syn- (sin-): combining form meaning *with, together with.* ➤Best restricted to words of Greek origin.—*Var.* **sym-, syl-, sys-.**

synapse (sin'aps) *n., pl.* **synapses** (-ap'sēz): (*neurol.*) the region, or locus of points, at which a nervous impulse passes from the **axon** of one **neuron** to the **dendrite** or to the cell body of another.—*Var.* **synapsis** (si·nap'səs).—*adj.* **synaptic.**

synaptic junction: a redundant expression for **synapse.**

synaptic knob: an irregular thickening in the unmyelinated part of an axon near its ending, believed to play an important part in the firing of one cell by another.—*Syn.* TERMINAL BULB, END FOOT, END BUTTONS (all misleading, since the knobs are not always at the end of the axon), BOUTON.

synaptic resistance: the relative ease or difficulty with which a neuron can be excited or fired across a synapse. ➤The phrasing tends to imply a certain theory of neuron activity which is not clearly established, but that implication need not be made.

synchiria (sin·kī'ri·ə): *n.* localization of a touch on one side as being on both sides of the body.

syncope (sing'kō·pi): *n.* (*med.*) a brief suspension of consciousness; a swoon or faint. —*adj.* **syncopal, syncopic** (-kop'ik).

syncretism (sing'krə·tiz·əm): *n.* **1.** the relatively indiscriminate collection of concepts and ideas into what pretends to be a **system,** without serious attempt to resolve contradictions. ➤**Eclecticism** is often, but erroneously, given this meaning. **2.** (*J. Piaget*) the naïve assumption (usually by young children) that objects or events thought of together belong together, in the absence of any reason to attribute time, space, or causal relationships to them.— *adj.* **syncretistic, syncretic** (-kret'ik).— *v.* **syncretize.**

syndrome (sin'drōm; -drə·mi): *n.* **1.** the pattern of **symptoms** that characterizes a particular disorder or disease. ➤Any single symptom may be found in other diseases; it is the combination that differentiates. A **symptom cluster** need not be differentiating; a syndrome is. But the two are often interchanged. **2.** loosely, a cluster of characteristics; a set of behaviors believed to have a common cause or basis.—*adj.* **syndromic** (-drom'ik).

synergic: *adj.* exerting force together or in combination, or upon the same point. ➤SYNERGIC MUSCLES usually work together to move a member. A SYNERGIC ADJUSTMENT is either altogether **adient** or altogether **abient** toward a single situation. The SYNERGIC THEORY holds that the tendency toward unification of behavior is due to the tendency of excitatory factors operative at a given time to converge upon a single response mechanism.—*Distg. fr.* **cooperative,** which refers to social behavior; and *fr.* **coordinated,** which implies a more complex pattern.—*Var.* **synergetic, synergistic.**—*n.* **synergy, synergism.**—*v.* **synergize.**

synesthesia: *n.* a condition, found in some individuals, in which perception of a certain type of object is regularly linked with particular **images** from another sensory mode. Thus, in colored hearing **(chromesthesia)** certain sounds regularly evoke imagery of certain colors, often spread out in space in a precise way. **Number form** is imagery of numbers in definite geometrical positions according to their serial order.— *Var.* **synaesthesia, syn(a)esthesis.**—*adj.* **synesthetic.**

synkinesis: *n.* an involuntary and useless movement accompanying a voluntary movement.—*adj.* **synkinetic.**

synoptic: *adj.* **1.** reduced to a brief sketch, as in a synopsis. **2.** pertaining to SYNOPSIA, or colored hearing.—See **synesthesia.**

syntality: *n.* the nature of a social group as revealed by consistent behavior of the group as such; whatever it is about a group that makes possible prediction of group performance. ➤It is conceived, not as a sort of algebraic sum of the relevant characteristics of its members, but as a property of the whole group.

syntaxic: *adj.* (*H. S. Sullivan*) characterizing a mode of experience that can be communicated by means of concepts having reference to objectively observable or **consensual** data.

synthesis: *n.* putting data together to form a whole; or the whole thus formed. ➤*Syn.* **fusion** (in which the parts cannot be identified); **integration** (which implies a compact and lasting union).—*Distg. fr.* **association,** which implies relatively little interaction between the parts.—*Ant.* **analysis.** —*adj.* **synthetic** (which has also acquired the meaning of artificial).

synthesizing type: proposed term for a classification of persons who attack a problem by attempting to see it as a whole. They tend to neglect details that do not clearly affect the whole. Analysis is little used.—*Contr. w.* **analytic type.**—*Cp.* **type.**

synthetic trainer: a mechanical device that provides a substitute for practice under actual operating conditions: e.g., the Link Instrument Trainer, which gives practice in controlling a simulated airplane without leaving the ground.

syntonia: *n.* a personality **syndrome** manifesting a high degree of emotional responsiveness to the environment, and proneness to **manic-depressive** illness.—*pers. n.* **syntone.**—*adj.* **syntonic.**

system: *n.* 1. the set of orderly and persisting interrelations between parts of a whole. 2. all the elements that work together to perform a given function. ➤Such a system may be of any level of complexity, from a world-wide organization down, and may include organisms (or their parts) and machines.—*Cp.* **system/dynamic.** 3. a group of concepts that serve as the framework for holding in orderly arrangement the data of a science. ➤A system is generally made up of a number of interlocking theories, hence **theoretical** and **systematic** are nearly synonymous; but the latter puts sharper emphasis upon orderly and logical structure or arrangement. CLOSED SYSTEM is derogatory for one not open to change. (*Distg. fr.* a closed **dynamic** *system.) The opposite of a closed system is **eclectic.** A scientific school is held together by a single system.—*adj.* **systematic, systemic** (which see for its very special meaning).—*v.* **systematize.**

system/activity: a number of separate or distinct behaviors that can be substituted for each other in relation to a certain function or goal: e.g., the several kinds of behavior—such as walking, hopping, crawling —any of which serves for locomotion.— *Syn.* BEHAVIOR SYSTEM.

system analysis: (*human eng.*) the discovery and identification of sources of error or variability in a system, the measurement of these errors, and the arrangement of elements to improve system performance.

systematic: *adj.* 1. pertaining to a system. —*Syn.* theoretical (see **system 3**). 2. having the orderly character of a system; occurring regularly and in predictable fashion.—*Distg. fr.* **systemic.**

systematic distortion: a falsification of perception or memory having a consistent character or direction.—*Distg. fr.* mere incompleteness or vagueness.—*Cp.* **leveling, sharpening.**

systematic error: see **error/systematic.**

systematized delusions: false beliefs that are internally consistent and form a connected and more or less permanent set of ideas.

system/closed or **/open:** 1. see **system** (3). 2. see **system/dynamic.**

system/dynamic: a persisting set of interrelations among the parts of a whole that determines the pattern of energy interchange among the parts, the pattern remaining the same within wide variations of the level of energy. ➤*Cp.* **gestalt, stationary state, homeostasis, region.** Such systems may be relatively OPEN to the entry of energy from without (as in the case of living organisms) or relatively CLOSED (as in the case of the atom); but a *completely* closed system could not affect anything outside itself and hence could not be known.

system equation: a mathematical description of the dynamic characteristics of a **system** based upon the analysis of the relation between **input** and **output.**

systemic (sis·tem'ik): *adj.* pertaining to a system; specif., pertaining to the system of the body or its internal organs.—See **sense/ systemic.**

systemic sense: see **sense/systemic.**

system/open: see **system/closed.**

system research: (*human eng.*) investigation directed toward discovering general principles applicable to the design and development of new systems, including those of which men are a part, and therefore including the characteristics of men in relation to the instruments and machines utilized.

systole (sis'tō·li): *n.* the period in which the heart muscle is in active contraction. ➤SYSTOLIC pressure is the maximal pressure reached in the arteries during the contraction of the heart: a measure of blood pressure.—*adj.* **systolic** (sis·tol'ik).

Szondi Test (zon'di): a projective test using pictures of psychiatric patients: the testee selects the two he likes most, the two he dislikes most.

T

T: 1. = (*phys.*) (not *ital.*) temperature, in degrees absolute. 2. = (not *ital.*) transition point. 3. (*Ror.*) total time required for response to all **inkblots.** 4. = (*Ror.*) **texture response.** 5. = (*info. theory*) *T* **function.**

$_{8}T_{R}$ = (*C. Hull*) reaction **latency (2); reaction time.**

t: 1. any case in a series (used in general formulas). 2. = time lapse since a stipulated event. 3. (*stat.*) the ratio of a statistic to its standard error; a critical ratio in which a more refined estimate of σ is used. It is the appropriate statistic to use when *N* is small. ➤The statistical significance or stability of *t* depends both upon its size and the number of **degrees of freedom.**—*Syn. t* function, *t* distribution, STUDENT'S TEST. (*Student* is the pseudonym of a prominent statistician.)

t$_{AB}$: (*stat.*) theoretical cell frequency at intersection of Ath row and Bth column.

$_{8}t_{R}$ = (*C. Hull*) median reaction latency (see **latency 2**).

tabes (tā'bēz): *n.* (*med.*) degeneration of the posterior column of the spinal cord, resulting in locomotor **ataxia.**—*Syn.* TABES DORSALIS (dôr·sā'lis).

table: *n.* an arrangement of scores that displays their relations to each other. ➤For various kinds of tables, see under the qualifying term: e.g., **frequency table.**—*adj.* **tabular.**—*v.* **tabulate,** to arrange data in a table.

table/two-way = **scatter diagram.**

taboo: *n.* a solemn social prohibition of act or word. ➤Originally there were religious sanctions for violation; but the term is now used, somewhat metaphorically, for any social prohibition with irrational support and rather drastic penalties.—*Var.* **tabu, tapu.**

taboo/incest: see **incest taboo.**

*tabula rasa***/doctrine of** (tab'ū·lə rā'sə): the view that the mind at birth is a blank tablet to be written upon by experience.

tabulation: *n.* the making of a **table;** or, data arranged in tabular form.

tach (tak): lab slang for **tachistoscope,** tachistoscopic.

tachistoscope (tə·kis'tə·skōp): *n.* an instrument for providing a very brief timed exposure (usually 1/10 second) of visual material such as pictures, letters, or digits. The exposure may be regulated by a shutter, a falling screen, or an interrupted illumination.—*adj.* **tachistoscopic** (-skop'ik), presented only for a very brief instant.

tachy- (tak'i-): combining form meaning *rapid, swift.*

tachycardia: *n.* rapid pulse.—*adj.* **tachycardiac.**

tachylalia (-lā'li·ə): *n.* excessively rapid speech.—*Syn.* TACHYPHEMIA, TACHYPHRASIA.

tacit: *adj.* not stated in words but silently assumed, often without awareness or assuming anything.

tact function: (*B. F. Skinner*) a vocal utterance of naming. In the young child it is rewarded by parents, esp. by approval.

tactile: *adj.* having to do with **touch.**—*Syn.* TACTUAL.

tactile circle: an area on the skin within which two pressure points are perceived as one. The size of the area varies greatly in different parts of the body.—*Cp.* **two-point threshold.**—*Syn.* (*hist.*) SENSORY CIRCLE.

tactual = **tactile.**

tail: *n.* (*stat.*) the part of a frequency curve or frequency distribution above or below any given **abscissa.** ➤*Cp. w.* the BODY OF THE DISTRIBUTION, which is the rest. It is unusual to set the cutting point for a tail to include as much as one third.

tail assumption: (*psychophys.*) in computing an **absolute *threshold,** the assumption that the class interval just beyond the stimulus value last presented at each end of the series contains all the remaining frequencies.

Talbot-Plateau law: If a surface is illuminated by a light that is interrupted so rapidly that no flicker is perceived, its brightness will be reduced (from that of steady illumination) by the ratio between the period during which the light actually reaches it and the whole period.

talent: see **ability.**

talion (tal'i·ən): *n.* (*psychoan.*) the principle of retribution in intrapsychic behavior. ➤The **id** is said to exact retribution (in symbolic forms) for repression; or the **superego** is said to impose a psychic disability in retaliation for violation of its requirements. TALION DREAD is a neurotic symptom; it refers to the symbolic representation of an unconscious dread of the penalties for an offense—e.g., the symbolic anxieties (taking many forms) that represent the unconscious dread of being castrated as punishment for unconscious Oedipal wishes.

talking out: the full and spontaneous discussion of a problem of personal adjustment with a counselor. ➤In general, the counselor is **nondirective,** and emotional as well as intellectual expression is accepted.

tally: *v.* to make a simple mark for each occurrence of a specified datum. ➤The commonest method is to make a vertical line for each of four occurrences, a diagonal from right to left for the fifth, and to repeat for successive groups of five. (The right to left diagonal results in fewer errors than a left to right, since the striking point is more likely to be precise.)

tambor (tam′bůr): *n.* a recording device. It consists of a chamber closed at one end by an elastic membrane. Pressure changes are communicated to the air or other fluid in the chamber by a tube and these are transmitted by the membrane to a writing lever which rests upon it.—*Var.* **tambour.**

tame: *adj.* of an animal that is tractable and useful or amusing to man; not ferocious or timid with man, as in the wild state.

tantrum: *n.* an uncontrolled display of anger and ill-temper: wild crying, striking, stamping, bumping the head, kicking the floor, etc.—*Syn.* TEMPER TANTRUM.

tanyphonia (tan″i·fō′ni·ǝ): *n.* abnormally thin, weak, metallic voice quality, resulting from excessive tension in the vocal muscles. —*Syn.* THIN VOICE.

tapping test: one in which the task is to make, with a stylus or pencil, as many taps as possible in a given time.—See also **Knox Cube Test.**

tarantism: *n.* a disorder characterized primarily by an uncontrollable desire to dance.

Tarchanoff phenomenon: see **electrodermal response.**

Tartini's tone = **difference tone.**

task: *n.* an act, or the result of an act, that is required or demanded of an individual, usually by another but often by himself. ➤The simplest voluntary movement or a lifelong endeavor alike may be called a task, and the act may be an overt response or a "mental" act; but there is always some degree of specification of what is required or acceptable as fulfillment of the task. The requirement is often largely implicit in the total situation.—See *Aufgabe.*

task-demand: *n.* a somewhat overfull expression emphasizing that a particular kind of task is explicitly requested or required.

task/developmental: see **developmental task.**

task-orientation: *n.* the attitude of a person when attention and effort are centered upon achievement of a task, rather than upon the satisfactions (or feelings) of other persons or upon one's own pleasure.

task-set: *n.* an emphasis upon the responses to be made rather than upon the goal to be reached.

taste: *n.* **1.** the sensory mode that depends upon adequate stimulation of the **taste** buds; the **gustatory** sense. ➤Four distinguishable and elementary taste qualities are usually recognized: sweet, sour, salt, bitter. Some add a metallic taste. These elementary tastes form more or less unitary fusions with odors to yield the characteristic flavors of substances taken into the mouth. **2.** (*pop.*) the sensory qualities of food and drink. In addition to flavors, these include other qualities such as temperature and texture of food in the mouth. **3.** ability to make valid or acceptable esthetic judgments; esp., the ability to select personal adornments and decorations for the home, etc., that are in accord with prevailing esthetic judgments of a cultural group.

taste buds: small end organs or sensory receptors in the mouth cavity, chemically activated and giving rise to sense data analyzable into varying compounds of four qualities: sweet, sour, salty, bitter.

taste tetrahedron: (*H. Henning*) a figure to represent schematically the four elementary taste qualities and their various combinations.

TAT = **Thematic Apperception Test.**

tau: *n.* (*M. G. Kendall*) an index of the congruence of a number of measures or tests of an individual.

tau coefficient of correlation: (*M. G. Kendall*) a rank order correlation for which the equation is

$$\tau = \frac{S}{\frac{1}{2}n(n-1)}$$

where S is a score based on the comparison of the rank of each item compared with each other.

tau effect: a misjudgment of spatial intervals resulting from the differing time spent on judging them.

tautology: *n.* needless repetition of the same or equivalent words, as if to add to the thought or feeling: e.g., *necessary essentials.* ➤Repetition for emphasis is not tautology, nor is saying the same thing in a different way for the sake of clarity.—*Syn.* **redundancy,** which is more general and includes use of excess words whether equivalent or not, and is also used technically in information theory.—*adj.* **tautologic(al).**

tautology/neural: a restatement of an observed behavior fact in terms of a speculative neural process that is not inferred independently but is posited specifically for the observed behavior. ➤*Cp.* the **conceptual nervous system,** in which many of the elements are independently known.

tautophone: *n.* a **projective** device consisting of a phonograph record that gives forth sounds so indistinct as to be not really intelligible, the subject being asked to say what the sounds suggest.

taxis (tak′sǝs): *n.* **1.** (*hist.*) ǝ **tropism.**

➤This meaning survives in the combinations: e.g., *geotaxis* = **geotropism. 2.** a movement elicited by a stimulus and constituting a direct and immediate adaptation to it: e.g., the quick grasp that catches an overturned goblet. ➤The term does not connote innateness or rigidity, as does **reflex;** and it is not limited to spatial orientation, as is **tropism.**

taxonomy (taks·on′ǝ·mi): *n.* the classification of data according to their natural relationships; or the principles governing such classification.—*adj.* **taxonomic** (tak″sǝ·nom′ik).—*pers. n.* **taxonomist.**

Taylorism or **Taylor system:** the first important system of **scientific management;** or the movement for scientific management.

Taylor-Russell tables: (*stat.*) tables permitting a determination of the net gain in selection accuracy attributable to use of a test.

t **distribution** = *t* (3).

TE: 1. = trial-and-error *learning. **2.** = time error.

teacher-made test = test/teacher-made.

teaching: *n.* the art of assisting another to learn. It includes the providing of information (**instruction**) and of appropriate situations, conditions, or activities designed to facilitate learning.

technic = **technique.**

technical: *adj.* **1.** pertaining to a branch of science; characterizing details that concern, or are understandable only by, persons learned in the field. **2.** characterizing the special vocabulary of a learned discipline.—*Ant.* **lay,** of statements not couched in the special language. **3.** pertaining to **technology.**—*Syn.* **technological** (*prefd.*). **4.** pertaining to **technique. 5.** pertaining to practical details rather than to theory.

technical term: any word or phrase used only, or in a specific way, in a specialized branch of knowledge (including manual skills, etc.).

technique (tek·nēk′): *n.* **1.** the formal aspect of a specialized kind of behavior, esp. one involving expertness; or, the degree of expertness. ➤Most techniques are nonverbal; but skill in using the voice, or in pronunciation and other formal aspects of speech, are also included. **2.** (*exper.*) the overt activities used to manipulate the independent or experimental variable and to measure both that and the dependent variables. ➤It includes the activities of managing the instruments used in experimentation or measurement.—*Syn.* **procedure,** a broader term. TECHNIC is sometimes a synonym, but its plural (TECHNICS) usually designates the study or principles of an art or of a special skill.—*adj.* **technical.**

technology: *n.* **1.** a systematic body of facts and principles related to a comprehensive practical and useful end. ➤The term is not limited to industry or engineering; the principles of effective teaching (pedagogy), e.g., comprise a technology. The term is somewhat more general than applied science.—See **psychotechnology. 2.** the actual processes of manufacture in a given industry or plant.

technopsychology = **psychotechnology.**

tele (tē′li): *n.* (*J. L. Moreno*) **1.** a feeling process projected into space and time, hence distant; the attraction (POSITIVE TELE) or repulsion (NEGATIVE TELE) of two people for each other on the basis of actual characteristics of both. **2.** the smallest unit of attitude or feeling measured by **sociometric tests.**

tel(e)-: combining form meaning *far, distant.*

telebinocular: *n.* a variety of **stereoscope** used in testing visual efficiency.

teleceptor: *n.* a distance receptor.—*Var.* **teleoceptor.**

telegnosis (tel″eg·nō′sǝs): *n.* (*parapsych.*) knowledge of distant events unobtainable by known normal means: a more general term than **clairvoyance.**—For related terms, see **cryptesthesia.**—*adj.* **telegnostic** (-nos′tik).

telekinesis (tel″e·ki·nē′sǝs): *n.* (*parapsych.*) movement of objects without the intervention of any known physical means.—*Cp.* **cryptesthesia.**—*adj.* **telekinetic.**

telencephalon (tel″en·sef′ǝ·lon) = **endbrain.**

teleoceptor = **teleceptor.**

teleological: *adj.* **1.** pertaining to ends, purposes, or goals.—*Syn.* **telic, hormic. 2.** pertaining to the doctrine of **teleology.** ➤In some quarters, the adjective seems to mean "admitting the reality of ends, hence tainted with the heresy of teleology," thus combining (**1**) and (**2**) and condemning the first because of the second. But one does not escape heresy hunters by speaking of telic or hormic.

teleology: *n.* **1.** the study of acts considered as being related to purposes or as being **purposive;** the study of behavior from the standpoint of its reference to a future situation. **2.** the point of view that behavior is defined and set off from other phenomena by the fact that it is purposive.—*Cp.* **hormic theory.**—See **psychology/divisions and schools of,** V. **3.** (*philos.*) the doctrine that ends sought for have causal influence on present events, that the future no less than the past affects the present. **4.** (*theol.*) the doctrine that a universal Purpose pervades all reality and that all events tend to its ultimate fulfillment.

teleonomic: *adj.* (*F. H. Allport*) pertaining to those patterns of behavior which are a function of an apparent or inferred purpose. ➤E.g., a child's disobedience may be classified teleonomically as attention-getting. Moreover, even apparently contradictory behaviors may be teleonomically the same: both obedience and disobedience can be attention-getting.

teleoreceptor = distance receptor.

telepathy: *n.* the knowledge by one person, not gained by any known perceptual process, of the mental processes of another person.—*Distg. fr.* **telegnosis** and **clairvoyance,** which refer to knowledge of objective events.—See also **cryptesthesia.**—*adj.* **telepathic.**

telephone theory: see **hearing theories.**

teleplasm: *n.* (*parapsych.*) a substance of unknown character supposed to be exuded from the person of a **medium (3)** and to be one of the means to **telekinesis.**—*Syn.* ECTOPLASM.

telesis (tel'ə·sis): *n.* the assumption of certain values as ends, to be attained by deliberate consciously planned conduct toward those ends.

telestereoscope (tel″ə·ster'i·ō·skōp): *n.* an instrument that causes the object or picture viewed to be seen in exaggerated relief or solidity. The most usual form brings images to the eyes from mirrors placed farther apart than the distance between the two eyes.—*Var.* **teleostereoscope.**

telesthesia: *n.* (*parapsych.*) supposed perception of objects or events that are beyond the range of normal sense perception. ➤It includes **clairvoyance** (properly limited to visual telesthesia), but also supranormal sense perception in other sense fields.—See **cryptesthesia.**

teletactor: *n.* an instrument for amplifying sound waves and transmitting them to the skin. It is used in teaching speech to the deaf.

telic (tel'ik): *adj.* characterizing that which has an end or purpose; purposive.

telic continuum: (*F. H. Allport*) the curve representing the frequency with which a purpose, or an institutional or customary prescription, is carried out in overt behavior. The curve measures the strength of the prescription or purpose relative to the constraints of circumstances. It is said to be usually a **J curve.**

telodendrion (tel″ə·den'dri·ən) *n., pl.* **telodendria:** (*neurol.*) the terminal filament of an **axon.**—*Var.* **telodendron** (-drən).—*Syn.* **end brush.**

temper: *n.* 1. a display of **anger,** esp., an unwarranted display. 2. (*W. McDougall*) a personality characteristic expressive of the *general* way in which impulses are manifested: strength or urgency, persistence, affectability by pleasure or unpleasure. ➤**Temper** is conceived as being inde-

pendent of the strength of particular impulses; it is a general trait.—*Cp.* **temperament.**

temperament: *n.* 1. the susceptibility of the person to emotive situations; the tendency to experience changes in mood. ➤**Temperament** is generally believed to be the correlate of metabolic and chemical changes in bodily tissues, esp. of the endocrines, but the relation of metabolic factors to experience factors has been little explored empirically.—*adj.* **temperamental,** given to extreme or unpredictable shifts of mood. 2. the system of tuning an instrument in a tempered *scale.

temperature/color: see **color temperature.**

temperature sense: the senses of **warmth** and **coolth.**

temperature spots: regions of specific sensitivity to warm and cold. ➤It is now known that they do not always directly overlie the **receptors** for temperature.

temper tantrum = **tantrum.**

template (tem'plət): *n.* a thin plate or board with cutout spaces, or a light frame, used as a guide for cutting, stamping, or drawing.

tempo: *n.* 1. time. 2. rate of movement or performance. 3. a characteristic rate of activity in general. ➤A general trait or PERSONAL TEMPO is found in some factor studies.

temporal: *adj.* 1. pertaining to time, or to time relations. 2. (*anat.*) pertaining to the temples or to the adjacent side of the head (TEMPORAL REGION). In neuroanatomy, **temporal** refers to the portions of the cerebral hemispheres that underlie the temples.

temporality: *n.* the time aspect of an experience; duration.

temporal lobe: that part of the cerebral hemisphere lying below the **lateral *fissure** and in front of the **occipital lobe.**

temporal summation: see **summation (2)** and **(3).**

temptation: *n.* an immediately attractive goal that conflicts with a goal that is socially approved or in accord with one's own ideals.—*v.* **tempt.**

tendency: see **disposition.**

tendency/central: see **central tendency/ index of.**

tendency/determining: see **determining tendency.**

tendency/final: (*psychoan.*) the truly central or ultimate goal imposed on a person by his neurosis. ➤Intermediate goals may be means or instruments, or (more often) **symbolic** substitutes. For many psychoanalysts, the final tendency in all neuroses is defined by the **Oedipal** situation.

tendency-in-situation: (*W. Coutu*) a proposed unit for the analysis of behavior or of any energy process: it emphasizes dynamic contingency as related to a whole field.—*Abbr.* **tinsit.**

tendentious: *adj.* conforming to a tendency; guided by a tendency rather than by the objective facts. ➤Tendentious perception or apperception is perceiving what one expects to perceive.

tender feeling: (*W. McDougall*) the specific emotion that correlates with the tendency to protect and cherish the young and helpless. ➤It is only one component in love or affection, which are often used as its synonyms.

tender-minded: see **tough-minded.**

tendon: *n.* an inelastic fibrous cord that attaches a muscle to a bone.—*adj.* **tendinous.**

tendon reflex: a muscular contraction elicited by tapping the tendon: e.g., the **knee jerk.**

tendon sensation: the sense data associated with stimulation of receptors in the tendon. ➤The usual stimulation is pressure due to movement; hence these data are kinesthetic.—*Var.* **tendinous sensation.**

tendon sense: see **kinesthesis.**

tenet: *n.* a principle, doctrine, or belief, esp. one held by an organization or by a scientific or philosophical school.

tension: *n.* 1. (*physiol.*) the strain by which a cord, membrane, or tissue is kept stretched; esp., the total condition of muscular strain at any one time. 2. the sensations that accompany local or general muscular strain. 3. a condition of the organism marked by unrest or uneasiness, by partly restrained restless activity, by pressure to act and readiness to act (but with no necessary implication of directed action). 4. an emotional state resulting when needs are unsatisfied or goal-directed behavior is blocked. ➤It is not clear how far (3) and (4) are to be regarded as the same phenomenon.—*Syn.* EMOTIONAL TENSION, PSYCHIC TENSION, (*pop.*) NERVOUS TENSION. 5. a hypothetical construct that ascribes the condition of (3) or (4) to an actual physical tension (1, above) in certain tissues or, somewhat more broadly, to a state of disequilibrium in tissue activity in general. ➤*Syn.* **drive** or **drive state.** As so often happens when empirical fact and hypothetical construct share the same name, the undeniable existence of one lends fictitious certitude to the other. ¶In most contexts, tension probably refers metaphorically to the phenomena of (3) and (4). 6. SOCIAL TENSION, an interpersonal or intergroup relationship in which antagonistic or hostile emotions are easily aroused, and friendly cooperative relations are difficult.—*adj.* **tense, tensional.**—*v.* **tense.**

tension movement: see **movement/tension.**

tension reduction: the lessening of **tension,** in any of its meanings, whether general or specific to certain tissues or action systems.—*Cp.* **drive reduction, need reduction,** both partial synonyms.

tension-relaxation: (*W. Wundt*) one of the three dimensions hypothesized for feeling.

tension system: 1. the behavioral mechanisms that control the alterations of a particular organic or tissue **tension.** ➤In current motivational theory the alteration referred to is nearly always a reduction, but such limitation of meaning is arbitrary. 2. (*K. Lewin*) a part region of a person wherein the degree of tension can change somewhat independently of tension changes in other regions or systems.

tensive: *adj.* 1. tending to create **tension.** 2. pertaining to a tendency in a given direction.—*Cp.* **extratensive.**

tensor tympani: a muscle attached to the **malleus** bone and the eardrum. Its function is to tighten the membrane of the eardrum.

teratology: *n.* the study of organic malformations and monstrosities.—*adj.* **teratological.**

term: *n.* 1. a symbol—generally a word or phrase—standing for a definite concept or idea. 2. (*math.*) a component or member of a compound quantity: a in $(a + b)$. 3. (*logic*) the subject or predicate of a proposition; or, a substantive word or phrase designating either of the items (the **fundaments**) between which a relation subsists. —See **terminology.**

Terman-Merrill Revision: see **Stanford-Binet.**

Terman-Miles Attitude-Interest Blank: an inventory designed to show the differences between the interests of men and women. ➤The inventory is standardized in terms of the American culture and does not imply that the interests are innately determined.

terminal bulb = **synaptic knob.**

terminal lag: see **inertia.**

terminal sensitivity: the greatest intensity of sensation of which a given organ is capable.—*Contr. w.* **liminal sensitivity,** the least intensity.

terminal stimulus: the maximal stimulus (along any given dimension) to which an organism can respond; the maximum **absolute *threshold.** E.g., in pitch, the maximum stimulus frequency is about 20,000 c.p.s.—*Cp.* **terminal sensitivity,** limited to the intensity dimension.

terminology: *n.* the system of terms, esp. of technical terms, used in a given learned discipline, art, craft, or technology; or the study of the effectiveness of such a system.

terminology/traditional: see **traditional terminology.**

terror: *n.* extreme fear, normal or pathological.

tertile: see **partile.**

test: *n.* 1. (*logic*) any criterion or operation used to determine the truth, correctness, precision, or accuracy of a proposition or hypothesis. 2. any measurement that yields quantitative data for judgment: e.g., an examination in a scholastic subject, an X ray of the chest, a test of **statistical *significance.** 3. = PSYCHOLOGICAL or MENTAL TEST, a set of standardized or controlled occasions for response presented to an individual with design to elicit a representative sample of his behavior when meeting a given kind of environmental demand. The occasion for response most often takes the form of a question or similar verbal stimulus. ➤Many authorities still restrict **test** to the **test of maximum performance,** in which each unit is a **task** (which see) challenging the individual to his best execution. But it is now common usage to include as a test any set of situations or occasions that elicit a characteristic way of acting, whether or not a task, and whether or not characteristic of the individual's best performance. Thus, even a self-inventory or an attitude survey is called a test. As *distg. fr.* **experiment,** the test seeks to measure differences between individuals, whereas in experiment differences are eliminated or held constant. But tests often form an essential part of experimentation in its wider sense.

Test alone is often used for **test battery, test *form, test instrument, test item, test scale, testing.** Definitions dealing with different kinds of test forms and with tests in general are found under subsequent entries: e.g., **test/selective answer.** See also **scale.** Tests for different purposes or in a special field are listed under the qualifying term: e.g., **achievement test.** The proper or proprietary names of tests are listed only if they are commonly used in such a way that the reference is obscure for one unfamiliar with the test: thus, the **Terman-Merrill test** is listed, but the Terman Group Test of Mental Ability is not. Commonly used initials **(CAT, S-B)** are included.

testable: *adj.* of propositions that can be put to the test—i.e., that permit prediction that a certain event will occur under stated conditions.

test/accuracy: a test that emphasizes accuracy as the criterion of excellence, the testee being allowed as much time as he needs to do as well as he can.

test age: the score obtained on an **age (equivalent) scale.**

test/alternate-response: a test in which each question offers a choice between two items. The commonest form is a True-False or Yes-No choice.—See **selective answer *test.**

test/altitude: a test to measure the maximum difficulty of test items with which a testee can cope.—*Contr. w.* **test/rate.**

test/analogies: see **analogies test.**

test/aptitude: see **aptitude test.**

test battery: 1. a group of tests combined to yield a single total score that is of maximal efficiency in measuring for a specified purpose or ability or trait. 2. a group of related tests to be administered at one time.

test/best answer = **test/selective answer.**

test/best reason: a **selective answer *test** in which the task is to select the best reason for an action or belief.

test blank: the paper upon which test items are printed, with or without spaces or symbols for answers.

test/cause-and-effect: one in which the task is to state (or to choose from the presented options) the presumed cause of a specified effect, or vice versa. ➤In form, this closely resembles the **best reason *test.**

test/central thought: a test in which the task is to analyze a paragraph for its theme or central idea, either restating it or checking one of several options as in a **selective answer *test.**

test chart: a chart for the measurement of visual **acuity:** e.g., the **Snellen chart.**

test/class-free: see **test/culture-free.**

test/completion: a test having blanks in a printed text for which the testee must supply the missing letter, word, or phrase; or an analogous test with nonverbal material.—*Cp.* **sentence completion test, incomplete pictures test.**—*Syn.* (*obsoles.*) COMBINATION TEST.

test/culture-free: a test of general ability from which have been eliminated, as far as possible, all items depending upon experiences that are more commonly found in one culture than another. ➤Such tests must eliminate language, and the information or skills selectively employed in one culture more than in others. The term is sometimes extended to CLASS-FREE TESTS, which are designed to be equally fair to persons from different socioeconomic classes (or subcultures) within the same culture.—*Syn.* CROSS-CULTURE TEST, *prefd.* as not implying complete freedom from cultural factors.

test/cycle omnibus: see **test/omnibus.**

testee: *n.* the person taking a test.

testes: *pl.* of **testis.**

test form: see **form/test.**

test/free recall = **association test.**—

Distg. fr. **test/recall,** in which the response is restricted.

test/free response: a test in which no restriction is placed on the kind of response the testee is to make, so long as it is to the task or situation presented.—*Cp.* **test/recall.**—*Contr. w.* **selective answer *test;** and *w.* free recall test (= **free association test**), in which one merely calls words to mind freely.

test/group: a test that can be given simultaneously to more than one person, generally to upwards of 20.—*Contr. w.* **test/individual.**

test/individual: a test designed for administration to only one person at a time.

test/informal: a series of tasks or questions designed to show the level of a person's ability. There are no norms, but the tester evaluates the testee's performance by some sort of intuitive standard.

testing: *n.* the administration of a **test** or tests.

testing the limits: 1. an attempt to discover what limits have been placed by authority (or by society) upon one's behavior and how far one can go without suffering undue punishment. **2.** (*Ror.*) a phase of testing in which the examiner exerts pressure in a systematic and controlled way in order to provoke reactions in directions avoided or not clarified by the subject in his spontaneous reactions.

test/instructional: see **instructional test.**

test/inventory: a test that systematically (usually somewhat superficially) covers the major areas of a pupil's achievement. It yields a **profile** of his strengths and weaknesses.—*Contr. w.* **diagnostic test,** which seeks to locate the underlying causes of a weakness.

testis *n., pl.* **testes:** one of the two ball-shaped structures containing the sex glands of the vertebrate male.—*Syn.* TESTICLE.

test item: in a **test** (3), an occasion or stimulus situation designed to elicit a response measurable as a single unit; a unit task worked at by itself and having a separate score for its performance. ➤Each test item meets the requirements of **test** (2) and is often treated as being a test by itself; more often many items are collected into a set which is called a **test** (3).

test/mastery: a test designed to discover whether a pupil has attained a required level of proficiency in an academic subject, or in a vocational or avocational skill.

test/matching: one in which the task is to select from one group of items the appropriate or matched items from a second list. The matching may be made according to a prescribed criterion or left to the subject.

test/mental: 1. = **intelligence test** (much

prefd.). **2.** any test of psychological function.—See **test** (3) and **scale/psychological.**

test/multiple-choice: see **test/selective answer.**

test/multiple-response: one in which the testee is to select more than one of the optional answers as correct.—*Distg. fr.* multiple-choice (or **selective answer**) *test, in which the *one* best answer is chosen. (The distinction is often missed.)

test/nonlanguage = **test/nonverbal.**

test/nonverbal: 1. a test that does not use words in the formulation of the task, nor require them in the solution; a test that does not ostensibly require use of verbal symbols.—*Syn.* **performance** *test. **2.** a test in which most of the **variance** between persons is not caused by differences in ability to manipulate verbal symbols. ➤The issue is not the use or nonuse of words in the test. Some performance tests are greatly aided by verbal ability, some tests using words are not. A test should be called nonverbal in this sense only when **factor analysis** has shown that it is not heavily loaded with a verbal factor (but in some current usages the factor analysis is apparently purely intuitive).

test/objective: 1. a means of measuring individual differences in behavior that eliminates, as far as possible, the influence of the examiner's bias or opinion. **2.** a test that can be routinely scored by the application of simple rules requiring a minimum of judgment. ➤The answers are usually recorded in some simple form (e.g., checking a prescribed space, writing *yes* or *no*) which is then compared with the standard answer. Many objective tests can be machine-scored. Note that **objective** in this sense means *objectively scored.* Devices to make a test objective in other respects are implied in the term **standardized** *test.—*Cp.* **selective answer** *test.—*Contr. w.* **test/subjective.**

test of maximum performance: a test in which the testee is challenged to make the best response he can to its several items. ➤This is sometimes referred to as "test in the strict sense," and most measures of performance fall within this definition. But other means of evaluation are now sometimes called **test**—e.g., a measure of a person's normal or usual handwriting (rather than of his best), a **rating,** a **behavior check list.**—See **test.**

test/omnibus: a test in which the various kinds of tasks are distributed throughout the test instead of being grouped (as is more usual) by kind, and from which only a single score is derived. In a CYCLE OMNIBUS TEST, the kinds of items are arranged in a recurrent pattern: *a, b, c, d; a', b', c', d';*

etc. In a SPIRAL OMNIBUS TEST, the several cycles are of increasing difficulty.

test/option = **test/selective answer.**

test/oral: any test in which the response is oral, usually to task questions also propounded orally.—*Distg. fr.* AURAL TEST, a test of ability to hear; and *fr.* ORAL SPEECH TEST, a test of the excellence with which one speaks.

testosterone (tes·tos′tə·rōn): *n.* an *androgenic *hormone, sometimes produced synthetically.

test/paper-and-pencil: a test in which the tasks set are printed, written, or drawn, and the reply is made by pen or pencil on paper. ➤It contrasts with **oral *test,** and in general with **performance *test.** (But some of the latter are nonlanguage tests on paper.)

test/performance: a test in which the role of language is minimized, the task requiring overt motor responses other than verbal. ➤Strictly speaking, every test is a test of performance—i.e., it requires the testee to produce a certain overt result. **Performance test,** however, has been specialized for those tests in which the score is based on a nonverbal response.

Usage is not very precise. Three degrees of "nonverbalness" may be distinguished: (*a*) everything completely nonverbal (rare or nonexistent for man); (*b*) instructions and task requirement nonverbal, but use of words not ruled out (e.g., the subject in a form-board test tells himself he needs a "smaller block to fill this hole"); (*c*) only the final task requirement nonverbal, instructions being given orally and (as in *b*) intermediate use of words not being ruled out. Tests of arithmetical calculation are not correctly called performance tests, nor are picture-pointing tests ("Show me the horse").—See **test/nonverbal.**

test/power: a test in which ability is measured by the difficulty of the tasks that the testee can perform when time is not limited. ➤In physics, power is rate of work; in a power test the *rate* is disregarded.—*Ant.* **speed *test, work-limit *test, time-limit procedure.**

test/power of: see **power function.**

test/preference: see **Kuder Preference Record.**

test profile: see **profile chart.**

test/psychological: see **test (3)** and **scale/psychological.**

test/rate: a test performed within a stringent time limit and containing many items of similar difficulty, no testee being expected to finish all items. The score depends on the number of correct answers.— *Syn.* SPEED TEST.—*Contr. w.* **test/accuracy, /altitude, /timed, /power.**

test/rearrangement: one in which each item presents several disarranged parts, the task being to rearrange them into a correct or meaningful sequence or whole: e.g., words to be arranged in a sentence, a jigsaw puzzle.

test/recall: a test in which the task is to say or write specific items previously studied.—*Syn.* SIMPLE RECALL TEST.—*Contr. w.* **test/selective answer.**—*Distg. fr.* **test/free recall,** and *fr.* **test/free response.**

test/recognition = **test/selective answer.**

test representativeness: see **representativeness/test.**

test-retest coefficient: the coefficient of correlation between two administrations of the same test, whether the same form or **comparable *forms** are used.—See **reliability coefficient.**

test scale: a number of tasks considered to be measures of a given variable, sufficient in number to be of some degree of reliability, and each having a **scale value.** A single score is obtained, either by adding the scale values of all correct items or by taking the scale value of the most difficult correct item or of the least difficult incorrect item.

test/scaled: 1. a test submitted to empirical analysis to insure that items are assigned numbers or values according to a working rule. **2.** a test in which items are arranged in order of increasing difficulty.

test scaling: assigning the test elements or items to a position on a dimension or scale, usually by trying them out on a sample of testees.

test score: the quantitative (usually numerical) value assigned to the performance of a test item or a test.

test/selective answer: a form of test in which a question or problem is presented together with a plurality of answers for the testee's choice of the best answer. ➤The question may be directly posed and a yes-no choice offered. Or a statement may be presented for characterization as true or false (TRUE-FALSE TEST). Or an incomplete statement may require completion by one of the suggested answers. A test that gives more than two suggested answers is often called a MULTIPLE-CHOICE TEST.—*Syn.* OPTION TEST (*recom.* but less common), BEST ANSWER TEST.—*Contr. w.* **test/free response** and **test/multiple response.**

test/self-administering: one in which such clear directions are given in the test itself that the tester needs only to keep order and to stop the entire test at the right time.

test/self-marking: a test so designed that the response of the testee is automatically recorded as right or wrong. ➤The response may be made by pressing a recording key; the written response may be transmitted by carbon paper to "right" or "wrong" spaces; or chemo-color reactors may reveal the correctness of response. The correctness may or may not be made known immediately to the testee.

test/short-answer: see **examination/short-answer.**

test/socioeconomic-free = test/class-free (see **test/culture-free**).

test/speed: a form of test in which achievement is measured by the number of tasks performed in a given time. ➤It is assumed that the differences in difficulty of the several items are random for each testee.— *Contr. w.* **test/power.**—*Syn.* **test/timed.**

test/spiral: a test having items of several different kinds which regularly recur in the same order but with different and more difficult content. ➤Thus, a test may have an arithmetic item, a spelling item, a reading item, a geography item; the cycle then repeats with different content at a higher level of difficulty.—*Syn.* SPIRAL OMNIBUS TEST.

test/standard: see **test/standardized.**

test/standardized: a test composed of empirically selected materials. It must have definite directions for use, adequately determined **norms**, and data on **reliability** and **validity.** ➤Note that it is norms, not standards, that are required for a standardized test.—*Syn.* STANDARD TEST (not *prefd.*).

test/subjective: a test that does not have **objective** and communicable standards for scoring. ➤*Ant.* objective *test.* Note the limited meaning of **subjective** (or **objective**) when applied to tests: it refers to the actual scoring of a particular answer, not to the prior decision on which answers are to be considered correct if and when given, nor to the way the test was drawn up. In many teacher-made tests of the short-answer variety, the teacher's relatively unaided judgment may decide which of alternative answers are to be scored correct or incorrect; but if there are explicit rules for applying that judgment in the scoring, the test is classified as objective. ¶Classification of essay tests or examinations as necessarily subjective is incorrect. Although it is true that many graders of such examinations have no explicit criteria and that the grading must therefore be called largely subjective, it is possible with care to make the grading of essays fairly objective. And even at worst, utter whimsicalness and lack of communicable standards (purely subjective grading) are surely rare.

test/teacher-made: a test prepared by a teacher for her own classes. ➤While such

tests lack the advantages of standardization, they may better reflect the actual teaching purposes.

test/timed: a test in which speed of performance is a major criterion of excellence. In one form of the timed test, record is made of the time required for each item or unit of performance. In another form (the TIME-LIMIT PROCEDURE), the testee is allowed a limited time, either on each unit of performance or on the whole test; the score is then the number successfully dealt with. —*Syn.* **test/speed.**—*Cp.* **test/work-limit.**

test/trade: a test designed to measure a person's actual present proficiency in a skill, trade, or vocation. It usually presents for performance a sample of the tasks actually performed in the trade.—*Cp.* **aptitude test.**

test/true-false: a form of examination in which the task is to say whether the presented statements are true or false. A variant form puts the question as a direct interrogation to be answered Yes or No.

test value: a tentative value, obtained from only a few observations, used to set the quantitative limits within which to vary an experimental variable.

test vector: see **vector/test.**

test-wise: *adj.* experienced in taking tests; knowing how to increase one's scores by evasion of some of the standard requirements.

test/work-limit: a form of test, in which each subject performs the same tasks, differences between them being based on the time required.—*Cp.* **test/timed.**—*Syn.* WORK-LIMIT PROCEDURE.

tetanus: *n.* (*med.*) **1.** a state of continued muscular contraction. **2.** an infectious disease, usually fatal, characterized by **tetanus** (1).—*Syn.* lockjaw.—*Distg. fr.* **tetany.**— *adj.* **tetanic.**—*v.* **tetanize,** to make tense (often metaphorically).

tetany: *n.* (*med.*) an abnormal condition or disease characterized by intermittent **tetanus** (1), chiefly in the extremities.—*Distg. fr.* **tetanus** (2).

tetartanopia: *n.* a form of color blindness in which blue or yellow stimuli are confused. ➤The existence of this form is disputed.

tetra-: combining form meaning *four,* having *four parts.*

tetrachoric correlation: see **correlation/tetrachoric.**

tetrachromatism = four-color theory (see **color theories**).

tetrad difference criterion: (*C. Spearman*) an early method for determining whether there is a single mathematical factor common to all the intercorrelations of a set of tests. The criterion is that all the tetrad differences shall be zero (within the limits of chance variation). ➤If there are four tests, *a, b, c, d,* then ($r_{abr_{cd}} - r_{ac}r_{bd}$) is one tetrad difference, ($r_{ad}r_{bc} - r_{ab}r_{cd}$) is another, and so for all combinations. The criterion has been replaced by other means of **factor analysis.**—*Cp.* **factor theory** of mental organization.

texture response or *T*: (*Ror.*) a response referring to the apparent texture of the **inkblot.**

TF: a test item that is to be marked T for True or F for False.—See **test/selective answer.**

***T* function:** (*info. theory*) a measure of the relatedness or association or contingency of the **classifications** of an ensemble. It is a measure of the reduction in the amount of information required to locate an **element** in a given classification if it has already been located in one or more other classifications.—See **redundancy.**

***t* function = *t* (3).**

thalamic theory of emotion: (*Cannon-Bard*) the view that stresses the role of the **thalamus,** directly and in interaction with the cortex, in releasing emotional responses and in adding a peculiar quality, based on this release, to simple sensory processes.

thalamus (thal′ə·məs): *n.* (*neurol.*) a mass of gray matter in the **diencephalon** which is an important relay center between various sensory organs and the cortex. ➤The expression THALAMIC REGION usually includes the entire diencephalon, not just the thalamus.—*Syn.* OPTIC THALAMUS.—*adj.* **thalamic** (thə·lam′ik).

thalamus/extrinsic: those dorsal thalamic nuclei which have **afferent** or input connections with other mechanisms. ➤The INTRINSIC THALAMUS consists of those dorsal thalamic nuclei that have their input from other thalamic nuclei. The EXTRINSIC CORTEX is the cortical area to which go the fibers from the extrinsic thalamus; the INTRINSIC CORTEX is the cortical area for fibers from the intrinsic thalamus.

thalamus/intrinsic: see **thalamus/extrinsic.**

thanato-: combining form meaning *death*: e.g., THANATOPHOBIA, fear of death.

Thanatos (than′ə·tos): *n.* (*Gk., death*) (*psychoan.*) the **death instinct** (which see).

theism: *n.* belief in the existence of a god or gods, esp. of personal gods.—*adj.* **theistic.**—*pers. n.* **theist.**

thema (thē′mə): *n.* (*H. A. Murray*) a description of a psychological event in terms of the way a particular **press** is interacting with a particular **need** to bring satisfaction or nonsatisfaction. ➤In a TAT, the thema attributed by the testee to the event in which the chief actor takes part is supposed to reveal the dominant needs or motivations of the testee—i.e., to reveal what the thema of his own actions would be in like circumstances.

Thematic Apperception Test or **TAT:** a **projective test** in which a person is asked to tell a story suggested by each of 19 pictures. ➤The pictures are sufficiently vague to leave much to the imagination of the testee. The test assumes that **themas** apperceived by the testee in the pictured behavior are those which are important in his own life.

theorem: *n.* **1.** a logically proved proposition, or a corollary thereof. **2.** a proposition that can be proved (or disproved) by relatively few steps; a proposition put into form for the application of logical rules for proof. ➤A complex hypothesis is broken down into a number of propositions or theorems, so stated that they preserve formal consistency and make clear the empirical facts needed to verify this part of the hypothesis. **3.** a proposition expressed in abstract mathematico-logical symbols. ➤If words are used, they are few and either point expressly to a particular objectively identified object or merely indicate operations to be performed.—*Distg. fr.* **postulate, definition, hypothesis, theory.**

theoretical frequency curve = frequency curve/normal.

theory: *n.* **1.** a general principle, supported by considerable data, proposed as an explanation of a group of phenomena; a statement of the relations believed to prevail in a comprehensive body of facts. ➤Theory is more solidly supported by evidence than is hypothesis. It is less firmly established than law; and it generally covers a wider range than a single law, which is usually limited to a single kind of relationship. **2.** (*pop.*) an abstract principle that is not considered practicable in application, despite the fact that the reasoning and the facts advanced are not (at least directly) challenged: That's a good *theory* but it won't work.—*adj.* **theoretical.**—*v.* **theorize.**

theory-begging: *n.* a variant of the logical fallacy of question-begging. It takes a term that refers to established fact as the name also for a controversial theory, thereby seeming to imply the correctness of the latter. It is the "labeling of a theoretical assumption as a behavior fact." (*G. Razran*) ➤The fallacy is very prevalent in psychology, probably because the science is a highly conceptual one. When certain facts are beyond dispute, the theory bearing the same name comes to seem equally certain. ¶Thus, **internal speech** is sometimes used as a synonym for thinking. Now there are undeniable, empirically observed data which are properly called internal speech; but their relation to thinking is a matter of far-from-certain theory. Again, in conditioning experiments there is an operation called **reinforcement,** whereby a response is strengthened again—i.e., literally reinforced. (The defining operation generally is: "*E* gives the animal food.") This fact is interpreted by some theorists in terms of a certain kind of inferred process. The inferred process, being also *called* reinforcement, is likely to seem as much a matter of fact as the objective strengthening of the response. ¶Such theory-begging is more than mere bad manners; it is lexical sin. It denies to opponents of the theory the obvious term by which to refer to the objective fact. Moreover, the fallacy of theory-begging is frequently combined with that of nominalism. An actually observed reinforcing operation is said by the unwary to be "explained in terms of reinforcement," forgetting that reinforcement is merely a restatement of the operation. ¶Fact and interpretation are always to some extent commingled, but that does not absolve us from the effort to keep them as distinct as possible. The avoidance of a theory-begging terminology is one means to that end.

theory of knowledge = epistemology.

therapeutic: *adj.* curative.

therapeutics: *n.* the branch of science dealing with the treatment of disease or **organismic** disorder.

therapist: *n.* one skilled in the employment of treatment techniques.

therapy: *n.* treatment intended to cure or alleviate a disordered condition, so that normal functioning is brought about.

therapy/active: 1. treatment in which the therapist assumes much responsibility and often intervenes with directive questions, advice, and even management of the patient's conduct.—*Syn.* ACTIVE PSYCHOTHERAPY. — *Contr. w.* **client-centered *therapy. 2.** (*psychoan.*) a form of **analysis** in which the analyst imposes prohibitions, makes positive suggestions, or creates artificial situations in order to elude or break down resistances that are unduly retarding analysis.

therapy/activity group: carefully guided participation in appropriate social activities, as itself a means to improving adjustment, and as facilitating other forms of therapy.

therapy/adjuvant: subsidiary or supplemental devices used in treatment.

therapy/assignment: see **assignment therapy.**

therapy/attitude: the effort to improve attitudes as a means of therapy; esp., the effort to help parents change the attitudes that are related causally to their child's maladjustment.

therapy/client-centered: a therapy based on the doctrine that psychotherapy consists in helping the client to mobilize his own latent psychic resources in the solution of his own problems. ➤This is accomplished by an attitude of **acceptance** (which see) and the **nondirective procedure** (which see). The therapist seeks to understand the client on his own terms. He encourages, but does not guide, the client's exploration of his troublesome attitudes and feelings. It is usually implied that the problem is solved when appropriate emotional response is substituted for persistent inappropriate emotional response, but the decision about what is appropriate (or good) is left to the client. During therapy, the client comes to understand his problem (though not necessarily its origin, as in psychoanalysis) and to plan for its solution.—*Syn.* NONDIRECTIVE THERAPY.

therapy/convulsive: see **convulsive therapy.**

therapy/dilution: the effort to lessen a person's sense of guilt by convincing him that his misconduct or shortcoming is common or universal.

therapy/expressive: a form of treatment that encourages the client to express all his ideas and feelings. ➤There are several theoretical explanations of why such expression is deemed helpful.

therapy/milieu: see **milieu therapy.**

therapy/play: see **play therapy.**

therapy/puppet: **play therapy** that uses puppets.

therapy/relationship: a point of view about all psychotherapy (rather than a specific kind) that emphasizes the potential curative effect of the client's own growth in understanding himself and in ability to plan for the future—a growth resulting from his activities, thoughts, and feelings in the therapy relationship. **Client-centered *therapy** is a further development of this thesis.

therapy/relaxation: the alleviation of disorder by teaching the individual to relax his muscles. ➤It is supposed that emotional tensions are also thereby relaxed, but the therapy itself works directly with muscle tension.

therapy/release: see **release therapy.**

therapy/situation(al) = milieu therapy.

therapy/speech: corrective work with persons having any form of disordered speech. ➤While direct help with the speech itself is always part of speech therapy, an attack upon the basic causes is also included. Hence, speech therapy overlaps considerably with **psychotherapy.**

therblig: *n.* (*F. B. Gilbreth*) an identifiable unit part of a repeated work act, used in efficiency studies.

theriomorphism (thir″i·ō·môr′fiz·əm): *n.* the attributing to human beings of the qualities of subhumans; the refusal to describe human beings in any terms specifically human; the dehumanizing of the behavior sciences and the description of all behavior in terms of the behavior of animals. ➤The disorder is widespread and highly contagious.—*Syn.* **zoomorphism.**—*Contr. w.* **anthropomorphism.**

thermal: *adj.* pertaining to heat.

thermalgesia (thẻrm″al·jē′zi·ə): *n.* a state of the organism when a warmth stimulus causes pain.—*Cp.* **causalgia.**

thermalgia = causalgia.

thermal sense = temperature sense.

thermanesthesia: *n.* insensitivity to warm and cool stimuli.—*Var.* **thermoanesthesia.**

therm(o)-: combining form meaning *warmth, heat.*

thermocouple: *n.* an instrument used to measure temperature differences.

thermoreceptor: *n.* a **receptor** for warmth or coolth.

thermotropism (thẻr″mõ·trõ′piz·əm): *n.* a simple orienting response to a warm or cold stimulus.—*adj.* **thermotropic.**

thesis: *n.* **1.** a proposition formally set forth for proof or disproof. **2.** a systematic treatise dealing with a specific problem. **3.** specif., in American universities, such a treatise written in partial fulfillment of the requirements for the master's degree. ➤*Distg. fr.* DISSERTATION, a treatise in partial fulfillment for the doctorate. Formerly thesis and dissertation were interchangeable.

θ_1, θ_2: an angle.

they-group = out-group.

thigmo-: combining form meaning *touch.*

thing: *n.* **1.** any material substance having definite spatial boundaries; an object occupying a specific, limited space. **2.** that to which a person reacts; any object of perception, thought, feeling or action—in short, anything at all. **3.** an inanimate object as contrasted with an organism.

thing language: description of experience in terms of everyday objects, rather than analytically in terms of stimuli or stimulus patterns.

thinking: *n.* **1.** any process or activity not predominantly perceptual by which one apprehends an object or some aspect of an object or situation. ➤Judging, abstracting, conceiving, reasoning, and (in a somewhat extended sense) imagining, remembering, and anticipating are forms of thinking. Although thinking is thus negatively defined by reference to perceiving, the two processes are not antagonistic but supplemental. Either may merely predominate in any given **cognitive** process. **2.** problem-solving that involves primarily ideas rather than perceiving and overt manipulation. **3.** meditating or reflecting upon a problem in order to understand the relationships involved.

4. subvocal or covert speech behavior. ➤This meaning, though fairly common, is a theory about thinking that masquerades as a definition—i.e., it is **theory-begging.** For varieties or kinds of thinking, see qualifying term: e.g., for autistic thinking, see **autism;** for creative thinking, see **creativeness, creative imagination.**

thinking/associative: see **associative thinking.**

thinking type: see **type/thinking.**

thinking/wishful: see **wishful thinking.**

thirst: *n.* **1.** a perception in which dryness of the mouth is the chief constituent. **2.** a desire for water. **3.** a hypothetical **drive state** based on relative dehydration or loss of water from the bodily tissues. ➤The thirst of **(1)** and **(2)** is an observable fact: that of **(3)** is an inference from the fact of water deprivation and certain behaviors taken to be symptoms of a drive state.

thobbing: *n.* emotional thinking; thinking short-circuited by prejudice or bias.—*Cp.* **autism.** ➤A useful neologism made up from the words *thinking, opinion, belief.*

thoracolumbar (thô″rə·kõ·lum′bər): see **autonomic nervous system.**

thorax (thô′raks): *n.* in man and the higher vertebrates, the part of the body between neck and abdomen, containing the heart, lungs, etc.; the chest.—*adj.* **thoracic** (thô·-ras′ik).

Thorndike Handwriting Scale: samples of handwriting, arranged in classes differing from each other by steps of approximately equal general merit, with which a given bit of writing may be compared and thus graded.

thought: *n.* **1.** a single complex idea that results from thinking. **2.** a **covert** activity involving **symbols;** the operations of using symbols. **3.** the **thinking** process. **4.** (*obsoles.*) cognitive experience in general. **5.** any distinct part of a thinking activity.

thought-hearing: *n.* a delusion that one's thoughts are audible—to oneself, or to oneself and others.

thought / imageless: see **imageless thought.**

thought impulses: (*psychoan.*) those elements of dreams that are not the result of instinctual desires but result from the tensions of everyday living: unsolved problems, strong impressions, etc.

thought/laws of: the basic axioms or assumptions that underlie rational thinking; the axioms without which thinking would be impossible. ➤The laws are not empirically demonstrated or based on fact; they are *assumed* and form the basis for any rational demonstration. See, e.g., the **law of *contradiction.** But the laws of thought must be deemed to be related to experience, since children do not always accept them.—*Distg. fr.* the LAWS OF LOGIC, which are practical rules for *valid* thinking.

thought questions: questions, in an examination or test, that cannot be answered by memory alone but require independent thinking during the test.

thought/supervalent: an **obsessional** train of thought. It may have all the marks of rationality save one—it cannot be dissipated.

threat: *n.* **1.** verbal, gestural, or other **symbolic** expression of intent to injure or inflict evil on a person; a menace. **2.** a **sign** of evil or injury to come; a portent; a sign, situation, or object inducing fear or anxiety. **3.** an imagined event, believed likely to happen, that excites dread.

threat/homeostatic: any event that would, if it became actual, disturb **homeostasis.**

three-color theory = **trichromatic theory.**

three-component theory: 1. = **trireceptor theory. 2.** = **trichromatic theory.**

three-track plan: see **ability grouping.**

threshold: *n.* the statistically determined point at which a stimulus is just barely adequate to elicit a specified **organismic** response (ABSOLUTE THRESHOLD), or at which it differs enough from another stimulus to elicit a different response (DIFFERENCE or DIFFERENTIAL THRESHOLD). ➤Experiment in psychology is generally considered to have originated with the effort to determine the intensity threshold for sensation, and the concept of threshold is fundamental to all measurement, even when it is not explicitly mentioned. Originally limited to the **dimensions** of sensation, it is now freely applied to any aspect of the stimulus broadly conceived. Thus, it is proper to speak of the threshold of social mobility, meaning the point on a complex dimension of social conditions above which social mobility occurs, below which it does not. It is desirable, however, in technical discourse to use the term only for a point determined by careful measurement and statistical treatment of data. ¶The concept of the threshold belongs essentially to that which elicits response— i.e., to the stimulus. Both objective and mentalistic psychologists use the concept and arrive at the same value for the threshold, thus suggesting that their differences may not be fundamental. The **psychophysical** methods were developed as means of determining thresholds.—*Syn.* LIMEN (lī′mən), *L.* for *threshold.—adj.* **liminal** (lī′mə·nəl, lim′i·nəl), used as adjective for both limen and threshold.

threshold/absolute: 1. see **threshold** for the general meaning. **2.** the minimum intensity at which a stimulus becomes effective, as measured under optimal experimental conditions. (Often still abbreviated *RL* for

Reiz-Limen, Ger., stimulus limen.)—*Syn.* STIMULUS THRESHOLD.

threshold/difference or **/differential: 1.** see **threshold** for general meaning. **2.** the minimum difference between a pair of stimuli that can be perceived as different under optimal experimental conditions.— *Syn.* DIFFERENCE LIMEN or *DL.*

threshold/sensation = **threshold/absolute.**

threshold/terminal: the maximum stimulus that will produce a given type of sensory experience or elicit a given kind of response.—*Abbr.* **TR** (*R* for *Ger. Reiz* = stimulus).

threshold/two-point: see **two-point threshold.**

thrombosis (throm·bō′səs): *n.* the formation of a blood clot, or thrombus, within the heart or blood vessels.—*adj.* **thrombotic.**

Thurstone scale: an attitude scale constructed by the method of **equal-appearing intervals.** ➤Each of a series of statements is assigned, on the basis of the pooled judgments of a hundred or more raters, a scale value of favorableness in respect to a given attitude object. The subject's score on the attitude questionary is the mean value of those items with which he indicates he is in agreement. This rationale of scale construction is applicable to any dimension of preference or judgment.

thwart: *v.* to interrupt or prevent the goal-directed activities of a person or group.— *Syn.* **frustrate.**

thymergastic reaction (thī″mər·gas′tik) : (*A. Meyer*) pathological affective behavior.

-thymia, -thymic: combining forms, respectively for nouns and adjectives, meaning *soul*; or *temper, mood, affect, feeling tone*: e.g., **cyclothymia.**

thymus: *n.* a gland of uncertain function in the neck and upper thorax. It usually atrophies in the adult human.—*adj.* **thymic.**

thyroid (gland): an endocrine gland whose lobes lie on either side of the upper windpipe. Its secretions are important in growth and in the control of metabolic rate. THYROXIN, also prepared synthetically, forms part of the secretion. THYROIDISM is excessive functioning of this gland.

tic: *n.* **1.** a nervous twitching that cannot be voluntarily controlled; esp., a small stereotyped movement of face or voice. (The latter may somewhat resemble a stammer.) —*Syn.* HABIT CONTRACTION. **2.** any compulsive movement. (Poor usage.)—*n.* **tiqueur** (tē·kêr′) (*Fr.*), one suffering from a tic.

tic douloureux (tēk′ dü″lü·rœ′) (*Fr.*) facial neuralgia, characterized by excruciating short sharp pains.

tickle: *n.* a complex experience derived from lightly stroking the skin (especially in certain sensitive regions). Fused with the light pressure sensation is considerable feeling tone and impulses to laughter and to spasmodic withdrawal movements—which may be uncontrollable. Despite the tendency to involuntary withdrawal, tickle may be pleasant and the person often deliberately seeks it. The experience is much stronger when caused by others, especially if unexpected.

timbre (tim'bər; taN-): *n.* that subjective quality of a complex tone which depends primarily upon the overtone pattern of the physical sound; the quality that distinguishes, e.g., a clarinet from a violin tone of the same pitch and loudness.—*Syn.* TONE COLOR, TONAL QUALITY (*ambig.*).

time-binding: *n.* 1. reacting in the light of past or future, as well as of present, conditions: in man, a process usually involving imagining or ideation but possible in some degree without it. 2. the social transmission of experience through successive generations so that what happens in one generation is, to some extent, made available to later generations.

timed test: see **test/timed.**

time error: a tendency to be biased in judgments of objects by their relative positions in time; e.g., when the first of two equal tones is usually judged louder. The error is arbitrarily called *positive* when the first of two stimuli is preferred or judged stronger, *negative* when the second is so judged.

time-limit procedure: a procedure in which the test score is determined by the amount correctly performed within time limits that are so set as to preclude finishing all the tasks.—*Syn.* **timed *test,** speed *test.—*Ant.* **work-limit *test.**

time perception: the apprehension of the length of time occupied by a psychological process, of rate of change, of placement in time, of order of occurrence.

time perspective: see **perspective.**

time/psychological: time subjectively estimated, i.e., without the aid of clocks and without direct guidance by such external factors as the position of the sun. ➤ It includes both the direct awareness of **duration,** considered by some to be an elementary attribute of a sensory process; and judgment of time, based on the number (to some extent, the kind) of experiences that have intervened.

time score: the time required to perform a given number of operations.—*Cp.* **rate *score.—*Contr. w.* **accuracy score.**

time sense: 1. = **time perception.** 2. loosely, the ability to judge lengths of time passed.

time study: recording the time taken for each unit of an industrial operation.—*Syn.* TIME-AND-MOTION STUDY.

timidity: *n.* the tendency to fear and shrink from situations that most persons do not find significantly fearful. Though disproportionate to the situation, the fear is usually not very strong.—*Distg. fr.* **shyness,** which is specific to social situations and responses.

tinnitus (ti·nī'təs): *n.* ringing in the ears and other head noises caused by physiological activities in the sensory mechanism but in the absence of any corresponding external stimulus. It frequently follows prolonged exposure to a loud sound.

tinsit: *n.* a neologism for **tendency-in-situation.**

tint: see **color tint.**

tiqueur: *n.* (*Fr.*) a person with a **tic.**

tissue: *n.* any structure in an organism made up of similar elements or cells that perform a common function. ➤ Usually the tissue has a particular location and its elements are joined together. But blood is sometimes called a tissue, despite its wide dispersion.

tissue need: see **need/tissue.**

titillate: *v.* to tickle.

toilet training: teaching the infant to observe the proprieties of his culture in regard to urination and defecation. ➤ The proprieties differ widely, and the effort to teach them is made at different ages and with different methods in different cultures. Severity in toilet training is supposed by some to have more devastating effects on the child's development than other kinds of severity.

tolerance: *n.* 1. noninterference with beliefs, attitudes, or practices different from one's own or which one deprecates; or the attitude of such noninterference. ➤ Tolerance is more active than indifference, or even open-mindedness; it implies explicit inhibition of preventive efforts or objections. 2. ability to endure a certain injurious condition without serious damage: e.g., drug *tolerance,* the ability to take a stated amount without pathological results. 3. (*stat., mech.*) the amount of deviation from a standard that is permitted: the *tolerance* limit.

tolerance/ambiguity: see **ambiguity tolerance.**

tolerance/anxiety: see **anxiety tolerance.**

tolerance/frustration: see **frustration tolerance.**

-tomy: combining form denoting *cutting, a cutting operation.*

tonal attribute: a distinguishable characteristic of a tone that can be held constant while other attributes are changing. ➤ Tonal **pitch, loudness,** and **volume** are generally accepted as attributes; the status of tonal *density,* tonal **brightness,** and of **tonality** is less certain. The attributes do not correspond in one-to-one relation with the physical characteristics of the sound waves.

tonal bell: (*C. E. Ruckmick*) a bell-shaped model to illustrate the interrelations of the attributes of **tonal brightness, volume,** and **tonality.**

tonal brightness: see **density/tonal.**

tonal (or **tone**) **character** = **timbre.** ➤In German, however, the equivalent word *Toncharakter* means **tonality** (1).

tonal chroma = **tonality.**

tonal gap: a region in the pitch series in which, for a given person, auditory acuity is lost or greatly reduced, though tones on both sides of it can be heard.—*Contr. w.* **tonal island.**—*Syn.* TONAL LACUNA.

tonal intermittence = **flicker/auditory.**

tonal island: (*aud.*) a region of normal acuity (for a given person) in the pitch series, bounded on both sides by a **tonal gap.**

tonality: *n.* **1.** (*exper. psych.*) that attribute of **pitch** by which a tone sounds more closely related to its octave than, for instance, to the tone adjacent to it in the musical scale. ➤The quality of *C-ness* of a C, e.g., is thought to be distinguishable from its quality as high or low in ordinary pitch perception, and to be a factor in **absolute *pitch,** although terminology and experimental evidence are both somewhat confused and inadequate.—*Syn.* TONAL CHROMA, OCTAVE QUALITY. **2.** (*music*) the family relationships, among the tones and chords of a scale, to the keynote or tonic.

tonal pencil: a visual model displaying the relation of pitch to **tonal *volume.**

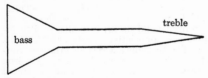

The horizontal dimension represents pitch, the vertical dimension volume. (Spatial representations including other tonal dimensions exist but are not pencil-like.)

tonal scale = TONAL RANGE, the entire extent of vibration frequencies perceptible to the average human ear—i.e., from about 20 to about 20,000 **c.p.s.**—*Distg. fr.* musical scale (see **scale 8**).

tonal volume: see **volume/tonal.**

tone: *n.* **1.** a sound whose physical stimulus consists of a regular or **periodic** vibration or wave in an elastic medium. ➤Tone is contrasted with **noise,** which is sound whose physical stimulus is irregular or non-periodic. PURE or SIMPLE TONES are heard when the stimulus is a simple **sine** wave; **compound *tones** are heard when the wave form is complex but still periodic—i.e., when the same complex form recurs at regular intervals.—*adj.* **tonal. 2.** = **whole**

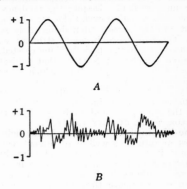

A. Pure tone wave
B. White noise

tone; a unit of measurement of musical intervals. ➤In the music of the Western world, the equal-tempered whole tone is 1/6 of an octave. **3.** the characteristic **timbre** of an instrument. **4.** = **tonus. 5.** a quality of total level of emotionality; mood: depressed *tone,* unpleasant feeling *tone.*

tone/beat = **difference tone.**

tone color = **timbre.**

tone/combination: see **combination tone.**

tone/compound: 1. (*psychol.*) any tone made up of simple or partial tones. ➤The component tones, if loud enough, can be directly heard as distinct. **2.** (*phys.*) = COMPOUND SOUND WAVE, a complex periodic sound wave that can be analyzed by **Fourier's law** into a number of **sinusoid** waves. It is the physical stimulus for the compound tone of (1).

tone deafness: see **deafness/tone.**

tone/difference: see **difference tone.**

tone/fundamental: see **fundamental tone.**

tone/intermittence = **interruption tone.**

tone/interruption: see **interruption tones.**

tone/otogenic: *prefd. syn.* for **tone/subjective** (which see).

tone/partial: see **partial tone.**

tone/pure: a sound whose physical stimulus is a simple vibration at a fixed rate (a **sinusoidal** vibration) in an elastic medium. It is not compounded with other tones and has no **partials.**—*Syn.* SIMPLE TONE.

tone/simple = **tone/pure.**

tone/subjective: a perceived tone whose primary stimulus is some activity within the auditory mechanism, not in sound waves outside the ear. Since there is an objectively real stimulus, *subjective* is misleading.

OTOGENIC TONE (originating in the ear) is recommended as more descriptive.

tone tint = timbre.

tone variator: an instrument for producing pure tones of variable pitch. ➤It consists of a **resonator** whose volume is controlled by a piston; blowing across the mouth of the resonator with a constant, moderate strength produces a fairly pure tone. The STERN VARIATOR is an early developed standard form.

tone/whole: see **whole tone.**

tonic: adj. 1. pertaining to **tonus.** 2. (music) characterizing the keynote or referring to it.—n. 3. (music) the first tone or keynote of a given scale, or a chord having this tone as its root. 4. (pop.) a medicine that increases appetite, promotes digestion, and/or gives tone to the whole body.

tonic immobility: a state of slight contraction of a large muscle group (or of the musculature generally) sufficient to keep the muscle taut but not sufficient to cause movement.

tonicity (tō·nis'ə·ti): n. 1. = **tonality** (poor usage). 2. the normal state of **tonus** of any organ or member, esp., of a muscle (MUSCLE or MUSCULAR TONUS).

tonic reflex: 1. a constant or immediately renewed **tonus** maintained by a designated stimulus state. ➤E.g., in many species, an animal placed on its back makes tonic extensor movements of its limbs (called TONIC VESTIBULAR REFLEXES because they are elicited by stimuli from the **vestibule**). 2. an abnormal continuation of tonus after a reflex action.

tonometer (tō·nom'ə·tər): n. any instrument for measuring the pitch of tones or for producing tones of known pitch; esp., a simple laboratory instrument that permits the damping of a sounding string in such a way as to bring out in isolation the several upper **partials.** ➤APPUNN'S TONOMETER is a reed organ carefully tuned to very small tonal intervals.

tonoscope: n. an instrument that converts sound waves into light and, by means of the **stroboscopic effect,** measures changes in pitch.

tonus (tō'nəs): n. (physiol.) a continuing slight stretching usually present in muscles when not in active movement. ➤Tonus is the regular condition of smooth muscle; in striate muscle, efferent impulses of low frequency are required to maintain it.—Syn. tonicity (2), MUSCULAR or MUSCLE TONUS, TONE (not recom.).—adj. **tonic.**

tonus/induced: see **induced tonus.**

tonus/plastic: a muscular tonus such that a limb remains fixed in the position given it by a manipulator.—Cp. **catalepsy** (2).

tool: n. any object, esp. a physical object, used by an animal to make direct changes in the environment: e.g., a stick used to poke food out of a box. ➤A box climbed on in order to obtain food is not a tool since the box itself does not change the environment. It may be called an instrument or instrumentality. Only rudimentary tool-using seems to be found below the apes and monkeys.—Distg. fr. MACHINE, which usually refers to a power-driven device.

tool subjects: school subjects which, in a given context at least, are thought of as valuable chiefly because of service to other subjects or to practical pursuits.

topectomy (tō·pek'tə·mi): n. a modified form of **lobotomy** wherein small incisions are made in the frontal lobe and thalamus, the surface of the brain being laid open to the surgeon.—See **lobotomy.**

topical flight = **flight of ideas.**

topographical principle: (neurol.) the hypothesis that the peripheral origins, including the spatial relations, of afferent excitation are reflected or continued in the organization of the tracts ascending to the brain, in the **thalamic** relay, and in the **cortex.** ➤In other words, differences in the receptor are represented by some sort of place relationships of the afferent impulses. This is a restatement of the old doctrine of **brain localization.** Contr. w. **functional principle of neural organization.** Facts consistent with both principles are established.

topography: n. (psychol.) 1. the mapping of regions or systems within which or between which psychic processes operate. ➤For psychoanalysis there are three regions: **conscious, unconscious,** and **preconscious.** Another division (also topographical but based on a different classification) is: **id, ego,** and **superego.** A topographic area is defined by the kinds of processes included in it, although a given process may cross from one area to another. An area or region may have many subregions. Some psychoanalysts conceive the preconscious as being only a subregion of the conscious. ¶Although Freud gave currency to both the concept and the term **topography,** other schools before and since have used topographic models and constructs.—Cp. **field theory, topological psychology.** 2. the full quantitative specification of all the relevant physically measurable dimensions of a response. PATTERN OF RESPONSE is sometimes used as a synonym but has other meanings.

topological psychology: (K. Lewin) the description and classification of psychological phenomena in terms of the formal relationships of the geometrical system called **topology** (which see). ➤E.g., certain phenomena are classified as "barriers." Since barriers have explicitly defined characteristics in topology, it is possible to make certain logical deductions: "If this phenomenon is a barrier, then such and such is true." The description in topological terms thus generates **hypotheses** for empirical testing; and topological psychology is to be conceived of as a very inclusive model.—See **model.**

topology: *n.* the systematic statement of the properties of spaces that do not change under one-to-one continuous transformation and are independent of magnitudes. ➤The familiar geometry of Euclid is the statement of the properties of spaces defined according to certain axioms and postulates about magnitude and direction. But a space can be defined by many other sets of relations. Topology, ignoring magnitude, considers the relations of invariance under continuous transformation. Suppose that a rubber sheet has drawn on it a figure with intersecting lines. Stretching the rubber will effect a continuous transformation of the figure—certain parts, e.g., may become relatively bigger. But many relations do not change, e.g., a certain part of the figure will remain next to another no matter how the sizes change. The totality of such relationships is the geometry of topology. Kurt Lewin proposed that the geometry of topology be the **model** for the description of psychological phenomena.—*adj.* **topological.**

torpor: *n.* temporary relative nonresponsiveness to ordinarily effective stimuli. ➤*Distg. fr.* **sleep,** though by what criteria it is difficult to say.—*Syn.* TORPIDITY, LETHARGY.—*adj.* **torpid.**

torsional movement/ocular: a rotation of the eyeballs about the front-to-rear axis. ➤It is of very limited extent and occurs as part of normal coordinated movements of the eyes. It is *not* an important component in what is popularly called "rolling the eyes."—*Syn.* TORSION.

total determination/coefficient of: (*stat.*) the proportion of the total **variance** in the dependent variable which may be accounted for by the variations in the independent variables included in the **multiple** *correlation;** the square of the multiple correlation coefficient.

totem (tō'təm): *n.* (*anthrop.*) an organism, or a representation of an organism, that is venerated as its symbol, its protective deity, or its spirit kin by a particular social group, community, or defined community division. ➤abstr. *n.* **totemism.**—*adj.* **totemic** (tō·tem'ik).

touch: *n.* **1.** contact of some object with a portion of the surface of another object, esp., of an animal body. ➤Touch may be ACTIVE (the animal moves into contact: the animal *touches*), or PASSIVE (the object moves into contact: the animal *is touched*).

—*Syn.* PALPATION. **2.** (*pop.* and *hist.*) = the SENSE OF TOUCH. ➤Since there are several qualitatively distinct discriminations and since these are mediated by several kinds of **receptors,** it is now less customary to speak of a single sense of touch than of **cutaneous** (or dermal) **senses.** FEELING SENSE is ambiguous. **3.** any of the several kinds of elementary sense data or sensations aroused by contact with an object. ➤It is generally agreed that pressure, warmth, coolth, and pain are qualitatively distinct. Heat is usually considered a fusion of warmth with pain. Whether tickle and itch are elementary sense data or fusions is uncertain.—*v.* **touch.**

touch/field of: the totality of stimulations (either potential or actual at any one time) caused by contact.

touch spot: a small area on the skin especially sensitive to faint point stimuli. ➤It is now believed that the touch spots are not *closely* related to underlying receptors.

tough-minded: *n.* a metaphorical description by W. James of a fundamental type of person, contrasted with TENDER-MINDED. ➤The tender-minded were said to be rationalistic, intellectualistic, idealistic, optimistic, religious, free-willist, monistic, dogmatical. The tough-minded were said to be empiricist, sensationalistic, materialistic, pessimistic, irreligious, fatalistic, pluralistic, skeptical. Although research does not find coherent clusters of behavior or unitary personal traits corresponding with James's two types, his description has been very influential in literary psychology.

toxemia: *n.* any pathological condition caused by poison in the blood.—*adj.* **toxemic.**

toxic: *adj.* pertaining to, or caused by, poison; poisonous.

toxic psychosis: see **psychosis/toxic.**

TR: abbr. for *terminalischer Reiz* (= *Ger.* terminal stimulus), the **terminal** *threshold.**

trace: *n.* a structural alteration inferred to be left in the nervous system as the result of any activity therein.—See **engram.**

trace conditional response: see **conditioned response/trace.**

trace/memory = engram.

trace/perseverative: (*C. Hull*) a neural impulse that continues with diminishing strength for a brief period after the cessation of firing of the neuron by receptor or other neuron. ➤When the impulse continues after the cessation of the *stimulus,* Hull used the symbol *s* and spoke of a PERSEVERATIVE STIMULUS TRACE.—*Cp.* **lag** (of sensation).

tracking: *n.* intermittent or continuous adjustment of an instrument or machine to maintain a normal or desired value (COM-

PENSATORY TRACKING), or to follow a moving reference marker (PURSUIT TRACKING). ➤Keeping a speedometer at 50 mph is compensatory tracking; keeping a moving object in the field of a telescope is pursuit tracking.

tracking/position: a **tracking** task in which movement of the operator's control is associated with a direct displacement or movement of the tracking indicator.—*Contr. w.* **tracking/rate.**

tracking/rate: a task in which the operator moves a control in such a way as to keep an indicator in line with a moving object, thus measuring the object's speed of motion.

tract: *n.* (*neurol.*) a bundle of nerve fibers having the same origin, terminus, or function.

tradition: *n.* **1.** a body of practices or beliefs handed down orally and supported on the grounds that they repeat earlier, hallowed practices. **2.** = the CUSTOMARY, that which has been done or believed and still is. ➤In this usage, there is no implication that the traditional is good. In scientific contexts, the implication is slightly derogatory: *It is traditional, yes, but is it sound?* Restriction to the orally transmitted has dropped out in this usage.

traditional terminology: 1. terms in popular speech referring to psychological phenomena. **2.** terms used in psychological writing before the revolt of **behaviorism.**

➤Many (but not all) traditional terms clearly implied a radical (or metaphysical) distinction between psychological and physiological phenomena—i.e., they were **dualistic** and **mentalistic.** To avoid the inner contradictions of the traditional terminology, behaviorism sought to describe behavior in strictly **objective** and **positivistic** terms.

It soon became apparent, however, that it is not possible (for the very long present at least) to describe more than a small fraction of the data of psychology in such objective terms. Now, rejection of a confused terminology does not justify a science in ignoring many of its data or its most significant problems. Confused as they undoubtedly were, the traditional terms referred to real data, though often to data badly analyzed or categorized. To abandon them is too often to leave ourselves with no language tools for grappling with real human problems.

The traditional terms, moreover, remained current not only in popular speech but in other scientific disciplines—remained with all their confusions uncorrected. Indeed, the great freedom with which some have been used in **psychoanalysis** has increased the confusion. Nor have the traditional terms profited by their halfhearted and often ambiguous acceptance in **neobehaviorism.** The arduous task of ensuring that they are not so used that they multiply confusion about *facts* cannot be dodged by those whose business it is to put the facts in order.

Fortunately, modern emphasis upon **constructs** and **intervening *variables** permits the reintroduction of many once-excluded terms. But merely to return to traditional terms, even after a serious effort to purge them of inner contradictions, is not enough. Behaviorism brought to a crisis a revolution not merely in terms but in concepts. (Ironically enough, early behaviorism, by insisting that a concept is nothing but a term, would make it impossible to state its own enduring contribution which—one insists—was to provide psychology with a new basic concept of its task.) The new conceptual wine was bound to burst many of the old terminological bottles.

Psychologists, therefore, have been busily engaged for a generation in inventing new terms conformable to the new conception of psychology as the science of behavior. Most of these, fortunately, have not been Greek **neologisms** but phrase combinations of more or less familiar English terms. The resulting somewhat Teutonic agglutinative stringing together of nouns (as in the title "Amount-set and the Length-Difficulty Function") is mildly offensive but is probably within the elastic boundaries of permissible English—if not overdone! Some of them have even achieved considerable currency.

But many psychologists have found themselves reverting more and more to the storehouse of traditional English terms to refer to psychic facts. Even though strongly suggestive of a metaphysical position, many nonetheless seem perfectly serviceable for behavior description. Particularly is this true of the verbs. "To be aware" or "to be conscious" do refer to a kind of behavior, however difficult it may be to specify it. (Some authors say that such terms refer to a particular relation of the person or organism to the environment.) Other terms, particularly some nouns such as "consciousness," seem to have unavoidable implications of a psychic realm that is distinct from behavior. Psychologists are beginning to pick and choose among these traditional terms; to this they must add critical reformation—a task in which the semanticist can be of help.

This dictionary must record both past and present usage. It is usually not too difficult to define a traditional term as the traditional psychologist used it. It is often possible also to translate its meaning into behavioral terms. There is real difficulty, however, in defining many still-current terms in strictly behavioral language. Few will doubt that **hallucination** refers to a real phenomenon. But it cannot be defined in behavioral terms without either intolerable paraphrase or much high theorizing, or both. (It is hard enough in any case to define.)

We shall, therefore, often have to define traditional expressions by using traditional terms, just as we define behaviorist expressions by using behavioral language so far as we can.

tradition-directed: (*D. Riesman*) of a person whose behavior is dictated by rules, rituals, and relationships laid down by past generations and modified only slightly by successive generations.—*Contr. w.* **inner-directed** and **outer-directed.**

train: *v.* to guide or direct the activities of another animal, the trainee, in such ways that the trainee learns to behave as desired by the trainer; also reflexively, to train oneself—i.e., to engage in activities designed to promote one's own learning.

trainability: *n.* the capacity for profiting from training.—*Syn.* **aptitude** (which see).

training: *n.* **1.** the totality of instructions, planned circumstances, and directed activity to which an animal or person is subjected in order to induce learning. **2.** a regime designed to render a person physically fit for strenuous activity, as in athletics. **3.** the care and education of the very young, or of animals. ➤Training, when conceived as leaving little scope to initiative or spontaneity of the trainee, is sometimes contrasted with **education,** which (presumably) stresses self-directed activity. As a corollary of this distinction, training is more often concerned with motor activities and skill and with the acquisition of such mental operations as have only few and simple alternatives (such as using correct grammar).

training analysis = **analysis/didactic.**

training device: an apparatus to be operated by one who is learning a skill. ➤The apparatus may or may not be a substitute for that used in actual practice of the skill.

training/escape: see **escape training.**

training/transfer of: see **transfer.**

trait: *n.* **1.** any enduring or persisting **character** or characteristic of a person by means of which he can be distinguished from another; that about a person which is consistently manifested, despite variation within a considerable range of circumstances. ➤This broad meaning includes physical appearance (or even those **somatic** characteristics known only by careful study and inference), consistent behavior characteristics, and inferred personality tendencies or dispositions. Usage, even by the same author, fluctuates between reference

to a consistently manifested pattern of behavior (= **surface *trait**) and to a part of the enduring structure of the person (inferred from behavior) which is the cause of the consistency (**source *trait**). ¶Trait tends to be used only for differentiating characteristics. When thus broadly defined, it includes many kinds of specific patterns— e.g., attitudes, virtues, even abilities or habits. Thus, the term **personality trait** is not wholly redundant since it attempts to distinguish a special class of traits, though unfortunately it is usually not clear just which traits are to be so named. ¶Biological and psychological usages of the term seem parallel, except that in some biological writing trait is equated with hereditary trait.—See **unit *trait, common *trait. 2.** (*stat.*) an isolated characteristic, quantitative or qualitative, of a group or class of items.—*Cp.* **variable.**

trait/character: 1. any trait by which persons are distinguished in respect to their **character** (4). **2.** = **personality trait** (an unnecessary usage). **3.** (*psychoan.*) an inherited tendency, either in its original form or as modified by the **ego, superego, or ego ideal.**

trait/common: 1. (*G. W. Allport*) a trait possessed in at least some strength by all persons in a given society or wider cultural group (e.g., by all persons in Western culture groups). ➤It is conceived as the result of **species *heredity** interacting with the universal environmental experiences to which all are exposed, such as the universal experience of helpless infancy. Proposed *syn.* UNIVERSAL TRAIT. **Common trait** is somewhat ambiguous, and it is needed for **(2)** below. *Universal* need not be taken absolutely: it can refer to all in a large population, with exception allowed for abnormal cases (just as two ears are "universal" though earless human beings occur). **2.** a trait possessed by many but not all individuals in a society. ➤This usage is proposed instead of Allport's usage above. It allows traits to be ordered on a continuum from **universal** through degrees of commonness to **unique.**

trait/common level: see **trait/compensatory.**

trait/compensatory: a trait, found in high degree, that helps to compensate for a low degree of another trait: e.g., the acuteness with which blind persons perceive certain sounds. ➤Such compensatory traits seem to be relatively uncommon, but a widely held folk theory asserts that they are the general rule. If this were so, correlations between traits would generally be negative. In fact they are generally positive. To express the fact of a considerable number of traits that correlate highly with each other the term COMMON LEVEL TRAIT has been proposed.

trait/constitutional: see **constitution.**

trait/culture: 1. a unit-characteristic of a culture: it may be a material object (a plow), a technique (plowing), or a belief (that plowing is women's work).—*Cp.* **culture complex. 2.** a characteristic of a person that is attributable to his having lived in a specific culture.—*Cp.* **trait/environmental-mold,** which is slightly more general.

trait difference: the difference between the relative strength of one trait and another trait in the same individual. ➤A person who is average in **aggression** but low in **frustration tolerance** shows a greater trait difference than one who is high in both.—*Cp.* **ipsative scaling.**

trait/dominant: see **dominant.**

trait/dynamic: a trait manifested in goal-directed behavior; one that operates as an enduring motive.

trait/environmental-mold: (*R. B. Cattell*) a source *trait whose unity has been built up in the individual by the action of certain unitary and persistent characteristics in his environment.

trait/ergic: an innate tendency to strive or act in a particular way.—*Syn.* **instinct, erg** (which see).

trait/generalized: one in which differences in an individual's behavior from situation to situation are small compared with differences between individuals in the same situations.

trait/metanergic = metanerg.

trait organization: the dynamic or cause-and-effect interrelationships between traits.

trait/orthogonal: a trait that correlates zero with, i.e., that varies independently of, the other traits under consideration.—*Syn.* INDEPENDENT TRAIT (*prefd.*), **unique *trait.**

trait/personal: a **structural** subdivision of the person, inferred to account for the persisting consistency of certain behaviors despite wide variations in stimulating circumstances.—*Syn.* **trait/source.**

trait profile: a chart on which the ratings or scores for a number of traits are plotted on a common scale in parallel rows, so that the pattern of traits can be visually perceived.—*Syn.* **psychograph (1).**

trait/recessive: see **recessive character.**

trait/source: an underlying trait (or factor) hypothesized to account for certain consistencies (or correlations) of behavior.

trait/surface: a pattern of behaviors consistently manifested in any of a class of similar circumstances; a cluster of behaviors all of which have appreciable positive correlations with each other. (In pathology, such a cluster is called a **syndrome.**)—See **trait** and **source *trait.**

trait/unique: 1. a trait peculiar to an individual, not found in quite the same form in other persons. ➤It has been held that any trait is inherently unique since its nature is determined by being part of a unique individual. Taken strictly, this view rules out scientific study or even description. Generally, however, *unique* is taken to mean "seldom found in exactly this form."—See **trait/common. 2.** (*stat.*) a trait that correlates zero (or nearly zero) with the other traits under consideration.—*Syn.* INDEPENDENT TRAIT (much *prefd.*), **orthogonal *trait.**

trait/unit or **/unitary:** a trait or characteristic of the organism, inferred from certain consistencies of behavior, that functions as a single whole, that is subject to increase or decrease as a whole, and that gives rise to behaviors that intercorrelate in person-to-person comparisons.—See **functional unity.**

trait/universal: preferred synonym for **trait/common (1).**

trait variability: the divergence or scatter from trait to trait within the individual, obtained by having him take a number of tests, scoring these on a common scale, and computing the variability of the scores around the mean of the tests.—See **ipsative scaling, trait difference.**

trance: *n.* a sleeplike state marked by reduced sensitivity to stimuli, loss or alteration of knowledge of what is happening, substitution of automatic for voluntary activity. ➤Trances are frequent in hysteria, and they may be hypnotically induced. In extreme form, trance resembles (or is) **coma.** Religious or emotionally marked trances are called ECSTASY.

transaction: *n.* a psychological event in which all the parts or aspects of the concrete event derive their existence and nature from active participation in the event. ➤Thus, a baseball batter—though in other events or transactions he may appear as a loving father or a good judge of cheese—derives his qualities *as a batter* from a transaction with 17 other players, the umpires, the coaches, the spectators, the rules of the game, the diamond, and all the paraphernalia of the game. All these other participants (including the inanimate ones) help make the batter what he is *as a batter* in this unique event. The transactional attributes derive from the unique event; but it is possible to generalize from many transactions so that, e.g., we have a man's batting average. And in virtue of man's ability to represent what is not objectively present, a transaction may involve the participation of absent elements—such as the batter's remembering his batting average or realizing that the eyes of the sporting world are upon him. Some psychologists hold that all psychological events are transactions.

transaction theory of perception: a doctrine that conceives of perceiving as a **transaction** (which see). ➤The out-thereness of the objects perceived and their significance are held to be created in the transaction—as indeed are all other properties of the perceived object. To be a normal perceptual transaction there must be sensory activity on the part of the perceiver.—*Cp.* **field theory.**

transcortical: *adj.* across the **cortex,** usually with special reference to the tracts that connect different parts of the cerebral cortex.

transection: *n.* the cutting across the long axis of a fiber or tissue.—*v.* **transect.**

transfer: *n.* 1. a general term for change in ability to perform a given act as a direct consequence of having performed another act relevant or related to it. ➤The unsatisfactory nature of the above reflects the unsatisfactory state of theory. The definition fails to distinguish **transfer** from such phenomena as **fatigue, sensory *adaptation,** and **stimulus** or **response *generalization.** Nor does it clarify what it is that makes the first act relevant to the second. Most important, transfer as thus defined seems almost to include everything that would be called learning, though most theories give different connotations to these two terms. ¶Despite these difficulties, transfer is, without undue ambiguity, the term for alterations in behavior brought about by certain specifiable operations: e.g., the easier learning of French following the study of Latin; the ease with which one may learn to roller skate as a result of learning to ice skate. The expression TRANSFER OF TRAINING, however, is redundant if training is broadly conceived, and is unnecessarily specialized if training is given its usual meaning. 2. = **transfer/applicational.** 3. any item moved from one category to another; specif., a student who has changed from one college or school to another.

transfer/applicational: improvement in one's performance in life situations as a result of having learned something in school.

transfer/bilateral: change of performance in a member on one side of the body as a result of training the corresponding member on the other side: e.g., a change in right-foot performance as a result of left-foot training.—*Syn.* CROSS-EDUCATION.

transfer by generalization: the hypothesis that improvement in one sort of performance as a result of learning in another sort is the consequence of mastering the applicable general rules or techniques useful in both tasks.—*Syn.* TRANSFER OF PRINCIPLES.

transference: *n.* (*psychoan.*) 1. displace-

ment of **affect** from one object to another. 2. specif., the process whereby a patient shifts affects applicable to another person onto the psychoanalyst. E.g., the patient directs upon the analyst the hatred he feels toward his father.

transference/negative: see **negative transference.**

transference neurosis: see **neurosis/ transference.**

transference resistance: (*psychoan.*) the repression of some of the manifestations of transferred affect. ➤The analysand transfers to the analyst the attitudes formerly associated with the parent, some of which are still inacceptable and must be repressed: e.g., a woman may show jealousy of the analyst, yet repress any direct sexual impulses toward him as father **imago.**

transfer/negative: a change for the worse in the performance of a task as a result of performing some other task. ➤The other task or performance is conceived to be somehow related and to interfere with the first, but the only evidence of the relation may be the worsening of performance in the first task when again attempted.—*Contr. w.* **transfer/positive,** a change for the better.

transfer of principles = **transfer by generalization.**

transfer of response: see **response *generalization.**

transfer of training: see **transfer.**

transfer/positive: an improvement in a performance as a result of a previous act.— See **transfer/negative.**

transformation: *n.* 1. a thorough change of form, structure, or composition. 2. (*math.*) a change of form in an equation or figure without changing its meaning or value; or the change of a mathematical group into an **isomorphic** group. 3. (*logic*) the substitution of one set of symbols for another, according to rules that make the two sets equivalent. 4. the process or processes accounting for **object *constancy.** ➤In color constancy, the actual retinal stimulus values (which differ very widely) are said to be transformed when, e.g., the fruit is perceived as orange-colored under a wide range of hue and intensity illumination. 5. the change of energy from one form to another: e.g., from heat to light. 6. (*psychoan.*) representation of a repressed feeling, in consciousness, by its opposite or in some other disguised form.

transformism: *n.* evolutionism, the doctrine that species are gradually changed under environmental influences.

transient situational personality disorders: (*Stan. Psychiat.*) a very general classification for disorders in which the symptoms do not reflect underlying personality disturbance but are merely the means taken by the individual in his struggle to deal with a very stressful situation.

ransitional cortex: a region of the cerebral **cortex,** extending as a band in the vicinity of the corpus **callosum,** and intermediate in architectural features between the phylogenetically new portions of the cortex and the older portions as seen in the **olfactory lobe.**

ransitive state: see **substantive state.**

ransitivity: *n.* (*logic*) a relationship such that if A stands in a certain relation to B, and B stands in the same sort of relation to C, then A stands in that relation to C. ➤Ordinary physical qualities are transitive, but psychological qualities or activities are not necessarily so. One may prefer A to B as dinner guest, and B to C, but not A to C. —*Cp.* **a fortiori.**—*adj.* **transitive.**

ransmission: *n.* **1.** moving something from one place or time or person to another. **2.** (*genet.*) passing a trait or characteristic from parent to offspring.—See **heredity. 3.** (*commun. theory*) the processes by which a **message** passes from the **input** to the **output;** or the average **amount of** ***information** coming from the input which reaches the output. ➤See **information** (3) for discussion. **4.** (*neurol.*) the firing in sequence of one neuron by another; neural conduction. **5.** (*sociol.*) = SOCIAL TRANSMISSION, the passing on from generation to generation (by such social means as teaching or other communication) of behavioral patterns, language, customs, traditions, mores, laws, etc. ➤It does not include the transmission of material products, even though socially produced, but does include the transmission of the technology or the ways of making such products.—*Syn.* SOCIAL HEREDITY, **social *inheritance** (both somewhat misleading).

ransmission/social: see **transmission** (5).

ransmission theory: the view that the conscious processes of the individual are the acts of an "oversoul" transmitted or retracted through the human body as a medium.

ransmission unit or **TU:** a logarithmic unit of sound intensity. The commonest instance is the **decibel.**

ransmitter: *n.* (*commun. theory*) any means by which a **message** is **encoded** and started on its way through a **channel.** ➤In face-to-face communication, the **transmitters** are the muscles that emit words, gestures, etc.

ransmutation of measures: changing a set of scores into an equivalent system: e.g., changing **raw *scores** into **standard *scores.**—*Cp.* **derived *scores.**

ransparency: *n.* the property of transmitting light in an image-forming state. ➤Transparency is lessened by whatever diffuses the light or reduces its **luminance.**

transparent surface color: a color seen in a two-dimensional mode and possessing (among others) the property of transparency which permits other objects to be seen beyond or behind it: e.g., the color of a clear glass pane perceived as a transparent plane.

transpose of a matrix: (*factor anal.*) a **matrix** whose successive rows are, in order, the successive columns of a given matrix.

transposition: *n.* **1.** the interchange of spatial, logical, or psychological relationships between two units of a system; the replacing of A by B and B by A.—See **transformation. 2.** (*music*) changing a musical composition from one key to another. **3.** = TRANSPOSITION BEHAVIOR, reacting in novel situations to similarities of relationship rather than to similarities of content. ➤E.g., an animal may be rewarded if he goes to B, an exit smaller than the A exit. He is said to show transposition behavior if, confronted with B and C, he selects C in preference to B, C being still smaller than B—i.e., if he reacts to the relationship "smaller" rather than to the concrete perceptual qualities (including absolute size) of the training object B.—*Syn.* TRANSPOSITION OF GESTALT. **4.** the theory of **transfer** that attributes the improvement in a second task to recognition of the existence in that task of patterned relationships already learned in the previous reaction period. **5.** in writing or reading, exchanging the positions of two letters, syllables, or words.—*n.* **transpose,** the system after a transposition has taken place.—*v.* **transpose.**

transposition behavior: see **transposition** (3).

transposition of affect: the attachment of feeling (with little or no change in quality) to a different and rationally inappropriate object.—*Syn.* **displacement,** which, however, is often used where the **affect** does not obviously resemble the original.

transvaluation of psychic values: a considerable shift in the system of values, amounting to the adoption of a new system if not the opposite of the older system. Psychoanalysts hold that this is a marked phenomenon in dreams.

transverse: *adj.* **1.** lying or moving across; specif., **2.** (*anat.*) at right angles to the **longitudinal** axis of the body.

transvestism: *n.* persistent desire to dress in those garments which in a given culture belong to the opposite sex, and to feel uncomfortable when dressed in the garments of one's own sex; or a persistent association of sex excitement with dressing in the clothes of the other sex. ➤The wearing of trousers by women in this century is not necessarily transvestism; in the last century it was.—*Syn.* TRANSVESTITISM.—*pers.* *n.* transvestite.—*v.* transvest.

trapezoid body: a strand of fibers in the pons which arise from the cells of the cochlear nucleus.

Traube-Hering waves (trou'bə-hā'ring): rhythmic and relatively long-period oscillations in blood pressure not correlated with the heartbeat nor with respiration.

trauma (trô'mə; trou'mə) *n.*, *pl.* traumata, traumas: injury or wound; any experience that inflicts serious damage upon the organism. The term is extensively used for psychological as well as somatic damage.—*adj.* traumatic (trô·mat'ik).—*v.* traumatize.

trauma/birth: see birth trauma.

trauma/primal: (*psychoan.*) a supremely important and stressful event in early life that inflicts permanent psychic injury. ➤Later psychic injuries are likely to be unconsciously associated with it. It is as if one unconsciously argued that the later injury is just a modification of the primal one. O. Rank held that birth is the primal trauma.

traumatic constitution: see traumatic psychosis.

traumatic delirium: delirium resulting from a brain or head injury.

traumatic neurosis: a neurosis (esp., hysteria or anxiety) precipitated by a trauma, either somatic or psychic, in which the symptoms are closely related to the original trauma.

traumatic psychosis: a mental disorder arising as direct result of a brain or head injury that produces psychotic symptoms. Three forms are distinguished: TRAUMATIC DELIRIUM, TRAUMATIC CONSTITUTION (in which there is a gradual change in the patient's make-up), and POSTTRAUMATIC MENTAL ENFEEBLEMENT.

treatment: *n.* 1. subjecting something or someone to an action or influence. 2. any measure to ameliorate an undesirable condition; an endeavor to help a person attain better health or better adjustment by whatever means: medical, surgical, psychotherapeutic, counseling, or direct aid. ➤The attempt to restrict the term to medical treatment is contrary to both historical and current usage. 3. (*stat.*) the systematic working over of data to discover relationships. 4. (*exper.*) the environmental stimuli that are systematically varied and brought to bear upon the subject of an experiment or test; the experimental or independent *variable.

treatment/convulsive: see convulsive therapy.

treatment/experimental: see experimental treatment.

treatment interview: see interview (2).

treatment variable = experimental variable (see experiment).

tree structure = (*neurol.*) dendrite.

Treffermethode: *n.* (*Ger.*) = retained members method, right associates procedure.

tremograph: *n.* an instrument for measuring the amount of involuntary fine movement made by a member or by the whole body—i.e., for measuring voluntary steadiness in maintaining a position.

tremolo (trem'ə·lō): *n.* rapid periodic variation in pitch and/or loudness of a tone, esp. an unpleasant variation. ➤*Syn.* vibrato, usually restricted to pitch changes, and to such changes as are less extreme.

tremor (trem'ər; trē'-): *n.* shaking or trembling; a repeated fine spastic movement ➤Tremors resulting from some form of neural impairment are classified as OF REST (or OF POSTURE) and OF INTENTION (i.e., taking place during voluntary movement) Trembling during excitement or emotion and shivering with cold may also be called tremor.

trend: *n.* 1. the direction manifested in a series of events. 2. a dynamic tendency or inclination to behave in a given way or in a certain direction. ➤Trend is perhaps the least qualified or restricted of the names for a psychophysical structure or mechanism having a dynamic effect. It carries no implication of lastingness, strength, unitariness origin, or causation. It is merely a slight extension of the basic meaning stated in (1) 3. (*psychiat.*) the pattern of ideas related to some pathological condition: e.g., a constellation of ideas related to incest, a delusional pattern, a group of autistic ideas ➤An unhappy usage, and becoming less common.

trend analysis: the statistical analysis of series of measurements of a variable, taken at several points in time, in order to discover whether there is a basic direction of change.

trend/malicious or /pernicious: 1. (*med.* a disorder that seems likely to become chronic. 2. marked behavior regression.

trend/neurotic: (*K. Horney*) a group of tendencies, usually developed in childhood oriented toward seeking the maximum security from the environment and so decreasing basic *anxiety.

trephine (tri·fin'; -fēn'): *v.* (*brain surgery* to cut a small circular disk out of the skull —*Syn.* TREPAN (trə·pan').

Treppe phenomenon = staircase phenomenon.

triad: *n.* a group of three; specif., in music

three tones forming a chord.—*adj.* **triadic** (trī·ad′ik).

triad/anal: see **anal triad.**

triads/method of: the presentation of three experimental stimuli with the requirement that the odd one be indicated. ➢The subject may be instructed in the basis of categorizing (e.g., "indicate which one differs most in size") or left free to select the odd member of the triad by any criterion that comes naturally.—*Cp.* **forced-choice technique.**

trial: *n.* **1.** a single effort, esp. one of a series of efforts, to accomplish a particular result. **2.** in experiments or tests, a single performance; a single complex response evoked by a particular stimulus complex. **3.** the process of putting something to the proof or the test.—*v.* **try.**

trial-and-error learning: see **learning/trial-and-error.**

trial response: a tentative response made to see how it will work. ➢The term is appropriate only when conditions make it possible to withdraw or seek alternatives if the trial response does not work.

trichotomy (trī·kot′ə·mi): *n.* a division into three parts, not necessarily equal.—*adj.* **trichotomous.**

trichromatic theory: a theory of color vision based on the facts of color mixture: that from the combinations of three **color primaries** all hues may be derived and that every change of combination gives rise to a different hue. The three primaries are usually considered to be a certain red, green, and violet.—See **color theories.**

trichromatism: *n.* that kind of vision in which all three of the primary colors are distinguished and may be used in color mixture to obtain the different hues. ➢It is contrasted with **dichromatism,** in which only two primaries are distinguished; and from ACHROMATISM, in which no hues can be distinguished. While trichromatism is the normal form of vision, there is an ANOMALOUS TRICHROMATISM in which the mixture of the three primaries yields for the subject any given hue, but the ratios required differ from the normal.

trick: *n.* (*indiv. psychol.*) a psychic mechanism by which a person keeps from recognizing his own deficiencies.—*Syn.* **defense mechanism.**

tridimensional theory of feeling: Wundt's theory that a feeling or affect has three dimensions: pleasantness-unpleasantness, excitement-quiescence, tension-relaxation.

trigeminal nerve (trī·jem′i·nəl): the Vth cranial nerve, which has both afferent and efferent fibers from face, nose, and tongue.

trigger action: the release of latent energy, the resulting action depending little upon the releasing force and chiefly upon the latent energy. ➢It is believed that nervous energy is the result of trigger action, each neuron being fired at full strength or not at all by action of the **receptor** or of the other neurons with which it is connected. Many psychological acts are clearly so disproportional to the stimulus that they must be supposed to be a case of trigger action.

triplet: *n.* one of three mammals gestated at the same time in the same uterus.—*Cp.* **twin.**

trireceptor theory: a theory that assumes three kinds of receptors in the retina corresponding with the three **color primaries** of the **trichromatic theory.**—See **color theories.**

triskaidekaphobia (tris·kī″dek·ə·fō′bi·ə): *n.* fear of the number 13. ➢A reduction to absurdity of Greek **neologisms.**

tristimulus value: the hue of a sample color stated in terms of the amounts of the primaries needed for a matching mixture.

tritanomaly (trit″ə·nom′ə·li): *n.* a rare type of anomalous **trichromatism.**

tritanopia (trit″ən·ō′pi·ə): *n.* a rare form of partial color blindness in which reddish blue and greenish yellow stimuli are confused. It is commonly a result of retinal disease but in rare cases may be inherited.—*Syn.* BLUE BLINDNESS.—*adj.* **tritanopic.**

tritone: *n.* (*music*) in an equal-tempered scale, an interval of half an octave (three whole tones); an augmented fourth.

trochlear nerve (trok′li·ər): the IVth cranial nerve, which controls the superior oblique **eye muscle.**—*Syn.* PATHETIC NERVE.

troland (trō′lənd): *n.* a unit of visual stimulation defined as that **illuminance** of the retina equal to that produced by viewing a surface whose **luminance** is one candle per square meter through an artificial pupil of one square millimeter area centered on the natural pupil. ➢Formerly called **photon,** but that term is now preferably used for a quantum of electromagnetic radiation.

trophic (trof′ik): *adj.* pertaining to the absorption of food, either by a single cell or by the whole organism.—*n.* **trophism,** the control of nutritive function.—*Distg. fr.* **tropism.**

tropism (trō′piz·əm): *n.* an automatic or forced orienting movement toward, or away from, a source of stimulation whose direction and extent is a direct function of the stimulus—e.g., the turning of a sunflower toward the sun. ➢The term tends to be broadened to include any mechanically or chemically forced movement. In compounds, the Greek name of the stimulus is prefixed: e.g., PHOTOTROPISM, a turning toward light. Unless explicitly noted, tropisms are POSITIVE—i.e., movements toward; but many are NEGATIVE, or away from the stimulus.—*Syn.* FORCED MOVEMENT, FORCED ORIENTATION,

taxis (which see).—*adj.* **tropistic; in com-** pounds, **-tropic** (as in PHOTOTROPIC).

truancy: *n.* absence without proper leave from home, school, or other place of duty, esp. in the case of children or adolescents. —*pers. n.* **truant.**

true: *adj.* **1.** characterizing a proposition or belief as corresponding with reality. ➤The philosophical question concerning what reality is and what correspondence with it means need not be raised, though some view is always implied.—*Ant.* ERRONEOUS, which emphasizes the human factor; FALSE. COR-RECT, often used as a synonym, properly re-fers to accordance with the rules of logic, mathematics, or some other standard. **2.** (*stat.*) corresponding with the entire uni-verse or total population under considera-tion, not merely with a sample.

true-false test: see **test/true-false.**

true measure: see **score/true.**

true value: see **score/true.**

truncated distribution: (*stat.*) a distribu-tion cut off by removal of, or by failure to obtain, certain classes of observations that would all fall at one extreme or the other of the frequency distribution; a distribu-tion cut off so that there are no cases at all beyond a certain point. The truncation may be unilateral or bilateral.

trunk/nerve: see **nerve trunk.**

trunk/sympathetic: (*neurol.*) the chain of interconnected **sympathetic ganglions** that extends along each side of the verte-bral column.

try/provisional: (*E. R. Hilgard*) the be-havior of an animal in a problem situation when trying to discover a route to the goal. ➤The term is less question-begging than **trial-and-error *learning.**

T scale: 1. one that has as its basis the standard *scores of the distribution of *unselected* 12-year-olds for any specified test or accomplishment. The mean of that distribution is given the value of 50; scores that are five times **SD** worse or better than the mean are given the values of 0 and 100 respectively, intermediate scores proceeding by steps of one for each 0.1SD. **2.** a similar scale based on any designated popu-lation. ➤The *T* scale is designed only for normal distributions.

***t*-test:** *n.* use of *t* (3) to determine whether a difference meets statistical criteria of **stability** or **reliability.**

T type: *n.* (*E. Jaensch*) a class of persons constitutionally inclined to **tetany**like con-tractions and to **eidetic imagery** of a pecu-liarly photographic character.—*Cp.* **B type.**

TU = transmission unit.

tubectomy = salpingectomy.

tuition: *n.* teaching; in learning experiments, any activity of another designed to help the learner to master the task more quickly.

tuitional analysis: an analysis (3) under-

taken for training but conducted by the analyst as usual and paid for by the analysand.

tumescence (tü·mes'əns): *n.* a swelling of any tissue, esp., of a genital tissue.—*adj.* **tumescent.**

tune: *v.* to adjust the frequency of a sound-ing body by mechanical means so that it emits a tone of required pitch.

tuning fork: a two-pronged piece of highly tempered metal that emits a tone of specific frequency. The overtones of the tuning fork are of almost negligible intensity so that its tone is almost pure.

tunnel vision: restriction of vision to the central area of the retina. Peripheral vision is lacking or very greatly restricted.

turnover/labor: in a labor force, the num-ber of persons hired to replace those who have quit or been fired within a given pe-riod, or the ratio of this number to the aver-age number on the payroll.

twilight attacks: in epilepsy, brief sudden changes in consciousness together with motor **automatisms,** meaningless action and speech. After the attack, the individual does not remember what has happened.

twilight vision: the kind of vision that takes place under conditions of faint illumination. ➤The retinal rods are thought to be the receptors for such seeing.—See **Purkinje effect.**—*Syn.* SCOTOPIC VISION.

twin: *n.* one of two mammals gestated in the same uterus at the same time.

twins/dizygotic = twins/fraternal.

twins/fraternal: twins that develop from two separate fertilized eggs or **zygotes** hence, are genetically no more alike than ordinary **sibs.** They may be of like or un-like sex.—See **twins/identical.**—*Syn.* DIZY-GOTIC TWINS, TWO-EGG TWINS.

twins/identical: twins formed by the divi-sion of a single fertilized ovum or **zygote** (hence, also called MONOVULAR or ONE-EGG TWINS, or MONOZYGOTIC TWINS), and devel-oping in one chorionic sac (hence, also called MONOCHORIONIC or ONE-SAC TWINS) ➤Such twins are presumed to have iden-tical heredity or genetic structure, whereas **fraternal *twins** are no more closely re-lated than ordinary **sibs.** Identical twins are always of the same sex.

twins/monochorionic (mon"ō·kôr·i·on" ik): one-sac twins; twins developing within a single sac.—*Syn.* **twins/identical** (which see).

twins/monovular: one-egg twins (see **twins/identical**).

twins/monozygotic = twins/identical.

twins/one-egg = twins/identical.

twins/one-sac = twins/identical.

twins/two-egg = twins/fraternal.

twitch: *n.* a sudden local convulsive con-traction.—See **muscle twitch.**

twitch/isometric: see **isometric twitch.**

two-aspect theory = double-aspect theory (see under **mind-body problem**).

two-factor theory: see **factor theory** (of mental organization).

two-point threshold: the distance apart at which two pointed objects, applied with simultaneous equal pressure to a given skin area, are perceived by touch as two. At lesser distances various ambiguous percepts result.

two-tailed test: a test for the **statistical *stability** (or **statistical *significance**) of a difference when it is assumed that the difference may be in either direction. ➤An actual situation and the method of data-gathering may permit A to be either less or more than B; the test is to see whether the actual obtained difference is of a magnitude likely to be found by chance. If the situation is such that A can be only more or only less than B, a ONE-TAILED TEST is used.

two-track plan: a form of **ability grouping** (which see).

two-way table = **scatter diagram.**

tympanic (tim·pan'ik): *adj.* pertaining to the eardrum.

tympanum (tim'pə·num) = eardrum.

type: *n.* **1.** a pattern of qualities that can be distinguished from other patterns and that serves as a model or exemplar in assigning individuals to a class or group; the defining pattern of a category. **2.** a real or, more often, an ideal or fictitious individual embodying the characteristics of a category in fullest measure; the central form about which all variations in the members of a class center. ➤This is a pre-Darwinian concept, but it is influential in much current thinking about type. **3.** all the members of a class or category considered as somehow collectively embodying the defining qualities of the group. ➤This meaning is quite common in biology. **4.** an individual having *most* of the defining qualities of the group— an average man, a typical dog. ➤This is a frequent meaning in **typologies. 5.** the extremes of a continuous variation: a *tall* vs. a *short type.* **6.** the peak instances of a bimodal distribution of a single variable: a *normal type* vs. a *pygmy type.* **7.** the modes of a bipolar distribution where the patterns at the two poles differ but with continuous intergradations; continuous species types: *business* vs. *artist type.* **8.** the modes of a bipolar distribution where the patterns at the poles are the central form about which variations center but the two patterns are discontinuous with each other: e.g., *dogs* and *ducks.* **9.** any pattern of qualities found frequently enough to seem a quasi node.

The operational means for distinguishing these different types differ considerably. But the term is often used indiscriminately, and in the absence of necessary factual data.

¶The underlying concept of type is statistical. But types are often freely postulated without any kind of statistics to support them: they are statistical concepts without statistics. Moreover, the several explicit statistical concepts (**5, 6, 7, 8**) are often confounded.

For kinds or varieties of types, see the qualifying part of the term: **affective reaction type, attitude type, rational type,** etc.

type/body: a scheme for classification of individuals according to the pattern of macroscopic anatomical characteristics, usually with the assumption that certain psychological characteristics are associated with each pattern; or, a particular kind of body build as thus classified.—See **body build** and **constitutional type;** also **type.**—*Syn.* SOMATOTYPE.

type/character: see **character.** Specific kinds of character appear under the qualifying term: e.g., **exploitive character.**

type fallacy: the unsupported belief that extremes constitute distinct types, not continuous with intermediate cases: e.g., the view that the feeble-minded, the insane, the genius constitute different "species" from the ordinary person. ➤However, there is also danger of an antitype fallacy, i.e., of denying discontinuities that are actually to be found in nature.

type/introvert: (*C. Jung*) see **introvert.**

type/motor reaction: see **reaction type.**

type/muscular: see **reaction type.**

Type I error: in tests of significance, rejecting the **null hypothesis** when it is true.

type/somatic = **type/body.**

types/psychological: 1. any type classification according to psychological variables. **2.** (*C. Jung*) classification of persons according to the psychic function most often depended on (**function type**), or according to the dominant attitude (**attitude type**). ➤There are four function types and two general attitude types (**introversion, extraversion**), thus yielding eight pure psychological types, besides intermediates. See **function type.**

type/thinking: (*C. Jung*) a classification category for persons whose psychological activities are dominated by thinking, and who tend to be motivated by reflective thinking.—See **types/psychological.**

type-token ratio or **TTR:** the ratio of the number of different words (types) to the total words (tokens) in a sample of language.

Type II error: in tests of significance, accepting the **null hypothesis** when it is false.

typify: *v.* to be an example; to stand as an example of other members of a class; to be a symbol for something similar.

typing: *n.* the determination of the **type (1)** to which a specimen or individual belongs.

typological: *adj.* pertaining to **typology;** making use of the type concept; character-izing a psychology strongly based on types (e.g., Jung's psychology).

typology: *n.* **1.** the study of **types. 2.** a particular system for the classification of types.

U

U: 1. = upper. **2.** = (*ital.*) number of un-like signs.

$_sU_R$: (*C. Hull*) the hypothetical innately pro-vided receptor-effector connections that make possible unlearned responses; an un-learned stimulus-response potentiality.

UCR or **UR** = **unconditioned response.** (**UR** *prefd.*).

UCS or **US** = **unconditioned stimulus.** (**US** *prefd.*).

Ucs.: (*psychoan.*) *abbr.* for **unconscious** or **unconsciousness.**

UCV = **uncontrolled** variable.

U **fibers:** short fibers by which adjacent cortical **gyri** are interconnected. ➤*Distg. fr.* the long **association fibers,** which make interconnections between widely separated regions.

U **hypothesis:** (*H. Helson*) the generaliza-tion that organisms can adapt to a fairly wide range of stimulus values and function optimally within this range.

ulstrith: *n.* (*H. A. Toops*) a group com-posed of all those in a given population who fall in the same class or category in each of the traits involved in the study. ➤E.g., if the traits are sex (*m* or *f*), com-plexion (*bl* for blond, *br* for brunet), and literacy (*l* or *il*), then the group of all who are *m, bl,* and *l* form one **ulstrith** for this study; those who are *m, bl,* and *il* form an-other. The traits need not be dichotomous, as in the above example; each defined class or category is the basis of sorting. The population need not be of persons, but of any items that are conceived as having two or more characteristics.

A STRITH is reached by adding all those alike on one trait throughout the popula-tion and may thus be described by one name. E.g., all the males in a population form one strith; in the above example the strith *males* is formed by combining the ulstriths (*m, br, l*), (*m, br, il*), (*m, bl, l*), (*m, bl, il*).

An AGGRITH is a heterogeneous combina-tion of ulstriths and striths, requiring a com-plex description. E.g., a population that is composed of the ulstrith (*m, br, il*) plus the strith "females" is heterogeneous. The popu-lations available for research are likely to be aggriths; but a research design based on ulstriths yields more usable data for the same size of population and the same ex-perimental treatment.

ultra- (ul'trə-): prefix meaning *beyond,* literally (in space) or figuratively.

ultrasonic (-son'ik): *adj.* beyond sound; of sound waves of higher frequency than can be heard by the human ear.—*Syn.* SUPER-SONIC.

ultraviolet: *adj.* characterizing radiant energy of wave lengths shorter than the ex-treme violet and lying beyond the ordinarily visible spectrum. (Usually assigned to vibrations below 400 or 390 millimicrons.)

umbilical cord (um·bil'i·kəl): the cord leading from the placenta to the navel of the fetus.

Umklammerung **response** (ùm·kläm'ər·-ùng): *n.* (*Ger.*) the **starting reflex.**

Umweg (ùm'väk): *n.* (*Ger.*) = **detour (be-havior** or **test).**

Umwelt (ùm'velt): *n.* (*Ger.*) the circum-scribed portion of the environment that is meaningful and effective for a given species and that changes its significance in accord-ance with the mood operative at a given moment.

unadjustment: *n.* the state of a person faced with a difficulty as yet unsolved. ➤When the difficulty is beyond the person's normally available resources, we have **maladjust-ment.**—See **adjustment.**

unambivalent: *adj.* (*psychoan.*) of two or more instinctual impulses harmoniously combined: e.g., initiative combined with love is unambivalent, whereas the combina-tion of love and hatred toward the same person is ambivalent.

unaware-need: *n.* a need that cannot be verbalized by the counsellee, manifesting it-self in vague anxiety and tenseness or other symptoms. The unaware-need is not neces-sarily unconscious; the inability to verbalize it may be due to the disorganization induced by an earlier basic **anxiety,** rather than to repression.

unbiased error = **error/chance (1)** or **error/compensating.**

unbiased estimate: (*stat.*) one based on a representative *sampling.

uncertainty: *n.* **1.** absence of full belief. ➤*Distg. fr.* DOUBT, which implies vacillation due to conflicting evidence (or conflicting valuation of the evidence). **2.** (*info. theory*) see **entropy.**

uncertainty/interval of: see **interval of uncertainty.**

uncial script (un'shi·əl) = **manuscript writing.**

unconditional response = **unconditioned response.**

unconditioned reflex: see **unconditioned response.**

unconditioned response: 1. a response evoked by a certain stimulus situation at the beginning of any given learning or conditioning period. ➤Pavlov worked with what he deemed to be an innately determined stimulus-response sequence and accordingly spoke of an UNCONDITIONED REFLEX. Current experimental work does not require that the unconditioned linkage be innately established but only that it be firmly established at the beginning of the experiment. **2.** the hypothetical or inferred mechanism whereby an unconditioned stimulus evokes an **unconditioned response (1).**—Symbols: UR, R_u.—See **conditioning.**

unconditioned stimulus: a stimulus that, at the beginning of a given learning or conditioning period, evokes a certain response. —See **conditioning, unconditioned response.**—Symbols: US, S_u.

unconscious: *adj.* **1.** characterizing any activity or **mental *structure** of which a person is not aware. ➤This usage is very inclusive. It includes purely physiological processes, such as the normal heartbeat or the secreting of cortisone, psychological structures such as a **set** or a **determining tendency** (which can often be consciously examined but more often are not), as well as the dynamic **mechanisms** postulated in psychoanalysis.—*Cp.* **subconscious,** characterizing processes or structures of which one is not clearly aware. **2.** of a person who is at the moment unaware of anything; of a person in a swoon, coma, or (in common usage) deep sleep. **3.** (*depth psychol.*) characterizing those processes that are in a broader sense psychic rather than "merely physiological" but cannot be brought to awareness by ordinary means (though they may be investigated by appropriate means).

➤**Unconscious** is one of the most troublesome terms in the psychological disciplines. One difficulty is that it is linked as a qualifier with terms that, when not so qualified, mean something intrinsically conscious: e.g., an *unconscious* wish. Wishing is a conscious process. *Unconscious* wishing is verbally self-contradictory; it seems to refer to an "unconscious conscious process." The difficulty may seem merely verbal but it has led to fallacious thinking.

A second difficulty is that the term is applied either to processes or to underlying structures or mechanisms in a way that often blurs distinctions between them. What is meant when a prejudice is called unconscious? "I do not like you, Dr. Fell; The reason why I cannot tell." The first clause asserts a highly conscious process, the second an unconscious cause or underlying mechanism.

A third difficulty is the paradox that a merely negative term should be attributive of positive properties. The unconscious is not merely the not-conscious; in the several depth psychologies, the fact that a process is unconscious is held to endow it with different, and even extra, dynamic effects.

It is said that there are no less than 39 distinct meanings of **unconscious;** it is certain that no author limits himself consistently to one. And nearly all meanings are closely linked to debatable theories. Any user of the term therefore risks suggesting agreement with theories that he may deplore.

Unfortunately, no single substitute can be suggested. In many contexts, *silent* or *unwitting* may serve. And it is usually possible to substitute a specific meaning for the frequently confused and general meaning. An unconscious determining tendency may be described as *unverbalized.* An unconscious attitude is *unreflective.* Secreting thyroxin is better described as *physiological* than as unconscious. An unconscious wish is better described as *repressed.* The primal processes postulated in psychoanalysis may be referred to as **id** processes.

But there is little prospect that **unconscious** can now be dislodged from either popular or technical vocabulary. All that is possible is to be wary of an inherently confusing term.

unconscious: *n.* **1.** a collective name for unconscious psychic activities.—See **unconscious** (*adj.*). **2.** (*depth psychol.*) a part or region of the psyche or person defined by the character of the activities ascribed to it. The activities are not open to direct conscious scrutiny but have dynamic effects on conscious process and behavior. ➤Two classes of activities are generally postulated: formerly conscious processes (or the representative of those processes) that have been expelled from the realm of the conscious; and certain primordial and infantile wishes and impulses that have never gained access to the conscious realm. ¶The expression the UNCONSCIOUS PROPER is sometimes employed to point up a distinction from the **preconscious,** whose contents are not at the time in the conscious but may be brought to consciousness without **resistance.** In later psychoanalysis, the term **id** has largely replaced the **unconscious** and is somewhat differently defined, but the two are regularly interchanged. See **id, collective *unconscious, repression.** (As a noun, **unconscious** is sometimes capitalized.)—*Syn.* UNCONSCIOUSNESS.

unconscious cerebration: an activity of the cerebrum unaccompanied by mental process.

unconscious/collective or **/racial:** (*C. Jung*) that part of the individual's unconscious which is inherited and which the individual shares with other members of the species. ➤Other psychoanalytic schools also postulate such inherited psychic mechanisms, but the term—and in general the great emphasis—is characteristic of the Jungians.—*Contr. w.* **personal *unconscious.**

unconscious desire: see **unconscious (3).**

unconscious inference: a judgment, generally not put into words but acted upon, that is arrived at without awareness of any reasoning process. ➤Helmholz introduced the term to explain such phenomena as color contrast.

unconscious/personal: that part of the **unconscious** which develops as a result of individual experience.—*Contr. w.* **collective *unconscious.**

uncontrolled: *adj.* not regulated or measured by the experimenter.

UnCS = US (*prefd.*), the **unconditioned stimulus.**

undefined concept: (*C. Hull*) an operationally defined experimental variable that forms a starting point in Hull's **hypothetico-deductive method.**

underachievement: *n.* performance poorer than predicted from an **aptitude** measurement.—See **overachievement.**

underachiever: *n.* a person who does not perform in specified ways as well as expected from certain known characteristics or previous record; specif., a student who does not accomplish as much in school as would be expected from his measured intelligence.

underage: *adj.* of a pupil who is younger than the normal age for the grade or form in which he is enrolled.

underproductive: *adj.* (*Ror.*) characterizing markedly meager statements in response to the inkblots.—*n.* **underproductivity.**

understanding: *n.* **1.** the process of apprehending or grasping a meaning. ➤*Contr. w.* **comprehension,** the process of apprehending the concrete event. (But the distinction is often ignored.) **2.** (*obs.*) the **mental *faculty** whereby meaning is apprehended. **3.** sympathy resulting from considering a person's behavior from his standpoint. **4.** (in the school of *Verstehende Psychologie*) an intuitive process whereby the true nature of a psychic process is directly

grasped. ➤Understanding is said to consider, not cause-and-effect relations, but the inner significance of a psychic process.

undifferentiated: *adj.* of any whole or aggregate whose parts do not greatly differ ➤The implication usually is that they may become more different.—See **differentiation.**

undoing: *n.* an infantile **defense mechanism** (found also in neuroses) wherein performing a certain activity is intended to cancel out a prior activity as if it had never happened. ➤A child is said to act on the belief that a faulty action can be *replaced,* just as a faulty object can. If a series of actions has hurt a brother and brought on a scolding, the damage can be undone by repeating the whole sequence up to the point where the brother was hurt but at that point, switching to an acceptable kind of action which now replaces the old This is also supposed to be the mechanism behind the ritualistic activities of **obsessive-compulsive reaction.** The rituals are often condensed symbolizations of the repeating process.

undulatory: *adj.* having the form of a wave.—*n.* **undulation.**—*v.* **undulate.**

unequivocal (un″i·kwiv′ə·kəl): *adj.* unambiguous; susceptible to but a single interpretation.

unfinished business: a descriptive term for a person's continuing concern over any unresolved problem, whether or not the problem is relevant to the present situation.—*Cp.* **Zeigarnik phenomenon, conative perseveration.**

Ungestalt (ùn′ge·shtält): *n.* (*Ger., not gestalt*) not a unitary whole or totality ➤In English it is sometimes an adjective but in German it is a noun.

ungraded class: a small class providing special opportunities for pupils who are retarded in school and need much individual attention along with some group activities The pupils are generally classed as mentally inferior but not as mentally deficient.

uni- (ū″ni-): combining form meaning *one single, unity.*

uniaural (ū″ni·ô′rəl): *adj.* pertaining to one ear alone.—*Syn.* MONAURAL (commonly used, although etymologically bastard).—*Contr. w.* **binaural.**

unicellular: *adj.* of an organism having only one cell.

unidextrality: *n.* use of one hand (or side) in preference to the other.—*Cp.* **ambilaterality, dextrality.**—*adj.* **unidextral.**

unidimensional: *adj.* of a variable that has but one dimension: all the change lies along a single line. ➤*Contr. w.* MULTIDIMENSIONAL. Unidimensional does not mean having a single cause but a singleness of measurement.

uniformity: *n.* similarity or identity, in a

relevant respects, of two or more events or processes, so that a statement about one applies equally to the others.

unilateral: *adj.* pertaining to one side only; esp., to one side of the body.—*Cp.* **ambilateral.**—*n.* **unilaterality.**

unimanual: *adj.* one-handed; pertaining to one hand.

unimodal: *adj.* of a **frequency** distribution having but a single **mode**—i.e., only one peak.

uniocular (ū″ni·ok′ū·lər): *adj.* one-eyed; pertaining to a single eye.—*Syn.* **monocular,** etymologically bastard but more common.

unique: *adj.* idiosyncratic; characterizing an object or event as unlike anything else, as the only one of its kind or class. ➤Properly speaking, *perfectly* or *absolutely unique* is redundant, and *relatively unique* is linguistically self-contradictory. If anything were absolutely unique—completely unlike anything else—it could never be compared with anything else, could in fact never be known or talked about sensibly. In actual use, therefore, the word usually refers to that which differs greatly from other objects with which it might be compared. Thus, each person is said to be unique, truly different from all other persons. Yet all are human, have certain human qualities in common. In many discussions unique carries overtones of superior worth.—*See* **trait/unique.**—*n.* **uniqueness.**

unique code number: (*stat.*) a code number, formed from **addends,** such that the two following criteria are met: (*a*) every possible pattern has a different code number; and (*b*) every possible code number, from the lowest to the highest, has a corresponding pattern—i.e., there is no potential code number without a corresponding pattern. ➤A nonunique code number meets the first of the above criteria but not the second.

unique factor: see **factor/unique.**

uniqueness: *n.* (*stat.*) that portion of the **variance** of a variable not accounted for by the factors contained in the other variables in the set; the complement of **communality.**—See also **unique.**

uniqueness/correction for: (*factor anal.*) a correction for the fact that *h* rarely equals unity. It is made by multiplying the original coordinates of each test by 1/*h*.

unison: *n.* the relation of identity in pitch. ➤Tones played or sung in octaves (high and low instruments or voices) are also loosely said to be IN UNISON, as *contr. w.* IN HARMONY.

unit: *n.* **1.** any item or datum taken by itself, disregarding any component parts of which it may be composed; an item treated as a uniform whole.—*adj.* **unitary. 2.** = UNIT OF MEASUREMENT; a magnitude used in determining the magnitude of other objects—i.e., how many unit magnitudes constitute the magnitude to be measured. ➤Most physical measurements are transformed into spatial units—time, e.g., is measured by the space traversed by a clock hand. Many psychological units represent relative frequency of occurrence of a performance. — See **scale.** — *adj.* (for 2) **unit.**

unitary function: see **functional unity.**

unitary hues = **color principals.**

unitary type: a person whose **eidetic imagery, aftersensations,** and **memory** *images are very similar.

unitas multiplex: (*W. L. Stern*) an entity in which many characteristics or members are integrated as a firm unity.

unit character: see **character/unit.**

unit factor: a **factor** that functions as a whole. Its influence is not attributable to any of its several parts but to all of them; and if it functions at all, all the parts function.—See **functional unity.**

unit operation: a particular response, or a group of responses occurring together, that counts as one in estimating the magnitude of an operation, esp. in industry.

unit plan: a method of organizing school instruction: carefully prepared assignments are given out, covering certain large areas of the subject under study, with detailed instructions for work. Each pupil works by himself, conferring occasionally with the teacher, but presents himself for evaluation of progress at stated intervals.

unit/standard: 1. a conventional unit of measurement: e.g., the meter, the second, the gram. **2.** = **standard *score.**

unity: *n.* **1.** the state in which all the parts of an object or system work together as a whole without interfering with each other. **2.** = SIMPLICITY, the state of a complex system in which all the parts may be regarded as alike for a given investigation. **3.** a state of such similarity in a number of items that they all fall into one class or category. **4.** (*esth.*) the characteristic of a work of art whose parts are so related that they seem to form one whole or system.

unity/functional: see **functional unity.**

unity thema: (*H. A. Murray*) a compound of interrelated dominant **needs** that are related to a **press** formed in early childhood and that play a major part in the individual's behavior.

univariate: *adj.* composed of one variable.

universal: *adj.* **1.** pertaining to a **universe;** or to (practically) all instances of a given category, e.g. to all persons. **2.** characterizing behavior common to all human societies despite the variations in their culture.—*n.* **3.** (*logic*) a generalization or proposition that asserts something to be true of all instances of a class: the proposition *All triangles have three sides* has the form of a universal.

universal complex: (*psychoan.*) a complex derived from fundamental instincts.—*Ant.* PARTICULAR COMPLEX, one whose characteristic features result specifically from individual features of a person's experience.

universalism: *n.* (*T. Parsons and E. Shils*) the tendency to define social and ethical standards in completely general terms without regard to the nature of the individual or the circumstances. ⇒*Ant.* PARTICULARISM, in which standards do take account of the individual and the circumstances.

universality: *n.* **1.** the quality of being **universal. 2.** the criterion for validity or acceptability of an idea that it is accepted by all men everywhere and everywhen.

universal rationality/principle of: see **sufficient reason/principle of.**

universe: *n.* **1.** the totality of all existing things. **2.** the totality of all existing things in a definable and very large system: e.g., everything in a stellar galaxy. **3.** = **universe of discourse** or **statistical** ***universe.**—*adj.* **universal.**

universe/attitude: see **attitude universe.**

universe of discourse: all that is under consideration in a particular investigation or discussion.—*Cp.* **universe/statistical.**

universe/statistical: the totality about which statistical inferences are to be made; the total **population** from which a sample is selected for measurement and statistical calculation.—*Syn.* REFERENCE POPULATION, PARENT POPULATION, **population.**—See **population (2).**

univocal (ū·niv′ō·kəl): *adj.* (*logic*) of a term that refers to only one object or class of objects; of a term that does not refer to objects from different classes as if they belonged to the same class.—*Syn.* **unequivocal,** unambiguous.—*Ant.* **equivocal, ambiguous.** ⇒Univocal tends to be used for singleness of denotation (i.e., singleness of reference to things), *unambiguous* for singleness of connotation (i.e., for singleness of meaning).

unlearned behavior: any act that comes about without any training or learning. ⇒Unlearned behavior may be "acquired" as a result of growth of bodily structure; hence, it is not the same as genetically determined or hereditary behavior.

unlearning: *n.* an intentional effort to reverse the effect of prior learning.

unmoral: *adj.* of a person to whom moral considerations do not apply, or who is ignorant of morality.—See **immoral.**

unnatural: *adj.* contrary to **nature.** ⇒Since nothing contrary to nature can exist, unless "nature" is surreptitiously given a value connotation, the word **unnatural** has no place in science.—*Syn.* UNCUSTOMARY, ARTIFICIAL, UNUSUAL (all *prefd.* in special contexts).

unpleasant: *adj.* **1.** characterizing an external state of affairs, a situation, an event, or an object that is disliked or disagreeable. **2.** characterizing a particular personal reaction that one dislikes and wishes to have terminated: an *unpleasant* experience. ⇒It is supposed that all emotions, affects, or feelings may be characterized on the dimension from pleasant to unpleasant.—*n.* **unpleasantness, unpleasure.**

unpleasure: *n.* a feeling tone, the opposite of **pleasure;** an attribute, probably elementary and unanalyzable, of the experience when one dislikes the situation or the object of experience and wishes it terminated.—*Syn.* UNPLEASANTNESS.

unreality = **irreality level.**

unreality/feeling of: a feeling that something experienced is not "real," is **illusory.** ⇒In extreme or persistent form this is a pathological symptom, but flashes of such feeling are not uncommon.

unreasonable: *adj.* **1.** of a conclusion or hypothesis contrary to logic. **2.** of a person who resists logical conclusions. **3.** of a person who makes unfair or unjustified demands upon associates; or of the demands themselves.—*Cp.* **unreasoning.**

unreasoning: *adj.* of a person or of behavior not controlled by reflective thinking. ⇒There is an implication of impulsive action—i.e., of immediate response to the situation—be the response adequate or inadequate.—*Distg. fr.* **unreasonable.**

unreflective: *adj.* impulsive; pertaining to action not guided by reflective thinking.

unreliable: *adj.* (*stat.*) not meeting a specified criterion of **reliability.** ⇒Without the specification, this term is so vague as to be useless.

unresolved: *adj.* of a problem, contradiction, or conflict not solved; still to be worked out. ⇒In psychoanalysis the term refers to inner conflicts, to the situation in which the impulses of different developmental stages have not been harmonized. Thus, although everyone is said to have some **Oedipal** difficulties, most persons come to terms with ambivalent feelings toward the father; if they do not, the Oedipal situation is unresolved.

unrest: *n.* a state characterized by a feeling of uneasiness and a tendency to acts that have no particular relation to comprehensive goals: e.g., the state in which a person takes a drink or lights a cigarette "just to be doing something."

UnS = **US** (*prefd.*), the **unconditioned stimulus.**

unselected: *adj.* characterizing a sample drawn from a larger population at random, or in such a way as to avoid bias or any constant factor influencing the sample. ➤The term is something of a misnomer, since it is frequently necessary to do quite a lot of selecting to obtain an unselected sample—i.e., a **representative** *sample (which is a better term).

unsociable = unsocial (1).

unsocial: *adj.* 1. disinclined to seek the company of others.—*Syn.* UNSOCIABLE. 2. of a person or a practice that does not conform to contemporary custom or social rules.— *Syn.* UNSOCIALIZED. ➤E.g., wild-swinging fighting is *unsocial* or unsocialized; boxing is socialized. 3. not directed to a socially desirable end.—*Syn.* asocial.—*Cp.* ANTISOCIAL, directed at ends that are socially undesirable.

unsocialized = unsocial (2).

unspaced learning or **repetition:** a procedure in learning experiments in which study or practice is pursued without interruption until the learning is complete.—*Syn.* **massed** *practice.—*Ant.* SPACED REPETITION or LEARNING, spaced *practice.

unstable: *adj.* 1. of a person given to unpredictable shifts in moods. 2. of a person likely to slip intermittently from normality into abnormality; of a person whose adjustment, currently fairly satisfactory, is precarious. 3. (*stat.*) of a value that is subject to an unallowable amount of chance variation.—See **stability/statistical.**

unstriped muscle: see **striate** *muscle.

unstructured: *adj.* characterizing an object or situation whose elements or attributes are not clearly distinguishable or do not form a clearly marked pattern. ➤*Cp.* **ambiguous,** used when the elements or attributes tend to elicit more than one interpretation. An object may be unstructured but, for a given person, not ambiguous. Thus, a Rorschach inkblot is relatively unstructured but may be unambiguously seen as a butterfly.—See **structure.**

unthinkable: *adj.* 1. of a proposition that is self-contradictory, or that is so inconsistent that it cannot be either affirmed or denied. 2. (*pop.*) of a proposal that is so distasteful or so unlikely to succeed that it cannot be seriously considered.

unweighted: *adj.* (*stat.*) of a datum or score that is not ostensibly multiplied by a weight when combined with others. ➤The term is a misnomer: such scores are not truly *un*weighted; they have the WEIGHT COEFFICIENT of unity, and they may not have equal weight in the combined scores. —See **weight** (2) and (3).

upgrading: *n.* 1. promotion to a higher-level job. 2. the process of preparing an employee for a higher job.

upper category: (*psychophys.*) the kind of report (in the method of single stimuli) that is more frequently given when the stimulus magnitude is sufficiently increased. ➤E.g., if, at a low intensity level, the report on a light is either *red* or *yellow,* and with intensity increase *red* becomes more frequent, *red* is the upper category.

upset: *n.* a disorganization of behavior that occurs when the animal is under an environmental demand to which it is unready to respond. ➤The demand must be one effectively recognized by the animal: ultrasonic waves, or a social situation of which one is blandly unaware, do not constitute environmental demands and hence do not lead to upset.

UQ: (*stat.*) = upper quartile, the value exceeded by one-fourth of the measures or obtained values in the distribution.

UR = **unconditioned response** or **UCR.**

$_sU_R$ = (*C. Hull*) unlearned stimulus-response connections.

uranism (yū′rən·iz·əm): *n.* male homosexuality.

Urban's constant process = **constant process.**

Urban's tables: tables of the **Müller-Urban weights.**

urethra (yū·rē′thrə): *n.* the duct that discharges urine from the bladder.—*adj.* **urethral.**

urethral erotism: the centering of sex feeling upon the urethral zone.

urge: *n.* a strong and continuing **impulse** or **motivation** toward an activity or toward attaining a certain goal: an *urge* to become famous. ➤The term carries no implication of being conscious.—See **desire.**—*Syn.* **drive.**

urning (ûr′ning): *n.* (*obsoles.*) a male homosexual.

urolagnia (yū″rō·lag′ni·ə): *n.* association of sex excitement with urine or urination.

US = **unconditioned stimulus.**

use/law of: the hypothesis that, other things being equal, a function is facilitated by being used or exercised, is weakened by disuse.—*Syn.* **law of** *exercise, **law of** *facilitation, law of **habit,** law of *frequency.

U-shaped curve: (*stat.*) a distribution shaped like the letter **U,** almost the inversion of the normal curve. ➤Such distributions have been obtained with measurements of suggestibility.

uterine theory: (*Hippocrates*) the completely discredited belief that **hysteria** is solely a feminine disturbance caused by displacement of the uterus.

uterus: *n.* the saclike structure in which the embryo of mammals develops within the mother's body.—*Syn.* WOMB.—*adj.* **uterine.**

U test: *n.* (*stat.*) a **nonparametric** test of the significance of the differences between means for unmatched groups.

utilitarianism: *n.* the philosophical doctrine that makes practical usefulness the criterion of value. ➤The unwitting acceptance of this view by common sense affects psychological thinking.

utility: *n.* **1.** the fitness of an organ or a process to promote biological survival or psychological adjustment of an organism. ➤Biological utility is more often meant when the term is unqualified. **2.** (of a test) a combined measure that includes validity, reliability, pertinence, economy, and acceptability.

utricle (ū'tri·kəl): *n.* a saclike structure in the **vestibule** of the inner ear containing the receptors that are stimulated by the inclination of the head.—*Syn.* UTRICULUS (ū·trik'ū·ləs).—*adj.* **utricular** (-trik'-).

utterance: *n.* a unit of vocal expression by one person, preceded and followed by silence on his part. An utterance may be made up of words, phrases, clauses, or sentences.

uvula (ū'vyə·lə): *n.* the cone-shaped appendage that hangs from the soft palate.—*adj.* **uvular.**

V

V: 1. = verbal comprehension factor (see **abilities/primary mental**). **2.** (*C. Hull*) (*ital.*) the magnitude of the intensity component of a **reaction potential. 3.** = (*Ror.*) (*ital.*) **vista response. 4.** (*psychophys.*) the **variable stimulus;** any value of the variable stimulus. (Also symbolized by *v*.)

v: **1.** = volt. **2.** = **variation/coefficient of. 3.** = **variable stimulus** (also **V**). **4.** = volume (also *abbr.* vol.).

VA = Veteran's Administration.

vacuum response: a behavior that appears in the absence of its usual releasing stimulus. ➤It is believed to be the result of very high **drive state.**

vagina: *n.* the canal from the uterus to the exterior of the body.

vaginism (vaj'ə·niz·əm): *n.* a painful involuntary spasm in the vagina. It may prevent intromission or withdrawal of the penis and is often associated with aversion to coition.—*Syn.* VAGINISMUS (-niz'məs).

vagotomy (və·got'ə·mi): *n.* cutting of the **vagus** nerve.

vagotonia (vä″gō·tō'ni·ə): *n.* the condition resulting from overaction of the **vagus** nerve.

vagus (nerve): the Xth cranial nerve.—*Syn.* **pneumogastric nerve** (which see).

valence: *n.* (*K. Lewin*) that property of an object or **region** in the **life space** by virtue of which the object is sought (POSITIVE VALENCE) or avoided (NEGATIVE VALENCE). ➤*Cp.* **goal**, which usually means the whole object, whereas valence means the attractive property of the goal. Hull says **valence** plus **field force** roughly equal **reaction potential.**—*Cp.* **cathexis.**

valence/chromatic: see **chromatic valence.**

valence/substitute: the attractiveness of one goal because some other goal has not been attained.

validation: *n.* **1.** the process of determining the degree of **validity** of a measuring instrument. **2.** making evident the correctness of a proposition or of a reasoning process.—For compound terms with **validation**, see also compounds with **validity**; e.g., validation/a priori = **validity/a priori.**

validation/consensual: see **consensual validation.**

validation/cross-: see **cross-validation.**

validation/external: determining the **validity** of a set of measures by comparing them with another set, the criterion, that has been independently obtained and is known (or believed) to approximate the true measure.—*Syn.* EMPIRICAL VALIDATION.

validation/internal: an attempt to determine or to improve the **validity** of a test by studying the test items and the total make-up of the instrument. ➤Internal validation, when checked by **empirical** *validity*, can greatly improve a test; without outside check it is not very trustworthy even when done by skilled test constructors.

valid exclusion or **valid inclusion:** see **false negative.**

validity: *n.* **1.** the quality of being founded on truth, fact, or law. **2.** (*logic*) the attribute of an argument that conforms with logical laws. ➤Validity in this sense is formal: it means that the reasoning process is correct. Whether the premises correspond with reality is not in question; hence, an argument may have logical validity even when based on a misstatement of facts. **3.** (*stat.*) a property of the whole measuring or testing process, but esp. of the test instrument, that insures that the obtained test scores correctly measure the variable they are supposed to measure; the property of the measuring process that makes the obtained scores useful in predicting a given variable. ➤Validity is always *validity for the measurement of a particular variable;* there is no such thing as general validity.

Nor is there absolute validity—we determine the *degree* of validity. And the validity index has no meaning apart from the particular operations by which it is determined. ¶There are two basic kinds of operation: those that compare the test items with some classification of test items (**content *validity,** which see) and those that compare the actual test scores with some outside criterion (**empirical *validity,** which see). The latter is meant when no qualifying expression is used with **validity.**—*n.* **validation.**—*v.* **validate,** to determine the degree of validity; or to show that a satisfactory degree of validity is present.

validity/a priori: a guess at the validity of a test from the apparent similarity of the items to the behaviors that one assumes are those of the variable to be measured: a primitive form of **content *validity.**—*Syn.* LOGICAL VALIDITY.

validity/assumption = **validity/commonsense.**

validity/coefficient of: an estimate of the degree to which a test measures what it is supposed to measure. It is the coefficient of correlation between (*a*) a set of scores and (*b*) an independently obtained set of scores (called the criterion scores) which are believed to represent the variable to be measured. ➤E.g., if success in academic studies is the variable to be measured, point-hour ratios or marks may be taken as the criterion scores—i.e., as sufficient approximation to the true measure of academic success. The correlation of test results with these scores is a validity correlation for the test. Correlation may be computed by any method appropriate to the data.—See **correlation.**—*Syn.* EMPIRICAL VALIDITY COEFFICIENT.

validity/common-sense: a guess about **content *validity** based on "obvious" relationships between the test items and what the test is supposed to measure. ➤It is usually the product of confident ignorance. —*Syn.* VALIDITY BY ASSUMPTION, **validity/a priori.**

validity/concurrent: a measure of the correspondence between test results and the present status or classification of individuals; a form of **empirical *validity.** ➤E.g., for a trade test, one may correlate test scores with trade skills previously rated in actual performance, or with standing in the trade as apprentice, journeyman, or expert. Concurrent validity differs from **predictive *validity** chiefly in respect to the time when the criterion measure is obtained. The former asks how well people score who have achieved a certain status; the latter asks how well the scores on the test correspond with some future achievement.

validity/congruent = **construct *validity** (*prefd.*).

validity/construct: a sophisticated form of **content *validity** that reflects the degree to which each test item is a sample of the behaviors defined by the **construct** in question, and the degree to which the items collectively are representative of the whole range or class of behaviors thus defined. ➤The construct must be made so explicit that one can determine whether each answer to a test item is a behavior belonging in the class in question. Thus, for a test of manual skill, one needs to know exactly what kinds of behaviors exemplify manual skill. The tentative selection of test items nearly always rests on construct validation, though, unfortunately, too often on a casual use thereof. Only when construct validity is perfect is there no necessity for **empirical *validity.**

validity/content: a general term for methods of ascertaining the validity of a test by studying the contents of its several test items, in contrast with **empirical *validity,** which studies how the test actually works when given to a sample population. ➤Two criteria are critical: Is each item an example of the kind of performance the test is intended to measure? And are they collectively a representative sample of the class of performances that constitute the variable to be tested? In an arithmetic test, e.g., it is necessary to insure that ability to perform arithmetically is the chief determiner of each item: an arithmetic problem should not test reading rather than arithmetic. It is further necessary to insure that the items cover fairly the range of arithmetic tasks intended: a test may be overloaded with multiplication as compared with addition. Content validity is especially useful for appraising achievement tests. In experimentation, the content validity of the measures of the several variables is usually taken for granted.—*Cp.* **validity/face.** For various aspects of content validity, see **validity/ construct, /curricular, /definitional, /face, /logical, /sampling**—all varieties of content validity.

validity criterion: any independent measure that is believed to be an approximately true measure of a variable.

validity/criterion-oriented: a validity measure based upon correspondence with a criterion: both **predictive** and **concurrent *validity** are criterion-oriented.—*Syn.* **validity/empirical.**

validity/curricular: the degree to which test items are representative of the knowledge, skills, or attitudes supposed to be learned in a given course of study—a form of **content *validity.** ➤A number of techniques, from simple inspection to elaborate sampling studies, are used.

validity/definitional: the postulated validity of a test when the items making up the test are taken as the definition of the variable to be measured. ➤If a test contains items x', x'', x''', we can arbitrarily call it a test of x, if x is rigorously restricted to mean only what is common to x', x'', x'''. This it seldom is. E.g., if the three items all require skillful manipulation, we may call it a "test of manipulation," but we cannot actually restrict *manipulation* to mean only the three performances actually measured. Definitional validity, therefore, turns out in practice to be more than merely definitional.—See **validity/logical; validity/construct.**

validity/ecological: (*E. Brunswik*) an established relationship (within a given **habitat** or set of environmental circumstances), between a **proximal** sensory impact and a **distal** variable in the more remote environment, such that the presence of the proximal stimulus implies a strong probability that the distal stimulus is operative and vice versa. ➤E.g., if there is a certain small image on the retina (a proximal stimulus), it is probable that there is an object in the environment (a distal stimulus) somewhat like the image.

validity/empirical: the validity of a measuring process determined by how well it works in practice with a sample population; the degree to which the actually obtained scores correspond with an independent set of scores (called **criterion scores** or **measures**) obtained from the same sample. The criterion scores are supposed to be an approximation to the true scores on the variable being measured. ➤See **validity coefficient** for the most common method of determining empirical validity.

validity/face: 1. = **validity/content** (which see). 2. the extent to which a test is made up of items that, to casual inspection, seem related to the variable to be tested. ➤This is hardly validity at all, though it may contribute to getting a test accepted.—*Syn.* ASSUMPTION VALIDITY, **common-sense *validity.**

validity/factorial: validity measured by correlating the test with a **factor** found by factor analysis. ➤Factorial validity is useful only in proportion as the factor is theoretically clear or known to be practically significant.

validity/intrinsic: validity arising from the fact that the items of a test inherently and necessarily call for the behavior that the test as a whole is designed to measure. E.g., in a test of arithmetical addition, the test item *How much are* $6 + 3$? has intrinsic validity.—*Cp.* **validity/face.**

validity/logical: an estimate of **content *validity** based on a comparison of the behavior demanded by the test with the behavior that, by a priori analysis, belongs to the variable to be measured. ➤E.g., if the variable to be measured is "aggression," it is necessary to be sure just which kinds of behaviors are included; logical validity then compares the behaviors elicited by the test items to see whether there is correspondence. —*Syn.* **validity/construct, /a priori,** /RATIONAL.

validity/predictive: an empirical ***validity** measure based on the correspondence actually found for a representative sample of persons between their test scores and their actual behavior, at a given interval after testing, in the tasks in question. ➤E.g., test scores may be compared with the academic marks or grades received the following year; the correlation is a measure of the validity with which grades can be predicted a year later.—*Cp.* **validity/concurrent.**

validity/rational = **validity/logical.**

validity/sampling: a measure of **content *validity** obtained by determining how far the test items are a representative sample of the universe of behaviors that define the variable to be measured, or that may be deduced from the defined nature of the variable. ➤E.g., it might be shown that scores based on 25 per cent of all possible addition operations adequately represent a person's ability to add.—*Cp.* **validity/curricular, validity/construct.**

validity/status: correspondence between test scores and the concurrent status of testees; e.g., between a test of leadership and actual status in positions believed to require leadership. It is a form of **concurrent *validity.**

valid negative or **valid positive:** see **false negative.**

value: *n.* 1. the worth or excellence, or the degree of worth, ascribed to an object or activity or a class thereof. ➤Though ascribed to the object and reacted to as if external or objective, **value** is a function of the valuing **transaction,** not of the object. A **valence** is a specific embodiment of a value in a particular concrete situation. 2. an abstract concept, often merely implicit, that defines for an individual or for a social unit what ends or means to an end are desirable. ➤These abstract concepts of worth are usually not the result of the individual's own valuing; they are social products that have been imposed on him and only slowly **internalized**—i.e., accepted and used as his own criteria of worth. 3. a **goal object.** ➤Instead of saying that a goal *has* a value, in this usage a goal *is* a value. 4. (*math.*) the magnitude of something, or the number that represents that magnitude; any of the numbers representing the different magnitudes of a variable. ➤E.g., the several scores in shooting at a target may be treated as the values obtained by the individual on a variable of accuracy in shooting. Value, **measure, score,** or **magnitude** may often be used interchangeably for a number (or other symbol of quantity) though they refer to slightly different functions of the number. (See **score.**) **5.** = LIGHT VALUE: the position of a visual datum on the scale from white through gray to black; lightness, or brightness. It is one of the three dimensions of the Munsell color system. **6.** = **color saturation** (not *recom.*). **7.** (*econ.*) a judgment of what an object will bring in exchange; the basis of price; EXCHANGE VALUE.

value/absolute: (*math.*) a number (representing a magnitude), irrespective of its positive or negative sign. E.g., the absolute value of +5 and −5 is the same and is written |5|.—*Contr. w.* **algebraic** ***value.***—*Syn.* NUMERICAL VALUE, ARITHMETIC VALUE.

value/algebraic: (*math.*) a number, representing a magnitude, that has a plus or a minus sign.—*Contr. w.* **value/absolute.**—*Syn.* DIRECTED VALUE, SIGNED VALUE.

value analysis: a variety of **content analysis** in which one tabulates all expressions referring to a certain **value (2)** that occur in a piece of writing. ➤A check list of the values to be looked for is provided, together with directions for assignment to a given value. E.g., in tabulating the values appealed to in advertising, "restores the glamour of youth" would be tabulated under "sex appeal." A given expression may be classified in more than one way.

value/face: see **face value.**

value judgment: a reaction to persons, situations, or actions in terms that imply an assessment of their value or worth rather than of their objective characteristics. ➤To say that a child has a straight nose is—or may be—objective fact; to say that he has an adorable nose is a value judgment. Value judgments are difficult chiefly when they masquerade as objective. Characterizing a child as "troublesome" is seldom merely an objective assertion that he makes trouble; it nearly always implies that the child's behavior is condemned according to some system of values.

value system: 1. the more or less coherent set of **values** that regulate a person's conduct, often without his awareness that they do so. **2.** the set of values overtly accepted by a person or by a social group. ➤The value systems of **(1)** and of **(2)** are often quite divergent.

value/true: see **score/true.**

vandalism: *n.* careless or malicious destruction of property one has no right to destroy. SEXUAL VANDALISM is the destruction, usually **compulsive,** of anything representing sex in pictures, statues, etc.

vanity: *n.* excessive desire for praise of one's appearance or accomplishments. ➤It is generally implied that the desire focusses on matters of little real importance. One is proud of one's vocational accomplishment, vain about a handsome beard.—*adj.* **vain.**

variability: *n.* **1.** (*stat.*) the unlikeness of the scores in a set from each other or from some standard; the fact that the scores or measures or values differ; or the degree to which they differ. It is measured by the **mean *deviation,** the **standard *deviation,** or the **variance.** ➤SAMPLE VARIABILITY is the variability not of the actual scores but of the **representative measures** of a series of samples. This is estimated by the standard error of the representative measure—the sample variability of the mean is the **standard error of the mean,** or σ_M. **2.** (*biol., psychol.*) the capacity for change manifested by an individual or species; or the amount of change from one generation to another in a species.

variability/absolute: variability expressed in terms of the original units of measurement, rather than in relative terms. —*Contr. w.* **variability/relative.**

variability/coefficient of: see **dispersion/ coefficient of.**

variability/continuous: see **continuous variation.**

variability/index of = **standard *deviation.**

variability of individual differences: the scatter of scores obtained by measuring many persons in the same way or with the same test. The usual measure is the **standard deviation of the distribution** (SD_{distr}).

variability/presolution: the progressively reduced variety of acts that characterize the animal's behavior during the earlier stages of problem-solving.

variability/quotidian: the likelihood that a certain difference from the mean will be found from day to day. ➤The term is often used where DAILY VARIATION rather than daily variability is meant. In either case, why **quotidian** instead of *daily,* or *day-to-day*?

variability/relative: the variability of a series of observations relative to the magnitude of the observations.—*Ant.* **variability/absolute.**

variable: *adj.* **1.** changing; changeable; subject to change; able to vary in quantity or magnitude or in some qualitative aspect.— *Ant.* **constant.**—*n.* **2.** a quantity that may increase or decrease, continuously or discontinuously, without other essential change: e.g., the area of skin stimulated, the intensity of the stimulus, the number of correct answers on a test, the time taken to react. ➤Note that it is the area which is the variable, not the skin; the intensity, not the stimulus; the number, not the correct answer; the time, not the reaction. In this sense, a variable is always an abstraction, the quantity.—*Syn.* **variate. 3.** anything that can change; any distinct function, aspect, attribute, or property that can change; a trait or characteristic; anything appearing in changed amount (or quality) in different individual instances. ➤This extends the meaning of (2) from the abstracted characteristic, *quantity*, to the concrete entities that manifest change. Anything whatever that can be perceived or thought about as distinct may be called a variable when it is desired to call attention to the fact that it is subject to change. ¶Variable refers to the actual quantities that are data; **trait** refers to that to which the data are assigned. Thus, trait suggests an entity as variable does not. ¶In psychology three classes of variables are distinguished: R VARIABLES, responses or acts; S VARIABLES, properties of the physical or social environment; O VARIABLES, the OR-GANIC or ORGANISMIC or PERSONAL VARIABLES, the changeable properties of the person or organism. The R variable is always the dependent variable. See **variable/dependent** and **variable/independent.** **Variation** is the abstraction, the fact of change; **variable** is the concrete changing quantity, entity, object, or attribute.—*v.* **vary.**

variable/autochthonous: a change arising within a system, specif. within a psychophysiological system, not primarily elicited by outside influence or stimulus.—See **autochthonous (2).**

variable/continuous: When, between any two **values (4)** of a variable, it is possible always to find or to posit an intermediate value, the variable is called **continuous.** When change is by distinct leaps, i.e., by finite steps between which no values can be placed, the variable is DISCONTINUOUS.

variable/controlled = **variable/independent.**

variable/criterion: a variable considered as a standard to which a given variable may be compared: e.g., the set of scores used as a standard in **validity** studies.—See **criterion.**

variable/dependent: 1. a variable whose changes are treated as being consequent upon changes in one or more other variables called collectively the **independent** *variable.* ➤In psychology, the measured dependent value is always the response. A

change in the organism is sometimes *inferred* as corresponding with the response change, but it is the changes in response that are observed and measured. ¶In mathematics, the dependent variable is the symbol whose values are determined by the other variables linked with it in an algebraic equation. The fundamental relation of *all* variables may be expressed in the form $Y = f(X)$, which reads "Y is a function of X," and means that Y changes in a way to be discovered and/or stated whenever X changes. In this formula, Y is the dependent, X the independent, variable.—See **independent** *variable.* **2.** the variable that is estimated from another variable or variables.—See **regression (4).**

variable/discontinuous: the opposite of **variable/continuous** (which see).—*Syn* DISCRETE VARIABLE.

variable/discrete = discontinuous variable (see **variable/continuous**).

variable/distal: see **distal vs. proximal variables.**

variable error: the **deviation** of a measure from the **true** *score* arising from small uncontrolled errors of observation that occur unsystematically.—*Ant.* **constant** *error* —*Syn.* **chance** *error.*

variable/experimental: see **experiment.**

variable/hypothetical process: see **process variable/hypothetical.**

variable/hypothetical state: see **state variable/hypothetical.**

variable/independent or **I.V.: 1.** the variable whose changes are regarded as not dependent upon changes in another specified variable; the variable which is manipulated or treated in an experiment to see what effect changes in that variable bring about in the variables regarded as dependent upon it. ➤The independence asserted is not absolute; there is no such thing as an absolutely independent variable. In psychology either the S VARIABLES (stimulus variables—i.e., environmental conditions, physical or social), or the O VARIABLES (characteristics of the organism or person) may be taken as independent. The **dependent** *variable* for psychology is always a response. Investigations with O variables as the I.V. give us **differential psychology** those with S variables as the I.V. give us **experimental psychology (1).** Where the independent variable can be altered by the experimenter, it is called the TREATMENT or EXPERIMENTAL VARIABLE: e.g., the order in which questions are asked.—See **variable dependent. 2.** in simple and multiple correlation, the **criterion** *variable* with which the measured variable or a group of variables is to be correlated.

variable interval reinforcement: see **reinforcement schedule.**

variable/intervening or **I.V.: 1.** any variable that is functionally connected with a preceding and a following variable. ➤It is recommended that this general meaning give way to the restricted meaning of **(2)** below. **2.** the expression in condensed form of the relationship between the control conditions and the dependent variable. ➤The **I.V.** has no properties except those of the empirical data of which it is an abstraction. Gravitation is an I.V.; it has no meaning other than the series of quantitative relationships that describe the reciprocal movements toward each other of bodies having mass. Gravitation is not an entity and not a cause; it is simply the fact that bodies move toward each other. Similarly, for Hull, **habit strength** is an I.V. It is defined as the relation, other things being equal, between the number of **reinforced** repetitions of a stimulus-response sequence and the probability that the stimulus will be followed by the response. Habit strength means just that relation and nothing else.

In the general sense of **(1)**, **intervening variable** includes the **hypothetical *construct,** parallel and contrasted with **intervening variable** in the restricted sense of **(2)**. But differentiating terminology has not yet stabilized. Thus, the **intervening process *variable** is an I.V. only in sense **(1)**; a *process* can hardly be an I.V. in the highly abstract sense of **(2)**. The intervening process variable is indeed a kind of hypothetical construct and is better called **hypothetical *process variable.** (*Cp.* the parallel **hypothetical *state variable.**)

The relationships may be set forth thus:

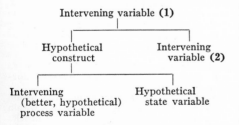

Intervening variable **(1)**

Hypothetical construct   Intervening variable **(2)**

Intervening (better, hypothetical) process variable   Hypothetical state variable

variable/intervening process = **process variable/hypothetical.**
variable/organic: see **organic variable.**
variable ratio reinforcement: see **reinforcement schedule.**
variable/response: see **response variable.**
variable stimulus: (*psychophys.*) any of the set of stimuli that are systematically compared with the **constant stimulus.**— Symbol: *s* or *V.*
variable/stimulus: see **stimulus variable.**

variable/treatment = experimental variable (see **experiment**).
variance = σ^2, the square of the **standard *deviation.** It is used as a measure of the extent to which individual scores in a set differ from each.—*Syn.* MEAN SQUARE DEVIATION, MEAN SQUARE ERROR.
variance/analysis of: see **analysis of variance.**
variance/error: see **error variance.**
variance/interaction: see **interaction variance.**
variance/true: individual differences in test scores that are attributable to true differences in characteristics under consideration.
variance/within-group: the variance that occurs *within* an experimental condition, as contrasted with variance caused by *different* experimental conditions; the variance that persists despite efforts made by the experimenter to control one or more potential sources of variance.
variate: *n.* **1.** = **variable** (2 or 3). **2.** the magnitude of a particular observation or measurement; a particular value of a variable.
variation: *n.* **1.** change. **2.** difference. **3.** dissimilarity in **homologous** organs. **4.** the extent to which the several values of a distribution depart from the mean; = **dispersion.**—*adj.* **variant.**
variational psychology = **differential psychology.**
variation/coefficient of: a measure of the relative **variability** of a distribution, equal to 100 times the standard deviation divided by the arithmetic mean.
variation/continuous: see **continuous variation.**
variation/mean = **deviation/mean.**
variation tone: the tone heard when a source of sound is rapidly interrupted.
variator /(Stern) = **tone variator.**
varied: *adj.* manifested in several forms; diversified. ➤VARIED RESPONSE consists of a series of responses to a problem situation that have little or no similarity to each other. Despite the differences, these responses relate to the same problem and hence **random activity** (which see) is not a good synonym, though commonly so used.
varied reaction/principle of: see **multiple response/principle of.**
variety: *n.* (*biol.*) a subdivision of a species.
vary: *v.* to change; esp., to change without losing identity. ➤Reds vary from a purplish crimson to a very orange red; and there is a corresponding continuous variation in the length of the light wave. But when the length of the light wave passes a certain point, the color is better said to alter or change to yellow, rather than to vary.
vas: *n.* (*L.*) (*anat.*) a duct for the conveyance of liquids.

vascular: *adj.* pertaining to ducts or vessels; or of a tissue rich in such ducts.

vascular theory: (*J. P. Nafe*) the hypothesis that coolth and warmth are merely sensations from constricting and dilating blood vessels.

vas deferens (vas def'ə·renz): *n.* (*L.*) the duct leading from the testis to the ejaculatory duct. Cutting of this tube is **vasectomy.**

vasectomy (vas·ek'tə·mi): *n.* the surgical severing or removal of a part of the *vas deferens,* the tube that conducts the sperm away from the testis. It is a method of sterilization of the male which does not affect the production and secretion of sex hormones nor interfere with sex activity or sexual feeling.—*Distg. fr.* **castration.**

vaso- (vas'ō-): combining form meaning *tube* or *vas,* and usually signifying *blood vessels.*

vasoconstriction: see **vasomotor.**

vasodilatation: see **vasomotor.**

vasomotor: *adj.* pertaining to the expansion (VASODILATATION) and contraction (VASOCONSTRICTION) of the blood vessels. The vasomotor nerves, which control these changes, form part of the sympathetic nervous system.

vector: *n.* **1.** (*math., phys.*) a directed magnitude; a force of given magnitude in a given direction. It is represented by a line with an arrowhead. The length represents the magnitude, the direction with respect to a system of coordinates indicates the direction of the force, and the arrow tip indicates the point of application of the force. **2.** (*topol.*) a directed magnitude in the life space; a force causing psychological locomotion. **3.** (*stat.*) the representation of a score for any variable as a line having length and direction, the length representing the size of the score, the direction the relation of the variable to other variables or to certain arbitrary axes.—See **vector/test, reference vector.**

vector psychology: (*K. Lewin*) the systematic delineation of dynamic psychological forces by means of **vectors.** ➤Vector psychology is neither a **school** nor a branch of psychology. Essentially, it refers to an expository method. It is much used in **topological psychology** and **field theory.** The use of vectors in factor analysis is a distinct approach.

vector/reference: see **reference vector.**

vector/test: (*stat.*) the representation of a test by a **vector** (3). ➤Two slightly different usages fall within the definition. **A.** The direction and length of the vector represent the compounded influence of the **factors** operative in the test or in a particular score. **B.** Each of several tests is represented by a vector whose length is the

variance; the angle between the vectors is that angle whose cosine equals the coefficient of correlation. A right angle represents zero correlation, and the smaller the angle the higher the correlation.

veg: *n.* (*psychophys.*) a unit in a scale for perceived weight, obtained by the halving method.

vegetative: *adj.* **1.** pertaining to plants, or to plant growth. **2.** pertaining to those animal activities that are also found in plants, esp. to those necessary to life and growth: e.g., breathing and digesting. ➤Locomotion is so seldom found in plants that it is deemed not vegetative. The VEGETATIVE FUNCTIONS are contrasted with RESPONSE FUNCTIONS, which are activities oriented toward the environment (seldom found in plants).

vegetative nervous system: an incorrect synonym for **autonomic nervous system.**

vegetative retreat: the tendency, when faced with difficulties, to revert to activities of the **vegetative** system such as were common in childhood: e.g., diarrhea when under stress.

velleity (və·lē'ə·ti): *n.* weak desire or volition.

velocity: *n.* rate of motion in a given direction, whether straight or curved. ➤*Cp.* speed, the rate of motion regardless of direction.

venereal: *adj.* **1.** pertaining to **coitus. 2.** pertaining to a disease usually transmitted by coitus.

venous (vē'nəs): *adj.* pertaining to the veins (the tubes leading toward the heart) or to their contents. ➤*Distg. fr.* ARTERIAL, pertaining to the tubes leading away from the heart.—*n.* **vein.**

ventilation: *n.* **1.** movement of air; hence, the supplying of oxygen to the blood. **2.** metaphorically, the activity of talking freely about a problem, expressing and exposing one's emotions with respect to it. ➤The term makes fewer assumptions than does **catharsis.**

ventral: *adj.* pertaining to the belly or to the belly-side of the body.—*Contr. w.* **dorsal.**—See **anterior.**

ventricle: *n.* (*anat.*) any small cavity within an organ; specif., one of the cavities within the heart or the brain. ➤The four ventricles of the brain form a system of communicating cavities that are continuous with the central canal of the spinal cord. Two (the LATERAL VENTRICLES) lie laterally, one in each hemisphere. Between them, and connecting with each, lies the THIRD VENTRICLE, which in turn leads by the **cerebral aqueduct** into the FOURTH VENTRICLE.—*adj.* **ventricular** (ven·trik'ū·lər).

ventro-: combining form denoting *the abdomen,* or *the anterior aspect.*

verbal: *adj.* pertaining to, taking the form

of, consisting of, words in any form: spoken, heard, seen, written, or thought. ➤When verbal is used for **oral** (i.e., for *spoken* words), we are left without a term covering all forms of communication by words. ("Wordy" has quite another meaning.) The misuse has become so common that no doubt in time it will prevail, but lest we be accessory to the crime we hereby inform against it. VERBAL BEHAVIOR includes both producing and responding to words.

verbalism: *n.* **1.** undue reliance upon words; the assumption that relationships suggested by facile habitual associations among words prevail in reality. **2.** the uncritical acceptance of definitions as if they were explanations. **3.** wordy expression lacking meaning.

verbalization: *n.* **1.** expression in words; or the capacity to express in words. **2.** expressing oneself in words when more directly instrumental behavior is called for. **3.** (*psychiat.*) verboseness; talking too much and in diffuse, random fashion.

verbal learning: learning to respond verbally to a verbal stimulus cue. It covers the range of tasks from learning to associate two nonsense syllables to learning to solve complex problems stated in verbal terms.— *Cp.* **perceptual-motor *learning.**

verbal scale or **test:** an intelligence test (or a part of one) in which ability to understand and use words plays a critical part in determining whether one can make the required responses. ➤No test can be entirely free of verbal influence. (*Cp.* **performance *test.**) A verbal scale is one in which ability with words is crucial.

verbal summator: a device that reproduces at low intensities various combinations of elementary vowel sounds to which the subject is invited to respond by telling what words he hears. It is used as a projective device and in studies of verbal perception.

verbatim: *adv.* word for word. VERBATIM RECALL is recalling in the exact words of the original.—*Cp.* **rote *learning.**

verbigeration (ver·bij"ə·rā'shən): *n.* **cataphasia,** a meaningless and stereotyped repetition of words or sentences.

verbomania = **logorrhea.**

verbomotor: *adj.* pertaining to the speaking of words.

vergence: *n.* a turning movement of the eyes.

veridical (və·rid'i·kəl): *adj.* corresponding to objective fact. ➤The term is used chiefly in **parapsychology** for revelations received by apparently supranormal means and objectively confirmed.

verification: *n.* **1.** the use of objective data to confirm or prove the truth or actuality of a hypothesis or theory; the process of establishing the correspondence between a theory and the facts. **2.** (*esth.*) a review or analysis by an artist to see whether he has obtained the artistic effect intended.

vermis (ver'məs): *n.* the median portion of the **cerebellum.**

vernier (ver'ni·ər): *n.* a subsidiary scaling device to permit reading off fractions of a larger scale.

Verstehende Psychologie (fer·shtā'ən·de): (*Ger., understanding psychology*) a school that holds that psychic processes are not to be described but to be intuitively understood. It is a variety of ***Geisteswissenschaftliche Psychologie*** (which see).

vertebra *n.*, *pl.* **vertebrae, -bras:** any of the bones in the spinal column.—*adj.* **vertebral.**

Vertebrata (ver"tə·brā'tə): *n.* *pl.* a comprehensive division of the animal kingdom comprising all the animals with a backbone. It was formerly ranked as a **phylum,** but now usually as a subphylum of the slightly larger phylum Chordata.—*n.* **vertebrate,** any animal of this division.

vertex: *n.* the uppermost point of a geometric or other figure; specif., the crown of the human or anthropoid head.—*adj.* **vertical.**

vertical: *adj.* **1.** of a direction parallel with that of the force of gravity; or, by extension, of a top-to-bottom direction, however defined. **2.** pertaining to the axis from head to foot of the human body. ➤For vertebrates who do not have upright posture, **cephalocaudal** axis is *prefd.*

vertiginous (vər·tij'ə·nəs): *adj.* dizzy.— *Var.* **vertiginal** (-nal).

vertigo: *n.* dizziness.

vesania (və·sā'ni·ə): *n.* any well-defined psychosis not somatic in origin; unsoundness of mind.—*adj.* **vesanic** (-san'ik).

vesical: *adj.* pertaining to the bladder.

vesicle: *n.* (*anat.*) a sac containing liquid. —*adj.* **vesicular** (və·sik'yə·lər) (not **vesical,** which is usually restricted to the bladder).

vestibule: *n.* a bony cavity in the **labyrinth (1)** containing two sacs (the **utricle** and **saccule**) filled with liquid. The term is sometimes extended to include also the semicircular canals (each with an enlarged or bulblike end called the **AMPULLA**), the whole constituting the VESTIBULAR APPARATUS. It is the sensory mechanism for the perception of acceleration and of the head's relation to gravity.—*Cp.* **static sense.**— *adj.* **vestibular** (ves·tib'yə·lər).

vestibule school: a factory training school through which beginners pass before admission to the regular workshops.

vestige: *n.* (*biol.*) a degenerate or imperfectly developed organ, more highly developed in the ancestry of the organism but thought to have no present function.—*Cp.* **rudiment,** *Anlage.*—*adj.* **vestigial.**

Vexierversuch (veks″ir·fer·züH′): *n.* (*Ger., vexation trial*) (*psychophys.*) a false stimulus—i.e., one not belonging in an experimental series—inserted at intervals to prevent the subject from responding according to a series set instead of to each stimulus as presented.

V factor = verbal comprehension factor (see **abilities/primary mental**).

viable (vī′ə·bəl): *adj.* **1.** of an organism capable of living or surviving; specif., of a premature organism capable of surviving outside the shell or uterus. **2.** figuratively, of a theory or movement capable of surviving. ➤A viable theory need not be **valid** but must at least seem plausible.—*n.* **viability.**

VIB = vocational interest blank: e.g., the **Strong Vocational Interest Blank.**

vibration: *n.* a regular or **periodic** motion to and fro of a particle or body. ➤The motion from one extreme to the other and back is called a VIBRATION CYCLE (for which ~ is a symbol). Formerly, a cycle was called a DOUBLE VIBRATION (d.v. or v.d.) in contrast with the single vibration (v.s.) which is the motion from one extreme to the other.

vibration/forced = **resonance.**

vibration frequency or **rate:** the number of vibration cycles per unit of time.—See **vibration.**

vibration/sympathetic or **/induced** = **resonance.**

vibrato (vi·brä′tō): *n.* (*music*) a pulsating effect consisting in slight and rapid variation in pitch (occasionally in intensity, or both) of a tone.—*Cp.* **tremolo.**

vibratory sensitivity: responsiveness to contact with a rapidly vibrating body.

VIBS: an abbreviated form of the **Wechsler-Bellevue Scale** consisting of the Vocabulary, Information, Block-design, and Similarities sections.

vicarious (vī·kăr′i·əs): *adj.* pertaining to a substitute. ➤It is said of the attempt of a person to satisfy frustrated desires by seeing them fulfilled in another person with whom he identifies: e.g., a parent may seek to satisfy his own frustrated ambition vicariously by his child's success. In escape literature, the reader experiences vicarious satisfaction. For VICARIOUS COMPENSATION, see **compensation.**

vicarious functioning: the substitution of one psychological process for another. ➤One sensory process S′ may be substituted for another S″ (**equipotentiality**) and one response R₁ for another R₂ (**equifinality**), so that, in learning for example, the stimulus situation may differ from that of the practice period, and the response likewise, yet a new relationship be demonstrated between S″ and R₂.—*Distg. fr.* **generalization,** either of stimulus or response, in which the stimuli S′ and S″ and the R₁ and R₂ must belong to the same "family" and be very similar. In vicarious functioning there need be equivalence only, with no similarity at all.

vicarious trial and error or **VTE:** (*K. Muenzinger*) the substitution of a mental performance for an **overt** performance in the tentative behaviors designed to solve a problem; the substitution of imagined responses for the overt in the tryouts of problem-solving.—See **learning/trial-and-error.**

vice: *n.* a habitual indulgence in a kind of behavior forbidden by the moral code.—*Ant.* **virtue.**

vicissitudes of libido: see **libido/vicissitudes of.**

Vienna Circle: a group of logicians studying the logic of science. They believe that such a logic will provide a unified science. **Physicalism** and **scientific** *empiricism (1) are among those of their tenets which strongly influence psychology.

Viennese School: the followers of Freud.

Vierordt's law (fir′ôrts): the generalization that the more mobile a part of the body, the lower is the **two-point threshold** of the part.

viewing angle: the angle formed by a line from the eye to the viewed surface. ➤A right angle is regarded as optimal.

viewing conditions: various conditions under which a visual observation is made, including size of the stimulus, characteristics of the surround, nature of the illuminant, area of the retina affected, etc.

vigilance: *n.* watchfulness; alertness to whatever may come; attentiveness.

vigilance function = **arousal function.**

vigilance/neural: (*H. Head*) a neurophysiological state of high readiness to discriminate and respond to stimulation.

Vigotsky test: a test of concept formation by use of colored blocks.

Vincent curve or **method:** a method for comparing the learning data of persons who require different times or numbers of trials to reach the stipulated level of proficiency. An equal fraction of the total time (or total number of equally spaced trials) required by any individual is treated as equivalent to the same fraction of another individual's total. Thus, the beginning and end of the learning curve are the same for all persons but the amount learned in any part or phase of the curve may differ.—*Cp.* **isochron.**

Vineland Social Maturity Scale: a rating scale of maturity based on presence or absence of certain everyday behaviors found to be characteristic of specified ages.

violet: *n.* the hue of visual sensations typically evoked by stimulation of the normal human eye with short-wave radiation around 433 millimicrons and shorter.

V IQ: an **intelligence quotient** calculated from scores on a verbal test.

viraginity (vir″ə·jin′ə·ti): the quality, in a woman, of being manlike in mental makeup.—*Cp.* **gynandrous.**—*adj.* **viraginous** (vi·raj′ə·nəs).—*pers. n.* **virago** (vi·rā′gō).

virgin: *n.* a female (usually only a matured female) who has not experienced sexual intercourse.—*adj.* **virgin,** which by extension means *untouched.*

virile: *adj.* manly; having the characteristics of a fully developed male, esp. the reproductive ability of the adult male.—*n.* **virility.**

virile reflex or **response:** erection in the male.

virilism (vir′ə·liz·əm): *n.* **1. viraginity. 2.** the development by a woman of the secondary sex characters of the male.—*Distg. fr.* **virility.**

virtual: *adj.* being so in essence or effect, even though not expressly: in *virtual* agreement.

virtue: *n.* a habit of voluntarily behaving according to the requirements of a moral code. ➤It is implied that the habit is not automatic, that virtuous action is always difficult.—*adj.* **virtuous.**

virulent: *adj.* **1.** poisonous; having dangerous or destructive properties. ➤Often used figuratively. **2.** of a class of smells of which morphine is typical.

vis a tergo (vis″ ä tèr′gō): (*L.*) a force from behind. ➤Used to express the idea that the present is determined by the past.

viscera: *n. pl.* the organs enclosed in any of the large cavities of the body; more specif., the organs of the abdomen. ➤In many psychological discussions, **viscera** is used not only for the organs but for the tissues inside the body wall (including the inner surface of the wall itself).—*n. sing.* **viscus** (not **viscera**).—*adj.* **visceral,** which see for extended meaning.

visceral: *adj.* **1.** pertaining to a viscus or the **viscera. 2.** loosely, pertaining to any organ or activity inside the body wall. ➤The term is badly misused in psychology; not only is the original anatomical reference stretched (as in sense **2**), but it is used to imply a number of vaguely conceived theories. Thus, a certain response may be characterized as "visceral rather than mental," meaning that the response is emotional. Now, although it is generally agreed that visceral activity occurs in emotion, no one seriously holds that emotion is merely an activity within the body wall; and no reasonably self-consistent meaning of "mental" excludes emotion. See **vis-**ceral **drive** for other examples. The extreme emphasis in theory on visceral phenomena has receded, but the loose and **theory-begging** use of the term is still with us. *Caveat lector!*

visceral drive: a **drive** based on physiological need; more accurately, a drive based on physiological processes within the body. ➤The term is loosely used. Thus, a drive to keep warm may be called visceral, though cutaneous elements are predominant. Fatigue, also often called visceral, is probably a muscular phenomenon.—*Syn.* **VISCEROGENIC DRIVE** (*prefd.*).

visceral sense: collective name for sensations derived from the **viscera.** ➤While the denotation is somewhat more restricted than that of **systemic *sense** or **interoceptive** sense, in context the same data are usually referred to.

visceroceptor: a **receptor** organ in one of the **viscera.**—*Syn.* **interoceptor** (somewhat broader).

viscerogenic (vis″ə·rō·jen′ik): *adj.* originating in the **viscera.**—See **visceral** and **visceral drive.**

viscerogenic motivation or **need:** motivation asserted to be based on nutritional, eliminative, and reproductive needs, or on processes taking place within the body. ➤*Syn.* **BIOGENIC MOTIVATION, VEGETATIVE MOTIVATION.** These are sometimes held to be the only *primary* sources of motivation, upon which all others are based.

viscerotonia: *n.* (*W. H. Sheldon*) a personality type marked by the tendency to general relaxation, love of comfort, sociability, conviviality, gluttony for food. It is correlated with the **endomorphic** bodily type.—See **ectomorphic.**

viscus: *n.* the singular of **viscera.**

visibility: *n.* **1.** that property of radiant energy which, when of adequate strength and lying within a certain range of wave lengths, excites a visual receptor process. **2.** the characteristic of a person's appearance and/or behavior that calls him to others' attention.

visibility coefficient: a numerical designation of the **visibility** of a given sample of radiant energy, generally of a single spectral wave length. The **RELATIVE VISIBILITY COEFFICIENT** takes as its standard the maximum visibility of a wave length of about 554 millimicrons.

visibility curve: a graphic representation of the relation of **brilliance** to **wave length.**

visible speech: the representation of each **phoneme** or unit of spoken sound by a pattern of black-gray-white. The sound waves of speech, transformed first into electrical impulses and these in turn into flashes of light, are photographed.

visile (viz′il): *n.* a visualizer; a person

whose **imagery** is predominantly of the visual kind.—*Syn.* **visual type.**

vision: *n.* **1.** the sense of seeing; the sense whose receptor is the eye and whose normal stimulus is light or radiant energy ranging from about 400 to 760 millimicrons. **2.** the act of seeing. **3.** that which is seen.

vision/alternating: use of the eyes alternately for brief periods instead of using them together in seeing. ➤Much of the time the data from one or other eye are simply suppressed, not used. The opposite process is binocular *vision, in which the data from both eyes are fused.—*Distg. fr.* **monocular** *vision, seeing with one eye exclusively over long periods.

vision/binocular: seeing with both eyes, usually fixated on the same point in space. ➤Normally, a fixated object is perceived as single, but, under some conditions, doubling **(diplopia)** or **retinal rivalry** occur. The fusion of the slightly different images as projected on the two retinas is an important factor in perception of depth. When (as with crossed eyes and in some other conditions) the two eyes cannot be fixed on the same point and the images cannot be fused, there is a tendency to suppress one image, with resulting **functional** UNIOCULAR VISION.

vision/central: seeing by means of the center portion of the retina, where all colors may be seen and where form and size discrimination are better than on the periphery. ➤Central vision is not limited to just the area of the **fovea** (FOVEAL VISION) but includes a small area around it.—*Cp.* **vision/paracentral, /peripheral.**

vision/daylight = photopic vision.

vision/distance: 1. seeing objects that are more than about 20 feet from the eye. **2.** ability to discriminate the relative distances of objects more than 20 feet away.

vision/double = diplopia.

vision/facial: see facial vision.

vision/field of: see visual field.

vision/foveal: seeing with the **foveal** area of the retina; or the field that can thus be seen.—*Cp.* **vision/indirect, /paracentral, /peripheral.**

vision/indirect: seeing with any portion of the retina except the central portion. It includes **paracentral** and **peripheral** *vision.

vision/line of = direction/line of.

vision/monochromatic: see **monochromatic vision.**

vision/monocular: usable vision in only one eye; seeing (permanently or for long periods) with only one eye.—See **vision/binocular.**—*Syn.* UNIOCULAR VISION, etymologically *prefd.*

vision/near: viewing something that lies at a distance of about 26 inches or less.

vision/paracentral: seeing by means of the area immediately surrounding the **fovea centralis.** ➤*Distg. fr.* peripheral *vision, which lies farther out toward the margin. INDIRECT VISION includes both.

vision/perimacular: vision using the portions of the eye lying in a ring area around the **macula.**

vision/peripheral: seeing by means of the outermost portions of the retina; seeing "out of the corner of the eye."—*Cp.* **vision/central, /paracentral, color zones.**

vision/persistence of: the tendency of visual excitation to outlast the stimulus; or, more generally, the tendency of changes in visual sensory response to lag behind changes in the stimulus.—See **lag (of sensation).**

vision/photopic: see photopic vision.

vision/recurrent: a succession of positive and negative afterimages or **aftersensations.**

vision/theory of = color theory. ➤Properly speaking, **theory of vision** should be somewhat broader; in practice the two terms are synonymous.

vista response: (*Ror.*) an **inkblot** response interpreting shading as depth, the differences in shading nuances being interpreted as differences in distance from the observer's eye.—Symbols *FK* or *V.*

visual: *adj.* pertaining to **vision** or seeing; characterizing an experience as belonging to the sense of vision.

visual acuity: see acuity/visual.

visual adaptation: adjustive change in visual sensitivity caused by continued visual stimulation or lack of stimulation. The three recognized types are scotopic or **dark adaptation,** photopic or **brightness** *adaptation, and color or **chromatic** *adaptation.

visual agnosia: see agnosia/visual.

visual aids: photographs, models, slides, motion pictures, etc., used in education as adjuncts to the learning process.—*Cp.* **aid/ audio-visual.**

visual angle: the angle subtended by an object in the visual field at the **nodal point** of the eye. ➤This angle determines the size of the image on the retina. Objects of different sizes or distances have the same-sized image on the retina if they subtend the same angle.

visual aphasia: see aphasia/visual.

visual axis: the straight line from the point of fixation through the **nodal point** to the point of clearest vision on the retina.—*Syn.* SIGHT(ING) LINE.—*Distg. fr.* **optical axis** and **line of** *direction. ➤For any position of the eye, there is only one visual axis. There is a whole pencil of lines passing from various points on the retina through the nodal point to the object viewed: these are the **lines of** *direction.

visual cells: (*anat.*) the neuroepithelial

cells: the rods, cones, and outer nuclear layer of the retina; the cells whose stimulation directly initiates the process of seeing; the **receptor** cells proper of vision.

visual field: 1. the totality of perceived objects visible to the unmoving eye of a particular observer at a given moment. **2.** the perceived three-dimensional space that forms a frame of reference for perceived objects, forms, distances, and movements. ➤Visual objects are perceived as lying or enclosed in space—not the conceptual space of mathematics but the space of direct perception. ¶The above two meanings are usually distinguished, but the terminology is confused: one authority restricts **visual field** to (1), another to (2); and FIELD OF VISION is employed with similar ambiguity. The analogy of **perceptual field** makes visual field the more appropriate term for (1). It is recommended that FIELD OF VISION be used for, if possible restricted to, (2). The addition of **subjective** or **phenomenal** to either term is not strictly necessary but serves to emphasize that the terms do not apply to the objective field, for which **field of** *regard is the term.—Syn.* **visual space** (which see).

visual hearing = **speech reading.**

visual induction: the effect of stimulation coming from one part of the **field of** *regard** upon the perceptual response to another part. ➤E.g., a pinpoint of light makes the surrounding darkness darker.—*Distg. fr.* **induction** (2), in which a direct spread of excitation is observed or hypothesized. Such physiological induction may or may not be the correlate of visual induction.

visualization: *n.* the capacity for visual imagery; the picturing of objects and events in one's mind.

visual line: a loose synonym for either **line of** *direction** or **visual axis.**

visual organization: the complex relationships between the elements in the **visual field**; a name for the fact that the phenomenal visual field always exhibits pattern, though sometimes much more than at other times. ➤Any kind of relationship may contribute to organization: figureground, similarity, all manner of spatial relationships, etc. Whatever may be the role of the viewer, the visual organization is perceived as a property of the field.

visual process: 1. any activity of the organism that contributes directly to seeing; any operation of the eye and of the nerve tracts and brain centers directly involved in seeing. **2.** the operation of seeing in general.

visual purple: a substance in the rods of the retina which bleaches in white light. It is believed to be the substance responsible for the reception of faint visual stimuli.

visual righting reflex: a change in the orientation of the head when shifting from one fixation point to another. ➤Its status as a **reflex** is doubtful.

visual space = field of vision (see **visual field** 2). ➤Visual space is spoken of in discussions of space perception; *field of vision* is used concretely for an actual perceived space.

visual type: a visualizer; a person given to thinking in visual terms; one prone to effective visual imagery.—*Syn.* **visile.**

visual yellow: a yellow substance sometimes found in the retina when **visual purple** has been bleached by light.

vital: *adj.* **1.** pertaining to life. **2.** essential to the continued existence of something; hence, crucially important.—*n.* **vitality.**

vital capacity: the greatest amount of air that can be exhaled after a maximum inhalation.

vital index: the **vital capacity** in cubic centimeters divided by the person's weight in kilograms.

vitalism: *n.* the doctrine that living substance has a "plus" in addition to, or over and above, its physicochemical constituents.

vitality: *n.* **1.** the quality of being alive. **2.** the property of an organism of being able to stay alive. **3.** biological vigor, energy, endurance. **4.** a complex personality pattern manifested by lively gestures and movements and by low threshold for the pleasant emotions.—*adj.* **vital.**

vita sexualis (vī″tə sek″shü·al′əs): (*L.*) the sexual life.

vitreous humor: the transparent jellylike substance that fills the eyeball between the retina and the lens.—*Syn.* VITREOUS BODY, VITREOUS.

vividness: *n.* **1.** = **clearness (1). 2.** impressiveness; strikingness.

vocabulary: *n.* **1.** a list of **words. 2.** the stock of words employed in a language or a passage, or by a person or group of persons.

vocabulary/active: see **language/passive.**

vocabulary burden or **load:** the number of different words or of word meanings occurring in a given spoken or written passage.

vocabulary/passive = **vocabulary/recognition.**

vocabulary/potential = **vocabulary/recognition.**

vocabulary/recognition: the words a person can understand when they appear in a context but that he may or may not be able to use in his own speech or writing.—*Syn.* PASSIVE VOCABULARY.

vocabulary test: a measure of the number of words a person understands or can use in some way. ➤Several criteria of understanding or use are employed (recognition in, or out of, context; ability to define; ability to use in a sentence, etc.) and yield very different scores. The test words are a sample either of general vocabulary or of a special vocabulary (e.g., of a branch of science or of a foreign language). Obtaining a representative sample is subject to many technical difficulties.

vocal: *adj.* 1. pertaining to voice; having a voice; uttered. ➤**Vocal** is often used also as the missing adjective for **speech,** but **oral** or *spoken* is to be preferred. 2. of a person given to audible expression of his feelings or opinions.

vocal cords: the ligaments in the larynx that are involved in the production of voice sounds.

vocality: *n.* the voiced or vowel-like character of a sound. ➤Different pitches have different vocality: low tones, e.g., somewhat resemble *oo* (*ü*).

vocalization: *n.* the animal activity of uttering sounds, including speaking, screaming, singing, babbling, and meaningless sounds. ➤Subhuman animals vocalize but have very limited (if any) speech.

vocalization/socialized: the use of vocal sounds to communicate, even though the sounds are not formed into words: e.g., the barking of a dog to be let out.

vocal language = *oral *language.

vocal organs: the entire mechanism for the production of voice sounds.

vocal register: the pitch range of an individual's voice; or a particular part of the range within which the tones have similar quality: e.g., the chest register vs. falsetto.

vocation: *n.* 1. originally, a task in life to which one was "called" either by Providence or by Nature. It implied both an imperious inclination and the necessary **aptitude** for the work. ➤This meaning is still current for those called to a special religious employment (ministers, priests, nuns, etc.), or for one who feels an imperious urge to meet a social need. 2. the way in which one earns his living. ➤The notion of "calling" is certainly almost wholly gone in this usage: few can be said to be "called" to their jobs.

vocational adjustment: having a position or job suited to one's abilities and inclinations.—*Cp.* **maladjustment/vocational.**

vocational aptitude: such present abilities and other personality qualities as justify prediction that, with adequate education and development, success and satisfaction in a given vocation are likely.—See **aptitude.**

vocational aptitude test: a test designed to predict how quickly and well a person can learn to perform the necessary tasks of a given vocation; or a series of tests designed to discover for which vocation a person has **aptitude.**

vocational counseling: any or all counseling procedures centered about the problems of selecting a vocation and preparing for it. ➤See **counseling.** While questions

of ability and of opportunities open to the counselee are foremost, they by no means constitute the whole process. Motivation and planning, e.g., may in a given case be more important.

vocational education: any form of education, whether given in a school or elsewhere, whose purpose is to fit an individual for effective pursuit of a recognized profitable employment.

vocational guidance = **vocational counseling.**

vocational selection: see **selection/vocational.**

vocomotor: *adj.* pertaining to, or characterizing, the movements of talking or singing.

voice: *n.* 1. sound produced by lungs and larynx (for birds, the syrinx). ➤It includes speech sounds, the cries and barks of animals, and the songs of birds, but is not usually applied to the so-called singing of insects, which is not wind-produced. 2. a vocal sound such as is heard in a vowel.—*n.* **vocalization,** the production of such sounds.—*v.* **vocalize.**

voice disorder: see **speech disorder.**

voice key: *n.* an instrument that automatically starts or stops a timing device when a person speaks. It is a very simple microphone.

volar (vō'lər): *adj.* pertaining to the palm of the hand or the sole of the foot.—*n.* **vola.**

volition: *n.* 1. the act of deciding upon and initiating a course of action; action without external compulsion. 2. = **voluntary activity.** 3. (*content psychol.*) a complex experience composed chiefly of kinesthetic sensations and an image of a goal or end.—*Syn.* **will,** now almost never used technically in psychology.—See **voluntary activity.**—*adj.* **voluntary,** of the concrete behavior or experience; **volitional,** of the topic.

volley: *n.* (*neurol.*) a synchronized discharge of neural impulses.

volley theory: see **hearing theories.**

volt: *n.* the electromotive force required to produce a current of one **ampere** through a resistance of one **ohm.**

volume = **voluminousness.**

volume/auditory: see **voluminousness.**

volume color: see **color/volume.**

volume of sound: see **voluminousness.**

volume/tonal: a **tonal** attribute that has thresholds distinct from those for **pitch** and **loudness.** It is the immediately apprehended bigness or **extensity** of a tone: the quality by which, e.g., the tone of a bass voice is heard as "bigger" than that of a coloratura soprano, even though the tones are of the same intensity (loudness).

voluminousness: *n.* an elementary or unanalyzable **attribute** or **dimension:** the immediately apprehended bigness or extensity of a sensory datum, esp., of a sound or a smell.—See **volume/tonal.**

voluntarism (vol′un·tər·iz″əm): *n.* **1.** the doctrine that makes **volition** the defining character of **mental process**: an extreme form of **purposive psychology. 2.** the doctrine that attributes causal efficacy to volition, that supposes the course of events can be influenced to some extent by volition.— *Ant.* **determinism.**—See **psychology/divisions and schools of, V.**

voluntary: *adj.* pertaining to **volition.**

voluntary activity: 1. activity unopposed by any other activity or **impulse** of the self or organism. **2.** activity preferred by the self. ➤The preference or choice may be immediate and effortless, or it may follow prolonged deliberation and be attended with effort. **3.** activity preceded by the idea of that activity, or of the end result to be achieved, together with a feeling of desire for the activity or end; action with intent. **4.** activity oriented toward an end. ➤**Purposive psychology** holds that this is true of all psychic activity. **5.** activity not forced upon a person.

➤Popular psychology has a pretty complete doctrine of **will** and **voluntary activity.** Scientific psychology has scarcely reached the point where it is possible to define how the terms are to be used. It is probable that a number of quite distinct sets of facts have been brought together under the one term. However, it does not yet seem possible to dispense with the concept of a class of behaviors, to be called **voluntary,** that differ from other behaviors in a number of ill-defined ways. Though it is not easy to say how, voluntary movement does seem to be empirically different from involuntary movement.

voluntary muscle: one that can be contracted voluntarily. ➤A person cannot voluntarily contract the **smooth *muscles.** He can voluntarily contract most **striate *muscles,** possibly can learn to contract voluntarily *any* striate muscle. But **voluntary** and **striate,** while thus overlapping, are not synonymous.

voluptuous: see **sensuous.**

voyeur (vwə·yėr′): *n.* one who seeks sex gratification by peeping; a Peeping Tom. —*n.* **voyeurism.**

v.s.: *abbr.* for *single vibration.*

VTE = vicarious trial and error.

V test: (*stat.*) a modification of the *t* **test,** used when the samples are large and the **variance** of the two samples is unequal.

vulva: *n.* the external **genitals** of the female.—*adj.* **vulvar.**

Vygotsky test (vĭ·got′ski): a sorting test with blocks of varied size, shape, and color. ➤Different restrictions on the sorting make this a test of ability to conceptualize, though it is not clear how far one can generalize from the rather special form of conceptualizing required.

W

W: 1. = (*phys.*) work in **joules. 2. =** (*psychophys.*) **Weber fraction. 3. =** (*stat.*) (*ital.*) a **weight** (also *w*). **4. =** (*stat.*) (*ital.*) **coefficient of *concordance. 5. =** word fluency factor (see **abilities/primary mental**). **6. =** (*Ror.*) (*ital.*) **whole response.**

w: **1. =** will factor. **2.** (*stat.*) a **weight.**

w: (*Ror.*) scoring code for a response to a part only of the inkblot area, whether or not that part is perceived as a whole.

WAIS = Wechsler Adult Intelligence Scale.

waking center: a brain center in the posterior part of the **hypothalamus** supposed to regulate sleep and waking.

Wallerian degeneration (wä·lir′i·ən): (*neurol.*) the breakdown of the **myelin** sheath tissue of those portions of the **axon** that have been severed from the cell body.

walleyed: *adj.* having a divergent squint.— See **divergence (2).**

wanderlust: *n.* desire for change; longing to leave home and to travel.

want: see **desire** (*v.*).

warming-up period: a brief time at the beginning of a task during which preliminary adjustments are made.

warm spot: a pointlike spot on the skin that is particularly sensitive to warm stimuli.

warmth: *n.* a sense datum whose normal stimulus is an object warmer than the skin and touching it.—*Syn.* WARMTH SENSATION. —*adj.* **warm.**

Wassermann test: a test of blood, or of the **cerebrospinal fluid,** for syphilitic infection.

wat (wot): *n.* (*C. Hull*) the unit for measuring **reaction potential.** The term is derived from the name J. B. Watson.

watch test: a rough test for **acuity** of hearing: the watch is moved toward or away from the subject until the **threshold** for its tick is established.

watt: *n.* a unit for measuring power, being the energy expended in doing one **joule** of work per second. It is most often used for electric measurements.

wave: *n.* the motion described by an advancing point that is simultaneously moving to and fro, either at a right angle to the direction of advance (a TRANSVERSE WAVE as found in water waves and in light) or LONGITUDINAL with it (as in sound waves).

wave amplitude: the extent of the to and fro pulsation of a wave.—See **amplitude.** —*Syn.* WAVE BREADTH.

wave frequency: the number of times a complete wave pattern from one crest to the next is completed per unit of time.— *Syn.* **frequency** (1), VIBRATION RATE.

wave length: the distance, at any instant, between two adjacent crests (or identical phases) of a series of waves which are advancing through a uniform medium. The wave length varies inversely with the vibration rate or frequency.

wave of excitation: 1. an electrochemical change propagated through living tissue in a wave form. **2.** a neural impulse, esp. when conceived as being an electrochemical change.

waxy flexibility: see **catalepsy** (2).

wayward: *adj.* unruly; disobedient; stubborn; seeking one's own way.

WB = **Wechsler-Bellevue Scale.**

W compulsion: (*Ror.*) tendency to use all the inkblot material on one card within the framework of one **content** whenever possible, or as far as is possible.

weak: *adj.* of low intensity. ➤Preferably used of stimuli. With reference to sensory response, FAINT is preferred.

weaning/psychological: 1. breaking a child's ties of psychological dependence upon a parent. **2.** dissolution of the **transference** situation at the end of a psychoanalysis; attaining independence of the psychotherapist.

Weber-Fechner law: see **Fechner's law** and **Weber's law.**

Weber fraction: the expression of **Weber's** law in the form $\Delta R/R$, where ΔR is the change of stimulus that is just perceptibly different and R is the value of the stimulus. The fraction is a constant over the middle range of intensity.—*Syn.* WEBER RATIO, WEBER FUNCTION.

Weber's law: the original psychological law of relativity of judgment of sensation: it states that the least added difference of stimulus that can be noticed is a constant proportional part of the original stimulus. ➤See **Fechner's law**, an extension and, in part, an interpretation of Weber's. Weber's law holds quite closely in the middle range of intensity.

Wechsler-Bellevue Scale: a test battery for intelligence, standardized for adults but usable for adolescents and older children. ➤The MA and IQ scores for this test are derived somewhat differently from the usual practice. Also called BELLEVUE SCALE. —*Cp.* **WISC** and **WAIS.**

Wedensky effect: At a certain frequency of excitation, a nerve-muscle preparation responds with a series of rapid twitches; beyond that frequency there is a single contraction followed by complete relaxation. ➤The expression WEDENSKY INHIBITION (sometimes used as *syn.*) implies a theory and should not be used for the data.

we-feeling: *n.* the awareness, by members of an **in-group,** that other members have similar ideas, feelings, and purposes, and that these feelings are caused, in large measure, by the group; the feelings of loyalty, common purpose, esprit de corps, in a group that has good morale.

we-group = **in-group.**

weight: *n.* **1.** the relative importance of some item or datum; the amount it contributes to some whole or combination in comparison with other items. **2.** = (*stat.*) NOMINAL WEIGHT, a multiplier (or **coefficient**) of a variable designed to modify its relative contribution to a total score or to the **variance** of the total. ➤E.g., it may be decided that a test battery better predicts a criterion if subtest L has greater relative influence than it would have if the raw scores were simply added to give a total; the scores on L are accordingly multiplied by some number greater than unity. (There are many ways of determining the size of the multiplier.) If no coefficient or multiplier of the subscores is explicitly written, the score is called **unweighted;** but this is a misnomer —in this case its NOMINAL WEIGHT is unity. (For the EFFECTIVE WEIGHT, see **3.**)—*Syn.* WEIGHT COEFFICIENT (*recom.*). **3.** = (*stat.*) EFFECTIVE or FUNCTIONAL WEIGHT, the actual relative contribution of a variable to the **variance** of a given composite variable. ➤The effective weight depends on the size of the **standard *deviation** of the nominally weighted variable and on its correlation with each of the other nominally weighted variables. (If no nominal weight is assigned, the weight is unity.—See **2.**)

It is impossible to use a score in a computation without its having an actual or effective weight. This fact is obscured by speaking of unweighted scores or of weights in sense (2). It is therefore recommended that the multipliers which have been called weights in sense (2) be always called WEIGHT COEFFICIENTS. (**Nominal** has other connotations that make it less useful for sense 2.) The unqualified term *weight* should be reserved for sense (3). Both WEIGHT COEFFICIENT and EFFECTIVE WEIGHT are strictly relative to a particular combination or computation.—See **factor loading.**—*Syn.* (for **2** and **3**) **load.**—*adj.* **weighted.**—*v.* **weight.**

weight age: see **age/weight.**

weight/arbitrary: a **weight coefficient** assigned to a variable upon a priori considerations regarding its importance. ➤Failure to assign any weight coefficient (so-called **unweighted** scores) is actually to assign the arbitrary weight of unity.

weight/beta or **/beta regression = beta weight.**

weight coefficient: see **weight (2).**

weight/effective: see **weight (2 and 3).**

weight experiment: (*psychophys.*) an experiment in which the subject judges small differences between freely lifted weights of moderate amount.—*Syn.* LIFTED WEIGHT EXPERIMENT.

weight/factor = factor loading.

weight/functional: see **weight (3).**

weighting: *n.* the determination of the relative influence each element of a composite score should have in the total by assigning a constant multiplier to each kind of element. ➤Simple addition of part-scores is a kind of weighting; the constant multiplier is simply unity.—See **weight.**

weighting/equal: (*stat.*) **1.** allowing two or more variables to have the same influence in determining a composite score. **2.** employing the same constant multiplier or coefficient in combining two or more variables to obtain a composite score. ➤This is an incorrect usage. If the variables have different **dispersions,** multiplying by the same constant gives them unequal influence.

weight/natural: the relative weight of a series of data when entered into a composite without ostensible **weighting.** ➤The natural weight then depends on the deviation of the series and its correlations with the other variables.

weight/nominal: see **weight (2).**

Weigl-Goldstein-Scheerer Test: a test of concept formation that requires the subject to sort 12 blocks according to likeness. There are 3 shapes and 4 colors for each shape. After one sorting, the *S* is asked to sort the pieces in another way.

we/I ratio: a measure of morale in a group situation, based on the proportion of conversational "we"s to "I"s.

Weismannism: *n.* a genetic theory that denies the inheritance of acquired characteristics, and postulates the continuity of the germ plasm through the generations.

well-adjusted: *adj.* tending to respond to one's environment in a way beneficial to oneself and to society. ➤This definition, though apparently easy to understand, is very vague.—See **adjustment.**

Weltanschauung (velt′än·shou·ŭng): *n.* (*Ger.*) view of the universe; one's total outlook on life, society, and its institutions; a value system having as its object the whole or what is known or knowable.

Weltschmerz (velt′shmerts): *n.* (*Ger.*) literally, world sorrow; sentimental sorrow over the woes of the world.

Wernicke's area or **center** (ver′ni·kəz): a cerebral area in the temporal region (of the left hemisphere in right-handed persons, of the right hemisphere in left-handed persons) that was formerly supposed to be the center for understanding spoken language. The relation of this area to speech is now known to be exceedingly complex.—*Cp.* **Broca's convolution.**

Wetzel grid: a device for plotting the interrelations of height, weight, and age over a period of years, with norms of development based on the interrelations.

Wever-Bray phenomenon: the **aural microphonic** (i.e., the electrical response generated in the **cochlea** when stimulated) combined with the action potential of the auditory nerve. This phenomenon is believed to reflect the properties of the stimulus as delivered to the cochlea.

***w* factor = will factor.**

Wherry-Doolittle method: (*stat.*) a short-cut method for selecting, from a larger number, a small number of tests that will yield a correlation with a criterion only slightly lower in validity than the multiple correlation of all the tests with the criterion.

whisper test: a rough test for hearing loss. The subject stands 20 feet away from the examiner with one ear toward him, the other ear being plugged with cotton or a fingertip. He must not see the examiner's lips. Words are pronounced in a distinct whisper.

white: *n.* an **achromatic color** of maximum lightness which represents one limit of the series of grays and which is the complement or antagonist of black, the other extreme of the gray series. ➤White is typically evoked by any mixture of wave lengths from a high-reflectance mat surface which approximates average daylight or the equivalent color temperature; but white depends also upon surrounding contrast.

white matter: those parts of the brain or spinal cord that are a very light gray from the myelin covering of the nerve fibers.—*Distg. fr.* **gray matter.**

whiteness constancy: see **constancy/object.**

white noise: see **noise/white.**

white space response: (*Ror.*) any response to the nonblot portion of the inkblot card; a response to a test card in which the white space is regarded as part of the pattern.—Symbol *S.*

whole: *n.* that which, though it may have distinguishable parts or members, yet may be thought about as a unit; a union of parts that may affect something else, the effect proceeding not from the parts singly but from all of them in combination.—*Syn.* TOTALITY, **gestalt.**—See **part, member.**—*adj.* **whole, entire.**

whole child: the individual child considered as a functioning unit, not as a collection of independent traits. ➤The term is a reaction against a tendency to consider the child in terms of some one aspect of his behavior, neglecting its relation to other behaviors. But it is often a mere slogan for those who fear that we may lose emotional warmth if we attempt an intelligent analytic appraisal of a child.

whole learning: see **learning/whole vs. part.**

whole-meaning test = **paragraph-meaning test.**

whole-object: *n.* (*psychoan.*) a person as a love object. ➤*Contr. w.* **part-object** (which see).

whole response or *W*: (*Ror.*) a response showing a reaction to the inkblot as a whole, or to almost all of the inkblot with no reference to anything in the omitted part. ➤There are several varieties of *W*. *W%* is a symbol for the percentage of whole responses in the entire examination.

whole tone: an interval between two tones whose exact size varies in different musical scales but which is roughly twice the smallest interval in the scale. In the Western musical scale, the whole tone is one-sixth of an octave, or two semitones.—*Syn.* WHOLE STEP.

wholism = **holism.**

wiggly-block test: the task of reassembling nine blocks cut by irregular wavy lines from a rectangular block.

wild: *adj.* **1.** of an organism not domesticated by man; of a plant or animal in its native habitat. **2.** of an animal that flees from man. **3.** of an animal that attacks others savagely, esp., one that attacks not from hunger but in anger; savage. **4.** of a human who acts like such an animal.

Wild Boy of Aveyron: the supposedly feral child studied by the physician Itard.

will: *n.* **1.** the capacity for voluntary activity; the ability to hold in check certain impulses and to release others. **2.** (generally *cap.*) the whole self active. ➤It is not clear to what extent these and related definitions refer to the same set of facts, nor whether the facts form a proper homogeneous group. The term is little used in contemporary psychology, though in the psychoanalytic school of O. Rank it has a central place. In popular use, will is conceived as a **faculty,** for which reason the synonym **volition** is preferred.

will factor: (*factor anal.*) the factor found in tests that require purposive striving or persistence and effort.—*Syn. w* **factor, *w*.**

will/free: see **free will.**

will-temperament tests: (*J. Downey*) a pioneer attempt to measure certain temperamental differences, chiefly on the basis of controlled handwriting tasks.

will to power: striving for the goal of being superior to others and able to dominate them. ➤The will to power was held by A. Adler to be central in both normal and neurotic behavior.

windmill illusion: the illusion of apparent *motion in which, without change in the stimulus, the apparent direction of rotating blades or spokes (or, esp., of their shadows) is intermittently reversed. ➤*Distg. fr.* the apparent reversal of direction of a wheel, occasionally seen in motion pictures, which is correlated with an actual change of speed and is an example of the **stroboscopic effect.**

window/oval: an opening between the middle and inner ear, closed by the **stapes** bone, through which vibration is transmitted to the inner ear.—*Syn.* FENESTRA OVALIS, FENESTRA VESTIBULI or VESTIBULARIS.

window/round: an opening between the inner and middle ear, closed by a flexible membrane that absorbs the alternating pressures coming from the **stapes** via the fluid of the inner ear.—*Syn.* FENESTRA ROTUNDA, FENESTRA COCHLEAE.

WISC test: the Wechsler Intelligence Scale for Children.

wish: *n.* a desire or longing, without overt attempt to attain; the mental representation of something as desirable. ➤The word strongly suggests a conscious process, but psychoanalysts posit an **unconscious** wish that functions much like a conscious wish. —See **desire** (*v.*).

wish fulfillment: *n.* **1.** (*psychoan.*) the discharge of a tension by imagining a satisfying or tension-reducing situation. ➤It is held that the **id** does not distinguish **image** from reality; the forming of the image is therefore wish fulfilling. The postulated process would be more fittingly called WISH DECEPTION. **2.** loosely, any indirect satisfaction, esp. one that is accepted after frustration.

wishful thinking: a thinking process guided more by one's wishes and desires than by a logical consideration of facts. It generally has the superficial appearance, however, of logical thinking.—*Syn.* AUTISTIC THINKING (see **autism**).

witch's milk: a milklike secretion sometimes exuded from the mammary glands of newborn infants of either sex.

withdrawal: *n.* **1.** leaving school permanently. **2.** the retraction of the penis before orgasm in order to prevent conception.—*Syn.* COITUS INTERRUPTUS. **3.** a pattern of action, induced by persistent frustration, in which a person removes himself from the realm of conflict and obtains satisfactions in less strenuous ways such as day-dreaming, drowsiness, alcoholism, narcotics, or escape into work where personal problems can be forgotten.—*Distg. fr.* **withdrawn behavior. 4.** (*E. Fromm*) exaggerated indifference or active destructiveness toward a world which makes a person feel isolated and powerless. ➤This includes **withdrawn behavior** and the behaviors of **(3)** but stresses lack of affectional relation as cause.

withdrawal symptoms: a wide range of symptoms shown by addicts when the usual habit-forming drug is not taken.

withdrawn behavior: lack of responsiveness, esp. of emotional responsiveness, in social relations.

wit work: (*psychoan.*) the psychological processes, mostly unconscious, that produce wit. ➤The processes are similar to those of **dream work.**

wolf child: see **feral child.**

Wonderlic Personnel Test: a shortened form of the Otis Self-Administering Test for Mental Ability.

Woodworth-Mathews Personal Data Sheet: a self-inventory designed for rapid screening of children or adolescents suspected of being **neurotic.** It calls for *yes* or *no* answers to questions about common complaints.

word: *n.* the smallest linguistic unit that can stand alone.

word association test: see **association test.**

word blindness = alexia.

word-building test: a test, similar to anagrams, in which the testee is asked to form as many words as possible from a certain set of letters.

word calling: in reading, the pronouncing of individual words without evidence that the meaning has been grasped.

word configuration: the general visual shape or pattern of a printed or written word; the more quickly seen over-all features of a word as long or short, as having letters extended above or below the line, etc. Sensitivity to configuration is a help in rapid reading.

word count: a study of the frequency with which given words occur in a representative sample of written or spoken speech. The count may be restricted to certain kinds of speech (e.g., that of nine-year-olds, or of Portuguese immigrants) or may sample the speech of a nation.

word deafness = aphasia/auditory.

word family: 1. a group of words having a common root. **2.** words having similar phonetic elements. ➤Both groupings may be used in teaching reading, esp. by those

who emphasize the ability to pronounce words **(word calling).**

word method: in teaching reading, a procedure that emphasizes recognition of the word as a whole rather than analysis into parts, either syllables or letters.

word salad: a jumble of words possessing no meaning—at least for the listener.—*Syn.* **paraphrasia, jargon.**

word sentence: a single word functioning as a whole unit of thought, therefore as a sentence: e.g., "Yes!", or a child's "Me!" meaning, "Let me do it by myself."

work: *n.* **1.** (*phys.*) the action of a force against a resistance, resulting in a change of place. **2.** (*physiol.*) the expenditure of energy derived from metabolism during bodily activity. **3.** (*psychol.*) the accomplishment of a psychological task. ➤Any attempt at a rigorous distinction between **(2)** and **(3)** leads to metaphysical theorizing. Most psychologists prefer to speak in more specific terms: so many eye movements, so many arithmetical problems solved.—*Cp.* **output.**

work decrement: loss in **output,** or in accomplishment of a specified task per unit of time.

working mean = mean/assumed.

working through: (*psychoan.*) the process of having the client face the same conflicts over and over again, under the analyst's supervision, until he can independently face and master the conflicts in ordinary life.

work/law of maximum: (*phys.*) A maximum amount of energy, for any given set of conditions, will be expended in the course of maintaining balance in an energy system. ➤Since a person is an energy system, this is held by some to be a basic law of behavior.

work-limit procedure or **test:** see **test/work-limit.**

work/mental: 1. the expenditure of energy to attain a result that is defined in mental terms—learning something, solving problems, thinking. ➤One need not imply that the energy in question is either mental or physical. This usage is preferred as being relatively theory-free. **2.** goal-directed expenditure of mental effort or energy. **3.** goal-directed expenditure of energy upon **covert behavior.** ➤Meanings **(2)** and **(3)** imply opposed metaphysical positions and are thus **theory-begging.**

work method: the way, esp. a habitual way, in which a person's psychophysiological equipment is used to attain an end result. ➤Levels of efficiency in work methods or work habits are distinguished.— *Cp.* **higher level *skills.**

work sample: a brief operation that includes selected typical acts performed in a job. It may be used as a selection test, or as a criterion for the validation of aptitude or job placement tests.

world/external: see **external world.**

World Test: see **Bolgar-Fisher World Test.**

world view: any comprehensive explanation of external reality and of man's relations to it.

worry: *n.* the emotional attitude characterized by uncertainty of one's ability to prevent the occurrence of an unsatisfactory state of affairs. EXCITED and DEPRESSED WORRY are spoken of.

worry inventory: a check list of things about which many persons worry. ➤It is usually employed as a self-inventory. Norms and scoring weights for items may be furnished, but the list is chiefly valued as a basis for interview and counseling.

worship: *n.* the act of honoring and adoring a deity; or the complex system of practices which, in any given religion, con-

stitute the mode of showing honor and veneration to deity.

worth: *n.* the value placed by a given person upon something, esp. (perhaps necessarily) its relative value. ➤**Value** is broader, since it includes what seems to be objective importance; but some believe that all supposedly objective value is really only worth.

W%: (*Ror.*) see **whole response.**

W response = (*Ror.*) **whole response.**

writing accent: those peculiar features of a person's, or of a cultural group's, handwriting which set it off from that of others. ➤The term is formed on the analogy of oral accent.

writing/automatic: see **automatic writing.**

Würzberg School: a group of psychologists at Würzberg University who, by means of introspective analysis, found evidence for **imageless thought,** *Aufgabe,* and **determining tendency,** which they believed were not composed of image and sensation.

X

$X:$ **1. range** of possible score. **2.** any gross or **raw *score** of the x distribution, or of the **independent *variable.**

X_o = **dependent *variable.**

$\overline{X}$ = **arithmetic *mean** of the x variable.

$\overline{X}_1, \overline{X}_2$ = predicted **raw *score.**

$x:$ **1. deviation** of a class or class interval from the mean value of the x variable. **2.** (*Ror.*) an uncommon response that imputes the likeness of a part of an animal or human being to an area of the inkblot to which the usual response is that of seeing a whole animal or human being.

$x':$ (*stat.*) a **deviation** from an **assumed *mean.**

$x^2:$ incorrectly used for **chi square** or χ^2.

xanthocyanopsia (zan″thō·sī″ən·op′si·ə): *n.* seeing everything as yellow or blue; redgreen **color blindness.**

xanthopsia (zan·thop′si·ə) = **yellowsightedness.**

X **axis** = abscissa (1).—See **axis.**

X **chromosomes:** see **chromosomes /X and Y.**

X **coordinate** = abscissa (1).—See **axis.**

x **distance** = abscissa (2).—See **axis.**

xeno- (zen′o-): combining form meaning *strange, foreign.*

xenoglossophilia: *n.* a disorder that leads to the use of strange, pretentious words, or those having a foreign origin, when simpler words from one's own vernacular would serve better. ➤The very term is itself the product of this probably incurable—certainly chronic—disorder. Inclusion of such foreignisms in this dictionary does not imply approval of their use.

xenoglossophobia: *n.* a morbid fear of foreign languages. ➤A very common affliction of graduate students.

xenophobia: *n.* abnormal fear of strangers.

xi or ξ (ksī; sī): (*psychophys.*) the point of subjective equality; the stimulus value at which the probability of a judgment "greater" equals the probability of a judgment "less."

X-O test: (*S. Pressey*) a pioneering test of attitudes and interests.

x **value:** see **axis.**

X-Y-Z grouping: (*educ.*) grouping pupils according to ability into three sections for separate instruction. ➤To conceal the basis of grouping, the slow learners are usually made the Y rather than the Z group.—See **ability grouping** for discussion.

Y

Y: 1. (*stat.*) *dependent criterion *variable; that which is being estimated or predicted by other variables singly or in combination. **2.** (*stat.*) any gross or **raw** *score of the *y* distribution. **3.** the dependent *variable in curve-fitting by the method of least squares. **4.** (*Ror.*) an inkblot response in which flat gray is the determinant.

y: 1. (*math.*) a value of an **ordinate**; the numerical value representing a distance from the *X* axis along any line parallel to the *Y* axis.—See **axis. 2.** (*stat.*) deviation of a value or class interval from the mean ordinate value.

y array = column (1).

Y axis = ordinate.—See **axis.**

Y chromosomes: see **chromosomes /X and Y.**

Y coordinate = ordinate.—See **axis.**

year scaling: see **age equivalent scale.**

yellow: *n.* the hue of visual sensations typically evoked by stimulation of the normal human eye with radiation of wave length approximately 582 millimicrons; or any color manifesting a hue predominantly similar to the typical yellow so produced.

yellow-sighted: *adj.* characterizing a heightened color sensitivity for yellow, or a tendency to see all objects tinged with yellow. ➤The phenomenon occurs (*a*) in individuals who possess a peculiar pigmentation of certain tissues of the eye, (*b*) in normal individuals following blue-adaptation, or (*c*) following the use of certain drugs.

yellow spot = macula lutea.

yellow/visual: see **visual yellow.**

Yerkes-Bridges Point Scale: an early adaptation of the **Binet Scale** to American conditions.

yes reaction = confirming reaction.

Young-Helmholtz theory: see **color theories.**

youth: *n.* **1.** a person from about age 16 to age 25. **2.** an adolescent. ➤The term is not sharply limited as to age. It properly refers to both sexes, but some restrict it to males. Its synonym, **juvenile,** tends to be more inclusive, extending downward into childhood.—See **development/levels of.**—*adj.* **youthful.**

y value or **y distance:** see **axis.**

Z

Z: 1. (*Ror.*) a response imputing organization to the inkblot pattern: two or more portions of the figure are seen in relation to one another, and the meaning reported depends on this organization. **2. = z** (2).

z: (*stat.*) **1. = standard** *score. **2.** a transformation of the product-moment correlation, *r*, for which the formula is

$$z = \frac{1}{2}[\log_e (1 + r) - \log_e (1 - r)]$$

➤The transformation has the advantage that it is approximately normally distributed. It may also be symbolized by *Z*, *Z'*, *z'*. **3.** the difference between two standard deviations expressed in logs:

$$z = \log_e \sigma_1 - \log_e \sigma_2$$

z₁, z₂ . . . z_t = standard *scores.

Zeigarnik phenomenon or **effect** (tsī·gär'nik): the experimental finding that names of tasks that were interrupted before completion are better recalled than names of completed tasks. ➤The term has been loosely applied to many phenomena having in common only that the person is interrupted.—*Syn.* (for the broader concept) **unfinished business.**

Zeitgeist (tsīt'gīst): *n.* (*Ger.*) the spirit of the times; the complex of ideas that, in a given era and culture, are charged with strong emotion.

Zeno's arrow: an argument, resting on the assumption that time is made up of discrete units, that motion is impossible or at least unthinkable.

zero/absolute: that point on a measuring scale at which a variable ceases to exist, at which nothing of the variable remains. ➤Absolute zero temperature is that point at which all molecular motion ceases. It is peculiarly difficult even to estimate the absolute zero point for any psychological variable.

zero/(absolute) ontogenetic = developmental zero.

zero/developmental: see **developmental zero.**

zero-order: *adj.* (*stat.*) referring to a correlation coefficient computed from the original data; thus, to one having no variables held constant. ➤The ordinary correlation r_{12} is a zero-order correlation, in contrast with a partial correlation of the first order $r_{12\cdot3}$ which has one variable, 3, held constant; or with one of the second order $r_{12\cdot34}$ which has two variables, 3 and 4, held constant.

zero/physiological: see **physiological zero.**

zero/true = **zero/absolute.**

zest: *n.* taking a hearty interest in living and seeking out opportunities for useful activity, recreation, and good fellowship.

zeta or ζ (zā′tə; zē′-): the difference between the squares of the **correlation ratio (eta)** and the **correlation coefficient,** $\zeta = (\eta^2 - r^2)$. ➤This variable is used in determining whether the regression is linear, which it will be if $\zeta = 0$. When the **C.R.** of zeta (which is $\zeta/2\sqrt{\zeta/N}$) is more than 2.5, the relation is considered *non*linear.

zoetrope (zō′ə·trōp): *n.* an old instrument, prototype of the motion picture, by which a series of still pictures passing rapidly in front of a narrow aperture are seen in motion.—See **phi-phenomenon.**

Zöllner illusion: an illusion of space perception in which two actually parallel lines seem divergent when one is crossed at a

sharp angle by a number of short lines slanting in one direction and the other by lines slanting in the opposite direction.

zone/erogenous or **/erotogenic:** an area whose stimulation arouses sexual or erotic feeling.

zone/primacy: (*psychoan.*) that area which, at a given period of development, yields greatest satisfaction to the **libido,** and which therefore tends to draw off satisfaction from other zones onto itself. ➤The typical order of primacy is said to be **oral, anal, phallic, genital;** but development may be arrested at, or may regress to, any stage.

zones/color: see **color zones.**

zones/retinal: see **color zones.**

zo(o)-: combining form meaning *animal.*

zoöerasty (zō′ə·er·as″ti): *n.* sexual intercourse with an animal.

zoology (zō·ol′ə·ji): *n.* the study of animal organisms. ➤Taken broadly, it includes psychology; but in practice zoology is limited to the study of animal structure and physiology.—*adj.* **zoological.**

zoomorphism (zō″ə·morf′iz·əm): *n.* the interpretation of man's behavior exclusively in the descriptive terms appropriate to infrahuman animals; the implicit denial to man of behavior that distinguishes him from infrahumans.—*Syn.* **theriomorphism.**—*Cp.* **anthropomorphism.**

zoophilia: *n.* unusually strong attraction to animals.—*adj.* **zoophilic.**

z score = **standard *score.**

z-test: *n.* a **projective test** consisting of three pictures successively projected on a screen: they are plain, colored, and cut into ribbons. Subjects write out responses, and interpretation in the main follows the pattern set by Rorschach.

Zürich School: the psychiatrists who follow the leadership of C. G. Jung.—*Syn.* **analytic psychology,** ANALYTIC PSYCHIATRY (*prejd.*).

zygote (zī′gōt): *n.* a cell formed by union of two gametes; in higher animals, the union of sperm and egg cell into the fertilized egg that begins a new individual; or the groups of cells produced by fission from that union in the first two weeks. ➤*Cp.* **gamete,** either of the two cells that unite to form the zygote.—*adj.* **zygotic** (-got′ik).

Zyve test: a test of scientific aptitude.

zyz: a **nonsense syllable** (such as is used in memory experiments) with which it seems suitable to end this dictionary.

$$z\ z\ Z\ z\ z$$